Portugal

The Minho (p428)

Porto, the Douro & Trás-os-Montes (p358)

The Beiras (p301)

Estremadura & Ribatejo (p264)

Lisbon & Around (p60)

The Alentejo (p211)

The Algarve (p152)

THIS EDITION WRITTEN AND RESEARCHED BY

Regis St Louis, Kate Armstrong, Kerry Christiani, Marc Di Duca, Anja Mutić, Kevin Raub

PLAN YOUR TRIP

MATT MUNRO / LONELY PLANET ©

PORTO P363

MATT MUNRO / LONELY PLANET ©

LISBON P61

ON THE ROAD

Contents

Welcome to Portugal

Medieval castles, cobblestone villages, captivating cities and golden beaches: the Portugal experience can be many things. History, great food and idyllic scenery are just the beginning...

Ghosts of the Past

Celts, Romans, Visigoths, Moors and Christians all left their mark on the Iberian nation. Here, you can gaze upon 20,000-year-old stone carvings in the Vila Nova de Foz Côa, watch the sunset over megaliths outside Évora or lose yourself in the elaborate corridors of Unesco World Heritage Sites in Tomar, Belém, Alcobaça or Batalha. You can pack an itinerary visiting palaces set above mist-covered woodlands, craggy clifftop castles and stunningly preserved medieval town centres.

The Portuguese Table

Freshly baked bread, olives, cheese, red wine or crisp *vinho verde* (young wine), chargrilled fish, *cataplana* (seafood stew), smoked meats – the Portuguese have perfected the art of cooking simple, delicious meals. Sitting down to table means experiencing the richness of Portugal's bountiful coastline and fertile countryside. Of course, you don't have to sit; you can take your piping-hot *pastel de nata* (custard tart) standing up at an 1837 patisserie in Belém, or wander through scenic vineyards sipping the velvety ports of the Douro Valley. You can shop the produce-filled markets, or book a table in one of the country's top dining rooms.

Cinematic Scenery

Outside the cities, Portugal's beauty unfolds in all its startling variety. You can go hiking amid the granite peaks of Parque Nacional da Peneda-Gerês or take in the pristine scenery and historic villages of the little-explored Beiras. Over 800km of coast offers more places to soak up the splendour. Gaze out over dramatic end-of-the-world cliffs, surf stellar breaks off dune-covered beaches or laze peacefully on sandy islands fronting calm blue seas. You'll find dolphin watching in the lush Sado Estuary, boating and kayaking along the meandering Rio Guadiana, and memorable walks and bike rides all across the country.

Rhythms of Portugal

Festivals pack Portugal's calendar. Drink, dance and feast your way through all-night revelries like Lisbon's Festa de Santo António or Porto's Festa de São João. There are kick-up-your-heels country fairs in the hinterlands, and rock- and world-music fests all along the coast. Any time of year is right to hear the mournful music of fado in the Alfama, join the dance party in Bairro Alto or hit the bars in Porto, Coimbra and Lagos.

Why I Love Portugal

By Regis St Louis, Writer

I'm enamoured by the scenery, the rhythms of village life and Portugal's outstanding (and underrated) food and wine. I love exploring the hidden beaches along the Costa Vicentina, taking picturesque walks in the Serra da Estrela (where I still bump into shepherds during a day's outing), and roaming in less-visited corners of the Alentejo – such a magical place for discovering the traditional soul of Portugal. But it's the Portuguese themselves who make this country so special. Despite the sometimes dour exterior (it's just a facade!), they're among the kindest and most warm-hearted people on earth.

For more about our writers, see p544

Above: Parque Nacional da Peneda-Gerês (p460)

Portugal

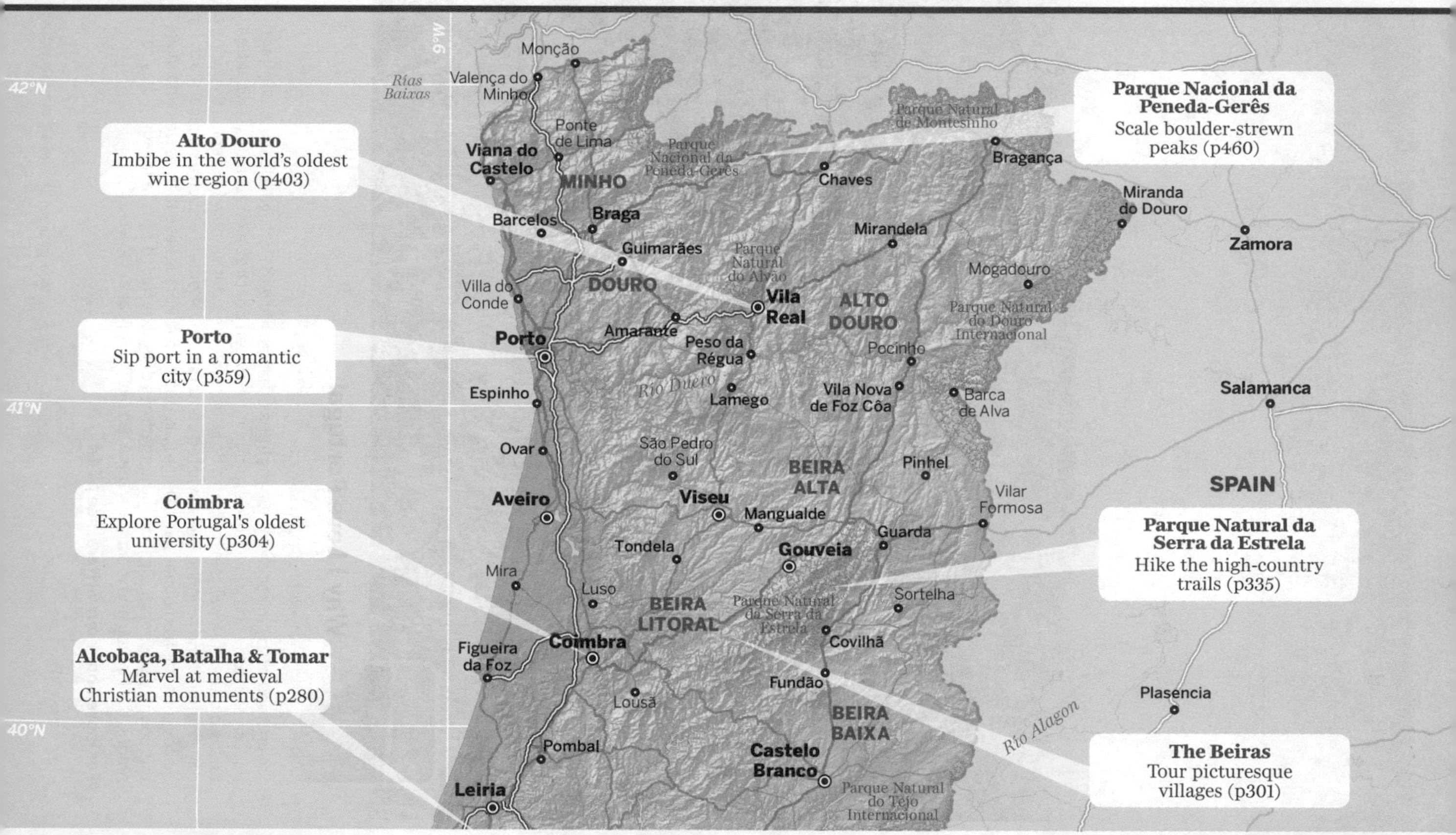
0 80 km
0 40 miles
Alto Douro
Imbibe in the world's oldest wine region (p403)
Porto
Sip port in a romantic city (p359)
Coimbra
Explore Portugal's oldest university (p304)
Alcobaça, Batalha & Tomar
Marvel at medieval Christian monuments (p280)
Parque Nacional da Peneda-Gerês
Scale boulder-strewn peaks (p460)
Parque Natural da Serra da Estrela
Hike the high-country trails (p335)
The Beiras
Tour picturesque villages (p301)
42°N
41°N
40°N
9°W
Rías Baixas
Monção
Valença do Minho
Ponte de Lima
Viana do Castelo
MINHO
Braga
Barcelos
Guimarães
DOURO
Villa do Conde
Porto
Amarante
Parque Nacional da Peneda-Gerês
Chaves
Parque Natural de Montesinho
Bragança
Miranda do Douro
Zamora
Mirandela
Parque Natural do Alvão
Vila Real
ALTO DOURO
Mogadouro
Parque Natural do Douro Internacional
Peso da Régua
Pocinho
Espinho
Rio Duero
Lamego
Vila Nova de Foz Côa
Barca de Alva
Salamanca
Ovar
São Pedro do Sul
BEIRA ALTA
Pinhel
Aveiro
Viseu
Mangualde
Vilar Formosa
SPAIN
Guarda
Tondela
Gouveia
Mira
Luso
BEIRA LITORAL
Parque Natural da Serra da Estrela
Sortelha
Covilhã
Coimbra
Figueira da Foz
Fundão
Lousã
BEIRA BAIXA
Plasencia
Río Alagon
Pombal
Castelo Branco
Leiria
Parque Natural do Tejo Internacional

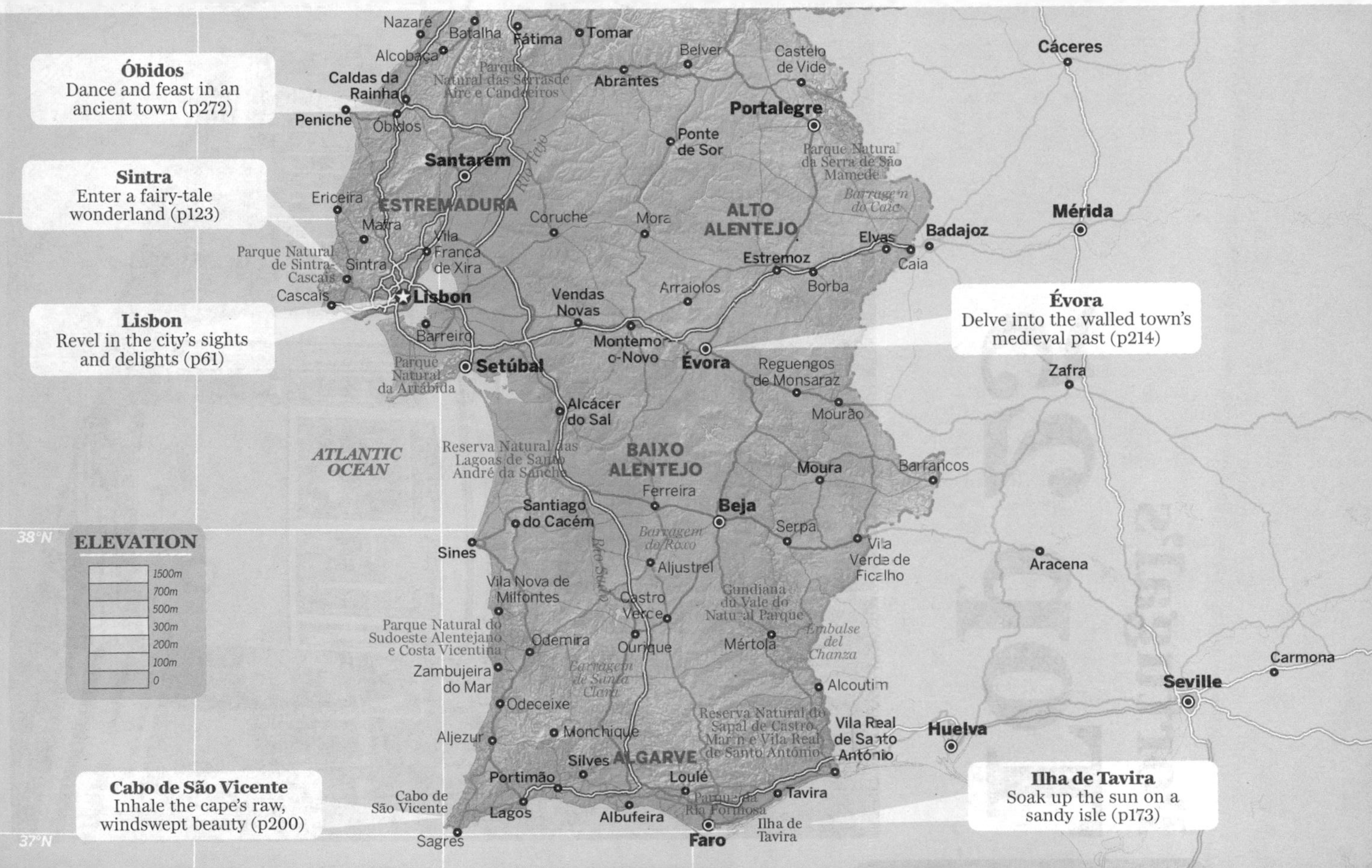
Óbidos
Dance and feast in an ancient town (p272)
Sintra
Enter a fairy-tale wonderland (p123)
Lisbon
Revel in the city's sights and delights (p61)
Évora
Delve into the walled town's medieval past (p214)
Cabo de São Vicente
Inhale the cape's raw, windswept beauty (p200)
Ilha de Tavira
Soak up the sun on a sandy isle (p173)
ELEVATION
1500m
700m
500m
300m
200m
100m
0
38°N
37°N
ATLANTIC OCEAN
ESTREMADURA
ALTO ALENTEJO
BAIXO ALENTEJO
ALGARVE
Nazaré
Batalha
Fátima
Tomar
Alcobaça
Caldas da Rainha
Peniche
Óbidos
Santarém
Ericeira
Mafra
Vila Franca de Xira
Parque Natural de Sintra-Cascais
Sintra
Cascais
Lisbon
Barreiro
Setúbal
Parque Natural da Arrábida
Abrantes
Belver
Castelo de Vide
Portalegre
Ponte de Sor
Parque Natural da Serra de São Mamede
Coruche
Mora
Vendas Novas
Montemor-o-Novo
Arraiolos
Estremoz
Borba
Elvas
Caia
Badajoz
Évora
Reguengos de Monsaraz
Mourão
Alcácer do Sal
Reserva Natural das Lagoas de Santo André da Sancha
Moura
Barrancos
Ferreira
Beja
Serpa
Vila Verde de Ficalho
Santiago do Cacém
Sines
Aljustrel
Vila Nova de Milfontes
Castro Verde
Parque Natural do Sudoeste Alentejano e Costa Vicentina
Odemira
Ourique
Mértola
Zambujeira do Mar
Odeceixe
Alcoutim
Monchique
Aljezur
Silves
Portimão
Lagos
Cabo de São Vicente
Sagres
Albufeira
Loulé
Faro
Tavira
Ilha de Tavira
Vila Real de Santo António
Huelva
Cáceres
Mérida
Zafra
Aracena
Seville
Carmona

Portugal's Top 25

1

The Alfama

1 Lisbon's Alfama district (p71), with its labyrinthine alleyways, hidden courtyards and curving, shadow-filled lanes, is a magical place in which to lose all sense of direction and delve into the soul of the city. You'll pass breadbox-sized grocers, brilliantly tiled buildings and cosy taverns filled with easygoing chatter, accompanied by the scent of chargrilled sardines and the mournful rhythms of fado drifting in the breeze. Round a bend and catch sight of steeply pitched rooftops leading down to the glittering Tejo, and you'll know you're hooked...

Porto

2 It would be hard to dream up a more romantic city than Portugal's second largest. Laced with narrow pedestrian laneways, Porto (p359) is blessed with baroque churches, epic theatres and sprawling plazas. Its Ribeira district – a Unesco World Heritage Site – is just a short walk across a landmark bridge from centuries-old port wineries in Vila Nova de Gaia, where you can sip the world's best port. And though some walls are crumbling, a sense of renewal – in the form of modern architecture, cosmopolitan restaurants, burgeoning nightlife and a vibrant arts scene – is palpable.

FÁBREGAS HARELUYA / SHUTTERSTOCK ©

VICTOR OVIES ARENAS / GETTY IMAGES ©

Historic Évora

3 The Queen of the Alentejo and one of Portugal's most beautifully preserved medieval towns, Évora (p214) is an enchanting place to spend several days delving into the past. Inside the 14th-century walls, Évora's narrow, winding lanes lead to striking architectural works: an elaborate medieval cathedral and cloisters, Roman ruins and a picturesque town square. Historic and aesthetic virtues aside, Évora is also a lively university town, and its many attractive restaurants serve up excellent, hearty Alentejan cuisine.

Beaches of the Algarve

4 Along Portugal's south coast, the Algarve (p174) is home to a wildly varied coastline. There are sandy islands reachable only by boat, cliff-backed shores, rugged rarely visited beaches and people-packed sands near buzzing nightlife. Days are spent playing in the waves, taking oceanfront strolls and surfing memorable breaks. For endless days of sun and refreshing ocean temperatures, come in summer; but to escape the crowds, plan a low-season visit, when prices dive and crowds disperse. Bottom: Albufeira (p182)

3

OLIVIER BIGOT / 500PX ©

4

SAIKO3P / SHUTTERSTOCK ©

Seafood

5 Always a seafaring culture, the Portuguese know a thing or two about cooking fish. Taste the culinary riches of Portugal's coast in dishes like *caldeirada de peixe* (fish stew layered with tomatoes, potatoes and rice), *açorda de camarãoes* (a tasty stew of shrimp, garlic and cilantro thickened with breadcrumbs) or *cataplana* (seafood stew). Algarve luminaries like A Eira do Mel (p202) are memorable settings for a seafood feast. Top left: *cataplana*

Sintra

6 Less than an hour by train from the capital, Sintra (p123) feels like another world. Resembling an illustration from a fairy tale, it is sprinkled with stone-walled taverns and has a whitewashed palace looming over it. Forested hillsides form the backdrop to the village's storybook setting, with imposing castles, mystical gardens, strange mansions and centuries-old monasteries hidden among the woodlands. The fog that sweeps in by night adds another layer of mystery, and cool evenings are best spent fireside in one of Sintra's many charming B&Bs.
Top right: Palácio Nacional da Pena (p125)

Cabo de São Vicente

7 There's something thrilling about standing at Europe's most southwestern edge, a headland of barren cliffs (p200) to which Portuguese sailors bid a nervous farewell as they sailed past, venturing into the unknown during Portugal's golden years of exploration. The windswept cape is redolent of history – if you squint hard (really hard), you'll see the ghost of Vasco da Gama sailing past. These days, a fortress and lighthouse perch on the cape and a new museum beautifully highlights Portugal's maritime-navigation history.

8

MATT MUNRO / LONELY PLANET ©

9

MATT MUNRO / LONELY PLANET ©

Sipping the Douro

8 The Alto Douro wine country (p403) is the oldest demarcated wine region on earth. Its terraced hills, with craggy vines that have produced luscious wines for centuries, loom either side of the Rio Douro. Whether you get here by driving the scenic back roads, or by train or boat from Porto, take the time to hike, cruise and taste. Countless vintners receive guests for tours, tastings and overnight stays, and if you find one that's still family owned, you may sample something very old and very special. Top: Quinta Nova (p404)

Fado

9 Born in a working-class Lisbon neighbourhood, the melancholic music of fado has been around for centuries. Despite its years, fado remains a living art, heard in tiny restaurants, like A Baîuca (p113), and music halls alike. A lone voice coupled with the 12-string Portuguese *guitarra* are all the tools needed to bring some listeners to tears, as songs recall broken hearts and the lost days of youth. In fado, raw emotion often conveys more than mere lyrics can; even non-Portuguese speakers find themselves moved by great *fadistas*. Bottom: A Baîuca (p113)

10

11

Ilha de Tavira

10 Ilha de Tavira (p173) has the lot for sunseekers, beach bums, nature lovers (and naturists): kilometre after kilometre of golden beach (think sand, sand, sand, as far as the eye can see), a designated nudist area, transport via miniature train, busy restaurants and a campground. To top it off, it's part of the protected Parque Natural da Ria Formosa. Outside the high season, the island feels wonderfully remote and empty, but be warned: during high season (July and August) the hordes descend.

Parque Natural da Ria Formosa

11 This special spot (p165) feels like it's in the middle of the wilderness, yet it's right off the Algarvian coast. Enclosing a vast area of *sapais* (marshes), *salinas* (salt pans), creeks and dune islands, the protected lagoon system stretches for an incredible 60km and encompasses 18,000 hectares. And it's all accessible from various towns – have a boat drop you at a deserted beach, or amble along the nature trail among the precious wetland bird life.

Megaliths Around Évora

12 Spiritual, historical, incredible – the ancient megaliths (p225) around Évora will make your hair stand on end. As a traveller, you often have these sites to yourself – and what better way to ponder the mysteries of places so ancient they cannot fully be explained? How did such massive rocks get hauled into place? Were they fertility symbols or proprietorial land boundaries? They beg questions, yet – refreshingly in a world of reasoning – provide few answers. Somehow, their appeal lies in not knowing.

Top: Cromeleque dos Almandres (p226)

Staying in a Pousada

13 Portugal has its share of boutique hotels and beach resorts, but some of its most memorable lodging is found in its *pousadas* (upmarket inns). The settings are jaw-dropping: clifftop mansions, 300-year-old castles and former monasteries – like the Pousada Convento de Évora (p221) – are among the 40 *pousadas* sprinkled across the country. Where else can you lodge in antique-filled rooms where dukes once slept, contemplating the age-old beauty of the landscape? Pulling aside curtains, you'll gaze upon vineyards, mountains or the coastline.

Bottom: Pousada Convento de Évora (p221)

12

INACIO PIRES / SHUTTERSTOCK ©

13

SABINE LUBENOW / GETTY IMAGES ©

MINEMERO / GETTY IMAGES ©

STOCKPHOTOSART / SHUTTERSTOCK ©

JOEL SANTOS / GETTY IMAGES ©

Nightlife in Lisbon

14 Lisbon's dizzying nightlife (p106) is a mix of old-school drinking dens, jazz clubs and stylish lounges. The challenge is where to begin. You can start the evening with sunset drinks on a terrace overlooking the city, then head to Bairro Alto for tapas and early evening cocktails on people-packed, bar-lined streets. Then head downhill to Cais do Sodré, a former red-light district turned hipster playground, or to Bica for a lively local bar scene. At the end of the night there's always riverside Lux, still one of Portugal's best nightspots.

Top left: Rua Nova do Carvalho

Alcobaça, Batalha & Tomar

15 These medieval Christian monuments – all Unesco World Heritage Sites – constitute one of Portugal's greatest national treasures. Each has its own magic: Manueline adornments and the roofless shell of the unfinished Capelas Imperfeitas at Batalha's monastery (p282); the kitchen at Alcobaça's monastery, where a multistorey chimney and fish-stocked river once tended to the appetites of monks; and the labyrinthine courtyards and 16-sided chapel of the Knights Templar at Tomar's Convento de Cristo.

Top right: Capelas Imperfeitas (p283)

Parque Natural da Serra da Estrela

16 Portugal's highest mountains (p335) blend rugged scenery, outdoor adventure and vanishing traditional ways. At Torre, the country's highest point (artificially pushed up to 2000m by the addition of a not-so-subtle stone monument!), you can slalom down Portugal's only ski slope. Hikers can choose from a network of high country trails with stupendous vistas. Oh, and did we mention the furry sheep-dog puppies that frolic by the roadside? You'll long to take one home.

17

ZACARIAS PEREIRA DA MATA / SHUTTERSTOCK ©

18

RENATO SEJI KAWASAKI / SHUTTERSTOCK ©

Villages of the Beiras

17 From schist-walled communities spilling down hillsides to sentinels that once guarded the eastern border against Spanish incursions, the inland Beiras (p301) are filled with picturesque and historical villages: Piódão, Trancoso, Sortelha, Monsanto, Idanha-a-Velha... Today mostly devoid of residents but not yet overwhelmed by mass tourism, they are some of the country's most appealing destinations. String a few together into the perfect road trip – or, better yet, don your walking shoes and experience these ancient places at a medieval pace. Top left: Piódão (p328)

Festivals

18 There's always something to celebrate in Portugal. For Easter, head to Braga (p434). Romantics will love Lisbon's Festa de Santo António, with locals plying sweethearts with poems and pots of aromatic basil. In August, catch Viana do Castelo's Romaria de Nossa Senhora d'Agonia, where *gigantones* (giants) parade down sawdust-painted streets alongside gold- and scarlet-clad women. And, in winter, young lads wear masks and colourful garb in Trás-os-Montes' villages during the pagan-derived Festa dos Rapazes.

Top right: Street decorations, Viana do Castelo (p444)

Coimbra

19 Portugal's atmospheric college town, Coimbra (p304) rises steeply from the Rio Mondego to a medieval quarter housing one of Europe's oldest universities. Students roam the streets clad in black capes, while fado musicians give free concerts beneath the Moorish town gate or under the stained-glass windows of Café Santa Cruz. Kids can keep busy at Portugal dos Pequenitos, a theme park with miniature versions of Portuguese monuments; grown-ups will appreciate the upper town's student-driven nightlife and the new bars and restaurants in the riverside park below.

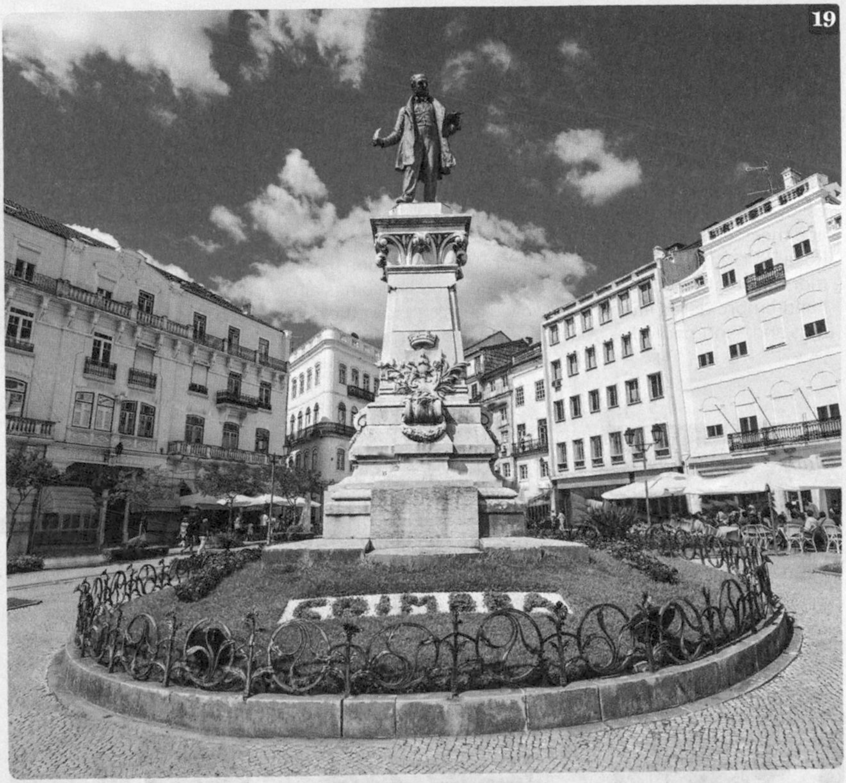

19

Óbidos

20 Wandering through the tangle of ancient streets and whitewashed houses of Óbidos (p272) is enchanting any time of year, but come during one of its festivals and you'll be in for a special treat. Whether attending a jousting match or climbing the castle walls at the medieval fair, searching for the next Pavarotti at the Festival de Ópera or delving into the written world at Fólio – Portugal's newest international literature festival – you couldn't ask for a better backdrop.

20

Barcelos Market

21 The Minho is famous for its sprawling outdoor markets, but the largest, oldest and most celebrated is the Feira de Barcelos (p437), held every Thursday in this ancient town on the banks of the Rio Cávado. Most outsiders come for the yellow-dotted *louça de Barcelos* ceramics and the gaudy figurines à la local potter Rosa Ramalho, while rural villagers are more interested in the scrawny chickens, hand-embroidered linen, hand-woven baskets and hand-carved ox yokes.

Azulejos

22 Some of Portugal's most captivating works of art are out on the streets. A great legacy of the Moors, the *azulejo* (hand-painted tile) was adopted by the Portuguese and put to stunning use over the centuries. Exquisite displays cover Porto's train station and churches, with stories painted on the ceramic surfaces. Lisbon has even more *azulejo*-adorned buildings all over town. The best place to start the hunt: Museu Nacional do Azulejo (p65), home to *azulejos* dating back 400 years. Bottom: Museu Nacional do Azulejo (p65)

ALAN COPSON / GETTY IMAGES ©

KRZYSZTOF DYDYNSKI / GETTY IMAGES ©

MATT MUNRO / LONELY PLANET ©

CALLE MONTES / GETTY IMAGES ©

MATT MUNRO / LONELY PLANET ©

Parque Nacional da Peneda-Gerês

23 The vast, rugged wilderness of Portugal's northernmost park (p460) is home to dramatic peaks, meandering streams and rolling hillsides covered with wildflowers. Its age-old stone villages seem lost in time and, in remote areas, wolves still roam. As always, the best way to feel nature's power is on foot along one of more than a dozen hiking trails. Some scale peaks, a few link to old Roman roads, others lead to castle ruins or waterfalls.

Braga

24 Portugal's third-largest city is blessed with terrific restaurants, a vibrant university and raucous festivals, but when it comes to historic sites it is unparalleled in Portugal. Braga (p430) has not one but two sets of Roman ruins, countless 17th-century plazas and an 18th-century palace turned museum. Then there's that splendid baroque staircase: Escadaria do Bom Jesus, the target of penitent pilgrims who come to make offerings at altars on the way to the mountaintop throughout the year.

Top right: Bom Jesus do Monte (p438)

Pastries

25 One of the great culinary wonders of Portugal, the cinnamon-dusted *pastel de nata* (custard tart), with its flaky crust and creamy centre, lurks irresistibly behind pastry counters across the country; the best are served piping hot in Belém (p79). Of course, when it comes to dessert, Portugal is more than a one-hit wonder, with a dazzling array of regional sweets – from the jewel-like Algarve marzipan to Sintra's heavenly almond-and-egg *travesseiros* to Serpa's cheesecake-like *queijadas*.

Bottom right: *pastel de nata*

Need to Know

For more information, see Survival Guide (p505)

Currency
Euro (€)

Language
Portuguese

Visas
Generally not required for stays of up to 90 days; some nationalities will need a Schengen visa.

Money
ATMs are widely available, except in the smallest villages. Credit cards accepted in midrange and high-end establishments.

Mobile Phones
Local SIM cards can be used in unlocked European, Australian and quad-band US mobiles.

Time
GMT/UTC in winter, GMT/UTC plus one hour in summer.

When to Go

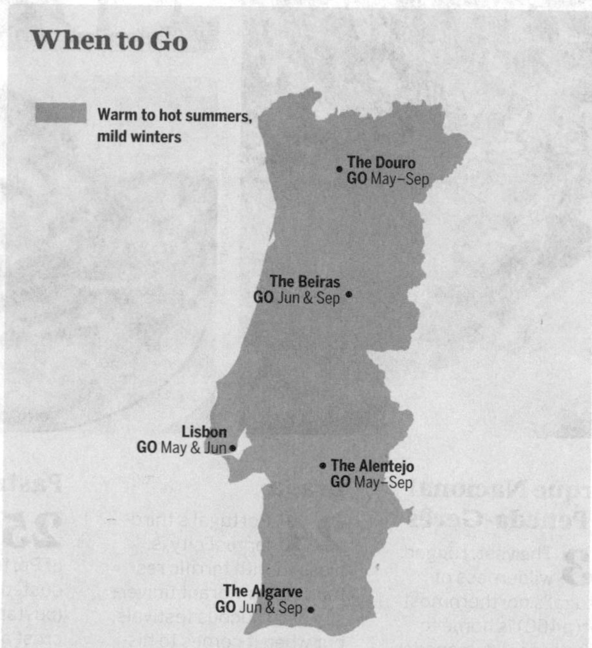

High Season (Jul & Aug)

➡ Accommodation prices increase 30%.

➡ Expect big crowds in the Algarve and coastal resort areas.

➡ Sweltering temperatures are commonplace.

➡ Warmer ocean temperatures.

Shoulder (Apr–Jun & Sep–Nov)

➡ Wildflowers and mild days are ideal for hikes and outdoor activities.

➡ Lively festivals take place in June.

➡ Crowds and prices are average.

➡ Colder ocean temperatures.

Low Season (Dec–Mar)

➡ Shorter, rainier days with freezing temperatures at higher elevations.

➡ Lower prices, fewer crowds.

➡ Attractions keep shorter hours.

➡ Frigid ocean temperatures.

Useful Websites

Lonely Planet (www.lonelyplanet.com/portugal) Destination information, hotel bookings, traveller forum and more.

Portugal Tourism (www.visitportugal.com) Portugal's official tourism site.

Portugal News (www.theportugalnews.com) The latest news and gossip in Portugal.

Wines of Portugal (www.winesofportugal.info) Fine overview of Portugal's favourite beverage, covering wine regions, grape varieties and wine routes.

Important Numbers

Country Code	☎351
International Access Code	☎00
Ambulance, Fire & Police	☎112

Exchange Rates

Australia	A$1	€0.66
Canada	C$1	€0.70
Japan	¥100	€0.83
New Zealand	NZ$1	€0.63
UK	£1	€1.27
USA	US$1	€0.89

For current exchange rates see www.xe.com.

Daily Costs

Budget: Less than €50

- Dorm bed: €15–22
- Basic hotel room for two: from €30
- Lunch special at a family-run restaurant: €7–9
- Second-class train ticket from Lisbon to Faro: from €22

Midrange: €50–120

- Double room in a midrange hotel: €50–100
- Lunch and dinner in a midrange restaurant: €22–35
- Admission to museums: €2–6

Top End: More than €120

- Boutique hotel room: from €120
- Dinner for two in a top restaurant: from €80
- Three-day surf course: €150

Opening Hours

Opening hours vary throughout the year. We provide high-season opening hours; hours will generally decrease in the shoulder and low seasons.

Banks 8.30am–3pm Monday to Friday

Bars 7pm–2am

Cafes 9am–7pm

Clubs 11pm–4am Thursday to Saturday

Restaurants noon–3pm & 7–10pm

Shopping malls 10am–10pm

Shops 9.30am–noon & 2–7pm Monday to Friday, 10am–1pm Saturday

Arriving in Portugal

Aeroporto de Lisboa (Lisbon) Metro trains allow convenient access to downtown (€1.90, 20 minutes to the centre, frequent departures from 6.30am to 1am). The AeroBus (€3.50) departs every 20 minutes from 7am to 11pm, while a taxi to the centre will cost around €15 and take around 15 minutes.

Aeroporto Francisco Sá Carneiro (Porto) Metro trains run frequently to the city centre (€2.45, including €0.50 Andante card) and take about 45 minutes. A taxi will cost €20 to €25 and take around 30 to 60 minutes.

Aeroporto de Faro (Faro) Buses run to the city centre (€2.20) every 30 minutes on weekdays and every two hours on weekends. A taxi will cost around €13 (20 minutes).

Getting Around

Transport in Portugal is reasonably priced, quick and efficient.

Train Extremely affordable, with a decent network between major towns from north to south. Visit **Comboios de Portugal** (p521) for schedules and prices.

Car Useful for visiting small villages, national parks and other regions with minimal public transport. Cars can be hired in major towns and cities. Drive on the right.

Bus Cheaper and slower than trains. Useful for more remote villages that aren't serviced by trains. Infrequent service on weekends.

For much more on **getting around**, see p516

First Time Portugal

For more information, see Survival Guide (p505)

Checklist

➡ Check whether you can use your phone in Portugal and ask about roaming charges.

➡ Book your first night's accommodation.

➡ Check the calendar to see which festivals to visit (or avoid!).

➡ Organise travel insurance.

➡ Check airline baggage restrictions.

➡ Inform your debit-/credit-card company of your travel plans.

What to Pack

➡ Phrasebook

➡ Travel plug

➡ Good walking shoes

➡ Earplugs for thin-walled guest houses and noisy weekend nights

➡ Sunscreen

➡ Swimming towel

➡ Rain jacket (especially in winter)

➡ English-language reading material

Top Tips for Your Trip

➡ Sample Portugal's culinary bounty at its *mercados* (markets). You'll find fruit, vegetables, breads, cheeses and smoked meats for picnics.

➡ Get off the main highways and take to the back roads. Sleepy villages, roadside fruit stands and tiny lanes lead to remote beaches.

➡ Do learn a few phrases in Portuguese. You'll earn respect and more than a few smiles with a well-placed '*bom dia*' or '*muito obrigado*'.

➡ Along those lines, don't try to use Spanish, which can rub some folks the wrong way. You're better off just using English.

➡ Don't be put off by the sometimes dour-looking Portuguese. Make the effort to approach people and you'll find a warm-hearted country.

What to Wear

Portugal is a fairly casual destination, though most Portuguese tend to wear trousers (rather than shorts) outside resort areas. For upscale dining, smart casual is all that's required – no restaurant will insist on jackets or ties, and nor will any theatre or concert hall.

Nights can get windy or chilly, so bring a lightweight jacket in summer, and be prepared for rain and cooler temperatures in winter.

Sleeping

Although you can usually find a room on the spot in any town, it's worth booking ahead, especially for July and August.

Guesthouses Small, often family-run places, some set in historic buildings; amenities range from simple to luxurious.

Hostels Portugal has a growing network of hostels around the country, with many choices in Lisbon and Porto.

Turihab Properties Options to stay in characterful manor houses, restored farmhouses or self-contained stone cottages.

Pousadas Unique accommodation inside former castles, monasteries and estates; nearly three dozen pousadas are spread across the country.

➡ **Private rooms and apartments** Loads of online listings throughout Portugal.

Money

ATMs are the easiest way to get cash in Portugal, and they are easy to find in most cities and towns. Tiny rural villages probably won't have ATMs, so it's wise to get cash in advance. Most banks have a Multibanco ATM, with menus in English (and other languages), that accepts Visa, Access, MasterCard, Cirrus and so on. You just need your card and PIN. Keep in mind that the ATM limit is €200 per withdrawal, and many banks charge a foreign transaction fee (typically around 2% to 3%).

Most hotels and smarter restaurants accept credit cards; smaller guesthouses, budget hotels and smaller restaurants might not, so it's wise to have cash with you.

Tipping

Restaurants In touristy areas, 10% for exceptional service. Elsewhere, tipping is rare.

Bars Not expected unless table service is provided, then no more than the loose change.

Snack bars It's courteous to leave a bit of spare change.

Taxis Not expected, but it's polite to round up to the nearest euro.

Hotels One euro per bag is standard; gratuity for cleaning staff is at your discretion.

Language

English is spoken in larger cities and in popular tourist areas (especially the Algarve), but is less common in rural areas and among older Portuguese. Many restaurants have English-language menus, though smaller family-run places typically do not (but may have English-speaking staff on hand to help out). Smaller museums are likely to have signs in Portuguese only. The Portuguese always appreciate the effort: a few key words, such as *'bom dia', 'boa tarde', 'obrigado/obrigada'* and *'por favor',* can go a long way.

See the Language chapter (p522), for more information.

Etiquette

Greetings When greeting females or mixed company, an air kiss on both cheeks is common courtesy. Men give each other a handshake.

Visiting churches It is considered disrespectful to visit churches as a tourist during Mass. Taking photos at such a time is definitely inappropriate.

'Free' appetisers Whatever you eat, you must pay for, whether or not you ordered it. It's common practice for restaurants to bring bread, olives, cheese and other goodies to the table, but these are never free and will be added to your bill at the end. If you don't want them, a polite 'No, thank you' will see them returned to the kitchen.

If You Like...

Food

Renowned for its seafood, hearty country cooking and many regional specialities, Portugal offers plenty of temptation for the food-minded traveller. Celebrated new chefs have brought attention to a host of dining rooms, while those who enjoy the simple things – olives, cheeses, roast meats, fish sizzling on the grill, freshly baked bread – will enjoy memorable meals in traditional restaurants all across the country.

Belcanto Serving up some of Lisbon's best dishes in the foodie-loving neighbourhood of Chiado. (p99)

Food festivals The Algarve elevates its seafood and regional delicacies to high art in these food-minded celebrations. (p166)

Vila Joya Overlooking the beach, this two-Michelin-starred restaurant is one of Portugal's finest. (p184)

Cataplana This decadent seafood stew is a south-coast speciality; it's available across the Algarve and almost always feeds two. (p165)

DOC Serves delectable haute cuisine in a beautiful setting on the Douro. (p406)

Wine & Port

Home to some of the oldest vineyards on earth, Portugal has some fantastic (and deliciously affordable) wines. Each region has its enticements, from full-bodied Alentejan reds to Minho's refreshing *vinho verde* (young wine), along with the famous ports from the Douro. Stylish wine bars and bucolic vineyards provide memorable settings in which to taste Portugal's great fruits of the vine.

BA Wine Bar do Bairro Alto Sample the country's finest quaffs at this atmospheric spot in Lisbon. (p107)

Herdade do Esporão An acclaimed winery outside Reguengos de Monsaraz, with vineyards dating back hundreds of years. (p226)

Casa de Mateus At this shop inside a palace, drink in the grandeur while sipping distinctive and rare Alvarelhão. (p408)

Solar do Vinho do Porto With views over the Douro, this elegant garden bar serves an astounding variety of ports. (p108)

Douro Vineyards Breathtaking views from 18th-century manors and velvety rich wines make the Douro a requisite stop for wine lovers. (p403)

Graham's Port wine lodges are two a penny in Gaia, but Graham's stands out with its stellar cellar tours, tastings and big views. (p371)

Beaches

With 830km of coastline, Portugal has sun-kissed shores of every type, from festive, people-packed coves to remote, windswept shores that invite endless wandering.

Ilha de Tavira This sandy island off the southern coast is a remarkable getaway. (p173)

São Jacinto To escape the crowds, head to this wild beach backed by dunes west of Aveiro. (p325)

Vila Nova de Milfontes Star of the Alentejo coastline is this lovely and vibrant village overlooking several pretty beaches. (p260)

Costa da Caparica Just across the Tejo from Lisbon is 8km of pretty coastline with stylish beach bars sprinkled along it. (p142)

Lagos This popular Algarve resort town offers a mix of lively surfing beaches and secluded sandstone-backed shorelines further out of town. (p191)

Top: Convento de Cristo (p295)
Bottom: Douro vineyards (p403)

Architecture

Taking in Portugal's wildly varied architecture involves delving into the past as you gaze upon medieval monasteries, imposing hilltop castles and ancient ruins.

Fortaleza de Sagres Contemplate Portugal's seafaring past from this clifftop perch over the Atlantic. (p199)

Casa da Música Rem Koolhaas' stunning music hall, completed in 2005, is an architectural gem. (p388)

Mosteiro dos Jerónimos Dom Manuel I's fantastical tribute to the great explorors of the 15th century. (p79)

Convento de Cristo Former headquarters of the Knights Templar, this Unesco World Heritage Site is stunning to behold. (p295)

Conímbriga The best-preserved Roman ruins on the Iberian Peninsula provide a window into the rise and fall of the once great empire. (p315)

Palácio Nacional de Mafra The construction of this exuberant palace with its 1200 rooms nearly bankrupted the nation. (p140)

Music

The national music of Portugal is undoubtedly fado, that stirring, melancholic sound that's so prevalent in Lisbon (its birthplace) and Coimbra. Other genres also have their followers, and you can catch live rock, jazz and a wide range of world sounds.

Alfama The birthplace of fado has many authentic places in which to hear it live – as well as tourist traps to avoid. (p75)

Á Capella Coimbra also has a fado-loving heart; this converted

14th-century chapel is the best place to hear it live. (p314)

Festival do Sudoeste One of Portugal's biggest music fests erupts each August in the seaside town of Zambujeira do Mar. (p29)

Casa da Música Rem Koolhaas' concert hall is both an architectural masterpiece and a vibrant set piece for year-round music events. (p388)

Musicbox This long-standing Lisbon space hosts an eclectic line-up of rock, folk, funk and more. (p108)

Art

In the Portuguese art world, quality trumps quantity. You may not find massive art institutions here, but you will find galleries showcasing unique works from the past and present – including homegrown Portuguese legends.

Museu Calouste Gulbenkian One of Lisbon's finest museums houses an epic collection of magnificent artwork from East and West. (p79)

Museu Colecção Berardo In Belém, this free museum hosts some of Portugal's most daring exhibits. (p82)

Casa das Histórias Paula Rego Cascais' best exhibition space celebrates the artwork of Paula Rego, one of Portugal's finest living painters. (p133)

Casa de Serralves Porto's art lovers never miss the cutting-edge exhibits inside this art-deco mansion in the park. (p374)

Museu da Tapeçaria de Portalegre Guy Fino Be dazzled by colour at this fine tapestry museum in the Alentejo. (p238)

Museu de Lamego This museum houses a superb collection of works by 16th-century luminary Grão Vasco. (p399)

Nightlife

When the sun goes down, things start to get interesting. Whether you want to party like a rock star or sip cocktails with a more laid-back, bohemian crowd, you'll find these and dozens of other scenes in Portugal.

Lagos Packed with music-filled bars and lounges, Lagos is the nightlife centre of the Algarve. (p196)

Forte São João Baptista In a striking 17th-century fort, this hotel, restaurant and nightclub throws some of the best summer parties in the north. (p397)

Cais do Sodré Lisbon's newish nightlife epicentre has colourful bars, tapas joints and DJ-spinning clubs that stay open till the early morning. (p96)

Porto Nightlife has exploded in recent years, with revellers packing the bar- and gallery-lined streets near Rua das Carmelitas. (p384)

Historic Villages

Portugal is home to many enchanting villages, where a stroll along peaceful cobblestone lanes is like a trip back in time.

Óbidos Medieval architecture, lively festivals and charming guest houses await in this fortified town an hour north of Lisbon. (p272)

Mértola Set high above the Rio Guadiana, this remarkably well-preserved Alentejo town is considered an open-air museum. (p251)

Monsanto A forlorn village surrounding an age-old, boulder-strewn castle, Monsanto has great walking trails through the rolling countryside nearby. (p331)

Miranda do Douro This remote fortress town on the edge of Spain has an imposing 16th-century castle and street signs in the ancient language of Mirandês. (p424)

Castelo de Vide Wander the medieval Jewish quarter and take in sweeping views over the surrounding cork and olive groves. (p241)

Month by Month

TOP EVENTS

Semana Santa, April

Serralves em Festa, May

Festa de Santo António, June

Festa de São João, June

Romaria de Nossa Senhora d'Agonia, August

February

Winter sees fewer crowds and lower prices along with abundant rainfall, particularly in the north. Coastal temperatures are cool but mild, while inland there are frigid days. Many resorts remain shuttered until spring.

Carnaval

Portugal's Carnaval features much merrymaking in the pre-Lenten celebrations. Loulé boasts the best parades, but Lisbon, Nazaré and Viana do Castelo all throw a respectable bash.

Fantasporto

Porto's world-renowned two-week international festival (www.fantasporto.com) celebrates fantasy, horror and just plain weird films.

Essência do Vinho

Oenophiles are in their element at this wine gathering (www.essenciadovinhoporto.com), held in late February in the sublime setting of Palácio da Bolsa. Some 3000 wines from 350 producers are available for tasting.

March

March days are rainy and chilly in much of Portugal, though the south sees more sunshine. Prices remain low, and travellers are few and far between.

Festival Internacional do Chocolate

For several days early in the month Óbidos celebrates the sweet temptation of the cacao bean (www.festivalchocolate.cm-obidos.pt).

April

Spring arrives, bringing warmer temperatures and abundant sunshine in both the north and the south. Late April sees a profusion of wild flowers in the south.

Semana Santa

The build-up to Easter is magnificent in the Minho's saintly Braga. During Holy Week, barefoot penitents process through the streets, past rows of makeshift altars, with an explosion of jubilation at the cathedral on the eve of Easter.

Ovibeja

This huge five-day agricultural fair in Beja features concerts every night, with handicrafts booths and abundant food stalls.

May

Lovely sunny weather and the lack of peak-season crowds make May an ideal time to visit. The beaches of the Algarve awake from their slumber and see a smattering of travellers passing through.

Feira das Cantarinhas

This huge three-day street fair of traditional handicrafts takes place in Bragança.

Queima das Fitas

Join the mayhem of the Burning of the Ribbons at the University of Coimbra (Portugal's Oxford), as students celebrate the end of the academic year with concerts, a parade and copious amounts of drinking (www.queimadasfitas.org).

Festa das Cruzes

Barcelos turns into a fairground of flags, flowers, coloured lights and open-air concerts at the Festival of the Crosses. The biggest days are 1 to 3 May. Monsanto, in the Beiras, also celebrates, with singing and dancing beside a medieval castle.

Festa do Mar

Celebrating the age-old love of the sea (and the patron saints of fishers), this festival brings a flotilla of fishing boats to Nazaré's harbour, as well as a colourful parade of elaborately decorated floats. There's plenty of eating and drinking.

Fátima Romaris

Hundreds of thousands make the pilgrimage to Fátima each year to commemorate the apparitions of the Virgin that occurred on 13 May 1917. The pilgrimage also happens on 12 and 13 October. (p491)

Serralves em Festa

This huge cultural event (www.serralvesemfesta.com) runs for 40 hours non-stop over one weekend in late May. Parque de Serralves hosts the main events, with concerts, avant-garde theatre and kids' activities. Other open-air events happen all over town.

June

Early summer is one of the liveliest times to visit, as the festival calendar is packed. Warm, sunny days are the norm, and while tourism picks up, the hordes have yet to arrive.

Fado no Castelo

Lisbon's love affair with fado reaches a high point at this annual songfest held at the cinematic Castelo de São Jorge over three evenings in June.

Festa do Corpo de Deus

This religious fest happens all across northern Portugal on Corpus Christi but is liveliest in Monção, with an old-fashioned medieval fair, theatrical shows and over-the-top processions.

Festival Med

Loulé's world-music festival (www.festivalmed.pt), held over three days, brings more than 50 bands playing an incredible variety of music. World cuisine accompanies the global beats.

Vaca das Cordas & Corpus Christi

Ponte de Lima gets rowdy during this unusual event, which features a bull on a rope let loose on the streets. A more solemn event follows, with religious processions along flower-strewn streets.

Festas de Junho

Amarante goes wild for its favourite saint and patron of lovers, São Gonçalo. All-night music, fireworks, markets and processions mark the occasion.

Festa de Santo António

The lively Festival of St Anthony is celebrated with fervour in Lisbon's Alfama and Madragoa districts, with feasting, drinking and dancing in some 50 *arraiais* (street parties).

Festa de São João

St John is the favourite up north, where Porto, Braga and Vila do Conde celebrate with elaborate processions, music and feasting, while folks go around whacking each other with plastic hammers.

Feira Nacional da Agricultura

One of Portugal's biggest country fairs, this family-fun event (www.cnema.pt) turns Santarém into an oversized playground for horse racing, bullfights, live music, feasting and dancing; there's loads of entertainment for kids.

Festas Populares

Celebrating the feast days of São João and São Pedro, Évora hosts a lively 12-day event that kicks off in late June. There's a traditional fairground, art exhibitions, gourmet food and drink, cultural events and sporting competitions.

July

The summer heat arrives, bringing sunseekers who pack the resorts of the Algarve. Lisbon and Porto also swell with crowds and prices peak in July and August.

Festival Internacional de Folclore

The week-long International Folk Festival in late July brings costumed dancers and traditional groups to Porto.

Mercado Medieval

Don your armour and head to the castle grounds for this lively two-week medieval fair (www.mercadomedievalobidos.pt) in Óbidos. Attractions include wandering minstrels, jousting matches and plenty of grog. Other medieval fairs are held in Silves and other castle towns.

Marés Vivas

Over a weekend in mid-July, Afurada dusts off its party clothes to host the Marés Vivas (http://maresvivas.meo.pt), which welcomes big rock and pop names to the stage. Headliners in recent years have included the Prodigy, Lenny Kravitz, Skrillex and *fadista* Ana Moura.

August

The mercury shoots up in August, with sweltering days best spent at the beach. This is Portugal's busiest tourist month, and reserving ahead is essential.

Festas de Cidade e Gualterianas

The old city of Guimarães brings revellers from across the region to its colourful processions, with allegorical floats, folk dancing, fireworks and bands (www.aoficina.pt).

Festival do Sudoeste

The Alentejan Glastonbury, in Zambujeira do Mar, attracts a young, surfy crowd with huge parties and big-name bands headlining (www.meosudoeste.pt).

Festival do Marisco

Seafood-lovers should not miss this fest (www.festivaldomarisco.com) in Olhão. Highlights include regional specialities like chargrilled fish, *caldeirada* (fish stew) and *cataplana* (a kind of Portuguese paella); there's also live music.

Romaria de Nossa Senhora d'Agonia

The Minho's most spectacular festival (www.festas-agonia.com), in Viana do Castelo, has street paintings, folk costumes, drumming and much merrymaking.

Feira de São Mateus

Folk music, traditional food and fireworks rule the day at St Matthew's Fair (www.feirasaomateus.pt) in Viseu.

Folkfaro

A musician's treat, Folkfaro (www.folkfaro.com) brings local and international folk performers to the city of Faro for staged and impromptu performances across town. Street fairs accompany the event.

Noites Ritual Rock

Towards the end of summer, Porto hosts a free weekend-long rock bash that sees up-and-coming bands from around Portugal work big crowds at the Jardins do Palácio de Cristal.

September

Peak tourist season officially runs until mid-September, when ongoing warm weather ensures beaches remain packed. Things cool down a bit, and prices dip, as the crowds dissipate by late September.

Festa de Nossa Senhora dos Remédios

Head to Lamego, in the Douro, for a mix of religious devotion and secular revelry. In early September, rock concerts and all-night celebrations coincide with pious processions winding through the streets.

Nossa Senhora da Nazaré

The festival of Our Lady of Nazaré brings much life to this eponymous town in Estremadura, with rich processions, folk music and dancing, bullfights and other competitions.

Feiras Novas

One of Portugal's oldest ongoing events, the New Fairs festival has a massive market and fair, with folk dances, fireworks and brass bands at Ponte de Lima.

December

December means rain and colder temperatures. Few travellers venture south, where many resorts close for the winter. Christmas and New Year's Eve bring merriment to the somewhat dreary season.

Festa dos Rapazes

Just after Christmas, the so-called Festival of the Lads is a rollicking time of merrymaking by young unmarried men, who light bonfires and rampage around in rags and wooden masks. Catch it in Miranda do Douro.

Plan Your Trip
Itineraries

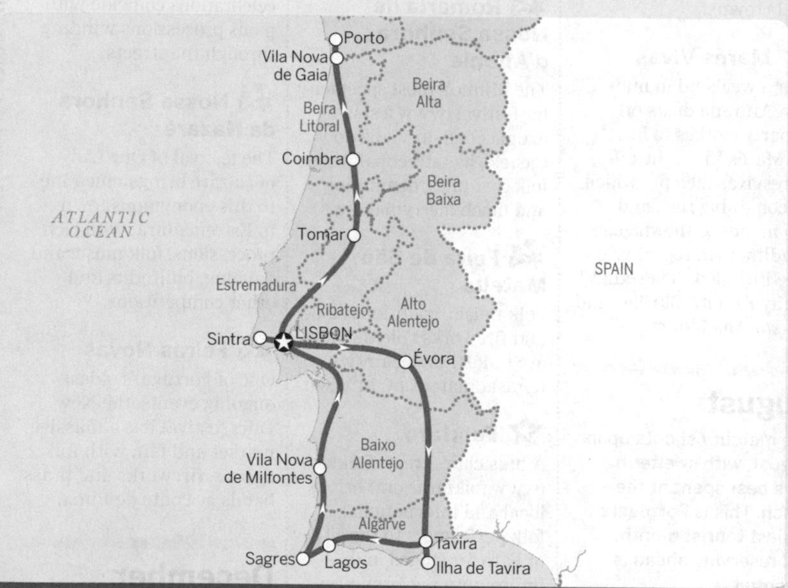

Highlights of Portugal

This grand journey takes you from the vibrant Portuguese capital to the sunny beaches of the Algarve and up north to striking, riverside Porto. Along the way, you'll visit Unesco World Heritage Sites, stroll medieval town centres and sample the varied cuisines of the north, south and centre.

Start in **Lisbon**, spending two days exploring the city's enchanting neighbourhoods, fado-filled taverns, atmospheric cafes and restaurants, and late-night street parties. Take vertiginous tram rides, and visit the hilltop castle and viewing points, museums and historic sites. On day three, head to nearby **Sintra**, for quaint village life amid woodlands and palaces. Next, enjoy two days exploring fascinating **Évora** and its nearby megaliths. From there, go south and spend a day in peaceful **Tavira**, one of the Algarve's prettiest towns, and then take the ferry out to car-free **Ilha de Tavira**. Continue west to beach- and nightlife-loving **Lagos**. Don't miss the pretty beaches (Batata, Dona Ana and Camilo) south of town. Keep going west until you hit laid-back **Sagres**, where you can

Sunset over Porto (p359)

visit its dramatically sited fort, surf good waves and contemplate the endless horizon at the cliffs near town. Go north back to Lisbon, stopping en route in the coastal town of **Vila Nova de Milfontes**, a great spot for uber-fresh seafood grilled to perfection. You can eat it right on the waterfront. Spend a day in **Tomar**, a sleepy river town that's home to the staggering Convento de Cristo. Then book two nights in the venerable university town of **Coimbra**, wandering the old quarters, visiting medieval convents and churches, and enjoying good meals, lively bars (during the academic year) and live music. Spend your last two days in **Porto**, Lisbon's rival in beauty. Enjoy a day exploring the Ribeira, visiting avant-garde galleries and museums, and taking in the nightlife in the city centre. Then head across the river to **Vila Nova de Gaia** for an introduction to the country's great ports. If time allows, take a boat trip along the Rio Douro, passing through dramatic gorge scenery and alongside centuries-old vineyards.

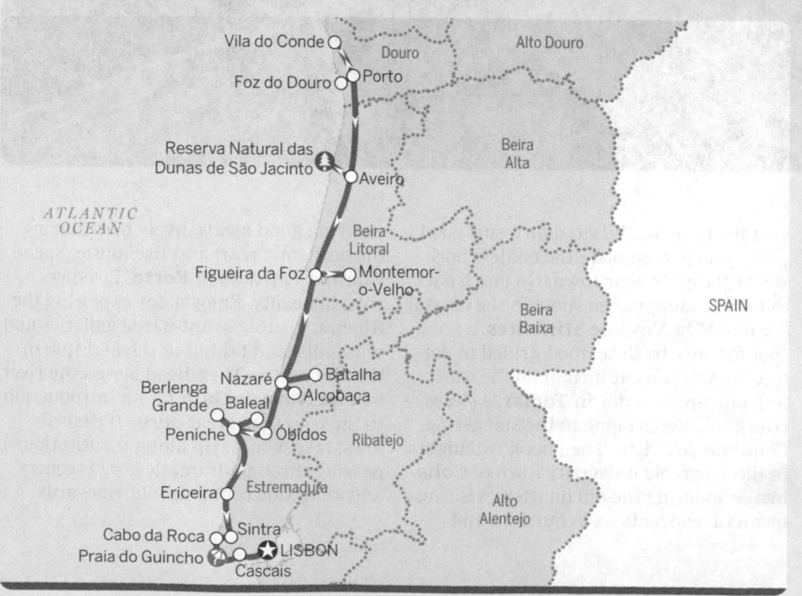
Vila do Conde
Douro
Alto Douro
Foz do Douro
Porto
Reserva Natural das
Dunas de São Jacinto
Aveiro
Beira
Alta
ATLANTIC
OCEAN
Beira
Litoral
Figueira da Foz
Montemor-
o-Velho
Beira
Baixa
SPAIN
Nazaré
Batalha
Berlenga
Grande
Baleal
Alcobaça
Peniche
Óbidos
Ribatejo
Ericeira
Estremadura
Alto
Alentejo
Sintra
Cabo da Roca
Praia do Guincho
LISBON
Cascais

ALBERTO LOTO / SHUTTERSTOCK ©

SAIKO3P / SHUTTERSTOCK ©

Top: Aveiro (p323)
Bottom: Mosteiro de Santa Maria de Alcobaça (p280)

3 WEEKS Exploring the Atlantic Coast

Scenic shorelines, captivating towns and staggering architectural monuments set the stage for this memorable journey down the Atlantic coast.

Begin in **Porto**, the port-wine capital at the mouth of the Douro. Spend two days exploring its historic centre, museums, parks and gardens, plus the beach neighbourhood of **Foz do Douro**. On the third day go north to the seaside town of **Vila do Conde**, a quick and popular beach getaway. Next, head south to **Aveiro**, for rides along its scenic canals from high-prowed *moliceiros* (traditional boats). For a fine day trip from here, take a bus and ferry out to the **Reserva Natural das Dunas de São Jacinto**, a scenic nature reserve and birdwatching site. The popular resort town of **Figueira da Foz** is the next stop; you'll find prime surfing, a touch of nightlife and wide people-packed beaches, with more isolated sands out of town. After a day of sunbaking, make an inland day trip to the striking mountaintop castle of **Montemor-o-Velho**. The picturesque and fun-loving beach town of **Nazaré** is next and here you can frolic in the waves, enjoy traditional seafood restaurants and take the funicular to a clifftop promontory for superb views. Nazaré is also a good base for exploring the architecturally stunning monasteries (and Unesco World Heritage Sites) in **Alcobaça** and **Batalha**. From there, head south to **Óbidos**, with its cobblestone lanes and upmarket inns. Go west back to the coast to reach **Peniche**, where you'll find excellent beaches, particularly in nearby **Baleal**. From Peniche, be sure to take a boat out to the remote island of **Berlenga Grande**. You can even stay overnight (reserve well ahead). Continue south to **Ericeira**, a whitewashed village perched atop sandstone cliffs. Explore the beaches, feast on seafood, then continue on to the fairy-tale setting of **Sintra**, where picturesque guest houses make a fine overnight stay. Take the road to the coast, and follow it out to the dramatically set **Cabo da Roca** and down to the windswept beach of **Praia do Guincho**. The next stop is the pretty village of **Cascais**, home to narrow pedestrian lanes, lively outdoor restaurants and leafy gardens. End your journey in **Lisbon**, spending a few days exploring Portugal's vibrant capital.

Circling the Centre

Dramatic scenery, frozen-in-time villages and clifftop castles make for a charming journey on this loop around Portugal's often overlooked interior.

From **Lisbon** head 200km southeast to the historic village of **Castro Verde**. Visit the royal basilica in town then the LPN Interpretative and Environmental Centre, a great spot for birdwatching some 5km north of town. Drive east to **Mértola**, a picturesque medieval settlement perched high above the placid Rio Guadiana. Wander the old streets, go kayaking on the river, sample wild boar (a local speciality) and overnight in one of the area's charming inns. From Mértola, drive north to **Beja**, a lively town with a walled centre, intriguing museums and a 13th-century castle with sweeping views over golden wheat fields beyond town. Keep north to reach **Évora**, the most vibrant town in the Alentejo. Its large cobblestone centre is a great place to wander, and is packed with history (don't miss the Bone Chapel and Roman temple). Évora has great traditional restaurants and makes a good base for visiting Neolithic sites in the countryside. Head northeast to the marble town of **Vila Viçosa**, home to a staggering palace and a peaceful town centre. Next up is **Castelo de Vide**, a wildly remote-feeling town set on a clifftop. Wander through the sleepy streets, have lunch, and then continue to Monsanto, another photogenic castle-in-the-sky town. Leave early for the two-hour drive to **Vila Nova de Foz Côa**, gateway to some of Iberia's most extensive petroglyphs. From here, it's an easy detour to the vineyards along the Douro. Otherwise, head southwest into the **Parque Natural da Serra da Estrela**, a scenic, mountainous area with great hiking, and peaceful guest houses where you can soak up the scenery. **Manteigas** makes a great base. After a day or two in the mountains, head west to the lively university town of **Coimbra**. Visit the historic campus, stroll the riverbank, feast on hearty Portuguese cooking and catch live Coimbra-style fado. Visit **Conímbriga**, southwest of Coimbra, for a look at Roman ruins, then continue to **Santarém**, with its Gothic architecture, atmospheric restaurants and panoramic views, before finishing the tour in Lisbon.

AITORMMFOTO / SHUTTERSTOCK ©

MATT MUNRO / LONELY PLANET ©

Top: Mértola (p251)
Bottom: Sardines, Castelo de Vide (p241)

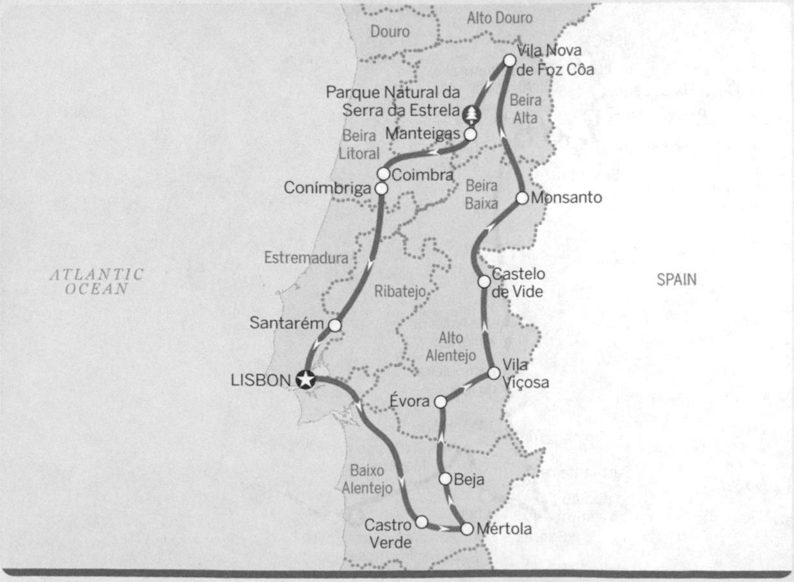

Alto Douro
Douro
Vila Nova de Foz Côa
Parque Natural da Serra da Estrela
Beira Alta
Manteigas
Beira Litoral
Coimbra
Conímbriga
Beira Baixa
Monsanto
Estremadura
ATLANTIC OCEAN
Castelo de Vide
SPAIN
Ribatejo
Santarém
Alto Alentejo
Vila Viçosa
LISBON
Évora
Baixo Alentejo
Beja
Castro Verde
Mértola

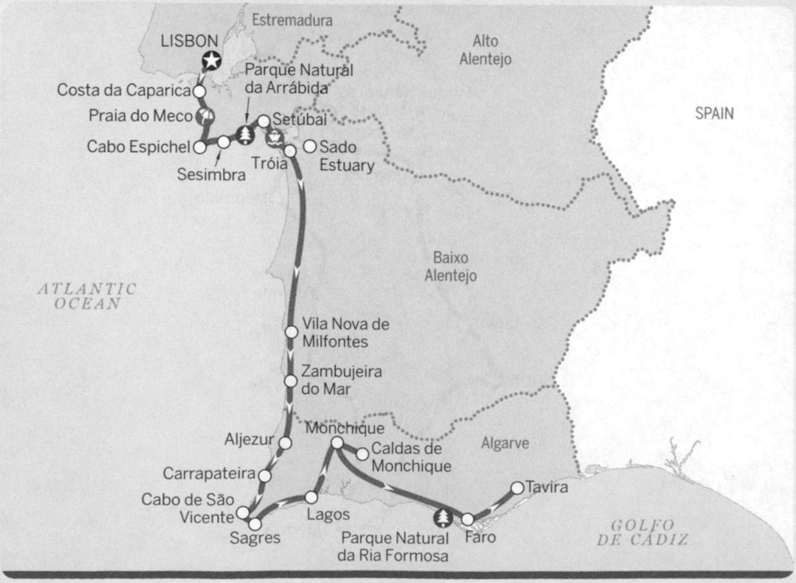

Estremadura
LISBON
Alto Alentejo
Parque Natural da Arrábida
Costa da Caparica
Praia do Meco
Setúbal
SPAIN
Cabo Espichel
Sesimbra
Tróia
Sado Estuary
Baixo Alentejo
ATLANTIC OCEAN
Vila Nova de Milfontes
Zambujeira do Mar
Monchique
Aljezur
Caldas de Monchique
Algarve
Carrapateira
Tavira
Cabo de São Vicente
Lagos
Sagres
Parque Natural da Ria Formosa
Faro
GOLFO DE CÁDIZ

STOCKPHOTOSART / SHUTTERSTOCK ©

RENAUD VISAGE / GETTY IMAGES ©

Top: Festival, Sesimbra (p144)
Bottom: Lisbon (p61) at night

Southern Beauty

This trip will give you a chance to see spectacular contrasts in scenery by following Portugal's southern rivers, beaches and ridges.

From **Lisbon** head to the **Costa da Caparica**, taking in the festive beaches near the town, and then escaping the crowds on wilder beaches to the south. Next head down to **Praia do Meco** for more sandy action and some great seafood. Keep going south to reach the desolate cliffs of **Cabo Espichel**. A good place to stay for the night is at a rural guest house outside **Sesimbra**, a fishing village turned resort with open-air restaurants and family-friendly beaches. On the next day, continue east, stopping for a picnic on the forest-lined shores of **Parque Natural da Arrábida**. At night, stay in **Setúbal** for more seafood feasting and a wander through the sleepy old-town quarters. The next day, book a dolphin-watching boat trip along the **Sado Estuary**. From Setúbal, take the ferry across to handsomely sited **Tróia**. Continue south to overnight in **Vila Nova de Milfontes**, a lovely seaside town with fine beaches and charming places to stay. Next is **Zambujeira do Mar**, a tiny village perched above a pretty beach. Follow the coast to **Aljezur**, with its unspoilt, cliff-backed sands, and into the rustic town of **Carrapateira**, with more wild, untouched beaches, plus cafes and guest houses catering to the surf-loving crowd. Head south, and you'll reach the southern coast at pretty, laid-back **Sagres**, another surfers town. Visit Sagres' sea-cliff fortress, then the surreal cliffs of **Cabo de São Vicente**. Go east to **Lagos**, one of the Algarve's liveliest towns, with loads of good sleeping, eating and drinking options. Afterwards, go inland to **Monchique**, with its densely wooded hillsides that offer picturesque walking, cycling and pony-trekking opportunities, followed by a spa visit in **Caldas de Monchique**. Back on the coast, stay overnight in the old town centre of lively **Faro**, before journeying out to the **Parque Natural da Ria Formosa**, a lagoon system full of marsh, creeks and dune islands. From there, head to **Tavira**, set with genteel 18th-century buildings straddling the Rio Gilão.

Off the Beaten Track: Portugal

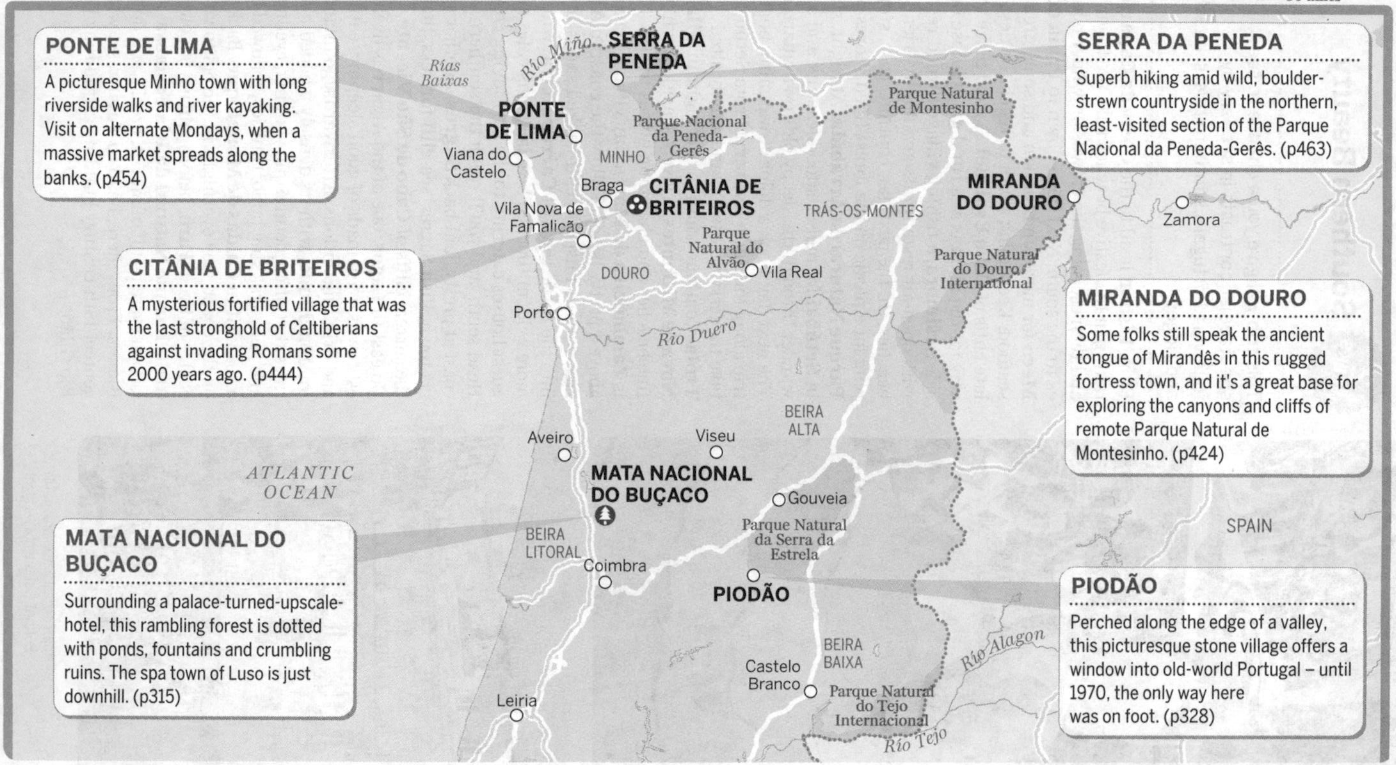

PONTE DE LIMA

A picturesque Minho town with long riverside walks and river kayaking. Visit on alternate Mondays, when a massive market spreads along the banks. (p454)

CITÂNIA DE BRITEIROS

A mysterious fortified village that was the last stronghold of Celtiberians against invading Romans some 2000 years ago. (p444)

MATA NACIONAL DO BUÇACO

Surrounding a palace-turned-upscale-hotel, this rambling forest is dotted with ponds, fountains and crumbling ruins. The spa town of Luso is just downhill. (p315)

SERRA DA PENEDA

Superb hiking amid wild, boulder-strewn countryside in the northern, least-visited section of the Parque Nacional da Peneda-Gerês. (p463)

MIRANDA DO DOURO

Some folks still speak the ancient tongue of Mirandês in this rugged fortress town, and it's a great base for exploring the canyons and cliffs of remote Parque Natural de Montesinho. (p424)

PIODÃO

Perched along the edge of a valley, this picturesque stone village offers a window into old-world Portugal – until 1970, the only way here was on foot. (p328)

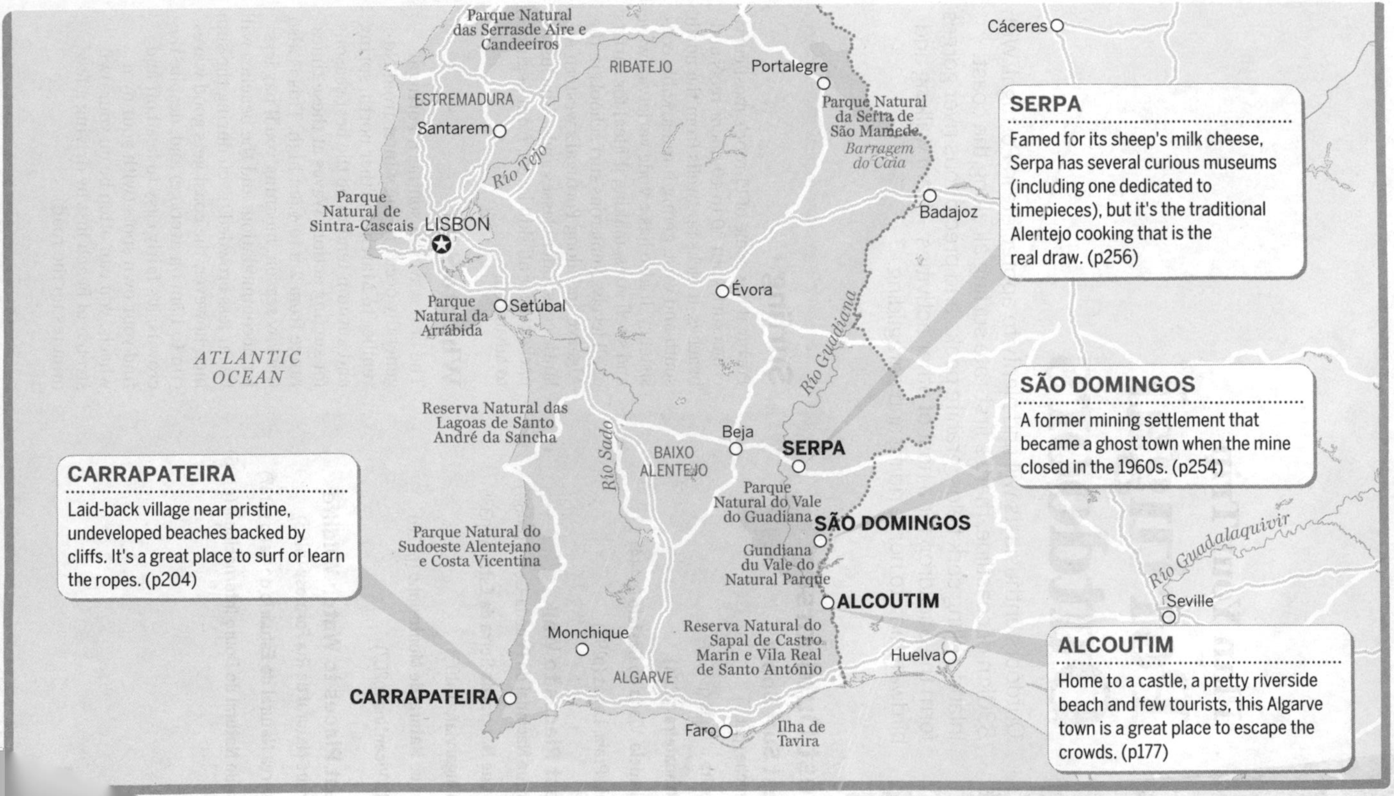

SERPA

Famed for its sheep's milk cheese, Serpa has several curious museums (including one dedicated to timepieces), but it's the traditional Alentejo cooking that is the real draw. (p256)

SÃO DOMINGOS

A former mining settlement that became a ghost town when the mine closed in the 1960s. (p254)

CARRAPATEIRA

Laid-back village near pristine, undeveloped beaches backed by cliffs. It's a great place to surf or learn the ropes. (p204)

ALCOUTIM

Home to a castle, a pretty riverside beach and few tourists, this Algarve town is a great place to escape the crowds. (p177)

Parque Natural das Serrasde Aire e Candeeiros
RIBATEJO
Portalegre
Cáceres
ESTREMADURA
Santarem
Parque Natural da Serra de São Mamede
Barragem do Caia
Río Tejo
Badajoz
Parque Natural de Sintra-Cascais
LISBON
Évora
Parque Natural da Arrábida
Setúbal
ATLANTIC OCEAN
Río Guadiana
Reserva Natural das Lagoas de Santo André da Sancha
Beja
BAIXO ALENTEJO
SERPA
Río Sado
Parque Natural do Vale do Guadiana
SÃO DOMINGOS
Parque Natural do Sudoeste Alentejano e Costa Vicentina
Gundiana du Vale do Natural Parque
ALCOUTIM
Río Guadalaquivir
Seville
Monchique
Reserva Natural do Sapal de Castro Marin e Vila Real de Santo António
Huelva
ALGARVE
CARRAPATEIRA
Faro
Ilha de Tavira

Plan Your Trip
Portugal Outdoors

Outdoors enthusiasts will find plenty to appreciate in Portugal. With 830km of coastline, there's first-rate surfing all along the coast. Inland, rolling cork fields, granite peaks and precipitous river gorges form the backdrop for a host of other activities – from walking and birdwatching to horse riding and paragliding.

Best Outdoors

Best Surf Spots

Peniche (p269)

Ribeira d'Ilhas (p266)

Carrapateira (p204)

Cabedelo, Viana do Castelo (p444)

Meia Praia, Lagos (p193)

Best Places to Walk

Parque Nacional da Peneda-Gerês (p460)

Parque Natural da Serra da Estrela (p335)

Via Algarviana (p195)

Parque Natural de Montesinho (p420)

Rota Vicentina (p207)

Best Places to Watch Wildlife

Parque Natural da Ria Formosa (p165)

Reserva Natural do Estuário do Sado (p147)

Parque Natural do Douro Internacional (p426)

Surfing

Portugal has some of Europe's most curvaceous surf, with 30 to 40 major reefs and beaches. It picks up swells from the north, south and west, giving it remarkable consistency. It also has a wide variety of waves and swell sizes, making it ideal for surfers of all levels. Numerous surf schools in the Algarve and along Portugal's western Atlantic coast offer classes and all-inclusive packages for all skill levels, from beginners to advanced.

When to Surf

The best waves in southern Portugal generally occur in the winter from November to March. Further north, spring and autumn tend to be the best seasons for surfing action. Waves at these times range from 2m to 4.5m high. This is also the low season, meaning you'll pay less for accommodation, and the beaches will be far less crowded. Even during the summer, however, the coast gets good waves (1m to 1.5m on average) and, despite the crowds, it's fairly easy to head off and find your own spots (with your own wheels, you can often be on your own stretch of beach just by driving a few minutes up the road).

WORLD CHAMPIONSHIP WAVES

In 2009 Portugal's surf scene got a real shot in the arm when Supertubos beach near Peniche was chosen as one of 10 stops on the ASP World Tour, the most prestigious international competitive surfing event. For 12 days in October, the beach was packed with surfers from around the world showing off their best moves. The event's organisers apparently liked what they saw – Supertubos has hosted the international contest (today known as the WSL Championship Tour) every year since then.

Supertubos isn't the only spot in Portugal with legendary breaks. Some 60km north of Peniche, you'll find some of the world's tallest waves, thanks to a deep-water canyon connected to the shoreline. Pro Hawaiian surfer Garrett McNamara set the world record for the largest wave ever ridden in 2011, when he surfed a wave reportedly 30.5m (100ft) high.

Essential Gear

The water temperature here is colder than it is in most other southern European countries, and even in the summer you'll probably want a wetsuit. Board and wetsuit hire are widely available at surf shops and surf camps; you can usually score a discount if you rent long-term – otherwise, you'll be paying around €20 to €30 per day for a board and wetsuit, or €15 to €25 per day for the board only.

Prime Spots

One of Portugal's best breaks is around Peniche (p269), where you can count on good waves with just about any wind. An excellent hostel and several residential surf camps make this an affordable base. Supertubos and Baleal are the most popular local beaches.

Other fabled surf spots include Ribeira d'Ilhas in Ericeira (p266) and Praia do Guincho near Cascais, which often host international championships. Another break that's famous among the global surfing community is Carrapateira (p204) in the western Algarve. Schools and clubs head over this way from Lagos and further afield to take advantage of the crashing waves. Nearby, the area around Praia do Penedo is a good choice for beginners.

There are countless other good surf spots up and down the coast including, but by no means limited to, the following, from north to south: Viana do Castelo, Praia da Barra, Costa Nova, Figueira da Foz, Nazaré, Costa da Caparica, Sesimbra, Vila Nova de Milfontes and Zambujeira.

Surf Schools & Operators

There are dozens of schools that can help you improve your surfing game. Most offer weekly packages including simple accommodation (dorms, bungalows or camping), meals and transport to the beach.

Recommended surf camps north of Lisbon include Ericeira's Rapture Surf Camp (p266) and the camps at Baleal (p270).

In the Algarve you will have your pick of countless operators, many of them concentrated around Lagos, Sagres and Carrapateira.

Online Resources

For information on wave conditions, competitions and more, surf on over to one of these helpful sites.

www.magicseaweed.com International site with English-language surf reports for many Portuguese beaches.

www.surfingportugal.com Official site of the Portuguese Surfing Federation.

www.surftotal.com Portuguese-language site with news about the national surf scene and webcams showing conditions at a dozen popular beaches around Portugal.

Walking

Portugal's wonderful walking potential is all the better because so few people know about it. Most organised walking clubs are in the Algarve, with marked trails and regular meetings. There is a cluster of organisations around the Monchique

Portugal Outdoors

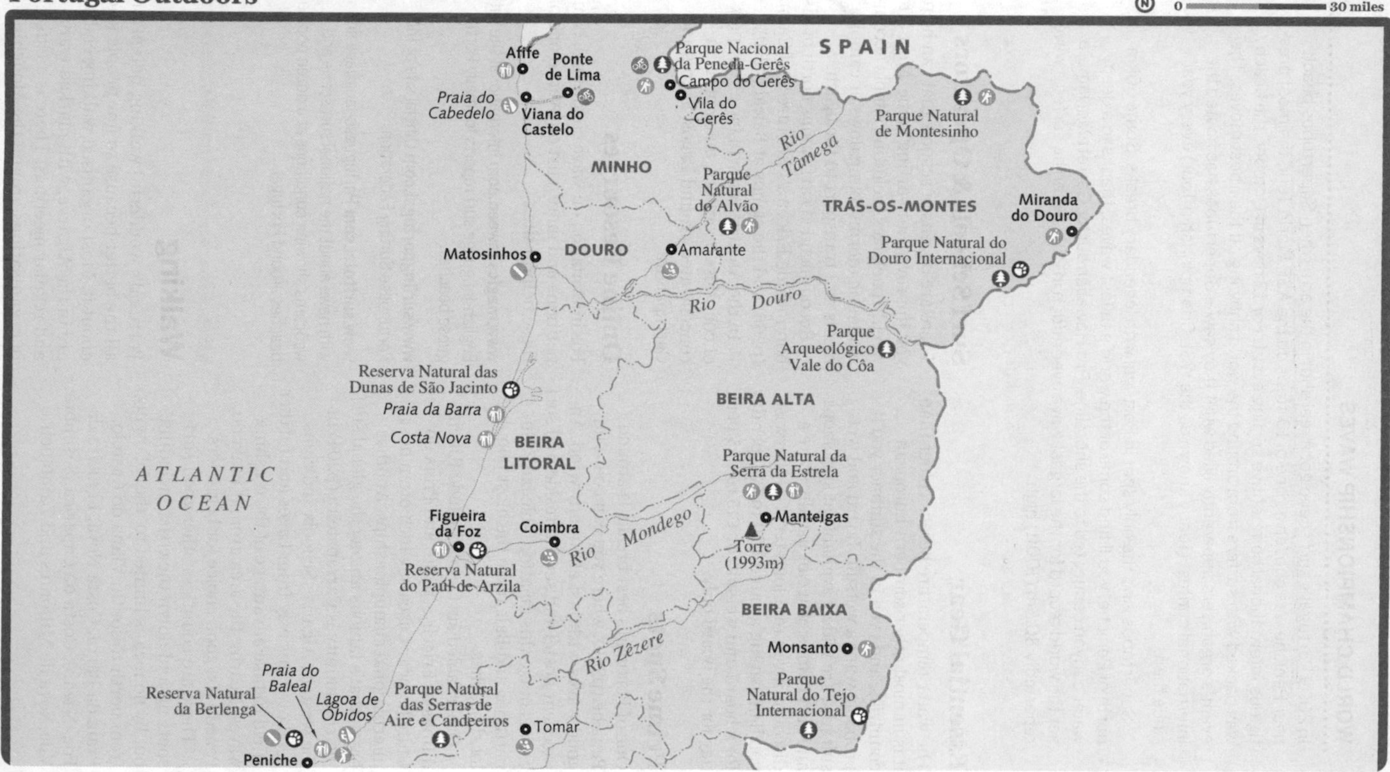

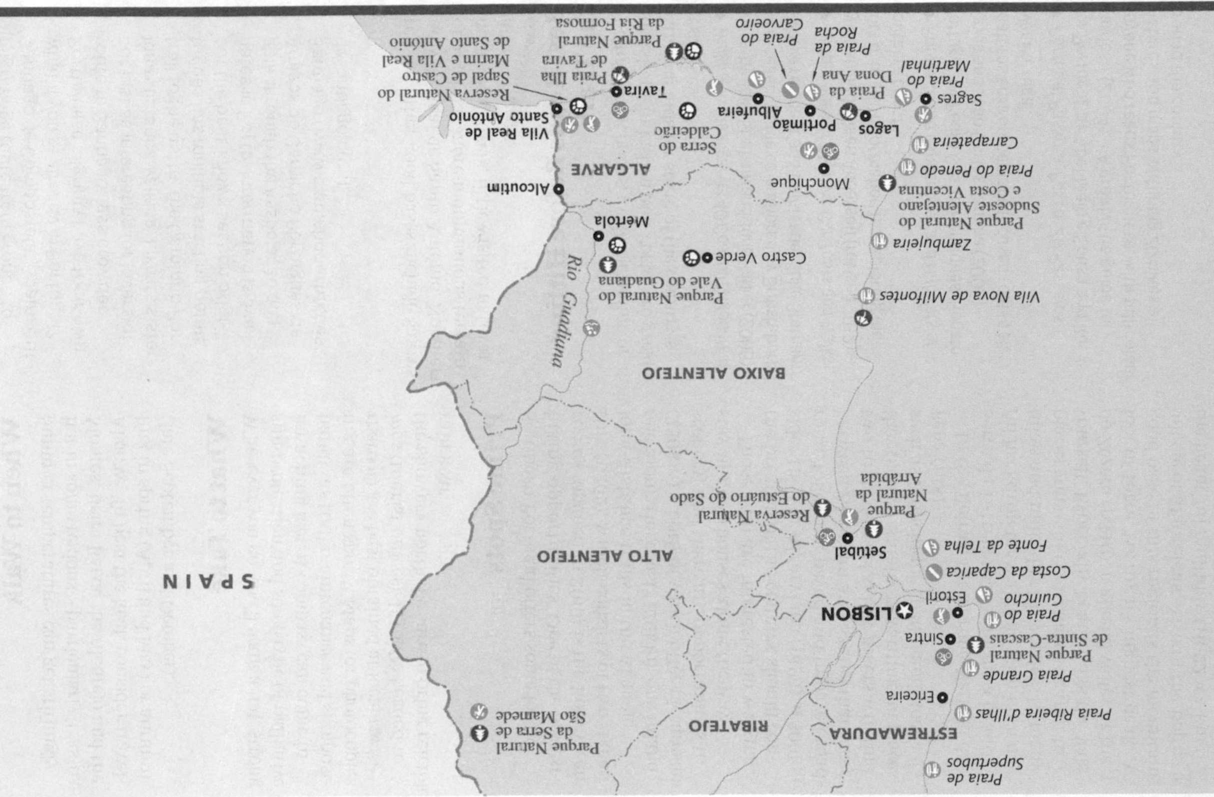
SPAIN
ESTREMADURA
RIBATEJO
ALTO ALENTEJO
BAIXO ALENTEJO
ALGARVE
Praia de Supertubos
Praia Ribeira d'Ilhas
Ericeira
Praia Grande
Parque Natural de Sintra-Cascais
Sintra
Praia do Guincho
Estoril
LISBON
Costa da Caparica
Fonte da Telha
Setúbal
Parque Natural da Arrábida
Reserva Natural do Estuário do Sado
Parque Natural da Serra de São Mamede
Vila Nova de Milfontes
Zambujeira
Parque Natural do Sudoeste Alentejano e Costa Vicentina
Praia do Penedo
Carrapateira
Sagres
Praia do Martinhal
Lagos
Praia da Dona Ana
Praia da Rocha
Portimão
Monchique
Albufeira
Praia do Carvoeiro
Castro Verde
Parque Natural do Vale do Guadiana
Mértola
Rio Guadiana
Alcoutim
Serra do Caldeirão
Tavira
Parque Natural da Ria Formosa
Praia Ilha de Tavira
Vila Real de Santo António
Reserva Natural do Sapal de Castro Marim e Vila Real de Santo António

SANTIAGO DE COMPOSTELA

Every year thousands of walkers from around the world hike the Camino de Santiago, the classic pilgrimage route from France to Santiago de Compostela, Spain. But what if you're already in Portugal? Portuguese pilgrims have their own route to Santiago, less crowded but just as interesting for lovers of long-distance walking. Like its sister trail to the north, the Caminho Português has multiple starting points, but the best-known section originates in Porto. Information is available through the Associação dos Amigos do Caminho Português de Santiago (www.caminhoportuguesdesantiago.com).

area but other good bases include Sagres and Vila Real de Santo António. Northern Portugal has more mountainous terrain and several lovely, little-visited natural parks.

Best Reads Before Hitting the Trail

The following books, available online or at bookshops in Lisbon and Porto, are great planning aids for some of the country's best hikes.

- *Walking in the Algarve: 40 Coastal & Mountain Walks*, by Julie Statham and June Parker (2006) – An excellent guide co-authored by British-born Algarve resident and tour leader Julie Statham.
- *Landscapes of Algarve: Car Tours and Walks*, by Brian and Eileen Anderson (revised 2012) – Lots of useful information for exploring the southern coast.
- *Routes to the Landscapes and Habitats of Portugal*, by Pedro Castro Henriques, Renato Neves and João Carlos Farinha (2005) – Features environmentally focused routes all over Portugal.
- *Portugal Passo-a-Passo: 20 Passeios por Portugal*, by Abel Melo e Sousa and Rui Cardoso (2004) – A great little guide for anyone who reads Portuguese, with full-colour pictures and maps outlining 20 hikes all around the country.
- *Guide to Walking Trails in the Algarve* (www.iltm.com/_novadocuments/62282) Published by Turismo de Portugal, this free downloadable guide has info on dozens of walks in the south.

When to Walk

Summer temperatures can get stiflingly hot in some regions – particularly Trás-os-Montes, Beira Baixa, the Alentejo and the Algarve. To beat the heat, consider travelling in spring (April and May) or autumn (late September and October).

What to Take

Wherever you go, you'll want a hat, strong sun protection and some type of palliative for aching feet. A compass can come in handy, as trail maintenance and signposting are often spotty. Maps (or photocopies thereof) are best obtained at local *turismos* (tourist offices). If you're headed to the showery north, be sure to bring reliable rain gear.

Prime Spots

Southern Portugal offers some lovely hiking opportunities. One of the newest routes (opened in 2013) is the Rota Vicentina (p262), which consists of two signed long-distance trails in the Alentejo – one along the coast (120km), one inland (230km) – both of which offer picturesque scenery, and there are opportunities to stay in guesthouses along the way.

Those who are interested in walking the breadth of the country should consider the Via Algarviana (p195), a 300km route following paved and unpaved roads between Alcoutim and Sagres that takes two to three weeks. Day hikers will find the Algarve equally rewarding, in places such as Monchique (p208) and Rocha da Pena (p181).

In the Beiras, the Parque Natural da Serra da Estrela (p335) forms a beautiful backdrop for walking, with both day hikes and multiday itineraries. In many places you're likely to have the trail to yourself. Especially beautiful is the Vale do Zêzere (p340), a glacial valley at the foot of Torre, Portugal's highest peak. A good base in this region is the mountain village of Manteigas. Also in the Beiras is the beautiful multiday GR-22 walking route, a 540km circuit of *aldeias históricas* (historic villages) including medieval hill towns such as Sortelha, Linhares and Monsanto.

Perhaps the country's best walking is in the far north, where Parque Nacional da Peneda-Gerês (p460) offers gorgeous hikes over mountainous terrain, encompassing forests, villages, high-altitude boulder fields, archaeological sites and ancient Roman milestones. A quiet base for adventure is Campo do Gerês (p468), while a busier touristy base (but with lots of services) is Vila do Gerês (p466). In neighbouring Trás-os-Montes, the natural parks of Montesinho (p420), Alvão (p411) and Douro Internacional (p426) also have some splendid trails connecting the region's remarkably picturesque stone villages.

Closer to civilisation, there are some great day hikes in prime tourist areas, including the walk along the top of Évora's 16th-century aqueduct (p219) and the climb from Sintra to its 9th-century Moorish castle (p124).

Walking Tours

If you love to walk but hate to plan, why not consider an organised walking tour? The companies listed here offer both group walking tours – complete with tour leader – and self-guided tours where you walk independently, following an itinerary provided by the tour company, with prearranged meals and lodging included in the price.

About 10km north of Sagres, walking-guide author Julie Statham runs **Portugal Walks** (☎965 753 033; www.portugalwalks.com), which offers week-long packages (€640 to €945), as well as self-guided walks (seven days from €560, 14 days from €870) in mainland Portugal, as well as in Madeira and the Azores.

Another dependable Portuguese outfitter offering guided walks throughout the country is **A2Z Adventures** (☎917 946 653; www.a2z-adventures.com).

Ecotourism company Sistemas de Ar Livre (p149), in Setúbal, arranges activities including three-hour guided walks.

Three noteworthy outfitters that are based out of the UK also run tours. **ATG Oxford** (www.atg-oxford.co.uk) offers week-long guided walking holidays between Sintra and Cascais; **Headwater** (www.headwater.com) leads week-long walking trips as well as cycling jaunts; and **Ramblers Holidays** (www.ramblersholidays.co.uk) has guided seven- to 10-day walking holidays in the Minho, the Douro and the Algarve.

Resources

Many *turismos* and natural-park offices offer free brochures about local walks, although materials frequently go out of print due to insufficient funding. Other organisations that produce free maps of their own trails include **Odiana** (www.odiana.pt) in the Algarve and the Centro de Interpretação da Serra da Estrela (p337) in the town of Seia in the Serra da Estrela.

Portugal uses a system of coloured blazes to mark its trails. White and red are the colours of choice for the major multiday trails known as Grandes Rotas, while red and yellow blazes indicate Pequenas Rotas (shorter day hikes).

Natural Parks & Reserves

Portugal's mixed bag of natural parks and reserves is worth the effort. The Parque Nacional da Peneda-Gerês is the country's only bona fide *parque nacional* (national park), but there are 24 other *parques naturais* (natural parks), *reservas naturais* (nature reserves) and *paisagens protegidas* (protected landscape areas). These areas total some 6500 sq km – just over 7% of Portugal's land area.

The Instituto da Conservação da Natureza e da Biodiversidade (p120) is the government agency responsible for the parks. It has general information, but detailed maps and English-language materials are sometimes hard to come by. Standards of maintenance and facilities vary wildly, but trails and resources within the parks are showing signs of improvement.

Other Outdoor Activities

While walking and cycling can be done at the drop of a hat, many other outdoor activities need a bit more organisation – and often specialist gear, as well as guides or instructors. Below are a few ideas to inform and inspire. If you need more details while you're travelling in

PARK/RESERVE	FEATURES
Parque Nacional da Peneda-Gerês (p460)	lushly forested mountains, rock-strewn plateaus, deer, birds of prey, hot springs, wolves, long-horned cattle
Parque Natural da Arrábida (p146)	coastal mountain range, birds of prey, diverse flora, damaged by wildfire
Parque Natural da Ria Formosa (p165)	salty coastal lagoons, lakes, marshes, dunes, rich bird life, beaches, Mediterranean chameleons
Parque Natural da Serra da Estrela (p335)	pristine mountains – Portugal's highest, rich bird life, rare herbs
Parque Natural das Serras de Aire e Candeeiros (p290)	limestone mountains, cave systems, covered in gorse & olive trees
Parque Natural de Montesinho (p420)	remote oasis of peaceful grassland & forest, last wild refuge for Iberian wolf
Parque Natural de Sintra-Cascais	rugged coastline & mountains, diverse flora
Parque Natural do Alvão (p411)	granite basin, pine forest, waterfalls, rich bird life, deer, boar
Parque Natural do Douro Internacional (p426)	canyon country with high cliffs & lakes, home to many endangered birds of prey
Parque Natural do Vale do Guadiana (p253)	gentle hills & plains, rivers, rare birds of prey, snakes, toads, prehistoric sites
Parque Natural do Sudoeste Alentejano e Costa Vicentina (p204)	coastal cliffs & remote beaches, unique plants, otters, foxes, 200 bird types
Reserva Natural da Berlenga (p272)	remote islands in clear seas, rock formations, caves, seabirds
Reserva Natural das Dunas de São Jacinto (p325)	thickly wooded coastal park, rich in bird life
Reserva Natural do Estuário do Sado (Sado estuary; p147)	estuary of mud, marshes, lagoons & dunes, bird life including flamingos, molluscs, bottlenose dolphins
Reserva Natural do Sapal de Castro Marim e Vila Real de Santo António (p177)	marshland & salt pans, flamingos, spoonbills, avocet, Caspian terns, white storks

Portugal, *turismos* can advise about specialist local operators and adventure centres.

Wildlife Watching

Portugal provides excellent opportunities for birdwatching, especially in Atlantic coastal lagoons and the deep river canyons along the Spanish border. In the south, prime birdwatching spots include the Serra do Caldeirão (p181), Parque Natural da Ria Formosa (p165), Parque Natural do Vale do Guadiana (p253) and the Reserva Natural do Sapal de Castro Marim e Vila Real de Santo António (p177). In the Alentejo, Castro Verde is near good birdwatching – in particular the LPN Interpretative and Environmental Centre (p256) – while the nature reserve of the Sado Estuary, Reserva Natural do Estuário do Sado (p147), near Setúbal is also a big draw.

The local environmental organisation **Formosamar** (☎918 720 002; www.formosamar.com) offers tours from Olhão in the Algarve, including a 2½-hour trip for €35 per person (minimum four people) in Parque Natural da Ria Formosa, employing marine biologists and raptor specialists as guides.

North of Lisbon, the Ilhas Berlengas make a perfect place to observe seabirds. Other good places for birdwatching include Reserva Natural do Paúl de Arzila near Coimbra; Dunas de São Jacinto (p328) near Aveiro; and the Tejo and Douro gorges, where vultures and eagles nest in the Parque Natural do Tejo Internacional and Parque Natural do Douro Internacional (p426).

Portugal's leading ornithological society is the **Sociedade Portuguêsa para o Estudo de Aves** (Map p82; ☎213 220 430; www.spea.pt; Avenida João Crisóstomo 18, Lisbon; ⏲9.30am-1pm & 2-6pm Mon-Fri), which runs government-funded projects to map the distribution of Portugal's breeding birds.

For birdwatching and other nature-oriented guided excursions in the Algarve, Natura Algarve (p159) offers boat-based trips through the Parque Natural da Ria Formosa.

UK-based Naturetrek (www.naturetrek.co.uk) runs an eight-day birdwatching excursion around southern Portugal starting at £1295.

Various companies in the Algarve and around the Sado estuary offer dolphin-spotting trips, including Mar Ilimitado (p200), Dolphins Driven (p183), Dizzy Dolphins (p194) and **Algarve Dolphins** (☎282 788 513; www.algarve-dolphins.com; adult/child from €35/25).

Cycling

Portugal has many exhilarating opportunities for mountain biking (*bicicleta todo terreno;* BTT). Monchique (p208) and Tavira (p167) in the Algarve, Sintra (p123) and Setúbal (p147) in central Portugal and Parque Nacional da Peneda-Gerês (p460) in the north are all popular starting points.

Bicycle trails are also growing in popularity. Rio Lima in the north has a handful of short greenways (ranging from 8km to 13.3km) that are popular with cyclists, walkers and runners. Another rail-to-trails initiative, the 49km **Ecopista do Dão** (www.ecopista-portugal.com) between Viseu and Santa Comba Dão in the Beiras, opened in 2011; there are even places to rent bikes near the start in Santa Comba Dão. Down south, the ambitious Ecovia do Litoral is a 220km cycling route across the Algarve that connects Cabo de São Vicente at Portugal's southwestern tip to Vila Real de Santo António on the Spanish border. For more information on the *ecovia* and other *ecovias* around Portugal, the *Ecovias Portugal Road Book* with maps and other key info is available for purchase online at www.ecoviasportugal.wix.com/ecovias portugal.

Meanwhile, bike paths have become fixtures of the urban landscape around Lisbon and in northern cities such as Porto, Coimbra and Guarda; popular bike trails have also cropped up in coastal venues such as the Estremadura's Pinhal de Leiria (p287) and the Lisbon coast between Cascais and Praia do Guincho.

PENNILESS PEDALLING

Fancy a ride without spending a euro-cent? An increasing number of Portuguese towns have adopted free bike programs. In places such as Aveiro and Cascais you can show up at the local free-bike agency, provide a photo ID, fill out a short form and hey, presto! – off you go on your very own bicycle.

Cycling Tours

If you're looking for a good day trip or a longer cycling holiday, there are a number of excellent companies that can point you in the right direction.

In Lisbon, **Portugal Bike** (☎214 783 153; www.portugalbike.com) has an excellent selection of bike tours. Trips go through the Algarve, the Minho or the Alentejo. There's also a route that follows the Camino de Santiago through northern Portugal and into Spain. Tours run five to 10 days and are available guided or self-guided.

Pedal Portugal (www.pedalportugal.com) is a well-established company offering both guided and self-guided bike tours throughout Portugal.

Based out of the USA, **Easy Rider Tours** (www.easyridertours.com) features several guided cycling itineraries in the Minho, Alentejo and Algarve, and along the Lisbon coast near Sintra.

From the UK, **Saddle Skedaddle** (www.skedaddle.co.uk) has both guided and self-guided tours lasting seven to nine days. Trips go through the eastern Beiras and the Alentejo (with a coastal and an inland route).

Rock Climbing, Paragliding & Adrenalin Sports

In the far north, the granite peaks of Parque Nacional da Peneda-Gerês (p460) are a climber's paradise. Other popular places are the schist cliffs at Nossa Senhora do Salto, east of Porto; the rugge

500m-tall granite outcropping of Cántaro Magro in the Serra da Estrela (p335); the limestone crags of Reguengo do Fetal near Fátima; the sheer rock walls of Penedo da Amizade, just below Sintra's Moorish castle; the dramatic quartzite ridge of Penha Garcia, near Monsanto in Beira Baixa; and Rocha da Pena (p181) in the Algarve.

Useful organisations for climbers include **Clube Nacional de Montanhismo** (☎917 827 472; www.cnm.org.pt) and **Grupo de Montanha e Escalada de Sintra** (www.gmesintra.com).

Paragliding is also popular in the north. Two prime launch sites are Linhares (p352) in the Serra da Estrela and Alvados in the Parque Natural das Serras de Aire e Candeeiros (p290).

Eco-aware, Sesimbra-based Vertente Natural (p145) offers trekking, canyoning, canoeing, diving and rappelling, while Porto-based Detours (p371) offers waterfall treks and canyoning, as well as off-track tours around the Douro in 4WD vehicles.

Located outside of Coimbra, **Capitão Dureza** (☎239 476 701; www.capitaodureza.com) is a one-stop shop for high-adrenalin activities including rafting, canyoning, abseiling (rappelling), mountain biking and trekking.

Porto-based **Trilhos** (☎225 504 604; www.trilhos.pt) is another reputable outfitter, offering climbing, caving, canyoning, trekking and other adventure sports.

Boating

Along the coast, especially in the Algarve, pleasure boats predominate, offering everything from barbecue cruises to grotto tours to dolphin-spotting excursions. Inland, Portugal's rivers, lagoons and reservoirs offer a wide variety of boating opportunities, including kayaking, sailing, rafting and canoeing. Rivers popular for boating include the Guadiana, Mondego, Zêzere, Paiva, Minho and Tâmega.

Companies that rent boats and/or operate boat trips can be found in Lagos, Mértola, Barragem do Alqueva, Tomar, Coimbra, Ponte de Lima, Rio Caldo and Amarante, just to name a few.

Diving

Portugal's best dive sites are concentrated in the Algarve. The water temperature is a bit crisp (around 14°C to 16°C, though it doesn't vary much between summer and winter); most divers prefer a 5mm suit. Visibility is usually between 4m and 6m; on the best days, it can range from 15m to 20m.

One of the best places for beginners to learn to dive is off Praia do Carvoeiro, with several operators offering PADI-

GREAT OUTDOOR ADVENTURES FOR FAMILIES

➡ Mountain bike through the outback to see the Palaeolithic petroglyphs at Parque Arqueológico do Vale do Côa (p406).

➡ Kayak with your kids down the Rio Mondego (p310) from Penacova to Coimbra.

➡ Learn to surf with the whole family at Hooked Surf School (p135) in Cascais.

➡ Take the invigoratingly bouncy boat ride (p272) from Peniche to Berlenga Grande, then stay overnight in a 17th-century fort converted into a hostel (p272).

➡ Look for dolphins (p200) – and learn about them from an onboard marine biologist – as you ply the Atlantic waters off the Algarve coast.

➡ Walk through a landscape of dramatic mountains and stone shepherds' huts as you climb the glacial Zêzere Valley, then cool off with icy water from a natural spring in Parque Natural da Serra da Estrela.

➡ Scan the horizon for pirates from the 17th-century fort (p145), play king of the castle at the Moorish *castelo*, or build sandcastles of your own on the beach at Sesimbra.

➡ Take the narrow-gauge train to the lovely, wild beaches along Costa da Caparica (p142).

➡ See dinosaur footprints – yes, *real* dinosaur footprints! – at Cabo Espichel (p144) or Monumento Natural das Pegadas dos Dinossáurios (p290).

accredited courses in English. PADI-accredited courses are also offered in Peniche (p270), as well as in Lagos (p194) and Sagres (p200), among other Algarve locations.

Closer to Lisbon, there are diving outfits at Costa da Caparica (p142), Sesimbra (p145) and Reserva Natural da Berlenga (p272).

Windsurfing & Kitesurfing

Praia do Guincho (p41), west of Sintra, and Portimão (p189) in the Algarve are both world-championship windsurfing sites. Other prime spots include (from north to south) Viana do Castelo's Praia do Cabedelo (p444); Lagoa de Óbidos, a pretty lagoon that draws both sailors and windsurfers; and (closer to Lisbon) the Costa da Caparica's Fonte da Telha. In the Algarve, Sagres (p200) attracts pros (its strong winds and fairly flat seas are ideal for free-riding), while Lagos (p193), Albufeira (p182) and Praia da Rocha (p190) cater to all.

Popular venues for windsurfing and kitesurfing lessons include the beaches that are around Viana do Castelo (p444), Foz do Arelho (p275), Peniche (p270), Praia do Guincho (p41), Lagos (p193) and Tavira (p170).

Horse Riding

Horse riding is a fantastic way to experience Portugal's countryside. Lusitano thoroughbreds hail from Portugal, and experienced riders can take dressage lessons at the **Escola de Equitação de Alcainça** (www.eealcainca.pt), near Mafra, in Estremadura. Otherwise, there are dozens of horse-riding centres – especially in the Alentejo, and in the Algarve at places such as Silves, Lagos, Portimão and Albufeira. Northern Portugal also offers some pleasant settings for rides, including Campo do Gerês (p468) at the edge of Parque Nacional da Peneda-Gerês. Rates are usually around €20 to €30 per hour.

Switzerland-based **Equitour** (www.equitour.com) offers eight-day riding holidays costing €1045 to €1800 per person, including accommodation and some meals. Its signature tour follows the Alentejo Royal Horse Stud Trail, with stays at grand country estates. Other destinations include the Alentejo coast and the rugged terrain of northern Portugal.

SKI PORTUGAL?

This isn't Switzerland – or even Spain for that matter – but believe it or not, Portugal has a downhill ski run. The country's highest peak, 1993m-high Torre in Parque Natural da Serra da Estrela (p336), offers basic facilities including three lifts and equipment rental. Truth be told, Torre offers more curiosity value than actual skiing excitement, and the mountain landscape is so fragile that it's hard to recommend this as sustainable tourism. If you're really hard-up, and want a (slightly) less environmentally damaging alternative, you can always hit the rather surreal 'dry ski' run at SkiParque (p340) east of Manteigas.

The Wyoming-based outfit **Equitours** (www.equitours.com), America's largest and oldest, offers a year-round classical dressage program on Lusitano horses at the Escola de Equitação de Alcainça. Rates including accommodation plus up to three hours of riding per day start at US$205 in the low season, and up to US$250 in the high season. Equitours also offers several different multiday rides around the country starting from around US$1700 (for an eight-day trip along the Alentejo coast) including lodging and food.

Golf

Portugal is a golf mecca, and its championship courses are famous for their rolling greens and ocean vistas. Although many courses are frequented mainly by club members and local property owners, anyone with a handicap certificate can play here. Greens fees run from €35 to over €120 per round.

Vidago Palace (p415), situated in Trás-os-Montes, has become one of the premier golfing destinations in Portugal. Estoril (p138) has nearly a dozen spectacular courses. Golf do Estoril, one of Portugal's best-known, has hosted the Portuguese Open Championship 20 times. It's 5262m long and set among eucalyptus, pine and mimosa trees. Two other Portuguese Open venues lie nearby: Oitavos Dunes, which rolls over windblown dunes and rocky outcrops; and Penha Longa, ranked one of Europe's best courses, with superb views of the Serra de Sintra. See www.estorilsintragolf.net or the Estoril and Cascais *turismos* for full details of all courses.

Two courses that are well-regarded around Lisbon are Troia Golf near Setúbal and Praia d'El Rey Golf & Beach Resort near Óbidos.

The Algarve has three-dozen courses at last count – including the renowned Vilamoura Oceânico Victoria, San Lorenzo, Monte Rei and Vale do Lobo courses. For a general overview, see the complete course guide at www.algarve-golf.com.

For golfing packages around Lisbon and in the Algarve, try UK-based **Your Golf Travel** (www.yourgolftravel.com).

Bear in mind that golf courses' toll on the environment can be significant, especially in dry and fragile coastal settings such as the Algarve.

The **Pestana** (www.pestanagolf.com) hotel group runs several of the Algarve's more affordable courses.

Bacalhau (dried salt-cod) served with potatoes

Plan Your Trip

Eat & Drink Like a Local

Settling down to a meal with friends is one of life's great pleasures for the Portuguese, who take pride in simple but flavourful dishes honed to perfection over the centuries. Seafood, roast meats, freshly baked bread and velvety wines are key staples in the everyday feast that is eating in Portugal.

The Year in Food

Spring

In late spring and early summer, you'll see signs advertising *caracois* (snails). These little delicacies are cooked in olive oil, garlic and herbs and are quite tasty. They go nicely with a cold beer.

Summer

Head to the market for bountiful fruits and vegetables: plump tomatoes, juicy peaches, *nísperos* (loquats), strawberries and other delights. Sardines, much loved along the coast (especially in Lisbon), are available from May through October, and are generally bigger and juicier in July and August.

Autumn

In September the Douro Valley begins its annual grape harvest; it's a festive time to visit, and some wineries allow visitors to take part.

Winter

During cold days Portuguese hunker down over hearty dishes such as *cozido à portuguesa*, a dish of mixed roast meats, potatoes, cabbage and carrots. Rich soups like *canja* (chicken soup) and *sopa de peixe* (fish soup) are also popular. In the Minho, January to March is the season for tender grilled eels.

Food Experiences

Meals of a Lifetime

➡ **Vila Joya** (p184) Delightful two-Michelin-star restaurant by the sea.

➡ **Alma** (p99) Brilliantly creative dishes in Lisbon by culinary superstar Henrique Sá Pessoa.

➡ **Botequim da Mouraria** (p222) Fantastic traditional Alentejan cooking in a tiny bar-seating-only tavern in Évora.

➡ **Tasca do Celso** (p261) Wonderful cuisine and a charming rustic ambience on the Alentejo coast in Vila Nova de Milfontes.

➡ **Restaurante O Barradas** (p188) Some 3km from Silves, this delightful converted farmhouse restaurant sources organic fish, meat and fruits in season.

➡ **DOC** (p406) Delectable fare and an unmatched wine list at an indoor-outdoor restaurant that has a great location right on the Douro.

➡ **Esplanada Furnas** (p268) Seafood feasts served on a cliff overlooking the waves in Ericeira.

➡ **Pedra de Sal** (p317) A cosy dining room that serves phenomenal Iberian pork dishes.

➡ **O Albertino** (p352) The superb traditional fare is well worth the drive to this spot tucked away in the mountainous northern reaches of Portugal.

➡ **Belcanto** (p99) Prepare for a dazzling meal at this celebrated restaurant of José Avillez in Lisbon.

➡ **Adraga** (p132) Excellent fresh fish served just steps from the ocean in a famous, but unfussy spot west of Sintra.

➡ **Restaurante António Padeiro** (p282) An atmospheric spot with legendary cooking in the historic town of Alcobaça.

➡ **O Paparico** (p377) A slice of rustic romance, just north of Porto, serving wonderfully authentic Portuguese food.

Cheap Treats

➡ **Pastel de nata** Custard tart, ideally served warm and dusted with cinnamon.

➡ **Travesseira** A rolled puff pastry filled with almond-and-egg-yolk custard. Find them in Sintra.

➡ **Tinned fish** Sardines, mackerel and tuna served with bread, olives and other accompaniments are the latest snack craze in Lisbon. Try Sol e Pesca (p97).

➡ **Francesinha** Porto's favourite hangover snack is a thick open-faced sandwich covered in melted cheese.

➡ **Marzipan** In the Algarve, this very sweet almond-infused confectionary is a local favourite.

PRICE RANGES

The following price ranges refer to a main course.

€ less than €10

€€ €10–20

€€€ more than €20

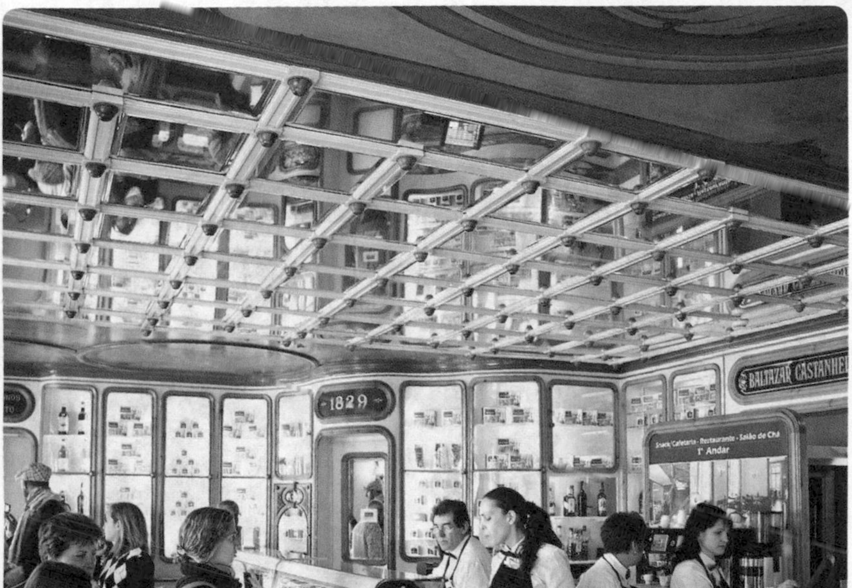

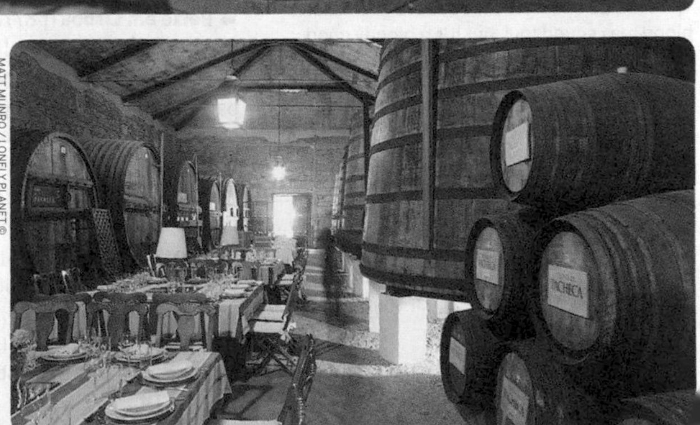

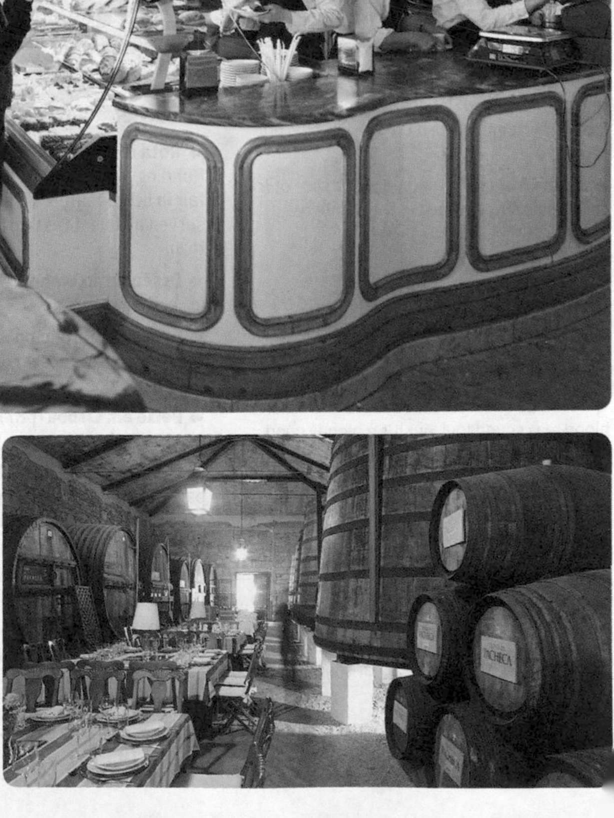

Top: Lisbon shop selling *pastel de nata*

Bottom: Wine barrels at Quinta da Pacheca (p403)

MATT MUNRO / LONELY PLANET ©

Mercado da Ribeira (p96)

➡ **Grilled chicken** Rotisserie chicken is an art form in Portugal. Spice it up with *piri-piri* (hot sauce).

➡ **Bifana** A bread roll served with a slice of fried pork inside. They're best in the Alentejo.

Dare to Try

➡ **Tripe** People from Porto aren't called *tripeiros* (tripe-eaters) for nothing. Try the surprisingly tasty *tripas à modo do Porto*, made of tripe, beans and sausage.

➡ **Arroz de cabidelo** Rice soaked in chicken's blood may sound foul, but it's a bloody good delicacy. The pork variant is called *arroz de sarrabulho*.

➡ **Morcela** Blood sausage made with pig's blood and perhaps rice and pork.

➡ **Caracois** Smaller and less fancy than escargots, these are snails, plain and simple. Toothpick prying skills required.

➡ **Torresmos** Slices of pig skin and fat served up deep-fried. Makes a great bar snack.

Food & Wine Festivals

➡ **Rota de Sabores Tradicionais** (p220) Running from January to May, this culinary fair in Évora features traditional specialities served at select restaurants throughout the town.

➡ **Essência do Vinho** A wine fest in Porto held in February.

➡ **Festival Internacional do Chocolate** (p273) Chocolate lovers descend on the pretty medieval town of Óbidos in March.

➡ **Peixe em Lisboa** (p87) A week of seafood feasting in April at top restaurants in Lisbon.

➡ **Festa de Santo António** Lisbon's lively street party in June is a great opportunity to feast on chargrilled sardines and roast suckling pig.

➡ **Feira do Alvarinho** (p453) In July, Monção in the Minho pays its respects to its most famous produce, the refreshing Alvarinho white wine.

➡ **Festival do Marisco** (p166) A sinful seafood festival held in August in the Algarve.

➡ **Cozinha dos Ganhões** (p231) The lively culinary festival held in Estremoz happens in late November or early December.

Carapaus de escabeche (fried marinated mackerel)

Local Specialities

Bread remains integral to every meal, and it even turns up in some main courses. Be on the lookout for *açorda* (bread stew, often served with shellfish), *migas* (bread pieces prepared as a side dish) and *ensopados* (stews with toasted or deep-fried bread).

Seafood stews are superb in Portugal, particularly *caldeirada*, which is a mix of fish and shellfish in a rich broth, not unlike a bouillabaisse. *Bacalhau* (dried salt-cod) is bound up in myth, history and tradition, and is excellent in baked dishes.

Lisbon

Simplicity, pristine ingredients and creativity mark Lisbon's gourmet scene. Chefs such as Henrique Sá Pessoa at Alma (p99), João Rodrigues at Feitoria (p106), José Avillez at Belcanto (p99) and Ljubomir Stanisic at 100 Maneiras (p100), among others, have put the Portuguese capital on the gastronomic map with ingredient-focused tasting menus that often put a spin on comfort foods such as slow-cooked suckling pig and *bacalhau*.

Algarve

This is a bivalve zone, with hordes of fresh clams, oysters, mussels, cockles and whelks. Don't go past the seafood *cataplana* (a Portuguese version of the Spanish paella) and *xerém* (corn mash made with cockles).

Alentejo

Warning to vegetarians: pork will confront you at every repast. Bread also figures heavily; you'll find it in gazpacho or *açorda*. During hunting season, *perdiz* (partridge), *lebre* (hare) and *javali* (wild boar) are the go. The Alentejo also has surf-and-turf blends such as *carne de porco à alentejana* (braised pork with baby clams).

Estremadura & Ribatejo

Seafood dominates the culinary palate in Estremadura; *caldeiradas de peixe* (fish stews) rule the menus, closely followed by *escabeche* (marinated vinegar fish stew) and *sopas de mariscos* (shellfish soups). Carnivores should head to Ribatejo – this is meat and tripe country.

Beiras

There's plenty of *bacalhau* and *ovos moles* (thickened sweet egg yolks), egg cakes and *chanfana* (goat or lamb stews), plus Atlantic seafood. Sausages are popular, as are cheeses, especially Rabaçal cheese and *Queijo Serra da Estrela* (Serra cheese).

NOTHING IS FREE

Throughout the country, waiters bring bread, olives and other goodies to your table when you sit down. This unordered appetiser is called the *couvert* and it is never free (*couvert* can cost €1.50 for some olives and bread to upwards of €8 per person for cheeses and high-quality fixings at flashier places). If you don't want it, send it away – or simply ignore it – and make sure it isn't accidentally added to your bill.

Minho

The Minho produces the famous *vinho verde* (green wine – 'green' because it's made from immature grapes, either red or white), *caldo verde* (Galician kale and potato soup), *broa de Milho* (golden corn loaf), thrifty *sopa seca* (dry soup) and seasonal eel-like lamprey, trout and salmon dishes.

Douro & Trás-os-Montes

The north is known for its pork dishes, *cabrito assado* (roast kid) and *posta de barrosã* (beef from a rare breed of cattle). The pork-free *alheira* (a bread and meat sausage) was invented by the Jewish people during the Inquisition. Crops of figs, cherries, almonds, chestnuts and oranges abound.

Dining Basics

When to Eat

➡ *Café da manhã* (breakfast; 8am to 10am) is generally a simple affair with coffee and a bread roll or pastry.

➡ *Almoço* (lunch; noon to 3pm) can be a two-course fixed price special, or something that is more casual, depending on the locale.

➡ *Jantar* (dinner; 7pm to 10pm) generally features more elaborate (and slightly pricier) dishes, though some places specialise in *petiscos* (sharing plates).

TOP MARKETS

Every sizable town has a local produce market where you can assemble a feast of a picnic (breads, cheeses, olives, fruits, vegetables, smoked meats and more) for very little cash. Here are a few of our favourites:

➡ **Mercado da Ribeira** (p96), Lisbon

➡ **Mercado do Livramento** (p150), Setúbal

➡ **Mercado Municipal** (p178), Loulé

➡ **Mercado Municipal** (p222), Évora

➡ **Mercado Municipal Dom Pedro V** (p312), Coimbra

➡ **Mercado Municipal** (p435), Braga

➡ **Mercado do Bolhão** (p363), Porto

Mercado do Bolhão (p363)

Where to Eat

➡ **Tasca** (tavern) Old-fashioned place with daily specials, fair prices and a local crowd.

➡ **Churrasqueira** (grill house) Specialising in chargrilled meats.

➡ **Marisqueira** (seafood restaurant) Serves up fish and crustaceans, often priced by the kilo.

➡ **Cervejaria** (beer house) Good for snacking and socialising.

➡ **Adega** (wine tavern) Usually decorated with wine casks and boasting a rustic, cosy ambience; expect hearty inexpensive meals.

Menu Decoder

➡ **Couvert** The bread, olives and other nibbles brought to your table; note that these are not free.

➡ **Dose** Portion, big enough for two people.

➡ **Ementa turística** Tourist menu.

➡ **Meia dose** Half-portion, enough for one person.

➡ **Petiscos** Tapas/snacks.

➡ **Postre** Dessert.

➡ **Prato do dia** Daily special or dish of the day.

➡ **Serviço** Service charge.

Regions at a Glance

Lisbon & Around

History
Food & Wine
Nightlife

Ghosts of the Past

History lurks around every corner, from roofless cathedrals that bore witness to Europe's most devastating earthquake to the 1000-year-old castle on the hill – the scene of bloody Crusades battles. There are Roman ruins, medieval churches, 16th-century convents and more.

Culinary Powerhouses

Ever-inventive chefs showcase the bounty of field and ocean, and traditional restaurants serve Spanish, Italian, Indian, French and other cuisines. Cinematic views, al fresco meals and buzzing dining rooms complete the experience.

Music-Fuelled Nights

Nights out range from curbside drinking in Bairro Alto to live fado shows in Alfama. Put your hands in the air at club Lux, listen to up-and-coming bands at Musicbox – the options are limitless.

p60

The Algarve

Beaches
Seafood
Activities

Captivating Coasts

Sun-kissed shores come in many forms in the Algarve: scenic coves, family-friendly bays, pounding surf. Beaches along the rugged west coast are more remote and natural. Those further east swell with holidaymakers in summer.

Seafood Feasts

Seafood plays a starring role in the Algarve – with superb *cataplanas* (seafood stews) and a vast range of grilled fish. You'll find all levels of restaurant, from Michelin-starred to beachside shack.

Outdoor Adventures

The Algarve offers a plethora of organised activities, especially for children, with water parks, horse riding and pirate-ship cruises. There's also birdwatching, thermal baths and surfing.

p152

The Alentejo

Medieval Villages
Food & Wine
Scenery

Relics of the Past

Medieval villages proliferate in the Alentejo. Marvão, Monsaraz, Mértola, Estremoz and Elvas all have eye-catching castles that played a role in shaping Portugal's history.

Traditional Cuisine

The Alentejo is known for its produce, especially *porco preto* (black pork) and its *doces conventuais* (sweets). Vineyards cover the region, and there's a good network of wineries.

Mesmerising Landscapes

This region boasts great walks and scenic drives. Highlights include mountains, rivers, gorges, and hillsides dotted with cork trees, olive groves and wild flowers. Parque Natural do Vale do Guadiana is particularly striking.

p211

Estremadura & Ribatejo

Architecture
Seafood
Surfing

Monasteries

A cluster of Unesco World Heritage Sites, Tomar, Batalha and Alcobaça are splendid religious monuments easily reached from Lisbon. With soaring arches, Manueline ornamentation and pretty courtyards, these Renaissance masterpieces are *the* reason to visit central Portugal.

Coastal Feasts

Ask a *lisbôeta* where to go for seafood, and they'll point you to Ericeira. This coastal village is full of restaurants where you choose the catch of the day and it is grilled on the spot.

Legendary Breaks

The waves of Baleal and Supertubos draw throngs from around the globe, and national championships are often held here.

p264

The Beiras

Castles
Scenery
Culture

Fortified Frontier

The inland Beiras are filled with castles and fortresses that once guarded the country's eastern frontier with Spain. From Folgosinho's minicastle to the elaborate star-shaped ramparts of Almeida, they tell tales of a rambunctious time in Portugal's history.

Grand Views

The rocky heights of the Serra da Estrela are a revelation of cool air, magnificent vistas and great walks. Portugal's highest mountains, once the domain of shepherds, now see a stream of outdoor enthusiasts.

University Life

Portugal's oldest university town, Coimbra, wears its tradition proudly, as evidenced by its medieval architecture and the black capes still worn by students.

p301

Porto, the Douro & Trás-os-Montes

Scenery
Wine & Port
Nightlife

Rivers & Rocks

Porto captivates with its pretty squares and riverside setting. Other stars include stone villages, natural parks and 30,000-year-old rock carvings at Vila Nova de Foz Côa.

Tastings & Wine Country

Taste the world's best ports in Vila Nova de Gaia, followed by a wine-tasting ramble through vineyard country in the Douro and southern Trás-os-Montes.

Drinking & Revelry

Porto's bar-crammed Galerias is the party hub, with retro-cool bars and live-music haunts. Try Ribeira for mellow wine bars and beachside Foz do Douro for drinks with Atlantic views.

p358

The Minho

History
Food & Wine
Activities

Medieval Wonders

Head to medieval Guimarães to discover Portugal's birthplace. Even more stunning is Braga, with its 1000-year-old cathedral and colourful festivals. Then there's the Celtic settlement of Citânia de Briteiros, atmospheric Viana do Castelo and the cinematic Valença do Minho citadel.

Fine Dining

Braga has first-rate restaurants, while Viana do Castelo and Guimarães also have gems. Home to *vinho verde* (young wine), the Minho produces some great wines, including the refreshing Alvarinho.

Surfing & Hiking

There's top surfing in Minho, particularly off Praia do Cabedelo. Parque Nacional da Peneda-Gerês has great hiking.

p428

On the Road

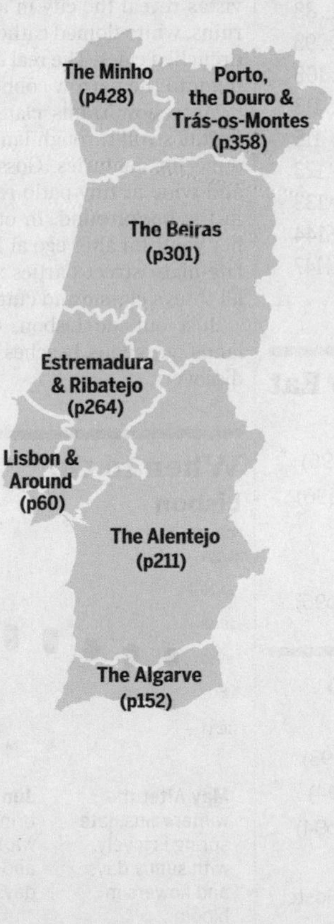

The Minho (p428)

Porto, the Douro & Trás-os-Montes (p358)

The Beiras (p301)

Estremadura & Ribatejo (p264)

Lisbon & Around (p60)

The Alentejo (p211)

The Algarve (p152)

Lisbon & Around

Includes ➡

Best Places to Eat

- Belcanto (p99)
- Cervejaria Ramiro (p96)
- Mercado da Ribeira (p96)
- Alma (p99)
- Ti-Natércia (p100)
- Solar dos Presuntos (p96)

Best Places to Sleep

- Palácio Belmonte (p93)
- Casa do Príncipe (p94)
- Santiago de Alfama (p94)
- Lisbon Calling (p92)
- Lisbon Destination Hostel (p88)

Why Go?

Spread across steep hillsides that overlook the Rio Tejo, Lisbon has captivated visitors for centuries. Windswept vistas reveal the city in all its beauty: Roman and Moorish ruins, white-domed cathedrals, grand plazas lined with sun-drenched cafes. The real delight of discovery, though, is delving into the narrow cobblestone lanes.

As yellow trams clatter through tree-lined streets, *lisboêtas* stroll through lamplit old quarters, much as they've done for centuries. Gossip is exchanged over fresh bread and wine at tiny patio restaurants as fado singers perform in the background. In other parts of town, Lisbon reveals her youthful alter ego at bohemian bars and riverside clubs, late-night street parties and eye-catching boutiques selling all things classic and cutting-edge.

Just outside Lisbon, there's more – enchanting woodlands, gorgeous beaches and seaside villages – all ripe for discovery.

When to Go

Lisbon

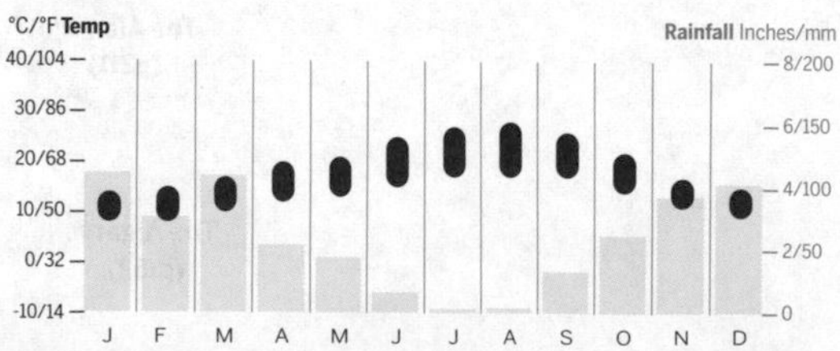

May After the winter rains, late spring is lovely, with sunny days and flowers in bloom.

Jun Early summer brings festivals, warm weather and perfect beach days.

Sep Lisbon is pure magic, with cooler days and nights and a lack of summer crowds.

LISBON

POP 547,700

History

Imperial riches, fires, plague, one of the most destructive and deadly earthquakes in recorded human history, revolutions, coups, Europe's longest dictatorship and the most severe financial crisis since the Great Depression – Lisbon has certainly had its ups and downs. But come hell or high water, Europe's second-oldest capital soldiers on, improbably emerging from each crisis better and more beautiful than before.

It's said that Ulysses was here first, but the Phoenicians definitely settled here 3000 years ago, calling the city Alis Ubbo (Delightful Shore). Others soon recognised its qualities: the Greeks, the Carthaginians and then, in 205 BC, the Romans, who stayed until the 5th century AD. After some tribal chaos, the city was taken over by North African Moors in 714. They fortified the city they called Lissabona and fended off the Christians for 400 years.

But in 1147, after a four-month siege, Christian fighters (mainly British crusaders) under Dom Afonso Henriques captured the city. In 1255, Afonso III moved his capital here from Coimbra, which proved far more strategic given the city's excellent port and central position.

In the 15th and 16th centuries Lisbon boomed as the opulent centre of a vast empire after Vasco da Gama found a sea route to India. The party raged on into the 1800s, when gold was discovered in Brazil. Merchants flocked to the city, trading in gold, spices, silks and jewels. Frenzied, extravagant architecture held up a mirror to the era, as seen in Manueline works such as Belém's Mosteiro dos Jerónimos.

At 9.40am on All Saints' Day, 1 November 1755, Lisbon was forever changed. Three major earthquakes hit, as residents celebrated Mass, in what is considered one of the most powerful earthquake sequences in recorded human history, measuring between an estimated 8.5 and 9.1 on the moment magnitude scale. The tremors brought an even more devastating fire and tsunami. Some estimate that as many as 90,000 of Lisbon's 270,000 inhabitants died. Much of the city was ruined, never to regain its former status. Dom João I's chief minister, the formidable Marquês de Pombal, immediately began rebuilding in a simple, cheap, earthquake-proof style that created today's formal grid around the Pombaline downtown area known as Baixa.

In 1908, amid social and economic turmoil, the Portuguese monarchy came to an abrupt and violent end when King Dom Carlos I, along with his heir apparent,

LISBON IN...

Two Days

Take a ride on tram 28 from **Praça do Comércio** (p64), hopping off to scale the ramparts of **Castelo de São Jorge** (p73). Sample some of Portugal's finest at **Wine Bar do Castelo** (p110) before trolling the picturesque lanes of Alfama and stopping for sizzling grilled sardines at open-air **Páteo 13** (p101) for a late lunch. In the afternoon, continue on to the fortress-like **Sé de Lisboa** (p75) cathedral en route to shopping in pedestrianised Baixa. Round things out with a fado-fuelled evening back in lantern-lit Alfama.

On day two, breakfast on pastries in Belém, then explore the fantastical **Mosteiro dos Jerónimos** (p79), the riverfront **Torre de Belém** (p81) and the avant-garde **Museu Colecção Berardo** (p82). Head for dinner at **100 Maneiras** (p100) and bar-crawling back in Bairro Alto. End the night at **Pensão Amor** (p107) in Cais do Sodré.

Four Days

Window-shop and cafe-hop away your morning in hip Príncipe Real (p77) or well-heeled Chiado (p67), before booking a walking or street-art tour for the afternoon. That night, dine at **Belcanto** (p99) or **Taberna Ideal** (p103), then go dancing in clubbing temple **Lux-Frágil** (p110).

On day four, catch the train to Sintra for walks through boulder-speckled woodlands to fairy-tale palaces. Back in Rossio, toast your trip with cherry liqueur at **A Ginjinha** (p106) and a seafood feast at **Cervejaria Ramiro** (p96).

Lisbon & Around Highlights

1. Get lost in the narrow village-like lanes of the **Alfama** (p71), searching for the soul of fado.
2. Bar-hop your way through the cobblestone streets of nightlife-loving **Bairro Alto** (p67).
3. Take in the pleasant outdoor cafes and restaurants of elegant **Chiado** (p67).
4. Take a rattling, roller-coaster ride through the city aboard **tram 28** (p85).
5. Gaze upon the Manueline fantasy of **Mosteiro dos Jerónimos** (p79).
6. Check out the burgeoning new bar scene in **Cais do Sodré** (p96).
7. Stride through enchanted forests to above-the-clouds palaces and castles in **Sintra** (p123).
8. Spend the day taking in the village lanes and outdoor eateries of laid-back **Cascais** (p133).
9. Frolick in the waves off the beautiful beaches around **Aldeia do Meco** (p144).

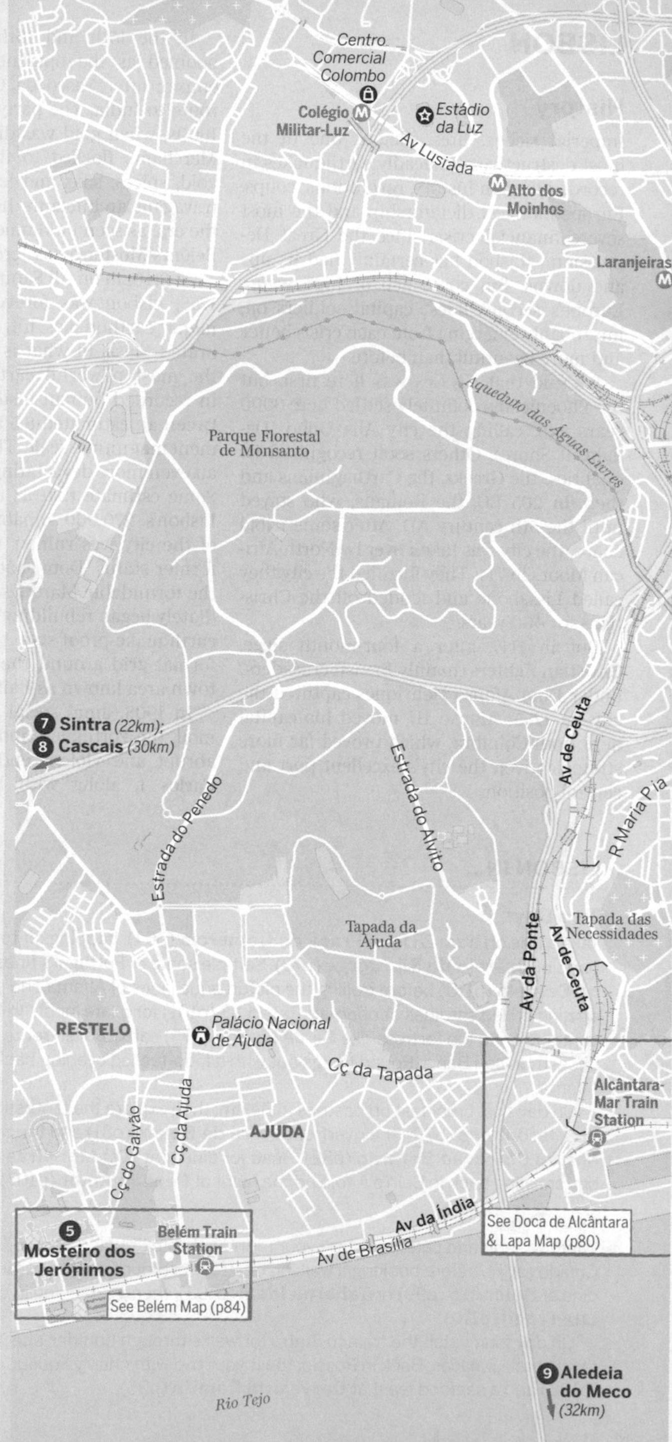

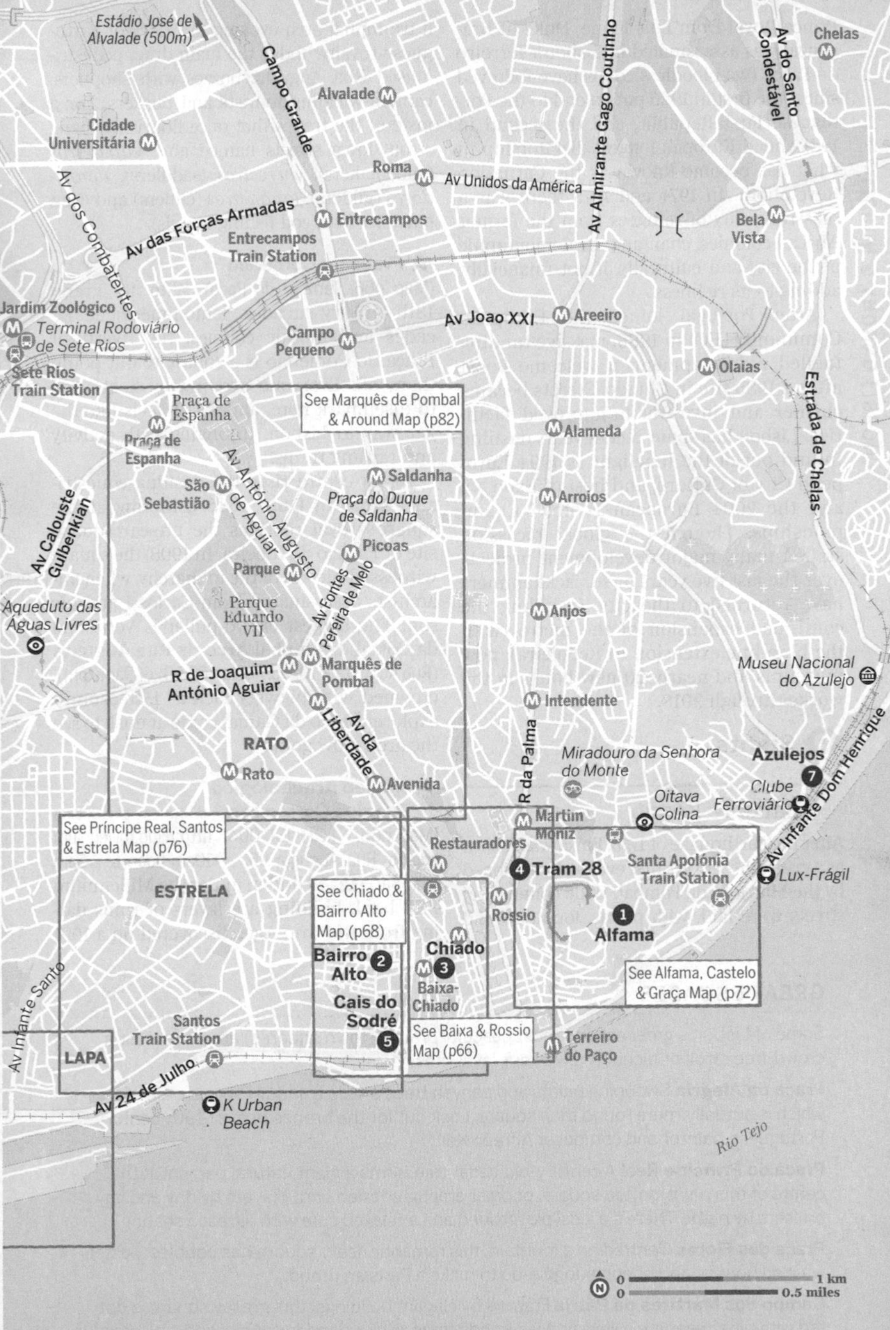
Estádio José de Alvalade (500m)
Campo Grande
Alvalade
Av Almirante Gago Coutinho
Av do Santo Condestável
Chelas
Cidade Universitária
Roma
Av Unidos da América
Av dos Combatentes
Av das Forças Armadas
Entrecampos
Entrecampos Train Station
Bela Vista
Jardim Zoológico
Terminal Rodoviário de Sete Rios
Sete Rios Train Station
Campo Pequeno
Av Joao XXI
Areeiro
Olaias
Estrada de Chelas
See Marquês de Pombal & Around Map (p82)
Praça de Espanha
Praça de Espanha
Alameda
São Sebastião
Av António Augusto de Aguiar
Saldanha
Praça do Duque de Saldanha
Arroios
Av Calouste Gulbenkian
Picoas
Parque
Av Fontes Pereira de Melo
Parque Eduardo VII
Aqueduto das Águas Livres
Anjos
Museu Nacional do Azulejo
R de Joaquim António Aguiar
Marquês de Pombal
Intendente
Av da Liberdade
RATO
Rato
Avenida
R da Palma
Miradouro da Senhora do Monte
Azulejos
7
Av Infante Dom Henrique
Clube Ferroviário
Oitava Colina
Martim Moniz
See Príncipe Real, Santos & Estrela Map (p76)
Restauradores
4 Tram 28
Santa Apolónia Train Station
Lux-Frágil
ESTRELA
See Chiado & Bairro Alto Map (p68)
Rossio
1 Alfama
Chiado
Bairro Alto 2
3
Baixa-Chiado
Cais do Sodré 5
See Alfama, Castelo & Graça Map (p72)
Av Infante Santo
Santos Train Station
See Baixa & Rossio Map (p66)
Terreiro do Paço
LAPA
Av 24 de Julho
K Urban Beach
Rio Tejo
0 1 km
0 0.5 miles

Prince Royal Dom Luís Filipe, Duke of Braganza, was assassinated in Lisbon's Terreiro do Paço. Two bloodless coups have followed since (the first in 1926 put an end to the Portuguese First Republic, and the second in 1974 ended Europe's longest dictatorship in what has become known as the Carnation Revolution). In 1974 and 1975 there was a massive influx of refugees from the former African colonies, changing the demographic of the city and culturally, if not financially, adding to its richness.

After Portugal joined the European Community (EC) in 1986, massive funding fuelled redevelopment, a welcome boost after a 1988 fire in Chiado. Streets became cleaner and investment improved facilities. Lisbon has spent recent years dashing in and out of the limelight as 1994 European City of Culture, and host of Expo '98 and the 2004 European Football Championships. Though the global recession stalled many major development projects over the last five years or so, jackhammers have returned to the city, including the continued expansion of the metro (with the blue-line extension to Reboleira), new museums and nearly 20 new hotels in the works through 2018.

Sights

Baixa & Rossio

After the earthquake of 1755, Baixa was reborn as a grid – the world's first ever – as envisioned by the Marquês de Pombal. Wide commercial streets were laid, with plazas, fountains and a triumphal arch evoking the glory of Portuguese royalty. Today the main drag, pedestrianised Rua Augusta, buzzes with shoppers, camera-wielding tourists and buskers. For a taste of the trades that once flourished here, stroll down streets named after *sapateiros* (shoemakers), *correeiros* (saddlers), *douradores* (gilders), *fanqueiros* (cutlers) and even *bacalhoeiros* (cod-fishing vessels).

★Praça do Comércio PLAZA

(Map p66; Terreiro do Paço) With its grand 18th-century arcades, lemon-meringue facades and mosaic cobbles, the riverfront Praça do Comércio is a square to out-pomp them all. Everyone arriving by boat used to disembark here, and it still feels like the gateway to Lisbon, thronging with activity and rattling trams.

At its centre rises the dashing equestrian **statue of Dom José I**, hinting at the square's royal roots as the pre-earthquake site of Palácio da Ribeira. In 1908, the square witnessed the fall of the monarchy, when anarchists assassinated Dom Carlos I and his son. The biggest crowd-puller is Verissimo da Costa's triumphal **Arco da Rua Augusta** (Rua Augusta 2-10; admission €2.50; 9am-7pm), crowned with bigwigs such as 15th-century explorer Vasco da Gama; come at dusk to see the arch glow gold.

★Núcleo Arqueológico da Rua dos Correeiros RUINS

(Map p66; 211 131 004; http://ind.millenniumbcp.pt; Rua Augusta 96; 10am-noon & 2-5pm Mon-Sat) FREE Hidden under the Millennium BCP bank building are layers of ruins dating from the Iron Age, discovered on a 1991

GREAT ESCAPES

Some of Lisbon's greenest and most peaceful *praças* (town squares) are perfect for a crowd-free stroll or picnic. A few of our favourites:

Praça da Alegria Swooping palms and banyan trees shade tranquil Praça da Alegria, which is actually more round than square. Look out for the bronze bust of 19th-century Portuguese painter and composer Alfredo Keil.

Praça do Príncipe Real A century-old cedar tree forms a giant natural parasol at the centre of this palm-dotted square, popular among grizzled card players by day and gay cruisers by night. There's a kids' playground and a relaxed cafe with alfresco seating.

Praça das Flores Centred on a fountain, this romantic, leafy square has cobbles, pastel-washed houses and enough doggie-do to make a Parisian proud.

Campo dos Mártires da Pátria Framed by elegant buildings, this grassy square is dotted with pine, weeping willow and jacaranda trees, with a pond for ducks and a pleasant indoor-outdoor cafe. *Lisboêtas* in search of cures light candles before the statue of Dr Sousa Martins, who was renowned for his healing work among the poor.

parking-lot dig. Fascinating archaeologist-led tours, run by Fundacão Millennium (booking ahead year-round is highly advisable), descend into the depths in English (departing on the hour). The extremely well-done site is now rightfully a National Monument.

★Igreja de São Domingos CHURCH
(Map p66; Largo de São Domingos; ⏲1-5pm) FREE It's a miracle that this baroque church still stands, having barely survived the 1755 earthquake, then fire in 1959. Dating to 1241, its sea of tea lights illuminates gashed pillars, battered walls and ethereal sculptures in its musty, yet enchanting, interior. Note the Star of David memorial outside marking the spot of a bloody anti-Semitic massacre in 1506.

Elevador de Santa Justa ELEVATOR
(Map p68; www.transporteslisboa.pt; cnr Rua de Santa Justa & Largo do Carmo; return trip €5; ⏲7am-11pm, to 10pm Oct-May) If the wrought-iron Elevador de Santa Justa seems familiar, it's probably because the neo-Gothic marvel is the handiwork of Raul Mésnier, Gustave Eiffel's apprentice. It's Lisbon's only vertical street lift, built in 1902 and steam-powered until 1907. Get there early to beat the crowds and zoom to the top for city views.

Bear in mind, however, some call the €5 fee Santa Injusta! You can save €3.50 by entering the platform from the top (behind Convento do Carmo) and paying just €1.50 to access the viewing platform.

Museu do Dinheiro MUSEUM
(Map p66; www.museudodinheiro.pt; Largo de São Julião; ⏲10am-6pm Wed-Sat) FREE Pop into Banco do Portugal's new money museum to see the stunning €34-million interior renovation of the once mighty São Julião church (closed in 1933); and the more notable Interpretation Centre for King Dinis' Wall, a preserved 30m expanse of the 13th-century medieval city wall, located in the church's former crypt and discovered during a 2010 excavation.

Ribeira das Naus PROMENADE
(Map p66) This riverfront promenade between Praça do Comércio and Cais do Sodré is a focal point along Lisbon's continually regenerating waterfront. With broad views over the river, it's a fine place for strolling, lounging, reading, cycling and kicking back with a coffee at the kiosk. This is the closest Lisbon gets to an urban beach.

DON'T MISS

MUSEU NACIONAL DO AZULEJO

You haven't been to Lisbon until you've been on the tiles at **Museu Nacional do Azulejo** (Map p62; www.museudoazulejo.pt; Rua Madre de Deus 4; adult/child €5/2.50, free 1st Sun of the month; ⏲10am-6pm Tue-Sun). Housed in a sublime 16th-century convent, the museum covers the entire *azulejo* spectrum, from early Ottoman geometry to zinging altars, scenes of lords a-hunting to Goan intricacies. Star exhibits are a 36m-long panel depicting pre-earthquake Lisbon, a Manueline cloister with web-like vaulting and exquisite blue-and-white *azulejos*, and a gold-smothered baroque chapel. Food-inspired *azulejos* – ducks, pigs and the like – adorn the restaurant opening onto a vine-clad courtyard.

Lisbon Story Centre MUSEUM
(Map p66; www.lisboastorycentre.pt; Praça do Comércio 78; adult/child €7/3; ⏲10am-8pm) This museum takes visitors on a 60-minute journey through Lisbon's history, from its early foundation (pre-ancient Roman days) to modern times. An audioguide and multimedia exhibits describe key episodes, including New World discoveries, the 1755 earthquake (with a vivid film re-enacting the horrors) and the reconstruction that followed.

Museu de Design e da Moda MUSEUM
(Map p66; Mude; www.mude.pt; Rua Augusta 24; ⏲10am-6pm Tue-Sun) This Baixa star, set in a cavernous former bank, contains furniture, industrial design and couture dating from the 1930s. Free since 2009, it's closed for renovations until September 2017 and will reopen with an admission fee. Highlights include iconic furniture by Charles Eames, Frank Gehry and Brazil's Campana Brothers; plus haute couture by the likes of Givenchy, Christian Dior and Balenciaga.

Rossio PLAZA
(Map p66; Praça Dom Pedro IV) Simply Rossio to locals, Praça Dom Pedro IV has 24-hour buzz. Shoeshiners and lottery-ticket sellers, hash-peddlers and office workers drift across its cobbles, gazing up to its ornate fountains and **Dom Pedro IV** (Brazil's first emperor), perched high on a marble pedestal.

And these cobbles have seen it all: witch burnings and bullfights, rallies and 1974

Baixa & Rossio

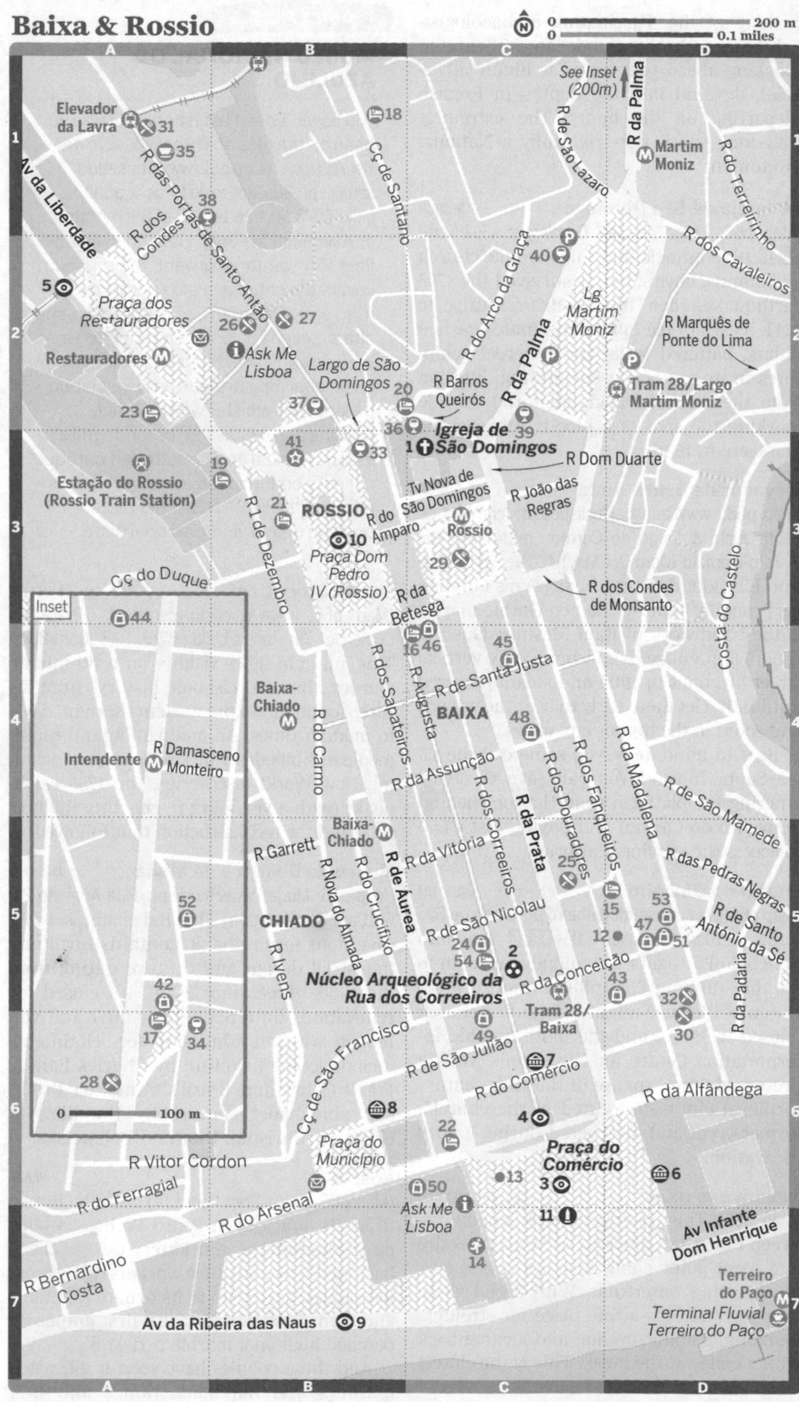

Baixa & Rossio

Top Sights
1 Igreja de São Domingos........................C3
2 Núcleo Arqueológico da Rua dos Correeiros........................C5
3 Praça do Comércio........................C6

Sights
4 Arco da Rua Augusta........................C6
5 Ascensor da Glória........................A2
6 Lisbon Story Centre........................D6
7 Museu de Design e da Moda........................C6
8 Museu do Dinheiro........................B6
9 Ribeira das Naus........................B7
10 Rossio........................B3
11 Statue of Dom José I........................C7

Activities, Courses & Tours
12 GoCar Touring........................D5
13 Lisbon Walker........................C6
14 ViniPortugal........................C7

Sleeping
15 Home Lisbon Hostel........................D5
16 Internacional Design Hotel........................C4
17 Largo Residencias........................A6
18 Lavra Guest House........................B1
19 Lisbon Destination Hostel........................B3
20 Lisbon Story Guesthouse........................B2
21 My Story Rossio........................B3
22 Pousada de Lisboa........................C6
23 Residencial Restauradores........................A2
24 Travellers House........................C5

Eating
25 Bebedouro........................C5
26 Bonjardim........................B2
27 Casa do Alentejo........................B2
28 Cervejaria Ramiro........................A6
29 Mercado da Baixa........................C3
30 Nova Pombalina........................D6
31 Solar dos Presuntos........................A1
32 Tasca Kome........................D5

Drinking & Nightlife
33 A Ginjinha........................B3
34 Casa Independente........................A6
35 Fábrica Coffee Roasters........................A1
36 Ginjinha Rubi........................C2
37 Ginjinha Sem Rival........................B2
38 Primeiro Andar........................A1
39 Rooftop Bar........................C2
40 Topo........................C2

Entertainment
41 Teatro Nacional de Dona Maria II........................B3

Shopping
42 A Vida Portuguesa........................A6
43 Espaço Açores........................D5
44 Feira das Almas........................A3
45 Garrafeira Nacional........................C4
46 Manuel Tavares........................C4
47 Napoleão........................D5
48 Outra Face da Lua........................C4
49 Papabubble........................C6
50 Pátio da Galé Lisbon Shop........................C6
51 Queijaria Nacional........................D5
52 Retrox........................A5
53 Santos Ofícios........................D5
54 Typographia........................C5

revolution carnations. Don't miss the **Estação do Rossio**, a frothy neo-Manueline station that has horseshoe-shaped arches and swirly turrets. Trains depart here for Sintra.

Ascensor da Glória FUNICULAR

(Map p66; www.transporteslisboa.pt; Praça dos Restauradores; €3.60; 7am-midnight Mon-Thu, 7am-12.30pm Fri, 8.30am-12.30am Sat, 9am-midnight Sun) Lisbon's second-oldest funicular has been taking folk from Praça dos Restauradores to Rua São Pedro de Alcântara since 1885. From the *praça* (town square), it climbs up to a viewpoint atop one of Lisbon's seven hills, Miradouro de São Pedro de Alcântara, and is a less tiring way of reaching Bairro Alto.

Bairro Alto & Chiado

Framed by the arches of Convento do Carmo, well-heeled Chiado harbours old-world cafes with literary credentials, swish boutiques, grand theatres and elegant 18th-century town houses. Designer divas who are seeking Portuguese couture, art buffs hunting Rodin originals and those content to people-watch from a cafe terrace flock here.

Sidling up to Chiado is the party-loving Bairro Alto, whose web of graffiti-slashed streets is sleepy by day. The district comes alive at twilight when hippie chicks hunt for vintage glitz in its retro boutiques and revellers hit its wall-to-wall bars and bistros.

★Convento do Carmo & Museu Arqueológico RUINS, MUSEUM

(Map p68; Largo do Carmo; adult/child €3.50/free; 10am-7pm Mon-Sat, to 6pm Oct-May) Soaring above Lisbon, the Convento do Carmo was all but devoured by the 1755 earthquake and that's what makes it so captivating. Its shattered pillars and arches are completely exposed to the elements. The Museu Arqueológico shelters treasures,

Chiado & Bairro Alto

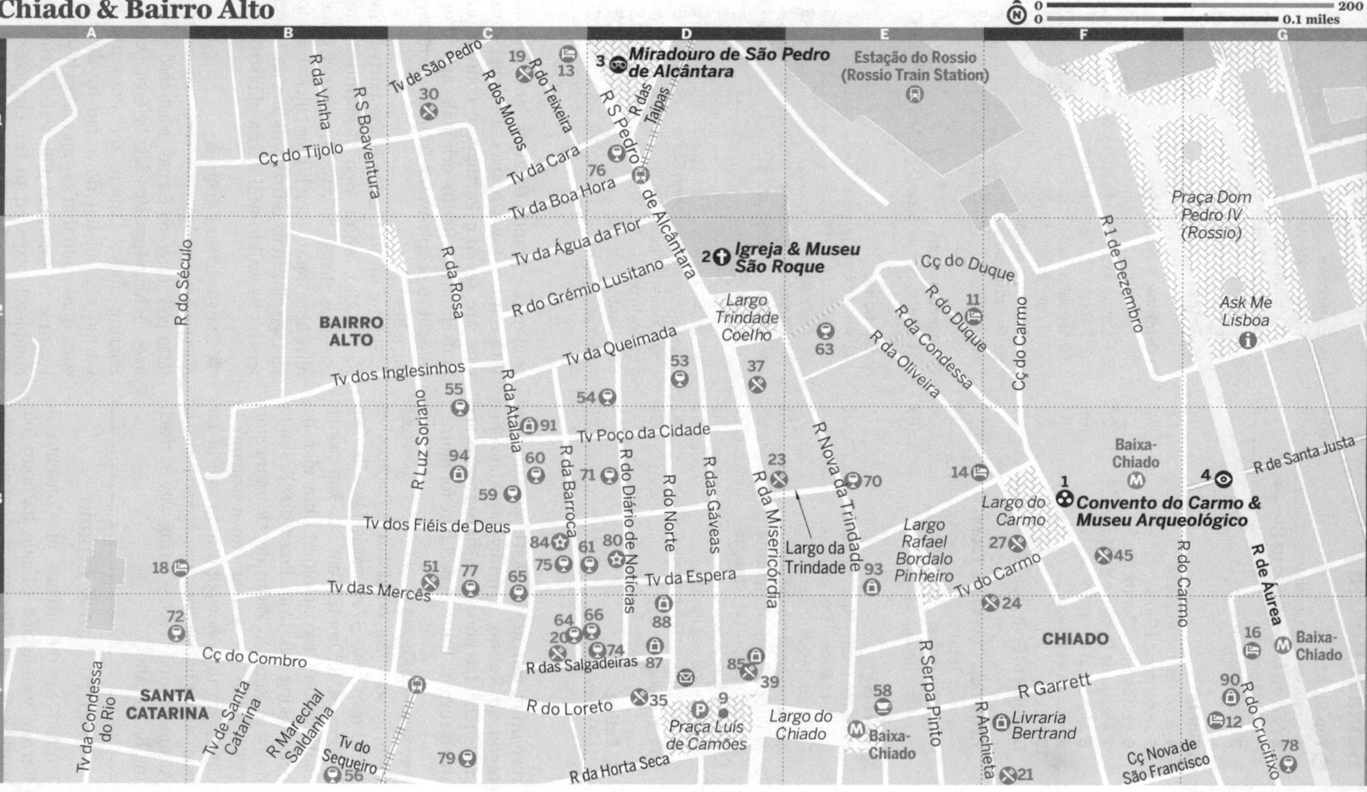

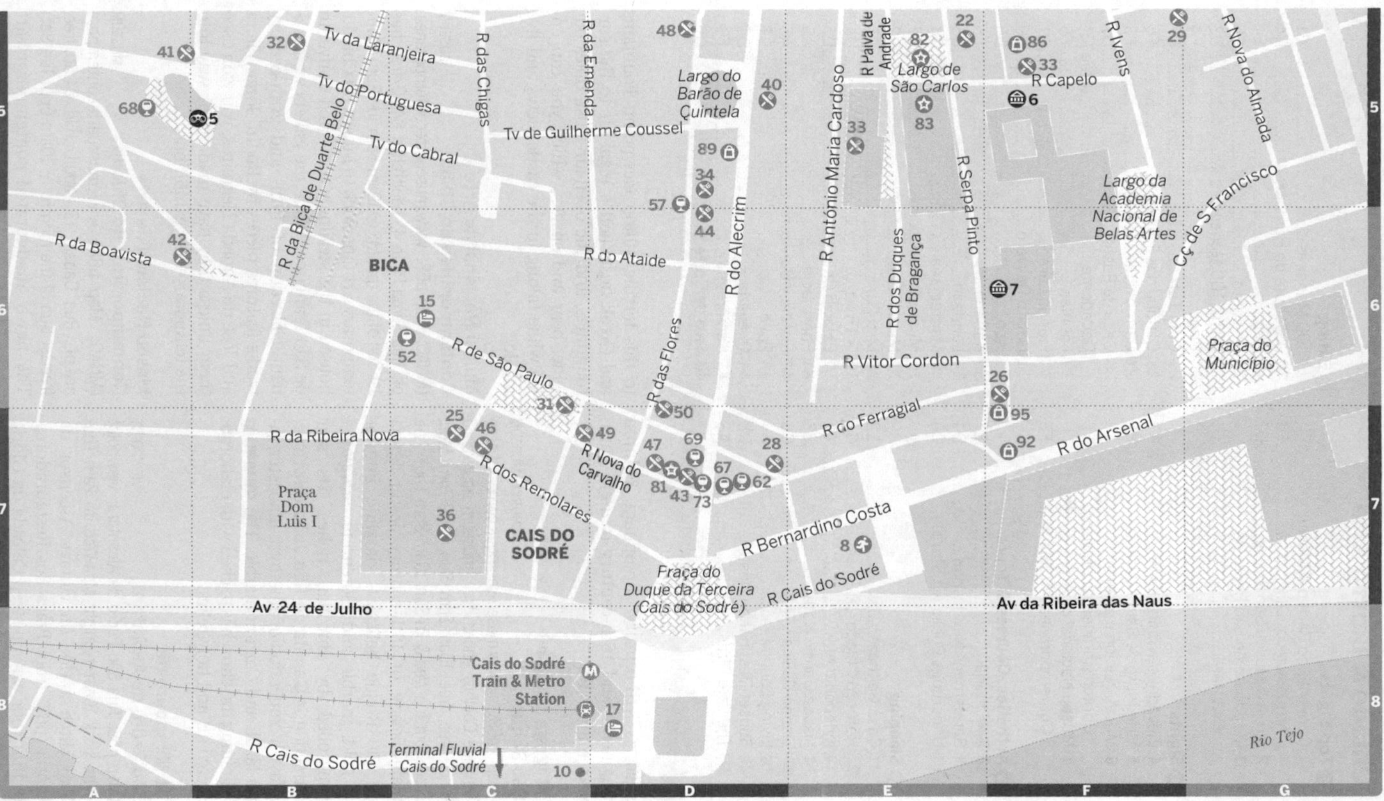
Tv da Laranjeira
R das Chigas
R da Emenda
Largo do Barão de Quintela
R Paiva de Andrade
Largo de São Carlos
R Capelo
R Ivens
R Nova do Almada
Tv do Portuguesa
Tv de Guilherme Coussel
R António Maria Cardoso
Tv do Cabral
R da Bica de Duarte Belo
R Serpa Pinto
Largo da Academia Nacional de Belas Artes
Cç de S Francisco
R da Boavista
BICA
R do Ataide
R do Alecrim
R dos Duques de Bragança
Praça do Município
R de São Paulo
R Vitor Cordon
R das Flores
R do Ferragial
R da Ribeira Nova
R Nova do Carvalho
R dos Remolares
R do Arsenal
Praça Dom Luis I
CAIS DO SODRÉ
R Bernardino Costa
Praça do Duque da Terceira (Cais do Sodré)
R Cais do Sodré
Av 24 de Julho
Av da Ribeira das Naus
Cais do Sodré Train & Metro Station
Rio Tejo
R Cais do Sodré
Terminal Fluvial Cais do Sodré

Chiado & Bairro Alto

Top Sights

1 Convento do Carmo & Museu Arqueológico F3
2 Igreja & Museu São Roque D2
3 Miradouro de São Pedro de Alcântara D1

Sights

4 Elevador de Santa Justa G3
5 Miradouro de Santa Catarina B5
6 Museu Nacional de Arte Contemporânea do Chiado F5
7 Museu Nacional de Arte Contemporânea do Chiado F6

Activities, Courses & Tours

8 Bike Iberia E7
9 Sandemans New Lisbon D4
10 Underdogs Public Art Store C8

Sleeping

11 Casa Balthazar E2
12 Hotel do Chiado G4
13 Independente C1
14 Lisboa Carmo Hotel E3
15 Lisbon Calling C6
16 Living Lounge G4
17 Sunset Destination Hostel D8
18 The Late Birds A3

Eating

19 100 Maneiras C1
20 A Cultura do Hamburger C4
21 Alma F4
22 Belcanto E5
23 Bistro 100 Maneiras D3
24 Brio F4
25 Cafe Tati C7
26 Cantina das Freitas F6
27 Carmo F3
28 Casa de Pasto D7
Decadente .... (see 13)
29 Fábulas F5
30 Flor da Laranja C1
31 Gelato Davvero C6
32 Isco B5
33 Kaffeehaus F5
34 Landeau D5
35 Manteigaria D4
36 Mercado da Ribeira C7
37 Mercantina D2
38 Mini Bar E5
39 O Trevo D4
40 Palácio Chiado D5
41 Pharmacia A5
42 Pistola y Corazon A6
43 Povo D7
44 Queijaria D6
45 Sacramento F3
46 Sala de Corte C7

such as 4th-century sarcophagi, column fragments and 16th-century *azulejo* Peruvian mummies.

★Igreja & Museu São Roque — CHURCH, MUSEUM

(Map p68; www.museu-saoroque.com; Largo Trindade Coelho; church free, museum adult/child €2.50/free, free 10am-2pm Sun; ⏲2-7pm Mon, 10am-7pm Tue-Wed & Fri-Sun, 10am-8pm Thu) The plain facade of 16th-century Jesuit Igreja de São Roque belies its dazzling interior of gold, marble and Florentine *azulejos* – bankrolled by Brazilian riches. Its star attraction is **Capela de São João Baptista**, a lavish confection of amethyst, alabaster, lapis lazuli and Carrara marble. The **museum** adjoining the church is packed with elaborate sacred art and holy relics.

★Miradouro de São Pedro de Alcântara — VIEWPOINT

(Map p68; Rua São Pedro de Alcântara; viewpoint 24hr, kiosk 10am-midnight Mon-Wed, to 2am Thu-Sun) Hitch a ride on vintage Ascensor da Glória (p67) from Praça dos Restauradores, or huff your way up steep Calçada da Glória to this terrific hilltop viewpoint. Fountains and Greek busts add a regal air to the surroundings, and the open-air kiosk doles out wine, beer and snacks, which you can enjoy while taking in the castle views and live music.

Museu Nacional de Arte Contemporânea do Chiado — MUSEUM

(MNAC; Map p68; www.museuartecontemporanea.pt; Rua Serpa Pinto 4; adult/child €4.50/free, free 1st Sun of the month; ⏲10am-6pm Tue-Sun) Contemporary-art fans flock to Museu do Chiado, housed in the strikingly converted Convento de São Francisco. While the gallery's permanent collection of 19th- and 20th-century works features pieces by Rodin, Jorge Vieira and José de Almada Negreiros, you won't see them unless they have made their way into the temporary-only exhibitions.

Museu Nacional de Arte Contemporânea do Chiado — MUSEUM

(MNAC; Map p68; www.museuartecontemporanea.pt; Rua Capelo 13; adult/child €4.50/free, free 1st Sun of the month; ⏲10am-6pm Tue-Sat) The newly inaugurated contemporary-art

47 Sol e Pesca D7
48 Taberna da Rua das Flores D5
49 Taberna Tosca C7
50 Vicente by Carnalentejana D7

Drinking & Nightlife

51 A Tabacaria C6
52 Alface Hall D2
53 Artis D2
54 BA Wine Bar do Bairro Alto C3
55 Bar Bicaense B4
56 By the Wine D5
57 Café a Brasileira E4
58 Capela C3
59 Club Carib C3
60 Clube da Esquina D3
61 Discoteca Jamaica D7
62 Duque Brewpub E2
63 Lisbon Winery C4
64 Majong C3
65 Maria Caxuxa D4
66 Musicbox D7
67 Noobai Café A5
68 Ô Bom O Mau e O Vilão D7
69 O Purista Barbiere E3
70 Old Pharmacy D3
71 Park A4
72 Pensão Amor D7
73 Purex D4
74 Sétimo Céu C3
75 Solar do Vinho do Porto D1
76 Tasca Mastai C3
77 The George G4
78 Zymology C4

Entertainment

79 A Tasco do Chico D3
80 Bar da Velha Senhora D7
81 Festival ao Largo E5
82 Teatro Nacional de São Carlos E5
83 Zé dos Bois C3

Shopping

84 A Carioca D4
85 A Vida Portuguesa F5
86 Cork & Company D4
87 El Dorado D4
88 Fábrica Sant'Ana D5
89 FNAC G4
90 Lena Aires C3
91 Loja das Conservas F7
92 Louie Louie E3
93 Oficina Irmãos Marques C3
94 Story Tailors F7

extension of Museu Nacional de Arte Contemporânea do Chiado is housed inside the former monk's sleeping quarters of the Convento de São Francisco.

Miradouro de Santa Catarina VIEWPOINT
(Map p68; Rua de Santa Catarina; 24hr) FREE
Students bashing out rhythms, pot-smoking hippies, stroller-pushing parents and loved-up couples all meet at this precipitous viewpoint in boho Santa Catarina. The views are fantastic, stretching from the river to the Ponte 25 de Abril and Cristo Rei.

Alfama, Castelo & Graça

Unfurling like a magic carpet at the foot of Castelo de São Jorge, Alfama is Lisbon's Moorish time capsule: a medina-like district of tangled alleys, palm-shaded squares and skinny, terracotta-roofed houses that tumble down to the glittering Tejo. These cobbles have been worn smooth by theatre-going Romans, bath-loving Moors who called it *al-hamma* (Arabic for 'springs'), and stampeding Crusaders.

Here life is literally inside out: women dish the latest *mexericos* (gossip) over strings of freshly washed laundry, men gut sardines on the street then fry them on open grills, plump matrons spontaneously

BEST PANORAMIC VIEWS

Largo das Portas do Sol Stunning angles over Alfama's jumble of rooftops, with the Tejo beyond.

Miradouro de Santa Luzia A fountain, bougainvillea and *azulejos* depicting the Siege of Lisbon in 1147.

Miradouro da Graça Pine-fringed square, with cafe, that makes a great spot for sundowners.

Miradouro da Senhora do Monte Relaxed vibe and the best views of the castle on the hill opposite.

Jardim do Torel Little visited with a concealed indoor-outdoor cafe (go down the steps on the right) with a DJ or live music on most summer weekend nights.

Miradouro de São Pedro de Alcântara Great views, drinks and people-watching just below Bairro Alto.

Alfama, Castelo & Graça

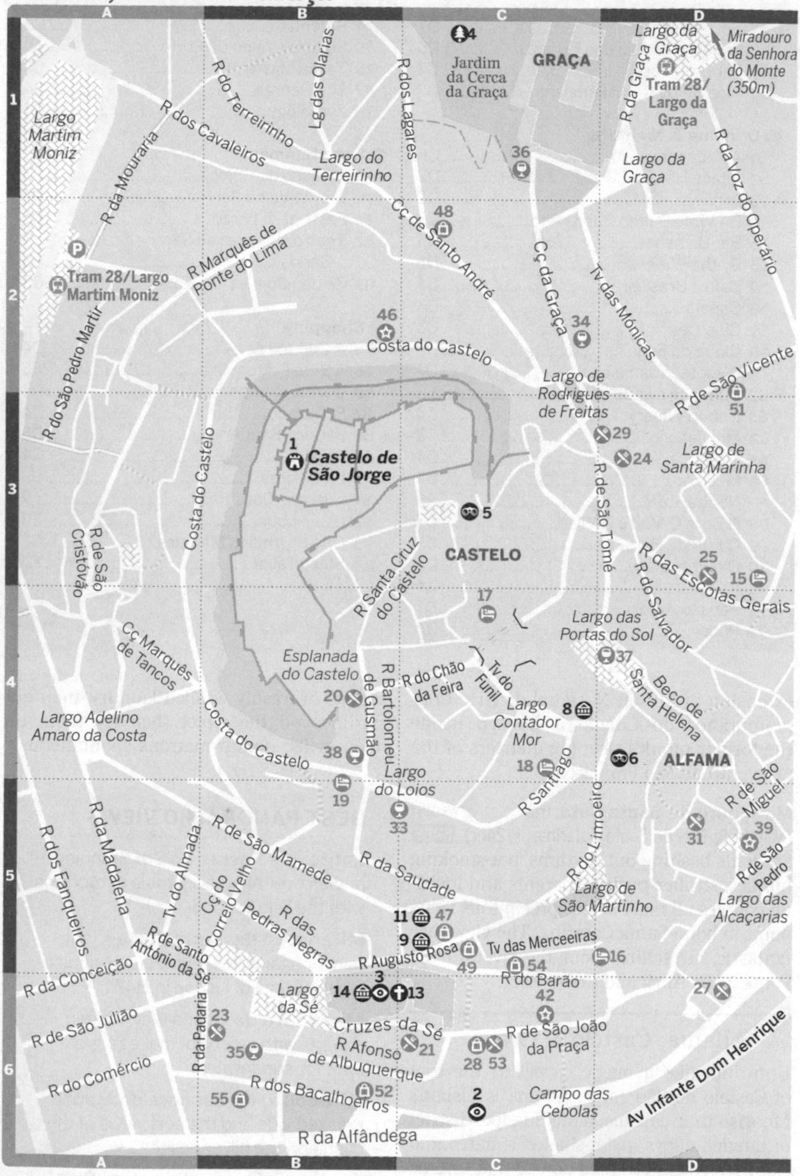

erupt into wailful fado, kids use chapel entrances as football goals, babies cry, budgies twitter, trams rattle and in the midday heat the web of steep lanes falls into its siesta slumber.

Add some altitude to your sightseeing by edging north to Graça, where *miradouros* (lookouts) afford sweeping vistas and the pearly-white Panteão Nacional and Igreja de São Vicente de Fora punctuate the skyline.

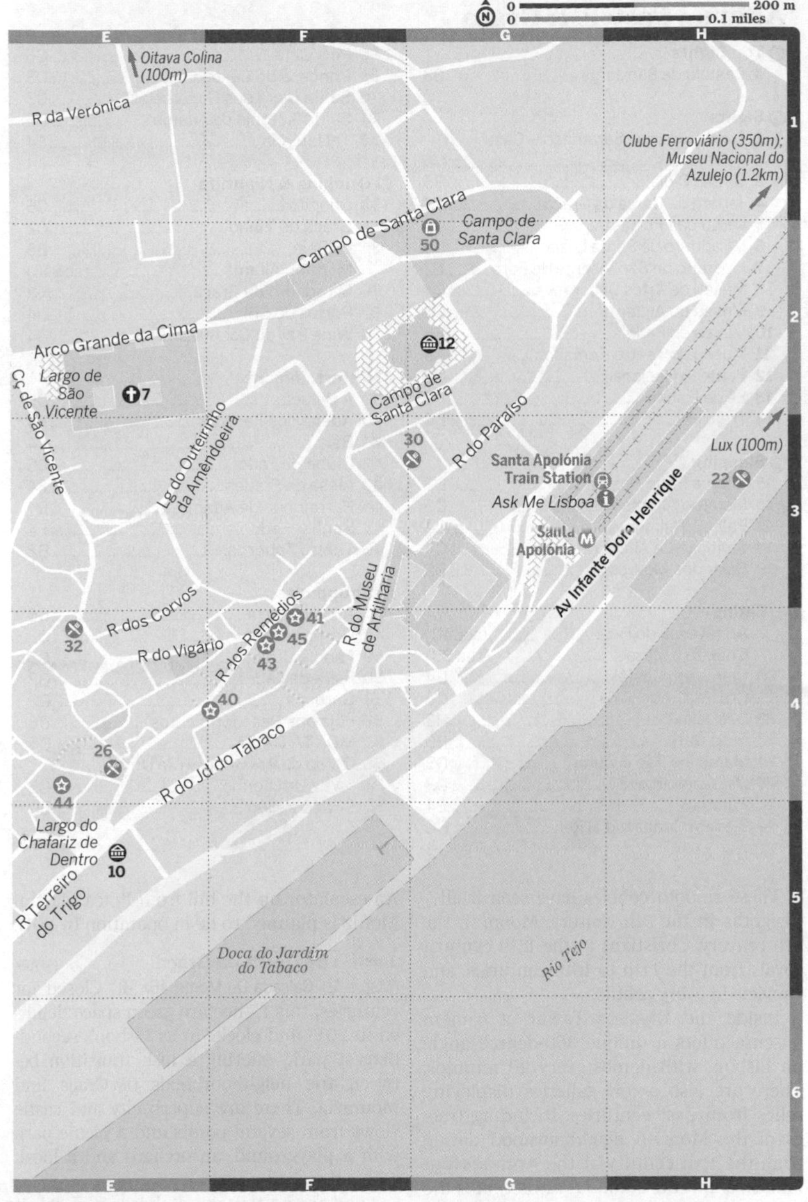

★Castelo de São Jorge CASTLE

(Map p72; www.castelodesaojorge.pt; adult/student/child €8.50/5/free; ⊙9am-9pm Mar-Oct, to 6pm Nov-Feb) Towering dramatically above Lisbon, the mid-11th-century hilltop fortifications of Castelo de São Jorge sneak into almost every snapshot. Roam its snaking ramparts and pine-shaded courtyards for superlative views over the city's red rooftops to the river. Three guided tours daily (Portuguese, English and Spanish) at 1pm and 5pm are included in the admission price.

Alfama, Castelo & Graça

Top Sights
1 Castelo de São Jorge B3

Sights
2 Fundação José Saramago – Casa dos Bicos C6
3 Gothic Cloister B6
4 Jardim da Cerca da Graça C1
5 Largo das Portas do Sol C3
6 Miradouro de Santa Luzia D4
7 Mosteiro de São Vicente de Fora E2
8 Museu de Artes Decorativas C4
9 Museu do Aljube C5
10 Museu do Fado E5
11 Museu do Teatro Romano C5
12 Panteão Nacional G2
13 Sé de Lisboa C6
14 Treasury B6

Sleeping
15 Alfama Patio Hostel D3
16 Memmo Alfama D5
17 Palácio Belmonte C4
18 Santiago de Alfama C4
19 Solar dos Mouros B5

Eating
A Travessa do Fado .... (see 10)
Chapitô à Mesa .... (see 33)
20 Claras em Castelo B4
21 Cruzes Credo Café C6
22 DeliDelux H3
23 India Gate B6
24 Marcelino Pão e Vinho D3
25 Os Gazeteiros D3
26 Páteo 13 .... E4
27 Placete Chafariz d'el Rei D6
28 Pois Café C6
29 Princesa do Castelo D3
30 Santa Clara dos Cogumelos G3
31 Santo António de Alfama D5
32 Ti-Natércia E4

Drinking & Nightlife
33 Chapitô C5
34 Graça do Vinho C2
35 LisBeer B6
Memmo Alfama .... (see 16)
36 Miradouro da Graça C1
37 Portas do Sol D4
38 Wine Bar do Castelo B4

Entertainment
39 A Baîuca D5
40 Adega dos Fadistas F4
41 Bela F4
42 Clube de Fado C6
43 Mesa de Frades F4
44 Parreirinha de Alfama E4
45 Senhor Fado F4
46 Teatro Taborda B2

Shopping
47 Arte da Terra C5
48 Cortiço & Netos C2
49 Fabula Urbis C5
50 Feira da Ladra G2
51 Garbags D2
52 Loja dos Descobrimentos B6
53 MO&TA CA.SA C6
54 O Voo da Andorinha/Era Uma Vez Um Sonho C5
55 Silva & Feijóo B6

These smooth cobbles have seen it all – Visigoths in the 5th century, Moors in the 9th century, Christians in the 12th century, royals from the 14th to 16th centuries, and convicts in every century.

Inside the **Ulysses Tower**, a camera obscura offers a unique 360-degree angle on Lisbon, with demos every 20 minutes. There are also a few galleries displaying relics from past centuries, including traces of the Moorish neighbourhood dating from the 11th century at the **Archaeological Site**. But the standout attraction is the view – as well as the anachronous feeling of stepping back in time amid fortified courtyards and towering walls. There are a few cafes and restaurants to while away time in as well.

Bus 737 from Sé or Praça da Figueira goes right to the gate. Tram 28 also passes nearby. An escalator up the hill from Praça Martim Moniz is planned to be in operation by 2017.

Jardim da Cerca da Graça PARK

(Map p72; Calçada Do Monte 46;) Closed for centuries, this 1.7-hectare green space debuted in 2015 and clocks in as Lisbon's second-biggest park, offering a lush transition between the neighbourhoods of Graça and Mouraria. There are superb city and castle views from several points and a picnic park with a playground, an orchard and a kiosk with a terrace.

Load up on wine and cheese and call it an afternoon!

Museu do Aljube MUSEUM

(Map p72; www.museudoaljube.pt; Rua do Augusto Rosa 42; 10am-6pm Tue-Sun) FREE Both poignant and haunting, this new and highly important museum has turned the former

Portuguese dictatorship's political prison of choice into a museum of truth and consequence, memorial and remembrance.

Museu de Artes Decorativas MUSEUM
(Museum of Decorative Arts; Map p72; www.fress.pt; Largo das Portas do Sol 2; adult/child €4/free; ⏲10am-5pm Wed-Mon) Set in a 17th-century palace, the Museu de Artes Decorativas creaks under the weight of treasures including blingy French silverware, priceless Qing vases as well as Indo-Chinese furniture, a collection amassed by a wealthy Portuguese banker from the age of 16. It's worth a visit alone to admire the lavish apartments that are embellished with baroque *azulejos,* frescoes and chandeliers.

It's a particularly atmospheric spot to watch a live **fado** performance on Wednesday evenings at 6pm.

Sé de Lisboa CATHEDRAL
(Map p72; Largo de Sé; ⏲9am-7pm Tue-Sat, to 5pm Mon & Sun) FREE One of Lisbon's icons is the fortress-like Sé de Lisboa, built in 1150 on the site of a mosque soon after Christians recaptured the city from the Moors.

It was sensitively restored in the 1930s. Despite the masses outside, the rib-vaulted interior, lit by a rose window, is calm. Stroll around the cathedral to spy leering gargoyles peeking above the orange trees.

History buffs shouldn't miss the less-visited **Gothic cloister** (Map p72; Largo de Sé; admission €2.50; ⏲10am-5pm Mon, to 6.30pm Tue-Sat Apr-Sep, 10am-5pm Mon-Sat Oct-Mar), which opens onto a deep pit full of archaeological excavations going back more than 2000 years. You have to squint hard to imagine it, but you'll see remnants of a Roman street and shopfronts, an Islamic-era house and dump, as well as a medieval cistern. The **Treasury** (Map p72; Largo de Sé; admission €2.50; ⏲10am-5pm Mon-Sat) showcases religious artwork.

Museu do Fado MUSEUM
(Map p72; www.museudofado.pt; Largo do Chafariz de Dentro; adult/child €5/3; ⏲10am-6pm Tue-Sun) Fado (the traditional Portuguese melancholic song) was born in the Alfama district. Immerse yourself in its bittersweet symphonies at the Museu do Fado. This engaging museum traces fado's history from its working-class roots to international stardom.

Mosteiro de São Vicente de Fora CHURCH
(Map p72; Largo de São Vicente; adult/child €5/free; ⏲10am-6pm Tue-Sun) Graça's Mosteiro de São Vicente de Fora was founded in 1147 and revamped by Italian architect Felipe Terzi in the late 16th century. Since the adjacent church took the brunt of the 1755 earthquake (the church's dome crashed through the ceiling of the **sacristy**, but emerged otherwise unscathed), elaborate blue-and-white *azulejos* dance across almost every wall, echoing the building's architectural curves.

Panteão Nacional MUSEUM
(Map p72; www.patrimoniocultural.pt; Campo de Santa Clara; adult/child €4/free, free 1st Sun of the month; ⏲10am-6pm Tue-Sun, to 5pm Oct-Mar) Perched high and mighty above Graça's Campo de Santa Clara, the porcelain-white Panteão Nacional is a baroque beauty. Originally intended as a church, it now pays homage to Portugal's heroes and heroines, including 15th-century explorer Vasco da Gama and *fadista* (singer of traditional Portuguese song) Amália Rodrigues.

Lavishly adorned with pink marble and gold swirls, its echoing dome resembles an enormous Fabergé egg. Trudge up to the 4th-floor viewpoint for a sunbake and vertigo-inducing views over Alfama and the river.

Oitava Colina BREWERY
(Map p62; ☎218 278 528; www.oitavacolina.pt; Travessa da Pereira 16A; tour & tasting €10) One of the top brewers in Lisbon's budding microbrew scene, Oitava Colina opens its brewery door for tours and tasting on Saturdays by appointment. You'll taste their standards (a lager, porter and IPA) plus any one-offs they

GET LOST IN THE ALFAMA

There's no place like the labyrinthine Alfama for ditching the map and getting lost in sun-dappled alleys and squares full of beauty and banter. Its narrow *becos* (cul de sacs) and *travessas* (alleys) lead you on a spectacular wild-goose chase past chalk-white chapels and tiny grocery stores, patios shaded by orange trees, and João's freshly washed underpants. The earthy, working-class residents, *alfacinhas*, fill the lanes with neighbourly chatter, wafts of fried fish and the mournful ballads of fado. Experiencing Alfama is more about luxuriating in the everyday than ticking off the big sights. Take a serendipitous wander through lanes fanning out from Rua de São Miguel, Rua de São João da Praça and Rua dos Remédios.

Príncipe Real, Santos & Estrela

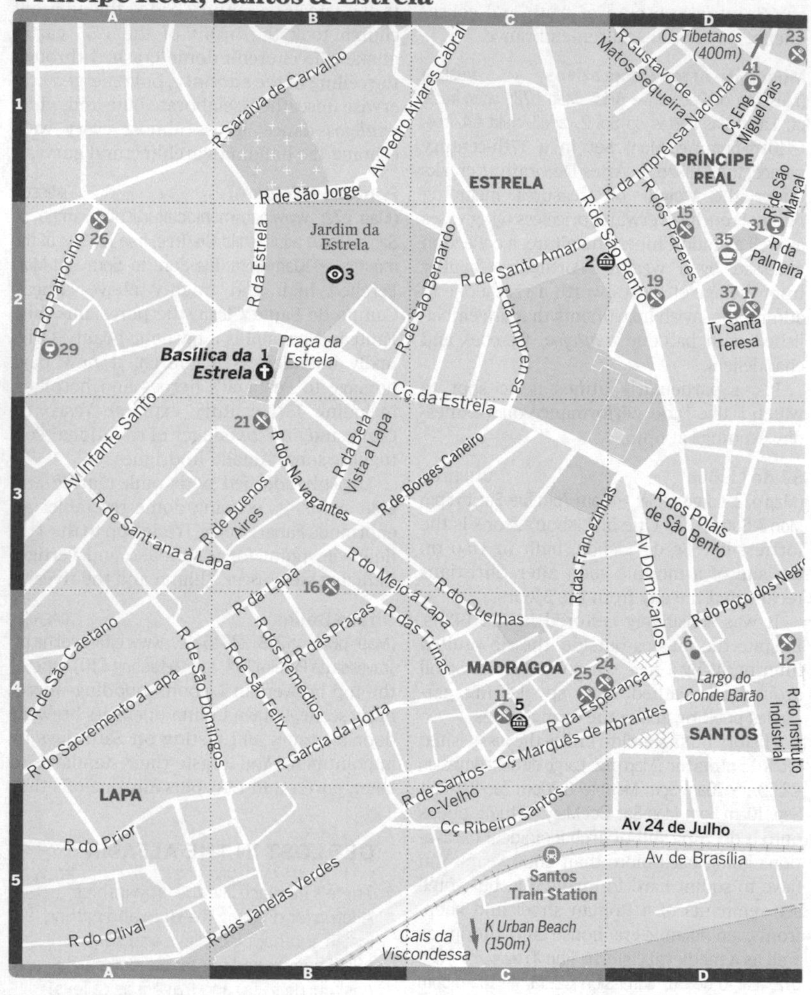

have going. It's a great insight into a truly micro operation.

Fundação José Saramago – Casa dos Bicos LANDMARK, MUSEUM

(Map p72; www.josesaramago.org; Rua dos Bacalhoeiros 10; adult/child €3/free; ⏲10am-6pm Mon-Sat) The pincushion facade of the Casa dos Bicos, the eccentric 16th-century abode of Afonso de Albuquerque, former viceroy to India, grabs your attention with its 1125 diamond-shape spikes *(bicos)*. The *casa* houses a small **museum** which is dedicated to José Saramago (1922–2010), Portugal's most famous writer; as well as a newly added ground-floor excavation of Roman ruins (which are free of charge).

Museu do Teatro Romano MUSEUM

(Roman Theatre Museum; Map p72; www.museuteatroromano.pt; Rua de São Mamede 5A; adult/child €1.50/free; ⏲11am-6pm Tue-Sun) FREE The ultramodern Museu do Teatro Romano, reopened in 2015 after a two-year renovation and further excavation, catapults you back to Emperor Augustus' rule in Olisipo (Lisbon). The star attraction is a ruined Roman **theatre** extended in AD 57, buried in

the 1755 earthquake and finally unearthed in 1964 (which you can enter for free).

Príncipe Real, Santos & Estrela

West of Bairro Alto, these serene and affluent tree-fringed neighbourhoods slope down to the Rio Tejo, and are dotted with boutique hotels, art galleries, vine-clad courtyards and antique shops. This offbeat corner of Lisbon harbours a handful of must-sees including a neoclassical basilica, exotic gardens, a cavernous ancient art museum, plus the neoclassical Palácio da Assembleia da República, home to Portugal's parliament.

★Basílica da Estrela CHURCH

(Map p76; Praça da Estrela; basilica free, nativity scene €1.50, roof €4; ⏲basilica 7.30am-7.45pm, terrace 10am-6.40pm, presépio 10-11.30am & 3-5pm, closed Mon afternoon & Sun morning) The curvaceous, sugar-white dome and twin belfries of Basílica da Estrela are visible from afar. The echoing interior is awash with pink-and-black marble, which creates a kaleidoscopic effect when you gaze up into the cupola. The neoclassical beauty was completed in 1790 by order of Dona Maria I (whose tomb is here) in gratitude for a male heir.

Museu da Marioneta MUSEUM

(Puppet Museum; Map p76; www.museudamarioneta.pt; Rua da Esperança 146; adult/child €5/3, free 10am-1pm Sun; ⏲10am-1pm & 2-6pm Tue-Sun) Discover your inner child at the surprisingly enchanting Museu da Marioneta, a veritable Geppetto's workshop housed in the 17th-century Convento das Bernardas. Alongside superstars such as impish Punch and his Portuguese equivalent Dom Roberto are rarities: Vietnamese water puppets, Sicilian opera marionettes and intricate Burmese shadow puppets. Check out the fascinating exhibit of the making of the animation film, *A Suspeita*.

Casa Museu de Amália Rodrigues MUSEUM

(Map p76; www.amaliarodrigues.pt; Rua de São Bento 193; adult/child €5/3.50; ⏲10am-1pm & 2-6pm Tue-Sun) A pilgrimage site for fado fans, Casa Museu de Amália Rodrigues is where the Rainha do Fado (Queen of Fado) Amália Rodrigues lived; note graffiti along the street announcing it as Rua Amália. Short tours take in portraits, glittering costumes and crackly recordings of her performances.

Jardim da Estrela GARDENS

(Map p76; Praça da Estrela; ⏲gardens 7am-midnight) FREE Seeking green respite? Opposite the Basílica da Estrela, this 1852 green space is perfect for a stroll, with paths weaving past pine, monkey puzzle and palm trees, rose and cacti beds and the centrepiece – a giant banyan tree. Kids love the duck ponds and animal-themed playground. There are several open-air cafes where you can recharge.

Príncipe Real, Santos & Estrela

Top Sights
1 Basílica da Estrela ... B2

Sights
2 Casa Museu de Amália Rodrigues ... C2
3 Jardim da Estrela ... B2
4 Jardim do Príncipe Real ... E1
5 Museu da Marioneta ... C4

Activities, Courses & Tours
6 We Hate Tourism Tours ... D4

Sleeping
7 Casa de Santos ... E4
8 Casa do Príncipe ... E1
9 Hotel Alegria ... F1
10 Memmo Príncipe Real ... F1

Eating
11 A Travessa ... C4
12 Água no Bico ... D4
13 As Velhas ... F1
14 Bettina & Niccolò Corallo ... E1
15 Cantinho Lusitano ... D2
16 Clube das Jornalistas ... B3
17 Dona Quitéria ... D2
18 Esplanada do Príncipe Real ... E1
19 Gelataria Nannarella ... D2
20 Jardim dos Sentidos ... F1
21 Loco ... B3
22 Mercearia do Século ... E2
23 O Prego da Peixaria ... D1
24 Petiscaria Ideal ... C4
25 Taberna Ideal ... C4
26 Tasca da Esquina ... A2
27 Terra ... E2
28 ZeroZero ... E1

Drinking & Nightlife
29 A Paródia ... A2
30 Bar TR3S ... E2
31 Cerveteca Lisboa ... D2
32 Chafariz do Vinho ... F1
33 Cinco Lounge ... E2
34 Construction ... E1
35 Copenhagen Coffee Lab ... D2
36 Finalmente ... E2
37 Foxtrot ... D2
38 Lost In ... F1
39 Loucos & Sonhadores ... F2
40 Pavilhão Chinês ... F1
41 Trumps ... D1
42 WoofLX ... E2

Shopping
43 Embaixada ... E1
44 Entre Tanto ... E1
45 Espaço B ... E1
46 Loja Real ... E1
47 Nuno Gama ... E1
48 Solar ... F1
49 Verso Branco ... E4

Jardim do Príncipe Real PLAZA
(Map p76) Shaded by a giant cedar tree, Jardim do Príncipe Real is a relaxing shady plaza with an alfresco cafe for watching the world go slowly by. The surrounding district is perfect for lazy days spent exploring markets, antique stores, edgy boutiques and design stores. Creatives, hipsters and the gay community love this boho pocket of Lisbon.

Lapa & Alcântara

Near the scenic but gratingly noisy suspension bridge (and Golden Gate lookalike) Ponte 25 de Abril, the reborn Alcântara dock is sprinkled with outdoor restaurants and drinking spots. For sightseers, the star attraction is the impressive Museu do Oriente; this spectacularly converted warehouse turns the spotlight on Portugal's links with Asia.

Getting here on westbound tram 28 or 25 is fun. You can also get here by taking the riverside bike path from Cais do Sodré.

Museu do Oriente MUSEUM
(Map p80; www.museudooriente.pt; Doca de Alcântara; adult/child €6/2, admission free 6-10pm Fri; 10am-6pm Tue-Sun, to 10pm Fri) The beautifully designed Museu do Oriente highlights Portugal's ties with Asia, from colonial baby steps in Macau to ancestor worship. The museum occupies a revamped 1940s *bacalhau* (dried salt-cod) warehouse – a €30-million conversion. Strikingly displayed in pitch-black rooms, the collection focuses on the Portuguese presence in Asia, and Asian gods.

Marquês de Pombal & Around

Up north, Lisbon races headlong into the 21st century with gleaming high-rises, dizzying roundabouts, shopping malls and the Parisian-style boulevard Avenida da Liberdade, which poet Fernando Pessoa dubbed 'the finest artery in Lisbon'. The contrast to the old-world riverfront districts is startling.

Though often overlooked, these parts reveal some gems: from René Lalique glitterbugs at the Museu Calouste Gulbenkian to Hockney masterpieces at Centro de Arte Moderna, hothouses in Parque Eduardo VII to the lofty arches of Aqueduto das Águas Livres.

★Museu Calouste Gulbenkian MUSEUM
(www.museu.gulbenkian.pt; Av de Berna 45; adult/child €5/free, Sun free; ⌚10am-6pm Wed-Mon) Famous for its quality and breadth, the world-class Museu Calouste Gulbenkian showcases an epic collection of Western and Eastern art – from Egyptian treasures to Old Master and Impressionist paintings.

The chronological romp kicks off with highlights such as gilded Egyptian mummy masks, Mesopotamian urns, elaborate Persian carpets, Qing porcelain (note the grinning *Dogs of Fo*) and a fascinating Roman gold-medallion collection. Going west, art buffs admire masterpieces by Rembrandt (*Portrait of an Old Man*), Van Dyck and Rubens (including the frantic *Loves of the Centaurs*). Be sure to glimpse Rodin's passionate *Eternal Springtime*. The grand finale is the collection of exquisite René Lalique jewellery, including the otherworldly *Dragonfly*.

Centro de Arte Moderna MUSEUM
(Modern Art Centre; CAM; www.cam.gulbenkian.pt; Rua Dr Nicaulau de Bettencourt; adult/chilld €5/free, free Sun; ⌚10am-6pm Wed-Mon) Situated in a sculpture garden, the Centro de Arte Moderna reveals a stellar collection of 20th-century Portuguese and international art.

Casa-Museu Medeiros e Almeida MUSEUM
(www.casa-museumedeirosealmeida.pt; Rua Rosa Araújo 41; adult/child €5/free, free 10am-1pm Sat; ⌚1-5.30pm Mon-Fri, 10am-5.30pm Sat) Housed in a stunning early-19th-century mansion, this little-known museum presents António Medeiros e Almeida's exquisite fine- and decorative-arts collection. Highlights include Han ceramics and Ming- and Qing-dynasty porcelain, Thomas Gainsborough paintings, a 300-strong stockpile of watches and clocks (one of the best private collections in Europe), and a dinner service that once belonged to Napoleon Bonaparte.

Parque Eduardo VII PARK
(Alameda Edgar Cardoso; ⌚daylight) FREE An urban oasis with British roots, Parque Eduardo VII is named after his highness Edward VII, who visited Lisbon in 1903. The sloping parterre affords sweeping views over the whizzing traffic of Praça Marquês de Pombal to the river.

Mãe d'Água HISTORIC BUILDING
(Mother of Water; www.epal.pt; Praça das Amoreiras 10; adult/child €3/1.50; ⌚10am-12.30pm & 1.30-5.30pm Tue-Sat, 1.30-5.30pm Sun) The king laid the aqueduct's final stone at Mãe d'Água, the city's massive 5500-cu-metre main reservoir. Completed in 1834, the reservoir's cool, echoing chamber is a fine place to admire 19th-century technology. Climb the stairs for a fine view of the aqueduct and the surrounding neighbourhood. Admission is €5 if there is an exhibition on.

Belém

As well as Unesco World Heritage–listed Manueline stunners such as Mosteiro dos Jerónimos and the whimsical Torre de Belém, this district 6km west of the centre offers a tranquil botanical garden, fairy-tale golden coaches, Lisbon's tastiest *pastéis de nata* (custard tarts) and a whole booty of other treasures.

The best way to reach Belém is on the zippy tram 15 from Praça da Figueira or Praça do Comércio.

★Mosteiro dos Jerónimos MONASTERY
(Map p84; www.mosteirojeronimos.pt; Praça do Império; adult/child €10/5, 1st Sun of month free; ⌚10am-6.30pm Tue-Sun, to 5.30pm Oct-May)

WATER FEATURE

The 109 arches of the **Aqueduto das Águas Livres** (Map p62; Aqueduct of the Free Waters; ☎218 100 215; www.epal.pt; Campolide) lope across the hills into Lisbon from Caneças, more than 18km away; they are most spectacular at Campolide, where the tallest arch is an incredible 65m high. Built between 1728 and 1835, by order of Dom João V, the aqueduct is a spectacular feat of engineering and brought Lisbon its first clean drinking water. Its more sinister claim to fame is as the site where 19th-century mass murderer Diogo Alves pushed his victims over the edge. One of the best places to see the aqueduct is in the leafy **Praça das Amoreiras** next to the Mãe d'Água.

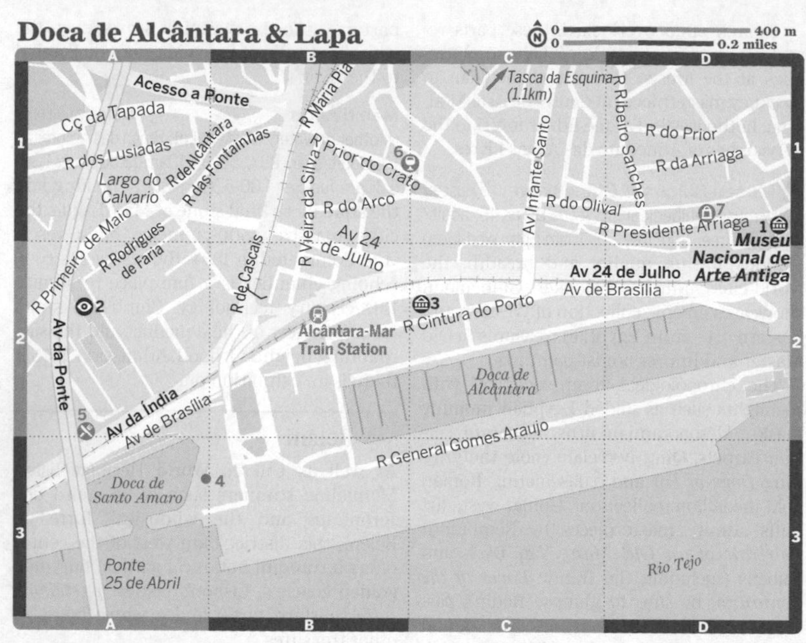

Doca de Alcântara & Lapa

Top Sights
1 Museu Nacional de Arte Antiga............D1

Sights
2 LX Factory............A2
3 Museu do Oriente............C2

Activities, Courses & Tours
4 HIPPOtrip............A3
Kiss the Cook............(see 2)

Eating
1300 Taberna............(see 2)
5 Cafetaria Village............A2
Landeau............(see 2)
Rio Maravila............(see 2)

Drinking & Nightlife
Bosq............(see 2)
6 Chimera Brewpub............B1

Shopping
Kare Design............(see 2)
Ler Devagar............(see 2)
LX Market............(see 2)
7 Portugal Gifts............D1

Belém's undisputed heart-stealer is this Unesco-listed monastery. The *mosteiro* is the stuff of pure fantasy; a fusion of Diogo de Boitaca's creative vision and the spice and pepper dosh of Manuel I, who commissioned it to trumpet Vasco da Gama's discovery of a sea route to India in 1498.

Wrought for the glory of God, Jerónimos was once populated by monks of the Order of St Jerome, whose spiritual job for four centuries was to comfort sailors and pray for the king's soul. When the order was dissolved in 1833, the monastery was used as a school and orphanage until about 1940.

Entering the **church** through the western portal, you'll notice tree-trunk-like columns that seem to grow into the ceiling, which is itself a spiderweb of stone. Windows cast a soft golden light over the church. Superstar Vasco da Gama is interred in the lower chancel, just left of the entrance, opposite venerated 16th-century poet Luís Vaz de Camões. From the upper choir, there's a superb view of the church; the rows of seats are Portugal's first Renaissance woodcarvings.

There's nothing like the moment you walk into the honey-stone Manueline **cloisters**, dripping with organic detail in their delicately scalloped arches, twisting auger-shell turrets and columns intertwined with leaves, vines and knots. It will simply wow. Keep an eye out for symbols of the age such as the armillary sphere and the cross of the Military Order, plus gargoyles and fantastical beasties on the upper balustrade.

If you plan to visit both the monastery and Torre de Belém, you can save a little by purchasing a €12 admission pass valid for both, or €16 including the **Museu Nacional de Arqueologia** (National Archaeology Museum; Map p84; www.museuarqueologia.pt; Praça do Império; adult/child €5/free, free 1st Sun of the month; ⏲10am-6pm Tue-Sun).

★Museu Nacional dos Coches MUSEUM

(Map p84; www.museudoscoches.pt; Av da Índia 136; adult/child €6/3, free 1st Sun of month; ⏲10am-6pm Tue-Sun) Cinderella wannabes delight in Portugal's most visited museum, which dazzles with its world-class collection of 70 17th- to 19th-century coaches in a new ultramodern (and some might say inappropriately contrasting) space that debuted in 2015. Don't miss Pope Clement XI's stunning ride, the scarlet-and-gold *Coach of the Oceans,* or the old royal riding school, **Antigo Picadeiro Real** (Map p84; Praça Afonso de Albuquerque; adult/child €4/free, free 1st Sun of month; ⏲10am-6pm Tue-Sun), across the street.

Torre de Belém TOWER

(www.torrebelem.pt; adult/child €6/3, 1st Sun of month free; ⏲10am-6.30pm Tue-Sun, to 5.30pm Oct-Apr) Jutting out onto the Rio Tejo, this Unesco World Heritage–listed fortress epitomises the Age of Discoveries. You'll need to breathe in to climb the narrow spiral staircase to the tower, which affords sublime views over Belém and the river.

Museu de Arte, Arquitetura e Tecnologia MUSEUM

(Art, Architecture & Technology Museum; MAAT; Map p84; www.maat.pt; Av Brasília, Central Tejo; from €5; ⏲noon-8pm, closed Tue) Lisbon's latest riverfront star is this low-rise, glazed-tiled structure that intriguingly hips and sways into ground-level exhibition halls. Visitors can walk over and under its reflective surfaces, which play with water, light and shadow and pay homage to the city's intimate relationship with the sea.

Museu da Presidência da República MUSEUM

(Museum of the Presidency of the Republic; Map p84; www.museu.presidencia.pt; Praça Afonso de Albuquerque, Palácio de Belém; adult/child €2.50/free; ⏲10am-6pm Tue-Sun) Portugal's small presidential museum is worth a look for its fascinating state gifts exhibit – note the outrageous 1957 offering from Brazil's Juscelino Kubitschek, a massive tortoiseshell depicting handpainted Brazilian scenes, Saudi swords and a gorgeous traditional Japanese dance depiction scene. Don't miss the official presidential portrait of Mário Soares.

Palácio Nacional da Ajuda PALACE

(Map p62; ☎213 637 095; www.palacioajuda.pt; Largo da Ajuda; adult/child €5/free, free 1st Sun of month; ⏲10am-6pm Thu-Tue) Built in the early 19th century, this staggering neoclassical palace served as the royal residence from the 1860s until the end of the monarchy (1910). You can tour private apartments and state rooms, getting an eyeful of gilded furnishings and exquisite artworks dating back five centuries; and, since 2014, the queen's chapel, home to Portugal's only El Greco painting.

DON'T MISS

A WONDROUS ART COLLECTION

Set in a lemon-fronted, 17th-century palace, the **Museu Nacional de Arte Antiga** (Ancient Art Museum; Map p80; www.museudearteantiga.pt; Rua das Janelas Verdes; adult/child €6/3, 1st Sun of month free; ⏲10am-6pm Tue-Sun) is Lapa's biggest draw. It presents a star-studded collection of European and Asian paintings and decorative arts. Keep an eye out for highlights such as Nuno Gonçalves' naturalistic *Panels of São Vicente,* Albrecht Dürer's *St Jerome,* Lucas Cranach's haunting *Salomé,* as well as period furniture pieces such as King Afonso V's ceremonial 1470s armchair and the elaborate lacquered wood, silver-gilt and bronze late-16th-century casket. Other gems include the golden wonder that is the *Monstrance of Belém*, a souvenir from Vasco da Gama's second voyage, and 16th-century Japanese screens depicting the arrival of the Namban (southern barbarians), namely big-nosed Portuguese explorers.

Marquês de Pombal & Around

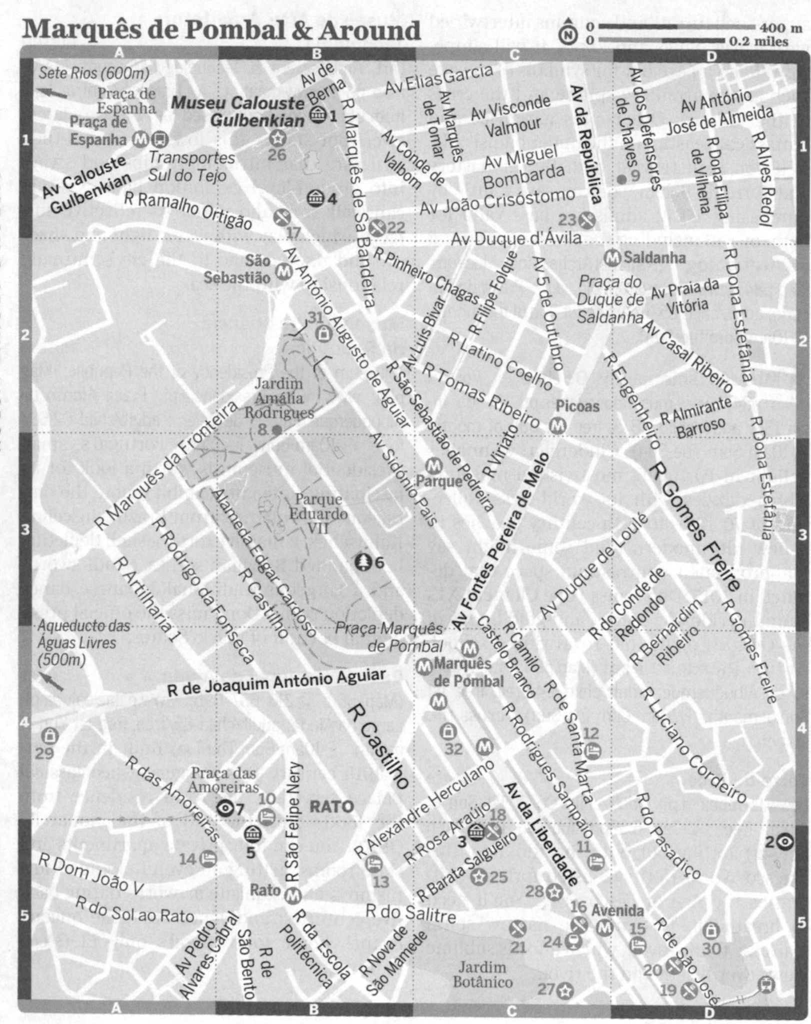

It's a long uphill walk from Belém, or you can take tram 18 or several buses from downtown, including 760 from Praça do Comércio.

Museu Colecção Berardo MUSEUM

(Map p84; www.museuberardo.pt; Praça do Império; ⏲10am-7pm Tue-Sun) FREE Culture fiends get their contemporary-art fix for free at the Museu Colecção Berardo, the star of the Centro Cultural de Belém. The ultrawhite, minimalist gallery displays millionaire José Berardo's eye-popping collection of abstract, surrealist and pop art, including Hockney, Lichtenstein, Warhol and Pollack originals.

Temporary exhibitions are among the best in Portugal. Also in the complex is a cafe-restaurant that faces a grassy lawn, a bookshop and a crafty museum store.

Palácio de Belém HISTORIC BUILDING

(Belém Palace; Map p84; ☎213 614 660; www.presidencia.pt; Praça Afonso de Albuquerque; €5/free; ⏲10am-6pm Sat) The salmon-slabbed 16th-century Belém Palace is Portugal's official presidential residence (though the country's last president, Cavaco Silva,

Marquês de Pombal & Around

Top Sights
1 Museu Calouste Gulbenkian B1

Sights
2 Campo dos Mártires da Pátria D5
3 Casa-Museu Medeiros e Almeida C5
4 Centro de Arte Moderna B1
5 Mãe d'Água B5
6 Parque Eduardo VII B3
7 Praça das Amoreiras B4

Activities, Courses & Tours
8 Lisbon Bike Tour B2
9 Sociedade Portuguêsa para o Estudo de Aves D1

Sleeping
10 Casa Amora B4
11 Hotel Britania C5
12 Inspira Santa Marta C4
13 Lisbon Dreams B5
14 O Bigode do Rato A5
15 Valverde D5

Eating
16 Cervejaria Ribadouro C5
Cinemateca Portuguesa .... (see 25)
17 Ground Burger B1
18 Guilty C5
19 Jesus é Goês D5
20 Maria Mil Reis D5
21 Os Tibetanos C5
22 Velocité B1
23 Versailles C1

Drinking & Nightlife
24 Red Frog C5

Entertainment
25 Cinemateca Portuguesa C5
26 Fundação Calouste Gulbenkian B1
27 Hot Clube de Portugal C5
28 São Jorge C5

Shopping
29 Amoreiras Shopping Center A4
30 Carbono D5
31 El Corte Inglês B2
32 Luis Onofre C4

chose to live in his own home) and office. Tours in Portuguese, English and French are available on Saturday only, with just 150 spots up for grabs (book in advance via email). Alternatively, a small but fascinating museum (p81) is open throughout the week.

Jardim Botânico Tropical GARDENS
(Map p84; www2.iict.pt; Largo dos Jerónimos; adult/child €2/1; ⏲10am-8pm May-Aug, shorter hours in winter) Far from the madding crowd, these botanical gardens bristle with hundreds of tropical species from date palms to monkey puzzle trees. Spread across 7 hectares, it's a peaceful, shady retreat on a sweltering summer's day. A highlight is the Macau garden, complete with minipagoda, where bamboo rustles and a cool stream trickles.

Padrão dos Descobrimentos MUSEUM
(Discoveries Monument; Map p84; www.padraodosdescobrimentos.pt; Av de Brasília; adult/child €4/2; ⏲10am-7pm, to 6pm Oct-Feb) Like a caravel frozen in midswell, the Padrão dos Descobrimentos was inaugurated in 1960 on the 500th anniversary of Henry the Navigator's death. The 56m-high limestone giant is full of Portuguese bigwigs. At the prow is Henry, while behind him are explorers Vasco da Gama, Diogo Cão, Fernão de Magalhães (Ferdinand Magellan) and 29 other greats.

Do take the lift (or puff up 267 steps) to the windswept **miradouro** for 360-degree views over the river. The mosaic in front of the monument charts the routes of Portuguese mariners.

Museu de Marinha MUSEUM
(Naval Museum; Map p84; www.museu.marinha.pt; Praça do Império; adult/child €6.50/free, free 1st Sun of month; ⏲10am-6pm Tue-Sun, to 5pm Oct-Apr) The Museu de Marinha is a nautical flashback to the Age of Discoveries with its armadas of model ships, cannonballs and shipwreck booty. Dig for buried treasure like Vasco da Gama's portable wooden altar, 17th-century globes (note Australia's absence) and the polished private quarters of UK-built royal yacht *Amélia*. A separate building houses royal barges, 19th-century firefighting machines and seaplanes.

Parque das Nações

A model of urban regeneration, Parque das Nações has almost single-handedly propelled the city into the 21st century since Expo '98. Here you'll find an impressive aquarium, riverside gardens, public-art

Belém

Belém

Top Sights
1 Mosteiro dos Jerónimos B1
2 Museu Nacional dos Coches D1

Sights
3 Antigo Picadeiro Real C1
4 Jardim Botânico Tropical B1
5 Museu Colecção Berardo A2
Museu da Presidência da República .... (see 10)
6 Museu de Arte, Arquitetura e Tecnologia D2
7 Museu de Marinha A1
8 Museu Nacional de Arqueologia A1
9 Padrão dos Descobrimentos B2
10 Palácio de Belém C1

Sleeping
11 Jerónimos 8 .... B1
12 Pensão Residencial Setúbalense C1

Eating
13 Alecrim & Manjerona C1
14 Antiga Confeitaria de Belém B1
15 Enoteca de Belém C1
16 Espaço Espelho d'Água A2

Entertainment
17 Centro Cultural de Belém A2

installations, and outdoor dining options galore.

To reach Parque das Nações, take the train or metro to Gare do Oriente and follow the signs to the waterfront. The riverside promenade is great for two-wheel adventures. To rent your own set of wheels, there are well-worn bikes at the reception of **Marina Parque das Nações** (☎218 949 066; www.marinaparquedasnacoes.pt; bike hire per 1/4/8hr €5/10/12; ⏲9am-9pm, to 7pm Oct-Apr) or head to **Ring-A-Bike** (☎964 442 027; www.ringabike.pt; Rua do Armistício 24, Moscavide; bike hire 1-/4-/8hr from €5/10/20; ⏲9am-8.30pm Wed-Mon), 1.6km northwest of Parque das Nações in Moscavide. For a bird's-eye view of the park, take a ride on the **Teleférico** (Telecabine Lisboa; www.telecabinelisboa.pt; Passeio do Tejo; 1-way adult/child €3.95/2; ⏲10.30am-8pm, 11am-7pm off season), which glides above the river's edge.

Oceanário AQUARIUM
(www.oceanario.pt; Doca dos Olivais; adult/child €14/9, incl temporary exhibition €17/11; ⏲10am-8pm, to 7pm winter) The closest you'll get to scuba diving without a wetsuit, Lisbon's Oceanário is mind-blowing. No amount of hyperbole, where 8000 marine creatures splash in 7 million litres of seawater, does it justice. Huge wrap-around tanks make you feel as if you are underwater, as you eyeball zebra sharks, honeycombed rays, gliding mantas and schools of neon fish.

Pavilhão do Conhecimento MUSEUM
(Pavilion of Knowledge; www.pavconhecimento.pt; Living Science Centre; adult/child €9/5; ⏲10am-6pm Tue-Fri, 11am-7pm Sat & Sun) Kids won't grumble about science at the interactive Pavilhão do Conhecimento, where they can experience the gravity on the moon (or lack thereof, rather) and get dizzy on a high-wire bicycle. Budding physicists have

fun whipping up tornadoes and blowing massive soap bubbles, while tots run riot in the adult-free unfinished house.

Gare do Oriente NOTABLE BUILDING
(Oriente Station; Av Dom João II) Designed by acclaimed Spanish architect Santiago Calatrava, the space-age Gare do Oriente is an extraordinary vaulted structure, with slender columns fanning out into a concertina roof to create a kind of geometric forest.

Activities

ViniPortugal WINE
(Map p66; www.winesofportugal.info; Praça do Comércio; ⏲11am-7pm Tue-Sat) Under the arcades on Praça do Comércio, this viticultural organisation offers €6 themed wine tastings, if booked in advance. Otherwise, pop in and grab a €3 enocard, which allows you to taste between two and four Portuguese wines, from Alentejo whites to full-bodied Douro reds.

Walking Tours

Sandemans New Lisbon WALKING
(Map p68; www.newlisbontours.com; ⏲10am, 11am & 2pm) FREE For the inside scoop on the city, Sandemans' fun, informative and free 2½-hour walking tours of downtown Lisbon are hard to beat. You'll do the rounds of all the major landmarks and get versed in history and city tips as you stroll. The tours begin at the scheduled time (book online) at the monument on Praça Luís de Camões.

Underdogs Public Art Store TOURS
(Map p68; www.under-dogs.net; Rua da Cintura do Porto de Lisboa, Armazém A; tours from €35; ⏲11am-8pm Mon-Sat) Witness the strength of street knowledge at this part gallery, part Montana-street-art paint store and cafe behind Cais do Sodre. Underdogs specialises in high-profile public art and is the go-to guy for Lisbon's street-art tours, the best of which hit the road via e-bike. Themes include central Lisbon, greater Lisbon and Vhils, the artist behind the underdogs.

Lisbon Walker WALKING
(Map p66; ☎218 861 840; www.lisbonwalker.com; Rua dos Remédios 84; 3hr walk adult/child €15/free; ⏲10am & 2.30pm) This excellent company, with well-informed, English-speaking guides, offers themed walking tours through Lisbon, which depart from the northwest corner of Praça do Comércio.

Lisbon Explorer WALKING
(☎213 629 263; www.lisbonexplorer.com; tour per person/group from €60/150) English-speaking guides peel back the many layers of Lisbon's history during the three-hour walking tours offered by this highly rated outfit. Fees do not include admissions but often include public-transport costs during the tour. Tours typically depart from Praça do Comércio or other central locations. You'll receive the meeting point upon booking.

Bike Tours

Lisbon Bike Tour CYCLING
(☎912 272 300; www.lisbonbiketour.com; adult/child €32.50/15; ⏲9.30am-1pm) It's all downhill on this 3½-hour guided bike ride from Marquês de Pombal to Belém.

Speciality Tours

We Hate Tourism Tours TOURS
(Map p76; ☎913 776 598; www.wehatetourismtours.com; Rua da Silva 27; per person from €30; ⏲11am-7pm Mon & Thu) One memorable way to explore the city is aboard an open-topped UMM (a Portuguese 4WD once made for the

DON'T MISS

HITCH A RIDE ON TRAM 28

Vintage **tram 28** (Rua da Conceição) offers the ultimate spin of Lisbon's blockbuster sights – from Basílica da Estrela to the backstreets of **Baixa** (Rua da Conceição) – for the price of a €2.85 ticket. The route from Campo Ourique to Martim Moniz is 45 minutes of astonishing views and absurdly steep climbs. The most exciting bit is when the tram commences its rattling climb to Alfama, where passengers lean perilously out of the window for an in-motion shot of the *sé* (cathedral) or hop out for postcard-perfect views from **Miradouro de Santa Luzia** (Map p72; Largo Santa Luzia). The final stretch negotiates impossibly narrow streets and hairpin bends up to Graça, where most folk get out to explore **Mosteiro de São Vicente de Fora** (p75). Keep in mind that many locals use this as their only transport; be kind and offer a seat, and avoid riding at peak hours. Beat the heavy crowds by going early in the morning or in the evening – otherwise they won't stop when full.

Walking Tour
Exploring the Alfama

START MIRADOURO DA SENHORA DO MONTE
END PRAÇA DO COMÉRCIO
LENGTH 3KM; TWO TO THREE HOURS

This scenic route starts on tram 28 from Largo Martim Moniz or the Baixa, taking in the city's best tram route *and* avoiding uphill slogs. Take the tram up to Largo da Graça. From here, stroll north and turn left behind the barracks for breathtaking views from Lisbon's highest lookout, **1 Miradouro da Senhora do Monte**. Next, walk south and turn right to pine-shaded **2 Miradouro da Graça**, where central Lisbon spreads out before you. Retrace your steps and head east to admire the exquisitely tiled cloisters of **3 Mosteiro de São Vicente de Fora** (p75), and the cool, echoing **4 Panteão Nacional** (p75). If it's Tuesday or Saturday, make a detour to the buzzy **5 Feira da Ladra** (Thieves Market; p118) to hunt for buried treasure. Otherwise, go west along Arco Grande da Cima until you reach Largo de Rodrigues de Freitas. Take the Costa do Castelo fork, continuing west to skirt the castle battlements along narrow cobbled streets affording stunning views. Pass in front of **6 Solar dos Mouros**, then turn left up to the **7 Castelo de São Jorge** (p73) and its **8 viewpoint**. Next, head down the steep lanes to Largo das Portas do Sol, and another fine vista from bougainvillea-clad **9 Miradouro de Santa Luzia** (p85). From here wander northward, past whitewashed **10 Igreja de Santa Luzia** and turn right into the atmospheric lane of Beco de Santa Helena, threading through labyrinthine Alfama to Largo das Alcaçarias. Take Rua de São João da Praça westward, pausing for a bite or a drink at **11 Cruzes Credo Café**, before continuing on to the fortress-like **12 Sé de Lisboa** (p75) and **13 Igreja de Santo António**. Continue downhill, stopping for a look at the intricate Manueline facade of **14 Igreja da Conceição Velha**, before ending at **15 Praça do Comércio** (p64), Europe's largest square.

army). In addition to the weekend King of the Hills tour, this alternative outfit organises dinners followed by a night tour around Lisbon, plus responsible walks, longer city tours and excursions to Sintra. Most trips depart from Praça Luís de Camões.

You can always find these folks hanging out and drinking wine at their quirky HQ, dubbed the Armazém Geral, on Mondays and Thursdays.

HIPPOtrip ADVENTURE
(Map p80; ☎211 922 030; www.hippotrip.com; Doca de Santo Amaro; adult/child €25/15; ⏰9am-6pm) This fun 90-minute tour takes visitors on a land and river tour in an amphibious vehicle that drives straight into the Tejo! It begins and ends at Doca de Santo Amaro. From April to September, tours depart at 10am, noon, 2pm, 4pm and 6pm (the last departure falls off the schedule from October to March).

GoCar Touring DRIVING
(Map p66; ☎210 965 030; www.gocartours.pt; Rua dos Douradores 16; per hr/day €29/89; ⏰9.30am-6.30pm) These self-guided tours put you behind the wheel of an open-topped, two-seater minicar with a talking GPS that guides you along one of several predetermined routes. Helmets included.

Culinary Activities

Culinary Backstreets FOOD
(☎963 472 188; www.culinarybackstreets.com/culinary-walks/lisbon; 3/6hr tour €85/118) *Eat Portugal* co-author Célia Pedroso leads epic culinary walks through Lisbon, a fantastic way to take in some of the best treats in town. Try *ginjinha* (cherry liqueur) followed by *pastel de nata* (custard tarts) and *porco preto* (Iberian black pork), paired with killer local wines. Tours are available Monday to Saturday. Expect tantalising multiple foodgasms followed by a debilitating food coma.

Kiss the Cook COOKING
(Map p80; ☎968 119 652; www.kissthecook.pt; Rua Rodrigues Faria 103, LX Factory; class €65; ⏰noon-3pm) If you're into Portuguese food in a big way and fancy picking up a few tips and tricks from the experts, why not pass by Kiss the Cook? Here you can prepare (and devour) traditional dishes. The cookery classes are totally hands-on and the price includes lunch and wine.

Festivals & Events

February

Lisbon Carnival CULTURAL
(www.visitlisboa.com) From Friday to Tuesday before Ash Wednesday, Lisbon celebrates with abandon at music-filled street parties and big events (including costume balls) at nightclubs.

April

Indie Lisboa FILM
(☎213 158 399; www.indielisboa.com; ⏰Apr & May) This spring filmathon brings 10 days of indie features, documentaries and shorts to Lisbon's big screens.

Peixe em Lisboa FOOD
(☎222 088 500; www.peixemlisboa.com; Terreiro de Paço; €15; ⏰Apr) Seafood lovers won't want to miss this week-long culinary extravaganza, put on by a dozen restaurants (including chefs with Michelin stars).

Dias da Música MUSIC
(☎213 612 400; www.ccb.pt; Praça do Império; ⏰Apr) Classical-music buffs see world-renowned orchestras perform at this three-day festival held in April at **Centro Cultural de Belém** (CCB; Map p84; ☎213 612 400; www.ccb.pt; Praça do Império; ⏰8am-8pm Mon-Fri, 10am-6pm Sat-Sun).

May

Meo Out Jazz MUSIC
(www.ncs.pt; ⏰May-Sep) One of the best free events of summer, Out Jazz happens on Fridays and Sundays from May through September, with a band playing at a different park around the city each week. DJs follow the live music. Bring a picnic blanket and join the festive summer crowds.

Rock in Rio – Lisboa MUSIC
(www.rockinriolisboa.sapo.pt; Bela Vista Park; ⏰May) This Brazilian import, which bounces between Rio, Madrid, Las Vegas and Lisbon, is one of the world's largest music festivals and tends to arrive in the Portuguese capital with the world's biggest bands in tow every other year, including 2018 and 2020.

June

Fado no Castelo FADO
(www.castelodesaojorge.pt; Praça de Armas, Castelo de São Jorge; ⏰10pm, Jun) FREE Lisbon's love affair with fado takes centre

SAINTLY CELEBRATIONS

Come all ye faithful lovers of *vinho*-swigging, sardine-feasting, dancing and merrymaking to June's **Festas dos Santos Populares** (Festivals of the Popular Saints), three weeks of midsummer madness. In Lisbon, the key saintly festivities are:

Festa de Santo António (Festival of St Anthony) This lively fest is celebrated with particular fervour in Alfama and Madragoa from 12 to 13 June, with feasting, drinking, *bailes* (balls) and some 50 *arraiais* (street parties). St Anthony has a bit of a reputation as a matchmaker. *Lisboêtas* declare their undying love by giving *manjericos* (basil plants) with soppy poems. Around 300 hard-up couples get hitched for free!

Festa de São Pedro (Festival of St Peter) Lisbon pulls out all the stops for St Peter, the patron saint of fisher folk, from 28 to 29 June. There are slap-up seafood dinners and river processions in his barnacled honour.

stage at this newly inaugurated annual song-fest held at the cinematic Castelo de São Jorge (p73) over three evenings in June, with a different singer performing each night in the square at the castle entrance. Admission is free; a limited number of tickets are available and must be picked up in advance.

Festival ao Largo MUSIC
(www.festivalaolargo.pt; late Jun-late Jul) Free outdoor performances including classical concerts, ballet recitals and opera take place in front of the Teatro Nacional de São Carlos (p115).

July

NOS Alive MUSIC
(www.nosalive.com; Passeio Marítimo de Algés; Jul) This three-day music and arts shindig, held annually in July along the river in Algés, is one of the best and most popular events on the European summer-festival circuit. The 10th anniversary 2016 edition drew headliners such as Radiohead, Arcade Fire and the Chemical Brothers.

BaixAnima PERFORMING ARTS
(Jul-Sep) Baixa's summertime shindig entertains the crowds for free on weekends from July to September with circus acts and live music, improvised theatre and mime.

Super Bock Super Rock FESTIVAL
(www.superbocksuperrock.pt; Jul) One of Portugal's premier music festivals, held in July. It jumps locations frequently – the 2016 edition saw artist such as Iggy Pop, Kendrick Lamar and The National rocking Parque das Nações.

August

Jazz em Agosto MUSIC
(217 823 000; www.musica.gulbenkian.pt; Aug) Both established and fresh talent are welcomed to the stage at this soulful jazz fest, which is held at **Fundação Calouste Gulbenkian** (Av de Berna 45A).

Sleeping

Lisbon has an array of boutique hotels, upmarket hostels and both modern and old-fashioned guesthouses. Be sure to book ahead for high season (July to September). A word to those with weak knees and/or heavy bags: many guesthouses lack lifts, meaning you'll have to haul your luggage up three flights or more. If this disconcerts, be sure to book a place with an elevator.

Baixa & Rossio

Sandwiched between the Alfama and Bairro Alto, this central area is packed with options, including high-end hotels, modest and upper-end guesthouses and first-rate hostels. You can walk everywhere and there's great public transit.

Lisbon Destination Hostel HOSTEL €
(Map p66; 213 466 457; www.destinationhostels.com; Rossio train station, 2nd fl; dm/s/d from €23/40/80;) Housed in Lisbon's loveliest train station, this world-class hostel has a glass ceiling lighting the spacious plant-filled common area. Rooms are crisp and well-kept, and there are loads of activities (bar crawls, beach day trips, etc). Facilities include a shared kitchen, game consoles, movie room (with popcorn) and 24-hour self-service bar. Breakfast is top-notch with crêpes and fresh fruit.

Home Lisbon Hostel HOSTEL €
(Map p66; ☎218 885 312; www.homelisbonhostel.com; Rua São Nicolau 13; dm €26-30) Situated in the heart of Baixa, this dorm-only hostel is one of the best maintained you'll come across. Facilities are above and beyond, from the professional-grade bar/reception to dark hardwood bunks spread across various floors with privacy curtains that might as well be luxury drapes. It's a family-run oasis, with the doting matriarch, known affectionately as Mamma, even cooking for guests.

Living Lounge HOSTEL €
(Map p68; ☎213 461 078; www.livingloungehostel.com; Rua do Crucifixo 116, 2nd fl; dm/s/d from €26/37/64; ❄@📶) The Living Lounge is steeped in style – vintage barber chairs, suspended tables, vinyl on the speakers – and offers spic-and-span mixed dorms with lockers, various hang lounges, friendly staff and excellent amenities (full kitchen, bicycle hire, an obvious cocktail emphasis). The nightly dinners and wide range of tours provide a fine opportunity to meet other travellers.

Travellers House HOSTEL €
(Map p66; ☎210 115 922; www.travellershouse.com; Rua Augusta 89; dm €28-30, s/d without bathroom €40/70, d €80-90; ❄@📶) Travellers enthuse about this super-friendly hostel set in a converted 250-year-old house on Rua Augusta. As well as cosy dorms and a wealth of comfortable privates (some more minimalist than others), there's a retro lounge with beanbags, an internet corner and a communal kitchen. Newly installed CCTV and heaters keep everyone safe and warm.

Residencial Restauradores GUESTHOUSE €
(Map p66; ☎213 475 660; www.residencialrestauradores.pt; Praça dos Restauradores 13, 4th fl; d €35; ❄) Run by a kindhearted old soul, this convent-evoking guesthouse has clean, old-fashioned rooms with homey furnishings and private bathrooms. The best have fine views over the plaza. French, English and Spanish spoken.

★ Lisbon Story Guesthouse GUESTHOUSE €€
(Map p66; ☎218 879 392; www.lisbonstoryguesthouse.com; Largo de São Domingos 18; d €80-100, without bathroom €50-70, apt €120; @📶) Overlooking Largo de São Domingos, Lisbon Story is a small, extremely welcoming guesthouse with nicely maintained, light-drenched rooms, all of which sport Portuguese themes (the Tejo, tram 28, fado etc) and working antique radios, record players and the like. The shoe-free lounge, with throw pillows and low tables, is a great place to chill.

My Story Rossio BOUTIQUE HOTEL €€
(Map p66; ☎213 400 380; www.mystoryhotels.com; Praça Dom Pedro IV 59; s/d from €127/137; ❄📶) This 2015 newcomer gets a gold star for its central location right on Rossio Sq. Carpeted hallways depicting Google Maps views of Lisbon lead to rooms (and bathrooms) that tend to be cramped (you'll be happier in a roomier superior), but travellers enjoy hi-tech mod cons such as TV/mirror hybrids, quirky themes (Fado, Amor, Lisboa) and value for money.

Lavra Guest House GUESTHOUSE €€
(Map p66; ☎218 820 000; www.lavra.pt; Calçada de Santano 198; d not incl breakfast €55-75; ❄📶) Set in a former convent that dates back two centuries, this 30-room guesthouse has stylishly set rooms with wood floors and tiny balconies. Some bathrooms are cramped. It's a short stroll from the Ascensor da Lavra, or a steep climb from Largo de São Domingos. Breakfast is €5.

Pousada de Lisboa BOUTIQUE HOTEL €€€
(Map p66; ☎210 407 650; www.pestana.com/en/hotel/pousada-lisboa; Praça do Comércio 31; r from €210; ❄@📶🏊) Location, location, location! Portugal's Pestana chain hit triple 7s with this 2015 newcomer's privileged position on Praça do Comércio. A €70-million renovation turned the former Ministry of Internal Affairs into a cosy *pousada* with museum-like qualities. Sculptures throughout represent epic moments in Portuguese history and, yes, you can sit on those 13th-century *liteiras* (litters).

Internacional Design Hotel BOUTIQUE HOTEL €€€
(Map p66; ☎213 240 990; www.idesignhotel.com; Rua da Betesga 3; s/d from €150/165; P❄@📶) This high-concept hotel has four types of rooms, each conjuring a radically different aesthetic. Urban rooms have brightly coloured artwork and duvets; Tribu rooms have wood details and burlap wallpaper; Zen aim for simple elegance; while Pop feature eye-catching art and bubblegum-coloured floors and walls. The best? Room 407 (Pop), with its tiny balcony staring straight over Rossio.

Lisbon's Architectural Highs

Lisbon is packed with stunning architectural works that span more than five centuries. You'll find wildly intricate Unesco World Heritage sites commemorating Portugal's Golden Age of Discoveries, whimsical works of wrought-iron elegance (with grand views over the old city) and cutting-edge designs of the late 20th century.

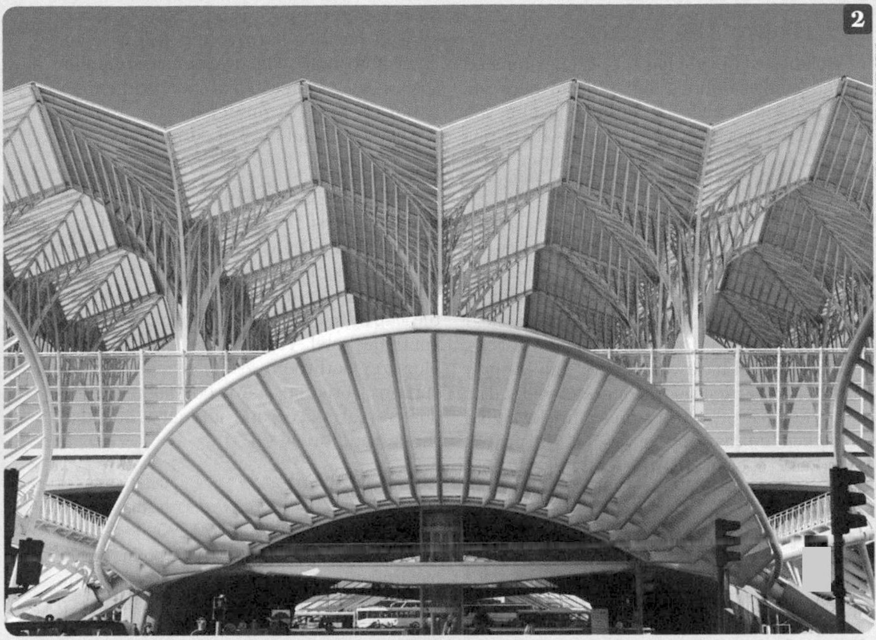

2

3

1. Torre de Belém (p81), Belém
Built in 1515, the Manueline-period architecture of Torre de Belém epitomises the Age of Discoveries era.

2. Gare do Oriente (p85), Parque das Nações
The futuristic Gare do Oriente was built by Spanish architect Santiago Calatrava for Expo '98.

3. Elevador de Santa Justa (p65), Baixa
Ride this neo-Gothic street lift for views of the city.

4. Sé de Liboa (p75), Alfama
This iconic Lisbon cathedral was built on the site of a mosque in 1150.

4

Bairro Alto & Chiado

Well-heeled Chiado has high-quality top-end and budget options, but little in between. Bairro Alto is nightlife central, meaning you won't get much rest amid the late-night revelry. The hip Santa Catarina district has a few options.

Lisbon Calling HOSTEL €
(Map p68; 213 432 381; www.lisboncalling.net; Rua de São Paulo 126, 3rd fl; dm/d with shared bathroom €16/55, d €75;) This fashionable, unsigned backpacker favourite near Santa Catarina features original frescoes, *azulejos* and hardwood floors – all lovingly restored by friendly Portuguese owners. The bright, spacious dorms and a brick-vaulted kitchen are easy on the eyes, but the private rooms – specifically room 1812 – will floor you: boutique-hotel-level dens of style and comfort that thunderously out-punch their price point.

Sunset Destination Hostel HOSTEL €
(Map p68; 210 997 735; www.destinationhostels.com; Cais do Sodré train station; dm €21-28, s/d without bathroom €35/70, d from €75;) This beautifully designed river-facing hostel is awash in antiquated art deco swank. It has comfy dorm rooms with electronic lockers and a high-style dining room, but it outclasses its peers with its roof pool terrace (with winter dome bar) and impressive river views. Organised street-art tours, pub crawls and fado excursions provide dependable good times.

Independente HOSTEL €
(Map p68; 213 461 381; www.theindependente.pt; Rua de São Pedro de Alcântara 81; dm €21-24, ste without/with view €80-100;) On the edge of the Bairro Alto, this super-stylish hostel has 11 dorm rooms (with six to 12 beds in each) and four Mid-Century Modern–leaning, minimalist suites with original exposed Pombaline Cage support beams and balconies overlooking the Tejo. Next door, **Suites & Terrace** offers more heterogeneously decorated private rooms (Indian tapestries, tattered antiques, classic Portuguese film posters).

Late Birds GUESTHOUSE €€
(Map p68; 926 713 331; www.thelatebirdslisbon.com; Travessa André Valente 21-21A; d €150-200;) Billed as a 'gay urban resort', these fabulous new Bairro Alto sleeps are better described as a high-style guesthouse where gay couples (and those that are straight but not narrow) can feel welcome and comfortable. The design-forward public spaces (sexy lounge, small pool and garden patio) are perfectly minimalist; the 12 whitewashed rooms all have desktop iMacs.

Hotel Alegria GUESTHOUSE €€
(Map p76; 213 220 670; www.alegrianet.com; Praça da Alegria 12; s/d not incl breakfast from €75/85;) Overlooking a palm-dotted plaza, this lemon-fronted belle-époque gem was completely made over in 2016, making the leap from midrange *residencial* to almost boutique hotel. New rooms feature muted blue-grey bathroom *azulejos* and matching curtains; original hardwood-floored corridors reveal stucco and antiques. Breakfast runs an additional €9.50.

★Casa Balthazar GUESTHOUSE €€€
(Map p68; 213 243 000; www.casabalthazarlisbon.com; Rua do Duque 26; r €170-290;) Tucked down a quiet lane, Casa Balthazar has undeniable appeal with spacious, beautifully furnished rooms that bridge art deco with the 21st century; friendly service and a grassy courtyard with a pool. Each of the 17 rooms has been appointed with high-end fittings (iPod docks, big flat-screen TVs, luxury bedding), and pricier rooms have magnificent views (some with private terraces).

★Lisboa Carmo Hotel HOTEL €€€
(Map p68; 213 264 710; www.lisboacarmohotel.com; Rua da Oliveira ao Carmo 1; r €154-203;) On the edge of one of Lisbon's prettiest plazas, this 45-room hotel has classically designed rooms, the best of which have sweeping Lisbon views. It earns high marks for its use of Portuguese products both in the rooms (bed linens, towels, bath products) and in the pleasant ground-floor restaurant.

Hotel do Chiado HOTEL €€€
(Map p68; 213 256 100; www.hoteldochiado.com; Rua Nova do Almada 114; s/d from €280/300;) Fusing 19th-century charm with 21st-century cool, the well-located Hotel do Chiado offers carpeted, well-appointed rooms that come in three styles: classics (small and boxy, with no view), superiors (brighter, roomier with French balconies) and premiums (top-floor rooms that open onto grassy, bougainvillea-clad terraces with views to the river and castle). The 7th-floor bar (open 11am to midnight) offers superb vistas.

LISBON FOR CHILDREN

Even little things in Lisbon spark the imagination – from bumpy rides on bee-yellow trams to gooey *pastéis de nata*(custard tarts). There are free or half-price tickets for little ones at major sights, half-portions at many restaurants and free transport for under-fives.

Parque das Nações

Parque das Nações is prime kiddie territory, where little nippers love to spot toothy sharks and sea otters at the eye-popping Oceanário (p84), experience zero-gravity and ride the high-wire bicycle at the hands-on Pavilhão do Conhecimento (p84), then get utterly soaked at the splashy **Jardins d'Água** (Water Gardens; Passeio de Neptuno; ⌚24hr).

Parque Eduardo VII

Most of Lisbon's squares and parks have playgrounds for little tykes to let off excess energy, including Parque Eduardo VII (p79) and an animal-themed one at Jardim da Estrela (p77).

Museu de Marinha

Go west to relive the nautical adventures of the Age of Discoveries in Belém's barge-stuffed Museu de Marinha (p83).

Museu da Marioneta

Marvel at the puppets in Lapa's enchanting Museu da Marioneta (p77).

Around Lisbon

When the weather warms up, take the train to Cascais (p133) for some ice-cream-licking, bucket-and-spade fun. Kids can make finny friends on a dolphin-watching tour in Setúbal (p147), or play king-of-the-castle in the fantastical turrets and woodlands of Sintra (p123).

Alfama, Castelo & Graça

Alfama's cobbled lanes generally offer peaceful slumber, though choose wisely or else you might find yourself being serenaded to sleep by a warbling *fadista*. On its hilltop perch above Lisbon, leafy Graça has dramatic views.

Alfama Patio Hostel HOSTEL €
(Map p72; ☎218 883 127; www.alfama.destinationhostels.com; Rua das Escolas Gerais 3; dm €18-24, s/d without bathroom from €30/45, d €60; @ 📶) In Alfama's heart, this beautifully run hostel offers custom-made, Cappadocia-inspired particle-board dorms with privacy curtains and lockable drawers. From the upper-floor rooms, you can practically file your fingernails across the top of the tram as it rattles past. A bevy of activities (fado, street art and surfing tours) and barbecues on the garden-like patio mean it's notably social.

But the open-air terrace and resulting views are what seals the deal.

Largo Residencias GUESTHOUSE €
(☎218 885 420; www.largoresidencias.com; Largo de Intendente 19, 3 esq; s/d without bathroom €28/45, s/d €45/65; 📶) Cool and quiet, this artsy multifloored guesthouse sits in the thick of it on Largo de Intendente. Rooms are simple but feature custom-made beds from reclaimed wood, plus piecemeal antiques and other flea-market-found furniture and accoutrements. There's a bohemian cafe on the ground floor.

Palácio Belmonte BOUTIQUE HOTEL €€€
(Map p72; ☎218 816 600; www.palaciobelmonte.com; Páteo Dom Fradique 14; ste €450-2500; P ❄ 📶 🏊) Nestled beside Castelo de São Jorge, this 15th-century palace, formerly belonging to the family of Brazil discoverer Pedro Álvares Cabral, turns on the VIP treatment with its nine suites, named after Portuguese luminaries and lavishly adorned with 18th-century *azulejos*, silks, marble and antiques.

There's a pool framed by herb gardens, a wood-panelled library where classical music plays and numerous other luxuries, including the privilege of sleeping amid original castle walls and towers. A new *sous-vide* **restaurant**, Leopold at Belmonte, opened in 2016.

★**Memmo Alfama** BOUTIQUE HOTEL €€€
(Map p72; ☎210 495 660; www.memmoalfama.com; Travessa Merceeiras 27; r €170-350;) Slip down a narrow alley to reach these gorgeous boutique Alfama sleeps, a stunning conversion of a shoe-polish factory and former bakery. The rooms are an ode to whitewashed minimalism and staff are as sleek as the decor with their uniform-issued Chuck Taylor All-Stars and hipster aura. The view down to the Tejo from the roof terrace is phenomenal.

Santiago de Alfama BOUTIQUE HOTEL €€€
(Map p72; ☎213 941 616; www.santiagodealfama.com; Rua de Santiago 10; r €220-486;) In 2015, Dutch hospitality dreamer Heleen Uitenbroek turned a ruined 15th-century palace into Lisbon's latest luxury sleeps at this 19-room bastion of style. Airy and awash in light pinewoods and contemporary art, her exquisite attention to detail is everywhere, from the Santiago cross-inspired tile flooring to textured bathroom tiling to an encased glass hallway revealing uncovered Roman steps.

Príncipe Real, Santos & Estrela

Leafy neighbourhoods and plenty of style set the scene for an overnight stay in the top-notch boutique hotels here. It's ideal for escapists who prefer pin-drop peace to central bustle.

★**Casa do Príncipe** B&B €€
(Map p76; ☎218 264 183; www.casadoprincipe.com; Praça do Príncipe Real 23; r €99-150;) Perfectly located, exquisitely restored and priced to shock, this new nine-room B&B is housed inside what once was the same 19th-century neo-Moorish palace as Embaixada (p118) next door. Original frescoes, *azulejos* and ornate moulded ceilings adorn the hardwood halls and spacious rooms, which are themed after the life of King Dom Pedro V. Indeed, you'll sleep like a king here yourself.

Casa de Santos GUESTHOUSE €€
(Map p76; ☎915 216 335; www.casadesantos.net; Rua da Boavista 102; d with/without bathroom from €89/55;) Casa de Santos has appealing wood-floored rooms decorated with artwork and eclectic furnishings, including pieces from Asia and Africa. The location is good for those interested in exploring the less touristy neighbourhoods of Santa Catarina and Santos. If you don't mind the shared bathrooms (20 rooms share eight bathrooms), it's excellent value.

Memmo Príncipe Real BOUTIQUE HOTEL €€€
(Map p76; ☎213 514 368; www.memmohotels.com; Rua Dom Pedro V 56; r from €234;) Príncipe Real's hottest new hotel is this 41-room cradle of cool steeped in a corresponding high-design ethos with its sister property in Alfama. Rooms contrast vintage furniture with modern artworks, many featuring terraces complete with outdoor firepits, a real coup for a city-centre hotel. Similarly impressive 180-degree city views beckon from the private rooftop terrace and pool.

Marquês de Pombal & Around

O Bigode do Rato B&B €
(☎938 282 199; www.obigodedorato.com; Rua Dom João V 2A, 4th fl; r per person €25;) Independently minded travellers will find great value at this Rato budget choice. Friendly Italian host Arianna has cutely gussied up a four-bedroom, two-bath apartment with eco-touches such as lampshades made from old cassette tapes and vintage suitcases. You can even get an astounding view (especially from the Metallica room). Arianna pops in for breakfast but it's otherwise all yours.

★**Casa Amora** GUESTHOUSE €€
(☎919 300 317; www.casaamora.com; Rua João Penha 13; d €90-180, apt €120-220;) Casa Amora has 11 beautifully designed guestrooms and studio apartments, with eye-catching art and iPod docks. There's a lovely garden patio where the first-rate breakfast is served. It's located in the peaceful neighbourhood of Amoreiras, a few steps from one of Lisbon's prettiest squares.

Lisbon Dreams GUESTHOUSE €€
(☎213 872 393; www.lisbondreamsguesthouse.com; Rua Rodrigo da Fonseca 29; s/d without bathroom €50/60, d €90;) On a quiet street lined with jacaranda trees, Lisbon Dreams offers excellent value for its bright, modern rooms with high ceilings and excellent mattresses. The green apples are a nice touch, and there are attractive common areas to unwind in. All bathrooms are shared except one, but are spotlessly clean.

Valverde BOUTIQUE HOTEL €€€
(☎210 940 300; www.valverdehotel.com; Av da Liberdade 164; d €200-325, ste €305-600; P❄@🛜🏊) Exquisite Valverde feels like a boutique town house (which of course it once was). Its facade is not showy, but once inside, an urban oasis of discerning design and personalised service is subtlety unveiled. The 25 rooms, reached by black-dominated, hushed hallways, are awash in cultured European art and unique Mid-Century Modern pieces, and elicit style, form and function.

Inspira Santa Marta HOTEL €€€
(☎210 440 900; www.inspirasantamartahotel.com; Rua de Santa Marta 48; r from €144; ❄@🛜) 🍃 The 89-room Inspira Santa Marta is an ecofriendly designer hotel set in a converted 19th-century building. Rooms are stylish but functional with five different feng-shui themes, including earth-toned Terra rooms and cork-floored Arvore (tree) rooms with sky-blue details. An inviting Mediterranean brasserie showcases locally grown ingredients, plus there's a bar with fireplace, games room with billiards table, and a spa.

Hotel Britania HOTEL €€€
(☎213 218 200; www.heritage.pt; Rua Rodrigues Sampaio 17; d €125-400; P❄@🛜) Art deco rules the waves at the 33-room Britania, a boutique gem near Avenida da Liberdade. Cassiano Branco put his modernist stamp on the rooms with chrome lamps, plaid fabrics and shiny marble bathrooms. Hobnob over a G&T at the bar, chat with the affable staff and let this time capsule take you back to 1942.

Belém

Pensão Residencial Setúbalense GUESTHOUSE €
(Map p84; ☎213 636 639; www.setubalense.pt; Rua de Belém 28; s/d not incl breakfast from €45/50; ❄🛜) A short toddle east of the Mosteiro dos Jerónimos, this 17th-century guesthouse has 55 twee but comfy rooms with tiled floors, floral fabrics and modern bathrooms (along with 25 new rooms on the way). Corridors are a tad dark, but *azulejos* and potted plants add a homely touch.

Jerónimos 8 BOUTIQUE HOTEL €€
(Map p84; ☎213 600 900; www.jeronimos8.com; Rua dos Jerónimos 8; s €95-235, d €105-250; ❄🛜) Belém's first boutique hotel, the 65-room Jerónimos 8 harbours style with clean lines, floor-to-ceiling windows and designer flourishes aplenty. Slick rooms are dressed in cream and caramel hues with natural fabrics (four include balconies with monastery views). Chill in the pepper-red bar or grab a drink and take it to the 2nd-floor deck.

Eating

Creative new-generation chefs at the stove, first-rate raw ingredients and a generous pinch of world spice has transformed Lisbon into a buzzing culinary capital. Reservations, even early in the week and in off-season, are a good idea – getting turned away without them is all too common.

Baixa & Rossio

Many of Baixa's old-school bistros and outdoor cafes heave with tourists, but tiptoe away from the main drag, Rua Augusta, and you'll find some gems in streets such as Rua dos Correiros and Rua dos Sapateiros.

★**Mercado da Baixa** MARKET €
(Map p66; www.adbaixapombalina.pt; Praça da Figueira; ⏲10am-10pm Fri-Sun) This tented market/glorious food court on Praça da Figueira has been slinging cheese, wine, smoked sausages and other gourmet goodies since 1855. It takes place on the last weekend of each month and it is fantastic fun to stroll the stalls eating and drinking yourself into a gluttonous mess.

Nova Pombalina PORTUGUESE €
(Map p66; www.facebook.com/anovapombalina; Rua do Comércio 2; sandwiches €2.20-4; ⏲7am-7.30pm, closed Sun) The reason this bustling traditional restaurant is always packed around midday is its delicious *leitão* (suckling pig) sandwich, served on freshly baked bread in 60 seconds or less by the lightning-fast crew behind the counter.

Tasca Kome JAPANESE €€
(Map p66; ☎211 340 117; www.kome-lisboa.com; Rua da Madalena 57; mains €7-15, sushi plates from €15; ⏲noon-2.30pm & 7-10pm Mon-Thu, noon-3pm & 7-10pm Fri, 12.30-3pm & 7-10pm Sat; 🛜) This blink-and-you'll-miss-it Japanese *tasca* is one of Lisbon's few turning out authentic cuisine from the Land of the Rising Sun. The menu doesn't overwhelm with options; instead, there's exquisite sushi, *tonkatsu* (breaded pork cutlets), *shime saba* (mackerel ceviche), slow-cooked pork belly and the like (eggplant bolognese for vegetarians), all

nicely washed down with sake or *mugi-cha* (roasted barley tea).

Bebedouro TAPAS €€
(Map p66; ☎218 860 376; www.facebook.com/bebedourowineandfood; Rua de São Nicolau 24; €4-13; ⏲noon-11.45pm, closed Tue; 📶) Wine-bottle lights illuminate stylish Bebedouro, where full-bodied Douro wines are nicely paired with tasting platters of regional cheese and sausage, creative salads and *petiscos* (tapas or small plates). The small, shotgun-style place has just five tables and five bar seats plus a little pavement terrace.

Bonjardim PORTUGUESE €€
(Map p66; ☎213 424 389; Travessa de Santo Antão 11; roast chicken for 2 €13.50; ⏲noon-11pm, closed Wed & Thu lunch) Juicy, spit-roast *frango* (chicken) is served with a mountain of fries at this no-frills joint. Add *piri-piri* (hot sauce) for extra spice. The pavement terrace is elbow-to-elbow in summer.

Casa do Alentejo PORTUGUESE €€
(Map p66; www.casadoalentejo.com.pt; Rua Portas de Santo Antão 58; mains €11-14; ⏲lunch & dinner Mon-Sat; 📶) Hidden behind a plain facade, the Casa do Alentejo has a museum-quality, Moorish-style interior that some say is even more impressive than the food – pork with clams, lamb stew and other Alentejan favourites served upstairs in two palatial 17th-century tile-filled dining rooms. The changing €8 lunch specials are good value.

★**Cervejaria Ramiro** SEAFOOD €€€
(Map p66; www.cervejariaramiro.pt; Av Almirante Reis 1; seafood per kg around €11.73-89.25; ⏲noon-12.30am Tue-Sun) Opened in 1956, Ramiro has legendary status among Lisbon's seafood lovers. Here you can feast on rich plates of giant tiger prawns, *percebes* (goose barnacles), lobster, crab and clams – and a juicy steak sandwich for nonpescatarians. Despite the high prices, the atmosphere is bustling and informal, with garrulous crowds quaffing more beer than wine.

Ramiro doesn't take reservations after 7.30pm, so arrive early and prepare to queue.

Solar dos Presuntos PORTUGUESE €€€
(Map p66; ☎213 424 253; www.solardospresuntos.com; Rua das Portas de Santo Antão 150; mains €16-27.50, seafood per kg €29-70; ⏲12.30-3.30pm & 7-11pm Mon-Sat; 📶) Don't be fooled by the smoked *presunto* (ham) hanging in the window, this iconic restaurant is renowned for its excellent seafood too. Start with the excellent *pata negra* (cured ham), *paio* smoked sausage and cheese *couvert* (stew), then dig into a fantastic lobster *açorda* (nibbles), delectable seafood paella or crustacean curry. Go easy on their homespun *piri-piri* – it bites back!

Chiado & Cais do Sodré

★**Mercado da Ribeira** MARKET €
(Map p68; www.timeoutmarket.com; Av 24 de Julho; ⏲10am-midnight Sun-Wed, to 2am Thu-Sat; 📶) Doing trade in fresh fruit and veg, fish and flowers since 1892, this oriental-dome-topped market hall is the word on everyone's lips since *Time Out* transformed half of it into a gourmet food court in 2014. Now it's like Lisbon in microcosm, with everything from Garrafeira Nacional wines to Conserveira de Lisboa fish, Arcádia chocolate and Santini gelato.

Follow the lead of locals and come for a browse in the morning followed by lunch at one of 35 kiosks – there's everything from Café de São Bento's famous steak and fries to a stand by top-chef Henrique Sá Pessoa. Do not miss it.

Landeau SWEETS €
(Map p68; www.landeau.pt; Rua das Flores 70; cake €3.50; ⏲noon-7pm; 📶) The Portuguese love to self-proclaim (by name, no less!) their product to be the Best This or the Best That in the World, but this don't-miss cafe puts its chocolate where its mouth is, serving up as flawless a piece of chocolate cake as you'll ever encounter.

Gelato Davvero ICE CREAM €
(Map p68; www.gelatodavvero.com; Praça São Paulo 1; mini/medium/large €1.50/2.50/3.50; ⏲12.45-8pm Sun & Tue-Thu, to midnight Fri-Sat; 📶) Owner Filippo Licitra defected from Lisbon's Gelataria Nannarella after a divorce. His rival *gelataria*, Davvero, boasts 35 flavours on the board, so there's room for wackiness (avocado, salmon, curried mango), but the creamilicious classics are all here. Take a seat on the striking stacked-hardwood booths and don't forget to top it with the delicious in-house whipped cream. When in Rome!

O Trevo PORTUGUESE €
(Map p68; Praça Luís de Camões 48; snacks €0.80-2.50; ⏲7am-10pm Mon-Sat) Despite a posh address on Praça Luís de Camões, O Trevo is a bustling and surly local joint deeply rooted in the daily grind. Working-class Lisbon bellies up to the counter for *bifanas* –

thinly sliced pork, precooked in boiling seasoned lard and slapped on the griddle, then served between two slices of warmed *biju* bread with mustard and/or chilli oil.

Pistola y Corazon MEXICAN €
(Map p68; www.pistolaycorazon.com; Rua da Boavista 16; tacos €6.50-7; noon-3pm & 6pm-midnight Mon-Fri, 6pm-midnight Sat-Sun;) This lively hipster *taquería* (taco stand) is a Godsend of authentic Mexican street tacos (*carnitas, cochinita pibil, carne asada, al pastor* etc, served in sets of three), served among tweaked *El Tri* kitsch (Frida Kahlo rocking a Daft Punk T-shirt!). The creative mescal- and tequila-laced cocktail list is equally outstanding. Write your name on the wait list – it's always packed.

Sol e Pesca PORTUGUESE €
(Map p68; www.solepesca.com; Rua Nova do Carvalho 44; tinned fish €3-5; noon-2am Sun-Thu, to 3am Fri-Sat) Rods, nets, hooks and fish charts give away this tiny bar's former life as a fishing-tackle shop. Cabinets are stacked with vintage-looking tins of sardines, tuna, mackerel and other preserved delicacies. Grab a chair, order a tin or two, and accompany it with bread, olives and wine, and you have the makings of a fine and quite affordable meal.

Povo PORTUGUESE €
(Map p68; www.povolisboa.com; Rua Nova do Carvalho 32; small plates €7-11; 6pm-2am Mon-Wed & Sun, to 4am Thu-Sat) On bar-lined Rua Nova do Carvalho, Povo serves tasty Portuguese comfort food in the form of *petiscos*. There's also outdoor seating, plus live performances a few times per week from in-house *fadista* Marta de Sousa (Thursdays are best; from 9.30pm).

Cafe Tati CAFE €
(Map p68; 213 461 279; www.cafetati.blogspot.com; Rua da Ribeira Nova 36; mains €7-8; 11am-1am Tue-Sun;) Cafe Tati has bohemian charm amid its smattering of well-lit stone-arched rooms with stencilled walls. Along with inventive *tibornas* (elaborate Portuguese-style bruschetta with toppings such as *presunto* dry-cured ham, green apple and brie) and salads (marinated tuna with sesame seeds and capers), there are appetising daily specials.

Cantina das Freitas PORTUGUESE €
(ACISJF; Map p68; www.juntanacionalacisjf.blogspot.pt; Travessa do Ferragial 1, top fl; mains €7; noon-3pm Mon-Fri) Sweet nuns dressed as lunch ladies run this small, sunny cafeteria inside a Catholic association, dishing up a daily soup (the gazpacho is great!), several mains – of the beef, sardines or codfish variety – and fresh fruit for dessert. The river views from the sun-drenched terrace are astounding.

Brio SUPERMARKET €
(Map p68; www.brio.pt; Travessa do Carmo 1; 9am-8pm Mon-Fri, 10am-8pm Sat, noon-7pm Sun) If you're self-catering or simply after a picnic, this organic, reasonably priced grocer stocks the essentials: wines, yoghurts, granolas, cold drinks, chocolates, cheeses, breads and more. There's also a small cafe with outdoor tables in front.

Mini Bar FUSION €€
(Map p68; 211 305 393; www.minibar.pt; Rua António Maria Cardoso 58; small plates €2.40-12.50, tasting menus €39-48.50; 7pm-2am;) Trendy and fun, Mini Bar is the most approachable and hippest entry point into the innovative cuisine of Michelin-starred chef José Avillez, who has several restaurants in the vicinity. Billed as a gourmet bar amid theatre-inspired decor, it's a trendy mash-up of nightlife and fine dining, where you'll enjoy exceptional craft drinking alongside small, chef-driven *petiscos*.

Palácio Chiado GASTRONOMIC €€
(Map p68; www.palaciochiado.pt; Rua do Alecrim 70; mains €7-28; noon-midnight Sun-Wed, to 2am Thu-Sat;) The ravishing former home of Portuguese barons and French generals is Lisbon's stunning new address for foodies, a gourmet-food court wrapped in exquisitely renovated 18th-century packaging. A breathtaking grand staircase, swamped by original stained glass and archetypal frescoes, invites you to explore seven gastronomic concepts spread over two floors, from burgers and grills to sparkling wine and seafood.

Taberna Tosca TAPAS €€
(Map p68; 218 034 563; www.tabernatosca.com; Praça São Paulo 21; tapas €7-15.50; noon-midnight) A peaceful retreat from nearby Rua Nova do Carvalho mayhem, Tosca is an enticing spot for Portuguese tapas and bold Douro reds (but don't be afraid to spring for a pitcher of fabulous port sangria). Open-air seating is on leafy Praça São Paulo in front, opposite an 18th-century church, making it feel like a hidden Lisbon highlight.

Vicente by Carnalentejana ALENTEJANO €€
(Map p68; 218 237 126; www.restaurantecarnalentejana.com; Rua das Flores 6; mains €9-14; noon-11pm;) This sexy newcomer dishes up succulent beef and pork dishes made with ultra-premium Carnalentejana DOP-certified meat from the Alentejo along with wines, cheeses, olive oils and other treats produced by the same artisan farmers. A former coal shop turned carnivore's den of decadence, the original low-slung stone walls, exposed air ducts and filament light bulbs are notably atmospheric.

Sacramento PORTUGUESE, MEDITERRANEAN €€
(Map p68; 213 420 572; www.sacramentodochiado.com; Calçada Sacramento 40; mains €13-38.50; noon-3pm & 7.30pm-midnight;) If you drop your *céntimos* at one touristy restaurant in Lisbon, choose contemporary Sacramento, a fun and festive restaurant gorgeously set inside a 17th-century former palace. Both the decor (soothing maroon and chocolate-framed mirrors and suspended red luminaires spread among several rooms) and the food (lovely wild mushrooms with *presunto*, a perfectly charred octopus *à lagareiro*) are real crowd-pleasers.

Queijaria CHEESE €€
(Map p68; www.queijaria.wix.com/queijaria; Rua das Flores 64; 1/3/5 cheese tasting €4.70/11.70/14.70; 1-10pm Tue-Fri, from noon Sat-Sun;) What started as Lisbon's only dedicated cheese shop has evolved into a fantastic place to sample top homespun cheeses from small regional producers otherwise inaccessible in the capital. Plop yourself down for a creamy, barnyardy five-cheese plate paired with wines or craft beer (serves two; €42.50 to €47.50). No regrets!

Sala de Corte STEAK €€
(Map p68; 213 460 030; www.saladecorte.pt; Rua da Ribeira Nova 28; steaks €11.50-29; noon-3pm & 7pm-midnight Mon-Fri, noon-midnight Sat-Sun;) The not-to-be-missed 'cut room' in Cais do Sodré dishes out succulent, perfectly seasoned imported beef in six cuts (entrecôte, *picanha*, sirloin, chateaubriand etc), which are chargrilled in a small, world-class Josper grill/oven hybrid, then prepped and beautifully presented on wooden planks in an intimate open kitchen. When you're sick of seafood, run here – but not without a reservation!

Taberna da Rua das Flores PORTUGUESE €€
(Map p68; 213 479 418; Rua das Flores 103; small plates €2.50-14; noon-midnight Mon-Fri, 6pm-midnight Sat) You'll have to get past the owner's unfortunate 'My way or the highway' attitude, but if you do, this tiny throwback tavern does a daily-changing, locally sourced chalkboard menu of creative small plates, all market-fresh and fantastic. Sweet staff offer in-depth, mouth-watering descriptions for each dish, which are chased with Lisbon-area-only wines and select cocktails mixed with hardcore Portuguese firewaters.

Mercantina PIZZA €€
(Map p68; 231 070 013; www.mercantina.pt; Rua da Misericórdia 114; pizza €8.70-14, pasta €10.80-13.40; noon-3.30pm & 7.30-11.30pm Mon-Thu, noon-3.30pm & 7pm-midnight Fri, 12.30-3.30pm & 7pm-midnight Sat, 12.30-3.30pm & 7-11.30pm Sun;) You'll find Lisbon's best pizza – uncut, certified by Napoli's strict *Associazione Verace Pizza Napoletana* – at this cosy Chiado hotspot whose hardwood-heavy decor vaguely approaches ski-lodge territory. The spicy *diavola* (tomato, mozzarella, ventricina, Parmesan and basil) and *mercantina* (tomato, mozzarella, ham, salami, mushrooms and Parmesan) are both showstoppers, but don't discount the phenomenal lasagne. Reserve ahead online.

Fábulas CAFE €€
(Map p68; www.fabulas.pt; Calçada Nova de São Francisco 14; mains €9-16; 10am-midnight, to 1am Fri-Sat;) Inside, exposed stone walls, soft lighting, vaulted ceilings and twisting corridors that open onto cosy nooks do indeed conjure a *fábula* (storybook fable). Vintage armchairs and sofas are fine spots for a snack, drink or classic dishes such as black-pork cheeks. Outside, there's a divine drinking patio for warm weather. Either way, the vibe is delightfully mellow.

Casa de Pasto PORTUGUESE €€
(Map p68; 963 739 979; www.casadepasto.com; Rua do São Paulo 20, 1st fl; mains €10-22; 12.30-3pm & 6-11pm Mon-Wed, to midnight Thu-Sat;) Up the stairs behind a not-very-triumphant facade lays this surprising treasure trove of 19th-century Portuguese bric-a-brac – seashell nightlights, ceramic taxidermy, gaudy mirrors – which fascinate while Diogo Noronha, a former Per Se intern and one of Lisbon's top upstart chefs, does decidedly delightful things with his charcoal oven. The tuna? The pork cheeks? The grilled veggies? Perfect.

Carmo PORTUGUESE €€
(Map p68; ☎213 460 088; www.restaurantecarmo.com; Largo do Carmo 10; mains €11-16, 3-course lunch €12; ⊙9.30am-midnight, closed Tue; 📶) On picturesque Largo do Carmo, this fan favourite is solid for elegantly presented Portuguese classics (monkfish rice, *bacalhau à Brás)* but not without somewhat rarer surprises (cuttlefish *feijoada* stew, Mirandela-style *alheira* pork sausage), all served under ornate ceilings and chandeliers. The best seats in the house are the window nooks with views across the plaza to Convento do Carmo.

Kaffeehaus CAFE €€
(Map p68; www.kaffeehaus-lisboa.com; Rua Anchieta 3; mains €5.50-17, Sun brunch €8.50-12; ⊙noon-midnight Tue-Sat, to 8pm Sun) Kaffeehaus has a bright interior with classic lines and big windows overlooking a peaceful corner of the Chiado, and it's a favourite eating and drinking spot among a cool but unpretentious crowd. Check the chalkboard for daily specials, including big salads, tasty schnitzels and sausages, strudels, cakes and more. Expect big crowds (and great food) at weekend brunches.

★**Alma** CONTEMPORARY, PORTUGUESE €€€
(Map p68; ☎213 470 650; www.almalisboa.pt; Rua Anchieta 15; mains €25-29, tasting menus €60-80; ⊙noon-3pm & 7-11pm Tue-Sun; 📶) Henrique Sá Pessoa, one of Portugal's most talented chefs, moved his flagship Alma from Santos to more fitting digs in Chiado in 2015. The casual space exudes understated style amid its original stone flooring and gorgeous hardwood tables, but it's Pessoa's outrageously good nouveau Portuguese cuisine that draws the foodie flock from far and wide.

★**Belcanto** PORTUGUESE €€€
(Map p68; ☎213 420 607; www.belcanto.pt; Largo de São Carlos 10; mains €45, tasting menu €125-145, with 5/7 wines €50/60; ⊙12.30-3pm & 7.30-11pm Tue-Sat; 📶) Fresh off a 2016 intimacy upgrade, José Avillez' two-Michelin-starred cathedral of cookery wows diners with painstaking creativity, polished service and first-rate sommelier. Standouts among Lisbon's culinary adventure of a lifetime include suckling pig with orange purée, sea bass with seaweed and bivalves and a stunning roasted butternut squash with miso; paired wines sometimes date to the '70s! Reservations essential.

Bistro 100 Maneiras FUSION €€€
(Map p68; ☎910 307 575; www.restaurante100maneiras.com; Largo da Trindade 9; mains €17-33; ⊙7.30pm-2am Mon-Sat; 📶) The Bosnian mastermind behind Bairro Alto's 100 Maneiras (p100) also oversees this creatively charged Chiado bistro. Start with the namesake 100 Maneiras Strong cocktail in the beautiful downstairs bar, then head upstairs for beautifully prepared dishes showcasing high-end Portuguese ingredients. Classics such as truffled mushroom risotto with wild shrimp are astounding; and options for braver souls include lamb brains.

Bairro Alto & Santa Catarina

Manteigaria PATISSERIE €
(Map p68; www.pt-br.facebook.com/manteigariacamoes; Rua do Loreto 2; pastel de nata €1; ⊙8am-midnight) Baking *pastéis de nata* really *is* rocket science in Lisbon. But this born-again butter factory gets it just right – crisp tarts that flake just so are filled with luscious cream and served with good strong coffee and smiles at this bright and tight modern cafe. This isn't Lisbon's most famous *pastel de nata*, but some say it's the best.

A Cultura do Hamburger CAFE €
(Map p68; www.facebook.com/aculturadohamburguer; Rua das Salgadeiras 38; burgers €6-9; ⊙noon-3.30pm & 6pm-midnight Mon-Fri, noon-4pm & 6.30pm-midnight Sat-Sun; 📶) In what is surely a legendary culinary coup, the owners of A Cultura do Chá woke up one morning and flipped the script. A Cultura do Hamburger was born in the same quiet Bairro Alto nook, with no tea in sight. Instead, some of Lisbon's most perfectly charred burgers emerge among these stone walls and arches and reclaimed-door tables.

Isco SEAFOOD €€
(Map p68; ☎213 461 376; www.restauranteisco.pt; Rua do Almada 29; small plates €7.50-12; ⊙12.30pm-12.30am Sun-Thu, to 2am Fri-Sat; 📶) Take a number (like at the deli counter) and prepare to wait at this Bica newcomer, a trendy *and* tasty maritime-themed hotspot dishing out daily-changing seafood *petiscos* to a fun and festive crowd. Fish tacos with mango salsa, cod and sweet-potato crisps, fresh ceviche – it's a catch-of-the-day free-for-all that doesn't disappoint.

Pharmacia MEDITERRANEAN €€
(Map p68; ☎213 462 146; www.chef-felicidade.pt; Rua Marechal Saldanha 2; tapas €4.50-16; ⊙1pm-

1am Tue-Sun; 📶) In Lisbon's apothecary museum, chef Susana Felicidade (Algarvian grandmother-trained!) dispenses tasting menus and tapas singing with flavours that are both market-fresh and Mediterranean influenced at this wonderfully quirky restaurant. Appetisers served in test tubes, and cabinets brimming with pill bottles and flacons – it's all part of the pharmaceutical fun. The terrace is a great spot for cocktails.

Flor da Laranja MOROCCAN €€
(Map p68; ☎964 781 122; Rua da Rosa 206; mains €14-16; ⏰7-11.30pm Mon-Sat; 📶) Casablanca native Rabea Esserghini runs a one-woman show at the wonderful Flor da Laranja, which means service is slow, but the cosy North African ambience and delicious Moroccan cuisine more than make up for it. Top picks include dolmas, mouth-watering couscous dishes, lamb, shrimp and veggie tagines, chicken with lemon confit and fresh berry crêpes for dessert.

Decadente PORTUGUESE €€
(Map p68; ☎213 461 381; www.thedecadente.pt; Rua de São Pedro de Alcântara 81; mains €9-16; ⏰noon-11pm Sun-Wed, to midnight Thu-Sat; 📶) This beautifully designed restaurant inside a boutique hotel overlooking the stunning São Pedro de Alcântara lookout, with touches of industrial chic, geometric artwork and an enticing back patio, serves inventive dishes showcasing high-end Portuguese ingredients at excellent prices. The changing three-course lunch menu (€10) is first-rate. Start with creative cocktails in the front bar.

Zé Varunca PORTUGUESE €€
(Map p68; ☎210 151 279; www.zevarunca.com; Travessa das Mercês 16; mains €8.50-14.50; ⏰noon-3pm & 7-11pm Mon-Sat; 📶) Fans of this small Alentejan icon were aghast when it disappeared from Lisbon's foodie map in 2015. Thankfully, Zé resurfaced a year later in improved Bairro Alto digs. Regional classics (*cozido de grão*, a chickpea and meat stew; bread-based cod dish *migas de bacalhau*) and products lugged from Estremoz incite riotous delight – appalling service is immediately forgiven. Reservations essential.

Jardim dos Sentidos VEGETARIAN €€
(Map p76; ☎213 423 670; www.jardimdosentidos.com; Rua Mãe d'Água 3; mains €8.50-9.50, lunch buffet €8.90; ⏰noon-3pm & 7-10pm Mon-Fri, 7-10.30pm Sat; 📶🖉) Vegetarian-minded diners flock to this attractive restaurant and wellness centre with a back garden/spa, an extensive lunch buffet and à la carte dinners. Among the globally inspired vegetarian offerings: four-cheese lasagne, vegetarian chilli, warm goat's-cheese salad and stuffed eggplant, plus a substantial tea menu.

★100 Maneiras FUSION €€€
(Map p68; ☎910 307 575; www.restaurante100maneiras.com; Rua do Teixeira 35; tasting menu €58, with classic/premium wine pairing €93/118; ⏰7.30pm-2am; 📶) How do we love 100 Maneiras? Let us count the 100 ways... The nine-course tasting menu changes twice yearly and features imaginative, delicately prepared dishes. The courses are all a surprise – part of the charm – though somewhat disappointingly, the chef will only budge so far to accommodate special diets and food allergies. Reservations are essential for the elegant and small space.

Alfama, Castelo & Graça

★Ti-Natércia PORTUGUESE €
(Map p72; ☎218 862 133; Rua Escola Gerais 54; mains €5-12; ⏰7pm-midnight Mon-Fri, noon-3pm & 7pm-midnight Sat) A decade in and a legend in the making, 'Aunt' Natércia and her downright delicious Portuguese home cooking is a tough ticket: there are but a mere six tables and they fill up fast. She'll talk your ear off (and doesn't mince words!) while you devour her excellent take on the classics. Reservations essential (and cash only).

Pois Café CAFE €
(Map p72; www.poiscafe.com; Rua de São João da Praça 93; mains €7-10; ⏰noon-11pm Mon, 10am-11pm Tue-Sun; 📶) Boasting a laid-back vibe under dominant stone arches, atmospheric Pois Café has creative salads, sandwiches and fresh juices, plus a handful of heartier daily specials (salmon quiche, sirloin steak). Its sofas invite lazy afternoons spent reading novels and sipping coffee, but you'll fight for space with the laptop brigade.

Princesa do Castelo CAFE €
(Map p72; Rua do Salvador 64A; snacks €1.50-5, mains €8.50; ⏰noon-midnight Tue-Sun; 📶🖉) 🍃 This bright and chirpy vegetarian cafe positively radiates good health with vegetarian, vegan, macrobiotic and sattvic dishes that play up the wild and the organic. Besides lunch specials such as Mexican quinoa chilli with fried bananas and tofu red curry, it's a nice place to stop for a juice, smoothie or just some positive vibes.

Claras em Castelo PORTUGUESE €
(Map p72; ☎218 853 071; Rua Bartolomeu de Gusmão 31; mains €10.50-14.50; ⊙10.30am-2am Thu-Tue) Just steps from the castle entrance, this tiny restaurant enjoys a loyal following for its warm service and solid home cooking. Dishes such as *bacalhau com natas* (cod in a creamy sauce) pair nicely with reasonably priced wines. Booking ahead is highly advisable.

Marcelino Pão e Vinho PORTUGUESE €
(Map p72; Rua do Salvador 62; mains €5-14; ⊙10am-midnight Mon-Tue, to 2am Thu-Sun; 📶) What this narrow cafe lacks in space it makes up for in atmosphere, with local artworks on the walls, occasional live music, traditional hats suspended from the ceiling and wine-crate-lined walls. It's a cosy space for refreshing sangria, and salads, sandwiches, quiches, fondue (cheese *and* chocolate!), desserts and other tapas.

Páteo 13 PORTUGUESE €
(Map p72; www.facebook.com/pateo13; Calçadinha de Santo Estêvão 13; mains €7-9; ⊙11am-11pm Tue-Sun, closed Nov-Feb; 📶) Follow the scent of chargrilled fish to this local favourite tucked away on a small, festively decorated plaza in the Alfama. Join buzzing crowds hunkered over picnic tables as they feast on barbecued seafood and meats, washed down with ever-flowing Alentejan reds.

Os Gazeteiros MODERN EUROPEAN €€
(Map p72; ☎939 501 211; www.osgazeteiros.pt; Rua das Escolas Gerais 114-116; prix-fixe lunch/dinner €14/20; ⊙noon-3pm Tue-Wed, noon-3pm & 6pm-2am Thu-Fri, 11am-3pm & 6pm-2am Sat-Sun; 📶) French chef David Eyguesier honed his skills at Pois Café, then his own underground restaurant at home before opening this sorely needed Alfama gem whose name loosely translates as 'The Truants' (he 'skipped' culinary school!). His daily-changing, market-fresh set menus delight under a spiderweb of modern lighting, beautiful geometric cabinetry and an open kitchen. No microwave. No freezer!

Chapitô à Mesa PORTUGUESE €€
(Map p72; ☎218 875 077; www.facebook.com/chapitoamesa; Rua Costa do Castelo 7; mains €18-21; ⊙noon-11pm Mon-Fri, 7.30-11pm Sat-Sun; 📶) Up a spiral iron staircase from this circus school's casual cafe, the decidedly creative menu of Chef Bertílio Gomes is served alongside views worth writing home about. His modern takes include classic dishes (*bacalhau à Brás*, stewed veal cheeks, suckling pig), plus daring ones (rooster testicles – goes swimmingly with a drop of Quinta da SIlveira Reserva).

Placete Chafariz d'el Rei BREAKFAST €€
(Map p72; ☎218 886 150; www.chafarizdelrei.com; Tv do Chafariz de El-Rei 6; brunch €19; ⊙noon-6pm Wed-Fri, 11am-6pm Sat-Sun; 📶) Entering the stained-glass-draped and palm-covered entrance hall of this hidden 20th-century mansion feels like a discovery, though the secret that this is one of Lisbon's top brunches is certainly out. The exquisite tearoom books up fast with socialites and foodies gnawing on towers of creamy cheeses and house-baked breads, savoury cold cuts, warm croissants and fresh-squeezed juices.

A Travessa do Fado PORTUGUESE €€
(Map p72; Largo do Chafariz de Dentro 1; mains €6.50-16; ⊙12.30-11.30pm Wed-Sun; 📶) Non-touristy restaurants are hard to come by in Alfama, but this one, the more casual sister restaurant to high-end **A Travessa** (Map p76; ☎213 902 034; www.atravessa.com; Travessa do Convento das Bernardas 12; mains €20-35; ⊙7.30pm-midnight Mon-Sat; 📶), gets a nod for its sun-drenched, flower-draped terrace, which is quite a nice spot for chasing classics such as stuffed squid or sea-bass rice with a refreshing *vinho verde* (young wine).

India Gate INDIAN €€
(Map p72; Rua da Padaria 18; mains €8-11.50; ⊙noon-3pm & 6-10pm Mon-Sat; 📶) If you just can't deal with any more *bacalhau*, Gujarati owners at this classy curry house oversee some of Lisbon's best Indian cuisine and are unafraid to give it a bit of bite if you beg. The solid menu of chicken, lamb, shrimp and veg classics (including some Goan specialities), served sizzling in traditional cookware, is a welcome respite.

Santa Clara dos Cogumelos INTERNATIONAL €€
(Map p72; ☎218 870 661; www.santaclaradoscogumelos.com; Campo de Santa Clara 7; petiscos €5-8, mains €14-17; ⊙7.30-11pm Tue-Fri, 1-3.30pm & 7.30-11pm Sat; 🖉) If you're a mushroom fan, this novel restaurant in the old market hall on Campo de Santa Clara is simply magic. The menu is an ode to the humble *cogumelo* (mushroom). Go for *petiscos* such as organic shitake with garlic and coriander, mains like risotto with porcini and black trumpets, and perhaps mushroom ice cream with brownies for dessert.

Santo António de Alfama PORTUGUESE €€
(Map p72; ☎218 881 328; www.siteantonio.com; Beco de São Miguel 7; mains €13.50-19.50; ⊙12.30-7pm & 8pm-2am; 📶) This bistro wins the award for Lisbon's loveliest summer courtyard: all vines, twittering budgies and fluttering laundry (though you'll struggle to find it at all in winter). The interior is a silver-screen shrine, while the menu stars tasty *petiscos* (appetisers): breaded brie with raspberry compote, blood sausage with apple purée, as well as more filling traditional Portuguese dishes.

DeliDelux CAFE
(Map p72; www.delidelux.pt; Av Infante Dom Henrique, Armazém B, Loja 8; mains €6.90-10.40; ⊙10am-10pm Sun-Thu, to midnight Fri-Sat; 📶) Besides a bounty of wine, cheeses, olive oils and other gourmet goodies, this deli's wonderful waterfront patio has yet to be discovered by tourists (despite this string of converted warehouses being attached – though not accessible from – the cruise-ship terminal). The charcuterie plates, salads, sandwiches and other light bites are all of exceptional quality.

Príncipe Real, Santos & Estrela

★**Gelataria Nannarella** ICE CREAM €
(Map p76; www.facebook.com/gelaterianannarella; Rua Nova da Piedade 68; small/medium/large €2/2.50/3; ⊙noon-10pm) This is where you'll get Lisbon's best gelato. Seatless Nannarella is squeezed into little more than a doorway, where Roman transplant Constanza Ventura churns out some 25 perfect, spatula-slabbed flavours of traditional gelato/sorbet daily to anxious lines of *lisboêtas*. Nailing both consistency and flavour, this sweet, sweet stuff from which heaven is made seemingly emerges straight from Ventura's kitchen.

★**Bettina & Niccolò Corallo** SWEETS €
(Map p76; www.claudiocorallo.com; Rua da Escola Politécnica 4; chocolate per kg from €90; ⊙10am-7pm Mon-Sat) Few chocolates command such undying devotion, but this family-run transplant from São Tomé and Príncipe elicits freakish enthusiasm for their thin artisan chocolate bars. Indeed, in ginger, orange, sea salt and pepper, sesame, and toffee and sea salt varieties, this is heart-stoppingly good stuff. Try a free sample with the excellent espresso before committing.

Dona Quitéria PORTUGUESE €
(Map p76; ☎213 951 521; Travessa de São José 1; small plates €5-12; ⊙7pm-midnight Tue-Sun) Locals do their best to keep this quaint corner *petiscaria* (small plates restaurant), a former grocery store from 1870, all to themselves – no such luck. Pleasant palette surprises such as tuna *pica-pau* instead of steak, or a pumpkin-laced cream-cheese mousse for dessert, put tasty creative spins on tradition. It's warm, welcoming and oh so tiny – so reserve ahead.

O Prego da Peixaria PORTUGUESE €
(Map p76; www.opregodapeixaria.com; Rua da Escola Politécnica 40; sandwiches €8.50-13; ⊙12.30pm-midnight, to 1am Fri-Sat; 📶) Grab a seat on rustic, reclaimed-hardwood cinema seats at this hotspot specialising in gourmet *pregos* (steak sandwiches). A perfect lunch here starts with the best *pica-pau* we've found in Lisbon (these bite-size pieces of steak are swimming in garlic-white-wine

CERCA VELHA: LISBON'S MEDIEVAL WALL

There are vestiges of Lisbon's medieval defensive wall scattered about Alfama and around – but you might walk right past them if you aren't paying attention or don't know where to look. Enter Lisbon city hall, which has teamed up with the Museu de Lisboa and Centro de Arqueologia de Lisboa, to create the free walking tour, *Muralhas de Lisboa: Cerca Velha*, based on intense historical and archaeological investigations of the city's pre-1147 fortified defence system (and later construction of the Fernandina wall from 1373–75).

There are 16 signposted points of interest along the circular 1500m path, beginning and ending near Castelo de São Jorge from Rua do Chão da Feira, down to the water and back around up to Porta de Alfofa. Notable stops include No 2 (Pátio Dom Fradique) – this 186m stretch of the wall is the longest intact section – and No 4 (Rua Norberto de Araújo), where the only Islamic portion of the wall is visible.

You'll need to pick up the city hall's helpful brochure and map, available in several languages at **Casa dos Bicos** (p76), and **Castelo de São Jorge** (p73), among other points.

sauce and then sopped up with garlic-butter-slathered *bolo de caco* bread), followed by the excellent Azores tuna sandwich with sweet-potato fries.

Cantinho Lusitano PORTUGUESE €

(Map p76; ☎218 065 185; www.cantinholusitano.com; Rua dos Prazeres 52; petiscos €4-8.50; ⊗7-11pm Tue-Sat; 📶) Sharing is what this unassuming little place is all about. Its appealing menu of *petiscos*, such as Azeitão cheese, chorizo, garlic shrimps, *pica-pau* beef and fava-bean salad, pairs nicely with Portuguese wines; and husband-wife team Silvia and João are consummate hosts. Reservations are a good idea at all times.

Esplanada do Príncipe Real CAFE €

(Map p76; Jardim do Príncipe Real; mains €8-15, cocktails from €7; ⊗9am-11pm Sun-Wed, to 2am Thu-Sat; 📶) This indoor-outdoor cafe is ideal for a coffee or cocktail break among the massive rubber tree palms and twittering birds in the pleasantly redone Jardim do Príncipe Real (p78). On the menu are fresh juices, a variety of mains (from quiche to steaks), salads, toasties, tapas and some lovely sweets (light cheesecakes, a chocolate, caramel and sea salt pie etc).

Água no Bico CAFE €

(Map p76; www.facebook.com/aguanobico.gaivotas; Rua das Gaivotas 8; mains €5-10; ⊗10am-9pm Tue-Wed, 10am-midnight Thu-Sat, 11am-6pm Sun; 🖉) Lisbon's first Paleo-focused cafe is tucked away on the grounds of elementary-school-turned-cultural-hub Polo Cultural Gaivotas Boavista under a sculpted wall by famed street-artist Vhils. A daily-changing menu of raw and Paleo delights draw consistent crowds. Think thick, savoury tarts and stews (wild boar and mushroom, ratatouille, venison etc) and lighter vegetarian/vegan fare. No sugar. Nothing processed.

Mercearia do Século DELI €

(Map p76; ☎216 062 070; www.facebook.com/merceariadoseculo; Rua de O Século 145; 2-course lunch €10; ⊗9am-6pm Tue-Thu, 10am-11pm Fri-Sat) Anthropologist and Portuguese cookbook writer Fernanda runs this sweet little deli and grocery store with love and an eye for careful sourcing. Lunch menus are wholesome and big on unorthodox flavour – be it baby mackerel with garlic, pork cheeks with chocolate sauce or eggplant cheesecake. You can also stock up on foodie gifts – fig bread, preserves, honey, olive oil etc.

ZeroZero PIZZA €€

(Map p76; ☎213 420 091; www.pizzeriazerozero.pt; Rua da Escola Politécnica 32; pizza €7.50-17.50; ⊗noon-midnight Sun-Thu, to 1am Fri-Sat; 📶) Just arriving at your table is a memorable ride, sliding past an enormous illustration from Ana Gil, a beautiful Prosecco bar and minimalist copper lamps and muted grey walls leading to an impressive, oak-fired pizza oven. Attention to Italian detail is fierce and the thin-crusted, uncut pies are memorable. And the patio! A stacked, bougainvillea-draped haven for pizza lovers.

Taberna Ideal FUSION €€

(Map p76; ☎213 962 744; Rua da Esperança 112-114; small plates €9.80, mains €16.80; ⊗7pm-2am Wed-Sat, 1.30pm-2am Sun) In a cosy, atmospheric dining room, Taberna Ideal (aka Taberna da Esperança) wows diners with flavourful dishes that blend Alentejan recipes with a modern edge. The inventive menu changes daily and features plates designed for sharing. Recent favourites include goat cheese, honey and rosemary bruschetta; sautéed mushrooms with chestnuts; and rabbit rice. Reserve ahead. Cash only for nonresidents.

Tasca da Esquina FUSION €€

(Map p76; ☎210 993 939; www.tascadaesquina.com; Rua Domingos Sequeira 41C; mains €8.60-22, tasting menu 3/5/7 courses €16.50/26.50/38; ⊗7.30-11.30pm Mon, 12.30-3.30pm & 7.30-11.30pm Tue-Sat; 📶) Headed by celebrated chef Vitor Sobral, the 'tavern on the corner' serves rich and inventive dishes featuring classic Portuguese ingredients. It's a small place in cool and contained Campo de Ourique, with a sizzling grill in front and a cheery sunroom where well-dressed diners fill the tables most days.

Petiscaria Ideal FUSION €€

(Map p76; ☎213 971 504; Rua da Esperança 100; small plates €9-13; ⊗7.30pm-2am, closed Sun; 📶) This small, buzzing spot serves delicious *petiscos* – octopus with peppers, olives and capers, roasted tomatoes stuffed with goat cheese and nuts, pork stew with pepper compote – followed by chocolate cake with fresh cream and wild berries. Walls are clad with mismatching *azulejos*, dining is at long communal tables, and there's a spirited rock-and-roll vibe to the place.

Terra VEGETARIAN €€

(Map p76; ☎213 421 407; www.restauranteterra.pt; Rua da Palmeira 15; buffet €13-16; ⊗12.30-3.30pm & 7.30-10.30pm Tue-Sun; 📶🖉) 🌿 Vegetarians sing the praises of Terra for its superb buffet (including vegan options) of salads, kebabs and curries, plus organic wines and juices. A fountain gurgles in the tree-shaded courtyard, lit by twinkling lights after dark.

Os Tibetanos VEGETARIAN €€
(213 142 038; www.tibetanos.com; Rua do Salitre 117; mains €10-12; 12.15-2.45pm & 7.30-10.30pm Mon-Fri, 12.30-3.30pm & 8-11pm Sat;) Part of a Tibetan Buddhism school, the mantra at Lisbon's oldest herbivore temple is fresh vegetarian food, with daily specials such as quiche and curry. Sit in the serene courtyard if the sun's out and save room for rose-petal ice cream.

Loco PORTUGUESE €€€
(Map p76; 213 951 861; www.facebook.com/locorestaurant; Rua dos Navigantes 53B; tasting menu €70-85) In the shadow of the Basílica da Estrela, Lisbon's latest hot table comes courtesy of chef Alexandre Silva, whose bold and modern take on Portuguese cuisine taps both tradition and travel on its way to a personality-rich gastronomic adventure. It offers two daily-changing, description-free tasting menus (you choose 14 or 18 'moments'), each steeped in sustainability and seasonality.

Lapa & Alcântara

Cafetaria Village CAFE €
(Map p80; www.vulisboa.com; Rua Primeiro de Maio 103, Village Underground Lisboa; mains €2.50-8.50; noon-8pm, to 6pm Tue-Sun Oct-Mar;) Located inside a raised antique double-decker city bus resting on shipping containers, this small cafe is part of Village Underground Lisboa, a London cultural-hub concept sprung up in Lisbon inside the grounds of the Carris complex in Alcântara. It does fantastic *tostas* and salads, good weekend brunches, and monthly specials such as *feijoada* and *cozida portuguesa,* both types of Portuguese stews.

Clube das Jornalistas MEDITERRANEAN, €€
(Map p76; 213 977 138; www.restauranteclubedejornalistas.com; Rua das Trinas 129; mains €15.50-33; 12.30-2.30pm & 7.30-10.30pm Mon-Sat;) You have to be determined to find hilltop Clube das Jornalistas, but persevere. This 18th-century house, opening onto a tree-shaded courtyard, has oodles of charm and serves Med-style and Portuguese dishes such as creamy Brazilian-style shrimp-stew risotto and truffled black pork. The service is faultless, the food a worthy runner-up.

Marquês de Pombal & Around

Ground Burger BURGERS €
(www.facebook.com/groundburger; Avenida António Augusto de Aguiar 148; burgers €7.90-10.90; noon-midnight, closed Sun & Mon;) Trendy Ground Burger is a strong contender in Lisbon's ongoing gourmet-burger war, tucked away almost discreetly around the side of an office building near the Museu Calouste Gulbenkian and sticking to perfectly executed classics (cheeseburger, bacon-cheese, chilli-cheese) and great hand-cut chips and onion rings. The local and international craft-beer list is one of Lisbon's most impressive.

Cinemateca Portuguesa CAFE €
(www.cinemateca.pt; Rua Barata Salgueiro 39; mains €7.50-13, films €3.20; 12.30pm-1am Mon-Sat;) Hidden on the 2nd floor of the indie-loving cinema and museum, this bright, wood-filled cafe with sunny terrace makes a fine retreat for an afternoon or evening pick-me-up. Menu features light snacks, drinks and daily specials.

Versailles PATISSERIE €
(Av da República 15A; pastries €0.80-1.70; 7.30am-midnight;) With a marble chandelier and icing-sugar stucco confection, this sublime patisserie is where well-coiffed ladies come to gossip and devour cream cakes (or scones with jam), espresso with *sortidos Húngaros* (chocolate-covered cookies) and a decadent house-chocolate-cake recipe.

Velocité CAFE €
(www.velocitecafe.com; Av Duque de Ávila 120; mains €5.80-9; 10am-8pm;) One for the bike lovers, design-forward Velocité is perfectly sited off a bike path. Stop in for healthy salads, soups, *tostas*, burgers, veggie burgers and artisanal beers. There's outdoor seating and a bright, open interior. Bike hire is available (per hour/day €5/15).

As Velhas PORTUGUESE €€
(Map p76; 213 422 490; www.facebook.com/restaurante.as.velhas; Rua da Conceição da Glória 21; mains €17-23; noon-3pm & 7-10pm) No airs, no graces, just hearty helpings of Portuguese soul food served by delightfully old-school servers are what you can expect at this beamed restaurant. The monkfish and clams in garlic and coriander sauce is superb, and so is the duck rice. Don't skip that dessert cart!

WORTH A TRIP

CRISTO REI

The sleepy seaside suburb of Cacilhas lies just across the Rio Tejo from the capital. Its star attraction – visible from almost everywhere in Lisbon – is 110m-high **Cristo Rei** (www.cristorei.pt; Alto do Pragal, Av Cristo Rei, Almada; adult/child €4/2; ⌚9.30am-6pm). Perched on a pedestal, the statue of Christ with outstretched arms is a slightly more baroque version of Rio de Janeiro's Christ the Redeemer. It was erected in 1959 to thank God for sparing Portugal from the horrors of WWII. A lift zooms you up to a platform, from where Lisbon spreads magnificently before you. It's a fantastic place for photos.

To reach the statue from Lisbon, take the breezy commuter ferry from Terreiro do Paço ferry terminal across the Tejo to Cacilhas (€1.20, 15 minutes), then bus 101 (€2 return). And make an afternoon of it: *lisboêtas* also flock to Cacilhas for the *cervejarias* (beer halls) serving fresh seafood, refreshing brews and fine views of the sun setting over the river.

Guilty INTERNATIONAL €€
(☎211 913 590; www.guilty.olivier.pt; Rua Barata Salgueiro 28A; mains €15-39, pizza €14.50-22; ⌚12.30-3.30pm & 7.30pm-midnight Mon-Fri, 12.30-4pm & 7.30pm-midnight Sat-Sun; 📶) Midway between restaurant and clubby lounge-bar, Guilty is the casual stalwart of Lisbon master-chef Olivier. With its bare brick walls, leather sofas, cowhides and young, good-looking crowd, it's sexy and it knows it, but this is the place to come for thick, perfectly juicy Black Angus or Wagyu burgers, pasta, speciality pizzas and DJ beats.

Jesus é Goês INDIAN €€
(☎211 545 812; Rua de São José 23; mains €8-17.50; ⌚noon-3pm & 7-11pm Tue-Sat; 📶) At one of Lisbon's best Indian restaurants, jovial chef Jesus Lee whips up contemporary Goan delicacies. Rice-sack tablecloths and colourful murals (note the playful Christian-Hindu imagery) set the scene for feasting on starters such as onion-coriander chickpea fritters or potato *bhaji* with *puri*; followed by mushroom and chestnut or shrimp curries, shrimp *biryani* or 11-spices goat – all fiery-fantastic.

Cervejaria Ribadouro SEAFOOD €€
(☎213 549 411; www.cervejariaribadouro.pt; Rua do Salitre 2; mains €10-28, seafood per kg €41-180; ⌚noon-12.30am; 📶) Bright, noisy and full to the gills, this bustling beer hall is popular with local seafood fans, some of whom just belly up to the bar, chase their fresh shrimp and *tremoços* (Lupin beans) with an ice-cold *imperial* (draught beer) and call it a night. The shellfish are plucked fresh from the tank, weighed and cooked to lip-smacking perfection.

Maria Mil Reis PORTUGUESE €€
(☎213 460 176; www.facebook.com/mariamilreis; Rua São José 71; mains €11-22; ⌚6pm-midnight; 📶) Small, unassuming and fun, Maria Mil Reis offers great-value Portuguese standards among the sea of ritzier options around Avenida da Liberdade. There is a distinct Brazilian vibe both with staff (chef and serving staff are *brasileiros),* some of the food (the house codfish is served Brazilian *moqueca*-style, with coconut milk and shrimp) and the giant goblets of wine.

Belém

Pastelaria Restelo BAKERY €
(www.pastelariaocareca.pt; Rua Duarte Pacheco Pereira 11D; croissants €1.20; ⌚8am-8pm Mon & Wed-Sat, 8.30am-8pm Sun) Better known as Pastelaria O Careca ('The Bald Guy') among locals, this simple *pastelaria* (pastry and cake shop) flanking a small plaza has been dishing out Lisbon's sweetest croissants since 1954. It's definitely worth heading a few blocks inland from the tourist onslaught along Belém's waterfront for the doughy, sugar-coated goodness.

Antiga Confeitaria de Belém PATISSERIE €
(Map p84; ☎213 637 423; www.pasteisdebelem.pt; Rua de Belém 84-92; pastries from €1.05; ⌚8am-11pm Oct-Jun, to midnight Jul-Sep) Since 1837, this patisserie has been transporting locals to sugar-coated nirvana with heavenly *pastéis de belém*. The crisp pastry nests are filled with custard cream, baked at 200°C for that perfect golden crust, then lightly dusted with cinnamon. Admire *azulejos* in the vaulted rooms or devour a still-warm tart at the counter and try to guess the secret ingredient.

Alecrim & Manjerona CAFE €

(Map p84; ☎213 620 642; www.facebook.com/alecrimmanjeronamercearia; Rua Embaixador 143; light meals & lunches €2.50-6; ⏱10am-7pm Tue-Sat) Tucked away from the crowds on a side street, Alecrim & Manjerona ('Rosemary & Marjoram') is a cute grocery store, cafe, deli and wine bar rolled into one. Besides delicious homemade cakes and tarts, it rustles up wallet-friendly day specials – from quiches to *bacalhau espiritual* (codfish gratin).

Enoteca de Belém PORTUGUESE, WINE BAR €€

(Map p84; ☎213 631 511; www.travessadaermida.com; Travessa do Marta Pinto 10; mains €16.50-18; ⏱1-11pm Tue-Sun; 📶) Tucked down a quiet lane just off Belém's main thoroughfare, this casual wine bar serves modernised Portuguese classics (fantastic octopus, Iberian pork), matched by an excellent selection of full-bodied Douro reds and refreshing Alentejan whites. The experience – led by well-trained servers particularly adept at gravitating you towards a juice that marries with your tastes – is distinctively memorable.

Espaço Espelho d'Água FUSION €€

(Map p84; ☎213 010 510; www.espacoespelhodeagua.com; Av de Brasília, Espelho d'Água; light mains €9-13.50; ⏱10am-midnight; 📶) Reviews are mixed on food and service but everyone agrees that the riverside terrace of this part gallery, restaurant and cultural space is a beautiful spot to take a load off. With its Age of Discoveries-nodding cuisine and Padrão dos Descobrimentos views, the menu offers Portuguese dishes with Brazilian and Angolan-heavy pinches of colonial sugar and spice.

★**Feitoria** MODERN PORTUGUESE €€€

(☎210 400 208; www.restaurantefeitoria.com; Altis Belém Hotel, Doca do Bom Sucesso; mains €33-38, tasting menus €75-120, with wine €110-175; ⏱7.30-11pm Mon-Sat; 📶) A defining dining experience awaits at chef João Rodrigues' slick, contemporary Michelin-starred restaurant overlooking the riverfront. Rich textures and clean, bright flavours dominate throughout three tasting menus (Land, Tradition and Travel) showcasing Portugal's rich and vibrant bounty. Egg-yolk, cheese and spinach ravioli with mushrooms and truffles, and Iberian pork neck with smoked eel, progressively exhilarate on every bite.

Parque das Nações

Bota Feijão PORTUGUESE €

(☎218 532 489; Rua Conselheiro Lopo Vaz 5; half/whole portion €8.50/12; ⏱noon-3pm Mon-Fri) Don't be fooled by the nondescript decor and railroad-track views – when a tucked-away place is this crowded with locals at lunchtime midweek, they must be doing something right. They're all here for one thing and one thing only: *leitão* – suckling pig spit-roasted on an open fire until juicy and meltingly tender, doused in a beautiful peppery garlic sauce.

Old House CHINESE €€€

(☎218 969 075; www.theoldhouseportugal.pt; Rua Pimenta 9; mains €8-40; ⏱noon-3pm & 7pm-midnight; 📶) Transport yourself to China at this authentic Szechuan powerhouse (tamed for local tastes), a Chinese chain restaurant that chose Parque das Nações as their first foray outside the motherland. The daunting list of specialities, including Beijing duck (€26.90 for two), hotpots and plenty of garlic- and pepper-loaded dishes, are a welcome taste-bud change-up.

River Lounge LOUNGE €€€

(☎211 107 600; www.myriad.pt; Cais das Naus, Myriad by Sana Hotel; mains €18-39; ⏱restaurant 7.30-10.30pm, bar 10am-2am) This slinky, monochrome, glass-walled restaurant-lounge has upped the style ante in Parque das Nações. Seasonal, Med-inspired cuisine is given a light touch of sophistication in dishes such as braised lobster with apple and pear *vol-au-vent,* or half-cured cod with dried fruits and veal *jus.*

Drinking & Nightlife

Baixa & Rossio

★**A Ginjinha** GINJINHA BAR

(Map p66; Largo de Saõ Domingos 8; ⏱9am-10pm) Hipsters, old men in flat caps, office workers and tourists all meet at this microscopic *ginjinha* (cherry liqueur) bar for that moment of cherry-licking, pip-spitting pleasure (€1.40 a shot).

Topo COCKTAIL BAR

(Map p66; www.topo-lisboa.pt; Commercial Center Martim Moniz, 6th fl, Praça Martim Moniz; cocktails from €7; ⏱12.30pm-midnight Tue-Thu, to 2am Fri-Sat) This hipster hang-out is yet another excellent rooftop lounge with extraordinary

LOCAL KNOWLEDGE

GINJINHA BARS

Come dusk, the area around Largo de São Domingos and the adjacent Rua das Portas de Santo Antão buzzes with locals getting their cherry fix in a cluster of *ginjinha* (cherry liqueur) bars. **A Ginjinha** (p106) is famous as the birthplace of the sugary-sweet tipple thanks to a quaffing friar from Igreja de Santo António who revealed the secret to an entrepreneurial Galician by the name of Espinheira. Order your €1 *ginjinha sem* (without) or – our favourite – *com* (with) the alcohol-soaked cherries. Other postage-stamp-sized bars nearby include **Ginjinha Sem Rival** (www.facebook.com/ginjasemrivaleeduardino; Rua das Portas de Santo Antão 7; ⌚8am-midnight Mon-Fri, 9am-midnight Sat-Sun) and **Ginjinha Rubi** (Rua Barros Queirós 27; ⌚7am-10.30pm Mon-Sat).

views over lively Praça Martim Moniz and the whole of Lisbon. It features loungey open-air wooden benches for sipping coffee, cocktails and noshing on light bites, and a covered indoor lounge, all set to a vibey soundtrack, often courtesy of DJs.

Fábrica Coffee Roasters CAFE

(Map p66; www.fabricacoffeeroasters.com; Rua das Portas de Santo Antão 136; coffee €1.20-5; ⌚9am-9pm) Keep on walking past the touristy restaurants that are situated along pedestrianised Rua das Portas de Santo Antão to this sublime coffee temple, where serious caffeine is served amid a hodgepodge of exposed brick, hardwood floors and mismatched vintage furniture. Single-origin arabica beans from Brazil, Ethiopia and Colombia are roasted in-house and churned into distinctly third-wave cups of joe. Connoisseurs rejoice!

Primeiro Andar BAR

(Map p66; Rua das Portas de Santo Antão 110, Ateneu Comercial de Lisboa; ⌚7pm-2am; 📶) Although it's right above a touristy pedestrian street, this delightful cafe-bar remains well-concealed from the masses. Despite initial appearances, it's a welcoming, laid-back place. To get here, follow the small alley about 30m south of the Ateneu Comercial de Lisboa building, go to the end and head inside the dark entrance and cross a basketball court: *voila!* Local's secret jackpot!

Rooftop Bar BAR

(Map p66; www.hotel-mundial.pt; Praça Martim Moniz 2, Hotel Mundial; ⌚6.30-12.30pm, to 11.30pm Nov-Mar) Grab a table at sundown on the Hotel Mundial's roof terrace for a sweeping view of Lisbon and its hilltop castle. Its backlit bar, white sofas and ambient sounds set the stage for evening drinks and sharing plates.

Bairro Alto & Chiado

★**Park** BAR

(Map p68; www.facebook.com/00park; Calçada do Combro 58; cocktails €6.50-8; ⌚1pm-2am Tue-Sat, 1-8pm Sun; 📶) If only all multistorey car parks were like this... Take the elevator to the 5th floor, and head up and around to the top, which has been transformed into one of Lisbon's hippest rooftop bars, with sweeping views reaching right down to the Tejo and over the bell towers of Santa Catarina Church.

The vibe is cool and creative and DJs spin hip hop, jazz and house at all hours. Plopping yourself down on the sunset-facing wooden chairs in the late afternoon is a Lisbon must.

★**Pensão Amor** BAR

(Map p68; www.pensaoamor.pt; Rua do Alecrim 19; cocktails €5.50-13; ⌚noon-3am Mon-Wed, to 4am Thu-Sat, to 3am Sun) Set inside a former brothel, this cheeky bar pays homage to its passion-filled past with colourful wall murals, a library of erotic-tinged works, and a small stage where you can sometimes catch burlesque shows. The Museu Erótico de Lisboa (MEL) was on the way at time of research.

★**BA Wine Bar do Bairro Alto** WINE BAR

(Map p68; ☎213 461 182; bawinebar@gmail.com; Rua da Rosa 107; wines from €3, tapas from €12; ⌚6-11pm Tue-Sun; 📶) Reserve ahead unless you want to get shut out of Bairro Alto's best wine bar, where the genuinely welcoming staff will offer you three fantastic choices to taste based on your wine proclivities. The cheeses (from small artisanal producers) and charcuterie (melt-in-your-mouth black-pork *presuntos*) are not to be missed, either. You could spend the night here.

Tasca Mastai BAR

(Map p68; www.facebook.com/tascadomastai; Rua da Rosa 14; cocktails €3.50-9; ⏲1pm-midnight Tue-Sun; 📶) This artsy, Italian-run bar-cafe is (literally) a refreshing change of pace for Bairro Alto – the long list of speciality Aperol Spritzes are worth a trip (try the tart and appley Hugo, summer drink perfection in a glass). It's a small, corner spot, with old sewing tables and tightly spun corrugated-cardboard bar stools. Bruschettas help soak up all those cocktails.

Lisbon Winery WINE BAR

(Map p68; ☎218 260 132; www.lisbonwinery.com; Rua da Barroca 9; wines from €4; ⏲noon-midnight; 📶) A commanding 16th-century cistern is the focal point at this hot new wine bar opened by two ex-journalists shunning the status quo. It purposely bypasses more-famous labels for lesser-known boutique wines. To pair, fantastic artisanal cheeses, grilled chorizos, *pata negra* hams and house-made jams.

A Tabacaria BAR

(Map p68; Rua de São Paulo 75; cocktails €7.50-16; ⏲4pm-2am) Small and intimate (and simultaneously sleek and grungy), this Cais do Sodré newcomer boasts a beautiful hardwood back bar and stained glass originally from this space when it opened as an exchange bureau in 1885. No tourists are here (well, until now, anyway...) and it serves mostly beer and gin and tonics (made with unique house-macerated tinctures).

Duque Brewpub BREWERY

(Map p68; www.duquebrewpub.com; Duques da Calçada 49; pints €5.50-8.90; ⏲noon-1am; 📶) Lisbon's first brewpub debuted in 2016 with 10 taps, five of which will be eventually dedicated to on-site suds (under the banner of Cerveja Aroeira) brewed in true craft-beer style: no two batches are the same. Additional taps feature invited Portuguese craft beers such as Passarola, Dois Corvos and Letra.

Alface Hall LIVE MUSIC

(Map p68; www.facebook.com/alface.music.hall; Rua do Norte 96; ⏲4pm-midnight; 📶) With one wall covered in LPs and another with old cinema chairs, there's an old-time feel to this jazz and blues bar in Bairro Alto. Free concerts happen nightly at 9.30pm on the minuscule stage (OK, it's just a spot on the floor).

Artis WINE BAR

(Map p68; www.facebook.com/artiswinebar; Rua Diário de Notícias 95; ⏲5.30pm-2am Sun & Tue-Thu, to 3am Fri & Sat) Down a few steps from street level, Artis is a warmly lit place with old wood details, a jazzy soundtrack and an excellent selection of wines by the glass or bottle. Nicely turned out *petiscos* such as Galician-style octopus and flambéed Portuguese sausage add to the appeal.

O Bom O Mau e O Vilão COCKTAIL BAR

(Map p68; www.facebook.com/obomomaueovilao; Rua do Alecrim 21; cocktails from €7.50; ⏲7pm-2am Mon-Thu, to 3am Fri-Sat) 'The Good, the Bad and the Ugly' is an artsy drinking den sprung from a refurbished Pombaline townhouse. It's divided among several rooms draped in contemporary artworks and period furnishings. DJs throw down funk, soul, acid jazz and vintage beats to an eclectic, easy-on-the-eyes crowd that is mingle-friendly and more highbrow than average for the neighbourhood.

Loucos & Sonhadores BAR

(Map p76; Travessa do Conde de Soure 2; ⏲10pm-4am Mon-Sat) Though it's in Bairro Alto, this smoky, bohemian drinking den feels secreted away from the heaving masses on nearby streets. Kitschy decor, free (salty) popcorn and eclectic tunes – it's a great place for eclectic conversation in the various rooms rather than pounding shots.

Musicbox CLUB

(Map p68; www.musicboxlisboa.com; Rua Nova do Carvalho 24; ⏲11pm-6am Mon-Sat) Under the brick arches on Rua Nova do Carvalho lies one of Lisbon's hottest clubs. The pulsating Music Box hosts loud and sweaty club nights with music shifting from electro to rock, plus gigs by up-and-coming bands.

Capela BAR

(Map p68; www.facebook.com/acapelabar; Rua da Atalaia 45; ⏲8pm-2am Sun-Thu, to 3am Fri-Sat) According to (questionable) legend this was once a Gothic chapel, but today Capela's gospel is an experimental line-up of electronica and funky house. Get there early (before midnight) to appreciate the DJs before the crowds descend. Frescoes, Renaissance-style nude murals and dusty chandeliers add a boho-chic touch.

Solar do Vinho do Porto WINE BAR

(Map p68; ☎213 475 707; www.ivdp.pt; Rua São Pedro de Alcântara 45; ports by the glass €1.50-

22.50; ⏲11am-12.30am Mon-Fri, 3-11.30pm Sat) The glug, glug of a 40-year-old tawny being poured is music to port-lovers' ears. Part of an 18th-century mansion, the low-lit, beamed cavern is ideal for nursing a glass from their 180-plus inventory of Portugal's finest.

Majong BAR
(Map p68; Rua da Atalaia 3; cocktails €7-9; ⏲5pm-2am Sun-Thu, to 3am Fri-Sat) Long-time favourite Majong oozes shabby chic with cabbage-shape lights, deep-red walls and school chairs, all atmospherically candlelit. Mojitos and imported beers flow as DJs spin minimalist techno and house.

Bar Bicaense BAR
(Map p68; www.facebook.com/bicaensereloaded; Rua da Bica de Duarte Belo 42A; ⏲7pm-2am, to 3am Fri-Sat) Indie kids have a soft spot for this chilled Bica haunt, kitted out with a minimalist array of retro light fixtures. It's a less rowdy scene than nearby Bairro Alto and there's contemporary fado interspersed with DJs spinning Brazilian and Cabo Verdean rhythms and sounds on Tuesday's Fado Redux (9.30pm).

O Purista Barbiere COCKTAIL BAR
(Map p68; www.opurista.pt; Nova da Trindade 16A; cocktails €9, haircuts €17; ⏲3pm-2am Mon-Thu, to 4am Fri-Sat; 📶) How about a cocktail with that haircut? Luckily, it's the patrons knocking back fantastic gin and tonics at this hipster bar and barbershop, not the bearded coiffeurs. It's a decidedly male, speakeasy environment, but after the barbers pack up at 11pm, a beautiful mixed crowd converges over pool, Belgian beers and solid tunes.

The George PUB
(Map p68; www.thegeorgelisbon.com; Rua do Crucifixo 58; ⏲noon-2am; 📶) This popular pub is the top choice for a classier pint among 200-year-old stone archways made all the more atmospheric by strategic lighting and chandeliers. The 15 taps include three you won't see often (London Pride, Peroni and Carling) and better-than-average local choices (such as Super Bock's craftier selections); and there's Euro-league footy on the TV.

By the Wine WINE BAR
(Map p68; www.facebook.com/bythewinejosemariadafonseca; Rua das Flores 41; wines by the glass €2.30-32; ⏲noon-midnight; 📶) Venture beyond Alentejo and Douro wines at this excellent wine bar, where some 65 offerings from the glass can be sipped under an impressive arched main hall ceiling strewn with 3200 wine bottles. You can thank the bar's owners winery, José Maria da Fonseca (p149), for the Setúbal-heavy liquid education.

Zymology ALCOHOL
(Map p68; www.facebook.com/zymologyshop; Rua das Chagas 31; ⏲1-7pm Mon-Fri, from 3pm Sat) At its heart, Zymology is an excellent craft beer shop, owned by Rolim Carmo, the head brewer from Mean Sardine brewery, focusing on artisanal beers from Portugal, Europe (Netherlands, Sweden, Denmark, Estonia) and the American Pacific Northwest. It's another epicentre for local and visiting beer nerds.

Old Pharmacy WINE BAR
(Map p68; Rua Diário de Notícias 83; wine by the glass €2.20-11; ⏲5.30pm-midnight; 📶) True to name, this dimly lit space was once a pharmacy, its backlit built-in cabinets lined with dozens of Portuguese wines. There's outdoor seating and a more grown-up vibe than most other Bairro Alto spots and, with around 120 wines by the glass, it's pretty ideal for tasting your way through a wine region or two.

Club Carib BAR
(Map p68; Rua da Atalaia 78; ⏲10pm-2am Sun-Thu, to 3am Fri-Sat) A dance-loving crowd has flocked to Carib for years, drawn by DJs spinning a dizzying variety of world beats – Afro-Cuban jazz, Brazilian MPB and samba, African funk, salsa, tango and more.

Discoteca Jamaica CLUB
(Map p68; www.jamaica.com.pt; Rua Nova do Carvalho 6; ⏲midnight-6am Tue-Sat) Gay and straight, black and white, young and old – everyone has a soft spot for this offbeat club. It gets going at around 2am at weekends with DJs pumping out reggae, hip hop and retro.

Café a Brasileira CAFE
(Map p68; Rua Garrett 120; espresso €0.70; ⏲8am-2am) All gold swirls and cherubs, this art-deco cafe has been a Lisbon institution since 1905. Sure it's touristy, but the terrace is brilliant for watching street entertainers beside the bronze statue of poet Fernando Pessoa. Order a *bica*, which takes its name from A Brasileira's 1905 catchphrase: *beba isto com açúcar* (drink this with sugar).

Maria Caxuxa BAR
(Map p68; Rua da Barroca 6; ⏲7pm-2am Mon-Thu, to 3am Fri-Sat; 📶) Set in a former bakery,

Maria Caxuxa has effortless style reminiscent of late '90s Berlin – its several rooms are decked with giant mixers, 1950s armchairs and sofas, marble and *azulejo*-lined walls and incongruous photos. Funk-laden jazz plays overhead during the week with alternative- and rock-spinning DJs adding to the eclectic weekend setting.

Chafariz do Vinho WINE BAR

(Map p76; ☎213 422 079; www.chafarizdovinho.com; Rua Mãe d'Água; ⏲6pm-midnight Tue-Sun) In the centuries-old vaults of Lisbon's famed Aqueduto das Águas Livres (p79), this beautiful *enoteca* (wine bar) pops the cork on wines handpicked by writer João Paulo Martins. Taste from 250 of Portugal's finest along with excellent accompanying tapas (try the 'PanTomato', a Catalan speciality given a Portuguese spin with the addition of *presunto*).

Noobai Café BAR

(Map p68; www.noobaicafe.com; Miradouro de Santa Catarina; cocktails €2.80-7.50; ⏲noon-10pm Tue-Thu, to midnight Fri-Sat, to 8pm Sun) Great views, winning cocktails and a festive crowd make Noobai a popular draw for a sundowner at Miradouro de Santa Catarina (p71). The vibe is laid-back, the music is funky jazz and the views over the Tejo are magical.

Alfama, Castelo & Graça

★Wine Bar do Castelo WINE BAR

(Map p72; ☎218 879 093; www.winebardocastelo.blogspot.pt; Rua Bartolomeu de Gusmão 13; wines by the glass €4-30; ⏲1-10pm) Located near the entrance to the Castelo de São Jorge (p73), this laid-back wine bar serves more than 150 Portuguese wines by the glass, along with gourmet smoked meats, cheeses, olives and other tasty accompaniments. Nuno, the multilingual owner, is a welcoming host and a fount of knowledge about all things wine-related.

Memmo Alfama BAR

(Map p72; www.memmoalfama.com; Travessa das Merceeiras 27; cocktails €8-9.50; ⏲noon-11pm; 📶) Wow, what a view! Alfama unfolds like origami from the stylishly decked roof terrace of the Memmo Alfama hotel. It's perfect sundowner material, with dreamy views over the rooftops, spires and down to the Rio Tejo.

Portas do Sol BAR

(Map p72; www.portasdosol.pt; Largo das Portas do Sol; cocktails €6; ⏲10am-1am, to 2am Fri-Sat; 📶) Near one of Lisbon's iconic viewpoints, this spacious sun-drenched terrace has a mix of sofas and white patio furniture, where you can sip cocktails while taking in magnificent river views. DJs bring animation to the darkly lit industrial interior on weekends.

Lux-Frágil CLUB

(Map p62; www.luxfragil.com; Av Infante Dom Henrique, Armazém A - Cais de Pedra, Santo Apolónia; ⏲11pm-6am Thu-Sat) Lisbon's ice-cool, must-see club, Lux hosts big-name DJs spinning electro and house. It's run by ex-Frágil maestro Marcel Reis and part-owned by John Malkovich. Grab a spot on the terrace to see the sun rise over the Tejo; or chill like a king on the throne-like giant interior chairs.

LisBeer BEER HALL

(Map p72; www.facebook.com/lisbeerbar; Beco do Arco Escuro 1; pints €4-7; ⏲4am-1am Thu-Thu, to 3am Fri-Sat; 📶) The loungiest and least beer-geeky of Lisbon's craft beer bars, Sé's LisBeer offers six artisanal brews on tap and another 250 or so in the bottle, divided by style and country with an obvious emphasis on Portugal's rising scene. It's a good spot to get hopped up among various rooms of tattered leather sofas and mismatched tables.

Graça do Vinho WINE BAR

(Map p72; www.facebook.com/gracadovinholx; Calçada da Graça 10; ⏲noon-11pm Mon-Fri, 12.30pm-12.30am Sat) This former pharmacy serves a refreshing variety of wines (at least 50 by the glass), which go nicely with cheeses, sardines, smoked meats and other appetisers.

Chapitô BAR

(Map p72; ☎218 875 077; www.chapito.org; Costa do Castelo 7; mains €18-24; ⏲terrace noon-2am, restaurant 7pm-2am; 📶) This alternative theatre/circus school occupies a former female prison and offers fantastic views from its bar. It's a top choice for a sundowner or a late-night drink overlooking the city. More serious foodies will want to book a table at the restaurant, Chapitô à Mesa (p101), in the hands of Bertílio Gomes, one of the city's top chefs.

Clube Ferroviário CLUB

(Map p62; www.clubeferroviarioblog.com; Rua de Santa Apolónia 59; ⏲5pm-2am Mon-Wed, 4pm-4am Thu & Fri, noon-4am Sat, noon-midnight Sun) Above Santa Apolónia train station, this former social club of Lisbon's railworkers has been transformed into an intriguing nightspot with DJs and occasional concerts; the best feature is the roof terrace with Tejo views.

Príncipe Real, Santos & Estrela

★Foxtrot BAR
(Map p76; www.barfoxtrot.com; Travessa Santa Teresa 28; cocktails €7-15; ⏲6pm-3am Mon-Sat, 8pm-2am Sun; 📶) A cuckoo-clock doorbell announces new arrivals to this dark, decadent slither of art-nouveau glamour, in the bar business since 1978. Foxtrot keeps the mood mellow with jazzy beats, excruciatingly attentive mixology detailed on a tracing-paper menu and a chilled feline that isn't afraid to belly up to the bar. It's a wonderfully moody spot for a chat.

★Cinco Lounge LOUNGE
(Map p76; www.cincolounge.com; Rua Ruben António Leitão 17; cocktails from €7.50; ⏲9pm-2am) Take an award winning London-born mixologist, Dave Palethorpe, add a candlelit, turquoise-kissed setting and give it a funky twist – *et voilà* – you have Cinco Lounge. Come here to converse, sip legendary cocktails or join a cocktail-mixing workshop. Cash only.

★Cerveteca Lisboa BEER HALL
(Map p76; www.cervetecalisboa.com; Praça das Flores 62; draught beer €2-7; ⏲3.30pm-1am; 📶) Lisbon's best craft-beer bar is a boozy godsend: a dozen oft-changing taps focusing on local and Northern European artisanal brews, including 10 local microbreweries, none of which are named Sagres or Super Bock. Not only will hopheads rejoice at IPAs from Lisbon standouts such as Dois Corvos and Oitava Colina, but having choice alone inspires cartwheels. *Adeus*, tasteless lagers!

Copenhagen Coffee Lab CAFE
(Map p76; www.cphcoffeelab.pt; Rua Nova da Piedade 10; coffee €1-7; ⏲8am-6pm Mon-Fri, from 10am Sat-Sun; 📶) Serious caffeine aficionados should make a beeline to this Danish import just off lovely Praça das Flores, where properly trained baristas know their way around strong espressos and creamy flat whites, plus a bastion of fiendish preparation methods (V60, Aeropress etc). The clean-lined, blindingly white space screams Denmark, but sometimes you have to transport yourself for java transcendence.

A Paródia BAR
(Map p76; www.aparodia.com; Rua do Patrocínio 26B; ⏲9pm-2am; 📶) This delightful bar time-warps you back to the more glamorous age of art nouveau, with its dark wood, red velvet walls, soft lamp lighting and vintage knick-knacks. It's a wonderfully cosy and intimate place for a tête-à-tête over cocktails, with jazz playing softly in the background.

Lost In BAR
(Map p76; www.facebook.com/lostin.esplanada; Rua Dom Pedro V 56; ⏲4pm-midnight Mon, 12.30pm-midnight Tue-Sat) For drinks and light bites with knockout views of the castle and downtown Lisbon, head to the Indo-chic patio at Lost In, shaded by colourful parasols and a new enclosed terrace. There's live jazz at 9.30pm on Thursdays.

K Urban Beach CLUB
(Map p62; www.grupo-k.pt; Cais da Viscondessa; ⏲midnight-6am Wed-Sun) Jutting out over the Tejo and skewing to world-is-our oyster-20-somethings, this airy club has three lively dance floors and nine bars, including outdoor seating and a summer pool that only enhances its scenic riverside setting. Get your house-charge card upon entry and hold onto it; there is no negotiation or reasoning with bouncers if you can't produce one when exiting.

Pavilhão Chinês BAR
(Map p76; www.facebook.com/pavilhaochineslisboa; Rua Dom Pedro V 89-91; cocktails from €9.50; ⏲6pm-2am, from 7pm Sun) Pavilhão Chinês is an old curiosity shop of a bar with oil paintings and model spitfires dangling from the ceiling, and cabinets brimming with glittering Venetian masks and Action Men. Play pool or bag a comfy armchair to nurse a port or an exquisitely mixed classic cocktail. Prices are higher than elsewhere, but such classy kitsch doesn't come cheap.

OFF THE BEATEN TRACK

CUTTING-EDGE CRAFT BREWS

One of the anchors helping make artsy Marvila Lisbon's next 'It' neighbourhood, the **Dois Corvos** (www.doiscorvos.pt; Rua Cap Leitão 94; ⏲2-9pm Sun-Thu, to midnight Fri-Sat; 📶) informal taproom is little more than a few tables from the brewery floor. Seattle microbrewer Scott Steffens brews the city's best craft beer, sold fresh from the 12 taps here and considerably cheaper than elsewhere. The Martiné Session IPA and Finisterra Porter are particularly worth the trip.

GAY & LESBIAN LISBON

The gay and lesbian community had much to celebrate in 2010, with the passing of a bill that legalised gay marriage. The big events worth looking out for are **Lisbon Pride** (www.portugalpride.org) in June, and the **Festival de Cinema Gay e Lésbico** (www.queerlisboa.pt) in late September.

The Scene

From camp to cruisy, Praça do Príncipe Real, just north of Bairro Alto, is king of Lisbon's gay and lesbian scene. It's worth being in town for DJ sets from **DMA** (www.discomyass.tumblr.com) or hot occasional party events such as **Spit & Polish**, usually held at Ministerium Club (www.ministerium.pt), and **Lesboa Party** (www.facebook.com/lp.international.lgbt). Most nightclubs around town, especially **Lux** (p110), draw a mixed gay-straight crowd. New gay guesthouse the **Late Birds** (p92) also does a bar night in its intimate lobby lounge Thursday to Saturday, as well as a bimonthly Sunday brunch.

For more listings, check out *Time Out* (http://timeout.sapo.pt), with a gay section updated weekly; and **Lisbon Beach** (☎964 457 981; www.lisbonbeach.com), which also does gay-centric tours.

WoofLX (Map p76; www.facebook.com/wooflx; Rua da Palmeira 44A; ⊙10pm-4am) Príncipe Real's bear-ish gay bar (though it attracts all shapes and sizes). It's part of the Woof empire that now includes the naughtier, more hardcore option Woof X.

Bar TR3S (Map p76; www.areismarcos.wix.com/tr3slisboa; Rua Rubén A Leitão 2; ⊙4pm-2am Sun-Thu, to 3am Fri-Sat) Real men and bears flock to this hopping bar, especially for its daily happy hour and outdoor seating.

Clube da Esquina (Map p68; www.facebook.com/clubedaesquina.bairroalto; Rua da Barroca 30; cocktails €5.50-8.50; ⊙6pm-2am Sun-Thu, to 3am Fri-Sat; 📶) DJs play hip hop and house to an eye-candy crowd. It's the anchor of Lisbon's gay corner at Rua da Baroca with Travessa da Espera ('Hope Alley', irony not lost) in Bairro Alto.

Construction (Map p76; ☎213 430 040; www.constructionlisbon.com; Rua Cecílio de Sousa 84; ⊙midnight-6am Thu-Sat) The top club of the moment among 30-somethings; with somewhat industrial design, pumping house music and a dark room.

Finalmente (Map p76; ☎213 479 923; www.finalmenteclub.com; Rua da Palmeira 38; ⊙midnight-6am) This popular club has a tiny dance floor, nightly drag shows and wall-to-wall crowds.

Purex (Map p68; www.facebook.com/purexclub; Rua das Salgadeiras 28; ⊙10pm-3am Fri & Sat) One for the girls, this unsigned Bairro Alto spot draws a lesbian and mixed crowd, with DJ nights and a small dance floor.

Sétimo Céu (Map p68; www.facebook.com/setimoceubar; Travessa da Espera 54; ⊙10pm-2am Mon-Thu, 9pm-3am Fri-Sat) A mainstay of the Bairro Alto scene, this old-school bar attracts a young festive crowd. Excellent caipirinhas.

Trumps (Map p76; ☎915 938 266; www.trumps.pt; Rua da Imprensa Nacional 104B; admission €10; ⊙midnight-6am Fri & Sat) Lisbon's hottest younger-skewing gay club with cruisy corners, a sizeable electro-house and pop-fuelled dance floor, and events from live music to drag.

Lapa & Alcântara

Bosq CLUB

(Map p80; ☎210 938 029; www.facebook.com/bosqlx; Rua Rodrigues Faria 103, LX Factory; ⊙11pm-5am Fri-Sat) The newest tenant for LX Factory (p114) is this cool two-storey nightclub, which features a 120-sq-metre vertical garden above the upstairs bar and duelling environments that bounce between dance, R&B and hip hop. Lisbon's bold and beautiful flock here to dance under the guise of nightlife-ready animal portraits and 3D wallpaper.

Chimera Brewpub BREWERY

(Map p80; www.chimera.kitchen; Rua Prior do Crato 6; half/pint €2.50-4; ⊙5.30pm-2am Tue-

Sat; [wifi icon]) Two chefs (one American, the other a Portuguese-raised Brazilian) launched Lisbon's second brewpub in 2016 with 12 brews, including rarer choices such as a Belgian blonde ale and American dark lager. Four taps are devoted to invited *lisboêta* suds from Dois Corvos and Oitava Colina. Downing proper pints within the Palácio das Necessidades' stone-walled 18th-century carriage tunnel feels vaguely medieval.

Marquês de Pombal & Around

★Red Frog COCKTAIL BAR
(www.facebook.com/redfrogspeakeasy; Rua do Salitre 5A; cocktails €8-12.50; 6pm-2am Sun-Thu, to 4am Fri-Sat) In true speakeasy fashion, sign-less Red Frog is accessed via a 'Press Here for Cocktails' doorbell. Enter a sophisticated world of mixology, where craft cocktails are king and appropriate behaviour, dress and glassware are tenants. The exquisite seasonal cocktail menu is perfectly balanced and the dark and classy room (including the intriguing secret one) is a perfect accompaniment. Connoisseurs only.

Casa Independente BAR
(www.casaindependente.com; Largo do Intendente 45; 2pm-midnight Tue-Thu, to 2am Fri, noon-2am Sat) There's always something going on at this creative space overlooking a sleepy plaza just north of Largo Martim Moniz. You can wander through rooms looking at strange and curious artwork, join the smokers on the plant-filled back patio, or nurse drinks in quiet corners of this rambling old space.

Belém

Darwin's Café CAFE
(210 480 222; www.darwincafe.com; Av Brasília Ala B; mains €13.50-26; 12.30-4pm Mon, 12.30-3.30pm, 4.30-6.30pm & 7.30-11pm Tue-Sun) This trendy, evolution-themed cafe suffers from a bit of scholarly overreach inside (though the big, round banquettes are great for groups), but its elevated terrace affords postcard-perfect views of the Tejo and Torré de Belém. It draws a fashion-forward local crowd for sophisticated pastas, risottos etc as well as an extensive list of bubbly by the flute.

☆ Entertainment

Fado

Mesa de Frades FADO
(Map p72; 917 029 436; www.facebook.com/mesadefradeslisboa; Rua dos Remédios 139A; 8pm-2.30am Mon-Sat) A magical place to hear fado, tiny Mesa de Frades used to be a chapel. It's tiled with exquisite *azulejos* and has just a handful of tables. The show begins around 11pm. Skip the food (which is hit-or-miss) and stick to drinks.

Bela FADO
(Map p72; 926 077 511; Rua dos Remédios 190; 8pm-3am Tue-Sun) This intimate spot features live fado on Wednesday, Friday, Saturday and Sunday, and eclectic cultural fare (poetry readings, jazz nights) on other nights. Although there is a €15 minimum consumption, unlike most fado houses, you won't have to buy a pricey meal as it's an appetisers-and-drinks kind of place. Fado begins at 9.15pm.

Senhor Fado FADO
(Map p72; 218 874 298; www.sr-fado.com; Rua dos Remédios 176; 8pm-2am Wed-Sat) Small and lantern-lit, this is a cosy spot for *fado vadio* (street fado). *Fadista* Ana Marina and guitarist Duarte Santos make a great double act.

A Baîuca FADO
(Map p72; 218 867 284; Rua de São Miguel 20; 8pm-midnight Thu-Mon) On a good night, walking into A Baîuca is like gate-crashing a family party. It's a special place with *fado vadio*, where locals take a turn and spectators hiss if anyone dares to chat during the singing. There's a €25 minimum spend, which is as tough to swallow as the food, though the fado is spectacular. Reserve ahead.

Parreirinha de Alfama FADO
(Map p72; 218 868 209; www.parreirinhadealfama.com; Beco do Espírito Santo 1; minimum €30; 8pm-2am) Owned by fado legend Argentina Santos, this place offers good food amid candlelit ambience; it attracts an audience that often falls hard for the top-quality *fadistas* (three singers and two guitarists per night, sometimes appearing straight from the crowd). Book by 4pm.

Adega dos Fadistas FADO
(Map p72; 211 510 368; Rua dos Remédios 102; noon-2am Tue-Sun) One of the top newer fado houses in the Alfama, the Adega dos Fadistas

DON'T MISS

FACTORY OF THE ARTS

Set in a converted 19th-century industrial complex, **LX Factory** (Map p80; www.lxfactory.com; Rua Rodrigues de Faria 103) is Lisbon's coolest hub of creativity. In 2007 some 23,000 sq metres of abandoned warehouses were transformed into art studios, galleries, and printing and design companies. Creative restaurants, bars and shops have added to the energy, and today LX Factory is a great spot to check out an alternative side of Lisbon. It's liveliest on weekend nights, though it's also worth stopping by the open-air market (vintage clothes, crafts) held on Sundays from 11am to 7pm. Get there on tram 15 or 18.

Other highlights:

Kiss the Cook (p87) Offers cooking classes (the chef speaks English).

Kare Design (Map p80; www.kare-design.com; Rua de Rodrigues Faria 103; ⌚noon-8pm Tue-Fri, 11am-8pm Sat, 10am-2pm Sun) Imaginative home-design store.

Ler Devagar (p119) Great bookshop and cosy cafe. Don't miss the wild exhibits on upper floors.

1300 Taberna (Map p80; ☎213 649 170; www.1300taberna.com; Rua Rodrigues de Faria 103, LX Factory; mains €16-22, 5-course menu with drinks €55; ⌚12.30-3pm & 8pm-midnight Tue-Sat; 📶) Excellent restaurant featuring creative takes on Portuguese fare.

Landeau (Map p80; www.landeau.pt; Rua Rodrigues de Faria 103, LX Factory; cake €3.50; ⌚11am-7pm; 📶) Wondrously gooey, perfectly moist, just-sweet-enough chocolate-cake perfection.

Rio Maravila (Map p80; ☎966 028 229; www.riomaravilha.pt; Rua Rodrigues de Faria 103, LX Factory; small plates €5-20; ⌚6pm-2am Tue, 12.30pm-2am Wed-Sat, 12.30pm-6pm Sun) Chef Diogo Noronha's good-time Portuguese-Brazilian *petiscos* (tapas) with outstanding river views.

serves up first-rate fado in a medieval-like stone-walled dining room. Mains cost around €17, and the added music charge is €10. Shows start at 9pm most nights.

A Tasco do Chico FADO
(Map p68; ☎961 339 696; www.facebook.com/atasca.dochico; Rua Diário de Notícias 39; ⌚noon-2am, to 3am Fri-Sat) This crowded dive (reserve ahead), full of soccer banners and spilling over with people of all ilk is a fado free-for-all. It's not uncommon for taxi drivers to roll up, hum a few bars, and hop right back into their cabs, speeding off into the night. Portugal's most famous fado singer, Mariza, brought us here in 2005. It's legit.

Clube de Fado FADO
(Map p72; ☎218 852 704; www.clube-de-fado.com; Rua de São João da Praça 92; admission before/after 10.30pm €7.50/10; ⌚8pm-2am) Clube de Fado hosts the cream of the fado crop in vaulted, dimly lit surrounds. Big-name *fadistas* performing here include Cuca Rosetta and Maria Ana Bobone, alongside celebrated guitarists such as owner Mario Pacheco. The food is less outstanding, so come for drinks, which is allowed after 10.30pm. Fado starts at 9.30pm.

Football

Estádio da Luz STADIUM
(Map p62; Estádio do Sport Lisboa e Benfica; ☎707 200 100; www.slbenfica.pt; Av General Norton de Matos) SL Benfica plays at this 65,000-seat stadium in the Benfica district, which also houses the club's **museum** (http://museubenfica.slbenfica.pt). It hosted the 2014 Champions League Final and was voted the most beautiful stadium in Europe that same year by French sporting newspaper, *L'Équipe*. The nearest metro station is Colégio Militar-Luz.

Estádio José de Alvalade STADIUM
(www.sporting.pt; Rua Prof Fernando da Fonseca) This state-of-the-art 50,000-seat football stadium hosts sporting matches. Just north of the university; take the metro to Campo Grande.

Music, Theatre & Dance

Hot Clube de Portugal JAZZ
(☎213 460 305; www.hcp.pt; Praça da Alegria 48; ⌚10pm-2am Tue-Sat) As hot as its name suggests, this small, poster-plastered cellar (and newly added garden) has staged top-drawer jazz acts since the 1940s. It's considered one of Europe's best.

Bar da Velha Senhora LIVE MUSIC
(Map p68; www.facebook.com/bardavelhasenhora; Rua Nova do Carvalho 40; ⏲6pm-2am Tue-Thu, to 3am Fri-Sat) The fabulously burlesque Bar da Velha Senhora whisks you back to those crazy days of the 1920s, with its low-lit interior and glittering revue shows. Tapas and cocktails with risqué names get the crowd in the mood for fado, cabaret, Latin jazz, flamenco, erotic poetry recitals and more.

Zé dos Bois LIVE MUSIC
(ZDB; Map p68; www.zedosbois.org; Rua da Barroca 59; cover €6-10; ⏲expositions 6-11pm Wed-Sat, concerts from 10pm) Focusing on tomorrow's performing-arts and music trends, Zé dos Bois is an experimental venue that has a graffitied courtyard, and an eclectic line-up of theatre, film, visual arts and live music acts.

Teatro Taborda THEATRE
(Map p72; ☎218 854 190; www.teatrodagaragem.com; Costa do Castelo 75) This cultural centre shows contemporary dance, theatre and world music. It also has spectacular views from its cafe-restaurant.

Teatro Nacional de São Carlos THEATRE
(Map p68; ☎213 253 045; www.saocarlos.pt; Rua Serpa Pinto 9; ⏲1-7pm Mon-Fri) Worth visiting just to see the sublime gold-and-red interior, but it also has opera, ballet and theatre seasons. The summertime **Festival ao Largo** (Map p68; www.festivalaolargo.pt; Largo de São Carlos; ⏲late Jun–late Jul) features free outdoor concerts on the plaza facing the theatre.

Teatro Nacional de Dona Maria II THEATRE
(Map p66; ☎800 213 250; www.teatro-dmaria.pt; Praça Dom Pedro IV; ⏲box office 11am-10pm Wed-Fri, 2-10pm Sat, 10.30am-7pm Tue & Sun) Rossio's graceful neoclassical theatre has a somewhat hit-and-miss schedule due to underfunding. Guided tours on Mondays (except August) at 11.30am (€6).

Cinema

Cinemateca Portuguesa CINEMA
(www.cinemateca.pt; Rua Barata Salgueiro 39; films €3.20) Screens offbeat, art-house, world and old films.

São Jorge CINEMA
(☎213 103 402; www.cinemasaojorge.pt; Av da Liberdade 175; films €4; ⏲10am-midnight) The grand São Jorge is a traditional cinema.

Shopping

Baixa & Rossio

★**Garrafeira Nacional** WINE
(Map p66; www.garrafeiranacional.com; Rua de Santa Justa 18; ⏲9.30am-7.30pm Mon-Fri, to 7.30pm Sat) This Lisbon landmark has been slinging Portuguese juice since 1927 and is easily the best spot to pick up a bevy of local wines and spirits. It is especially helpful and will steer you towards lesser-known boutique wines and vintage ports in addition to the usual suspects. The small museum features vintages dating to the 18th century.

★**Typographia** CLOTHING
(Map p66; www.typographia.com; Rua Augusta 93; T-shirts €16-24; ⏲10am-9pm) With shops in Porto and Madrid as well, this T-shirt shop is one of Europe's best. It features a select, monthly-changing array of clever and artsy, locally designed T-shirts, which everyone else won't be wearing once you get back home.

Retrox VINTAGE
(Map p66; www.facebook.com/retroxcoisasvintage; Rua dos Anjos 4C; ⏲2-7pm Wed-Mon) Stylish Brazilian Josiane Lima has assembled a funky collection of vintage kitsch from the '50s to '70s, from Portugal and abroad, at this hip Intendente shop. The ever-changing bounty might feature Abba 45s, West German scales, Cuban cigar boxes, framed 1940 Comboios de Portugal train schedules or old-school Japanese Super 8 cameras.

Espaço Açores FOOD
(Map p66; www.espacoacores.pt; Rua de São Julião 58; ⏲10am-2pm & 3-7pm Mon-Sat) The closest you can get to actually visiting the Azores is this attractive shop, where a taste of the islands comes in the form of cheeses, honeys, preserves, passion-fruit liqueurs and, apparently, the oldest tea produced in Europe.

Napoleão WINE
(Map p66; www.napoleao.co.pt; Rua dos Fanqueiros 70; ⏲9am-8pm Mon-Sat, 1-8pm Sun) Of the two Napoleão shops on this corner, this friendly, English-speaking cellar specialises in Portuguese-only wines, ports and spirits with hundreds of bottles to choose from (and other homegrown gourmet products). Ships worldwide.

Feira das Almas MARKET
(Map p66; www.feiradasalmas.org; Regueirão Dos Anjos 70; ⏲2-10pm) This rambling alternative

market takes place on the first weekend of each month and draws a young-leaning, eclectic crowd of freaks and geeks who gobble up alternative designs and vintage clothing, jewellery, rare vinyl, funky art, handmade soaps, artisan chocolates, tea with DJs, performance art and a bar fuelling the fun. No two days are the same.

Queijaria Nacional FOOD
(Map p66; www.queijarianacional.pt; Rua da Conceição 8; ⏲10am-7pm) A one-stop cheese shop with varieties from all over Portugal – from pungent and creamy Serra da Estrela to Azores and Alentejo varieties. You can also pair cheese and charcuterie with Portuguese wines during a tasting here.

A Vida Portuguesa GIFTS & SOUVENIRS
(Map p66; www.avidaportuguesa.com; Largo do Intendente 23; ⏲10.30am-7.30pm) The second outlet of Catarina Portas' made-in-Portugal boutique has turned a 19th-century ceramics factory into another must-visit Lisbon shop, this time also helping revitalise the Intendente neighbourhood.

Pátio da Galé Lisbon Shop GIFTS & SOUVENIRS
(Map p66; www.askmelisboa.com; Rua do Arsenal 15; ⏲9.30am-7.30pm) Housed in the Pombaline Pátio da Galé complex, this shop is crammed with 100% Portuguese gifts, from tram Ts to cockerel mugs and cork bags to speciality foods. It's run by Ask Me Lisboa, the public face of Lisbon tourism.

Papabubble CANDY
(Map p66; www.papabubble.com; Rua da Conceição 117; ⏲10am-7pm Mon-Sat) Papabubble makes and sells very tasty old-fashioned hard candy in a variety of classic and creative flavours (including raspberry-lime, kiwi and aniseed). Kids might enjoy seeing the candymakers in action behind the counter.

Manuel Tavares FOOD & DRINKS
(Map p66; www.manueltavares.com; Rua da Betesga 1A; ⏲9.30am-7.30pm Mon-Sat) For a lingering taste of Lisbon, nip into this wood-fronted store, which has been tempting locals since 1860 with *pata negra*, pungent cheeses, *ginjinha*, port and other Portuguese treats.

Santos Ofícios ARTS & CRAFTS
(Map p66; www.santosoficios-artesanato.pt; Rua da Madalena 87; ⏲10am-8pm Mon-Sat) If you have always fancied a hand-embroidered fado shawl, check out this brick-vaulted store. Santos is a must-shop for Portuguese folk art including Madeira lace, blingy Christmas decorations and glazed earthenware.

Outra Face da Lua VINTAGE
(Map p66; www.aoutrafacedalua.com; Rua da Assunção 22; ⏲10am-8pm Mon-Sat, noon-7pm Sun; 📶) Vintage divas make for this retro boutique in Baixa, crammed with puff ball dresses, lurex skirts and wildly patterned '70s shirts. Jazz and electronica play overhead. Revive over salads, sandwiches, cocktails and cosmic iced tea at the in-store cafe.

Bairro Alto & Chiado

★Loja das Conservas FOOD
(Map p68; www.facebook.com/lojadasconservas; Rua do Arsenal 130; ⏲10am-9pm Mon-Sat, noon-8pm Sun) What appears to be a gallery is on closer inspection a fascinating temple to tinned fish (or *conservas* as the Portuguese say), the result of an industry on its deathbed revived by a savvy marketing about-face and new generations of hipsters. The retro-wrapped tins, displayed along with the history of each canning factory, are the artworks.

A Vida Portuguesa GIFTS & SOUVENIRS
(Map p68; www.avidaportuguesa.com; Rua Anchieta 11; ⏲10am-8pm Mon-Sat, from 11am Sun) A flashback to the late 19th century with its high ceilings and polished cabinets, this former warehouse and perfume factory lures nostalgics with all-Portuguese products from retro-wrapped Tricona sardines to Claus Porto soaps, and heart-embellished Viana do Castelo embroideries to Bordallo Pinheiro porcelain swallows. Also located in Intendente.

Cork & Company GIFTS & SOUVENIRS
(Map p68; www.corkandcompany.pt; Rua das Salgadeiras 10; ⏲11am-7pm Mon-Thu, to 9pm Fri-Sat) 🍃 At this elegantly designed shop, you'll find cork put to surprisingly imaginative uses, with well-made and sustainable cork handbags, pens, wallets, journals, candleholders, hats, scarves, place mats, umbrellas, iPhone covers and even chaise longues!

Fábrica Sant'Ana ARTS & CRAFTS
(Map p68; www.santanna.com.pt; Rua do Alecrim 95; azulejos from €5; ⏲9.30am-7pm Mon-Fri, 10am-7pm Sat) Handmaking and painting *azulejos* since 1741, this is the place to get some eye-catching porcelain tiles for your home.

Oficina Irmãos Marques ART
(Map p68; www.oficinairmaosmarques.com; Rua Luz Soriano 71; ⏰10am-7pm Wed-Sat) Even if you don't buy anything, it's worth popping into Brazilian-born, Portuguese-transplanted Gezo Marques' gallery/workshop, mainly for his striking woodwork which channels the maze-like tapestries of Brazilian favela construction into one-of-a-kind cabinetry and wood art. You will also find provocative paintings, *objets d'art*, chandeliers and unique interior-design pieces – perhaps easier to lug home than a chest of drawers.

A Carioca FOOD
(Map p68; Rua da Misericórdia 9; ⏰9am-7pm Mon-Fri, to 1pm Sat) Little has changed since this old-world store opened in 1924: brass fittings still gleam, the coffee roaster is still in action and home blends, sugared almonds and toffees are still lovingly wrapped in green paper.

Louie Louie MUSIC
(Map p68; www.louielouie.biz; Rua Nova da Trinidade 8; ⏰11am-7.30pm Mon-Sat, 3-7.30pm Sun) Clued-up DJs head for this funky music store stocking secondhand vinyl and the latest house, dance and electronica grooves. Its tiny cafe does a mean chocolate cake.

Story Tailors CLOTHING
(Map p68; www.storytailors.pt; Calçada do Ferragial 8; ⏰11am-7pm Tue-Sat) Mirror, mirror…undoubtedly one of Lisbon's fairest boutiques is this chandelier-lit enchanted forest of fashion, where design duo Luís Sanchez and João Branco bewitch with fairytale dresses, floaty ruffle skirts, quirky reversible coats and their latest catwalk creations.

El Dorado VINTAGE COTHING
(Map p68; ☎213 423 935; Rua do Norte 23; ⏰noon-9pm Mon-Sat, 5-9pm Sun) A gramophone plays vinyl classics as divas bag vintage styles from psychedelic prints to 6in platforms and pencil skirts at this Bairro Alto hipster. There's also a great range of club wear.

Livraria Bertrand BOOKS
(Map p68; ☎213 476 122; www.bertrand.pt; Rua Garrett 73; ⏰9am-10pm Mon-Sat, 11am-8pm Sun) The world's oldest operating bookshop, open since 1732 according to *Guinness World Records*, Bertrand has excellent selections, including titles in English, French and Spanish.

LOCAL KNOWLEDGE

CATWALK QUEENS

Make way for Lisbon's trio of catwalk queens, revamping wardrobes with their majestic collections.

Fátima Lopes (☎213 240 550; www.fatimalopes.com; ⏰8am-10pm Mon-Sat) Divas love Fátima's immaculate collection of figure-hugging, Latin-inspired threads – from slinky suits to itsy-glitzy prom dresses and hot-pink ball gowns.

Lena Aires (Map p68; ☎213 461 815; Rua da Atalaia 96; ⏰2pm-midnight Mon-Sat) Lena's funky Bairro Alto boutique brims with citrus-bright knits and fresh-faced fashion.

Luis Onofre (www.luisonofre.com; Avenida da Liberdade 247; shoes from €208; ⏰10am-7pm Mon-Sat) For sexy women's shoes fit for a princess, it doesn't get any bigger than Portugal's Luis Onofre, whose designs have graced the soles of Michelle Obama, Naomi Watts and Paris Hilton.

FNAC BOOKS, MUSIC
(Map p68; ☎707 313 435; www.fnac.pt; Rua do Carmo 2, Armazéns do Chiado; ⏰10am-10pm; 📶) One of the city's biggest book and music stores. You can buy tickets for many concerts and events here as well.

Alfama, Castelo & Graça

★**Cortiço & Netos** HOMEWARES
(Map p72; www.corticoenetos.com; Calçada de Santo André 66; ⏰10am-1pm & 2-7pm Mon-Sat) A wonder wall of fabulous *azulejos* greets you as you enter this very special space. It's the vision of brothers Pedro, João, Ricardo and Tiago Cortiço, whose grandfather dedicated more than 30 years to gathering, storing and selling discontinued Portuguese industrial tiles. Reviving the family trade, they are experts on the *azulejo* and how it can be interpreted today.

★**Arte da Terra** GIFTS & SOUVENIRS
(Map p72; www.aartedaterra.pt; Rua Augusto Rosa 40; ⏰11am-8pm) In the stables of a centuries-old bishop's palace, Arte da Terra brims with authentic Portuguese crafts including Castello Branco embroideries, nativity figurines, hand-painted *azulejos*, fado CDs and quality goods (umbrellas, aprons, writing

SHOPPING MALLS

When you need a break from the heat, step into air-conditioned splendour. All of the following malls have cinemas, good food courts and, of course, shops.

Centro Comercial Colombo (www.colombo.pt; Av Lusíada; ⊙9am-midnight)

Amoreiras Shopping Center (Complexo das Amoreiras; www.amoreiras.com; Av Duarte Pacheco; ⊙10am-11pm)

El Corte Inglês (www.elcorteingles.pt; Av António Augusto de Aguiar 31; ⊙10am-10pm Mon-Thu, to 11.30pm Fri & Sat, to 8pm Sun; 📶)

Dolce Vita Tejo (www.dolcevitatejo.pt; Avenida Cruzeiro Seixas 5 e 7, Amadora; ⊙10am-11pm Sun-Thu, to midnight Fri-Sat)

journals) made from cork. Some goods are beautifully lit in former troughs.

Garbags BAGS

(Map p72; www.garbags.eu; Rua São Vicente 17; ⊙10am-8pm Mon-Sat, to 6pm Sun) This eco-friendly Graça outfit sells messenger bags, iPhone cases, wallets, handbags and zipper pouches cleverly made from former coffee sacks, potato-chip bags, juice containers and other recycled materials. The gear seems durable (and waterproof) and the look is somewhat sleek, if you don't mind the corporate logos.

MO&TA CA.SA FASHION & ACCESSORIES

(Map p72; ☎937 133 093; Rua São João da Praça 97, 1st fl; ⊙9am-10pm) To meet Portuguese designer Jorge Moita and see the full array of his La.Ga bags – which he affectionately calls his UFOs – visit his new design workshop in Alfama. The striking tear-shaped handbags made of super-lightweight, incredibly resistant Tyvek, bear the creatively unique hallmarks of female prisoners, designers and artists.

O Voo da Andorinha/ Era Uma Vez Um Sonho GIFTS & SOUVENIRS

(Map p72; Rua do Barão 22; ⊙10am-8pm Mon-Sat) Candy-bright beads, hand-stitched swallows, embroidered accessories and quirky furnishings made with recycled junk – you'll find all of this and more at this adorable boutique near the cathedral. It shares space with the unique handcrafted puppets, stuffed animals, puzzles and illustrated books of Era Uma Vez Um Sonho. It's great for kids.

Loja dos Descobrimentos ARTS & CRAFTS

(Map p72; www.loja-descobrimentos.com; Rua dos Bacalhoeiros 14A; ⊙9am-7pm Mon-Sat) Watch artisans carefully painting handmade *azulejos* (hand-painted tiles) at this workshop and store near the Casa dos Bicos (p76). Fruits and flowers, boats, culinary motifs or geometric – tiles are available in myriad colours and designs.

Fabula Urbis BOOKS

(Map p72; www.fabula-urbis.pt; Rua Augusto Rosa 27; ⊙10am-1pm & 3-8pm) A great little bookshop that celebrates works about Portugal, both by home-grown and expat authors. All the best works by Lobo Antunes, Saramago, Pessoa, Richard Zimler and Robert C Wilson are here and available in English, French, Spanish, Italian, German and, of course, Portuguese.

Silva & Feijóo FOOD

(Map p72; www.facebook.com/silvaefeijoo; Rua dos Bacalhoeiros 117; ⊙10am-7pm Mon-Sat) Planning a picnic? Stop by this nearly 100-year-old brand's shop, one of several in the area, for sheep's cheese from the Seia mountains, sardine pâté, rye bread, *salsichas* (sausages) and other Portuguese goodies.

Feira da Ladra MARKET

(Map p72; Campo de Santa Clara; ⊙6am-5pm Tue & Sat) Browse for back-of-the-lorry treasures at this massive flea market. You'll find old records, coins, baggy pants, dog-eared poetry books and other attic junk. Haggle hard and watch your wallet – it isn't called 'thieves market' for nothing.

Príncipe Real, Santos & Estrela

★Embaixada SHOPPING CENTRE

(Map p76; www.embaixadalx.pt; Praça do Príncipe Real 26; ⊙noon-8pm, restaurants to 2am) Take an exquisite 19th-century neo-Moorish palace and fill it with fashion, design and concept stores on the cutting-edge of cool and you have one of Lisbon's most exciting new shopping experiences: Embaixada. Centred on a grand sweeping staircase and courtyard are boutiques selling everything from vintage records to organic cosmetics, eco-homewares, contemporary Portuguese ceramics and catwalk styles.

There is a wonderful gin-centric bar-cafe in the atrium (Gin Lovers) and a good steakhouse hidden below, to the back (O Talho).

Solar ANTIQUES
(Map p76; www.solar.com.pt; Rua Dom Pedro V 70; azulejos €15-200; ⏲10am-7pm, closed Sat & Sun Jul-Aug) Hawking antique *azulejos* for seven decades, Solar offers row after row and pile after pile of precious Portuguese tiles dating from the 1500s to 1900s, many of which were salvaged from old churches and palaces.

Verso Branco DESIGN
(Map p76; www.versobranco.pt; Rua da Boavista 132-134; ⏲11.30am-8pm Tue-Sat) 'Free verse' is the name of this split-level design store, where Fernando has a story for every object. The high-ceilinged space showcases Portuguese contemporary arts, crafts and furnishings, from Burel's quality wool creations to limited edition La.Ga bags by designer Jorge Moita – the beautifully crafted bags made from Tyvek weigh just 40g and can hold 55kg.

Entre Tanto DESIGN
(Map p76; www.entretanto.pt; Rua do Escola Politécnica 42; ⏲noon-8pm) Inside the 17th-century Castilho Palace, this concept store is divided into fashion, lifestyle, design and food, and features locally leaning designers where possible. Don't miss the gorgeous Alentejan woollen blankets and scarves from Stró, leather sneakers from Jak and that Banoffie cheesecake from LXeesecake!

Nuno Gama FASHION & ACCESSORIES
(Map p76; www.nunogama.pt; Rua do Século 171; ⏲10am-8pm) One of the country's most feted fashion designers, Nuno Gama is Portugal's catwalk king. His sleek flagship store showcases Nuno's hallmarks, including a love of blue, contemporary, figure-hugging tailoring, as well as a subtle use of heritage motifs, such as coats of arms and *azulejo* patterns. There's also a barber shop here should you fancy revamping your locks.

Loja Real DESIGN
(Map p76; www.facebook.com/lojareal.Lisboa; Praça do Príncipe Real 20; ⏲10.30am-8pm Mon-Sat) A showcase for largely Portuguese designers, Loja Real features a wide assortment of unique, high-quality products that run the gamut of home decor (cushions, teapots, vases), fashion (clothing, jewellery) and artwork to items for children (clothing, books and toys). The emphasis is 'slow retail': nothing mass-produced or made with plastics or cheap materials.

Espaço B FASHION & ACCESSORIES
(Map p76; www.espaco-b.com; Rua Dom Pedro V 120; ⏲10.30am-7.30pm Mon-Sat) This high-end boutique offers well-tailored men's and women's fashions, including designer sneakers from Y-3 and Premiata, hip Stutterheim raincoats and locally designed +3251 T-shirts.

Clothing aside, Espaço B stocks scarves, artfully designed jewellery, fashion and design books and other collectables.

Lapa & Alcântara

LX Market MARKET
(Map p80; http://lxmarket.com.pt; Rua Rodrigues de Faria 103, LX Factory; ⏲11am-6pm Sun) Vintage clothing, antiques, crafts, food, and weird and wonderful plants – the LX Factory (p114) market is the place to find them. Live music entertains Sunday shoppers.

Ler Devagar BOOKS
(Map p80; ☎213 259 992; www.lerdevagar.com; Rua Rodrigues de Faria 103, LX Factory; ⏲noon-9pm Mon, noon-midnight Tue-Thu, noon-2am Fri-Sat, 11am-9pm Sun) Late-night bookworms and anyone who likes a good read will love this floor-to-ceiling temple of books at the LX Factory (p114). Art, culture and foreign-language titles are well represented.

Portugal Gifts GIFTS & SOUVENIRS
(Map p80; www.facebook.com/portugalgifts; Rua Presidente Arriaga 60; ⏲10am 7pm Mon-Fri) This craft shop puts a contemporary spin on Portuguese souvenirs, with everything from funky Barcelos cockerel mugs to *azulejo* coffee coasters and chocolate sardines.

Marquês de Pombal & Around

Carbono MUSIC
(www.carbono.com.pt; Rua do Telhal 6B; ⏲11am-7pm Mon-Sat) The staff may be grumpy, but it's hard not to like Carbono, with its impressive selection of new and secondhand vinyl and CDs. World music – West African boogaloo, Brazilian tropicalia – is especially well represented.

Information

DANGERS & ANNOYANCES

Lisbon is generally a safe city with a low crime rate.

➡ Mind your wallet on tram 28 – a major hotspot for pickpockets – and at other tourist hubs such as Rua Augusta.

➡ Be wary of your surroundings at night around metro stations such as Anjos, Martim Moniz and Intendente, where there have been muggings. Take care in the dark alleys of Alfama and Graça.

➡ Ward off hash and cocaine offers from swarthy characters in Baixa – especially around Rossio – and in Bairro Alto with a firm but polite 'no' (PS: the drugs are fake).

EMERGENCY

Police ☎112

Fire ☎112

Ambulance ☎112

Lisbon Tourist Police ☎213 421 623

INTERNET ACCESS

The majority of cafes and restaurants in Lisbon offer free wireless access, though it's not always obvious as few bother changing the name of their wi-fi network from the ones that come with the router. Ask your server.

MEDIA

Popular Portuguese newspapers include *Diário de Notícias* (www.dn.pt) and the tabloid bestseller *Correiro da Manhã* (www.cmjornal.xl.pt). The *Portugal News* (http://theportugalnews.com) is an English-language daily.

MEDICAL SERVICES

British Hospital (☎800 271 271; www.british-hospital.pt; Rua Tomás da Fonseca) English-speaking staff and English-speaking doctors.

Clínica Médica Internacional (☎213 513 310; www.cmil.pt; Avenida Sidónio Pais 14) A quick (though not cheap) private clinic with English-speaking doctors.

Farmácia Estácio (Praça Dom Pedro IV 62; ⏲8.30am-8pm Mon-Fri, 10am-7pm Sat-Sun) A central pharmacy.

> **ℹ LISBOA CARD**
>
> If you're planning on doing a lot of sightseeing, the **Lisboa discount card** represents excellent value. It offers unlimited use of public transport (including trains to Sintra and Cascais), entry to all key museums and attractions, and up to 50% discount on tours, cruises and other admission charges. It's available at **Ask Me Lisboa** tourist offices, including the one at the airport. The 24-/48-/72-hour versions cost €18.50/31.50/39. You validate the card when you want to start it.

MONEY

Multibanco ATMs are widespread throughout the city; look for the MB logo. International credit cards – referred to as Visa, even when they are MasterCard and others! – can be problematic. Smaller family-run shops, restaurants and guesthouses will only accept Portuguese-issued debit cards as far as plastic goes.

Nova Câmbios (www.novacambios.com; Praça Dom Pedro IV 42; ⏲8am-8pm Mon-Sat, 9am-8pm Sun) The best bet for changing cash or travellers cheques is a private exchange bureau like this one.

POSTAL SERVICES

Correios, Telégrafos e Telefones (CTT; www.ct.pt) is the national postal service of Portugal.

Main Post Office (CTT; www.ctt.pt; Praça dos Restauradores 58; ⏲8am-10pm Mon-Fri, 9am-6pm Sat)

Post Office (CTT; www.ctt.pt; Praça do Município 6; ⏲8.30am-6.30pm) Central post office.

Post Office (CTT; Map p68; www.ctt.pt; Praça Luís de Camões 20; ⏲8.30am-6pm Mon-Fri) Handy location on Praça Luís de Camões.

TOURIST INFORMATION

Ask Me Lisboa (www.askmelisboa.com) The largest and most helpful tourist office in the city faces Praça dos Restauradaures inside the Palácio Foz. Staff dole out maps and information, book accommodation and reserve rental cars. The smaller branch on Rua Jardim do Regedor (☎213 472 134; Rua Jardim do Regedor 50; ⏲11am-6pm) near Praça Restauradores offers tourist info, left luggage and charged internet access. There is another helpful branch on Praça do Comércio (☎210 312 810; Praça do Comércio; ⏲9am-8pm).

Ask Me Lisboa also runs several information kiosks, which are handy places for maps and quick information: Airport (☎218 450 660; Aeroporto de Lisboa, Arrivals Hall; ⏲7.30am-9.30am Tue-Sat); Belém (Map p84; ☎213 658 435; Largo dos Jernónimos, Belém; ⏲10am-1pm & 2-6pm Tue-Sat); Santa Apolónia (Map p72; ☎910 517 982; Door 48, Santa Apolónia train station; ⏲7.30am-9.30pm Tue-Sat); Rossio Square (Map p68; ☎910 517 914; Praça Dom Pedro IV; ⏲10am-1pm & 2-6pm); Parque das Nações (☎910 518 028; Alameda dos Oceanos; ⏲10am-1pm & 2-7pm Apr-Sep, to 6pm Oct-Mar).

These are all run by the city's official tourism arm, Turismo de Lisboa, but bear in mind it is member-driven so not impartial when it comes to recommendations.

Instituto da Conservação da Natureza e da Biodiversidade Portugal's governmental body responsible for the management of protected and state forested areas in Portugal.

Getting There & Away

AIR

Situated around 6km north of the centre, the ultramodern **Aeroporto de Lisboa** (Lisbon Airport; 218 413 700; www.ana.pt; Alameda das Comunidades Portuguesas) operates direct flights to major international hubs including London, New York, Paris and Frankfurt. Several low-cost carriers (EasyJet, Ryanair, Transavia, Norwegian etc) leave from the less-efficient terminal 2 – you'll need to factor in extra time for the shuttle ride if arriving at the airport on the metro.

BOAT

The **Transtejo ferry line** (213 500 115; www.transtejo.pt) has several riverfront terminals. Services are less frequent on weekends and may increase in summer.

Estação Fluvial de Belém (Map p84; 213 500 115; www.transtejo.pt) offers service to Trafaria and Porto Brandão (€1.15, every 30 to 60 minutes), about 3.5km and 5km respectively from Costa da Caparica town.

Terminal Fluvial Cais do Sodré (Map p76; 213 500 115; www.transtejo.pt) offers service to Cacilhas (€1.20, 10 minutes, every 10 minutes, 5.35am to 1.40am), Montijo (€2.75, 30 minutes, 6.30am to 11.15pm) and Seixal (€2.35, 30 minutes, 6.35am to 11.15pm).

Terminal Fluvial Terreiro do Paço (213 500 115; www.transtejo.pt; Rua da Cintura do Porto de Lisboa) offers service to Barreiro (€2.30, 30 minutes, every 10 to 30 minutes, 5.45am to 2am), for rail connections to the Alentejo, Algarve and Setúbal.

BUS

Information and tickets for international departures are scarce at weekends, so try to avoid that last-minute Sunday dash out of Portugal.

Sete Rios

Lisbon's main long-distance bus terminal is **Rodoviário de Sete Rios** (Praça General Humberto Delgado, Rua das Laranjeiras), adjacent to both Jardim Zoológico metro station and Sete Rios train station. The big carriers, **Rede Expressos** (707 223 344; www.rede-expressos.pt) and **Eva** (707 223 344; www.eva-bus.com), run frequent services to almost every major town. You can buy your ticket up to seven days in advance.

Domestic services include:

Coimbra €14.50, 2½ hours, 15 to 25 daily
Évora €12.50, 1½ hours, 10 to 20 daily
Faro €20, 3½ hours, four to eight daily
Porto €20, 3½ hours, 10 to 20 daily

Buses to Sesimbra and Costa da Caparica also leave from here.

Intercentro (707 200 512; www.intercentro.pt; Gare do Oriente) runs coaches to destinations all over Europe, beginning at Sete Rios and stopping at Gare do Oriente 15 minutes later. In addition to Madrid, there are direct connections to Paris (€91, 28 hours, 9.15am) and Amsterdam (€147, 35 hours, 7am).

Gare do Oriente

The large bus terminal, **Gare do Oriente** (p85), concentrates on services to the north and onto Spain and beyond. On the 1st floor are bus-company booths (mostly open from 9am to 5.30pm Monday to Saturday, and to 7pm Friday, closed for lunch; smaller operators only open just before arrival or departure).

The biggest companies operating from here are **Renex** (218 956 836; www.renex.pt; Gare do Oriente), which heads to the Algarve, Porto and Minho; **Citiexpress** (707 223 344; www.citiexpress.eu; Gare do Oriente), which heads to Coimbra, Porto and Guimarães; and Spanish operator **Avanza** (912 722 832; www.avanzabus.com), which heads to Madrid.

Services include:

Braga €20.50, 4½ hours, eight to 12 daily
Guimarães €20.50, 4½ hours, eight to 12 daily
Lagos €19.50, 4½ hours, seven to eight daily
Madrid €43, eight hours, 9.15am, 8.15pm Monday to Saturday, plus 12.15pm Monday to Friday

Terminal Campo Grande

Regional operators in the north – including **Mafrense** (707 201 371; www.mafrense.pt) for Ericeira and Mafra – operate from **Terminal Campo Grande** (217 928 180; www.rodoviariadelisboa.pt) outside Campo Grande metro station.

CAR & MOTORCYCLE

Motorbikes, ranging from 50cc to 700cc, are available for hire from **LX Rent a Scooter** (917 249 806; www.lxrentascooter.pt; Campo das Cebolas 21; 9.30am-6.30pm). Prices start at €32 for 24 hours. **Free Spirit Campers** (964 492 955; www.freespiritcampers.com; Rua Rodrigues de Faria 103, LX Factory; per day €80-120; 10am-5pm Mon-Fri) inside LX Factory rents fully equipped converted Fiat Ducato campervans.

The big-name car-hire companies are all on hand, though you can often save by using local agencies; most offer pick-up and delivery service to the Palácio Foz tourist office on Praça dos Restauradores. The tourist offices have loads of car-rental fliers where you can compare prices. Staff will even call and book a vehicle for you.

Autojardim (218 463 187; www.auto-jardim.com; Aeroporto de Lisboa)
Avis (800 201 002; www.avis.com.pt)
Europcar (219 407 790; www.europcar.pt)
Hertz (808 202 038; www.hertz.com)
Holidays Car (217 150 610; www.holidayscar.com; Urbanização de São Marcos 61)

TRAIN

Lisbon is linked by train to other major cities. Check the **Comboios de Portugal** (☎707 210 220; www.cp.pt) website for schedules. Express services include:

Évora €12, 1½ hours, three to four daily

Coimbra €20, two hours, 10 to 20 daily

Faro €21, three hours, three to six daily

Porto €24, three hours, seven to 18 daily

Lisbon has several major train stations.

Do not forget to validate your ticket/transport card (at some train stations, it's possible to hop on the train without doing so) – the fine is 100 times the price of your journey if caught (and checks are frequent!).

ℹ Getting Around

TO/FROM THE AIRPORT

Metro

The Aeroporto metro station allows convenient access to downtown. Change at Alameda (green line) to reach Rossio and Baixa.

Bus

The **AeroBus** (www.aerobus.pt; 1-way adult/child €3.50/2) departs from outside arrivals (adult/child €3.50/2, 25 to 35 minutes, roughly every 20 minutes from 7am to 11pm). It goes via Marquês de Pombal, Avenida Liberdade, Restauradores, Rossio and Praça do Comércio to Cais do Sodré. The ticket gives free passage on the entire city bus network for the rest of the day. You'll save 10% by purchasing your tickets online in advance.

Taxi

Expect to pay about €15 for the 15-minute taxi ride into central Lisbon, plus €1.60 if your luggage needs to be placed in the boot. Avoid long queues by flagging down a taxi outside the departures hall. Make sure the cabbie switches on the taxi meter, and that you pay the listed fare.

CAR & MOTORCYCLE

Lisbon can be quite stressful to drive around, thanks to heavy traffic, maverick drivers and narrow one-way streets and tram lines. There are two ring roads useful for staying out of the centre: the inner Cintura Regional Interna de Lisboa (CRIL) and the outer Cintura Regional Externa de Lisboa (CREL).

Once in the centre, parking is the main issue. Spaces are scarce, parking regulations are complex, pay-and-display machines are often broken and car-park rates can be expensive (up to €25 per day). On Saturday afternoon and Sunday parking is usually free.

There are a few good places for free parking. Campo de Santa Clara, near the Alfama, is good every day except Saturday and Tuesday, when the Feira da Ladra (p118) takes over the lot. You can also find free parking on Avenida 24 de Julho west of Cais do Sodré. Always lock up and don't leave any valuables inside, as theft is a risk.

PUBLIC TRANSPORT

Bus, Tram & Funicular

Companhia Carris de Ferro de Lisboa (Carris; ☎213 500 115; www.carris.transporteslisboa.pt) operates all transport in Lisbon proper except the metro. Its buses and trams run from about 5am or 6am to about 10pm or 11pm; there are some night bus and tram services.

Pick up a transport map, *Rede de Transportes de Lisboa*, from tourist offices. The Carris website has timetables and route details.

Don't leave the city without riding popular **tram 28** (Largo Martim Moniz) from Largo Martim Moniz or **tram 12** from Praça da Figueira through the narrow streets of the Alfama. Go early in the morning or at night to avoid the tourist mobs.

BIKING THE TEJO

With its steep, winding hills and narrow, traffic-filled lanes, Lisbon may not seem like the ideal place to hop on a bicycle, though the city added a biking/jogging path in 2010 to the delight of pedallers. Coursing along the Tejo for nearly 7km, the path connects Cais do Sodré with Belém, and has artful touches – including the poetry of Pessoa printed along parts of it. It passes beside a rapidly changing landscape – taking in ageing warehouses that are being converted into open-air cafes, restaurants and nightspots. In 2013, an additional path opened connecting Santa Apolónia with Parque das Nações, an additional 8km jaunt.

A handy place to rent bikes a short stroll from Cais do Sodré is **Bike Iberia** (Map p68; ☎969 630 369; www.bikeiberia.com; Largo Corpo Santo 5; bike hire per hr/day from €5/14; ⊙9.30am-7pm). True enthusiasts will also want to pick up their indispensable and extremely well-done *Lisbon Bike Map* (€5), which not only details all the bike trails in the Lisbon region, but notes terrain, inclines, points of interest and traffic etiquette.

Those looking for a longer ride can bike out to Belém, catch the ferry to Trafaria, and then continue on another bike path (separate from traffic) that runs for about 6km down to the pretty beach of Costa da Caparica.

TICKETS & TRANSPORT CARDS

You'll pay more for transport if you buy your ticket on board rather than purchasing a prepaid card. On-board one-way prices are €1.80 for buses, €2.85 for trams and €3.60 (return) for funicular rides (one-way tickets not available). Santa Justa, however, costs €5 return.

Viva Viagem card €0.50 from metro-station kiosks (add credit in €5 denominations). Each ride will then deduct €1.40 per trip from the card for buses and metro and €1.80 for suburban Comboios de Portugal trains.

Zapping Allows for pay-as-you-go fares of €1.25 on buses and metro; add credit between €5 and €40 denominations.

Day passes €6 and allows unlimited travel over a 24-hour period on the entire transport network. If you will take more than five trips on the bus or metro on any given day, this is the best and easiest choice.

Lisboa Card Good for most tourist sights as well as bus, tram, funicular and metro travel.

Bilhete Train & Bus Hop-on, hop-off, one-day travel card valid on Comboios de Portugal trains and Scotturb suburban buses between Lisbon, Cascais and Sintra for €15.

Two other useful lines are **tram 15**, which runs from Praça da Figueira and Praça do Comércio via Alcântara to Belém, and **tram 18** from Praça do Comércio via Alcântara to Ajuda. Tram 15 features space-age trams with on-board machines for buying tickets and passes. Tram stops are marked by a small yellow *paragem* (stop) sign hanging from a lamp post or from the overhead wires.

Metro

The **metro** (www.metro.transporteslisboa.pt; single/day ticket €1.40/6; ⏲6.30am-1am) is useful for short hops, and to reach the Gare do Oriente and nearby Parque das Nações.

Buy tickets from metro ticket machines, which have English menus. The Lisboa Card is also valid.

Entrances are marked by a big red 'M'. Useful signs include *correspondência* (transfer between lines) and *saída* (exit to the street). There is some impressive contemporary art on the metro, including Angelo de Sousa at Baixa-Chiado and Friedensreich Hundertwasser at Oriente.

Watch out for pickpockets in rush-hour crowds.

TAXI

Táxis in Lisbon are reasonably priced and plentiful. If you can't hail one, try the ranks at Rossio and Praça dos Restauradores, near stations and ferry terminals, and at top-end hotels, or call **Rádio Táxis** (☎218 119 000; http://taxislisboa.pt) or **Autocoope** (☎217 932 756; www.autocoope.pai.pt).

The fare on the meter should read €3.25 (daytime flagfall). You will be charged extra for luggage and an additional 20% for journeys between 9pm and 6am, plus more if they cross municipalities or if you call. Rip-offs occasionally occur (the airport route is the main culprit). If you think you may have been cheated, get a receipt from the driver, note the registration number and talk to the tourist police.

Taxi apps have been slow to catch on in Lisbon, but **99Taxis** (www.99taxis.com), **MyTaxi** (www.pt.mytaxi.com) and **Uber** (www.uber.com) are available.

AROUND LISBON

Sintra

POP 26,000

With its rippling mountains, dewy forests thick with ferns and lichen, exotic gardens and glittering palaces, Sintra is like a page torn from a fairy tale. Its Unesco World Heritage–listed centre, Sintra-Vila, is dotted with pastel-hued manors folded into luxuriant hills that roll down to the blue Atlantic.

Celts worshipped their moon god here, the Moors built a precipitous castle, and 18th-century Portuguese royals swanned around its dreamy gardens. Even Lord Byron waxed lyrical about Sintra's charms: 'Lo! Cintra's glorious Eden intervenes, in variegated maze of mount and glen', which inspired his epic poem *Childe Harold's Pilgrimage*.

It's the must-do day trip and, if time's not an issue, has more than enough allure to seize you for days.

Sintra has become quite popular, and it's hard to escape the tourist masses (especially in summer). Go early in the day midweek to escape the worst of the crowds.

Sights

★ **Palácio Nacional de Sintra** PALACE
(Map p128; www.parquesdesintra.pt; Largo Rainha Dona Amélia; adult/child €10/8.50; ⏲9.30am-7pm, shorter hours in low season) The star of

Around Lisbon

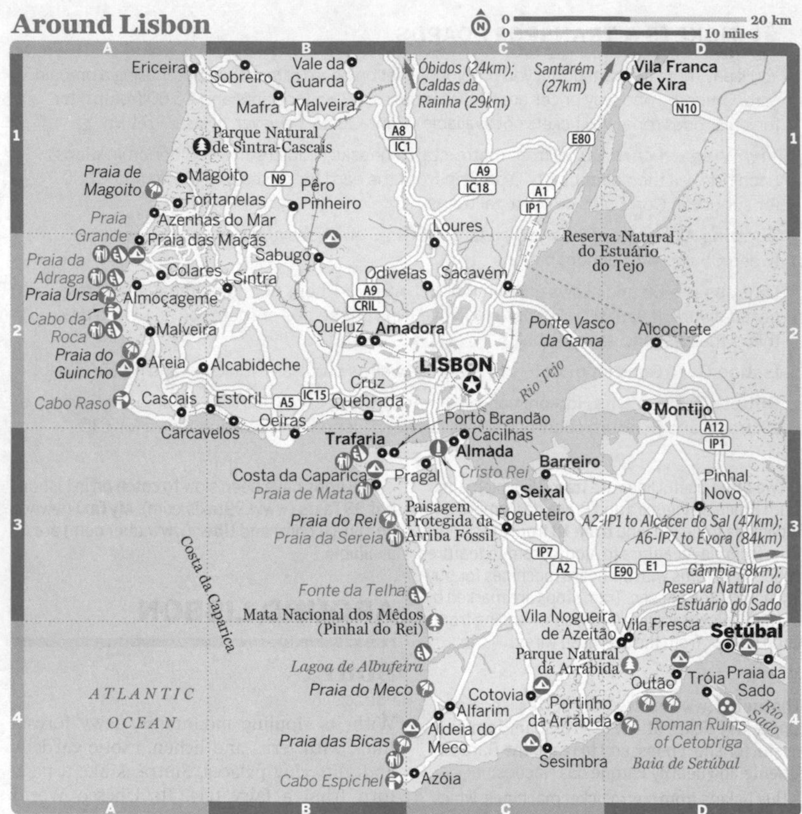

Sintra-Vila is this palace, with its iconic twin conical chimneys and lavish interior. The whimsical interior is a mix of Moorish and Manueline styles, with arabesque courtyards, barley-twist columns and 15th- and 16th-century geometric *azulejos* that figure among Portugal's oldest.

Of Moorish origins, the palace was first expanded by Dom Dinis (1261–1325), enlarged by João I in the 15th century (when the kitchens were built), then given a Manueline twist by Manuel I in the next century.

Highlights include the octagonal **Sala dos Cisnes** (Swan Room), adorned with frescoes of 27 gold-collared swans; and the **Sala das Pegas** (Magpie Room), with its ceiling emblazoned with magpies. Lore has it that the queen caught João I kissing one of her ladies-in-waiting. The cheeky king claimed the kisses were innocent and all '*por bem*' ('for the good'), then commissioned one magpie for every lady-in-waiting.

Other standouts are the wooden **Sala dos Brasões**, bearing the shields of 72 leading 16th-century families, the shipshape **Galleon Room** and the Palatine **chapel** featuring an Islamic mosaic floor. Finally, you reach the restored **kitchen** of twin-chimney fame, where you can almost hear the crackle of a hog roasting on a spit for the king.

★Castelo dos Mouros CASTLE

(Map p126; www.parquesdesintra.pt; adult/child €8/6.50; ⏲10am-6pm) Soaring 412m above sea level, this mist-enshrouded ruined castle looms high above the surrounding forest. When the clouds peel away, the vistas over Sintra's palace-dotted hill and dale, across to the glittering Atlantic are – like the climb – breathtaking.

The 10th-century Moorish castle's dizzying ramparts stretch across the mountain ridges and past moss-clad boulders the size of small buses.

The best walking route here from Sintra-Vila is not along the main road but the quicker, partly off-road route via Rua Marechal Saldanha. The steep **trail** is around 2km, but quiet and rewarding.

Tickets and info are available at the **entrance** (Map p126; ⌚10am-6pm).

★ Palácio Nacional da Pena PALACE

(Map p126; www.parquesdesintra.pt; combined ticket with Parque Nacional da Pena adult/child €14/12.50; ⌚10am-6pm) Rising from a wooded peak and often enshrouded in mist, Palácio Nacional da Pena is a wacky confection of onion domes, Moorish keyhole gates, stone snakes and crenellated towers in pinks and lemons. It is considered the greatest expression of 19th-century romanticism in Portugal.

Ferdinand of Saxe Coburg-Gotha, the artist-husband of Queen Maria II, and later Dom Ferdinand II, commissioned Prussian architect Ludwig von Eschwege in 1840 to build the Mouresque-Manueline epic (and as a final flourish added an armoured statue representing a medieval knight overlooking the palace from a nearby peak). Inspired by Stolzenfels and Rheinstein castles and Potsdam's Babelsberg Palace, a flourish of imagination and colour commenced.

The eclectic, extravagant interior is equally unusual, brimming with precious Meissen porcelain, Portuguese-style furniture, trompe l'oeil murals and Dom Carlos' unfinished nudes of buxom nymphs.

There are daily guided tours at 2.30pm. Buses depart from the entrance to the palace every 15 minutes (€3); otherwise it's a 10- to 15-minute walk uphill.

Parque da Pena GARDENS

(Map p126; ☎219 237 300; www.parquesdesintra.pt; adult/child €7.50/6.50, combined ticket with Palácio Nacional da Pena €14/12.50; ⌚10am-6pm) Nearly topped by King Ferdinand II's whimsical Palácio Nacional da Pena (only Cruz Alta, at 529m, is higher), these romantic gardens are filled with tropical plants, huge redwoods and fern trees, camellias, rhododendrons and lakes (note the castle-shaped duck houses for web-footed royalty!). Save by buying a combined ticket if you want to visit Palácio Nacional da Pena too.

While the crowds descend on the palace, another less-visited but fascinating site within the park is the *Snow White & the Seven Dwarfs*-evoking **Chalet da Condessa d'Edla** (adult/child €9.50/8.50), an Alpine-inspired summer getaway cottage commissioned by King Ferdinand II and his future second wife, Elise Hensler (the Countess of Edla).

Buses to the **park entrance** (www.parquesdesintra.pt) leave from Sintra train station and near Palácio Nacional de Sintra, among other spots around town. A taxi costs around €10 one-way. The steep, zigzagging walk through pine and eucalyptus woods from Sintra-Vila is around 3km to 4km.

Palácio & Parque de Monserrate PALACE

(www.parquesdesintra.pt; adult/child €8/6.50; ⌚10am-6pm) At the centre of a 30-hectare park, a manicured lawn sweeps up to this whimsical, Moorish-Gothic-Indian *palácio*, the 19th-century romantic folly of English millionaire Sir Francis Cook. The wild and rambling gardens were created in the 18th century by wealthy English merchant Gerard de Visme, then enlarged by landscape painter William Stockdale (with help from London's Kew Gardens).

Its wooded hillsides bristle with exotic foliage, from Chinese weeping cypress to dragon trees and Himalayan rhododendrons. Seek out the Mexican garden nurturing palms, yuccas and agaves, and the bamboo-fringed Japanese garden abloom with camellias.

The park is 3.5km west of Sintra-Vila.

Convento dos Capuchos MONASTERY

(Capuchin Monastery; ☎219 237 300; www.parquesdesintra.pt; adult/child €7/5.50; ⌚10am-8pm) Hidden in the woods is this bewitchingly hobbit-hole-like convent, which was originally built in 1560 to house friars who lived in incredibly cramped conditions, their tiny cells having low, narrow doors. Byron mocked the monastery in his poem *Childe Harold's Pilgrimage*, referring to recluse Honorius who spent a staggering 36 years here (before dying at age 95 in 1596).

It's often nicknamed the Cork Convent, because its cells are lined with cork. Visiting here is an *Alice in Wonderland* experience as you squeeze through to explore the warren of cells, chapels, kitchen and cavern. The monks lived a simple, touchingly well-ordered life in this idyllic yet spartan place, hiding up until 1834 when it was abandoned after all religious orders were abolished.

You can walk here – the monastery is 7.3km from Sintra-Vila (5.1km from the turn-off to Parque da Pena) along a remote, wooded road. There is no bus connection to the convent (taxis charge around €35 return; arrange for a pick-up ahead). Well-worth-it audioguides are available for €3.

Sintra

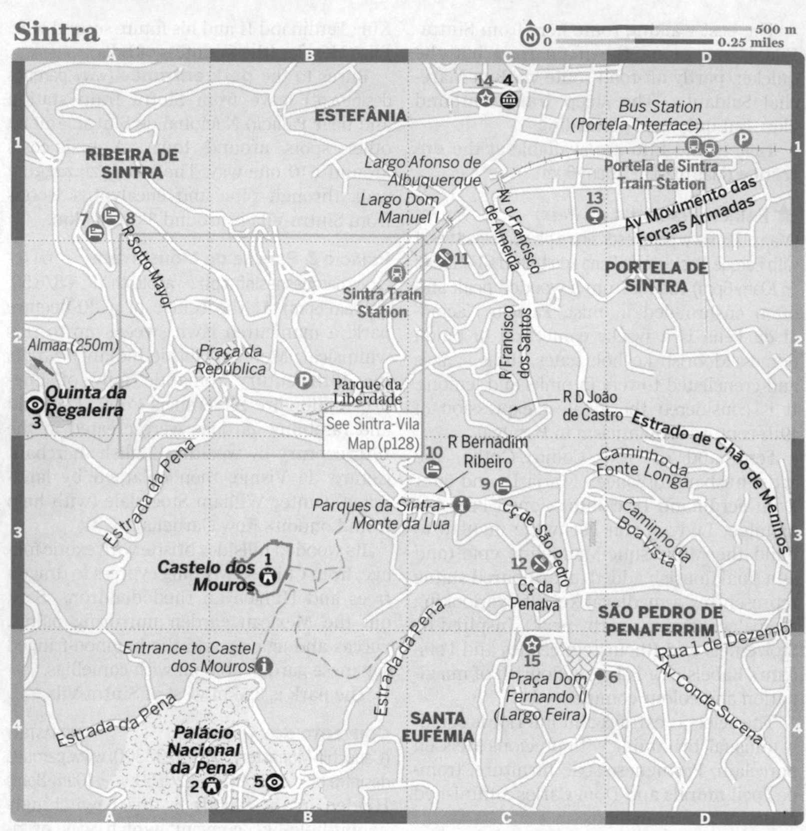

Sintra

Top Sights
1 Castelo dos Mouros B3
2 Palácio Nacional da Pena B4
3 Quinta da Regaleira A2

Sights
4 Museu das Artes de Sintra C1
5 Parque da Pena B4

Activities, Courses & Tours
6 MuitAvenutra C4

Sleeping
7 Casa do Valle A1
8 Casa Miradouro A1
9 Hotel Sintra Jardim C3
10 Quinta das Murtas C3

Eating
11 Dom Pipas C2
12 Nau Palatina C3

Drinking & Nightlife
13 Saloon Cintra C1

Entertainment
14 Centro Cultural Olga Cadaval C1
15 Taverna dos Trovadores C4

Museu das Artes de Sintra MUSEUM
(MU.SA; Map p126; www.cm-sintra.pt; Av Heliodoro Salgado; adult/child €1/free; ⏲10am-8pm Tue-Fri, 2-8pm Sat-Sun) This new museum took over the former Museu de Arte Moderna space in 2014 and features a small and manageable collection of contemporary and modern art, 80% or so of which is dedicated to local works. The permanent collection features some of Portugal's best-known artists, most notably painters Columbano Bordalo Pinheiro and António Carneiro and sculptor Dorita de Castel-Branco.

Museu Anjos Teixeira MUSEUM
(Map p128; Alameda Volta do Duche; ⏲10am-6pm Tue-Fri, noon-6pm Sat & Sun) FREE Set in a former watermill, this small museum displays works by the father-and-son duo of Anjos Teixeira – two of Portugal's greatest sculptors. Most of the pieces here are the work of Pedro Augusto (1908–97), the son, who enjoyed greater success than his father, and was connected to the neorealism of the 1940s.

Activities

Sintra is a terrific place to get out and stride, with waymarked **hiking trails** (look for red and yellow stripes) that corkscrew up into densely wooded hills strewn with giant boulders. Justifiably popular is the gentle 50-minute trek from Sintra-Vila to Castelo dos Mouros. You can continue to Palácio Nacional da Pena (another 15 minutes). From here you can ascend Serra de Sintra's highest point, the 529m Cruz Alta (High Cross), named after its 16th-century cross, with amazing views all over Sintra. It's possible to continue on foot to São Pedro de Penaferrim and loop back to Sintra-Vila. You can print off maps and info on various hiking trails from the municipality's website under 'Percursos Pedestres' (www.cm-sintra.pt).

Horse riding is available in the Parque da Pena, from 30-minute teasers (€10) to six-hour excursions (€100).

Go2Sintra Tours CYCLING
(Map p128; ☎917 855 428; www.go2cintra.com; Av Dr Miguel Bombarda 37; ⏲10.30am-7pm) Offers highly recommended electric-bike tours (from €35) as well as eBike rental (take our word for it – you'll want the motorised option in Sintra!). A full day's rental with support starts at €30. Its office is across from the Sintra train station inside the SintraCan shop.

MuitAvenutra ADVENTURE
(Map p126; ☎967 021 248; www.muitaventura.com; Rua Marquês Viana 31) This adventure outfitter has a regular schedule of organised activities, including mountain biking, rappelling, jeep tours, trekking and nighttime hikes. It's based in São Pedro.

Festivals & Events

Festival de Sintra CULTURAL
(www.festivaldesintra.pt; ⏲May or Jun) Usually in May or June, the three-week-long Festival de Sintra features classical recitals, ballet and modern dance, world music and multimedia events, plus concerts for kids.

Sleeping

It's worth staying overnight, as Sintra has some magical guesthouses, from quaint villas to lavish manors. Book ahead in summer.

★**Moon Hill Hostel** HOSTEL €
(Map p128; ☎219 243 755; www.moonhillhostel.com; Rua Guilherme Gomes Fernandes 19; dm €19, d with/without bathroom €89/59; ❄@🛜) This design-forward, minimalist newcomer easily outshines the Sintra competition. Whether you book a boutique-hotel-level private room, with colourful reclaimed-wood headboards and wall-covering photos of enchanting Sintra forest scenes (go for 10 or 14 for Pena National Palace views, 12 or 13 for Moorish castle views) or a four-bed mixed dorm (lockers), you are sleeping in high style.

Nice Way Sintra Palace HOSTEL €
(Map p128; ☎219 249 800; www.nicewaysintra.com; Rua Sotto Mayor 22; dm €19-21, d with/without bathroom €70/60; P@🛜) In a rambling but recently refreshed mansion north of the main square, you'll find stylishly outfitted rooms with newly installed heaters, great countryside views and a lovely garden. There's an intriguing, old-fashioned shared kitchen and a friendly vibe, making it a good place to meet other travellers.

Almaa HOSTEL €
(☎219 240 008; www.almaasintrahostel.com; Caminho dos Frades; dm €18, r with/without bathroom €58/52; @🛜) Sustainably minded Almaa is an idyllic spot to recharge, with a quirky design scheme (featuring recycled furniture) and an attractive setting. The surrounding 3.5 hectares of lush grounds has walking paths and an old spring-fed reservoir for swimming. It's not without imperfections (a little mould-proof paint would work wonders) but as the name suggests, it has soul. It's a 10-minute walk from the village centre.

★**Sintra 1012** B&B €€
(Map p128; ☎918 632 997; www.sintra1012.com; Rua Gil Vicente 10; d €60-120; ❄@🛜) You'll probably need to go to war to book one of the four spacious and smart rooms in this highly recommended guesthouse run by a young Portuguese-American couple. Behind original medieval walls, it's a modern minimalist retreat which, in Roman times, was Sintra's first theatre. Today, it's all comfort and class right down to the basement studio, an astonishing deal (€60).

Sintra-Vila

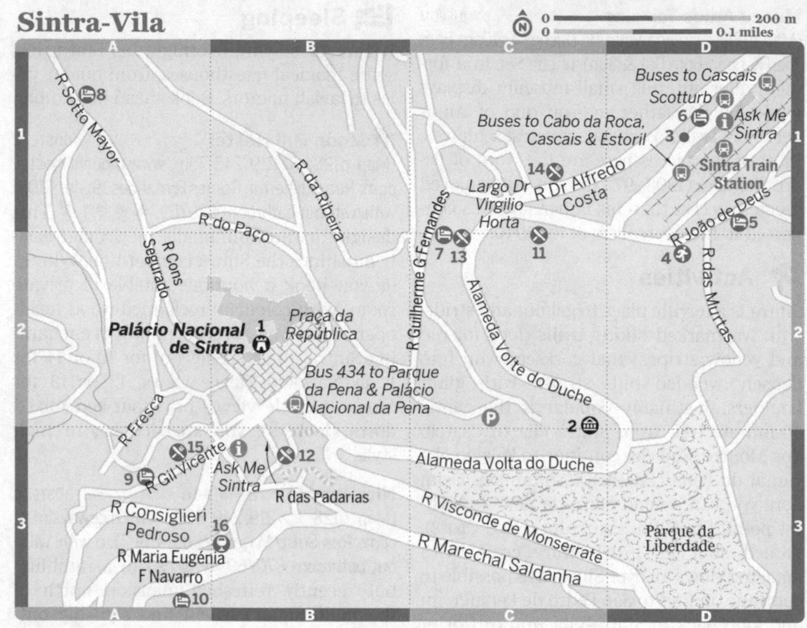

Villa Mira Longa B&B €€
(Map p128; ☎219 244 502; www.villamiralonga.com; Estrada da Pena 4; d €110-135; P@☎) A fabulous and gay-friendly choice, this restored 1898 baby-blue villa is a short walk from the centre and offers comfortable rooms (the best with panoramic views) and beautiful common areas (including an antique-filled dining room and an exquisitely manicured garden). The kind Belgian-Brazilian hosts have a wealth of knowledge about Sintra and spread a first-rate breakfast.

Casa Miradouro GUESTHOUSE €€
(Map p126; ☎914 232 203; www.casa-miradouro.com; Rua Sotto Mayor 55; d €110-140, without breakfast €90-120; ☎) Lovely Belgian Charlotte is your consummate host at this imposing Battenberg cake of a house, built in 1893, with eight elegant, stuccoed rooms stocked with bathrobes, Egyptian-cotton sheets and panoramic views. The best have small balconies.

Casa do Valle B&B €€
(Map p126; ☎219 244 699; www.casadovalle.com; Rua da Paderna 5; d €90-120; P@☎≋) Just downhill from the historical centre, Casa

do Valle has spacious rooms set around a garden with an inviting pool. Some rooms lack an en suite. It has fine views of the lush hillsides rising above the valley, friendly multilingual service courtesy of the Finnish owner and two monstrous Great Danes.

Hotel Sintra Jardim GUESTHOUSE €€

(Map p126; 219 230 738; www.hotelsintrajardim.pt; Largo Sousa Brandão 1; s & d €75-80;) This stately 1880s manor overlooks rambling gardens and offers partial castle views from some of its 16 rooms (they are bright, high-ceilinged affairs but slightly underwhelming – the real coups here are the gardens and spectacular pool). Wake up to birdsong and a hearty breakfast.

Quinta das Murtas GUESTHOUSE €€

(Map p126; 219 240 246; www.quintadasmurtas.com; Rua Eduardo Van Zeller 4; s/d/apt from €70/75/120;) A grand manor surrounded by lush greenery, this retreat charms with sweeping views, a trickling fountain and a grand lounge room with carved columns, traditional, tiled-flooring and original Italian frescoes. The rooms are light and spacious and there are seven roomier apartments with kitchenettes spread about the property.

Monte da Lua GUESTHOUSE €€

(Map p128; 210 121 659; www.montedalua.org; Av Dr Miguel Bombarda 51; s/d without breakfast from €55/65;) Opposite the train station, this warm and welcoming marshmallow-pink villa offers clean and simple wood-floored rooms; the best overlook the wooded valley at the back. Friendly new owners hope to eventually add espresso machines and dorm beds.

Casa de Hóspedes Dona Maria da Parreirinha GUESTHOUSE €€

(Map p128; 219 232 490; www.dmariaparreirinha.com; Rua João de Deus 12-14; s/d/tr €55/65/75;) A short walk from the train station, this 15-room, family-run affair has old-fashioned rooms with big windows, dark-wood furnishings and floral fabrics. Friendly and enthusiastic Tanya is the family face these days, ensuring guests feel welcome in her grandfather's home.

Eating

Café Saudade CAFE €

(Map p128; www.saudade.pt; Av Dr Miguel Bombardo 6; mains €5.50-8; 8.30am-8pm;) This former bakery, where Sintra's famous *queijadas* (crisp pastry shells filled with a marzipan-like mix of fresh cheese, sugar, flour and cinnamon) were made, has cherub-covered ceilings and a rambling interior. It's a fine spot for pastries (the massive scones are a travel highlight in the making) or lighter fare (with a changing soup, salad, fish and meat dish of the day) or an evening glass of wine.

Fábrica das Verdadeiras Queijadas da Sapa PATISSERIE €

(Map p128; www.facebook.com/queijadasdasapa; Alameda Volta do Duche 12; pastries from €0.85; 9am-6pm Tue-Fri, 9.30am-6.30pm Sat & Sun) This place has been rotting the teeth of royalty since 1756 with bite-sized *queijadas*.

Casa Piriquita PATISSERIE €

(Map p128; www.facebook.com/pastelaria.piriquita; Rua das Padarias 1-5; travesseiros €1.30; 9am-9pm Thu-Tue) This busy cafe is a popular destination for inexpensive bites as well as Sintra's famous *queijadas* and *travesseiros* (almond pastries). If you're here on a Wednesday, Piriquita II just up the street at Rua das Padarias 18 is open.

Nau Palatina PORTUGUESE €€

(Map p126; 219 240 962; www.facebook.com/barnaupalatina; Calçada São Pedro 18; tapas €5.50-9.90; 6pm-midnight Wed-Sat, 3-9pm Sun;) Sintra's friendliest and most-welcoming restaurant is a travel-highlight-reel star-in-the-making. Congenial owner Zé's creative tapas are as slightly off-centre as his location, a well-worth-it 1km walk from the centre. Spice Route undertones are weaved throughout the small but tasty menu of small (€1.50) and medium (from €5.50) tidbits strongly forged from local and regional ingredients.

LOCAL KNOWLEDGE

SWEET DREAMS

Sintra is famous for its luscious sweeties. **Fábrica das Verdadeiras Queijadas da Sapa** has been fattening up royalty since 1756 with *queijadas* – crisp pastry shells filled with a marzipan-like mix of fresh cheese, sugar, flour and cinnamon. Since 1952, **Casa Piriquita** has been tempting locals with another sweet dream: the *travesseiro* (pillow), light puff pastry turned, rolled and folded seven times, then filled with delicious almond-and-egg-yolk cream and lightly dusted with sugar.

INcomum PORTUGUESE €€
(Map p128; ☎219 243 719; www.incomumbyluis-santos.pt; Rua Dr Alfredo Costa 22; mains €14.50-15.50; ⏲noon-midnight; 📶) Chef Luis Santos is shaking up the scene in Sintra with his modern upgrades to Portuguese cuisine, served amid the muted greys and greens of his synchronic dining room. INcomum quickly established itself as the anti-traditional choice among serious foodies, first by dangling an unbeatable €9.50, three-course lunch carrot, then by letting the food seal the deal.

Tulhas PORTUGUESE €€
(Map p128; Rua Gil Vicente 4; mains €10-18; ⏲noon-11pm, to 10pm winter; 📶) This converted grain warehouse is dark, tiled and quaint, with wrought-iron chandeliers and a relaxed, cosy atmosphere. It's rightfully renowned for its *bacalhau com natas* (creamy bechamal with shredded cod, served au gratin) but the tasty *arroz de pato* (duck rice) is worth your consideration as well.

Dom Pipas PORTUGUESE €€
(Map p126; www.restaurantedompipas.com.pt; Rua João de Deus 62; mains €8.50-15.50; ⏲noon-3pm & 7-11pm Tue-Sun; 📶) A local favourite, Dom Pipas serves excellent Portuguese dishes, amid *azulejos* and rustic country decor. It's behind the train station (left out of the station, first left, then left again to the end).

Drinking & Nightlife

Saloon Cintra BAR
(Map p126; www.facebook.com/barsaloon.cintra; Av do Movimento das Forças Armadas 5, Portela da Sintra; ⏲8pm-2am Mon-Fri, from 3pm Sat-Sun; 📶) Sintra's best bar isn't in the Vila, but that shouldn't stop seasoned drinkers from checking it out. A potpourri of antiques and Portuguese bric-a-bric hovering over mismatched vintage sofas makes for an atmospheric spot to take in the Belgian-heavy beer list (including Mc Chouffe on tap), good cocktails and a cool local crowd.

Fonte da Pipa BAR
(Map p128; www.facebook.com/barfontedapipa; Rua Fonte da Pipa 11-13; ⏲9pm-3am) A tiled bar, this has craggy, cave-like rooms and comfy seats. A Sintra mainstay.

☆ Entertainment

Taverna dos Trovadores LIVE MUSIC
(Map p126; ☎219 233 548; www.tavernadostrovadores.pt; Praça Dom Fernando II 18; ⏲noon-4pm & 7pm-2am Mon-Sat, to 4pm Sun) This atmospheric restaurant and bar features live music (folk and acoustic) on Friday and Saturday nights – an institution that's been around for more than two decades. Concerts run from 11.30pm to 2am. Nearby, their new Sabores de Sintra offers dinner andfado. It's located in São Pedro de Penaferrim.

Centro Cultural Olga Cadaval CULTURAL CENTRE
(Map p126; ☎219 107 110; www.ccolgacadaval.pt; Praça Francisco Sá Carneiro) Sintra's major cultural venue stages concerts and theatre.

ℹ Information

There's an ATM at the train station and in the tourism office as well as others aroud town. Sintra offers free wi-fi access points around town. Look for the green ConnectedCity Sintra signs.

Ask Me Sintra (Turismo; Map p128; ☎219 231 157; www.askmelisboa.com/sintra; Praça da República 23; ⏲9.30am-6pm), near the centre of Sintra-Vila, is a helpful multilingual office

DON'T MISS

A SURREAL MANSION & GARDENS

Exploring the **Quinta da Regaleira** (Map p126; www.regaleira.pt; Rua Barbosa du Bocage; adult/child €6/3; ⏲10am-8pm high season, shorter hours in low season) is like delving into another world. This neo-Manueline extravaganza was dreamed up by Italian opera-set designer Luigi Manini under the orders of Brazilian coffee tycoon, António Carvalho Monteiro, aka 'Monteiro dos Milhões' ('Moneybags Monteiro'). Enter the villa to begin the surreal journey, with ferociously carved fireplaces, frescoes and Venetian-glass mosaics. Keep an eye out for mythological and Knights Templar symbols.

The playful gardens are fun to explore – footpaths wriggle through the dense foliage to follies, fountains, grottoes, lakes and underground caverns. All routes seem to eventually end at the revolving stone door leading to the initiation well, **Poço Iniciático**, plunging some 27m. You walk down the nine-tiered spiral (three by three – three being the magic number) to mysterious hollowed-out underground galleries, lit by fairy lights.

with expert insight into Sintra and the surrounding areas. There's also a small **train station branch** (Map p128; ☎211 932 545; www.askmelisboa.com/sintra; Sintra train station; ⊙10am-noon & 2.30-6pm), often overrun by those arriving by rail. **Parques da Sintra – Monte da Lua** (Map p126; ☎219 237 300; www.parquesdesintra.pt; Largo Sousa Brandão; ⊙9.30am-6pm, shorter hours in winter), which manages the majority of top Sintra sites, also has a friendly information centre.

Cintramédica (☎219 100 080; www.cintramedica.pt; Travessa da Portela, Edifício Cintramédica, Portela da Sintra; ⊙7am-9pm Mon-Fri, to 1pm Sat) Private medical clinic in Sintra. Consultations without insurance run €80.

Police Station (Guarda Nacional Republicana; ☎213 252 620; www.gnr.pt; Rua João de Deus 6)

Getting There & Away

Scotturb (Map p128; ☎219 230 381; www.scotturb.com; Av Dr Miguel Bombarda 59; ⊙9am-6pm) buses 403 and 417 leave regularly for Cascais (€4.10, one hour), the latter via Cabo da Roca (€4.10). Bus 418 heads to Estoril (€3.50, 40 minutes). Most services leave from **Sintra train station** (which is *estação* on timetables) and travel via Portela de Sintra. Scotturb's useful information office, open 9am to 1pm and 2pm to 8pm, is opposite the station.

Mafrense (☎261 816 152; www.mafrense.pt) buses head to Mafra (€3.40, 45 minutes) and Ericeira (€3.40, 45 minutes) from the **Portela Interface** (Map p126; Largo Vasco da Gama) on the north side of Portela da Sintra station.

Comboios de Portugal (p122) trains (€2.15, 40 minutes) run every 15 minutes between Sintra and Lisbon's Rossio station.

If arriving by train, go to the last stop – Sintra – from where it's a pleasant 1km walk (or short bus ride) into the village.

Buses to Cabo da Roca, Cascais & Estoril (Map p128; Av Dr Miguel Bombarda)

Buses to Cascais (Map p128; Av Dr Miguel Bombarda)

Getting Around

BUS

From the train station it's a 1km scenic walk into Sintra-Vila, or you can hop on **bus 435**, which goes from the station to Sintra-Vila (€1). This bus continues on to Quinta da Regaleira and Palácio de Monserrate.

A handy bus for accessing the Castelo dos Mouros is **Scotturb bus 434** (Map p128; Praça da República) (€5), which runs from the train station via Sintra-Vila to the castle (10 minutes), Palácio Nacional da Pena (15 minutes) and back. One ticket gives you hop-on, hop-off access (in one direction; no backtracking).

SPEEDY TRANSPORT

If you have limited time and you'd like to see some of the attractions beyond Sintra-Vila, **Sight Sintra** (Map p128; ☎219 242 856; www.sightsintra.pt; Rua João de Deus; tour €35-45; ⊙10am-7pm) rents out tiny two-person buggies that guide you by GPS along one of three different routes. The most popular takes you to Castelo dos Mouros and Palácio da Pena among other sites. It's located around the corner from the train station. You can also create your own itinerary, and hire a buggy for €25 per hour.

You can also purchase a daily €12 **hop-on, hop-off Scotturb ticket** that works across the entire network and is valid in any direction until midnight. Be prepared to wait – even in winter the bus lines outside major attractions can be long.

CAR

Driving can be a challenge on the narrow roads around Sintra. Parking is limited around town and there are very few spaces at Palácio Nacional da Pena, so it's better to avoid driving there in busy times. For parking near town, there's a free car park below Sintra-Vila; follow the signs by the *câmara municipal* (town hall) in Estefânia. Alternatively, park at Portela Interface and take the bus.

TAXI

Taxis are available at the train station or opposite Sintra-Vila post office. They are metered, so fares depend on traffic. Count on about €10 one-way to Palácio Nacional da Pena; if you want them to wait, the meter runs at €15 per hour; expect to pay about €25 to €30 for a return visit to Convento dos Capuchos.

TRAM

On weekends, Sintra's restored electric tram, the **Elétrico de Sintra** (www.cm-sintra.pt; one-way €3; ⊙Fri-Sun 8 May-21 Jun) offers access to the coast, running from Rua Alves Roçadas near Portela de Sintra train station, arriving at Praia das Maçãs 45 minutes later. Trams depart hourly from 10.20am to 5pm from Friday to Sunday (11.55am to 6.45pm Saturday and Sunday). The last tram back leaves the beach at 5.45pm during the week and 6pm on weekends.

West of Sintra

Precipitous cliffs and crescent-shaped bays pummelled by the Atlantic lie just 12km west of Sintra. Previous host of the European Surfing Championships, **Praia Grande** lures surfers and bodyboarders to its big sandy beach with ripping breakers, and you can clamber over the cliffs to spot dinosaur fossils. Family-friendly **Praia das Maçãs** has a sweep of gold sand, backed by a lively little resort. **Azenhas do Mar**, 2km further, is a cliffhanger of a village, where a jumble of whitewashed, red-roofed houses tumble down the crags to a free saltwater pool (only accessible when the sea is calm).

En route to the beaches, quaint **Colares** makes a worthwhile pit stop with its panoramas, stuck-in-time village charm and wines dating to the 13th century. The vines grown today are the only ones in Europe to have survived the 19th-century phylloxera plague, saved by their deep roots and sandy soil. To taste or purchase some of the venerable wines, visit **Adega Regional de Colares** (☎219 291 210; www.arcolares.com; Alameda Coronel, Linhares de Lima 32; tastings €3.70-9.85, tours €12.30; ⏲9am-1pm & 2-6pm Mon-Fri, 9am-1pm Sat), which also offers tours with the winemaker if arranged in advance.

Wild and wonderful **Cabo da Roca** (Rock Cape) is a sheer 150m cliff, facing the roaring sea, 18km west of Sintra. It's Europe's westernmost point and a terrific sunset spot. Though a steady trickle of visitors come to see the **lighthouse** (open Wednesday between 2pm and 5pm only) and buy an €11 'I've-been-there' certificate at the **Turismo** (☎219 280 081; www.sintraromantica.net; Cabo da Roca; ⏲9am-7.30pm, to 6.30pm Oct-Apr), it still has an air of rugged, windswept remoteness, best seen on a 10km-loop hike (maps available at Turismo).

Just before reaching Cabo da Roca, there's a small sign indicating the turn-off to **Praia Ursa**. From here it's a 20-minute descent along a treacherous path (take care!) to a beautiful deserted beach (bring your own food and drinks). You might see a few nudists here in summer. From here you can continue walking along the coast another 5km to Praia Grande.

Sleeping

Quinta Beira-Mar — B&B €

(☎219 283 353; www.quintabeiramar.com; Rua Da Vigia No 12, Praia Pequena; dm/s/d without bathroom €25/30/65, d with bathroom €75; ⏲closed Jan-Feb; 📶🏊) Friendly haff-Brit Suzanna oversees this six-room working farm complete with horses, ducks, dogs and cats. It feels like the countryside yet is steps from Praia Pequena, Praia Grande and Praia das Maçãs. Wooden-accented rooms are spacious while bathrooms are surprisingly modern. It's a cosy option for those who want a rural element to their sun-worshipping. Horse riding is available.

Hotel Arribas — HOTEL €€

(☎219 289 050; www.arribashotel.com; Av Alfredo Coelho 28, Praia Grande; d €90-141, ste from €141; P❄@📶🏊) While this 59-room, scallop-shaped relic of a family hotel isn't a pretty face, its sea views over Praia Grande and 100m-long, 5-million-litre ocean-water pool are quite a show. Its light, breezy rooms were updated in 2016 and feature fridges, TVs and balconies that are ideal for watching surfers ride the waves.

Eating

Many cafes and seafood restaurants are scattered along Praia Grande; Praia das Maçãs also has a few options.

★ Adraga — SEAFOOD €€

(☎219 280 028; www.restaurantedaadraga.com; Praia da Adraga; seafood €32-85 per kg; ⏲12.30-10.30pm; 📶) This legendary seafood restaurant sits on the edge of a small beach below Almoçageme. No fancy techniques or overdressed dining room here – just incredibly fresh fish and seafood cooked to perfection, served in a casual, yellow-tableclothed setting with framed sea views. Call ahead to reserve a table by the window. Parking can be tough in summer.

Restaurante Central — PORTUGUESE €€

(☎219 290 071; Rua da Liberdade 100, Colares; mains €7.50-15; ⏲noon-3.30pm & 7-10pm, closed Wed dinner & Thu; 📶) Drawing a healthy mix of village old-timers and hip travellers, the authentic Portuguese cuisine of Mrs Dalila takes centre stage at this simple but charming local haunt. You'll find staples such as whole *bacalhau* (dried salt-cod) and *bitoque* (steak and egg with fries) along with a daily-changing array of excellent dishes.

Azenhas do Mar — SEAFOOD €€€

(☎219 280 739; www.azenhasdomar.com; Azenhas do Mar; mains €18-37, seafood per kg €45-120; ⏲12.30-10pm; 📶) Shake the table and your plate might just fall into the sea at this top seafood place, perched above the saltwater pool in Azenhas do Mar. The sea views are stunning, especially from the deck. Skip the overpriced and underwhelming tuna tartar and spend that €18 on the delicious grilled octopus. A taxi from Sintra costs about €13.

Getting There & Away

Bus 441 from Sintra's Portela Interface runs frequently via Colares to Praia das Maçãs (€3.25, 25 minutes) and on to Azenhas do Mar (€4.10, 30 minutes), sometimes stopping at Praia Grande (€4.10, 25 minutes) six times daily (more in summer). Bus 440 also runs from Sintra to Azenhas do Mar (€4.10, 35 minutes). On weekends, the Elétrico de Sintra (€3) goes from Sintra to Praia das Maçãs via Colares.

Bus 403 to Cascais runs regularly via Cabo da Roca (€4.10, 45 minutes) from Sintra station.

Cascais

POP 35,000

Cascais (kush-*kaish*) has rocketed from sleepy fishing village to much-loved summertime playground of wave-frolicking *lisboêtas* ever since King Luís I went for a dip in 1870. Its trio of golden bays attracts sun-worshipping holidaymakers, who come to splash in the ice-cold Atlantic. Don't expect to get much sand to yourself at the weekend, though.

There's plenty of post-beach life, with winding lanes leading to small museums, cool gardens, a shiny marina and a pedestrianised old town dotted with designer boutiques and alfresco fish restaurants. After dark, lively bars fuel the party. There's also great surfing at Praia do Guincho, 9km northwest, and running or cycling along the shoreline path.

Sights

Palácio da Cidadela de Cascais MUSEUM
(www.museu.presidencia.pt; Cidadela de Cascais, Av Dom Carlos I; adult/child €4/free; 10am-1pm & 2-6pm) Commissioned as a summer palace in 1870 by King Dom Luís I, this captivating museum remains the official residence of visiting heads of state in Portugal. When Putin isn't present, it's yours for the touring. Contemporary Portuguese tapestries, rare Lincrusta wall coverings, striking hardwood ceilings and fascinating gilded wood dragon/cherub chandeliers stand out among myriad Asian and European antiques.

Duna da Cresmina VIEWPOINT
(Núcleo de Interpretação; 918 847 421; www.dunadacresmina.com; Rua da Areia; 9am-6pm) Built in 2013, this nature interpretation centre was built to educate (and protect) the fragile flora and fauna of the coastal dune system around Guincho. To lure folks in, they built a cafe serving excellent crêpes, salads and *tostas* with a postcard-ready outdoor terrace that dramatically frames 180-degree views of Cabo Raso, Praia da Cresmina and Praia do Guincho.

Walk off lunch on the well-built plankway system that extends into the dunes (guided tours available in advance). It's located 6km northwest of Cascais on the way to Guincho; and bus 415 from Cascais passes by.

Boca do Inferno VIEWPOINT
Atlantic waves pummel craggy Boca do Inferno (Mouth of Hell), 2km west of Cascais. It's about a 20-minute walk along the coast, or you can catch the BusCas (427) from Cascais station (€1, every 10 to 15 minutes). Expect a mouthful of small splashes unless a storm is raging.

Casa das Histórias Paula Rego MUSEUM
(www.casadashistoriaspaularego.com; Av da República 300; adult/child €3/free; 10am-6pm Tue-Sun, to 7pm summer) The Casa das Histórias Paula Rego showcases the disturbing, highly evocative paintings of Portugal's finest living artist. Biannually changing exhibits span Rego's career, from early work with collage in the 1950s to the twisted fairy tale–like tableaux of the 1980s, and up to the disturbing realism of more recent years.

Cidadela de Cascais FORTRESS
The citadel is where the royal family used to spend the summer. Today it houses a luxury hotel – the **Pestana Cidadela Cascais** (214 814 300; www.pestana.com; Av Dr Dom Carlos I; r from €286;) – a courtyard restaurant, bookshop, art gallery, chapel and the Palácio da Cidadela de Cascais. Beyond lies the modern **Marina de Cascais** (214 824 800; www.mymarinacascais.com; Casa de São Bernardo) with its postcard-perfect lighthouse, sleek yachts and lounge bars.

Parque Marechal Carmona PARK
(www.cm-cascais.pt/equipamento/parque-marechal-carmona; Av Rei Humberto II; 8.30am-6pm, to 8pm summer) The wild Parque Marechal Carmona provides a shady retreat from the seaside crowds, with a duck pond, birch and pine trees, palms and eucalyptus, rose gardens and flowering shrubs.

The grounds harbour the **Museu Condes de Castro Guimarães** (www.cm-cascais.pt/equipamento/museu-condes-de-castro-guimaraes; adult/child €3/free; 10am-5pm Tue-Sun), the whimsical early-19th-century mansion that comes complete with castle turrets and

Cascais

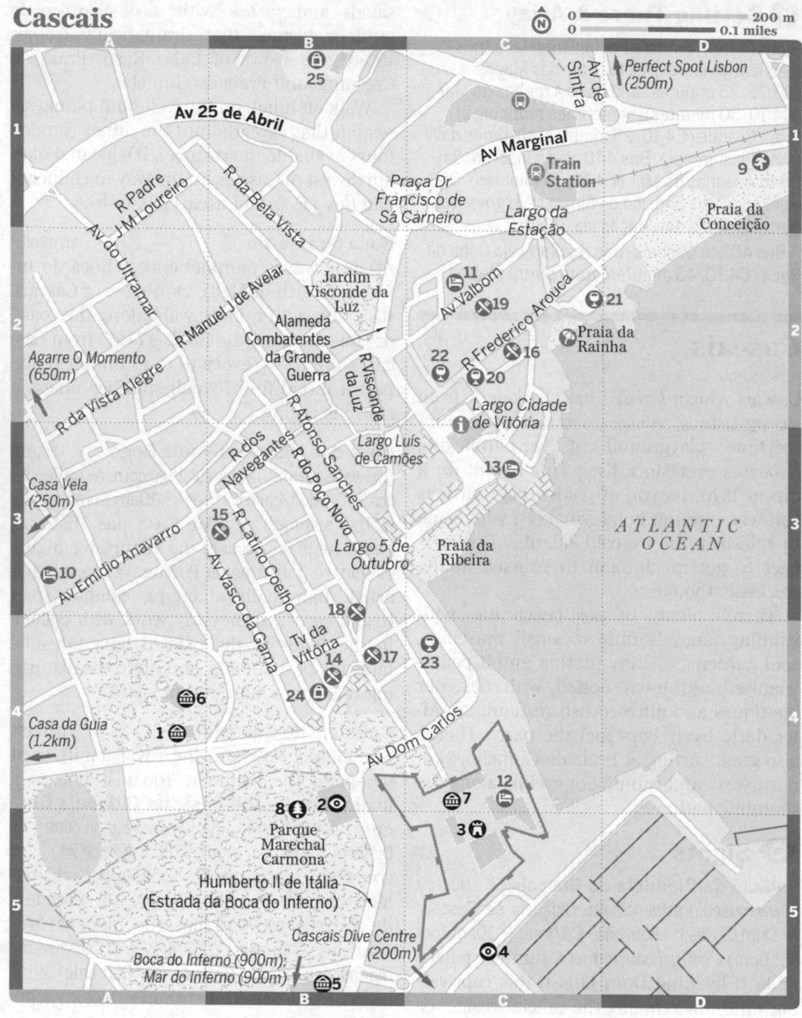

Arabic cloister. The lavishly decorated interior houses some 17th-century Indo-Portuguese cabinets, oriental silk tapestries and 350-year-old *azulejos*.

Centro Cultural de Cascais CULTURAL CENTRE
(www.fundacaodomluis.pt; Av Rei Humberto II de Itália; adult/child €3/free; 10am-6pm Tue-Sun) The colourful Centro Cultural de Cascais, in what was a Carmelite convent, hosts contemporary exhibitions and cultural events.

Museu do Mar Rei Dom Carlos MUSEUM
(www.cm-cascais.pt/museumar; Rua Júlio Pereira de Mello; adult/child €3/free; 10am-5pm Tue-Fri, 10am-1pm & 2-5pm Sat-Sun) The small, brightly accented Museu do Mar spells out Cascais' maritime history with costumes, tools, nets and boats, accompanied by quotes (in English) from the fisherfolk.

Beaches

Cascais' three sandy bays – Praia da Conceição, Praia da Rainha and Praia da Ribeira – are fine for a sunbake or a Atlantic dip, but don't expect much towel space in summer.

The best beach is wild, windswept Praia do Guincho, 9km northwest, a mecca to surfers and windsurfers with massive crash-

Cascais

Sights

1 Casa das Histórias Paula Rego A4
2 Centro Cultural de Cascais.................... B4
3 Cidadela de Cascais C5
4 Marina de Cascais C5
5 Museu Condes de Castro Guimarães B5
6 Museu do Mar Rei Dom Carlos A4
7 Palácio da Cidadela de Cascais C4
8 Parque Marechal Carmona B4

Activities, Courses & Tours

9 Cascais Watersports Centre................D1

Sleeping

10 Ljmonade Hostel.................................... A3
11 Pergola House.. C2
12 Pestana Cidadela Cascais C4
13 Villa Cascais... C3

Eating

14 5 Sentidos B4
15 Apeadeiro B3
16 Café Galeria House of Wonders C2
17 Confraria Sushi..B4
18 Os Bordallos...B3
19 Santini C2

Drinking & Nightlife

20 Crow Bar C2
21 Esplanada Rainha....................................C2
22 O Luain's C2
23 Paradigma C4

Shopping

24 Ceramicarte B4
25 Mercado da Vila B1

ing rollers. The strong undertow can be dangerous for swimmers, but Guincho still lures nonsurfers with powder-soft sands, fresh seafood and magical sunsets.

Activities

If you're keen to ride the waves, grab your boardies and check out the surfing courses available at **Moana Surf School** (☎964 449 436; www.moanasurfschool.com; Estrada do Abano, Praia do Guincho; private per hr €40, group lesson €25, 4-lesson course €85), which also rents boards and wetsuits. **Guincho Surf School** (☎914 024 400, 917 535 719; www.guinchosurfschool.com; 1/2/5 group lessons €30/50/100, private €50/90/135) also offers classes. South African-run **Hooked Surf School** (☎913 615 978; www.hookedsurf.com; intro lesson €25, 4 lessons €80) holds classes here as well as on other beaches along A Linha – the train line from Lisboa – such as Carcavelos and around Sintra.

But Cascais is not limited to water sports. **Cascais Routes** (☎919 860 899; www.cascaisroutes.pt; Av da Charneca; tours from €40) specialises in land adventures such as rock climbing and mountain biking.

Cascais Dive Center DIVING
(☎211 328 265; www.cascaisdive.com; Marina de Cascais; single dive incl equipment €55; ⊙9am-6pm, 10am-12.30pm & 2.30-5pm Oct-Apr) At the Marina de Cascais (p133), this outfit can take you scuba-diving around the Cascais coastline and beyond with equipment rental and courses.

Cascais Watersports Centre WATER SPORTS
(Praia da Duquesa; ⊙10am-7.30pm) At Praia da Duquesa, midway between Cascais and Estoril, you can rent pedaloes and canoes, and arrange waterskiing jaunts and windsurfing. Summer only.

Festivals & Events

Festival de Estoril Lisboa MUSIC
(www.festorilisbon.com) This festival, founded in 1975 as the Festival de Música da Costa do Estoril, brings classical and jazz concerts to both Cascais and Estoril in July. Some concerts are free.

Festas do Mar CULTURAL
This festival in late August, Portugal's only free summer festival, celebrates Cascais' maritime heritage with outdoor concerts, nautical parades and fireworks.

Sleeping

Perfect Spot Lisbon HOSTEL €
(☎924 058 643; www.perfectspot-lisbon.com; Av de Sintra 354; 3-/4-/7-day packages from €155/205/365; P 📶) New parents Jon and Rita run this lovely hostel – perfect for families in addition to surfers and climbers – in a large home just a smidgen outside the tourist zone. Spacious rooms and dorms are themed with unique art, but the real coup is the closed-in garden, a supreme hang space with day beds and a BBQ lounge.

Ljmonade Hostel HOSTEL €
(☎214 865 671; www.ljmonade.com; Rua Manuel Joaquim Gama Machado 4A; dm from €22, r with/

FREE WHEELS

For a spin out along the coast, take advantage of **BiCas** (9am-5pm winter, 8am-7pm summer), Cascais' free bike-hire scheme. The well-worn bikes are available from 8am to 7pm daily at various points around town, including Largo da Estação near the train station. Demand is naturally high, so arrive early and bring some form of ID. There's a bicycle path that runs the entire 9km stretch from Cascais to Guincho. A shorter route is along the attractive seafront promenade to Estoril, 2km east.

without bathroom €85/65;) In a quiet neighbourhood some 900m southwest of the train station, this Ukrainian-run hostel has the best traveller vibe of Cascais' budget options. Dorms come in four-, six- or seven-bed varieties (mixed and separate) but low vaulted ceilings may be tough on basketball and volleyball players. A sunny terrace, big shared kitchen and free nightly wine are big pluses here.

Camping Orbitur do Guincho CAMPGROUND €
(214 870 450; www.orbitur.pt; EN 247-6, Lugar de Areia; bungalows with/without bathroom from €93/49, sites per adult/tent/car €6.90/9.40/7.10;) Set back behind the dunes of Praia do Guincho, 9km from Cascais, this pine-shaded site is one of the Lisbon area's finest. It has a new swimming pool, restaurant, tennis court and even solar-powered showers in some cases. It gets busy in July and August. Buses run frequently to Guincho from Cascais.

Agarre o Momento GUESTHOUSE €€
(214 064 532; www.agarreomomento.com; Rua Joaquim Ereira 458; d/tr/q with shared bathroom €60/75/85;) This inviting guesthouse in a peaceful residential neighbourhood has bright, airy rooms amid kitschy signage plus a garden, shared kitchen and bike rental. It's a 15-minute walk (1.5km) north of the station, or a short taxi ride.

Casa Vela GUESTHOUSE €€€
(218 093 996; www.casavelahotel.com; Rua dos Bem Lembrados 17; d from €145;) The friendly Casa Vela has it all: 18 bright and attractive rooms set with modern furnishings in decor schemes set to either spice or colonial themes; deceptively large and grand gardens with trickling fountains, hidden nooks and a tranquil pool; and a Portuguese-by-birth, Mozambican-by-upbringing manager, João Paulo, who is the epitome of jovial hospitality. Paradise found.

Villa Cascais BOUTIQUE HOTEL €€€
(214 863 410; www.thealbatrozcollection.com; Rua Fernandes Tomás 1; d from €145;) If you like your hotels with a jolting dose of personality, the newly made-over, so-very-blue Villa Cascais (blue walls, blue couches and blue ceilings!) should sit quite well. Striking brass staircases lead to 11 beautiful and spacious rooms in three colours (two of which are not blue), each with discerning lounge furniture. Trendy, bright and beautiful!

Pergola House B&B €€€
(214 840 040; www.pergolahouse.pt; Av Valbom 13; s/d from €84/131;) An oasis of calm with a lush garden and bougainvillea-draped facade, this century-old manor is a family heirloom. A marble staircase sweeps up to 10 classically elegant rooms with stucco, dark-wood trappings and sparkling bathrooms; several have garden-facing balconies. Relax in the antique-filled sitting room or with a glass of complimentary port in the evening.

Eating

You'll find a glut of restaurants with alfresco seating along pedestrianised Rua Frederico Arouca and cobbled Largo Cidade de Vitória. For seafood and sunsets, make for the ocean-facing restaurants in Guincho.

Os Bordallos BURGERS €
(Rua Marques Leal Pancada 430; burgers €4.80-12; noon-3pm & 7-11pm Tue-Sat, noon-3pm Sun;) Humbly tucked away in the narrow alleyways above town, this cosy joint does good gourmet Portuguese-style burgers amid a bit of history – it's owned by and named after a descendant of Rafael Bordalo Pinheiro, a famous Portuguese cartoonist and ceramist (that's his work on the wall). Service is a delight, too. Save room for the lime pie!

Santini ICE CREAM €
(www.santini.pt; Av Valbom 28F; 2/3/4 scoops €2.60/4.50/5.80; 11am-midnight) All hail Lisbon's favourite gelato. Santini's creamy, rich, 100% natural version is made to the age-old family recipe of Italian immigrants, dating to 1949. Join the line at this tiny outlet, grab a cone and eat quickly before it melts.

★Bar do Guincho PORTUGUESE €€
(www.bardoguincho.pt; Estrada do Abano, Praia do Guincho; mains €8.50-17.50; noon-7pm Sun & Tue-Thu, noon-midnight Fri-Sat, to late Jul-Aug;) Sweeping the awards for most dramatic location in Cascais, this good-time bar/restaurant sits tucked behind a craggy ridge on the northern end of Guincho. From the sand, you would never know it's there, but it is – *a*nd it is packed! Revellers rake in the beach-friendly burgers, seafood and salads washed down with cold *cerveja* (beer). Settle in for the afternoon.

★Café Galeria House of Wonders CAFE €€
(www.facebook.com/houseofwonders; Largo da Misericórdia 53; buffet 1/2 people €14.95/24.50, light meals €2.50-9.75; 10am-midnight;) This fantastically whimsical, Dutch-owned cafe is tucked away in the old quarter. Its astonishingly good Middle Eastern/Mediterranean vegetarian meze buffet downstairs includes a hot-dish add-on for €9.95 (aubergine moussaka, zucchini lasagne etc) amid a warm, welcoming ambience and artwork-filled interior. Don't miss it!

Upstairs, you'll find set plates of similar food for €6.95 as well as delightful cakes (always at least one vegan and gluten-free option), juices, cocktails and coffee, which can be taken on the rustic rooftop terrace, with picturesque views over Cascais. A true traveller's delight.

5 Sentidos PORTUGUESE €€
(961 571 194; www.restaurante5entidos.com; Largo Assunção 6; mains €12.50-25.10; 12.30-3pm & 6.30-11pm, closed Tue;) In a colourful and cosy home known around town as Casa do Largo (the site of a legendary bar of the same name), 5 Sentidos is popular with expats and in-the-know tourists, who come for sophisticated meat and seafood that move beyond *bitoques* and grilled fish.

Páteo do Petisco PORTUGUESE €€
(214 820 036; www.facebook.com/pateodopetiscocascais; Travessa das Amoreiras 5; tapas €2.90-6.50, mains €8-13.50; noon-11.30pm Tue-Sun) To escape the high prices and tourist masses in the old town, head out to this local favourite in the Torre neighbourhood. It's a buzzing place, with a friendly, tavern-like vibe and good-value Portuguese-style tapas – ideal for sharing with friends. It's about 3km northwest of the old town centre, best reached by taxi (around €5). Reserve ahead.

If you don't feel like making the trek, it serves an identical menu at its newer location inside Mercado da Vila (p138).

Confraria Sushi JAPANESE €€
(214 834 614; www.confrariasushi.pt; Rua Luís Xavier Palmeirim 14; salads €9-15, sushi plates €13-48; noon-midnight Sun-Thu, to 2am Fri-Sat;) It's hard to know where to look first at this bright, art-slung cafe, with hipster servers and candlelight at night. It's jazzed up with flower prints, zebra stripes and technicolour glass chandeliers. It's a fun spot for sushi and salads, albeit pricey – you're paying for an added cool quotient here. There are a handful of tables on the sunny patio.

Apeadeiro SEAFOOD €€
(Av Vasco da Gama 252; mains €7-14; noon-3pm & 7-10pm Tue-Sat, noon-3pm Sun) With simple decor, this sunny neighbourhood restaurant is known for its superb chargrilled fish served at reasonable prices. It has particularly good *couvert* (optional appetisers).

Casa da Guia INTERNATIONAL €€
(www.casadaguia.com; Av Nossa Senhora do Cabo 101) Among palm and pine trees, this lush waterfront complex contains a handful of shops, cafes and restaurants with outdoor terraces overlooking the deep blue Atlantic. It's located on the main coastal road, about 3km west of the historic centre (and 1.3km west of Boca do Inferno).

Mar do Inferno SEAFOOD €€€
(214 832 218; www.mardoinferno.com; Av Rei Humberto II de Itália; seafood per kg €49-137.50; noon-11pm Tue-Thu;) Near the Boca do Inferno, this humble-looking place serves superb seafood dishes to ocean views. Its mouth-watering mixed platters for two (€39.50 to €88 – they'll do the cheapest one for one person!) are legendary. The service can be hit or miss. Reserve ahead to score a table on the terrace.

Drinking & Nightlife

The pub-like bars huddling around Largo Luís de Camões fill with a good-time crowd after sunset.

Crow Bar BAR
(www.facebook.com/crowbarcascais; Travessa da Misericórdia 1A; pints €3-5; 8pm-2am Mon-Thu, from 6pm Fri-Sat;) Sitting unsuspectingly above one the most atmospheric and touristy streets in Cascais is this alternative drinking den, a tatted-up dive bar with a rock and roll

attitude, mead on draught and Motörhead vodka. No sea views. No sunsets. It offers the best selection of local craft beer left of Lisboa (25 or so in the bottle, six on draught).

Paradigma COCKTAIL BAR
(www.facebook.com/paradigmacascais; Av Dom Carlos I 48; cocktails €5.50-15; 12.30pm-2am Mon-Fri, 6pm-2am Sat;) While there's no shortage of bars in Cascais, proper mixology can be hard to come by. This upscale cocktail lounge does a commendable job with both classic and inventive cocktails and is a sophisticated spot to enjoy sea views as well.

O Luain's PUB
(Rua da Palmeira 4A; noon-2am;) For the craic in Cascais, it has to be this cheery Irish watering hole. Pull up a stool for Guinness, Premiere League footy or live jam sessions on weekends (nightly in summer).

Esplanada Rainha BAR
(www.facebook.com/esplanadarainha.cascais; Largo da Praia da Rainha; sangria pitchers €12-20; 10am-6pm, closed Thu) For sundowners with a sea view, head to this outdoor place with a vista overlooking Praia da Rainha beach.

Shopping

Mercado da Vila MARKET
(Av Dom Pedro I & Rua Padre Moisés da Silva; 6.30am-5pm Mon-Sat) Completely revamped and modernised in recent years, Cascais' municipal market tempts with not only fresh local produce such as juicy Algarve nectarines, glossy olives, wagon wheel-sized cheeses and bread on various days (check the schedule online), but also with a new line-up of bars, restaurants and gourmet-takeaway stalls surrounding an inviting outdoor plaza.

Ceramicarte FINE ART
(214 840 170; www.ceramicarte.pt; Largo da Assunção 3; 10.30am-1.30pm & 3-6pm Mon-Fri, 10.30am-1pm Sat) This eye-catching gallery showcases Luís Soares' bright, fused-glass creations, from jewellery to tableware.

Information

Ask Me Cascais (Turismo; 912 034 214; www.visitcascais.com; Largo Cidade Vitória; 9am-8pm summer, to 6pm winter) The official Cascais tourist information booth has a handy map and events guide (*What's in Cascais*), and is helpful to an extent.

Hospital de Cascais (214 653 000; www.hospitaldecascais.pt; Av Brigadeiro Victor Novais Gonçalves) In a new location in Alcabideche, 6km north of Cascais. Offers emergency service with English-speaking doctors.

Multibanco (Rua Sebastião José de Carvalho e Melo 6) Handy ATM across from the train station.

Tourist Police Station (214 814 067; www.psp.pt; Largo Mestre Henrique Anjos; 10am-noon & 1-10pm) Located in the plaza across from Praia da Ribeira.

Getting There & Away

The **train station** (www.cp.pt; Largo da Estação) and nearby **bus station** (www.scotturb.com) are about 250m north of the main pedestrianised drag, Rua Frederico Arouca.

Scotturb (214 699 125; www.scotturb.com) runs the Cascais bus system. Bus 417 goes about hourly from Cascais to Sintra (€4.10, 40 minutes). For a more scenic view take bus 403 (€4.10, 1¼ hours), which goes via Cabo da Roca (30 minutes).

Comboios de Portugal (p122) trains run from Lisbon's Cais do Sodré station to Cascais via Estoril (€2.15, 40 minutes, every 20 to 30 minutes, 5.30am to 1.30am).

It's only 2km to Estoril, so it doesn't take long to walk the seafront route.

Getting Around

Buses 405 and 415 go to Guincho (€3.25, 20 minutes, about hourly from 6.50am to 7.50pm). Scotturb's 427 (BusCas; €1) leaves every 10 to 20 minutes from just outside the train station and wiggles its way around most of the city's most important tourist sites.

For a taxi, call 214 659 500.

Estoril

POP 24,000

With its swish hotels, turreted villas and glitzy casino, Estoril (shtoe-*reel*) once fancied itself as the Portuguese Riviera. The rich and famous came here to frolic in the sea, stroll palm-fringed landscaped gardens and fritter away their fortunes. Though it still has a whiff of faded aristocracy, those heady days of grandeur have passed. Today, Estoril remains a well-to-do, less touristy option than Cascais with a nice beach and casino. While some overnight guests may end up wishing they'd stayed in livelier Cascais, those looking for more peace and quiet will find a burgeoning guesthouse scene that yields some of the area's most memorable options.

Estoril was where Ian Fleming hit on the idea for *Casino Royale,* as he stalked Yugoslav double-agent Dusko Popov at the casino.

During WWII, the town heaved with exiles and spies (including Graham Greene, another British intelligence man and author).

Sights

Estoril's sandy Praia de Tamariz tends to be quieter than the bays in Cascais and has showers, cafes, beachside bars and a free ocean swimming pool, east of the train station.

Estoril has a world-famous golf scene, including the acclaimed **Golf do Estoril**.

Estoril Casino CASINO
(214 667 700; www.casino-estoril.pt; Av Dr Stanley Ho; 3pm-3am) Bond fans after a spritz of espionage head for glitzy Casino Estoril, the inspiration for Ian Fleming's *Casino Royale*. Fritter away your euros on a high-stakes poker tournament or check out the spangly Las Vegas–style shows. There's a first-rate **Chinese restaurant** on the ground floor.

Sleeping

★ **Blue Boutique Hostel** HOSTEL €
(214 663 006; www.blueboutiquehostel.com; Av Marginal 6538; dm from €20, r with/without bathroom from €50/89) You can't miss this gorgeous aquamarine belle of the ball, a sky-blue bright mansion restored into A Linha's best hostel. The design-forward space, with marble staircases, retro furniture and local art installations, offers an above-bar shared kitchen, colourful dorms with lockers and a near wrap-around porch. There's an emphasis on water sports (surfing, windsurfing and stand-up paddleboarding) but why leave?

Hotel Smart GUESTHOUSE €€
(214 682 164; www.hotel-smart.net; Rua Maestro Laçerda 6; s/d from €75/85;) The affable Bandarra family runs this 26-room colonial-orange guesthouse with pride – think manicured lawns, a clean swimming pool, gleaming marble floors and new modernised bathrooms (part of a 2016 renovation). The light-filled rooms have lots of polished wood and tiny balconies.

Eating

Pastelaria Garrett PORTUGUESE €
(214 680 365; www.pastelariagarrettestoril.pt; Av de Nice 54; snacks €3-5, mains €10-26.50; 8am-7pm Wed-Mon) A block west of the park, this handsomely set *pastelaria* and restaurant is one of Lisbon's most storied, a destination bakery when it comes to *Bolo Rei* (a Christmas-like fruitcake served year-round), *palmiers cobertos* (puff pastry covered with sweet egg icing) and croissants, but everything is good, including the savoury lunch fare.

Cozinha do Mar PORTUGUESE €€
(214 689 317; Av São Pedro 9; mains €8-19; noon-3pm & 7-10.30pm Mon-Sat) This small, classy locals' haunt also receives its fair share of tourists who come for great-value Portuguese staples such as grilled fish, *dourada* (sea bream) cooked with rock salt, *bacalhau à Brás* (salted cod with eggs and potatoes) and *açorda de camarão* (shrimp over mashed day-old bread with garlic and herbs) served over kitschy seashell tablecloths. Friendly service, too.

It's about a 350m walk north of Monte Estoril station.

Drinking & Nightlife

Deck Beer Garden BEER GARDEN
(www.deckbeerlab.pt; Arcadas do Parque 21; beer €1.50-7.90; 8am-2am, closed Wed;) The owner of a decades-old *restaurante típico* facing the Estoril's pretty Jardim do Estoril realised he needed to get hip to craft brewing to keep up with the cool kids. The result is a clash of two eras, the artisanal draught brews are a work-in-progress but are surely better summer-heat beaters than Super Bock. The outdoor seating is ideal.

Queluz

Versailles' fanciful cousin-once-removed, the powder-puff **Palácio de Queluz** (219 237 300; www.parquesdesintra.pt; adult/child €10/8.50; 9am-5.30pm, to 7pm high season) was once a hunting lodge, converted in the late 1700s to a royal summer residence. It's surrounded by queen-of-hearts formal gardens, with oak-lined avenues, fountains (including the Fonte de Neptuno, ascribed to Italian master Bernini) and an *azulejo*-lined canal where the royals went boating.

The palace, whose facade was restored to its original 'enamel blue' during a massive 2015 restoration, was designed by Portuguese architect Mateus Vicente de Oliveira and French artist Jean-Baptiste Robillon for Prince Dom Pedro in the 1750s. Pedro's niece and wife, Queen Maria I, lived here for most of her reign, going increasingly mad. Her scheming Spanish daughter-in-law, Carlota Joaquina, was quite a match for eccentric British visitor William Beckford. On one occasion she insisted that Beckford run a race with her maid in the garden and then dance a bolero, which he did 'in a delirium of romantic delight'.

Inside it's like a chocolate box, with a gilded, mirror-lined Throne Room and Pedro IV's bedroom where he slept under a circular ceiling, surrounded by *Don Quixote* murals. The palace's vast kitchens now house a palatial restaurant, **Cozinha Velha** (☎214 356 158; www.pousadas.pt; mains €17-30; ⊙1-3pm & 7.30-10pm), where you can feast on original palace recipes such as the steamed Dover sole.

Once you've seen the palace, live the life: the Royal Guard of the Court quarters have been converted into the dazzling **Pousada de Dona Maria I** (☎214 356 158; www.pousadas.pt; Largo do Palácio de Queluz; s/d from €120/130; ❄📶), with high-ceilinged rooms that will make you feel as if you're at home with the royals.

Getting There & Away

Queluz is 12km northwest of Lisbon and makes an easy day trip. Frequent trains from Lisbon's Rossio station stop at Queluz-Belas (€1.55, 18 minutes).

Mafra

POP 11,000

Mafra, 39km northwest of Lisbon, makes a superb day trip from Lisbon, Sintra or Ericeira. It is home to Palácio Nacional de Mafra, Portugal's extravagant convent-palace hybrid with 1200 rooms. Nearby is the beautiful former royal park, Tapada Nacional de Mafra, once a hunting ground and still teeming with wild animals and plants.

The monumental palace facade dominates the town. Opposite is a pleasant square, Praça da República, which is lined with cafes and restaurants.

Sights

Palácio Nacional de Mafra PALACE

(☎261 817 550; www.palaciomafra.pt; Terreiro Dom João V; adult/child €6/free, free 1st Sun of the month; ⊙palace 9am-6pm Tue-Sun, basilica 9.30am-1pm & 2-5.30pm) Wild-spending Dom João V poured pots of Brazilian gold into this baroque palace, covering a mind-boggling 4 sq km and comprising a monastery and basilica. Begun in 1717 and finished by 1746, the exuberant mock-marble confection is the handiwork of German master Friedrich Ludwig, who trained in Italy and clearly had a kind of Portuguese Vatican in mind.

No expense was spared: around 45,000 artisans worked on building its 1200 rooms and two bell towers, which shelter the world's largest collection of bells (97 in total, 92 of which are original).

When the French invaded Portugal in 1807, Dom João VI and the royals skedaddled to Brazil, taking most of Mafra's furniture with them. Imagine the anticlimax when the French found nothing but 20 elderly Franciscan friars. General Junot billeted his troops in the monastery, followed by Wellington and his men. From then on the palace became a military haven. Even today, much of it is occupied by the military as an academy.

On a self-guided visit, you'll take in treasures such as the antler-strewn hunting room, a striking infirmary, the gorgeous Blessing Room, awash in colorful *Lioz* stone and a walled bed for mad monks (maybe sent over the edge by all those corridors!). The biggest stunner is the 83.6m-long barrel-vaulted library, housing some 36,000 book volumes encasing an as-yet-uncounted 100,000-plus 15th- to 18th-century books, many handbound by the monks. It's an appropriate fairy-tale coda to all this extravagance that they're gradually being gnawed away by rats. The basilica of twin bell-tower fame is strikingly restrained by comparison, featuring multihued marble floors and Carrara marble statues.

Aldeia Típica José Franco MINIATURE VILLAGE

(Estrada Nacional 116; ⊙9.30am-7pm, to 6pm Oct-Mar) FREE At the village of Sobreiro, 4km northwest of Mafra (take any Ericeira-bound bus), sculptor José Franco has created an enchanting miniature, vaguely surreal craft village of windmills, watermills and traditional shops. Kids love it here; as do some adults, especially when they discover the rustic *adega* (winery) serving red wine and snacks. Most folks, however, bring a picnic.

Tapada Nacional de Mafra FOREST

(☎261 814 240; www.tapadademafra.pt; Portão do Codeçal; activities €4.50-20; ⊙9.30am-5.30pm) The 819-hectare Tapada Nacional de Mafra is where Dom João V used to go hunting. Enclosed by an original 21km wall, the grounds are now an environmentally aware game park, home to free-roaming wild boar and red deer, plus smaller numbers of foxes, badgers and eagles.

WORTH A TRIP

A WOLF IN THE WOODS

There's no need to be afraid of the wolves at the **Centro de Recuperação do Lobo Ibérico** (Iberian Wolf Sanctuary; 261 785 037; http://lobo.fc.ul.pt; Vale da Guarda, Picão; adult/concession €6/4; 4pm & 6pm Sat-Sun May-Sep, 3pm & 4.30pm Sat & Sun Oct-Apr) located near Malveira, 10km east of Mafra. The centre is home to around 16 wolves that can no longer live in the wild. Visits are by 90-minute guided tours.

Set in a forested valley, the centre aims to boost the rapidly dwindling numbers of the Iberian wolf population (now just 300 in the wild in Portugal, along with an additional 1700 in Spain) by affording them safe shelter in a near-to-natural habitat inside five 1-hectare enclosures. As the wolves are free to roam in their large enclosures, there's no guarantee that you'll spot them, but encounters are frequent. There are volunteering opportunities as well. The sanctuary is best reached by private transport (call ahead for directions as GPS will take you an impassable way). Cash only (no strollers and no wheelchairs).

To appreciate the different ecosystems, hike through its woodlands of Portuguese oak, cork oak and pine; don't miss the 350-year-old cork oak saved from fire in 2003. The 4km trail is a good introduction to the park, but you have a greater chance of spotting animals on one of the more remote 7.5km routes. Also on the grounds is a simple but pleasantly furnished **guesthouse** (s/d €45/55). On weekends, many activities are on offer, including horse riding (by advance reservation), archery and wagon rides, among others. You can also take a tourist 'train' around the park, which, unfortunately, leads to organised feedings to guarantee spottings.

The Tapada is about 7km north of Mafra, along the road to Gradil. It's best reached by private transport, as buses are erratic; from Mafra, taxis charge around €10 one way.

Sleeping

★**Aldeia da Mata Pequena** RURAL INN €€
(219 270 908; www.aldeiadamatapequena.com; Rua São Francisco de Assis; €75-160;) Located 9km south of Mafra, this unique rural tourism option is the forward-thinking vision of *lisboêta* Diogo Batalha, who managed to buy and restore 18 ruined structures of a 300-year-old village, 13 of which so far have been turned into fabulous, historically accurate stone cottages, each with a kitchen, living room and sleeping area.

Eating

★**João da Vila Velha** PORTUGUESE €
(261 811 254; Rua Pedro Julião 4; mains €7-10; noon-10pm Fri-Wed) Located just enough off the tourist path, old school Chef João runs this authentic and colourful neighbourhood *tasca* (tavern). There's a wealth of simple but honestly cooked classics (octopus, *bacalhau* etc) and a good bit of wilder and gamier meat dishes (wild boar, rabbit and the like). Standouts include a wild-boar *chanfana* (stew) and a curried-shrimp *moqueca* (shrimp stew).

Adega de Covento PORTUGUESE €€
(261 814 185; www.adegadoconvento.pt; Rua Moreira 11; mains €8-15; noon-4pm Sun-Mon, to 11pm Tue-Wed, to 2am Fri-Sat;) This classy option, a short walk from the palace but tucked away down a seldom-used side street, does an incredibly tender and tasty octopus rice (*arroz de polvo*) on special and a host of other classic menu staples. Portions are hefty and more gourmet than expected, with an emphasis on seafood (but plenty of *carne* as well).

Information

Turismo (261 817 770; www.cm-mafra.pt; Av das Forças Armadas 28; 10am-1pm & 2-6pm) Mafra's new tourist information centre is just off the south side of the palace and full of information, maps and helpful staff.

Getting There & Around

Mafra's bus terminal is at Parque Intermodal on Rua Santa Casa da Misericórdia, 1.2km west of the palace, but buses also stop in front of the palace. Regular **Mafrense** (707 201 371; www.mafrense.pt; Rua Santa Casa da Misericórdia, Parque Intermodal) buses to Sintra (€3.40, one hour) and Lisbon's Campo Grande terminal (€4.20, 75 minutes, at least hourly) leave from the bus stop across from the palace in front of the Mafricentro shop. For Ericeira (€2.30, 20 minutes, at least hourly), go to the stop on the palace side of the street next to Turismo.

Mafra's train station is 6km away from the town centre but, with infrequent transport, it's not a recommended option (though taxis charge around €10 from the station to the town centre). Go to Malveira station instead for easier connections (20 minutes) to Mafra.

There is a **taxi point** (☎ 261 815 512) on Praça da República, just off the north side of the palace in front of the Cartório Notarial.

SETÚBAL PENINSULA

As the mercury rises, the promise of sun, sea and mouth-watering grilled fish lures *lisboêtas* south to the Setúbal Peninsula for weekends of ozone-enriched fun. Beach bums make for the Costa da Caparica's 8km sweep of golden sand to laze on a lounger, surf the chilly Atlantic and unwind over sundowners in beachside cafes. Further south sits Cabo Espichel, a vertiginous cape thrashed by the Atlantic, where you can trace the footprints of dinosaurs.

The main hub of the region is the vibrant port of Setúbal, a fine place to munch *choco frito* (fried cuttlefish) and spot bottlenose dolphins on a breezy cruise of the marshy Sado estuary. To the west lies Parque Natural da Arrábida, lined with scalloped bays flanked by sheer cliffs that are home to birds of prey. It leads to the cobbled backstreets of the fishing town of Sesimbra, overshadowed by a Moorish castle.

Costa da Caparica

Costa da Caparica's seemingly never-ending beach attracts sun-worshipping *lisboêtas* craving all-over tans, surfers keen to ride Atlantic waves, and day-tripping families seeking clean sea and soft sand. It hasn't escaped development, but head south and the high-rises soon give way to pine forests and mellow beach-shack cafes. The town has the same name as the coastline, and is a cheery place with shops and lots of inflatable seaside tack, done up in 2009 under a now-bankrupt government-sponsored revitalisation project that was responsible for building the town's 24 boxy seaside bar and restaurant structures.

Costa da Caparica town focuses on Praça da Liberdade. West of the *praça*, pedestrianised Rua dos Pescadores, with hotels and restaurants, leads to the seaside and a helpful tourist office. The main beach (called Praia do CDS, or Centro Desportivo de Surf), with cafes, bars and surfing clubs along its promenade, is located a short walk north.

Beaches

During summer a narrow-gauge railway runs most of the length of the beach and you can jump off at any one of 20 stops. The nearer beaches, including **Praia do Norte** and **Praia do Santo Antonio**, are great for families (as is **Praia da Cabana do Pescador** at stop 12, which boasts a playground), while the further ones are younger and trendier. **Praia 19** (stop 19) is a more-secluded gay and nudist haven.

Activities

Among the best **surfing** spots for beginners are **São João da Caparica**, **Praia da Mata** and **Praia da Sereia**. Locals prefer Praia do Barbas and bodyboarders tend towards **Cova do Vapor** for its big barrels. **Fonte da Telha** (where the train terminates) and **Praia da Bela Vista** are the best beaches for **windsurfing** and **kitesurfing** with numerous water-sport facilities. Check the handy *Tabela de Marés* booklet (available at the *turismo*), listing tide times, surf shops and clubs.

Da Wave (p143) rents out surfboards, bodyboards, wetsuits and beach gear (footballs, Frisbees and in-line skates).

Cabana Divers DIVING
(☎ 919 390 278; www.cabanadivers.pt; Av Primeiro de Maio s/n, Fonte da Telha; dive with/without equipment from €45/35; ⏰ 9am-7pm) Cabana Divers, with a nicely set-up bar and wicker basket chairs by the beach, provides scuba-diving lessons and all the necessary equipment.

Centro Internacional de Surf SURFING
(☎ 212 919 078; www.caparicasurf.com; Praia do CDS; group/private lesson €20/40; ⏰ 9am-6pm) The main surfing school.

Five Sevens CYCLING
(☎ 212 962 278; www.fivesevens.pt; Av General Humberto Delgado 31; per hr/day €4/10; ⏰ 10am-1pm & 3-7pm Mon-Sat) Rents the most reliable bikes in town, for both adults and children year-round. It's right in the centre across the avenue from the tourist information office.

Sleeping

★ Lost Caparica Surf House B&B €€
(☎918 707 779; www.lostcaparica.com; Rua Dr Barros de Casro 17; dm/s/d with shared bathroom €25/55/65;) Your charming and stylish host Filipa has turned this former architect's home into an upscale surfers' crash pad. Her keen eye for vintage design ensures a Mid-Century Modern ethos throughout the space, a welcome retreat for weary but discerning sand addicts. Hot outdoor showers, an open-air solarium and a modern guest kitchen are highlights. The six-bed dorm has a fireplace.

Surf lessons and yoga are on offer, as is puppy time with the adorable beagle, Serra.

Residencial Mar e Sol GUESTHOUSE €€
(☎212 900 017; www.residencialmaresol.com; Rua dos Pescadores 42; s/d/tr €45/55/80;) The friendly, family-run Mar e Sol offers just-renovated rooms (simple but comfy) in warm hues with parquet floors. This family also has a gastronomy empire: it also runs popular Italian restaurant **Napoli** (☎212 903 197; www.facebook.com/restaurantenapoli-costacaparica; Rua dos Flores 1; mains €7.50-14; noon-midnight;) on the premises, Portugal's first burger joint, **Sandwich Bar** (www.facebook.com/sandwichbarcostacaparica; Praça da Liberdade 5; burgers €2.40-4; noon-2am), opened in 1974, and the tapas-style TascaRica, all within a shout. There is bike hire too (summer only).

Eating

In Costa da Caparica town, seafood restaurants line Rua dos Pescadores.

TascaRica TAPAS €
(Praça da Liberdade 7; tapas €1.90-10; noon-midnight Tue-Sun) Cheap and quick, belly up to the counter and take a turn on Portuguese-style tapas. Make sure to use the restroom before you go – they've caused quite a stir in town!

O Mercado PORTUGUESE €€
(☎218 235 099; www.facebook.com/omercadocc; Av 1 de Maio 36D; mains €8-12; noon-midnight Mon-Sat, to 5pm Sun;) Oozing rustic charm, this savvy Portuguese-fusion gastropub is a pleasant escape from beach-bum Babylon. The select menu ranges from classics (*bitoque à portuguesa*) to modern takes on pork cheeks and a lovely stewy octopus. There's a good wine list and better beers on offer than usual. A nice night out.

Da Wave CAFE €€
(www.da-wave.com; Praia Nova; mains €2.60-12; 11.30am-7.30pm Oct-Mar, to 2am Apr-Sep;) One of many open-sided cafe-restaurants along the beach, Da Wave has a laid-back, seaside-diner vibe with its beanbag chairs, loungers and reggae playing overhead. American-style breakfasts, sandwiches, pizzas and juices make up the menu. Find it by heading 500m from town in the direction of the narrow-gauge train.

Drinking & Nightlife

Bar Waikiki BAR
(☎212 962 129; www.waikiki.com.pt; Praia da Sereia; sandwiches/burgers/salads from €3.80/3/10; 10am-7.30pm Apr-May & Sep-Oct, 9.30am-4am Jun-Aug, closed Oct-Mar) Nicely on its own, this beachfront bar is popular with surfers and has a cool lounge vibe. Great for sundowners, you'll find it at stop 15 on the train.

Information

Alamada Turismo (☎212 900 071; www.m-alamada.pt; Frente Urbana de Praias, Edifício da Polícia Marítima; 9.30am-1pm & 2-5.30pm Mon-Fri, to 1pm Sat Apr-Sep) Very helpful staff in the modern brown building on the beach.

Getting There & Away

Transportes Sul do Tejo (TST; ☎211 126 200; www.tsuldotejo.pt) runs buses 153 and 161 several times daily in summer to Costa da Caparica from Lisbon's Praça de Espanha (€3.25, 40 minutes) and Praça do Areeiro (€4.10, one hour), respectively. Service drops off quite a bit in winter. The **bus terminal** (Av General Humberto Delgado) is 400m northwest of the Praça da Liberdade; additional stops are by the *praça*.

The best way to get here is by ferry to Cacilhas (every 15 minutes) from Lisbon's Cais do Sodré, where bus 135 runs to Costa da Caparica town (€3.25, 20 minutes, every 30 to 60 minutes).

Those who prefer to cycle can do a bike-ferry-bike combo from Lisbon. Take the bike path along the Tejo out to Belém, board the ferry to Trafaria, and continue another 3km by bike from there along a bike path to Costa da Caparica.

Getting Around

The **train** (adult/child €7.50/3 return, cheaper if you go a shorter distance) along the beach runs every half-hour from 9am to 7.30pm departing from Praia Nova (Praia da Saúde) and making more than a dozen stops before reaching Fonte da Telha, about 1km before the end of the county beach. The town is also ideal for biking.

Aldeia do Meco

This tiny village, 12km northwest of Sesimbra, is famous for its seafood restaurants.

Praia do Meco is an unspoilt sweep of golden sand, flanked by low-rise cliffs; try to catch one of its mesmerising sunsets.

In a quiet wooded setting 1.4km north of the village, big, fairly modern, whitewashed **Country House** (964 072 470; www.countryhouse-meco.com; Rua Alto da Carona 34, Alfarim; d €50, 2-/4-person apt €65/85;) offers four spacious rooms (with coffeemakers and fridge) and three apartments, most with balconies. It's located 2km from the beach and is well signposted.

Beachfront **Bar do Peixe** (212 684 732; Praia do Meco; fish per kg €40-55; 10.30am-7pm Mon-Thu, to 11pm Fri-Sun), north of Praia das Bicas, has a chilled vibe and a sea-facing terrace. It serves good grilled fish and refreshing carafes of white-wine sangria. Other top restaurants are scattered throughout the village, particularly on the main street Rua do Comércio.

Transportes Sul do Tejo (707 508 509; www.tsuldotejo.pt; Praça de Espanha) buses 223 and 231 run from Sesimbra to Aldeia do Meco (€2.30, 25 minutes, four to eight daily).

Cabo Espichel

At strange, bleak Cabo Espichel, frighteningly tall cliffs – some met by swaths of beach – plunge into piercing blue sea. The only buildings on the cape are a huge church, the 18th-century **Nossa Senhõra do Cabo**, flanked by two arms of desolately empty pilgrims' lodges, and the 1790 lighthouse.

It's easy to see why Wim Wenders used this windswept spot, with its lonely, brooding atmosphere, as a location when he was filming *A Lisbon Story*. It's worth your while trying to catch the Cabo Espichel Festival (p145) if you are visiting in September.

Transportes Sul do Tejo (p144) buses 201 and 205 to Cabo Espichel run direct from Sesimbra (€2.45, 25 minutes, two daily), while more frequent buses terminate at the village of Azóia (€2.35, 10 daily Monday to Saturday, six Sunday), about 3km before the cape.

DINO PAWS

Step back 150 million years while hunting for the footprints of dinosaurs on the craggy limestone cliffs just north of Cabo Espichel. The clearly visible imprints are near the small cove of Praia dos Lagosteiros. Rare and remarkably well preserved, the tracks date to the Late Jurassic age when this area was the stomping ground of four-legged, long-necked, herbivorous sauropods. Apparently, they were first discovered in the 13th century by fishermen who believed they were made by a giant mule that carried Our Lady of the Cape. Kids and dinosaur fans should take a short ramble to see how many footprints they can find.

Sesimbra

POP 35,000

As well as fine sands, turquoise waters and a Moorish castle slung high above the centre, this former fishing village offers excellent seafood in its waterfront restaurants.

Though the beach gets packed in summer, the town has kept its low-key charm with narrow lanes lined with terracotta-roofed houses, outdoor cafes and a palm-fringed promenade for lazy ambles. Cruises, guided hikes and scuba-diving activities here include trips to Cabo Espichel, where dinosaurs once roamed. It's 30km southwest of Setúbal, sheltering under the Serra da Arrábida at the western edge of the beautiful Parque Natural da Arrábida.

Sights

Castelo CASTLE

(7am-8pm summer, to 7pm winter) FREE For sweeping views over dale and coast, roam the snaking ramparts of the Moorish castle, rising 200m above Sesimbra. It was taken by Dom Afonso Henriques in the 12th century, retaken by the Moors, then snatched back by Christians under Dom Sancho I.

The ruins harbour the 18th-century, chalk-white **Igreja Santa Maria do Castelo**; step inside to admire its heavy gold altar and exquisite blue-and-white *azulejos*. The shady castle grounds are ideal for picnics and a few small historical exhibitions on history offer brief distractions. To get here from town, any outbound bus can drop you at the start of the pedestrian path, a 1km walk up to Castelo.

Fortaleza de Santiago CASTLE
(9.30am-8pm, to midnight summer) FREE In the town centre, the grandest castle on the sand is 17th-century Fortaleza de Santiago, once part of Portugal's coastal defences and the summertime retreat of Portuguese kings. It was reopened to much fanfare in 2014 and now includes a stunning cafe, a new maritime museum, tourist information and the renovated governor's quarters. Audio tours are available for €3.

Activities

Sesimbra is a great place to get into the outdoors with a backyard full of cliffs for climbing, clear water for scuba diving, Atlantic waves for windsurfing, and kilometers of unspoiled coastal trails for hiking and cycling. Adrenaline junkies get their thrills with vigorous pursuits from canyoning to rappelling.

Vertente Natural ADVENTURE SPORTS
(210 848 919; www.vertentenatural.com; Porto de Abrigo 6; tours from €20; 10am-7pm Jun-Sep) An eco-aware, one-stop shop for adventure sports, this Sesimbra-based outfitter offers trekking, canyoning, canoeing, diving and rappelling. The summer office is seasonal, but activities are offered year-round from its headquarters in the village of Almoinha, 4km north of Sesimbra.

Anthia Diving Center DIVING
(965 225 787; www.anthiadivingcenter.com; Porto de Abrigo, Loja 1; single dive incl equipment €45, tours from €35; 9am-6pm) This friendly, highly recommended SSI-affiliated dive centre has legions of fans and is open year-round. In addition to diving, it offers dolphin tours from April to October.

Aquarama CRUISE
(965 263 157; www.aquarama.com.pt; Av dos Náufragos; adult/child from €20/12; Jun-Sep) Runs at least one trip per day to Cabo Espichel on a glass-bottomed partially submerged boat. Buy tickets at the office or on the boat.

SSB Surf Academy SURFING
(917 027 327; www.ssbsurfacademy.com; Rua Cândido dos Reis 8; intro lesson €20, 4 lessons €60) Offers lessons and board hire, which runs €12 for two hours or €27 for the day.

Festivals & Events

Senhor Jesus das Chagas RELIGIOUS
(4 May) On 4 May, a procession stops twice to bless the land and four times to bless the sea, carrying an image of Christ that is said to have appeared on the beach in the 16th century (usually kept in Misericórdia church).

Cabo Espichel Festival RELIGIOUS
(Sep) Spectacularly set, this festival celebrates an alleged apparition of the Virgin Mary during the 15th century; an image of the Virgin is carried through the parishes, ending at the Cape. It takes place on the last Sunday in September.

Sleeping

A Bela Piscosa GUESTHOUSE €
(210 897 821; www.abelapiscosa.com; Travessa Xavier da Silva 2, 4, 6; s/d with shared bathroom €25/40, d €60;) This budget find in the centre of the action is bursting with personality – brace yourself for blinding colour schemes – and it was all dreamed up by the friendly family who turned a dilapidated old house into the whimsical life of the party. Rooms 8, 9 and the attic boast sea views, and bathrooms are modern and clean. No breakfast.

Quinta do Rio RURAL INN €
(212 189 343; www.estalagemquintadorio.com; Alto das Vinhas; s/d from €40/50; May-Nov;) Nestled among orange groves and vineyards, this converted *quinta* (estate), 7km from Sesimbra, is a calm hideaway with mostly light, spacious rooms and mountain views. It's a bit run-down, but families will enjoy the minigolf at any rate.

Forte do Cavalo CAMPGROUND €
(212 288 508; www.cm-sesimbra.pt; Parque Municipal de Campismo, Forte do Cavalo; campsites per adult/tent/car €3.55/5.25/2.35; closed 5 Jan-1 Feb;) Camp under the pines at this hilltop municipal site, 1km west of town. It has sea views, a restaurant as well as a kids' playground.

Sana Sesimbra HOTEL €€€
(212 289 000; www.sesimbra.sanahotels.com; Av 25 de Abril 11; d with/without sea view €210/160, ste from €270; P) Overlooking the sea, the modern Sana has attractive violet-trimmed rooms with big windows that overlook the ocean or the town and hills beyond (it's worth paying an extra €50 for the sea views). The newly renovated rooftop pool, bar and hot tub add to the appeal – and it's worth stopping for a drink even if you don't stay here.

It's in a good central location, a short stroll east of Fortaleza de Santiago.

WORTH A TRIP

PARQUE NATURAL DA ARRÁBIDA

Thickly green, hilly and edged by gleaming, clean, golden beaches and chiselled cliffs, the Parque Natural da Arrábida stretches along the southeastern coast of the Setúbal Peninsula from Setúbal to Sesimbra. Covering the 35km-long Serra da Arrábida mountain ridge, this is a protected area rich in Mediterranean plants, from olive, pistachio and strawberry to lavender, thyme and chamomile, with attendant butterflies, beetles and birds (especially birds of prey such as eagles and kestrels), and 70 types of seaweed. Its pine-brushed hills are also home to deer and wild boar.

Highlights of Parque Natural da Arrábida are the long, golden beaches of windsurfer hotspot **Figueirinha** and the sheltered bay of **Galapo**. Most stunning of all is **Portinho da Arrábida** with fine sand, azure waters and a small 17th-century fort built to protect the monks from Barbary pirates.

Local honey is delicious, especially that produced in the gardens of the whitewashed, red-roofed **Convento da Arrábida** (212 197 620; arrabida@foriente.pt; admission €5; Wed-Sun), a 16th-century former monastery overlooking the sea just north of Portinho (call ahead to schedule a visit). Another famous product is Azeitão ewe's cheese, with a characteristic flavour that owes much to lush Arrábida pastures and a variety of thistle used in the curdling process.

Public transport through the middle of the park is nonexistent; some buses serve the beach from July to September (around four daily to Figueirinha).

Your best option is to rent a car or motorcycle, or take an organised trip by jeep and/or boat. Be warned: parking is tricky near the beaches, even in low season.

Eating

Sea-foodies are in heaven in Sesimbra. Here, what swims in the Atlantic in the morning, lands on plates by midday. Check out the fish restaurants by the waterfront just east of the fort.

Isaías SEAFOOD €

(914 574 373; Rua Coronel Barreto 2; mains €7-10; noon-3.30pm & 7-10pm Mon-Sat;) No menu, no frills, just *the* tastiest grilled fish and cheapest plonk in town at this *tasca* run with love and prowess by Senhor Isaías, his son Carlos and chip-maven Maria. Sole, sardines, swordfish (your boneless choice) – it's all uniformly delicious. Simple perfection.

Casa Mateus SEAFOOD €€

(963 650 939; www.casamateus.pt; Largo Anselmo Braamcamp 4; mains €11-16; noon-4pm & 7-11pm;) Upgrade from ubiquitous grilled fish at this cosy dining room drenched in hardwood and old stone. Husband and wife team Mateus and Cristina do wonderful things with seafood – our stone bass with bacon, clams and sweet potatoes was stunning, but order envy will abound over the seafood rice and the razor clams with lemon, olive oil and cilantro!

Ribamar SEAFOOD €€€

(212 234 853; www.restauranteribamar.pt; Av dos Náufragos 29; mains for 2 €32-46; noon-4pm & 7-11pm) One of Sesimbra's best, this sleek restaurant faces the beach. Feast away on large seafood platters for two. Choosing a bottle from the long wine list is quite a challenge.

Information

The helpful **tourist office** (212 288 540; www.visitsesimbra.pt; Fortaleza de Santiago; 9.30am-6pm) is located inside Fortaleza de Santiago.

Getting There & Away

There are numerous buses operated by **Transportes Sul do Tejo** (www.tsuldotejo.pt; Av da Liberdade) leaving from Lisbon's Praça de Espanha (€4.30, 60 to 90 minutes); from Setúbal (€3.60, 45 minutes); and from Cacilhas (€3.85, around one hour). There are less-frequent runs to Cabo Espichel (€2.45, 25 minutes, two daily) and the village of Azóia (€2.35, 20 minutes), about 3km before the cape, from Sesimbra.

The bus terminal is a straight-shot 250m north of the Fortaleza on Av da Liberdade.

You can hire bikes or scooters from **Badger** (212 686 001; Av 25 de Abril; bike per hour/full day €2.50/15; 8am-1pm & 2.30pm-midnight summer, to 7pm winter), near the Sana Sesimbra hotel.

Setúbal

POP 114,000

The thriving port town of Setúbal (*shtoo-bahl*) makes a terrific base for exploring the region's natural assets. Top of the must-do list is a cruise to the marshy wetlands of the Sado estuary, the splashy playground of bottlenose dolphins, flocks of white storks (spring and summer), and wintering flamingos that make the water fizz like pink champagne. You can hike or bike along the dramatic, pine-brushed coastline of Parque Natural da Arrábida, or simply soak up rays on nearby sandy beaches.

Back in town, it's worth taking a stroll through the squares in the pedestrianised old town and clambering up to the hilltop fortress for views over the estuary. The fish reeled the Romans to Setúbal in 412, so it's no surprise that seafood here is delicious. On Avenida Luísa Todi, locals happily while away hours polishing off enormous platters of *choco frito* and carafes of white wine.

Sights

Reserva Natural do Estuário do Sado NATURE RESERVE
(www.icnf.pt) FREE This natural reserve protects the Sado Estuary, a biologically rich area of wetlands extending east and south of Setúbal. With more than 250 avian species, this is a prime spot for birdwatching. The little-visited **Moinho de Maré das Mouriscas** (265 783 090; 9.30am-7.30pm Wed-Sun Apr-Sep, 10am-6pm Oct-Mar) FREE, 8km east of Setúbal, has short walking trails and a bird observatory across the mudflats.

It's set beside a former tide mill built in 1601, which also houses a gallery and cafe. You'll need a car to get here. Stop in the Municipal Turismo (p151) for exact directions.

Casa da Cultura CULTURAL CENTRE
(265 236 168; www.casadacultura-setubal.pt; Rua de Trás da Guarda 26; 10am-midnight Tue-Thu, to 1am Fri-Sat, to 10pm Sun) FREE This newish art space has a packed calendar. Wander through exhibitions on the main floor, or stop in for an evening concert of jazz, classical quartets and world music. The cinema upstairs has a mix of European art-house fare, children's films and documentaries.

Prices are reasonable: exhibitions are free; films and concerts range from free to €7. Stop in the **Cafe das Artes** for a drink and to see what's on.

Igreja de Jesus CHURCH
(Praça Miguel Bombarda; 9.30am-1pm & 2-5.30pm Tue-Sun) FREE Setúbal's architectural wonder is this sand-coloured stunner, the first known example of Manueline architecture, adorned with gargoyles and twirling turrets. Around the altar, 18th-century blue-and-white geometric *azulejos* contrast strikingly with the curling arches of the roof. Constructed in 1490, the church was designed by Diogo de Boitaca, better known for his later work on Belém's fantastical Mosteiro dos Jerónimos.

Castelo de São Filipe CASTLE
(7am-10pm) Worth the 500m schlep uphill to the west, the castle was built by Filipe I in 1590 to fend off an English attack on the invincible Armada. Converted into a *pousada* (upmarket inn) in the 1960s, its hulking ramparts afford precipitous views and its chapel is festooned in blue-and-white 18th-century *azulejos*.

At time of research, it had been shuttered for 24 months, awaiting EU funding to help fix its unstable hillside foundation.

Praça do Bocage PLAZA
All streets in the pedestrianised old town seem to lead to this mosaic-cobbled square, presided over by the arcaded pink-and-white town hall. It's a sunny spot for a wander amid the palms and fountains, or for coffee and people-watching on one of the pavement terraces.

Museu do Trabalho Michel Giacometti MUSEUM
(Largo Defensores da República; adult/child €1.50/free; 9.30am-6pm Tue-Fri, 3-6pm Sat 1 Jun-15 Sep, 9.30am-6pm Tue-Fri, 2-6pm Sat-Sun 16 Sep-31 May) How does the sardine get in the tin and 1001 other fishy mysteries are solved at this quirky, rarely visited museum, set in a former sardine-canning factory. There's also an entire 1920s grocery, transported from Lisbon wholesale.

Museu de Arqueologia e Etnografia MUSEUM
(Museum of Archaeology & Ethnography; www.maeds.amrs.pt; Av Luísa Todi 162; 9am-12.30pm & 2-5.30pm Tue-Sat) FREE This small, rambling museum showcases prehistoric, protohistoric and Roman collections as well traditional artefacts of fishing, gathering and salt exploitation, among other popular art and handicrafts.

Setúbal

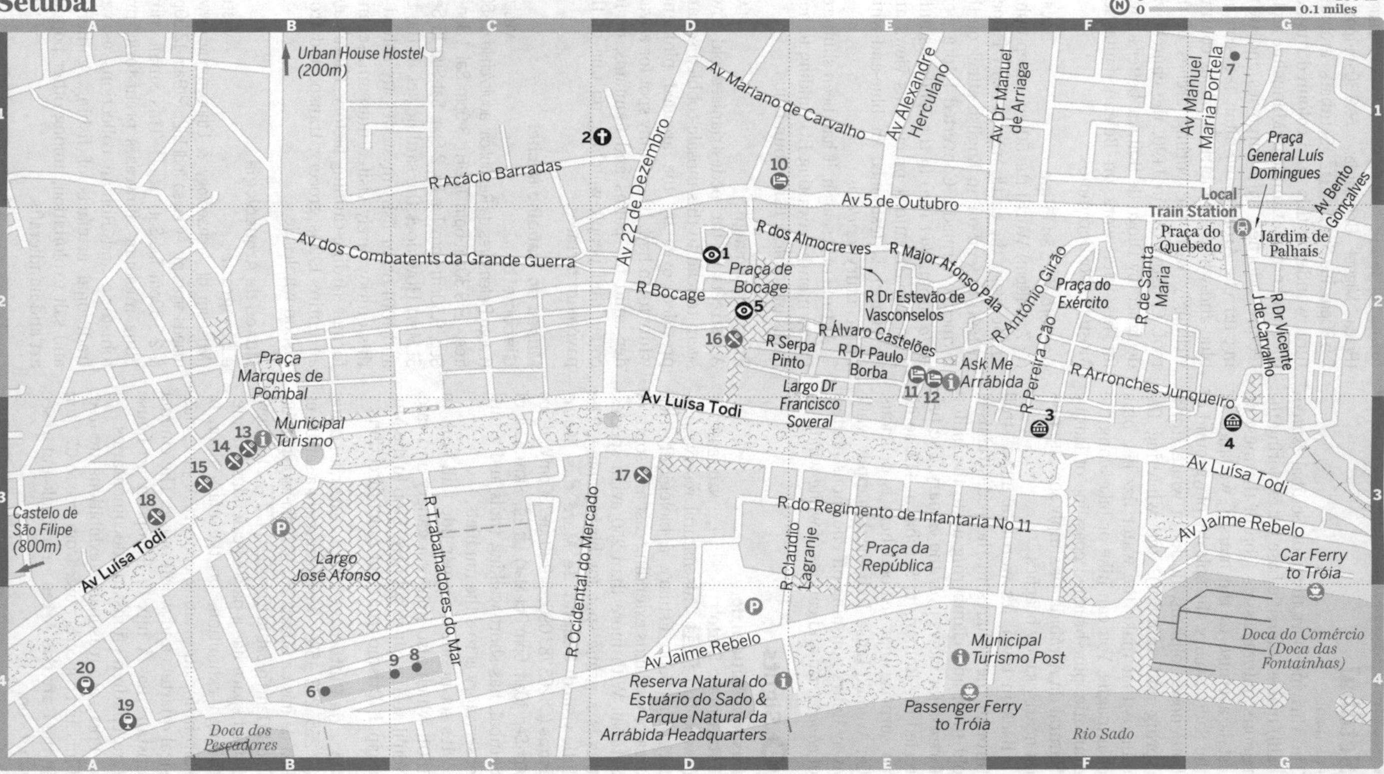
0 200 m
0 0.1 miles
Urban House Hostel (200m)
Av Mariano de Carvalho
Av Alexandre Herculano
Av Dr Manuel de Arriaga
Av Manuel Maria Portela
Praça General Luís Domingues
Av Bento Gonçalves
Local Train Station
Praça do Quebedo
Jardim de Palhais
R Acácio Barradas
Av 22 de Dezembro
Av 5 de Outubro
Av dos Combatents da Grande Guerra
R dos Almocre ves
R Major Afonso Pala
Praça de Bocage
R Bocage
R Dr Estevão de Vasconselos
R António Girão
Praça do Exército
R de Santa Maria
R Dr Vicente J de Carvalho
R Álvaro Castelões
R Serpa Pinto
R Dr Paulo Borba
Ask Me Arrábida
R Pereira Cão
R Arronches Junqueiro
Praça Marques de Pombal
Largo Dr Francisco Soveral
Av Luísa Todi
Municipal Turismo
Castelo de São Filipe (800m)
R Trabalhadores do Mar
R Ocidental do Mercado
R do Regimento de Infantaria No 11
R Cláudio Lagranje
Praça da República
Av Jaime Rebelo
Car Ferry to Tróia
Largo José Afonso
Doca do Comércio (Doca das Fontainhas)
Municipal Turismo Post
Reserva Natural do Estuário do Sado & Parque Natural da Arrábida Headquarters
Passenger Ferry to Tróia
Rio Sado
Doca dos Pescadores
1
2
3
4
5
6
7
8
9
10
11
12
13
14
15
16
17
18
19
20
A
B
C
D
E
F
G

Setúbal

Sights

1 Casa da Cultura....D2
2 Igreja de Jesus....D1
3 Museu de Arqueologia e Etnografia....F3
4 Museu do Trabalho Michel Giacometti....G3
5 Praça do Bocage....D2

Activities, Courses & Tours

6 Nautur....B4
7 Sistemas de Ar Livre....G1
8 Troiacruze....C4
9 Vertigem Azul....C4

Sleeping

10 Blue Coast Hostel....D1
11 Guest House Bocage....E2
12 Hotel Bocage....E2

Eating

13 490 Taberna STB....B3
14 Amburgaria & Pregaria Tradicional....B3
15 Baluarte da Avenida....B3
16 Delice Garden....D2
17 Mercado do Livramento....D3
18 Taifa....A3

Drinking & Nightlife

19 Absurdo....A4
20 Corktale....A4

Beaches

While Setúbal itself is a little underwhelming, the coastal scenery outside town is spectacular. Don't miss the chiselled cliffs, pine-brushed hills and picturesque beaches of Parque Natural da Arrábida.

Alternatively, it's an easy 20-minute ferry ride – look out for dolphins on the way – to **Tróia** (and its nouveau-rich playground of a marina) where the soft, sandy beaches are flanked by dunes.

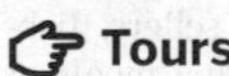

Tours

Cruises & Dolphin Watching

A highlight of any trip to Setúbal is the chance to spot resident bottlenose dolphins on a cruise of the Reserva Natural do Estuário do Sado (p147). The frolicsome fellas show off their dorsal fins to a happy-snappy crowd; listen for their high-pitched clicking. Plenty of companies run half-day trips around the estuary (leaving from Doca do Comércio, aka Doca das Fontainhas).

Vertigem Azul DOLPHIN WATCHING
(265 238 000; www.vertigemazul.com; Rua Praia da Saúde 11D; 8am-7pm) Offers sustainable three-hour dolphin-watching tours in the Sado estuary (€35).

Troiacruze BOATING
(265 228 482; www.troiacruze.com; Rua do Praia da Saúde 11; 9am-1pm & 2-5pm daily summer, Mon-Fri winter) Offers regular dolphin-spotting (€30) and summer sunset cruises; other cruises, such as a sailing galleon along the Sado estuary, are by reservation.

Nautur BOATING
(265 532 914; www.nautur.com; Rua Praia do Saúde 15E; cruises €30-55; 9am-1pm & 2-6pm Mon-Fri, 9am-1pm Sat summer, 9am-1pm & 2-6pm Mon-Fri winter) Offers a variety of cruises, starting on the Sado estuary, then visiting Arrábida beach, before returning to the river for some dolphin-spotting.

Rotas do Sal DOLPHIN WATCHING
(967 066 072; www.rotasdosal.pt; Rua dos Comediantes 9) Runs dolphin-spotting river tours (€30 per person) as well as birdwatching and other cultural tours.

Walking Tours

Sistemas de Ar Livre WALKING
(SAL; 265 227 685; www.sal.pt; Av Manuel Maria Portela 40; per person from €6; 10am Sat & Sun Sep-Jun) The ecotourism company Sistemas de Ar Livre arranges activities including three-hour guided walks in or around Setúbal, Lisboa and Alentejo.

Cycling Tours

GoPerSports (265 501 621; www.gopersports.pt; Estrada de Palmela 15; ½/full day €12/15) offers several half-day bike tours in the surrounding nature.

Wine Tours

For detailed info on all the wine producers you can visit in the area, the tourist office usually has a free leaflet from the *Rota de Vinhos Península de Setúbal*. If not, check online at www.rotavinhospsetubal.com.

José Maria da Fonseca WINE
(266 197 500; www.jmf.pt; Rua José Augusto Coelho 11, Vila Nogueira de Azeitão; visits €3; 8am-5pm) Wine lovers shouldn't miss the cellar tours of José Maria da Fonseca, the oldest Portuguese producer of table wine and Moscatel de Setúbal, in nearby Vila Nogueira de Azeitão. The winery is now run by the sixth generation of the family. Ring ahead to arrange a visit.

From Setúbal, buses leave frequently to Vila Nogueira de Azeitão (20 minutes).

Sleeping

Blue Coast Hostel HOSTEL €
(☎265 417 837; www.bluecoasthostel.com; Av 5 de Outubro 140; dm/d from €16/45;) Blue Coast has colourful dorm rooms with all kinds of surprising recycled design touches (lampshades fashioned from cake pans and wine crates) that marry nicely with atmospheric original accents such as hardwood floors and marble bathroom flooring. There's a lounge, a sociable back patio and free bikes available. Daily meals (€7.50 each) are a good place to meet other travellers.

Urban House Hostel HOSTEL €
(☎917 813 089; www.facebook.com/urbanhouse.setubal; Av Gen Daniel de Sousa 75; dm €15;) Inside a converted family home dating to the '60s a few clicks north of the centre, is this design-forward nautical-themed hostel. Friendly owner Augusto runs a tight ship. There isn't a rowdy party vibe, but it's a good bet for those looking for longer-term accommodation surrounded by a thoughtfully curated, family atmosphere.

Hotel Bocage HOTEL €
(☎265 543 080; www.hoteisbocage.com; Rua São Cristovão 14; s €25-40, d €35-80;) For the same price as more run-down budget options in the vicinity, you can sleep in this modern and clean hotel that dwarfs the others for value. It's less noisy as well, being a block back from the main road into the old town. Rooms are spread among here and their nearby **guesthouse** (☎265 543 080; www.hoteisbocage.com; Rua de José António Januário da Silva 29; s €25-40, d €35-80;), but facilities are equal. Downside: frustrating wi-fi.

Tróia Design Hotel RESORT €€€
(☎265 498 000; www.troiadesignhotel.com; Marina de Tróia, Tróia; s/d from €220/254;) From its jarring, nonlinear glass facade to its ubermodern vibe, this 236-room luxury resort is Tróia's attempt at high style. It has a vertigo-inducing glass atrium and a gigantic high-heel art installation by Joana Vasconcelos, made with pots and pans. It can feel forced, but trendsetters won't baulk at the sleek rooms with deep, free-standing bathtubs and impressive sea views.

Eating

Head to the western end of Av Luísa Todi, where al fresco restaurants serve up lip-smacking, fresh seafood. Be sure to sample local specialities such as *caldeirada,* a hearty fish stew, and *choco frito* washed down with sweet Moscatel de Setúbal wine.

Taifa THAI €
(☎265 231 642; www.facebook.com/taifa.setubal; Av Luísa Todi 558; mains €7-15; ⊙11am-2am Sun & Tue-Thu, to 4am Fri-Sat;) A nice break from seafood, Taifa is a jazzy little cafe with outdoor tables and an eclectic menu that includes fiery Thai curries from a Bangladeshi chef, Belgian beers and fragrant gin and tonics. The soundtrack is equally diverse, encompassing blues, folk, swing, soul and salsa, and there's live music at least twice a month. Reserve ahead on weekends.

Amburgaria & Pregaria Tradicional SANDWICHES €
(www.facebook.com/amburgariaepregaria; Av Luísa Todi 510; items €7.50-9.70; ⊙noon-3pm & 7-11pm Tue-Sun;) Trendiness meets country kitsch at this restaurant for burgers and *pregos* (traditional Portuguese steak sandwiches). Popular burgers include *caco* (with garlic butter, cheddar and a fried egg on traditional bread from Madeira); for *pregos*, try *chico fininho* (with fried onions, bacon and cheese). Excellent fries.

Delice Garden CAFE €
(www.facebook.com/delicegarden; Praça do Bocage; mains €2-6.95; ⊙8.30am-midnight, to 7pm winter;) This cute little cafe on Praça do Bocage offers the best vantage point for optimal people-watching and Instagram-ready plaza views. It does good crepes, paninis, croissants, pitchers of sangria and other cocktails.

Mercado do Livramento MARKET €
(Av Luísa Todi; ⊙7am-2pm Wed-Sun) Amid life-size statues of vendors (fruit sellers, fishmongers etc), you can assemble a picnic at this enticing market: cheese, olives, bread, seasonal fruits and more.

★ **490 Taberna STB** PORTUGUESE €€
(☎265 109 960; Av Luísi Todi 490; mains €11-25.50; ⊙12.30-11.30pm, closed Tue;) Probably Setúbal's best restaurant, this contemporary *taberna* is where in-the-know foodies go for revamped Portuguese cuisine with a modern edge. The *bacalhau* with poached eggs will completely reformat your idea of salted cod and the pork cheeks in *moscatel*

are a rich and succulent delight with slightly charred *migas* (side dish made from leftover bread). Reservations? *Sim!*

Baluarte da Avenida SEAFOOD €€
(☎265 573 470; www.facebook.com/restaurantebaluartedaavenida; Av Luísa Todi 524; mains €8-18, fish per kg €23-50; ⌚lunch & dinner; 📶) Baluarte serves excellent fish and seafood dishes cooked to perfection without a lot of fuss. Start with local Azeitão cheese, followed by grilled fish or *caldeirada* for two, and finish with a glass of Setúbal *moscatel*. The downside: smoking is allowed inside the restaurant – quite aggravating for nonsmokers – though technically in a separate space.

Drinking & Nightlife

★Corktale WINE BAR
(www.cordtale.pt; Rua Plácido Stichini 2; wines by the glass €3-8; 📶) This wine bar is the domain of the air-traffic controller-turned-sommelier Gonçalo Patraquim, who will suss out your palate and introduce you to something brilliant from his meticulously curated inventory of 200 boutique wines by the glass (60 from Setúbal), paired with exquisite regional cheeses and tapas (€3 to €9.50).

Absurdo LOUNGE
(www.facebook.com/barabsurdo; Av José Mourinho 24; cocktails €5.50-14; ⌚4pm-midnight Tue-Thu, to 6am Fri-Sat; 📶) The trendiest spot in town is your weekend must, when the outdoor patio here rocks until sunrise. Absurdo is where you'll find Setúbal's bold and beautiful, sipping excellent cocktails while live cover/tribute bands (last Friday of the month) or DJs (every Friday and Saturday) play. One drink minimum after 10pm.

Information

Hospital São Bernardo (☎265 549 000; www.hsb-setubal.min-saude.pt; Rua Camilo Castelo Branco) Near the Praça de Touros, off Avenida Dom João II.

Multibanco (Praça do Bocage) Handy ATM.

Police Station (☎265 522 022; www.psp.pt; cnr Avs 22 de Dezembro & Luísa Todi)

TOURIST INFORMATION

Ask Me Arrábida (Regional Turismo; ☎265 009 993; www.askmelisboa.com/arrabida; Travessa Frei Gaspar 10; ⌚9.30am-12.30pm & 2-6pm Mon-Sat) Has a glass floor revealing the remains of a Roman *garum* (fish-condiment) factory.

Municipal Turismo (Casa da Baía Setúbal; ☎265 545 010; www.visitsetubal.com.pt; Av Luísa Todi 468; ⌚9am-8pm Sun-Wed, to midnight Thu-Sat 1 Jun–15 Sep 15, 9am-8pm 16 Sep–31 May) Excellent information about Setúbal and attractions in the surrounding countryside.

Municipal Turismo Post (www.visitsetubal.com.pt; Av Jaime Rebelo; ⌚10am-1pm & 2-5pm) Small municipal tourism information booth near the passenger ferry to Tróia.

Reserva Natural do Estuário do Sado & Parque Natural da Arrábida Headquarters (☎265 544 140; www.icnf.pt; Praça da República; ⌚9am-1pm & 2-6pm Mon-Fri) Stop here for information books and souvenirs.

Getting There & Away

BOAT

Passenger-only catamarans (☎265 235 101; www.atlanticferries.pt; adult/child return €6.55/4.40; 📶) to Tróia depart half-hourly to hourly every day (adult/child return €6.55/4.40) from 6.20am to 4am. **Car ferries** (☎265 235 101; www.atlanticferries.pt; car/additional passengers €14.75/3.45; 📶) (car and driver €14.75, additional passenger €3.45) run from 7.30am to 10pm. Note that car ferries, catamarans and cruises all have different departure points.

BUS

Transportes Sul do Tejo (p144) buses 561 (express) and 755 (normal) run between Setúbal and Lisbon's Praça de Espanha (€4.30, 45 to 90 minutes, at least hourly) – or bus 783 from Cacilhas (€4.10, 50 minutes, every 15 minutes Monday to Friday, every two hours Saturday and Sunday). Services drop off considerably in winter.

Setúbal's bus terminal, operated by Transportes Sul do Tejo, is 650m or so north of Praça da República.

TRAIN

From Lisbon's Sete Rios station at least six **Comboios de Portugal** (p122) IC trains run daily to Setúbal (from €9.65, one hour), with a change at Pinhal Novo. You can also catch a frequent ferry from Lisbon's Terreiro do Paço terminal to Barreiro station (€2.30, 30 minutes), from where there are cheaper, frequent *urbano* (urban) trains to Setúbal (€2.15, 30 minutes).

Getting Around

Most sights are within easy walking distance of the pedestrianised centre. The bus station is about 150m north of the centre; the main train station is 700m north of the centre. Frequent ferries shuttle across the Rio Sado to the Tróia peninsula from terminals around Doca do Comércio.

Cycling is a great way to discover the coast at your own pace. Hire a bike from **GoperSports** (p149).

Car-rental agencies include **Avis** (☎265 538 710; www.avis.com; Av Luísa Todi 96; ⌚9am-1pm & 3-7pm Mon-Fri).

The Algarve

Includes ➡

Best Places to Eat

- ➡ Vila Joya (p184)
- ➡ A Eira do Mel (p202)
- ➡ Restaurante O Barradas (p188)
- ➡ Pastelaria Chicca (p198)

Best Places to Sleep

- ➡ Casa d'Alagoa (p159)
- ➡ Pousada do Palácio de Estoi (p163)
- ➡ Tavira House Hotel (p171)
- ➡ Vila Monte (p166)
- ➡ Mareta View Boutique B&B (p202)

Why Go?

The alluring coast of the Algarve receives much exposure for its breathtaking cliffs, golden beaches, scalloped bays and sandy islands. But 'sun, surf and sand' is far from the end of the Algarve story; there's no shortage of other attractions, activities, beach bars (and discos), castles (both sand and real), diving, entertainment, fun...

Let's be frank: Portugal's premier holiday destination sold its soul to tourism in the '60s and never really looked back. Behind sections of the south coast's beachscape loom massive conglomerations of bland holiday villas and brash resorts. However, the west coast is another story – one more about nature and less about development.

Yet the coastal Algarve is a 'drop in the ocean' for any visitor. The enchanting inner Algarve boasts pretty castle towns and historic villages, cork tree– and flower-covered hillsides, birdlife, and the wonderful Via Algarviana hiking trail crossing its breadth.

When to Go

Lagos

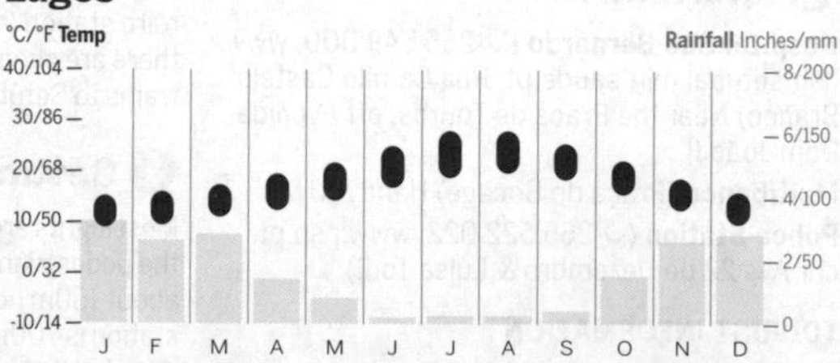

Any time The region is blessed with good weather – a mild winter, and sun almost year-round.

Feb–Mar See and smell the abundance of almond and orange blossoms.

Apr–May Hike inland amid the wild flowers and leafy hillsides or get in pre-season swims.

History

The Algarve has a long tradition of settlement. Phoenicians came first and established trading posts some 3000 years ago, followed by the Carthaginians. Next came the industrious Romans who, during their 400-year stay, grew wheat, barley and grapes and built roads and palaces. Check out the remains of Milreu, near Faro.

Then came the Visigoths and, in 711, the North African Moors. They stayed 500 years, although later Christians obliterated what they could. Many place names come from this time and are easily recognised by the article 'al' (eg Albufeira, Aljezur, Alcoutim). The Syrian Moors called the region in which they settled (east of Faro to Seville, Spain) 'al-Gharb al-Andalus' (western Andalucía), later known as 'Algarve'. Another Arabic legacy is the flat-roofed house, originally used to dry almonds, figs and corn, and to escape the night heat.

Trade, particularly in nuts and dried fruit, boomed, and Silves was the mighty Moorish capital, quite independent of the large Muslim emirate to the east.

The Reconquista (Christian reconquest) began in the early 12th century, with the wealthy Algarve the ultimate goal. Though Dom Sancho I captured Silves and territories to the west in 1189, the Moors returned. Only in the first half of the 13th century did the Portuguese claw their way back for good.

Two centuries later the Algarve had its heyday. Prince Henry the Navigator chose the appropriately end-of-the-earth Sagres as the base for his school of navigation, and had ships built and staffed in Lagos for 15th-century explorations of Africa and Asia – seafaring triumphs that turned Portugal into a major imperial power.

Dangers & Annoyances

This is Portugal's most touristed area, and petty theft is prevalent. Never leave valuables unattended in the car or on the beach.

Swimmers should be aware of coastal conditions, especially on the west coast; these include dangerous ocean currents, strong winds and sometimes fog. Check the coloured flags: chequered means the beach is unsupervised, red means don't even dip your toe in as it's currently unsafe to do so, yellow means paddle but don't swim, and green means it's safe to swim. Blue is an international symbol that means the beach is smashing – safe, clean and with good facilities.

Cliff instability is a problem, especially heading westwards from Lagos. Erosion is ongoing and serious rock falls and smaller landslides do occur. Heed the signs at the beaches and along the cliffs.

Getting Around

BUS

A good bus network runs along the Algarve coast and to Loulé. From here, you can access inland Algarve, although services become more limited. Two big bus companies, **Eva Transportes** (www.eva-bus.com) and **Rede Expressos** (www.rede-expressos.pt), zip frequently between the Algarve and elsewhere in Portugal. Smaller lines include **Renex** (www.renex.pt) and **Frota Azul** (www.frotazul-algarve.pt).

CAR

Most main towns have reliable car-hire outlets.

TRAIN

Trains run along the coast between Faro and Vila Real de Santo António, and Faro and Lagos (and Loulé). Express trains run to/from the region's main towns to Lisbon. Both the national train company and the various bus companies all have easily searchable online timetables.

Faro

POP 50,000

The Algarve's capital has a more distinctly Portuguese feel than most resort towns. Many visitors only pass through this underrated city, which is a pity, as it makes for an enjoyable stopover. It has an attractive marina, well-maintained parks and plazas, and a historic old town full of pedestrian lanes and outdoor cafes. Its student population of 8000 ensures a happening nightlife, and its theatre scene is strong. Marvellously preserved medieval quarters harbour curious museums, churches and a bone chapel. The lagoons of the Parque Natural da Ria Formosa and nearby beaches, including the islands of Ilha de Faro to the southwest and Ilha da Barreta (aka Ilha Deserta) to the south, add to Faro's allure.

INFORMATION GUIDES

Algarve Tourism has produced some excellent full-colour information guides covering the Algarve – everything from wine trips, driving routes, the best beaches and the Via Algarviana walking track, among others. These are available from tourist offices for €7 (the full-colour waterproof diving booklet is €25).

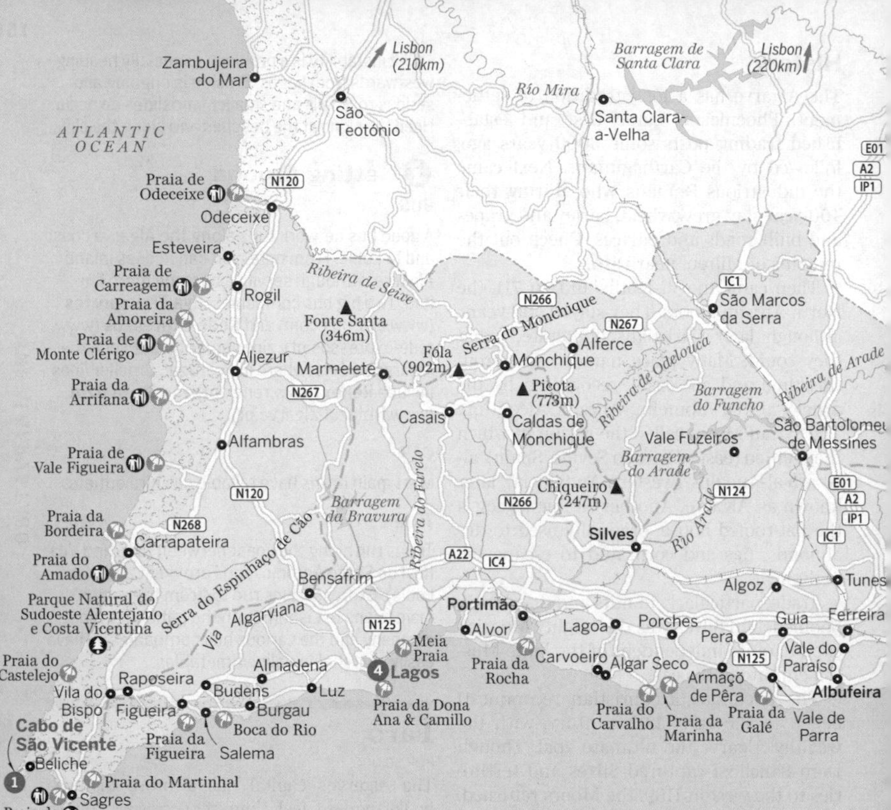

The Algarve Highlights

1 Wind your way up the stunning – and secluded – west coast, after peering over the cliffs of **Cabo de São Vicente** (p200), Portugal's most southwesterly point.

2 Lounge in waters off the untouched sand islands of **Parque Natural da Ria Formosa** (p165).

3 Explore the **Inner Algarve** on foot, by bicycle or in a car, especially the villages of **Alte and Salir** (p181) in and around the **Serra do Caldeirão** (p181).

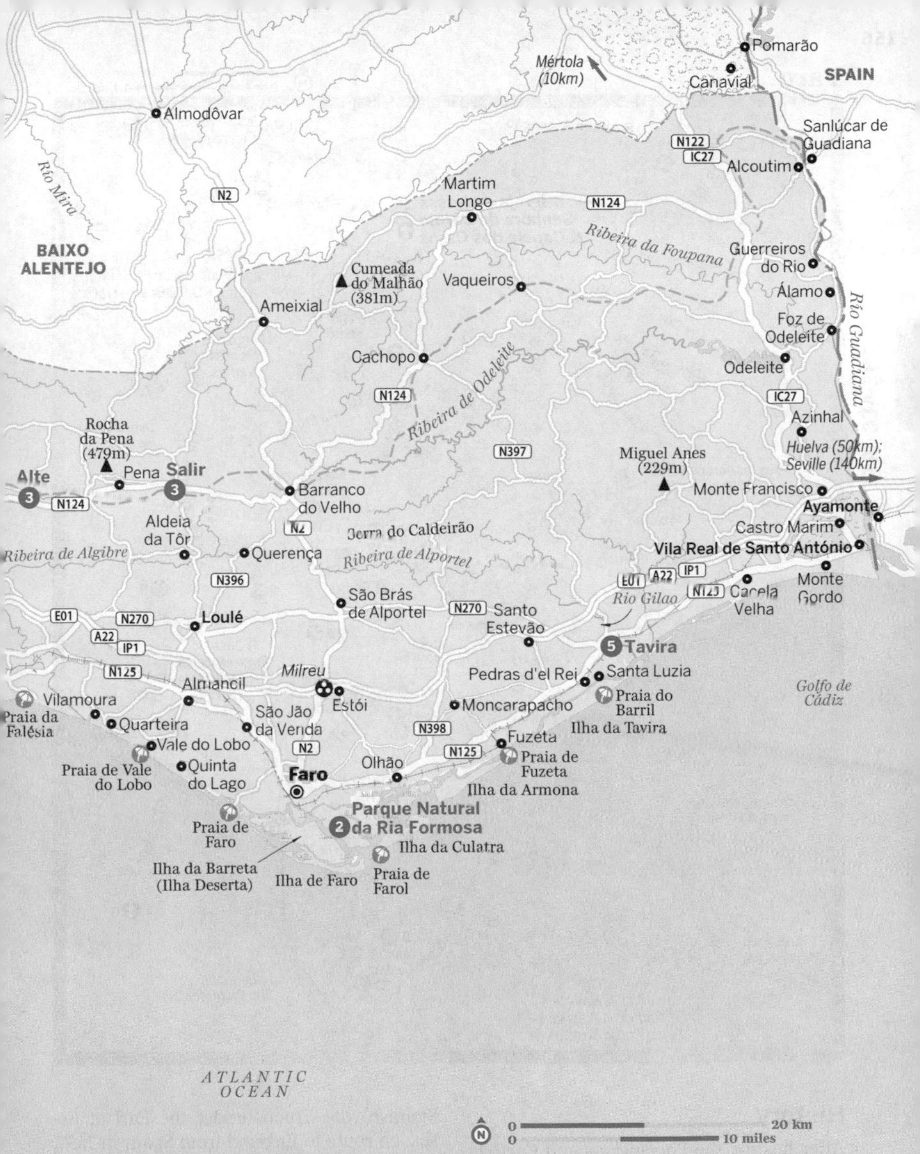

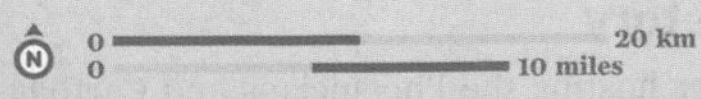

4 Find your inner hedonist at **Lagos'** (p191) beaches and nightclubs.

5 Explore **Tavira** (p167), the Algarve's most attractive town.

Faro

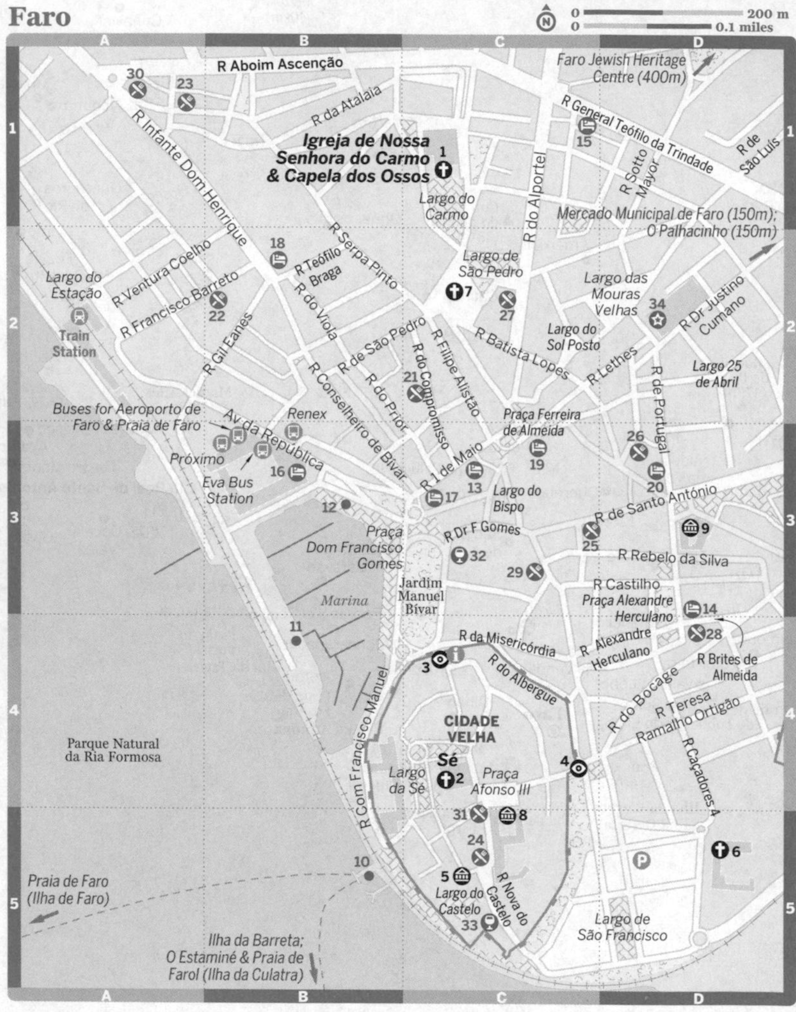

History

After hosting the Phoenicians and Carthaginians, Faro boomed as the Roman port Ossonoba. During the Moorish occupation it became the cultured capital of an 11th-century principality.

Afonso III took the town in 1249 – making it the last major Portuguese town to be recaptured from the Moors – and walled it.

Portugal's first printed works – books in Hebrew made by a Jewish printer – came from Faro in 1487.

A city from 1540, Faro had a brief golden age that ground to a halt in 1596, during Spanish rule. Troops under the Earl of Essex, en route to England from Spain in 1597, plundered the city and carried off hundreds of priceless theological works from the bishop's palace, now part of the Bodleian Library in Oxford.

Battered Faro was rebuilt, only to be shattered by an earthquake in 1722 and then almost flattened by another in 1755. Most of what you see today was built post-quake, though the historic centre largely survived. In 1834 Faro became the Algarve's capital.

Faro

Top Sights
1 Igreja de Nossa Senhora do Carmo & Capela dos Ossos....C1
2 Sé....C4

Sights
3 Arco da Vila....C4
4 Arco de Repouso....C4
5 Galeria Trem....C5
6 Igreja de São Francisco....D5
7 Igreja de São Pedro....C2
8 Museu Municipal....C5
9 Museu Regional do Algarve....D3

Activities, Courses & Tours
10 Animaris....B5
11 Formosamar....B4
12 Natura Algarve....B3

Sleeping
13 A Doca....C3
14 Casa d'Alagoa....D3
15 Hotel Dom Bernardo....C1
16 Hotel Eva....B3
17 Hotel Faro....C3
18 Hotel Sol Algarve....B2
19 Pensão Residencial Central....C3
20 Stay Hotels Faro....D3

Eating
21 A Venda....C2
22 Adega Nova....B2
23 Chefe Branco....A1
24 Faz Gostos....C5
25 Gardy....C3
26 Gengibre e Canela....D3
27 Maktostas....C2
28 Pastelaria Coelho....D4
29 Restaurante Madeirense....C3
30 Santo António Atelier de Comida....A1
31 Vila Adentro....C5

Drinking & Nightlife
32 Columbus Bar....C3
33 O Castelo....C5

Entertainment
34 Teatro Lethes....D2

Sights

Cidade Velha

Within medieval walls, the picturesque Cidade Velha (Old Town) consists of winding, peaceful cobbled streets and squares, reconstructed in a melange of styles following successive batterings – first by marauding British and then by two big earthquakes.

Arco da Vila LANDMARK

(9am-6pm) Enter the Cidade Velha through the neoclassical Arco da Vila, built by order of Bishop Francisco Gomes (Faro's answer to the Marquês de Pombal), who oversaw the city's reconstruction after the 1755 earthquake. The tower above it is accessed from within the tourist office and inside there's a small exhibition on the building; from the top you can admire the views and also the industry of the couple of storks that have built their huge nests up there.

★**Sé** CATHEDRAL

(www.paroquiasedefaro.org; Largo da Sé; adult/child €3.50/free; 10am-6.30pm Mon-Fri, 9.30am-1pm Sat Jun-Aug, slightly shorter hours Sep-May) The centrepiece of the Cidade Velha, the *sé* was completed in 1251 but heavily damaged in the 1755 earthquake. What you see now is a variety of Renaissance, Gothic and baroque features. Climb the tower for views across the walled town and estuary islands. The cathedral also houses the **Museu Capitular**, with an assortment of chalices, priestly vestments and grisly relics (including both forearms of St Boniface), and a small 18th-century shrine built of bones.

The blocky, castle-like cathedral occupies what was probably the site of a Roman temple, then a Visigoth cathedral and then a Moorish mosque. Only the tower gate and several chapels remain of the original Romanesque-Gothic exterior – the rest was obliterated in 1755. The interior has very elaborate baroque side altarpieces, and the altar itself is flanked by matching vaulted Gothic chapels. The baroque organ is worth noting.

Museu Municipal MUSEUM

(289 897 400; Praça Dom Afonso III 14; adult/student €2/1; 10am-6pm Tue-Fri, 10.30am-5pm Sat & Sun Jun-Sep, 10am-7pm Tue-Fri, 11.30am-6pm Sat & Sun Oct-May) Faro's domed 16th-century Renaissance **Convento de Nossa Senhora da Assunção**, in what was once the Jewish quarter, houses the Museu Municipal. Highlights include the 3rd-century *Mosaic of the Ocean,* found in 1976; 9th- to 13th-century domestic Islamic artefacts; and works by a notable Faro painter, Carlos Filipe Porfírio, depicting local legends. Informative pamphlets in English detail key exhibits,

including the interesting *Paths of the Roman Algarve*, an atmospheric display of monumental stones. The museum hosts regular fado (traditional song) performances.

Galeria Trem GALLERY
(www.cm-faro.pt; Rua do Trem; 12.30-7pm Tue-Sat Jun-Sep, 11.30am-6pm Tue-Sat Oct-May) FREE This attractively converted building houses temporary exhibitions by known local and international artists – painters, photographers, installation artists and sculptors. It's worth popping by to see what's on.

Arco de Repouso LANDMARK
You can leave the Cidade Velha through the medieval Arco de Repouso (Gate of Rest). Apparently Afonso III, after taking Faro from the Moors, put his feet up and heard Mass nearby. Around the gateway are some of the town walls' oldest sections – Afonso III's improvements on the Moorish defences.

Elsewhere in Faro

★Igreja de Nossa Senhora do Carmo & Capela dos Ossos CHURCH
(Largo do Carmo; €3.50; 10am-6.30pm Mon-Fri, 9.30am-1pm Sat, last admission 1hr before closing, mass 7pm Mon-Fri, 6pm Sat, 10am Sun) This twin-towered baroque church was completed in 1719 under João V. The spectacular facade was completed after the 1755 earthquake. Brazilian gold paid for it, and the interior is gilded to the extreme. The numerous cherubs seem comparatively serious and sober, no doubt contemplating the ghoulish attraction behind the church: the 19th-century Capela dos Ossos, built from the bones and skulls of over 1000 monks as a blackly reverent reminder of earthly impermanence. It's quite a sight.

Museu Regional do Algarve MUSEUM
(289 827 610; Praça da Liberdade; adult/concession €1.50/1; 10am-1.30pm & 2.30-6pm Mon-Fri) Three of the four halls at this worthwhile museum house exhibitions on rural life in the Algarve. This includes mock-ups of 19th-century shops and rooms, a real fishing boat, some impressively woven creations in wicker, bamboo and palm leaves, and lots of rag rugs and fishing nets. The fourth hall is always given over to a temporary show on a folksy local theme.

Igreja de São Francisco CHURCH
(Largo de São Francisco; mass 8.30am & 6.30pm) Features a blinding white facade, dazzling woodwork and a frenzied 18th-century baroque interior with tiles depicting the life of St Francis. Part of the monastery now houses the Algarve's tourism and hospitality school.

Igreja de São Pedro CHURCH
(Largo de São Pedro; from 9am) This tri-nave 16th-century church can be found at the southern end of Largo do Carmo. The plain exterior hides an interesting interior of 18th-century *azulejos* (hand-painted tiles) and fine-carved woodwork.

Faro Jewish Heritage Centre CEMETERY
(www.cilisboa.org/faro; Estrada da Penha; tour €3; 9am-1pm & 2-4.30pm Mon-Fri) The last vestiges of the first post-Inquisition Jewish presence in Portugal are found at the extraordinary Jewish cemetery, here which has 76 beautiful marble gravestones. The small site also has a tiny museum and recreated synagogue (complete with a reconstructed wedding). Knowledgeable caretaker António starts you off with a long-winded DVD, then gives a detailed, interesting tour. You'll find the place tucked behind the football stadium – look for the cypresses – 1km from the centre.

Beaches

The town's beach, **Praia de Faro**, with miles of sweeping sand, windsurfing operators and a few cafes, is on the Ilha de Faro, 10km away. It's crammed in July and August. Take bus 14 or 16 from Próximo bus station (€2.22, half-hourly June to August, via the airport).

Ferries go out to **Praia de Farol** (on Ilha da Culatra) and **Ilha da Barreta** (aka Ilha Deserta), a remote strip of sand just off the mainland. Here, you will find Estaminé (p161), an environmentally friendly restaurant built on boardwalks and run by solar power.

Tours

★Animaris BOATING
(918 779 155, 917 811 856; www.animaris.pt) Runs trips to Ilha da Barreta (Ilha Deserta). Boats (€10 to €15 return) leave from southeast of the marina, in front of the Cidade Velha (Old Town) walls. There's a ticket kiosk by the marina. The same company runs 1½-hour year-round boat trips (€25) through Parque Natural da Ria Formosa. Boats leave from the pier next to Arco da Porta Nova.

★Formosamar BOATING
(918 720 002; www.formosamar.com; Clube Naval, Faro Marina) This recommended outfit

genuinely embraces and promotes environmentally responsible tourism. Among the excellent tours it provides are two-hour birdwatching trips around the Parque Natural da Ria Formosa (€25), dolphin watching (€45), cycling (€37), and a two-hour small-boat trip that penetrates some of the narrower lagoon channels (€25). All trips have a minimum number of participants (usually two or three).

Formosamar also runs kayaking trips and rents out kayaks and bikes. It has departures from Olhão and Tavira, too, and various ticket offices around the Faro waterfront.

Natura Algarve BOATING
(☎918 056 674; www.natura-algarve.com; Stand 2, Avenida da República) This eco-responsible operator offers a range of mainly boating activities, from all-day tours exploring the Ria Formosa (5½ hours, €52 excluding lunch) to two-hour dolphin trips (€45), 2½-hour birdwatching trips (€35) and the popular 'Natura' trip – a 2½-hour interpretative tour covering history, traditions and the local economy. You explore the canals as well as nearby Ilha da Culatra.

Festivals & Events

Festa da Ria Formosa FOOD
(www.cm-faro.pt; late Jun-early Aug) This event held at the height of summer is one for pescatarians and seafood-lovers. Fishers and others set up stalls and prepare their wares, from crustaceans to other ocean delights. Concerts add to the fun atmosphere.

FolkFaro MUSIC
(www.folkfaro.com; mid-Aug) The city's big folk festival features lots of dance (with local and international folk groups), live music and street fests. Held at various venues around town.

Feira de Santa Iria RELIGIOUS
(www.cm-faro.pt; late Oct) Faro's biggest traditional event honours St Irene with fairground rides, stalls and entertainment. It takes place in a temporary fairground to the northeast.

Sleeping

Faro has it all, from four-star comfort to crash-pad *residenciais*. Outside high season, prices can more than halve.

★Casa d'Alagoa HOSTEL €
(☎289 813 252; www.farohostel.com; Praça Alexandre Herculano 27; dm not incl breakfast €22-30, d €80;) Housed in a renovated mansion on a pretty square, this commendable budget option has all the elements of today's sophisticated hostel: it's funky, laid-back and cool (and clean!). There's a range of spacious dorms, a great lounge and an upstairs terrace, plus a communal kitchen…but hey, why do you need it when dinner is on offer? Bike rental also available.

A Doca GUESTHOUSE €
(☎289 820 716; www.residencialadoca.com; Rua 1 de Maio 21; s/d €40/50;) This superbly run, spotless guest house does the basics well – the wi-fi is strong, the beds are comfortable and there are staff members on hand 24 hours a day. Rooms are small – the double beds fill them out – and the showers could run a little hotter in winter, but the location, near the waterfront, is superb. Handy coffee machine at reception.

Pensão Residencial Central GUESTHOUSE €
(☎289 807 291; Largo do Bispo 12; s/d not incl breakfast €40/50;) The eight rooms at this small guest house are cool and tiled, and vary in size. They come with small bathrooms and gentle courtesy from the owners. Rooms with balconies overlook the pretty

ALGARVIAN GEOGRAPHY 101

The Algarve – both along the coast and inland – comprises different areas. The coastline is 155km long and can be roughly categorised into distinct areas: the leeward coast (Sotavento), from Vila Real de Santo António to Faro, is largely fronted by a chain of sandy offshore *ilhas* (islands); the central coast, from Faro to Portimão, features the heaviest resort development; the progressively rockier windward coast (or Barlavento) from Lagos to Sagres culminates in the wind-scoured grandeur of the Cabo de São Vicente, Europe's southwesternmost corner; the Costa do Ouro (Golden Coast) borders the Costa de Sagres (Bay of Sagres), while the Costa Vicentina stretches for 110km north of Sagres and is part of the windy, wild Parque Natural do Sudoeste Alentejano e Costa Vicentina. Elsewhere, in the hilly, thickly green interior, are two high mountain ranges, the Serra de Monchique and less-visited Serra do Caldeirão.

FINDING A BED

During July and August thousands of Portuguese and foreign visitors flock to the Algarve. Faro airport – the region's main transport hub – experiences multiple daily inbound and outbound flights. During this time, most visitors have prebooked package accommodation. For the independent traveller, it can be tricky to front up and expect to find a bed with no reservation; try to reserve a night or two in advance. Prices, too, are at their highest. In most places you can expect to pay considerably less in *mais tranquilo* (quieter) times. Check hotel websites for special deals.

square; rooms at the back are quieter. Prices can drop substantially in low season.

Stay Hotels Faro HOTEL €€
(☎289 898 080; www.stayhotels.pt; Rua de Portugal 17; d €75-130; ❄ 📶) This revamped, re-branded hotel (formerly the Santa Maria) has a trendy design lobby, but the rooms are pretty standard, with the building's previous no-frills incarnation coming through in the bathrooms in particular. Breakfast is an extra €6 and there's a 24-hour bar with snacks available.

Hotel Sol Algarve HOTEL €€
(☎289 895 700; www.hotelsolalgarve.com; Rua Infante Dom Henrique 52; s/d €55/75; P ❄ 📶) This central, efficiently run hotel has bright, spick-and-span motel-style rooms, some with balconies. It's nothing special, but it will do the job and offers decent value outside of high summer. Look for deals on the website.

Hotel Dom Bernardo HOTEL €€
(☎289 889 800; www.bestwesternhoteldombernardo.com; Rua General Teófilo da Trindade 20; s/d €78/85; P ❄ 📶) The Dom Bernardo's rooms are spotless and modern, if a little '80s (although some have been renovated). Beware: it's a popular group option and normally booked solid from June to September. Free parking available. Prices are significantly reduced during low season.

Hotel Eva HOTEL €€
(☎800 8585 1234; www.hotel-eva-faro.h-rez.com; Avenida da República 1; d €88-105; P ❄ 📶 🏊) Upmarket Eva has 134 spacious, pleasant rooms, with rates varying according to whether the view from the window is of sea, marina or city. There's a rooftop swimming pool for more marina gazing and various meal plans are available for a fairly reasonable cost.

Hotel Faro HOTEL €€€
(☎289 830 830; www.hotelfaro.pt; Praça Dr Francisco Gomes 2; s/d €108/128; P ❄ 📶) We're not sure how this modern cubist block made it past the town planners, but it has comfortable, sleek rooms with large beds, marble-filled bathrooms and flat-screen TVs. The small top-floor bar-restaurant with terrace is great for a sunset cocktail and there's a small gym for sunrise workouts.

Eating

Faro's restaurants are big on seafood, though there's also plenty for those who like their food without fins and tentacles. Faro's big, daily *mercado municipal* (municipal market) is in Largo Mercado.

Chefe Branco PORTUGUESE €
(Rua de Loulé 9; mains €4.50-13.50; ⏲noon-11pm) A fabulous local spot with appealing street-side seating and a slightly tacky but cosy interior. The delightful staff serves honest, homestyle fare including rabbit, goat and seafood dishes. The half portions are the biggest this side of the Rio Tejo. Finish with an excellent Algarvian dessert.

Gengibre e Canela VEGETARIAN €
(Travessa da Mota 10; buffet €7.50; ⏲noon-3pm Mon-Sat, groups only evenings; 📶 🌿) Give the taste buds a break from meat and fish dishes and veg out (literally) at this Zen-like restaurant. The buffet changes daily; there may be vegetable lasagne, vegetarian *feijoada* (bean casserole) and tofu dishes, but there's only the occasional curry. Wine and desserts are extra.

Maktostas CAFE €
(Rua do Alportel 29; dishes €4-9; ⏲9am-2am; 📶) This worthwhile spot has an understatedly downbeat retro interior where students and Faro bohemians of all ages gather for the delicious and enormous open toasties, the daily specials or a few beers. The tree-shaded terrace out the front, looking over a peaceful square, is even better.

Pastelaria Coelho PORTUGUESE €
(Rua Brites de Almeida 2; mains €4-7; ⏲7.30am-12.30am) This has to be the most deceptive spot in Faro. It looks like a *pastelaria* (pastry and cake shop) from the outside, yet inside it morphs into a restaurant, serving up some hearty daily specials for a Portuguese song,

including tuna steaks, seafood *açorda* (stew) and roast pork. Locals rate it very highly.

Gardy PATISSERIE €
(Rua de Santo António 16; pastries €0.50-4; 8.30am-7.30pm Mon-Sat;) This is the place to head for your patisserie fix, which can be taken under brick vaulting or in the grandly columned space behind. It has a wide variety of homemade specialities but is slow to get going at breakfast time.

Mercado Municipal de Faro MARKET €
(289 897 250; www.mercadomunicipaldefaro.pt; Largo Dr Francisco Sá Carneiro; stalls 7am-3pm Mon-Sat;) Faro's impressive modern market building makes a great place to wander, people-watch, buy fresh produce, sit down on a terrace with a coffee or have lunch at one of several worthwhile eateries.

★ **A Venda** PORTUGUESE €€
(Rua Do Compromisso 60; mains €6-15; noon-11pm Tue-Sat) Sit down to a plate of honest, homestyle Portuguese food like *avó* (granny) used to make at this trendily retro backstreet place everyone's talking about. 'The Shop' has an ancient tiled floor, mismatched furniture and antique glass display cases, plus a loyal following that comes for the food and the occasional session of live music.

★ **Faz Gostos** PORTUGUESE, FRENCH €€
(289 878 422; www.fazgostos.com; Rua do Castelo 13; mains €13-19.50; noon-3pm & 7-11pm Mon-Fri, 7-11pm Sat;) Elegantly housed in the old town, this restaurant offers high-class French-influenced Portuguese cuisine in a spacious, comfortably handsome dining area. There's plenty of game, fish and meat on offer with rich and seductive sauces, and a few set menus are available.

Restaurante Madeirense MADEIRAN €€
(967 168 140; Rua 1 Dezembro 28; mains €8-17; noon-10.30pm Tue-Sun) For an exotic take on Portuguese cuisine, this small Madeiran restaurant bangs down plates loaded with specialities you'll only get on the Island of Eternal Spring. *Espada* (scabbard fish), *bolo de caco* (potato bread) and *pudim de maracuja* (maracuja pudding) are just some of the treats on offer; round things off with a poncha (sugar-cane liqueur) or sweet Madeira wine.

Estaminé SEAFOOD €€
(917 811 856; www.animaris.pt; Ilha da Barreta; mains €9-15; 10.30am-7pm Jun-Sep, 11am-5.30pm Oct-May) Like a spaceship landed on an alien planet, this remote restaurant rises up on boardwalks from the Ilha da Barreta as its sole building. It's an entirely self-sufficient operation, using 100% solar power and desalinated water. As you might expect, it specialises in fish and seafood. It has an adjoining snack bar serving cocktails.

Santo António Atelier de Comida PORTUGUESE €€
(289 802 148; www.atelierdecomida.com; Praça Largo Camões 23; mains €6-15; 8am-midnight;) Modern in design rather than cuisine, this place has a confusing entrance and an open kitchen. Trendy seating abounds, but there are few fripperies on the lengthy menu, which excels with juicy cuts of pork and delicious barbecued whole fish. Quality tastes are sometimes paired with curious presentation, but once it's in your mouth, who minds?

Vila Adentro PORTUGUESE €€
(933 052 173; www.vilaadentro.pt; Praça Dom Afonso III 17; mains €12-18; 9am-midnight) With street-side tables in old Faro and a handsome dining area decorated with bright furniture and lovely tiled panels, this conversion of a historic building has a lot going for it. Service is multilingual and well meaning, and the kitchen turns out interesting and tasty flavour combinations drawing on local traditions and inspiration from further afield.

Adega Nova PORTUGUESE €€
(289 813 433; www.restauranteadeganova.com; Rua Francisco Barreto 24; mains €7-12; noon-3pm & 5-11pm; P) Dishing up simply grilled fish and meat, this popular place has plenty of country charm, with a beamed ceiling, rustic cooking implements on display, and long, communal tables and bench seats creating one of Faro's most atmospheric dining rooms. Service is efficient.

Drinking & Nightlife

Faro's student-fuelled nightlife clusters in Rua do Prior and the surrounding alleys, with bars and clubs open most days till late, though things pick up considerably on the weekends.

★ **Columbus Bar** BAR
(www.barcolumbus.pt; Praça Dom Francisco Gomes 13; noon-4am;) Definitely the place to be, this popular central place has a street-side terrace in the heart of town and an attractive brick-vaulted interior. The bar staff

does a fine job mixing cocktails, and there's a pleasing range of spirits. Gets lively from around 11pm.

O Castelo BAR
(Rua do Castelo 11; ⏲10.30am-4am Wed-Mon winter, from 10am summer; 📶) O Castelo is all things to all people: bar, restaurant, club and performance space. Start your day here with a coffee, grab a light meal for lunch or take in sunset over a cocktail. In summer the outside morphs into a party space, and there are regular fado (traditional song) nights. Its location atop the historic old-town walls is superb.

☆ Entertainment

Teatro Lethes THEATRE
(☎289 878 908; www.actateatro.org.pt/teatro-lethes; Rua Lethes; ⏲box office 2-6pm Tue-Fri, 8-9.30pm performance days) This tiny and exquisite Italianate theatre hosts drama, music and dance performances. Adapted into a theatre in 1874 (from a building dating to 1603), it was once the Jesuit Colégio de Santiago Maior. Check its website or ask the tourist office for a list of what's on; you can buy tickets online.

ℹ Information

Turismo (www.visitalgarve.pt; Rua da Misericórdia 8; ⏲9am-1pm & 2-6pm) This efficient, busy place offers information on Faro.
Turismo de Aeroporto Internacional (☎289 818 582; ⏲8am-10pm) Based at Faro airport and one of a series of offices run by Algarve Tourism around the region; good for basic information on arrival.

ℹ Getting There & Away

AIR

TAP (Air Portugal; ☎707 205 700; www.flytap.com) has multiple daily Lisbon–Faro flights (40 minutes). There's an office at the airport. Internationally there are many flights a day to/from regional airports across the UK and Germany.

For flight enquiries call the **airport** (FAO; ☎289 800 800; www.ana.pt; 📶).

BUS

Buses arrive at and depart from **Eva bus station** (☎289 899 760; www.eva-bus.com; Av da República 5). Eva services run to Seville in Spain (€20, 3½ hours, four daily) via Huelva (€16, 2½ hours).
Renex (☎289 812 980; www.renex.pt; Avenida da República 106), located opposite the bus terminal, has express coaches to Lisbon (€20, five hours, at least hourly).
Buses for Aeroporto de Faro and Praia de Faro depart from a stop next to the bus station.

Services include the following.
Albufeira (€4.70, 1½ hours, at least hourly). Some go on to Portimão (€5.50, 1¾ hours) and Lagos (€5.90, two hours).
Loulé (€3.25, 40 minutes, at least hourly).
Olhão (€3.25, 20 minutes, every 20 minutes weekdays, every 45 minutes weekends).
São Brás de Alportel (€4.10, 40 minutes, 11 daily) via Estói (€3.25, 20 minutes).
Vila Real de Santo António (€5.50, 1¾ hours, nine daily) via Tavira (€4.60, one hour).

CAR

The most direct route from Lisbon to Faro takes about five hours. An alternative to the motorway is the often traffic-clogged N125. Tolls apply.

Faro's easiest parking is in Largo de São Francisco (free).

Major car-rental agencies are at the airport.
Auto Jardim (☎289 818 491; www.auto-jardim.com; Aeroporto de Faro)
Auto Rent (☎282 417171; www.autorent.pt; Aeroporto de Faro)
Guerin (☎289 889 445; www.guerin.pt; Aeroporto de Faro)

TRAIN

There are three direct trains from Lisbon daily (€21.20 to €22.20, 3¾ hours); 1st-class fares are slightly higher. You can also get to Porto (€41.70, six to eight hours, four daily), sometimes changing at Lisbon.

Regional services include the following.
Albufeira (€3.30, 30 minutes, hourly).
Lagos (€7.30, 1¾ hours, hourly).
Vila Real de Santo António (€5.20, 1¼ hours, hourly) via Olhão (€1.40, 10 minutes).

ℹ Getting Around

TO/FROM THE AIRPORT

Próximo (☎289 899 700; www.proximo.pt) city buses 14 and 16 run to the bus station (€2.22, 20 minutes, half-hourly June to August, slightly less frequently in low season). From here it's an easy stroll to the centre.

A taxi into town costs around €13 (20% more after 10pm and on weekends), plus around €2 for each luggage item.

BICYCLE

You can rent bikes (including kids' bikes) from Formosamar (p158; per hour/day €6/20).

BOAT

Animaris (p158) operates four ferries a day to/from Ilha da Barreta (€10 return).

TAXI

Ring for a **taxi** (☎ 289 895 795) or find one at the taxi rank outside the train station.

Milreu & Estói

POP 3650

Ten kilometres north of Faro, the Roman ruins at Milreu make a pleasant excursion when you need a break from the beaches. Several hundred metres up the road is the sleepy but attractive village of Estói, which boasts a derelict but charming 18th-century rococo palace and gardens, some of which has been renovated into a *pousada* (upmarket inn).

Sights

Milreu Ruins RUINS

(€2; ⏲9.30am-1pm & 2-6.30pm Tue-Sun May-Sep, 9am-1pm & 2-5.30pm Tue-Sun Oct-Apr) Set in beautiful countryside just outside of Estói, north of Faro, these ruins of a Roman villa are so large and grand they were originally thought to have been a town. The villa, inhabited from the 1st century AD, has the characteristic peristyle form, with a gallery of columns around a courtyard. The highlight is the temple, the fish mosaics and former central pool of which suggest that it was devoted to a water cult.

The fish mosaics in the bathing chambers (to the west of the villa's courtyard) provide a tantalising glimpse of the villa's former glory. The remains of the bathing rooms also include the *apodyterium* (changing room; note the arched niches and benches for clothes and post-bath massage) and the *frigidarium*, which had a marble basin to hold cold water for cooling off after a bath.

Other luxuries included underground heating and marble sculptures (now in Faro and Lagos museums).

In the 6th century the temple was converted into a church, and a small mausoleum was added, and in the 8th century it was converted into a mosque. In the 10th century it collapsed, possibly due to an earthquake, and the site was abandoned. In the 15th century, a farmhouse was constructed within the abandoned site (the house, much modified, is still there today).

At the entrance to the site, a small museum gives some context, including a scale model of the temple in its glory days.

Sleeping & Eating

Simple local cafes front Estói's small main square.

★Pousada do Palácio de Estoi HISTORIC HOTEL €€€

(☎ 210 407 620; www.pousadas.pt; Rua São José; r from €135; P ❄ @ ✈ ≋) This sumptuous rococo-style palace is quite a sight with its Versailles-style gardens and pink facade. Nonguests are allowed to visit its public areas: a succession of delightful rooms ending in a very tempting terrace for a drink or a light meal. The hotel rooms are spacious and comfortable, set in a modern wing.

Getting There & Away

Eva buses (p162) run from Faro to Estói, passing through Milreu (€3.25, 20 minutes, 10 daily Monday to Friday), continuing on to São Brás de Alportel. At weekends there is a skeleton service. Estói is nearly 1km from Milreu.

São Brás de Alportel

POP 10,600

Seventeen kilometres north of Faro, this quiet country town provides a welcome break from the coast. São Brás de Alportel (SBA) has few attractions in the town proper, but it's a pleasant place to stroll. There are some excellent activities in the surrounding area, including walks and a guided cork route. SBA was a hot spot in the 19th-century heyday of cork and there are still 10 prospering factories around the town. It lies in a valley in the olive-, carob-, fig- and almond-wooded Barrocal region, a lush limestone area sandwiched between the mountains and the sea.

Sights

★Museu do Traje MUSEUM

(☎ 289 840 100; www.museu-sbras.com; Rua Dr José Dias Sancho 61; €2; ⏲10am-1pm & 2-5pm Mon-Fri, 2-5pm Sat & Sun) This beautifully maintained museum, 300m east of the town square, is a labour of love for the curator and Friends of the Museum. It's housed in a former cork magnate's mansion (stunning in itself – note the original kitchen). The building displays an ever-changing exhibition of local costumes, of which there are

WORTH A TRIP

ALMANCIL

It's worth making a detour to Almancil, 13km northwest of Faro and about 6km south of Loulé, to visit the marvellous **Igreja de São Lourenço de Matos** (Church of St Lawrence; Rua da Igreja; €2; ⌚10am-1pm & 3-5pm Mon-Sat). The church was built on the site of a ruined chapel after local people, while digging a well, had implored the saint for help and then struck water.

The resulting baroque masterpiece, which was built by fraternal master-team Antão and Manuel Borges, is smothered in *azulejos* (hand-painted tiles) – even the ceiling is covered in them. The walls depict scenes from the life of the saint. In the earthquake of 1755, only five tiles fell from the roof.

Buses between Albufeira (40 minutes) and Loulé (15 minutes) stop in Almancil.

15,000 in the museum store – it's Portugal's second-largest collection.

Igreja Matriz CHURCH
(Largo do Igreja) You'd be lucky to find this 16th-century church open outside Mass time, but the breezy views of the orange groves and surrounding valleys are worth heading this way for. At Easter the church is the central point of the Festa das Tochas Floridas, which sees the roadway heading into the town centre covered in a carpet of flowers.

Jardim de Verbena PARK
(Rua do Matadouro; ⌚8am-8pm Apr-Sep, to 6pm Oct-Mar) FREE Below what was once a bishop's palace, this pretty garden is a shady place for a picnic. It's now dominated by the municipal swimming pool.

Centro da Calçadinha MUSEUM
(Rua do Matadouro 2; ⌚9am-5.30pm Tue-Sat) FREE This surprisingly large and empty centre has information on an ancient footpath used since Roman times. In winter you might be the day's only visitor.

Activities

Calçadinha de São Brás de Alportel WALKING
This is an ancient road constructed during Roman times, possibly linking Faro (Ossonoba) with Beja (Pax Julia). It was used by mules and shepherds until the 19th century. You can wander along two branches – one is around 100m, the other 500m. Ask for directions at the Centro da Calçadinha or tourist offices.

Cork Route WALKING
(☎918 204 977; www.algarverotas.com; short/medium/full tour €19/36/42) English-speaking guides lead a fascinating interpretative tour along a cork route that might include visiting a traditional cork factory or viewing cork stacks in the surrounding countryside, known as the *barrocal* (limestone) coastal region. Participants learn about the industry, from the extraction of cork from the trees to its production, the processes and use.

Festivals & Events

Feira da Serra FIESTA
(http://feiradaserra.cm-sbras.pt; ⌚ late Jul) This down-home country fair sells locally produced cheese and meats, cakes, wine and other belly fillers; there are also games for the kids and plenty of folkloric song and dance performances.

Sleeping

Hospedaria São Brás GUESTHOUSE €
(☎919 999 756; Rua Luís Bívar 27; s/d €35/55; ❄📶) Around the corner from the bus station (along the Loulé road), this guest house in a tiled mini-mansion is jam-packed with attractive antiques (note the gramophone), pretty *azulejos* (hand-painted tiles) and plants. The owner is delightful.

Eating

Pastelaria O Ervilha CAFE €
(Largo de São Sebastião 7; pastries from €0.75; ⌚8am-8pm Tue-Sun; 📶) In the centre of town and overlooking the square, this São Brás institution (it's been around since 1952) sells tasty pastries made on the premises as well as fresh sandwiches and the usual A–Z of Portuguese coffee.

Ysconderijo INTERNATIONAL €€
(☎289 849 520; Rua Gago 47; mains €13-19; ⌚6.30pm-1am Tue-Sat) The best place to eat in SBA is this contemporary, evenings-only almost gourmet spot near the *turismo*. The menu is an eclectic mix of flavoursome duck, lamb and seafood, kids eat for €5 a head and you can start or finish with a €4 cocktail.

Reservations are recommended in summer and you can't pay by card.

Information

Ponte de Informacão Turística (289 840 000; www.cm-sbras.pt; Rua Dr Victorino Passos Pinto 1-5; 9am-1pm & 2-5pm Mon-Fri) The municipality's tourist point is next to the municipal swimming pool.

Turismo (289 843 165; www.visitalgarve.pt; Largo de São Sebastião; 9am-12.30pm & 1-4pm Mon-Fri) Distributes maps and information on the region and town.

Getting There & Away

Buses run to/from Faro (via Estói, €4.10, 30 minutes, nine daily) and to Loulé (€3.25, 25 minutes, four weekdays). There are fewer services at weekends.

Olhão

POP 15,000

A short hop east of Faro, Olhão (pronounced *ol-yowng*) is the Algarve's biggest fishing port, with an active waterfront and pretty, bustling lanes in its old quarters. There aren't many sights, but the flat-roofed, Moorish-influenced neighbourhoods and North African feel make it a pleasant place to wander. The town's fish restaurants draw the crowds, as does the morning fish and vegetable market on Avenida 5 de Outubro, best visited on Saturday.

Olhão is also a springboard for those wishing to head out to the Parque Natural da Ria Formosa's sandy islands, Culatra and Armona, plus the park's environmental centre at Quinta de Marim. For fans of Portuguese football, until recently this small town had the Algarve's only Primeira Liga team – Olhanense.

Sights

★Parque Natural da Ria Formosa NATURE RESERVE

(www.icnf.pt) This sizeable system of lagoons and islands stretches for 60km along the Algarve coastline from west of Faro to Cacela Velha. It encloses a vast area of *sapal* (marsh), *salinas* (salt pans), creeks and dune islands. The marshes are an important area for migrating and nesting birds. You can see a huge variety of wading birds here, along with ducks, shorebirds, gulls and terns. This is the favoured nesting place of the little tern and the rare purple gallinule.

Quinta de Marim NATURE RESERVE

(www.icnf.pt; 8am-8pm Mon-Fri, 10am-8pm Sat & Sun Apr-Oct, 9am-noon & 2-5pm daily Nov-Mar) Located three kilometres east of Olhão is the beautiful 60-hectare Centro Educação Ambiental de Marim (commonly known as Quinta de Marim). A 3km trail takes you through various ecosystems – dunes, salt marshes, pine woodlands – as well as to a wildlife rescue centre and a historic water mill. Chameleons are among the local species of interest. The Parque Natural da Ria Formosa headquarters and interpretation centre is also here.

To get here, take a municipal bus to the campground (200m before the visitor centre).

Mercados Municipais MARKET

(Avenida 5 de Outubro; 7am-2pm Mon-Sat) By the water, these two noble centenarian red-brick buildings are excellent examples of industrial architecture and house picturesque traditional fruit and fish markets that are worth a look at any time but are especially appealing on a Saturday morning. A string of simple seafood eateries and cafes makes them an atmospheric spot for a bite with water views.

Beaches

Island Beaches BEACH

The island beaches that are offshore form part of the Parque Natural da Ria Formosa and make an appealing summer destination for strolling or sunbathing. Boats (€3.70 to €4.30 return) run to Armona, Culatra and Farol at least three times a day (more frequently in summer) from the quay just east of the Mercados Municipais on Avenida 5 de Outubro.

Activities

Caminho das Lendas WALKING

(Legends Rte; www.cm-olhao.pt) An interesting 300m walking route winds its way through the knot of alleyways and tiny squares just back from the seafront. Info boards relate myths and legends associated with the area.

Tours

For around €12 per hour, you can grab a ride on a traditional boat through one of several private boat operators. Formosamar (p158), based in Faro, has tours departing from Olhão.

Festivals & Events

Festival do Marisco FOOD

(www.festivaldomarisco.com; mid-Aug) This lively seafood festival features all the great Algarvian oceanic dishes, including *caldeirada* (fish stew) and *cataplana* (seafood stew). Bands playing live music add to the fun; it's one of southern Portugal's livelier festivals.

Sleeping

Camping Olhão CAMPGROUND €

(289 700 300; www.sbsi.pt; sites per adult/tent/car €4.20/3.10/3.40, family bungalows €50-80;) This large, well-equipped, shady campground is 2km east of Olhão by the train line, and pleasantly close to the nature walk at Quinta de Marim. To get here, you can catch a municipal bus from the bus station.

O Tartufo B&B €€

(289 791 218; www.otartufo.com; Sitio do Gião 41, Moncarapacho; s/d with shared bathroom €58/70, d €75-90, apt €100; mid-Apr–mid-Oct;) Enthusiastic expatriates Michelle and Theo have converted this old *quinta* (farmhouse) into eight pleasant rooms – a creative blend of traditional Moorish with a touch of contemporary hippy. The B&B is set within a lovely garden, complete with hammocks, mosaic paths and fountains. A communal kitchen is a handy addition. It's located in Moncarapacho, 4km inland from Fuzeta. Call for directions.

Pensão Bicuar GUESTHOUSE €€

(289 714 816; www.pensionbicuar.com; Rua Vasco da Gama 5; s/d €39/66;) This guest house offers a range of pleasant rooms featuring old-fashioned details and quirky idiosyncrasies that visitors enjoy. Some rooms have bathrooms, others don't. A guest kitchen, a roof terrace and a book exchange are handy inclusions. It's right in the heart of town.

★ **Vila Monte** BOUTIQUE HOTEL €€€

(289 790 790; www.vilamonte.com; Sitio dos Caliços, Moncarapacho; s/d from €100/120;) Stay in whitewashed splendour at this farmhouse boutique hotel near the village of Moncarapacho, around 8km northeast of Olhão. Traditionally fashioned rooms are all terracotta floors, white wood and cosy fabrics, while the hotel stands in 9 hectares of olive groves and orange-tree orchards. Two swimming pools, tennis courts and a superb restaurant complete the picture. Room rates are very reasonable.

Eating

Avenida 5 de Outubro has a market (p165) and is lined with seafood restaurants open for lunch and dinner (closed in between). Follow your whim – nearly all serve good *cataplanas* (seafood stews) and *xerém* (similar to polenta).

Tasca o Galo PORTUGUESE €€

(Rua a Gazeta de Olhão 7; mains €8-16; 5pm-midnight Mon-Sat) In a converted merchant's store in an alley just back from the seafront, this tiny 22-seat affair serves a brief menu of homemade dishes including *cataplana* (seafood stew) and cuttlefish. Begin with a simple €2 starter of award-winning olive oil and bread while you admire the mishmash of furniture, colourful Portuguese tablecloths and light, breezy dining room. Friendly Portuguese-Swedish owners.

Tacho à Mesa PORTUGUESE €€

(289 096 734; Rua Lavadouros 46; mains €8-15; 11am-3pm Mon-Sat, 7.30-10.30pm Tue-Sat;) The white, modern interior in this spot set back from the main drag, Avenida da República, plays host to excellent traditional cooking accompanied by a cordial welcome. With fresh produce purchased twice a day, it produces a great *cataplana* (seafood stew), super-juicy *bochechas de porco* (pork cheeks) and other Algarvian-Alentejan delights.

Sabores do Churrasco BARBECUE €€

(www.saboresdochurrasco.pt; Avenida 5 de Outubro 162; buffet €10-16; noon-4pm & 7pm-midnight;) On offer here is an authentic-as-they-come Brazilian *churrasqueira*, and an incredible all-you-can-eat carnivorous extravaganza – five kinds of grilled meat or, for an even greater protein injection, 12 kinds in one sitting.

Information

Turismo (289 713 936; www.visitalgarve.pt; Largo Sebastião Martins Mestre 6; 9am-6pm Tue-Thu, 9am-1pm & 2-6pm Fri-Mon)

Getting There & Away

BUS

Eva express buses run to Lisbon (€20, 3¾ hours, four to five daily), as do Renex services.

Buses run frequently to/from Faro (€3.25, 20 minutes).

TRAIN

Regular trains run to Faro (€1.40, 10 minutes, hourly) and east to Fuzeta (€1.40, 10 minutes) and Tavira (€2.35, 30 minutes).

Getting Around

Handy municipal buses run 'green and yellow routes' around town, including to the campground and supermarkets.

Ferry services run out to the *ilhas* from the pier at the eastern end of Jardim Patrão Joaquim Lopes.

Ilha da Armona (€3.70 return, 15 minutes) At least nine daily June to mid-September, hourly July and August, around four daily mid-September to May. The last trip back from Armona in July and August leaves at 8.30pm.

Ilha da Culatra (€3.70 return, 30 minutes) Six daily from June to September and four daily from mid-September to May.

Praia de Farol (€4.30 return, one hour) Six daily from June to September and four daily from mid-September to May.

Tavira

POP 15,100

Set on either side of the meandering Rio Gilão, Tavira is arguably the Algarve's most charming town. The ruins of a hilltop castle, an old Roman bridge and a smattering of Gothic and Renaissance churches are among its historic attractions. An enticing assortment of restaurants and guesthouses makes it an excellent base for exploring the Algarve's eastern reaches.

Tavira is ideal for wandering; the warren of cobblestone streets hides pretty, historic gardens and shady plazas. There's a small, active fishing port and a modern market. Only 3km from the coast, Tavira is the launching point for the stunning, unspoilt beaches of Ilha de Tavira.

History

The Roman settlement of Balsa was just down the road from Tavira, near Santa Luzia (3km southwest). The seven-arched bridge the Romans built at Tavira (which was then called Tabira) was an important link in the route between Baesuris (Castro Marim) and Ossonoba (Faro).

In the 8th century the Moors occupied Tavira. They built the castle, probably on the site of a Roman fortress, and two mosques. In 1242 Dom Paio Peres Correia reconquered the town. Those Moors who remained were segregated into the *mouraria* (segregated Moorish quarter) outside the town walls.

As the Portuguese port closest to the Moroccan coast, Tavira became important during the Age of Discoveries, serving as a base for expeditions to North Africa, with a hospital and supplying provisions (especially salt, wine and dried fish). Its maritime trade also expanded, with exports of salted fish, almonds, figs and wine to northern Europe. By 1520 it had become the Algarve's most populated settlement and was raised to the rank of city.

Decline began in the early 17th century when the North African campaign was abandoned and the Rio Gilão became so silted up that large boats couldn't enter the port. Things got worse when the plague struck in 1645, followed by the 1755 earthquake.

After briefly producing carpets in the late 18th century, Tavira found a more stable income in its tuna fishing and canning industry, although this too declined in the 1950s. Today, tourists have taken the place of fish as the biggest source of town income.

Sights

Old Town

Enter the old town through the **Porta de Dom Manuel**, built in 1520 when Dom Manuel I made Tavira a city. **Largo da Porta do Postigo** is by another old town gate and is in the town's Moorish quarter.

Torre da Tavira CAMERA OBSCURA

(www.torredetavira.com; Calçada da Galeria 12; adult/child €4/2; 10am-5pm Mon-Fri, to 1pm Sat Jul-Sep, 10am-5pm Mon-Fri Feb-Jun, to 4pm Oct-Jan) The Torre da Tavira, which was formerly the town's water tower (100m), houses a camera obscura. A simple but ingenious object, the camera obscura reveals a 360-degree panoramic view of Tavira, its monuments and local events, in real time – all while you are stationary.

Igreja de Santa Maria do Castelo CHURCH

(Calçada da Galeria; Mass 7.15pm Mon-Sat, 11.30am Sun) Built in Gothic style over a mosque, but rebuilt by an Italian neoclassicist following earthquake damage 500 years later, this church by the castle retains original elements – namely the main doorway,

Tavira

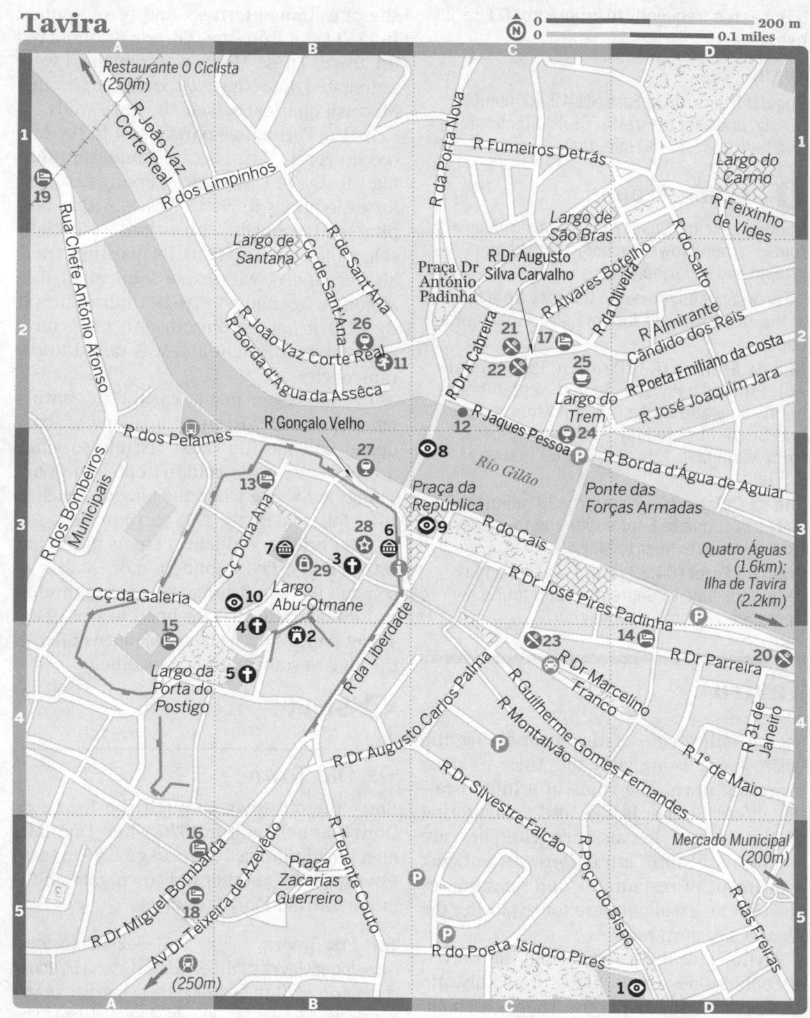

two side chapels and Arabic-style windows in the clock tower. Inside is a plaque marking the tomb of Dom Paio Peres Correia, who took the town back from the Moors, as well as those of the seven Christian knights whose killing by the Moors precipitated the final attack on Tavira.

Igreja da Misericórdia CHURCH

(Largo da Misericórdia; ⌚9.30am-1pm & 2-6pm Mon-Sat) Built in the 1540s, this church is the Algarve's most important Renaissance monument, with a magnificent carved, arched doorway. Inside, the restrained Renaissance arches contrast with the cherub-heavy baroque altar; tiled panels depict the works of mercy. Behind is a museum with a rather effeminate St John, salvers, chalices, and a hall with an interesting 18th-century applewood ceiling and elegant furniture.

Castelo CASTLE

(Largo Abu-Otmane; ⌚8am-5pm Mon-Fri, 9am-7pm Sat & Sun, to 5pm winter) FREE Tavira's ruined castle rises high and mighty above the town. Possibly dating back to Neolithic times, the structure was rebuilt by Phoeni-

Tavira

Sights
1 Biblioteca Municipal Álvaro de Campos ... D5
2 Castelo ... B4
3 Igreja da Misericórdia ... B3
4 Igreja de Santa Maria do Castelo ... B4
5 Igreja de Santiago ... B4
6 Núcleo Islâmico ... B3
7 Palácio da Galeria ... B3
8 Ponte Romana ... C3
9 Praça da República ... C3
10 Torre da Tavira ... B3

Activities, Courses & Tours
11 Abílio Bikes ... B2
12 Tourist Train ... C2

Sleeping
13 Calçada Guesthouse ... B3
14 Casa Beleza do Sul ... D4
15 Pousada Convento de Tavira ... A4
16 Pousada de Juventude Tavira ... A5
17 Residencial Lagôas ... C2
18 Tavira House Hotel ... A5
19 Tavira Inn ... A1

Eating
20 A Barquinha ... D4
21 Aquasul ... C2
22 O Tonel ... C2
23 Pastelaria Tavirense ... C4

Drinking & Nightlife
24 Pessoa's Cafe ... C3
25 Sítio Cafe ... C2
26 Tasca do Zé André ... B2
27 Tavira Lounge ... B3

Entertainment
28 Fado Com História ... B3

Shopping
29 Casa do Artesão ... B3

cians and later taken over by the Moors; most of what now stands is a 17th-century reconstruction. The interior holds a pleasantly exotic botanic garden, and the octagonal tower offers fine views over Tavira. Note that the ramparts and steps are without railings, so parents beware.

Igreja de Santiago CHURCH
(Rua Dom Paio Peres Correia; Mass 8.45am Tue & Thu, 5pm Sat) Just south of Tavira's castle is the whitewashed 17th-century Igreja de Santiago, built where a small mosque probably once stood. The area beside it was formerly the Praça da Vila, the old town square.

Palácio da Galeria MUSEUM
(281 320 540; Calçada da Galeria; adult/child €2/1, with Núcleo Islâmico €3/1.50; 10am-12.30pm & 3-6pm Tue-Sat Apr-Oct, 9am-4.30pm Nov-Mar) This elegant palace puts on a variety of exhibitions on a wide range of artistic and historical topics.

Elsewhere in Tavira

Praça da República SQUARE
For centuries this sociable town square on the riverfront served as promenade and marketplace, where slaves were traded along with fish and fruit. Today a large part of it has been remodelled as an open amphitheatre, cars squeezing between it and the cafe tables that tumble out of the square's many cafes.

Ponte Romana BRIDGE
This seven-arched bridge that loops away from Praça da República may predate the Romans but is so named because it linked the Roman road from Castro Marim to Tavira. The structure you see dates from a 17th-century reconstruction. The latest touch-up job was in 1989, after floods knocked down one of its pillars. The view upriver is one of the prettiest in the region; downriver things are spoilt a bit by the modern flyover nearer the coast.

Núcleo Islâmico MUSEUM
(Praça da República 5; adult/child €2/1, with Palácio da Galeria €3/1.50; 10am-12.30pm & 3-6pm mid-Jun–mid-Sep, 10am-4.30pm Tue-Sat mid-Sep–mid-Jun) Built around the globulous remains of an Islamic-era structure, this small 21st-century museum exhibits impressive Islamic pieces discovered in various excavations around the old town. There's a six-minute introductory video downstairs; one of the most important finds on display upstairs is the Tavira vase, an elaborate ceramic work with figures and animals around the rim. Multilingual handouts are available at reception.

The top floor of the museum is dedicated to temporary exhibitions with a local theme.

Biblioteca Municipal Álvaro de Campos LIBRARY
(www.cm-tavira.pt; Rua da Comunidade Lusíada 21; ⏲2-6.30pm Mon & Sat, 10am-6.30pm Tue-Fri) Aspiring architects and anyone who appreciates modern design should pay a visit to Tavira's municipal library, which was originally the town prison. Architect João Luís Carrilho da Graça sympathetically and cleverly converted the former prison's facade and cells into a modern, harmonious cultural space. Opened in 2006, the building houses books, exhibitions and computers.

Arraial Ferreira Neto Museum MUSEUM
(Hotel Vila Galé Albacora; ⏲9am-6pm Mar-Oct) FREE The original name of a former fishing community (between 1943 and around 1970) and now incorporated within the **Hotel Vila Galé Albacora** (☎281 380 800; www.vilagale.pt; Quatro Águas; s/d from €140/165; ⏲Mar-Oct; P❄📶🏊), the site has original buildings as well as this tiny tuna-fishing museum. It has little in the way of description but does have a diorama of the complex tuna-netting system and some impressive black-and-white photos.

Quatro Águas VILLAGE, OUTDOORS
You can walk 2km east along the river, past the fascinating, snowlike salt pans to Quatro Águas. The salt pans produce tip-top table salt and attract feeding birds in summer, including flamingos. As well as being the jumping-off point for Ilha de Tavira, the seaside hub of Quatro Águas has a couple of seafood restaurants. Buses run here in summer.

Santa Luzia VILLAGE
The fishing village of Santa Luzia is effectively a district of Tavira these days, and it's a recommended place to wander to get a feel for typical Algarve life. Overlooking the channel that separates the mainland from the Ilha de Tavira, the village is famous for its *polvo* (octopus), which you can try in several restaurants. Have a nose around the fishers' storage huts, where you'll see them mending nets. Boat trips also leave from the waterfront here.

Activities

Passeios Ria Formosa BOATING
(☎962 156 922; www.passeios-ria-formosa.com) Offers various boat trips in the Ria Formosa protected area, with departures from Santa Luzia and Cabanas near Tavira, as well as from Olhão and Fuseta. Choices range from hour-long cruises (€12.50) to all-day explorations of the offshore islands and ecosystems (€60).

Kitesurf Eolis KITESURFING
(☎962 337 285; www.kitesurfeolis.com; Centro Comercial, Shop 33, Ria Formosa 38, Cabanas de Tavira) Highly professional outfit based at Cabanas de Tavira, around 6km east of Tavira, offering kitesurfing classes and a range of other water sports.

Festivals & Events

Festa de Cidade CULTURAL
(⏲23 & 24 Jun) You can't go wrong with free sardines and that's what you'll get at Festa de Cidade, Tavira's biggest festival. Myrtle and paper flowers decorate the streets, and the dancing and festivities carry on till late.

Sleeping

★ **Pousada de Juventude Tavira** HOSTEL €
(☎281 326 731; www.pousadasjuventude.pt; Rua Dr Miguel Bombarda 36; dm €17, d €38-47; ⏲Jan-Nov; 📶) Forget the stereotypical youth hostel: this hip, modern spot is a comfortable haven for the budget traveller. It features a lovely living room decked out in a Moorish theme, spacious four-bed dorms, a fabulous kitchen and a laundry. Its ingenious design even allows for attractive hotel-style doubles. What's more, it's bang in the centre of town.

Residencial Lagôas GUESTHOUSE €
(☎281 328 243; Rua Almirante Cândido dos Reis 24; s/d €25/45; ❄📶) For those who prefer a bit more privacy than hostels provide, this is one of the few true budget options in town. It offers small (some cramped), spotless rooms, some with their own bathroom, some without. There's a plant-filled courtyard and a sunny roof terrace with views. Very cheap in the low season.

★ **Casa Beleza do Sul** APARTMENT €€
(☎960 060 906; www.casabelezadosul.com; Rua Dr Parreira 43; apt €90-120; 📶) A gorgeous historic house in central Tavira is showcased to full advantage in this beautiful conversion. The result is a cute studio and three marvellous suites of rooms, all different, with original tiled floors and modern bathrooms. All

have a kitchenette and there are numerous thoughtful touches that put this well above the ordinary. Minimum stays apply.

The roof terrace and patio make sublime spots for relaxation.

★Tavira Inn GUESTHOUSE €€
(Casa do Rio; 917 356 623; www.tavira-inn.com; Rua Chefe António Afonso 39; d €60-110;) Run by a genial owner, whose artworks and offbeat design enliven things, this is a quirky spot nestled by the train bridge and in front of the river. Comfortably rustic rooms come in two categories; the upper ones have balconies. There's a delightful saltwater pool and plenty of charm. Children are not permitted.

Calçada Guesthouse GUESTHOUSE €€
(927 710 771, 926 563 713; www.calcadaguesthouse.com; Calçada de Dona Ana 12; r not incl breakfast €85-100;) Two British expats renovated and run this stylish, centrally located spot. It has bright, homey rooms and a gorgeous roof terrace for gazing out across Tavira's rooftops. Breakfast costs €8.50, and children are welcome. Minimum stays sometimes apply.

Quinta do Caracol GUESTHOUSE €€
(281 322 475; www.quintadocaracol.com; Rua do São Pedro; s/d from €100/120;) This unpretentious, rambling 17th-century farmhouse is set in a lovely garden, despite the surrounding suburban development. Each of its apartments is uniquely kitted out with traditional Algarve furnishings and rustic artwork; all have kitchenettes. It's child- and pet-friendly.

From Tavira's train station, cross the railway and turn left at Rua de Sao Pedro. The entry is 200m further on the left – look for the blue-and-white arch.

Tavira House Hotel BOUTIQUE HOTEL €€€
(281 370 307; www.tavirahousehotel.com; Rua Dr Miguel Bombarda 47-49; d/ste €106/155;) If this boutique number were an American movie icon, she'd be Zsa Zsa Gabor. It's tastefully campish and the unique rooms beautifully incorporate the mansion's original features. Each room is named after a flower, and the design reflects this in colour and quirky touches. Oh, and there's even a tiny Roman-style dipping pool and a fabulous roof terrace.

It's virtually unmarked, so keep a look out for the house number.

Pousada Convento de Tavira HISTORIC HOTEL €€€
(210 407 680; www.pousadas.pt; Rua Dom Paio Peres Correia; d/superior d €175/210;) Located right in the historic part of town, this elegant converted convent has attractive and plush rooms – some with modern four-poster beds – a pool and a pricey restaurant. It's a stylish retreat that can offer real value in low season. Ask staff to show you the excavations that have revealed the remains of Moorish-era houses.

Quinta da Lua BOUTIQUE HOTEL €€€
(281 961 070; www.quintadalua.com.pt; Bernardinheiro, Santo Estevão; d/ste €205/275;) Peace and serenity are included in the room rates at this tranquil converted manor house set among orange groves 4km northwest of Tavira. This delightful place has eight bright and very stylish rooms set around a large saltwater swimming pool. The extensive gardens feature an outdoor lounge area. The superb breakfasts feature anything from homemade muesli to eggs.

Eating

You can take your pick of eateries along the waterfront's well-trodden taste-bud path, Rua Dr José Pires Padinha.

A couple of reasonable, slightly more upmarket restaurants are in Quatro Águas.

For tasty, alternative, off-the-beaten-track eating experiences, head to the fishing village of Santa Luzia, situated 3km southwest of Tavira. Here, *marisqueiras* (seafood restaurants) serve up the local speciality, *polvo* (octopus).

Pastelaria Tavirense DESSERTS €
(Rua Dr Marcelino Franco 17; pastries €0.50-3; 8am-midnight;) Tavira's most popular *pastelaria,* among locals at least, this unmarked place serves up all the usual custardy treats plus the full spectrum of Portuguese coffees in a busy, bright setting, painted some unfortunate shades of orange.

O Tonel PORTUGUESE €€
(963 427 612; Rua Dr Augo Silva Carvalho; mains €9.50-14; noon-3pm & 7-11pm Wed-Mon) Gourmet-style food for a decent price is the mantra at this new restaurant where traditional dishes such as codfish *cataplana* (stew) and grilled meat and seafood dominate the menu. Dishes are served with

hipster-esque imagination, though some may not appreciate their food served on slates and in jars.

A Barquinha PORTUGUESE €€
(Rua Dr José Pires Padinha 142; mains €7-13; noon-3pm & 7-10.30pm Thu-Tue) One of the better choices on this restaurant-heavy riverside street, this cluttered, narrow eatery is hospitable and cosy. A Barquinha does simple things well, with tasty salads and grilled local fish the way to go. You may have to try knocking at the door to be admitted.

Aquasul INTERNATIONAL €€
(281 325 166; Rua Dr Augo Silva Carvalho 13; mains €11-19; 6.30-10pm Tue-Sat;) You won't hear too much Portuguese spoken here, given this restaurant's popularity among foreigners and expats, but this Dutch-run place serves up some tasty international dishes in a cosy, art-and-mosaic-filled setting. The owners make an effort to source sustainably from the market.

Restaurante O Ciclista PORTUGUESE €€
(281 325 246; www.restauranteociclista.pt; Rua João Vaz Corte Real; mains €7-14, fish per kilogram €25-55; noon-3pm & 7-10pm;) Just beyond the N125 bridge, this isolated, barn-like spot stands out on its own but pulls the local crowds. Seafood here is fresh, grilled and served by the kilo, and meat dishes are also well prepared. Good value and generous portions.

Drinking & Nightlife

Bars are found throughout town; most are on the northern bank, with a couple along Rua Dr José Pires Padinha.

For a higher-velocity night, head to the *mercado municipal*, which hosts a row of dancier, pre-club bars that play music from hands-in-the-air house to African. The area buzzes in July and August.

Sítio Cafe BAR
(Largo do Trem; 8am-midnight Mon-Sat;) This is a popular local spot for a light lunch or an evening drink, and one of the few places with any atmosphere out of season. Divided into three parts – outside, light-inside and dark-inside – it has decent house wine and does tasty toasted sandwiches.

Tasca do Zé André BAR
(Rua João Vaz Corte Real 36; 10am-midnight Wed-Mon) It's a real pleasure to drop into this tiny, authentic place with its cordial boss and range of ageing liqueur bottles under the Portugal scarves behind the bar. It's great for an ice-cold *imperial* (small draught beer) or a coffee, but it also puts on good-value salads, as well as toasts and deli tapas.

Tavira Lounge BAR
(281 381 034; www.taviralounge.com; Rua Gonçalo Velho 16-18; noon-2am Mon-Sat Jun-Sep, reduced hrs Oct-May;) By day it's a cafe-restaurant, by night a cafe-bar. Whatever it is, it's cosy and a lovely place to chill over delicious tapas snacks, or to kick back with a cocktail or a smoothie. Several inviting spaces ensure a long and comfortable visit.

Pessoa's Cafe BAR
(Rua Jacques Pessoa 22; 6pm-2am) A colourful, arty place with outdoor seating on the river bank, Pessoa's has a menu of snacks, tapas and drinks. In the cooler months sit inside and admire the abstract oils that are on the walls; in the summertime take your drink outside for some south-facing sipping.

☆ Entertainment

★Fado Com História FADO
(968 774 613; www.fadocomhistoria.wix.com; Rua Damião Augo de Brito Vasconcelos 4; €5; 5 shows 10am-6pm Mon-Sat) If you've not had the pleasure of experiencing fado (traditional song) before, this comprehensive introduction is very worthwhile. It's popular and there's limited space, so try to buy your ticket a couple of hours ahead. The roughly 30-minute show begins with an interesting film about fado's roots and history, followed by three live songs with explanations in English.

Shopping

Casa do Artesão ARTS & CRAFTS
(www.asta.pt; Calçada da Galeria 11; 10am-1pm & 2-5.30pm) This handicrafts collective in the heart of the old town makes a fine spot to shop for traditional basketware, cloth, ceramics and *aguardente* (distilled fruit spirit).

Mercado Municipal MARKET
(Av Dom Manuel I; 8am-2pm Mon-Sat) This large, modern food market is near the bridge at the eastern edge of town.

WORTH A TRIP

CACELA VELHA

Enchanting, small and cobbled, Cacela Velha is a huddle of bright-bordered whitewashed cottages. The town has a pocket-sized fort, orange and olive groves, and gardens blazing with colour. It is located about 14km east of Tavira, above a gorgeous stretch of sea, with a couple of excellent cafe-restaurants, splendid views and a meandering path down to the long, white beach. Busy in summer, it's a very quiet retreat during the rest of the year.

A kilometre by road from Cacela Velha, the waterside **A Fábrica do Costa** (☎281 951 467; www.fabricadocosta.pt; Sítio da Fábrica; mains €10-17; ⏲noon-4pm & 7-10pm) has a stunning setting and a magical outlook over the bobbing boats on the estuary and to the sand island beyond. The food is predictably maritime, with good seafood-rice dishes, succulent oysters and a decent *cataplana* (seafood stew).

Unfortunately, there's no direct bus from Tavira, but Cacela Velha is located only 1km south of the N125 (2km before Vila Nova de Cacela; €1.80), which is on the Faro–Vila Real de Santo António bus route.

Information

Banks with ATMs lie around Praça da República and Rua da Liberdade.

SOS Clinic (☎281 380 660; Rua Almirante Cândido dos Reis 226; ⏲8am-midnight) Private clinic. Between midnight and 8am doors are closed, but ring in an emergency as there's an on-duty practitioner.

Turismo (☎281 322 511; www.visitalgarve.pt; Praça da República 5; ⏲9am-6pm Mon-Wed, 9am-1pm & 2-6pm Thu-Sat Sep-Jun, 9am-6pm daily Jul & Aug) Provides local and some regional information and has accommodation listings.

Getting There & Away

BUS

The **bus station** (☎281 322 546; Rua dos Pelames) has the following services:

Faro €4.30, one hour, seven daily.

Lisbon €20, up to five hours, four to five daily.

Huelva (Spain) €15, 1½ hours, twice daily.

Seville (Spain) €19, three hours, twice daily.

Vila Real de Santo António €4.30, 40 minutes, six daily.

TRAIN

Trains run daily to Faro (€3.15, 35 minutes, hourly) and Vila Real (€2.65, 30 minutes, hourly).

Getting Around

BICYCLE

Abílio Bikes (☎281 323 467; www.abiliobikes.com; Rua João Vaz Corte Real 23; city bike per day/week €7/35; ⏲9.30am-1pm & 3-7pm Mon-Sat Jun-Sep, closed Sat afternoon Oct-May) Tavira's oldest bike shop rents out all kinds of bikes. Staff members can give advice on great rides in the area.

TAXI

Taxis (☎281 325 746, 281 321 544) A reliable rank is located on Rua Dr Marcelino Franco.

TOURIST TRAIN

Tourist Train (45min tour adult/child €4/3; ⏲hourly 10am-midnight Jul & Aug, to 8pm Jun, to 7pm Sep-May) Starts from the northern side of Ponte Romana and visits the main sights.

Ilha de Tavira

Sandy islands (all part of the Parque Natural da Ria Formosa) stretch along the coast from Cacela Velha to just west of Faro, and this is one of the finest. Made up of dunes, gently shelving sand and a strip of woodland, this is the Algarve at its best, a real hideaway only reachable by boat. Beach time and swimming are obvious attractions, and you can even enjoy a camping holiday on the island.

Beaches

Ilha de Tavira BEACH

The huge beach at Ilha de Tavira's eastern end, opposite Tavira, has water sports, a **campground** (☎281 321 709; pitches per 1/2 people incl tent €12/17.50; ⏲Jun-Sep) and cafe-restaurants. Reached by ferry from Quatro Águas, 2km from Tavira, the island usually feels wonderfully remote and empty, but during July and August things get busy. A kilometre west of the jetty is an unofficial nudist area.

1

JOHN HARPER / GETTY IMAGES ©

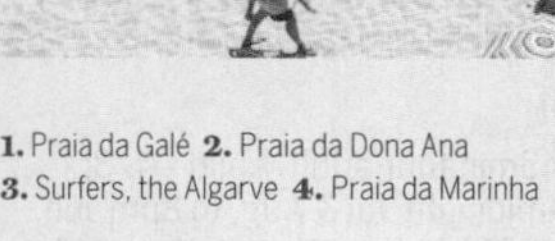

1. Praia da Galé **2.** Praia da Dona Ana
3. Surfers, the Algarve **4.** Praia da Marinha

3

2

JUAMPITER / GETTY IMAGES ©

4

Beaches of the Algarve

The Algarve's extraordinary coastline – stretching for over 150km along the Atlantic ocean – is incredibly diverse, and offers an abundance of enticing choices.

Small, secluded coves to wide stretches of rugged, dune-backed shores. Simple rock-backed nooks with calm waters (great for kids) to rugged coasts with huge swells.

The coast's varied geography changes dramatically along its length and makes for some quirky beachscapes. From Vila Real de Santo António to the tiny village of Cacela Velha, the beaches are a dune system. The central coast sees kilometres of limestone cliffs. Think eroded rock towers, and plenty of nooks and caves.

The increasingly rocky coast, from Lagos to Sagres, culminates in the wind-scoured grandeur of the Cabo de São Vicente. Here, dramatic black cliffs, bordered by beautiful sandy stretches, head north along the Costa Vicentina Natural Park. This stretch is made for serious surfers.

Top 10 Beaches of the Algarve

Our (highly subjective) picks include:

Odeceixe This beach has a river on one side and the ocean on the other.

Praia da Falésia A posh 'resort' beach backed by high ochre-hued cliffs.

Praia da Marinha Great snorkelling, with a novel entry via a long staircase.

Meia Praia Vast, popular and scenic, with options for water sports.

Praia do Barril Crown jewel of Ilha de Tavira, with an anchor cemetery.

Ilha da Barreta (Ilha Deserta) Accessed by boat through nature-filled lagoons.

Praia de Vale Figueira Long stretch of wild, little-frequented coast.

Praia da Bordeira Wild untamed beauty (with surfing).

Praia da Dona Ana & Praia do Camilo Enchanting, golden rock formations.

Praia de Vale do Lobo Has all the tourist services within reach and on tap.

Praia do Barril BEACH

(⌚ train 8.30am-10pm Jun-Sep, 9am-5pm Oct-May) From Pedras d'el Rei – a resort 4km southwest of Tavira – cross a narrow bridge to the Ilha de Tavira, then walk 1.5km, or take the miniature train, to find a glorious beach and the remnants of a fishing settlement, with a bar-restaurant and a cemetery of anchors from the former tuna-fishing fleet.

Getting There & Away

Ferries make the five-minute hop to the *ilha* (€1.80 return) from Quatro Águas, 2km southeast of Tavira. Check with the crew when the last one runs! In July and August they usually operate until midnight and can be very busy.

In addition to the local ferry, **Sequa Tours water taxi** (☎ 966 615 071; www.sequatours.com/watertaxiservice.html) operates 24 hours a day from July to mid-September, and until midnight from May to June. The fare from Quatro Águas-Tavira to the island is around €18 for five people.

A bus goes to Quatro Águas from the Tavira bus station from July to mid-September (eight daily). A taxi to Quatro Águas costs around €5.

For Praia do Barril, take a bus from Tavira to Pedras d'el Rei (10 minutes, around eight daily weekdays), from where the little train runs regularly to the beach (it runs all year, though the timetable varies out of high season).

Vila Real de Santo António

Perched on the edge of wide Rio Guadiana, low-key but pleasant Vila Real de Santo António stares across into Spanish eyes. Its small pedestrian centre is architecturally impressive: within five months in 1774, the Marquês de Pombal stamped the town with his hallmark gleaming grid pattern of streets (like Lisbon's Baixa district) after it was destroyed by floods. The town's square named in his honour – Praça Marquês de Pombal – is the lively focal point of the centre, cobbles radiating out from a statue of King Don José I, who was on the throne at the time of Pombal's efforts. The impressive fortress of Castro Marim lies just to the north and the large, sandy Monte Gordo beach is 4km away.

Sleeping

Residência Matos Pereira GUESTHOUSE €

(☎ 281 543 325; www.residenciamatospereira.com; Rua Dr Sousa Martins 57; s/d €25/40; ❄ 📶) Contained within a conspicuously green building, this family-home guest house has benevolent owners and small rooms, each of them very different, some with a terrace and very steep steps.

Villa Marquez HOTEL €€

(☎ 281 530 420; Rua Dr José Barão 61; s/d €55/70; ❄ 📶) Two streets back from the waterfront, near the bus station, this modern, yellow place has bright and airy – if a little cramped – rooms and a rooftop terrace with views over town. The best value in town, and substantially cheaper in low season.

Eating

★ **Sem Espinhas Guadiana** SEAFOOD €€

(☎ 281 544 605; www.semespinhas.net; Avenida da República 51; mains €12-23.50; ⌚ noon-10.30pm) One of four sister eateries in the area, this large, clean-cut restaurant, done out in crisp brown, white and blood-red livery, serves excellent seafood such as razor clams, shrimp and octopus with gourmet-like panache. There's a kids' play area and a huge wine selection; service, though slightly unsmiling, is efficient.

Os Arcos PORTUGUESE €€

(Avenida da República 45; mains €7-15; ⌚ lunch & dinner) Unpretentious, with rows of tables under whitewashed arches (hence the name), Os Arcos is a large eatery for holidaying Spanish and Portuguese families. There's a 50/50 split between meat and fish on the menu, and service is efficient if typically gruff.

Information

Turismo (☎ 281 544 495; Avenida Marginal, Monte Gordo) The nearest tourist office is located in Monte Gordo, 4km away.

Getting There & Away

BOAT

Ferries cross the river border every hour to whitewashed Ayamonte; buy tickets (adult/child €1.80/1.15) from the waterfront **office** (⌚ 9am-6.30pm Mon-Sat, 9.15am-5.40pm Sun). Note: there is a one-hour time difference between Portugal and Spain.

BUS

Buses (☎ 281 511 807; www.eva-bus.com) service the following destinations:

Faro €5.50, 1¾ hours, nine daily.

Lisbon €20, 4¾ hours, around nine daily.

Mértola €11, two hours, daily.

Monte Gordo €2.25, seven minutes, at least twice hourly.
Seville €18, 2½ hours, daily.
Tavira €4.30, 40 minutes, nine daily.

TRAIN

Vila Real is the eastern terminus of the Algarve line. Trains run to Faro (€5.20, 70 minutes, 13 daily), where you may or may not have to change to a connecting service to Lagos (€10.40, three hours).

Castro Marim

POP 3200

Slumbering in the shadows of a 14th-century castle, Castro Marim is a picturesque village that sees few foreign visitors. It has a quaint, tree-shaded centre, a few cafes, and impressive fortifications. These afford views across the surrounding salt pans, the bridge to Spain and the marshes of the Reserva Natural do Sapal de Castro Marim, which is famous for its flamingos. For walkers, there are some good trails around the area. It's 3km north of Vila Real de Santo António.

Sights

Castelo FORT

(€1.10; 9am-7pm Apr-Oct, to 5pm Nov-Mar) Castro Marim's huge castle has an intriguing borderland history. Much of the area was destroyed in the 1755 earthquake, but the ruins of the main fort are still impressive. Inside the wonderfully derelict castle walls stands a 14th-century church, the Igreja de Santiago, where Prince Henry the Navigator is said to have prayed. A small museum displays dusty artefacts dating back to the Iron Age. But it's the views into Spain and across the salt flats that will stick in the memory.

In the 13th century, Dom Afonso III built this castle over Moorish and Roman foundations in a dramatic and strategic position for spying on the Spanish frontier. In 1319 it became the first headquarters of the religious military order known as the Order of Christ, formerly the Knights Templar. Until they moved to Tomar in 1334, they used this castle to keep watch over the estuary of the Rio Guadiana and Spain.

Most of the grand stretch of ruins today, however, dates from the 17th century, when Dom João IV ordered the addition of vast ramparts. At the same time Forte de São Sebastião, a smaller fort (closed to the public), was built on a nearby hilltop.

A well-known medieval fair takes place in and around the castle over the last weekend in August.

Reserva Natural do Sapal de Castro Marim e Vila Real de Santo António NATURE RESERVE

(9am-12.30pm & 2-5.30pm Mon-Fri) Established in 1975, this nature reserve is Portugal's oldest, covering 20 sq km of marshland and salt pans bordering the Rio Guadiana north of Vila Real. Important winter visitors include greater flamingos, spoonbills and Caspian terns; in spring it's busy with white storks.

The park headquarters is 2km east of the N122 from a signposted turnoff 1.5km north of Castro Marim. Here there's a 500m walking trail with faded interpretative signboards.

Information

Turismo (281 531 232; Mercado Local, Rua de São Sebastião; 9am-1pm & 2-5pm) Small office housed in the the village's tiny whitewashed market building.

Getting There & Away

Buses from Vila Real run to Castro Marim (€2.25, eight minutes, eight daily) and go on to Monte Francisco, a short distance north. Weekend buses are extremely limited. If coming from the west by train, don't get off at the station called Castro Marim – it's miles from the village.

Alcoutim

POP 2900

Strategically positioned along the idyllic Rio Guadiana, Alcoutim (ahl-ko-*teeng*) is a small village just across the river from the Spanish town of Sanlúcar de Guadiana. What-are-you-looking-at fortresses above both villages remind visitors of testier times. Phoenicians, Greeks, Romans and Arabs have barricaded themselves in the hills here, and centuries of tension have bubbled across the river, which forms the Algarve's entire eastern boundary. In the 14th century, Dom Fernando I of Portugal and Don Henrique II of Castile signed a tentative peace treaty in Alcoutim. Tragically, today Alcoutim is struggling to stay on the map, its population slowly diminishing. Nevertheless, it's worth a quick visit if you're passing between the Algarve and Alentejo, even if just for the quirky riverside beach and fascinating castle and churches.

Sights

Castelo CASTLE

(€2.50; ⏱9.30am-7pm Apr-Sep, 8.30am-4.30pm Oct-Mar) The flower-ringed, 14th-century *castelo* has sweeping views. Inside the grounds is the **Núcleo Museológico de Arqueologia** (Archaeological Museum), displaying ruined medieval castle walls and other artefacts, and an exhibition on Islamic board games.

The entrance fee to the castle also includes entry to the tiny themed museums (*núcleos museológicos*) in Alcoutim and around.

Activities

Praia Fluvial BEACH

(www.cm-alcoutim.pt) The main attraction for most day trippers is this small riverside beach, equipped with sand, cafe, palm-leaf umbrellas and even a very bored lifeguard! The setting on a narrow tributary of the Rio Guadiana is lovely, but in summer it's baking hot. At the bridge, follow the signs to Praia Fluvial.

Inland Adventures BOATING

(☎922 173 183, 289 388 857; www.inland-adventures.com) This small Alcoutim-based company offers riverboat trips and bicycle tours along the Rio Guadiana and in the surrounding area.

Sleeping

Brisas do Guadiana GUESTHOUSE €

(☎967 531 064; visitaralcoutim@gmail.com; Rua do Bairro das Casas Pré-Fabricadas; s €35, d €40-45) Contrary to the odd street name ('Prefabricated Houses St'), this smart yellow place on top of the hill behind the castle offers spic-and-span rooms that are very well maintained.

Pousada da Juventude HOSTEL €

(☎281 546 004; www.pousadasjuventude.pt; dm €13, d €35-40, apt €70; ⏱reception 8am-noon & 6pm-midnight; ❄@📶🏊) On the river, 1km north of the square, past the new town, is this well-appointed hostel, a cluster of random whitewashed buildings with an excellent pool and kitchen facilities, plus bikes and canoes for rent. Look for the white dome.

Eating

O Soeiro PORTUGUESE €

(☎281 546 241; Rua do Município 4; daily specials €6.50-10.50; ⏱lunch Mon-Fri) A cheap and cheerful lunch spot, this family-run place is good for its grilled chicken, succulent steaks and occasional fresh fish, and its setting near the river.

O Camané PORTUGUESE €€

(Rua 1 de Maio; mains €8-15; ⏱lunch & dinner Wed-Mon) In the heart of things, this popular spot is bursting with a range of Algarvian and Alentejan dishes, including *porco preto* (Iberian pig) and *açorda* (bread soup). There's always a good selection of daily specials.

Information

Turismo (☎281 546 179; Rua 1 de Maio; ⏱9am-1pm & 2-6pm Tue-Sat) Located just above the riverside, this office distributes maps and other information.

Getting There & Away

Without your own wheels, Alcoutim is tricky to reach. Bus services run to/from Vila Real de Santo António (€4.25, 1¼ hours, one on Monday, Wednesday and Friday); on Monday and Friday these go to/from Beja (around €5, two hours) via Mértola (50 minutes).

Loulé

POP 26,700

One of the Algarve's largest inland towns, and only 16km northwest of Faro, Loulé (lo-*lay*) is a reasonable base from which to explore the inland Algarve. A busy commercial centre, it's a fast-growing place in which service employees live while working (or seeking work) in the Algarve. Loulé has an attractive old quarter and Moorish castle ruins, and its history goes back to the Romans. A few of Loulé's artisan traditions still survive; crafty folk toil away making wicker baskets, copperworks and embroidery in hole-in-the-wall workshops about town. Loulé's small university lends it some verve, as does its wild Carnaval and FestivalMed, an annual music festival.

Sights

Mercado Municipal MARKET

(Praça da Republica; ⏱6.30am-3pm Mon-Sat) Loulé's most impressive piece of architectural heritage is its art-nouveau market, a 1908 revivalist neo-Arab confection with four oriental-looking cupolas at the four corners and Moorish features picked out in raspberry red against cream walls. Inside it's a mix of blood-and-guts fish market, cheap cafes and local produce such as orange-blossom

Loulé

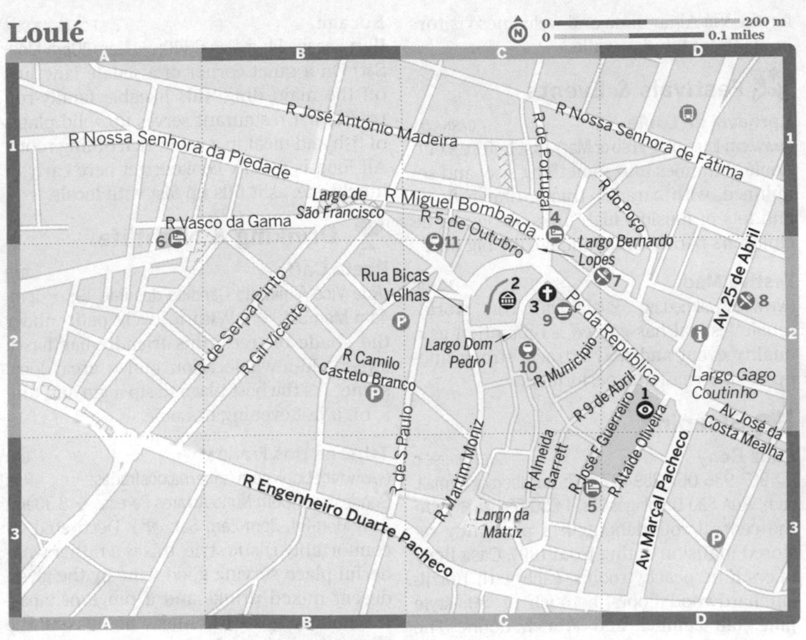

Loulé

Sights
1 Mercado Municipal D2
2 Museu Municipal C2
3 Nossa Senhora da Conceição C2

Sleeping
4 Casa Beny C1
5 Hospedaria Dom Fernando C3
6 Loulé Jardim Hotel A1

Eating
7 Bocage D2
8 O Beco D2

Drinking & Nightlife
9 Café Calcinha C2
10 Poeta Caffe C2
11 Taberna dos Frades C2

honey, fig 'cheese' (not cheese at all) and Cliff Richard's wine.

Nossa Senhora da Conceição CHAPEL
(Rua Dom Paio Peres Correia; 9.30am-5.30pm Tue-Fri, to 4pm Sat) Situated opposite Loulé's castle, and dating from the mid-17th century, the small chapel of Nossa Senhora da Conceição possesses three impressive elements: a heavily gilded baroque altar, floor-to-ceiling *azulejos* (hand-painted tiles) and a whitewashed stucco ceiling. During excavations, an Islamic door dating from the 3rd century was uncovered under the floor, where it now remains, protected by glass.

Museu Municipal MUSEUM
(Castelo; 289 400 600; www.cm-loule.pt; Largo Dom Pedro I; €1.62; 10am-6pm Tue-Fri, to 4.30pm Sat) Housed in Loulé's restored castle, the archaeology section at this museum takes it right from the beginning: *Homo erectus* kicks things off, and via dusty collections of pottery and bone we arrive at the Roman and Islamic periods. Medieval house ruins can be viewed under a glass floor, and the admission fee includes entry to a stretch of square-towered **castle walls** and the **Cozinha Tradicional Algarvia**, a re-creation of a traditional Algarve kitchen, featuring a hearth, archaic implements and burnished copper.

Activities

Almargem WALKING
(289 412 959; www.almargem.org) The environmental group Almargem is responsible

for the Via Algarviana and welcomes visitors on its (free) Sunday walks.

Festivals & Events

Carnaval de Loulé CARNAVAL
(www.cm-loule.pt; Feb or Mar) Just before Lent, Loulé shimmies into something sexy and sequinned, with parades, tractor-drawn floats and lots of musical high jinks. Friday is the children's parade and Sunday's the big one.

FestivalMed MUSIC
(www.festivalmed.pt; late Jun) This world-music festival has gained a reputation as a quality event and now attracts strong line-ups of international performers.

Sleeping

Casa Beny GUESTHOUSE €
(967 936 067, 289 417 702; casabeny.g@gmail.com; Rua São Domingos 13; d €50-55;) On the central roundabout in a pleasantly restored mansion dating from 1897, Casa Beny offers nine peachy rooms, each with Brazilian hardwood floors, a touch of '80s-style pine, tall ceilings and French doors. The rooftop terrace has castle views.

Loulé Jardim Hotel HOTEL €€
(289 413 095; www.loulejardimhotel.com; Praça Manuel D'Arriaga 25; s/d €79/99, d with terrace €109;) A late-19th-century building with spacious, tasteful, airy rooms, this well-run place overlooks a pretty square. Book ahead for a terrace. There's a small outdoor pool with sunloungers, and breakfast is a substantial affair. Prices are normally much lower than the high-season prices listed here.

Hospedaria Dom Fernando GUESTHOUSE €€
(289 415 553; Travessa do Mercado; s/d €45/65;) Despite its mere '*hospedaria*' rating, this sound choice offers simple, fairly up-to-date rooms in an excellent location behind the market. There's a great restaurant on the premises, staff members are friendly and the continental breakfast includes fresh fruit.

Eating

O Beco PORTUGUESE €
(Travessa do Beco; mains €6-10; noon-3pm & 7-9pm Mon-Sat) There's no gourmet nonsense at this Portuguese eatery, with its platters of filling meat and fish, and its striking interior of whitewashed walls, dark-timber ceiling and tiny, neatly laid tables. Hearty soup, grilled critter (with wine), custardy dessert, coffee – you're done.

Bocage PORTUGUESE €
(Rua Bocage 14; mains €6-10; 11am-10pm Mon-Sat) On a quiet corner of a sedate lane just off the main drag, this likeable family-run traditional restaurant serves up solid plates of fish and meat in a wood-rich dining room. All food is freshly cooked; get here early at lunchtime, as it fills up fast with locals.

Drinking & Nightlife

Poeta Caffe BAR
(Rua Vice Almirante Cândido dos Reis 19; 1pm-4am Mon-Sat;) With a lovely patio under the shade of trees, this friendly bar has a sweet old-town location and a great local scene. It's the best place to sip a gin and tonic on a hot evening in Loulé.

Taberna dos Frades BAR
(www.facebook.com/taberna.dosfrades; Rua Condestável Dom Nuno Alvares Pereira; 8.30am-2am Mon-Fri, 3pm-2am Sat;) Decorated in comfortably rustic style, this is a rather wonderful place serving good wine by the glass, decent mixed drinks and a range of tapas. It regularly hosts live-music nights, and the atmosphere is nearly always great.

Café Calcinha CAFE
(289 415 763; Praça da República 67;) Loulé's oldest cafe is a replica of an old Brazilian coffee shop, opened in 1928 and virtually unchanged since. Closed at the time of research, this important piece of the town's heritage is certain to reopen soon, and you'll once again be able to enjoy a brew at one of the period marble-topped tables.

Information

Turismo (289 463 900; www.visitalgarve.pt; Avenida 25 de Abril 9; 9am-6pm) Staff availability determines whether this helpful office stays open over lunchtime.

Biblioteca Municipal de Loulé (www.cm-loule.pt; Rua José Afonso; 2.30-7pm Mon, 9.30am-7pm Tue-Fri, 10am-5.30pm Sat mid-Sep–mid-Jun, 9.30am-7pm Mon-Fri mid-Jun–mid-Sep;) Library with free internet.

Getting There & Away

If you're arriving by train, note that the station is 5km southwest of town (take any Quarteira-bound bus).

Daily **bus** (289 416 655; Rua Nossa Senhora de Fátima) connections head to the following towns:

Albufeira €4.30, 55 minutes, five daily.

Faro €3.25, 40 minutes, hourly weekdays, fewer at weekends.

If you're heading to Portimão on a weekday, change at Albufeira. At weekends there are four direct buses (€5.50, 1½ hours). Express buses head to Lisbon (€20, four hours, four to five daily).

Getting Around

Parking can be tricky in Loulé – park on the edge of town.

Serra do Caldeirão

Lying around 30km north of Loulé is the wonderful region of Serra do Caldeirão, a beautiful protected area of undulating hills, cork trees and harsh scrubland. The area is renowned for its bird varieties. It's an excellent place to hike – the Via Algarviana passes through – and a great spot to base yourself to meander through some ancient villages and enjoy the local cuisine. A feature of the region is its *fontes* (traditional water sources, many of which comprise exquisite taps and fountains), highlighted by signs that have been erected over the years.

Alte & Salir

Perched on a hillside on the edge of the Serra do Caldeirão, **Alte**, located 45km northwest of Loulé, is a quaint and very pretty little village. In high season visitors are disgorged from buses for a quick-see experience. Boasting flower-filled streets, whitewashed buildings and several *fontes* (traditional water taps and streams), it's a pleasant place to wander for an hour or so. The *fontes* were traditionally used for the mills and former wells; a main *fonte*, Fonte Grande, passes through dykes, weirs and watermills. *Artesanatos* (handicrafts shops) are dotted around town, as are several restaurants and cafes.

If travelling by car, pass through the small, sleepy and attractive town of **Salir**. It's a pleasant, very authentic village set on two hills, with castle walls dating from the 12th century and an attractive church.

Sights

Fábrica de Brinquedos WORKSHOP

(Torre/Tôr; 9am-1pm Mon-Fri) The school in this hamlet near Alte had fallen into disuse because there weren't enough children. There wasn't much work around, either, so three local women decided to learn a craft and put the building to use. It's now a workshop where they make charming wooden toys, and it's a heart-warming place to visit. From Alte, head up the hill, past the Hotel Alte on the road to Santa Margarida, then take a left turn.

Pólo Museológico de Salir MUSEUM

(Largo Pedro Dias, Salir; 9am-1pm & 2-5pm Mon-Fri) FREE Within the area encompassed by what remains of Salir's ruined castle, this little museum displays local archaeological finds and offers tourist information.

Pólo Museológico Cândido Guerreiro e Condes de Alte MUSEUM

(289 478 058; Rua Condes de Alte, Alte; 12.30-3pm Mon-Fri) FREE This museum-cultural space pays homage to Alte's famous poet, Cândido Guerreiro, along with the Counts of Alte who once lived here. It displays books and paraphernalia and also offers tourist information.

Sleeping

Quinta do Coração GUESTHOUSE €

(289 489 959; www.algarveparadise.com; Carrasqueiro; s/d €35/55, self-catering studios €60, 2-person cottages €65;) The setting of this converted farmhouse in Carrasqueiro (7km east of Salir) is lovely: on a wooded hill, encircled by a eucalyptus, olive-grove and cork-tree paradise. This ain't your gleaming white-tiled experience: the rooms, studios and cottage (with kitchenette) are

> **WALKS IN THE SERRA DO CALDEIRÃO**
>
> The most worthwhile short walk in the area is to climb **Rocha da Pena**, a limestone rock between Alte and Salir, off the N124, by means of a well-signposted 4.7km circuit (follow the road signs to the mountain). A return walk takes about two to three hours. The museums in **Salir**, **Alte** and **Querença** (p182) usually stock a basic map-guide.
>
> Carry water and snacks; there's a small shop-cafe at the base and another in Pena village but no other refreshment stops for miles. Note fire-danger times – bushfires occur in this area.

rough and rustic, in a pleasant sort of way. It's on the Via Algarviana.

★B&B Candelária B&B €€
(☎969 097 399; www.casa-candelaria.com; Monte Seco; s/d/f €55/70/105; P 📶) A labour of love by the delightful multilingual owner has created an enchanting place to stay in this hill village a few kilometres north of the N270. Five petite rooms are rustic and comfortable, with thick adobe walls providing natural coolness. Upstairs are a lovely deck and a great guest kitchen-lounge area. If you can't relax here you'd better see a medic.

Quinta do Freixo FARMSTAY €€
(Casa d'Alvada; ☎289 472 185; www.quintadofreixo.org; Benafim; s/d/ste €48/65/78; P 📶) This pleasant place, a converted barn, is located on a functioning farm well known for producing traditional foodstuffs. From the pleasant communal areas you can look out to see farm animals without leaving the complex's green lawns and swimming pool. The 10 comfortable rooms feature Alentejan (painted wooden) furniture. Don't rely on its being open if you haven't booked.

It's about 3.5km north of the roundabout in the centre of Benafim. Popular with small European groups.

Eating

Agua Mel CAFE €
(www.facebook.com/aguamel; Largo José Cavaco Veira, Alte; pastries €1-4; ⏲9am-7pm; 📶) Alte doesn't have great restaurants, but it makes up for it with this cafe. An exceedingly friendly place, it has a lovely outlook and turns out absolutely scrumptious cakes, pies and other sweet treats; it does the odd savoury snack, such as toasted sandwiches, too. The boss is a good source of local info and the coffee is excellent.

Monte da Eira PORTUGUESE €€
(☎289 438 129; www.restaurantemontedaeira.com; Clareanes; mains €12-18; ⏲12.30-2.30pm & 7-10.15pm; 📶) On Rte 396, 5km north of Loulé in the village of Clareanes, is this smart restaurant, housed in the stables of a converted threshing mill, with several rooms and two outdoor terraces. People come from afar to feast on dishes of *javali* (wild boar), lamb and bean casserole, and stewed rabbit. To top it off, pick from a wine list of hundreds.

Getting There & Away

Buses depart Loulé for Alte (€3.60, 45 minutes, twice daily on weekdays) and Salir (€2.45, 30 minutes, six daily on weekdays, one Saturday).

Querença

Though perhaps a little over-restored, this is one of the region's prettiest villages, with whitewashed buildings set around a square dignified by a lovely church.

There are plenty of good walks hereabouts; you can grab maps at the Pólo Museológico da Água.

Pólo Museológico da Água MUSEUM
(☎289 422 495; ⏲9am-1pm & 2-5pm Mon-Fri) FREE This small, modern museum, located on the square, has a model of a waterwheel as well as information panels (in Portuguese) on water use. There's also a tourist office here, and it holds the keys to the church opposite. Despite official opening hours, you'll often find staff members here at weekends.

Tasquinha do Lagar PORTUGUESE €
(Rua da Escola; mains €8.50-10; ⏲lunch & dinner Thu-Tue) On the left as you come to the village proper, this place offers hearty, no-frills country cooking with valley views. Dishes change daily but regularly feature heart-warmers such as lamb stew.

Albufeira

POP 40,800

Once a scenic fishing village, Albufeira has all but lost the vestiges of its past – fishing boats are now moored at the ultramodern marina southwest of the centre. These days, the place is devoted to mass-market tourism; the old town – with its pretty cobblestone streets and Moorish influences – is concealed by gaudy signs, English menu boards and rowdy bars. It is the destination for cheap package deals, mainly catering to Brits and Germans and focused on cheap food, ale and beach fun for the kids.

But even if this isn't your sort of place, don't give up on Albufeira – it has good transport links to lovely beaches, such as Praia da Galé to the west, there are heaps of activities to enjoy and there's a relaxed holiday atmosphere away from the British pubs. To explore the pretty inland villages and the area's high-quality restaurants, you will need your own transport.

Sights

Museu de Arte Sacra MUSEUM

(Praça Miguel Bombarda; €2; 10.30am-4.30pm & 8-11pm Jul & Aug, 10.30am-4.30pm Sep-Jun) This tiny museum is housed in the beautifully restored 18th-century Chapel of San Sebastian and exhibits sacred art from the surrounding churches that survived the 1755 earthquake. The main eye-catchers are the gilded wooden altar and the old *azulejos* (hand-painted tiles) along the walls.

Museu Municipal de Arqueologia MUSEUM

(www.cm-albufeira.pt; Praça da República 1; €1; 9.30am-12.30pm & 1.30-5.30pm Tue, Sat & Sun, 9.30am-5.30pm Wed, 2-10pm Thu & Fri Apr-Sep, slightly shorter hours Oct-Mar) This small museum showcases items excavated from the municipality and surrounds (such as the castle in the village of Paderne). Pieces date from the prehistoric era to the 16th century. Highlights include a beautifully complete Neolithic vase from 5000 BC and a Roman mosaic from Retorta. The upper floor hosts interesting temporary exhibitions.

Beaches

Albufeira became as popular as it did due to its beaches of sharp, red-gold sand. **Praia do Peneco**, through the tunnel near the *turismo*, is usually head-to-toe with sunloungers. East and west of town are beautifully rugged coves and bays, though the nearest are heavily developed and often crowded. These include **Praia da Oura**, at the bottom of 'the Strip' 3km to the east and accessible by the blue (*azul*) line bus (catch it above the escalators by the old fishing quarter); **Praia da Falésia**, a long beach 10km to the east; **Balaia** and **Olhos de Água**. Buses run to Olhos de Água (10 minutes, half-hourly), mostly continuing to Praia da Falésia (20 minutes).

One of the best beaches to the west, **Praia da Galé**, about 6km away, is long and sandy, not so crowded and a centre for jet-skiing and waterskiing. Eva buses run to Praia da Galé (€2.25 one way, 20 minutes, seven daily) or the red line (bus 1 or 2) heads there every half-hour in summer (€1.40).

Activities

Krazy World WATER PARK

(282 574 134; www.krazyworld.com; Algoz; adult/child €13/8; 10am-6pm or 6.30pm Mar-Oct, plus most weekends Nov-Feb) Near São Bartolomeu de Messines, about 17km northwest of Silves, this much-touted animal and crocodile park also has minigolf, ponies and two swimming pools and is a diverting day away from the beach for kids. Transport is available from Albufeira and other resorts.

Dolphins Driven BOATING

(913 113 094; www.dolphins.pt; Marina de Albufeira; tours adult/child €35/20) Offers three excellent excursions from Albufeira: a 2½-hour exploration of the local sea caves and dolphin-watching; dolphin spotting off the coast; and a kayak trip into the local caves.

Festivals & Events

Fiesa ART

(www.fiesa.org; mid-Mar–Oct) On the beach at Armação de Pêra, this is the biggest sand-sculpture contest in the world. Artists are given 40,000 tons of sand to play with and their truly amazing creations can be admired throughout the season.

Sleeping

Dianamar GUESTHOUSE €€

(289 587 801; www.dianamar.com; Rua Latino Coelho 36; s/tr €50/75, d €60-65; Apr-Oct;) Happily a little removed from the central hubbub, but very close to the beach, friendly Dianamar has lovely details such as fresh flowers, and attractive rooms, many with balconies and two with sea views. Excellent and very generous breakfasts and afternoon teas are on offer. It's best to reserve ahead.

★**Vila São Vicente** BOUTIQUE HOTEL €€€

(289 583 700; www.hotelsaovicentealbufeira.com; Largo Jacinto D'Ayet; d €120-155;) This peaceful, classically decorated boutique hotel has 25 handsome rooms with polished-wood floors, helpful staff, and a great back deck and pool area. Most rooms have small balconies; rooms are naturally cheaper on the landward side. A welcome relief from the town's theme-park atmosphere, and great value in low season. No children are allowed.

Vila Joya RESORT €€€

(☎289 591 795; www.vilajoya.com; Estrada da Galé; small d from €310, d from €470; P ❄ @ 📶 ≋) Vila Joya is a luxury resort and spa close to Albufeira yet a planet away in every respect, located right on the beachfront near Praia da Galé. Pool areas, lush green lawn, views of the sea and a health spa create an ultra-plush and relaxing experience. If your purse strings don't stretch to staying here, consider a meal at the excellent restaurant.

Eating

Veneza PORTUGUESE €€

(☎289 367 129; www.restauranteveneza.com; Estrada de Paderne 560A, Mem Moniz; mains €10-20; ⊙12.30-3pm Wed-Mon, 7.30-10.30pm Thu-Tue; 📶) This restaurant is famed for serving what many consider to be the Algarve's finest *cataplana* (seafood stew) – here, a delicious pork and clam combination – but in truth almost all of its dishes taste so good you'll want to return. It also has one of the region's finest cellars. It's 11km north of Albufeira; you'll need a car to get there.

Casa da Fonte PORTUGUESE €€

(Rua João de Deus 7; mains €6.50-18.50; ⊙noon-midnight) A short uphill walk from the *turismo*, this popular place serves everything from sandwiches to scabbard fish in a beautiful courtyard lined with *azulejos* (hand-painted tiles) and set around a lemon tree. The staff are friendly, and the atmosphere is relaxed and more authentically Portuguese than at many of Albufeira's other eateries.

★**Vila Joya Restaurant** MODERN EUROPEAN €€€

(☎289 591 795; www.vilajoya.com; Estrada da Galé; degustation menu €175; ⊙sittings 1-1.45pm & 7.30-8.45pm; 📶) Run by Austrian expat chef Dieter Koschina, this is one of Portugal's best fine-dining restaurants, located in the Vila Joya resort (p183). Koschina draws on a variety of culinary influences and sources the best Portuguese produce to create dishes of rich elegance. There's excellent service to match.

Dom Carlos PORTUGUESE €€€

(☎289 541 224; Rua Alves Correia 100; 5-course menu €49; ⊙from 7.15pm Wed-Sun) If you want to splash out a bit but walk back to your hotel, the Dom Carlos has the best dining in town. The elegant but intimate interior dressed in white and baby blue feels a world away from the central feeding frenzy, and the five-course menus are a taste-bud delight.

Information

TOURIST INFORMATION

Municipal Tourism Office (☎289 515 973; www.cm-albufeira.pt; Estrada de Santa Eulália N395; ⊙9am-6pm Mon-Fri) Helpful local tourist office with maps and info; on one of the main entrance roads into town.

Things To Do (☎966 130 256; Avenida da Liberdade 63; ⊙10am-midnight Mar-Oct) A handy one-stop shop for booking any experience in the Albufeira area, including all theme parks, dolphin watching, bike hire and 4WD safaris.

Turismo (☎289 585 279; www.visitalgarve.pt; Rua 5 de Outubro 8; ⊙9.30am-7pm Jul & Aug, 9am-6pm Sep-Jun) Algarve Tourism office; by the tunnel that leads to the beach.

Getting There & Away

BUS

The **main bus station** (☎289 580 611; Rua Paul Harris) is 2km north of town. Passengers travelling to Lisbon can purchase tickets at a more conveniently located **bus shop** (Avenida da Liberdade 27; ⊙6.45am-7.45pm Mon-Fri, from 8am Sat & Sun), outside of which buses leave for the main bus station (€1.40) every 30 minutes from 7am to 10pm.

Faro €4.70, 1½ hours, half-hourly.

Lagos €5.50, one hour 20 minutes, 12 daily.

Lisbon €20, three hours, six daily.

Loulé €4.30, 40 minutes, seven daily.

Silves €4.30, 40 minutes, seven daily.

Buses also head to Huelva in Spain (€16, three hours, via Faro), and on to Seville (€20, four hours).

TRAIN

Services from Albufeira:

Faro €3.30, 30 minutes, nine daily.

Lagos €4.80, 1¼ hours, nine daily.

Getting Around

To reach the train station, take the '*giro*' city bus (€1.40). The *giro* (red line; bus 1 or 2) also leaves half-hourly for Praias de São Rafael, Galé and Guia (€1.40). These depart from the top of the escalators above the fishing quarter. Blue-line buses head to Praia Ouro, though you return on the green line.

For car hire, try one of the following.

Auto Jardim (☎289 580 500; www.auto-jardim.com; Edifício Brisa, Avenida da Liberdade)

Auto Prudente (☎289 542 160; www.auto-prudente.com; Estrada de Santa Eulália, Edifíccio Ondas do Mar, Loja 1)

THE ALGARVE FOR KIDS

The Algarve is a fun, kid-focussed area with loads of attractions, family-friendl[illegible] and cultural activities. Try thrilling water parks such as **Slide & Splash** (p186) [illegible] **Krazy World** (p183); the great **zoo** (☎282 680 100; www.zoolagos.com; Quinta Fi[illegible] adult/child €16/12; ⏰10am-7pm Apr-Sep, to 5pm Oct-Mar;) in Lagos; and, at Silve[illegible] the imagination-firing **castle** (p187).

There are some excellent museums, too: in São Brás de Alportel there's a simple cork display in the **Museu do Traje** (p163), and in Portimão the wonderful **Museu de Portimão** (p189) re-creates a former fish cannery.

Many towns along the coast run boat trips, and several have little trains.

Albufeira is particularly child friendly, with a plethora of agencies in the area selling a variety of trips, from horse riding to cruising on pirate ships. Most boat trips leave from the marina. Other kid-oriented activities include the following:

Albufeira Riding Centre (☎961 269 526; www.albufeiraridingcentre.com; Vale Navio Complex) On the road to Vilamoura. Offers one- to three-hour horse rides for all ages and abilities.

Aqualand (☎282 320 230; www.aqualand.pt; N125, Sítio das Areias, Alcantarilha; adult/child €22.50/16.50; ⏰10am-6pm Jul-Sep, to 5pm from mid-Jun) Huge loop-the-loop slide and rapids.

Aquashow (☎289 315 129; www.aquashowparkhotel.com; Quarteira; adult/child €29/19; ⏰10am-7pm Aug, to 6.30pm Jul, to 5.30pm Jun & Sep, to 5pm May) In Quarteira, 10km east of Albufeira, with parrots, reptiles and a wave pool.

Carvoeiro

POP 2700

Carvoeiro is a cluster of whitewashed buildings atop tawny, gold and green cliffs and backed by hills. Shops, bars and restaurants rise steeply from the small arc of beach that is the focus of the town, and beyond lie hillsides full of sprawling holiday villas. This diminutive seaside resort 5km south of Lagoa is prettier and more laid-back than many of the bigger resorts, but its size means that it gets full in summer.

Beaches

The town's handkerchief-sized sandy beach, **Praia do Carvoeiro**, is surrounded by the steeply mounting town. About 1km east on the coastal road is the bay of **Algar Seco**, a favourite stop on the tour-bus itinerary thanks to its dramatic rock formations.

If you're looking for a stunning swimming spot, continue east along the main road, Estrada do Farol, to **Praia de Centianes**, where the secluded cliff-wrapped beach is almost as dramatic as Algar Seco. Buses heading for **Praia do Carvalho** (nine per day weekdays and three per day on weekends from Lagoa, via Carvoeiro) pass nearby – get off at Colina Sol Aparthotel, the Moorish-style clifftop hotel.

Praia da Marinha BEACH

One of a few nearby beaches with karstic rock stacks, this is perhaps the most beautiful. As it's also a little hard to get to, it can be low in crowds, though these things are relative in summer. It's 8km southeast of Lagoa, but the nicest way to get to it is via the Percurso dos Sete Vales Suspensos path.

Activities

Percurso dos Sete Vales Suspensos WALKING

This spectacular clifftop walk connects the beaches east of Carvoeiro. Beginning at Praia Vale Centianes, 2.3km east of town, it heads 5.7km to Praia da Marinha, with its picturesque rock stacks, via the beach at Benagil. It's one of the Algarve's most memorable walks.

Divers Cove DIVING

(☎282 356 594; www.divers-cove.com; Quinta do Paraíso; 3hr introduction €80, 1-day discovery €135, 2-day scuba dive €270, 4-day open water €450; ⏰9am-7pm) This multilingual family-run diving centre provides equipment, dives and PADI certification.

Slide & Splash WATER PARK

(282 340 800; www.slidesplash.com; Estrada Nacional 125; adult/child 5-10yr €27/19; 10am-5pm, 6pm or 6.30pm daily May-Sep, Mon-Sat Apr & Oct) Touted across the Algarve, this popular place is 2km west of Lagoa. It's widely considered Portugal's best; visitors rave about the sheer quantity of attractions, including slides, toboggans and more. There's enough here to keep kids and adults entertained for most of a day, though with no family ticket available it can be quite an expensive outing.

Golf

Golfers can take their pick: there's the **Pestana Gramacho** (282 340 900; www.pestanagolf.com) and **Pestana Vale da Pinta** (282 340 900; www.pestanagolf.com), both at Pestana Golf Resort; and **Vale de Milho** (282 358 502; www.valedemilhogolf.com; Praia do Carvoeiro) near Praia de Centianes.

Sleeping

Casa Luiz GUESTHOUSE €

(282 354 058; www.casaluiz.com; Rampa da Nossa Senhora da Encarnação; d/studios/apt not incl breakfast €70/80/95;) These four clean and modern rooms and studios (with kitchenette) all overlook the beach and face the sunset. Three of the rooms have balconies.

★**O Castelo** GUESTHOUSE €€

(919 729 259; www.ocastelo.net; Rua do Casino 59; d without view €65, with view €90-110;) West of the bay, this standout guest house with a welcoming and justifiably proud owner is fully renovated and gleamingly well maintained. Rooms are most inviting; some share a large terrace and sea views (with sunrises), and one has a private balcony. This property gets all the details right, the breezy decor complementing the refracted light from the glittering sea.

Eating

Le Crô Portugal PORTUGUESE €

(Estrada do Farol 77; tapas €5-7, mains €6-12; 11am-10pm) Run by a friendly couple, this tiny tapas and wine place turns out some of Carvoeiro's tastiest Portuguese food and stocks a connoisseur's selection of wine. The hosts are friendly, knowledgeable and committed to providing such a great experience that you'll come back a second time. Many do.

A Marisqueira SEAFOOD €€

(Estrada do Farol 95; mains €12-25; noon-2.30pm & 6.30-10pm Mon-Sat) This simple, well-established place has an outdoor terrace and is known for its seafood and grilled dishes. It's about 500m up the main road east of Carvoeiro beach.

Drinking & Nightlife

Restaurante Boneca Bar BAR

(282 358 391; 10am-midnight) Hidden in the rock formations out at Algar Seco, just over 1km east of the beach in Carvoeiro, this long-standing place is a novel spot for a cocktail, a great venue to be at sunset, and a decent retreat for a light meal or beer at any time.

Information

The post office and several banks are located on Rua dos Pescadores (the one-way road in from Lagoa).

Turismo (282 357 728; 9am-1pm & 2-6pm Tue-Sat) Just back from the beach in the centre of town.

Getting There & Away

Buses run on weekdays between Carvoeiro and Portimão (€3.25, 35 minutes, eight daily) and Lagoa (€2.25, 10 minutes, 14 daily).

Getting Around

Several car-rental agencies are located along the road back to Lagos. Parking is difficult in summer – you are best to head to Estrada do Farol and walk.

Silves

POP 11,000

Silves is an attractive town of jumbling orange rooftops scattered above the banks of the Rio Arade. It boasts one of the best-preserved castles in the Algarve, attractive red-stone walls and winding, sleepy backstreets on a hillside. Not much happens around town, but it's a good base if you're after a less hectic, non-coastal Algarvian pace. It's 15km northeast of Portimão.

History

The Rio Arade was long an important route into the interior for the Phoenicians, Greeks and Carthaginians, who wanted the copper and iron action in the southwest of the country. With the Moorish invasion from the 8th century, the town gained prominence due to its strategic hilltop, riverside site. From the mid-11th to the mid-13th centuries, Shelb (or Xelb), as it was then known, rivalled Lisbon in prosperity and influence: according to the 12th-century Arab geographer Idrisi, it had a population of 30,000, a port and shipyards, and 'attractive buildings and well-furnished bazaars'.

The town's downfall began in June 1189, when Dom Sancho I laid siege to it, supported by a horde of (mostly English) crusaders, who had been persuaded (with the promise of loot) to pause in their journey to Jerusalem and give Sancho a hand. The Moors holed up inside their impregnable castle, but after three hot months of harassment they ran out of water and were forced to surrender. Sancho was all for mercy and honour, but the crusaders wanted the plunder they were promised, and stripped the Moors of their possessions (including the clothes on their backs) as they left, tortured those remaining and wrecked the town.

Two years later the Moors recaptured the town. It wasn't until 1249 that Christians gained control once and for all. But by then Silves was a shadow of its former self. The silting up of the river – which caused disease and stymied maritime trade – coupled with the growing importance of the Algarvian ports hastened the town's decline. Devastation in the 1755 earthquake seemed to seal its fate. But in the 19th century, local cork and dried-fruit industries revitalised Silves, hence the grand bourgeois architecture around town. Today tourism and agriculture are its lifeblood.

Sights

★Sé CATHEDRAL

(Rua da Sé; €1; 9am-12.30pm & 2-5pm Mon-Fri, 9am-1pm Sat Jun-Aug) Just below the castle is the *sé* (cathedral), built in 1189 on the site of an earlier mosque, then rebuilt after the 1249 Reconquista and subsequently restored several times following earthquake damage. In many ways, this is the Algarve's most impressive cathedral, with a substantially unaltered Gothic interior. It's dramatically high and simple inside, with elegant vaulting, beautiful windows and several fine tombs. The Christ sculpture, the *Senhor dos Passos*, is one of the main processional figures of the town's Easter celebrations.

★Castelo CASTLE

(282 440 837; adult/concession/under 10yr €2.80/1.40/free, joint ticket with Museu Municipal de Arqueologia €3.90; 9am-8pm Jun-Aug, to 6.30pm Mar-May & Sep-Nov, to 5pm Dec-Feb) This russet-coloured, Lego-like cast ly occupied in the Visigothic great views over the town and countryside. What you see toda ly from the Moorish era, thou was heavily restored in the 20th Walking the parapets and admiring the vistas is the main attraction, but you can also gaze down on the excavated ruins of the Almohad-era palace. The whitewashed 12th-century water cisterns, 5m deep, now host temporary exhibitions.

Museu Municipal de Arqueologia MUSEUM

(282 444 838; Rua das Portas de Loulé; adult/under 10yr €2.10/free, joint ticket with Castelo €3.90; 10am-6pm) Built tight against the defensive walls, this archaeological museum has a mix of finds from the town and around. The modern building was constructed around an 18m-deep Moorish well with a spiral staircase heading into the depths that you can follow for a short stretch. Otherwise this is another Algarve museum that starts at the prehistoric beginning but soon moves on to focus on the Almohad period of the 12th and 13th centuries.

Casa da Cultura Islâmica e Mediterrânica ARTS CENTRE

(282 440 895; www.cm-silves.pt; Largo da República) Even if there is no exhibition, lecture or performance taking place here, it's still worth the 600m walk west of the centre to view this wonderfully restored neo-Moorish cultural centre, built with art-nouveau flourish in 1914.

Activities

Country Riding Centre HORSE RIDING

(917 976 992; www.countryridingcentre.com; 1/3hr rides €40/80; 9am-1pm & 3.30-7pm Mon-Sat) Located about 4km east of Silves, left off the road to Messines (it's signposted), this riding centre offers lessons and hour-long to half-day rides for all levels.

Festivals & Events

Feira Medieval HISTORICAL

(www.cm-silves.pt; mid-Aug) Held over a week each August (precise dates vary annually), the Medieval Fair brings the Silves of old to life. The town's important events and people are represented, from Silves governor Al Muthamid to the town being awarded its charter. Bawdy costumes, dances, jesters, feasts, traditional food and handicrafts all evoke life in the 11th to 13th centuries.

leeping

sa das Oliveiras INN €
(282 342 115; www.casa-das-oliveiras.com; Montes da Vala; s €45-53, d €55-65;) This welcoming, peaceful place offers an old-style B&B with a British flavour, with five great-value rooms in a relaxed setting. There's a lovely garden and pool area. It's 4km from Silves train station and a little tricky to find: grab the map or GPS coordinates from the website. No cards.

Quinta da Figueirinha INN €
(282 440 700; www.qdf.pt; 2-/4-/6-person apt from €55/89/129;) This 36-hectare organic farm and botanic garden, run by a kindly agronomist, offers simple apartments in peaceful farm-like surroundings. Orchards (with more than 50 species of plant) are yours for picking and wandering. Leave Silves and cross the bridge, taking the first left to Fragura then continue for 4km. You can self-cater, or there's a basic restaurant serving delicious, wholesome buffet-style food.

Duas Quintas INN €€
(282 449 311; www.duasquintas.com; Santo Estevão; d/studios €105/130;) Set among orange groves and rolling hills, this utterly charming converted farmhouse has six pleasant rooms, a living space, terraces and a pool. Some of the furniture is antique and there are big discounts for staying a week or more. It's 6km northeast of Silves along the N124.

Eating

Pastelaria Rosa CAFE, DESSERTS €
(Largo do Município; pastries €1.50-3; 7.30am-10pm Mon-Sat;) On the ground floor of the town-hall building, this quaint, tile-lined place is Silves' oldest cafe and the best place to try Algarvian sweets. The table service is excellent and the extra you pay for the coffee and cakes here is worth it for the location and atmosphere. It's next to the tourist office.

Recanto dos Mouros PORTUGUESE €€
(282 443 240; www.recantodosmouros.com; Rua Estrada do Monte Branco; mains €9-14; lunch & dinner Thu-Tue) Situated 1km or so behind the castle (follow the signs), this is one of Silves' most popular places. As the Portuguese attest, it's *bom preço-qualidade* (damn good value) for lots of hearty Algarvian delights.

Marisqueira Rui SEAFOOD €€
(282 442 682; www.marisqueirarui.com; Rua Conselheiro Vilarinho 27; mains €10-16.50; noon-11pm Wed-Mon) Situated in the old town, with a unfancily dated interior of yellow and cork, this place is Silves' finest seafood restaurant. Join the locals – it gets busy – and savour plates from cockles, clams and crabs to bass and seafood rice. You can dine cheaply on bream or sea bass here, or blow the budget on a crustacean feast.

Café Inglês INTERNATIONAL €€
(282 442 585; Rua do Castelo 11; mains €10-23; 9am-5.30pm Mon, to midnight Tue-Sun Mar-Oct;) Located below the castle entrance, Café Inglês has a wonderful, shady terrace. The food is excellent (don't miss the chocolate St Emilion dessert). One of the Algarve's liveliest restaurants north of the coast, it boasts an elegant interior, and has live jazz, fado (traditional song) and African music at weekends.

★ **Restaurante O Barradas** PORTUGUESE €€€
(282 443 308; www.obarradas.com; Palmeirinha; mains €8.50-25; 6-10pm Thu-Tue;) The star choice for foodies is this delightful converted farmhouse run by Luís and his German wife, Andrea. They take pride in careful sourcing, and use organic fish, meat and fruit in season. Luís is a winemaker, so you can be assured of some fine wines. Follow the road to Lagoa and then to Palmeirinha; it's 3km from Silves.

Information

Centro de Interpretaçao do Património Islâmico (282 440 800; Largo do Município; 9am-1pm & 2-5pm Mon-Fri) This interesting little spot promotes the network of Islamic routes through Portugal, Spain and Morocco and also acts as the municipal tourism office. Knowledgeable overseer Miguel knows a lot about the town and its Islamic cultural heritage. It contains a small but interesting exhibition on traditional mud-brick production.

Turismo (282 098 927; www.visitalgarve.pt; Parque das Merendas; 9am-1pm & 2-6pm Tue-Sat) Next to the main car park and bus stops.

Getting There & Away

BUS

There are no direct buses between Lagos and Silves; change at Portimão (40 minutes).

Albufeira €4.30, 45 minutes, four to seven daily.

Portimão €3.30, 20 minutes, five to nine daily. For Faro you must change at Lagoa (€4.50). All buses leave from the riverfront.

TRAIN

The train station is located 2km south of the town, but you'll need to take a local bus (three to five daily) or catch a cab, as it's along a major highway.

Train services from Silves:

Lagos €2.90, 35 minutes, nine daily.
Faro €5.15, one hour, nine daily.

Getting Around

Much of the hilly, compact centre of Silves is easily navigated on foot; many streets are pedestrianised areas only. Drivers are advised to park in the large car parks on the city side (north) of the river and southwest of the city centre (no charge).

Portimão

POP 55,000

Bustling Portimão is the western Algarve's main commercial centre and the second-most-populous city in the Algarve. Those expecting a gritty port town will be disappointed/relieved – the centre is a small, friendly hub with a pleasant waterfront, an assortment of outdoor cafes, and sizzling fish restaurants in the old quarter and quayside. You can also arrange a boat trip up the Rio Arade. Most people only pass through en route to Praia da Rocha.

History

Portimão was an important trading link for Phoenicians, Greeks and Carthaginians (Hannibal is said to have visited). The Romans called it Portos Magnus and it was fought over by Moors and Christians. In 1189 Dom Sancho I and a band of crusaders sailed up the Rio Arade from here to besiege Silves. Almost destroyed in the 1755 earthquake, it regained its maritime importance in the 19th century. It became the region's fishing and canning centre before this, too, declined.

Sights

★Museu de Portimão MUSEUM
(www.museudeportimao.pt; Rua Dom Carlos I; adult/child €3/free, 10am-2pm Sat free; ⌚2.30-6pm Tue, 10am-6pm Wed-Sun Sep-Jul, 7.30-11pm Tue, 3-11pm Wed-Sun Aug) The ultra-modern, award-winning Museu de Portimão, housed in a 19th-century fish cannery, is one excellent reason to visit Portimão. The museum focuses on three areas: archaeology, underwater finds and, the most fascinating, a re-creation of the fish cannery (mackerel and sardines). You can see former production lines, complete with sound effects – clanking and grinding and the like. An excellent video (in Portuguese) of the fishing industry reveals each step in the process, from netting the shoals to packaging.

Activities

Operators galore line the riverside promenade offering **boat trips**. These include cruises up the coast and/or the Rio Arade, visiting caves along the way. Prices start at around €30. There are also **dolphin-spotting** opportunities. Some trips are in fishing boats for 10 people, others are in sailing boats for 35.

Santa Bernarda BOATING
(☎967 023 840; www.santa-bernarda.com; adult/child from €35/20) Santa Bernarda runs trips visiting the caves and coast on a 23m wooden sailing ship with wheelchair access and a pirate theme. The full-day trip includes a beach barbecue and time to swim.

Festivals & Events

Festival da Sardinha FOOD
(www.festivaldasardinha.pt; ⌚mid-Aug) A celebration of Portugal's favourite fish, the sardine, with associated music, dance and festivities.

Sleeping

Alameda Hostel HOSTEL €
(☎968 696 499; www.alamedahostel.com; Rua do Comércio 9; dm €20; ❄📶) Right in the heart of the city centre, this new hostel is basic, clean and bright, and puts you within easy walking distance of everything. There are two funky kitchens for self-caterers.

Globo Hotel HOTEL €€
(☎282 405 030; www.hoteisalgarvesol.pt; Rua 5 de Outubro 26; r €97; ❄📶) Rooms here have a snazzy design, with contemporary fittings and abundant natural light. Each floor has a colour scheme, from lilac to green. It's central and rates more than halve outside July and August.

Eating

Casa da Isabel PATISSERIE €
(Rua Direita 61; pastries €1-5; ⌚9am-midnight Jul & Aug, to 8pm Sep-Jun; 📶) This delightfully

elegant little tearoom is housed in a cute, tile-fronted mansion and churns out a mouth-watering array of desserts, of a type traditionally invented and made by nuns in convents. Although it serves a range of teas and infusions, most prefer coffee to go with their tooth-rotters.

Carvi SEAFOOD **€€**
(282 417 912; Rua Direita 34; mains €8-14.50; noon-midnight Wed-Mon) Famous hereabouts for its seafood, Carvi is a short walk down Rua Direita from the *turismo*. Service isn't always as warm as it could be, but the quality of the food, served at communal rows of tables dressed in white linen, makes up for it. There's also a very long wine list.

Clube Naval do Portimão PORTUGUESE **€€**
(Restaurante do Cais; 282 432 325; Zona Ribeirinha; mains €13.50-17; noon-3pm & 7-11pm Tue-Sun;) Near the municipal museum on the waterfront, the Naval Club has a fancy upstairs restaurant with unsurpassed views over the water. Go for the fish of the day, tuna steaks, or skewers. The downstairs cafe is great for a coffee or beer waterside.

Drinking & Nightlife

Taska Porta Velha BAR
(918 053 169; Travessa Manuel Dias Barão; tapas €5-10; 10pm-4am Mon-Sat;) This atmospheric bar has been lovingly restored and decorated, with antique knick-knacks and modern artworks spread throughout several rooms. Tables are made of wood and stone slabs; it's *petiscos* (tapas/snacks) and drinks only. Head up the road opposite Rua Direita number 63.

Entertainment

Bar Marginália LIVE MUSIC
(Rua Arco Maravilhas; 9pm-2am Tue & Wed, to 3am Thu, to 4am Fri & Sat;) This charismatic backstreet bar is one of Portimão's best locations for live music, with weekend concerts (normally on the heavier side of the spectrum), plus Thursday karaoke sessions.

Information

Turismo Municipal (282 402 487; www.cm-portimao.pt; Plaza 1 de Dezembro; 9.30am-5.30pm Mon-Fri) Portimão's information office is housed in the wonderful Teatro Municipal de Portimão ('Tempo').

Getting There & Away

BUS

Local bus 33 shuttles between Praia da Rocha and Portimão's Largo do Dique (€1.50) every half-hour. The walk is miserable, passing the deserted port and convent ruins en route, though many do it.

To head further afield, Portimão has excellent bus connections. **Frota Azul** (www.frotazul-algarve.pt) has services to Monchique (€4.30, 45 minutes, six to eight daily), Silves (€3.25, 35 minutes, five to nine daily) and Lagos (€4.10, 40 minutes, hourly).

Eva buses leave from near the petrol station along the riverside on Avenida Guanaré. Services include:

Albufeira €4.60, one hour, at least hourly.

Cabo São Vicente €6.35, 1½ hours, one daily.

Faro €5.50, 1¾ hours, seven daily.

Lagos €4, 35 minutes, hourly.

Lisbon €20, 3¼ hours, six daily.

Loulé €5.50, 1¾ hours, five services, weekends only.

For Sagres and Salema you must change in Lagos.

TRAIN

Eight daily trains connect Portimão with Tunes (€2.95, 45 minutes). Change at Tunes for Lisbon. Services also go to Silves (€1.50, 20 minutes, nine daily) and Lagos (€2, 20 minutes, 11 daily).

BOAT

Until fairly recently Portimão was the departure point for a ferry that serviced Madeira and the Canary Islands (by all accounts a harrowing ordeal on the open Atlantic lasting days). There have been rumblings recently that this heavily subsidised service might be restarted.

Getting Around

If you have your own wheels, the easiest parking is a free riverside area by the Repsol petrol station.

Praia da Rocha

POP 200

Five minutes' drive from Portimão, Praia da Rocha has one of the Algarve's best beaches, backed by ochre-red cliffs and the small 16th-century Fortaleza da Santa Catarina.

Behind the beach looms the town; this has long known the hand of development, with high-rise condos and luxury hotels sprouting along the cliffside, and a row of restaurants, bars and clubs packed along the main thoroughfare. If you look hard beyond the concrete facade, Praia da Rocha has several vestiges of an elegant past, including some 19th-century mansions, which are now atmospheric guest houses.

There's also the sleek Marina de Portimão, painted autumnal colours (to match the cliffs), and a well-known casino where you can fritter away your holiday money.

Sleeping

Accommodation is almost impossible to find during the high season if you don't have a prior reservation.

Albergaria Vila Lido GUESTHOUSE €€
(282 241 127; www.hotelvilalido.com; Avenida Tomás Cabreira; d €100-150;) Near the fort, this sturdy white-with-blue-trim hotel is housed in a converted 19th-century mansion and features super-welcoming hosts and bright, optimistic rooms, most of which have a verandah and sea views. Breakfast is served on the terrace overlooking the Atlantic.

Bela Vista BOUTIQUE HOTEL €€€
(282 460 280; www.hotelbelavista.net; Avenida Tomás Cabreira; r €270-410, ste €450-550; Mar-Nov;) This beautiful spot – a renovated former mansion with two modern wings – adds a touch of class to Praia da Rocha. Portuguese interior-design team Graça Viterbo has gone to town here, using a quirky blend of contemporary and antique, all in a blue-and-yellow colour theme. It's uber-luxurious yet not so snobby you can't sneeze, and professional yet fun.

The restaurant is open to the public and is worth checking out. Prices are significantly lower outside high season.

Eating

The marina has a row of romantic, upmarket dining and drinking spots, some of which stare across at the beautiful Praia Meia Grande. In summer, grab a sundowner at one of the beachside eateries.

F Restaurante PORTUGUESE €€
(919 115 512; Avenida Tomás Cabreira; mains €13-20; 3-10.30pm Mon-Sat;) A large and rather cheeky Facebook-style 'F' on a pink background (and possibly a tout) greet you at this classier-than-most-here restaurant on the strip. There are super views over the beach and a quality menu of Portuguese dishes; service can't be faulted. A rare treat is the *cataplana* (seafood stew) for solo diners (normally it's only for two to share).

Marisqueira Praia da Rocha PORTUGUESE €€
(Rua Bartolomeu Dias; mains €8.40-20; 10am-11pm Mon-Sat) An unusually traditional restaurant for Praia da Rocha, this popular, low-key place opposite Algarve Mor hotel offers decent Portuguese fare, with a hearty array of daily specials. The exotic fish in the aquariums are not for consumption.

Drinking & Nightlife

Praia da Rocha bristles with bars that are packed with sun-reddened British faces, satellite TV, live music and karaoke. Many are owned or run by foreign residents. These and the town's plethora of Irish pubs are open all day (and nearly all night).

Nana's Bar BAR
(Rua José Bivar; 2pm-4am;) The best bar in town by some distance, Nana's has much more local character than the others, pours better drinks and keeps it real with Portuguese lingua franca.

Information

Turismo (282 419 132; Avenida Tomás Cabreira; 9am-6pm) Large office strategically positioned on the strip.

Lagos

POP 22,000

As far as touristy towns go, Lagos (*lahgoosh*) has got the lot. It lies along the bank of the Rio Bensafrim, with 16th-century walls enclosing the old town's pretty, cobbled lanes and picturesque piazzas and churches. Beyond these lies a modern but not overly unattractive sprawl. The town's good restaurants and the range of fabulous nearby beaches add to the allure. With every activity under the sun (literally) on offer, plus a pumping nightlife, it's not surprising that people of all ages are drawn here.

Aside from its hedonistic appeal, Lagos has historical clout, having launched many naval excursions during Portugal's extraordinary Age of Discoveries.

History

Phoenicians and Greeks set up shop at this port (which later became Roman Lacobriga) at the mouth of the muddy Rio Bensafrim. Afonso III recaptured it from the Moors in 1241. In 1415 a giant fleet set

Lagos

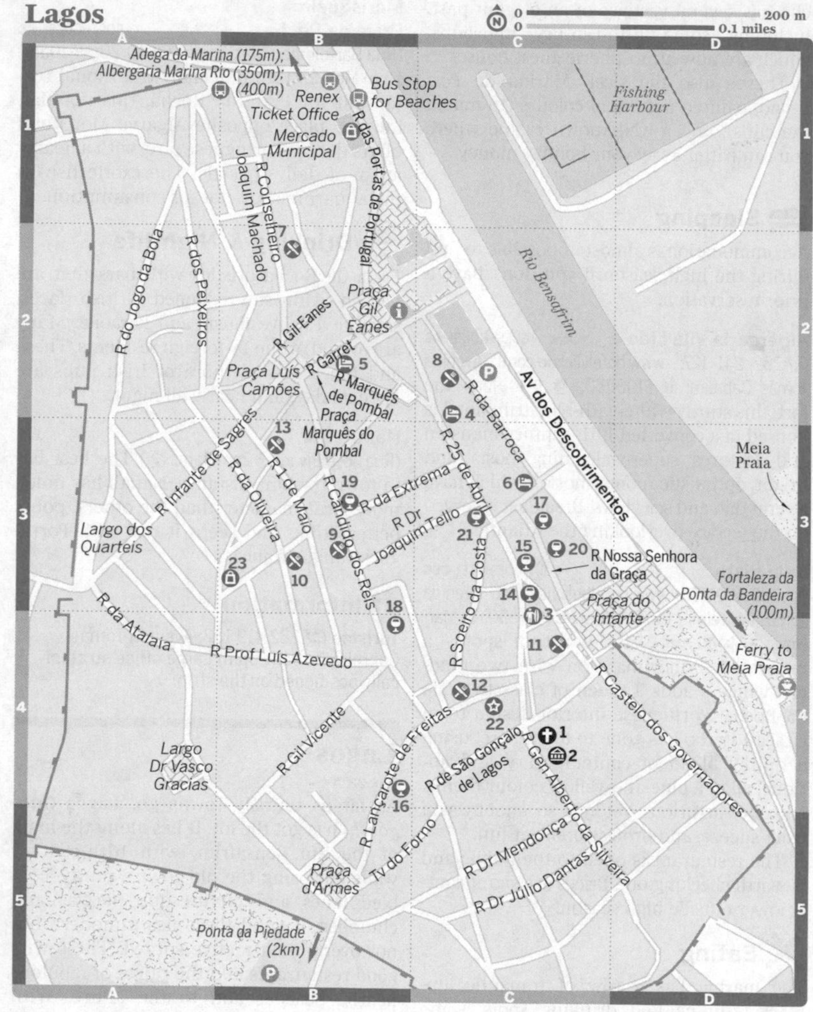

sail from Lagos under the command of the 21-year-old Prince Henry the Navigator to seize Ceuta in Morocco, thereby setting the stage for the Age of Discoveries.

The shipyards of Lagos built and launched Prince Henry's caravels, and Henry split his time between his trading company here and his navigation school at Sagres. Local boy Gil Eanes left Lagos in 1434 as commander of the first ship to round West Africa's Cape Bojador. Others continued to bring back information about the African coast, along with ivory, gold and slaves. Lagos has the dubious distinction of having hosted (in 1444) the first sale of Africans as slaves to Europeans, and the town grew into a slave-trading centre.

It was also from Lagos in 1578 that Dom Sebastião, along with the cream of the Portuguese nobility and an army of Portuguese, Spanish, Dutch and German buccaneers, left on a disastrous crusade to Christianise North Africa, which ended in a debacle at Alcácer-Quibir in Morocco. Sir Francis Drake inflicted heavy damage on Lagos a few years later, in 1587.

Lagos was the Algarve's high-profile capital from 1576 until 1755, when the earthquake flattened it.

Lagos

Sights
1 Igreja de Santo António C4
2 Museu Municipal C4

Activities, Courses & Tours
3 Lagos Surf Center C4

Sleeping
4 Hotel Mar Azul C2
5 Inn Seventies B2
6 Old Town Hostel C3

Eating
7 A Forja B2
8 Arribalé C2
9 Café Gombá B3
10 Casinha do Petisco B3
11 Cervejaria Dois Irmãos C4
12 Dom Vinho II C4
13 Mimar Café B3

Drinking & Nightlife
14 Bon Vivant C3
15 Eddie's Bar C3
16 Garden B4
17 Grand Café C3
18 Inside Out B4
19 Red Eye Bar B3
20 Stevie Ray's Blues Jazz Bar C3
21 Taberna de Lagos C3

Entertainment
22 Centro Cultural C4

Shopping
23 Owl Story B3

Sights

Lagos is planning to open a museum dedicated to the slave trade in the old slave market. Ask at the tourist office (p197) to see whether this is up and running when you visit.

Igreja de Santo António CHURCH
(Rua General Alberto da Silveira; adult/child incl museum €3/1.50; ⊙10am-12.30pm & 2-5.30pm Tue-Sun) This little church, bursting with gilded, carved wood, is a stupendous baroque extravaganza. Beaming cherubs and ripening grapes are much in evidence. The dome and *azulejo* (hand-painted tile) panels were installed during repairs after the 1755 earthquake. Enter the church from the adjacent Museu Municipal.

Ponta da Piedade VIEWPOINT
(Point of Piety) Protruding south from Lagos, Ponta da Piedade is a dramatic wedge of headland. Three windswept kilometres out of town, the point is well worth visiting for its contorted, polychrome sandstone cliffs and towers, complete with lighthouse and, in spring, hundreds of nesting egrets. The surrounding area is brilliant with wild orchids in spring. On a clear day you can see east to Carvoeiro and west to Sagres. The only way to reach it is by car or on foot.

Museu Municipal MUSEUM
(☎282 762 301; Rua General Alberto da Silveira; adult/concession €3/1.50; ⊙10am-12.30pm & 2-5.30pm Tue-Sun) Lagos' town museum, an old-fashioned but lovably curious collection, holds a bit of everything: swords and pistols, landscapes and portraits, minerals and crystals, coins, china, miniature furniture, Roman mosaics, African artefacts, stone tools, model boats, and an intriguing model of an imaginary Portuguese town. The museum is also the entry point for the baroque Igreja de Santo António.

Beaches

Meia Praia, the vast expanse of sand to the east of town, has outlets offering sailboard rental and waterskiing lessons, plus several laid-back restaurants and beach bars. South of town the beaches – **Batata, Pinhão, Dona Ana** and **Camilo**, among others – are smaller and more secluded, lapped by calm waters and punctuated with amazing grottoes, coves and towers of coloured sandstone. An informal boat service shuttles back and forth from the waterfront in Lagos to Meia Praia.

Activities

Water Sports

Lagos is a popular surfing centre and has good facilities; surfing companies head to the west coast for the waves.

Lagos Surf Center SURFING
(☎282 764 734; www.lagossurfcenter.com; Rua da Silva Lopes 31; 1-/3-/5-day courses €55/150/225) Will help you catch a wave and head to where there are suitable swells. Children must be accompanied by a family member over 14 years of age. It also rents out wetsuits (€5 per day) and boards (€15 to €25) and offers beach kayaking and paddle-boarding trips.

Windsurf Point WINDSURFING
(☎282 792 315; www.windsurfpoint.com; Bairro 1 Maio, Meia Praia; ⏰9am-7pm) Offers windsurfing courses (beginners full day €190) at Meia Praia, along with kitesurfing, paddle-boarding, board rental (per hour/day €35/70) and a shop.

Kayak Adventures KAYAKING
(☎913 262 200; www.kayakadventureslagos.com; 3hr tour €25) Offers kayaking trips, including snorkelling, from Batata Beach.

Blue Ocean DIVING
(☎964 665 667; www.blue-ocean-divers.de) For those who want to go diving or snorkelling. Offers a half-day discovery experience (€30), a full-day dive (€90) and a Divemaster PADI scuba course (€590). It also offers kayak safaris (half-/full day €30/45, children under 12 half price).

Axessextreme KAYAKING
(☎919 114 649; www.axessextreme.com; 3hr tour €25) Offers recommended sea-kayaking trips in the Algarve as well as mountain biking and surfing.

Boat Trips & Dolphin Safaris

Numerous operators have ticket stands at the marina or along the promenade opposite. They operate a bit like sausage factories but offer some fun outings. Local fishers offering jaunts to the grottoes by motorboat trawl for customers along the promenade and by the Fortaleza da Ponta da Bandeira.

Bom Dia BOATING
(☎282 087 587; www.bomdia-boattrips.com) The oldest operator, and based at the marina, Bom Dia runs trips on traditional schooners, including a five-hour barbecue cruise with a chance to swim (adult/child €49/25), a two-hour grotto trip (adult/child €25/10) and a family fishing trip (adult/child €40/25).

Dizzy Dolphins BOATING
(☎938 305 000; www.dizzydolphin.com) Run by a former BBC wildlife-documentary producer, this small outfit offers excellent 90-minute summer dolphin-spotting trips on a rigid inflatable.

Other Activities

Mountain Bike Adventure CYCLING
(☎918 502 663; www.themountainbikeadventure.com; Porta da Vila; rides €20-55) Bike fanatics will have some fun with this company, which offers a range of outings from shorter scenic trips to full-on technical rides with shoots, drops and jumps.

Tiffany's HORSE RIDING
(☎282 697 395; www.teamtiffanys.com; Vale Grifo, Almádena; ⏰9am-dusk) Seven kilometres west of Lagos, this outfit charges €33 for an hour's horse riding. Other options include a three-hour trip (€85) and an all-day forest trip that includes a luxury picnic (€140).

Sleeping

Old Town Hostel HOSTEL €
(☎282 087 221; Rua da Barroca 70; dm €23; @ 📶) If you're in town to party, this highly rated hostel is the place to sleep it all off during the day. Located in atmospheric Rua da Barroca, it has kitchen, terrace and small common room, but the dorms are a little cramped and often full. The friendly staff is more than willing to show you the best bars.

★**Inn Seventies** GUESTHOUSE €€
(☎967 177 590; www.innseventies.com; Rua Marquês de Pombal; d €90-129; P ❄ 📶 ≈) Though the entrance and stairwell don't give a great first impression, the rooms here are sexy suites with a vaguely '70s theme. They come well equipped with big TV, fridge and Nespresso machine, and there's a nice rooftop deck with views and plunge pool. The central location is fabulous and prices include the town's best buffet breakfast.

★**Hotel Mar Azul** GUESTHOUSE €€
(☎282 770 230; www.hotelmarazul.eu; Rua 25 de Abril 13; s €50-60, d €60-85; ❄ @ 📶) This little gem is one of Lagos' best-value spots. It's a central, well-run and delightfully welcoming place, with tidy, modern, compact rooms, some even boasting sea views. The simple breakfast is a mean €5 extra.

Albergaria Marina Rio HOTEL €€
(☎282 780 830; www.marinario.com; Avenida dos Descobrimentos; s €100-125, d €103-128; P ❄ @ 📶 ≈) Overlooking the harbour, this hotel has comfortable rooms with smart modern decor and balconies. On the downside, it faces the road and backs onto the bus station. Most rooms are twins. There's a tiny pool and roof terrace.

Vila Galé Lagos RESORT €€€
(☎282 771 400; www.vilagale.com; Meia Praia; s/d from €168/198; P ❄ 📶 ≈) This large place, part of a national chain, offers all the creature comforts for resort-loving visitors and

business clients. Everything seems to come in multiples – pools, restaurants, activities and zeros (as in the price, but deals are available).

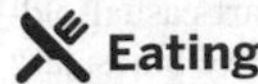

Eating

Café Gombá CAFE €
(☎282 762 188; Rua Cândido dos Reis 56; ⏰8am-7pm Mon-Sat, Sun mid-Jun–mid-Sep; ❄) Although around since 1964, this traditional cafe-bakery with 21st-century decor looks more like it opened in 2016. Elderly locals hang out here for the best cakes, coffees and sandwiches in town, and it's correspondingly cheap.

Bar Quim PORTUGUESE €
(Meia Praia; mains €7-12; ⏰10am-10pm Fri-Wed; 📶) Around for decades, this is perhaps the best of the sand-side eateries on Meia Praia. It's a fair stroll along the beach, but it's well worth it for the welcoming service, delicious fish soup and toothsome prawns sizzled in butter and garlic.

Mimar Café CAFE €
(Rua António Barbosa Viana 27; snacks €3.50-8.50; ⏰8am-midnight Mon-Sat Jun-Aug, to 10pm Sep-May; 📶) One of the town's best-value casual eateries, Mimar is excellent for coffees and breakfasts, plus home-baked meals (accompanied by scrumptious salads). Daily lunch specials are great deals for around €4. There's an attached *pastelaria* (pastry and cake shop) and by night it's a tapas and wine bar.

★A Forja PORTUGUESE €€
(☎282 768 588; Rua dos Ferreiros 17; mains €8-17.50; ⏰noon-3pm & 6.30-10pm Sun-Fri) Like an Italian trattoria, this buzzing *adega tipica* pulls in the crowds – locals, tourists and expats – for its hearty, top-quality traditional food served in a bustling environment at great prices. Plates of the day are always reliable, as are the simply prepared fish dishes.

Dom Vinho II INTERNATIONAL €€
(Rua Lançarote de Freitas 18; mains €8.50-24; ⏰12.30pm-1.30am Mon-Sat, 7pm-1.30am Sun; 📶) Removed from the main-street bustle where its parent restaurant stands, this elegant upstairs dining area boasts solid dark-wood furniture and a refined feel. Service is truly excellent, and there's a top list of vintage wines. The long menu features dishes unusual for Portugal, such as lamb in mint sauce and spaghetti bolognese. Limited availability after 11pm.

WALKING ACROSS THE ALGARVE

If you like a good walk, by far the best way to appreciate the magnificent landscapes of the inland Algarve is to hike part (or all) of the 300km **Via Algarviana** (www.viaalgarviana.org) that crosses the region from northeast to southwest. Some of the most beautiful sections are around Monchique, where splendid vistas open up as you climb through cork groves to the Algarve's highest hilltops.

Download route information on the website; grabbing the GPS points is also a good idea, as signposting isn't always clear. The official Via Algarviana route booklet (€7) is available from the Algarve Tourist Association's tourist offices.

The best two-day taster of the trail is to stay in Monchique, walk up to Picota and back one day, and up to Fóia and back the next.

Arribalé PORTUGUESE €€
(☎918 556 618; www.arribale.com; Rua da Barroca 40; mains €9.50-19.50, tapas around €5; ⏰7pm-midnight Tue-Sat) Tucked away on an atmospheric street, this super-compact place offers a short, simple menu of mostly salads and grilled meat, though it also does a vegetarian dish of the day. The owners are friendly, quality is high, and there's an appealing, homey vibe. There aren't many tables, so it's worth booking.

O Camilo SEAFOOD €€
(Praia do Camilo; mains €8-15; ⏰10am-10pm; 📶) Just north of Ponta da Piedade, perched on the cliffs above pretty Praia do Camilo, this place is synonymous with excellent seafood dishes. Specialities such as clams, sea bream and tuna steak are on offer daily. The setting is light, bright and airy, and there's a large terrace. This is definitely a place to linger.

Casinha do Petisco SEAFOOD €€
(Rua da Oliveira 51; mains €8-14.50; ⏰10am-3pm & 6-10.45pm Mon-Sat) Blink (or be late) and you'll miss this tiny traditional gem. Cosy and simply decorated, it comes highly recommended for its seafood grills and shellfish dishes.

Cervejaria Dois Irmãos TAPAS €€

(☎282 181 100; Travessa do Mar 2; mains €6.60-18; ⏰11am-midnight; 📶) Locals and passing tourists alike head to this relaxing and stylish place housed in a quaint old building on Praça do Infante. The sublime selection of *petiscos* (tapas) includes everything from pipis to pork ear. *Cataplana* (seafood stew) and good, if somewhat pricey, grilled fish are available, too. There's lovely outdoor seating on the pretty square.

Adega da Marina PORTUGUESE €€

(☎282 764 284; Avenida dos Descobrimentos 35; mains €6-14, fish per kilogram €34-55; ⏰noon-2am; 📶) This barn-like place is a bit like a Portuguese grandmother: she hasn't changed her hairstyle in a while, but she still dishes out generous portions of reliable (and economical) grilled chicken and seafood favourites to grateful guests (who sometimes queue to eat here in summer). Her accessories include iron chandeliers and random farming implements.

Atlântico PORTUGUESE €€€

(☎282 792 806; www.restauranteatlantico.com; Estrada da Meia Praia; mains €14-29; ⏰lunch & dinner Mon-Sat; 📶) Head to Meia Praia to experience this restaurant, where the owner is a bit of a character and the food is expertly prepared. There's a bar, a stunning terrace with beach views and a very old wine collection. The menu, with both Portuguese and international dishes, is extensive. An excellent retreat.

Drinking & Nightlife

★**Bon Vivant** BAR

(www.facebook.com/bonvivant.lagos; Rua 25 de Abril 105; ⏰2pm-4am; 📶) This long-standing central bar is far classier than some of the nearby options, takes some care over its mainly R&B music and makes an effort to keep patrons entertained. Spread across several levels with various terraces, Bon Vivant shakes up some great cocktails and is pretty hot once it gets going (usually late). Look out for the bartenders' juggling feats.

Linda's Bar BAR

(www.lindabeachbar.pt; São Roque, Meia Praia; ⏰10am-11pm Thu-Tue summer, 11am-6pm Thu-Tue winter; 📶) A madly popular beach hang-out, with fab food, good salads, cocktails and tunes.

Stevie Ray's Blues Jazz Bar BAR

(www.stevie-rays.com; Rua da Senhora da Graça 9; ⏰Tue-Sat 9pm-6am; 📶) This intimate two-level candlelit joint is the best live-music bar in town, attracting a smart-casual older crowd. At weekends it has live blues, jazz and oldies. Admission is free, but a €5 minimum consumption is applied.

Red Eye Bar BAR

(www.redeyebarlagos.com; Rua Cândido dos Reis 63; ⏰8pm-2am Tue-Sun) This straight-up rock 'n' surf bar makes a top spot to kick off the night, with drink specials, a pool table and friendly staff.

Garden BEER GARDEN

(Rua Lançarote de Freitas 29; ⏰1pm-midnight; 📶) This appealingly decorated beer garden makes a great spot to lounge around on a sunny afternoon with a beer or cocktail. Once you smell the barbecuing meat, you might decide to stay for a meal, too. To find it, look for the kissing-snails mural on the outside wall.

Inside Out BAR

(www.facebook.com/insideoutFace; Rua Cândido dos Reis 19; ⏰8pm-4am; 📶) This late opener has good DJs and a lively atmosphere, fuelled by enormous fishbowl cocktails.

Duna Beach Club BAR

(Meia Praia; ⏰bar 9pm-2am, restaurant hours vary; 📶) Chill out with the smart set at this hotel bar-restaurant, open day and night. It's located bang on Meia Praia beach, with a pool and attitude. At night it's the bar for the 'resort-chic' folk.

Taberna de Lagos BAR

(www.tabernalagos.pt; Rua Dr Joaquim Tello 1; ⏰noon-2am; 📶) Boasting a stylish space and brooding electronic music in a historic central building, this airy and atmospheric bar and restaurant attracts a somewhat savvier bar-goer than the typical Lagos drinking den (higher cocktail prices also keep some punters away). It has live fado (traditional song) on Monday night.

Grand Café CLUB

(Rua da Senhora da Graça; ⏰10pm-6am; 📶) This classy place has three bars and lots of gold leaf, kitsch, red velvet and cherubs, over which are draped dressed-up local and foreign hipsters. Given its central location, it's a popular spot to end up.

Eddie's Bar BAR

(Rua 25 de Abril 99; ⌚2pm-4am) A good-natured and buzzing local beer stop, this busy dark-wood bar gathers plenty of surfers and backpackers, who spill out onto the street-side tables.

☆ Entertainment

Centro Cultural PERFORMING ARTS

(☎282 770 450; https://centroculturaldelagos.wordpress.com; Rua Lançarote de Freitas 7; ⌚10am-6pm Sep-Jun, 3-11pm Jul & Aug; 📶) This is Lagos' main venue for performances and contemporary-art exhibitions. It's always worth dropping by to see what's on.

Shopping

Owl Story BOOKS

(☎917 414 386; Rua Marreiros Neto 67; ⌚10am-5.30pm Mon-Fri, to 2pm Sat) Run by a friendly English couple, Owl Story has an excellent supply of secondhand books in English.

Mercado Municipal MARKET

(Avenida dos Descobrimentos; ⌚7am-2pm Mon-Sat) Lagos' characterful municipal market is an intriguing place to wander and a great spot to stock up on fresh produce, including excellent seafood.

ℹ Information

Turismo (☎282 763 031; www.visitalgarve.pt; Praça Gil Eanes; ⌚9am-7pm Jul & Aug, to 6pm Easter-Jun & Sep, to 5pm Oct-Easter) The very helpful staff offer excellent maps and leaflets.

ℹ Getting There & Away

BUS

From the **bus station** (☎282 762 944; www.eva-bus.com; Rua Vasco da Gama) buses travel to the following:

Albufeira €5.50, 1½ hours, six daily.

Cabo de São Vicente €4.20, one hour, one on weekdays only.

Faro €5.90, two hours 10 minutes, six daily.

Lisbon €20, four hours, 10 expresses daily.

Portimão €4.30, 25 to 40 minutes, hourly.

Sagres €3.85, one hour, nearly hourly on weekdays, nine on Saturday and Sunday.

To get to/from Carrapateira or Monchique, change at Aljezur (€3.85, 50 minutes, four daily) or Portimão. Buses to Aljezur serve Odeceixe (€4.35, 1½ hours).

Renex also operates an express service from Lagos to Lisbon (€20); tickets are available from the **Renex ticket office** (☎282 768 932, 282 768 931; Rua das Portas de Portugal 101).

Buses also go to Seville (via Huelva) in Spain (€21, 5½ hours, two to three times daily Monday to Friday, more frequently in summer).

TRAIN

Lagos is at the western end of the Algarve line, and has the following direct connections:

Faro (€7.30, 1¾ hours, nine daily), via Albufeira (€4.80, one hour).

Vila Real de Santo António (€10.40, 3¼ hours, seven daily) .

Trains go daily to Lisbon (all requiring a change at Tunes; €22.70, four hours, five daily).

ℹ Getting Around

BOAT

In summer, locals run a **boat** (€0.50; ⌚Apr-Oct) to and fro across the estuary to the Meia Praia side from a landing near the Forte da Ponta da Bandeira.

BUS

Local Onda bus 2 links the city centre with all the surrounding beaches – the main city-centre **stop** is near the market on the riverfront. The tourist office can provide information. Tickets cost €1, a day ticket €3.50. Buses run from Monday to Saturday between 7am and 8pm (7pm on Saturday). A few run on Sunday.

CAR

Drivers are advised to leave their cars in one of the free car parks on the outskirts of Lagos (look for the large parking signs). An alternative is the underground car park on Avenida dos Descobrimentos, but this road can get congested in summer. Street parking spaces close to the centre are metered – watch out or you'll be wheel-clamped.

Local agencies offering competitive car- and scooter-rental rates include the following.

Auto Jardim (☎282 769 486; www.auto-jardim.com; Rua Victor Costa e Silva 18A)

Luzcar (☎282 761 016; www.luzcar.com; Largo das Portas de Portugal 10)

Motorent (☎282 769 716; www.motorent.pt; Rua Victor Costa e Silva; 3-day bicycle/motorcycle/scooter hire from €21/60/60)

TAXI

You can call for **taxis** (☎282 460 610) or find them on Rua das Portas de Portugal where buses stop.

ST VINCENT

Although not much is known about the life of the Spanish-born St Vincent, his death is so legendary that both Spain and Portugal claim him as their own. In Portugal he is considered the patron saint of wine and sea voyages.

St Vincent was a Spanish preacher who was killed by the Romans in 304. During his torturous death (he was burnt at the stake), he is said to have maintained such composure, praising God all the while, that he converted several of his torturers on the spot. Following his martyrdom, his remains were gathered, at which point two differing accounts emerge. Spain claims his final resting place is in Ávila. Portugal claims that his remains washed up on the shores of the Algarve, near Sagres, in a boat watched over by two protective ravens. A shrine in his honour, which Muslim chronicles refer to as the Crow Church, became an object of Christian pilgrimage, though it was destroyed by Muslim fanatics in the 12th century.

Afonso Henriques, Portugal's first king, had the remains moved by ship to Lisbon in 1173, again accompanied by ravens. St Vincent became Lisbon's patron saint (his remains now rest in the **Igreja de São Vicente de Fora**, p110). A raven features in the city's coat of arms – some *lisboêtas* claim that ravens inhabited the church's bell tower for years afterwards.

Lagos to Sagres

To the west of Lagos, the coastline is sharp and ragged, and much less developed, though the area is certainly not undiscovered. Once-sleepy fishing villages set above long beaches have now woken up to the benefits of tourism and, in some cases, developers have moved in. Out of the high season, these places remain bewitchingly calm.

Luz

Six kilometres west of Lagos, the small resort of Luz – fronted by a sandy beach that's ideal for families – is packed with Brits. Most accommodation is prebooked by those on a package deal. Luz is a convenient side trip from Lagos.

Praia da Luz is well known in the UK as the place from where Madeleine McCann disappeared in May 2007.

★**Pastelaria Chicca** INTERNATIONAL €€
(☎282 761 334; www.pastelariachiccaluz.com; Rua da Várzea 3; mains €13-15; ⏲5-11pm Sun-Fri summer, lunch & dinner daily winter; 📶✍) 🌿 You could visit Luz for no other reason than to dine here. Among the superb offerings are savoury bread-and-butter pudding, vegetable stacks (and other veggie options), amazing salads, fish and meats, and top-notch desserts (don't miss the white-chocolate-and-raspberry tart) and cakes. All ingredients are organic. Come with time to spare and an empty stomach.

Getting There & Away

Lagos' **Onda** (www.aonda.pt) bus 4 runs frequently from Lagos (around €2, 15 minutes) and arrives by the village church on the waterfront.

Salema

This charmingly small coastal resort has an easy-going atmosphere; it's set on a wide bay 17km west of Lagos, surrounded by developments that manage not to overwhelm it. It's ideal for families, and there are several small, secluded beaches within a few kilometres – **Praia da Salema** by the village, **Praia da Figueira** to the west and **Boca do Rio** to the east.

Sleeping

Quinta dos Carriços CAMPGROUND €
(☎282 695 201; www.quintadoscarricos.com; sites per adult/tent/car €5/5/4, studios/apt €65/90; P@📶) Just 1.5km north of Salema, this campground is in a peaceful, tree-filled setting with abundant birdlife (no radios allowed!). It has studios and apartments and a designated nudist camping area.

A Maré GUESTHOUSE €€
(☎282 695 165; www.the-mare.com; s/d incl breakfast €64/80, self-catering apt €75-90; ❄📶) Just off the main road into town, this blue-and-white beach house has slightly dated but bright rooms, some with sea views, a pretty garden and a handy guest kitchen. It's a short stroll downhill to the beach. Two-night minimum stay may apply in summer.

Hotel Residencial Salema HOTEL €€

(☎282 695 328; www.hotelsalema.com; Rua 28 de Janeiro; s/d €85/90; ⏲Apr-Oct; P❄📶) Fifty metres from the beach, the Salema offers bright rooms with terraces (most with sea views) in a modern whitewashed building. Guests praise the egg-rich breakfasts and families the quick access to the sand.

Eating

For a place of its size, Salema boasts several excellent eateries.

Água na Boca SEAFOOD €€

(☎282 695 651; Rua dos Pescadores 82; mains €14-18; ⏲5.30-11pm Mon-Sat; 📶) This is a top-notch choice in Salema, with glass sea-view frontage, cellar dining room and a good range of daily seafood specials. You'll find it uphill to the east of the central car park.

Restaurante O Lourenço SEAFOOD €€

(☎282 698 622; Rua 28 de Janeiro; mains €9-16; ⏲lunch & dinner Mon-Sat) Just west of the central car park, this compact and unpretentious place is recommended for its fish (the owner happens to be a keen fisherman). The day's catch will be brought out on a plank for you to select from.

Getting There & Away

At least six buses daily connect Lagos and Salema (€2.65, 30 minutes). Many more stop at the crossroads, from where it's a 3km walk along the main road – these services are marked on timetables as Salema(x).

Sagres

POP 1900

Overlooking some of the Algarve's most dramatic scenery, the small, elongated village of Sagres has an end-of-the-world feel with its sea-carved cliffs and empty, wind-whipped fortress high above the frothing ocean. Despite its connection to Portugal's nautical past, there isn't much of historical interest in town. Its appeal lies mainly in its sense of isolation, plus access to some fine beaches. The village has a laid-back vibe and simple, cheery cafes and bars, and it's become particularly popular in recent years with a surfing crowd. Outside town, the cliffs of Cabo de São Vicente make for an enchanting visit.

One kilometre east of the square, past holiday villas and restaurants, is the port, still a centre for boat building and lobster fishing, and the marina.

Sagres has milder temperatures than other parts of the Algarve, with Atlantic winds keeping the summers cool.

History

Sagres is where dashing Prince Henry the Navigator built a new, fortified town and a semi-monastic school of navigation that specialised in cartography, astronomy and ship design, steering Portugal towards the Age of Discoveries.

At least, that's according to history and myth. Henry was, among other things, governor of the Algarve and he had a residence in its primary port town, Lagos, from where most expeditions set sail. He certainly did put together a kind of nautical think tank, though how much thinking went on out at Sagres is uncertain. He definitely had a house somewhere near Sagres, where he died in November 1460.

In May 1587 the English privateer Sir Francis Drake, in the course of attacking supply lines to the Spanish Armada, captured and wrecked the fortifications around Sagres. The Ponta de Sagres was refortified following the earthquake of 1755, after which there was little of verifiable antiquity left standing.

Sights

Fortaleza de Sagres FORT

(☎282 620 140; adult/child €3/1.50; ⏲9.30am-6.30pm Apr, 9am-8pm May, Jun & Sep, 9am-8.30pm Jul & Aug, 9am-5pm Oct-Mar) Blank, hulking and forbidding, Sagres' fortress offers breathtaking views over the sheer cliffs, and all along the coast to Cabo de São Vicente. According to legend, this is where Prince Henry the Navigator established his navigation school and primed the early Portuguese explorers. It's quite a large site, so allow at least an hour to see everything.

Inside the gate is a huge, curious stone pattern that measures 43m in diameter. Named the **rosa dos ventos** (literally, a pictorial representation of a compass), this strange configuration is believed to be a mariner's compass or a sundial of sorts. Excavated in 1921, the paving may date from Prince Henry's time but is more likely to be from the 16th century.

The precinct's oldest buildings include a cistern tower to the east, a house, and the small, whitewashed, 16th-century **Igreja de Nossa Senhora da Graça**, a simple barrel-vaulted structure with a gilded

17th-century altarpiece. Take a closer look at the tiled altar panels, which feature elephants and antelopes.

Many of the gaps you will see between buildings are the result of a 1960s spring clean of 17th- and 18th-century ruins that was organised to make way for a reconstruction (later aborted) that was to coincide with the 500th anniversary of Henry's death.

It's a great walk around the perimeter of the promontory, information boards shedding light on the rich flora and fauna of the area. Don't miss the limestone crevices descending to the sea, or the labyrinth art installation by Portugal's famous sculpture-architect Pancho Guedes. Near the southern end of the promontory is a **lighthouse**. Death-defying anglers balance on the cliffs below the walls, hoping to land bream or sea bass.

At the time of research a huge, new and incongruously 21st-century visitors centre was being bolted together opposite the entrance. This will contain a gift shop, an exhibition centre and a cafe.

Cabo de São Vicente LANDMARK

Five kilometres from Sagres, Europe's southwesternmost point is a barren headland, the last piece of home that Portuguese sailors once saw as they launched into the unknown. It's a spectacular spot: at sunset you can almost hear the hissing as the sun hits the sea. A red **lighthouse** houses the small but excellent **Museu dos Faróis** (adult/child €1.50/1; ⏲10am-6pm Tue-Sun Apr-Sep, to 5pm Oct-Mar), showcasing Sagres' role in Portugal's maritime history.

The cape – a revered place even in the time of the Phoenicians and known to the Romans as Promontorium Sacrum – takes its present name from a Spanish priest martyred by the Romans. The old fortifications, trashed by Sir Francis Drake in 1587, were later pulverised by the 1755 earthquake.

A kilometre before reaching the lighthouse, you'll pass **Fortaleza do Beliche**, built in 1632 on the site of an older fortress. The interior, once a hotel, is off-limits, but you can descend a pretty pathway down to near the water. The sheltering walls here make for a more appealing picnic spot than the wind-whipped cape.

Beaches

There are four good beaches a short drive or long walk from Sagres: **Praia da Mareta**, just below the town; lovely **Praia do Martinhal** to the east; **Praia do Tonel** on the other side of the Ponta de Sagres, and good for surfing; and the isolated **Praia de Beliche**, on the way to Cabo de São Vicente.

Surfing is possible at all beaches except Praia do Martinhal and nearby Praia da Baleeira. Several places offer surfing and bodyboarding lessons.

Activities

Boating & Diving

★**Mar Ilimitado** BOATING

(☎916 832 625; www.marilimitado.com; Porto da Baleeira) Mar Ilimitado, a team of marine biologists, offers a variety of highly recommended, ecologically sound boat trips, from dolphin spotting (€35, 1½ hours) and seabird watching (€45, 2½ hours) to excursions up to Cabo de São Vicente (€25, one hour).

Cape Cruiser BOATING

(☎919 751 175; www.capecruiser.org; Porto da Baleeira) Offers a range of boat trips, including dolphin watching (€35, 1½ hours), seabird watching (€45, 2½ hours), trips to Cabo São Vicente (€25, one hour) and various fishing excursions.

DiversCape DIVING

(☎965 559 073; www.diverscape.com; Porto da Baleeira) The PADI-certified DiversCape organises snorkelling expeditions (€25, two hours), plus dives of between 12m and 30m around shipwrecks. A dive and equipment costs €50/240/380 for one/six/10 dives, while the four-day PADI open-water course is €395. Beginners' courses (from €80) are available and there are even sessions for children aged over eight (€60).

Surfing

Sagres Natura SURFING

(☎282 624 072; www.sagresnatura.com; Rua São Vicente) This recommended surf school also rents out bodyboards (€15 per day), surfboards (€20) and wetsuits (€10). It has bikes for hire (€10) and the same company also runs a surf-equipment shop and hostel.

Free Ride Sagres Surfcamp SURFING

(☎916 089 005, 965 780 252; www.frsurf.com; Hotel Memmo Baleeira, Sítio da Baleeira; 1-/3-/5-day lessons €60/165/250) One of several surf schools in the area, this set-up offers lessons, packages and hire, as well as free transport from Sagres and Lagos to wherever the surf's good that day.

Sagres

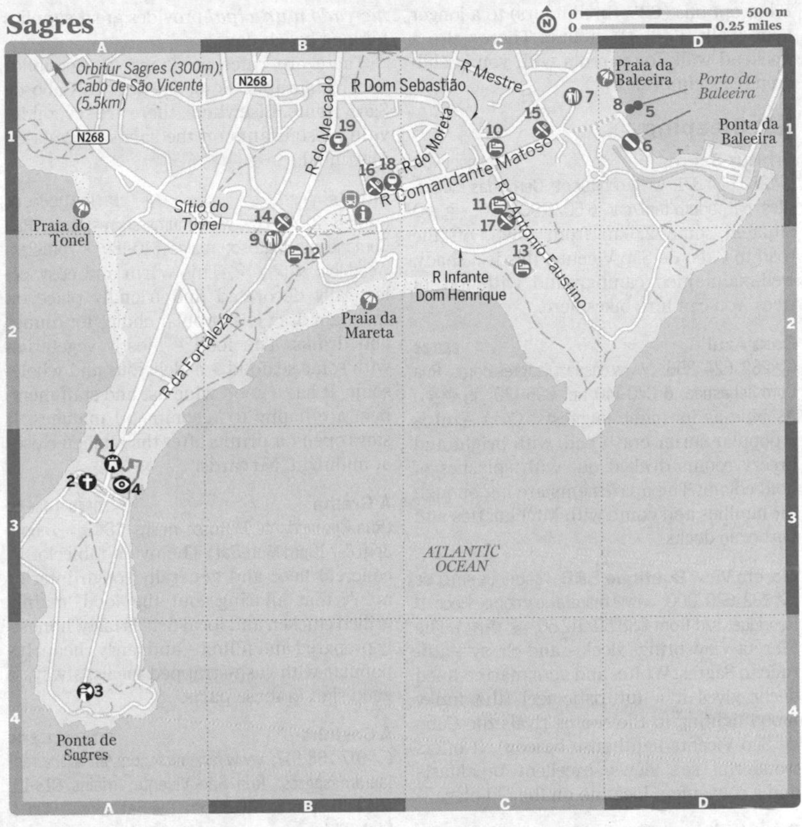

Sagres

Sights

- 1 Fortaleza de Sagres A3
- 2 Igreja de Nossa Senhora da Graça A3
- 3 Lighthouse A4
- 4 Rosa dos Ventos A3

Activities, Courses & Tours

- 5 Cape Cruiser D1
- 6 DiversCape D1
- 7 Free Ride Sagres Surfcamp C1
- 8 Mar Ilimitado D1
- 9 Sagres Natura B2

Sleeping

- 10 Casa Azul C1
- 11 Casa do Cabo de Santa Maria C1
- 12 Mareta View Boutique B&B B2
- 13 Pousada do Infante C2

Eating

- 14 A Casínha B1
- 15 A Grelha C1
- 16 Mum's B1
- 17 Vila Velha C1

Drinking & Nightlife

- 18 Dromedário B1
- Pau de Pita .... (see 18)
- 19 Warung B1

Walking

★ Walkin'Sagres WALKING

(☎ 925 545 515; www.walkinsagres.com) Multilingual Ana Carla offers recommended guided walks in the Sagres area, explaining the history and other details of the surrounds. The walks head through pine forests to the cape's cliffs, and vary from shorter

7.7km options (€25, three hours) to a longer 15km walk (€40, 4½ hours). There's also a weekend walk for parents with young children (€15, children free).

Sleeping

Orbitur Sagres CAMPGROUND €
(282 624 371; www.orbitur.pt; Cerra das Moitas; sites per adult/tent/car 6.50/6.90/6.10;) Situated some 2.5km from town, off the road to Cabo de São Vicente, this is a shady, well-maintained campground with lots of trees. You can hire bikes here.

Casa Azul B&B €€
(282 624 856; www.casaazulsagres.com; Rua Dom Sebastião; d €70-140, apt €95-120;) As blue as its name suggests, Casa Azul is a popular surfer crash pad, with bright and breezy rooms decked out with splashes of bold colour. The apartments are big enough for families and come with kitchenettes and barbecue decks.

Mareta View Boutique B&B BOUTIQUE HOTEL €€
(282 620 000; www.maretaview.com; Beco D Henrique; s/d from €88.50/112.50;) The Mareta View brings sleek – and classy – attitude to Sagres. White- and aquamarine-hued decor gives it a futuristic feel (the funky mood lighting in the rooms rivals the Cabo de São Vicente lighthouse beacon). It offers wonderful sea views, excellent breakfasts and a convenient location on the old plaza.

Casa do Cabo de Santa Maria GUESTHOUSE €€
(282 624 722; www.casadocabodesantamaria.com; Rua Patrão António Faustino; not incl breakfast d €60-80, apt €80-120;) These immaculately kept, welcoming rooms and apartments might not have sweeping views, but they are colourfully furnished and are cleaned daily. They're excellent value.

Pousada do Infante HOTEL €€€
(282 620 240; www.pousadas.pt; Rua Patrão António Faustino; r from €150;) Possibly the most pleasant place to stay in Sagres, this modern *pousada* (upmarket inn) boasts large rooms in a great setting near the clifftop. Count on bright interiors with splashes of fruity colour, public areas with an air of colonial grandeur and picture-perfect views from the terraces.

Eating

Many places close or operate shorter hours during low season (November to April). The *mercado municipal* provides great supplies for long beach days.

There are cafes on Praça de República and restaurants along the way to Cabo de São Vicente. Elsewhere, there are several inviting restaurants on the sands of Praia do Martinhal.

Mum's INTERNATIONAL €€
(968 210 411; www.mums-sagres.com; Rua Comandante Matoso; mains €10-18; 7pm-2am Wed-Mon;) This warm and cosy, eclectically decorated and friendly place on the main drag is a popular choice for dinner and drinks. The food – mostly vegetarian with some seafood – is delicious and wholesome. It has a good wine list and staff members are happy to recommend matches. It stays open for drinks after the kitchen closes at midnight. No cards.

A Grelha PORTUGUESE €€
(Rua Comandante Matoso; mains €8-13; noon-3pm & 7-10pm Mon-Sat) The nylon tablecloths, concrete floor and generally rough interior aren't that alluring, but the food, mainly grilled chicken and local fish, is tasty, honestly prepared and filling – and fairly cheap. It's popular with cash-strapped locals, always a good sign in these parts.

A Casínha PORTUGUESE €€
(917 768 917; www.facebook.com/acasinha.restaurantesagres; Rua São Vicente; mains €13-19; 12.30-3pm & 7-10.30pm Tue-Sat, closed Jan & Feb) This cosy terracotta-and-white spot – built on the site of the owner's grandparents' house – serves up some fabulous Portuguese cuisine, including stand-out barbecued fish, a good variety of *cataplanas* (seafood stews) for two (€34) and *arroz de polvo* (octopus rice). High quality, with a pleasant atmosphere.

★ **A Eira do Mel** PORTUGUESE €€€
(282 639 016; Estrada do Castelejo, Vila do Bispo; mains €16-22; noon-2.30pm & 7.30-10pm Tue-Sat) It's worth driving 10km north of Sagres to Vila do Bispo to enjoy José Pinheiro's creations at this much-lauded slow-food restaurant. The meat leans towards the Algarvian; the seafood has a more contemporary touch. Think rabbit in red-wine sauce (€16), octopus *cataplana* (seafood stew) with sweet potatoes (€35 for two people), curried Atlantic wild shrimps (€22) and *javali* (wild boar; €17). Mouth-watering.

Vila Velha INTERNATIONAL €€€
(☎282 624 788; www.vilavelha-sagres.com; Rua Patrão António Faustino; mains €13-30; ⌚6.30pm-midnight Tue-Sun;) In a stylish old house with a lovely mature garden in front, the upmarket, Dutch-owned Vila Velha offers consistently good seafood mains (go for the catch of the day), plus meat dishes such as rabbit and pork in mango sauce. It's more internationally flavoured than all of Sagres' other restaurants.

Drinking & Nightlife

It's Groundhog Day (albeit a pleasant one) along Rua Comandante Matoso, with several atmospheric, good-value cafe-bars located cheek-to-cheek, the centre of Sagres' post-surfing nightlife scene.

Warung BAR
(☎282 624 432; www.warung.eu; Rua do Mercado; ⌚6pm-2am;) This popular post-surf spot plays a good variety of music, does decent food, offers a range of drinks and has a relaxed but upbeat atmosphere. Worth seeking out.

Pau de Pita CAFE
(Rua Comandante Matoso; ⌚10am-2am;) The funkiest of its neighbours in the bar strip (at least in terms of its design), this place has great salads, crêpes and juices (snacks €4 to €10), all enjoyed to a chilled-out soundtrack. At night, it mixes decent drinks and is as lively as any of the other bars, with a good post-surfing vibe.

Dromedário BAR
(☎282 624 219; Rua Comandante Matoso; ⌚10am-late;) Sagres' original cafe-bar, Dromedário is still going strong (it's been here for well over 30 years). There's good food (try the burgers), karaoke and 'mixology', aka creative cocktails. The spacious, mildly Moorish-themed interior is a cool spot to hang out after a day on the waves.

Information

Bank & ATM (Rua Comandante Matoso)
Turismo (☎282 624 873; www.cm-viladobispo.pt; Rua Comandante Matoso; ⌚9am-1pm & 2-6pm Tue-Sat, extended hours summer) Situated on a patch of green lawn, 100m east of Praça da República. Buses stop nearby.

Getting There & Around

The **bus stop** (Rua Comandante Matoso) is by the *turismo*. You can buy tickets on the bus.

Buses come from Lagos via Salema (€3.85, one hour, six daily). On weekends there are fewer services. It's only 10 minutes to Cabo de São Vicente (twice daily on weekdays only; €2). Handy bike rental is available at **Sagres Natura** (p200) and also at **Maretta Shop** (☎282 624 535; www.marettashop.com; Rua Comandante Matoso; ⌚9.30am-10.30pm).

WILDLIFE OF THE ALGARVE

With five special protection areas (a birding initiative), eight special areas of conservation, two natural parks and one natural reserve – not to forget its sea life – the Algarve is one of the most flora- and fauna-rich regions of the country. The **purple gallinule** (aka the purple swamp-hen or sultan chicken) is one of Europe's rarest and most nattily turned-out birds – a large violet-blue water creature with red bill and legs. In Portugal it only nests in a patch of wetland spilling into the exclusive Quinta do Lago estate, at the western end of the Parque Natural da Ria Formosa (p165), 12km west of Faro. Look for it near the lake at the estate's São Lourenço Nature Trail.

Another eye-catching Algarve resident is the **Mediterranean chameleon**, a 25cm-long reptile with independently moving eyes, a tongue longer than its body and skin that mimics its environment. It's the only chameleon found in Europe, its habitat limited to Crete and the Iberian Peninsula. Your best chance of seeing this shy creature is on spring mornings in the Quinta Marim area of the Parque Natural da Ria Formosa or in Monte Gordo's conifer woods, now a protected habitat for the species.

Bird-lovers should consider a trip to the Serra do Caldeirão foothills. The dramatic Rocha da Pena, a 479m-high limestone outcrop, is a classified site because of its rich flora and fauna. **Orchids**, **narcissi** and **native cistus** cover the slopes, where **red foxes** and **Egyptian mongooses** are common. Among many bird species seen here are the huge **eagle owl**, the **Bonelli's eagle** and the **buzzard**.

There's a *centro ambiental* (environmental centre) in Pena village, and you can walk up to the top of Rocha itself.

North of Sagres

Heading north along the Algarve's western coast, you'll find some amazing beaches, backed by beautiful wild vegetation. Thanks to building restrictions imposed to protect the **Parque Natural do Sudoeste Alentejano e Costa Vicentina**, it's relatively well preserved. This protected area is rarely more than 6km wide, and runs for about 120km from Burgau to Cabo de São Vicente and up nearly the entire western Algarve and Alentejo shore. Here there are at least 48 plant species found only in Portugal, and around a dozen or so found only within the park.

The region is home to otters, foxes and wildcats, and some 200 species of bird enjoy the coastal wetlands, salt marshes and cliffs, including Portugal's last remaining ospreys. Although the seas can be dangerous, the area has a growing reputation for some of Europe's finest surf and attracts people from all over the world.

Carrapateira

Surf-central Carrapateira is a tranquil, pretty, spread-out village, with two exhilarating nearby beaches whose lack of development, fizzing surf and strong swells attract both a hippy, surf-dude crowd and, more recently, *Lisboetas*. The coast along here is wild, with copper-coloured and ash-grey cliffs covered in speckled yellow and green scrub, backing creamy, wide sands.

Sights

Museu do Mar e da Terra da Carrapateira MUSEUM

(☎282 970 000; Rua de Pescador; adult/child €2.50/1; ⏲10am-1pm & 1.30-4.30pm Tue-Sat) The Carrapateira Land & Sea Museum is a must for visitors – surfers or otherwise. Up a steep hill near the top of town, its contemporary design space has small exhibits covering everything from the fishing industry to the daily life of locals, and intriguing photographic collages depict the Carrapateira of yesteryear (there's minimal English labelling). The vista from the museum's ingenious viewing window over the dunes is sublime.

Activities

For surfing courses (packaged with accommodation) contact **Algarve Surf School** (☎962 846 771; www.algarvesurfschool.com; Praia do Amado; day lesson €50) or **Amado Surfcamp** (☎927 831 568; www.amadosurfcamp.com; 1-week package incl accommodation, breakfast, equipment hire & lessons €425-525, camping €325).

★Beach Hike WALKING

The 9km circuit of Carrapateira's two fabulous beaches, Praia da Bordeira and Praia do Amado, from the town is a visually stunning hike (or drive), with lookouts over the beaches and the rocky coves and cliffs between them.

Praia da Bordeira BEACH

(Praia Carrapateira) Beautiful Praia da Bordeira is a mammoth swathe of sand merging into dunes 2km from the north side of town.

Praia do Amado BEACH

Known for its surf, stunning Praia do Amado is at the southern end of the village.

Praia de Vale Figueira BEACH

One of the more remote west-coast beaches, this wide, magnificent stretch of whitish sand has an ethereal beauty, backed by stratified cliffs hazy in the ocean spray. It's reached by a rough, partly paved road that runs some 5km from the main road at a point 10km north of Carrapateira (take the northern of the two turn-offs). There are no facilities.

Sleeping

Despite the number of campervans you see around the place, camping here is definitely illegal – please think twice before joining the camping fray; the dune system is particularly fragile.

Monte do Sapeiro B&B €€

(☎282 973 108; www.montedosapeiro.pt; Vilarinha; r €100; P❄📶) You'll settle in here like a pig in a sty…which is exactly what these two rooms formerly were. Now they're contemporary and very sleek accommodation, set on a lawn with lounging areas and views of fields beyond. The stunning kitchen is for communal use (and breakfasts with homemade goodies). It's located in Vilarinha, a small inland village just south of Carrapateira.

There's a minimum stay of a week in July and August, and two nights at other times.

Bamboo GUESTHOUSE €€

(☎969 009 988, 282 973 323; Sítio do Rio; d/tr €60/85, 2-person apt €90; 📶) 🍃 About 800m from Praia da Bordeira, on the main road, this friendly, ecologically-minded guest house has four decent, colourful rooms and friendly owners. It also has a great open-plan apartment.

Casa Fajara BOUTIQUE HOTEL €€€
(282 973 134; www.casafajara.com; Bordeira; r €105-172;) Looking like a Greek villa, this secluded boutique hideaway offers real relaxation. The rooms vary in size and outlook – some have balconies – but all are extremely well kept, with excellent facilities. It's 500m down the road opposite the turnoff to Praia da Bordeira.

Eating

Cafes and snack bars line the town's tiny plaza and keep long hours.

Microbar Carrapateira CAFE €
(Largo do Comercio; meals €5-11; 10am-10pm) The name certainly conceals just how much this excellent place on the square has to offer. Whatever you feel like, it's got it. That includes surfer comfort food, including tasty bruschetta, generous hamburgers and vegetarian options; an ice-cold *imperial* (small draught beer); moist cakes; soy coffee; and a cocktail in the sun.

Sítio do Forno SEAFOOD €€
(282 973 914; Praia do Amado; mains €8-17; noon-10pm;) On the cliff overlooking Praia do Amado, this large eatery evolved from a tiny fisher's cabana. The value is in the setting (with its magnificent ocean views), not so much in the cuisine (though some fish dishes are delicious, depending on what's available).

Getting There & Away

One bus a day on weekdays links Carrapateira with Aljezur (€3.25, 25 minutes), where you can change for Lagos.

Aljezur

Some 20km north of Carrapateira, Aljezur is an attractive village that straddles a river. The western part is Moorish, with a collection of cottages below a ruined 10th-century hilltop castle; the eastern side, called Igreja Nova (New Church), is 600m up a steep hill. Aljezur is close to some fantastic beaches, edged by black rocks that reach into the white-tipped, bracing sea – surfing hot spots. The surrounding countryside, which is part of the natural park, is a tangle of yellow, mauve and green wiry gorse and heather.

Sights & Activities

Hidden in the narrow backstreets of Aljezur is a string of quaint museums (one admission price of €2 permits you to visit all four museums!). All are well worth a visit.

Museu Municipal MUSEUM
(www.cm-aljezur.pt; Largo 5 de Outubro; €2; 9am-1pm & 2-6pm Tue-Sat) This small but likeable museum has three rooms. Downstairs is an archaeological collection displaying everything from Stone Age axes to a 16th-century whipping post, while across the hall the Islamic section has a good selection of locally produced ceramics. Upstairs is an ethnographic display with everything from clocks to carts. Information is in Portuguese. An English video explains the area's attractions, which include three nearby museums that you can enter on the same ticket.

Museu de Arte Sacra MUSEUM
(Rua do Castelo; €2; 9am-1pm & 2-6pm Tue-Sat) Built in the 16th century and damaged in the 1755 earthquake, the modest Igreja da Misericórdia church was reconstructed in the 18th century. Its small religious-art museum houses items donated by a locally born Monsignor. The highlights are the old church bell and a 14th-century crown. Visit the museum first, and the guardian will open the church for you. Admission includes entry to three other Aljezur museums.

Castelo CASTLE
(24hr) FREE The polygonal castle, on the site of an Iron Age fort, was built by the Moors in the 10th century, conquered by the Christians in 1249, then abandoned in the late 15th century. The walls and a couple of towers survive, as well as a cistern. Great views of the surrounding area can be had from the rock in the middle of the fortress.

Museu Antoniano MUSEUM
(www.cm-aljezur.pt; Rua de Santo António; €2; 9am-1pm & 2-5pm Tue-Sat Oct-May, to 6pm Jun-Sep) Housed in a former chapel built in the 17th century (which was destroyed in the 1755 earthquake), this is now a museum devoted to St Anthony, with paintings, books, coins and icons all relating to the saint. Admission includes entry to three other Aljezur museums. Ask at the Museu Municipal for entry.

Casa Museu Pintor José Cercas MUSEUM
(www.cm-aljezur.pt; Rua do Castelo; €2; 9am-1pm & 2-5pm Tue-Sat Oct-May, to 6pm Jun-Sep)

This quaint house belonged to Portuguese painter José Cercas (1914–92) who left his home and belongings – a collection of furniture, artworks and personal objects – to the town. Ask at the Museu Municipal (p205) for entry. Admission includes entry to three other Aljezur museums.

Burros e Artes TOUR
(☎967 145 306, 282 995 068; www.burros-artes.blogspot.com; Vale das Amoreiras) For those who believe 'slow is beautiful', this might be your kind of travel – covering 10km to 15km per day on foot with nothing but you, stunning nature and your *burro* (donkey), which carries your luggage. This company coordinates trips – generally from two days to two weeks – including accommodation, food and optional multilingual guides.

Beaches

Wonderful, unspoilt beaches near Aljezur include **Praia da Arrifana** (10km southwest, near a tourist development called Vale da Telha), a dramatic, curved black-cliff-backed bay with one restaurant, balmy pale sands and some big northwest swells (a surfer's delight); and **Praia de Monte Clérigo**, about 8km northwest. **Praia de Amoreira**, 6km away, is a wonderful beach where the river meets the sea. More difficult to reach but worth the effort is the more remote **Praia de Vale Figueira**, about 15km southwest of Aljezur via rugged dirt roads.

Surfing lessons are available through **Arrifana Surf School** (☎917 862 138; www.arrifanasurfschool.com; Praia da Arrifana; 1-/3-/4-/5-day course €55/150/200/225; ⏲Mar-Oct).

Sleeping

Amazigh Hostel HOSTEL €
(☎282 997 502; www.amazighostel.com; Rua da Ladeira 5; dm/d €15/59; @📶) This hip and happening hostel is clean and intelligently designed, with inbuilt lockers under the bunks, steel staircases, surfboard and gear storage, a cool living area (including a sun terrace with lovely views), plus a communal kitchen. It's all about the waves here: it's a great place for tips on local conditions, and there's summer transport to nearby beaches.

Pousada da Juventude HOSTEL €
(☎282 997 455; www.pousadasjuventude.pt; Praia da Arrifana; dm/d €17/64; P) This grey-and-yellow hostel is decked out in plastic furniture of cutting-edge design. The hostel offers light and airy rooms, great communal areas including a sunny terrace, a storeroom for surf gear, and a washing and drying room. The location is superb, a few minutes' walk from Praia da Arrifana.

Parque de Campismo Serrão CAMPGROUND €
(☎282 990 220; www.campingserrao.com; per adult/tent/car €5.50/5/4; P@📶🏊) This tranquil, shaded site is 4km north of Aljezur, then 1km off the main road. It has wheelchair access, tennis courts, a playground and apartments, plus bike rental. There are also house apartments for rent.

Restaurante-Bar A Lareira GUESTHOUSE €€
(☎282 998 440; Rua 3 de Janeiro; d/tr €70/85; 📶) Located in Igreja Nova, this guest house boasts 12 clean and tidy rooms with wood details, and each opens onto a shared terrace with lovely views. There's a good restaurant below.

Eating

Cafe-bars overlook the main square around Igreja Nova. In Praia da Arrifana there's a string of seafood restaurants (packed with Portuguese at weekends) on the road above the beach, where you can expect to pay around €10 for grilled fish.

O Paulo SEAFOOD €€
(☎282 995 184; www.restauranteopaulo.com; Arrifana; mains €12-20; ⏲9.30am-10pm; 📶) Spectacularly set by the ruined fortress of Arrifana, with majestic clifftop views as far as Cabo de São Vicente, O Paulo has a covered terrace that makes a romantic spot for a meal. The vistas are hard to live up to, but it does a pretty good job here, with plates – just about all seafood – packed with Algarve flavour and colour.

Bistrot Gulli ITALIAN €€
(☎282 994 344; Sítio de Santa Susana, N120; mains €11-18; ⏲12.30pm-midnight Tue-Sun) On the main road 4km south of Aljezur, this looks like a standard driver's lunch stop until you enter and discover a handsome modern interior and a menu of not just pizzas but rather innovative, quality Mediterranean staples using excellent ingredients. There are various degustation options, so kick back, order some wine, designate a driver and enjoy.

Restaurante-Bar A Lareira PORTUGUESE €€
(Rua 3 de Janeiro; mains €9-15; ⏲9am-11pm) Warning: walk past here with a rumbling

tummy and you'll be in like a shot, lured by the wonderful aromas emanating through the doors. It's unpretentious and family run, and (you guessed it) it serves up authentic Portuguese meat and fish dishes.

Shopping

Mercado Municipal MARKET

(8am-2pm Mon-Sat) Located near the bridge, the municipal market is a good place to buy fresh fruit and veggies, and it has a very appealing fish counter.

Information

Turismo (282 998 229; Rua 25 de Abril 62; 9am-6pm Tue-Thu, 9am-1pm & 2-6pm Fri-Mon) On the main road through town; helpful.

Getting There & Away

If you're driving, there's a free car park next to the *turismo*. Eva buses run between Lagos and Aljezur (€3.85, four on weekdays, one on Saturday). One bus runs on weekdays to/from Carrapateira (30 minutes). **Rede Expressos** (www.rede-expressos.pt) buses run north to Lisbon (€18, two daily) and south to Lagos (€8, two daily) and Portimão (€9, one daily). No buses run to/from Praia da Arrifana.

Odeceixe

Around here the countryside rucks up into rolling, large hills. As the Algarve turns into the Alentejo, the last coastal settlement is Odeceixe, an endearing small town clinging to the southern side of the Ribeira de Seixe valley, and so snoozy it's in danger of falling off, except during high season, when Portuguese and European visitors pack the place out.

Activities

Rota Vicentina HIKING

(www.rotavicentina.com) This long-distance walking route enters the Algarve at Odeceixe and continues right down the west coast to Cabo de São Vicente. The day walk from Odeceixe to Aljezur (18km) is an easy introduction to the trail, heading through mostly flat local farmland. It's a picturesque glimpse of Portuguese rural life. Optional detours take you right to the coast for clifftop stretches.

Praia de Odeceixe BEACH

This tongue of sand is winningly set at a river mouth and flanked by imposing cliffs. It's a good family option, as smaller kids can paddle on the peaceful river side of the strand. It's 3.5km from the endearing whitewashed village of Odeceixe, a hub of budget accommodation. The beach itself has eating, sleeping and surfing options.

Odeceixe Surf School SURFING

(963 170 493; www.odeceixesurfschool.com; Praia de Odeceixe; 1-/3-/5-day courses €55/150/225; 10.30am-7pm) This friendly setup offers surfing classes (and board and wetsuit rental), with sites both on and just above the beach; look for the octopus sign. It'll transport you to whatever local beach has the best waves that day and can arrange packages with accommodation.

Sleeping

Pensão Luar GUESTHOUSE €

(282 947 194; www.pensaoluar.blogspot.com; Rua da Várzea 28; d/tr €65/75;) At the western edge of the village, this friendly place is good value (prices are almost half outside high season), with modern, white spic-and-span rooms with traditional dark-wood furniture and tiled floors. A basic breakfast is included.

Parque de Campismo São Miguel CAMPGROUND €

(282 947 145; www.campingsaomiguel.com; sites per adult/tent/car €6.75/6.20/5.70, bungalows from €85;) Not technically in the Algarve, but close enough to be very handy, this campground-miniresort is 1.5km north of Odeceixe. Shaded by pines, it has bags of facilities, including a proper restaurant and a large pool area. Wooden bungalows are also available. Very quiet in low season.

Casa Hospedes Celeste GUESTHOUSE €

(282 947 150; www.casahospedesceleste.com; Rua Nova 9; d €50-60;) Run by delightful owners, this renovated, clean and bright spot is excellent value and located in a great central location. Rooms are smallish but have colourful bedspreads and TV. Hikers and surfers are welcome. Considerably lower rates outside July and August.

Casa Vicentina INN €€€

(282 947 447; www.casavicentina.pt; Monte Novo; d/ste €125/165;) For a touch of indulgence head to this stylish complex set in tranquil, rural surrounds. The interior-decorator owner has gone to town in the rooms and suites; these are arranged around a lush green lawn with pool and lily

ponds. Some rooms have kitchenettes. It's 2km from Odeceixe, near Maria Vinagre, and is well signposted.

Eating

Chaparro PORTUGUESE **€€**
(Rua da Estrada Nacional; mains €7.50-12.50; ⌚noon-midnight) A great choice for tasty no-nonsense Portuguese grilled meat and seafood, which can be enjoyed in the smoky dining room or outside when the mercury is high. Watch your food cook before your very eyes on the huge grill inside or chill with a drink until the waiter bangs it down.

Taberna do Gabão PORTUGUESE **€€**
(☎282 947 549; Rua do Gabão 9; mains €7-13; ⌚10am-midnight) Odeceixe's best dining option, this welcoming restaurant features good-value traditional dishes served in a charming old-fashioned wooden dining room. There's also a small patio for outdoor seating.

Getting There & Away

Express buses run between Lagos and Odeceixe (€4.45, 80 minutes, four on weekdays) via Aljezur (35 minutes). Buy tickets at the *papelaria* (newsagent; open 9am to 1pm) next to the market.

Monchique

POP 2800

High above the coast, in cool mountainous woodlands, the picturesque hamlet of Monchique makes a lovely base for exploring the surrounding area, with some excellent options for walking, biking and canoeing. Nearby Caldas de Monchique, a locally famous spa town, is another alluring factor.

Set in the forested Serra de Monchique, the Algarve's mountain range, lying some 24km north of Portimão, Monchique is also known for having the best brews of the fiery *medronho*, a locally made liqueur.

Fires regularly affect this area during summer. These cause widespread damage and ongoing frustration at the lack of measures to prevent the devastation.

Sights

A series of brown pedestrian signs starting near the bus station directs visitors up into the town's narrow old streets and major places of interest.

Nossa Senhora do Desterro CHAPEL
Overlooking the town from a wooded hilltop are the ruins of a 17th-century Franciscan monastery. It is on the path of the Via Algarviana and you can climb up here.

Igreja Matriz CHURCH
(Rua da Igreja; ⌚9am-6pm) The local church has an extraordinary, star-shaped Manueline porch decorated with twisted columns that look like lengths of knotted rope. The side door is also impressive. Inside you'll find a simple interior, with columns topped with ropey capitals, and a side chapel that contains beautiful 17th-century glazed tiles showing St Francis, sinners in hell, and St Michael roughing up the devil. Behind the church is a small **museum of sacred art** (www.cm-monchique.pt; Rua da Igreja; €1; ⌚10am-1pm Mon-Fri).

Activities

Walks around Monchique HIKING
The Via Algarviana (p195) passes through Monchique between spectacular climbs to the hills of Picota and Fóia, making Monchique a great base for hiking. It's around 10.5km return to the top of Picota, and 8km one way to the summit of Fóia. There are several other reasonably well-marked walks in the vicinity.

From Monchique, the Trilha dos Moinhos is a 10.3km circuit of the hills above town, offering some fabulous views. From the top of Fóia, there are loop trails of 6.5km and 17km, while Caldas de Monchique, Picota and Monchique are linked by an 18km circular trail.

Alternativtour OUTDOORS
(☎965 004 337; www.alternativtour.com; tours €50-75) Alternativtour runs guided walks, mountain-biking tours, canoeing trips and combined mountain-biking and canoeing trips. Tours require a minimum of two people; per-person prices decrease the larger the group gets. Bike hire costs €20 per day.

Outdoor Tours OUTDOORS
(☎282 969 520; www.outdoor-tours.com; Rua Francisco Bivar 142A, Mexilhoeira Grande; tours from €20) This Dutch-run company offers biking (€48), kayaking (from Lagos; €25) and walking trips (day walks €38) in and around the Algarve and Serra de Monchique.

WORTH A TRIP

FÓIA

The 902m Fóia peak, 8km west of Monchique, is the Algarve's highest. The road to the summit climbs through eucalyptus and pine trees and opens up views over the hills. On the way are numerous piri-piri pit stops offering spicy chicken. Telecommunication towers prickle the summit, but ignore them and look at the panoramic views. On clear days you can see to the corners of the western Algarve – Cabo de São Vicente to the southwest and Odeceixe to the northwest.

We know that you shouldn't use the word 'gorgeous' too much. But that's all that comes to mind when describing **O Luar da Fóia** (282 911 149; Estrada da Fóia; mains €7-14.50; 10am-11pm Tue-Sun) – this 'g' word applies to the setting (slightly rustic), the view (cliff-edge expansive) and the cuisine (full-on traditional Portuguese using quality produce). Of course, chicken piri-piri is the go here, as is suckling pig, cow's cheek in a pot and some excellent-value wines. It's well worth the extra grunt to get here.

Sleeping

Miradouro da Serra GUESTHOUSE €
(282 912 163; Rua dos Combatentes do Ultramar; s/d €36/44; P) Up steep Rua Engenheiro Duarte Pacheco (signposted to Portimão), near the *turismo,* this 1970s hilltop place, run with great seriousness, offers sweeping, breezy views and neat rooms, some with balcony. It's popular with hikers who appreciate the day-launching breakfast.

Villa Vina INN €€
(965 753 393; www.villavina.pt; Rua de Caldas de Monchique; r €79; P) Hidden up a tiny pathway (note: the only access is by steps) and signed as you cross the Ribeira do Banho, around 500m after the turn-off to Caldas de Monchique, this lovely rural villa with a pretty garden is perfect for those who crave seclusion rather than village infrastructure. Reservations are required.

Vilafoìa HOTEL €€€
(282 910 110; www.vilafoia.com; Corte Pereiro Apartado 241; s/d not incl breakfast €91/119; P) Efficiently run and quite up to date, this rural hotel enjoys an enchanting location in a hillside cork grove, with splendid views south over the Algarvian coast. Downstairs rooms are bright, with balconies, while upstairs are good family suites; a couple of self-catering cottages are further up the hill. It's a good base for walkers.

To find it, head out of Monchique towards Fóia and turn left after 1km: it's signposted from there.

Eating

Ó Chá Lá CAFE €
(Rua Samora Gil 12; light meals €2-6; 9am-7pm Mon-Fri, to 2pm Sat;) Teahouses are a bit like puppies: it's very difficult to dislike them. And this calming spot is no exception, doing light meals such as soups and quiches, and turning out excellent cakes and tarts in a bright, tiled-floor space.

A Charrete PORTUGUESE €€
(282 912 142; Rua Samora Gil 30-34; mains €11-16; lunch & dinner Thu-Tue) Touted as the area's best eatery for its wide menu of regional dishes, this likeably old-fashioned, though slightly pricey place offers reliably good cuisine amid country-rustic charm. A house speciality is the cabbage with spicy sausages. The unusually long list of desserts includes an award-winning honey flan.

Drinking & Nightlife

Barlefante BAR
(Travessa das Guerreiras; noon-2am Mon-Thu, 1pm-4am Fri & Sat, 1pm-2am Sun;) Monchique's coolest haunt, this fun cave-like place has a touch of the burlesque, with hot-pink walls, red-velvet alcoves, ornate mirrors and chandeliers. The outdoor tables on this narrow alley are also a prime spot.

Shopping

Leonel Telo CERAMICS
(Rua Engenheiro Duarte Pacheco; 11am-5pm) Located on the main road, by the big bend in the centre of town, this studio lets you watch potter Leonel at work and browse his bright, quality ceramics.

Information

Turismo (282 911 189; www.cm-monchique.pt; Largo de São Sebastião; 9.30am-1pm & 2-5.30pm Mon-Fri) A useful spot for picking up maps, and has some information on walks.

Getting There & Away

Frota-Azul (www.frotazul-algarve.pt) buses run to/from Portimão (€4.30, 45 minutes, five to eight daily).

Caldas de Monchique

Caldas de Monchique is a bit like the set of *The Truman Show*. It's a slightly sanitised, faintly fantastical hamlet with a therapeutic calm, its pastel-painted buildings nestled above a delightful valley full of birdsong and eucalyptus, acacia and pine trees. Located 6km south of Monchique, it's 500m below the main road.

It has been a popular spa for over two millennia – the Romans loved its 32°C, slightly sulphurous waters, which are said to be good for rheumatism, and respiratory and digestive ailments. Dom João II came here for years in an unsuccessful attempt to cure his dropsy.

Floods in 1997 led to the closure of the spa hospital, after which it was redeveloped into a spa resort and its picturesque buildings repainted pale pink, green and yellow.

Activities

Termas de Monchique Spa SPA
(282 910 910; www.monchiquetermas.com; adult/hotel guest €15/12; mid-Feb–Dec) In the wooded valley below town; admission allows access to the sauna, steam bath, gym, and swimming pool with hydromassage jets. You can then indulge in special treatments, from a Cleopatra bath to a chocolate-mask wrap.

Sleeping

Albergaria do Lageado HOTEL €
(282 912 616; www.albergariadolageado.com; s/d €45/55; May-Oct;) In the village, Albergaria do Lageado is an attractive hotel with a red-sloped roof and a cosy ambience. It has spotless rooms and a small pool surrounded by plants. There's also a simple restaurant. Packages including board are available.

Termas de Monchique Hotels HOTEL €€
(www.monchiquetermas.com; d €75-95; mid-Feb–Dec;) There are four hotels in the Termas de Monchique complex. All have the same room rates. You can book weekend or week-long packages that include treatments. Prices are cheaper in low season.

Situated next to the Termas de Monchique spa, **Hotel Termal** is the oldest, biggest (and least modern) of the spa's four hotels. Next to the spa's main reception, **Hotel Central** has 13 beautifully furnished rooms. **Estalagem Dom Lourenço** is the most luxurious option, but for style, **Hotel Dom Carlos** is the newest and most contemporary.

Eating

Café Império PORTUGUESE €
(282 912 290; Largo dos Chorões; mains €6-12; lunch & dinner Wed-Mon;) Locals adore this place as it reputedly serves up the best piri-piri chicken in the region. While you tuck in enjoy the lovely views of the valley. Heading north, it's 700m on the left-hand side past the turn-off to Caldas – look for the old tiled 'Schweppes' sign on the wall.

Restaurante 1692 PORTUGUESE €€
(282 910 910; www.monchiquetermas.com; mains €9-18; 12.30-3pm & 7-10pm mid-Feb–Dec;) This upmarket place has tables in the tree-shaded central square, and a classy interior. Service is a bit hit-and-miss, and the setting is perhaps a little better than the decent, but overpriced, food.

Getting There & Away

The Monchique–Portimão bus service (run by Frota Azul) goes via Caldas de Monchique (€4.30, eight daily); the bus stop is on the road above the hamlet near Restaurant Rouxinol. It's easy to miss – ask the driver to alert you.

The Alentejo

Includes ➡

Best Places to Eat

- ➡ Tasca do Celso (p261)
- ➡ Confraria (p243)
- ➡ Alecrim (p232)
- ➡ Restaurante Sever (p246)
- ➡ Sabores de Monsaraz (p228)

Best Places to Sleep

- ➡ Trainspot (p246)
- ➡ Albergaria do Calvario (p221)
- ➡ Convento da Provença (p240)
- ➡ São Lourenço do Barrocal (p228)
- ➡ Casa do Colégio Velho (p233)

Why Go?

Go to be bewitched. Portugal's largest region, covering a third of the country, truly captivates. Think dry, golden plains, rolling hillsides and lime green vines. A rugged coastline, traditional whitewashed villages, marble towns and majestic medieval cities. Plus a proud if melancholic people, who valiantly cling to their local crafts.

Centuries-old farming traditions – and cork production – continue here. Alentejo's rich past offers Palaeolithic carvings, fragments from Roman conquerors and solid Visigothic churches. There are Moorish-designed neighbourhoods and awe-inspiring fortresses built at stork-nest heights.

And the cuisine? Alentejo is the destination for traditional food. Gastronomic delights are plentiful – pork, game, bread, cheese, wine, and seafood along the coastline. Bird life and rare plants are prolific, and walking opportunities abound.

The world is (finally) catching on to Alentejo. Get there before it does.

When to Go

Évora

°C/°F **Temp** — **Rainfall** Inches/mm

40/104 – 30/86 – 20/68 – 10/50 – 0/32 – -10/14 | 8/200 – 6/150 – 4/100 – 2/50 – 0

J F M A M J J A S O N D

Apr & May Red and yellow flowers mingle with golden plains, and it's baby stork time!

Sep & Oct Enjoy festival frenzy while missing the crowds and the heat.

Jun & Jul Pre-August beaches await, plus Festas Populares, Évora's bounciest country fair.

The Alentejo Highlights

1 Sample the history, culture and cuisine of the historically rich Unesco World Heritage–listed **Évora** (p214).

2 Gaze out over the countryside from **Marvão** (p244), one of the Alentejo's most enchanting hilltop fortress villages.

3 Admire the view over the sea cliffs along **Rota Vicentina** (p262), one of Portugal's most captivating multiday treks.

4 Watch the shadows play on the mysterious **Cromeleque dos Almendres** (p226) megaliths outside of Évora.

5 Stroll with the spirits of past civilisations and religions in the riverside enclave of **Mértola** (p251).

Tróia
Sesimbra
Alcácer do Sal
ATLANTIC OCEAN
Río Sado
Grândola
Reserva Natural das Lagoas de Santo André da Sancha
Santiago do Cacém
Sines
São Topes
Porto Côvo
Praia do Malhão
Cercal
Vila Nova de Milfontes
Parque Natural do Sudoeste Alentejano e Costa Vicentina
Rota Vicentina
Odemira
Río Mira
Zambujeira do Mar
São Teotónio
Odeceixe
Ribeira de Seixe
Rogil
Lagos (35km)
Monchique
Albufeira (40km)
São Marcos da Serra
Casa Branca
Barragem de Pego do Altar
Alvito
Barragem do Alvito
Barragem de Odivelas
Ferreira do Alentejo
BAIXO ALENTEJO
Barragem do Roxo
Aljustrel
Funcheira
Ourique
Castro Verde
Entradas
Santa Clara-a-Velha
Barragem de Santa Clara
Almodôvar
Serra do Caldeirão
Faro (50km)
Ameixial
Cachopo
ALGARVE
Martim Longo
Alcoutim
Vila Real de Santo António (35km)
Beja
Portel
São Pedro do Corval
Reguengos de Monsaraz
Outeiro
Telheiro
Monsaraz
Mourão
Luz
Barragem do Alqueva
Alqueva
Moura
Rio Guadiana
Serpa
Vila Verde de Ficalho
Amareleja
Barrancos
Villanueva de la Fresno
Jerez (20km)
Rosal de la Frontera
Seville (130km)
Pulo do Lobo
Parque Natural do Vale do Guadiana
Mértola
São Domingos
Moreanes
Ribeira de Ceiras
Embalse del Chanza
Pomarão
Canavial
Santa Bárbara de Casa
Paymogo
Cabezas Rubias
SPAIN
Puebla de Guzmán
Villanueva de los Castillejos
0 40 km
0 20 miles
N380
N2
N261
IC1
IP8
N259
N121
E01
A2
IP1
IC4
N120
N393
N263
N123
N266
E802
IP2
N18
N384
N258
N255
N260
N385
N386
N256
N265
N122
N124

History

Prehistoric Alentejo was a busy place, and even today it is covered in megaliths. But it was the Romans who stamped and shaped the landscape, introducing vines, wheat and olives, building dams and irrigation schemes and founding huge estates called *latifúndios* to make the most of the region's limited rivers and poor soil.

The Moors, arriving in the early 8th century, took Roman irrigation further and introduced new crops such as citrus and rice. By 1279 they were on the run to southern Spain or forced to live in *mouraria* (segregated Moorish quarters) outside town walls. Many of their hilltop citadels were later reinforced by Dom Dinis, who created a chain of spectacular fortresses along the Spanish border.

Despite Roman and Moorish development, the Alentejo remained agriculturally poor – increasingly so when the Age of Discoveries led to an explosive growth in maritime trade, and seaports became sexy. Only Évora flourished, under the royal patronage of the House of Avis, but it too declined once the Spanish seized the throne in 1580.

During the 1974 revolution Alentejo suddenly stepped into the limelight: landless rural workers who had laboured on the *latifúndios* for generations rose in support of the communist rebellion and seized the land from its owners. Nearly 1000 estates were collectivised, although few succeeded and all were gradually reprivatised in the 1980s. Most are now back in the hands of their original owners.

Today Alentejo remains among Europe's poorest and emptiest regions. Portugal's entry into the EU (and its demanding regulations), increasing mechanisation, successive droughts and greater opportunities elsewhere have hit the region hard: young people have headed for the cities, leaving villages – and their traditions – to die out. Although its cork, olives, marble and granite are still in demand, and the deep-water port and industrial zone of Sines is of national importance, this vast region contributes only a small fraction to the gross national product. Locals are still waiting for the benefits that were promised by the construction of the huge Barragem do Alqueva (Alqueva Dam) and its reservoir.

ALTO ALENTEJO

The northern half of the Alentejo is a medieval gem, with a scattering of walled fortress towns (such as Elvas and Estremoz) and remote cliff-top castles (such as Marvão and Castelo de Vide). Only a handful of visitors to Alto Alentejo travel beyond Évora, so once outside the city you'll see traditional life at its most authentic.

Évora

POP 49,000

One of Portugal's most beautifully preserved medieval towns, Évora is an enchanting place to delve into the past. Inside the 14th-century walls, Évora's winding lanes lead to striking architectural works: a medieval cathedral and cloisters; the cinematic columns of the Templo Romano (near the intriguing Roman baths); and a picturesque town square, once the site of some rather gruesome episodes courtesy of the Inquisition. Aside from its historic and aesthetic virtues, Évora is also a lively university town, and its many attractive restaurants serve up hearty Alentejan cuisine. Outside of town, Neolithic monuments and rustic wineries make for fine day trips.

Évora climbs a gentle hill above the Alentejo plain. Around the walled centre runs a ring road from which you can enter the town on one of several 'spoke' roads. The town's focal point is Praça do Giraldo, 700m from the bus station to the southwest.

History

The Celtic settlement of Ebora had been established here before the Romans arrived in 59 BC and made it a military outpost, and an important centre of Roman Iberia, when it was known as 'Ebora Liberalitas Julia'.

After a depressing spell under the Visigoths, the town got its groove back as a centre of trade under the Moors. In AD 1165 Évora's Muslim rulers were hoodwinked by a rogue Portuguese Christian knight known as Giraldo Sem Pavor (Gerald the Fearless). The story goes like this: Giraldo single-handedly stormed one of the town's watchtowers by climbing up a ladder of spears driven into the walls. From there he distracted (some say killed) municipal sentries while his companions took the town with hardly a fight.

Évora's golden age was from the 14th to 16th centuries, when it was favoured by the Alentejo's own House of Avis, as well as by scholars and artists. Declared an archbishopric in 1540, it got its own Jesuit university in 1559.

When Cardinal-King Dom Henrique, last of the Avis line, died in 1580 and Spain seized the throne, the royal court left Évora and the town began wasting away. The Marquês de Pombal's closure of the university in 1759 was the last straw. French forces plundered the town and massacred its defenders in July 1808.

Ironically, it was decline itself that protected Évora's very fine old centre – economic success would have led to greater redevelopment. Today its population is smaller than it was in the Middle Ages.

Sights

Capela dos Ossos CATACOMB

(Chapel of Bones; Praça 1 de Maio; 9am-6.30pm Jun-Sep, 9am-12.30pm & 2.30-5pm Oct-May) One of Évora's most popular sights is also one of its most chilling. The walls and columns of this mesmerising *memento mori* (reminder of death) are lined with the bones and skulls of some 5000 people. This was the solution found by three 17th-century Franciscan monks for the overflowing graveyards of churches and monasteries.

There's black humour to the way the bones and skulls have been arranged in patterns, and the whole effect is strangely beautiful, though probably not one you'd be inspired to recreate at home. An inscription over the entrance translates as 'We bones that are here await yours'. Above the chapel, a museum contains works of religious art and a terrace with views over town. The former Chapter House (which currently houses the ticket counter for the chapel) contains a fine collection of *azulejos* (hand-painted tiles).

Igreja de São Francisco CHURCH

(Praça 1 de Maio) Évora's best-known church is a tall and huge Manueline-Gothic structure, completed around 1510 and dedicated to St Francis. Legend has it that the Portuguese playwright Gil Vicente is buried here.

Praça do Giraldo PLAZA

The city's main square has seen some potent moments in Portuguese history, including the 1483 execution of Fernando, Duke of Bragança; the public burning of victims of the Inquisition in the 16th century; and fiery debates on agrarian reform in the 1970s. Nowadays it's still the city's focus, host to less dramatic activities such as sitting in the sun and drinking coffee.

The narrow lanes to the southwest were once Évora's *judiaria* (Jewish quarter). To the northeast, Rua 5 de Outubro, climbing to the *Sé* (cathedral), is lined with handsome town houses wearing wrought-iron balconies, while side alleys pass beneath Moorish-style arches.

Sé CATHEDRAL

(Largo do Marquês de Marialva; €1.50, with cloister & towers €3.50, with museum €4.50; 9am-5pm) Guarded by a pair of rose granite towers, Évora's fortress-like medieval cathedral has fabulous cloisters and a museum jam-packed with ecclesiastical treasures. It was begun around 1186, during the reign of Sancho I, Afonso Henriques' son; there was probably a mosque here before. It was completed about 60 years later. The flags of Vasco da Gama's ships were blessed here in 1497.

You enter the cathedral through a portal flanked by 14th-century stone apostles, flanked in turn by asymmetrical towers and crowned by 16th-century roofs. Inside, the Gothic influence takes over. The chancel, remodelled when Évora became the seat of an archdiocese, represents the only significant stylistic change since the cathedral was completed. Golden light filters through the window across the space.

The cool **cloister** is an early-14th-century addition. Downstairs are the stone tombs of Évora's last four archbishops. At each corner of the cloister, a dark, circular staircase (at least one will be open) climbs to the top of the walls, from where there are good views.

Climb the steps in the south tower to reach the choir stalls and up to the **museum**, which demonstrates again the enormous wealth poured into the church, with ecclesiastical riches, including a revolving jewelled reliquary (containing a fragment of the true cross). Encrusted with emeralds, diamonds, sapphires and rubies, it rests on gold cherubs and is flanked by two Ming vases and topped by Indo-Persian textiles.

Museu do Évora MUSEUM

(266 730 480; Largo do Conde de Vila Flor; adult/child €3/free; 9.30am-5.30pm Tue-Sun) Adjacent to the cathedral, in what used to be the archbishop's palace (built in the 16th century), is this elegant museum. The cloistered courtyard reveals Islamic, Roman and medieval remains. In polished rooms upstairs are former Episcopal furnishings and a gallery of Flemish paintings. Most memorable is *Life of the Virgin*, a 13-panel series originally

Évora

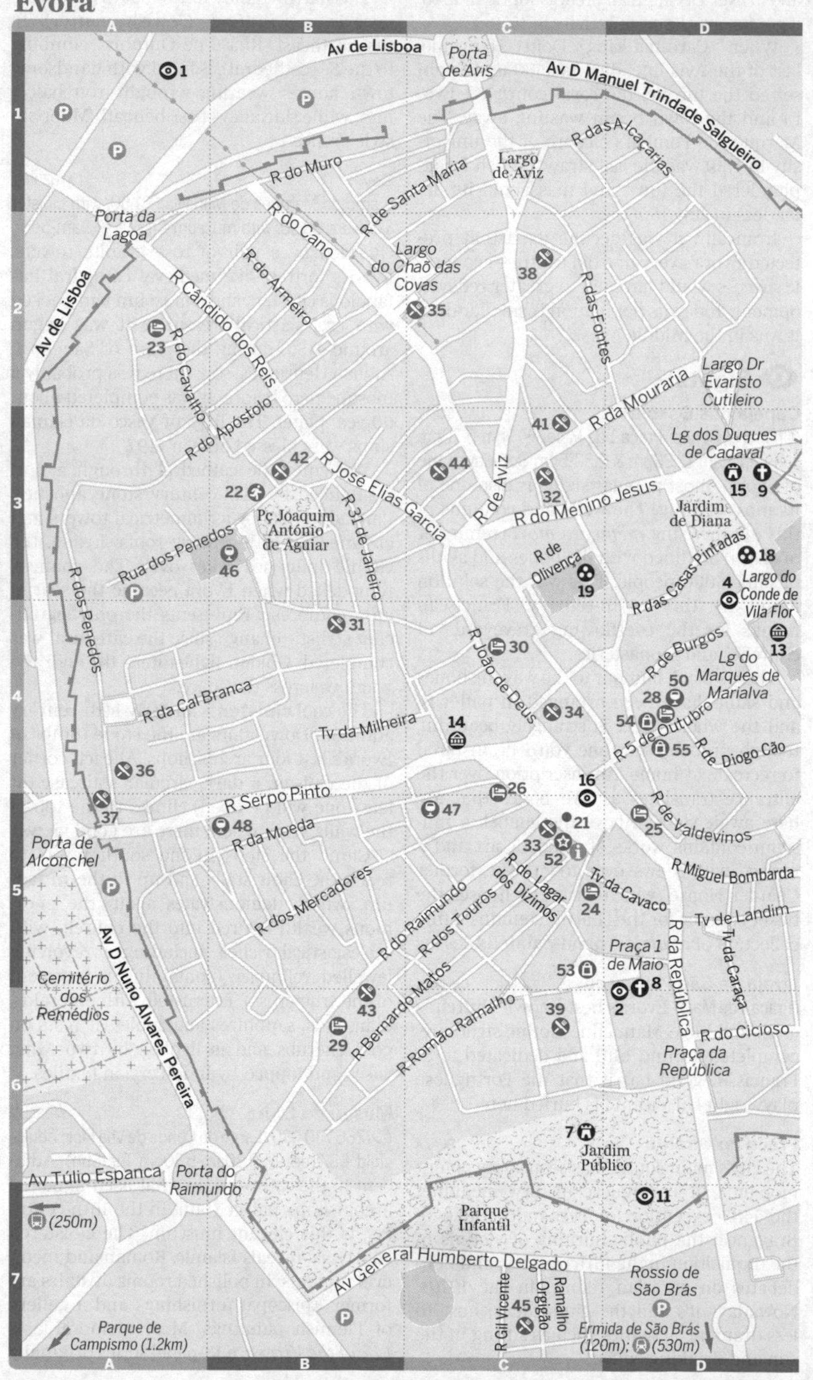

THE ALENTEJO ÉVORA

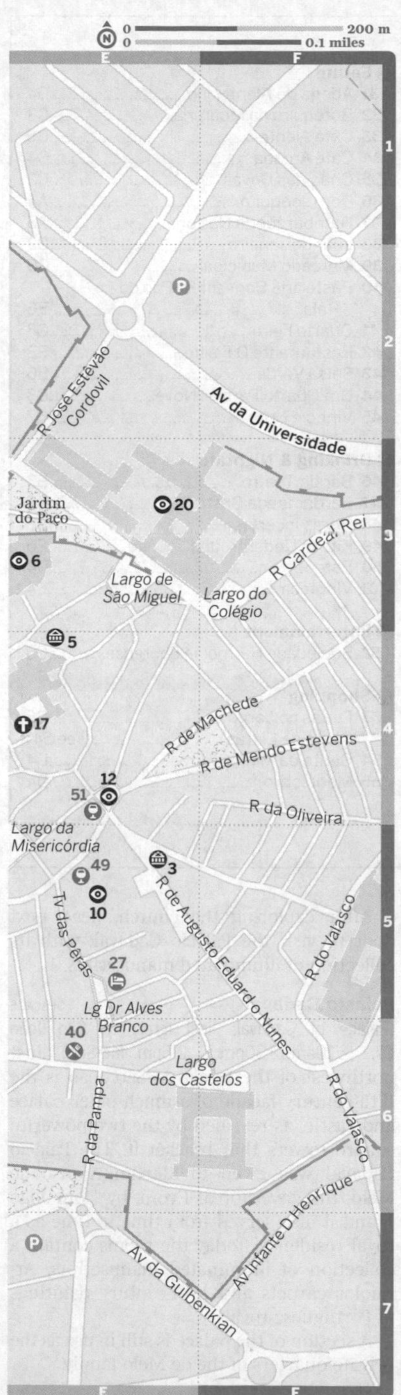

part of the cathedral's altarpiece, created by anonymous Flemish artists working in Portugal around 1500.

Templo Romano RUINS
(Temple of Diana; Largo do Conde de Vila Flor) Once part of the Roman Forum, the remains of this temple, dating from the 2nd or early 3rd century, are a heady slice of drama right in town. It's among the best-preserved Roman monuments in Portugal, and probably on the Iberian Peninsula. Though it's commonly referred to as the Temple of Diana, there's no consensus about the deity to which it was dedicated, and some archaeologists believe it may have been dedicated to Julius Caesar.

How did these 14 Corinthian columns, capped with Estremoz marble, manage to survive in such good shape for some 18 centuries? The temple was apparently walled up in the Middle Ages to form a small fortress, and then used as the town slaughterhouse. It was uncovered late in the 19th century. Obviously these unwitting preservation techniques worked, as the imposing colonnade is stunningly complete.

Fórum Eugénio de Almeida MUSEUM
(www.fundacaoeugeniodealmeida.pt; Largo do Conde de Vila Flor; adult/child €4/free, Sun free; ⌚10am-6pm Tue-Sun) In a building that once housed the Holy Office of Inquisition, this centre of arts and culture hosts some of Évora's most thought-provoking art exhibitions throughout the year. Also part of the foundation is the Casas Pintadas, a small collection of outdoor murals facing a little garden.

Casas Pintadas HISTORIC SITE
(admission €1; ⌚10am-6pm Tue-Sun) Painted on the garden walls of an open vaulted gallery are a series of unusual 16th-century murals that were once part of a noble's residence. Recently restored, these paintings depict creatures real and imagined, such as birds, hares, foxes, a basilisk, a mermaid and a harpy. Access is via the Fórum Eugénio de Almeida.

Coleção de Carruagens MUSEUM
(Carriage Collection; Largo Dr Mário Chicò 4; €1, Sun before 12.30pm free; ⌚10am-12.30pm & 1.30-6pm Tue-Sun) Part of the Eugénio de Almeida Foundation, this pint-sized museum houses an intriguing collection of old carriages. It's hidden away behind the *Sé* (cathedral), and is largely overlooked by most visitors.

Évora

Sights

1 Aqueduto da Água de Prata A1
2 Capela dos Ossos D6
3 Casa Cordovil E5
4 Casas Pintadas D3
5 Coleção de Carruagens E4
6 Convento dos Lóios E3
Fórum Eugénio de Almeida .... (see 4)
7 Galeria das Damas C6
8 Igreja de São Francisco D5
9 Igreja de São João D3
10 Igreja do Carmo E5
11 Jardim Público D7
12 Largo da Porta de Moura E4
13 Museu do Évora D4
14 Museu Relogio C4
15 Palácio Cadaval D3
16 Praça do Giraldo C5
17 Sé E4
18 Templo Romano D3
19 Termas Romanas C3
20 Universidade de Évora E3

Activities, Courses & Tours

21 Agia C5
22 Rota dos Vinhos do Alentejo B3

Sleeping

23 Albergaria do Calvario A2
24 Casa dos Teles C5
25 Évora Inn D5
26 Évora Terrace Hostel C4
27 Hostel Namaste E5
28 Hotel Riviera D4
29 Moov Hotel B6
Pousada Convento de Évora .... (see 6)
30 Stay Inn Ale-Hop C4

Eating

31 Adega do Alentejano B4
32 Botequim da Mouraria C3
33 Café Alentejo C5
34 Café Arcada C4
35 Chão das Covas C2
36 Dom Joaquim A4
37 Hamburgueria Nacional A5
38 Luar de Janeiro C2
39 Mercado Municipal C6
40 Pastelaria Conventual Pão de Rala E6
41 Quarta Feira C3
42 Restaurante O Fialho B3
43 Salsa Verde B6
44 Um Quarto Para as Nove C3
45 Vinho e Noz C7

Drinking & Nightlife

46 Bar do Teatro B3
47 Bardamoeda Gastropub C5
48 Horas Incertas B5
49 Kitsch Underground Lounge E5
50 Páteo D4
51 Vinoteca E4

Entertainment

52 Sociedade Harmonia Eborense C5

Shopping

53 Feiras no Largo C5
Fonte de Letras .... (see 54)
54 Gente da Minha Terra D4
55 Montsobro D4

Igreja de São João CHURCH

(Church of St John the Evangelist; €7; ⌚10am-12.30pm & 2-5pm Tue-Sun) The small, fabulous Igreja de São João, which faces the Templo Romano, was founded in 1485 by one Rodrigo Afonso de Melo, count of Olivença and the first governor of Portuguese Tangier, to serve as his family's pantheon. It is still privately owned, by the Duques de Cadaval, and notably well kept.

Behind its elaborate Gothic portal is a nave lined with fantastic floor-to-ceiling *azulejos* produced in 1711 by one of Portugal's best-known tile-makers António de Oliveira Bernardes. The grates in the floor expose a surprising underworld: you can see a deep Moorish cistern that predates the church and an ossuary full of monks' bones. In the sacristy beyond are fragments of even earlier *azulejos*.

After exploring the church, head next door to visit the Palácio Cadaval, with its collection of illuminated manuscripts.

Palácio Cadaval PALACE

(Palace of Cadaval; incl Igreja de São João €7; ⌚10am-12.30pm & 2-5pm Tue-Sun) Just northwest of the Igreja de São João is the 17th-century facade of a much older palace and castle, as revealed by the two powerful square towers that bracket it. The Palácio Cadaval was given to Martim Afonso de Melo, the governor of Évora, by Dom João I, and it also served from time to time as a royal residence. Today the rooms contain a collection of illuminated manuscripts, Arraiolos carpets and 18th-century paintings of Portuguese royals.

A section of the palace is still in use as the private quarters of the de Melo family.

Convento dos Lóios NOTABLE BUILDING
(Largo do Conde Vila-Flor) The former Convento dos Lóios, to the right of Igreja de São João, has elegant Gothic cloisters topped by a Renaissance gallery. A national monument, the convent was converted into a top-end *pousada* (upmarket inn) in 1965. If you want to wander around, wear your wealthy-guest expression – or have dinner at its upmarket restaurant.

Jardim Público GARDENS
(⌚8am-9pm May-Aug, to 7pm Mar, Apr, Sep & Oct, to 5.30pm Nov-Feb) For a lovely tranquil stroll, head to the light-dappled public gardens (with a small outdoor cafe) south of the Igreja de São Francisco. Inside the walls of the 15th-century Palácio de Dom Manuel is the **Galeria das Damas** (Ladies' Gallery; ⌚10am-noon & 2-6pm Mon-Fri, 2-6pm Sat) FREE, an indecisive hybrid of Gothic, Manueline, neo-Moorish and Renaissance styles. It's open when there are (frequent) temporary art exhibitions. From the town walls you can see, a few blocks to the southeast, the crenellated, pointy-topped Arabian Gothic profile of the **Ermida de São Brás** (Chapel of St Blaise; Avenida Dr Barahona).

Aqueduto da Água de Prata AQUEDUCT
(Aqueduct of Silver Water) Jutting into the town from the northwest is the beguilingly named Aqueduto da Água de Prata, designed by Francisco de Arruda (better known for Lisbon's Tower of Belém) to bring clean water to Évora and completed in the 1530s. At the end of the aqueduct, on Rua do Cano, the neighbourhood feels like a self-contained village, with houses, shops and cafes built right into its perfect arches, as if nestling against the base of a hill.

It's possible to walk for around 8.5km alongside the aqueduct, starting outside town, on the road to Arraiolos. There are three access points; the tourist office provides maps. Unfortunately, it's not a circuit walk and heads in one direction only, so transport back can be a problem if you don't have your own wheels. Take plenty of liquids – ironically, there's no potable water along the way.

Universidade de Évora UNIVERSITY
(☎266 740 800; €3; ⌚main bldg 9am-8pm Mon-Fri, to 6pm Sat) Just outside the walls to the northeast is the university's main building (Colégio do Espírito Santo), a descendent (reopened in 1973) of the original Jesuit institution founded in 1559 (which closed when the Jesuits got shooed out by Marquês de Pombal in 1759). Inside are arched, Italian Renaissance-style cloisters, the Mannerist-style Templo do Espírito Santo and beautiful *azulejos* (hand-painted tiles).

Largo da Porta de Moura PLAZA
The Moura Gate Square stands just southeast of the cathedral. Near here was the original entrance to town. In the middle of the square is a strange-looking, globular 16th-century Renaissance fountain. Among the elegant mansions around the square is **Casa Cordovil** (Largo da Porta de Moura), built in Manueline-Moorish style. Have a look across the road to the west at the extraordinary knotted Manueline stone doorway of the **Igreja do Carmo** (Our Lady of Carmo Church; Rua Dom Augo Eduardo o Nunes).

Museu Relogio MUSEUM
(☎266 751 434; www.museudorelogio.com; Rua Serpa Pinto 6; €2; ⌚2-6pm Tue-Fri, 10am-12.30pm & 2-6pm Sat & Sun) This is one of two watch museums that houses one family's extraordinary private collection (the other is in Serpa). You name it – if it ticks, chimes, beeps and tells the time in some form or another, it's here. The highlight is watching a master watch repairer at work.

Termas Romanas RUINS
(Praça do Sertório; ⌚9am-5.30pm Mon-Fri) FREE Inside the entrance hall of the *câmara municipal* (town hall) are more Roman vestiges, only discovered in 1987. These impressive Roman baths, which include a *laconicum* (heated room for steam baths) with a superbly preserved 9m-diameter circular pool, would have been the largest public building in Roman Évora. The complex also includes an open-air swimming pool, discovered in 1994.

Tours

Ebora Megalithica TOURS
(☎964 808 337; www.eboramegalithica.com; per person €25, maximum 7 people; ⌚tours 10am & 2.30pm Mon-Sat) If you're interested in the megaliths – Almendres, Zambujeiro and the Menir dos Almendres – this three-hour tour is a must. Young archaeologist enthusiast Mário makes the megalithic sites accessible in every sense, providing the where, what, why and how. He succeeds in making the experience an educational yet relaxed one.

Cartuxa Winery WINE
(☎266 748 383; www.cartuxa.pt; Estrada da Soeira; from €5; ⌚tours 10.30am, 11.30am, 3pm & 4.30pm) For a taste of history, this is a fun visit – Cartuxa is one of the oldest wineries in Alentejo. Run by the well-known local philanthropic foundation Eugénio de Almeida, it produces some good wines at all prices, along with olive oils and other products. You must reserve a tour (strictly at the times given); prices start at €5 and then vary according to how many wines you want to taste.

The winery is located about 2km northwest of the old city walls.

Rota do Fresco CULTURAL
(☎284 475 413; www.rotadofresco.com; per person €25) Offers fascinating cultural tours led by an art historian to local baroque sites filled with frescos and *azulejos* (hand-painted tiles). Reservations required.

Agia WALKING
(☎963 702 392; www.alentejoguides.com; adult/under 12yr €15/free, minimum 2 people; ⌚10am) Agia offers daily two-hour guided walking tours of Évora, departing from outside the *turismo* (tourist office) on Praça do Giraldo.

Rota dos Vinhos do Alentejo WINE
(Wine Route of the Alentejo; ☎266 746 498; www.vinhosdoalentejo.pt; Praça Joaquim António de Aguiar 20-21; ⌚2-7pm Mon, 11am-7pm Tue-Fri, 10am-1pm Sat) Head here to sample some of the great wines of the Alentejo. Every Monday new wines are on offer, with more than 70 wineries represented. Tastings of the dozen varieties on hand are free (try them all!). Bottles will set you back anywhere from €3.50 to €9.

Festivals & Events

Rota de Sabores Tradicionais FOOD
A gastronomic festival that lasts for months, celebrating game in January, pork in February, soups in March, lamb in April and desserts in May. Traditional restaurants in the city serve specialities accordingly.

Queima das Fitas FIESTA
Like the famous celebrations in Coimbra, the Queima das Fitas features a riotous end-of-year celebration for University of Évora students finishing the term. Expect a week of outdoor concerts and dance parties.

Festas Populares CULTURAL
(⌚Jun) Évora's biggest, bounciest annual bash, and one of Alentejo's best country fairs, held in late June.

Sleeping

Hostel Namaste HOSTEL €
(☎266 743 014; www.hostelnamasteevora.pt; Largo Doutor Manuel Alves Branco 12; dm/s/d €17/30/45;) Maria and Carla Sofia are the kind souls that run these welcoming digs in the historic Arabic quarter. Rooms are bright, spotlessly clean and decorated with splashes of art and colour, and there's a lounge, library, kitchen and bike hire. Breakfast costs €4.

Moov Hotel HOTEL €
(☎266 240 340; www.hotelmoov.com; Rua do Raimundo 99; d €45-70;) Once home to Évora's first bullring, Moov Hotel features attractive modern rooms with a minimalist design and a lounge adorned with B&W photos of prancing ponies and handsome horsemen. The multilingual staff are friendly. The bone-white courtyard with trickling fountain could use some trees (or other shade).

Évora Terrace Hostel HOSTEL €
(☎266 701 650; www.evoraterracehostel.com; Praça do Giraldo 83, 2nd fl; dm/d/tw incl breakfast €15/34/34;) A good old-fashioned hostel with small neat dorms with bunk beds (and a separate female dorm), plus one double and one twin room. It sleeps only 20 in total so it's not overwhelming. There's also a communal kitchen and small roof terrace. It's located right on the plaza, up a couple of flights of stairs.

Casa dos Teles GUESTHOUSE €
(☎266 702 453; www.casadosteles.planetaclix.pt; Rua Romão Ramalho 27; s/d €30/35, with shared bathroom €20/25;) These eight mostly light and airy rooms are simply furnished but good value for their central location. The quarters are clean and quiet, though the vibe might seem a little sombre for some.

Parque de Campismo CAMPGROUND €
(☎266 705 190; www.orbitur.pt; sites per adult/tent/car €6.50/7/6.10) Flat, grassy and tree-shaded, with disabled access, Orbitur's well-equipped campground is 2km southwest of town. Yellow line bus 41 from Praça do Giraldo, via Avenida de São Sebastião and the bus station, goes close by.

Évora Inn HOSTEL €
(☎266 744 500; www.evorainn.com; Rua da República 11; s/d/ste €45/59/65;) This friendly nine-room guesthouse in a 120-year-old building brings a serious dose of style to Évora. Pop art adorns the rooms and corridors, along with eye-catching wallpaper, modular chairs, a bold colour scheme and

WORTH A TRIP

ARRAIOLOS: THE GREAT CARPETS OF PORTUGAL

About 20km north of Évora is the small town of Arraiolos, famed for its exquisite *tapetes* (carpets). These handwoven works have been in production here since the 12th century and show a marked influence from Persian rugs. It seems half the town is involved in this artistry, and on a casual stroll, you might encounter several locals stitching in front of their homes. Rug patterns are based on abstract motifs, *azulejo* designs or flower, bird or animal depictions.

Shops selling *tapetes* are abundant, and you can pay anything from €50 for a tiny runner to €2000 for the most beautiful pieces, which feature more elaborate designs.

The village itself dates from the 2nd or 3rd century BC and is laid out along traditional lines, with whitewashed blue-trimmed houses topped with terracotta roofs and the ruins of a castle overlooking the town. The plain facade of the **Igreja da Misericórdia** hides a beautiful interior with a golden altar and 18th-century *azulejo*-lined walls.

Take a peak at the centuries-old dye chambers in the main square, which is also where you'll find the **turismo** (tourist office; 266 490 254; www.cm-arraiolos.pt; Praça do Municipio 27; 10am-1pm & 2-6pm Tue-Sun).

There's a flashy **pousada** (upmarket inn; 266 419 340; www.pousadas.pt; off N370; d €110-230;) just outside town.

unusual features (including a telescope in the Mirante room up top). Rooms are bright, if a bit boxy, and staff have loads of great tips on discovering the hidden gems of Évora.

Stay Inn Ale-Hop HOTEL €

(910 852 255; www.stayinn.pt; Rua João de Deus 86; r €45-60;) In the heart of town, this place offers spacious, attractively set modern rooms, the best of which have big windows over the street. There's a kitchen for guests (with free coffee and tea), a small terrace and a little play area for kids. It's located above the Ale-Hop store (check in at the shop).

Hotel Riviera HOTEL €€

(266 737 210; www.riviera-evora.com; Rua 5 de Outubro 49; s/d/ste €65/80/98;) Only one block from the *praça* (town square), this charming and well-renovated place has bright, stylish rooms with *boveda* (brick-arched) ceilings as well as carved bedheads. Bathrooms are gleamingly tiled. Prices are significantly less outside high season.

★ **Albergaria do Calvario** BOUTIQUE HOTEL €€€

(266 745 930; www.albergariadocalvario.com; Travessa dos Lagares 3; r €116-133;) Unpretentiously elegant, discreetly attentive and comfortable, this beautifully designed guesthouse has an ambience that travellers adore. The staff leave no service stone unturned and breakfasts are among the region's best, with locally sourced organic produce, homemade cakes and egg dishes.

Gorgeous lounge areas are decked out with a tasteful melange of antique and modern furniture. Comfortable beds, flat-screen TVs, books, heating and air-conditioning and a pleasant garden patio area ensure a homey, don't-want-to-leave kind of stay. It's located in a delightful part of town, near Porta Lagoa and the aqueduct. Excellent insider tips for exploring the Alentejo.

Pousada Convento de Évora HERITAGE HOTEL €€€

(266 730 070; www.pestana.com; Largo do Conde de Vila Flor; r €140-260;) Occupying the former Convento dos Lóios opposite the Templo Romano, this beautiful *pousada* (upmarket inn) has a historic air, though the rooms are furnished in a contemporary style (mint green and white) and set around a pretty cloister. There's a flash restaurant (mains €18 to €24) on the ground floor of the cloister.

Eating

Salsa Verde VEGETARIAN €

(266 743 210; www.salsa-verde.org; Rua do Raimundo 93A; small plate €4.95 or per kg €14.40; noon-3pm & 7-9.30pm Mon-Fri, noon-3pm Sat;) Vegetarians (and Portuguese pigs) will be thankful for this veggie-popping paradise. Pedro, the owner, gives a wonderful twist to traditional Alentejan dishes such as the famous bread dish, *migas*, prepared with mushrooms. Low-playing bossa nova and a cheerful airy design make a fine complement to the dishes – all made from fresh, locally sourced products (organic when possible).

Chão das Covas PORTUGUESE €

(☎266 706 294; www.facebook.com/chaodascovascafe; Largo do Chão das Covas; sharing plates €4.50-6, mains €7-10; ⌚11am-3pm & 5.30-11pm Tue-Sun) Tucked away on a small plaza beside the aqueduct, this friendly, boxcar-sized eatery serves up tasty home-cooked Alentejan classics that change by day, as well as good-value *petiscos* (sharing plates) like fried squid, roasted peppers, cheese platters and the like. It's a fine place to linger, with a barrel-vaulted ceiling, B&W photos of Évora and terrace seating on warm days.

Hamburgueria Nacional BURGERS €

(Rua dos Penedos 13; mains €4-8; ⌚noon-3pm & 7-10.30pm) For decadent and deliciously gourmet burgers, stop by this hip little eatery, which serves up eight or so different varieties including a tasty vegetarian option, amid exposed lightbulbs, rockabilly tunes and a long bar perfect for solo diners. You can top with carmelised onions, cheese or bacon and add a side of sweet potato fries (or octopus salad) for a full meal.

Café Arcada CAFE €

(www.facebook.com/Cafe.Arcada.Evora; Praça do Giraldo 10; mains €7-10; ⌚8am-9.30pm Sun-Thu, to 10.30pm Fri & Sat) This busy, barn-sized cafe is an Évora institution serving coffee, crêpes and cakes. You can sit at an outdoor table on the lovely plaza.

Pastelaria Conventual Pão de Rala BAKERY €

(Rua do Cicioso 47; pastries €1.20-3; ⌚7.30am-8pm; 📶) The *azulejo*-covered walls (complete with a bakery scene) and low-playing fado create a fine setting for nibbling on heavenly pastries and convent cakes, all made on the premises. Don't miss the *pão de rala* (an egg yolk, sugar, lemon zest and almond cake) – it's sweet stuff and wonderfully sinful.

Mercado Municipal MARKET €

(Municipal Market; Praça 1 de Maio; ⌚7am-6pm Tue-Sun) You can pick up cheeses, olives, smoked meats, fruit and vegetables at the municipal market.

Botequim da Mouraria PORTUGUESE €€

(☎266 746 775; Rua da Mouraria 16A; mains €14-17; ⌚12.30-3pm & 7-10pm Mon-Fri, noon-3pm Sat) Poke around the old Moorish quarter to find some of Évora's finest food and wine – gastronomes believe this is Évora's culinary shrine. Owner Domingos will expertly guide you through the menu, which also features an excellent variety of wines from the Alentejo. There are no reservations and just nine stools at a counter. It is extremely popular, and lines are long. To have any chance of getting a seat, arrive before it opens.

Adega do Alentejano PORTUGUESE €€

(☎266 744 447; Rua Gabriel Victor Monte Pereira 21; mains €8-13; ⌚noon-3pm & 7-10pm Mon-Sat) Red-and-white checked tablecloths, rustic decor and a garrulous host named Carlos set the stage for a fun, casual night of Alentejo fare that won't break the bank. Start off with the rich *sopa de tomate* (tomato soup) served with sausages (good for sharing), then move on to hearty pork or codfish dishes. House wine comes straight from the barrel.

Um Quarto Para as Nove PORTUGUESE €€

(☎266 706 774; http://restaurante14pras9.pt; Rua Pedro Simões 9; mains €11-19; ⌚12.30-3pm & 7.30-10pm Thu-Tue) It will forever be 'a quarter to nine' at this jovial eatery (the owner bought the timepiece secondhand – it never worked). Broken appliances aside, the delightful place has clocked up 30 years experience and, with that, some of Évora's best seafood dishes. It's hard to go past the generous and tasty *arroz* (risotto) dishes; the daily specials are highlights.

THE WINE ROUTE

Wines here, particularly the reds, are fat, rich and fruity. But tasting them is much more fun than reading about them, so drop in on some wineries. The **Rota dos Vinhos do Alentejo** (Wine Route of the Alentejo) splits the region into three separate areas – the Serra de São Mamede (dark reds, full bodied, red fruit hints); Historic (smooth reds, fruity whites) around Évora, Estremoz, Borba and Monsaraz; and the Rio Guadiana (scented whites, spicy reds). Some wineries also have accommodation options.

You'll see brown signs all over the Alentejo announcing that you are on the wine trail, and you can pick up the booklet that lists wineries and their details at any local tourist office. Otherwise visit the helpful Rota dos Vinhos do Alentejo (p220) headquarters.

Vinho e Noz PORTUGUESE €€
(☎266 747 310; Ramalho Orgigão 12; mains €11-13; ⊙noon-10pm Mon-Sat) This unpretentious place is run by a delightful family and offers good service, a large wine list and good-quality cuisine. For over 30 years, it has been one of the best-value places in town.

Dom Joaquim PORTUGUESE €€
(☎266 731 105; www.restaurantedomjoaquim.pai.pt; Rua dos Penedos 6; mains €14-17; ⊙noon-3pm & 7-10.45pm Tue-Sat, noon-3pm Sun) Housed in a renovated building with stone walls and modern artwork, this restaurant offers fine dining in a smart, contemporary setting. Chef Dom Joaquim serves excellent traditional cuisine including meats (game and succulent, fall-off-the-bone lamb) and seafood dishes, such as *caçao* (dogfish).

And Chef Joaquim adores his clients as much as they love his skills. He serves big tastes with great enthusiasm. Desserts consist mainly of *doces conventuais* (traditional convent puddings). Oh so sweet.

Café Alentejo PORTUGUESE €€
(☎266 706 296; Rua do Raimundo 5; mains €9-15; ⊙12.30-3pm & 7.30-10.45pm Mon-Sat) Housed in a 16th-century building, Café Alentejo is full of arches and smart decor (with beautiful floors). You'll find classic Alentejan cooking with good regional wines to match. The amazing aromas – a heady mix of red wine and herbs – will hit you on entry.

Restaurante O Fialho PORTUGUESE €€
(☎266 703 079; http://restaurantefialho.pai.pt; Travessa dos Mascarenhas 16; mains €14.50-18; ⊙noon-3pm & 7-10pm Tue-Sun) An icon of Évora's culinary scene, O Fialho has been wowing diners since 1945 – as evidenced by the photos of visiting dignitaries lining the walls. Amid wood panelling and white tablecloths, professional wait staff serve up first-rate Alentejan cuisine. The appetisers steal the show, along with the extensive wine list.

Quarta Feira PORTUGUESE €€€
(☎266 707 530; Rua do Inverno 16; dinner per person incl appetisers, wine & dessert €25; ⊙12.30-2.30pm & 7.30-9.30pm Tue-Sat) Don't bother asking for the menu since there's just one dish on offer at this jovial eatery tucked away in the Moorish quarter. Luckily it's a stunner: slow-cooked black pork so tender it falls off the bone, plus fresh baked bread, cured ham (and other appetisers), dessert and ever-flowing glasses of wine – all served for one set price.

Luar de Janeiro PORTUGUESE €€€
(☎266 749 114; www.luardejaneiro.com; Travessa do Janeiro 13; mains €13-21; ⊙noon-3pm & 7-10pm Fri-Wed) We'll be upfront: you don't come here for the atmosphere (no soft lighting, no music). You do come here for attentive service and dishes made with the freshest, top-quality produce. It's run by a kind-hearted mother-and-son team, who serve first-rate *presunto* (ham), delectable *cabrito assado no forno* (oven-roasted kid) and a delicious, risotto-like *arroz de bacalhau* (codfish and rice).

Paulo lets the food do the talking; it will hit your hip pocket, but it's sustainable in every other sense.

Drinking & Nightlife

Art Cafe CAFE
(Rua Serpa Pinto 6; ⊙11am-midnight Tue-Sat, to 9pm Sun & Mon) Set in the cloisters of the old Palácio Barrocal, this bohemian cafe and drinking spot has outdoor tables, hipster wait staff and electronic grooves. The outdoor tables beneath are a fine spot to unwind with a sangria after a day exploring. Tasty veg-friendly snacks too (gazpacho, *tostas*, lasagna).

Bar do Teatro BAR
(www.facebook.com/bardoteatrogarciaderezende; Praça Joaquim António de Aguiar; ⊙4pm-2am) Next to the theatre, this small, inviting bar has high ceilings and old-world decor that welcomes a friendly mixed crowd. The music tends towards lounge and electronica.

Horas Incertas BAR
(☎266 092 491; www.bar-horasincertas.com; Rua Serpa Pinto 141; ⊙8pm-2am Tue-Sat) A stained-glass door and a few art-deco fixtures add a bit of class to this low-key lounge in a western corner of the old town. While it's usually empty during the week, things pick up on weekends, when you can catch live music (jazz, Brazilian acoustic, rhythms of Cape Verde) and the odd poetry night. Check the website for upcoming events.

Vinoteca WINE BAR
(☎266 098 365; Largo da Porta da Moura 25; ⊙10am-midnight Tue-Sun) Newly opened Vinoteca offers an excellent array of wines by the glass (from €2), plus cheeses, smoked meats and salads (like rocket, goat's milk cheese and walnuts) to accompany them. The setting is a little sedate, but it's still a fine choice if you want to sink into an armchair and linger over some of the Alentejo's finest.

Páteo WINE BAR
(☎919 549 745; Rua 5 de Outubro, Beco da Espinhosa; ⊙noon-2am; 📶) Right in Évora's medieval heart, this bar has a pretty tree-shaded patio for nursing a glass of Alentejo wine. The food is pretty good too.

Bardamoeda Gastropub BAR
(☎266 785 047; Rua da Moeda 55; ⊙7.30pm-3am Tue-Sun; 📶) Nestle in under the vaulted ceilings of this cool spot and order a great meal at a reasonable price (mains €7 to €10) and a drink, anything from beer on tap to spirits. It sometimes has live acoustic music.

Kitsch Underground Lounge COCKTAIL BAR
(Rua Miguel Bombarda 56A; ⊙10pm-3am Tue-Sat) Kitsch draws a young crowd to a two-room space on Rua Miguel Bombarda (a street with a few other bars nearby). DJs spin ambient grooves – deep house, electro jazz – while the bobbing crowd sips cocktails. It's fairly dead until after midnight.

☆ Entertainment

Sociedade Harmonia Eborense ARTS
(☎266 746 874; Praça do Giraldo 72) For theatre, film, concerts and art expositions, stop in at the imaginative cultural centre Sociedade Harmonia Eborense to see what's on.

Shopping

Rua 5 de Outubro has rows of *artesanatos* (handicrafts shops) selling pottery, knick-knacks and cork products. A couple of shops in the modern Mercado Municipal (p222) sell pottery. On the second Tuesday of each month a vast open-air market sprawls across the big Rossio de São Brás, just outside the walls south of Rua da República.

Fonte de Letras BOOKS
(www.facebook.com/fonteleletras; Rua 5 de Outubro 51; ⊙10am-7pm Mon-Fri, to 6pm Sat) Set on Évora's main shopping lane, this small bookstore stocks intriguing titles, including English-language versions of books by Portuguese authors (and top-rated books set in Portugal). The shop also sells CDs and has a small cafe for snacks and coffee. Don't miss the gumball machine in front that sells tiny poems (for a mere €0.50).

Gente da Minha Terra FOOD, CRAFTS
(www.gentedaminhaterra.pt; Rua 5 de Outubro 39; ⊙10am-7pm) On a boutique-lined street leading off the main plaza, this is a great one-stop shop for gifts. The shelves are packed with quality olive oils, *azulejos* (hand-painted tiles), textiles, ceramics and pretty packages of tinned sardines and other preserves.

Montsobro HOMEWARES
(www.montsobro.com; Rua 5 de Outubro 66; ⊙10am-6pm Mon-Sat) One of many shops along Rua 5 de Outubro, this was the first – and is still one of the best – that sells cork products.

Feiras no Largo MARKET
(Praça 1 de Maio; ⊙8am-2pm Sat & Sun) Each weekend sees the Feiras no Largo, one of four different markets held in the city. Expect antiquities, books and collectables, art and *artesenato*.

WORTH A TRIP

ÉVORAMONTE

Thirty-two kilometres northeast of Évora, this tiny village, with its quaint 16th-century castle, makes an interesting detour on your way through the region. There are fine views all around across the low hills.

The **Castelo** (adult/student €2/1; ⊙10am-1pm Wed-Sun, 2-5pm Tue-Sun, closed 2nd weekend of every month) dates from 1306, but was rebuilt after the 1531 earthquake. Exterior stone carving shows unwarlike small bows, the symbol of the Bragança family – the knot symbolises fidelity. The interior is neatly restored, with impressively meaty columns topped by a sinuous arched ceiling on each cavernous floor. The roof provides sweeping panoramas.

Most visitors have their own wheels. There are two buses a day, however, travelling between Évora (around €4, 50 minutes) and Évoramonte on weekdays. Schedules change depending on whether school is in session.

Information

MONEY

There are several banks with ATMs on and around Praça do Giraldo, including **Caixa de Crédito Agrícola** (Praça do Giraldo 13).

MundiTransfers (☎266 761 025; Rua Serpa Pinto 40A; ⏲10am-2pm & 3-7pm Mon-Fri) is the only place that changes travellers cheques.

TOURIST INFORMATION

Rota dos Vinhos do Alentejo headquarters (p220) Come here for details of a *rota dos vinhos* (wine route) to *adegas* (wineries) in the Alentejo, plus wine tastings and cellar visits.

Turismo (☎266 777 071; www.cm-evora.pt; Praça do Giraldo 73; ⏲9am-7pm Apr-Oct, to 6pm Nov-Mar) This helpful, central tourist office offers a great town map.

Getting There & Away

BUS

The **bus station** (☎266 738 120; Avenida São Sebastião) is located a short distance west of the walled centre.

DESTINATION	COST (€)	DURATION	FREQUENCY
Beja	express 8	1½hr	hourly
Coimbra	18.50	4½hr	4 daily (or change in Lisbon)
Elvas	express 12	1¼hr	3 daily Mon-Fri
Estremoz	express 8	30-50min	6 daily
Faro (via Albufeira)	17.50	4hr	3 daily
Lisbon	12.50	1½-2hr	hourly
Portalegre	12.50	1½hr	3-5 daily
Reguengos de Monsaraz	express 8	45min	2 daily Mon-Fri, 1 daily Sat-Sun
Vila Viçosa	9.50	1hr	3 daily

TRAIN

The **Évora station** (☎266 742 336) is outside the walls, 600m south of the Jardim Público (p219). There are daily trains to/from Lisbon (€12.20, 1½ hours, four daily). Trains also go to/from Beja (change in Casa Branca; €7.20, 2¼ hours, four daily), Lagos (€26.30, 4½ to five hours, three daily) and Faro (€25.30, four to five hours, two daily).

Getting Around

BICYCLE

Evora Adventure Bike (☎969 095 880, 266 702 326; Travessa do Barão 18; half-day/4 days €8/40; ⏲9am-9pm) Half-day and multiday bike rental.

CAR & MOTORCYCLE

If you're driving it's best to park outside the walls at a signposted car park (eg at the southern end of Rua da República in Parking Rossio de São Brás). Spaces inside the walls are limited and usually metered, and driving here can be tricky due to a web of narrow streets. Pricier hotels have some parking.

On the outskirts of town, in the direction of Viana, **Europcar** (☎266 742 627; Estrada de Viana, Lot 10; ⏲9am-1pm Mon-Fri, 3-6.30pm Mon-Sat) has cars for hire.

TAXI

Taxis (☎266 734 734) congregate in Praça do Giraldo. On weekdays expect to pay about €6 from the train station to Praça do Giraldo.

Around Évora

Megaliths are found all over the ancient landscape that surrounds Évora. These prehistoric structures, built around 5000 to 7500 years ago, dot the European Atlantic coast, but here in Alentejo there is an astounding amount of Neolithic remains. Dolmens (Neolithic stone tombs; *antas* in Portuguese) were probably temples and/or collective tombs, covered with a large flat stone and usually built on hilltops or valleys, near water lines. Menhirs (individual standing stones) point to fertility rites – as phallic as skyscrapers, if on a smaller scale; and cromeleques, organised sets of standing stones, seem to incorporate basic astronomic orientations related to seasonal transitions (equinoxes and solstices).

Megalith devotees can buy the book *Paisagens Arqueologicas A Oeste de Évora* (€13), which has English summaries, at the *turismo* in Évora.

There are more megaliths around Reguengos de Monsaraz, Elvas and Castelo de Vide.

Sights

Anta Grande do Zambujeiro

ARCHAEOLOGICAL SITE

The Great Dolmen of Zambujeiro, 13km southwest of Évora, is Europe's largest dolmen. Under a huge sheet-metal protective shelter in a field of wildflowers and yellow broom, stand seven stones and a 'closing slab' that connects the chamber with the corridor. Each is 6m high and together they form a huge chamber around 5m in diameter.

Unfortunately, the entrance is blocked and you cannot enter but you can peer in from the high mound behind. Archaeologists removed the capstone in the 1960s. Most of the site's relics are in the Museu do Évora (p215).

Cromeleque dos Almendres ARCHAEOLOGICAL SITE

(Almendres Cromlech) Set within a beautiful landscape of olive and cork trees – unfortunately the dirt road almost impinges onto the site – stands the Cromeleque dos Almendres. This huge, spectacular oval of standing stones, 15km west of Évora, is the Iberian Peninsula's most important megalithic group and an extraordinary place to visit. The site consists of a huge oval of some 95 rounded granite monoliths – some of which are engraved with symbolic markings – spread down a rough slope.

The megaliths were erected over different periods, it seems, with basic astronomic orientations and were probably used for social gatherings or sacred rituals back in the dawn of the Neolithic period.

Two and a half kilometres before Cromeleque dos Almendres stands **Menir dos Almendres**, a single stone about 4m high, with some very faint carvings near the top. Look for the sign; to reach the menhir you must walk a few hundred metres from the road.

DON'T MISS

SÃO PEDRO DO CORVAL

Known for its fine pottery traditions, the tiny village of **São Pedro do Corval**, 5km east of Reguengos de Monsaraz, has dozens of pottery workshops where you can see both the potters and artists in action and purchase a few pieces of cheap and cheerful plates, pots, jugs, candlesticks and floor tiles.

With more than 20 *olarias* (pottery workshops), the village is one of Portugal's largest pottery centres. It's difficult to recommend one *olaria* over another; wander along Rua da Primavera and the nearby streets (follow the '*olarias*' signs) and ask at the Reguengos and Monsaraz tourist offices for a map locating the *olarias*. Buses between Reguengos and Monsaraz stop here.

Getting There & Away

To get to this area, your only options are to rent a car or bike (though note that about 5km of the route is rough and remote), hire a taxi for the day (around €60), or go on a guided tour (p219).

With your own wheels, head west from Évora on the old Lisbon road (N114) for 10km, then turn south for 2.8km to Guadalupe, then follow the signs to the Cromeleque dos Almendres (4.3km).

Return to Guadalupe and head south for 5km to Valverde, home of the Universidade de Évora's school of agriculture and the 16th-century Convento de Bom Jesus. Following the signs to Anta Grande do Zambujeiro, turn into the school's farmyard and onto a badly potholed track. After 1km you'll see the Great Dolmen.

Reguengos de Monsaraz

POP 7300

This small working-class town, once famous for its sheep and wool, is a stopping point and transport hub for Monsaraz. It's also close to the pottery centre of São Pedro do Corval as well as to an impressive half-dozen dolmens and menhirs (out of around 150 scattered across the surrounding plains). It's worth a day trip for its excellent wineries alone, particularly the renowned Herdade do Esporão.

Sights & Activities

Herdade do Esporão WINERY

(☎266 509 280; www.esporao.com; wine tasting from €5; ⌚10am-7pm daily, restaurant closed Mon Nov-Mar) There are several wineries around Reguengos (part of the wine route), including the acclaimed Herdade do Esporão, 7km south of town. Under the direction of oenologist David Baverstock, it produces a wide variety of wines for the domestic and overseas markets. There are tours through the extraordinary wine cellars, among the largest in Portugal.

It's worth splurging at the wine cellar shop or the restaurant. Reservations are essential for dining at the restaurant (prix-fixe lunch menu €40 to €70), and recommended for booking a tour (which are sometimes booked solid by groups; there's typically one English-language tour each day). If you show up without a reservation, you can still enjoy wine tasting in the cafe. Charcuterie, cheeses and other snacks are available.

The small on-site **museum** features the original artwork done for the wine labels of Esporão's annual reserve collection; each year a famous Portuguese artist is given the honours. The property's border was defined in 1267 and it has vestiges of Roman times.

Shopping

Fabrica Alentejana de Lanificios ARTS & CRAFTS
(☎266 502 179; http://mizzete.pt; Rua Mendes; ⏲10am-4.30pm Mon-Fri) This is the last handloom producer of *mantas alentejanas* (woollen floor rugs). The owner and/or weavers are happy to show you around. The factory is southeast of the *praça* (town square; take the road to Monsaraz and turn right at Rua Mendes) and the factory's shop is in Monsaraz.

Getting There & Away

Buses run to Évora (€7, 45 minutes, several daily) and direct to Lisbon (€14.30, 2½ hours, two daily). There's also a weekday bus to Monsaraz.

Monsaraz

Perched high over the surrounding countryside, tiny Monsaraz is a charming village with a looming castle at its edge, great views over the Alqueva Dam and olive groves sprinkling the landscape. Its narrow streets are lined with uneven-walled, whitewashed cottages. Today, the village prospers on tourism, with a handful of restaurants, guesthouses and artisan shops. It's worth coming to taste a slice of traditional Portugal, wander the slumbering streets and sample Alentejan cuisine. It's at its best as it wakes up in the morning, in the quiet of the evening or during a wintry dusk.

Settled long before the Moors arrived in the 8th century, Monsaraz was recaptured by the Christians under Giraldo Sem Pavor (Gerald the Fearless) in 1167, and then given to the Knights Templar as thanks for their help. The castle was added in 1310.

Sights

Menhir do Outeiro ARCHAEOLOGICAL SITE
Situated 3km north of Monsaraz is the granite, 5.6m-tall Menhir do Outeiro, one of the tallest megaliths ever discovered.

Igreja Matriz CHURCH
(⏲9.30am-1pm & 2-5.30pm) The parish church, near the *turismo,* was rebuilt after the 1755 earthquake and again a century later. Inside is an impressive nave and a 14th-century marble tomb carved with 14 saints. An 18th-century *pelourinho* (stone pillory) topped by a Manueline globe stands outside.

The 16th-century **Igreja da Misericórdia** is opposite, but it is rarely open.

Museu do Fresco MUSEUM
(Fresco Museum; Praça Dom Nuno Álvares Pereira; €1; ⏲9.30am-1pm & 2-5.30pm) Housed inside a fine Gothic building beside the parish church, this museum houses a rare example of a 14th-century secular fresco. The striking work depicts a good judge (with angels perched behind his shoulder) and a bad judge, the latter appropriately two-faced (with a demon on his left shoulder).

A collection of photographs depict life in the rural Alentejo from the early 1900s to the 1950s – and cover the period of mass immigration from the countryside (in the 1960s, Monsaraz alone lost 4500 inhabitants). Unfortunately, the explanatory signage is in Portuguese only.

Castelo CASTLE
(⏲24hr) The weather-beaten castle at the southwestern end of the village was one in the chain of Dom Dinis' defensive fortresses along the Spanish border. It's now converted into a small bullring, and its ramparts offer a fine panoramic view over the Alentejan plains.

Activities

Dark Sky Alqueva OUTDOORS
(Rua das Flores 6A, Telheiro; per person €12; ⏲10.30pm Jun-Sep) Lack of light pollution and the often clear skies make this part of the Alentejo an excellent place for stargazing. During the summer, Sem Fim (p229) restaurant in Telheiro organises nightly viewing sessions, with a telescope and a guide to help you map out the star-filled skies.

Capitão Tiago BOATING
(☎962 653 711; www.sem-fim.com; Rua das Flores 6A, Telheiro; per person from €20) A great way to explore the Barragem do Alqueva is by boat. Capitão Tiago runs excellent voyages in his 17m Dutch sail boat. Several trips are available – the standard is a two-hour trip with the chance to swim and visit some of the islands. Other packages include a boat trip with a meal (€40). You can also rent bikes (€25 per day).

Festivals & Events

Museu Aberto MUSIC
(Open Museum; ⏲Jul) Monsaraz heaves with jollity during its weeklong Museu Aberto music festival, held in July in even-numbered years.

WORTH A TRIP

MEGALITHS AROUND MONSARAZ

Neolithic megaliths are scattered throughout the landscape around Monsaraz – it is great to explore and discover them (they're signposted, but finding each one is an adventure) amid the tangles of olive groves and open fields of wildflowers. Most spectacular is **Cromeleque do Xerez**, an ensemble with the triumphant 7-tonne menhir at its centre. The rocks once stood 5km south of Monsaraz but were moved before flooding by the massive Barragem do Alqueva. A remaining highlight is the **Menhir de Bulhoa**, another phallic stone with intriguing carved circles and lines; it's 4km north of Monsaraz off the Telheiro–Outeiro road. A map outlining the region's megalithic circuit is available at the tourist office (p229).

Festa de Nosso Senhor Jésus dos Passos CULTURAL
(Sep) Bullfights and processions feature in this festival around the second weekend of September.

Sleeping

Dom Nuno GUESTHOUSE €€
(964 304 078; www.dnunoth.com; Rua José Fernandes Caeiro 6; s/d from €46/60) Inside the old walls, this delightful, family-run guesthouse was one of Monsaraz' first lodging options when it opened back in 1983. Today this historic building (a pharmacy in the 1700s) is run by the second generation, and it offers eight spacious rooms with thick walls, terracotta floors and bright modern bathrooms. The best rooms have views over the countryside. Good breakfasts.

Casa Rural Santo Condestável B&B €€
(966 926 970; casacondestavel@gmail.com; Rua Direita 4; r €50-70, ste €70-85;) A rustic, pin-drop peaceful retreat, this whitewashed house dates to the 17th century and offers five cool rooms with heavy carved wooden beds. Some have fine views over the plains to the Alqueva Dam.

Casa Saramago de Monsaraz RURAL INN €€
(266 557 494; www.casasaramago-monsaraz.com.pt; Rua de Reguengos 9A, Telheiro; s/d €50/70; P) Based in Telheiro, at the foot of Monsaraz, this delightfully converted blue and white *quinta* (estate) is great value for money. Rooms are tastefully decorated in old-style furniture. The Portuguese owners are friendly and accommodating. Rooms in the former *celeiros* (silos) have verandahs and face Monsaraz.

Casa Dona Antónia B&B €€
(266 557 142; www.casadantonia-monsaraz.com; Rua Direita 15; s €50-55, d €65-75, ste €100;) The seven rooms in this traditional house vary in size, but all are pleasant and comfortable. The suite is huge and includes a terrace.

São Lourenço do Barrocal BOUTIQUE HOTEL €€€
(266 247 140; www.barrocal.pt; r €180-280, apt €275-350; P) Set on a 780-hectare estate of olive groves and vineyards, 7km west of Monsaraz, this rural tourism stay offers countryside charm that doesn't stint on high-end comforts. What was once a self-contained farming village has been transformed into lovely boutique accommodation, and the excellent restaurant uses many products grown or raised on-site.

Eating

Cafe-Restaurante Lumumba PORTUGUESE €
(Rua Direita 12; mains €8-10; noon-2.30pm & 7.30-10pm Tue-Sun) This small place has a more local, less touristy clientele who come for filling, inexpensive staples. Don't let dueling TVs and neon lights deter you, head to the terrace for a meal with a view.

★**Sabores de Monsaraz** PORTUGUESE €€
(969 217 800; www.saboresdemonsaraz.com; Largo de S Bartolomeu; mains €12-15; 12.30-3.30pm Tue, 12.30-3.30pm & 7.30-10.30pm Wed-Sun;) Perched high above the plains, with views reaching as far as Spain, this stone-built tavern is a rustic, wonderfully family-friendly spot. Good honest Alentejano home cooking stars on the menu, with dishes like meltingly tender black pork and *migas com bacalhau e coentros* (codfish with bread and coriander). Don't pass up dessert – the rich *sericaia* (an egg custard tart) with sugared plums is magnificent.

Taverna Os Templarios PORTUGUESE €€
(266 557 166; Rua Direita 22; mains €11-18; noon-3pm & 7-10.30pm Wed-Mon) Step back in time with this Knights Templar–themed eatery, complete with iron chandeliers, wall-mounted weapons and banners strung from the rafters. The food is classic Alentejan fare, and it's one of Monsaraz' more reliable eateries. Don't miss the view from the back terrace.

Sem Fim PORTUGUESE €€
(☎962 653 711; www.sem-fim.com; Rua das Flores 6A, Telheiro; mains €10-16; ⊙11am-2am Fri-Sun Mar-Dec) In Telheiro this former olive oil factory has been transformed into an atmospheric eating and drinking space. The changing menu features a small selection of good Alentejo classics as well as options for vegetarians.

Xarez INTERNATIONAL €€
(www.xarez-monsaraz.com; Rua de Santiago 33; mains €8-14; ⊙11am-8pm Fri-Wed Sep-Oct & Dec-May, to midnight Jun-Aug) A tourist magnet for its views and reasonable *petiscos* (snacks) and mains. It gets mixed reviews for food, so we prefer to come in between meal times for a drink on the terrace.

Shopping

Casa Tial FOOD
(Rua dos Celeiros 10; ⊙10am-7pm Wed-Mon Oct-May, daily Jun-Sep) Run by a French expat, this charming little shop is a fine spot to browse for gifts, with artfully wrapped tins of sardines, high-quality olive oils, unique wines and rich chocolates. You can also stop by for coffee and dessert. The jazzy soundtrack invites lingering.

Loja da Mizette ARTS & CRAFTS
(☎266 557 159; http://mizzete.pt; Rua do Celeiro; ⊙10am-6pm Oct-May, to 7.30pm Jun-Sep) At this Monsaraz shop, you can purchase handsome Alentejano *mantas* (woollen rugs and blankets) that are still made entirely by handloom. The factory in Reguengos where these are produced – the Fabrica Alentejana de Lanificios (p227) – is the only one still in existence.

Information

Multibanco ATM (Travessa da Misericórdia 2) Located off the main square.

Turismo (tourist office; ☎927 997 316; Rua Direita; ⊙9.30am-1pm & 2-5.30pm) Stocked with some regional information, including bus timetables and basic maps of the area's megalithic monuments.

Getting There & Away

Buses run to/from Reguengos de Monsaraz (€3.10, 35 minutes, four daily weekdays). The last bus back to Reguengos, where you can pick up connections to Évora, is around 6pm (check, however, as this changes).

Estremoz

POP 7500

Along with neighbouring Borba and Vila Viçosa, the very authentic, active town of Estremoz is one of the region's well-known marble hotspots and is worth visiting. The region's marble – rivalling that in Carrara, Italy – is used all over the place: even the cobbles are rough chunks of marble.

Ringed by an old protective wall, Estremoz has a centre set with orange tree-lined lanes, a 13th-century hilltop castle enclosed in an old quarter, and peaceful plazas (the main one being Rossio Marquês de Pombal, or 'the Rossio'). This simple provincial town is a busy trading centre, with lots of shops selling farm tools, though visitors can also load up on crafts, earthenware pottery and gourmet delights – all of which are available at the great market that fills the huge central square on Saturday. The town also boasts some excellent eateries.

Sights

Lower Town

On the fringes of the Rossio are imposing old churches, former convents and, just north of the square, monastic buildings converted into **cavalry barracks**. Opposite these, by Largo General Graça, is a marble-edged water tank, called the **Lago do Gadanha** (Lake of the Scythe) after its scythe-wielding statue of Neptune. Some of the prettiest marble streets in town are south of the Rossio, off Largo da República.

Palácio dos Marqueses da Praia e Monforte MUSEUM
(Rua da Vasco da Gama 13; ⊙9am-12.30pm & 2-5.30pm) FREE This former royal palace was recently restored and reopened to the public in 2015. It houses a changing array of exhibitions showcasing talented artists from the Alentejo – easily the best works in Estremoz – with three to four shows annually. Regardless of what's on, it's well worth strolling the marble-lined corridors, past stained-glass windows beneath lovely decorative ceilings.

Upper Town

The upper town is surrounded by dramatic zigzagging ramparts and contains a gleaming white palace. The easiest way to reach it on foot is to follow narrow Rua da Frandina from

Estremoz

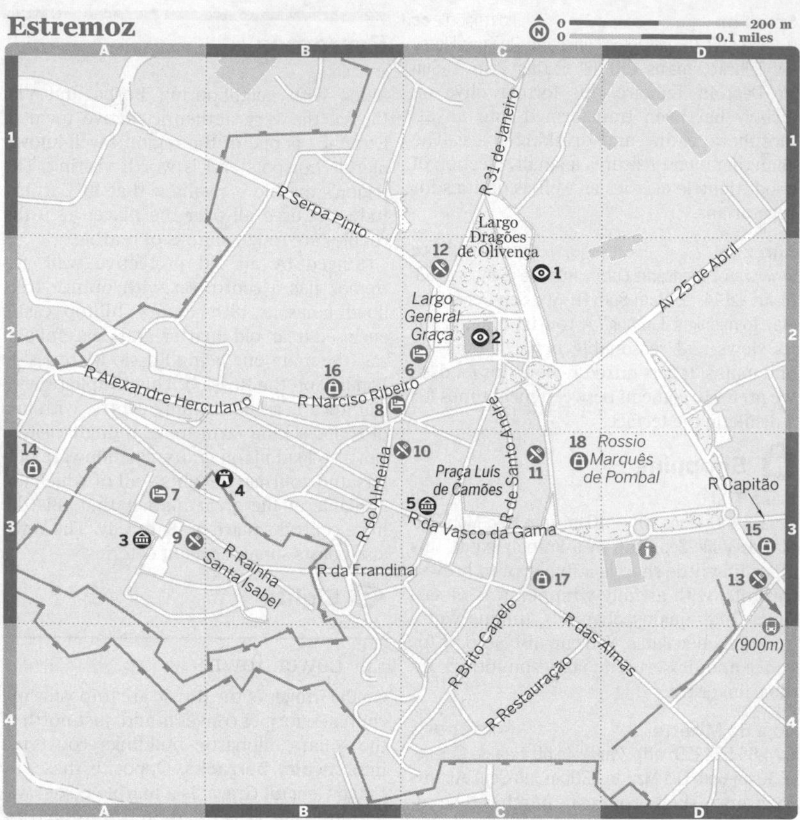

Estremoz

Sights

1 Cavalry Barracks C2
2 Lago do Gadanha C2
3 Museu Municipal A3
4 Paço Reial B3
5 Palácio dos Marqueses da Praia e Monforte C3

Sleeping

6 Hotel O Gadanha C2
7 Pousada de Rainha Santa Isabel A3
8 Residencial Jose Miguel B2

Eating

9 A Cadeia A3
10 Adega do Isaías C3
11 Alecrim C3
12 Gadanha Mercearia e Restaurante C2
13 Venda Azul D3

Shopping

14 Afonso Ginja A3
15 Casa Galileu D3
16 Fátima Estróia B2
17 Irmãs Flores C3
18 Saturday Market C3

Praça Luís de Camões and pass the inner castle walls through the Arco da Frandina.

Paço Reial PALACE

(Royal Palace; 9am-7pm) FREE At the top of the upper town is the stark, glowing-white, fortress-like former royal palace, now the Pousada de Santa Rainha Isabel. Dom Dinis built the palace in the 13th century for his new wife, Isabel of Aragon. Visitors are welcome to view the public areas of the *pousada* and climb the keep, which offers a superb panorama of the old town and surrounding plains. The holes at the keep's edges were channels for boiling oil – a good way of getting rid of uninvited guests.

After Isabel of Aragon's death in 1336 (Dinis had died 11 years earlier), the palace was used as an ammunition dump. An inevitable explosion, in 1698, destroyed most of the palace and the surrounding castle, though in the 18th century João V restored the palace for use as an armoury. The 27m-high keep, the **Torre das Três Coroas** (Tower of the Three Crowns), survived and is still the dominant feature. It's so called because it was apparently built by three kings: Sancho II, Afonso III and Dinis.

Museu Municipal MUSEUM
(☎268 339 219; Largo D Dinis; €1.55; ⊙9am-12.30pm & 2-5.30pm Tue-Sun) This museum is housed in a beautiful 17th-century almshouse near the former palace. Pretty hand-painted furniture sits alongside endearing, locally carved wooden figures (charming rural scenes by Joaquim Velhinho) and a collection of typical 19th-century domestic Alentejan items.

Festivals & Events

Feira Internacional de Artesanato e Agro-Pecuária de Estremoz FERIA
(FIAPE; ⊙Apr) The town's biggest event is the Feira Internacional de Artesanato e Agro-Pecuária de Estremoz, a baskets, ceramics, vegetables and livestock bonanza, held for several days at the end of April.

Cozinha dos Ganhões FOOD
(Festival de Gastronomia Alentejana; ⊙Nov) Held late November to early December, this four-day culinary festival features traditional dishes, game meats and heavenly desserts. Later in the evening, live music, a bar area and a dance floor keep thing interesting.

Sleeping

Residencial Jose Miguel GUESTHOUSE €
(☎268 322 326; Travessa da Levada 8; s/d/tw €25/38/40;) In a central location, you'll find this family-run, powder-blue guesthouse that hides a warren of rooms. All are quite clean, with dark-wood furniture and white crocheted bedspreads. Some rooms in back have smaller windows, while those facing the street are brighter, with sizeable windows.

Hotel O Gadanha HOTEL €
(☎268 339 110; www.hotelogadanha.com; Largo General Graça 56; s/d/tr €23/38/50;) This whitewashed house is excellent value. It has bright, fresh, white and clean rooms (with satellite TV and even hairdryers) overlooking the square. Disappointingly, there are no single rates Friday to Sunday. It's popular, so it's worth reserving ahead.

★ **Pousada de Rainha Santa Isabel** LUXURY HOTEL €€€
(☎268 332 075; www.pousadas.pt; Largo Dom Dinis; d €130-180;) In the restored former palace, this lavish *pousada* (upmarket inn) offers spacious rooms with antique furnishings and views over the Alentejo plains. There are lovely palace gardens, a pool with views and common areas set with museum-quality tapestries.

Eating

Gadanha Mercearia e Restaurante PORTUGUESE €€
(☎268 333 262; www.merceariagadanha.pt; Largo Dragões de Olivença 84A; sharing plates €6-17, mains €15-20; ⊙10am-11pm Tue-Sat, to 8pm Sun) This foodie-loving spot brilliantly merges traditional local products with contemporary touches. Extraordinary *petiscos* (snacks) include *linguiça de porco preto* and *farinheira* with quail eggs (*farinheira* is a local speciality made of pork fat, herbs and flour). The daily lunch menu is highly recommended.

Venda Azul PORTUGUESE €€
(☎961 941 394; Largo de São José 26; mains €7-17; ⊙noon-2.30pm & 7-10pm Mon-Sat) Just south of the main square, Venda Azul serves up delicious Alentejan fare at unbeatable prices – a feast for two, including wine and dessert, can be had for under €30. Never mind the bustling, unpretentious atmosphere, this place is universally loved by locals and visitors alike. Call ahead to be sure of scoring a table. The *porco preto* (black Iberian pig) is legendary.

A Cadeia INTERNATIONAL, PORTUGUESE €€
(☎268 323 400; www.cadeiaquinhentista.com; Rua Rainha Santa Isabel; sharing plates €6-18, mains €13-19; ⊙12.30-3pm & 7.30pm-midnight) Unlock your purses at this place, housed in the former judicial jail, which dates from the 16th century; the two storeys of the quadrangle separated male and female prisoners. The restaurant serves *petiscos* and main dishes. There's also an area for coffee and drinks under the building's arch and a classy, romantically lit bar upstairs.

Adega do Isaías PORTUGUESE €€
(☎268 322 318; Rua do Almeida 21; mains €12-18; ⏰noon-3pm & 7-10pm Mon-Sat; ✎) To enter this delightful rustic *tasca* (tavern), you pass by a sizzling grill cooking up tender fish, meat and Alentejan specialities. Inside, a wine cellar awaits, with tables and huge wine jars.

★**Alecrim** PORTUGUESE €€€
(☎268 324 189; www.facebook.com/AlecrimEstremoz; Rossio Marquês de Pombal 31; mains €14-20; ⏰9am-11pm Thu-Tue) Alecrim is one of the best places in town for a meal, no matter the time of day. Come at lunchtime for excellent multicourse daily specials (creamy codfish dishes and tender Alentejan pork), or stop by in the morning for croissants, eggs or pancakes. By evening, you can nibble on creative tapas plates or heartier servings of roast lamb with grilled vegetables.

Shopping

The *turismo* can provide a list of artisans who work with cork, clay, wood and iron, making figurines, bells, sculptures and unique pieces. Most work from their homes, but many are happy to receive customers – it makes a great visit. Those who make *bonecas,* the clay dolls for which the town is famous, include **Irmãs Flores** (☎268 323 350; Largo da República 16; ⏰9am-1pm Mon-Sat, 2-7pm Mon-Fri), **Afonso Ginja** (☎268 081 618; afonsoginja@gmail.com; Rua Direita 5; ⏰9am-1pm & 3-7pm) and **Fátima Estróia** (Rua Narciso Ribeiro).

Saturday Market MARKET
(Rossio Marquês de Pombal; ⏰8am-1.30pm) The weekly Saturday market held on the Rossio provides a great display of Alentejan goodies and Estremoz specialities, from goat's and ewe's milk cheeses, to a unique style of unglazed, ochre-red pots.

Casa Galileu ARTS & CRAFTS
(☎268 323 130; Rua Victor Cordon 16; ⏰7am-8pm) If you miss the Saturday market, visit this shop southeast of the Rossio. It is crammed with locally made items, including essentials such as flat caps, drinking horns and cowbells.

Information

Caixa Geral de Depósitos (Rossio Marquês de Pombal 43) Has a handy ATM.

Turismo (☎268 339 227; www.cm-estremoz.pt; Casa de Estremoz, Rossio Marquês de Pombal; ⏰10am-1pm & 2-6pm) Office on the southern side of Rossio Marquês de Pombal.

Getting There & Away

All buses stop at and depart from a smart new, modern 'marble-mobic' **bus station** (☎938 876 333; Avenida Rainha Santa Isabel), located off Avenida 25 de Abril (behind the *azulejo*-covered former train station).

DESTINATION	COST (€)	DURATION	FREQUENCY
Elvas	9	60-80min	5 daily
Évora	8	1¼hr	6 daily Mon-Fri, 1 Saturday
Évoramonte	4.60	21min	4 daily Mon-Fri
Portalegre	8.50	45min	at least 4 daily
Vila Viçosa	3	30min	3 daily Mon-Fri

Regular buses also head further afield to Faro (€18.10; change in Albufeira or Évora) in the Algarve, and Lisbon (€15, at least six daily).

Vila Viçosa

POP 4900

If you visit just one marble town in the region, Vila Viçosa is the one to hit. It features Praça da República, a long attractive plaza set with orange trees, a marble palace (one of the country's largest) and a castle.

This was once home to the Bragança dynasty, whose kings ruled Portugal until it became a republic – Dom Carlos spent his last night here before his assassination; it was also the birthplace of Catarina de Bragança (1638), who married Charles II to become Queen of England (and after whom Queens in New York was named). There are many sites and sights of marble (and nonmarble) and a friendly laid-back citizenry who are proud of their sparkling town.

Sights

Paço Ducal PALACE
(☎268 980 659; www.fcbraganca.pt; Terreiro do Paço; adult/under 10yr €6/free; ⏰2-5pm Tue, 10am-1pm & 2-5pm Wed-Fri, 9.30am-1pm & 2-5pm Sat & Sun, to 5.30pm or 6pm Apr-Sep) The dukes of Bragança built their palace in the early 16th century when the fourth duke, Dom Jaime, decided he had had enough of his uncomfortable hilltop castle. The wealthy Bragança family, originally from Bragança in Trás-os-Montes, had settled in Vila Viçosa in the 15th century. After the eighth duke

became king in 1640, it changed from a permanent residence to just another royal palace, but the family maintained a special fondness for it and Dom João IV and his successors continued to visit the palace.

The palace's best furniture went to Lisbon after Dom João IV ascended the throne, and some went on to Brazil after the royal family fled there in 1807, but there are still some stunning pieces on display, such as a huge 16th-century Persian rug in the Dukes Hall. Lots of royal portraits put into context the interesting background of the royal family.

The private apartments hold a ghostly fascination – toiletries, knick-knacks and clothes of Dom Carlos and his wife Marie-Amélia are laid out as if the royal couple were about to return (Dom Carlos left one morning in 1908 and was assassinated in Lisbon that afternoon).

A Portuguese-speaking guide leads the compulsory hour-long tours. English tours are offered at 11am on Wednesday, Thursday and Friday. Other parts of the Ducal Palace, including the 16th-century cloister, house more museums containing specific collections and with separate admission fees (armoury/coach collection/Chinese Porcelain/treasury €3/3/2.50/2.50).

Castelo CASTLE

FREE The fascinating Dom Dinis walled hilltop castle was where the Bragança family lived before the palace was built. Part of it has been transformed into the Museu de Arqueologia and Museu de Caça – a must-visit. Surrounding the castle is a cluster of village houses and peaceful overgrown gardens. There's a 16th-century Manueline *pelourinho* (pillory), with sculpted frogs.

Igreja de Nossa Senhora da Conceição CHURCH

(8.30am-12.30pm & 2.30-6.30pm) Within the castle walls is this brilliantly tiled 15th-century church. It is also known as *Solar da Padroeira,* Home of the Patron Saint – the Virgin's image is within. It was here that in 1646 Dom João IV offered the kingdom to Nossa Senhora Da Conceição who became then the patron saint of Portugal. From that time on, the kings of Portugal never wore the crown again, as it was now the Virgin's. Celebrations take place on 8 December.

Museu de Arqueologia & Museu de Caça MUSEUM

(Archaeological Museum and Game & Hunting Museum; €3; 2-5pm Tue, 10am-1pm & 2-5pm Wed-Fri, 9.30am-1pm & 2-5pm Sat & Sun, to 5.30pm or 6pm Apr-Sep) Inside the historic *castelo* looming above Vila Viçosa, you'll find an intriguing collection of relics from days past, as well as some less appealing animal skins and assorted other taxidermy. Nevertheless, a visit to these museums is a must – if only for an excuse to wander through the castle itself (think 'secret' tunnels, giant fireplaces and wonderful vaulted ceilings). The extraordinary (and under-promoted) archaeological collection is housed in the castle's many rooms and spans various eras from the Palaeolithic to the Roman. It even has ancient Egyptian treasures.

Sleeping

Hospedaria Dom Carlos GUESTHOUSE €

(268 980 318; hospedariadcarlos@hotmail.com; Praça da República 25; s/d/tr €30/40/50;) In an excellent location on the main square, the Dom Carlos offers tidy and comfortable rooms with wood finishing and fine views over the plaza. The towels (and mattresses) are a bit stiff, but it's a peaceful spot.

Casa do Colégio Velho GUESTHOUSE €€

(268 889 430; www.casadocolegiovelho.com; Rua Dr Couto Jardim 34; d €75-95, ste €110-125;)

USING YOUR MARBLES

The marble towns gleam with rosy-gold or white stone and the effect is enhanced by the houses, which have a Hollywood-smile brightness. As if locals hadn't found enough uses for the stone stuff, with their marble doorsteps, pavements and shoes (OK, we made that last one up), a process has been cooked up to create marble paint: marble is recrystallised limestone, so if you heat marble chips in a clay oven for three days they turn into calcium oxide, which is mixed with water to become whitewash. Cheaper than paint. People take pride in the whiteness of their houses and retouch them annually.

While we're on the subject of colour, apparently the yellow borders keep away fever, while blue is the bane of flies (you can add these colours to the oxide). The blue theory may have some truth, or at least international adherents – in Rajasthan (India) local people also apply pale blue to their houses to ward off mosquitoes.

You'll feel like Catarina de Bragança herself in one of the seven plush rooms in this former family residence, which was home to the Jesuits in the 17th century. Decoration embraces a melange of styles, including modern art deco and even rare rose marble in one of the bathrooms. The helpful English-speaking owner is handy with recommendations. The *casa* overlooks a lovely, neat garden, with lilies and a pool.

Solar dos Mascarenhas HOTEL €€
(☎268 886 000; www.solardosmascarenhas.com; Rua Florbela Espanca 125; r €65-105; ❄📶🏊) This upscale charmer in a heritage building in the centre of town has stylish, contemporary rooms filled with natural light and boasting spotless marble bathrooms. There's an enticing lounge area filled with lavender sofas.

Herdade da Ribeira de Borba RURAL INN €€
(☎268 980 709; www.hrb.com.pt; Ciladas; r €90-130; ❄🏊) Five kilometres out of Vila Viçosa and on a working farm (think rural tranquillity, walks, birdwatching), this lovely option offers everything from contemporary apartments with kitchens in former workers' cottages, to plainer but pleasant rooms in the main building. Perfect for longer-term stays.

Pousada de Dom João IV LUXURY HOTEL €€€
(☎268 980 742; www.pousadas.pt; Terreiro do Paço; d €105-220; ❄📶🏊) Next to the Paço Ducal, this former royal convent was once the 'House of the Ladies of the Court'. Today, this regal spot offers spacious rooms, terraces and classic furnishings. Rooms open onto a striking inner courtyard.

Eating

Taverna dos Conjurados PORTUGUESE €€
(☎268 989 530; Largo 25 de Abril 12; mains €10-19; ⊙12.30-3pm & 7.30-10pm Tue-Sun Apr-Oct, weekends only Nov-Mar) More upmarket than the average taverna, this inviting eatery serves excellent regional cooking. The attentive host is proud of his classic Portuguese dishes, with some recipes going back to the Dukes' times (complete with time-consuming preparation). Salted codfish, duck with plum sauce, and stewed partridge with saffron sauce are favourites.

Cafe Restauração PORTUGUESE €€
(Praça da República; mains €8-12; ⊙noon-3pm & 7-10pm) Facing the main plaza in town, this local favourite draws a garrulous crowd of young families, old timers and out-of-towners, who come for drinks and snacks at the well-placed outdoor tables. The food is fairly standard Alentejan fare, but it's hard to beat the setting.

Os Cucos PORTUGUESE €€
(☎268 980 806; mains €7-15; ⊙noon-3pm & 7.30-10pm; 📶) Hidden in the pretty gardens near the *mercado municipal,* this is the pick for quality food and shady location. It has an airy, semicircular interior, and you can eat snacks at garden tables. The changing specials – Wednesday *arroz de pato* (duck with rice); Thursday *borrego assado* (roast lamb) – feature unique regional dishes.

Drinking & Nightlife

Tertúlia Perfeita CAFE
(Rua de Éstremoz 3; ⊙9.30am-8pm Sun-Thu, to 3am Fri & Sat; 📶) Inside the castle walls, and a few steps from the Igreja de Nossa Senhora da Conceição, Tertúlia Perfeita has a terrace that makes a fine spot for an afternoon pick-me-up or a cocktail later in the evening. On weekends, it's popular with the student crowd and the beats get louder as the night progresses.

Entertainment

Paço Ducal CLASSICAL MUSIC
(☎268 980 659; www.fcbraganca.pt) Classical concerts are held in the chapel of the Paço Ducal on the last Friday of the month at 9pm year-round.

Information

Turismo (☎268 889 317; www.cm-vilavicosa.pt; Praça da República 34; ⊙9am-1pm & 2.30-5.30pm Oct-May, 9.30am-1pm & 2.30-5.30pm Jun-Sep) For town maps and information.

Getting There & Away

There are limited buses to/from Évora (1¾/one hour, two to three on weekdays), and Estremoz (35 minutes, two to three on weekdays).

Elvas

POP 25,000

Elvas' claim to fame is that it boasts the largest group of bulwarked dry-ditch land fortifications in the world. The impressive fortifications zigzagging around this pleasant little town – declared a Unesco World Heritage Site town in 2012 – reflect an extraordinarily sophisticated military technology. Its moats, fort and heavy walls would indicate a certain paranoia if it weren't for

Elvas' position, only 15km west of Spain's Badajoz. Inside the stout town walls, you'll find a lovely town plaza, some quaint museums and very few foreign visitors – aside from the occasional flood of Spanish day trippers. Although there's not much to hold your attention beyond a day, Elvas is an interesting place to visit, with its evocative frontier-post atmosphere, narrow medina-like streets, and extraordinary, forbidding walls and buttresses.

History

In 1229 Elvas was recaptured from the Moors after 500 years of fairly peaceful occupation. The following centuries saw relentless attacks from Spain, interrupted by occasional peace treaties. Spain only succeeded in 1580, allowing Felipe II of Spain (the future Felipe I of Portugal) to set up court here for a few months. But the mighty fortifications were seldom breached: in 1644, during the Wars of Succession (1640–68), the garrison held out against a nine-day Spanish siege and, in 1659, just 1000 – an epidemic had wiped out the rest – withstood an attack by a 15,000-strong Spanish army. The fortifications saw their last action in 1811, when the Duke of Wellington used the town as the base for an attack on Badajoz during the Peninsular War.

Sights

Torre Fernandina TOWER

(Fernandina Tower; 268 636 470; Rua da Cadeia; 3-6pm Tue, 10am-1pm & 3-6pm Wed-Sun) The Fernandina Tower was the result of alterations undertaken in the 14th century to the second Muslim wall. It served as a jail from the end of the 15th century. These days, you can climb the spiral staircase to the top for wonderful views. Note: the lighting is poor and it's a steep and winding climb up three levels.

Aqueduto da Amoreira AQUEDUCT

It took an unsurprising 100 years or so to complete this breathtakingly ambitious aqueduct. Finished in 1622, the huge cylindrical buttresses and several tiers of arches stalk from 7km west of town to bring water to the marble fountain in Largo da Misericórdia. It's best seen from the Lisbon road, west of the centre.

Castelo CASTLE

(adult/student/child €2/1/free; 9.30am-1pm & 2-6pm May-Sep, to 5pm Oct-Apr) You can walk around the battlements at the castle for dramatic views across the baking plains. The original castle was built by the Moors on a Roman site and rebuilt by Dom Dinis in the 13th century, then again by Dom João II in the late 15th century.

Museu de Arte Contemporânea de Elvas GALLERY

(MACE; 268 637 150; Rua da Cadeia; €2; 2-6pm Tue, 11am-6pm Wed-Sun) The Museu de Arte Contemporânea de Elvas is a must-see if the right exhibition is showing. Opened in 2007, the museum is housed in a cleverly renovated baroque-style building from the 1700s, formerly the Misericórdia Hospital, and houses exhibitions of modern Portuguese artists from the collection of António Cachola.

Forte da Graça FORT

(Monte de Nossa Senhora da Graça; €5, guided tour €8; 10am-5pm Tue-Sun, guided visits 10.30am & 3pm Tue-Sun, plus 11am & 2.30pm Sat & Sun) Looming high over the arid countryside, about 3km north of town, this old military fort has a commanding presence. From the *castelo,* the fort is just visible on a distant hillside. Partially restored in 2015, the thick-walled corridors provide a window into the past – particularly if you take part in one of the guided tours. There are splendid views over Elvas and the surrounding countryside.

Forte de Santa Luzia FORT

(268 628 357; €2; 2-6pm Tue, 11am-6pm Wed-Sun) Dating from the 1640s, this miniature, zigzag-walled fort lies just 1.4km south of the *praça* (town square). Today its houses a military museum with displays of weaponry dating back to the 18th century.

Igreja das Domínicas CHURCH

(Largo de Santa Clara; 9.30am-12.30pm & 2-5pm Oct-May, 10am-1pm & 3-6pm Jun-Sep) This plain church hides a thrilling interior. There are painted marble columns under a cupola, gilded chapels and fantastic 17th-century *azulejos* covering the surface. The unusual octagonal design was inspired by the Knights Templar chapel, which stood on a nearby site before this church was built in the mid-16th century. It was once the church of the Dominicans, and is all that is left of the original monastery.

Igreja de Nossa Senhora da Assunção CHURCH

(Praça da República; 9.30am-12.30pm & 2-5pm Oct-May, 10am-1pm & 3-6pm Jun-Sep) Francisco de Arruda designed this sturdy fortified church

Elvas

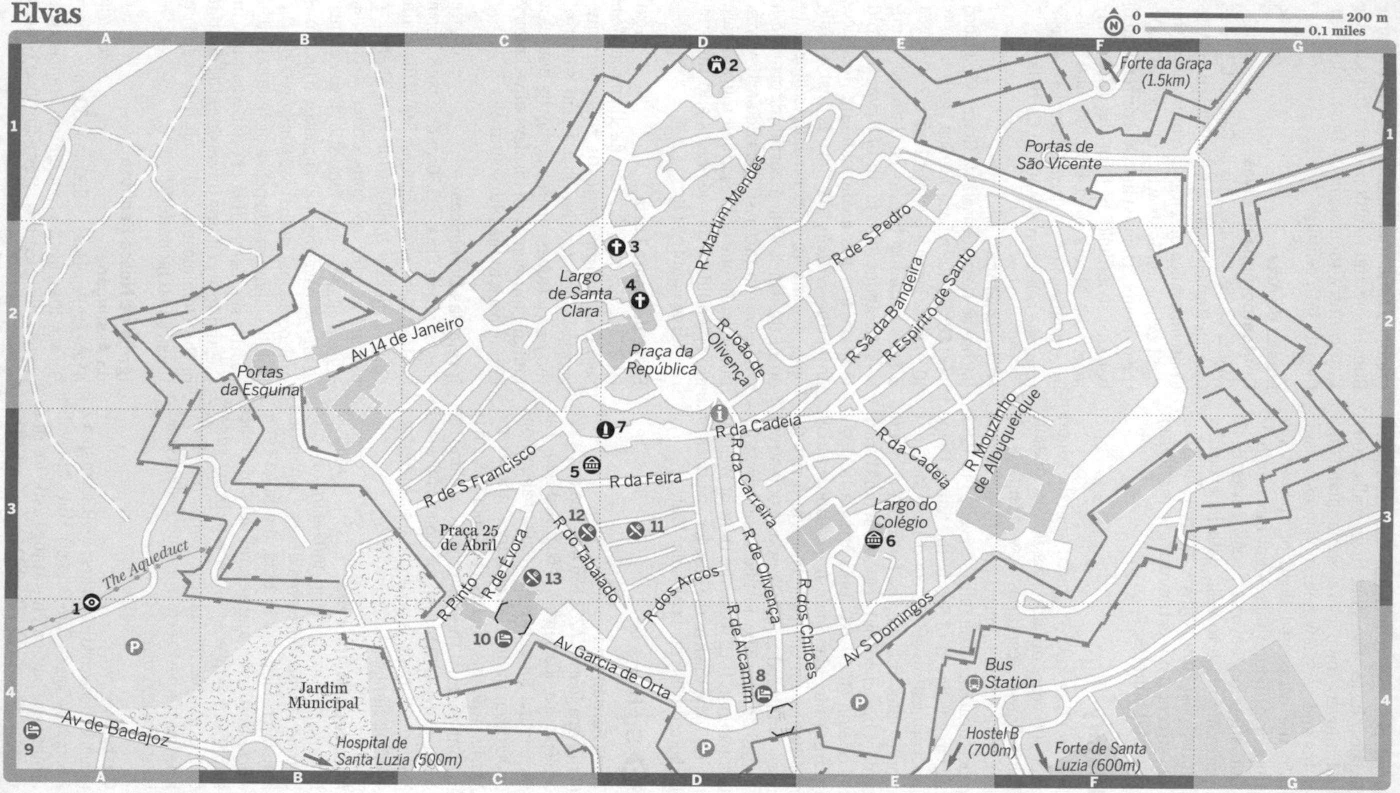

0 200 m
0 0.1 miles
Forte da Graça (1.5km)
Portas de São Vicente
2
3
4
Largo de Santa Clara
R Martim Mendes
R de S Pedro
R Sá da Bandeira
R Espirito de Santo
R João de Olivença
Praça da República
Av 14 de Janeiro
Portas da Esquina
7
R da Cadeia
R da Cadeia
R Mouzinho de Albuquerque
5
R de S Francisco
R da Feira
R da Carreira
Largo do Colégio
6
12
11
R do Tabalado
Praça 25 de Abril
R de Évora
R Pinto
13
R dos Arcos
R de Olivença
R dos Chilões
R de Alcamim
The Aqueduct
1
10
Av Garcia de Orta
8
Av S Domingos
Bus Station
Jardim Municipal
Av de Badajoz
9
Hospital de Santa Luzia (500m)
Hostel B (700m)
Forte de Santa Luzia (600m)

Elvas

Sights

1 Aqueduto da Amoreira........................A4
2 Castelo........................D1
3 Igreja das Domínicas........................D2
4 Igreja de Nossa Senhora da Assunção........................D2
5 Museu de Arte Contemporânea de Elvas........................C3
6 Museu Fotográfico João Carpinteiro........................E3
7 Torre Fernandina........................D3

Sleeping

8 Garcia de Orto........................D4
9 Hotel Dom Luís........................A4
10 Hotel São João de Deus........................C4

Eating

11 A Coluna........................D3
12 Adega Regional........................C3
13 O Lagar........................C3

in the early 16th century, and it served as the town's cathedral until Elvas lost its episcopal status in 1882. Renovated in the 17th and 18th centuries, it retains a few Manueline touches, such as the southern portal. Inside is a sumptuous 18th-century organ and some pretty, but somewhat lost, 17th- and 18th-century tiling.

Museu Fotográfico João Carpinteiro MUSEUM
(☎268 638 470; Largo Luis de Camões; adult/child €2/1; ⏲10am-1pm & 2-7pm Wed-Sun, 2-7pm Tue Jun-Sep, 10am-1pm & 2-5pm Wed-Sun, 2-5pm Tue Oct-May) Housed in the old town cinema is this tiny museum that contains a collection of vintage cameras, the oldest a pocket-vest number dating from 1912. Unless you're a camera buff, you'll probably find the changing art exhibitions (free) in the small gallery in front more interesting.

Tours

Agia WALKING
(☎933 702 392; www.alentejoguides.com) This licensed guide association organises two-hour walking tours (€15) that explore Elvas' historic sites. Contact Agia in advance for meeting places and times.

Festivals & Events

Festas do Senhor da Piedade e de São Mateus MUSIC
(⏲Sep) Elvas starts to tap its blue suede shoes in late September, celebrating the Festas do Senhor da Piedade e de São Mateus, with everything from agricultural markets and bullfights to folk dancing and religious processions (especially on the last day).

Sleeping

Hostel B HOSTEL €
(☎933 498 227; www.hostelb.net; Avenida Colégio Luso-Britânico 6; dm €15; P❄📶) Although well outside the centre, to the south of the city, this art-filled house is a great option for budget-minded travellers. It has four bunk rooms, with four beds in each, and guests can hang out in the common areas around the house (living room, dining room, kitchen) or enjoy the fine view from the verandah. The ruins of an old fort (São Pedro) are a few steps from the front door.

Garcia de Orta GUESTHOUSE €
(☎963 176 380; www.rgarciadeorta.com; Avenida Garcia de Orta 3A; s/d/tr/q €27/35/45/60; 📶) Straight downhill from the Praça da República, this welcoming, family-run guesthouse provides excellent value for money, with nine bright rooms set with quality furnishings. The whole place is very well maintained. Book ahead, as it's often full.

Hotel São João de Deus LUXURY HOTEL €€
(☎268 639 220; www.hotelsaojoaodeus.com; Largo do Hospital; s/d from €60/70; ❄@🏊) Spanish-owned and -operated since 2004, this is Elvas' grandest hotel. It's a pleasant, although not always sympathetic, conversion of a 17th-century convent. Each room is different in size and decor – the larger ones are lovely, a couple of smaller ones less so. Most have handsome wood floors and heavy fabrics; one has a bedhead made of tiles.

Hotel Dom Luís LUXURY HOTEL €€
(☎268 636 710; www.hoteldluis-elvas.com; Avenida de Badajoz; s/d €55/70; ❄📶) This modern 88-room establishment earns high marks for friendliness, although the design is a touch uninspiring – with rooms set in a contemporary decor of browns and beiges. It's 700m west of the centre, just outside the town walls, and it has a pleasant outdoor cafe with great views of the aqueduct.

Eating

On weekends, the restaurants are packed at lunchtime with visitors arriving from Spain. Call ahead or go early to beat the crowds. For alfresco dining and snacks, head to one of the outdoor cafes on the Praça da República.

A Coluna PORTUGUESE **€€**
(268 623 728; Rua do Cabrito 11; mains €10-14; noon-2.30pm & 7-10pm Wed-Mon) Fancying itself as the town's 'gourmet' number, this tavern-cavern offers an elegant space with *azulejos* on the walls. Pork and *bacalhau* (codfish) dishes are its forte.

Adega Regional PORTUGUESE **€€**
(268 623 009; www.adegaregional-elvas.com; Rua João Casqueiro 22B; mains €9-13; 11am-4pm & 7-10pm Wed-Mon;) Locals love this small place where it's all about the food – lashings of *plumas de porco preto* (pork), and *marisco* (shellfish) dishes of all kinds, or a good-value three-course daily meal for €10.

O Lagar PORTUGUESE **€€**
(966 038 995; Rua Nova da Vedoria 7; mains €8-15; noon-3pm & 7-10pm Fri-Wed) Smart and buzzing, O Lagar dishes up excellent regional cooking, with good-value, high-quality *açorda* (a kind of bread soup) and *bacalhau* Service can be a bit slow, but it's a pleasant enough place to linger over a meal.

Information

Banco Espirito Santo (268 939 240; Praça da República) One of many banks with ATMs around town.

Turismo (268 622 236; www.cm-elvas.pt; Praça da República; 9am-7pm Apr-Oct, 9am-6pm Mon-Fri, 9am-12.30pm & 2-5.30pm Sat & Sun Nov-Mar) Usually has a town map and pamphlets.

Getting There & Away

The **bus station** is outside the city walls, on the road to Spain. It's an 800m walk mostly uphill (or a €6 taxi ride) to the main *praça*. Popular bus routes:

Estremoz (€8.50, 45 minutes, one weekdays) Or change at Vila Viçosa.

Évora (€12, 1¼ to 1¾ hours, four weekdays)

Faro (€22, 6½ hours, one daily)

Lisbon (around €18, 3¼ to 3½ hours, seven daily)

Portalegre (€14, 1¼ hours, two weekdays)

Getting Around

Drivers be aware: it's possible to find central parking, but it's not always easy (and most spots inside the walls are paid). If you don't like narrow one-way streets, park on the outskirts of town (or just inside Portas de Olivença).

Portalegre

POP 15,200 / ELEV 520M

Alto Alentejo's capital Portalegre is bunched up on a hilltop at the foot of Serra de São Mamede. This pretty, whitewashed, ochre-edged city makes for a charming, low-key, off-the-beaten-track experience. It's worth stopping here, at the very least, en route to mountaintop villages.

Inside the city walls are faded baroque mansions and relics of the town's textile-manufacturing heyday – wool was the mainstay in the 18th century, cork in the 19th century and tapestries in the 20th. Even today Portalegre stays true to its legacy of natty threads – the Portalegre Tapestry Factory still produces extraordinary tapestries of artworks by famous modern artists, and there's a fabulous museum showcasing the work.

The town's former glory is recorded in stone: faded 17th-century baroque town houses and mansions dot Rua 19 de Junho to the southeast.

Sights

Museu da Tapeçaria de Portalegre Guy Fino GALLERY
(Rua da Figueira 9; adult/child €2.10/1; 9.30am-1pm & 2.30-6pm Tue-Sun) If there's one thing you must visit in Portalegre, it's this splendid museum. Opened in 2001, it contains brilliant contemporary creations from Portalegre's unique tapestry factory. It's named after the factory founder, who created an innovatory 'stitch' by hand weaving. The museum shows a selection of the 7000 colours of thread used.

French tapestry artist Jean Lurçat at first dismissed the technique, until the factory made a copy of one of his works – a cockerel – and asked him to identify the one made at Aubusson, in France. He chose the more perfect Portalegre copy – you can see them juxtaposed here. The huge tapestries are vastly expensive, and the museum includes works by some of the most famous names in Portuguese 20th-century art, including Almada Negreiros and Vieira de Silva. They are all hand-signed on the back by the artist, attesting their quality and authenticity.

Aficionados can visit the **factory** (245 301 400; www.mtportalegre.pt; Rua de Iria Gonçalves 2; 9am-5pm Mon-Fri) where the tap-

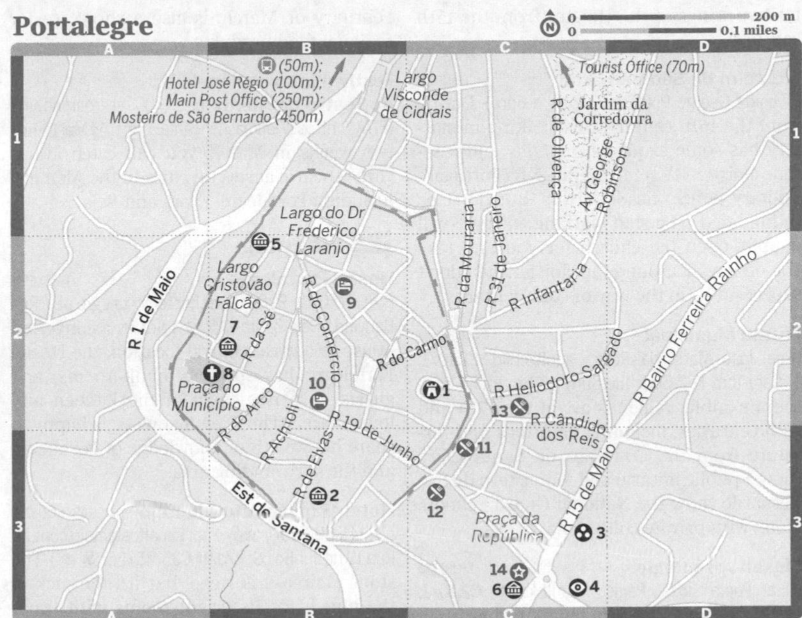

Portalegre

Sights

1 Castelo C2
2 Convento de Santa Clara B3
3 Fabrica de Cortiça Robinson C3
4 Manufactura de Tapeçarias de Portalegre C3
5 Museu da Tapeçaria de Portalegre Guy Fino B2
6 Museu José Regio C3
7 Museu Municipal B2
8 Sé B2

Sleeping

9 Hostel Portalegre B2
10 Hotel Mansão Alto Alentejo B2

Eating

11 Lagóia C3
12 O Poeiras Restaurante C3
13 Solar do Forcado C2

Drinking & Nightlife

Pátio da Casa Café Concerto .... (see 9)

Entertainment

14 Centro de Artes do Espectáculo de Portalegre C3

estries are made (its walls are also adorned with examples). Photography is prohibited and advance reservations are required.

Fabrica de Cortiça Robinson RUINS

(Rua 15 de Maio) This abandoned cork factory is slowly being turned into a cultural centre. Until that happens, however, you can peer inside and wander through a warren of rooms where old machinery lies rusting. Founded in 1835 by an Englishman named Thomas Reynolds, the factory was a major employer in Portalegre (with more than 2000 workers at its peak). Production declined in the second half of the 20th century, and the place only closed for good in 2009.

Convento de Santa Clara HISTORIC BUILDING

(Rua de Elvas; 9am-1pm & 2-6pm Mon-Fri, 2-6pm Sat) FREE Yet another of Portalegre's hidden treasures, this former convent is now part of the municipal library, meaning you can freely wander around at will. It has an impressive cloister and a few *azulejo*-covered walls. Though the original convent dates back to the 14th century, most of the structure dates from the 18th century, save for two wings of the cloister from the 15th century.

Mosteiro de São Bernardo CHURCH

(Avenida George Robinson; 9am-6pm) Dating from the 16th century, this striking monastery has some exquisite *azulejos* and a serene cloister. It's set inside a GNR (Portugal's military police) headquarters, but don't be intimidated. The staff working the gate will happily open the church for you and take you on a walk around the cloister. Just don't expect much in the way of commentary.

Museu Municipal MUSEUM

(Rua José Maria da Rosa; adult/child €2.10/1; 9am-1pm & 2-6pm Tue-Sun) The local museum exhibits religious art of the 17th and 18th centuries, including paintings and furniture from the Convento de Santa Clara (now a public library) and Monastero de São Bernardo (now the National Guard School), along with private collections.

Museu José Régio MUSEUM

(Rua Poeta José Régio; adult/child €2.10/1; 9.30am-1pm & 2.30-6pm Tue-Sun) This small museum in poet José Régio's former house shows his magpie-like collection of popular religious art, with around 400 Christ figures. There are lots of rustic ceramics from Coimbra, which 18th-century migrant workers used to swap for clothes.

Sé CATHEDRAL

(Praça do Município; 2.30-6pm Tue, 9am-noon & 2.30-6pm Wed-Sun) In 1550 Portalegre became the seat of a new diocese and soon got its own cathedral. The pyramid-pointed, twin-towered 18th-century facade sombrely presides over the whitewashed Praça do Município. The sacristy contains an array of fine *azulejos*.

Castelo CASTLE

(9.30am-1pm & 2.30-6pm Tue-Sun) FREE Portalegre's castle, off Rua do Carmo, dates from the time of Dom Dinis. Its three restored towers offer good views across the town. There is a temporary exhibition gallery on the 1st floor.

Festivals & Events

Portalegre JazzFest MUSIC

(http://caeportalegre.blogspot.com; Mar/Feb) Rising stars of the jazz world descend on Portalegre every year, with a mix of classic and cutting-edge sounds. The fest, held in February or March, is also a showcase for regional food products.

Festival Internacional do Teatro do Alentejo PERFORMING ARTS

(FITA; https://lendiasdencantar.org; Mar) For two weeks in March, you can catch avant-garde theatre at several cities in the Alentejo, including Portalegre, Évora and Beja.

Sleeping

Hostel Portalegre HOSTEL €

(967 002 998; www.hostelportalegre.pt; Rua Benvindo Ceia 2; dm €15;) Set in a converted house in a great central location, the Hostel Portalegre has spacious bunk rooms, and guests have free reign of the kitchen and lounge area. The friendly owner is happy to share his wealth of knowledge of Portalegre and the surrounding area.

Hotel Mansão Alto Alentejo GUESTHOUSE €

(245 202 290; www.mansaoaltoalentejo.com.pt; Rua 19 de Junho 59; s/d/tr €35/45/55;) The stone staircase is steep, but it's the pick of the bunch for its bright rooms with traditional hand-painted Alentejan furniture and lounge area. It has a good, central location.

★ **Convento da Provença** LUXURY HOTEL €€

(245 337 104; www.provenca.pt; Monte Paleiros; s/d/ste €75/85/95; P) Mother Superior may not have approved of this out-of-town luxury sleeping option, but we do. This renovated former convent has an austere white exterior, but its interior is another story. Shiny sabres and suits of armour fill the grand lounge room and entrance hall. The spacious rooms and suites are decked out in masculine hues and stylish wooden trimmings. All have lovely green views.

Hotel José Régio HOTEL €€

(245 009 190; www.hoteljoseregio.com; Largo António José Lourinho; s/tw/d €63/75/80;) Named after the city's favourite native son, this stylish 35-room hotel has obvious appeal, with attractive rooms, each with a poem of José Régio's (in Portuguese of course) on the wall. All the rooms have light grey colour schemes with high-end mattresses, a small work desk, an armchair and big windows.

Quinta da Dourada RURAL INN €€

(937 218 654; www.quintadadourada.pt; d €75-85; P) Seven kilometres northeast of Portalegre, in the Parque Natural da Serra de São Mamede, this picture-perfect, modern-looking place is surrounded by glorious

vegetation – lime trees and flowers. The individual rooms are smartly furnished and have granite floors.

Eating

★ Solar do Forcado PORTUGUESE €€
(☎245 330 866; Rua Cândido dos Reis 14; mains €9-14; ⏲12.30-3.30pm & 7.30-10.30pm Mon-Fri, 7.30-10.30pm Sat) The current owner and his late father were former *forcados* (performers of a specific style of Portuguese bullfighting), as attested by the many photos and paraphernalia that cover the walls of this atmospheric spot. Meat lovers should charge in here for hefty regional delights of *bovino* (bull meat), wild pig and deer, plus great *doces conventuais* (convent desserts).

Lagóia TAPAS €€
(☎245 092 410; Rua Garrett 24; sharing plates €6-14; ⏲11am-3pm & 5-11pm Wed-Mon; 📶) For a different take on Portuguese cooking, head to this small eatery near the Praça da República, where you can assemble a first-rate meal from the varied sharing plates. Oven-baked Camembert with *presunto* (ham), shrimp with garlic, and chickpeas with codfish are among the hits. Good cocktail choices, too, with over a dozen gins on hand.

O Poeiras Restaurante PORTUGUESE €€
(☎245 201 862; Praça da República 9-15; mains €8-13; ⏲noon-3pm & 7-10pm Tue-Sat, noon-3pm Sun) Step into this cheerfully tiled eatery for satisfying plates of Alentejano cuisine that won't break the bank. Standout dishes include chicken *piri-piri* (chilli), *borrego assudo* (roast lamb) and *porco preto* (Alentejan pork). Wine starts at €5 a bottle.

Drinking & Nightlife

Pátio da Casa Café Concerto CAFE
(Rua Benvindo Ceia 1; ⏲10am-2am Mon-Sat, 3pm-2am Sun; 📶) A bohemian air pervades this hidden glass-roofed patio cafe, with its chunky wooden tables, Moroccan glass lamps and world music soundtrack. Changing artwork adorns the walls, and there's live music most weekends. At other times, it draws a local crowd who stop in for coffee or sangria, snacks (*tostas,* crêpes, veggie burgers) and free wi-fi.

Entertainment

Centro de Artes do Espectáculo de Portalegre THEATRE
(☎245 307 498; www.caeportalegre.blogspot.com; Praça da República 39) Overlooking Praça da República is Portalegre's major performance space, hosting fado singers, rock, jazz and acoustic groups, as well as dance and theatre. Ask at the tourist office for current shows.

Information

Turismo (☎245 307 445; Rua Guilherme Gomes Fernandes 22; ⏲9.30am-1pm & 2.30-6pm) Helpful staff dole out information and a town map. Also free internet access.

Getting There & Away

The **bus station** (☎245 330 723) has regular bus services that run to the following destinations:

DESTINATION	COST (€)	DURATION	FREQUENCY
Castelo Branco	9.50	1hr 50min	1 daily
Castelo de Vide	5	30min	2 daily Mon-Fri
Elvas	14	1½hr	1 daily Mon-Fri
Estremoz	8	50min	1 daily Mon-Fri
Évora	12.50	1½hr	1 daily Mon-Fri
Lisbon	15	4hr	1 daily
Marvão	4	45min	2 daily Mon-Fri

Castelo de Vide

POP 2400 / ELEV 570M

High above lush, rolling countryside, Castelo de Vide is one of Portugal's most attractive and underrated villages. Its fine hilltop vantage point, dazzlingly white houses, flower-lined lanes and proud locals are reason alone to visit. There aren't many attractions in town, but there doesn't need to be. Absorb this pleasant place for a day and a night; at dusk and early morning you can experience the town at its most disarming. You'll see elderly women crocheting on doorsteps, children playing in the narrow streets and neighbours chatting out of upper-storey windows.

Castelo de Vide is famous for its crystal-clear mineral water, which spouts out of numerous pretty public fountains; several of these are surrounded by hedged gardens.

Castelo de Vide

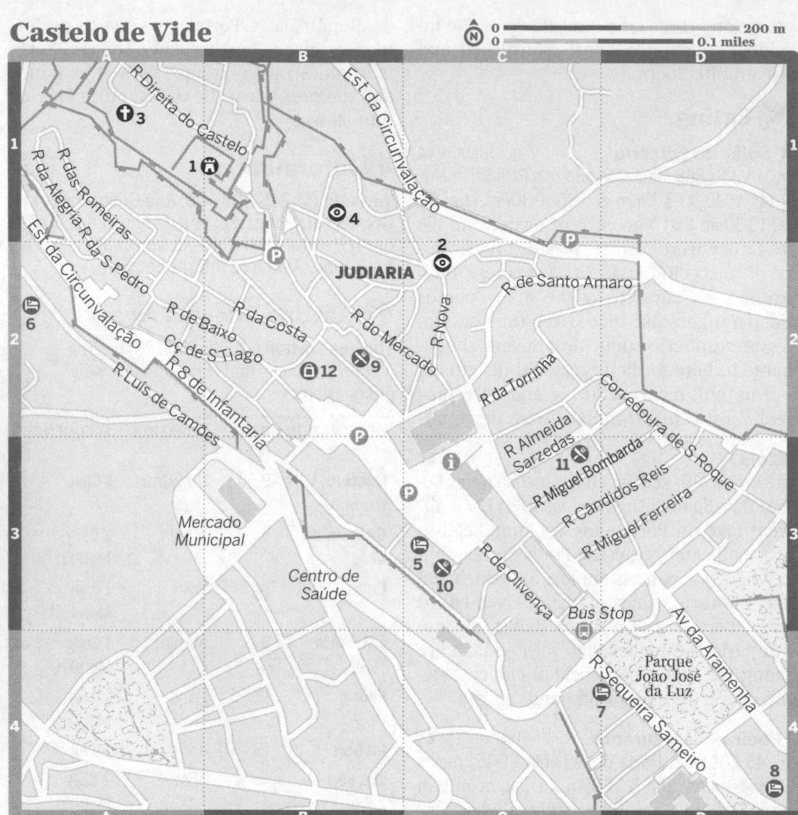

Castelo de Vide

Sights
1 Castelo B1
2 Fonte da Vila C2
3 Igreja da Nossa Senhora da Alegria A1
4 Judiaria B1
Synagogue & Museum .... (see 4)

Sleeping
5 Casa Amarela C3
6 Casa de Hóspedes Machado A2
7 Inatel D4
8 Sol e Serra D4

Eating
9 Confraria B2
10 Doces & Companhia C3
11 O Miguel C3

Shopping
12 Toca do Chocolate B2

Sights

Synagogue & Museum MUSEUM
(9am-1pm & 2-5pm Tue-Sun Sep-May, to 6pm Jun-Aug) FREE Reopened in 2009 after being converted into a museum, the site comprises the original synagogue – two rooms (one for women and one for men), a wooden tabernacle and Holy Ark for Torah scrolls. The remaining rooms (part of the village home from which the synagogue was originally converted) house a superb collection of items illustrating the history of the Jewish communities of Castelo de Vide. Following Manuel I's convert-or-leave edict in 1496, many Jews returned to Spain, though some headed to Évora.

Castelo CASTLE
(⏲9.30am-1pm & 2-5.30pm Sep-May, to 6pm Jun-Aug) FREE Originally Castelo de Vide's inhabitants lived within the castle's sturdy outer walls; even now there remains a small inner village with a church, the 17th-century **Igreja da Nossa Senhora da Alegria**. You can take in some brilliant views from here over the town's red roofs, surrounded by green and olive hills. Also in the castle walls is a small armoury museum, and a one-room gallery devoted to the Inquisition.

Judiaria HISTORIC SITE
By the castle is a small *judiaria* – the former Jewish district. A sizeable community of Jews settled here in the 12th century, then larger waves came in the early 15th century after the expulsion of the Jews from Spain. At first they didn't have an exclusive district, but Dom Pedro I restricted them to specific quarters. The highlight of this area is the synagogue and museum.

Fonte da Vila FOUNTAIN
(Rua da Fonte) In a pretty square just below and east of the *judiaria* is the worn-smooth 16th-century marble Fonte da Vila, with a washing area. This, along with several other fountains in the village, spouts the delicious mineral water for which Castelo de Vide is known.

Activities

Keen walkers should ask at the tourist office for walking trail maps such as those headed to Torrinha and Serra de S Paulo. These wonderful three- to four-hour sojourns around the area pass old churches, fountains, and megaliths and dolmens.

Festivals & Events

Carnaval CARNIVAL
(⏲Feb/Mar) Held in February/March, this festival is great fun, with everyone out to watch processions of those in their homemade fancy dress.

Easter Festival RELIGIOUS
Castelo de Vide's big bash – and one of the most traditional of its festivals – is the four-day fair on Good Friday to Easter Monday when a couple of lambs go through the highs and lows of blessings and slaughter. Processions, folk dances, band music and revelry take place.

Sleeping

Inatel HOTEL €
(☎245 900 240; www.inatel.pt; Rua Sequeira Sameiro 6; s/d from €34/45; 📶) Overlooking a leafy park in the town centre, this Portuguese chain offers excellent value for money. Rooms have terracotta floors, heavy carved-wood furniture, comfortable beds and spacious bathrooms (the vanity mirror is a nice touch). Grab a table in the back of the breakfast room for pretty mountain views (with swallows flittering about).

Sol e Serra HOTEL €
(☎245 900 000; www.grupofbarata.com/solserra; Av da Europa 1; s/d from €30/40; ❄📶🏊) The facade is showing its age, and the rooms could use a bit of an update, but on other fronts, the Sol e Serra is not a bad option. Most rooms have a clean and simple look, with painted furniture and balconies overlooking the greenery in front. There's also a pool.

Casa de Hóspedes Machado GUESTHOUSE €
(☎245 901 515; www.casamachado.com.pt; Rua Luís de Camões 33; s/d/tr €25/30/35; 📶) On the western edge of town, this friendly and efficiently run place has airy, modern and spotless rooms, some of which offer fine views. There's a small, shared kitchen and outdoor patio.

Casa Amarela GUESTHOUSE €€
(☎245 905 878; www.casaamarelath.pt; Praça Dom Pedro V 11; s/d from €70/80; 📶) This beautifully restored 18th century building on the main square, with views over the *praça,* is a luxurious choice. It has stone staircases and common areas filled with antiques. The 11 rooms drip with rich fabrics and feature massive, marble-filled bathrooms.

Eating

Doces & Companhia CAFE €
(☎245 901 408; Praça Dom Pedro V 6; snacks €3-6; ⏲8.30am-7.30pm Mon-Sat, to 11pm Jul-Sep; 🌿) Serving great cakes and ice cream, this is the place to ease your sugar cravings. Also on offer are light meals (quiche, crêpes, burgers), teas, coffees and set-menu lunches (around €8). There are usually vegetarian options. When the weather clears, head to the back terrace to enjoy the view.

★**Confraria** PORTUGUESE €€
(☎916 603 652; Rua Santa Maria 10; mains around €11; ⏲10am-10pm Tue-Sun) This outstanding

WORTH A TRIP

MIGHTY MEGALITHS

In the wild, boulder-strewn landscape around Castelo de Vide are dozens of ancient megaliths. The two most impressive are the **Anta da Melriça**, northwest of town, and the 7m-high **Menhir da Meada**, around 13km north of town. This is supposedly the tallest menhir in the Iberian Peninsula – a large phallus for keeping the fields fertile and acting as a territory marker (one of the few believed to have done both jobs). The so called **Parque Megalítico dos Coureleiros** is a collection of five different arrangements.

These megaliths are best accessible by car. Ask for a map from the tourist office.

restaurant serves up delectable plates of regional fare showcasing whatever is fresh and seasonal. The menu is limited and mostly meat-centric (think tender beef cheeks, wild partridge and rich roast pork), but plates are beautifully turned out and the wines on offer (all from the Alentejo) are outstanding.

O Miguel PORTUGUESE **€€**
(☎961 341 109; Rua Almeida Sarzedas 32-34; mains €9-13; ⊙noon-2.30pm & 7.30-10pm Mon-Sat) This long-standing down-to-earth spot whips up regional dishes including *migas de batata* (potato dumplings), tripe and traditional flavours of the season in a convivial atmosphere. Set lunches for around €9 are served on weekdays.

Shopping

Toca do Chocolate FOOD
(Rua Mouzinho da Silveira 14; ⊙3-7pm Wed-Fri, 11am-1pm & 3-7pm Sat & Sun) If you have a weakness for chocolate, don't miss this heavenly shop and cafe hidden on a narrow lane on the way to the castle. You'll find plenty of temptations here, from rich hot chocolate to chocolate-covered fruit, decadent tarts and even chocolate liqueurs.

Information

Caixa Geral de Depósitos (☎245 339 100; Praça Valéncia de Alcántara) Centrally located bank and ATM.

Turismo (☎245 908 227; www.cm-castelo-vide.pt; Praça Dom Pedro V; ⊙9am-12.30pm & 2-5.30pm Nov-Apr, 9am-1pm & 3-6pm May-Oct) Stocks some reasonable printed matter, including maps and leaflets.

Getting There & Away

From the **bus stop** (☎245 901 510) at Praça Valéncia de Alcántara, buses run to/from Portalegre (€5, 20 minutes, one to three daily) and Lisbon (€18, 4¼ hours, two daily). For Marvão you must change in Portagem. Ask at the *turismo* for bus times.

Marvão

On a jutting crag high above the surrounding countryside, the narrow lanes of Marvão feel like a retreat far removed from the settlements below. The whitewashed village of picturesque tiled roofs and bright flowers has marvellous views, a splendid castle and a handful of low-key guesthouses and restaurants. Since the 16th century, the town has struggled to keep inhabitants, and today the friendly locals survive mainly on tourism. It's worth spending a night here.

Arriving by car or bus you'll approach Portas de Ródão, one of the four village gates, opening onto Rua de Cima, which has several shops and restaurants. Drivers can park outside or enter this gate and park in Largo de Olivença, just below Rua de Cima.

History

Not surprisingly, this garrison town just 10km from the Spanish frontier has long been a prized possession. Romans settled here, and Christian Visigoths were on the scene when the Moors arrived in 715. It was probably the Moorish lord of Coimbra, Emir Maraun, who gave the place its present name.

In 1160 Christians took control. In 1226 the town received a municipal charter, the walls were extended to encompass the whole summit, and the castle was rebuilt by Dom Dinis.

Marvão's importance in the defence against the Castilians was highlighted during the 17th-century War of Restoration, when further defences were added. But by the 1800s it had lost its way, a garrison town without a garrison, and this lack of interest is why so many 15th- and 16th-century buildings have been preserved. Its last action was at the centre of the tug-of-war between the Liberals and Royalists; in 1833 the Liberals used a secret entrance to seize the town – the only time Marvão has ever been captured.

Sights

Castelo CASTLE
(9am-9pm summer, 10am-7pm winter) FREE
The formidable castle, built into the rock at the western end of the village, dates from the end of the 13th century, but most of what you see today was built in the 17th century. The views from the battlements are staggering. There's a huge vaulted cistern (still full of water) near the entrance and it's landscaped with hedges and flowerbeds. The *torre de menagem* (keep) has displays on the castle's history even predating its founding in the 13th century.

Museu Municipal MUSEUM
(adult/student €1.90/1; 9am-12.30pm & 1.30-5pm Tue-Sun) Just southeast of the castle, the Igreja de Santa Maria provides graceful surroundings for this one-room museum. Its newly renovated exhibition hall offers a brief overview of regional history, from the Paleolithic era to more recent centuries.

Casa da Cultura CULTURAL CENTRE
(Largo do Pelourinho; 10am-1pm & 2-5pm) FREE
In a restored building, this cultural centre hosts changing exhibitions. You can also check out the rustic upstairs courtroom, dating from 1809, and there's a small handicrafts shop on-site (in what was a former prison).

Activities

Caballos Marvão HORSE RIDING
(964 594 202; www.caballosmarvao.com;) For equestrian adventures, get in touch with this friendly, professionally run outfit, which offers a wide range of outings. You can head out on a one-hour ride (€20) through typical Alentejan scenery, explore the little-visited landscapes along the Rio Sever or ride along old smuggler routes past vulture colonies near the Spanish border (€80, five hours). The stables are located about 5km northeast of Marvão. Call for directions.

Rio Sever SWIMMING
(Portagem) A favourite local way to cool off in the summer is to take a dip in the Rio Sever. From June to September, a short stretch of river in Portagem is netted off so you can swim safely. Portagem is about 6km southwest of Marvão.

Visiting Megaliths
You can make a brilliant 30km round-trip via Santo António das Areias and Beirã, visiting nearby *antas* (dolmens). Follow the '*antas*' signs through a fabulously quiet landscape of cork trees and rummaging pigs. Some megaliths are right by the roadside, while others require a 300m to 500m walk. Be sure to bring refreshments: there's no village en route. You can continue north of Beirã to visit the megaliths in the Castelo de Vide area.

Walking
Ask at the tourist office (p246) for instructions on the interesting 7.5km circuit walk from Marvão to Portagem via Abegoa and Fonte Souto (or 2.5km direct to Portagem), following a medieval stone-paved route. Note: the return journey is steep.

Sleeping

Casa da João GUESTHOUSE €
(245 993 437; joao_carlos64@sapo.pt; Travessa de Santiago 1; r €30) One of two budget options in town, this offers two double rooms with cork floors and a shared bathroom.

WORTH A TRIP

ROMAN RUINS

The excellent little Roman museum **Cidade de Ammaia** (245 919 089; www.ammaia.pt; Estrada da Calçadinha 4; €2; 9am-12.30pm & 2-5.30pm) lies between Castelo de Vide and Marvão in São Salvador de Aramenha. From São Salvador head 700m south along the Portalegre road, then turn left, following the signs to Ammaia.

In the 1st century AD this area was a huge Roman city called Ammaia, flourishing from the area's rich agricultural produce (especially oil, wine and cereals). Although evidence was found (and some destroyed) in the 19th century, it wasn't until 1994 that thorough digs began.

Here you can see some of the finds, including engraved lintels and tablets, jewellery, coins and some incredibly well-preserved glassware. You can also follow paths across the fields to where the forum and spa once stood and see several impressive columns.

★Trainspot GUESTHOUSE €€
(☎963 340 221; http://trainspot.pt; Largo da Alfândega, Beirã; r with shared/private bathroom €45/65; P 📶) Located some 11km north of Marvão in the tiny village of Beirã, this extraordinary place offers lodging in a beautifully converted building that was once part of the now inactive train station. It's a designer's dream with lovely tilework, a spacious lounge with fireplace and intriguing details (including a bicycle dangling from the ceiling). The rooms are bright and quite comfy. The patio faces onto the old train tracks.

The guesthouse makes a fine base for exploring the area. There are lesser known megaliths and lovely walks (or horse rides) in the countryside nearby.

★Quinta do Barrieiro GUESTHOUSE €€
(☎936 721 199; www.quintadobarrieiro.pt; r €55-130, 6-person apt €150-230; P ❄ 📶 🏊) Special occasion anyone? Bah! You shouldn't need an excuse to come to this rural tourism abode. Home to two creative Portuguese – a sculptor and an architect – this superb place, made up of several *casinhas* (little houses) and rooms, provides comfort, creativity and the outdoors (there are some great walks around the property and to a dam).

The garden is full of the owner's sculptures, as are the airy communal living areas. Continental breakfasts are excellent and cost €15 per double room. Ring for directions as it's 13km from Marvão, 10km from Portalegre.

Estalagem de Marvão GUESTHOUSE €€
(☎968 147 862; http://innmarvao.com; Rua do Espírito Santo 1; s/d/f €40/60/80; ❄ 📶) In the heart of the village, you'll find six simple but attractively decorated rooms and kind staff. The inn also operates a shop, where you can browse gourmet food items and a few crafts.

Hotel El Rei Dom Manuel HOTEL €€
(☎245 909 150; www.turismarvao.pt; Largo da Olivença; s €45-65, d €55-95; 📶) The pick for reliability. This charming, friendly and professional hotel has comfortable rooms with tiled floors, drapes and puffy pillows. The best rooms are the suites with a view. Breakfast is served in the hotel restaurant.

Casa da Árvore GUESTHOUSE €€
(☎245 993 854; www.casadaarvoremarvao.com; Rua Dr Matos Magalhães 3; s/d from €50/65; ❄) This elegant guesthouse has five country-home-style rooms and an attractive, comfortable lounge area with a stunning view. Great for kicking back after pounding the streets. It's worth paying a bit extra (€5) for a room with a verandah.

Dom Dinis GUESTHOUSE €€
(☎245 909 028; www.domdinis.pt; Rua Dr Matos Magalhães 7; s/d from €50/60; ❄ 📶) Dom Dinis has nine smallish but modern rooms with whitewashed walls and heavy wood furnishings. The largest has a balcony with lovely views over the castle walls. Even if you don't score a room with a view, you can enjoy the sweeping expanse from the terrace.

Eating

O Castelo PORTUGUESE €
(www.facebook.com/cafeloungemarvao; Rua Dr Matos Magalhães 7; lunch special €9; ⏲9am-11pm) This cafe has outdoor tables and a cosy interior where you can warm up by the fireplace on frosty afternoons. It has changing lunch specials throughout the week as well as lighter fare – tostas, sandwiches, soups – hot chocolate, Alentejan wines and the like.

★Restaurante Sever PORTUGUESE €€
(☎245 993 318; Estrada Rio Sever, Portagem; mains €11-19; ⏲noon-3pm & 7-10pm) The pick of the restaurants for miles around, this smart place is in a beautiful location, just over the bridge in Portagem, on the Rio Sever. It comes highly recommended by locals and serves first-class Alentejan cuisine. Specials include roast leg of lamb and wild rabbit with mushrooms. The grilled vegetables are great for vegetarians.

Varanda do Alentejo PORTUGUESE €€
(☎245 909 002; www.varandadoalentejo.com; Praça do Pelourinho 1; mains €9-13; ⏲noon-3pm & 7-10pm Mon-Sat, noon-3pm Sun) This popular place serves up lots of pork-based regional specialities, which you can enjoy with a sangria on the terrace. You'll also find classic *bacalhau* (codfish) dishes, octopus and several vegetarian plates.

Information

Caixa Geral do Depósitos (Rua do Espiríto Santo) Has an ATM.

Turismo (☎245 909 131; www.cm-marvao.pt; Rua de Baixo; ⏲9am-1pm & 2-6pm Jun-Sep, to 5pm Oct-May) After the gate entrance (not to be confused with a small information booth on the left as you enter the walls) is the helpful *turismo*, which has a complete list of accommodation options and free internet access. Pick up jams and souvenirs here too.

Getting There & Away

Buses run between Portalegre and Marvão (45 minutes, two daily weekdays). There is also a service to/from Castelo de Vide (22 minutes), but it may require a change of bus at Portagem, a key road junction 6km southwest of Marvão.

For taxi trips, contact the owner of the restaurant **Varanda do Alentejo** (☎245 909 002; Praça do Pelourinho 1). A taxi to Castelo de Vide costs around €16.

BAIXO ALENTEJO

The southern half of the Alentejo is packed with history. The scenic hilltop town of Mértola has an old centre that's something of a living museum with its archaeological sites dating back to Islamic period. Beja has Roman and Visigoth ruins, including recently excavated sites that will be showcased in a new museum; Moura has its share of artifacts and a small Moorish street pattern. For something a little different, don't miss the abandoned mining buildings of São Domingos.

Beja

POP 24,000

Baixo Alentejo's principal town is easy-going, welcoming and untouristed, with a walled centre and some beguiling sights, all of which are within an easy walk of each other; these often follow old Roman routes. Often dismissed as Évora's 'plainer cousin', Beja has an inferiority complex, but it shouldn't. Its inexpensive guesthouses, quaint plazas and excellent eateries make for a relaxing stop and a very genuine Portuguese experience.

Beja is at the heart of the regional tourist area called Planície Dourada (Golden Plain) – meaning it's surrounded by a sea of wheat fields. On Saturday there's the bonus of a traditional market, spread around the castle.

Sights

Centro de Arqueologia e Artes MUSEUM
(Praça da República) Under construction at time of research, this new museum will house some of the great archaeological finds unearthed in Beja in recent years. Pieces date back to the Iron Age (the 7th century BC) and include relics from Islamic and medieval times, though the highlight will be the Roman collection. In fact, the museum will incorporate features of a Roman temple and a Roman forum discovered here in 2008. The opening date for the museum is slated for late 2017.

Igreja de Nossa Senhora dos Prazeres e Museu Episcopal MUSEUM
(Largo dos Prazeres 4; ⏰10am-12.30pm & 2-5.30pm Wed-Sun) FREE Several museums of religious artworks opened in Beja some years back. So great was the wealth of the Catholic Church that no single space can display all of the paintings and other items. The most attractive is housed in this restored church. While the church is stunning, perhaps only those interested in religious art might appreciate the museum (enter from near the altar).

Castelo CASTLE
FREE Dom Dinis built this castle on Roman foundations in the late 13th century. Eventually, the **Torre de Menagem** may (re)open to visitors. The *turismo* is located here.

Convento de Nossa Senhora da Conceição MUSEUM
(Largo da Conceição; adult/child €2/free; ⏰9.30am-12.30pm & 2-5.30pm Tue-Sun) Founded in 1459, this Franciscan convent was the location for the romance between a nun and soldier that inspired *Letters of a Portuguese Nun*. Indeed a romantic setting, it's a delicate balance between no-nonsense Gothic and Manueline flights of fancy. The interior is lavish – amazing highlights are the rococo chapel with 17th- and 18th-century gilded woodwork, and a chapel inlaid with intricate marble. The **Museu Regional** (adult/child €2/1; ⏰9.30am-12.30pm & 2-5.30pm Tue-Sun) is inside the convent.

Praça da República PLAZA
This renovated attractive town square with a *pelourinho* (stone pillory) is the historic heart of the old city. Dominating the square is the 16th-century **Igreja de Misericórdia**, a hefty church with an immense porch – its crude stonework betrays its origins as a meat market. The **Planície Dourada** building features an elegant Manueline colonnade.

Museu Visigótico MUSEUM
(Largo de Santo Amaro; adult/student €2/1; ⏰9.30am-12.30pm & 2-5pm Tue-Sun) Found just beyond the castle, the unusual Visigothic museum is housed in the former Igreja de Santo Amaro, parts of which date from the early 6th century when it was a Visigothic church – meaning it's one of Portugal's oldest standing buildings. Inside, the original columns display intriguing, beautiful carvings. The admission fee includes entry to the Museu Regional.

Beja

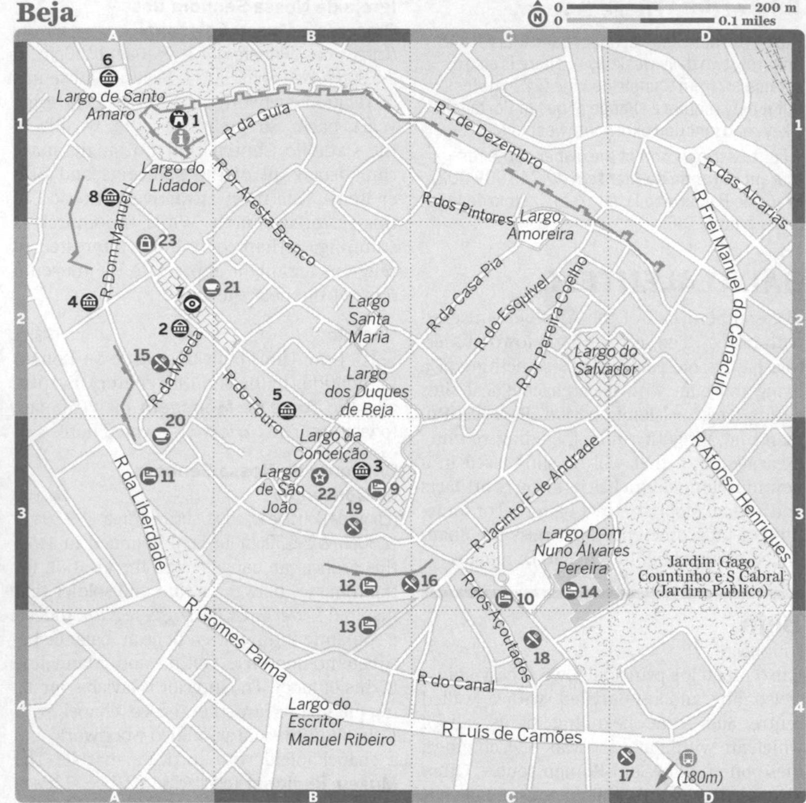

Museu Jorge Vieira MUSEUM

(Rua do Touro 33; 9.30am-12.30pm & 2-6pm Tue-Sun) FREE A charming, small museum, devoted to exhibiting the work of the renowned Portuguese sculptor Jorge Vieira, who donated his works to Beja. His monumental bulbous figures and strange creatures capture the imagination, calling to mind Maurice Sendak's *Where the Wild Things Are*. Look out for Viera's linked ellipses on Praça Diogo Fernandes de Beja.

Santa Casa da Misericórdia HISTORIC BUILDING

(Rua Dom Manuel I 19) FREE For a dip into history, take a stroll through the fascinating corridors of this once grand hospital. It opened back in the early 1500s (only closing to patients in 1969), and you can still see some of the painstakingly carved Manueline-style stone arches and columns. Take a peek inside the old pharmacy, which is preserved as an intriguing relic from decades past.

Sleeping

Hospedaria Rosa do Campo GUESTHOUSE €

(284 323 578; www.rosadocampo.pt; Rua da Liberdade 12; s/d/tr from €30/40/52;) This sparkling guesthouse has polished floors (wood or granite) and spacious rooms, each utterly spotless with a small refrigerator. The owner loves a bit of greenery, keeping plants in the foyer and in most of the rooms. Incredible value.

Hospedaria Dona Maria HOTEL €

(284 327 602; www.hospedariadonamaria.com; Largo Dom Nuno Álvares Pereira 12; s/d/ste from €28/38/45;) In a pretty, half tile-covered building just outside the walls, the Hospedaria Dona Maria has trim, modern, but somewhat small rooms, with comfy mattresses, tiny desks and a light colour scheme – apart from the lavender duvets and pillows that add a dash of colour. The service is

Beja

Sights

1 Castelo ... A1
2 Centro de Arqueologia e Artes ... A2
3 Convento de Nossa Senhora da Conceição ... B3
4 Igreja de Nossa Senhora dos Prazeres e Museu Episcopal ... A2
5 Museu Jorge Vieira ... B2
Museu Regional ... (see 3)
6 Museu Visigótico ... A1
7 Praça da República ... A2
8 Santa Casa da Misericórdia ... A1
Torre de Menagem ... (see 1)

Sleeping

9 Beja Hostel ... B3
10 Hospedaria Dona Maria ... C3
11 Hospedaria Rosa do Campo ... A3
12 Hotel Bejense ... B3
13 Hotel Santa Bárbara ... B4
14 Pousada de São Francisco ... C3

Eating

15 A Pipa ... A2
16 Luiz da Rocha ... B3
17 Sabores do Campo ... D4
18 Smiles ... C4
19 Vovó Joaquina ... B3

Drinking & Nightlife

20 Estoriastantas ... A3
21 JCCC ... A2

Entertainment

22 Pax Julia Teatro Municipal ... B3

Shopping

23 Igreja de Misericórdia ... A2

friendly and there's a decent Italian restaurant on the ground floor.

Beja Hostel GUESTHOUSE €
(☎961 934 618; www.hostelfreimanuel.com; Rua Alexandre Herculano 7; s/d/q €20/30/60; 📶) This new guesthouse in the centre of town is a good choice for budget travellers. Despite the name, there are no dorms, just clean and simple private rooms, with an appealing lounge, pool table and cafe.

Hotel Bejense GUESTHOUSE €
(☎284 311 570; www.hotelbejense.com; Rua Capitão João Francisco de Sousa 57; s/d/tr €35/45/60; ❄📶) This pleasant family-run option has bright rooms, each slightly different in design – some have murals, others elaborately painted bedheads. Front rooms have small balconies and the hallways are trimmed with tiles. You might have flashbacks to your own childhood while walking up the stairs, which are lined with family photos. Breakfast is a small but excellent buffet.

Hotel Santa Bárbara GUESTHOUSE €
(☎284 312 280; www.hotelsantabarbara.pt; Rua de Mértola 56; s/d/tr €35/45/60; ❄📶) This reliable and good-value choice has neat, motel-style rooms with artwork and colourful throws on the bed. Front rooms have balconies over the lane. In winter you can warm up beside the small fireplace in the lounge. It's well located in the pedestrianised town centre.

Pousada de São Francisco LUXURY HOTEL €€€
(☎284 313 580; www.pousadas.pt; Largo Dom Nuno Álvares Pereira; s/d from €130/140; P❄📶🏊) Located in the 13th-century São Francisco Convent, this *pousada* provides gorgeous rooms, formerly cells, and a restaurant (open all day) with a magnificent vaulted ceiling. A Gothic chapel, former chapter house and pleasant lounge areas add to the unique and luxurious atmosphere.

Eating

★**Sabores do Campo** VEGETARIAN €
(Rua Bento de Jesus Caraça 4; per kg €14; ⊙noon-9.30pm Mon-Fri; 🌱) If you're a vegetarian, or simply need a break from pork and codfish, this cheerful cafeteria-style eatery will come as a godsend. Fresh fruit (papaya, mango, strawberries), stuffed mushrooms, oven-baked enchiladas, cabbage-wrapped 'sausage' (from soy), vegetarian lasagna and honey-drizzled filo pastry filled with goat's milk cheese and walnuts are just a few of the recent delicious hits of the ever-changing daily menu. Prices are by weight.

Smiles CAFE €
(Rua da Infantaria 17; desserts around €3; ⊙7.30am-7pm Mon-Fri, 8am-1pm Sat) This little spot whips up delicious desserts – think chocolate tort drizzled with caramel, vegan banana cake and strawberry tart. Indie rock plays softly in the background, there's art on the walls, and the kind-hearted staff make decent coffees.

Luiz da Rocha CAFE €
(☎284 323 179; www.luizdarocha.com; Rua Capitão João Francisco de Sousa 63; snacks €2-3; ⊙8am-11pm Mon-Sat, to 8pm Sun) Founded in 1893,

this is one of Beja's oldest cafes and best-known institutions. It gathers a chatty neighbourhood crowd day and night and is justly famous for its cakes: *trouxas de ovos* (literally 'sweet egg yolks') and *porquinhos de doce* ('sweet little pigs'). There's a more polished sit-down restaurant upstairs that serves up Alentejan staples (mains €7 to €10).

Taberna do Arrufa TAPAS €
(☎967 229 487; www.facebook.com/TabernaDoArrufa; Travessa das Francas 3, Cuba; tapas €4-8; ⏲noon-2am Thu-Mon, 5pm-2am Wed) This eating and drinking den has some of the best atmosphere for miles around – a mix of old-fashioned charm and bohemian style, though it's located 20km north of Beja. Sharing plates are the name of the game, with Serpa cheese, roasted pork cheeks, grilled octopus, steaming pots of clams and sweet potato fries best washed down with a jug of the local wine.

Vovó Joaquina INTERNATIONAL €€
(☎284 322 140; www.facebook.com/VovoJoaquina; Rua do Sembrano 57; mains €7-13; ⏲noon-2.30pm & 7.30-11pm Tue-Sat) Modern meets traditional in this delightfully quirky place where old photos, chandeliers, marble-topped bales and a piano are the backdrops. It serves up a reasonable selection of pasta, French dishes and local favourites. Despite its cavernous size, the space is warm and inviting, and if there's a crowd, the buzz takes precedence over the good but not dazzling Alentejan cuisine.

A Pipa PORTUGUESE €€
(☎284 327 043; Rua da Moeda 8; mains €6-13; ⏲noon-3pm & 7-10.30pm Mon-Sat) This rustic eatery has a wood-beamed ceiling, bright blue wooden chairs, checked tablecloths and serves excellent daily dishes. The meat – such as *febras de porco* (pork steaks) and *lombinhos de porco preto* – is delicious.

LOVE LETTERS FROM BEJA

A series of scandalous, passionate 17th-century love letters came from Beja, allegedly written by one of the nuns of **Convento de Nossa Senhora da Conceição** (p247), Mariana Alcoforado, to French cavalry officer Count Chamilly. The letters immortalised their love affair while the count was stationed here during the time of the Portuguese war with Spain.

The *Letters of a Portuguese Nun* first emerged in a French translation in 1669 and subsequently appeared in English and many other languages. Funnily enough, the originals were never found.

In 1972 three Portuguese writers, Maria Isabel Barreno, Maria Teresa Horta and Maria Velho da Costa, published *The Three Marias: New Portuguese Letters*, a collection of stories, poems and letters that formed a feminist update of the letters – for which they were prosecuted under the Salazar regime.

Drinking & Nightlife

JCCC CAFE
(Praça da República 7; ⏲8am-10pm) Though the food is nothing to write home about, this lively spot makes a fine destination for an afternoon pick-me-up or evening cocktail, especially if you grab one of the outdoor tables on the peaceful Praça da República.

Estoriastantas CAFE
(☎964 443 202; www.facebook.com/estoriastantas; Rua das Portas de Aljustrel 22; ⏲9am-1pm & 3.30-6pm Mon-Fri, 10am-1pm & 4-6pm Sat) Checkered floors, vintage furnishings and quirky artwork draw a creative crowd to this charming cafe and event space.

Entertainment

Pax Julia Teatro Municipal CINEMA, THEATRE
(☎284 315 090; http://paxjuliateatromunicipal.blogspot.com; Largo de São João 1) This cinema and theatre hosts regular concerts, dance performances and film screenings. A program guide is available at the theatre's box office.

Shopping

Igreja de Misericórdia ARTS & CRAFTS
(Praça da República; ⏲10am-1pm Mon-Sat, 2-5.30pm Mon-Fri) An *artesenato* cooperative has a range of goods for sale within the Igreja de Misericórdia – a unique style of store. You'll find hand-painted ceramics, cork products, strawberry preserves and more.

Information

Turismo (☎284 311 913; Rua Capitão João Francisco de Sousa 25; ⏲9.30am-12.30pm & 2-6pm) Located within the castle premises. Provides a city map but not much else.

Getting There & Away

BUS

From the **bus station** (☎284 313 620) buses run to regional towns and villages. Weekends

WORTH A TRIP

ALVITO

Situated only 38km northwest of Beja and 37km southwest of Évora in Baixa Alentejo, beautiful Alvito is well worth visiting, at least for half a day. Be aware, though, such is its appeal, it's the kind of place you get to and wish you'd packed your toothbrush. The town was the home of the Portuguese barons; the first baron, Dom João Fernandes da Silveira, decided to make Alvito an artistic landmark.

You can visit parts of a 15th-century former castle, now a luxury **pousada** (284 480 700; www.pousadas.pt; s/d from €120/130;), and several important churches. The 16th-century **Ermida de Sao Sebastião** has some extraordinary revived frescos.

Throughout the village, you can see beautiful Manueline features – pick up a map from the **turismo** (284 480 808; www.cm-alvito.pt; Rua dos Lobos 13; 9am-12.30pm & 2-5.30pm Mon-Fri, 10am-12.30pm & 2-5.30pm Sat) and play 'spot the Manueline doorway' (these are stunning).

Public transport is very limited in these parts. It's most convenient to arrive with your own wheels.

If you decide to stay the night in Alvito, our pick is the delightful **Horta do Padre** (961 865 052, 284 485 400; fernandadamaso@hotmail.com; Quinta da Esperança, Apartado 16; s/d €30/40;), a renovated blue-and-white traditional Alentejan farmhouse 1km east of Alvito's centre (direction down Estrada de São Roman), with comfortable rooms and excellent breakfasts. The multilingual owners Fernanda and Lino are passionate about preserving Portuguese traditional practices and are fountains of knowledge about the region. Call in advance.

see fewer services. The bus station is in the southern part of town, about 600m from the historic centre.

Buses run from Beja to local destinations and those further afield:

Albufeira (€14, two hours, three daily)
Évora (€8, 1¼ hours, hourly)
Faro (€14.20, three hours, three daily)
Lisbon (€13.30, three hours, eight daily)
Mértola (€11, one hour, one daily)
Serpa (€6, 40 minutes, three daily) From Serpa, some continue to Moura (€8, 65 minutes).

CAR

Drivers are advised to park their cars in the clearly marked car parks outside the walled centre.

TRAIN

Trains head to Lisbon (€14 to €18, three hours, three daily). You change to a connecting train at Casa Branca.

Mértola

POP 2000

Spectacularly set on a rocky spur, high above the peaceful Rio Guadiana, the cobbled streets of medieval Mértola are a delightful place to roam. A small but imposing castle stands high, overlooking the jumble of dazzlingly white houses and a picturesque church that was once a mosque. A long bout of economic stagnation in this remote town has left many traces of Islamic occupation intact, so much so that Mértola is considered a *vila museu* (open-air museum). To let Mértola's magic do its thing, you need more than a quick visit here. Every two years in May Mértola comes to life during the town's Islamic Festival.

History

Mértola follows the usual pattern of settlement in this area: Phoenician traders, who sailed up the Guadiana, then Carthaginians, then Romans. Its strategic position, as the northernmost port on the Guadiana, and the final destination for many Mediterranean routes, led the Romans to develop Mértola (naming it Myrtilis) as a major agricultural and mineral-exporting centre. Cereals and olive oil arrived from Beja, copper and other metals from Aljustrel and São Domingos. It was a rich merchant town.

Later the Moors, who called it Martulah and made it a regional capital, further fortified Mértola and built a mosque. Dom Sancho II and the Knights of the Order of Santiago captured the site in 1238. But then, as commercial routes shifted to the Tejo, Mértola declined. When the last steamboat service to Vila Real de Santo António ended and the copper mines of São Domingos (the area's main employer) closed in 1965, its port days were over.

Sights

Alcáçova ARCHAEOLOGICAL SITE

(9.15am-12.30pm & 2-5.15pm Tue-Sun) FREE This recently opened site contains the ruins of what was once a thriving Islamic neighbourhood. Some 20 dwellings were here, each with a classic Mediterranean layout – a main entry patio, kitchen, storage area, sleeping quarters and latrine. You can wander around the site on raised platforms, with signage (in English and Portuguese) pointing out key details.

Also on the site is an even older find – the ruins of a portico with mosaic tiles that was once part of a 5th-century Episcopal Palace. Below lies an impressive 32m-long underground gallery dating from the same period. Shortly after the reconquest by the Knights of Santiago in the 13th century, the neighbourhood was destroyed and turned into a cemetery.

Casa Islâmica HISTORIC SITE

(9.15am-12.30pm & 2-5.15pm Tue-Sun) FREE Next to the Alcáçova, this interpretation centre is an accurately sized replica of an Islamic residence dating from the 12th century. Key features include an open central patio with a rainwater collection tank in the center, small sleeping alcoves, a storage area, kitchen with fireplace and a toilet that was linked to the sewers that emptied outside the town walls.

Castelo CASTLE

(9am-6pm Tue-Sun) FREE Above the parish church looms Mértola's fortified castle, most of which dates from the 13th century. It was built upon Moorish foundations next to an Islamic residence, the *alcáçova* (citadel), which itself overlaid the Roman forum. For centuries the castle was considered western Iberia's most impregnable fortress. From the walls, there are fabulous views – the *alcáçova* is on one side, and the old town and the river on the other.

The castle's prominent tower, the **Torre de Menagem** (adult/student/child €2/1/free; 9.15am-12.30pm & 2-5.15pm Tue-Sun), has exhibitions related to the history of Mértola, with several worthwhile (if dramatically scored) videos in both English and Portuguese on Mértola's strategic location and the reconquest by the Knights of Santiago in 1238.

Igreja Matriz CHURCH

(Rua da Igreja; 9.15am-12.30pm & 2-5.15pm Tue-Sun) Mértola's striking parish church – square, flat-faced and topped with whimsical little conical decorations – is known because in a former incarnation it was a mosque, one of the few in the country to have survived the Reconquista. It was reconsecrated as a church in the 13th century. Look out for an unwhitewashed cavity in the wall, behind the altar; in former times this served as the mosque's *mihrab* (prayer niche).

Note also the goats, lions and other figures carved around the peculiar Gothic portal and the typically Moorish horseshoe arch in the north door.

Attached to the church is a small underground **museum** (head out the rear door of the church and turn right) that has displays of items dating back to the Moorish period found during excavations – including lovely Islamic tiles, 6th-century marble pediments and carved, twisted columns.

Casa Romana RUINS

(Roman House; Largo Luís de Camões; 9am-1pm & 2-6pm Mon-Fri, 9.45am-1pm & 2-5.45pm Sat & Sun) FREE The enchanting Casa Romana is located in the cellar of the *câmara municipal* (town hall). The clever display allows visitors to walk 'through' the foundations of the Roman house upon which the building rests, and brings it to life with its small collection of pots, sculpture and other artefacts.

Museu Paleocristão RUINS, MUSEUM

(Palaeo-Christian Museum; Rossio do Carmo; 9am-12.30pm & 2-5.30pm Tue-Sun) FREE This museum, north of the old town, features a partly reconstructed line of 6th-century Roman columns and poignant funerary stones, some of which are beautifully carved with birds, hearts and wreaths. It was the site of a huge Palaeo-Christian basilica, and the adjacent cemetery was used over the centuries by both Roman-era Christians and medieval Moors.

MÉRTOLA'S MUSEUMS

Mértola's wonderful group of museums open only from Tuesday to Sunday (generally from 9.15am to 12.30pm and from 2pm to 5.15pm) and form an excellent tour of the town. Most museums are free, though there is talk of reinstating fees (of €2 per museum), and offering a discounted pass (around €5) to visit the whole lot.

Museu Islâmico MUSEUM
(Largo de Misericordia; adult/student €2/1; ⏲9am-12.30pm & 2-5.30pm Tue-Sun) At the southern end of the old town, the Islamic Museum is a small but dramatic display of inscribed funerary stones, jewellery, pots and jugs from the 11th to 13th centuries.

Convento de São Francisco GARDENS
(☎286 612 119; www.conventomertola.com; €5; ⏲10am-6pm Sun) This 400-year-old former convent, across the Ribeira de Oeiras, 500m southwest of Largo Vasco da Gama, has been owned since 1980 by Dutch artist Geraldine Zwanikken and her family. In a true labour of love, they have gradually transformed the ruins into an extraordinary place, most simply described as an organic nature reserve full of herbs, rare plants and flowers, watered by a restored Islamic irrigation system. Locals have their vegetable gardens here.

It's also an art gallery. Highlights include Geraldine's modern artworks and, gracing the former chapel (if they are not being shown in temporary exhibitions elsewhere), the kinetic installations of renowned artist Christiaan Zwanikken. The nearby riverside is devoted to specially constructed nests for storks and lesser kestrels.

Activities

Beira Rio Náutica KAYAKING, BICYCLE HIRE
(☎913 402 033, 286 611 190; www.beirario.pt; Rua Dr Afonso Costa 108; kayak rental 1hr/day from €5/15, bike 1hr/day from €5/10) You can rent kayaks for trips down the lazy river at Beira Rio Náutica. It also offers boat tours (minimum four; €10 per person) and you can hire bicycles here.

Parque Natural do Vale do Guadiana WALKING TRAILS
Created in 1995, this zone of hills, plains and deep valleys around Serpa and Mértola shelters the Rio Guadiana, one of Portugal's largest and most important rivers. Among its rich variety of flora and fauna are several rare or endangered species, including the black stork (sightings of the shy creatures are rare), lesser kestrel (most likely around Castro Verde and at Convento do São Francisco), Bonelli's eagle, royal owl, grey kite, horned viper and Iberian toad. The park also has many prehistoric remains.

Ask at the **park headquarters** (☎286 610 090; Rua Don Sancho II; ⏲9am-noon & 2-5pm Mon-Fri), in smart premises by the *câmara municipal* (town hall), for details of walking trails and where to spot wildlife – they can advise you and provide you with a basic map.

DON'T MISS

ENTRADAS

The tiny village of Entradas is a photo-stop must. Entradas' main street features tiny, whitewashed homes and is a wonderful example of a working rural village. The name is said to have come from the fact that it was the *entrada* (gateway) to the Campos de Ourique, sought-after winter pastures for herds and herders.

In the village centre, the beautifully laid out **Museu da Ruralidade** (☎286 915 329; Rua da Santa Madalena; ⏲9.30am-12.30pm & 2-6pm Wed-Sun) showcases elements of local cultural and agricultural practices.

Festivals & Events

Islamic Festival RELIGIOUS
(⏲May) Mértola comes to life every two years in May (dates change but it's uneven numbered years) during the town's Islamic Festival, when it is decorated to resemble a souk. Music, handicrafts and festivities continue for several days.

Sleeping

Casa Rosmaninho GUESTHOUSE €
(☎966 948 616; www.casarosmaninho.com; Rua 25 de Abril 23; r €25-35; 📶) Inside a yellow, two-storey house in the town centre (just outside the old walls), you'll find four cheerfully decorated rooms (purple being the colour accent of choice) that are a great value for the money. The small roof terrace has fine views of the castle. Ana, the host, does a great job of making guests feel at home.

Casa do Funil GUESTHOUSE €
(☎934 187 455; www.casadofunil.com; Rua Prof Batista da Graça 19; s €35-45, d €40-50) Just inside the old walls, this appealing place has four lovely rooms with wood floors, nice furniture and shuttered windows with views over the river. Rui and Paola make their guests feel at home, and they can advise on outdoor activities (birdwatching, canoeing, day trips) in the area.

WORTH A TRIP

SÃO DOMINGOS

The ghost town of São Domingos, 15km east of Mértola, consists of desolate rows of small mining cottages. Once the mine closed in the 1960s, many miners emigrated or moved to Setúbal. But the nearby village is set amid beautiful countryside and next to a huge lake, where you can swim or rent a paddleboat or canoe.

The São Domingos mine itself is over 150 years old – though mining has been taking place here since Roman times – and is a deserted, eerie place to explore, with crumbling old offices and machinery. The rocks surrounding it are clouded with different colours, and the chief mine shaft is filled with deep, unnatural dark-blue water, shot through with substances that don't bear thinking about (read: contaminated). Locals have no fondness for the firm that established the mines, which kept its workers in line with a private police force.

On the main road leading into town, the **Cine Teatro da Mina de São Domingos** (Rua Catarina Eufémia; €1; 2-5.30pm Tue-Sun) provides a suitable introduction to life during the mining days. Tucked away on one of the narrow streets of the village, **Casa do Mineiro** (Rua Santa Isabel 31-33; 9am-12.30pm & 2-5.30pm Mon-Fri, plus Sat & Sun Jun & Aug) FREE recreates a typical miner's cottage.

São Domingos is best visited with your own transport.

Casa da Tia Amalia HOSTEL €

(918 918 777, 286 612 336; www.casadatiaamalia.com; Estrada dos Celeiros 16, Além Rio; dm/d with shared bathroom €17/43;) Across the river from Mértola in Além Rio, this delightful guesthouse offers sweeping views of the village and the castle rising above it. The rooms have homey touches, and the living room (with fireplace) is a fine spot to relax. There's also a four-bed dorm (and a shared kitchen), making it a good option for budget travellers.

Hotel Museu HOTEL €

(286 612 313; www.hotelmuseu.com; Rua Dr Afonso Costa 112; s €45, d €55-60;) On the road leading down to the river, this sleek modern hotel has attractive, comfortably furnished rooms with black-and-white print on the wall and big windows – the best of which offer sweeping views over the riverside. Roman ruins were found in the foundations and anyone can visit (thus the hotel name).

Convento de São Francisco GUESTHOUSE €€

(286 612 119; www.conventomertola.com; apt €70) For those who are happy with rustic and a more laissez-faire approach, this former convent overlooking Mértola and the Rio Guadiana is a lovely spot for hardier, artistic and/or tranquil souls. The fully equipped apartments are converted from former stables, ateliers and the like. There's a cottage (solar powered) on the grounds for those looking for complete seclusion. Single-night stays are not offered. An artist-in-residence program is also available.

Monte do Alhinho RURAL INN €€

(286 655 414; www.omontedoalhinho.com; Estrada Nacional 265; s/d €50/60;) Try the appealing Monte do Alhinho, 8km from Mértola on the road to São Domingos. This tastefully converted farmhouse-cum-hacienda has massive rooms, fluffy white towels and a superb kitchen, where breakfast – an onslaught of Alentejan delights – is served. Discounts apply for two or more nights.

Eating

Café-Restaurante Alentejo PORTUGUESE €

(286 655 133; Rua Grande 3, Moreanes; mains €8-12; 11.30am-3pm & 7-9.30pm Tue-Sun) This attractive place in Moreanes, 10km from Mértola on the way to São Domingos, is almost a museum thanks to its antique exhibits (including the local clients themselves!). It serves great-value, hearty helpings of true Alentejan cuisine, with standout dishes like *javali* (boar), *veado* (venison) and *migas com entrecosto* (a bread dish with ribs).

Tamuje PORTUGUESE €

(286 611 115; Rua Dr Serrão Martins 34; mains €7-11; noon-3pm & 7-11pm Mon-Sat) This welcoming two-room restaurant serves up excellent traditional plates, all made with care. Grilled pork ribs, fried squid with garlic, and fava beans with pork, along with game meat (wild boar, rabbit venison) are among the standouts. Don't overlook the rich desserts.

Casa Amarela TAPAS €€
(☎918 918 777; www.facebook.com/EspacoCasaAmarelaMertola; Estrada dos Celeiros 25, Além Rio; mains €10-15; ⏲8-11.45pm Fri & Sat, noon-3.30pm Sat & Sun) Although it's only open on weekends, this place makes a great spot for inventive Portuguese fare. Outdoor tables on the verandah have magnificent views of Mértola – all of it, since this place is located across the river in Além Rio. There's typically live music every other Saturday night.

O Brasileiro PORTUGUESE €€
(www.obrasileiro.pt; Cerro de São Luís; mains €8-14; ⏲noon-2.30pm & 7-10pm) Set on a hill above Mértola, this pleasant spot serves great quality traditional cuisine. Known for its game dishes, including *javali* (wild pig) and *migas* (meat and bread stew) dishes.

Restaurante Alengarve PORTUGUESE €€
(☎286 612 210; Avenida Aureliano Mira Fernandes; mains €7-14; ⏲noon-3pm & 7-10pm Thu-Tue; 📶) Run by the same family for over 40 years, this place is well loved by locals and extremely consistent for its home-style Alentejan dishes. There's outdoor seating on the front patio.

Drinking & Nightlife

Lancelote BAR
(Rua Nossa Senhora da Conceição 3; ⏲10.30am-6.30pm Wed-Sun, 9pm-4am Fri & Sat) This vaguely medieval-feeling bar has friendly barkeeps and eclectic decor (colourful paintings and a wall of skeleton keys), with a shaded wooden terrace attached.

Shopping

Mercado Municipal MARKET
(Municipal Market; Praça Vasco da Gama; ⏲7am-7pm Mon-Fri, 6am-7pm Sat, 8am-7pm Sun) Self-caterers should head to the *mercado municipal,* which sells fresh fruit and vegetables, olives and cheeses.

Oficina de Tecelagem ARTS & CRAFTS
(Rua da Igreja 35; ⏲9.30am-5pm) A small wool-weaving workshop next to the *turismo,* this place hangs on by a thread through tourist sales of beautiful handmade products, including rugs and ponchos. Weaving is done on-site.

Information

Millennium BCP Bank (Rua Dr Afonso Costa) Has an ATM.

Turismo (☎286 610 109; Rua da Igreja 31; ⏲9am-12.30pm & 2-5.30pm mid-Sep–Jun, 9.30am-12.30pm & 2-6pm Jul–mid-Sep) Just inside the walled town, the *turismo* has a town map, list of *quartos* (private rooms) and free internet access. Also stocks brochures outlining nine different *percursos pedestres* (walking trails) in the area, varying from one- to five-hour walks.

Getting There & Away

Rede Expressos (☎286 611 127; www.rede-expressos.pt) has services to Lisbon (€17, four hours, one daily), Beja (€11, one hour, one daily) and Vila Real de Santo António/Monte Gordo (€11, 1½ hours, one daily). **Rodoviária do Alentejo** (www.rodalentejo.pt) offers a slower local Vila Real (€6, two hours) service via Alcoutim (50 minutes), which runs on Monday and Friday. It also has three weekday services to/from Beja (€6, 75 minutes).

Castro Verde

POP 4200

The thriving village of Castro Verde has a big history – once an ancient hill fort, it soon grew into a settlement. The village is located near the site where the Battle of Ourique was fought (1139), when Afonso Henriques defeated the Moors and declared himself the first King of Portugal. In the 18th century Dom João V ordered the construction of the stunning Basílica Real, whose tiles replicate the battle scenes. These days, its inhabitants are fiercely proud of the local traditions; their annual fair – **Feira de Castro** – is held on the third weekend of October. It's worth the detour here, especially if en route from Beja to Mértola or the Algarve.

Sights

Museu da Lucerna MUSEUM
(Largo Vitor Prazeres; ⏲10am-12.30pm & 2-5.30pm Tue-Sun) FREE The building – a former factory – that houses this museum is as interesting as the beautiful collection of ancient Roman oil lamps from the 1st century that were found in the region. It also has exhibitions.

Basílica Real CHURCH
(Royal Basilica; ☎286 328 550; Praça do Município; church/museum free/€1; ⏲10am-1pm & 2-5.30pm Wed-Sun) The 18th-century Royal Basilica features extraordinary gilded woodcarvings and a set of tiled panels depicting the Battle of Ourique. A small museum shows religious art. The highlight is the unique 13th-century silver head of Saint Fabian.

Activities

LPN Interpretative & Environmental Centre BIRDWATCHING
(League for the Protection of Nature; ☎286 328 309; www.lpn.pt; Herdade de Vale Gonçalinho; ⏰9am-1pm & 2-6pm Tue-Sat) This environmental organisation is responsible for overseeing the protected area (85,000 hectares) known as the steppe – the flat, grassy land that distinguishes this area – and for implementing protection measures for the incredible steppe birds, including the great bustard and lesser kestrels. Staff at the information office are particularly welcoming; you can view displays and pick up information.

This is the place for birdwatchers and the departure point for walks in the steppe; ask at the office. It's located 8km northeast of Castro Verde (on E802, the main road to Beja).

Information

Turismo (☎286 328 149; www.cm-castroverde.pt; Rua Dom Afonso I; ⏰9am-12.30pm & 2-5.30pm Tue-Fri, 10am-1pm & 3-6pm Sat & Sun) Has maps, information and a selection of local products for sale.

Getting There & Away

Castro Verde is connected by bus to Beja (€6, one hour, three daily), Évora (€13.30, 2¼ hours, two daily) and Lisbon (€16, 4¼ hours, two daily).

Serpa

POP 7100

Planted among the rolling hills of vineyards and dusty fields, Serpa is a sleepy, atmospheric town of bleached-white walls and narrow cobblestone streets. At its medieval heart is a small, pretty plaza carefully guarded by the elderly folk who have long called Serpa home. Locals are renowned for their love of food, and several factory outlets produce the town's culinary jewel, *queijo Serpa*, a cheese made from curdled sheep's milk.

It's worth a quick visit, or even an overnight stay if you want to experience life in the Portuguese slow lane.

Sights

Walls still stand around most of the inner town. Along the west side (follow Rua dos Arcos) run the impressive remains of an 11th-century **aqueduto**. At the southern end is a huge 17th-century wheel pump (aka *noria*), once used for pumping water along the aqueduct to the nearby **Palácio dos Condes de Ficalho**.

Castelo CASTLE
(Largo dos Santos Próculo e Hilarião; ⏰9am-5pm Tue-Sun) FREE Dating from the 14th century, this imposing castle affords long views from the battlements: flat plains, the aqueduct, town walls, rooftops and orange trees, and the slow life of Serpa residents. Inside the walls, the **Museu Municipal de Arqueologia de Castelo** houses a small collection of archaeological exhibitions, with information on Neolithic sites near Serpa.

Museu Etnográfico MUSEUM
(Ethnographic Museum; Largo do Corro; ⏰9am-12.30pm & 2-5.30pm Tue-Sun) FREE No traditional rural trade is left unturned in the exquisite exploration of Alentejan life found at Serpa's Museu Etnográfico. Occupying the former town market (in use from 1887 to 1986), the museum beautifully presents restored items donated by locals. Polished tools used by former wheelwrights, saddle makers, cheese makers, barrel makers and ironmongers – among others – are on display.

Museu do Relógio MUSEUM
(Watch Museum; ☎284 543 194; www.museudorelogio.com; Rua do Assento 31; adult/under 10yr €2/free; ⏰2-6pm Tue-Fri, 10am-12.30pm & 2-6pm Sat & Sun) The Watch Museum houses an amazing collection of watches and clocks (shared with its sister museum in Évora), dating from a 1630 Edward East clock to the museum's own present-day wristwatch model. Napoleonic gilded timepieces and Swiss cuckoo clocks are among the 2000 pieces ticking away in the cool surroundings of the former Convento do Mosteirinho.

Festivals & Events

Festas de Senhora de Guadalupe RELIGIOUS
Celebrations of Serpa's patron saint take place over Easter from Good Friday to the following Tuesday – there is a pilgrimage to bring the saint's image down to the parish church, and on the last day a procession takes it back to the chapel. On Easter Tuesday, roast lamb is the traditional meal.

Noites na Nora THEATRE
(⏰Jul) This festival features nightly local theatre and music shows on a terrace tucked behind the aqueduct. It usually runs for two weeks in July, but check with the tourist office as dates can change.

Serpa

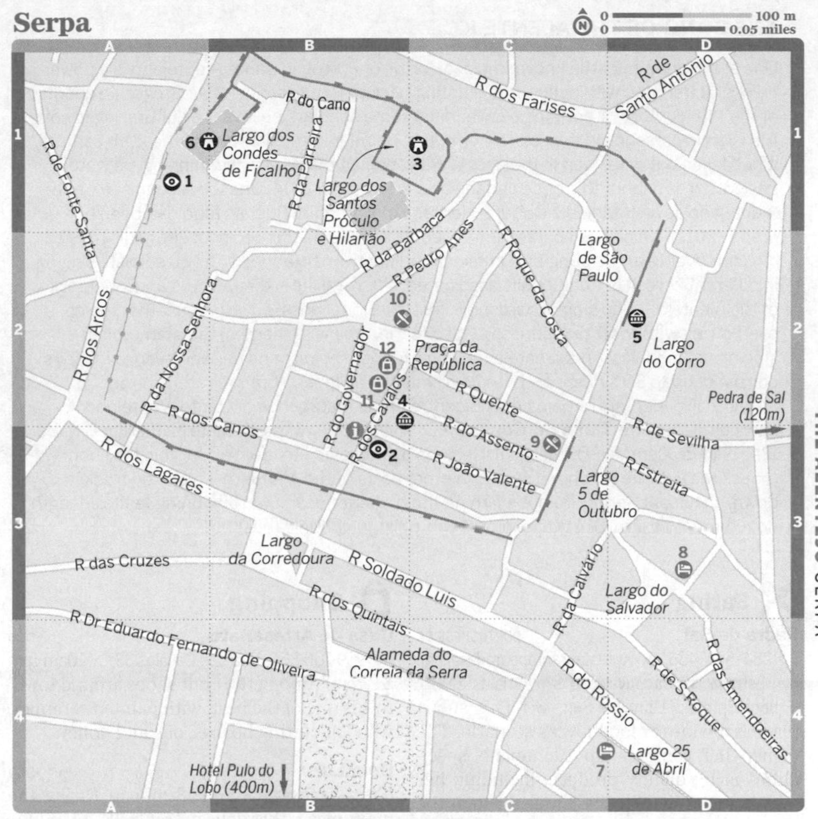

Serpa

Sights

1 Aqueduto A1
2 Casa do Cante B3
3 Castelo C1
4 Museu do Relógio B2
5 Museu Etnográfico D2
6 Palácio dos Condes de Ficalho A1

Sleeping

7 Casa Virgínia C4
8 Residencial Beatriz D3

Eating

9 Molhó Bico C3
10 Restaurante O Alentejano B2

Shopping

11 Casa de Artesenato B2
12 Dom Luis B2

Sleeping

Residencial Beatriz GUESTHOUSE €
(☎284 544 423; www.residencialbeatriz.com; Largo do Salvador 10; s/d €35/45, apt €50-75; P ❄ wi-fi) Overlooking the pretty square, this small guesthouse provides simple but comfortable rooms of varying sizes. If there's more than two of you, the apartments provide good-value stays.

Hotel Pulo do Lobo HOTEL €
(☎284 544 664; www.residencialpulodolobo.com; Estrada de São Brás 9A; s/d €30/45; wi-fi) Handy to the bus station, this sparkling place and its house-proud owners provide plain but modern rooms. Excellent value if you don't mind being slightly out of the centre.

Casa Virgínia GUESTHOUSE €
(☎284 549 145; Largo 25 de Abril; s/d €20/30; wi-fi) This guesthouse has basic but spotless rooms as well as en suite bathrooms.

THE SONG OF THE ALENTEJO

One of the great but little known musical forms of Portugal, Cante Alentejano is a powerful choral tradition with deep roots – dating back to Renaissance-style Gregorian chants of the 15th century or perhaps even earlier (some scholars believe it a cultural legacy of the Islamic presence in the country). Though popular in the first half of the 20th century, it had fallen out of fashion in the post WWII years. All that is slowly changing, as word has gotten out about this once endangered art form. In 2014, Unesco recognised Cante Alentejano as an Intangible Cultural Heritage of Humanity (just as fado had been honored in 2011), which has sparked interest both far and near in rediscovering this music.

Cante Alentejano is sung by a choir without instrumentation, with two soloists singing in different keys. It is traditionally associated with rural life – the farmers and labourers of the Alentejo – who sing of hardships, lost love, loneliness, poverty and other topics overflowing with *tristeza* (sadness). Despite the sorrowful themes, the many voices singing polyphonic works create a moving experience, full of power and even joy. Choirs consist of up to 30 singers and can be all male or all female but are rarely mixed.

The Baixo Alentejo remains the epicentre of the resurgence of Cante Alentejano. A new cultural centre, **Casa do Cante** (284 540 108; www.casadocante.pt; Rua dos Cavalos 12; 9am-5.30pm Mon-Fri) FREE, in Serpa is a good place to learn about this tradition (check the website for choral events in other parts of the Alentejo). If you can track it down, check out Sérgio Tréfaut's film *Alentejo, Alentejo*, an award-winning feature-length documentary from 2014 that explores this rich, polyphonic music.

Eating

Pedra de Sal PORTUGUESE €€
(284 543 436; www.restaurantepedradesal.pai.pt; Estrada da Circunvalaçao s/n; mains €9-15; noon-3pm & 7-11pm Tue-Sun;) This smart place is a win-win food-lover's scenario. The owner-chef conjures up Alentejano specialities using quality produce, including her own home-grown greens. Enter through the plant-rimmed courtyard into a soaring space that evokes farmhouse chic, complete with artfully hung farm implements on the thick stone walls. Courtyard dining in the summer.

It's located about a seven-minute walk east of the walls (take Rua da Sevilha).

Restaurante O Alentejano PORTUGUESE €€
(284 544 335; Praça da República; mains €9-13; noon-3pm & 7-10.30pm Tue-Sun) This handsome place, above a cafe of the same name, in a former mansion, serves local cuisine. Go for the daily specials – anything from braised hare in red wine to pigs' trotters.

Molhó Bico PORTUGUESE €€
(284 549 264; www.molhobicoserpa.com; Rua Quente 1; mains €8-15; noon-3pm & 7-10pm Thu-Tue) With its wagon-wheel lights, huge wine urns and friendly ambience, this enticing place pulls a crowd. Eating here is a traditional gastronomic experience – the kitchen odours will hit you as soon as you enter its arched, rustic space. Hearty half serves are available.

Shopping

Casa de Artesenato FOOD
(969 706 366; Rua dos Cavalos 33; 10am-1pm & 2-7pm) Among the craft shops around town, this is one of the best, with painted ceramics, wooden cutting boards, oils and honey.

Dom Luis FOOD
(Praça da República 15; 8am-7pm) Facing the main plaza, this delicatessen sells *queijadas* (pastry shells with marzipan-like filling), olive oils, cheeses and other edible items.

Information

Caixa Geral de Depósitos (Praça da República) Located on the main square in town. Has an ATM.

Turismo (284 544 727; www.cm-serpa.pt; Rua dos Cavalos 19; 10am-1pm & 2-6pm) Provides a map of the old town with good listings and sells CDs of local folk music.

Getting There & Away

BUS

The **bus station** (284 544 740) is several kilometres south of town; head south along Avenida da Paz to get here. Buses run to/from Lisbon (€15.20, four hours, three to five daily) via Beja (€4). There are no direct buses to Évora (head to Beja first).

CAR

If arriving by car it's best to park outside the wall, or risk tight gateways into the old town and breathtakingly narrow streets.

Moura

POP 8200

This pleasant working-class city, a flattish fortified town, has an ageing castle, graceful buildings and a well-preserved Moorish quarter. Well placed near water sources and rich in ore, Moura has been a farming and mining centre and a fashionable spa in previous incarnations. More recent developments? The world's largest solar-power generation plant is located nearby and it's the nearest large town to the Barragem do Alqueva, 15km to the north.

The Moors' 500-year occupation came to an end in 1232 after a Christian invasion. Despite the reconquest, Moorish presence in the city remained strong – they only abandoned their quarter in 1496 (after Dom Manuel's convert-or-leave edict).

The town's name comes from a legend related to the 13th-century takeover. Moorish resident Moura Salúquiyya opened the town gates to Christians disguised as Muslims. They sacked the town, and poor Moura flung herself from a tower.

Sights

Castelo CASTLE

(9am-12.30pm & 2.30-5.30pm) FREE The castle offers fabulous views across the countryside. One of the towers is the last remnant of a Moorish fortress. Rebuilt by Dom Dinis in the 13th century and again by Dom Manuel I in 1510, the castle itself was largely destroyed by the Spanish in the 18th century. There's a ruined convent inside the walls.

You can visit the *torre de menagem* (keep) on guided visits only (offered daily at 10am, noon, 3pm and 5pm). It contains a small collection of weaponry, some dating back to the 16th century. You can also climb up the winding steps for a fine view over the castle and the arid landscape just beyond town.

Museu Municipal MUSEUM

(285 253 978; Rua da Romeira 19; 9.30am-12.30pm & 2-5.30pm Tue-Sun) FREE In an appealing residential quarter off a lane about 200m east of the *praça* (head up Rua do Espírito Santo, behind the tourist office), this tiny museum contains local prehistoric and Roman remains, such as 1st- and 2nd-century needles, as well as Moorish funerary tablets.

Jardim Dr Santiago & Spa GARDENS

(thermal spa 9am-noon) The lovely, shady Jardim Dr Santiago, at the eastern end of Praça Sacadura Cabral, is a delightful place. There are good views, a bandstand, shady, flowering trees and it's a favourite spot for elderly men to sit and chat.

At the **thermal spa**, at the entrance to the garden, you can join the locals for a soak in a basic bath (open May to October). Bicarbonated calcium waters, said to be good for rheumatism, burble from the richly marbled **Fonte das Três Bicas** (Fountain with Three Spouts) by the entrance to the *jardim*.

Lagar de Varas do Fojo MUSEUM

(Museu do Azeite; Rua João de Deus 20; 9.30am-12.30pm & 2-5.30pm Tue-Sat) FREE With a system of production that would have been similar to that of Roman times, an oil press here re-creates the oil-pressing factory that functioned on this spot between 1841 and 1941, with giant wooden and stone-wheel presses, vats and utensils.

Jardim das Oliveiras GARDENS

(9am-12.30pm Tue-Sat) FREE Opposite the Lagar de Varas do Fojo is the Jardim das Oliveiras, with various varieties of olive trees and herbs, and reflective space. It's dedicated to Miguel Hernández, a Spanish poet and revolutionary who, upon fleeing Spain, entered the Moura district, only to be returned by Salazar to Franco's troops. He later died in prison.

Mouraria AREA

(Poço Árabe) The old Moorish quarter lies at the western end of Praça Sacadura Cabral. It's a well-preserved tight cluster of narrow, cobbled lanes and white terraced cottages with chunky or turreted chimneys.

Núcleo Árabe MUSEUM

(Travessa da Mouraria 11; 9.30am-12.30pm & 2.30-5.30pm Tue-Sun) FREE Just off Largo da Mouraria, the Núcleo Árabe has a pocket collection of Moorish ceramics and other remains, such as carved stone inscriptions and a 14th-century Arabic well. Visits here must be arranged through the Museu Municipal.

Sleeping

Hotel de Moura HOTEL €

(285 251 090; www.hoteldemoura.com; Praça Gago Coutinho 1; s/d €39/49) Overlooking a leafy plaza, the Hotel de Moura has comfortable if rather sparsely furnished rooms; be sure to get a room in the front with a view onto the greenery. The lounge with a small bar in this handsome tile-covered building (a former convent) is quite inviting: arched brick ceilings, big windows and rustic Alentejan decorations on the walls.

Hotel Santa Comba HOTEL €
(☎285 251 255; www.hotelsantacomba.com; Praça Sacadura Cabral 34; s/d/tr €25/38/45; ❄) In a great location overlooking the main square, the Hotel Santa Comba has pleasant rooms with painted wrought-iron beds, heavy woven drapes and bedspreads, and some rather curious artwork. The nicest rooms have French doors with decorative balconies that open onto the square. The pretty breakfast room/lounge has striking ornate ceilings.

Eating

Taberna o Liberato PORTUGUESE €
(☎285 254 171; 2A Rua da Mouraria 3; ⏲11am-3.30pm & 6.30pm-midnight Mon-Sat) Just off the main square, Praça Sacadura Cabral, this cosy tavern is a lively spot for a bite and a drink. There's not much of a menu, but the owner whips up delicious tapas plates – including a very rich *presunto* (cured ham) – served with his first-rate wine selection.

O Trilho PORTUGUESE €€
(☎285 254 261; www.otrilho.com; Rua 5 de Outubro 5; mains €7-14; ⏲noon-3pm & 7-10pm Tue-Sun; 👪) Three streets east of Rua Serpa Pinto, O Trilho is a local favourite, with excellent regional mains and well-prepared daily specials (like monkfish rice and roast black pork dishes), set in pleasant, starched-tablecloth surroundings. Don't neglect the homemade desserts – the meringue-like *molotof* is excellent.

Information

Turismo (☎285 251 375; www.cm-moura.pt; ⏲9am-12.30pm & 2-5.30pm) The tourist office is located on the castle grounds. It provides information and internet access.

Getting There & Away

Buses run to/from Beja (around €5, one hour, six daily weekdays) via Serpa (€3.50, 40 minutes). Rede Expressos runs to Lisbon (€16.20, four hours, daily) via Évora (€11, 1½ hours); these leave from Praça Sacadura Cabral.

COASTAL ALENTEJO

Coastal Alentejo (Alentejo Litoral in Portuguese) has undeniable appeal. Beautiful beaches, whitewashed villages and seafood feasts are among the chief draws. This is also a great place for outdoor lovers, with first-rate surfing, kayaking and mountain biking, as well as scenic walks along the coast – including two well-marked walking treks totalling 400km that go all the way down to Cabo de São Vicente in the Algarve.

Vila Nova de Milfontes

POP 3200

One of the loveliest towns along this stretch of the coast, Vila Nova de Milfontes has an attractive, whitewashed centre, sparkling beaches nearby and a laid-back population who couldn't imagine living anywhere else. Milfontes remains much more low key than most resort towns, except in August when it's packed to the hilt with surfers and sun-seekers (up to 50,000 people in town). It's located in the middle of the beautiful Parque Natural do Sudoeste Alentejano e Costa Vicentina and is still a port (Hannibal is said to have sheltered here) alongside a lovely, sand-edged limb of estuary.

Beaches

Praia do Farol BEACH
Praia do Farol, the lighthouse beach just by the town, is sheltered but gets busy. Beaches on the other side of the estuary are less crowded. Be careful of the strong river currents running through the estuary.

Praia do Malhão BEACH
If you have your own transport, head 7km north of town to the fantastic Praia do Malhão, backed by rocky dunes and covered in fragrant scrub. The sea can be quite wild here, but the rugged coast is strikingly empty of development. To get here, travel 2.5km to Bruinheras, turn left at the roundabout just before the primary school, then travel another 3km – at the time of research it was signed to the left.

Activities

Sudaventura SURFING
(☎916 925 959; www.sudaventura.com; Rua Custódio Brás Pacheco 38A; ⏲10am-7pm, closed Sun Dec-Feb) Offers a range of excursions, including canoe trips, and kayak, surfboard, stand-up paddleboard and bike rentals. A two-hour stand up paddleboarding/surfing lesson costs €35/45.

Sleeping

Sol da Vila GUESTHOUSE €
(☎962 574 157; www.soldavila.com; Rua Custódio Brás Pacheco 4; d/apt €55/90; 📶) A centrally located, unpretentious spot with bright, spotless rooms and a lovely patio with a

prolific lemon tree. The friendly owner on the premises can provide tips on exploring the town. Three apartments are also available. Bike rental is €10 per day.

Campiférias CAMPGROUND €
(☎283 996 140; www.campingcampiferias.com; Rua da Praça; sites per adult/tent/car €4.30/3.60/4.40;) Shady and situated only 800m from the beach. There's a games room and restaurants on-site.

Casa Amarela GUESTHOUSE €€
(☎283 996 632; www.casaamarelamilfontes.com; Rua Dom Luis Castro e Almeida; dm/d/tr/q €20/65/80/92.50; @) This cheery yellow place is set with eclectic knick-knacks belonging to the genial English-speaking owner, Rui. In the main building you'll find seven bright rooms and a lounge space. Nearby the new, handsomely furnished annexe has 17 appealing rooms with brick floors, blond woods and artwork from Rui's world travels. The spacious courtyard is a lovely place to unwind.

Hotel Casa dos Arcos GUESTHOUSE €€
(☎933 890 264, 283 998 767; Rua dos Carris; d/tr €70/85;) Jauntily painted in blue and white, this airy and spotless (if dated) guesthouse has comfortable beds, tiled floors and small balconies. The best rooms have waterfront views.

Casa do Adro GUESTHOUSE €€
(☎283 997 102; www.casadoadro.com.pt; Rua Diário de Notícias 10; d €90;) Set in a house dating from the 17th century, this special option is filled with antiques and artwork. It has six elegantly furnished bedrooms, some with private balcony or shared terrace. Hospitality abounds and foodies will love the breakfasts – and you can turn up to this scrumptious spread at any time in the morning.

Eating

Mabi CAFE, ICE CREAM €
(Largo de Santa Maria 25; ice cream from €2; 8am-10pm Tue-Sun) Famed for its ice cream, Mabi is one of the icons of town, and it serves up creamy rich decadence to an often packed house (go early to beat the lines). This buzzing bakery and dessert spot also offers massive croissants and other snacks.

Ritual TAPAS €€
(☎914 440 404; www.facebook.com/RitualRestauranteTapasBar; Rua Barbosa Viana 4; tapas €6-16, mains €12-17; 6-11pm Mon-Sat;) With its tall ceilings and colonial-like ambience, Ritual is one of the most atmospheric settings for a meal in town. The eclectic tapas menu features creative combinations like sun-dried tomato hummus, garlic and ginger sauteed shrimp, and cured sausage fired in *aguardente* (distilled spirits). The global influence extends to main courses, including Thai curry, fresh gnocchi and salmon tataki.

Porto das Barcas PORTUGUESE €€
(☎283 997 160; Estrada do Canal; mains €12-16; noon-10pm Wed-Mon) With a wonderful outlook over the water and cliffs, this is a great place to kick back for a seafood lunch. Its light and airy ambience in a dreamy location are winners whatever your impression of the cuisine (which locals love). It's 2.5km north of town along the canal road.

Conversas com Sal CONTEMPORARY €€
(☎283 998 078; Avenida Marginal Edifício Milfontes; tapas around €4-6, mains €12-15; noon-3pm & 7-10pm Tue-Sun;) There's a hip vibe to this laid-back spot that feels more southern California than coastal Alentejo. It has surfboards on the wall, table football, retro sofas and guitars, though the waterfront views from the terrace are the real draw. The menu has good sharing plates (sausage croquettes, clams, flambeed shrimp), juicy burgers and heartier plates of lamb chops and seafood dishes.

Restaurante A Fateixa SEAFOOD €€
(☎283 996 415; Largo do Cais; mains €8-15; noon-3pm & 7-10pm Thu-Tue) A Fateixa delivers good grills and seafood dishes – try the *tamboril* (monkfish) rice for two – and it has breezy outdoor tables. It's excellent value given its perfect setting down by the river.

★**Tasca do Celso** PORTUGUESE €€€
(☎283 996 753; www.tascadocelso.com; Rua dos Aviadores; mains €13-25; noon-3pm & 7-11pm Tue-Sun) *The* choice. Locals and travellers from far and wide rave about the excellent cuisine produced within the kitchen of this charming, 'upmarket rustic' blue-and-white building. You're safe trying anything here, though the seafood is outstanding (and priced accordingly). Great service, open fires, and an appealing bar area too. Reservations essential at night.

Drinking & Nightlife

Manjedoura & Lua Cheia BAR
(☎283 998 282; Cerca do Arneirão; 10pm-4am Mon-Sat) One of Vila Nova's best spots for a night out, this place has fun parties

WALKING THE ALENTEJO

The **Rota Vicentina** comprises two walking trails – one coastal and one inland – and runs along the southwest coast to Cabo de São Vincente. The coastal walk (referred to as 'the fishermen's trail') begins in Porto Côvo. It uses paths forged by beachgoers and fisherfolk and passes through some of the harsher, yet stunning, coastal scenery and wilderness. The inland route (dubbed the 'historical way') is equally appealing. It runs through the Parque Natural do Sudoeste Alentejano e Costa Vicentina, plus rural towns and villages, cork tree forests and valleys.

Both trails are made up of sections, and it's never more than 25km between villages, where you can lodge for the night (thus no need to bring camping gear). The Fishermen's Trail comprises four sections, totalling 120km, and the walk is slightly more difficult with some passages on dunes and thigh-tiring sands. At times it runs along the cliffs, mostly single track, and only walkers are allowed. The longer Historical Way consists of 12 sections totalling 230km. Trails are wider and generally the walk is easier; mountain bikes are permitted.

Private companies have cottoned onto the route, providing luggage transfer between each night's lodging, but there's nothing to stop you from doing it alone, if you're prepared to carry your things. Numerous accommodation options are along both routes. For further information see www.rotavicentina.com.

(including the odd costume event), with DJs spinning wide-ranging sounds including Kizomba, the latest dance craze from Angola.

Bar Azul BAR
(Largo do Rossio 20; ⏲9pm-2am Fri & Sat) Always lively, whatever the time of year, even if the rest of the town is dead. This is a jovial bar with a pool table and lots of papier-mâché sharks, octopuses and squid hanging from the ceiling.

Information

Turismo (☎283 996 599; Rua António Mantas; ⏲9am-1pm & 3-6pm Oct-May, 9am-6pm Jun-Sep; 📶) Off the main road, opposite the police station. Buses stop 100m along the same road. There's free wi-fi and a computer if you need to get online.

Getting There & Away

Vila Nova has three bus connections daily on weekdays to/from Odemira (€6, 20 minutes). **Rede Expressos** (☎283 107 069; www.rede-expressos.pt) buses run daily from Lisbon (€16, 3½ hours, three daily, more in summer) via Setúbal (€14.20) and at least once daily to/from Portimão (€13.50, two hours) and Lagos (€13, two hours). There are summer services to Sagres (€13, two hours). The ticket agent for Rede Expressos is located in the sewing shop on Travessa dos Amadores.

Zambujeira Do Mar

POP 900

Enchantingly wild beaches backed by rugged cliffs form the setting of this sleepy seaside village. The main street terminates at the cliff and from there paths lead to the attractive sands below. Quieter than Vila Nova, Zambujeira attracts a backpacker, surfy crowd, though in August the town is a party place and hosts the massive music fest, **Festa do Sudoeste**. The high-season crowds obscure Zambujeira's out-of-season charms: fresh fish in family-run restaurants, blustering clifftop walks and a dramatic, empty coast.

Activities

A 3km-long walking and biking path runs between Zambujeira do Mar and Porto de Pesca.

Sleeping

Hakuna Matata HOSTEL €
(☎918 470 038; Rua da Fonte 16; dm/d €22/50; 📶) A great option for budget travellers, this charming spot has four- and six-bed dorms, as well as private rooms with shared facilities. Guests have access to the kitchen and lounge, and you can rent bikes. It's in a good location, a short walk to the village centre and the beach.

Rosa dos Ventos GUESTHOUSE €€
(☎283 961 391; www.rosadosventoszambujeira.com; Rua Nossa Senhora do Mar; d €75;) A short walk from the town centre (and 75m from the cliff over the ocean), this well-maintained guesthouse has airy modern rooms painted in light hues (including some in pastel shades), with mini-fridges and other mod cons that are set around a patio. Some rooms have partial ocean views.

★**Herdade do Touril** RURAL INN €€€
(☎937 811 627; www.herdadedotouril.pt; r from €130;) Four kilometres north of Zambujeira do Mar is this upmarket *quinta* (estate) building with rooms and apartments of the fluffy-pillow variety. Some are located within the original building (built in 1826), others are converted farm cottages. The rustic and contemporary design of this tranquil place has an African safari-lodge feel – without the lions of course.

Eating

Costa Alentejana SEAFOOD €€
(☎283 961 508; Rua Miramar 8; mains €12-18; ⊙noon-3pm & 7-11pm Tue-Sun) Everyone's favourite seafood restaurant in town serves up mouth-watering octopus, rice dishes, tender crab and other plates of uberfresh seafood. Wash it down with a first-rated bottle of Cortes de Cima.

A Barca SEAFOOD €€
(☎283 961 186; Entrada da Barca, Porto de Pesca; meals €10-16; ⊙noon-3pm & 7-11pm Tue-Sun Feb-Nov, daily Jul & Aug) The owner's father once cooked lunch for the local fisherfolk after they came into port; these days, the former kiosk is an upmarket restaurant that serves great fish and *marisco* (shellfish) dishes to discerning diners. Lovely outdoor area and view of the sea, but (of course) expect the odd seagull.

Restaurante Sacas SEAFOOD €€
(☎283 961 151; Entrada da Barca, Porto de Pesca; meals €9-16; ⊙noon-3pm & 7-10pm Thu-Tue, daily Jul & Aug) A family team add colour to this fun, laid-back 'cabana' – Dona Ana Maria even creates her own seafood dishes. The fresh fish and shellfish more than make up for the car-park view (many years ago the cabana was at the base of the cliffs, but it was destroyed by rough seas).

Information

Turismo (☎283 961 144; ⊙10am-6pm Tue-Sat) There's a small *turismo* providing basic information on the main street.

Getting There & Away

In summer, Rede Expressos (www.rede-expressos.pt) buses connect Zambujeira with Vila Nova de Milfontes (€8, 45 minutes, one daily) and Lisbon (€15, 3¾ hours, one daily). You can buy tickets at **Pastelaria Doce Tentaçao** (Rua da Palmira 101). Buses also run to Odemira (40 minutes) and Beja (three hours, one weekdays); for these you buy your ticket on the bus.

Porto Côvo

POP 1040

The appealingly 'traditional cute' Porto Côvo is worh a quick visit if you have the time. Perched on low cliffs with views over the sea, Porto Côvo is a former fishing village with a pretty square, cobbled streets lined with sun-bleached houses and a popular beach. It gets packed in summer.

Activities

In summer, a boat shuttles between Porto Côvo and the diminutive island of Ilha do Pessegueiro (Fishermen's Island). Diving trips can be arranged through **Ecoalga** (☎964 620 394; www.ecoalga.com; Rua 25 de Abril 5C).

Eating

Cervejaria Marquês SEAFOOD €€
(☎269 905 036; Largo Marquês de Pombal 10; mains €12-19; ⊙noon-3pm & 7-10pm Wed-Mon;) Porto Côvo's overwhelmingly favourite dining spot is set on the town's main square, with inviting outdoor tables, a smart tiled interior and scrumptious plates of grilled fish and seafood salads. No reservations.

Information

Turismo (☎269 959 124; Largo do Mercado; ⊙9am-noon & 1-5pm Mon-Fri Oct-May, 10am-1pm & 3-7pm Mon-Sat Jun-Sep) Located on the edge of the old town, just one block north of the main square and next to a car park.

Getting There & Away

During summer at least five buses a day travel to/from Lisbon (€16, three hours). There are also regular connections to Vila Nova de Milfontes (around €6, 20 minutes).

Estremadura & Ribatejo

Includes ➡

Best Places to Eat

- ➡ Mar à Vista (p268)
- ➡ Estrela do Mar (p287)
- ➡ Restaurante António Padeiro (p282)
- ➡ Casa Pires (p280)

Best Places to Sleep

- ➡ Casa das Marés (p270)
- ➡ Casa d'Óbidos (p273)
- ➡ Challet Fonte Nova (p282)
- ➡ Blue Buddha Beachhouse (p267)

Why Go?

Stretching from the Rio Tejo to the Atlantic Ocean, Estremadura and Ribatejo constitute Portugal's heartland, but their central importance goes beyond geography. These fertile lands have formed the backdrop for every major chapter in Portuguese history, from the building of key fortified settlements in the 12th century to the release of Salazar's political prisoners in 1974. Two of medieval Portugal's critical battles for autonomy – against the Moors at Santarém and the Spaniards at Aljubarrota – were fought and won here, and remain commemorated in the magnificent monasteries at Alcobaça and Batalha, both Unesco World Heritage Sites. A third Unesco site, Tomar's Convento de Cristo, was long the stronghold of the Knights Templar.

These days the region draws visitors not only to these renowned monasteries, but also to its vineyards, beaches, castles and historic villages – and Fátima, modern Portugal's premier religious shrine.

When to Go

Leiria

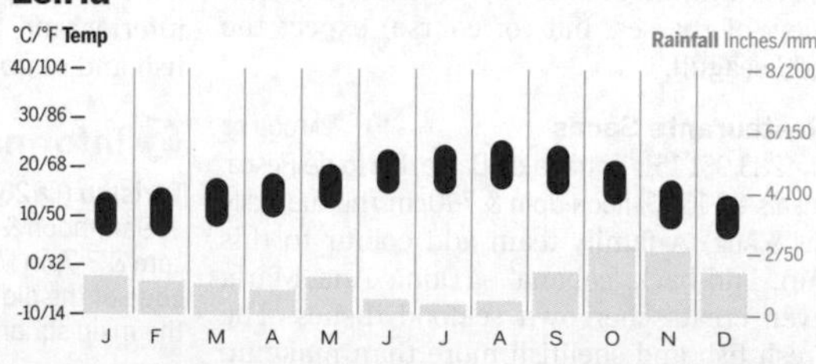

Apr & May Beat summer heat (and crowds) with a springtime visit to the region's World Heritage Sites.

Jun & Sep For warm beaches at cooler prices, visit the coast in early summer or autumn.

Oct World-class waves at Peniche, Ericeira and other prime surf spots.

Estremadura & Ribatejo Highlights

1. Travel back in time at an awe-inspiring monastery in **Batalha** (p282).

2. Wander around the limestone walls of **Parque Natural das Serras de Aire e Candeeiros** (p290).

3. Watch Supertubos pros at the prime surfing destination of **Peniche** (p269).

4. Survey the Rio Tejo from the heights of the 12th-century **Castelo de Almourol** (p294).

5. Cross the arched bridge to the island fort of **Berlenga Grande** (p269).

6. Sail across the **Foz do Arelho** (p275) lagoon at sunset.

7. Grab a book in the literary village of **Óbidos** (p272).

8. Catch Carnaval or New Year's fireworks at one of Estremadura's most picturesque beach-party settings in **Nazaré** (p277).

9. Feast on the region's best seafood in **Ericeira** (p266).

ESTREMADURA

Running up the Atlantic coast from the mouth of the Rio Tejo almost to the Rio Mondego, Estremadura has long been a land of plenty, its rolling hills and valleys offering up some of Portugal's richest farmland. For proof, visit the elaborate kitchens that fattened up the monks at Alcobaça's extraordinary monastery. The coast is blessed with miles-long strands of beach, which also catch some of Europe's best surf.

Estremadura earned its name the same way as Spain's Extremadura: for a time, it represented the furthest reaches of the Reconquista.

Ericeira

POP 10,260

Picturesquely draped across sandstone cliffs above the blue Atlantic, sunny, whitewashed Ericeira is popular with *lisboêtas* seeking a quick weekend getaway. It's equally renowned for spectacular ocean vistas and excellent seafood restaurants and is also a mecca for surfers, who come here for the great waves and camaraderie. The town's old centre is clustered around Praça da República, with the sprawl of newer development spreading south and north.

Beaches

As well as the small **Praia dos Pescadores** in the heart of town, there are three beaches within walking distance of the centre. **Praia do Sul**, also called Praia da Baleia, is easiest to get to and has a protected pool for children. **Praia do Norte** (also called Praia do Algodio) and **Praia de São Sebastião** lie to the north. Some 5km north is unspoilt **Praia de São Lourenço**, while **Praia Foz do Lizandro**, a big bite of beach backed by a small car park and a couple of restaurants, is 3km south.

Activities

The big attraction in Ericeira is surfing. Serious aficionados congregate 3km north of town at Praia da Ribeira d'Ilhas, a World Qualifying Series (WQS) site and frequent host to Portuguese national surfing championships; most amateurs will find the waves at the nearer Praia de São Sebastião challenging enough.

Surf schools (*escolas de surf*) abound in Ericeira. Most offer a week's package, which includes lessons, equipment and, in many cases, accommodation. A couple of outfits focus on stand-up paddle boards. Contact the turismo (p268) for a list of registered schools.

Rapture Surf Camp SURFING

(☎919 586 722; www.rapturecamps.com; Foz do Lizandro 6; surf lessons €30, board & wetsuit rental per day €10, dm incl half-board €29-39) Standing out among the surf camps in Ericeira, Rapture offers nicely chilled digs right on the beach and lessons with proficient instructors.

Activity Surf Center SURFING

(Rua de Santo António 3A; per day surfboard/wetsuit hire €20/10) Rents out surfboards, paddle boards, body boards and wetsuits. You can pick up bikes for rental here as well (€15 per day).

Sleeping

Book ahead in the peak season months of July and August. During the low season, expect discounts of 30% to 50%.

Residencial Fortunato GUESTHOUSE €

(☎261 862 829; www.pensaofortunato.com; Rua Dr Eduardo Burnay 45; d €55-70, with ocean view €65-80; P 📶) One of the best budget options around, this well-run, well-kept place has light, bright and all-white rooms in a nice location at the end of a pedestrian street. The best digs upstairs have small terraces with lovely sea views, for €10 extra. Parking under the building costs €3 per night.

Ericeira Camping CAMPGROUND €

(☎261 862 706; www.ericeiracamping.com; sites per adult/child/tent/car €6/3/6.50/3, cabins from €85; P @ 📶) Situated on the coastal highway 800m north of Praia de São Sebastião, this high-quality site has two-bedroom cabins, lots of trees, a playground, disabled access and a municipal swimming pool next door.

★ **Blue Buddha Beachhouse** GUESTHOUSE €€

(☎910 658 849; www.bluebuddhahostel.com; Rua Florêncio Granate 19; d/tr/f from €70/90/112; 📶) The nearest thing to your own modern beach house, this delightful spot has seven very smart rooms, plus an ocean vista to die for. A spacious communal living room with couches, cable TV, and mod cons adds

Ericeira

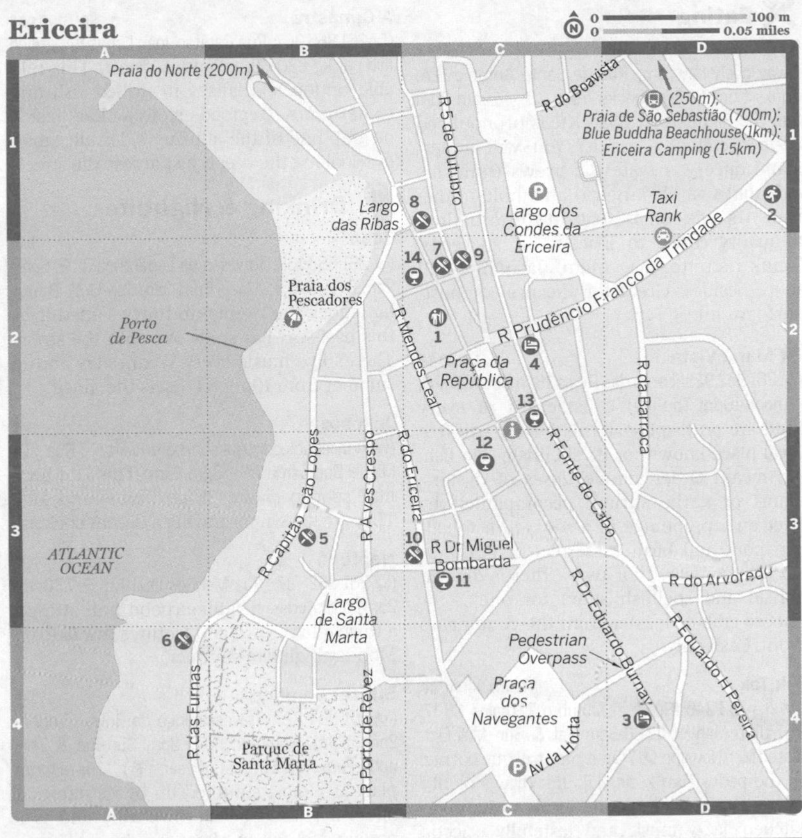

Ericeira

Activities, Courses & Tours
- 1 Activity Surf Center C2
- 2 Go Out D1

Sleeping
- 3 Residencial Fortunato D4
- 4 Residencial Vinnus C2

Eating
- 5 A Canastra B3
- 6 Esplanada Furnas A4
- 7 KFÉ C2
- 8 Mar à Vista C1
- 9 Tik Tak C2
- 10 Tik Tapas C3

Drinking & Nightlife
- 11 Jukebox C3
- 12 Neptuno C3
- 13 Sunset Bamboo C2
- 14 Tubo C2

to the appeal, plus there's a guest kitchen. Multilingual proprietress Luzia knows the lot, from surfing spots to the latest bars.

Residencial Vinnus GUESTHOUSE €€
(☎913 807 449; www.residencialvinnus.com; Rua Prudêncio Franco da Trindade 19; without breakfast d €55-70, tr €80, f €80;) Bright, with trendy, contemporary decor, the centrally located Residencial Vinnus offers great value, with simple and comfortable whitewashed rooms. It's worth the extra investment for the spacious ones with kitchenette, but the pretty corner doubles have great light. Excellent overall with a good attitude. In summer you might cop street noise from nearby bars.

Eating

KFÉ CAFE €
(www.lovely-bay.com; Rua de Santo António 12A; drinks from €1.50, snacks from €3; 9am-8pm Sun-Thu, 9am-1am Fri & Sat) Kfé is pronounced *ca-fay* (coffee) – get it? You will understand once you taste the brews from this cafe that's barely larger than a hole-in-the-wall. Its mission is to bring international-quality coffee to Ericeira. It succeeds. Think ristretto, macchiato, flat white and more besides. Great for the pre- or post-surf java hit.

★**Mar à Vista** SEAFOOD €€
(261 862 928; Largo das Ribas 16; mains €17-20; noon-10pm Thu-Tue) Crustaceans of every kind are on display at this hearty frill-free local place known for its shellfish. (No fish. No meat.) Order simple *doses* of oysters, clams or garlic shrimp accompanied by beer on tap, indulge in a *massada, feijoada* (pork and bean casserole) or *cataplana* (seafood stew) for two – there's *açorda* (bread and shellfish stew) for one! – or choose crab or lobster from the counter up front. Cash only.

Tik Tak INTERNATIONAL €€
(261 863 246; Rua 5 de Outubro 7; mains €8-17; 7-11pm Mon-Fri, 12.30-3pm Sat & Sun May-Oct, closed Mon Nov-Apr;) On a picturesque corner in the pedestrian zone, Tik Tak draws plenty of tourists and hip young locals to its open kitchen, jazzy music and tastefully eclectic interior. The varied menu offers a break for those unmoved by Ericeira's seafood fetish; there are more fresh vegetables than most other places, plus abundant nonfishy options.

Tik Tapas TAPAS €€
(261 869 235; Rua do Ericeira 15; tapas €3-9; 7pm-1am Tue-Fri, 12.30-3pm & 7pm-1am Sat & Sun;) Decked out with orange walls, colourful wooden tables and a blue bar, this place sells really tasty meat, fish and vegie tapas, full meals, sangria and draught beer.

★**Esplanada Furnas** SEAFOOD €€€
(261 864 870; www.restaurantefurnasericeira.com; Rua das Furnas; fish & seafood per kg €20-65, mains €16-30; noon-4pm & 5-10pm) Furnas is all about freshly caught fish and spectacular ocean views. They'll show you the catch of the day and then barbecue your choice on the spot. The per-kilogram price on the board covers the fish plus all the accompaniments.

A Canastra SEAFOOD €€€
(261 865 367; Rua Capitão João Lopes 8A; grilled fish per kg €20-60; lunch & dinner) This reliable option specialises in grilled fish and *caldeiradas* (seafood stews). Eat inside or grab one of the alluring sidewalk tables overlooking the ocean just across the street.

Drinking & Nightlife

Tubo BAR
(261 863 168; Travessa da Esperança 3; 6pm-2am Fri & Sat Nov-May, 6pm-3am Jun-Oct) Popular among the twenty- to thirty-somethings, this post-surf bar spills out onto the street. There's live music every Wednesday and in summer from 10pm a DJ sets the mood.

Jukebox BAR
(www.facebook.com/jukeboxbarericeira; Rua Dr Miguel Bombarda 7; 8pm-2am) This laid-back little spot specialises in jazz, blues and soul. They are known for mixing a decent cocktail.

Neptuno PUB
(261 862 017; Rua Mendes Leal 12; 7.30pm-2am) This cosy neighbourhood pub attracts a thirty-plus crowd and features live fado on Monday nights in summer.

Sunset Bamboo BAR
(261 864 827; Travessa Jogo da Bola; noon-2am nightly summer, noon-8pm Sun-Tue & Thu, noon-2am Fri & Sat rest of year;) This casual place is almost summed up by its name. It offers a relaxed beach-town vibe and is a perfect spot for an afternoon drink. There's a light menu of sandwiches and snacks.

Information

Turismo (261 863 122; www.cm-mafra.pt; Rua Dr Eduardo Burnay 46; 10am-6pm Sep–mid-Jul, 10am-10pm mid-Jul–Aug) Offers useful maps of the town, information on surfing (ask for the *Surf Guide* booklet), and maps and brochures for Lisbon and beyond.

Getting There & Away

Mafrense (261 862 717; www.mafrense.pt) buses stop at the bus station 500m north of the *praça* (town square), off the national road N247. Ask at the *turismo* for timetables.

Bus connections to northern destinations such as Peniche and Coimbra are best made through Torres Vedras (€3.85, one hour, six to 10 on weekdays, two on Saturday and one on Sunday). Other destinations, with services roughly hourly, are Lisbon–Campo Grande station (€6.10, 1¼ hours), Mafra (€2.30, 25 minutes) and Sintra (€3.40, 50 minutes).

Getting Around

Regular local buses to Torres Vedras go past Praia da Ribeira d'Ilhas (around €1). For Praia Foz do Lizandro (around €1), take any Sintra-bound bus to a stop on the N247 above the beach.

You can rent bicycles from **Go Out** (☎ 925 307 317; www.goout.com.pt; Rua Prudêncio Franco da Trindade 1; per day/week bicycle €12/56, scooter €28/140; ⏰10am-8pm Nov-May, to 10pm Jun-Oct).

There's a **taxi rank** on Rua Prudêncio Franco da Trindade, near the post office.

Peniche

POP 14,700

Popular for its long, fabulous town beach, nearby surf strands and also as a jumping-off point for the beautiful Ilhas Berlengas nature reserve, Peniche is spectacularly set on a headland surrounded by sea. It remains a working port, giving it a slightly grittier, more 'lived in' feel than its resort neighbours. The walled historic centre makes for pleasant strolling, and the seaside fort where Salazar's regime detained political prisoners is a must-see for anyone interested in Portuguese history. Artisan lovers will enjoy Peniche's speciality, handmade lace, and you can watch the nimble fingers of women at work. Outdoors enthusiasts will love the beaches east of town, where lessons and rentals for every sport under the sun are available.

Sights

Berlenga Grande — ISLAND

Sitting about 10km offshore from Peniche, and part of the Berlenga archipelago, Berlenga Grande is a spectacular, rocky and remote island, with twisting, shocked-rock formations and gaping caverns.

It's the only island of the archipelago you can visit; the group consists of tiny islands surrounded by clear, calm waters full of shipwrecks – great for snorkelling and diving.

Baleal — BEACH

About 5km to the northeast of Peniche is this scenic island-village, connected to the mainland village of Casais do Baleal by a narrow causeway (note: it's accessed through a car park). The fantastic sweep of sandy beach here offers some fine surfing. Surf schools dot the sands, as do several bar-restaurants.

Fortaleza — FORT

(☎ 262 780 116; ⏰9am-12.30pm & 2-5.30pm Tue-Fri, from 10am Sat & Sun) FREE Dominating the south of the peninsula, Peniche's imposing 16th-century fortress was used in the 20th century as one of dictator Salazar's infamous jails for political prisoners.

By the entrance where prisoners once received visitors – the stark booths with glass partitions are preserved – is the Núcleo-Resistência, a grim but fascinating display about those times including Resistance leaflets and prisoners' poignant, beautifully illustrated letters to their children.

Housed inside the fortress complex is the Museu Municipal.

Museu Municipal — MUSEUM

(☎ 262 780 116; €1.60; ⏰9am-12.30pm & 2-5.30pm Tue-Fri, from 10am Sat & Sun) Housed inside the fortress complex is this museum, whose most striking feature is the top floor, which has a row of cells for political prisoners from the dictatorship years, some used for solitary confinement. Floors below this contain a non-thrilling municipal mishmash, from Roman archaeological artefacts and shipwreck finds to shells and examples of local lace work.

Headland — HEADLAND

While in Peniche, make sure you do the 8km circuit of the whole headland (walking is hot going, however, as much of it is on the road). At Cabo Carvoeiro, the very tip, there's a lighthouse and spectacular views of a rock stack and the Berlenga islands, as well as an excellent restaurant.

Activities

Surfing

Long renowned as a prime surfing destination, Peniche burnished its celebrity status when **Supertubos** beach, south of town, was selected as a stop on the ASP World Tour, the most prestigious international circuit of competitive surfing.

Meanwhile, **Baleal** is a paradise of challenging but, above all, consistent waves that make it an ideal learners' beach.

Peniche is full of surfers' hostels and schools. Depending on the season, surf camps at Baleal charge from €300 to €545 for a week of classes, including equipment and shared self-catering lodging. You can also take individual two-hour classes for around €35 and rent boards (€20) and wetsuits (€20). Well-established operators include **Baleal Surfcamp** (262 769 277; www.balealsurfcamp.com; Rua Amigos do Baleal 2; 1-/3-/5-day course €60/95/145) and **Peniche Surfcamp** (962 336 295; www.penichesurfcamp.com; Avenida do Mar 162, Casais do Baleal; 1/2/10 surf classes €35/60/250).

Diving

There are good opportunities for diving, especially at Berlenga. Expect to pay about €65 to €75 (less around Peniche) for two dives with **Acuasuboeste** (918 393 444; www.acuasuboeste.com; Porto de Pesca; diving intro course €80, two dives €65) or **Haliotis** (262 781 160; www.haliotis.pt; Casal da Ponte S/N, Atouguia da Baleia; single-/double-dive trip €35/75). Both also offer a range of PADI certification courses.

Kitesurfing

Kitesurfing is big. On the far side of high dunes about 500m east of the walled town, **Peniche Kite & Surf Center** (919 424 951; www.penichekitecenter.com; Avenida Monsenhor Bastos, Praia de Peniche de Cima; surf & kitesurf lesson €40, 2-person minimum) offers surfing and kitesurfing lessons with equipment for €40 (minimum two persons).

Tours

Associação de Operadores Marítimo-Turística TOURS
(926 852 046; associacaopescadesportiva@gmail.com; Marina do Peniche, Cais de Belengas, Office No 8) The association is responsible for local tour boats and organises cruises on demand throughout the year (depending on conditions). These range from €9.50 per person for a trip to Cabo Carvoeiro, to €50 to head to the Farilhões, the twin outer islands of the Berlenga chain.

Viamar TOURS
(262 785 646; www.viamar-berlenga.com; return adult/child €20/10) Viamar makes the 40-minute boat trip to Berlenga, with up to three daily departures in high season.

Sleeping

Residencial Rimavier GUESTHOUSE €
(262 789 459; www.rimavier.com; Rua Castilho 6; s/d €40/50) This immaculate *pensão* (guest house) – run by the helpful, chatty family in the souvenir shop downstairs – has small but spruce rooms, nautically themed linens and hallways decorated with lovely tile paintings of Peniche. Note: prices do not include breakfast and you'll have to head elsewhere for your morning java fix.

Peniche Hostel HOSTEL €
(969 008 689; www.penichehostel.com; Rua Arquitecto Paulino Montês 6; dm €18-20, d €50;) This older-style little hostel run by friendly staff, only steps from the tourist office and a five-minute walk from the bus station, has colourfully decorated rooms with a hippie element. Front rooms have windows while some smaller, more claustrophobic rooms do not.

Parque de Campismo Peniche Praia CAMPGROUND €
(262 783 460; www.penichepraia.pt; Estrada Marginal Norte; sites per adult/child/tent/car €4.60/2.40/4.60/3.40;) On the high, windy, north side of the peninsula, 1.7km from town and the beach, and 2km from Cabo Carvoeiro, this compact site comprises an unattractive mix of bungalows, apartments, plus double rooms (€49 to €79 in high season).

★ **Casa das Marés** B&B €€
(Casa 1 262 769 200, Casa 2 262 769 255, Casa 3 262 769 371; www.casadasmares1.com; Praia do Baleal; d €80-89;) At the picturesque, windswept tip of Baleal stands one of the area's most unique accommodation options. Three sisters inherited this imposing house from their parents and divided it into three parts – each of which now serves as its own little B&B. Breezy, inviting rooms all have great close-up sea views, and the sound of the breaking waves below is magical.

Katekero II GUESTHOUSE €€
(262 787 107; www.feriaskatekero.com; Avenida do Mar 68; d or apt €60-80;) The appealing and spacious modern rooms here are simple but attractive, with comfortable bed platforms, a fridge, and in some cases, a small balcony. All have great views over the water, and are very reasonably priced for this location. There are also modern apartments with kitchen and options for sleeping up to four.

MH Hotel HOTEL €€€
(262 780 500; www.mh-hotels.pt; Avenida Monsenhor Manuel Bastos; s/d/tr €110/140/200;) It's hard to miss Peniche's brand-new, spiffy addition to the hotel scene; it stands out like a bright, white beacon on approach into town. With a view over the

sand dunes, it's like a massive (and very sleek) beach house and attracts everyone from business groups to surfers after comfort. Rooms are large, breezy and all have balconies.

Surfers Lodge DESIGN HOTEL €€€
(Avenida do Mar 132, Ferrel; s/d/f €139/191/323) This hip spot is all about the design. And experience. Given its apparent target (surfers who are riding a money wave, and are happy to spend it), it redefines the image of the hippie dude living out of a combi van. The funky decor incorporates polished concrete and recycled woods and comprises clean lines, whites and natural hues.

Eating

Restaurante A Sardinha SEAFOOD €
(262 781 820; Rua Vasco da Gama 81; mains €6-14; noon-4pm & 6-10.30pm) Once a simple fishing *tasca* (tavern), this popular place was given a makeover a couple of years back, and boasts everything from gold and white painted chairs and designer lighting. But it hasn't lost what it does best: simply grilled fish and *caldeirada*. Big portions, done well.

Taberna do Ganhão PORTUGUESE €€
(Largo dos Amigos do Baleal, Baleal; mains €8-15; 10am-10pm Thu-Tue) This 'new school tavern' is a reconstituted 'old school tavern' where fishermen bought wine and grocerics (plus it was the first in the area to have a telephone). The current owners have reinvigorated its spirit by maintaining its red-and-white-checked tables and traditional daily plates (*feijoada* on a Thursday, *açorda de camarãoes* on a Friday and so on).

★**Nau dos Corvos** MODERN PORTUGUESE €€€
(262 783 168; www.naudoscorvos.com; Marginal Norte, Cabo Carvoeiro; mains €19.50-37; noon-3pm & 7-10.30pm) It's just you and the sea out here at Cabo Carvoeiro, 2.5km from the town centre at the tip of the peninsula. But as you gaze out at the Atlantic from the windy platform, it's nice to know that under your feet is an excellent, upmarket seafood restaurant (and Peniche's best). It boasts some of the best sunset views in Portugal.

Drinking & Nightlife

The area around Igreja de São Pedro is the old town's drinking hub (think four walls, cold beer and a home stereo system). For nightlife, you're really better off in Baleal, where you'll find several laid-back surfer bars right on the beach.

3Ás PUB
(Treis Ás; www.tresasbar.pt; 1pm-2am Sun-Thu, to 4am Fri & Sat) This smoky but atmospheric pub is chock-a-block with old bikes, fishing paraphernalia and photos of Peniche from a bygone era. It pulls in the surfing and local crowds after anything from a toastie to a beer or cocktail.

Java House BAR
(Largo da Ribeira 14; 9am-3am Mon-Thu, to 4am Fri & Sat;) This popular place has an atmospheric exposed-rock interior and terrace. It deals in everything from early-morning coffees to sandwiches and crêpes. The lights dim later in the evening, and DJs strut their stuff.

Information

Turismo (262 789 571; www.cm-peniche.pt; Rua Alexandre Herculano; 9am-1pm & 2-5pm) Open longer hours in summer.

Getting There & Away

BUS

Peniche's **bus station** (968 903 861; Rua Dr Ernesto Moreira) is served by **Rodotejo** (www.rodotejo.pt) and **Rede Expressos** (www.rede-expressos.pt). Destinations include Coimbra (€14.70, 2¾ hours, hourly), Leiria (€12.80, two hours, three to four daily), Lisbon (€9, 1½ hours, every one to two hours) and Óbidos (€3.20, 40 minutes, six to eight daily).

CAR

Driving into Peniche, the main highway (N114/IP6) reaches a roundabout shortly before town, where you can bear left towards the centre, right for Baleal and the eastern beaches, or straight for 3km along the northern cliffs to Cabo Carvoeiro and its lighthouse. Most days you can find ample free parking on the road that runs along the harbour.

Getting Around

From the bus station, it's a 10-minute walk west to the historic centre. The fort, harbour and Avenida do Mar – where you'll find most of the seafood restaurants – are a short distance south.

Local buses connect Peniche with Baleal (€1.80, 10 minutes) during the week, but service is spotty on weekends outside summer. Bikes are a handy way to get around; hire them at **Wildside Campers** (262 785 318; www.wildsidecampers.com; Avenida Monsenhor Bastos 33; rental per day/week €15/70).

Reserva Natural da Berlenga

Sitting about 10km offshore from Peniche, Berlenga Grande is a spectacular, rocky and remote island, with twisting, shocked-rock formations and gaping caverns. It's the only island of the Berlenga archipelago you can visit – the group consists of three tiny islands surrounded by clear, calm, dark-blue waters full of shipwrecks that are great for snorkelling and diving.

In the 16th century Berlenga Grande was home to a monastery, but now the most famous inhabitants are thousands of nesting seabirds, especially guillemots. The birds take priority over human visitors: the only development that has been allowed includes housing for a small fishing community and a lighthouse. Paths are clearly marked to stop day trippers trespassing on the birds' domain.

Linked to the island by a narrow causeway is the 17th-century Forte de São João Baptista, now one of the country's most dramatic (but barren) hostels.

Sleeping & Eating

If you want to sleep on the island, you'll need to reserve ahead; places can be prebooked solid as early as May.

There's a small grocery store on the island for self-catering.

Forte de São João Baptista CAMPING €
(262 750 244, 916 876 403; www.facebook.com/aaberlenga; per person €20; Jun–mid-Sep) The original fort (built in 1666) was later remodelled as an inn but was then abandoned for many years. This is a dramatic but dead-basic spot that's essentially 'camping with walls': you sleep in rooms, but must bring all your own linen, food and drinking water. Wonderful bucket-nozzle showers from cistern water are on offer; bathrooms are shared.

Mar e Sol HOTEL €€
(919 543 105, 262 750 331; www.restaurantemaresol.pt; tw/f €100/150; May-Sep) The decent if simple rooms here would seem overpriced anywhere else, but when you consider the location just a few steps above Berlenga's boat dock and directly adjacent to its only restaurant, things appeal more. Prices halve at the beginning and end of the season.

Getting There & Away

Viamar (262 785 646; www.viamar-berlenga.com; day round-trip adult/child €20/10, one way €12/6; 20 May-15 Sep) is the longest-established of several harbourside outfits, all making the 45-minute trip to the island on roughly the same schedule and for the same round-trip fare. Viamar sails three times daily during July and August, at 9.30am, 11.30am and 5.30pm, returning at 10.30am, 4.30pm and 6.30pm. During the remainder of the season there's one trip per day, departing at 10am and returning at 4.30pm. Tickets tend to sell out quickly in summer, as only 300 visitors are allowed each day. All sailings are weather-dependent. Some companies also offer add-ons such as a guided hike on the island or a sea-cave visit.

If you're prone to seasickness, choose your day carefully – the crossing can be rough.

Óbidos

POP 3100

Surrounded by a classic crenellated wall, Óbidos' gorgeous historic centre is a labyrinth of cobblestoned streets and flower-bedecked, whitewashed houses livened up with dashes of vivid yellow and blue paint. It's a delightful place to pass an afternoon, but there are plenty of reasons to stay overnight, as there's excellent accommodation including a hilltop castle now converted into one of Portugal's most luxurious *pousadas* (upmarket hotels).

Hill-town aficionados looking to savour Óbidos' 'lost in time' qualities may find the main street ridiculously touristy, especially on weekends and during festivals. There are pretty bits outside the walls too.

The main gate, Porta da Vila, leads directly into the main street, Rua Direita, lined with chocolate and cherry-liqueur shops.

In recent years Óbidos has been reinventing itself as a literary centre: quirky and very atmospheric, themed bookshops abound and in 2015 it held Folio, its first literary festival, intended to be an annual event.

History

When Dom Dinis first showed Óbidos to his wife Dona Isabel in 1228, it must have already been a pretty sight because she fell instantly in love with the place. The king decided to make the town a wedding gift to his queen, initiating a royal tradition that lasted until the 19th century.

Any grace it had in 1228 must be credited to the Moors, who had laid out the streets and had only recently abandoned the strategic heights. The Moors had chased out the Visigoths, who in turn had evicted the Romans, who also had a fortress here.

Until the 15th century Óbidos overlooked the sea; the bay gradually silted up, leaving the town landlocked.

Sights

Castelo, Walls & Aqueduct HISTORIC SITE

FREE You can walk around the unprotected **muro** (wall) for uplifting views over the town and surrounding countryside. The walls date from Moorish times (later restored), but the **castelo** (castle) itself is one of Dom Dinis' 13th-century creations. It's a stern edifice, with lots of towers, battlements and big gates. Converted into a palace in the 16th century (some Manueline touches add levity), it's now a deluxe pousada (p274).

The impressive 3km-long **aqueduct**, southeast of the main gate, dates from the 16th century.

Igreja de Santa Maria CHURCH

(Praça de Santa Maria; 9.30am-12.30pm & 2.30-7pm summer, to 5pm winter) The town's elegant main church, near the northern end of Rua Direita, stands out for its interior, with a wonderful painted ceiling and walls done up in beautiful blue-and-white 17th-century *azulejos* (hand-painted tiles). Paintings by the renowned 17th-century painter Josefa de Óbidos are to the right of the altar. There's a fine 16th-century Renaissance tomb on the left, probably carved by French sculptor Nicolas Chanterène.

Santuário do Senhor da Pedra CHURCH

(Largo do Santuário; 9am-12.30pm & 2.30-7pm Tue-Sun May-Sep, to 5pm Oct-Apr) FREE Below town this imposing, if a little ramshackle, church is an 18th-century baroque gem in need of some tender loving care. It's worth the stroll down here for the unusual hexagonal interior; in the altar is the stone sculpture of Christ crucified that gives the place its name.

Museu Municipal MUSEUM

(262 955 500; Solar da Praça de Santa Maria; 10am-1pm & 2-6pm Tue-Sun) FREE Located in an 18th-century manor house just next to Igreja de Santa Maria, the town's museum houses a small collection of paintings spanning several centuries. The highlight is a haunting portrait by Josefa de Óbidos, *Faustino das Neves* (1670), remarkable for its dramatic use of light and shade.

Festivals & Events

Mercado Medieval FAIR

(www.mercadomedievalobidos.pt) This two-week medieval fair – held during July inside the castle grounds and below the town's western wall – includes live entertainment, jousting matches (yes, on horses!), plenty of grog and pigs roasting on spits, and the chance to try your hand at scaling the town walls with the help of a harness and rope.

Folio LITERATURE

(Literary Festival) In 2015 Óbidos hosted its first literary festival. At the time of research it was planning its second and had attracted 2001 Noble Prize winner VS Naipaul. If this is anything to go by, it could be one to watch. While the first festival focused on Portuguese and Brazilian writing, there are plans to become more international. Changing dates.

Festival Internacional do Chocolate FOOD

(www.festivalchocolate.cm-obidos.pt;) This scrumptiously decadent month-long celebration with varying dates draws over 200,000 people with events for every age and taste, including a kids' playhouse made entirely from chocolate.

Sleeping

Although touristy, Óbidos has an excellent array of accommodation, from an atmospheric *pousada* to cosy guest houses and some cutting-edge boutique hotels.

Hostel Argonauta HOSTEL €

(963 824 178, 262 958 088; www.hostelargonauta.com; Rua Adelaide Ribeirete 14; dm/d €25/50;) In a pretty spot just outside the walls, this feels more like a friend's place than a hostel. Run with good cheer, it has an arty, colourful dorm with wood-stove heating and beds as well as bunks; there's also a cute double with a great view.

★**Casa d'Óbidos** HOTEL €€

(262 950 924; www.casadobidos.com; Quinta de São José; s/d €75/90, 2-/4-/6-person apt without breakfast €90/140/175; P) In a whitewashed, 19th-century villa below town, this

WORTH A TRIP

BUDDHA EDEN

What have the Taliban got to do with a rural winery 12km south of Óbidos? Well, when they blew up the Buddhas of Bamiyan in Afghanistan in 2001, the millionaire art collector José Berardo was so incensed at the wanton destruction of culture that he decided to do something to balance it out and created a large sculpture park on the grounds of his winery. The result, **Buddha Eden** (www.buddhaeden.com; Carvalhal; €3; ⏲9am-6pm), is an astonishing sight, with monumental Buddhist statues standing proud above the cork trees, a phalanx of terracotta warriors looking down on a duck-filled lake, modern contemporary sculpture among the vines, and a little tourist train (adult/child €3/free) doing the rounds for the sore-of-foot. It's a great place to relax, and there's a cafe here, as well as a wine shop. To make a day of it, there's an appealing restaurant in the nearby village – **Mãe d'Água** (www.restaurantemaedagua.com; Rua 13 Maio 26, Sobral do Parelhão; mains €11-20; ⏲noon-4pm & 7pm-late Tue-Sun) does confident modern Portuguese fare in a contemporary setting within a noble old building.

To get here, take the A8 motorway south from Óbidos and exit at junction 12, then follow signs for Carvalhal.

delightful option features spacious, breezy rooms with good new bathrooms and period furnishings, plus a tennis court, swimming pool and lovely grounds with sweeping views of Óbidos' bristling walls and towers. Breakfast is served at a common dining table. Trails lead through orchards up to town.

Hotel Josefa d'Óbidos HOTEL €€
(☎262 959 296; http://josefadobidoshotel.com; Rua Dom João de Ornelas; s/d/tr from €55/75/85; ❄📶) One of Óbidos' best-value hotels, with friendly and efficient English-speaking staff, this pleasant and unpretentious place is well-located just outside the main gates. It offers two types of rooms in two different wings: from sleeker, more contemporary options to atmospheric, older-style rooms. Breakfast consists of an extremely generous buffet and there's a busy bar downstairs, plus a restaurant.

Casa do Relógio GUESTHOUSE €€
(☎262 959 282; www.casadorelogio.com; Rua da Graça 12; s/d/tr €45/60/80; 📶) Just east of the town walls this 18th-century house (named for a nearby sundial) has eight smallish but spotless rooms that have had a nearly-not-quite-there decor update. There's a pretty shared terrace and it's good value for money.

Literary Man DESIGN HOTEL €€
(☎262 959 217; www.theliteraryman.pt; Rua Dom João de Ornelas; r from €95) Billed as one of the first 'literary' hotels around, this new hotel, housed in a beautiful building (a former convent), is remarkable for its concept. It has a libary-cum-bar-cafe-cum-hotel-lounge, whose decor is a melange of funk and traditional, and wall-to-wall books (for sale). Guest rooms are contemporary and minimalist: all polished concrete and recycled wood. A book or two adds the colour accents.

Casas de São Thiago B&B €€
(☎262 959 587; www.casas-sthiago.com; Largo de São Thiago 1; s/d €65/80; 📶) This frilly labyrinth of snug, 18th-century rooms (choc-a-block with antiques) and tiled, flower-filled courtyards in the shadow of the castle has its own wine cellar and billiards room. Rooms vary, but all offer standard midrange comforts, plus some nice antique touches. There are an additional six slightly cheaper rooms in another building near the principal entrance to town.

Hotel Real d'Óbidos HOTEL €€€
(☎262 955 090; www.hotelrealdobidos.com; Rua Dom João de Ornelas; s €112-120, d €130-150; P❄📶≋) It's all medieval here, with suits of armour, shields riveted to the walls and staff in tunics, but modern comforts aren't lacking. Just outside the town walls, this is an atmospheric and well-equipped aristocratic dwelling converted to a small upmarket hotel. Rooms are spacious and commodious, and the summertime pool is great, as is the four-poster suite.

Pousada do Castelo HISTORIC HOTEL €€€
(☎262 955 080; www.pousadas.pt; d/ste from €220/350; ❄📶) One of Portugal's most unusual *pousadas* occupies the town's forbidding 13th-century castle. The rooms are within two sections – the castle (traditional decor), and the attached building known as 'the cottage' (more modern interiors). Reserve ahead for the split-level rooms in the

two castle towers (warning: cosy, and not for claustrophobes) – especially the King D Dinis room, popular with honeymooners.

Eating

★ Ja!mon Ja!mon TASCA €
(☎916 208 162; mains €5; ⏲10am-late Tue-Sun) Just outside Porta da Vila, before the tourism office, don't miss this cute little eatery. Six tables are crammed into a quaint room, a former *padeiria* (bakery), and fresh bread is baked in the wood-fired oven (along with other dishes). Each day brings a small selection of daily specials. We suggest just sitting back and letting the experience happen.

Senhor da Pedra PORTUGUESE €
(Largo do Santuário; mains €6-9; ⏲10am-10pm) Behind the striking church of Senhor da Pedra below town, this simple white-tiled eatery (the one on the right as you look at the row of restaurants) is a recommended place to try low-priced authentic Portuguese cuisine. It's a classic affair with mum in the kitchen, and dad on the tables. Don't expect fast service.

Tasca Torta INTERNATIONAL €€
(☎262 958 000; Rua Direita 81; mains €9-15; ⏲12.30-2.30pm & 7-9.30pm Wed-Mon) A pleasant hum, appealing aromas and colourful plates sum up this stylish, contemporary spot. There's a cosy line of tables down one side, a kitchen on the other, and black-and-white photos of Portuguese fishermen. As for the cuisine? Everything from delicious salmon lasagne to a trilogy of octopuses. Delicious starters are arranged on a slate plate.

Petrarum Domus PORTUGUESE €€
(☎262 959 620; www.petrarumdomus.com; Rua Direita; mains €9-19; ⏲noon-3.30pm & 7-9.45pm) Amid age-old stone walls, Petrarum has been churning out the same old menu for a while now. Think hearty dishes like pork with mushrooms, mixed seafood sautées and several *bacalhau* plates. There are plainer pastas for those wanting a change of Portuguese fare.

Alcaide PORTUGUESE €€
(☎262 959 220; Rua Direita 60; mains €12-17; ⏲noon-3pm & 7-10pm) Holding a place in history as Óbidos' first restaurant, this upstairs spot has windows overlooking the town and features creative dishes such as *requinte de bacalhau* (cod with cheese, chestnuts and apples). It's better than most of the main-street options.

Drinking & Nightlife

Bar Cave Do Vale (Toupeiro) BAR
(Rua Dom João de Ornelas; ⏲7pm-2am Mon-Fri, 4pm-2am Sat & Sun) A medieval drinking den (it's an underground 'cave') with dripping wax and stone walls. A fun bar on this street and as a place for a post-meal snifter. They serve their own '*toupeiro*' (a fruit and wine mix).

Troca Tintos BAR
(Rua Dom João de Ornelas; ⏲6pm-2am Mon-Sat) A fado shawl and guitar on the wall sets the precedent for what's to come in this intimate space, a former chapel: a friendly wine bar serving up a good selection of Portuguese wines, *petiscos* (tapas, snacks; €3 to €15) and live music, including fado on Monday evenings.

Information

Turismo (☎262 959 231; www.obidos.pt; ⏲9.30am-7.30pm summer, to 6pm winter) Just outside Porta da Vila, near the bus stop, with helpful multilingual staff offering town brochures and maps in five languages.

Getting There & Away

BUS

Buses stop on the main road just outside Porta da Vila. There are frequent departures for Peniche (€3.15, 40 minutes) and hourly buses on weekdays to Lisbon (€8.15, 65 minutes), plus five buses on Saturday and Sunday.

CAR

There is a fee-charging car park just outside the gate, while the one just across the road is free.

TRAIN

There are at least six daily trains to Lisbon (€8.45 to €9.30, 2½ hours) mostly via connections at Mira Sintra-Meleças station on the suburban Lisbon line. The station is located outside the northeastern section of the castle walls. It's a pretty, but uphill, walk to town.

Foz do Arelho

With a vast, lovely beach backed by a river-mouth estuary ideal for windsurfing, Foz do Arelho remains remarkably undeveloped. It makes a fine place to laze in the sun, and outside July and August it'll often be just you and the local fishermen. The beach has a row of relaxed bars and restaurants; the town is a 15-minute walk inland.

Activities

Escola de Vela da Lagoa WATER SPORTS
(☎962 568 005, 262 978 592; www.escoladevelada-lagoa.com; Rua do Penedo Furado; ⏲10am-sunset Jun-Sep, shorter hours in low season) Hires out sailboats (€16 per hour), canoes (€10), windsurfing boards (from €15) and catamarans (from €20). Gives windsurfing and sailing lessons (two hours, €60/90 for one/two) and group kayak lessons (three hours, €14 per person). From the Foz do Arelho village, it's 2.8km: turn left on the road that follows the lagoon's inland edge past the rock called 'Penedo Furado' and continue.

Sleeping

Parque de Campismo Foz do Arelho CAMPGROUND €
(☎262 978 683; www.orbitur.pt; sites per adult/child/tent/car €6.50/3.90/6.90/6.10, 5-person cabin €123; P 🛜 🏊) This good, shady campsite, 2km from the beach, is run by Orbitur. It has a restaurant, a bar, laundry facilities and a market.

Água d'Alma HOTEL €€
(☎262 979 610; www.aguadalma.pt; Rua dos Camarções 3; s/d from €55/68; P ❄ 🛜) Recently renovated, this friendly spot on the hill near the market offers neat, smart rooms. There's a small bar and lounge area for post-beach relaxation.

Eating

Tavola de Pedra PORTUGUESE €€
(www.tavoladepedra.pai.pt; Rua Francisco Almeida Grandela 135A; mains €9-18; ⏲noon-3pm & 7-10.30pm Wed-Mon Oct-Mar) In the village, at the entrance from the east, this place has no outlook but offers the town's best local cooking, with tasty seafood stews and soups plus good-quality meat dishes and, every Saturday, an Angolan *moamba* (chicken stew). The attached bar-cafe at the front (open 8am to 2am Wednesday to Monday) is decked out in contemporary decor and serves up a decent coffee.

Cais da Praia SEAFOOD €€
(www.caisdapraia.com; Avenida do Mar; mains €9-19; ⏲9am-3am Jun-Aug, 10am-2am Sep-May; 🛜 👪) The trendiest of Foz do Arelho's waterfront joints, this glassy place is right on the beach and serves everything from sandwiches to full meals, with great lagoon views and a cocktail list. It's full of European visitors and very family-friendly.

Cabana do Pescador SEAFOOD €€€
(☎262 979 451; Avenida do Mar; mains €13-26, fish per kg €30-50; ⏲noon-4pm & 7-10.30pm Tue-Sun Sep-Jul, daily Aug) This renowned restaurant with its ocean-view terrace serves excellent meals featuring every imaginable form of sea life. It's not a frilly place, but the fish on a slab and central fountain with crustaceans scuttling about show what it's all about.

Drinking & Nightlife

Trombone BAR
(Largo do Arraial 3; ⏲9pm-2am) In the village, this characterful, spacious jazz bar has tasty mixed drinks and a pleasant terrace. It may not be the liveliest bar in town, but it's the best.

Getting There & Away

In summer, regular buses connect Foz do Arelho with Caldas da Rainha (€2.20, 20 minutes), from where you can connect to larger towns.

São Martinho do Porto

POP 2700

In contrast to nearby Nazaré, São Martinho do Porto is no party town, but a happy place where families and older paddlers enjoy the gentle lap of the waves on the omega-shaped bay ringed by sheltered, safe, sandy beaches.

Sleeping

Colina do Sol CAMPGROUND €
(☎262 989 764; www.colinadosol.net; sites per adult/child/car €5/2.50/4, tent €5-7; P 🛜 🏊) This friendly campsite is 2km north of town, and about the same distance from the beach, with disabled access, a children's playground, a pool and some sections shaded by pine trees.

Palace do Capitão B&B €€
(☎262 985 150; www.hotelpalacecapitao.com; Rua Capitão Jaime Pinto 6; d €100-140, ste €180; P ❄ 🛜) This perfectly preserved, if ever-so-slightly tired 19th-century sea captain's home directly across from the beach is a place of distinction, with much of its original Victoriana still intact. Rooms are all different and beautiful, with character. Room 4 (the captain's former bedroom) is lovely and light. The upstairs suite (room 6) has a sun terrace, accessed by a whimsical spiral staircase.

Hotel Atlântica HOTEL €€
(☎262 980 151; www.hotelatlantica.pt; Rua Miguel Bombarda 6; d €80; 🛜) In a modern building,

this welcoming place has spotless white-and-blue rooms with tiled floors to match. Rooms have low beds, little balconies and a summery feel. Ultra-friendly, helpful owners. Downstairs, the restaurant has a great terrace and serves simple but good fish and meat dishes. Room rates drop dramatically outside July and August.

Eating

Seafood eateries line São Martinho do Porto's quay and beachfront. You are safe to take your pick; all prepare fresh seafood and the quality is good.

Pastelaria A Concha CAFE €
(Rua José Bento da Silve 39-41; cakes from €0.90; 8am-8pm Fri-Wed) In São Martinho do Porto's upper village, not far from the church, you'll find this nondescript little cafe that has served up big, sweet flavours since 1950. All cakes are made on the premises. Does a killer *pastel de nata* (custard tart).

Restaurante Royal Marina INTERNATIONAL €€
(www.restaurante-royal-marina.eu; Rua Cândido dos Reis 30A; mains €8-15; 11.30am-3pm & 7-10pm Fri-Tue, 7-10pm Thu Feb-Sep;) A Swiss owner-chef runs the kitchen and his friendly Portuguese wife runs the floor. This pleasant, unpretentious spot on the quay has a slightly old-time maritime feel and serves up great seafood. And (surprise!) it whips up international treats such as *nasi goreng*. They are happy to cater to vegetarians.

Boca do Mar SEAFOOD €€
(262 990 749; Avenida Marginal 26D; mains €13-20; noon-10pm Tue-Sun) The slickest of the seafood restaurants, with plastic designer-style chairs, white surrounds and a contemporary feel, this place comes recommended for its seafood dishes plus good steaks (€13 to €17).

Information

Turismo (262 989 110; www.cm-alcobaca.pt; Rua Vasco da Gama; 9.30am-1pm & 2-6.30pm Tue-Sat) In the heart of the village; in the same building is an elevator that takes you up to the top of the town (free of charge).

Getting There & Away

BUS

Rede Expressos (www.rede-expressos.pt) runs at least five buses daily to/from Lisbon (€11.20, 1½ hours). **Rodotejo** (www.rodotejo.pt) has buses heading to Óbidos, Batalha, Alcobaça and Nazaré. Check online for the ever-changing schedules or at the tourist office.

Rodotejo buses stop on Rua Conde de Avelar, a block inland from the waterfront, and outside Intermarché supermarket, 1km northeast of the centre. Rede Expressos buses depart from Intermarché only.

TRAIN

The train station is about 700m southeast of the centre. There are six daily trains northbound to Leiria (€4.20 to €4.60, 40 to 45 minutes) and around six southbound to Caldas da Rainha (€1.60 to €1.75, 15 minutes), with onward connections in both directions.

Nazaré

POP 10,500

With a warren of narrow, cobbled lanes running down to a wide, cliff-backed beach, Nazaré is Estremadura's most picturesque coastal resort. The sands are packed wall-to-wall with multicoloured umbrellas in July and August, but the party atmosphere isn't limited to the summer beach scene – Nazaré is one of Portugal's top draws for New Year's Eve and Carnaval celebrations as well.

The town centre is jammed with seafood restaurants, bars and local women in traditional dress (in summer, they're hawking rooms for rent, especially near seafront Avenida da República). To get a different perspective, take the funicular up to Promontório do Sítio, where picture-postcard coastal views unfold from the cliffs.

In 2011, Nazaré hit the headlines for the record-breaking feats of gutsy surfer Garrett McNamara, who rode the monster waves that roll in north of town. Note that high surf is in winter, so don't be disappointed if you witness summer's calmer swells.

Sights

Farol LIGHTHOUSE
(Sítio; €1; closes at 6pm) This amazing lighthouse (famous for its backdrop when Garrett McNamara and surfers are in the high seas) is a lovely place to visit, especially as the sun is setting. It has a small explanation of the geological reasons for the ocean's high seas.

Ascensor FUNICULAR
(Funicular; adult/child €1.20/0.90; 7.30am-8.30pm winter, to 2am summer) Departs to Promontório do Sítio every 15 minutes and every 30 minutes after 8.30pm.

Nazaré

Nazaré

Sights
1 Ascensor A1

Activities, Courses & Tours
2 Nazaré Surf School B3

Sleeping
3 Lab Hostel C2
4 Magic Art Hotel C2
5 Nazaré Hostel B1
6 Vila Conde Fidalgo D2

Eating
7 A Tasquinha B3
8 Conchinha da Nazaré B2
9 Xapa's Taberna B2

Drinking & Nightlife
10 Casa O Santo A2

Promontório do Sítio HISTORIC SITE

Until the 18th century the sea covered the present-day site of Nazaré; locals lived at this cliff-top area 110m above the beach. Today this tourist-filled promontory is popular for its tremendous views, the lighthouse and its religious associations. From Rua do Elevador, north of the *turismo*, an ascensor climbs up the hill to Promontório do Sítio; it's nice to walk back down, escaping the crowds of trinket-sellers. There are plenty of places to stay and eat up on the cliff-top too.

On a foggy day in 1182, local nobleman Dom Fuas Roupinho was in pursuit of a deer when the animal disappeared off the edge of the Sítio precipice. Dom Fuas cried out to the Virgin, whose sculpture was venerated in a nearby cave, for help, and his horse miraculously stopped right at the cliff's edge; the mark of one of its horseshoes is still visible. In what is a much-repeated story in the Iberian peninsula, Dom Fuas built the small Hermida da Memória chapel on the edge of the drop-off to commemorate the event and house the sculpture. It was later visited by a number of VIP pilgrims, including Vasco da Gama. The statue is now housed in the grander church across the square.

Igreja de Nossa Senhora da Nazaré CHURCH

(Sítio; 10am-7pm Apr-Sep, 10am-6pm Oct-Mar) FREE The 17th-century, baroque Igreja de Nossa Senhora da Nazaré, decorated with attractive Dutch *azulejos*, is on the Promontório do Sítio and holds the much-venerated sculpture of the Virgin, said to have been made by Joseph himself in Nazareth when Jesus was a baby: hence the name of the town. For €1, you can get up close and personal with the statue itself – it's not too often that you get the chance to appear in the middle of an altarpiece.

Look out for paintings of a deer in mid-air that refer to the legend of the Virgin's appearance here. Though the fall was tragic for the animal itself, its look of surprise is difficult not to be bemused by.

Activities

Nazaré Surf School SURFING
(916 386 907; www.nazaresurfschool.pt; Avenida da República S/N, Edificio S Miguel; 1/5/10 private classes €50/225/400) You can learn how to tap into your inner Garrett McNamara (or not) with this recommended surf school.

Festivals & Events

Carnaval MARDI GRAS
One of Portugal's brashest Mardi Gras celebrations, held in February, with lots of costumed parades and general irreverence. Many people dress up and the nights go loud and long.

Festa do Mar RELIGIOUS
Held every year on the first Sunday afternoon in May, this festival features a parade with floats dedicated to local patron saints and a procession of decorated boats that leave the harbour and head around Nazaré's beachfront.

Nossa Senhora da Nazaré RELIGIOUS
This annual pilgrimage, held in Sítio on 8 September (with celebrations until 23 September), sees a religious mass in the sanctuary and a procession with the image of Our Lady in the streets of Sítio. As Nazaré's big religious festival, it also features sombre processions, folkloric dances and bullfights.

Sleeping

You'll likely be hit up by local women offering rooms for rent. It never hurts to bargain and see what the going rate is. Expect a 30% to 50% discount on rates outside July and August.

Nazaré Hostel HOSTEL €
(918 622 893; www.nazarehostel.com; Rua Nova da Areia 24; dm/d €20/60) This renovated house has modern, pine and white interiors. Offers five airy doubles and two dorms, all with shared bathrooms. The communal kitchen and nice common area are attractive to a young, surfing crowd, especially those after a beach-house experience.

★ **Lab Hostel** HOSTEL €
(www.labhostel.pt; Rua de Rio Maior 4; dm €25-26, d €67-69;) One of Portugal's band of growing 'glostels' (glamorous hostels), this just about takes the cake. Stylish, clean design, attention to detail and some of the whitest, brightest and cleanest rooms around. There's a female dorm, a family room and breakfast is included. Prices here are for August only (they're reduced at other times).

★ **Vila Conde Fidalgo** GUESTHOUSE, APARTMENT €
(262 552 361; www.facebook.com/VilaCondeFidalgo; Avenida da Independência Nacional 21a; d/apt €50/65;) Built around flower-strewn courtyards and patios, this pretty family-run complex a few blocks up from the beach was a former fishermen's colony. Delightful English-speaking owner Ana offers 10 clean, colourful and comfortable rooms with mini-fridges, plus a dozen apartments of varying sizes. Breakfast is €5 extra, served in your room or on the terrace outside.

Parque de Campismo Valado CAMPGROUND €
(262 561 609; www.orbitur.pt; Rua dos Combatentes do Ultramar 2; sites per adult/child/tent/car €6.50/3.90/6.90/6.50; P) This shady, well-equipped year-round Orbitur site has a restaurant, bar and excellent swimming pool as well as bungalows and fixed tents available. It's 2km east of town, off the Alcobaça road.

Magic Art Hotel HOTEL €€
(262 569 040; http://hotelmagic.pt; Rua Mouzinho de Albuquerque 58; s/d €105/110; P) Close to the action, this hotel has gone for the standard current trend, the more ritzy and chic modern look. Clean-lined, well-equipped white rooms with artily presented photos of old-time Nazaré contrast with appealing black-slate bathrooms. It was being re-renovated at the time of research.

Eating

★ **A Tasquinha** SEAFOOD €
(262 551 945; Rua Adrião Batalha 54; mains €7-11; noon-3pm & 7-10.30pm Tue-Sun) This exceptionally friendly family affair has been running for 50-plus years, serving high-quality seafood in a pair of snug but pretty tiled dining rooms. Expect queues on summer nights.

THE BIGGEST WAVE

A tiny black dot on a massive wall of water: footage of surfers riding monster waves at Nazaré has captivated the world in recent years. Given the right conditions, the big ones here can be over 30m high – think an eight-storey office building. The official world record of 23.77m for the biggest wave surfed was set here in 2011 by Garrett McNamara, who nearly bettered the feat with another giant in 2013. The waves are so fast and tall that surfers get towed in by jet-ski.

Why so big? Storms and winds in the Atlantic can generate mighty waves by themselves, but Nazaré has a peculiarity that multiplies this potential: an offshore underwater canyon some 5km deep pointing right at Praia do Norte beach. The energy of the ocean swells is concentrated by this feature, producing the massive waves.

Conchinha da Nazaré SEAFOOD €
(☎262 186 156; Rua de Leiria 17D; mains €7-12; ⏰lunch & dinner) One of the most authentic experiences around, this simple place on a backstreet square serves good-value seafood, including wood-grilled fish and delicious *açorda de marisco* (thick bread soup with seafood; €12). Many nights there are more locals than tourists.

★**Casa Pires** SEAFOOD €€
(Largo de Nosso Sra da Nazaré 45, Sítio; fish per kg €40-50, mains €11-16; ⏰noon-3.30pm & 7-10.30pm Tue-Sun) Many locals think that this is the only place in Nazaré to eat grilled sardines. Enough said. When sardines are out of season, though (read frozen), you can always opt for a grilled fish instead. Stick to the suggestions of whatever is going that day.

Xapa's Taberna PORTUGUESE €€
(www.facebook.com/tabernaxapas; Rua Alexandre Herculano 18; mains €8-15; ⏰10am-2am; 🌶) A refreshing alternative to the local seafood eateries, here the owner-chef cooks up whatever he decides, using organic produce sourced that day. The diverse dishes incorporate traditional and modern cooking methods. On Thursdays and Fridays guitar music sets the mood. Vegetarians rejoice, there are options for you, too.

Drinking & Nightlife

To drink with the locals, check out the bars around Travessa do Elevador.

Casa O Santo BAR
(☎262 085 128; Travessa do Elevador 11; ⏰noon-late) An immensely enjoyable *cervejaria* (beer house) serving beer, wine and tasty seafood snacks (appetisers from €5) – especially recommended are the garlicky steamed *ameijoas* (clams). Grab a table on the pavement, or eat under the stone arches of the cosy interior rooms beside the bustling bar.

Information

Turismo (☎262 561 194; www.cm-nazare.pt; Avenida Vieira Giumarães, Edifício do Mercado Municipal; ⏰9.30am-1pm & 2.30-6pm Oct-Mar, 9.30am-12.30pm & 2.30-6.30pm Apr-Jun, 9am-9pm Jul & Aug) In the front offices of the food market. Helpful, multilingual staff.

Getting There & Away

BUS

Rodotejo (www.rodotejo.pt) and **Rede Expressos** (www.rede-expressos.pt) serve the following destinations several times daily from Nazaré's bus station, a couple of blocks in from the ocean: Alcobaça (€2.20, 20 minutes), Leiria (express/local €6.80/3.80, 40/60 minutes), Lisbon (€11, 1¾ hours) and Peniche (€9.80, 70 minutes).

TRAIN

The nearest train station is in Valado da Frades, 6km east of Nazaré.

Alcobaça

POP 17,800

Only 100km north of Lisbon, the little town of Alcobaça has a charming if touristed centre with a little river and bijou bridges. All, however, yields centre stage to the magnificent 12th-century Mosteiro de Santa Maria de Alcobaça, one of Portugal's memorable Unesco World Heritage Sites.

Sights

★**Mosteiro de Santa Maria de Alcobaça** MONASTERY
(☎262 505 120; www.mosteiroalcobaca.pt; church free, monastery adult/child/family €6, with Tomar & Batalha €15; ⏰9am-5pm Apr-Sep, 9am-5.30pm Oct-Mar) One

of Iberia's great monasteries utterly dominates the town of Alcobaça. Hiding behind the imposing baroque facade lies a high, austere, monkish church (free entry) with a forest of unadorned 12th-century arches. But make sure you visit the rest too: the atmospheric refectory, vast dormitory and other spaces bring back the Cistercian life, which, according to sources, wasn't quite as austere here as it should have been.

The monastery was founded in 1153 by Afonso Henriques, first king of Portugal, honouring a vow he'd made after the reconquest of Santarém in 1147. The monastery estate became one of the richest and most powerful in the country, apparently housing 999 monks, who held Mass nonstop in shifts.

In the 18th century, however, it was the monks' growing decadence that became famous, thanks to the writings of 18th-century travellers such as William Beckford, who, despite his own tendency to exaggerate, was shocked at the 'perpetual gormandising... the fat waddling monks and sleek friars with wanton eyes...'. The party ended in 1834 with the dissolution of the religious orders.

Much of the original facade of the **church** was altered in the 17th and 18th centuries. However, once you step inside, the combination of Gothic ambition and Cistercian austerity hits you immediately: the nave is a breathtaking 106m long but only 23m wide, with huge pillars and truncated columns. It is modelled on the French abbey of Clairvaux.

Occupying the south and north transepts are two intricately carved 14th-century tombs, the church's greatest possessions, which commemorate the tragic love story of Dom Pedro and Dona Inês de Castro. Although the tombs themselves were badly damaged by rampaging French troops in search of treasure in 1811, they still show extraordinary narrative detail. The tombs are inscribed Até ao Fím do Mundo (until the end of the world) and, on Pedro's orders, placed foot to foot so that, when the time comes, they can rise up and see each other straight away.

Nearby, look at the remarkable clay figures in the chapel of St Bernard and the unusual arching in the ambulatory.

The grand **kitchen**, described by Beckford as 'the most distinguished temple of gluttony in all Europe', owes its immense size to alterations carried out in the 18th century, including a water channel built through the middle to divert wild fish right into the kitchen.

The adjacent **refectory**, huge and vaulted, is where the monks ate in silence while the Bible was read to them from the pulpit, reached by a photogenic arched staircase. The monks entered through a narrow door on their way to the refectory; those too fat to pass through were forced to fast.

The beautiful **Claustro do Silencio** (Cloister of Silence) dates from two eras: Dom Dinis built the intricate lower storey, with its arches and traceried stone circles, in the 14th century; the upper storey, typically Manueline in style, was added in the 16th century. Off the northwestern corner of the cloister is the 18th-century **Sala dos Reis** (Kings' Room), so called because statues of practically all the kings of Portugal line the walls. Below them are *azulejo* friezes depicting stories relevant to the abbey's construction. Upstairs, make sure you see the vast vaulted dormitory.

LOVE, POLITICS & REVENGE

As moving as *Romeo and Juliet* – and far more gruesome – is the tragic story of Dom Pedro. Son of the king, Dom Afonso IV, Pedro fell madly in love with his wife's Galician lady-in-waiting, Dona Inês de Castro, with whom he had several children. Even after the death of Pedro's wife, his father forbade Pedro from marrying Inês, wary of her Spanish family's potential influence. Suspicious nobles continued to pressure Dom Afonso IV until finally he sanctioned Inês' murder in 1355, unaware that the two lovers had already secretly married.

Two years later, when Pedro succeeded to the throne, he exacted his revenge by ripping out and eating the hearts of Inês' murderers. He then exhumed and crowned her body, and ordered the court to pay homage to his dead queen by kissing her decomposing hand.

The couple are buried in elaborate tombs in the **Mosteiro de Santa Maria de Alcobaça** (p280). Inês' tomb rests, not on lions, but on the animal-like figures of the men that assassinated her.

Sleeping

Hostel Rossio Alcobaça HOSTEL €
(☎262 598 237; www.hostelrossioalcobaca.pt; Praça 25 de Abril 15; dm €17-18, d without/with bathroom from €32/40; 📶) There are not many places left where you can can enjoy a view of one of the world's top monastery sites, all from your hostel room. This new spot, bang on the main plaza, has been delightfully restored. Clean, bright, minimalist-style rooms are set around a hexagonal design. Shared kitchen and terrace are a bonus.

Hotel Santa Maria HOTEL €
(☎262 590 160; www.hotelsantamaria.com.pt; Rua Dr Francisco Zagalo 20-22; s/d/f €39/56/120; P❄📶) Popular with tour groups, this modern place sits just across from the Mosteiro de Santa Maria de Alcobaça. It's unexciting but has a great location and offers decent value. Book ahead for the front rooms with views of the monastery's facade and square.

★**Challet Fonte Nova** BOUTIQUE HOTEL €€€
(☎262 598 300; www.challetfontenova.pt; Rua da Fonte Nova 8; s/d/ste €85/120/130; P❄📶) Set amid pretty gardens, this elegant, charming, 19th-century chalet has grand common areas with gleaming wood floors, carpets and period furnishings. The main house is especially attractive: sumptuously decorated rooms with big plush beds, tall French windows, and a downstairs self-serve bar with billiard table. There's also a whitewashed modern annexe with suites and a small spa complex.

Eating

★**Restaurante António Padeiro** PORTUGUESE €
(☎262 582 295; www.facebook.com/restauranteantoniopadeiro.alcobaca; Rua Dom Maur Cocheril 27; mains €6-15; ⏲noon-3pm & 7-10pm) If the monks had not pigged out at the Alcobaça monastery (their gluttony was eventually noticed), they would have flocked to this wonderful elegant-but-not-snobby spot. It's clocked up 70 years and for good reason. It boasts a superb atmosphere (traditional trinkets minus the kitsch), super-quality fare from the kitchen and ultra-professional service. The owners know their cuisine. As do the regular locals.

O Cabeço PORTUGUESE €€
(☎914 500 202; www.ocabeco.pt; Rua Dona Elvina Machado 65; mains €9-15; ⏲12.30pm-late Tue-Sat) As the locals say, this is *bem posto* (well situated). And they don't mean just the view. This lovely spot, located on a hill behind Alcobaça, is an understated, modern, wooden and stone cabana with country-garden surrounds. It serves Portuguese dishes with contemporary flair, and is the perfect place to escape the monastery and plaza crowds.

Information

Turismo (☎262 582 377; www.cm-alcobaca.pt; Rua 16 de Outubro 7; ⏲10am-1pm & 2-6pm Oct-Apr, 10am-1pm & 3-7pm May-Sep) In a street near the monastery, providing assistance in multiple languages.

Getting There & Away

Coming from Leiria it's possible to see both Batalha and Alcobaça in a single, carefully timed day on **Rodotejo** (www.rodotejo.pt; Rua Manuel da Silva Carolino) and/or **Rede Expresso** (www.rede-expressos.pt) buses. Note: most buses run less frequently on weekends. Destinations include Batalha (€3.20, 30 minutes, six per weekday), Leiria (€3.85, 50 minutes, six per weekday), Porto do Mos (€3.20, one to three daily), Nazaré (€2.20, 20 minutes, four to six daily), and Lisbon (€11.50, two hours, six per weekday).

Batalha

POP 8500

Among the supreme achievements of Manueline architecture, Batalha's monastery transports visitors to another world, where solid rock has been carved into forms as delicate as snowflakes and as pliable as rope.

Sights

★**Mosteiro de Santa Maria da Vitória** MONASTERY
(☎244 765 497; www.mosteirobatalha.pt; adult/child €6/free, church free, with Alcobaça & Tomar €15; ⏲9am-6.30pm Apr-Sep, 9am-6pm Oct-Mar) The extraordinary abbey of Batalha was built to commemorate the 1385 Battle of Aljubarrota (fought just south of here). Most of the monument was completed by 1434 in Flamboyant Gothic, but Manueline exuberance steals the show, thanks to additions made in the 15th and 16th centuries (the 'unfinished chapels').

At the Battle of Aljubarrota, around 6500 Portuguese, commanded by Dom Nuno Álvares Pereira and supported by a few hundred English soldiers, repulsed a 30,000-strong force of Juan I of Castile, who had come claiming the throne of João d'Avis. João called on the Virgin Mary for help and vowed to build a superb abbey in return for victory. Two years later he made good on his promise, as work began on the Dominican abbey.

The glorious limestone **exterior** bristles with pinnacles and parapets, flying buttresses and balustrades, and late-Gothic carved windows, as well as octagonal chapels and massive columns. The spectacular western doorway's layered arches pack in apostles, angels, saints and prophets, all topped by Christ and the Evangelists.

The vast, vaulted Gothic **interior** is plain, long and high (the highest in Portugal), warmed by light from the deep-hued stained-glass windows. Some of the interior was originally painted. To the right as you enter is the intricate Capela do Fundador (Founder's Chapel), an achingly beautiful, lofty, star-vaulted square room lit by an octagonal lantern. In the centre is the joint tomb (the first pantheon to be built in Portugal) of João I and his English wife, Philippa of Lancaster, whose marriage in 1387 cemented the alliance that still exists between Portugal and England. The tombs of their four youngest sons line the south wall of the chapel, including that of Henry the Navigator (second from the right).

Afonso Domingues, master of works during the late 1380s, built the fabulous **Claustro Real** (Royal Cloister) in a Gothic style, but it's the later Manueline embellishments by the great Mateus Fernandes that really take your breath away. Every arch is a tangle of detailed stone carvings of Manueline symbols, such as armillary spheres and crosses of the Order of Christ, entwined with writhing vegetation, exotic flowers and marine motifs – corn and shells. Three graceful cypresses echo the shape of the Gothic spires atop the adjacent chapter house. (And we challenge you to spot the ancient graffiti on the walls!)

Anything would seem austere after the Claustro Real, but the simple Gothic **Claustro de Dom Afonso V** is like being plunged into cold water – sobering you up after all that frenzied decadence. Between the two cloisters is an interpretation centre.

To the east of the Claustro Real is the early-15th-century chapterhouse, **Sala do Capítulo**, containing a beautiful 16th-century stained-glass window. The huge vault was considered so potentially dangerous that prisoners on death row were employed to remove its supports. A guard of honour overwatches the tomb of unknown soldiers (a Mozambican soldier and Flemish soldier from WWI).

MULTI-MONASTERY TICKET

If you're planning to visit the monasteries at Alcobaça and Batalha, as well as the Convento de Cristo in Tomar, you can get (from any one of them) a combined ticket for €15 (a saving of €3) that will let you in to all three and is valid for a week.

The roofless **Capelas Imperfeitas** (Unfinished Chapels) are perhaps the most astonishing aspect of Batalha. Only accessible from outside the abbey, the octagonal mausoleum with its seven chapels was commissioned in 1437. However, the later Manueline additions by the architect Mateus Fernandes overshadow everything else.

Although Fernandes' plan was never finished, the staggering ornamentation is all the more dramatic for being open to the sky. Most striking is the 15m-high doorway, a mass of stone-carved thistles, ivy, flowers, snails and all manner of 'scollops and twistifications', as William Beckford noted. Dom Duarte can enjoy it for all eternity: his tomb, and that of his wife, lie opposite the door.

Batalha de Aljubarrota Centro de Interpretação BATTLEFIELD

(www.fundacao-aljubarrota.pt; adult/student/child/family €7/5/3.50/20; ⏲10am-5.30pm Tue-Sun) For Portuguese people Aljubarrota conjures up a fierce sense of national pride, a 1385 battle where they defeated an odds-on favourite Castilian force and established the foundations for the Portuguese golden age. We thought the entry fee to the modern interpretation centre here, 3km south of Batalha, was steep until we saw the multimedia show, a no-expenses-spared blood-and-thunder half-hour medieval epic (showing at 11.30am, 3pm and 4.30pm, audioguide €3) that brings the whole thing to vivid life.

The display on bones is also fascinating – one skull still has the tip of an arrowhead in it. The battlefield itself is freely accessible and has some English explanations, but to really understand what went on here, you'll want the audioguide from the interpretation centre. It's available in eight languages.

MCCB MUSEUM

(Museu da Comunidade Concelhia da Batalha; www.museubatalha.com; Largo Goa, Rua Damão e Diu 4; €2.50; ⏲10am-1pm & 2-6pm Wed-Sun) This modern, award-winning municipal museum in the centre of town is well worth the visit, taking you through the prehistory and history of the region, including some well-presented Roman remains and sections on the Battle of Aljubarrota and Mosteiro de Santa Maria da Vitória's construction.

Sleeping

Pensão Gladius GUESTHOUSE €
(244 765 760, 919 103 044; Praça Mouzinho de Albuquerque; d without breakfast €30) In the square right next to the abbey, friendly older proprietor Dona Eglantina runs this snug but attractive place (one of the 'old world' guest houses that's independent of 'official' lists). It's got a vaguely alpine feel, with flower-filled window boxes and three spotless, modern rooms tucked under the eaves. You might get wi-fi signal from the free council zone outside.

Hotel Mestre Afonso Domingues HOTEL €€
(244 765 260; www.hotel.mestreafonsodomingues.pt; Largo Mestre Afonso Domingues 6; s €95, d €105-120, ste €140;) It's smart, it's sleek, it's comfortable. And its positioning doesn't get better than this: smack in front of Batalha's extraordinary monastery (it was a former *pousada* – the official and very plush hotels owned by the Portuguese government). Many rooms have amazing vistas and balconies. The downside is that it's ultra-popular with groups. Good online deals. A reasonable restaurant is attached.

Hotel Casa do Outeiro HOTEL €€
(244 765 806; www.hotelcasadoouteiro.com; Largo Carvalho do Outeiro 4; s/d/tr/f from €60/65/80/135; P) This modern hotel with a guest-house feel was being renovated at the time of research. If past experience is anything to go by, it's an excellent bet. The rooms are all modern, commodious and attractive, and all a little different. Balconies, coffee tray and mini-fridge are standard, as is the excellent breakfast with home-made jams, and a welcome drink on arrival.

Eating

Churrasqueira Vitória GRILL HOUSE €
(244 765 678; Largo da Misericórdia; mains €7-10; noon-3pm & 7-10pm) Neither outstanding nor terrible, this simple, friendly place serves tasty grilled meat and other Portuguese standards. Grab half a chicken for €7 and go home happy. Good-value lunch menus are only €8.

Burro Velho PORTUGUESE €€
(244 764 174; www.burrovelho.com; Rua Nossa Sra do Caminho 6A; dishes €10.50-15.50; noon-3.30pm & 7-10pm Mon-Sat, noon-3.30pm Sun) The pick of Batalha's limited eating options, this bustling place serves up decent dishes. It's run by a young guy who not only works the floor but has established the recipe for success: service flair and quality products. Cuisine is full-on Portuguese, from *alheira* (sausage) to octopus rice, and there's plenty of other sea life in the tanks to choose from.

Information

Turismo (244 765 180; www.descobrirbatalha.pt; Praça Mouzinho de Albuquerque; 10am-1pm & 2-6pm) The very helpful, enthusiastic Nelia has worked here for years and knows the lot. The *turismo* faces the back side of the monastery.

Getting There & Away

Buses with **Rodotejo** (www.rodotejo.pt) and **Rede Expressos** (www.rede-expressos.pt) leave from the stop on Rua do Moinho da Via, near the Intermarché supermarket, behind the police station, very close to the abbey and *turismo*. Express services go to major cities, including Lisbon (€12, two hours) four to five times daily – buy tickets online or at Cafe Frazão behind the church nearby. For Alcobaça, Fátima, Leiria, Nazaré and Tomar, connections are few and schedules change frequently, though with forward planning it can be done. See helpful Nelia in the *turismo* for the rundown.

A taxi to Fátima costs around €25.

Leiria

POP 55,000

Leiria is an agreeable mixture of medieval and modern, a lively university town built at the foot of a promontory fortified since Moorish times. The town's dramatically sited castle is a commanding presence above the narrow streets and red-tiled roofs of the historic centre, built along the lazy curves of the Rio Lis.

Dom Afonso III convened a *cortes* (Portugal's early parliament) here in 1254; Dom Dinis established his main residence in the castle in the 14th century; and in 1411 the town's sizeable Jewish community built Portugal's first paper mill. Modern-day Leiria has a pleasant, low-key urban buzz and makes a convenient base for visiting nearby sights, including Alcobaça, Batalha, Fátima and the Pinhal de Leiria – all easily accessible by bus.

Leiria

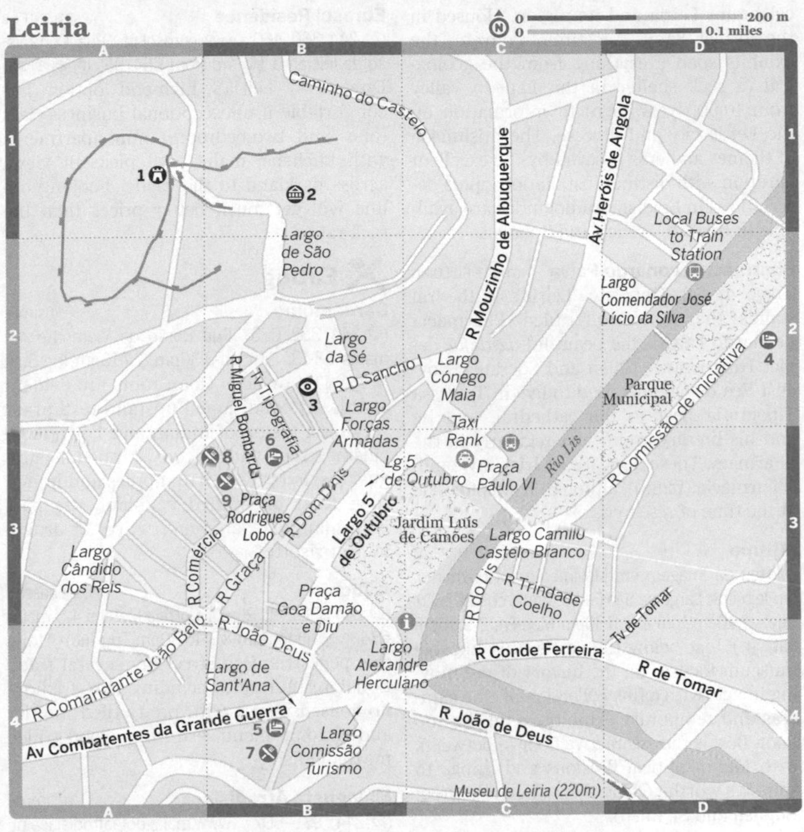

Leiria

Sights
1 Castelo A1
2 M|i|mo B1
3 Pharmácia Leonardo Paiva B2

Sleeping
4 Eurosol Residence D2
5 Hotel Leiria B4
6 Hotel Leiriense B3

Eating
7 A Toca B4
8 Cardamomo B3
9 Malagueta Afrodisíaca B3

Drinking & Nightlife
Pharmácia .... (see 3)

Sights

Castelo CASTLE

(☎244 813 982; www.cm-leiria.pt; adult/child €2.10/free; ⊙9.30am-6.30pm Apr-Sep, 9.30am-5.30pm Oct-Mar) Inside the castle walls is a peaceful garden, overgrown with tall trees, and the ruined but lovely Gothic **Igreja de Nossa Senhora da Penha**, originally built in the 12th century and rebuilt by João I in the early 15th century. It has beautiful leaflike carvings over one arch. The castle's most spectacular feature, however, is a gallery with stone seats. It provides a fantastic vantage point over the town's red-tiled roofs, though the structure is largely the result of restoration.

Museu de Leiria MUSEUM

(☎244 839 677; www.cm-leiria.pt; Santo Agostinho Convent, Rua Tenente Valadim 41; incl Museu do Moinho de Papel €5; ⊙9.30am-5.30pm) Opened in November 2015, this lovely museum celebrates Leiria and its region. Housed in the former Santo Agostinho Convent, the exhibits span everything from the geological (a rock shelter in the Lapedo Valley from 10,000 years ago) to information on the Leiria city and diocese. The mishmash of themes and eras is saved by the excellent curation with distinct installations, plus descriptions in English. Audioguides are available in English, French and Spanish.

Pharmácia Leonardo Paiva NOTABLE BUILDING
(Largo da Sé) Opposite Leiria's cathedral stands the wonderfully tiled Pharmácia Leonardo Paiva – the beautiful *azulejos* depict Hippocrates, Galen and Socrates. Novelist Eça de Queirós used to live in Travessa Tipografia next to the cathedral, and he and his literary group met regularly in the pharmacy. These days, it's an Irish-style pub (Pharmácia (p286)), although it was for sale at the time of research.

M|i|mo MUSEUM
(Museu da Imagem em Movimento; http://mimo.cm-leiria.pt; Largo de São Pedro; adult/child €2.10/free; 10am-1pm & 2-5.30pm Mon-Fri, 2-5.30pm Sat;) Just below the castle, this likeable museum focuses on the history of the moving image, with a fine collection of cine cameras and temporary exhibitions on the top floor. Best is the interactive floor in between, with lots of optical illusions and things to spin. It's worth getting the audioguide (free; English and Spanish).

Sleeping

Hotel Leiria HOTEL €
(244 812 802; hotelleiriaclassic.pt; Rua Dr Correia Mateus 30; s/d/tr from €27.50/37.50/47.50;) In a characterful 1920s blue building on a very central corner, this casual hotel is a curious mishmash of dated and new. However, prices are fair for the budget accommodation and it's smack in the middle of town. The elegance of public areas extends to the spacious rooms, which have balconies. The 'doormat' carpet means no street mud.

Hotel Leiriense HOTEL €
(244 823 054; www.hotelleiriense.com; Rua Afonso de Albuquerque 6; s/d €30/45;) On a cobbled street in the historic centre, this dignified place has a great location and 23 small but decent rooms with double-glazing to keep out street noise. There's a retro appeal to its marble steps, tiled hallways and parquet wood floors.

Eurosol Residence APARTMENT €€
(244 860 460; www.eurosol.pt; Rua Commissão de Iniciativa 13; s/d from €84/96;) Downtown Leiria's high-end option has comfortable if unexceptional business-class (one- and two-bedroom) mini-apartments with kitchens, many with pleasant views across parkland to the castle. Booking online will get much better prices than the rack rates.

Eating

Cardamomo FUSION €
(244 832 033; Rua Barão de Viamonte 43; mains €8-13; noon-3.30pm & 7-10pm Tue-Sun;) The owner's Goan roots are evident at this air-conditioned upstairs restaurant serving a fusion of Indian and Portuguese cuisine. Start with bacon-wrapped asparagus or salad greens with apples and honey, then feast on stuffed eggplant, sea bass with mango, Goan *xacuti* curry or arugula-beet risotto.

A Toca PORTUGUESE €
(244 832 221; Rua Dr Correia Mateus 42; mains €7-13; noon-3pm & 7-10.30pm Thu-Tue) Along this pedestrianised street are several traditional restaurants, including this friendly, no-nonsense spot with pretty tiled interior and a long menu featuring wood-grilled meat and fish.

Malagueta Afrodisíaca FUSION €€
(244 831 607; www.malaguetaafrodisiaca.pt; Rua Gago Coutinho 17; mains €12-15; 7pm-midnight;) For a rare deviation from standard Portuguese fare, head to this trendy, slinkily decorated place, tucked down a narrow street in the historic centre. The eclectic 10-page menu features aphrodisiac teas, flaming desserts, mixed drinks, and a dizzying collection of Brazilian, Mexican and other overseas-influenced dishes. This is a place to linger; service can be quite slow.

Drinking & Nightlife

Bars are scattered throughout the historic centre, and the student population keeps things hopping.

Pharmácia PUB
(Largo da Sé 9; 9.30pm-3.30am Mon-Sat) Set inside a marvellously tiled 19th-century pharmacy (p286) directly opposite the cathedral, this Irish-style bar features a mellow vibe, darts and a vast universe of drinks.

Information

Turismo (☎244 848 770; www.turismodocentro.pt; Jardim Luís de Camões; ⊙9am-6pm Mon-Fri, 9am-1pm & 2-6pm Sat & Sun) Provides a free town map. Might be moving location; check the website for the current address.

Getting There & Away

BUS

Rodotejo (www.rodotejo.pt) and **Rede Expressos** (www.rede-expressos.pt) both serve the **bus station** (Largo 5 de Outubro) in the heart of town. Buses run every hour or two to Alcobaça (€3.55, 50 minutes), Batalha (€1.95, 20 minutes), Coimbra (€9, 50 minutes), Fátima (€3.35 to €6, 25 to 45 minutes), Lisbon (€12.50, two hours) and Nazaré (express/local €6.80/3.80, 40/60 minutes).

TRAIN

Leiria is on the train line that runs about three times daily from Figueira da Foz (€5, one hour) to the Mira Sintra-Meleças station near Lisbon (€10.35 to €11.40, 2½ to 3½ hours). The station is 4km northwest; local bus 4 runs here frequently from Largo Comendador José Lúcio da Silva (€1.25, 10 minutes). A taxi costs about €5.

Pinhal de Leiria

First planted by a forward-looking monarch some 700 years ago, the Pinhal de Leiria is a vast forest of towering pines whose fragrance and stippled shade make this one of the loveliest stretches of Portugal's Atlantic coast. Dom Dinis expanded it significantly as a barrier against encroaching dunes and also as a source of timber for the maritime industry – a great boon during the Age of Discoveries.

Today, the protected forest covers more than 100 sq km along the coast west of Leiria. Narrow roads and well-maintained bike paths cut through it, leading to a number of really excellent beaches and three resort towns: São Pedro de Moel, 20km west of Leiria; Praia da Vieira, 16km north of São Pedro along the coastal highway; and Pedrógão, 2km further north.

Sleeping

São Pedro de Moel's accommodation is the most appealing of the three towns.

Orbitur CAMPGROUND €
(☎244 599 168; www.orbitur.pt; São Pedro de Moel; sites per adult/child/tent/car €6.40/3.20/8.40/5.90; P wi-fi pool) In among the pine trees but in the centre of town, this well-equipped, pretty site includes a swimming pool, disabled facilities and a playground. Two-/four-/five-person bungalows cost €92/102/107 in August or €67/77/82 the rest of the summer.

Hotel Mar e Sol HOTEL €€
(☎244 590 000; www.hotelmaresol.com; Avenida da Liberdade 1, São Pedro de Moel; r €85-130; air-con wi-fi) This well-refurbished hotel is comfortable and sparkling clean, with minimalist modern decor. It's showing ever-so-slight signs of wear, but is in a great position; the best rooms, with balconies and grand views over the tussling sea, cost €35 to €45 extra. There's a rooftop sun-deck and a gym and spa complex (costing extra) and good low-season discounts.

Eating

Bambi Café CAFE €
(Avenida da Liberdade, São Pedro de Moel; snacks €4-5.50; ⊙1pm-2am Jul-Sep, 1pm-2am Sat Oct-Jun; wi-fi) Portuguese beer on tap, wi-fi, and comfy couches on an outdoor deck overlooking the pine-tree-filled park are the big draws at this cool, glass-walled cafe.

O Pai dos Frangos PORTUGUESE €€
(☎244 599 158; Praia Velha; mains €13-20; ⊙10am-late Jun-Sep, 10am-10pm Tue-Sun Oct-May) 'The Father of Chickens' sits in splendid isolation right on the fabulous sands of Praia Velha, 1km north of São Pedro de Moel. Specialities include *arroz de marisco* (paella-like rice and seafood stew) and *terramar* (a massive dish of beef, lobster, clams and french fries for a minimum of two people; €25 per person). Plus, yes, there's grilled chicken.

★**Estrela do Mar** SEAFOOD €€€
(☎244 599 245; Avenida Marginal, São Pedro de Moel; mains €14-22, fish per kg €40-55; ⊙noon-2am summer, noon-midnight Wed-Mon winter) In an utterly memorable position on the water, this classic seafood place scores top marks for location: the dining room is right over the waves above São Pedro's town beach. Prices here partly reflect the unbeatable view, but the quality and atmosphere are great.

Getting There & Away

From Leiria there are at least six daily buses to São Pedro de Moel (€3, 40 minutes) and Praia da Vieira (€3.35, 45 minutes). If driving from Leiria, follow signs for Marinha Grande first.

Fátima

Whatever your beliefs, you can't help but be impressed by the vast reserves of faith that every year lead as many as six million people to the glade where, on 13 May 1917, the Virgin Mary is said to have first appeared to three awestruck peasant children. Where sheep once grazed there are now two huge basilicas on opposite ends of a vast 1km-long esplanade.

Before this event, there was nothing here (little can grow on limestone, which is what the area is comprised of). These days, it's another story.

For Catholic pilgrims Fátima has a magnetic appeal like few places on earth, and whatever your faith, or otherwise, a trip here will provide you with new insights into Portugal's religious culture.

Fátima is packed with boarding houses and restaurants for the pilgrim masses, plus hundreds of shops crowded with glow-in-the-dark Virgins and busts of the Pope.

Sights

Santuário de Fátima CHRISTIAN SITE
(☎249 539 600; www.fatima.pt) FREE It's difficult to believe that a century ago, this was rocky pastureland outside an insignificant village. This vast complex is now one of Catholicism's major shrines; the focus of enormous devotion and pilgrimage. At the eastern end is the 1953 **Basílica de Nossa Senhora do Rosário de Fátima**, a triumphantly sheer-white building with colonnade reminiscent of St Peter's. Nearby, the **Capela das Aparições** (Chapel of the Apparitions) marks the site where the Virgin appeared.

At the precinct's western end is the **Basílica da Santíssima Trindade**. In between is a massive space where the crowds gather.

The Capela das Aparições is the focus of the most intense devotion. Supplicants who have promised penance (for example, in return for helping a loved one who is sick, or to signify a particularly deep conversion) shuffle on their knees across the vast esplanade, following a long marble runway polished smooth by previous penitents. Near the chapel is a blazing pyre where people light candles in prayer. The sound of hundreds of candles is like a rushing waterfall.

Inside the older church, the Basílica de Nossa Senhora do Rosário de Fátima, attention is focused on the tombs of the three children, Os Três Pastorinhos (the three little shepherds): Francisco (died 1919, aged 11) and Jacinta (died 1920, aged 10), both victims of the flu epidemic, were beatified in 2000. Lúcia, the third witness of the apparition, entered a convent in Coimbra in 1928, where she died in 2005. Her beatification is underway.

The new basilica, Basílica da Santíssima Trindade, was inaugurated in 2007, and, while impressive, has something of a conference-centre feel. A central passageway hung with golden angels leads to a long etched-glass window spelling out scriptural verses in dozens of languages. Running around the edges of the monumental, round marble structure are 12 9m bronze doors, each with a biblical quote dedicated to one of Jesus' disciples. Inside, the impersonal feel is redeemed by Irish artist Catherine Green's striking altarpiece depicting a wild-haired and gaunt Crucifixion, backed by Slovenian artist Marko Ivan Rupnik's beautiful mosaic work.

At the sanctuary entrance is a segment of the Berlin Wall, a tribute to 'God's part in the fall of communism'.

Masses are held (in Portuguese) regularly, often in the Capelinha das Aparições; check at the information booth near the chapel.

Grutas da Moeda CAVE
(☎244 703 838; www.grutasmoeda.com; São Mamede; adult/child €6/3, joint ticket with Centro de Interpretação €8/2; 9am-5pm Oct-Mar, to 6pm Apr-Jun, to 7pm Jul-Sep) These underground caves, located 2km northwest of Fátima, are part of the surrounding limestone massif. They were discovered in 1971 when two hunters chased a fox that disappeared into a hole. Visitors can enter the caves (which are atmospherically lit and are an extraordinary 20°C), descending via steps to a depth of 45m on a 350m circuit. It won't ping the 'wow, the best thing ever' scale, though it's interesting. Tours are fully guided (English, German and French guides available; 30 minutes).

Sleeping

Avenida de Fátima HOTEL €
(☎249 534 171; www.hotelavenidadefatima.com; Avenida José Alves Correia da Silva; s/d €30/45; P ❄ ☎) Modern with spick-and-span rooms with every contemporary comfort, this is an excellent deal not far from the basilica. Prices are a steal for this standard, and there are convenient family rooms available.

Eating

O Crispim PORTUGUESE €€
(☎249 532 781; www.ocrispim.com; Rua S João Eudes 23; mains €10-20; ⊙lunch & dinner Tue-Sun) It's worth seeking this place out for an atmosphere full of good cheer without any ostentatious piety. It's a comfortably rustic sort of place serving house wine in wooden tankards and whose speciality is grilled meats – Iberian pork, and succulent beef from the north of Portugal, flame-grilled on the back patio. Prices are by weight, but are reasonable.

Getting There & Away

BUS

Fátima (sometimes called Cova da Iria on timetables) is a stop on most major north–south bus runs. The following destinations are served by regular buses with **Rede Expressos** (www.rede-expressos.pt): Coimbra (€11.30, one to 1¼ hours), Lisbon (€12, 1½ hours) and Porto (€17.50, two hours). **Rodotejo** (www.rodotejo.pt) has buses heading to Leiria (€3.20), mainly in mid-morning and late afternoon. Weekend services are severely limited.

TRAIN

Fátima's train station is 21km east: buses are a much better option.

Porto de Mós

POP 6000

Dominated by a 13th-century hilltop castle, Porto de Mós is an untouristy town on the little Rio Lena that makes a good launchpad for exploring the mountains and caves of the adjacent Parque Natural das Serras de Aire e Candeeiros.

Porto de Mós became a major Roman settlement whose residents used the Lena to ferry millstones from a nearby quarry. The region remains an important centre for quarrying the black-and-white stones used in *calçada portuguesa,* the mosaic-style pavements seen throughout Portugal.

Sights

Estrada Romana RUINS
About 15 minutes northeast of Porto de Mós by car (and signed from near the castle), a section of ancient Roman road has been converted into a walking trail. Marked with red and yellow blazes, the old road bed meanders through the hills for 9km; the most impressive section is at the signposted trailhead above the town of Alqueidão da Serra.

Castelo CASTLE
(www.municipio-portodemos.pt; over/under 25yr €1.50/0.75; ⊙10am-12.30pm & 2-6pm Tue-Sun May-Sep, to 5.30pm Oct-Apr) The green-towered castle was originally a Moorish stronghold. Conquered definitively in 1148 by Dom Afonso Henriques, it was largely rebuilt in 1450 and again after the 1755 earthquake. These days it's too pristine to be convincingly medieval, but is fun to climb around and has pleasant views across the valley to the Serras de Aire e Candeeiros. Stick around until closing and watch 'em lock up with a key the size of your forearm.

Activities

Ecopista WALKING
(https://pt-br.facebook.com/EcopistaPortodeMos) Opened in 2012, this neat, gravel trail heads along former railway tracks in the days when small trains shunted coal from the Mina São Pedro. It's around 3km one way (6km return along the same track), carved into the mountainside and providing great views over Porto de Mós and surrounds.

Sleeping

Quinta de Rio Alcaide RURAL APARTMENT €
(☎244 482 207, 968 434 115; www.rioalcaide.com; Rio Alcaide; d from €35; P ⛱) About 1km southeast of Porto de Mós, this rustic inn is set in a converted 18th-century paper mill. The rooms and apartments are charming, including one in a hilltop windmill, and another that, in 1973, served as a meeting place for Portuguese captains plotting the Revolution of the Carnations. The grounds feature a pool, citrus trees, hiking trails and a cascading stream.

Eating

Dom Lambuças PORTUGUESE €€
(Rua Monsenhor José Cacela, Alcaria; snacks €7-8; ⊙lunch & dinner Wed-Mon) In the small village of Alcaria, this welcoming and very genuine old-school *petisqueiria* (place selling huge portions of *petiscos,* or tapas) with its red awnings gets the thumbs up for all things local and of high quality. Fabulous value.

Tasquinha D'Maria PORTUGUESE €€
(Rua Principal 155, Livramento; mains €7-12; ⊙lunch & dinner Tue-Sun) This rustic spot, with traditional paraphernalia from rural workers, is nothing fancy. But it serves up honest

fare and great grills with excellent-quality local meats. And the locals rave about it.

Adega do Luis PORTUGUESE €€

(☎964 103 287; www.adegadoluis.pt; Rua Principal 650, Livramento; mains €13-20; ⏰12.30-3pm & 7-10pm Wed-Mon) Some 3km southeast of Porto de Mós, this delightful (if touristy) place with high ceilings, stone walls and a roaring fire in the brick oven serves grilled bacon, lamb chops, Iberian pork and *picanha* (rump steak), with pear tart for dessert. Call ahead outside summer as hours fluctuate according to demand.

Information

Turismo (☎244 491 323; www.municipio-portodemos.pt; Jardim Público; ⏰10am-1pm & 2-6pm Mon-Sat) Near the town's main roundabout in the building marked 'Espaço Jovem'; it has free internet terminals and a useful booklet on walks and bike paths.

Getting There & Away

There are two to three buses each weekday to/from Leiria (€3.20, 45 minutes) via Batalha (€2.20, 15 minutes). There are also up to four daily buses to Alcobaça (€3.20, 35 minutes).

Parque Natural das Serras de Aire e Candeeiros

With its barren limestone heights crisscrossed by hiking trails, this natural park east of Porto de Mós is a popular and very beautiful place for outdoor pursuits.

Once the haunt of dinosaurs, the park is famous for its cathedral-like caves, but above ground it's also scenic, particularly the high Planalto de Santo António (starting 2km south of the Grutas de Santo António). Gorse- and olive-grove-covered hills are divided by an irregular grid of dry-stone walls and threaded by cattle trails, all making for tempting rambles.

Sights

Fórnea CANYON

(www.municipio-portodemos.pt/page.aspx?id=405) FREE Don't miss stunning Fórnea, Europe's largest natural amphitheatre (around 1km in diameter) in the middle of the limestone park. You can enter from two directions but must go most of the way on foot. The first entrance is signed at Alcaria road. Park at the snack bar; it's a 20-minute walk to the base. To enter from the topside for incredible views, head to Chão das Pias village. A sign shows the way (best to ask); the site is due east – a 15-minute walk.

Monumento Natural das Pegadas dos Dinossáurios DINOSAUR FOOTPRINTS

(☎249 530 160; www.pegadasdedinossaurios.org; Estrada de Fátima, Bairro; adult/child €3/2; ⏰10am-12.30pm & 2-6pm Tue-Sun, to 8pm Sat & Sun end Mar-end Sep; 👪) On the N357 10km south of Fátima in the village of Bairro, this extraordinary quarry is one of the most important locations for sauropod prints in the world, with more than a thousand individual prints. Visits start with a 20-minute video in Portuguese, followed by a 1.5km walk around the quarry, first seeing the prints from above then walking among them.

These, the oldest and longest sauropod tracks in the world, record walks in the mud a trifling 175 million years ago. The dinos would have been stepping through carbonated mud, later transformed into limestone. As you walk across the slope you can clearly see the large elliptical prints made by the hind feet and the smaller, half-moon prints made by the forefeet.

Mira de Aire CAVE

(☎244 440 322; www.grutasmiradaire.com; Mira de Aire; adult/child €6.60/3.90; ⏰9.30am-8pm Jul & Aug, 9.30am-7pm Jun & Sep, 9.30am-6pm Apr-May, 9.30am-5.30pm Oct-Mar; 👪) Portugal's largest cave system, 14km southeast of Porto de Mós, is very commercial and old-fashioned, although the caves themselves are impressive. The 45-minute tour's spiralling 110m descent leads through psychedelically lit chambers to a final cavern containing a lake with a rather hokey fountain display. There's also a children's zoo and an aquapark here. There are three Rodotejo buses weekdays from Porto de Mós (€2.65, 35 minutes).

Grutas de Alvados & Grutas de Santo António CAVE

(☎249 841 876; www.grutasalvados.com; adult/child per cave €5.80/3.60, both caves €9/6; ⏰10am-6.30pm Jul & Aug, 10am-5pm Sep-Jun) Discovered in 1964, these caves are the spiky smaller cousins of Mira de Aire, with similarly disco-flavoured lighting. These caves are about 15km southeast of Porto de Mós, and 2km and 3.5km, respectively, south of the N243 from Porto de Mós to Mira de Aire.

Sleeping

Pousada de Juventude Alvados HOSTEL €
(☎244 441 202; www.pousadasjuventude.pt; Barreira de Água, Alvados; dm €13, d without/with bathroom €30/34, f without bathroom €45-50; ⏲Dec-Oct; P 📶) This friendly, sparkling, modern place 8km southeast of Porto de Mós has four-bed dorms, doubles with and without private bathrooms, kitchen and wheelchair-accessible facilities. The helpful and long-standing manager, Joana, can give you the rundown of what's in the area. Buses from Leiria (€4.50, 55 minutes) stop in front twice daily from Tuesday to Saturday.

Cooking & Nature Emotional Hotel DESIGN HOTEL €€€
(☎244 447 000; www.cookinghotel.com; Rua Asseguia das Lages 181, Alvados; d €159; P 📶 🏊) This boutique hotel is located in Alvados, a quaint rural village. Each of the rooms is whimsically decorated in line with an emotion: Meditation, Melancholy, Fun, Nostalgia etc. It's clever, though the design elements are hardly understated. The result is a blast of design gimmicks from the sublime (unique rooms with vistas) to the less so (plaques in English lettering).

Information

Park Headquarters (ICNF; Instituto da Conservação da Natureza e das Florestas; ☎243 999 480; www.icnf.pt; Rua Dr Augo César Silva Ferreira, Rio Maior; ⏲9am-12.30pm & 2-5.30pm Mon-Fri) In the town of Rio Maior, south of the park.

Getting There & Away

Parque Natural das Serras de Aire e Candeeiros can be tricky to get to and this is one spot you might like to explore with your own wheels.

RIBATEJO

Literally meaning 'Above the Tejo', Ribatejo is the only Portuguese province that doesn't border either Spain or the open ocean. A string of Templar castles are proof of its strategic importance, though these days its clout is economic, thanks to industry along the Tejo and the rich agricultural plains that spread out from the river's banks. This is also bull country – most of Portugal's fighters are bred in and around the capital, Santarém.

Santarém

POP 29,200

Contemplating the staggering views from Santarém's Portas do Sol atop the old town walls, it's easy to understand why Roman, Visigoth, Moorish and Portuguese armies all wanted to claim this strategic stronghold above the Rio Tejo. Dom Afonso Henriques' storming of these heights in 1147 marked a turning point in the Reconquista and quickly became the stuff of Portuguese national legend.

A group of beautiful Gothic buildings recalls Santarém's glory days, though it was quickly eclipsed by Lisbon. These days, the traditional centre with its venerable stores and workshops still functioning amid a general air of genteel decay makes it worth a visit, as do the heart-lifting vistas. What it lacks in accommodation options it makes up for with its atmospheric restaurants.

History

One of the most important cities of Lusitania under Julius Caesar, and prized by the Moors under the name Xantarim for almost 400 years, Santarém already had centuries of history under its belt before passing to Portuguese rule in 1147. So great was Dom Afonso Henriques' joy at conquering this legendarily impenetrable citadel that he built the magnificent Mosteiro de Santa Maria de Alcobaça in gratitude.

WINES OF RIBATEJO

For years, Ribatejo wines were considered good, honest jug stuff, while the really good vintages came from Alentejo. However, the 21st century has seen winemakers pursuing more experimental techniques and exploiting more labour-intensive, higher-quality terrains on the stony hillsides. In 2000 the region, now called simply Tejo, won DOC status (DOC stands for Denominação de Origem Controlada, the best wine certification in Portugal). For information about vineyards and suggested do-it-yourself itineraries, head to www.winesofportugal.info, or pick up one of ViniPortugal's free wine-route maps, available at tourist offices.

Santarém

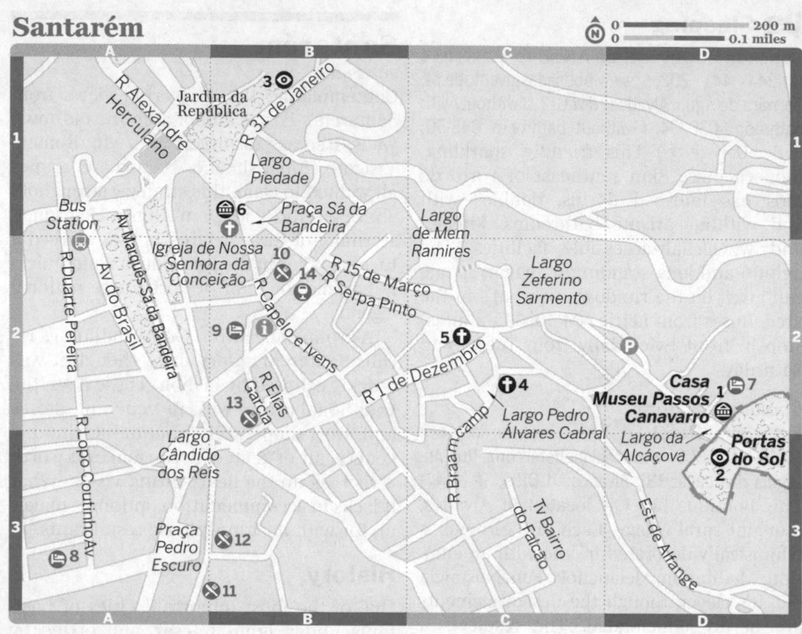

Santarém

Top Sights
1 Casa Museu Passos Canavarro D2
2 Portas do Sol D3

Sights
3 Convento de São Francisco B1
4 Igreja da Santa Maria Graça C2
5 Igreja de Marvila C2
6 Museu Diocesano de Santarém B1

Sleeping
7 Casa da Alcáçova D2
8 Hotel Vitória A3
9 Santarém Hostel B2

Eating
10 O Saloio B2
11 Taberna do Quinzena B3
12 Taberna O Balcão B3
13 Tascá B2

Drinking & Nightlife
14 Taberna e Mercearia Sebastião B2

Sights

★Casa Museu Passos Canavarro MUSEUM
(☎243 325 709; www.fundacaopassoscanavarro.pt; Largo da Alcáçova 1; adult/child €5/free; ⏱10am-1pm & 3-6pm Tue-Sun) Right by the Portas do Sol and sharing some of the same privileged views, this is a unique place to visit for lovers of art and beauty. The historic house, once home to 19th-century liberal politician Passos Manuel, is stocked with artistic treasures and curios, from Japanese furniture and *netsuke* (miniature sculptures) to 16th-century maps and collections of 20th-century art.

★Portas do Sol GARDENS
(Gates of the Sun; ⏱9am-11pm May-Sep, 9am-8pm Oct-Apr) FREE Occupying the site of the Moorish citadel, the Portas do Sol garden proffers utterly majestic views over the Rio Tejo and the great spread of plains that surround it. The garden's shady walks make a fine option for a picnic or afternoon linger. It's particularly spectacular at sundown.

Igreja de Marvila CHURCH
(Largo de Marvila; ⏲10am-12.30pm & 2-5.30pm) FREE Dating from the 12th century but with 16th-century additions, this endearing little church has a fine, twisted Manueline doorway, while the interior is completely awash in brilliant, dramatically patterned *azulejos* dating from the 17th century.

Museu Diocesano de Santarém MUSEUM
(www.museudiocesanodesantarem.pt; Praça Sá da Bandeira; €4; ⏲10am-1pm & 2-6pm Mon-Fri, to 7pm Sat & Sun) Recently reopened after five years of renovation, this small but excellent museum, in a former Jesuit college adjoining the cathedral, holds a lovely collection of restored religious artworks from its diocese. Around 200 works span the 13th to 19th centuries and descriptions are in English. The oldest piece is a tempera painting of the Annunciation and there is a most remarkable statue of Christ, depicted in a rare pose, half on and half off the cross.

Convento de São Francisco MONASTERY
(Rua 31 de Janeiro; €2; ⏲9am-12.30pm & 2-5.30pm Wed-Sun) This restored 13th-century Franciscan monastery is a fine example of Portuguese Gothic. Especially lovely is the cloister, with graceful twinned columns and arches. It's also a venue for temporary exhibitions.

Igreja da Santa Maria Graça CHURCH
(Largo Pedro Álvares Cabral; ⏲9am-12.30pm & 2-5.30pm) FREE This early-15th-century church, with its delicately carved facade of multilayered arches, is a Santarém jewel. Inside, a rose window spills light across the beautifully spare interior of stone columns and white walls. Note the tombs of Pedro Álvares Cabral (the 'discoverer' of Brazil, who lived in Santarém) and Dom Pedro de Menezes, the first governor of the *Ceuta e do Império* (City and of the Empire; Vila Real).

Igreja de Nossa Senhora da Conceição CATHEDRAL
(Sé; Praça Sá da Bandeira; €4 with Museu Diocesano de Santarém) FREE This baroque, 17th-century Jesuit church, built on the site of the former royal palace, looms over the town's most impressive square, Praça Sá da Bandeira. The church now serves as the town's cathedral. Inside is a lush baroque ceiling bursting with angels, plus a number of elaborately gilded altars. Unless a mass is underway, entry is via the recently opened Museu Diocesano de Santarém.

Festivals & Events

Feira Nacional da Agricultura FAIR
(www.cnema.pt) Promoting agricultural and food products, this is famous nationwide for its merriment, concerts, horse races, bullfights and night-time bull-running. It lasts 10 days in the first half of June and mostly takes place 2km west of the town centre.

Sleeping

★ **Santarém Hostel** HOSTEL €
(☎243 322 256; www.santaremhostel.blogspot.pt; Rua Eng António Júnior 26; dm/s/d €15/30/40, 4-person r €70) One of Portugal's best 'glostels' (glamorous hostels), this place is spot on: helpful owner Mario runs a great ship, from the neat, airy, brightly decorated rooms (each with en suite), to the massive home-away-from-home lounge room complete with TV, guitar and designer sofas. There's also a sunny patio and cosy bar (with Mario's amazing guitar collection). A top location in the historic centre.

Hotel Vitória GUESTHOUSE €
(☎243 309 130; hotelvitoriasantarem@gmail.com; Rua Segundo Visconde de Santarém 21; s €29, d €45-60; ❄📶) This night-at-your-great-aunt's-type place was due to have a big overhaul at the time of research. Friendly young owner. Should be worth checking the place out.

Casa da Alcáçova HISTORIC HOTEL €€€
(☎243 304 030; www.alcacova.com; Largo da Alcáçova 3; r €135-175; P❄📶🏊) With the atmosphere of a stylish country retreat, but right in the city, this secluded manor house is set by its own section of the city walls, offering spectacular views from the ramparts and many of the rooms. The interior, although lovely, is a bit can't-put-your-feet-up sumptuous and, crammed with antiques and attitude to match, it's not to everyone's taste.

Eating

★ **Taberna do Quinzena** PORTUGUESE €
(www.quinzena.com; Rua Pedro de Santarém 93; mains €6-9; ⏲lunch & dinner Mon-Sat) This fabulous, atmospheric neighbourhood hang-out is well worth a visit. Its theme is *forcadeiros* (Portuguese bullfighters) and it celebrates these through its posters, photos and paraphernalia. But as far as the cuisine goes – look at the walls' worth of awards. Dishes are very local – delicious plates of grilled

pork or fish, washed down with cheap, local Ribatejo wine straight from the barrel.

O Saloio PORTUGUESE €
(Travessa do Montalvo 11; mains €6.50-14; ⌚lunch & dinner Mon-Fri, lunch Sat) This cosy, tiled, family-friendly *tasca* is a neighbourhood favourite thanks to its authentic Portuguese dishes. Drop your inhibitions and discover the local specialities; ask owner Senhor Artur what the dish of the day is.

Taberna O Balcão PORTUGUESE €€
(Rua Pedro de Santarém 73; mains €12.50-16; ⌚noon-11pm Mon-Thu, noon-midnight Fri & Sat) This place has the flavour of Ribatejo, from traditional Portugal recipes to modern dishes such as a Black Angus beef hamburger. The decor – a mix of modern and old – is done with flair: marble-topped tables, ceramic plates on the walls, and stunning retro-Ribatejan tiles. It's traditional with a modern twist and appeals to those who enjoy well, nice things.

Tascá TAPAS €€
(facebook.com/TASCAnanet; Rua Arco de Manços 8; petiscos €4.50-7; ⌚noon-2am) Bright, fun and contemporary, this loosely Spanish-themed bar attracts a trendy, younger crowd. It does innovative *petiscos*, high on presentation and taste from its open kitchen. Most of the socialising goes on around the barrels or on the great terrace outside. Friday to Sunday brings on special main dishes (€8 to €12).

Drinking & Nightlife

Taberna e Mercearia Sebastião BAR
(www.tabernaemerceariasebastiao.blogspot.com; Travessa do Froes 13; ⌚noon-3pm & 7-11pm Mon-Sat) This 19th-century grocer's shop has had a sympathetic modern refit and now presents a cool, characterful, intimate space. You can eat well here (mains €8 to €16) – best are the specials – and for just a snack, the *petisco* plates with a quarter of wine go down a treat for €3.50. It opens for coffee from 10am.

Information

Turismo (☎243 304 437; www.cm-santarem.pt; Rua Capelo e Ivens 63; ⌚10am-8pm Mon-Fri, 9.30am-1pm & 2-5.30pm Sat & Sun)

Getting There & Away

The train station is 2.4km northeast and steeply downhill from the centrally located **bus station** (☎243 333 200; Avenida do Brasil). Local buses run regularly between the two stations on weekdays and Saturday mornings (€1.40, 10 minutes). Taxis charge about €5.

BUS

Rede Expressos (www.rede-expressos.pt) and **Rodotejo** (www.rodotejo.pt) operate at least three times daily (more frequently to Lisbon) to: Coimbra (€14, 2¼ hours), Fátima (€9.10, 45 minutes), Leiria (€12.20, 1¼ hours) and Lisbon (€7.60, one hour).

TRAIN

Very frequent IC (€11.70) and local (€7.35) trains go to Lisbon (45 minutes to one hour).

Constância & Castelo de Almourol

POP 1000

Constância's compact cluster of whitewashed houses, cobbled lanes and narrow staircases spills picturesquely down a steep hillside to the confluence of the Rios Tejo and Zêzere. It's a sleepy, pretty village whose leafy riverfront promenade, main square and gardens make a lovely place for lunch or a stroll before moving on to the biggest draw in these parts, nearby Castelo de Almourol.

Sights

Castelo de Almourol CASTLE
(⌚10am-1pm & 2.30-7.30pm Mar-Oct, 10am-1pm & 2.30-5.30pm Nov-Feb) Like the stuff of legend, 10-towered Castelo de Almourol stands tantalisingly close to shore but just out of reach in the Rio Tejo. The castle is 5km from Constância. Boats (€2.50, five minutes) leave regularly from a riverside landing directly opposite the castle. Once on the island, a short walk leads up to the ramparts, where you're free to linger as long as you like.

The island, almost jumping distance from land, was once the site of a Roman fort; the castle was built by Gualdim Pais, Grand Master of the Order of the Knights Templar, in 1171. It's no surprise that Almourol has long caught the imagination of excitable poets longing for the Age of Chivalry.

Buses run between Constância and Tancos, passing near the castle.

Sleeping

Casa João Chagas GUESTHOUSE €
(☎249 739 403; www.casajoaochagas.com; Rua João Chagas, Constância; s/d €34/50; P❄📶) Set in the former town hall and another

building opposite, this excellent place offers large, simple, modernised rooms with comfortable beds and a good attitude. It's right in the centre of things just off the main square near the river.

Information

Turismo (☎249 730 052; www.cm-constancia.pt; Avenida das Forças Armadas; ⊙10.30am-5pm Mon-Fri, noon-5pm Sat & Sun) In the municipal offices in the centre of town.

Getting There & Away

BUS

Constância is easily reached by bus from Tomar (€2.45, 40 minutes). **Rodotejo** (www.rodotejo.pt) runs four buses on weekdays to Tancos (20 minutes), which will drop you at the turn-off to the castle, from where it's a 10-minute walk.

CAR

If driving your own vehicle, exit the A23/IP6 at Constância and follow signs to the castle.

TRAIN

To visit the castle only, take a local train (changing at Entroncamento) from Tomar (€3.25, 55 minutes) or Santarém (€4, 45 minutes, some direct services) to tiny Almourol station, then walk 1km downhill to the ferry landing. The train station nearest Constância – known as Praia do Ribatejo – is 2km outside town, so the bus is a better option if you're only visiting Constância.

Tomar

POP 16,000

Tomar is one of central Portugal's most appealing small towns. With its pedestrian-friendly historic centre, its pretty riverside park frequented by swans, herons and families of ducks, and its charming natural setting adjacent to the lush Mata Nacional dos Sete Montes (Seven Hills National Forest), it wins lots of points for aesthetics.

But to understand what makes Tomar truly extraordinary, cast your gaze skyward to the crenellated walls of the Convento de Cristo, which forms a beautiful backdrop from almost any vantage point. Eight-and-a-half centuries after its founding, this venerable headquarters of the legendary Knights Templar is a rambling concoction of Gothic, Manueline and Renaissance architecture that bears extravagant witness to its integral role in centuries of Portuguese history, from the founding of Portugal as a nation-state to the Age of Discoveries.

Sights

★Convento de Cristo MONASTERY

(www.conventocristo.pt; Rua Castelo dos Templários; adult/under 12yr €6/free, with Alcobaça & Batalha €15; ⊙9am-6.30pm Jun-Sep, 9am-5.30pm Oct-May) Wrapped in splendour and mystery, the Knights Templar held enormous power in Portugal from the 12th to 16th centuries, and largely bankrolled the Age of Discoveries. Their headquarters sit on wooded slopes above the town and are enclosed within 12th-century walls. The Convento de Cristo is a stony expression of magnificence, founded in 1160 by Gualdim Pais, Grand Master of the Templars. It has chapels, cloisters and choirs in diverging styles, added over the centuries by successive kings and Grand Masters.

The **Charola**, the extraordinary 16-sided Templar church, thought to be in imitation of the Church of the Holy Sepulchre in Jerusalem, dominates the complex. Its eastern influences give it a very different feel to most Portuguese churches; the interior is otherworldly in its vast heights – an awesome combination of simple forms and rich embellishment. It's said that the circular design enabled knights to attend Mass on horseback. In the centre stands an eerily Gothic high altar while wall paintings date from the early 16th century. A huge funnel to the left is an ancient organ pipe (the organ itself is long gone).

Dom Manuel was responsible for tacking the nave on to the west side of the Charola and for commissioning a two-level **choir**. The *coro alto* (upper choir) is a fabulous Manueline work, with intricate decor on the vaulting and windows. The main western doorway into the nave is a splendid example of Spanish *plateresque* style.

Seeming to have grown from the wall, the window on the church's western side is the most famous and fantastical feature of the monastery. It's the ultimate in Manueline extravagance, a celebration of the Age of Discoveries: a Medusa tangle of snaking ropes, seaweed and cork boats, atop of which floats the Cross of the Order of Christ and the royal arms and armillary spheres of Dom Manuel. It's best seen from the roof of the adjacent Claustro de Santa Bárbara. Follow signs to the *janela* (window). Unfortunately obscured by the Claustro Principal is an almost-equivalent window on the southern side of the church.

Two serene, *azulejo*-decorated cloisters to the east of the Charola were built during the

Tomar

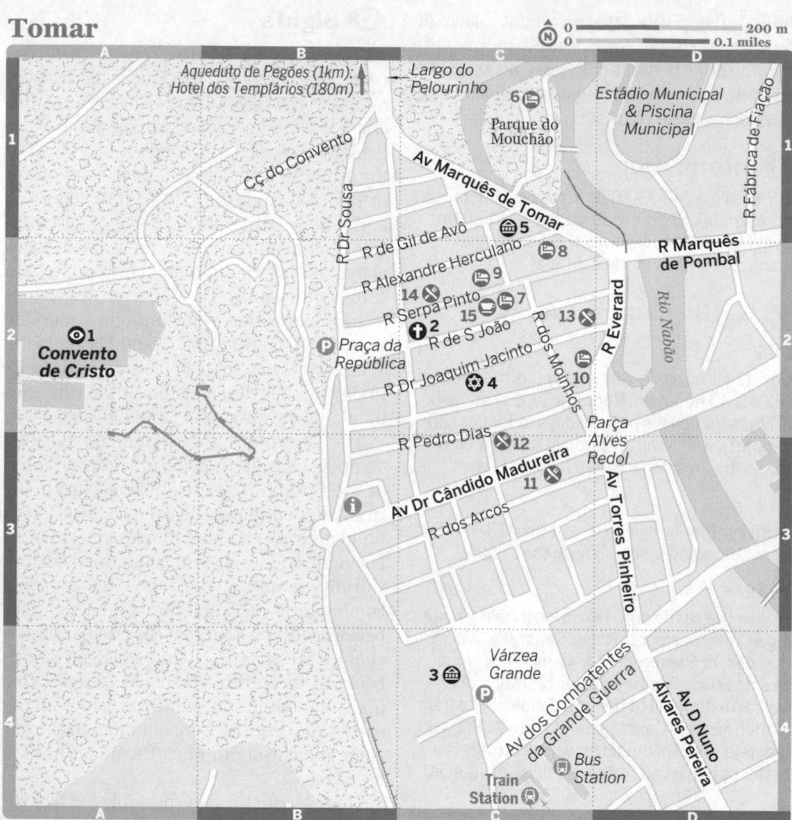

Tomar

Top Sights
1 Convento de Cristo ... A2

Sights
2 Igreja de São João Baptista ... C2
3 Museu dos Fósforos ... C4
4 Museu Luso-Hebraico Abraham Zacuto ... C2
5 Núcleo De Arte Contemporânea ... C1

Sleeping
6 Estalagem de Santa Iria ... C1
7 Hostel 2300 Thomar ... C2
8 Hotel Cavaleiros de Cristo ... C2
9 Residencial União ... C2
10 Thomar Story ... C2

Eating
11 Amor Lusitano ... C3
12 Calça Perra ... C3
13 Casa das Ratas ... C2
14 Restaurante Tabuleiro ... C2

Drinking & Nightlife
15 Café Paraíso ... C2

time when Prince Henry the Navigator was Grand Master of the order in the 15th century. The **Claustro do Cemitério** (Burial-Ground Cloisters) contains two 16th-century tombs and pretty citrus trees, while the two-storey **Claustro da Lavagem** (Ablutions Cloisters) affords nice views of the crenellated ruins of the Templars' original castle.

The elegant Renaissance **Claustro Principal** (Great Cloisters) stands in striking contrast to the flamboyance of the monastery's Manueline architecture. Commissioned during the reign of João III, the cloisters were probably designed by the Spaniard Diogo de Torralva but completed in 1587 by an Italian, Filippo Terzi. These foreign architects were among several responsible for introducing a delayed Renaissance style into Portugal. The Claustro Principal is arguably the country's finest expression of that style: a sober ensemble of Greek columns and pillars, gentle arches and sinuous, spiralling staircases.

Aqueduto de Pegões AQUEDUCT

FREE This impressive aqueduct, striding towards the monastery from the northwest, was built between 1593 and 1613 to supply water to thirsty monks. Its 180 arches, some of which are double-decker, are thought to have been designed by Italian Filippo Terzi. It's best seen just off the Leiria road, 2.3km from town.

Núcleo De Arte Contemporânea GALLERY

(Rua de Gil de Avô; 3-6pm Wed-Sun) FREE This modern museum showcases the work of 20th-century modernists and surrealists as well as contemporary artists from all over Portugal.

Museu Luso-Hebraico Abraham Zacuto SYNAGOGUE

(Rua Dr Joaquim Jacinto 73; 10am-noon & 2-5pm Tue-Sun winter, 10am-noon & 3-6pm summer) FREE On a charming cobbled lane in the old town, you'll find the country's best-preserved medieval synagogue. Built between 1430 and 1460, it was used for only a few years before Dom Manuel's convert-or-leave edict of 1497 forced most Jews to do the latter. The synagogue subsequently served as prison, chapel, hayloft and warehouse until classified as a national monument in 1921.

Museu dos Fósforos MUSEUM

(www.museudosfosforos.vidasmundanas.net; Avenida General Bernardo Faria; 10am-noon & 3-6pm Tue-Sun) FREE This museum, reached via the lovely courtyard of the Convento de São Francisco, contains Europe's largest collection of matchboxes. Amassed by local 'phillumenist' Aquiles da Mota Lima, the 40,000-plus matchboxes from countries around the world depict everything from bullfighters to bathing beauties, dinosaurs and French cuisine.

Igreja de São João Baptista CHURCH

(Praça da República; 10am-7pm Tue-Sun) FREE The old town's most striking church faces Praça da República, itself an eye-catching ensemble of 17th-century buildings alive with the echo of cooing pigeons. The church dates mostly from the late 15th century. It has an octagonal spire and richly ornamented Manueline doorways on its northern and western sides. Inside are 16th- and 17th-century *azulejos*. Gregório Lopes, one of 16th-century Portugal's finest artists, painted the church's six fine panels.

Festivals & Events

Nossa Senhora da Piedade RELIGIOUS

This important religious festival features a candlelit procession and a parade of floats decorated with paper flowers. It's held on the first Sunday in September.

Festa Templaria Tomar CULTURAL

(www.festatemplaria.pt) A fun medieval fair, celebrating the Templars, with lots of costumes, lectures and handicrafts. Held annually on different dates (check the website).

Sleeping

★ **Hostel 2300 Thomar** HOSTEL €

(249 324 256; www.hostel2300thomar.com; Rua Serpa Pinto 43; dm €18-20, d €40;) One of Portugal's funkiest hostels, this cleverly renovated mansion right in the heart of town celebrates Portugal, with each room brightly decorated in the country's theme: from the Lisbon tram to sardines. Airy dorms (and doubles), lockers, modern bathrooms and a cool and fun living space are enough to convert those after luxe experiences into a backpacker instead.

This is a standout for budget travellers. Even a light breakfast is included.

Camping Redondo CAMPGROUND €

(249 376 421; www.campingredondo.com; Poço Redondo; sites per adult/child/tent/car €4/2.50/4/2.50, 4-person safari tent €45, 4-person chalet €60-85;) This lovely Dutch- and British-run campground with four chalets plus two additional stone cottages is 9km northeast of Tomar at Poço Redondo. Amenities include a bar, pool and sun terrace (plus kid-friendly things such as a games room, playground and ponies).

Consult the website for transport details and driving directions in English.

Residencial União GUESTHOUSE €

(249 323 161; www.residencialuniao.pt; Rua Serpa Pinto 94; s/d €30/50;) Tomar's most atmospheric budget choice, this once-grand

TRAYS, VIRGINS & REVELRY

Tomar's **Festa dos Tabuleiros** (www.tabuleiros.org) – literally 'Festival of the Trays', also known as Festa do Espírito Santo ('Festival of the Holy Spirit') – is a weeklong celebration with music, drinking, dancing and fireworks. The festival is held every four years in June or July: upcoming years are 2019 and 2023.

The highlight is definitely the procession of some 400 young, white-clad women (traditionally virgins) bearing headdresses of trays stacked as tall as they are with loaves of bread and ears of wheat, decorated with colourful paper flowers and, finally, topped with a crown, cross or white paper dove. Young male attendants, dressed in black and white, help the girls balance the load, which can weigh up to 15kg. The following day, bread and wine are blessed by the priest and handed out to local families. The festival is believed to have roots in pagan fertility rites, though officially it's related to the saintly practices of 14th-century Dona Isabel (Dom Dinis' queen).

town house on the main pedestrian drag features large and sprucely maintained rooms with antique furniture and fixtures. Especially pleasant are the elegant breakfast room, serve-yourself bar and kindly owners. It's better value in summer than winter, when it can feel a little chilly.

Hotel Cavaleiros de Cristo HOTEL €

(☎249 321 203; Rua Alexandre Herculano 7; s/d €35/55; ❄📶) Down a side street near the river, this place offers comfortable, modern rooms with writing desks and minibars.

★**Hotel dos Templários** HOTEL €€

(☎249 310 100; www.hoteldostemplarios.pt; Largo Cândido dos Reis 1; s/d from €79/99, superior s/d from €99/132; P❄📶🏊) At the river's edge, just outside the historic centre, this spacious, efficient hotel offers excellent facilities including gym, sauna, and indoor and outdoor pools (the last adjacent to a small but stylish hotel bar). The rooms are large and very comfortable; most have balconies, some of which overlook the river. Service is five-star and the breakfast spread is great.

Room rates are normally lower than the rack rates that are listed here; check the hotel website.

Thomar Story BOUTIQUE HOTEL €€

(☎249 327 268; www.thomarstory.pt; Rua João Carlos Everard 53; s/d/tr €53/60/65; ❄📶) A major refurbishment of an old house has created 12 light and pleasant rooms along the lines of the current trend in Portugal: funky wall decorations and mirrors, bright accessories and modern bathrooms. The interior of each in some way reflects Tomar, from the town's convent to its synagogue. Breakfast costs €5.

Wooden floors means there can be some noise, but otherwise it's a safe bet.

Estalagem de Santa Iria INN €€

(☎249 313 326; www.estalagemsantairia.com; Parque do Mouchão; s/d/ste €45/62/102; P📶) Centrally located on an island in Tomar's lovely riverside park, this curious, slightly kitsch, old-fashioned inn is Portugal's answer to Britain's *Fawlty Towers* (in a good way). It has large, careworn, but comfortable rooms, most with balconies overlooking the leafy grounds or the river. Despite its glitches, it's a friendly place, and the location is great.

Downstairs are a restaurant and bar, both with roaring winter fireplaces.

Quinta do Valle HOTEL €€

(☎249 381 165; www.quintadovalle.com; 2-/4-person apt €77/98; P📶🏊) With parts dating back to the 15th century, this manor house 8km south of Tomar has been turned into rural accommodation, with large grounds, chapel, swimming pool and quaint two- to four-bedroom apartments featuring fireplaces and kitchenettes.

To get here from Tomar, take the N110 south, exit at Guerreira, pass through the village and turn right, following the *turismo de habitação* signs.

It's got a lovely out-of-the-way feel and is a venue for utter relaxation. Breakfast is available for €7.50 extra per person.

✕ Eating

Amor Lusitano PORTUGUESE €

(amorlusitano.pt; Avenida Dr Cândido Madureira 19; cakes €1-2, petiscos €4-5; ⏰9am-9pm Sun-Thu, to midnight Fri & Sat) This charming spot is part cafe, part wine bar, part elegant lounge room. Importantly, however, it celebrates all things *Lusitano* (Portuguese) so this is the place to come for *doces conventuais* (convent cakes) or some of Portugal's finest wine. It's the kind of place that you come for a cup of tea and *pão do lo* (sponge cake), and stay for a tipple.

Casa das Ratas PORTUGUESE €€
(Rua Dr Joaquim Jacinto 6; mains €8-12; ⌚noon-3pm & 7-10pm Tue-Sat, noon-3pm Sun) One of Tomar's fun experiences, where old meets new. Housed in a former *adega* (winery), the eatery is lined with wine vats. As grain was once here too, it used to attract rats (thus the name), but besides the jokey ones you'll see hanging off electric wires, you'll see nothing but delicious share plates and good wine.

Calça Perra PORTUGUESE €€
(www.calcaperra.pt; Rua Pedro Dias 59; mains €14-18; ⌚11am-3pm & 6.30pm-midnight Mon-Sat, plus 10.30am-3pm Sun summer) At this charming backstreet eatery you can partake in the elegant dining room or the breezy courtyard below. Seasonal specials like *dourada grelhada* (grilled bream) and *açorda de peixe* (a bread-filled fish stew) back up the list of reliable meat and fish dishes and a selection of tasty pastas.

Restaurante Tabuleiro PORTUGUESE €€
(Rua Serpa Pinto 140; mains €8-12; ⌚noon-3pm & 7-10pm Mon-Sat; ) Located just off Tomar's main square, this family-friendly local hangout features warm, attentive service, good traditional food and ridiculous (read: more-than-ample) portions. A great spot to experience local fare. The cod pie is a standout.

Drinking & Nightlife

Café Paraíso CAFE
(cafeparaisotomar.com; Rua Serpa Pinto 127; snacks from €2.50; ⌚8am-2am Mon-Sat, 9am-7pm Sun) More than 100 years old and frozen in time since its renovation in 1946, this old-fashioned, high-ceilinged deco cafe serves as a refuge for anyone in need of a mid-afternoon snack and a shot of caffeine or whisky.

Entertainment

Fatias de Cá THEATRE
(960 303 991; www.fatiasdeca.net) This Tomar-based theatre company presents highly innovative and entertaining monthly performances (more in summer) of works such as *The Name of the Rose* and *The Tempest,* often in amazing locations.

THE ORDER OF THE KNIGHTS TEMPLAR

Founded in about 1119 by French crusading knights to protect pilgrims visiting the Holy Land, the Templars got their name when King Baldwin of Jerusalem housed them in his palace, which had once been a Jewish temple. The Knights soon became a strictly organised, semireligious gang. Members took vows of poverty and chastity, and wore white coats emblazoned with a red cross – a symbol that eventually came to be associated with Portugal itself. By 1139 the Templars were the leading defenders of the Christian crusader states in the Holy Land.

In Portugal, Templar knights played a key role in expelling the Moors. Despite vows of poverty, they accepted land, castles and titles in return for military victories. Soon the order had properties all over Europe and the Middle East. This geographically dispersed network enabled them to take on another influential role: bankers to kings and pilgrims.

By the early 14th century, the Templars had grown so strong that French King Philip IV – eager for their wealth or afraid of their power – initiated an era of persecution (supported by the French pope Clement V). He arrested all of the knights, accusing many of heresy and seizing their property. In 1314 the last French Grand Maître (Master) was burned at the stake.

In Portugal, Dom Dinis followed the trend by dissolving the order, but a few years later he cannily re-established it as the Order of Christ, though now under the royal thumb. It was largely thanks to the order's wealth that Prince Henry the Navigator (Grand Master from 1417 to 1460) was able to fund the Age of Discoveries. In the 16th century, Dom João III took the order into a humbler phase, shifting it towards monastic duties. In 1834, with the dissolution of the monasteries, the order's lands were confiscated, but it still lives on to some extent: these days the Grand Master is the Portuguese president.

Information

Turismo (☎ 249 329 823; www.cm-tomar.pt; Avenida Dr Cândido Madureira; ⊙ 9.30am-12.30pm & 2-6pm) Offers a good town map, an accommodation list and information about a historical trail.

Getting There & Away

The **bus station** (☎ 249 312 738; Avenida dos Combatentes da Grande Guerra) and **train station** (www.cp.pt; Avenida dos Combatentes da Grande Guerra) are next door to each other, about 500m south of the *turismo*. You will also find several large car parks here.

BUS

Regular services go to Lisbon (€10, 1¾ hours) and Fátima (€3.85, one hour), and one weekday bus at 7.30am heads to Leiria (€4, one hour). At the time of research, incredibly, there were no services to Batalha or Alcobaça.

TRAIN

Trains run to Lisbon (€9.65 to €10.85, 1¾ to two hours) via Santarém (€5.05 to €5.55, 40 to 55 minutes), every hour or two between 6am and 10pm.

The Beiras

Includes ➡

Best Places to Eat

- ➡ Pedra de Sal (p317)
- ➡ Tres Pipos (p349)
- ➡ O Albertino (p352)
- ➡ Restaurante de Casa das Penhas Douradas (p342)
- ➡ Tapas Nas Costas (p312)

Best Places to Sleep

- ➡ Casa das Penhas Douradas (p341)
- ➡ Casa da Sé (p348)
- ➡ Casa Pombal (p311)
- ➡ Casa das Obras (p341)
- ➡ Universal Boutique Hotel (p319)

Why Go?

Three worlds rolled into one, the Beiras offer as much diversity as any region in Portugal.

Along the Atlantic, the Beira Litoral lures surfers and sunseekers with scores of sandy beaches. Here, the sophisticated university city of Coimbra and the brash casino-party town of Figueira da Foz arm-wrestle for visitors' attention.

Move inland to the Beira Alta highlands and the mood shifts entirely. Stoic stone villages cling to the slopes of Portugal's highest mountains – the Serra da Estrela – and cast their gaze down at the fertile wine country of the Dão valley.

East of the mountains, in the hypnotically beautiful Beira Baixa, vast expanses of olive and cork-oak forest spread across a hotter, lonelier landscape. Here, surveying the borderlands from the ramparts of nearly abandoned medieval fortress-towns, you'll feel centuries away from the coast you just left behind.

When to Go

Coimbra

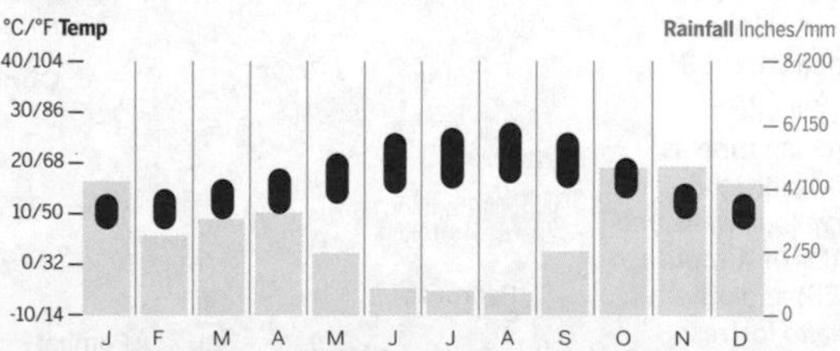

Early May Queima das Fitas fills Coimbra's streets with students in dashing capes.

Jun Before summer crowds descend, and beaches are warm enough for a swim.

Jul Clear mountain air and low-season prices in the Serra da Estrela.

The Beiras Highlights

1. Explore the hilltop labyrinth, home of fado, fabulous views and a marvellous historic university in **Coimbra** (p304).

2. Hike alongside the glistening Rio Zêzere outside **Manteigas** (p339), past shepherds' huts and soaring peaks.

3. Admire the art nouveau facades lining the canals of **Aveiro** (p323, and ride through history aboard a *moliceiro* (seaweed vessel).

4. Zigzag your way up terraced slopes to **Piódão** (p328), the most picturesque of the Beiras' stone villages.

5. Conjure up a vanished civilisation at the Roman ruins of **Conímbriga** (p315).

6. Sip fine Dão wine in the flowery civic gardens of **Viseu** (p345).

7. Savour the golden light in the cork-oak forest as you climb from ancient Idanha-a-Velha to the spectacular craggy clifftop village of **Monsanto** (p331).

8. Whistle a marching tune as you explore the marvellous walls and castles of **Almeida** (p356) and other *planalto* fortress-towns.

Quinta do Vallado
Pinhão
Mesão Frio
Peso da Régua
Vila Real (25km)
São João de Pesqueira
Rio Douro
Pocinho
Parque Natural do Douro International
Tabuaço
N108
Lamego
(906m)
Vila Nova de Foz Côa
TRÁS-OS-MONTES
N2
IP3
Parque Arqueológico Vale do Côa
Muxagata
Tarouca
Castelo Melhor
Barca de Alva
N226
Moimenta da Beira
SPAIN
N321
Penedono
Serra da Gralheira
Parque Natural do Douro Internacional
E802
IP2
Marialva
Castro Daire
Sernancelhe
Figueira de Castelo Rodrigo
BEIRA ALTA
N226
N221
IP3
Aguiar da Beira
Trancoso
Pinhel
Rio Águeda
N324
Almeida
N2
Linhares
N226
Rio Côa
Serra da Caramulo
Penalva do Castelo
Celorico da Beira
N221
Vilar Formosa
Viseu
Quinta da Boavista
Fornos de Algodres
E80
IP5
N231
E80
IP5
Santar
Mangualde
IP3
N17
Folgosinho
Guarda
Nelas
Rio Mondego
Videmonte
N324
A35
Gouveia
N231
Serra da Estrela
Benespera
Carregal do Sal
Parque Natural da Serra da Estrela
Río Zêzere
PORTUGAL
Seia
Manteigas
E802
IP2
N17
Bobadela
Torre (1993m)
Belmonte
Sabugal
Rio Alva
N18
Santo Amaro
Sortelha
N17
N231
Rio Côa
Três Entradas
Caria
Terreiro
Covilhã
Reserva Natural da Serra da Malcata
Piódão
Serra de Açor
Valverde del Fresno
Penamacor
Río Zêzere
SPAIN
Fundão
N112
N239
Orca
BEIRA BAIXA
Medelim
Monsanto
Penha Garcia
E802
IP2
N332
N239
Idanha-a-Velha
Lardosa
Barragem da Idanha
Rio Erges
N112
Oleiros
N238
N233
Castelo Branco
Cáceres (65km)
Rosmaninhal
Proença-a-Nova
Monforte da Beira
IC8
IP2
E802
Rio Ponsul
Ribeira do Aravil
Rio Tejo
Portalegre (65km)
Monte Barata
Parque Natural do Tejo Internacional
Alcántara

BEIRA LITORAL

Coimbra

POP 101,450

The medieval capital of Portugal for over a hundred years, and site of the country's greatest university for the past five centuries, Coimbra wears its weighty importance in Portuguese history with dignity. Its atmospheric, beautiful historic core cascades down a hillside in a lovely setting on the east bank of the Rio Mondego: it's a multicoloured collage of buildings spanning nearly a millennium.

During the academic year, you'll be sure to feel the university's influence. Students throng bars and cafes, and graffiti scrawled outside *repúblicas* (communal student dwellings) address the political issues of the day. On a summer evening, the city's old stone walls reverberate with the haunting metallic notes of the *guitarra* (Portuguese guitar) and the full, deep voices of fado singers.

Then there's the city's modern side – a contemporary riverfront park with terrace bars and restaurants, a spiffy pedestrian bridge across the Mondego, and vast shopping complexes.

History

The Romans founded a city at Conímbriga, though it was abruptly abandoned in favour of Coimbra's more easily defended heights. The city grew and prospered under the Moors, who were evicted definitively by Christians in 1064. The city served as Portugal's capital from 1139 to 1255, when Afonso III decided he preferred Lisbon.

The Universidade de Coimbra, Portugal's first university (and among the first in Europe), was actually founded in Lisbon by Dom Dinis in 1290 but settled here in 1537. It attracted a steady stream of teachers, artists and intellectuals from across Europe. The 16th century was a particularly heady time thanks to Nicolas Chanterène, Jean de Rouen (João de Ruão) and other French artists who helped create a school of sculpture here that influenced styles all over Portugal.

Today Coimbra's university remains Portugal's most prestigious – and one of its most traditional. Students still attend class in black robes and capes – often adorned with patches signifying course of study, home town or other affiliation – while a rigorously maintained set of rites and practices called the *codigo de praxe* governs all aspects of student life.

Sights

Crowning Coimbra's steep hilltop is the university, around and below which lies a tangle of old town lanes. The new town, locally called 'Baixa', spreads at the foot of the hill and along the Rio Mondego.

The city also makes a fine base for day visits to the remarkable Roman ruins at Conímbriga, the medieval hilltop fortress of Montemor-o-Velho or the outlandishly ornate Palace Hotel do Buçaco.

Upper Town

Long a Moorish stronghold and for a century the seat of Portugal's kings, Coimbra's upper town rises abruptly from the banks of the Rio Mondego. The most picturesque way to enter Coimbra's labyrinth of lanes is via **Arco de Almedina** – the city's heavy-duty Moorish gateway – and up the staggered stairs known as Rua Quebra Costas ('Backbreaker').

People have been gasping up this hill (and falling down it) for centuries; local legend says that it was the 19th-century writer Almeida Garrett who persuaded the mayor to install the stairs.

Up Rua Sub Ripas is the grand Manueline doorway of the early-16th-century **Palácio de Sub Ripas** (Rua Sub Ripas), signposted Torre da Contenda; its Renaissance windows and stone ornaments are the work of Jean de Rouen, whose workshop was nearby. Further on is the Torre de Anto (p307), a tower that once formed part of the town walls and recently opened as the Núcleo da Guitarra e do Fado de Coimbra (Guitar and Fado of Coimbra Centre).

For a glimpse of student life, stroll along any of the alleys around the Sé Velha (old cathedral) or below the Sé Nova (new cathedral). Flags, offbeat art and graffiti mark the cramped houses known as *repúblicas,* each housing a dozen or so students from the same region or faculty.

★**Universidade de Coimbra** UNIVERSITY

(☎239 242 744; www.uc.pt/en/informacaopara/visit/paco; adult/student €9/7, tower €1; ⏱9am-7.30pm mid-Mar–Oct, 9.30am-1pm & 2-5.30pm Nov–mid-Mar) The city's high point, the university nucleus, consists of a series of remarkable 16th- to 18th-century buildings, all set within and around the vast Páteo das Escolas ('patio' or courtyard). These include the Paço das Escolas (Royal Palace; p306), clock tower (p306), Prisão Acadêmica (prison; p307), Capela de São Miguel (chapel; p307) and Biblioteca Joanina (library; p307). To enter the library, visitors are admitted in small groups every 20 minutes. Buy your ticket at the university's visitor centre near the Porta Férrea. With the exception of the library, you can enter and explore the university on your own, or head off with a knowledgable tour guide on one of three different tours (€12.50/15/20). These take place daily at 11am and 3pm.

➡ Porta Férrea

One of the most symbolic aspects of the university, the main entrance (iron gate) was designed by architect António Tavares in 1634 on the orders of Rector D Álvaro da Costa. It occupies the same site as the main gate to Coimbra's Moorish stronghold and was the first major work following the acquisition of the Royal Palace by King Felipe I in 1597.

➡ Statue of João III

Located in the middle of the university square, João III turns his back on a sweeping view of the city and the river and faces the centre of learning. It was he who reestablished the university in Coimbra in 1537 and invited big-shot scholars to teach here in what had previously been a royal palace.

➡ Clock Tower

Another of the university's symbolic structures in Coimbra, the 18th-century tower – and its clock and bells – regulate academic life. Built between 1728 and 1733, on the premise that there could be no order without a clock, it was nicknamed '*a cabra*' ('goat'; or 'bitch' in contemporary lingo), as it rang out to end the day's classes, signifying the curfew (in the days when students had to be home by 7pm or face prison) and that there would be classes the following day. In fine conditions, you can climb the tower (€1).

➡ Paço das Escolas

(Royal Palace) The Schools Palace, the original Royal Palace, houses the university's iconic *salas*. Here, important traditional academic ceremonies still take place. To visit the palace, from the courtyard gate take the stairway on the right up to **Sala dos Capelos** (named after the academic cape used by the university's Doctors; also known as the Grand Hall), a former examination room hung with dark portraits of Portugal's kings, and heavy quiltlike decoration. Nearby is the private **Examination Room**, lined with paintings of the university rectors.

The adjacent passageway affords visitors excellent city views. In fine weather you may be permitted to enter the balcony, worth doing for fabulous vistas.

➡ Capela de São Miguel

(Universidade de Coimbra; ⌚9am-7.30pm mid-Mar–Oct, 9.30am-1pm & 2-5.30pm Nov–mid-Mar) This extraordinarily beautiful, ornate baroque chapel has a brightly painted ceiling, ornate tilework, Manueline features and a gilded organ. It was reopened (in March 2016) after a year of renovation. Concerts still take place here on occasion – ask at the *turismo*.

➡ Biblioteca Joanina

(João V Library; ☎239 859 818; Universidade de Coimbra; ⌚9am-7.30pm mid-Mar–Oct, 9.30am-1pm & 2-5.30pm Nov–mid-Mar) This extraordinary library, a gift from João V in the early 18th century, seems too extravagant and distracting for study, with its rosewood, ebony and jacaranda tables, elaborately frescoed ceilings and gilt chinoiserie bookshelves. Its 60,000 ancient books deal with law, philosophy and theology. A lower floor has more tomes and the Prisão Acadêmica.

➡ Prisão Acadêmica

Below the Biblioteca Joanina is this evocative place: a former lock-up for misbehaving students. Originally located beneath the Sala dos Capelos, the academic lock-up was later transferred back to the medieval jail of the Royal Palace below the library (incredibly, the university was able to operate its own separate laws). In 1834, after the liberal revolution in Portugal, the prison was used as a safe deposit for books and illuminated manuscripts of convents and monasteries.

★ Sé Velha CATHEDRAL

(Old Cathedral; ☎239825273; www.sevelha-coimbra.org; Largo da Sé Velha, Rua do Norte 4; €2.50; ⌚10am-6pm Mon-Sat, 1-6pm Sun) Coimbra's stunning 12th-century cathedral is one of Portugal's finest examples of Romanesque architecture. The main portal and facade are exceptionally striking. Its crenellated exterior and narrow, slit-like lower windows serve as reminders of the nation's embattled early days, when the Moors were still a threat. These buildings were designed to be useful as fortresses in times of trouble.

The church was financed by the first king of Portugal, Afonso Henriques. The high, barrel-vaulted nave preserves its main Romanesque features; side altars and well-preserved Gothic tombs of bishops are

Coimbra

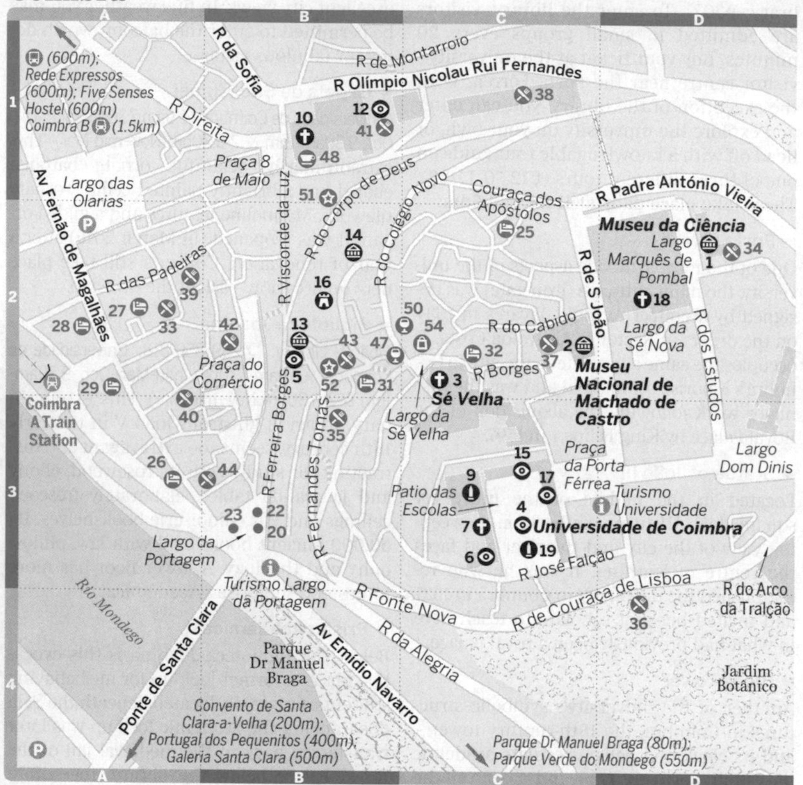

backed by bright Andalusian tiles. The high gilt retable is in ornate late-Gothic style and depicts the Assumption of Mary. Contrast this with the Renaissance Capela do Santíssimo Sacramento alongside. If you want to visit on a Sunday, note that Mass is at 11am.

★Museu Nacional de Machado de Castro MUSEUM

(☎239 853 070; www.museumachadocastro.pt; Largo Dr José Rodrigues; adult/child €6/free, cryptoportico only €3, with audioguide €7.50; ⌚2-6pm Tue, 10am-7pm Wed-Sun Apr-Sep, 2-6pm Tue, 10am-6pm Wed-Sun Oct-Mar) This great museum is a highlight of central Portugal. It's built over the Roman forum, the remains of which can be seen and cover several levels. Part of the visit takes you down to the vaulted, spooky and immensely atmospheric galleries of the cryptoportico that allowed the forum to be level on such a hilly site. The artistic collection is wide-ranging and superb. The route starts with sculpture, from the architectural (column capitals) through Gothic religious sculpture and so on.

Highlights include a section of the delicate cloister of São João de Almedina and some exquisite alabaster pieces from England. Renaissance masters arriving in Coimbra from other parts of Europe brought their own styles and contributed to the establishment of a distinctive Coimbra tradition. A whole chapel has even been reassembled here. The section downstairs includes impressive 16th-century terracotta figures from Hodart's *Last Supper*, while paintings on the higher floors include stunning Flemish panels by Metsys. A collection of gold monstrances, furniture and Moorish-influenced pieces are almost too much by the time you reach them.

★**Museu da Ciência** MUSEUM

(☎239 854 350; www.museudaciencia.org; Largo Marquês de Pombal; adult/student €5/3.50; ⏰10am-6pm Tue-Sun) This wonderful science museum occupies a centuries-old former monastery converted by Pombal into the university's chemical engineering building. It features intriguing state-of-the-art interactive science displays coexisting with 18th-century lab sinks; don't miss the giant glowing globe in a room paved with medieval stones, or the psychedelic insect's-eye view of flowers. Displays are in English/Portuguese. There's also a great cafe with terrace and views down to the new town.

The most extraordinary section, only reopened in 2016, is housed in a building opposite (guided visits only). The collection displays 17th- to 19th-century teaching aids of the former physics and zoology study laboratories. Think curiosity cabinets and some of the most simple, ingenious scientific contraptions around (we love the centaur used to measure the direction and velocity of an arrow). Part of the joy, too, is observing the exquisite craftsmanship.

Sé Nova CATHEDRAL

(New Cathedral; ☎239 823 138; www.senova.do.sapo.pt; Largo da Sé Nova; €1; ⏰8.30am-6.30pm Mon-Sat, 10am-12.30pm Sun) The large, severe 'new' cathedral, started by the Jesuits in 1598 and completed a century later, dominates the square of the same name high in the old town. Its sober Renaissance lines contrast with the gilt side panels and ornate baroque altarpiece. Down the side is a gallery of reliquaries featuring bones and worse from minor saints and bishops, including St Francis Xavier and St Luke (so it is claimed!). Climb to the platform for uplifting city views.

Núcleo da Guitarra e do Fado de Coimbra/Torre de Anto MUSEUM

(Guitar and Fado of Coimbra Centre; Rua Sub Ripas; ⏰10am-1pm & 2-6pm Tue-Sun) FREE On Rua Sub Ripas in Coimbra's upper town is the Torre de Anto, a tower that once formed part of the ancient city walls. The poet António Nobre (1867–1900) lived there in the late 19th century, thus the tower's name. Since 2015 the Torre de Anto has housed the Núcleo da Guitarra e do Fado de Coimbra, part of the Municipal Museum network.

Baixa & Around

Igreja de Santa Cruz CHURCH

(Praça 8 de Maio; adult/student €2.50/1.50; ⏰9am-5pm Mon-Fri, 9am-noon & 2-5pm Sat, 4-5.30pm Sun) From the trendy shops outside, this church plunges you back to Portugal's past. Step through the Renaissance porch and flamboyant 18th-century arch to discover some of the Coimbra School's finest work, including an ornate pulpit and the elaborate tombs of Portugal's first kings, Afonso Henriques and Sancho I. The most striking Manueline work is in the restrained 16th-century cloister.

Behind the church is **Jardim da Manga** (Rua Olímpio Nicolau Rui Fernandes), once part of the cloister, and its curious fountain: a lemon-yellow, four-buttressed affair.

Núcleo da Cidade Muralhada/Torre de Almedina MUSEUM

(☎239 833 771; www.cm-coimbra.pt; Pátio do Castilho; adult/student €1.80/1.20; ⏰10am-1pm & 2-6pm Tue-Sat) Housed in the medieval tower directly above the Arco de Almedina, this

Coimbra

Top Sights
1 Museu da Ciência ... D2
2 Museu Nacional de Machado de Castro ... C2
3 Sé Velha ... C2
4 Universidade de Coimbra ... C3

Sights
5 Arco de Almedina ... B2
6 Biblioteca Joanina ... C3
7 Capela de São Miguel ... C3
8 Casa Museu Bissaya Barreto ... F4
9 Clock Tower ... C3
10 Igreja de Santa Cruz ... B1
11 Jardim Botânico ... E4
12 Jardim da Manga ... B1
13 Núcleo da Cidade Muralhada/Torre de Almedina ... B2
14 Núcleo da Guitarra e do Fado de Coimbra/Torre de Anto ... B2
15 Paço das Escolas ... C3
16 Palácio de Sub Ripas ... B2
17 Porta Férrea ... C3
Prisão Académica ... (see 6)
18 Sé Nova ... D2
19 Statue of João III ... C3

Activities, Courses & Tours
20 Go Walks ... B3
21 Skygarden ... E4
22 Tuk a Day ... B3
23 Yellow Bus Tours ... B3

Sleeping
24 Alojamento Local Duarte's ... E3
25 Casa Pombal ... C2
26 Hotel Astória ... A3
27 Hotel Domus ... A2
28 Hotel Oslo ... A2
29 Hotel Vitória ... A2
30 Luggage Hostel & Suites ... F1
31 Quebra-Luz ... B2
32 Serenata Hostel ... C2

Eating
33 Adega Paço dos Condes ... A2
34 Cafetaria Museu da Ciência ... D2
35 Fangas Mercearia Bar ... B3
36 Justiça e Paz ... D4
37 Loggia ... C2
38 Mercado Municipal Dom Pedro V ... C1
39 Porta Larga ... A2
40 Restaurante Giro Churrasqueira ... A3
41 Restaurante Jardim da Manga ... B1
42 Restaurante Zé Neto ... B2
43 Tapas Nas Costas ... B2
44 Zé Manel dos Ossos ... B3

Drinking & Nightlife
45 AAC Bar ... E2
46 Aqui Base Tango ... F3
47 Bar Quebra Costas ... B2
48 Café Santa Cruz ... B1
49 Noites Longas ... F3
50 O Moelas ... C2

Entertainment
51 Á Capella ... B1
52 Fado ao Centro ... B2
53 Teatro Académico de Gil Vicente ... E2

Shopping
54 Carlos Tomás ... C2

historical museum displays a plaster reproduction of Coimbra's old-town layout, complete with castle. A multilingual audiovisual presentation takes you step by step around the 2km of walls. There's an exhibition and city views upstairs, but the real fun is looking down through the *matacães* (embrasures), through which hot oil was traditionally poured on enemies below.

Praça da República & Around

Leafy Praça da República is a social centre, especially for students. The surrounding neighbourhood, laid out in the 19th century and still dominated by prim bourgeois homes of the period, is a relaxing break from the high density of both the university and the Baixa area.

Jardim Botânico GARDENS
(☎239 855 233; www.uc.pt; ⊙9am-8pm Apr-Sep, 9am-5.30pm Oct-Mar) FREE A serene place to catch your breath, the lovely university-run botanic garden sits in the shadow of the 16th-century **Aqueduto de São Sebastião**. Founded by the Marquês de Pombal, the garden combines formal flower beds, meandering paths and elegant fountains.

The green-fingered can also visit the greenhouses (closed at the time of research) and the adjacent Museu Botânico, while Skygarden (p309) has a series of ziplines.

Casa Museu Bissaya Barreto MUSEUM
(☎239 853 800; www.fbb.pt; Rua Infantaria 23; adult €2.50, child & senior €1.25; ⊙11am-1pm Tue-Fri, 3-6pm Tue-Sun) Bissaya Barreto was a local surgeon, scholar and obsessive hoarder of fine arts, and his handsome, late-19th-

century mansion has been turned into an art museum. A guide (not necessarily English-speaking) accompanies guests through rooms jam-packed with Portuguese sculpture and painting, Chinese porcelain, old *azulejos* (hand-painted tiles) and period furniture.

Along & Across the River

In an ecclesiastical counterweight to the university, a cluster of convents, together with several other sights, sits on the far side of the Rio Mondego. Lovely green spaces stretch south from the Ponte de Santa Clara along the eastern bank of the river. **Parque Dr Manuel Braga** provides a haven of serene shade under stately rows of old sycamores, while the **Parque Verde do Mondego** (www.parqueverdedomondego.pt;) FREE features riverfront bars and eateries, a pedestrian bridge across the Rio Mondego and a small playground for kids.

Convento de Santa Clara-a-Velha CONVENT
(239 801 160; Rua das Parreiras; adult/student €4/2.50; 10am-7pm Tue-Sun Apr-Sep, 10am-6pm Tue-Sun Oct-Mar) This Gothic convent was founded in 1330 by the saintly Dona Isabel, Dom Dinis' wife; it served as her final resting place until flooding forced her to be moved uphill. The adjacent **museum** displays archaeological finds and shows two films, one about the nuns who lived here, the other documenting the 20-year renovation that cleared the river ooze that had drowned it since the 17th century.

Convento de Santa Clara-a-Nova CONVENT
(239 441 674; www.rainhasantaisabel.org; Calçada de Santa Isabel; cloister €2; 9am-6.45pm Mon-Fri Nov-Feb, 8.30am-7pm Mon-Sat, from 9am Sun Mar-Oct) Begun on higher ground in the 17th century to replace its flooded twin, this convent is devoted almost entirely to the saintly Queen Isabel's memory. Aisle panels tell her life story, while her solid-silver casket is enshrined above the altar, and even her clothes hang in the sacristy. Her statue is the focus of the Festa da Rainha Santa (p310).

Portugal dos Pequenitos AMUSEMENT PARK
(239 801 170; www.portugaldospequenitos.pt; Rossio de Santa Clara; adult/under 13yr/family €9.50/5.95/23.95; 10am-8pm mid-Jun–Sep;) The brainchild of local collector Bissaya Barreto, this is an impossibly cute theme park where kids clamber over, into and through doll's-house versions of Portugal's most famous monuments, while parents clutch cameras at the ready. There's an extra charge to visit marginally interesting minimuseums of marine life, clothing and furniture.

Quinta das Lágrimas GARDENS
(Rua Vilarinho Raposo; adult/under 15yr/f €2.50/1/5; 10am-5pm Tue-Sun mid-Oct–mid-Mar, 10am-7pm mid-Mar–mid-Oct) Legend says Dona Inês de Castro met her grisly end in the gardens of this private estate. It's now a deluxe hotel, although anyone can take a turn about the grounds and track down the Fonte dos Amores (Lovers' Fountain), which reputedly marks the spot where the prince's unwitting mistress was struck down. Also note the sequoia tree planted by the Duke of Wellington.

Activities

Several organisations offer tours on foot or tuk-tuk, plus kayaking and other outdoor activities.

Tuk a Day TOURS
(964 486 445, 962 826 855; per person €10; 9am-1pm & 3-7pm) Travellers love the passionate Sr Amando and his informative, 1¼-hour tours of Coimbra. He speaks many languages (around five at last count) and knows a lot. Minimum three people (or €30). Tours begin at the Portagem.

Go Walks WALKING
(910 163 118; www.gowalksportugal.com; Rua do Sargento Mor 4-6; from €12.50) Various themed walking tours – from fado to Jewish Coimbra – run by enthusiastic, knowledgable students who speak good English (French and Spanish also bookable).

Skygarden ZIPLINE
(910 230 797; www.skygardenadventure.com; Calçada Martim de Freitas; adult/child €17/13; 10am-8pm Tue-Sun Apr-Sep, 10am-5.30pm Tue-Sun Mar & Oct, weekends only Nov & Feb) It's not what you might associate with a historic seat of learning, but for an education of a different kind, you can fly through the lush green of the Jardim Botânico on a 200m valley slide, climb ropes or 'free fall' from an ancient tree.

Yellow Bus Tours BUS
(239 801 100; www.yellowbustours.com; adult/child €12/6; daily mid-Mar–Apr, Fri-Sun Apr–mid-May, Tue-Sun mid-May–mid-Oct) Hour-long hop-on, hop-off bus tours of Coimbra with recorded multilingual commentary. The double-decker open-top buses originate near the *turismo* at Largo da Portagem. Tours run hourly from 10am to 5pm, except between

noon and 3pm. You can pay on board or buy tickets online or at the *turismo* and hotels. An extra €4 buys a riverboat tour.

O Pioneiro do Mondego KAYAKING
(☎239 478 385; www.opioneirodomondego.com; guided tours per person €22.50) Rents out kayaks for paddling the Mondego between Penacova and Torres de Mondego, an 18km trip.

Festivals & Events

Queima das Fitas FIESTA
(www.queimadasfitas.org) Coimbra's biggest bash is Queima das Fitas, a boozy week of fado and revelry that takes place during the first week in May when students celebrate the end of the academic year.

Festival das Artes ART
(www.festivaldasartes.com) This two-week festival in June or July brings classical music to the Quinta das Lágrimas, jazz to the riverboats, guest chefs to local restaurants and other forms of merriment to Coimbra's streets.

Festa da Rainha Santa RELIGIOUS, FIESTA
(www.rainhasantaisabel.org) Held around 4 July in even-numbered years, this festival commemorates Santa Isabel. A Thursday-night candlelit procession carries her statue from the Convento de Santa Clara-a-Nova across the Ponte de Santa Clara to Largo da Portagem and through the streets to Igreja do Carmo; a second procession the following Sunday returns her to the convent.

Sleeping

★**Serenata Hostel** HOSTEL €
(☎239 853 130; www.serenatahostel.com; Largo da Sé Velha 21; dm/d without bathroom €15/38, d/ste/f with bathroom €49/55/79; 📶) In the pretty heart of the (noisy-at-night) old town, this noble building with an intriguingly varied history has been converted to a fabulous hostel, chock-full of modern comforts and facilities while maintaining a period feel in keeping with this historic zone. Great lounge areas, a cute, secluded sun terrace, spacious dorms and a modern kitchen complete a very happy picture.

Luggage Hostel & Suites HOSTEL €
(☎239 820 257; www.theluggagehostel.com; Rua Antero de Quental 125; hostel dm/d without bathroom €18/42, with bathroom s €45-90, d €50-98, f €110; 📶) This property (with an interesting history) has been converted into a stunning hostel-hotel. For those of you who don't mind sharing common rooms with dorm-room dwellers, the hotel floors feature seven private, beautifully decorated rooms. The decor is impressive with hip, mid-century-modern furniture and rooms are spacious and airy. Some have private (but external) bathrooms while others have en suites.

Alojamento Local Duarte's GUESTHOUSE €
(☎239 051 403; www.alojamentolocalduartes.com; Rua Castro Matoso 4; s/d €25/30) An old-style, simple, no-fuss spot with the odd sloping floor but clean yellow and white rooms. The friendly owners speak English and French. Great for families and anyone on a budget. Breakfast is not available but guests can use a communal kitchen.

Quebra-Luz GUESTHOUSE €
(☎912 278 779; www.quebra-luz.com; Rua Quebra Costas 18; s/d without bathroom €37/42, with bathroom €45/50; 📶) Right on the old town's 'back-breaking' stairs, this place isn't easy to find but makes a good central haven (though you won't be able to park close by). It's an apartment with four rooms decorated

FIRED UP

In the first week of May, Coimbra marks the end of the academic year with **Queima das Fitas**, a week-long party that serves as the country's biggest and best excuse to get roaring drunk. Literally, the name means 'Burning of the Ribbons', because graduates ritually torch the colour-coded ribbons worn to signify particular courses of study.

In the wee hours of Friday morning, the Queima kicks off with the Serenata Monumental, a hauntingly beautiful midnight fado performance on the steps of the Sé Velha. The agenda continues with sports events, private black-tie balls, nightly concerts at the so-called Queimodromo across the Ponte de Santa Clara, and a beer-soaked Sunday-afternoon parade called the Cortejo dos Grelados that runs from the university down to Largo da Portagem.

In their rush to sponsor the various festivities, Portuguese breweries provide ultra-cheap beer, which is distributed and drunk in liberal quantities.

with attractive fabrics that give the place an optimistic feel. Two share a bathroom (another has an exterior private bathroom) and there's a kitchen and book exchange.

Hotel Vitória HOTEL €
(☎234 824 049; www.hotelvitoria.pt; Rua da Sota 9-13; s/d/tr €45/55/75; ❄📶) This friendly family-run *residencial* (guesthouse) has had a makeover. The more renovated rooms have a clean-line Nordic feel and lots of light (not all are renovated though). Try for a 3rd-floor room for the best views of the old town or river. There's a great family room available too, and a downstairs restaurant.

Hotel Botânico de Coimbra HOTEL €
(☎239 714 824; residbotanico@gmail.com; Bairro de São José 15; s/d/tr €38/48/59; ❄📶) This simple, but irreproachably kept, guesthouse is a 15-minute stroll from the centre through the botanic gardens and boasts friendly staff and elegantly sparse rooms, including some family suites. Rooms vary in size – some are very spacious. The overall package is excellent, there's double-paned glass to keep out street noise and easy street parking around the corner.

Hotel Domus GUESTHOUSE €
(☎239 828 584; www.residencialdomus.com; Rua Adelino Veiga 62; s €40, d €48-50, tr €65; ❄📶) Clean, well-maintained Domus is a family-run place in a quiet pedestrian shopping zone near Coimbra A train station. There are some nice old features and furnishings, plus friendly management. The best rooms are the front-facing ones upstairs, which get plenty of natural light.

★**Casa Pombal** GUESTHOUSE €€
(☎239 835 175; www.casapombal.com; Rua das Flores 18; s with/without bathroom €55/40, d with/without bathroom €65/54; @📶) In a lovely old-town location, this winning, Dutch-run guesthouse squeezes tons of charm into a small space. You can forgive the odd blip for the delicious breakfast (served in a gorgeous blue-tiled room) and the friendly staff who provide multilingual advice. Nine cosy wood-floored rooms (five with shared bathroom) are individually decorated in historical style; a couple boast magnificent views.

Five Senses Hostel HOTEL €€
(☎239 094 135; facebook/fivesenseshostel; Rua da Figueira da Foz 51; dm €20, d €65-80, f €100-140; ❄📶) Handily located for the bus station, yet still accessible to the historic centre on foot, this lovely new hostel-cum-guesthouse is part of the new and contemporary breed of sleeping options. It's white, light and modern, and resembles a large and sleek holiday house.

Hotel Oslo HOTEL €€
(☎239 829 071; www.hoteloslo-coimbra.pt; Avenida Fernão de Magalhães 25; s/d €55/65; P❄📶) This comfortable, reliable hotel near the Coimbra A station has well-maintained rooms, a free garage with complimentary valet parking, satellite TV, double-paned windows and a popular 5th-floor bar (open 7pm to 1am) with views up to the university. For not much extra the 'superior' rooms have larger bathrooms, flatscreen TVs and balconies with views. The standards are compact but fine too.

Residencial Alentejana GUESTHOUSE €€
(☎239 825 903; www.residencialalentejana.com; Rua Dr António Henriques Seco 1; s €40-55, d €50-70; ❄📶) Worth the uphill walk, this prominent old town house offers wood-panelled, high-ceilinged rooms. It's an older-style, characterful place with kindly owners and a good-value local restaurant downstairs.

Hotel Astória HOTEL €€
(☎239 853 020; www.almeidahotels.com; Avenida Emídio Navarro 21; s/d/ste €72/92/130, superior s/d €97/117; ❄📶) The Astória's unmistakable art nouveau facade contemplates the river and Largo da Portagem. It has personality and professional staff; it's all delightfully old-fashioned but that goes for the very dog-eared rooms too. It won't be to everyone's taste. The round tower rooms have wraparound views and a little balcony in a prime location. Wi-fi is only in the lobby.

★**Quinta das Lágrimas** HOTEL €€€
(☎239 802 380; www.quintadaslagrimas.pt; Rua António Augusto Gonçalves; r €160-260; P❄📶🏊) This splendid historical palace is now one of Portugal's most enchanting upper-crust hotels. Choose between richly furnished rooms in the old palace, or Scandinavian minimalism in the modern annexe – complete with Jacuzzi. A few rooms look out on to the garden where Dona Inês de Castro reputedly met her tragic end. Discounts are sometimes available online, even in high season, and it's cheaper midweek.

Eating

The atmospheric narrow streets between Praça do Comércio and Coimbra A train station are full of characterful, older-style

Portuguese eateries; just wander down here and smell what's cooking. Many contemporary tapas-style places have opened in the old town (better for vegetarians). There's something to suit all budgets.

Cafetaria Museu da Ciência CAFE €
(☎ 910 575 151; Rua dos Estudos; light meals €4-9; ⏰ 10am-6.30pm; ✎) Tucked away in a remote part of the top of town, the science museum's cafe offers a large interior warmed by a log fire and an excellent terrace with views over the town below. Its light meals include quiches, salads and juices. It's renowned for its fabulous weekend breakfasts (from 11.30am to 4.30pm; €14.30). Daily plates Monday to Friday cost €6.

Justiça e Paz CAFETERIA €
(☎ 239 822 483; www.justicaepaz.com/restaurante-e-bar.php; Rua de Couraça de Lisboa 30; fixed menu €6; ⏰ 8.30am-11.30pm Mon & Tue, 8.30am-11pm Fri, 9am-7pm Sat; ✎) Part of the university's Law Faculty, this wonderful cafeteria is one of Coimbra's best-kept secrets. An excellent option for the budget traveller in need of a hearty meal, it offers plates of the day plus a soup for €6. And there are veggie options available, too. Another big plus is the sun terrace and views from heights over the town's botanic garden.

Adega Paço dos Condes PORTUGUESE €
(☎ 239 825 605; Rua do Paço do Conde 1; mains €5-10; ⏰ 11.30am-3pm & 7-11pm Mon-Sat) Usually crowded with students and Coimbra locals, this straightforward family-run grill, with its retro sign out the front, is one of the city's best budget eateries. It's like something from a bygone era: prices are great and there's a long list of daily specials, which are usually your best way forward.

Porta Larga SANDWICHES €
(☎ 239 823 619; Rua das Padeiras 35; sandwiches €4.50; ⏰ 9am-8pm Mon-Sat) For a quick snack with a hefty dose of local flavour, António's *sandes de leitão* (roast pork sandwiches) can't be beat. For over 76 years it's been serving up (let's not beat around the bush here) little piggies turning on spits.

Mercado Municipal Dom Pedro V MARKET €
(Rua Olímpio Nicolau Rui Fernandes; ⏰ 7am-7pm Mon-Sat) A colourful stop for self-caterers, this market is full of lively fruit and vegetable stalls and butcher shops displaying Portuguese cuts of meat (hooves, claws and all).

★ **Tapas Nas Costas** TAPAS €€
(☎ 239 157 425; www.tapasnascostas.pt; Rua Quebra Costas 19; tapas €3.50-6.60; ⏰ noon-midnight Tue-Sat) *The* 'hotspot' about town at the time of research, this sophisticated tapas joint delivers delicious tapas. Decor is stylish, as are the gourmet-style goodies, such as *ovo com alheira de caça e grelos* (sausage with turnip greens and egg; €5.60). What are 'small-to-medium' sized servings for Portuguese are possibly 'normal' for anyone else, so share plates are a satisfying experience.

Loggia PORTUGUESE €€
(☎ 239 853 076; www.loggia.pt; Largo Dr José Rodrigues, Museu Nacional de Machado de Castro; mains €13.50-16; ⏰ 10am-6pm Tue-Sun, 7.30-10.30pm Wed-Sat) This museum restaurant has one of the town's most enviable locations, with stunning views (thanks to the glass walls) over the cascading roofs of the old city. It's a romantic, candlelit dining scene by night, and great value for its confident modern Portuguese mains (the lunchtime €9.50 special is good value).

Zé Manel dos Ossos TASCA €€
(☎ 239 823 790; Beco do Forno 12; mains €7-15; ⏰ noon-3pm & 7.30-10pm Mon-Fri, noon-3pm Sat) Tucked down a nondescript alley, this little gem, papered with scholarly doodles and scribbled poems, serves all things cooked off the bone. Come early or be prepared to wait in line. The charismatic service makes dining here an experience.

Fangas Mercearia Bar TAPAS €€
(☎ 934 093 636; www.fangas.pt; Rua Fernandes Tomás 45; petiscos €3-9; ⏰ 12.30-4pm & 7.30pm-12.30am Sat & Sun, 7pm-12.30am; ✎) Top-quality deli produce is used to create delightful *petiscos* (tapas) in this bright, cheery dining room, the best old-town place to eat in. Service is slow but friendly and will help you choose from a delicious array of tasty platters – sausages, stuffed vegetables, conserves – and interesting wines. When closed during the week, head to the larger 'sister', Fangas Maior, (opn 7pm-12.30am) a few doors away.

Restaurante Giro Churrasqueira PORTUGUESE €€
(☎ 239 833 020; www.restaurantegiro.com; Rua das Azeiteiras 39; mains €9-15; ⏰ noon-4pm & 7-10.30pm Mon-Sat) This back-alley place serves toothsome traditional Portuguese fare in a pleasant, tiled carnations-on-the-table-style dining room. The grilled meats

and fish are excellent, and though portions aren't as large as in some places, that's probably a good thing.

Restaurante Zé Neto PORTUGUESE €€

(☎239 826 786; Rua das Azeiteiras 8; mains €9-14; ⏱9am-3pm & 7pm-midnight Mon-Sat) This marvellous family-run place specialises in homemade Portuguese standards, including *cabrito* (kid; half portions €6). Things have been modernised by the elderly owner's daughter, who is the chef (until recently her father used to tap out the menu on a vintage typewriter), but thankfully, it hasn't lost its flair for producing great meats.

Restaurante Jardim da Manga PORTUGUESE €€

(☎239 829 156; Rua Olímpio Nicolau Rui Fernandes; mains €11-14.50; ⏱8am-midnight Sun-Fri) This cafeteria-style restaurant serves up tasty meat and fish dishes, with pleasant outdoor seating beside the amazing Jardim da Manga fountain. Better-value specials during lunch than in the evening.

Drinking & Nightlife

Coimbra has some action-packed bars. In the old town, around Praça da Sé Velha, students spill onto the cobblestones outside classic pubs, while the area around Praça da República is chock-full of bars and clubs.

★Café Santa Cruz CAFE

(☎239 833 617; www.cafesantacruz.com; Praça 8 de Maio; ⏱7.30am-midnight Mon-Sat) One of Portugal's most atmospheric cafes, where the elderly statesmen meet for their daily cuppas. Santa Cruz is set in a dramatically beautiful high-vaulted former chapel, with stained-glass windows and graceful stone arches. The terrace grants lovely views of Praça 8 de Maio. Don't miss the *crúzios*, award-winning, egg- and almond-based conventual cakes for which the cafe is famous.

★Galeria Santa Clara BAR

(☎239 441 657; www.galeriasantaclara.com; Rua António Augusto Gonçalves 67; ⏱1pm-2am Mon-Fri, to 3am Sat & Sun) Arty tearoom by day and chilled-out bar by night, this terrific place across the Mondego has good art on the walls, a series of sunny rooms and a fine terrace. It's got a great indoor-outdoor vibe and can feel like a party in a private house when things get going.

DON'T MISS

TOP VIEWS IN COIMBRA

Coimbra's picturesque hillside position means there are some great spots to enjoy magnificent views. Our pick of the vistas:

- The Museu Nacional de Machado de Castro cafe, **Loggia** (p312)
- Cafe at the **Museu da Ciência** (p312)
- Top of the tower at **Paço das Escolas** (p306)
- Belvedere of **Convento de Santa Clara-a-Nova** (p309)

Aqui Base Tango BAR

(http://aquibasetango.com; Rua Venâncio Rodrigues 8; ⏱9pm-4am Tue-Sat) This offbeat house holds one of Coimbra's most enticing bars, a quirky space with extremely original decor and a relaxed, inclusive vibe. Music ranges from jazz to alternative rock and there's always something interesting going on or in the pipeline. Gay friendly, too.

Noites Longas CLUB

(☎239 835 167; Rua Almeida Garrett 11; ⏱midnight-6am Mon-Sat) This alternative club plays mainly rock and goes loud and very late. It's not subtle but it's a reliable local favourite. Gay friendly.

O Moelas BAR

(☎962 445 275; Rua dos Coutinhos 14; ⏱10pm-4am) A friendly family-run drinking spot for students – cheap drinks for big (and late) nights. Enough said.

AAC Bar BAR

(Bar Associação Académica de Coimbra; www.facebook.com/baraac; Av Sá da Bandeira; ⏱3pm-4am) Join the black-cape-clad students at their student-union bar, where beers are cheap and everyone is welcome. The esplanade out back, with wood decking and a grassy lawn, makes an agreeable refuge.

Bar Quebra Costas BAR

(☎239 841 174; Rua Quebra Costas 45; ⏱noon-4am Mon-Fri, 2pm-4am Sat) This Coimbra classic has a sunny, cobblestoned terrace, an artsy interior, friendly service, chilled-out tunes and the occasional jazz session. It's in the perfect position for sipping a cold beer as you watch people puff and pant up the Quebra Costas.

✩ Entertainment

★ **Fado ao Centro** FADO
(☎910 679 838; www.fadoaocentro.com; Rua Quebra Costas 7; show incl drink €10) At the bottom of the old town, this friendly fado centre is a good place to introduce yourself to the genre. There's a performance every evening at 6pm. Shows include plenty of explanation, in Portuguese and English, about the history of Coimbra fado and the meaning of each song. It's tourist-oriented, but the performers enjoy it and do it well.

Teatro Académico de Gil Vicente THEATRE, CONCERT VENUE
(TAGV; ☎239 855 630; www.tagv.info; Praça da República) This university-run auditorium is an important theatre, cinema and concert venue.

Á Capella FADO
(☎239 833 985; www.acapella.com.pt; Rua do Corpo de Deus; entry incl drink €10; ⏱shows 9.30pm daily Apr-Oct, Thu-Sun Nov-Mar) A 14th-century chapel turned candlelit cocktail lounge, this place regularly hosts the city's most renowned fado musicians. There's a show every night at 9.30pm (though it's opening, or otherwise, can be a bit unpredictable).

Shows cater directly to a tourist crowd, but the atmosphere and music are both superb. The setting is as intimate as the music itself, with heart-rendingly good acoustics.

Shopping

Carlos Tomás CERAMICS
(☎239 812 945; carlostomas_ceramicaartesanal@hotmail.com; Largo da Sé Velha 4) Lovely hand-painted ceramics (and more) by Senhor Tomás. Will even do custom-made orders of your own design.

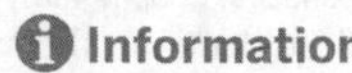

Information

MEDICAL SERVICES

Hospital da Universidade de Coimbra (☎239 400 400; www.chuc.min-saude.pt; Praceta Mota Pinto) Located 1.5km northeast of the centre.

POST

Post Office Praça da República (Praça da República; ⏱9am-6pm Mon-Fri, 10am-6pm Sat)

TOURIST INFORMATION

These offices offer good town maps as well as what's-on listings.

Turismo Largo da Portagem (☎239 488 120; www.turismodecoimbra.pt; Largo da Portagem; ⏱9am-6pm Mon-Fri, 9am-1pm & 2-6pm Sat & Sun mid-Sep–mid-Jun, 9am-8pm Mon-Fri, 9am-6pm Sat & Sun mid-Jun–mid-Sep) By the bridge, in the centre of things.

Turismo Praça República (☎939 010 084; www.turismodecoimbra.pt; Praça da República; ⏱9am-6.30pm Mon-Fri) On the eastern side of town.

Turismo Universidade (☎239 834 158; www.turismodecoimbra.pt; Praça da Porta Férrea; ⏱9am-7.30pm mid-Mar–Oct, 9am-1pm & 2-5.30pm Nov–mid-Mar) Adjacent to the Universidade de Coimbra ticket desk, just outside the Porta Férrea.

Getting There & Away

BUS

From the rather grim **bus station** (Av Fernão de Magalhães), a 15-minute walk northwest of the centre, **Rede Expressos** (☎239 855 270; www.rede-expressos.pt) runs at least a dozen buses daily to Lisbon (€14.50, 2½ hours) and to Porto (€12, 1½ hours), with almost as many to Braga (€14, 2¾ hours) and to Faro (€27, six to nine hours). There's also a regular service (more frequent in summer) that runs to Seia (€10, 1¾ hours), Guarda (€13.10, two to three hours) and other points around the Parque Natural da Serra da Estrela.

TRAIN

Long-distance trains stop only at **Coimbra B** station, north of the city. Cross the platform for quick, free connections to more-central **Coimbra A** (called just 'Coimbra' on timetables).

Coimbra is linked by regular Alfa Pendular (AP) and *intercidade* (IC) trains to Lisbon (AP/IC €22.80/19.20, 1¾/two hours) and Porto (€16.70/13.20, one/1¼ hours); IC trains also stop at intermediate destinations north and south. Trains run roughly hourly to Figueira da Foz (€2.65, one hour) and Aveiro (€5.25, one hour).

Getting Around

BICYCLE

Electronic bikes are available from **E.Tour** (☎926 646 711; www.etour.pt; per bike 3/6/12hr €12/20/35, 2-person minimum).

BUS

Between them, buses 27, 28 and 29 run about every half hour from the main bus station and the Coimbra B train station to Praça da República.

You can purchase multiuse tickets (three/five/10 trips €2.20/3.15/5.80; day ticket €3.50), which are also usable on the *elevador*, at the **SMTUC office** (www.smtuc.pt; Largo do Mercado; ⌚7am-7pm Mon-Fri, 8am-1pm Sat) at the foot of the *elevador*, at official kiosks and also at some *tabacarias* (tobacconists and newsagents). Tickets bought on board cost €1.60 per trip.

You'll also see *patufinhas* (electric minibuses) crawling around pedestrian areas in the centre of Coimbra, between Baixa and Alta Coimbra and through the medieval heart of the city. These accept the same tickets as other SMTUC buses.

CAR

If you come by car, prepare for snarled traffic and scarce parking. Convenient parking near the Baixa is on the west bank of the river, in a lot just across Ponte de Santa Clara from Largo da Portagem. Nearer the university, free street parking is available on side streets around Praça da República. You can hire cars from **Hertz** (☎219 426 300; www.hertz.pt; Edifício Tricana, Rua Padre Estevão Cabral, Shop 6).

ELEVADOR DO MERCADO

The **elevador** (1hr ticket €1.50, 3/5/10 trips €2.20/3.15/5.80; ⌚7.30am-9pm Mon-Sat, 10am-9pm Sun) – a double elevator connected by walkway, between the market and the university – can save you an uphill climb. Use city bus tickets or buy a ticket from the lift operator.

Around Coimbra

Conímbriga

★Roman Ruins RUINS

(ruins & museum adult/child €4.50/free; ⌚10am-7pm) In the rolling country southwest of Coimbra, Conímbriga boasts Portugal's most extensive Roman ruins, one of the best-preserved sites on the Iberian Peninsula. It tells the poignant tale of a town that, after centuries of security, was split in two by quickly erected walls and then entirely abandoned as the Roman Empire disintegrated.

Elaborate mosaics, heated baths and fountains evoke toga-clad dalliances. Through the middle of this runs a massive defensive wall, built in haste to fend off raids.

To get your head around Conímbriga's fascinating history, begin (or end) at the renovated four-room museum. Displays present every aspect of Roman life from mosaics (including the amazing minotaur mosaic) to medallions.

Conímbriga actually dates back to Celtic times (*briga* is a Celtic term for a defended area). But when the Romans settled here in the 1st century AD, it blossomed into a major city on the route from Lisbon (Olisipo) to Braga (Bracara Augusta). Its prosperity is revealed by well-to-do mansions carpeted with elaborate mosaics and scattered with fountains.

In the 3rd century the townsfolk, threatened by invading tribes, desperately threw up a huge defensive wall right through the town centre, abandoning the residential area. But this wasn't enough to stop the Suevi (Sueves) seizing the town in 468. Inhabitants fled to nearby Aeminius (Coimbra) – thereby saving Conímbriga from destruction.

Once in the ruins (50m from the museum), the disproportionately large wall will first draw your attention, followed by the patchwork of exceptional mosaic floors below it. Here you'll find the fabulous **Casa dos Repuxos** (House of Fountains); though partly destroyed by the wall, it contains cool pond-gardens, fountains and truly extraordinary mosaics showing the four seasons and various hunting scenes.

The site's most important **villa**, on the other side of the wall, is said to have belonged to one Cantaber, whose wife and children were seized by the Suevi in an attack in 465. It's a palace of a place, with baths, pools and a sophisticated underground heating system.

Excavations continue in the outer areas. Eye-catching features include the remains of a 3km-long **aqueduct**, which led up to a hilltop bathing complex, and the **forum**, once surrounded by covered porticoes.

Check bus schedules as these change seasonally, with fewer buses outside summer. At the time of research, buses run from Coimbra directly to the ruins (€2.30, 45 minutes) at 9am, 9.30am and 12.30pm Monday to Friday; 9.30am, 12.30pm and 3.30pm Saturday; and 9.30am, 12.30pm and 3pm Sunday. Return-trip departures are at 1pm and 6pm Monday to Friday; 1.30pm and 6.30pm Saturday; and 2pm and 6.30pm Sunday. There are also half-hourly buses to Condeixa-a-Nova, which is a half-hour stroll from the ruins.

Luso & Mata Nacional do Buçaco

A retreat from the world for almost 2000 years, the slopes of the Serra do Buçaco are now home to the walled, 105-hectare Mata Nacional do Buçaco (or Bussaco). Harbouring an astounding 700 plant species, from huge Mexican cedars to tree-sized ferns, this national forest is equally fecund in terms of the poetry it has inspired. Generations of Coimbra's literary types have enshrined the forest in the national imagination with breathless hymns to its mystical marriage of natural and spiritual beauty.

And in the midst of the forest stands a royal palace completed in 1907; despite the extravagance of its fairy-tale neo-Manueline facade, the dynasty fell just three years later.

The gateway is the quaint little spa town of Luso, whose spa waters are considered a balm. You can stay in Luso or the royal palace itself, otherwise it's an easy day trip from Coimbra.

History

The Luso and Buçaco area probably served as a Christian refuge as early as the 2nd century AD, although the earliest known hermitage was founded in the 6th century by Benedictine monks. In 1628 Carmelite monks embarked on an extensive program of forestation. They planted exotic species, laid cobbled paths and enclosed the forest within high stone walls. The forest grew so renowned that in 1643 Pope Urban VIII decreed that anyone damaging the trees would be excommunicated.

The peace was briefly shattered in 1810, when Napoleon's forces under Masséna were beaten here by the Anglo-Portuguese army of the future Duke of Wellington (the battle is re-enacted here every 27 September). In 1834, when religious orders throughout Portugal were abolished, the forest became state property.

Sights

★Mata Nacional do Buçaco — FOREST

(www.fmb.pt; car/cyclist/pedestrian €5/free/free; 8am-8pm Apr-Sep, to 6pm Oct-Mar) The aromatic forest is criss-crossed with trails, dotted with crumbling chapels and graced with ponds, fountains and exotic trees. The most accessible paths lead to pretty **Vale dos Fetos** and **Fonte Fria**, where swans swim beneath a grand staircase. Among several fine viewpoints is **Cruz Alta** (545m). But the most fascinating paths are those leading to tiny chapels and hermitages, plus those following the religious trail 'Way of the Cross'.

What most visitors come to see is the fairy-tale Palace Hotel do Buçaco (p317).

Now a luxury hotel, Palace Hotel do Buçaco was a royal summer retreat (completed in 1907) built on the site of a 17th-century Carmelite monastery. This wedding cake of a building is over the top in every way: outside, its conglomeration of turrets and spires is surrounded by rose gardens and swirling box hedges in geometrical patterns; inside (nonguests are more or less prohibited entry) are neo-Manueline carvings, suits of armour on the grand staircases and *azulejos* (tiles) illustrating scenes from *Os Lusiados* (The Lusiads), in which Portuguese armies win glorious battles at sea amid the dismayed looks of their stupefied opponents.

By road the Portas das Ameias, the nearest gate into the forest, is 900m from the centre. The hotel is 2.1km from the Portas das Ameias.

Santa Cruz do Bussaco — CHURCH

(www.fmb.pt; adult/child €2/1; 10am-1pm & 2-5pm Oct-Mar, to 6pm Apr-Sep) Tucked away behind the Palace Hotel do Buçaco, this is what remains of a convent where the future Duke of Wellington rested after the Battle of Bussaco in 1810. The atmospheric interior has decaying religious paintings, an unusual walkway right around the chapel, some guns from the battle, and the much-venerated image of Nossa Senhora do Leite (Our Lady of the Milk), with a raft of ex-voto offerings.

Activities

Maloclinic Spa — SPA

(www.maloclinictermasluso.com; Rua Álvaro Castelões; 8am-1pm & 2-7pm daily high season, 9am-1pm & 2-6pm Mon-Sat low season) Just the ticket after a long walk in the forest, the Termas de Luso welcomes drop-in visitors for therapies ranging from full-body massages (€60) and spinal steam baths (€15) to body wraps. People come from far and wide to fill their bottles for free at the adjacent natural spring.

Sleeping

Alojamento Local Imperial — HOTEL €

(231 937 570; www.residencialimperial.com; Rua Emídio Navarro, 25, Luso; d €32-42) Extremely good value, the 14 rooms here are small and ever so slightly dog-eared, but are light and pleasant. The hotel is conveniently located, with some rooms overlooking Luso's sweet little plaza.

Alegre Hotel — BOUTIQUE HOTEL €

(231 930 256; www.alegrehotels.com; Rua Emídio Navarro 2, Luso; s/d €45/55; P) This grand, atmospheric, pinkish-coloured 19th-century town house has large doubles with plush drapes, decorative plaster ceilings and polished period furniture. Its appeal is enhanced by an elegant entryway, formal parlour and pretty vine-draped garden with pool.

Palace Hotel do Buçaco HOTEL €€€
(☎231 937 970; www.themahotels.pt; Mata Nacional do Buçaco; s €148-199, d €169-225; P) This sumptuous royal palace was originally a hunting lodge (completed in 1907). It sits in the middle of the forest and offers a delightfully ostentatious place to stay. Common areas are stunning – particularly the tilework above the grand staircase – though some rooms feel a little musty and threadbare. Don't expect flatscreen TVs or period furniture, but do expect stunning marble bathrooms.

Eating

★**Pedra de Sal** PORTUGUESE €€
(☎231 939 405; www.restaurantepedradesal.com; Rua Francisco A Dinis 33, Luso; mains €4-16; ⊙noon-3.30pm & 7-9.30pm Wed-Mon) Winningly done out in dark wood, this is the best restaurant in Luso by quite a distance. It specialises in succulent cuts of pork from the Iberian pig, has some excellent wines to wash them down with and top service to boot. Book ahead at weekends.

Palace Hotel do Buçaco PORTUGUESE €€
(☎231 937 970; www.themahotels.pt; Mata Nacional do Buçaco; mains €11.50-15; ⊙8-10.30am, 1-3pm & 8-10pm;) For a truly memorable dinner, it's hard to beat the elegant spread at the Palace Hotel's dining room, itself a work of art, with natural light pouring over the parquet wood floors through a graceful faux-Manueline window studded with rosettes and overlapping arches. The menu includes vegetarian options. Or go all out with the Royal Tasting Menu (€50).

Information

Turismo (☎231 939 133; Rua Emídio Navarro 136, Luso; ⊙9.30am-1pm & 2.30-5.30pm) Has accommodation information, internet access, town and forest maps, and is helpful.

Getting There & Away

BUS

Buses (handier than the train) run five times each weekday (four only return from Luso) and twice daily on Saturdays from Coimbra's main bus station to Luso (around €4, 40 minutes). In July and August they head to the Palace Hotel do Buçaco (around €4, 50 minutes).

CAR

If driving from Coimbra, ignore your GPS and make sure you take the lovely, foresty N235, which comes off the IP3: you'll save a toll, too.

TRAIN

Trains run three times Monday to Saturday (two on Sunday) from Coimbra B station to Luso/Buçaco station (€2.60, 25 minutes), but the inconvenient schedule makes a same-day round trip nearly impossible. From Luso/Buçaco station it's a 15-minute walk to central Luso, plus another half hour uphill through the forest to the Palace Hotel.

Montemor-o-Velho

Today at the site of the historic Montemor-o-Velho, you can walk the crenellated battlements and survey lush rice fields lying alongside the Rio Mondego far below. Inside little remains but part of the ruined **Paço das Infantas** (Princesses' Palace), built by Afonso Henrique's aunt Urraca, and the beautifully tiled **Igreja de Santa Maria de Alcáçova**, a small Romanesque church with 16th-century Manueline touches. It conserves some 18th-century wall paintings. The site's strategic importance as a fortification dates back at least two millennia.

Sights

Castelo do Montemor-o-Velho CASTLE
(⊙9.30am-6pm Apr-Sep, 9.30am-5.30pm Oct-Mar) FREE Perched high atop a rugged hill 25km west of Coimbra, the glowering walls of the Castelo do Montemor-o-Velho dominate the surrounding marshland. Whether seen from a distance or from atop the castle walls themselves, it's easy to imagine this site as an early bastion in the Reconquista. Ferdinand I of Castile and León recaptured Montemor-o-Velho from the Moors in 1064, and within less than a century his great-grandson Afonso Henrique claimed it as part of his new Kingdom of Portugal.

Over the intervening centuries the castle was rebuilt and expanded several times, with most of the current structure dating from the 14th century.

Sleeping

Hotel Abade João HOTEL €
(☎239 687 010; http://abadejoao.com; Rua dos Combatentes da Grande Guerra 15; s €30, d €45-50; P❄) This cool and attractive option sits above the sleepy, pretty town square. Comfortable rooms are a steal at these prices and breakfast is included.

Information

Turismo (www.cm-montemorvelho.pt; Castelo do Montemor-o-Velho; ⏲9.30am-5.30pm Sep-May, 10am-8pm Jun-Aug) This modern block is housed within the castle walls.

Getting There & Away

Trains between Coimbra B and Figueira da Foz stop every hour or two at Montemor station (around €2.65), 4km southeast of the castle.

Moisés Correia de Oliveira (www.moises-transportes.pt) buses between Coimbra (€3.60, 50 minutes) and Figueira (around €3, 30 minutes) stop closer to the castle, five to eight times daily (fewer on Sunday).

Figueira da Foz

POP 27,740

Popular with Portuguese holidaymakers for over a century, the beach resort of Figueira da Foz (fi-*guy*-ra da *fosh;* Figueira) continues to attract big summer crowds – including Spaniards lured by easy motorway access, and surfers drawn to championship-calibre waves at Cabedelo. For most visitors, the star attractions are Figueira's outlandishly wide beach and a casino featuring big-name acts on summer evenings. The local sands are so vast that it takes a five-minute walk across creaky boardwalks simply to reach the sea. Out of season, the place has a more tranquil charm, but thanks to the increasing number of sophisticated eateries and bars it's not a lonely experience. In summer it's another matter: sizzling bodies and candy-striped beach huts fill every square inch of beach and evenings are upbeat.

Sights

Serra da Boa Viagem HEADLAND

For those with wheels, this headland, found 4km north of Figueira and carpeted in pines, eucalyptus and acacias, is a fine place for panoramas, picnics and cool walks. Take the coastal road to Buarcos, turn right at the lighthouse and follow the signs to Boa Viagem. Up here, Luso Aventura has a series of zipline-style routes between trees.

Museu Municipal Dr Santos Rocha MUSEUM

(☎233 402 840; Rua Calouste Gulbenkian; adult/child €2/free; ⏲9.30am-5pm Tue-Fri, 2-7pm Sat Sep-Jun) This modern museum, beside Parque das Abadias, houses a wonderfully wide-ranging collection featuring local archaeological finds, Roman coins, medieval statues, outlandish Indo-Portuguese furniture, objects documenting Portugal's early African explorations and rotating art exhibits.

Beaches

Despite its size, Figueira's main city beach gets packed in August. Families will enjoy the sheltered **Praia do Forte**, by the fort. For some terrific surf and more character than the main beach, head north to **Buarcos**, a 2km stroll along the pleasant beachfront promenade. Alternatively, **Transdev** (☎233 422 648; www.transdev.pt) runs buses there (€1.35) every 45 minutes or so.

For more seclusion, continue around Cabo Mondego headland to **Praia de Quiaios**, about 10km north of Figueira da Foz. Transdev buses run here from the bus station (€2.45, 30 minutes) six times every weekday.

South across the mouth of the Rio Mondego is **Praia de Cabedelo**, Figueira's prime surfing venue.

A little further is **Praia de Gala**. AVIC buses run from the train station via the centre to Cabedelo and Gala (both €1.35) every hour or so on weekdays (less often on weekends).

Activities

Escola de Surf da Figueira da Foz SURFING

(☎918 703 363; www.surfingfigueira.com; Rua do Cabedelo 36, São Pedro; group/individual classes €30/40, short-/paddle-board rental per day €20/30) Surf classes and rentals are available from Escola de Surf da Figueira da Foz.

Luso Aventura ZIPLINE

(☎915 536 555; www.lusoaventura.com; ⏲Apr-Oct) If you've had enough of the water, get some air thrills on one of several zipline courses (€10 to €17).

Festivals & Events

Festas da Cidade FIESTA

The town festival carries on for two weeks encompassing the 23rd and 24th June, with folk music, parades and concerts.

Sleeping

High season is July and August. Expect discounts of up to 40% in winter. You may be approached in summer by locals offering private rooms: while informal, they are often decent deals.

Paintshop Hostel HOSTEL €
(233 436 633; www.paintshophostel.com; Rua da Clemência 9; dm/d €20/50;) Set in a characterful blue house in the old part of town, this top-of-the-line hostel offers high-ceilinged dorms and quiet private rooms (also with shared bathrooms) at the top of the building. Facilities are great for backpackers and surfers; it offers bike, board and wetsuit rental, a DVD library, free wi-fi and breakfast, a kitchen, a pool table, and a great bar area out the back.

Orbitur Gala CAMPGROUND €
(233 431 492; www.orbitur.pt; Praia de Gala; sites per adult/child/tent/car €6.80/4.10/9/6.40;) The best of the local campgrounds, this flat, shady spot is next to a great beach. It's south of Foz do Mondego and 1km from the nearest bus stop. Bungalows cost €92 for two in high season, half that outside summer.

★**Universal Boutique Hotel** BOUTIQUE HOTEL €€
(233 090 110; www.universalboutiquehotel.pt; Rua Miguel Bombarda 50; d €102-139;) Figueira's new and lovely boutique option, only a few blocks back from the beach, is a luxurious and romantic spot, with a delightful lounge-bar area and rooms with all the modern trimmings. Each of the four floors is themed by colour and contemporary architectural touches are throughout (thinking 'hanging' balustrades, a glass floor and more).

Casa dos Suecos GUESTHOUSE €€
(233 040 483; www.casadossuecos.com; Rua Joaquim Sotto Mayor 73A; d €70-80, f €95;) Staying here is a bit like being a guest at a friend's house in a smart neighbourhood. Originally built for Swiss workers, it has maintained its name, and these days it continues as a guesthouse. Rooms feel Scandanavian – clean lines and blonde woods – and provide great value if you don't mind being out of the thick of things.

Hotel Wellington HOTEL €€
(233 426 767; www.lupahoteis.com; Rua Dr Calado 25; s/d/f €75/85/120;) Near the beach and casino action, this comfortable hotel is right in the heart of things and offers immaculate rooms with huge beds, minibars and writing desks, along with nearby off-street parking (€7 per night).

Hotel Aviz HOTEL €€
(233 422 635; Rua Dr A L Lopes Guimarães 16; s €45-50, d €55-65;) Run by a charming, well-travelled couple, this squeaky-clean guesthouse two blocks from the beach has lovely wood floors, high ceilings and some nice period details. Reserve ahead in summer. Prices are halved in off season.

Sweet Atlantic Hotel HOTEL €€€
(233 408 900; www.sweethotels.pt; Avenida 25 de Abril 21; r not incl breakfast €124;) Rising over the beachfront promenade, this excellent modern hotel contrasts chocolatey and dark cherry colours with the bright magnificence of the strand-and-sea views from its comfortable rooms. All have some sea view, those that are front on are stunning. Small kitchenettes, smart bathrooms, and a spa complex (€15 for a 90-minute circuit) are other good extras.

Eating

★**Núcleo Sportinguista** PORTUGUESE €
(233 434 882; Rua Praia da Fonte 14; mains €8-8.50; noon-3pm & 7-10pm) Sitting under the awning, surrounded by enthusiastic locals and a sea of tables draped in checked tablecloths, feels a bit like crashing a Portuguese family's private barbecue. Don your best green and white clothes – it's a supporters' club for the Lisbon football team Sporting Clube – and enjoy the delicious grilled meats and cheap pitchers of wine. A great deal.

Mar à Vista TASCA €
(Rua 5 de Outubro, Buarcos; mains €7-11; noon-5pm) Although touristy in summer, this taverna is as simple and genuine as they come, and is the spot for *sardinhas assadas* (grilled sardines) – as many as you can eat.

It's located in Buarcos at the northern end of Figueira da Foz.

Praça 18 CAFE €
(Praça General Freire de Andrade 18; mains €4.50-9; 11.30am-10pm Mon-Fri, 11.30am-3pm & 6.30-10.30pm Sat;) This gorgeous retro-hip cafe is run by young souls. The funky furniture mix reflects the menu that encompasses everything from gourmet hamburgers to salads. Great vegetarian options. You won't want to be in a hurry (service can be a bit disorganised), but it's not a place to rush anyway as it's a pleasant spot to chill. Daily plates cost between €4.50 and €6.50.

Emanha Geladeria ICE CREAM €
(Avenida 25 de Abril 62-64; ice cream from €2.20; 8am-midnight) Although it's a chain (there are three in Figueira da Foz and the company started here), this is Portugal's 'favourite'

Figueira da Foz

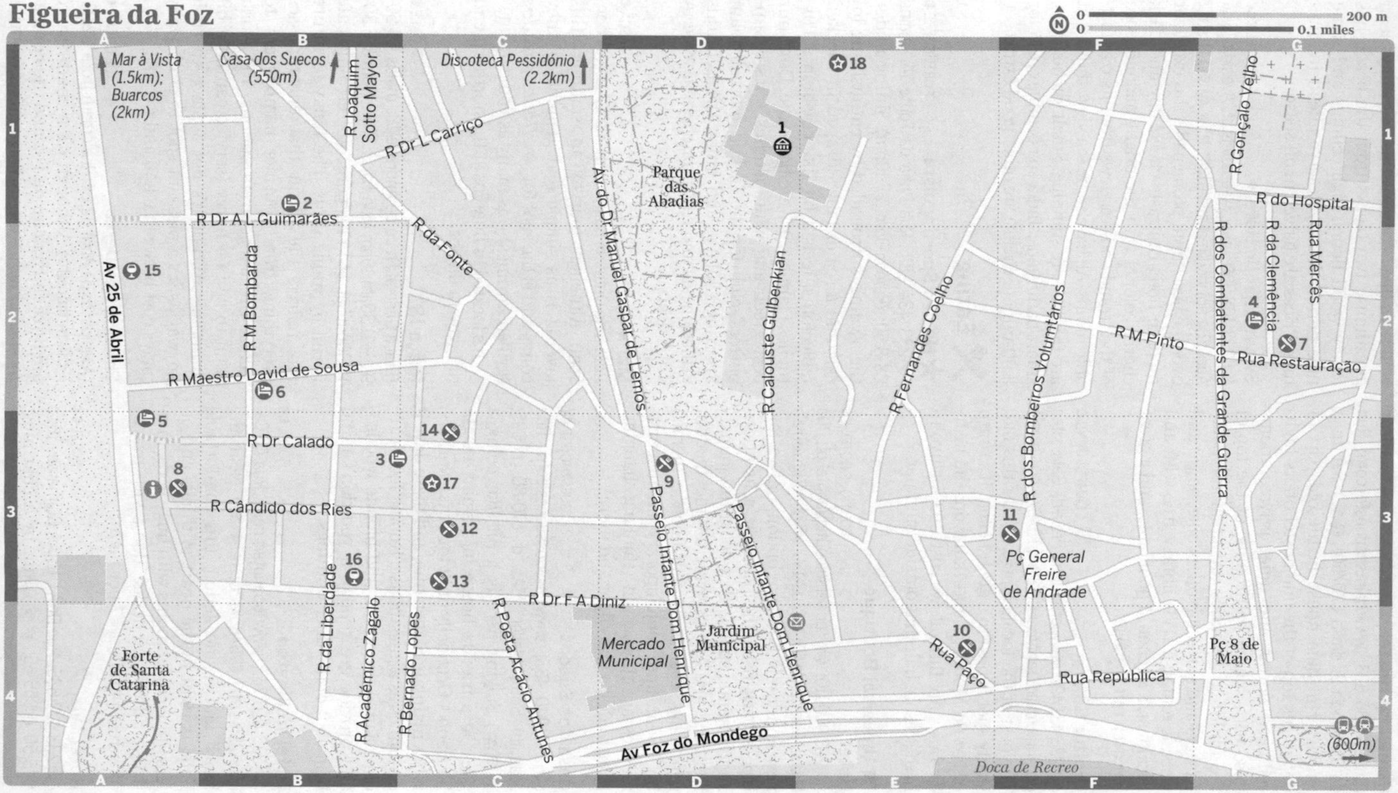

0 200 m
0 0.1 miles

Mar à Vista (1.5km); Buarcos (2km)
Casa dos Suecos (550m)
Discoteca Pessidónio (2.2km)
18
1
Parque das Abadias
R Joaquim Sotto Mayor
R Dr L Carriço
R Gonçalo Velho
R do Hospital
2
R Dr A L Guimarães
R da Fonte
R dos Combatentes da Grande Guerra
R da Clemência
Rua Mercês
15
Av 25 de Abril
R M Bombarda
Av do Dr Manuel Gaspar de Lemos
R Calouste Gulbenkian
R Fernandes Coelho
R dos Bombeiros Voluntários
4
7
R M Pinto
Rua Restauração
R Maestro David de Sousa
6
5
14
R Dr Calado
3
9
8
17
R Cândido dos Ries
Passeio Infante Dom Henrique
11
12
Pç General Freire de Andrade
16
13
R Dr F A Diniz
R da Liberdade
R Académico Zagalo
R Bernado Lopes
R Poeta Acácio Antunes
Mercado Municipal
Jardim Municipal
10
Rua Paço
Pç 8 de Maio
Rua República
Forte de Santa Catarina
Av Foz do Mondego
Doca de Recreo
(600m)

Figueira da Foz

Sights
1 Museu Municipal Dr Santos Rocha D1

Sleeping
2 Hotel Aviz B1
3 Hotel Wellington B3
4 Paintshop Hostel G2
5 Sweet Atlantic Hotel A3
6 Universal Boutique Hotel B2

Eating
7 A Grega G2
8 Emanha Geladeria A3
9 Núcleo Sportinguista D3
10 Pizzeria Claudio E4
11 Praça 18 .... F3
12 Restaurante Caçarola I C3
13 Volta e Meia C3
14 Wine Bar by Cristal C3

Drinking & Nightlife
15 Complexo Piscina de Mar A2
16 Zeitgeist Caffé B3

Entertainment
17 Casino Figueira C3
18 Centro de Artes e Espectáculos E1

ice cream (so the locals say) and a rite of passage for any ice-cream licker. It's on the terrace above the *turismo*.

A Grega PORTUGUESE €
(Rua Restauração 30; mains €7-9.50; 12.30-3pm & 7-10pm Tue-Sun) This simple, ultrafriendly neighbourhood restaurant does tasty grilled meats, including an Argentine-style *parrillada* (mixed grill; €16.50) that two will struggle to finish. There's also toothsome calamari and mixed fish dishes.

Pizzeria Claudio PIZZA €
(Largo do Carvão 11e; pizzas from €7; noon-2.30pm & 7-10.30pm Tue-Sun) Good pizzas. Join the lines out the door in summer.

★ **Wine Bar by Cristal** INTERNATIONAL €€
(Rua Dr Calado 24; mains €6-12; 8pm-4am Tue-Sun) This lovely bar-restaurant has lifted the quality of Figueira da Foz' local eating and bar scene. Tapas and other dishes are served creatively and with pizzazz. There's a great bar with an extensive wine, cocktail and spirits menu (gin lovers are in for a treat). And be sure to get down and dirty with Ricardo's, err, chocolate dessert.

Volta e Meia PORTUGUESE €€
(233 418 381; www.voltaemeia.com; Rua Dr Francisco António Diniz 64; mains €8-15; noon-3pm & 7-11pm Mon & Wed-Fri, to midnight Sat & Sun) It describes itself as an all-in-one restaurant-*tasca*-teahouse-bar-*petisqueira* (and more). Indeed, this cosy spot prepares lovely Portuguese plates with a gourmet flair. It's an arty space and a fun place to visit. Offers a changing weekly menu with a daily plate.

Restaurante Marisqueira Rosa Amélia SEAFOOD €€
(Av D João II 2, Buarcos; mains from €10; 12.30-3pm & 7-11pm) In Buarcos (within the Hotel Tamargueira complex) in a new, modern eatery, traditional 'fisherwoman' and personality about town, the proud, traditionalist Dona Rosa Amelia, does what she does best: whipping up *mariscos* (shellfish) dishes.

Restaurante Caçarola I SEAFOOD €€
(233 424 861; Rua Cândido dos Reis 65; specials €7.50-8, mains €12.50-15; 10am-2am) This popular seafood restaurant has been here for over 40 years and has managed to hang in there. Why? It's a quirky spot where locals belly up to the island bar all day long for good-value *combinados do dia balcão* (daily lunch-counter specials). In addition to the counter seating, there are tables on the pedestrian boulevard outside.

Drinking & Nightlife

Complexo Piscina de Mar BAR
(Av 25 de Abril; 10am-8pm Jul & Aug) Kick back on a lounger or dive into the pool at this waterfront bar with great beach views, resident DJ and a big-screen TV for those must-see football matches.

Discoteca Pessidónio CLUB
(233 435 637; Rua Estrada da Serra, Condados, Tavarede; 10pm-late Fri & Sat Jul & Aug) Still going strong after four decades, Pessidónio can be found in the suburbs east of the municipal campground. Its four distinct dance venues include the Capela Club, whose poolside Sala da Piscina is popular for tropical drinks on hot summer nights.

Zeitgeist Caffé BAR
(Rua Dr Francisco António Diniz 82; ⏲8pm-4am) Glamorous Zeitgeist features comfy couches and chairs, and windows overlooking the popular strip of bars that lines adjacent Rua Académico Zagalo. There's regular live music and DJs in a wide range of styles.

☆ Entertainment

Casino Figueira CASINO
(☎233 408 400; www.casinofigueira.pt; Rua Dr Calado 1; ⏲3pm-3am Sun-Thu, 4pm-4am Fri & Sat) Shimmering in neon and acrylic, Figueira's casino is the epicentre of the city's nightlife. Crawling with cash-laden holidaymakers in search of a quick buck, it has roulette and slot machines, and a sophisticated piano bar with live music after 11pm some evenings in summer. Dress up at night – beach attire, thongs (flip-flops) or sports shoes may keep you out.

Centro de Artes e Espectáculos ARTS CENTRE
(☎233 407 200; www.cae.pt) Behind the Museu Municipal Dr Santos Rocha, CAE hosts big-name bands, theatre and art-house cinema. Check the website or pick up a schedule at the *turismo*.

ℹ Information

Biblioteca Municipal (Rua Calouste Gulbenkian; ⏲2-7.30pm Mon, 9.30am-7.30pm Tue-Fri, 2-7pm Sat) Free internet at the town library.

Main Post Office (Passeio Infante Dom Henrique; ⏲9am-6pm Mon-Fri)

Turismo (☎233 422 610; www.figueiraturismo.com; Av 25 de Abril 19; ⏲9.30am-1pm & 2-5.30pm) Good maps and information plus the *Agenda* magazine with a list of what's on.

ℹ Getting There & Away

BUS

Figueira is served by two long-distance bus companies.

Moisés Correia de Oliveira (☎233 426 703; www.moises-transportes.pt) has regular departures (fewer on weekends), via Montemor-o-Velho, to Coimbra (€4.30, 1½ hours).

Rede Expressos (www.rede-expressos.pt) has buses to Lisbon (€15.50, 2¾ hours, at least three daily) via Leiria; and to Aveiro (€8.50, one hour, two to four daily).

TRAIN

Train connections to/from Coimbra (€2.65, one hour, hourly weekdays, fewer on weekends) are superior to buses. There are also direct trains to Leiria (€5.45, one hour, three daily), with connecting service to Mira Sintra-Meleças station on the suburban Lisbon line. For Porto, change in Coimbra.

Praia de Mira

For a few days of sunny, windblown torpor, head for Praia de Mira, the best-equipped town along the 50km coastal strip between Figueira da Foz and Aveiro. Sandwiched between a long, clean beach and a canal-fed lagoon, this small resort has little to distract you from the main business at hand: sun, sea and seafood.

Activities

Secret Surf School SURFING
(☎915 480 890; www.secretsurfschool.com; 1/5/10 classes per person €17.50/80/145; ⏲daily Jul & Aug, Mon-Sat Sep-Jun) Operated from Duna Bar, located on the beach in the centre of town; they can teach you how to get out there and ride the waves.

Sleeping

Orbitur CAMPGROUND €
(☎231 471 234; www.orbitur.pt; Estrada Florestal 1-Km 2, Dunas de Mira; sites per adult/child/tent/car €6.50/3.90/6.90/6.10; ⏲mid-Mar–end-Sep; P 📶) This well-equipped, shady site is at the southern end of the lagoon. Bungalows are available from €84 in August, or €59 the rest of the summer.

Maçarico Beach Hotel HOTEL €€
(☎231 471 114; www.macaricobeachhotel.com; Rua Raúl Brandão; r €85-95, with sea view €113-123; P ❄) This stylish seafront hotel, a refurbishment of an old favourite guesthouse, features a sudoku-like facade and a glitzy lobby. Rooms are neat and modern, some with excellent sea-view balconies. The pool deck has more great vistas.

Eating

Salgáboca SEAFOOD €€
(www.salgaboca.pt; Rua Furriel Henriques da Costa 19; mains €8.50-25; ⏲10.30am-3.30pm & 6.30pm-late Oct-May, 10am-late Jun-Sep; 📶) It's fun to come to this modern spot with dark wooden chairs and tables for the atmosphere – think noise (not great for the hard of hearing), buzz and wonderful fishy aromas. The name means 'salty mouth' so there's no prize for guessing the menu – seafood galore. Staff speak English and other languages and are happy to work through the menu.

DON'T MISS

ALIANÇA UNDERGROUND MUSEUM

Between Aveiro and Coimbra, in the village of Sangalhos in the Bairrada wine-producing region, the extraordinary **Aliança Underground Museum** (916 482 226, 234 732 045; www.alianca.pt; Rua do Comércio 444, Sangalhos; €3; 90min visits 10am, 11.30am, 2.30pm, 4pm) is part *adega* (winery), part repository of an eclectic, enormous and top-quality art and artefact collection. Under the winery, vast vaulted chambers hold sparkling wine, barrels of maturing *aguardente* (a distilled spirit), and a series of galleries displaying a huge range of objects.

The highlight is at the beginning: a superb collection of African sculpture, ancient ceramics and masks, but you'll also be taken by the spectacular mineral and fossil collection and the beauty of some of the spaces. Other pieces include *azulejos* (hand-painted tiles) and quirky animals by former ceramics company Bordallo Pinheiro (still an icon in Portugal), plus an upstairs gallery devoted to India.

Our only complaints are that there's no information on individual pieces, and you don't have time to linger at leisure. Phone ahead to book your visit, which can be in English and includes a glass of sparkling wine.

Restaurante Caçanito SEAFOOD €€
(231 472 678; Av Arrais Balista Cera; mains €10-15; 9am-midnight Apr-Sep, 10am-5pm Oct-Mar) Neighbourhood cats wait expectantly outside the door of this great little restaurant. Previously an old shack, it morphed into an unadorned wood and glass cube right on the beach. Caçanito wins universal acclaim from locals for its superb charcoal-grilled seafood. It's been going for 43 years, so it's doing something right.

Marisqueira Tezinho SEAFOOD €€
(231 471 162; Av da Barrinha 9; mains €13-25; 10am-3.30pm & 6.30-10pm, closed Tue Sep-Jun) Bustling and friendly, with only two small rooms, this place opposite the lagoon is recommended for its ultrafresh seafood.

Drinking & Nightlife

Sixties Irish Pub IRISH PUB
(231 472 475; Travessa Arrais Manuel Patrão 14; 8pm-2am Mon-Thu, 7.30pm-4am Fri & Sat, 3pm-2am Sun) Tucked into a classic pub-crawler's alley a block from the beachfront, this cosy spot has multiple beers on tap and a lively old-school Irish atmosphere.

Information

Turismo (231 480 550; www.cm-mira.pt; Avenida da Barrinha; 9am-1pm & 2-5pm, extended hours in high summer) The *turismo*, beside the lagoon 450m south of Avenida Cidade de Coimbra, shares a traditional wooden house with a little ethnographic exhibition.

Getting There & Away

Praia de Mira is 7km west of Mira on the N109, itself 35km north of Figueira da Foz.

Most transport only stops inland at Mira. **Transdev** (231 458 412; www.transdev.pt) runs buses from Coimbra to Praia de Mira via Mira three to five times daily, with extra services in summer. There are two buses on weekdays from Aveiro to Praia de Mira (around €4, one hour); otherwise you'll have to change (or get a taxi) in Mira. Buses also run regularly from Figueira da Foz to Mira (around €4, one hour).

Aveiro

POP 54,400

Hugging the edge of the Ria, a shallow coastal lagoon rich in birdlife, Aveiro (uh-*vey*roo), whose name might come from the Latin *aviarium* (place of birds), is a prosperous town with a youthful, energetic buzz. It's occasionally dubbed the Venice of Portugal thanks to its high-prowed boats, hump-backed bridges and small network of picturesque canals. It's a lovely little place best explored on foot or aboard a *moliceiro* – the traditional seaweed-harvesting boat now converted to tourist use.

History

A prosperous seaport in the early 16th century, Aveiro suffered a ferocious storm in the 1570s that blocked the mouth of the Rio Vouga, closing it to ocean-going ships and creating fever-breeding marshes. Over the next two centuries, Aveiro's population shrank by three-quarters. But in 1808 the Barra Canal forged a passage back to the sea, and

Aveiro

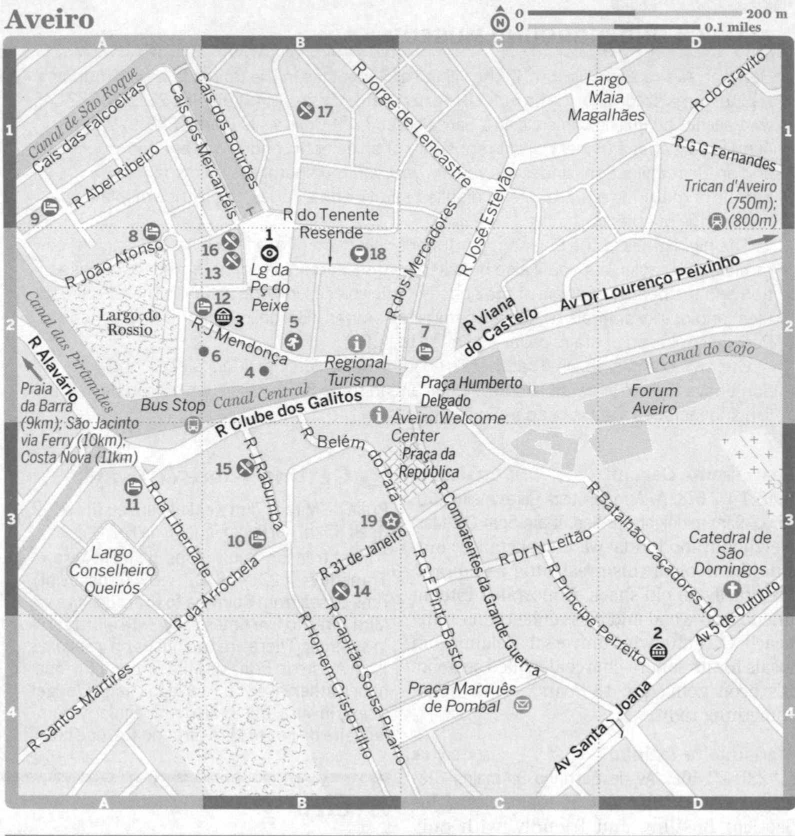

Aveiro

Sights
1 Mercado do Peixe B2
2 Museu de Aveiro/Santa Joana D4
3 Museu do Aveiro/Arte Nova B2

Activities, Courses & Tours
4 Ecoria B2
5 Oficina do Doce B2
6 Viva a Ria B2

Sleeping
7 Aveiro Palace Hotel C2
8 Aveiro Rossio Hostel A2
9 Aveiro Rossio Lodge A1
10 Hotel Aveiro Center B3
11 Hotel das Salinas A3
12 Hotel Moliceiro B2

Eating
13 Adega Típica O Telheiro B2
14 Ki B3
15 Maré Cheia B3
16 O Bairro B2
17 Tasca Palhuça B1

Drinking & Nightlife
Casa de Chá .... (see 3)
18 Decante Wine Bar B2

Entertainment
19 Teatro Aveirense B3

within a century Aveiro was rich once more, as evidenced by the spate of art nouveau houses that still define the town's old centre. Salt harvested here was taken to Newfoundland to preserve the cod that came back as *bacalhau* (dried salt-cod).

Sights

★Reserva Natural das Dunas de São Jacinto NATURE RESERVE

(www.rotadabairrada.pt) Stretching north from São Jacinto, between the sea and the lagoon west of Aveiro, is this supremely peaceful 6.7-sq-km wooded nature reserve, equipped with trails and birdwatching hides. A meandering 7km loop trail runs through the pines and dunes and can be walked at any time (you should register at the interpretative centre, however). The best birdwatching is from November to February.

At the trailhead, 1.5km north of the ferry on the N327, is a map, as well as a small, helpful interpretative centre (p328).

To get here, take a bus from Aveiro to Forte da Barra (one way/return €2.50/4), where there is a ferry to São Jacinto (passenger/car return €3/5). Schedules for boats are at www.moveaveiro.pt; bus schedules are at www.transdev.pt. Drivers can also circumnavigate the lagoon and arrive from the north via Ovar, but it's a much longer journey.

Museu de Aveiro/Santa Joana MUSEUM

(☎234 423 297; www.ipmuseus.pt; Avenida Santa Joana; €4, 10am-2pm Sun free; ⏲10am-6pm Tue-Sun) This fine museum in a beautiful space, the former Mosteiro de Jesus, owes its finest treasures to Princesa Joana (later canonised), daughter of Afonso V. In 1472, 11 years after the convent was founded, Joana 'retired' here and, though forbidden to take full vows, she stayed until her death in 1490.

The extraordinary painting collection spans the 10th to 15th centuries. Her tomb, a 17th-century masterpiece of inlaid marble mosaic, takes centre stage in an equally lavish room (the remodelled lower choir stalls). The adjacent gold-leafed chapel is decorated with *azulejos* depicting Princesa Joana's life. The museum's paintings include a late-15th-century portrait of her, attributed to Nuno Gonçalves.

Catedral de São Domingos CATHEDRAL

(www.paroquiagloria.org) Formerly part of a Dominican convent, with the Manueline stone cross of Saint Domingo displayed within. The facade has two pairs of unusual Doric pilasters. Note the three figures – Faith, Hope and Charity – along with the coat of arms of Infante D Pedro (the King's son).

Mercado do Peixe MARKET

(Largo da Praça do Peixe; ⏲7am-1pm Tue-Sat) A fun place to watch the fishmongers sell their seafood to the restaurateurs and more besides.

Museu do Aveiro/Arte Nova MUSEUM

(www.cm-aveiro.pt; Rua Dr Barbosa Magalhães 9; adult/child €2/free; ⏲9.30am-12.30pm & 2-6pm Tue-Fri, 2-6pm Sat & Sun) Set in Aveiro's most eye-catching art nouveau building, this small museum above a cafe has a modest one-room exhibition in Portuguese on art nouveau design and architecture. Larger temporary displays upstairs rotate every three months. Ask for the multilingual brochures detailing all the town's art nouveau highlights, or better still, the audioguides in Portuguese, English and Spanish outlining the same (€10 deposit).

Beaches

The surfing venues of **Praia da Barra** and **Costa Nova**, situated 13km west of Aveiro, are good for a day's outing. Prettier Costa Nova has a beachside street lined with cafes, kitsch gift shops and picturesque candy-striped cottages. Buses (one way/return €2.50/4, hourly) go from Aveiro's Rua Clube dos Galitos.

Wilder and more remote is **Praia de São Jacinto**, on the northern side of the lagoon. The vast beach of dunes is a 1.5km walk from São Jacinto port, through a residential area at the back of town. Be sure to visit the Dunas de São Jacinto Interpretative Centre (p328). Take a bus from Aveiro to Forte da Barra (one way/return €2.50/4), where there is a ferry to São Jacinto (passenger/car return €3/5). Schedules for boats are at www.moveaveiro.pt; bus schedules are at www.transdev.pt. Drivers can also circumnavigate the lagoon and arrive from the north via Ovar, a much longer trip.

Activities

Around 10 companies run trips in the *moliceiros*. Contact the Aveiro Welcome Center (p328) for a rundown.

Oficina do Doce FOOD

(☎234 098 840; www.oficinadodoce.com; Rua João Mendonça 23; tours €2; ⏲10am-7pm Jun-Sep, 10am-5pm Oct-May) Part living museum, part workshop, Oficina do Doce introduces visitors to Aveiro's proudest culinary tradition – *ovos moles:* eggy, sugary sweets originally developed by local nuns. You can

WORTH A TRIP

MUSEU MARÍTIMO DE ÍLHAVO

The wonderful **Museu Marítimo de Ílhavo** (234 329 990; www.museu-maritimo.cm-ilhavo.pt; Avenida Dr Rocha Madahil; €5; 10am-6pm Tue-Sat year-round, 2-6pm Sun Mar-Sep) is in a modern, award-winning building in the town of Ílhavo, 8km south of Aveiro. It covers the history of the maritime identity of the Portuguese, from cod fishing (with superb fishing vessels from the 19th and 20th centuries) to the oil paintings on the bows of the *moliceiros* (the traditional seaweed-harvesting boats). A highlight is the codfish aquarium, showcasing the Atlantic cod, which the Portuguese have been fishing (and munching on!) for centuries. Combined entry with the associated Santo André ship museum costs €6.50.

watch as modern-day confectioners work their magic, or learn about the process first-hand by filling your own. Reserve your visit ahead (tours are 45 minutes) by visiting their premises, or via email.

O Cicerone WALKING
(234 094 074; www.o-cicerone-tour.com; from per person €22.50) In summer, O Cicerone leads various (half- and full-day) tours in Aveiro and surrounds.

Viva a Ria BOATING
(969 008 687; www.vivaaria.com; adult/child €8/4) Offers trips in traditional seaweed-gathering boats on the Ria; also arranges trips to the Oficina do Doce (though you can arrange these directly).

Ecoria BOATING
(www.ecoria.pt; adult/child €8/4) Near the *turismo,* this is one of several canalside operators offering 45-minute trips daily on *moliceiros* around the Ria, with departures subject to passenger numbers.

Festivals & Events

Festa da Ria FIESTA
Aveiro celebrates its canals and *moliceiros* in late August. Highlights include folk dancing and a *moliceiros* race, plus competitions for the best *moliceiro* murals.

Festas do Município FIESTA
Aveiro sees two weeks of merrymaking around 12 May in honour of Aveiro's patron saint, Santa Joana.

Feira de Março FIESTA
(http://feirademarco.pt) Held from 25 March to 25 April, this festival dates back five and a half centuries. Nowadays it features everything from folk music to rock concerts.

Sleeping

★ **Aveiro Rossio Hostel** HOSTEL €
(234 041 538; www.aveirorossiohostel.com; Rua João Afonso de Aveiro 1; dm €21-25, r without/with bathroom €54/75;) One of Portugal's first 'funky' hostels, this lovely spot offers a relaxed and stylish decor, with family heirlooms, recycled furniture and found objects. It overflows with homey touches, such as the waffle (sandwich) iron, and splashes of colour. Dorm rooms come with individual reading lamps, and there are a couple of air-conditioned rooms under the eaves with beds rather than bunks.

Trican d'Aveiro GUESTHOUSE €
(Tricana de Aveiro; 234 423 366; Avenida Dr Lourenço Peixinho 259; without bathroom d €20-30, tr €45) This handsome art nouveau building is directly across from the train station, about a 15-minute walk from the centre. The owners, who also run the adjacent *pastelaria* (pastry and cake shop), have fixed up the bright, high-ceilinged rooms simply but tastefully. An excellent choice for budget travellers who don't want a hostel experience. Rooms with bathroom cost around €10 more per person.

★ **Hotel das Salinas** HOTEL €€
(234 404 190; www.hoteldassalinas.com; Rua da Liberdade 10; s/d €65/80, apt for 1/2/3/4 people €70/90/110/130;) This wonderful little spot, which had a complete overhaul in 2016, offers ultramodern, clean and white rooms. The 'studio' units have kitchenettes and plasma TVs for little more than a regular double: great for families. Some rooms offer nice canal views. A good breakfast is served in a pleasant indoor-outdoor patio.

Aveiro Rossio Lodge GUESTHOUSE €€
(234 041 538; www.aveirorossiohostel.com; Rua das Tricanas 5; d not incl breakfast €60-80;) A great option for couples, this nicely renovated house has compact but stylish rooms, created with an eye for colour

and design. The themed superior rooms on the top floor are worth the upgrade. It's an upmarket annexe of the nearby Aveiro Rossio Hostel. Check-in and admin is done through the hostel. The hitch? Tiny bathrooms, and breakfast isn't included.

Hotel Aveiro Center HOTEL €€

(234 380 390; www.hotelaveirocenter.com; Rua da Arrochela 6; incl breakfast s €48, d €70-80; P) This small hotel is a short stroll from the heart of town and has a quiet backstreet location. It was due for a complete overhaul at the time of research so is worth checking out. Little extras like tea trays in the rooms and a welcome drink back up the cordial service.

Aveiro Palace Hotel HOTEL €€

(234 423 001; www.hotelaveiropalace.com; Rua Viana do Castelo 4; s/d €75/85; P@) Aveiro's most central hotel, and one of its smartest, overlooks the heart of town. Four stars might be pushing it a bit, but the price is right and the location unrivalled. It's worth paying an extra €10 for a superior and getting views over the street and canal. There's a pretty 1st-floor lounge, and you can leave your car for only €5 a day in the nearby underground parking.

Hotel Moliceiro HOTEL €€€

(234 377 400; www.hotelmoliceiro.com; Rua Dr Barbosa de Magalhães 15; s/d €110/127.50; @) This central hotel is so well cared for it feels like it just opened. Solicitous staff run a stylish set-up in a primo position, with well-equipped chambers, sturdy but stylish furnishings and decent-sized bathrooms. The halls are dark, but the rooms are pleasantly light. Higher-grade rooms add views over the park and canal, more space and zippier decor.

Eating

Tasca Palhuça PORTUGUESE €

(Rua Antónia Rodrigues 28; daily plate half-portion €7; hours vary Sun & Mon) As '*tasca*-like' and genuine as they come, this place is largely shielded from travellers due to its side-street location. We think it's great – the type of place where clients have stuck to their (regular) seats longer than the tiles have been glued to the walls. The cuisine is meaty, fishy and plentiful. This is the place to try *caldeirada de enguias* (eel stew) for two (€20).

Ki VEGETARIAN €

(www.kimacrobiotico.com; Rua Capitão Sousa Pizarro 15; meals €8; 10am-6pm Mon-Fri;) Vegetarians, your prayers have been answered. This small, vegan-focused spot, tucked away in a street in a quiet part of town, offers a different set plate daily, plus soup and tea. Desserts cost an extra €3. Nothing from animals is used; everything is *vegan-licious*.

Adega Típica O Telheiro PORTUGUESE €

(234 429 473; Largo da Praça do Peixe 20-21; mains €7-9; noon-3.30pm & 7.30-11pm Tue-Sun) A charismatic old-style place with hanging curios and rather nifty stools at the bar for comfier eating (also a great spot to sit if dining solo). The food is reliably tasty, with cheap daily specials and abundant doses of fish and grilled meat.

★ A Peixaria SEAFOOD €€

(234 331 165; www.restauranteapeixaria.pt; Rua Mestre Jorge Pestana, São Jacinto; mains €14-18, fish per kg €30-60; noon-3pm & 7-10pm Tue-Sun) A block back from the waterfront in São Jacinto, this no-frills family restaurant has the best fish in town and, many say, the region. There's always a big variety of Atlantic species, simply and deliciously done – try the eel stew, too.

Maré Cheia SEAFOOD €€

(Rua José Rabumba 8-12; fish per kg €30-60; lunch & dinner Thu-Tue) *Maré cheia* means 'high tide' in Portuguese, but '*cheia*' (full) applies equally to this popular seafood eatery, complete with 'meet your meal' fish-tanks. You'll often have to elbow your way through a crowd of locals just to get your name on the waiting list. It's a great place to try the local *enguias* (eels), served fried, grilled or *caldeirada* (stewed).

O Bairro MODERN PORTUGUESE €€

(234 338 567; www.obairro.pt; Largo da Praça do Peixe 24; mains €13.50-17; lunch & dinner Tue-Sun) The decor artfully blends the traditional and the modern, the formal and the whimsical. At the time of research, a new owner had just taken the reins.

Drinking & Nightlife

Casa de Chá BAR

(www.casadechaartenova.com; Rua Dr Barbosa Magalhães 9; 9.30am-2am Tue-Fri, noon-2am Sat, noon-10pm Sun;) In the town's most striking art nouveau building, this casual cafe-bar has a fine range of tea and infusions and livens up at night with excellent caipirinhas, Friday night DJs and a perky summer scene.

Decante Wine Bar WINE BAR
(Rua do Tenente Resende 28; ⊙5pm-late) People congregate at the streetside tables to sip wine during the early evening, then move inside for live music most nights, including everything from Latin rhythms, rock and blues to jazz and world music.

☆ Entertainment

Teatro Aveirense THEATRE
(☎234 400 920; www.teatroaveirense.pt; Rua Belém do Para) Celebrating over 125 years at the heart of Aveiro's cultural scene, this recently renovated historic theatre regularly hosts dance, music and theatre performances.

ℹ Information

Aveiro Welcome Center (☎234 377 761; www.cm-aveiro.pt; Rua Clube dos Galitos 2; ⊙9am-6pm) Its helpfulness varies, although it can book some excursions.

Dunas de São Jacinto Interpretative Centre (☎234 331 282; www.rotadabairrada.pt; Estrada Nacional 327; ⊙9am-noon & 1-5pm Mon-Sat)

Hospital Infante Dom Pedro (☎234 378 300; www.hip.min-saude.pt; Av Artur Ravara)

Police Station (☎234 302 510; Praça Marquês de Pombal)

Post Office (Praça Marquês de Pombal; ⊙8.30am-6.30pm Mon-Fri)

Regional Turismo (☎234 420 760; www.turismodocentro.pt; Rua João Mendonça 8; ⊙9am-8pm Mon-Fri, 9am-6pm Sat & Sun Jun-Sep, 9am-1 & 2-6pm Oct-May) In an art nouveau gem beside the Canal Central; has some information on Portugal's central region.

ℹ Getting There & Away

BUS

Few long-distance buses terminate here – there isn't even a bus station. Catch buses at the **stop** on Rua Clube dos Galitos; many also stop at the train station.

Rede Expresso (www.rede-expressos.pt) has five to six daily services to/from Lisbon (€16, three to four hours), Coimbra (€6, 45 minutes) and Figueira da Foz (€8.30, 1¼ hours).

Transdev (www.transdev.pt) run a slower but cheaper coastal service to Figueira da Foz via some intermediate beaches. Other services run to Viseu (€8.30, one hour) and on to Guarda and Castelo Branco.

TRAIN

Trains run from the modern station, which has superseded the beautiful old tiled one alongside. Aveiro is within Porto's *urbano* network, which means there are commuter trains there at least every half hour (€3.40, one hour); much pricier IC/AP links (€11.70/14.20, 30 to 40 minutes) are only slightly faster. There are also at least hourly links to Coimbra (regional/intercity/AP €5.25/11.70/14.20, 30 to 60 minutes) and several daily IC (€21.45, 2½ hours) and AP (€27.55, two hours) trains to Lisbon.

ℹ Getting Around

BICYCLE

Loja BUGA (Bicicleta de Utilização Gratuita de Aveiro; www.moveaveiro.pt; Praça do Mercado 2; ⊙9am-6pm Mon-Fri, 10am-1pm & 2-6pm Sat & Sun) Provides bikes for use within the town limits, all for free. Bike quality can vary a bit. Leave an ID such as your driver's licence or passport.

BUS

Catch buses to the coast at the stop on Rua Clube dos Galitos (€1.90, or €9.40 for a 10-trip ticket). It's an easy 15-minute walk southwest from the train station into town.

Piódão

POP 178

Remote Piódão (pee-*oh*-downg) offers a chance to see rural Portugal at its most pristine. This tiny traditional village clings to a terraced valley in a beautiful, surprisingly remote range of vertiginous ridges, deeply cut valleys, rushing rivers and virgin woodland called the Serra de Açor (Goshawk Mountains).

Until the 1970s you could only reach Piódão on horseback or by foot, and it still feels as though you've slipped into a time warp. The village is a serene, picturesque composition in schist stone and grey slate; note the many doorways with crosses over them, said to offer protection against curses and thunderstorms.

⊙ Sights

Igreja Nossa Senhora Conceição CHURCH
This eclectic church stands out like a beacon against the schist of surrounding houses, for its colour (vivid white) and its cylindrical buttresses. It is believed to have been built on the site of a former chapel, though the current building, funded by locals, dates to the early 19th century.

Núcleo Museológico de Piódão MUSEUM
(Largo Cónego Manuel Fernandes Nogueira; €1; ⏲10am-1pm & 2-6pm Jun-Sep, 9am-1pm & 2-5pm Oct-May) This tiny museum displays reconstructions of typical rooms in local homes, complete with tools, pottery and furniture. There are also historical photos of Piódão and its residents.

Activities

A signposted network of **hiking trails** connects Piódão to the villages of Foz d'Égua (6.3km, two-hour loop hike) and Chãs d'Égua (4km, one hour each way).

Sleeping

Casa de Xisto Piódão COTTAGE €
(☎933 403 055; www.casadexistopiodao.com; Rua Francisco Pacheco; s/d/q not incl breakfast €50/55/75) This tall, narrow house in the heart of the village, next to the O Fontinha restaurant, sleeps up to six in comfort. There's not a lot of space, but it's colourful and cosy. Minimum two-night stay.

Casa da Padaria B&B €
(☎235 732 773; www.casadapadaria.com; d €50) On the far side of the village from where you arrive, this handsome house has an exceptionally friendly host and offers good value for simple rustic rooms.

Estalagem do Piódão HOTEL €€
(☎235 730 100; www.inatel.pt; r €80-95; P 📶 🏊) Looming unaesthetically on a ridge above the village, this government-run caricature of a local schist house has rather luxurious, modern rooms and a decent restaurant with vistas. It's a helpful, friendly place with an indoor pool. Rates vary according to demand and you'll usually get a cheaper deal online.

Eating

O Fontinha PORTUGUESE €
(mains €8; ⏲lunch & dinner) A schist house in the heart of the village, this is a good venue for simple, tasty, local food like *chanfana* (goat stew), grilled trout or *bacalhau* (cod).

Information

Turismo (☎235 732 787; www.visitarganil.pt; Largo Cónego Manuel Fernando Nogueira; ⏲10am-1pm & 2-6pm Jun-Sep, 9am-1pm & 2-5pm Oct-May) On the square; provides info on Piódão.

Getting There & Away

The only public transport is a bus from Arganil (41km west) to Piódão (€4.30, 1¼ hours) on Thursday and Sunday. Check current times with Piódão's *turismo*, as they change.

The area's breathtaking views, narrow roads and sheer drops are a lethal combination for drivers.

BEIRA BAIXA

Beira Baixa closely resembles the neighbouring Alentejo, with hospitable locals, fierce summer heat and rolling plains stretching to the horizon. It's also home to sprawling agricultural estates, humble farming hamlets and several stunning fortress towns that for centuries guarded the vulnerable plains from Spanish aggression.

Castelo Branco

POP 35, 240

Sweltering Castelo Branco isn't Portugal's most charming provincial capital but makes a good jumping-off point for outlying attractions such as Monsanto and Idanha-a-Velha. The best reasons to visit are the town's excellent, ever-increasing museums, the result of its efforts to become a centre of culture. There are some charming medieval streets clustered in its heart, and the town's modern development includes an attractive series of tree-lined squares and boulevards.

Sights

★**Centro de Cultura Contemporânea de Castelo Branco** MUSEUM
(☎272 348 170; www.facebook.com/oficialcentroculturacontemporaneacb; Campo Mártires da Pátria S/N; ⏲10am-1pm & 2-6pm Tue-Sun) FREE A recent addition to Castelo Branco's many museums, this cutting-edge building was designed by Spanish architect Josep Lluis Mateo in collaboration with Portuguese architect Carlos Reis de Figueiredo. It's a delightful space with a cantilevered floor that extends over the town plaza. Three of the four levels exhibit thought-provoking Portuguese and international modernist works. There are also temporary exhibitions to check out.

Museu Cargaleiro MUSEUM
(☎272 337 394; www.fundacaomanuelcargaleiro.pt; Rua dos Cavaleiros 23; adult/child €2/1;

DON'T MISS

PARQUE NATURAL DO TEJO INTERNACIONAL

Still one of Portugal's wildest landscapes, the 264-sq-km **Parque Natural do Tejo Internacional** (www.naturtejo.com/en) shadows the Rio Tejo and the watersheds of three of its tributaries. While not aesthetically remarkable, it shelters some of the country's rarest bird species, including black storks, Bonelli's eagles, royal eagles, Egyptian vultures, black vultures and griffon vultures. The park was established in 2000, after a major push by private environmental organisation Quercus.

The **park headquarters** in Castelo Branco can provide background information.

The best-marked hiking trail, the Rota dos Abutres (Route of the Vultures), descends from Salvaterra do Extremo (60km east of Castelo Branco) into the canyon of the Rio Erges.

Drivers can get a taste of the park's natural beauty by following the unnumbered road between Monforte da Beira and Cegonhas (southeast of Castelo Branco), which passes through a beautiful cork-oak forest on either side of the Ribeira do Aravil. It doesn't appear on all maps: pass through Monforte da Beira if coming from Castelo Branco, and turn right after 2km. Alternatively, a signposted turnoff to the park just short of Monforte takes you down a rough, circular route through part of the park, but the way's not well indicated.

10am-1pm & 2-6pm Tue-Sun) This extraordinary museum is spread over two buildings, a mid-18th-century home in Rua dos Cavaleiros (Knights Street) and an out-of-place but cutting-edge modern building nearby. It exhibits the collection of the Manuel Cargaleiro Foundation, including works by Cargaleiro (1927–), a celebrated Portuguese ceramicist and painter who settled in France, plus other Portuguese and international artists. Cargaleiro was influenced by the École de Paris (Paris School of artists).

Museu de Francisco Tavares Proença Júnior MUSEUM
(Paço Episcopal; Largo Dr José Lopes Dias; adult/student/under 10yr €2/1/free; 9am-5.30pm Tue-Sun Oct-Apr, 10am-7pm Tue-Sun May-Sep) The Museu de Francisco Tavares Proença Júnior is housed in the otherwise sober 18th-century bishop's palace. The centrepiece (downstairs) is an excellent display of local archaeological finds. Whether you're a fan of embroidery or not, don't miss the upstairs exhibition of Castelo Branco's famous *colchas:* silk-embroidered linen bedspreads and coverlets inspired by silks and motifs brought back by Portuguese explorers. There's a stunning collection of Asian originals.

After you visit, head 100m south to the School of Embroidery (opposite the cathedral) to see local embroiderers at work on stunning pieces (no photos permitted).

Jardim do Paço Episcopal GARDENS
(Rua Bartolomeu da Costa; €2; 9am-5pm Oct-Apr, to 7pm May-Sep) This delightful, unusual retreat is the garden of the bishop's palace, a baroque whimsy of clipped box hedges and little granite statues representing virtues, seasons, kings, saints, months and continents among other things. Notice that the statues of Portugal's Spanish-born kings Felipe I and II are smaller than those of the Portuguese monarchs.

At the bottom of the kings' stairway, there's a hidden, clap-activated fountain, sadly out of order at the time of research. It was built by a loutish 18th-century bishop who liked to surprise maidens by soaking their petticoats. Ask the attendant whether it's back in operation.

Castelo CASTLE
FREE There's little left of this castle, which was built by the Knights Templar in the 13th century and extended by Dom Dinis. A phone mast now stands where the chapel once was. However, the garden, which has supplanted the walls, offers grand views over town and countryside. The old lanes that lead back down to the town centre are also picturesque.

Sleeping

Império do Rei PENSION €
(272 341 720; www.imperiodorei.pt; Rua dos Prazeres 20; s/d/tr/f incl breakfast €35/50/65/75; P) The town's pick for the excellent price:quality ratio. There are

18 clean, appealing rooms, all individually decorated with themes based around the region. There's even in-room information about the region supplied in Portuguese and English. Friendly staff are an added bonus.

Hotel Rainha d'Amélia BUSINESS HOTEL €€
(☎272 348 800; hotelrainhadamelia.pt; Rua de Santiago 15; r €55-85; ❄📶) This nondescript place holds few surprises but has clean, warm rooms (some with the unfortunate odour from 'illegal' smokers). The staff are extremely helpful and a reasonable buffet breakfast is up for the taking. The hotel is centrally located and is good value if you can get internet deals.

Eating

O Pinguim PORTUGUESE €
(Rua Dadrá 7A; mains €7.50-10; ⊙8am-midnight Mon-Sat) Friendly and bright, fast and efficient, and the type of place where you join the locals for good 'home cooked' fare over a football game on the big screen. Don't be put off when you look through the small, plain cafe-bar entrance; the restaurant is through another door. Great veal and grilled octopus, and it's hard to resist the €2 desserts.

Retiro do Caçador PORTUGUESE €
(www.restauranteretirocacador.pai.pt; Rua Ruivo Godinho 15; mains €7-13; ⊙noon-3pm & 7-10.30pm Mon-Sat) Given that *'caçador'* means hunter, prepare yourself for some hearty meat dishes at this busy, bistro-style spot. Everything from deer stew to *javali* (boar), with *bacalhau* (salted cod) dishes to hook you in, too. Locals overwhelmingly recommend this place. And for good reason.

Information

Biblioteca Municipal (Centro Cívico; ⊙10am-6.30pm Mon-Fri) Free internet in the public library.

Cyber Centro Municipal (Praça 25 de Abril; internet per hr €1; ⊙9am-11pm Mon-Fri) Across the courtyard from the library.

Parque Natural do Tejo Internacional Office (☎272 348 140; http://natural.pt/portal/en; Avenida do Empresário, Praça Nercab; ⊙9am-12.30pm & 2-5.30pm Mon-Fri) This headquarters is the place for information on the park.

Turismo (☎272 330 339; www.cm-castelo branco.pt; cnr Av Nuno Álvares & Rua Cadetes de Toledo; ⊙9.30am-7.30pm Mon-Fri, 9.30am-1pm & 2.30-6pm Sat & Sun) Good brochures and city information.

Getting There & Away

BUS

Rede Expressos (www.rede-expressos.pt) services from Castelo Branco:

Coimbra (€14.50, two to three hours, one to four daily)

Covilhã (€6, 50 minutes, almost hourly daily)

Guarda (€11, 1½ hours, at least eight daily)

Lisbon (€14.90, 2¾ hours, one to four daily)

TRAIN

Castelo Branco is on the Lisbon–Covilhã line. Three daily IC trains to Lisbon (€14.70, 2¾ hours) are supplemented by a couple of slower regional services (€14.30, 3¾ hours). IC/regional services also serve Covilhã (€6.60/6.30, 50 minutes/one hour).

Monsanto

POP 200

Like an island in the sky, the stunning village of Monsanto towers high above the surrounding plains. A stroll through its steeply cobbled streets, lined with stone houses that seem to merge with the boulder-strewn landscape, is reason enough to come. But to fully appreciate Monsanto's rugged isolation, climb the shepherds' paths above town to the abandoned hilltop castle, whose crumbling walls command vertiginous views in all directions. Walkers will also appreciate the network of hiking trails threading through the vast cork-oak-dominated expanses below.

Sights

Castelo CASTLE
(⊙24hr) This formidable stone fortress seems almost to have grown out of the boulder-littered hillside that supports it. It's a beautiful site, windswept and populated by lizards and wildflowers. Immense vistas include Spain to the east and the Barragem da Idanha dam to the southwest.

There was probably a fortress here even before the Romans arrived, but after Dom Sancho I booted out the Moors in the 12th century it was beefed up. Dom Dinis refortified it, but after centuries of attacks from across the border it finally fell into ruin.

Just below the castle stands what's left of the Romanesque **Capela de São Miguel**,

> **WORTH A TRIP**
>
> **PENHA GARCIA**
>
> A good side trip from Monsanto takes you 14km north then east along the N239 towards the Spanish border to this little village. It's a picturesque spot with a dam and lake behind it. From the church, a charming 3km circular walking route, the **Rota dos Fósseis**, takes you through an extraordinary canyon where you visit old mills and millers' houses (incredibly, these were used until the 1960s; a delightful guide will show you around) and various fabulous fossil finds. You can also walk to Penha Garcia along the GR-12 path from Monsanto.

with its cluster of tombs carved into solid rock eerily lying just outside the chapel portal.

Activities

Monsanto is criss-crossed by long-distance hiking trails, including the GR-12 from Lisbon to Bulgaria, and the GR-22, a 540km circuit of Portugal's historic villages. For a beautiful, relatively easy walk (one hour return), descend the GR-12 along the stone road to the **Capela de São Pedro de Vira-Corça**, a medieval chapel surrounded by giant boulders. You can follow this same trail all the way to Idanha-a-Velha, a beautiful but exposed 10km walk best in cooler weather.

Festivals & Events

Festa das Cruzes CULTURAL

On 3 May each year Monsanto comes alive with the Festa das Cruzes, in honour of Nossa Senhora dos Cruzes and commemorating the invasion of the Moors. The story goes that the starving villagers threw their last lonely calf over the walls, taunting their besiegers as if they had plenty to spare. The hoodwinked attackers promptly abandoned the siege.

These days, young girls throw baskets of flowers instead, after which there's dancing and singing beside the castle walls.

Sleeping

Casa Pires Mateus GUESTHOUSE €

(casapiresmateus@gmail.com; Rua Fernando Namora 4; d from €50; wi-fi) You can forgive the odd shortcoming (no wall heating) of this otherwise charming, recently opened spot. It's in an old family house that's been converted to a spotless, comfortable abode, with spacious rooms and one smaller double. Some rooms have great views over the rooftops. Lovely female host but little English is spoken. Good breakfasts.

Casa da Tia Piedade GUESTHOUSE €

(966 910 599; www.casadatiapiedade.com; Rua da Azinheira 21; d/q without breakfast €60/70; air-con wi-fi) You've just about got your own house attached to this slightly dated but warmly welcoming spot in Monsanto's heart, with separate entrance, terrace and kitchen/lounge. There are two bedrooms (the smaller one has a view) but only one is let at a time unless you're a group, so the exterior bathroom is private. The owners are helpful and kind but also respect privacy.

Monsanto Geo-Hotel Escola DESIGN HOTEL €€

(277 314 061; www.monsantoghe.com; Rua da Capela 1; d from €85; air-con wi-fi) You'll see the modern lift tower on approach before you realise what it belongs to. It's part of a renovated mansion (previously one of Portugal's *pousadas*; upmarket inns), whose rooms are so modern, so white and bright, and so hip, that you'll wonder if you've landed somewhere other than 'traditional' Monsanto. But somehow it seems to work.

Eating

Adega Típica O Cruzeiro PORTUGUESE €€

(936 407 676; Rua Fernando Namora 4; mains €10.50-13; 12.30-3pm & 7-9pm Thu-Mon, 12.30-3pm Tue) Just below the old town, this likeable place is a rather surprising find as you descend into the bowels of a modern municipal building. The attractive dining area boasts spectacular views over the plains below, and the super-friendly staff serve very tasty meals from a seasonal menu – if you spot a dish with wild mushrooms *(cogumelos silvestres)* go for it (€11).

Petiscos e Granitos PORTUGUESE €€

(Rua Pracinha; mains €9-17.50; 12.30-4pm & 7.30-10pm Tue-Sun) Wedged within gigantic boulders, Petiscos e Granitos' back terrace provides a fantastic backdrop for sipping a *copo de vinho* (glass of wine) at sunset, with incomparable views over the plains below. With all the extra trimmings it can hit the wallet, but specialities like game dishes and grilled lamb chops with roasted potatoes are delicious. Closed Mondays in winter.

Information

Turismo (☎277 314 642; www.cm-idanhanova.pt; Rua Marquês da Graciosa; ⏰9.30am-1pm & 2-5.30pm Tue-Sun) See the website for details of accommodation in the area.

Getting There & Away

Without a car, Monsanto can be difficult to reach. **Rodoviária da Beira Interior** (RBI; ☎272 320 997; www.transdev.pt) has one direct bus daily between Castelo Branco and Monsanto (€5.90, one hour), leaving Castelo Branco at 5.15pm Monday to Friday, 12.25pm on Saturday and 11.40am on Sunday, with a bus returning from Monsanto at 7.15am daily. Ask at the *turismo* in either Monsanto or Castelo Branco for the latest schedules.

Idanha-a-Velha

POP 80

Extraordinary Idanha-a-Velha is a very traditional small village with a huge history. Nestled in a remote valley of patchwork farms and olive orchards, it was founded as the Roman city of Igaeditânia (Egitania). Roman ramparts still define the town, though it reached its apogee under Visigothic rule: they built a cathedral and made Idanha their regional capital. It's also believed that their legendary King Wamba was born here.

Moors were next on the scene, and the cathedral was turned into a mosque during their tenure. They, in turn, were driven out by the Knights Templar in the 12th century. It's believed that a 15th-century plague virtually wiped out the town's population, with survivors going on to found Idanha-a-Nova about 20km to the southwest. However, the townspeople's misfortune is our luck, since they left the town virtually intact. Today a small population of shepherds and farmers live amid the Roman, Visigothic and medieval ruins.

Sights

Ruins RUINS

FREE The only evidence of the Knights Templar is the Torre dos Templários, made of massive chunks of stone and now surrounded by clucking hens. It sits on top of what was likely the pedestal of a Roman temple. Other Roman remains include the gracefully arched bridge that is situated on the east side of town and the old wall and gate on the north side.

Catedral CATHEDRAL

(⏰10am-12.30pm & 2.45-4.30pm) FREE Tucked into a corner of the walled town sits the 6th-century Visigothic cathedral, surrounded by a jigsaw puzzle of scattered archaeological remains. The church has undergone heavy restoration, but its early roots are evident everywhere: foundation stones bearing Latin inscriptions, Moorish brick arches, salvaged Roman columns and Visigothic elements such as the baptistry visible through glass near the entrance. Of the frescos within, the best preserved features São Bartolomeu with a demon at his feet.

If the church is not open, ask for the key at the tourist office.

Lagar de Varas & Museu Epigráfico Egitaniense MUSEUM

(⏰9.30am-1pm & 2-5.30pm Tue-Sun) FREE The Lagar de Varas, near the cathedral, hosts an impressive olive-oil press made in the traditional way with ruddy great tree trunks providing the crushing power. In the same complex you'll find a narrow epigraphic museum densely packed with more than 200 stones from the area bearing Latin inscriptions. Touch-screen displays explain (in English and Portuguese) the context of the collection, with in-depth studies of three noteworthy stones.

Sleeping

Pousada de Juventude Idanha-a-Nova HOSTEL €

(☎277 208 051; www.pousadasjuventude.pt; Praça da República 32, Idanha-a-Nova; dm/f €12/50, d without/with bathroom €26/30; ⏰Dec-Oct; 📶) Very well-equipped modern hostel with a prime location in the attractive hill town of Idanha-a-Nova.

Information

Turismo (☎277 914 280; www.cm-idanhanova.pt; Rua da Sé; ⏰9.30am-1pm & 2-5.30pm Tue-Sun) Housed in the **Lagar de Varas**; the friendly staff will unlock the cathedral if they are free.

Getting There & Away

There's a daily bus service to/from Idanha-a-Nova (40 minutes), from where you can catch onward buses to Castelo Branco (around €4, 45 minutes, two to three daily). Alternatively, you can hike the beautiful but exposed 10km trail from Monsanto or get a pricey taxi from Idanha-a-Nova (around €30).

Sortelha

Perched on a rocky promontory, Sortelha is the oldest of a string of fortresses guarding the frontier east of Guarda and Covilhã. Its fortified 12th-century castle teeters on the brink of a steep cliff, while immense walls encircle a village of great charms. Laid out in Moorish times, it remains a winning combination of stout stone cottages, sloping cobblestone streets and diminutive orchards.

'New' Sortelha lines the Santo Amaro–Sabugal road. The medieval hilltop fortress is a short drive, or a 10-minute walk, up one of two lanes signposted '*castelo*'.

The town holds a medieval fair in the last weekend of September. You can join in the fun by hiring clothes and spending coins from the era.

Sights

Old Town HISTORIC SITE

FREE The entrance to the fortified old village is a grand, stone **Gothic gate**. From here, a cobbled lane leads up to the heart of the village, with a *pelourinho* (stone pillory) in front of the remains of a small **castle** to the left and the parish **church** to the right. Higher still is the **bell tower** – climb it for a view of the entire village. For a more adventurous and scenic climb, tackle the **ramparts** around the village (beware precarious stairways and big steps).

As you walk, keep your eyes open for the weather-worn Arabic script above the doorway of the **Casa Árabe** at the top of town.

Oh! And at the castle entrance, look for the *mata-cães,* the holes in the verandah through which hot oil was poured to repel the enemy.

Sleeping

Casas do Campanário & Casa da Vila COTTAGE €

(271 388 638; luispaulo55@sapo.pt; Rua da Mesquita; d €50, house for 4/6 people €100/150;) Nicely sited at the top of the village, near the bar of the same name, are Sortelha's 'inside the walls' lodging options: gorgeous, traditional houses with kitchenettes, living room and bedrooms. They're happy to rent out one double (of two double) rooms. Prices include heating in winter. Ask at Bar Campanário, just above the bell tower.

Casa da Lagariça & Casa da Calçada COTTAGE €€

(271 388 116; www.casalagarica.com; Calçada de Santo Antão 11; d €55 Sep-Jun, €80 Jul & Aug; P) These cute stone cottages just below the old town make fine bases. The larger, Lagariça, has two doubles and a twin as well as a sofa bed; the smaller has two doubles. You can rent out just a room or the whole house; the houses come with kitchen but breakfast is included.

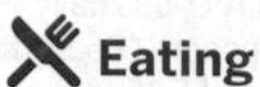

Eating

O Celta PORTUGUESE €€

(https://pt-br.facebook.com/RestauranteOCelta; Rua Dr Vitor Manuel Pereira Neves 10; mains €8-15; noon-2.30pm Wed-Mon) O Celta (The Celt) might not be in the old village (it's outside the old gates) but it serves up a medieval atmosphere and fabulous Portuguese favourites, including great *enchidos regionais* (regional smoked meats), and is a reliable bet. It's open all year. A small cafe is at the front and the helpful owner is used to tourists with queries.

Restaurante Dom Sancho PORTUGUESE €€

(271 388 267; Largo do Corro; mains €11-18; lunch & dinner Tue-Sat, lunch Sun) Sortelha's favourite, if tourist-oriented, eatery sits just inside the main Gothic gates. Prices for the regional cuisine – with several game options – are high, but the food is renowned and the dining room rustically elegant in a medieval-themed kind of way. For lighter snacks and drinks, head to the beamed, stone-walled bar downstairs (with cosy fireplace in winter).

Drinking & Nightlife

Bar Boas Vindas BAR

(noon-late Fri-Sun) Uphill and to the right of the *turismo,* this cosy little stone house with couches, rustic farm decor, a cat curled up by the fire and a well-stocked bar makes a great place to get cosy in winter, or to kick back on the cute terrace on a hot summer afternoon.

Information

Turismo (271 381 072; www.cm-sabugal.pt; Largo do Corro; 9am-1pm & 2-5.30pm winter, 10am-1pm & 2-6pm Tue-Sun summer) Located 50m within the old town gates; has some fun medieval-style items for sale.

Getting There & Away

You really need your own wheels to get to Sortelha. The only bus service is on school days, on a school bus that takes kids to and from Sabugal, from where you can connect to Guarda.

Regional trains on the Covilhã–Guarda line (three to four daily) stop at Belmonte-Manteigas station, 12km to the northwest, from where you can catch a **taxi** (☎ 936 259 107) to Sortelha (around €20 to €25).

PARQUE NATURAL DA SERRA DA ESTRELA

Fascinating for its natural and cultural history, Parque Natural da Serra da Estrela was one of Portugal's first designated parks, and at 888 sq km remains the country's largest protected area. The rugged boulder-strewn meadows and icy lakes of its high country form one of Portugal's most distinct and unexpected landscapes. It's a glorious, seasonal beauty: the *altiplano* (upland) area is stunning in the morning or evening light. On the slopes below, rushing rivers historically provided hydro power to spin and weave the Serra's wool into cloth. Nowadays traditional sheep-herding is giving way to a service economy catering to weekending tourists.

The presence of the 1993m Torre – Portugal's highest peak – at the park's centre is both a blessing and a curse. It forms a dramatic backdrop, but as the only place in Portugal where snow dependably falls, it also lures winter hordes with little consciousness of their impact on the high country's ecosystems.

Activities

Wildlife Watching

The park harbours many endangered or vulnerable species including the black stork, Montagu's harrier, chough, turtle dove and 10 species of bats. If you're lucky you may also catch a glimpse of high-altitude midwife frogs, mountain rock lizards or rare birds such as the peregrine falcon, eagle owl and rock thrush.

The flora, too, is interesting. Several of the park's plants have been put on the list of endangered or vulnerable species due to their popularity as medicinal remedies, including mountain thrift *(Armeria transmontana)*, great yellow gentian *(Gentiana lutea)* and juniper *(Juniperus communis)*.

Walking

The Serra abounds in walking and climbing opportunities; these mountains are one of Portugal's most alluring destinations for outdoors enthusiasts.

Crisp air and immense vistas make this a trekking paradise. In part because of limited infrastructure, surprisingly few people get off the main roads. Even in summer, walkers will generally feel they have the park to themselves.

While still very chilly and possibly damp, late April has the hillsides bright with wildflowers. The weather is finest from May to October. Winter is harsh, with snow at the higher elevations from November or December to April or May.

Whenever you come, be prepared for extremes: scorching summer days give way to freezing nights, and chilling rainstorms blow through with little warning. Mist is a big hazard not only because it obscures walking routes and landmarks, but because it can also stealthily chill you to the point of hypothermia.

There are three main 'official' routes through the park, as well as branches and alternative trails. The 90km TSE1 runs the length of the park. It's the easiest to follow, taking in every kind of terrain, including the summit of Torre. TSE2 and TSE3 (both around 80km) run respectively along the western and eastern slopes. All of the trails pass through towns and villages, each of which offers some accommodation. Many of the finest walks start around Manteigas. Other good routes head off the N339 south of Sabugueiro – the day walks along Lagoa Comprida or to Covão do Lagoacho are worthwhile at any time of year.

By far the best resource is Centro de Interpretação da Serra da Estrela (p337) in Seia. Multilingual staff here are experts on hiking in the Serra and are goldmines of route information. They'll give you personalised advice and can also organise guided hikes.

Within a zone of special protection, camping and fires are strictly prohibited except at designated sites, all of which are on the main trails.

Biking & Other Activities

The Vodafone Bike Park around Torre (half-/full day €15/20) has three runs, available once the snow has melted.

SkiParque (p340), east of Manteigas, offers many activities, including summertime 'dry skiing', paragliding, rock climbing, mountain biking and hiking.

Parque Natural da Serra da Estrela

Skiing

The ski season typically runs from January to March, with the best conditions in February.

Sleeping

While Seia, Gouveia, Manteigas, Covilhã and Guarda all provide useful bases with comfortable accommodation options, those wanting a true mountain experience should opt for Manteigas, because the others – situated on the Serra's outer slopes – are more a part of the surrounding plains.

High season here is December to March (winter), so many accommodations increase their rates (camping grounds are the exception; they drop their rates or close during this time).

Information

The recently opened **Centro de Interpretativo do Vale Glaciar do Zêzere** (CIVGLAZ; www.civglaz-manteigas.pt; adult/child €2.50/1.50; ⏲10.30am-12.30pm & 2-5pm Mon-Fri, from 10am Sat & Sun mid-Sep–mid-May, 10.30am-12.30pm & 2-5.45pm Mon-Fri, from 10am Sat & Sun mid-May–mid-Sep) provides a wonderful and visual insight into the surrounding glacial valley.

There are park offices at Manteigas (headquarters), Seia, Gouveia and Guarda; local *turismos* can also provide park information.

Getting There & Away

Express buses run daily from Coimbra to Seia, Guarda and Covilhã, and from Aveiro, Porto and Lisbon to Guarda and Covilhã. There are daily IC trains from Lisbon and Coimbra to Guarda (plus IR services calling at Gouveia) and from Lisbon to Covilhã (with IR services on to Guarda).

Driving can be hairy, thanks to mist and wet or icy roads at high elevations, and stiff winds. The Gouveia–Manteigas N232 road is one of the most tortuous in all of Portugal. Be prepared for traffic jams around Torre on weekends.

There are regular, though infrequent, bus services around the edges of the park but none directly across it.

Seia

At first, modern Seia might feel largely like a charmless strip of contemporary buildings slapped onto a hillside. But look again. It has sweeping views over the surrounding lowlands and some excellent local museums, especially the Centro de Interpretacão da Serra da Estrela. Plus it boasts attractive rural lodgings in the surrounding hills. The town itself is also a handy place to buy cheese, cured meats and woolly slippers.

Sights

Centro de Interpretacão da Serra da Estrela MUSEUM
(CISE; ☎238 320 300; www.cise.pt; Rua Visconde Molelos; adult/child €1/2.50; ⏲10am-6pm Tue-Sun) This regional museum provides an excellent introduction to the Serra da Estrela region. A nine-minute film in English or Portuguese takes you flying around the mountains' main points of interest. Multimedia displays include an interactive scale model of the Serra. As the organisation was responsible for marking the region's trails, CISE also has very helpful information on hiking and is the best place in the region to buy maps.

Museu do Brinquedo MUSEUM
(Toy Museum; ☎238 082 015; museu.brinquedo@cm-seia.pt; Largo de Santa Rita; adult/child €3/2; ⏲10am-6pm Tue-Sun; 👪) This museum traces the history of Portuguese toys, from the Victorian to the contemporary, and as such, provides an interesting cultural study of Portuguese society, past and present. On display are over 8000 toys made of everything from paper and clay to wood and cork, plus factory-made dolls and cars. There are two playrooms and a large collection of toys from around the world.

Museu do Pão MUSEUM
(☎238 310 760; www.museudopao.pt; adult/child €5/3; ⏲10am-6pm Tue-Fri & Sun, to 10pm Sat) This museum, set in a huge complex with mill wheels, a restaurant and rustic buildings, has all the information you'll ever need on local bread production. The highlight is the traditional-style shop. It's 1km northeast of the centre on the road to Sabugueiro.

Sleeping

Casa das Tílias HOTEL €€
(☎927 186 125; www.tilias.com; Rua das Tilias, São Romão; d €60-70, tr €65, f €70, apt €125; P 📶 🏊) This gorgeous 1850s-era mansion with polished wooden floors and high ceilings (some with lovingly restored friezework) has six rooms and a grand parlour in the main building, plus three self-catering apartments in the modern adjacent annexe. Service is efficient and businesslike, and there's a spacious garden area. It's 4km from Seia – follow signs to São Romão.

Casas da Ribeira COTTAGE €€
(☎238 311 221; www.casasdaribeira.com; Póvoa Velha; cottages 2-person €60-70, 4-person €80-120; 📶) Close to Seia's services but feeling a million miles away (and at an altitude of 1000m), this charming collection of vine-draped stone cottages sits in the hills above town. The eight houses are similar, rustic and beautifully restored with kitchens and fireplaces (firewood included). A delicious breakfast with home-baked bread is provided. There's normally a two-night minimum stay.

Casa do Vidoeiro APARTMENT €€
(☎238 085 502; www.casadovidoeiro.com; Av Dr Joaquim Guilherme 14; d from €60; P 📶) One of the only kinds of accommodation in the centre, and an excellent choice if you decide to use Seia as your base to explore Serra da Estrela, Casa do Vidoeiro is a large 19th-century mansion that has been converted into pleasant, bright apartments. It's handily located a five-minute walk from the centre. Has a 24-hour reception, too.

Hotel Eurosol Seia-Camelo HOTEL €€
(☎238 310 100; www.eurosol.pt; Av 1 de Maio 16; s/d €50/60, winter weekends €60/85; P ❄ @ 📶 🏊) This well-equipped, friendly hotel in the centre of town has large rooms, pink-marble bathrooms with abundant hot water, a large sandy children's play area, a summer pool with lounge chairs and free off-street parking. We list rack rates here, but you can normally get a better deal via the website. Two-night minimum on winter weekends. Wi-fi is extra.

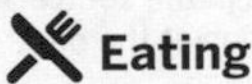

Eating

Restaurante Regional da Serra PORTUGUESE €
(☎238 312 717; Av dos Combatentes da Grande Guerra 14; mains €6-11; ⏲noon-3pm & 7-9.30pm)

WORTH A TRIP

SABUGUEIRO

Attracting tourists from far and wide thanks to its title as Portugal's highest village (at 1050m), Sabugueiro is more noteworthy as a place to shop for *queijo da serra* (mountain cheese) and Serra da Estrela dogs than as a destination in itself. You can buy some excellent cheese here, although it's mostly made with milk from outside the Serra da Estrela due to diminishing local supply and skyrocketing demand. If you like the centre runny, ask for a cheese that's *amanteigado* – delicious!

Dog lovers will find it hard to resist stopping to look at the impossibly cute Serra da Estrela puppies peering wistfully from their roadside cages. Local families also sell delicious smoked ham, rye bread, juniper-berry firewater and cosy fleece slippers for the chilly mountain nights.

Sabugueiro is a 15-minute drive uphill from Seia. A taxi from Seia costs around €12.

This trim place is well known for hearty regional specialities, including local cheeses and sausages as well as *chanfana à serrana* (highland goat).

Taberna da Fonte PORTUGUESE €€
(Largo da Misericórdia 1; mains €8-15; 7-10pm Tue-Sun) With a gourmet shop attached (selling everything from smartly packaged oils to local cheeses), it's no surprise that this bar-restaurant is one of Seia's trendier spots. That said, despite the smart chairs, modern lampshades and slate floor, it's great value for money, serving up rich daily specials such as *chanfana* (goat) and *bacalhau* (cod) and delicious *pão caseiro* (homemade bread).

Restaurante Borges PORTUGUESE €€
(238 313 010; Travessa do Funchal 7; mains €9-14; lunch & dinner Fri-Tue, lunch Wed) Tucked away in a tight corner off the main street, this country-style place offers large portions of delicious traditional Portuguese fare and is popular with locals celebrating special events. The TV conspicuously blaring in other Portuguese restaurants is blessedly absent here.

Information

Biblioteca (Rua da Caínha; 9am-noon & 2-6pm Mon-Fri) Free internet in the heart of town at the local library.

Parque Natural da Serra da Estrela Office (238 310 440; www.icnf.pt; Praça da República 30; 9am-12.30pm & 2-5.30pm Mon-Fri) Tough to spot, this park office is in the centre of town. There's better information at the park interpretation centre (p337) though.

Turismo (238 317 762; www.cm-seia.pt; Rua Pintor Lucas Marrão; 9am-12.30pm & 2-5.30pm Mon-Sat, 9am-1pm Sun) Helpful and central.

Getting There & Away

Marques (238 312 858; www.marques.pt) has buses to Viseu and local villages several times each weekday.

Rede Expressos (238 313 102; www.rede-expressos.pt) has buses going to Lisbon (€18.50, four hours), Coimbra (€10, 1½ hours) and Guarda (€10.50, 70 minutes). It also runs two direct buses weekly to Covilhã (€13.20, 1¾ hours).

Gouveia

POP 3800

Gouveia, draped across a hillside 5km from the N17, is a charming blend of the contemporary and historical in a small-town setting. Pleasantly laid out, with parks and public gardens, it offers sufficient accommodation, food and transport to be a good base for exploring the northwestern side of Serra da Estrela. Several interesting churches, including São Pedro, clad in gorgeous *azulejos* (tile; added as recently as 1940) keep the eyes keen, as do several quirky museums.

Recently, local tourist authorities have made a big effort to promote the area by introducing 20 themed walking routes, designed to stimulate all the senses.

Sights

Museu Municipal de Arte Moderna Abel Manta MUSEUM
(www.cm-gouveia.pt; Rua Direita 45; 9.30am-12.30pm & 2-6pm Tue-Sun) FREE This fascinating little museum pays homage to Abel Manta, a controversial 20th-century Portuguese modernist painter, who was born in Gouveia. Around 23 of his works are on display, along with other works by well-known Portuguese painters.

It's housed in a 17th-century building, previously home to the Counts of Caria, Vinhó and Almedina, and features fine baroque details (note the doors and windows).

Activities

Gouveia Pelos Sentidos WALKING
(Gouveia for the Senses; www.gouveiapelossentidos.pt) Unfortunate spoiler: this is for those able to read Portuguese. This otherwise wonderful initiative is a series of themed walking routes, covering everything from cheeses and bread to wine and oil, lovely villages and other sites. You can buy the complete set of route maps from the tourist office (€15) and get the GPS coordinates from an associated app.

Sleeping

Casas do Toural COTTAGE €€
(927 971 221; www.casasdotoural.pt; Rua Direita 74; cottages 2-person €65-75, 4-person €110-160;) This gorgeous ensemble of restored houses surrounds an immaculately kept hillside farm-garden in the centre of town. Most rooms feature exposed stone walls, kitchens, fireplaces and living rooms. Book in advance on weekends. For longer-term guests, owner Maria José offers guided hikes into the Serra da Estrela. Apartments are self-catering, but if you want breakfast, it's available for €5.

Hotel Monteneve HOTEL €€
(238 490 370; www.montenevehotel.com; Av Bombeiros Voluntários 12; s/d €45/65, not incl breakfast €40/55;) This old granite building in the heart of town has been converted into a rigorously clean hotel with comfortable rooms and a pleasant breakfast area. A good deal.

Quinta das Cegonhas CAMPGROUND €€
(238 745 886; www.cegonhas.com; Nabaínhos; sites 2 adults, tent & car €21.50, d €61, apt €69-91;) This restored 17th-century *quinta* (country estate), 6km northeast of Gouveia, has nice views, terraced tent sites, private rooms and self-catering apartments. The Dutch owners offer a wealth of information about local hikes. If you'd rather just kick up your feet and relax, head to the pool and lounge area. Sociable evening meals are available.

Madre de Água BOUTIQUE HOTEL €€€
(www.quintamadredeagua.pt; Vinhó; d €130;) This upmarket experience is for those who want to know where their bottled milk comes from. This boutique hotel is located in the middle of the owners' farm, which produces everything from grapes and olive oil to Serra da Estrela cheese. The 10 rooms are smart and sleek, but the wow factor comes with the sunny, glass-walled lounge areas.

Eating

Restaurante O Júlio PORTUGUESE €€
(Travessa do Loureiro 1; dishes €9-14.50; 12.30-3pm & 7-9pm Wed-Mon) Tucked away in a narrow downtown street, this place is popular for its regional cuisine. Local character Senhor Júlio holds the fort while the rest bustle around him. House specialities include *cabrito à serrana* (mountain-style kid) and *batatinhas do céu* (heavenly potatoes).

Information

Turismo (238 083 930; www.cm-gouveia.pt; Jardim da Ribeira; 9.30am-12.30pm & 2-6pm Tue-Sun) On a pleasant square five minutes' walk downhill from Praça de São Pedro.

Vergílio Ferreira Municipal Library (Praça de São Pedro; 9.30am-12.30pm & 2-6pm Mon-Fri, 9am-1.30pm Sat;) Free internet access is available here in a stunning 18th-century building.

Getting There & Away

BUS

Rede Expressos (238 493 675; www.rede-expressos.pt) and **Marques** (www.marques.pt) stop at Gouveia's **bus station** (238 493 675; Rua Cidade da Guarda), a 10-minute walk north of the centre. Marques runs to Seia (€2.75, 25 minutes, two per weekday) and Guarda (€4.50, 1½ hours, one daily at 7.30am). Rede Expressos goes two or three times daily to Coimbra (€12.80, two hours) and Lisbon (€19.50, 4¾ hours).

TRAIN

The Gouveia railway station, 14km north near Ribamondego, is on the Beira Alta line between Coimbra (€9, 1¾ hours) and Guarda (€5.65, 50 minutes) – regional trains stop here two to four times daily. A taxi between Gouveia and the station will cost around €12.

Manteigas

Sights

★Burel Factory MUSEUM
(www.burelfactory.com; Amieiros Verdes; free tours 11am Mon-Sat, noon Sun, shop 10am-6pm Mon-Fri, 10am-1pm Sat) The burel factory at

Manteigas originally opened in 1960 and employed 1000 people at its height (burel is a wool fabric similar to felt). After a decline in the industry it had to shut its doors last decade, but, having fallen in love with burel, a passionate investor decided to reconstitute the factory. You can now tour a part of the factory and see the burel production process from start to finish. Save your pennies for shop purchases.

Poço do Inferno
WATERFALL

In springtime, this waterfall in a craggy gorge makes a beautiful sight. From Manteigas, drive approximately 4km along the signposted main road towards Torre. Just beyond Caldas de Manteigas, turn left for Poço do Inferno (Hell's Well) and climb a further 6km to the falls through lush evergreen forest. In summer the waterfall slows to a trickle.

Activities

★Trilhos Verdes
WALKING

(www.manteigastrilhosverdes.com) This excellent network of marked trails in the Manteigas area makes the town a great base for hiking. There are 16 'themed' routes known as 'Trilhos Verdes'; each trail has its own leaflet. Obtain them from the park office in town or browse them online (available in English).

Penhas Douradas
WALKING

A medium-difficulty walk from Manteigas goes to Penhas Douradas, on a ridge high above. The track climbs northwest out of town via Rua Dr Afonso Costa to join a sealed, switchback forestry road and, briefly, a loop of the Seia-bound N232. Branch left off the N232 almost immediately, on another road to the Meteorological Observatory. From there it's a short, gentle ascent to Penhas Douradas.

You're about 700m above Manteigas here, and mustn't miss the stunning view from a stub of rock called Fragão de Covão; just follow the signs. You can also drive up the N232 just for the view.

Walking back the same way makes for a return trip of about eight hours.

Vale do Zêzere
WALKING

The relatively easy ramble through this magnificent, glacier-scoured valley, one of the park's most beautiful and noteworthy natural features, is a highlight of any trip to Manteigas. Its only drawback: the trail is shadeless and baking in clear summer weather.

From Manteigas, follow the N338 for 2.8km towards Caldas de Manteigas, leaving the road at the 'Roteiro Rural Palhotas' sign just beyond the spa hotel. From here, a part-cobbled, part-dirt road leads upstream through irrigated fields dotted with typical stone *casais* (huts). About 4km along, the unpaved road crosses the Rio Zêzere just above a popular local swimming hole.

From here, the 4km trail follows the Rio Zêzere upstream along its eastern bank, climbing gradually through a wide-open landscape dotted with stone shepherds' huts and backed by spectacular views of the looming mountains on either side. Eventually the path narrows and steepens as you scramble up to meet the N338 (11km from Manteigas).

Once at the N338, backpackers wanting to stay overnight amid this dazzling scenery can continue uphill on the paved road 1.1km to the Covão da Ametade campground. Thirsty day-trippers should descend 900m along the road to Fonte Paulo Luís Martins, a crystalline spring whose delightfully cold water (constantly 6°C) is bottled in Manteigas and sold nationally. If you've left a car at the swimming hole, you can walk an additional 3.2km back downhill along the N338, although it's usually easy to hitch a ride from someone filling bottles at the springs.

SkiParque
OUTDOORS

(☎275 980 090; www.skiparque.pt; N232; ⊙10am-6pm) A dry-ski run 8km east of Manteigas, friendly SkiParque has a lift, gear rental, snowboarding, a cafe and a treeless, functional campground. The price for lifts and equipment rental is €15/27 per one/four hours in high season. Lessons (one/two people €25/35) are also available.

SkiParque organises other outdoor activities such as rock climbing, hiking, mountain biking and paragliding lessons for first-timers.

Sleeping

Campismo Covão d'Ametade
CAMPGROUND €

(www.covaodametade.wix.com/home; Covão d'Ametade; sites €1.50-2.50 plus per adult/child €1.50/1; P) The wilder of two idyllic, bare-bones campgrounds tucked away in the mountains surrounding Manteigas, this rough camping (read tents-only) site sits in a grove of birch trees near the head of the Vale do Zêzere, with awe-inspiring views up to the looming Cántaro Magro. There are basic toilets, picnic tables and cement barbecues, but no electricity or hot water.

It's signposted at a hairpin bend 12km west of Manteigas along the N338.

Covão da Ponte CAMPGROUND €
(www.covaodaponte.com; sites per adult/child/tent/car €1.50/1/1.50/1; P) At this lovely, shaded spot along the Mondego, you can wade, picnic or simply relax by the river's tranquil headwaters. Hikers can also explore the surrounding fields and mountains on three loop trails of varying lengths. To get here, take the N232 5.4km uphill from Manteigas, then continue an additional 5km from the signposted turn-off. The poorly marked park entrance is on the right.

Pensão Estrela GUESTHOUSE €
(275 981 288; www.residencialestrela.web.pt; Rua Doutor Sobral 5; s/d from €25/35;) This recommended mother-and-son team in the heart of the village offers very clean, comfortable, heated rooms with good bathrooms at a great price. Breakfast is simple but decent, with tasty mountain *chouriço* (spicy sausage), and there's a sociable bar downstairs.

Pensão Serradalto GUESTHOUSE €
(275 981 151; paragem_serradalto@hotmail.com; Rua 1 de Maio 15; s €25, d summer/winter €35/45; Wed-Mon;) In the heart of town, the 'keep on keeping on' Serradalto offers basic rooms with wood floors and older furnishings, plus fine valley views from a sunny, grapevine-shaded upstairs terrace. There's a good, old-style Portuguese restaurant downstairs, also with amazing vistas (closed Tuesday; mains €9.90 to €15).

★Casa das Obras HOTEL €€
(275 981 155; www.casadasobras.pt; Rua Teles de Vasconcelos; r €68-70;) Elegant and friendly, Manteigas's nicest in-town lodging is a lovely 18th-century town house that has been carefully renovated to preserve its original grandeur and stone-walled charm. It's all historical feel and noble elegance but it's no shrine, rather a relaxed spot with a top welcome from the family that has owned this place for centuries.

Hotel Berne HOTEL €€
(275 981 351; www.hotelberne.com; Quinta de Santo António; s/d €45/65; P) Looking and feeling like a small, modern Swiss chalet, Berne packs a big punch considering there are only 17 rooms, all decked out in cheerful, modern blonde wood. It's perfect for families. Some rooms have balconies opening onto views of Manteigas and the mountains above.

★Casa das Penhas Douradas HOTEL €€€
(275 981 045; www.casadaspenhasdouradas.pt; Penhas Douradas; s €115-150, d €135-170, ste €270; P@) On its mountaintop perch between Manteigas and Seia, this hotel gets everything right, from its funky design (minimalist Scandinavian meets trendy retro Portuguese in an open-plan design) to its impeccable, seamless service (evening drinks, afternoon teas, fireplaces, various lounge areas). And that's before you plunge into the heated pool or grab a spa treatment (the massages are amazing).

A SHEPHERD'S BEST FRIEND

Any animal lover travelling through the Serra da Estrela will be hard-pressed to resist the 'take me home now' feeling prompted by the region's indigenous Cão da Serra da Estrela, or **Estrela mountain dog** (EMD). It's not just the adorable fuzzy golden and black puppies; the massive adults are as handsome as they are strong, smart, loving and loyal.

Widely recognised as one of the most ancient breeds on the Iberian Peninsula, the EMD is thought to have descended from dogs brought by the Romans or Visigoths. Over the centuries, shepherds chose the best dogs to guard their goats and sheep and perform in harsh mountain conditions. Fiercely resisting any predator daring enough to attack its flock, the EMD can also be gentle as a lamb, especially in its nurturing attitude towards the young of both the human and goat/sheep variety. Traditionally the dogs were outfitted with spiked collars to protect their throats against an attacking wolf or bear.

While today the EMD is a popular Portuguese pet, its traditional use has declined drastically. Ironically, the wolf-recovery organisation **Grupo Lobo** (http://lobo.fc.ul.pt) has become a leading advocate for reviving the EMD's role as herd guardian. Conservationists worldwide now see herd-guarding dogs as one of the best strategies for protecting flocks while promoting wolf recovery.

Eating

Pastelaria Padaria Floresta BAKERY, CAFE €
(Rua 1 de Maio; snacks €1.20-2.50; 6am-7pm Mon-Sat, 8am-1pm Sun) Open bright and early, this nondescript little bakery is a hiker's best friend, with simple sandwiches on home-made bread plus delicious trail snacks for around €1. Taste the *empadas de frango* (pastry dough filled with chicken), *queijadas de requeijão* (half-sweet half-savoury cheese tarts) and the house speciality *pastéis de feijoca* (bean cakes).

Santa Luzia PORTUGUESE €€
(963 968 013; Rua Dr Esteves Carvalho 4; mains €9-14; noon-3pm & 7-9pm) The crisp reds and whites of the dining area blend seductively with the dark-wood tables at this main-street eatery, whose bar is always buzzing with locals enjoying a beer or two. The menu is aimed more at visitors, but features tasty-enough mountain specialities like trout and roast goat. There's *javali* (wild boar) and a great outdoor terrace with mountainside perspectives.

Restaurant Vale do Zêzere HOTEL €€
(275 982 002; www.hotelvaledozezere.com; Quinta de Santo António; mains €8.50-11; noon-2.30pm & 7-9pm Wed-Mon) A drawcard for the locals and one of few decent eateries in town is this popular family-run eatery. It serves up local favourites, including *feijocas* (bean dishes) and *chanfana* (braised goat) and offers a dessert buffet. While still in Manteigas, it's slightly out of the town clutter.

Restaurante de Casa das Penhas Douradas GASTRONOMY €€
(Penhas Douradas; snacks €5-12, mains €15-25; 8.30-10am, 1-3pm & 8-10pm) This smart, trendy eatery (part of Casa das Penhas Douradas) is a world away from traditional village life, and its decor comprises streamlined, Scandinavian-style tables. It's smart, sophisticated and very good. However, tradition is not lost: the dishes use local products, served up with gourmet flair. This means portions are more modest than at the usual Portuguese eatery, and the quality is high.

Drinking & Nightlife

Grannitus BAR
(Rua Sobral 3) All you could want in a mountain-village bar is here: log fire, pool table, cheap drinks, good atmosphere. Just don't take on the locals at darts unless you're pretty good at it.

Information

Parque Natural da Serra da Estrela Office Headquarters (275 980 060; www.icnf.pt; Rua 1 de Maio 2; 9am-1pm & 2-6pm Mon-Fri) On the main road in the centre of town. Has useful leaflets on walking routes in the Manteigas area but that's about all (no English is spoken).

Turismo (275 981 129; www.cm-manteigas.pt; Rua Dr Esteves de Carvalho 2; 9am-12.30pm & 2-5.30pm Tue-Sat mid-Sep–Jun, Wed-Sun Jul–mid-Sep) Run by the friendly and helpful José; on the main road near the petrol station.

Getting There & Away

By car, from Seia or Gouveia you approach Manteigas down a near-vertical switchback, the N232. South of town, the N338 snakes up the Zêzere valley into the high country between Torre and Penhas da Saúde.

Two weekday buses connect Manteigas with Guarda. Check with Manteigas' *turismo* for up-to-the-minute details.

Torre

In winter, Torre's road signs are so blasted by freezing winds that horizontal icicles barb their edges. Outside the snow season (mid-December to mid-April), Portugal's pinnacle is rather depressing – tired and tacky, occupied by several ageing golf-ball radar domes and a sweaty, smelly shopping arcade. The 7m-high, neoclassical obelisk was erected by João VI in the early 19th century so that Portugal could cheekily claim its highest point was exactly 2000m.

Even if you give Torre (and the slight detour there) a miss, it's worth making the trip in this direction just to survey the dramatic surroundings. The drive from Manteigas or Covilhã is especially breathtaking, passing through the **Nave de Santo António** – a high-country sheep-grazing meadow – before climbing through a surreal moonscape of crags and gorges. Visible near the turn-off for Torre is **Cántaro Magro**, a notable rock formation. Rising 500m straight from the valley below, it's a spectacular spot popular with rock-climbers.

Activities

Portugal's highest peak, at 1993m, Torre (Tower) produces a winter freeze so reliable that it's got a small **ski resort** (275 314 727; www.skiserradaestrela.com; half/full day Sat & Sun

Nov-Apr €17.50/25, other times €12/15; 9am-5pm in ski season;), with mainly beginners' slopes.

Getting There & Away

Between July and September (and weekends throughout the year), **Autotransportes do Fundão** (275 336 448) runs a 2pm bus service from Covilhã's bus station to Torre (€3, 1½ hours), arriving around 3.30pm and returning down the mountain an hour later.

Penhas da Saúde

Penhas, the closest spot in which to hunker down near Torre (about 10km from Covilhã), isn't a town but a weather-beaten collection of chalets sited striplike along the N339 at an elevation of about 1500m.

Sleeping

Pousada da Juventude HOSTEL €

(275 335 375; www.pousadasjuventude.pt; winter dm €12, d €35-45; Oct-Aug;) Penhas' first-rate mountaintop hostel has a communal kitchen and cafeteria, giant stone fireplaces and a games room featuring billiards and table tennis. The deluxe doubles in the annexe are especially nice, but those in the main building are cosy too. Dorms have eight berths and plenty of space; meals are available. Book well ahead in winter.

Getting There & Away

Daily throughout August, and on weekends in late July and early September, buses with **Autotransportes do Fundão** (275 336 448) run from Covilhã's bus station to Penhas (€2.30) at 8.50am and 2pm, returning down the mountain at 5pm (check times as they may change).

A taxi from Covilhã to Penhas costs around €30.

Covilhã

POP 36,700

Modern Covilhã is awash in suburban sprawl, its 18th-century textile factories having given way to high-rise apartment blocks. Despite the dreary outskirts, Covilhã's pleasant historic core remains intact, and the presence of the Universidade da Beira Interior lends it an air of modern urban vitality. The city's geographic setting on steeply canted terraces provides phenomenal views eastward towards Spain.

Sights

Igreja de Santa Maria CHURCH

(Rua 1 Dezembro) FREE In the midst of the grittier streets west of Praça do Município is the Igreja de Santa Maria, with a startling facade covered in *azulejos* (tiles). Recently a local government initiative has encouraged (rather than frowned upon) works of graffiti; love them or hate them, several artworks on surrounding walls form an interesting juxtaposition with the stunning tiles.

Jardim Público PLAZA

(Av Frei Heitor Pinto) Commanding fabulous views, the leafy Jardim Público, north of Praça do Município, is a popular local gathering place and a pleasant spot for a drink at sunset.

Museu de Lanifícios MUSEUM

(Museum of Wool-Making; 275 319 724; www.museu.ubi.pt; Rua Marquês d'Ávila e Bolama; adult/16-25yr €5/2.50; 9.30am-noon & 2.30-6pm Sat & Sun) Covilhã used to be the centre of one of Europe's biggest wool-producing regions but stray outside the centre and you'll see the town's ghostly mills standing empty and forlorn. Sited in the former royal textile factory, this museum traces the proud but vanishing history of wool production and cloth dyeing in the Serra da Estrela.

Ponte Pedonal Penedos Altos BRIDGE

This striking pedestrian bridge spans the valley east of the old town. It's immediately noticeable for its loftiness (52m at its top point) and unusual zigzag trajectory. Built by João Luís Carrilho da Graça, it's won rave reviews in architecture circles since its opening in 2009. It links the town's public swimming pool and outer suburbs.

Sleeping

Hotel Covilhã Jardim HOTEL €

(275 322 140; www.hotelcovilhajardim.com; Jardim Público 40; s/d Apr-Dec €30/48, Jan-Mar €35/55;) This amiable, bright, modern, family-run place sits on the municipal gardens. All rooms have lots of natural light and leafy views of the park or sweeping panoramas of the surrounding mountains (room 110 has both), and one is wheelchair-accessible. The pleasant cafe downstairs is another plus.

Covilhã

Sights

1 Igreja de Santa Maria A3
2 Jardim Público B1

Sleeping

3 Casa com História A1
4 Hotel Covilhã Jardim B1
5 Hotel Solneve B3

Eating

6 ComFusão B4
7 Pastelaria Restaurante Montiel B3
8 Restaurante Zé do Sporting B3

Drinking & Nightlife

Covilhã Jardim Café-Bar ....(see 4)

Hotel Solneve HOTEL €
(275 323 001; www.solneve.pt; Rua Visconde da Coriscada 126; s/d €33/55;) With views of Covilhã's main square, this grand k hotel in the heart of town has spotless, high-ceilinged, modernish rooms. Facilities are good, with minibars, a decent restaurant and a swimming pool downstairs, plus off-street parking (€2.50). A good-value choice.

Casa com História GUESTHOUSE €€
(968 310 610, 275 322 493; www.casacomhistoria.pt; Rua Dr António Plácido da Costa 25; d €70-80, f €100) Like the confident new kid in high school, this is one of Covilhã's trendy additions: an old mansion, fitted out with contemporary style. Each room has a unique touch, from enlarged photographic wallpaper to bright refurb'ed furniture (note: some are loft rooms – think low beams). Stunning library-cum-lounge areas and breakfast are wonderful bonuses.

Eating

Varanda da Estrela PORTUGUESE €€
(www.varandadaestrela.pt; Penhas da Saúde; mains €11-15) This popular spot is 11km out of Covilhã, up the winding road en route to Penhas da Saude. It's a handsome eatery that celebrates Serra da Estrela (it's decked out in stone and features local artefacts), and serves up rich and filling Portuguese cuisine. Locals rave about the *javali* (wild boar) and the oven-baked delights.

ComFusão PORTUGUESE €€
(275 098 902; Rua de São Tiago 13; dishes €6-14; 4pm-2am Mon-Sat) This comfortable and convivial spot is winningly decorated in wood and stone and offers a short selection of typical northern Portuguese dishes and *petiscos* (tapas) presented with modern flair and design.

Restaurante Zé do Sporting PORTUGUESE €€
(Rua Comendador Mendes Veiga 19; mains €8-14; lunch & dinner Tue-Sat, lunch Sun) Head here for unpretentious comfort food. There's lots of grilled meats – including local favourites such as *coelho* (rabbit) and *cabrito* (kid) – and other Portuguese classics. If it's on the menu when you visit, try the *feijoada á transmontana,* a hearty stew of beans, cabbage, pork and smoky sausage.

Pastelaria Restaurante Montiel CAFE €€
(275 322 086; Praça do Município 33-37; snacks €2-5, mains €11-13; cafe 7.30am-late, restaurant noon-3pm & 5-10pm) The upstairs dining room serves decent regional cooking, with an emphasis on meat dishes. The downstairs cafe is a Covilhã's social hub (if a smoky one)

and serves tasty snacks: fabulous *empadas* (pies), sausage rolls and the like.

 Drinking & Nightlife

Companhia Club CLUB
(www.companhiaclub.com; Rua da Indústria 33) This surprisingly sleek and modern DJ bar and club is one of a cluster of late-night venues popular with students, set in the abandoned-looking mill zone in the north of town. To get there, head along Avenida Frei Heitor Pinto past the *turismo* and veer right down Rua da Indústria.

Covilhã Jardim Café-Bar CAFE
(275 322 140; Jardim Público 40; 8am-2am) With comfy couches inside and tree-shaded tables on its parkside terrace, this trendy little cafe makes for an enjoyable place to watch the world go by.

Information

Turismo (275 319 560; www.turismodocentro.pt; Av Frei Heitor Pinto; 9am-1pm & 2-6pm Mon-Sat) Has a good map of town and a few dusty pamphlets, but is of limited help.

Getting There & Away

BUS

From the long-distance **bus station** (275 313 506; Av da Anil), **Rede Expressos** (www.rede-expressos.pt) runs regularly to Guarda (€6, 45 minutes, nine daily Monday to Friday). Regular services go via Castelo Branco (€6, one hour) to Lisbon (€15.20, 3¾ hours). There are also multiple daily services to Porto (€16.60, 3¾ hours).

TRAIN

Three daily IC trains run to/from Lisbon (€17.20, 3¾ hours) via Castelo Branco (€6.60, 50 minutes). Regional trains serving Castelo Branco are slightly slower and slightly cheaper.

Getting Around

From the train and long-distance bus stations, it's a punishing 2km climb to Praça do Município, the town centre. A taxi up the hill from either station will cost about €6, or you can catch a **Covibus local bus** (275 098 097; www.covibus.com; tickets €1.30): take bus 10 or 11 for Praça do Município.

BEIRA ALTA

Heading north and west from the Serra da Estrela, mountains give way quickly to rolling plains that stretch up to the Douro valley and east to Spain. Threat of invasion from its not-always-friendly neighbour marks both the region's history and its landscape. A series of fearsome fortress-towns are the biggest draw for travellers, though the cities of Viseu and Guarda also have charms, from excellent local wines to troves of Renaissance art.

Viseu

POP 47,250

One of the Beiras' most appealing cities, Viseu rivals more-visited Coimbra for sheer charm and vitality. Its well-preserved historic centre offers numerous enticements to pedestrians: cobbled streets, meandering alleys, leafy public gardens and a central square – Praça da República, aka the 'Rossio' – graced with bright flowers and fountains. Sweeping vistas over the surrounding plains unfold from the town's highest point, the square fronting the cathedral, built on the site of a former mosque, while some of Portugal's standout Renaissance art is on show alongside. Viseu is also a great place to eat and drink: the reds from the surrounding Dão region are considered to be some of Portugal's finest.

Praça de Dom Duarte is named after the Portuguese monarch born in Viseu. Several noble mansions adorn the square.

History

According to legend, Viriato, chief of the Lusitani tribe, took refuge in a cave here before the Romans hunted him down in 139 BC. The Romans built a fortified camp just across the Rio Pavia from Viseu. The town, conquered and reconquered in the struggles between Christians and Moors, was definitively taken by Fernando I, king of Castilla y León, in 1057.

Afonso V completed Viseu's sturdy walls in about 1472. The town soon spread beyond them, and grew fat from agriculture and trade. An annual 'free fair', declared by João III in 1510, carries on today as one of the region's biggest agricultural and handicrafts expositions.

Sights

North of the cathedral along Rua Silva Gaio is the longest remaining stretch of the old **town wall**. Rua Augusto Hilário runs southeast through the former **judiaria** (14th- to 16th-century Jewish quarter). Rua Direita,

Viseu's most appealing street and once the most direct route to the hilltop, is a lively melee of shops, souvenir stands, restaurants and old town houses.

★Museu Grão Vasco MUSEUM
(www.imc-ip.pt; Adro da Sé; €4, Sun morning free; 2-5.30pm Tue, 10am-6pm Wed-Sun) Adjoining the cathedral, the severe granite box of the Paço de Três Escalões (Palace of Three Steps) was originally built as the bishop's palace. It's now a splendid museum featuring Viseu's own Vasco Fernandes, known as Grão Vasco (the Great Vasco; c 1475–1543) – one of Portugal's seminal Renaissance painters.

Azulejos PUBLIC ART
On the north side of the Rossio is a large and beautiful scene of fine *azulejos* (tiles) that depict scenes from regional life. These were painted in 1931 by Joaquim Lopes (1886–1956).

Parque do Fontelo PARK
A haven of woodland and open space sprawls beyond the Portal do Fontelo. Here is the 16th-century **Antigo Paço Episcopal** (former Bishop's Palace), now home to the Welcome Center - Solar do Vinho do Dão, together with once-lovely Renaissance gardens, a stadium and a recreation complex.

Museu Almeida Moreira MUSEUM
(apoio.municipe@cm-viseu.pt; Rua Soar de Cima; 10am-12.30pm & 2-5.30pm Tue-Sun) FREE The 19th-century, *azulejo*-adorned Museu Almeida Moreira, which was the genteel home to the first director of the Museu Grão Vasco, houses fine furnishings and an art collection.

Catedral de Viseu CATHEDRAL
(Sé; 9am-noon & 2-7pm) FREE Resplendent on a high rock is the 13th-century granite cathedral, whose gloomy Renaissance facade conceals a splendid 16th-century interior, including an impressive Manueline ceiling. The lower level, handsome with tiles, Ionic columns, tombstone fragments and round arches, is one of Portugal's earliest Italian Renaissance structures. Note the amazing Romanesque-Gothic portal on one corner, rediscovered during restoration work in 1918. The upper gallery of the adjacent cloister affords panoramas of Viseu's historic centre.

Casa da Rua Dom Duarte NOTABLE BUILDING
(Rua Dom Duarte) Lovely and narrow Rua Dom Duarte was the most direct path to reach the citadel. Along with many beautiful (sadly decaying) buildings, this house has a beautiful Manueline window and is regarded as the king's birthplace (it's closed to the public).

Igreja Dos Terceiros CHURCH
FREE At the southern end of Praça da República is the late-18th-century Igreja dos Terceiros, all heavy, gilded baroque but for the luminous *azulejos* portraying the life of St Francis.

Activities

Dão Ecotrail WALKING, CYCLING
(Ecopista do Dão; www.ciclovia.pt) You can cycle or walk along the ecotrail, a 50km stretch of former railway between Viseu and Santa Comba Dão.

Welcome Center – Solar do Vinho do Dão WINE
(232 410 060; www.rotavinhosdao.pt; Rua Aristides Sousa Mendes; 10am-12.30pm & 2-7pm Tue-Sat) This wonderful welcome centre, housed in a stunning building, a renovated 12th-century palace, showcases the vineyards of the Dão region and will set you on your way. As well as tastings (for a small fee), there's a video on the region and you can buy an excellent wine-route kit, outlining five different routes with details of each winery (in English and Portuguese).

Paço dos Cunos de Santar WINE
(232 945 452; Largo do Paço de Santar, Santar; 10am-10pm Tue-Sun) Top billing goes to the centrally located Paço dos Cunos de Santar, a 17th-century estate 17km south of Viseu, where you can tour the vineyard before a tasting of its noble wines and olive oils, many of which go nicely with the seasonal, creative takes on regional cuisine in the contemporary restaurant.

Casa de Santar WINE
(232 942 937; http://casadesantar.com; Santar; guided visits 11am & 3pm Tue-Sat, shop 10am-noon & 2-6pm Tue-Sat) One of the most accessible wineries from Viseu is Casa de Santar, situated about 15km southeast on the N231. It has fine grounds and lovely architecture.

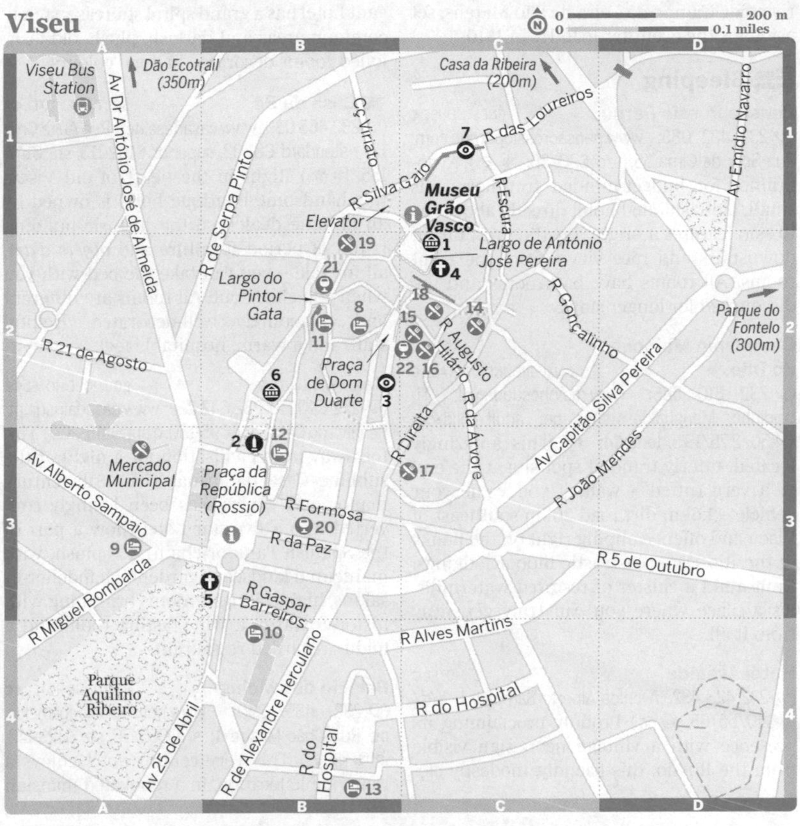

Viseu

Top Sights
1 Museu Grão Vasco C2

Sights
2 Azulejos B3
3 Casa da Rua Dom Duarte B2
4 Catedral de Viseu C2
5 Igreja Dos Terceiros B3
6 Museu Almeida Moreira B2
7 Town Wall C1

Sleeping
8 Casa da Sé B2
9 Hotel Avenida A3
10 Hotel Grão Vasco B4
11 Palácio dos Melos B2
12 Pensão Rossio Parque B3
13 Pousada de Viseu B4

Eating
14 Casa dos Queijos C2
15 O Cortiço C2
16 O Hilário C2
17 O Pateo C3
18 Restaurante Colmeia C2
19 Restaurante Muralha da Sé B2

Drinking & Nightlife
20 Brothers B3
21 Irish Bar B2
22 Palato Wine House C2

Festivals & Events

Feira de São Mateus CULTURAL

(www.feirasaomateus.pt) Viseu's biggest annual get-together is a jamboree of agriculture and handicrafts from mid-August to mid-September, augmented by folk music, traditional food, amusement-park rides and fireworks. This direct descendant of the town's old 'free fair' still takes place in the riverside Campo da Feira de São Mateus, set aside for the event by João III in 1510.

Sleeping

Pensão Rossio Parque GUESTHOUSE €
(232 422 085; www.pensaorossioparque.com; Rua Soar de Cima 55; s/d €30/35;) A no-brainer for budget-minded travellers, this small, old-fashioned hotel directly above the Rossio features a bright, bustling restaurant downstairs and nice views from the front rooms. All rooms have bathrooms and are discounted for longer stays.

Campismo Moinhos do Dão CAMPGROUND, COTTAGE €
(232 610 586; www.moinhosdodao.nl; Tibaldinho, Mangualde; sites per adult/child/car €4.50/2.75/1.75, tent €4; P) This amazingly located, utterly tranquil spot sits at the end of a very rutted – walk if you value your vehicle – 1.6km dirt road 20km southeast of Viseu and offers camping right on the banks of the Rio Dão, plus rustic indoor lodgings. Built amid a cluster of restored watermills, it's a place where you can truly get away from it all.

Hotel Avenida HOTEL €
(232 423 432; Avenida Alberto Sampaio 1; s/d/tr €40/55/65; @) Proudly proclaiming its presence with a vintage neon sign visible from the Rossio, this friendly, modestly elegant hotel has a grand spiral staircase, stately common areas and darkish, plush, old-fashioned rooms decorated in regal colours.

★ **Casa da Sé** BOUTIQUE HOTEL €€
(232 468 032; www.casadase.net; Rua Auga Cruz 12; r standard €81-92, superior €102-113, ste €147-155;) Right in the heart of old Viseu, this handsome boutique hotel is owned by an antique dealer, so the historic building is full of period furniture and *objets d'art,* all for sale – you can take the bed with you when you check out. All rooms are different and exceedingly well-decorated. Helpful staff, and a warm, hospitable feel.

Casa da Ínsua BOUTIQUE HOTEL €€
(232 640 110, 232 642 222; www.casadainsua.pt; Penalva do Castelo; r €95-150, q apt €145-200) Tiptoe away from civilisation for a night at the sublime Casa da Ínsua. This 18th-century manor and winery has been lovingly converted into a five-star hotel (now a part of the Spanish Parador chain). It's plush, with manicured landscape gardens, chandelier-lit salons, high-ceilinged rooms brimming with historic charm, a wine-tasting room and a highly regarded restaurant.

Palácio dos Melos BOUTIQUE HOTEL €€
(232 439 290; www.hotelpalaciodosmelos.pt; Rua Chão Mestre 4; s/d €65/76, ste €123-142; P@) This very central hotel enjoys a remarkable location, in a renovated mansion

WINES OF THE DÃO REGION

The velvety reds of the Dão region, south and east of Viseu, have been cultivated for over 2000 years, and are today among Portugal's best drops. Vineyards are mostly sheltered in valleys at altitudes of 200m to 900m just west of the Serra da Estrela, thus avoiding the rain of the coast but also the harsh summer heat that comes further inland. This, together with granitic soil, helps the wines retain their natural acidity. Dão wines are often called the Burgundies of Portugal because they don't overpower but, rather, are subtle and full of finesse.

Some three dozen Dão vineyards and producers offer multilingual cellar tours and tastings; most require advance booking. Two popular wineries near Viseu are at **Casa da Ínsua**, 30km east on the IP5 and N329-1, and **Casa de Santar** (p346), 15km southeast on the N231. Both have fine grounds and lovely architecture, and the former is also a plush five-star country hotel.

For those keen to learn about Dão wines, don't miss the new **Welcome Center – Solar do Vinho do Dão** (p346) in Viseu's 16th-century Antigo Paço Episcopal, run by the Comissão Vitivinícola Regional do Dão, the region's regulatory body. Here, the public can not only sample Dão wines, but get information on the region's excellent wine routes. Many of the wineries have excellent restaurants attached.

White Dão wines are also available, though the full-bodied reds are generally better and more prolific. But do try the sparkling white wines of the separate, small Lafões region, northwest of Viseu.

built right into the town walls. The 22 rooms incorporate all the modern comforts you'd expect from a five-star place, but the most atmospheric rooms in the original older building also have grand high ceilings, carpets and chandeliers that speak of a different time.

Guests have access to a small grassy yard where drinks are served, reached by a catwalk across the top of the old town gate. Look for money-saving packages online, including meals in the hotel's gourmet restaurant.

Quinta da Boavista FARMSTAY €€

(☎919 858 340; www.quintadaboavista.pt; Penalva do Castelo; apt from €80; P 📶 🏊) A shining example of enotourism, Quinta da Boavista is a winery run with passion by an English-speaking vigneron. The eco-aware farmhouse sits in a secluded spot and offers well-equipped apartments, wine tastings of its full-bodied reds and delicious home-cooked meals (if reserved ahead). There's also a swimming pool, horse riding and relaxation. It's 35km northeast of Viseu.

Hotel Grão Vasco HOTEL €€

(☎232 423 511; www.hotelgraovasco.pt; Rua Gaspar Barreiros; s/d €77/87; P ❄ 📶 🏊) It's a little retro (think black noticeboards with white clip-on letters), but there's something nice about this huge old-school place. The service is excellent and the low-bedded rooms are pretty comfortable. Go for one on the top floor if available – if not, grab one on the garden side of the building.

★**Pousada de Viseu** HOTEL €€€

(☎210 457 320; www.pousadas.pt; Rua do Hospital; s from €95, d €105-162; P ❄ @ 📶 🏊) This superbly refashioned *pousada* set in a monumental 19th-century hospital is a top luxury option. The original three floors, all with ridiculously high ceilings and spacious rooms, have been enhanced with a 4th floor dedicated to superior rooms with panoramic terraces. The enormous central courtyard, with bar, is a neoclassical delight, while the elegant former pharmacy has been converted into a cosy lounge.

Eating

Casa dos Queijos PORTUGUESE €

(Travessa das Escadinhas da Sé 7; mains €7.50-9.50; ⏲noon-3pm & 7-11pm Mon-Sat) Despite the owner's amusingly gruff attitude, this stone-walled old place, hidden up narrow stairs, gets top marks for atmosphere and for its carefully prepared grills and *cozidos* (stews). The shop downstairs, stacked high with tempting wines and cheeses, is a neighbourhood hang-out where locals chat all afternoon over glasses of wine.

O Hilário PORTUGUESE €

(Rua Augusto Hilário 35; mains €7.50-10; ⏲10am-10pm Mon-Sat; 🌶) Fantastically friendly and welcoming, this slice of old Portugal is named for the 19th-century fado star who once lived down the street. Great-value *doses* (portions) will feed one hungry person, but halves are available for lighter appetites. If your favourite grandparents owned a restaurant this would be it. Will organise vegetarian options if required.

Mercado Municipal MARKET €

(Rua 21 de Agosto; ⏲Mon-Sat) Self-caterers will find fruit, vegetables and other goodies at this market.

Restaurante Colmeia TASCA €€

(Rua das Ameías 12; mains €11-12; ⏲9am-3pm & 7-10.30pm Mon-Sat) For over 38 years this little *tasca*, now decorated with rural bits and bobs, has dished out regional Portuguese dishes. *Bacalhau à Tasca* (salted cod) and *cabrito assado* (roasted goat) are popular but the mixed grill is fabulous. It comes as no surprise that portions are large enough to share.

O Pateo PORTUGUESE €€

(www.pateo-restaurante.pt; Rua Direita 48; mains €8-13.50; ⏲10am-3.30pm Mon & Tue, 10am-3.30pm & 6.30-10.30pm Wed-Sat) This busy, cosy spot is oh so typical and the type of place where you are truly enveloped by cooking aromas. It's fun to come at lunchtime as you'll rub shoulders with everyone from businesspeople to elderly regulars out for their nosh. It's great value, too, with hearty plates of the day for around €7.

Tres Pipos PORTUGUESE €€

(☎232 816 851; www.3pipos.pt; Rua de Santo Amaro 966, Tonda; mains €10-17; ⏲noon-3pm & 7-10pm Tue-Sat, noon-3pm Sun) If you're opting out of the pricier winery restaurants in the area, head instead to Tres Pipos in the village of Tonda, 29km southwest of Viseu. It's a convivial, family-run affair, with spot-on hearty, regional dishes like *cabrito assado* and *polvo à lagareiro* (octopus with potatoes, garlic and olive oil) in atmospheric dining rooms with old wooden ceilings and thick stone walls.

O Cortiço PORTUGUESE €€
(☎ 232 423 853; Rua Augusto Hilário 45; mains €11-17; ⏱ noon-3pm & 7-10pm Tue-Sat, noon-3pm Sun) This heartily recommended stone-walled eatery specialises in traditional recipes collected from surrounding villages. Generous portions are served in heavy tureens, and the good house wine comes in medieval-style wooden pitchers. Finish your meal with a glass of the local firewater made from olives.

Restaurante Muralha da Sé PORTUGUESE €€€
(☎ 232 437 777; www.muralhadase.pt; Adro da Sé 24; mains €19-21; ⏱ noon-2.30pm & 7.15-10pm Tue-Sat, lunch Sun) This unabashedly upper-crust spot under the looming Igreja da Misericórdia boasts fine regional cuisine made with ingredients from the nearby Serra da Estrela, plus cathedral-square views from its terrace.

Drinking & Nightlife

Bars in the streets around the cathedral overflow, making for a merry atmosphere.

Palato Wine House WINE BAR
(☎ 232 435 081; Praça de Dom Duarte 1; ⏱ 8pm-4am Mon-Sat) In a trendy locale, this comfortably posh spot has a long list of Dão and Douro wines by the bottle, with 30-odd available by the glass at fair prices given the quantity they pour. The interior blends plush fabrics with exposed stone, and downstairs is cosy as well. Service is solicitous, and snacks and rolls are served until 3.30am.

Brothers BAR
(Rua da Paz 26; ⏱ hours vary) This stylish cafe-bar in an attractive area of the new town has a bohemian-style Parisian atmosphere, good beers and coffee, and regular live music.

Irish Bar PUB
(Largo do Pintor Gata 8; ⏱ 8.30am-2am Mon-Sat, 1pm-2am Sun) Smoky and atmospheric, this place offers Guinness on tap, occasional live Irish music and terrace seating on a charming square near the old town gate.

Shopping

Casa da Ribeira ARTS & CRAFTS
(☎ 232 429 761; Largo Nossa Senhora da Conceição; ⏱ 10am-1pm & 2-6pm Wed-Sat, 2-6pm Tue) In this municipal space, local artisans work and sell their products, including lace, ceramics and the region's distinctively black earthenware.

Information

Hospital de São Teotónio (☎ 232 420 500; Av Dom Duarte)

Tourism Kiosk (Rossio; ⏱ 10am-5pm) This kiosk provides basic information on Viseu, including maps.

Welcome Center Viseu (☎ 232 420 950; www.cm-viseu.pt; Adro da Sé; ⏱ 9am-6pm Mon-Fri, 9-1pm & 2-6pm Sat & Sun; 📶) Viseu's tourist office is by the cathedral square. There's free internet and wi-fi here, too. As well as maps, it has a useful brochure on walks in and around Viseu.

Getting There & Away

Rede Expressos (☎ 232 422 822; www.rede-expressos.pt) serves the following destinations regularly from the **bus station** (Centro Municipal de Transportes; Av Dr Antonio José de Almeida) at the western edge of town.

Coimbra (€8.70, 1¼ hours)
Guarda (€9, one hour)
Lisbon (€18.30, 3½ hours)
Porto (€12, 1¾ hours)
Vila Real (€10.30, 1¼ hours)

Guarda

POP 26,000 / ELEV 1056M

Forte, farta, fria, fiel e formosa (strong, rich, cold, loyal and handsome): such is the popular description of Portugal's highest fully fledged city. Hunkered down on a hilltop, it was founded in 1197 to guard young Portugal against both Moors and Spaniards (hence the name).

Nowadays this district capital is a delightful place to spend an afternoon. Old Guarda is perched on a steep hill, a rambling climb from the IP5 or the train station, both roughly 5km northeast of the old centre. From the bus station on Rua Dom Nuno Álvares Pereira, it's 800m northwest to the cathedral square and the heart of the old town.

Sights

Old Town HISTORIC SITE
FREE With its 16th- to 18th-century mansions and its overpowering cathedral, **Praça Luís de Camões** is the town's centrepiece. Plenty of medieval atmosphere survives in the cobblestone lanes and huddled houses north of the cathedral, centred around **Rua de São Vicente**.

Guarda

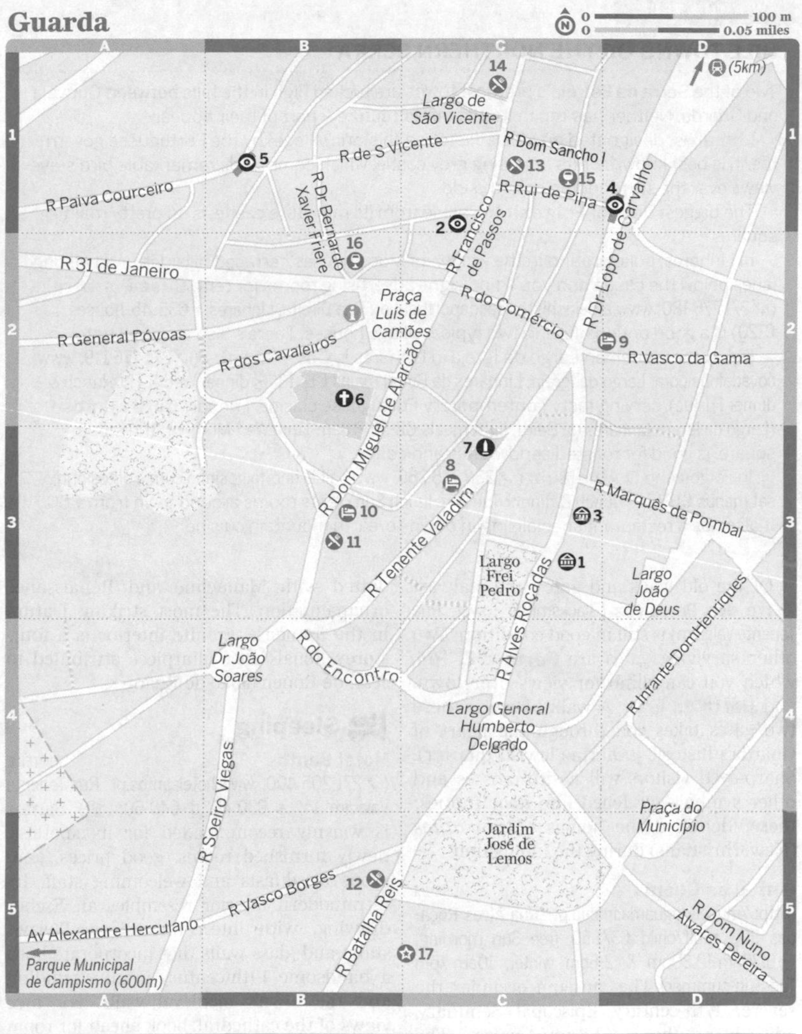

Guarda

Sights

1 Museu da Guarda C3
2 Old Town C1
3 Paço da Cultura C3
4 Porta da Erva D1
5 Porta d'El Rei B1
6 Sé B2
7 Torre dos Ferreiros C3

Sleeping

8 Hotel Santos C3
9 Residência Filipe D2
10 Solar de Alarcão B3

Eating

11 O Bule B3
12 O Caçador B5
13 Restaurante A Floresta C1
14 Restaurante Belo Horizonte C1

Drinking & Nightlife

15 Aqui Jazz C1
16 Praça Velha B2

Entertainment

17 Teatro Municipal da Guarda C5

WORTH A TRIP

HILL TOWNS OF THE NORTHERN SERRA

Two of the Serra da Estrela's prettiest towns are tucked high in the hills between Gouveia and Guarda. Neither has much tourist infrastructure – part of their appeal.

Linhares, designated an *aldeia histórica* (historic village) by the Portuguese government, is best known for its imposing grey castle, which commands remarkable bird's-eye views over the surrounding countryside.

The biggest draw of **Folgosinho**, aside from its miniature castle, is its pretty main square.

In Linhares, poke around in the warren of stone houses, terraced hillsides and twisting lanes below the castle and you'll find signs advertising rooms for rent; **Casa Pissarra** (☎271 776 180; www.aldeiashistoricasdeportugal.pt; Rua Direita, Linhares; r €35-45, houses €120) is a good option offering two typical village houses. There's also an Inatel hotel.

Below the church on Largo da Igreja in Linhares is **Cova da Loba** (☎271 776 119; www.covadaloba.com; Largo da Igreja, Linhares da Beira; mains €12-18; ⊙dinner Wed & Thu, lunch & dinner Fri-Tue), serving tasty contemporary Portuguese cuisine. Friendly **Cafe Mimoso** (Largo da Igreja, Linhares da Beira; light meals €2-5; ⊙8am-11pm Wed-Mon), on the same square, is good for toasted sandwiches and coffee.

In Folgosinho **O Albertino** (☎238 745 266; www.oalbertino-folgosinho.com; Folgosinho; set menus €11-16; ⊙lunch & dinner Tue-Sat, lunch Sun) rents rooms around town from €50. It also has a restaurant specialising in down-to-earth mountain cuisine.

Of the old walls and gates, the stalwart **Torre dos Ferreiros** (Blacksmiths' Tower; Rua Tenente Valadim) is still in good condition. Two other surviving gates are **Porta d'El Rei**, which you can climb for views over town, and **Porta da Erva**. A walk between these two gates takes you through the heart of Guarda's historic **judiaria** (Jewish quarter). Sharp-eyed visitors will notice crosses and other symbols scratched into door frames: these identified the homes of *marranos* (New Christians) during the Inquisition.

Museu da Guarda MUSEUM
(http://museudaguarda.imc-ip.pt; Rua Alves Roçadas 30; adult/child €3/1.50, free Sun morning; ⊙9.30am-12.30pm & 2-6pm winter, 10am-7pm Tue-Sun summer) The museum occupies the severe, 17th-century Episcopal Seminary, adjacent to the old bishop's palace. The collection runs from Bronze Age swords to Roman coins, from Renaissance sculpture to 19th- and 20th-century Portuguese painting.

In the adjacent, 18th-century courtyard, the handsome **Paço da Cultura** (⊙9am-12.30pm & 2-5.30pm Tue-Sat) FREE features temporary art exhibitions. Check out its beautiful patio.

Sé CATHEDRAL
(Praça Luís de Camões; ⊙9am-noon & 2-5pm) Powerful in its sobriety, this grey Gothic fortress squats heavily over the central square. The earliest parts date from 1390 but it's also dotted with Manueline and Renaissance ornamentation. The most striking feature in the immense, granite interior is a four-storey Renaissance altarpiece attributed to Jean de Rouen (João de Ruão).

Sleeping

Hotel Santos HOTEL €
(☎271 205 400; www.hotelsantos.pt; Rua Tenente Valadim 14; s €30-40, d €40-60; 📶) Santos is warmly recommended for its spotless, newly furnished rooms, good prices, generous breakfasts and welcoming staff. Its ultramodern interior resembles an Escher drawing, with interconnecting walkways, stairs and glass walls that incorporate both a handsome 19th-century granite building and the town's medieval walls. For nice views of the cathedral, book ahead for room 307 on the top floor.

Parque Municipal de Campismo CAMPGROUND €
(☎271 221 200; Rua do Estádio Municipal; sites per adult/child/car €2.50/2/3, tent €2.50-3.50; P) Very close to the town centre and next to a leafy park, this municipal site has free hot showers and plenty of shade. It's open all year but you'll freeze in winter.

Residência Filipe GUESTHOUSE €
(☎271 223 658; www.residenciafilipe.com; Rua Vasco da Gama 9; s/d/tr €20/35/45; P📶) This funny mix of old and new offers mostly bright,

attractive rooms, brisk service and breakfast. Very good value for the budget traveller.

Solar de Alarcão HOTEL €€
(☎962 327 177, 271 214 392; www.uk.solardealarcao.pt; Rua Dom Miguel de Alarcão 25-27; d €55-75; P 📶) Easily Guarda's most refined choice, this beautiful 17th-century granite mansion has its own courtyard and loggia, and sits within spitting distance of the cathedral. It offers a handful of lush rooms, oozing gold and red hues, that are stuffed with antique furniture and drapes.

Eating

O Bule CAFE €
(☎271 211 275; Rua Dom Miguel de Alarcão; ⊙8am-8pm Mon-Fri, 9am-8pm Sat, 10am-8pm Sun) This lovely, traditional cafe near the cathedral specialises in local pastries, including delicious *queijadas* (sheep's milk tarts) in a variety of flavours.

Restaurante Belo Horizonte PORTUGUESE €€
(☎271 211 454; Largo de São Vicente 1; mains €9-15; ⊙10.30am-3pm & 7-10pm Mon-Sat, lunch Sun) Granite-fronted Belo Horizonte comes highly recommended by locals. It does a great line in regional specialities such as *cabrito grelhado* (grilled kid). The solicitous husband-and-wife team here do everything right. There are *bacalhau* specials every day.

O Caçador SEAFOOD €€
(☎271 211 702; Rua Batalha Reis 121; mains €7-15; ⊙noon-3pm & 7-10pm Tue-Sun) Since 1985 this buzzy spot has been drawing in dinner guests with a happy red neon sign and a glass-walled front room vaguely reminiscent of Parisian brasseries. O Caçador, despite its name (the hunter), specialises in seafood brought straight from the coast.

Restaurante A Floresta PORTUGUESE €€
(☎271 212 314; Rua Francisco de Passos 40; mains €8-14; ⊙noon-3pm & 7-11pm Wed-Mon) This snug, friendly and elegant place serves hearty regional cuisine, including the marvellous *chouriçada,* a heaping portion of grilled sausages from the nearby Serra da Estrela.

Drinking & Nightlife

Praça Velha BAR
(Rua Augo Gil 17; ⊙10am-2am Mon-Sat; 📶) This cute little place is a fine spot for free wi-fi or an evening drink while you wait for the late-openers to get their act together. There's pleasant outdoor seating in a great location.

Aqui Jazz BAR
(Rua Rui de Pina 29; ⊙11pm-3am Wed-Sat) Attracts arty types with live jazz in its attractive stone-walled interior.

Entertainment

Teatro Municipal da Guarda THEATRE
(☎271 205 240; www.tmg.com.pt; Rua Batalha Reis 12) Guarda's shiny theatre complex, a boxy modern building of greyish-green glass just south of the historic centre, regularly hosts high-quality theatre, dance and music, including frequent international acts.

Information

Turismo (☎271 205 530; www.cm-guarda.pt; Praça Luís de Camões; ⊙9am-5.30pm Mon-Fri, 9am-1pm & 2-5pm Sat & Sun winter, 9am-6pm Mon-Fri, 10am-1pm & 2-6pm Sat & Sun summer) Helpful, with free internet access.

Getting There & Away

BUS

Rede Expressos (☎271 212 720; www.rede-expressos.pt) runs services at least three times daily to the following destinations:

Castelo Branco (€10.80, 1¾ hours)
Coimbra (€13.50, 2¾ hours)
Covilhã (€6, 45 minutes)
Lisbon (€17.50, 4½ hours)
Porto (€14, three hours)
Viseu (€8.90, one hour)

Rede Expressos also goes to Seia (€10.50, 70 minutes; at least once daily) and Gouveia (€11.40; Monday to Saturday).

CitiExpress (www.citiexpress.eu/agente/guarda) runs services to Covilhã, Viseu and Trancoso, among other smaller towns.

TRAIN

Guarda's modern train station is served by at least two fast IC trains daily from Lisbon (€20.70, 4¼ hours) and Coimbra (€16.70 to 19.20, 2¼ hours). For Porto change at Pampilhosa (frequent services).

Getting Around

Buses run by **Transportes Urbanos da Guarda** (www.mun-guarda.pt) between the train station and the centre (around €1) are infrequent; if one isn't waiting, you're probably better off taking a taxi (€4 to €5).

Trancoso

POP 3100

A warren of cobbled lanes squeezed within Dom Dinis' mighty 13th-century walls makes peaceful, hilltop Trancoso a delightful retreat from the modern world.

Although it's predominantly a medieval creation, the town's castle also features a rare, intact Moorish tower, while just outside the walls are what are believed to be Visigothic tombs.

Dinis underscored the importance of this border fortress by marrying the saintly Dona Isabel of Aragon here in 1282. But the town's favourite son is Bandarra, a lowly 16th-century shoemaker and fortune-teller who put official noses out of joint by foretelling the end of the Portuguese monarchy.

Sure enough, shortly after Bandarra's death, the young Dom Sebastião died, heirless, in the disastrous Battle of Alcácer-Quibir in 1558. Soon afterwards, Portugal fell under Spanish rule.

Sights

Old Town HISTORIC SITE

The **Portas d'El Rei** (King's Gate), surmounted by the ancient coat of arms, was always the principal entrance, whose guillotinelike door sealed out unwelcome visitors. The walls run intact for over 1km around the medieval core, which is centred on the main square, **Largo Padre Francisco Ferreira**. The square, in turn, is anchored by an octagonal *pelourinho* (pillory) dating from 1510. Another important gate, **Portas do Prado**, serves as the western entrance to the walled town.

Like many northern towns, Trancoso acquired a sizeable Jewish community following the expulsion of Jews from Spain at the end of the 15th century. As elsewhere along

A SECRET SECT IN BELMONTE

When the Moors ruled Portugal, it's estimated that 10% of the country's population was Jewish. Jews remained vital to the young Christian state, serving as government ministers and filling key roles in Henry the Navigator's school devoted to overseas exploration. The current Duke of Bragança, hereditary king of Portugal, proudly acknowledges his own Jewish parentage.

When Portugal embraced Spain's Inquisitorial zeal beginning in the 1490s, thousands of Jews from both Portugal and Spain fled to northeast Portugal, including the Beiras and Trás-os-Montes, where the arm of the Inquisitors had not yet reached. But it wasn't too long before the Inquisitors made their presence felt even here, and Jews once again faced conversion, expulsion or death.

However, in the 1980s it was revealed that in the town of Belmonte, 30km south of Guarda, a group of families had been practising Jewish rites in secret since the Inquisition – for over 500 years. While many such communities continued in secrecy well into the Inquisition, most slowly died out. But Belmonte's community managed to survive the centuries by meticulously ensuring marriages were arranged only among other Jewish families. The transmission of Jewish tradition was oral and passed from mother to daughter. Each Friday night families descended into basements to pray and celebrate the sabbath. Now that the community is out in the open, they have embraced male-dominated Orthodox Judaism, though the female elders have not forgotten the secret prayers that have been doggedly transmitted these past 500 years.

The **Museu Judaico de Belmonte** (Rua Portela 4; adult/child €2.50/1.50; ⊙9am-12.30pm & 2-5.30pm Tue-Sun mid-Sep–mid-Apr, 9.30am-1pm & 2.30-6pm Tue-Sun mid-Apr–mid-Sep) has a well-presented little display of Jewish artefacts, mostly modern, with some history about the 20th century re-establishment of Judaism in Portugal. Ask here about visits to the town's synagogue.

Other museums include one on olive oil, plus the **Museu dos Descobrimentos** (Belmonte; adult/child 6-18 yr €5/3.50; ⊙9am-12.30pm & 2-5.30pm mid-Sep–mid-Apr, 9.30am-1pm & 2.30-6pm mid-Apr–mid-Sep) covering Portugal's New World discoveries – the explorer Pedro Álvares Cabral, known as the discoverer of Brazil, was born here.

See www.cm-belmonte.pt for more details on visiting Belmonte.

There are several daily bus connections (fewer on weekends) between Belmonte and Guarda.

the border, you can generally spot Jewish houses by looking for a pair of doors: a smaller one for the private household and a larger one for a shop or warehouse. The old **judiaria** (Jewish quarter) covered roughly the southeast third of the walled town. Among dignified reminders of that time is a former rabbinical residence called the **Casa do Gato Preto**, decorated with the gates of Jerusalem and other Jewish images.

About 150m northward is Trancoso's prettiest church, the 13th-century **Capela de Santa Luzia**, with heavy Romanesque door arches and unadorned dry-stone construction. Trancoso abounds with other churches heavy with baroque make-up, most prominently the **Igreja de São Pedro**, behind the *pelourinho* on Largo Padre Francisco Ferreira.

Castelo CASTLE

(9am-12.30pm & 2-5.30pm Tue-Fri, 10am-5pm Sat, 10am-4.30pm Sun) FREE On a hill in the northeast corner of town is the tranquil castle, with its crenellated towers and the distinctively slanted walls of the squat, Moorish Torre de Menagem, which you can climb for views.

Visigothic Tombs TOMB

FREE Across the road from the Portas do Prado, beside the courthouse, is an untended rock outcrop carved with eerie, body-shaped cavities, thought to be Visigothic tombs dating to the 7th or 8th century.

Festivals & Events

Feira Medieval de Trancoso CULTURAL

In the last weekend of June Trancoso heads back to its past with lots of dressing up, a medieval market in the castle area, jousting and more. It's lots of fun.

Feira de São Bartolomeu FAIR

Held in mid-August (dates vary), this fair has artisan's stalls, exhibitions, music, food stands and fun family activities.

Sleeping

Residencial Dom Dinis GUESTHOUSE €

(271 811 525; www.domdinis.net; Av da República 10; s/d/tr €24/40/50; P) In a drab apartment block behind the post office, the Dom Dinis has a strong aroma of bleach (that is, squeaky clean) and 22 basic, remodelled rooms with wooden floors, plus a downstairs bar and restaurant.

Hotel Turismo de Trancoso HOTEL €€

(271 829 200; www.hotel-trancoso.com; Rua Professora Irene Avillez; s/d/tr €45/65/94; P) It's rather large and monolithic, but otherwise this welcoming modern hotel has comfortable, Nordic-style rooms with blonde wood and good space, some with balconies. It's attractively set around an interior atrium. Facilities are good, including an indoor pool and small gym. Deals are usually available online, with prices midweek or in winter especially attractive.

Eating

São Marcos Restaurante PORTUGUESE €

(Rua Frei João de Lucena 7; mains €7-12; noon-3pm & 6-10pm) This friendly little spot has been churning out Portuguese fare for 40 years. With its pretty lace curtains, white tablecloths and cosy decor, it's a pleasant place to dine. The cuisine is good, though not outstanding. It's not ridiculously priced, however, for its location in the historic zone near the *pelourinho*. Omelettes will please those who are tired of meaty fare.

Dom Gabriel PORTUGUESE €

(Av Engenheiro Frederico Ulrich 9A; mains €9-11; 8.30am-midnight Tue-Sun) Just outside the city walls, this is the town's best-value restaurant for solid local fare, with well-prepared meat dishes and a friendly attitude. The plate of the day is excellent value.

Casa da Prisca DELI €

(271 811 196; www.casadaprisca.com; Rua da Corredoura 1; 9am-7pm) This centenarian shop specialising in regional cheeses and smoked meats just inside the Portas d'El Rei is a fun place to browse. Try the *sardinhas doces* (sweet sardines), a local fish-shaped confection made with eggs, almonds, cinnamon and chocolate.

Drinking & Nightlife

Bar Água Benta BAR

(Rua dos Cavaleiros 36A; 10pm-3am Mon-Thu, to 4am Fri & Sat) Tucked away in the backstreets is this little cafe-bar, with a cheerful and youthful atmosphere, international beers, and live music and karaoke.

Information

Turismo (271 811 147; www.cm-trancoso.pt/turismo; 9am-12.30pm & 2-5.30pm Mon-Fri, 10am-5pm Sat, 10am-4.30pm Sun) Maps and brochures in English. Open longer hours in summer.

WORTH A TRIP

AROUND THE PLANALTO

While Trancoso and Almeida are the quintessential *planalto* fortress-villages, three other towns are well worth a gander, though only if you have your own wheels – bus connections would be maddening in this sparsely populated region. With a car, you could see all three in a single, long day.

Located 30km northwest of Trancoso, **Sernancelhe** has a wonderfully preserved centre fashioned out of warm, beige-coloured stone. Sights include a 12th-century church that boasts Portugal's only free-standing Romanesque sculpture; several grand 17th- and 18th-century town houses, one of which is believed to be the birthplace of the Marquês de Pombal; and hills that bloom with what are considered to be Portugal's best chestnuts.

Heading northeast another 16km, you arrive at little **Penedono**, with its small but splendid **castle** (www.cm-penedono.pt; 9am-5pm Mon-Fri, 10am-12.30pm & 2.30-5pm Sat, 2.30-5pm Sun) FREE. This irregular hexagon, with its picturesque crenellation, has fine views over the *planalto*. It probably dates back to the 13th century and is a remarkable sight. The **turismo** (www.cm-penedono.pt; 9am-5pm Mon-Fri, 10am-12.30pm & 2.30-5pm Sat, 2.30-5pm Sun) is below the castle. Penedono holds an impressive Medieval Fair at the beginning of each July (dates vary).

Perhaps most impressive of all is **Marialva**, 25km southeast of Penedono. The beautiful upper part of the old town is dominated by a forbidding, 12th-century **castle** (adult/15-25yr/under 15 yr €1.50/0.75/free; 9am-5pm Mon-Fri, 10am-12.30pm & 2.30-5pm Sat, 2.30-5pm Sun) that guards over the rugged valley of the Rio Côa. Below its walls lies a haunting little village populated almost exclusively by black-clad widows knitting in the timeless shade.

If you want to make an overnight trip of it, consider staying at **Residencial Flora** (254 504 411; flora.residencial@gmail.com; Bairro do Prazo, Penedono; s/d €20/35), a short walk downhill from Penedono's *castelo*, which offers plain but modern rooms with bathrooms. The hotel opposite the castle has a great location but mixed reviews from readers.

Marialva has several appealing options, including the cushiest digs of all at the luxurious **Casas do Côro** (www.casasdocoro.pt; Marialva; s/d/ste from €130/145/260;), with a great location on the cobbled square by the castle.

Getting There & Away

BUS

From Trancoso's **bus station** (Centro de Camionagem de Trancoso; 965 053 840; Av Calouste Gulbenkian), just northwest of the walled town, **Rede Expressos** (www.rede-expressos.pt) has services to Viseu (€7, 70 minutes, two to three daily), with connections via Celorico da Beira to Guarda (€9, 1¼ to 1¾ hours, daily).

TRAIN

The closest train stations are at Celorico da Beira, 27km to the south, and Vila Franca das Navas, 16km southeast.

Almeida

POP 1500

After Portugal regained independence from Spain in the 1640s, the country's border regions were on constant high alert. Almeida, along with Elvas and Valença do Minho, became a principal defence against Spanish incursions. Almeida's vast, star-shaped fortress – completed in 1641 on the site of its medieval predecessor, 15km from Spain – is the least famous but the most handsome of the three.

When its military functions were largely suspended in 1927, Almeida settled into weedy obscurity. Nowadays, the fortified old village – designated as a national monument and recently scrubbed up for tourism – is a place of great charm: the town may have the disquieting calm of a museum, but it also has enough history and muscular grandeur to set the imagination humming.

Sights

Museu Histórico Militar de Almeida MUSEUM

(adult/child €3.50/free, includes Sala de Armas & CEAMA entry; 9am-5.30pm Tue-Sun Oct-Jun,

10am-6.30pm Tue-Sun Jul-Sep) This interesting museum is built into the *casamatas* (casemates or bunkers), a labyrinth of 20 underground rooms used for storage, barracks and shelter for troops in times of siege. In the 18th century these *casamatas* also served as a prison. British and Portuguese cannons are strewn about.

Tickets include entry to CEAMA, an annex of the historical museum that has details on the construction of the fortress.

Sala de Armas MUSEUM
(adult/child €1/free; 9.15am-5.15pm Tue-Sun Oct-Jun, 10am-6.30pm Tue-Sun Jul-Sep) This small display of swords and muskets in the exterior entrance of the Portas de São Francisco is an annex of the town's historical museum.

Festivals & Events

Recriação Histórica do Cerco de Almeida CULTURAL
A lively (and very well choreographed) reenactment of the 1810 French invasion against the English and Lusitano troops, held at the end of every August.

Sleeping

Residencial-Restaurante A Muralha GUESTHOUSE €
(271 574 357; www.amuralha.pt; Bairro de São Pedro; s/d €25/40;) This functional, modern place sits 250m outside the Portas de São Francisco on the Vilar Formoso road. It has quiet and spotless rooms that offer decent value and a large restaurant serving excellent local food (mains €7 to €14). The owner is a South African–Portuguese man who speaks fluent English.

Hotel Fortaleza de Almeida HOTEL €€
(271 574 283; www.hotelparadordealmeida.com; s €73-98, d €85-125;) We're not sure how this got through the building regulations – it's a modern block within the old town, on the site of former cavalry quarters near the north bastion. A genuine personal welcome is offered, and rooms are large and comfortable with lovely parquetry floors, and giant windows and/or balconies; some have great views over the walls.

Casa de Pedra APARTMENT €€
(919 625 138; www.casadepedra.com.pt; Praça da Liberdade 9; apt €85-115;) On the same pretty square as Almeida's town hall, courthouse and post office, this comfortable apartment occupies a restored 17th-century stone house smack in the historic centre. It's full of natural light and smartly done up with modern furnishings. You can rent each floor separately or take the whole house. Breakfast is an extra €5.

Information

Turismo (271 570 020; www.cm-almeida.pt; 9am-12.30pm & 2-5.30pm Mon-Fri, from 10am Sat & Sun) The *turismo* is impressively located in an old guard-chamber within the Portas de São Francisco. Here you can get a map of the fortress.

Getting There & Away

Nondrivers will almost certainly have to stay the night due to limited bus connections. There's weekday bus service to Celorico da Beira, from where you can change for destinations like Coimbra and Viseu. There's also a daily bus to and from Guarda (€5.20, one hour).

Porto, the Douro & Trás-os-Montes

Includes ➡

Best Places to Eat

- Cantina 32 (p378)
- A Sandeira (p380)
- DOC (p406)
- Don Roberto (p419)
- Pedro Lemos (p384)

Best Places to Sleep

- 6 Only (p375)
- Casa Cimeira (p405)
- Morgadio da Calçada (p405)
- Pedras Salgadas (p415)
- Guest House Douro (p374)

Why Go?

It's the dynamic Rio Douro that brings diversity to the province it has defined, a province with granite bluffs, wine caves, medieval stone houses and steep, terraced vineyards. Romantic Porto, Portugal's second-largest city, is at its mouth; one of the world's oldest demarcated wine regions is close to the source; and scores of friendly villages in between have always relied on it for water, food and commerce. Alongside the river, the region also boasts intricately carved cathedrals, baroque churches, palatial *quintas* (estates), beaux arts boulevards and 18th-century wine cellars.

Sandwiched between the Rio Douro and the Spanish border in Portugal's extreme northeast corner, ruggedly beautiful Trás-os-Montes is named for its centuries-long isolation 'behind the mountains'. Life here unfolds at a different pace, dictated by harsh, pristine nature. Both its food and its people are hearty and no-frills, as you'll soon find out when travelling its towns and wilderness areas.

When to Go

Porto

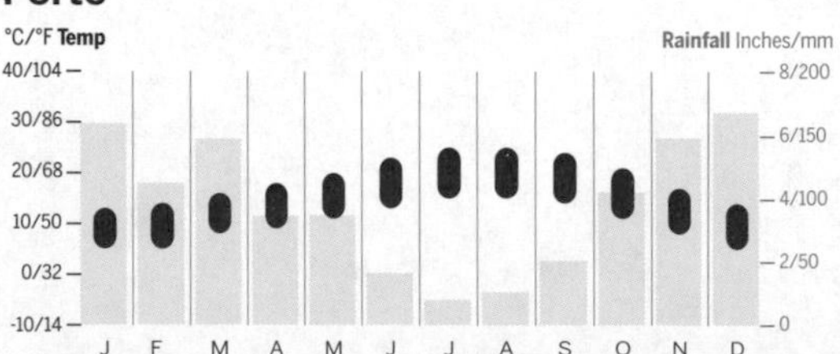

24 Jun Festa de São João, Porto's biggest party, with music, fireworks and plastic mallets.

Aug–Sep Lamego's Festa de Nossa Senhora dos Remédios runs for weeks.

Sep Hillsides of Trás-os-Montes hang heavy with grapes; hiking abounds in parks.

PORTO

POP 237,600

Opening like a pop-up book from the Rio Douro at sunset, humble-yet-opulent Porto entices with its medieval centre, divine food and wine, and charismatic locals.

Porto's charms are as subtle as the nuances of an aged tawny port, best savoured slowly on a romp through the hilly backstreets of Miragaia, Ribeira and Massarelos. It's the quiet moments of reflection and the snapshots of daily life that you'll remember most: the slosh of the Douro against the docks; the snap of laundry drying in river winds; the sound of wine glasses clinking under a full moon; the sight of young lovers discreetly tangled under a landmark bridge, on the rim of a park fountain, in the crumbling notch of a graffiti-bombed wall...

History

Porto put the 'Portu' in 'Portugal'. The name dates from Roman times, when Lusitanian settlements straddled both sides of the Rio Douro. The area was briefly in Moorish hands but was reconquered by AD 868 and reorganised as the county of Portucale, with Porto as its capital. British-born Henri of Burgundy was granted the land in 1095, and it was from here that Henri's son and Portuguese hero Afonso Henriques launched the Reconquista (Christian reconquest), ultimately winning Portugal its status as an independent kingdom.

In 1387 Dom João I married Philippa of Lancaster in Porto, and their most famous son, Henry the Navigator, was born here. While Henry's explorers groped around Africa for a sea route to India, British wine merchants – forbidden to trade with the French – set up shop, and their presence continues to this day, evidenced in port-wine labels such as Taylor's and Graham's.

Over the following centuries Porto acquired a well-earned reputation for rebelliousness. In 1628 a mob of angry women attacked the minister responsible for a tax on linen. A 'tipplers riot' against the Marquês de Pombal's regulation of the port-wine trade was savagely put down in 1757. And in 1808, as Napoleon's troops occupied the city, Porto citizens arrested the French governor and set up their own short-lived junta. After the British helped drive out the French, Porto radicals were at it again, leading calls for a new liberal constitution, which they got in 1822. Demonstrations in support of liberals continued to erupt in Porto throughout the 19th century.

Meanwhile, wine profits helped fund the city's industrialisation, which began in earnest in the late 19th century, at a time when the elite in the rest of Portugal tended to see trade and manufacturing as vulgar. Today the city remains the economic capital of northern Portugal and is surpassed only by much-larger Lisbon in terms of economic and social clout.

Sights

With the exception of the blockbuster Museu de Arte Contemporânea, Porto's must-sees cluster in the compact centre and are easily walkable. Many of the big-hitters huddle in the Unesco-listed Ribeira district and Aliados, while hilltop Miragaia has some peaceful pockets of greenery and knockout views. For port-wine lodges aplenty, cross the river to Gaia.

Ribeira

★Igreja de São Francisco CHURCH

(Map p366; Praça Infante Dom Henrique; adult/child €4/2; 9am-8pm Jul-Sep, to 7pm Mar-Jun & Oct, to 6pm Nov-Feb) Sitting on Praça Infante Dom Henrique, Igreja de São Francisco looks from the outside to be an austerely Gothic church, but inside it hides one of Portugal's most dazzling displays of baroque finery. Hardly a centimetre escapes unsmothered, as otherworldly cherubs and sober monks are drowned by nearly 100kg of gold leaf. If you see only one church in Porto, make it this one.

High on your list should be the nave, interwoven with vines and curlicues, dripping with cherubs and shot through with gold leaf. Peel back the layers to find standouts such as the Manueline-style Chapel of St John the Baptist, the 13th-century statue of St Francis of Assisi and the 18th-century Tree of Jesse, a polychrome marvel of an altarpiece. The church museum harbours a fine, well-edited collection of sacred art.

In the eerily atmospheric catacombs, the great and the good of Porto were once buried. Look out for sculptural works by Italian master Nicolau Nasoni and prolific Portuguese sculptor António Teixeira Lopes.

★Sé CATHEDRAL

(Map p366; Terreiro da Sé; cloisters adult/student €3/2; 9am-12.30pm & 2.30-7pm Apr-Oct, to 6pm Nov-Mar) From Praça da Ribeira rises a

Porto, the Douro & Trás-os-Montes Highlights

❶ Wine-taste your way around the vineyards of the **Alto Douro** (p403) region.

❷ Lose yourself amid the alleys of Porto's **Ribeira** (p359) neighbourhood.

❸ Relax beside the Rio Tâmega and its medieval bridge in **Amarante** (p397) .

❹ Come face to face with Palaeolithic artwork at the world-famous archaeological site of **Parque Arqueológico do Vale do Côa** (p406).

❺ Stroll the formal gardens and taste some fine wines at the stately 18th-century **Casa de Mateus** (p408).

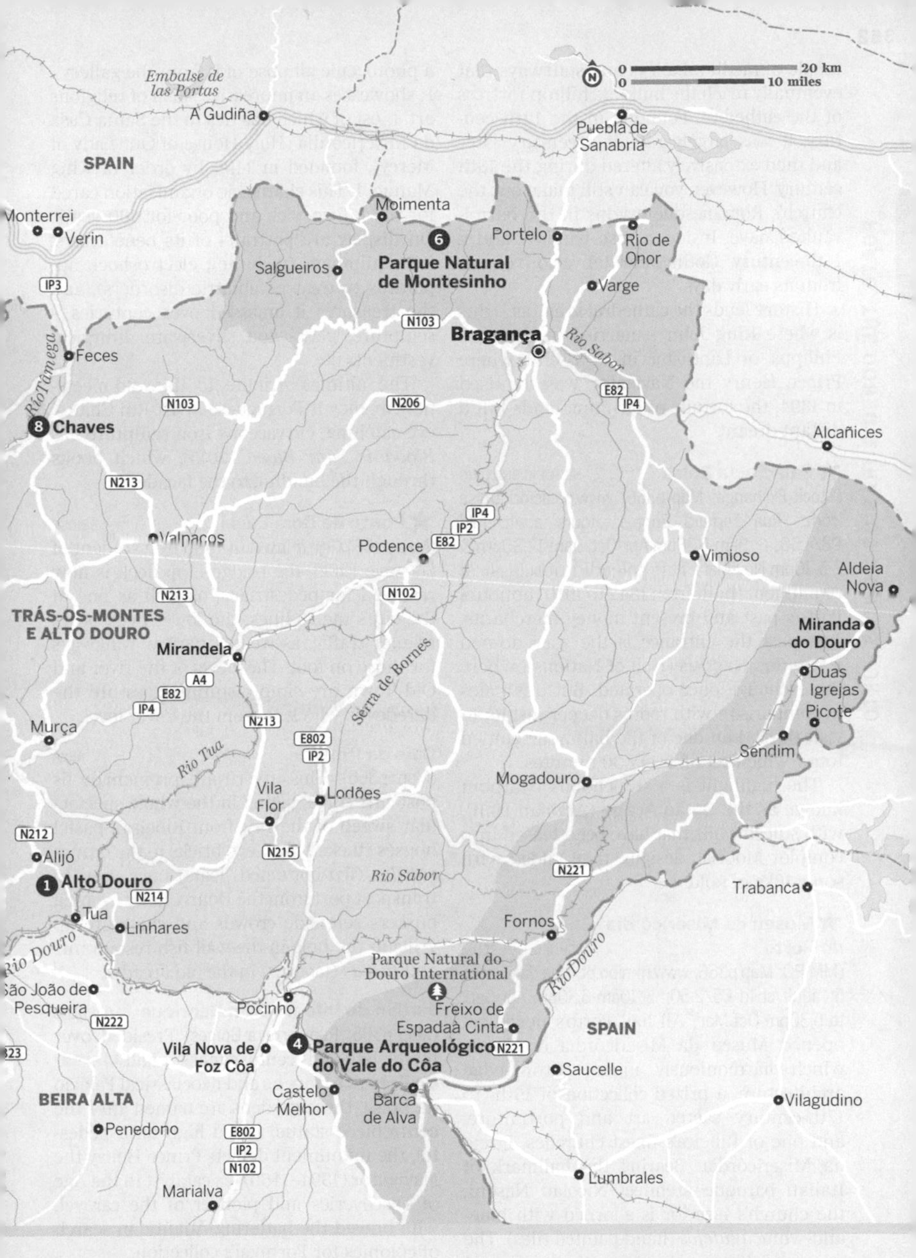

6 Hike across a medieval bridge or climb the park's heather-draped hills to 21st-century windmills in **Parque Natural de Montesinho** (p420).

7 Swim in natural pools above **Fisgas de Ermelo** (p411) waterfall in Parque Natural do Alvão.

8 Take in the medieval tower and the 17th-century fortifications from **Chaves'** (p413) Roman bridge.

tangle of medieval alleys and stairways that eventually reach the hulking, hilltop fortress of the cathedral. Founded in the 12th century, it was largely rebuilt a century later and then extensively altered during the 18th century. However, you can still make out the church's Romanesque origins in the barrel-vaulted nave. Inside, a rose window and a 14th-century Gothic cloister also remain from its early days.

History lends the cathedral gravitas – this is where King John I married his beloved Philippa of Lancaster in 1387, and where Prince Henry the Navigator was baptised in 1394, the fortune of far-flung lands but a distant dream.

★Palácio da Bolsa HISTORIC BUILDING

(Stock Exchange; Map p366; www.palaciodabolsa.com; Rua Ferreira Borges; tours adult/child €8/4.50; ⏲9am-6.30pm Apr-Oct, 9am-12.30pm & 2-5.30pm Nov-Mar) This splendid neoclassical monument (built from 1842 to 1910) honours Porto's past and present money merchants. Just past the entrance is the glass-domed **Pátio das Nações** (Hall of Nations), where the exchange once operated. But this pales in comparison with rooms deeper inside; to visit these, join one of the half-hour guided tours, which set off every 30 minutes.

The highlight is a stupendous ballroom known as the **Salão Árabe** (Arabian Hall), with stucco walls that have been teased into complex Moorish designs, then gilded with some 18kg of gold.

★Museu da Misericórdia do Porto CHURCH, MUSEUM

(MMIPO; Map p366; www.mmipo.pt; Rua das Flores 5; adult/child €5/2.50; ⏲10am-6.30pm Apr-Sep, to 5.30pm Oct-Mar) All hail Porto's newly reopened Museu da Misericórdia do Porto, which harmoniously unites cutting-edge architecture, a prized collection of 15th- to 17th-century sacred art and portraiture, and one of Ribeira's finest churches, Igreja da Misericórdia. Bearing the hallmark of Italian baroque architect Nicolau Nasoni, the church's interior is adorned with blue-and-white *azulejos* (hand-painted tiles). The museum's biggest stunner is the large-scale Flemish Renaissance painting, *Fons Vitae* (Fountain of Life), depicting Dom Manuel I and family around a fountain of blood from the crucified Christ.

The museum centres on a sky-lit atrium, and a visit begins on the 3rd floor, gradually working down to the church (be sure to get a photogenic glimpse of it from the gallery). It showcases an impressive stash of religious art, most of which has ties to the Santa Casa da Misericórdia (Holy House of Our Lady of Mercy), founded in 1499 by order of King Manuel I. This charitable organisation cared for the infirm, sick and poor for 500 years. On display are portraits of its benefactors, lab equipment (including electroshock apparatus to treat psychiatric disorders), and the treasures it amassed over centuries – sculpture, glass- and silverware, liturgical vestments etc.

The ultimate tribute to this old-meets-new medley is Portuguese artist Rui Chafes' eye-catching, curvaceous iron sculpture *My Blood is Your Blood* (2015), which hooks through the building to the facade.

★Ponte de Dom Luís I BRIDGE

(Map p366) Completed in 1886 by a student of Gustave Eiffel, the bridge's top deck is now reserved for pedestrians, as well as one of the city's metro lines; the lower deck bears regular traffic, as well as narrow walkways for those on foot. The views of the river and Old Town are simply stunning, as are the daredevils who leap from the lower level.

Cais da Ribeira AREA

(Map p366) This riverfront promenade is postcard Porto, taking in the whole spectacular sweep of the city, from Ribeira's pastel houses stacked like Lego bricks to the *barcos rabelos* (flat-bottomed boats) once used to transport port from the Douro. Early evening buskers serenade crowds and chefs fire up grills in the hole-in-the-wall fish restaurants and *tascas* (taverns) in the old arcades.

Jardim do Infante Dom Henrique GARDENS

(Map p366; Rua Ferreira Borges) Presided over by the late-19th-century market hall **Mercado Ferreira Borges** and neoclassical Palácio da Bolsa, these gardens are named after the centrepiece statue. Lifted high on a pedestal, the monument depicts Prince Henry the Navigator (1394–1460) – a catalyst in the Age of Discoveries and pioneer of the caravel, who braved the battering Atlantic in search of colonies for Portugal's collection.

Casa do Infante HISTORIC BUILDING

(Map p366; Rua Alfândega 10; adult/child €2.20/free; ⏲9.30am-1pm & 2-5.30pm Tue-Sun) Just back from the river is this handsomely renovated medieval townhouse where, according to legend, Henry the Navigator was born in 1394. The building later served as Porto's first customs house. Today it boasts three floors of exhibits. In 2002 the complex was excavated, revealing Roman foundations and some remarkable mosaics – all of which are now on display.

Aliados & Bolhão

★Mercado do Bolhão MARKET
(Map p366; Rua Formosa; ⏲7am-5pm Mon-Fri, to 1pm Sat) The 19th-century, wrought-iron Mercado do Bolhão does a brisk trade in fresh produce, including cheeses, olives, smoked meats, sausages, breads and more. At its lively best on Friday and Saturday mornings, the market is also sprinkled with inexpensive stalls where you can eat fish so fresh it was probably swimming in the Atlantic that morning, or taste or sample local wines and cheeses.

★Livraria Lello HISTORIC BUILDING
(Map p366; Rua das Carmelitas 144; €3; ⏲10am-7.30pm Mon-Sat, 11am-7pm Sun) Ostensibly a bookshop, but even if you're not after books, don't miss this exquisite 1906 neo-Gothic confection, with its lavishly carved plaster resembling wood and stained-glass skylight. Feels magical? Its intricately wrought, curiously twisting staircase was supposedly the inspiration for the one in the Harry Potter books, which JK Rowling partly wrote in Porto while working here as an English teacher from 1991 to 1993. The €3 entry is redeemable if you buy a book.

São Bento Train Station HISTORIC BUILDING
(Map p366; Praça Almeida Garrett; ⏲5am-1am) One of the world's most beautiful train stations, beaux arts São Bento wings you back to a more graceful age of rail travel. Completed in 1903, it seems to have been imported from 19th-century Paris with its mansard roof. But the dramatic *azulejo* panels of historic scenes in the front hall are the real attraction. Designed by Jorge Colaço in 1930, some 20,000 tiles depict historic battles (including Henry the Navigator's conquest of Ceuta), as well as the history of transport.

Rua Santa Catarina AREA
(Map p366) This street is absurdly stylish and romantic, with trim boutiques, striped stone footpaths and animated crowds. It's home to Porto's most ornate tearoom, the art nouveau Café Majestic (p387), and the extraordinary *azulejo*-bedecked Capela das Almas.

Torre dos Clérigos TOWER
(Map p366; www.torredosclerigos.pt; Rua de São Filipe de Nery; €3; ⏲9am-7pm) Sticking out on Porto's skyline like a sore thumb – albeit a beautiful baroque one – this 76m-high tower was designed by Italian-born baroque master Nicolau Nasoni in the mid-1700s. Climb its 225-step spiral staircase for phenomenal views over Porto's tiled rooftops, spires and the curve of the Douro to the port wine lodges in Gaia. It also harbours an exhibition that chronicles the history of the tower's architects and residents.

Capela das Almas CHURCH
(Map p366; Rua Santa Catarina 428; ⏲7.30am-1pm & 3.30-7pm Mon, Tue & Sat, 7.30am-7pm Wed-Fri, 7.30am-1pm & 6-7pm Sun) On Rua Santa Catarina stands the strikingly ornate, *azulejo*-clad Capela das Almas. Magnificent panels here depict scenes from the lives of various saints, including the death of St Francis and the martyrdom of St Catherine. Interestingly, Eduardo Leite painted the tiles in a classic 18th-century style, though they actually date back only to the early 20th century.

Miragaia

★Museu Nacional Soares dos Reis MUSEUM
(Map p366; www.museusoaresdosreis.pt; Rua Dom Manuel II 44; adult/child €5/free,1st Sun of the month free; ⏲10am-6pm Tue-Sun) Porto's best art museum presents a stellar collection ranging from Neolithic carvings to Portugal's take on modernism, all housed in the formidable Palácio das Carrancas.

Miradouro da Vitória VIEWPOINT
(Map p366; Rua São Bento da Vitória) Porto is reduced to postcard format at this *miradouro* (viewpoint), perched high and mighty above a mosaic of terracotta rooftops that tumble down to the Douro. It's a highly atmospheric spot at dusk when landmarks such as the Ponte Dom Luís I bridge are illuminated and the lights on Vila Nova de Gaia's wine lodges flick on one by one.

Igreja do Carmo CHURCH
(Map p366; Rua do Carmo; ⏲8am-noon & 1-6pm Mon & Wed, 9am-6pm Tue & Thu, to 5.30pm Fri, to 4pm Sat, to 1.30pm Sun) Dating to the late 18th century, this captivating *azulejo*-covered church is one of Porto's best examples of rococo architecture. The tiled panel on the facade pays tribute to Nossa Senhora (Our Lady

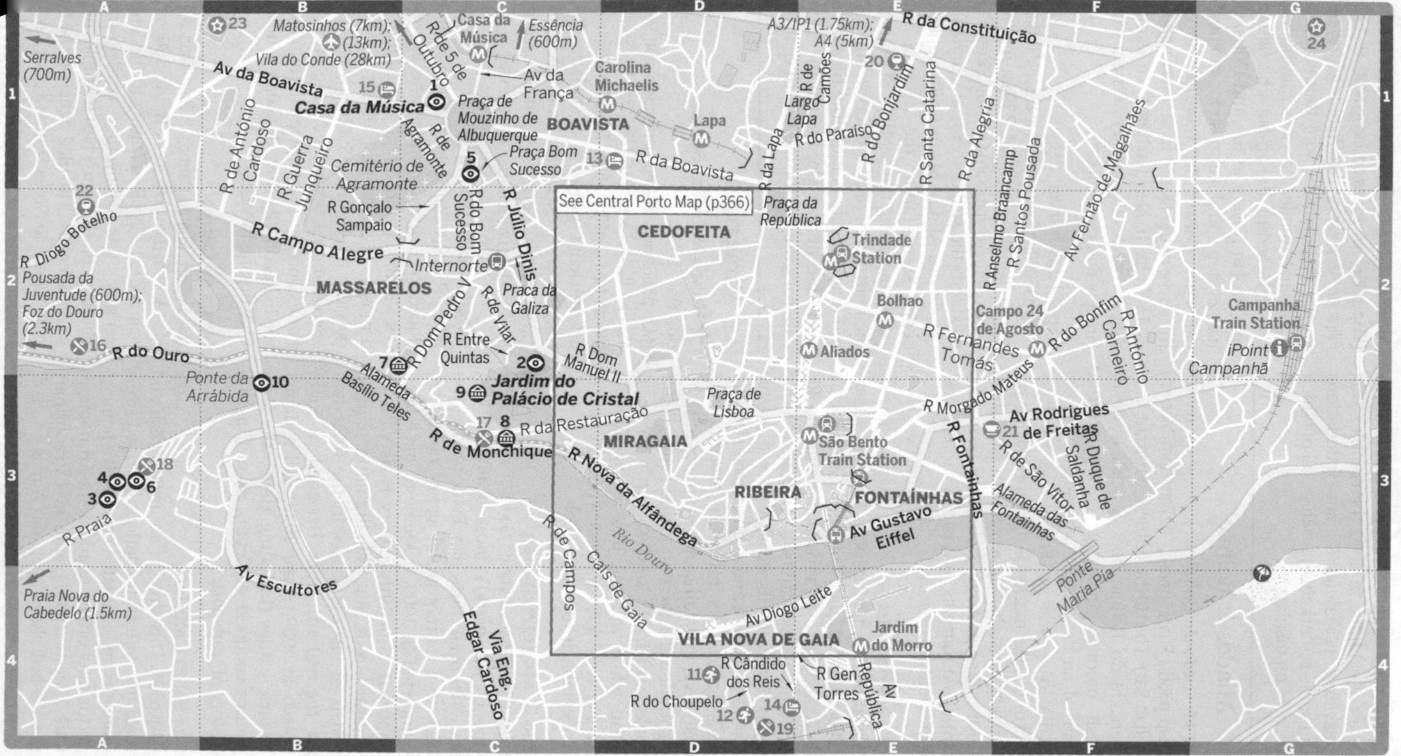
0 1 km
0 0.5 miles
Serralves (700m)
Matosinhos (7km); (13km); Vila do Conde (28km)
Casa da Música
Essência (600m)
A3/IP1 (1.75km); A4 (5km)
R da Constituição
Av da Boavista
R de 5 de Outubro
Av da França
Carolina Michaelis
Casa da Música
Praça de Mouzinho de Albuquerque
BOAVISTA
Lapa
Largo Lapa
R de Camões
R do Paraíso
R do Bonjardim
R Santa Catarina
R da Alegria
R Anselmo Braancamp
R Santos Pousada
Av Fernão de Magalhães
R de António Cardoso
R Guerra Junqueiro
Cemitério de Agramonte
R de Agramonte
Praça Bom Sucesso
R da Boavista
R da Lapa
R do Bom Sucesso
R Júlio Dinis
See Central Porto Map (p366)
Praça da República
CEDOFEITA
Trindade Station
R Gonçalo Sampaio
R Diogo Botelho
R Campo Alegre
Internorte
Pousada da Juventude (600m); Foz do Douro (2.3km)
MASSARELOS
R Dom Pedro V
R de Vilar
Praca da Galiza
Bolhao
Campo 24 de Agosto
R Fernandes Tomás
R do Bonfim
R António Carneiro
Campanha Train Station
iPoint
Campanhã
Aliados
R do Ouro
R Entre Quintas
R Dom Manuel II
Ponte da Arrábida
Alameda Basílio Teles
Jardim do Palácio de Cristal
Praça de Lisboa
R Morgado Mateus
Av Rodrigues de Freitas
R da Restauração
R de Monchique
MIRAGAIA
São Bento Train Station
R Fontainhas
R de São Vitor
R Duque de Saldanha
R Nova da Alfândega
RIBEIRA
FONTAÍNHAS
Alameda das Fontainhas
Av Gustavo Eiffel
R Praia
Rio Douro
Ponte Maria Pia
Av Escultores
R de Campos
Cais de Gaia
Av Diogo Leite
Praia Nova do Cabedelo (1.5km)
Via Eng. Edgar Cardoso
VILA NOVA DE GAIA
Jardim do Morro
R Cândido dos Reis
R Gen Torres
Av República
R do Choupelo
1 2 3 4 5 6 7 8 9 10 11 12 13 14 15 16 17 18 19 20 21 22 23 24
A B C D E F G

Porto

Top Sights
1 Casa da Música C1
2 Jardim do Palácio de Cristal C2

Sights
3 Douro Marina A3
4 Lavadouro Público A3
5 Mercado Bom Sucesso C1
6 Mercado de Peixe São Pedro da Afurada A3
7 Museu do Carro Eléctrico C2
8 Museu do Vinho do Porto C3
9 Museu Romântico C3
10 Ponte da Arrábida B3

Activities, Courses & Tours
11 Croft D4
12 Taylor's D4

Sleeping
13 Casa do Conto D1
14 Gaia Porto Hostel D4
15 Hospedaria Boavista B1

Eating
Casinha Boutique Café .... (see 15)
Em Carne Viva .... (see 15)
16 O Antigo Carteiro A2
17 Taberna Cais das Pedras C3
18 Taberna São Pedro A3
19 Yeatman D4

Drinking & Nightlife
Bar Casa da Música .... (see 1)
20 Pride Bar E1
21 Terraplana E3
22 Zenith Lounge Bar A2

Entertainment
23 Boavista FC B1
Casa da Música .... (see 1)
24 FC Porto G1

Centro Português de Fotografia MUSEUM
(Portuguese Photography Centre; Map p366; www.cpf.pt; Campo dos Mártires da Pátria; exhibition hall 10am-6pm Tue-Fri, 3-7pm Sat & Sun) FREE This stately yet muscular building (1796) once served as a prison and now houses a photography museum. You actually walk through the thick iron gates and into the cells to see the work, which lends the intriguing exhibits even more gravitas. On the 3rd floor is a collection of cameras spanning every decade; particularly fascinating are the espionage ones, discreetly hidden in everything from Pepsi cans to Marlboro packets.

Immediately south of the museum are the narrow, atmospheric lanes that were once part of Porto's *judiaria* (Jewish quarter).

Jardim da Cordoaria PARK
(Map p366; Rua Campo dos Mártires da Pátria) This pleasantly leafy park is known simply as 'Cordoaria'. Check out the four haunting **sculptures** by Spanish sculptor Juan Muñoz. The romantic, narrow lanes that run north from the Cordoaria are the domain of Porto's hippest bars.

Vila Nova de Gaia

Jardim do Morro GARDENS
(Map p366; Avenida da República) The cable car swings up to this hilltop park, which can also be reached by crossing the upper level of Ponte Dom Luís I. Shaded by palms, these gardens are all about the view. From here, Porto is reduced to postcard format, with the pastel-hued houses of Ribeira on the opposite side of the Douro and the snaking river below.

Espaço Porto Cruz WINERY, MUSEUM
(Map p366; www.myportocruz.com; Largo Miguel Bombarda 23; 11am-7pm Tue-Sun) This swank port-wine emporium inside a restored 18th-century riverside building celebrates all things port. In addition to a shop where tastings are held (€7.50 for three ports), there are exhibition halls, a rooftop terrace with panoramic views and the De Castro Gaia (p381) restaurant on the 3rd floor.

Teleférico de Gaia CABLE CAR
(Map p366; www.gaiacablecar.com; one-way/return €5/8; 10am-8pm May-Sep, to 6pm Oct-Mar) Don't miss a ride on the Teleférico de Gaia, an aerial gondola that provides fine views over the Douro and Porto on its short, five-minute jaunt. It runs between the southern end of the Ponte Dom Luís I and the riverside.

Mosteiro da Serra de Pilar MONASTERY
(Map p366; Rampa do Infante Santo; adult/child €3/1; 10am-6.30pm Tue-Sun Apr-Oct, to 5.30pm Nov-Mar) Watching over Gaia is this 17th-century hilltop monastery, with its circular cloister, church with gilded altar, and stellar river views. Requisitioned by the future Duke of Wellington during the Peninsular War (1807–14), it still belongs to the Portuguese military and can only be visited on 40-minute guided tours leaving hourly between 10.30am and 12.30pm and 2.30pm and 5.30pm.

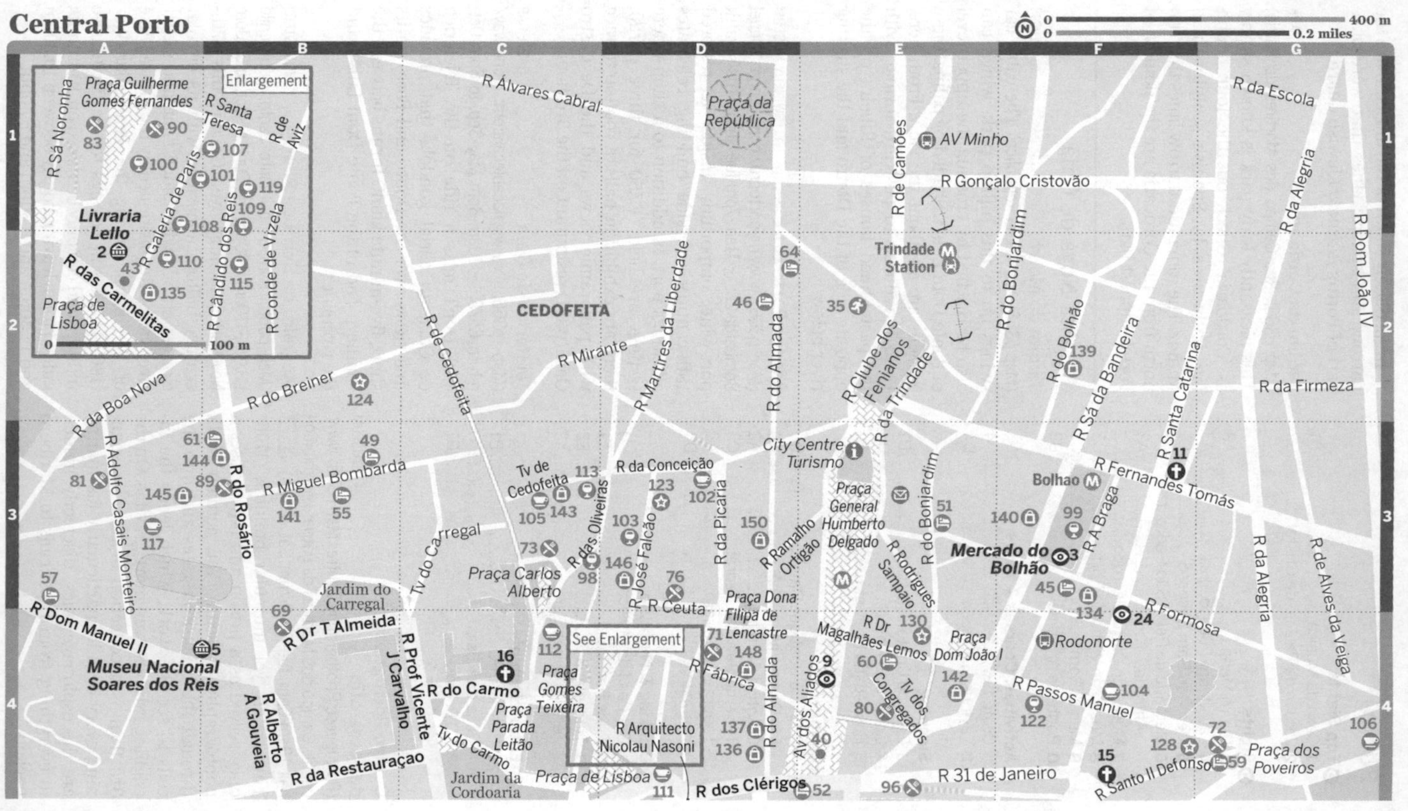
Central Porto
400 m
0.2 miles
Enlargement
R Sá Noronha
Praça Guilherme Gomes Fernandes
R Santa Teresa
R de Aviz
R Galeria de Paris
R Cândido dos Reis
R Conde de Vizela
Livraria Lello
R das Carmelitas
Praça de Lisboa
100 m
R Álvares Cabral
Praça da República
AV Minho
R de Camões
R Gonçalo Cristovão
R da Escola
R da Alegria
R Dom João IV
Trindade Station
R do Bonjardim
CEDOFEITA
R de Cedofeita
R Martires da Liberdade
R do Almada
R Clube dos Fenianos
R da Trindade
R do Bolhão
R Sá da Bandeira
R Santa Catarina
R da Firmeza
R Mirante
R do Breiner
R da Boa Nova
R Adolfo Casais Monteiro
R do Rosário
R Miguel Bombarda
Tv de Cedofeita
R das Oliveiras
R da Conceição
R José Falcão
R da Picaria
City Centre Turismo
Praça General Humberto Delgado
R Ramalho Ortigão
R Rodrigues Sampaio
Bolhao
R Fernandes Tomás
R A Braga
Mercado do Bolhão
R da Alegria
R de Alves da Veiga
Tv do Carregal
Praça Carlos Alberto
R Ceuta
Praça Dona Filipa de Lencastre
R Dr Magalhães Lemos
Praça Dom João I
R Formosa
Rodonorte
Jardim do Carregal
R Dom Manuel II
R Dr T Almeida
Museu Nacional Soares dos Reis
R Alberto A Gouveia
R Prof Vicente J Carvalho
R do Carmo
Praça Gomes Teixeira
Praça Parada Leitão
Tv do Carmo
See Enlargement
R Fábrica
R Arquitecto Nicolau Nasoni
Av dos Aliados
Tv dos Congregados
R Passos Manuel
R da Restauraçao
Jardim da Cordoaria
Praça de Lisboa
R dos Clérigos
R 31 de Janeiro
R Santo Il Defonso
Praça dos Poveiros

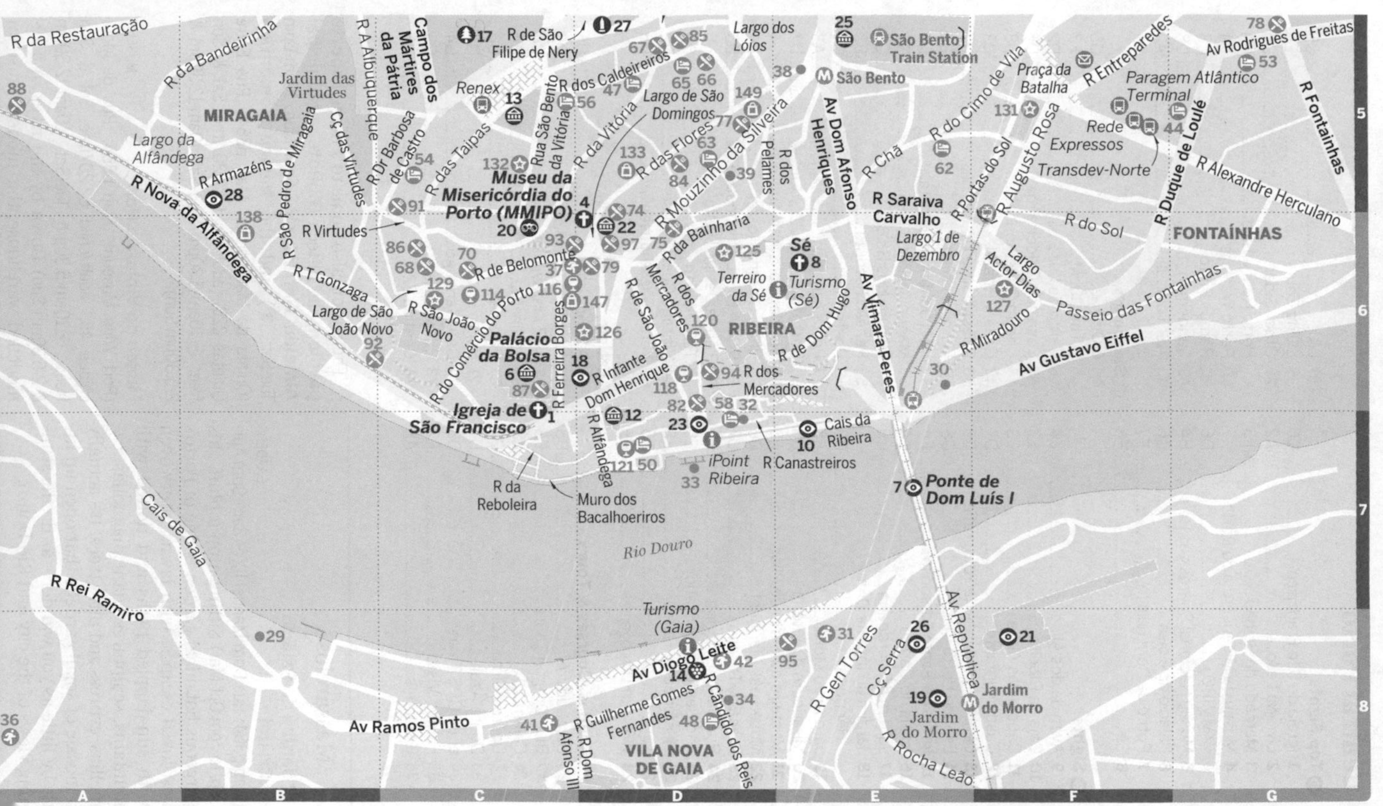
R da Restauração
R da Bandeirinha
Jardim das Virtudes
MIRAGAIA
Largo da Alfândega
R Armazéns
R Nova da Alfândega
R São Pedro de Miragaia
Cç das Virtudes
R A Albuquerque
Campo dos Mártires da Pátria
R Dr Barbosa de Castro
R das Taipas
Renex
R de São Filipe de Nery
Rua São Bento da Vitória
R dos Caldeireiros
Largo de São Domingos
R da Vitória
R das Flores
Mouzinho da Silveira
R dos Pelames
Largo dos Lóios
São Bento Train Station
São Bento
Av Dom Afonso Henriques
R Chã
R do Cimo de Vila
Praça da Batalha
R Entreparedes
Paragem Atlântico Terminal
Rede Expressos
Transdev-Norte
R Duque de Loulé
Av Rodrigues de Freitas
R Fontainhas
R Alexandre Herculano
FONTAÍNHAS
R do Sol
R Portas do Sol
R Augusto Rosa
R Saraiva Carvalho
Largo 1 de Dezembro
Largo Actor Dias
Passeio das Fontainhas
R Miradouro
Av Gustavo Eiffel
Museu da Misericórdia do Porto (MMIPO)
R Virtudes
R T Gonzaga
Largo de São João Novo
R São João Novo
R de Belomonte
R do Comércio do Porto
Palácio da Bolsa
R Ferreira Borges
R Infante Dom Henrique
R de São João
R dos Mercadores
R da Bainharia
Terreiro da Sé
Sé
Turismo (Sé)
RIBEIRA
R de Dom Hugo
Av Vímara Peres
Igreja de São Francisco
R Alfândega
R da Reboleira
Muro dos Bacalhoeiros
iPoint Ribeira
R Canastreiros
Cais da Ribeira
Ponte de Dom Luís I
Rio Douro
Cais de Gaia
R Rei Ramiro
Turismo (Gaia)
Av Diogo Leite
R Cândido dos Reis
R Guilherme Gomes Fernandes
R Dom Afonso III
VILA NOVA DE GAIA
Av Ramos Pinto
R Gen Torres
Cç Serra
Av República
Jardim do Morro
R Rocha Leão

Central Porto

Top Sights

1 Igreja de São Francisco........................C6
2 Livraria Lello........................A2
3 Mercado do Bolhão........................F3
4 Museu da Misericórdia do Porto (MMIPO)........................D6
5 Museu Nacional Soares dos Reis........................B4
6 Palácio da Bolsa........................C6
7 Ponte de Dom Luís I........................E7
8 Sé........................E6

Sights

9 Avenida dos Aliados........................E4
10 Cais da Ribeira........................E7
11 Capela das Almas........................F3
12 Casa do Infante........................D7
13 Centro Português de Fotografia........................C5
14 Espaço Porto Cruz........................D8
15 Igreja de Santo Ildefonso........................F4
16 Igreja do Carmo........................C4
17 Jardim da Cordoaria........................C5
18 Jardim do Infante Dom Henrique........................D6
19 Jardim do Morro........................E8
20 Miradouro da Vitória........................C6
21 Mosteiro da Serra de Pilar........................F8
22 Museu das Marionetas........................D6
23 Praça da Ribeira........................D7
24 Rua Santa Catarina........................F4
25 São Bento Train Station........................E5
26 Teleférico de Gaia........................E8
27 Torre dos Clérigos........................D5
28 World of Discoveries........................B5

Activities, Courses & Tours

29 Barcadouro........................B8
30 Blue Dragon Tours........................E6
31 Cálem........................E8
32 Douro Acima........................D7
33 Douro Azul........................D7
34 eFun GPS Tours........................D8
35 Fold 'n' Visit........................E2
36 Graham's........................A8
37 L&L........................C6
38 Living Tours........................E5
39 Other Side........................D5
Porto Rent a Bike........................(see 30)
40 Porto Walkers........................E4
41 Ramos Pinto........................C8
42 Sandeman........................D8
43 Tuk Tour........................A2

Sleeping

44 6 Only........................G5
45 B The Guest........................F3
46 Canto de Luz........................D2
47 Casa dos Caldeireiros........................D5
48 Charm Guesthouse........................D8
49 Gallery Hostel........................B3
50 Guest House Douro........................D7
51 In Porto Gallery........................E3
52 InterContinental Porto........................E4
53 Magnólia Hostel........................G5
54 Maison Nos B&B........................C5
55 Pensão Favorita........................B3
56 Poets Inn........................C5
57 Porta Azul........................A3
58 Porto River........................D7
59 Residencial Santo André........................G4
60 Rivoli Cinema Hostel........................E4
61 ROSA ET AL Townhouse........................B3
62 Tattva Design Hostel........................E5
63 Tiles Apartments........................D5
64 Vintage Guest House........................D2
65 Yours Guesthouse........................D5

Eating

66 A Sandeira........................D5
67 All In Porto........................D5
68 As 7 Maravilhas........................C6
69 Atelier........................B4
70 Belos Aires........................C6
71 Book........................D4
72 Cafe Santiago........................G4
73 Camafeu........................C3
74 Cantina 32........................D5

Massarelos

★Jardim do Palácio de Cristal GARDENS

(Map p364; Rua Dom Manuel II; 8am-9pm Apr-Sep, to 7pm Oct-Mar) Sitting atop a bluff, this gorgeous botanical garden is one of Porto's best-loved escapes, with lawns interwoven with sun-dappled paths and dotted with fountains, sculptures, giant magnolias, camellias, cypress and olive trees. It's actually a mosaic of small gardens that open up little by little as you wander – as do the stunning views of the city and Rio Douro.

The park is also home to a domed **sports pavilion**, the hi-tech **Biblioteca Municipal Almeida Garrett** (2-6pm Mon, 10am-6pm Tue-Sat;) and the **Museu Romântico** (Quinta da Macieirinha; Map p364; Rua Entre Quintas 220; adult/child €2.20/free, Sat & Sun free; 10am-5.30pm Mon-Sat, 10am-12.30pm & 2-5.30pm Sun).

Museu do Vinho do Porto MUSEUM

(Port Wine Museum; Map p364; Rua de Monchique 45; adult/child €2.20/free, Sat & Sun free; 10am-5.30pm Tue-Sat, 10am-12.30pm & 2-5.30pm Sun) Down by the river in a remodelled warehouse, this modest museum

75 Cantinho do Avillez........D6
76 Cultura dos Sabores........D3
77 Da Terra........D5
78 Dama Pé de Cabra........G5
De Castro Gaia........(see 14)
79 DOP........D6
80 Flor dos Congregados........E4
81 Frida........A3
82 Jimão........D6
83 Leitaria da Quinta do Paço........A1
84 Mercearia das Flores........D5
85 Miss'Opo........D5
86 O Caraças........C6
87 O Comercial........C6
88 Papavinhos........A5
89 Quintal Bioshop........B3
90 Stash........A1
91 Taberna de Santo António........C5
92 Taberna do Barqueiro........B6
93 Taberna do Largo........C6
94 Taberna dos Mercadores........D6
95 Taberninha Do Manel........E8
96 Tapabento........E4
97 Traça........D6

Drinking & Nightlife
360º Terrace Lounge........(see 14)
98 Aducla........C3
99 Bolhão Wine House........F3
100 Bonaparte Downtown........A1
101 Café Au Lait........A1
102 Café Candelabro........D3
103 Café Lusitano........D3
104 Café Majestic........F4
105 Casa de Ló........C3
106 Duas de Letra........G4
107 Era Uma Vez No Paris........B1
108 Galeria de Paris........A1
109 Gin House........B1
110 La Bohème........A2
111 Livraria da Baixa........D4
112 Moustache........C4
113 Museu d'Avó........C3
114 Pinguim Café........C6
115 Plano B........B2
116 Prova........C6
117 Rota do Chá........A3
118 Vinologia........D6
119 Wall........B1
120 Wine Box........D6
121 Wine Quay Bar........D7
122 Zoom........F4

Entertainment
123 Armazém do Chá........D3
124 Breyner 85........B2
125 Casa da Mariquinhas........D6
126 Hard Club........D6
127 Hot Five Jazz & Blues Club........F6
128 Maus Hábitos........F4
129 Restaurante O Fado........C6
130 Teatro Municipal Rivoli........E4
131 Teatro Nacional São João........F5
132 TNSJ Mosteiro de São Bento da Vitória........C5

Shopping
133 43 Branco........D5
134 A Pérola Do Bolhão........F3
135 A Vida Portuguesa........A2
águas furtadas........(see 141)
136 Almada 13........D4
137 Arcádia........D4
138 Armazém........B6
139 Azulima........F2
140 Casa Ramos........F3
141 CC Bombarda........B3
142 Central Conserveira da Invicta........E4
143 Coração Alecrim........C3
144 CRU........B3
145 Flapper........A3
146 Goodvibes........D3
147 Oliva & Co........C6
148 Touriga........D4
149 Tradições........D5
150 Workshops Pop Up........D3

traces the history of wine- and port-making with an informative short film, models and exhibits, though it doesn't offer much insight into the wine itself.

Museu do Carro Eléctrico MUSEUM
(Tram Museum; Map p364; www.museudocarroelectrico.pt; Alameda Basílio Teles 51; adult/child €8/4; 2-6pm Mon, 10am-6pm Tue-Sun) Housed in an antiquated switching-house, this museum is a tram-spotter's delight. It displays dozens of beautifully restored old trams – from early 1870s models once pulled by mules to streamlined, bee-yellow 1930s numbers.

Boavista

★Casa da Música LANDMARK
(Map p364; 220 120 220; www.casadamusica.com; Avenida da Boavista 604-610; guided tour €7.50; Portuguese/English guided tours 11am/4pm) At once minimalist, iconic and daringly imaginative, the Casa da Música is the beating heart of Porto's cultural scene and the home of the Porto National Orchestra. Dutch architect Rem Koolhaas rocked the musical world with this crystalline creation – the jewel in the city's European Capital of Culture 2001 crown.

LOCAL KNOWLEDGE

THE ART OF THE TILE

Azulejos (hand-painted tiles) greet you on almost every corner in Porto. One of the delights of taking a serendipitous stroll through the historic centre is the tiles you will encounter. Old and new, utilitarian and decorative, plain and geometrically patterned, they dance across the facades of medieval houses, the walls of cafes and bars, along metro-station tunnels and in opulent church interiors.

Some of the finest tiles grace Porto's churches. Among them is the large and exquisite panel of *azulejos* covering the **Igreja do Carmo** (p363). Silvestre Silvestri's 1912 magnum opus illustrates the founding of the Carmelite order and pays homage to Nossa Senhora (Our Lady).

On the Rua Santa Catarina, the **Capela das Almas** (p363) catches your eye with the astonishing feast of *azulejos* festooning its facade; this stunning frieze by Eduardo Leite recounts the lives of various saints, including the death of St Francis and the martyrdom of St Catherine. The blue-and-white tiles evoke the classic 18th-century style, but actually date to 1929.

Rising high above Praça da Batalha, the elegant baroque **Igreja de Santo Ildefonso** (Map p366; Praça da Batalha; ⏱9am-noon & 3-6.30pm Mon-Sat, 9am-1pm Sun) is another *azulejo*-bedecked wonder. Some 11,000 blue-and-white tiles, by Jorge Colaço (1932), grace the facade, depicting scenes from the life of Santo Ildefonso and allegories from the Eucharist.

But Porto's crowning glory when it comes to tiles is undoubtedly the resplendent **São Bento Train Station** (p363), a veritable ode to *azulejo* art. Spelling out momentous events in Portuguese history, including the Battle of Valdevez (1140), the arrival of King João I and Philippa of Lancaster in Porto (1387) and the Conquest of Ceuta (1415), the friezes designed by master Jorge Colaço in 1930 are so vivid and detailed you can almost here the fanfare and the stampeding cavalry.

The wonky cuboid conceals a shoebox-style concert hall lauded for some of the world's best acoustics. If your curiosity has been piqued, join one of the daily guided tours.

Mercado Bom Sucesso MARKET
(Map p364; www.mercadobomsucesso.com; Praça Bom Sucesso; ⏱10am-11pm Sun-Thu, to midnight Fri & Sat) For a snapshot of local life and a bite to eat, nip into Boavista's revamped Mercado Bom Sucesso. A complete architectural overhaul has brought this late 1940s market hall bang up to date. Now bright, modern and flooded with daylight, the striking curved edifice harbours a fresh produce market, a food court, cafes and the slick design hotel, Hotel da Música.

Foz do Douro

Parque da Cidade PARK
(Avenida da Boavista) The hum of traffic on the Avenida da Boavista soon fades as you enter the serene, green Parque da Cidade, Portugal's largest urban park. Laced with 10km of walking and cycling trails, this is where locals come to unplug and recharge, picnic (especially at weekends), play ball, jog, cycle, lounge in the sun and feed the ducks on the lake.

Jardim do Passeio Alegre GARDENS
(Rua Passeio Alegre) A joy for the aimless ambler, this 19th-century garden is flanked by graceful old buildings and dotted with willowy palms, sculptures, fountains and a bandstand that occasionally stages concerts in summer. Listen to the crash of the ocean as you wander its tree-canopied avenues. There's also crazy golf for the kids.

Tours

Porto Tours TOURS
(☎222 000 045; www.portotours.com; ⏱10am-7pm) This excellent municipal service provides details of all the recommended tour operators, from walking tours, Douro cruises and jaunts by Segway, bike and scooter to private taxi tours or helicopter rides over the city. As well as providing impartial advice, Porto Tours will make bookings for you.

★**Taste Porto Food Tours** TOURS
(☎967 258 750; www.tasteportofoodtours.com; food tour adult/child €59/39; ⏱food tours 10am, 10.30am & 4pm Tue-Sat) Loosen a belt notch for these superb half-day food tours, where you will sample everything from Porto's best slow-roasted-pork sandwich to éclairs, fine wines, cheese and coffee. Friendly, know-

ledgeable André and his team lead these indulgent 3½-hour walking tours, which take in viewpoints, historic back lanes and the Mercado do Bolhão en route to restaurants, grocery stores and cafes.

★Other Side TOURS
(Map p366; ☎916 500 170; www.theotherside.pt; Rua Souto 67; ⏲9am-8pm) Well-informed, congenial guides reveal their city on half-day walking tours of hidden Porto (€19), *petisco* (tapas) trails (€25), and e-bike tours of Porto and Foz (€29). They also venture further afield with full-day trips to the Douro's vineyards (€85) and to Guimarães and Braga (€69).

Porto Walkers WALKING
(Map p366; ☎918 291 519; www.portowalkers.pt; Praça da Liberdade, Avenida dos Aliados) Peppered with anecdotes and personality, these young and fun guided walking tours are a great intro to Porto, starting at 10.45am and 3.30pm daily. The tours are free (well, the guides work for tips, so give what you can). Simply turn up at the meeting point on Praça da Liberdade and look out for the guide in the red T-shirt.

Be My Guest WALKING
(☎938 417 850; www.bemyguestinporto.com; 3hr tours €20) To get better acquainted with Porto, sign up for one of Be My Guest's terrific themed walking tours of the city, skipping from an insider's peek at *azulejos* to belle époque architecture. Run by a passionate trio of guides – Nuno, Sabina and Fred – it also arranges four-hour cookery workshops (€30) and wine-tasting tours (€25). Meeting points vary.

Tuk Tour TOURS
(Map p366; ☎915 094 443; www.tuktourporto.com; Rua das Carmelitas 136) *Tuk-tuks* are maybe more Thailand than Porto, but these electric numbers are an eco-cool way to buzz around the city as your clued-up guide shares anecdotes. Tours skip from one-hour spins of Gaia and Afurada (€15) to 1½-hour night tours of the city illuminated (€20). Tours either depart from Rua das Carmelitas or Avenida Ramos Pinto.

Blue Dragon Tours TOURS
(Map p366; ☎222 022 375; www.bluedragon.pt; Avenida Gustavo Eiffel 280; tours from €15) This reputable outfit runs classic three-hour bike tours, which begin on Avenida dos Aliados and take in major sights such as the Sé and Mercado do Bolhão. It also offers several half-day walking tours, including Jewish Porto and a foodie tour (from €39), as well as three-hour Segway tours (from €55). Prices depend on group sizes.

eFun GPS Tours TOURS
(Map p366; ☎220 923 270; www.efungpstours.com; Rua Cândido dos Reis 55) One of the most fun and ecofriendly ways to zip about town is in a nippy Renault Twizy with eFun GPS tours on itineraries such as the 1½-hour By the River tour (€38), taking in riverfront attractions from Ponte da Arrábida to the fishing village of Afurada.

Living Tours TOURS
(Map p366; ☎228 320 992; www.livingtours.pt; Rua Mouzinho da Silveira 352-4; ⏲9am-8pm Apr-Oct, to 6pm Nov-Mar) A great range of sightseeing options are on offer at this friendly agency, from half-day city tours (€35) to fado tours with dinner (€65) and day trips to the Douro and Minho (€95).

Detours ADVENTURE
(☎966 054 152; www.detours.pt) In addition to waterfall treks and canyoning, Porto-based Detours offers off-track tours around the Douro in 4WD vehicles. It's a great way to avoid the crowds and get off the beaten trail (and right between the vineyards).

River Cruises

Several outfits offer cruises in ersatz *barcos rabelos,* the colourful boats that were once used to transport port wine from the vineyards. Cruises last 45 to 55 minutes and depart at least hourly on summer days. You can board at Porto's Cais da Ribeira or Cais da Estiva, or at Vila Nova de Gaia's Cais de Gaia or Cais Amarelo. By far the largest carrier is **Douro Azul** (Map p366; ☎223 402 500; www.douroazul.com; 6-bridges cruise adult/child €10/5; ⏲9.30am-6.30pm); **Barcadouro** (Map p366; ☎223 722 415; www.barcadouro.pt; Avenida Ramos Pinto 240, Cais de Gaia) and **Douro Acima** (Map p366; www.douroacima.pt; Rua dos Canastreiros 40; tours €12.50; ⏲10am-6.30pm Apr-Oct, to 4.30pm Mar) are also solid choices.

Port Tasting

★Graham's WINE
(Map p366; ☎223 776 484; www.grahams-port.com; Rua do Agro 141; tours incl tasting €10-100; ⏲9.30am-6pm) One of the original British-founded Gaia wine cellars, established way back in 1820, Graham's has been totally revamped and now features a small museum. It's a big name and a popular choice for

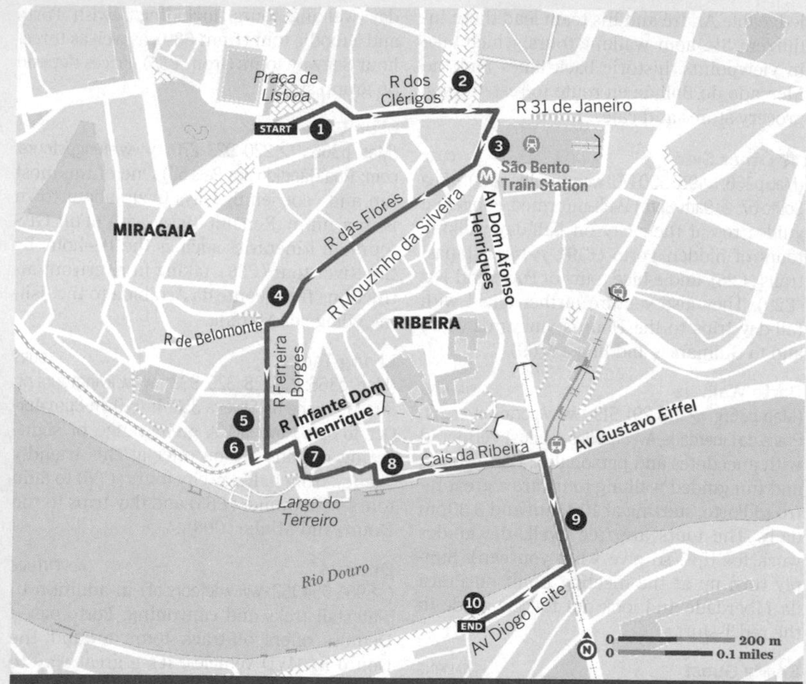

Walking Tour
Porto by Foot

START TORRE DOS CLÉRIGOS
FINISH VILA NOVA DE GAIA RIVERFRONT
LENGTH 2KM; TWO TO THREE HOURS

Begin at the baroque ❶ **Torre dos Clérigos** (p363), which offers unrivalled views over Porto from its 76m-high tower. Next, head down Rua dos Clérigos, passing the foot of grand ❷ **Avenida dos Aliados** and pausing to admire the avenue's beaux arts splendour. Just ahead, you'll see the French-inspired ❸ **São Bento Train Station** (p363). Check out the astounding *azulejos* (hand-painted tiles) in its main hall. Now cross over to Rua das Flores, a lovely street dotted with second-hand booksellers, old-fashioned stationers and some enticing cafes.

Near the end of the street is Nicolau Nasoni's baroque masterpiece, the ❹ **Igreja da Misericórdia** (p362), part of the stunning new Museu da Misericórdia do Porto. Cross Largo São Domingos to Rua Ferreira Borges, where you will pass the neoclassical ❺ **Palácio da Bolsa** (p362). You can check out its main courtyard – once Porto's stock exchange – for free or stay on for a tour of its elaborate interior, including its spectacular gilded ballroom. Just next door is the ❻ **Igreja de São Francisco** (p359), with a severe Gothic facade hiding a jaw-dropping golden interior.

Head back up Rua Infante Dom Henrique and turn right on Rua da Alfândega, where you'll find the medieval ❼ **Casa do Infante** (p362), the birthplace of Henry the Navigator and the site of some remarkable Roman ruins. Continue into the shadowy Ribeira district, following narrow, medieval Rua de Fonte Taurina as it opens onto the lovely ❽ **Praça da Ribeira**. From here, take a stroll along the Rio Douro, admiring Vila Nova de Gaia's port-wine lodges across the river. Next, walk across the Eiffel-inspired ❾ **Ponte de Dom Luís I** (p362) to Gaia's ❿ **waterfront esplanade**. Grab an outdoor table at one of the waterfront cafes and enjoy the splendid city views across the Douro over a well-deserved drink and some belly-filling *petiscos* (tapas).

tours, which last around 30 minutes, dip into atmospheric barrel-lined cellars and conclude with a tasting of three to eight port wines (tour prices vary according to quality).

★Taylor's WINE

(Map p364; ☎223 742 800, 223 772 956; www.taylor.pt; Rua do Choupelo 250; tours incl tasting €12; ⏱10am-6pm) Up from the river, British-run Taylor's boasts lovely, oh-so-English grounds with tremendous views of Porto. Its one-hour tours include a tasting of three top-of-the-range port wines – your reward for the short huff uphill. Its cellars are simply staggering, piled to the rafters with huge barrels, including the big one containing 100,000L of late bottled vintage.

Sandeman WINE

(Map p366; ☎223 740 533; www.sandeman.com; Largo Miguel Bombarda 3; museum free, guided tours incl tasting from €6; ⏱10am-12.30pm & 2-6pm Mar-Oct, 9.30am-12.30pm & 2-5.30pm Nov-Feb) Housed in an imposing granite building, Sandeman is a perfect first port of call for those who are new to port. It's free to visit the museum, showcasing port-related paintings and memorabilia whisking you back to 1790 when the young Scotsman George Sandeman started dabbling in the port and sherry trade. Guides dressed in black capes and hats lead the tours.

Cálem WINE

(Map p366; ☎223 746 660; www.calem.pt; Avenida Diogo Leite 344; tours incl tasting €6; ⏱10am-7pm May-Oct, to 6pm Nov-Apr) Going strong since 1859, these award-winning wine cellars are among Porto's most attractive. Available in several languages, the informative, entertaining guided tours last around 30 minutes and include a video screening in one of the huge oak vats used for port ageing. A visit concludes with a tasting of two port wines – usually a ruby and a white.

Festivals & Events

Festa de São João RELIGIOUS

(St John's Festival) Porto's biggest party. For one night in June, on the 24th, the city erupts into music, competitions and riotous parties; this is also when merrymakers pound each other on the head with squeaky plastic mallets (you've been warned).

Festa de São Pedro da Afurada FIESTA

The fishing village of Afurada pulls out all the stops for this festival in the days building up to 29 June. Dressed in traditional fishing garb, locals parade through the streets with statue-topped palanquins and give blessings to boats along the river. There's plenty of partying, with grilled sardines, *vinho,* live music, dancing and fireworks.

Marés Vivas MUSIC

(http://maresvivas.meo.pt) Over a weekend in mid-July, Afurada dusts off its party clothes to host the Marés Vivas, welcoming big rock and pop names to the stage. Headliners in recent years have included James Bay, Elton John, James, Tom Odell, Beth Orton and Foy Vance.

Serralves Em Festa CULTURAL

(www.serralvesemfesta.com) This huge (free) celebration runs for 40 hours nonstop over one weekend in early June. Parque de Serralves hosts the main events, with concerts, avant-garde theatre and kiddie activities. Other open-air events happen all over town.

Festival Internacional de Folclore de Gulpilhares MUSIC

(International Folk Festival of Gulpilhares) A week-long festival in late July/early August that attracts international groups.

Noites Ritual Rock MUSIC

A weekend rock extravaganza in late August.

Festival Internacional de Teatro de Expressão Ibérica THEATRE

(International Theatre Festival of Iberian Expressions; www.fitei.com) Two weeks of contemporary theatre in Spanish and Portuguese; held in late May/early June.

Fantasporto FILM

(Porto International Film Festival; www.fantasporto.com) Two weeks of fantasy, horror and just plain weird films in February/March.

Sleeping

Ribeira

Tiles Apartments APARTMENT €

(Map p366; ☎929 140 947, 929 140 938; portotilesapartment@hotmail.com; Rua Mouzinho da Silveira 195; apt €50-85; 📶) Cátia and David are your affable, clued-up hosts at this super-central apartment duo, glammed up with the namesake blue-and-white *azulejos*. The apartments are roomy, spotless, fitted with kitchenettes, and are big enough to squeeze in four (each with a double and a sofa bed). A welcome decanter of port on arrival is a nice touch. Minimum two-night stay.

DON'T MISS

THE ART & GREENERY OF SERRALVES

The fabulous cultural institution at **Serralves** (www.serralves.pt; Rua Dom João de Castro 210; adult/child museums & park €10/free, park only €5/free, 10am-1pm 1st Sun of the month free; ⌚10am-7pm Tue-Fri, to 8pm Sat & Sun May-Sep, reduced hours Oct-Mar) combines a museum, a mansion and extensive gardens. Cutting-edge exhibitions, along with a fine permanent collection featuring works from the late 1960s to the present, are showcased in the **Museu de Arte Contemporânea**, an arrestingly minimalist, whitewashed space designed by the eminent Porto-based architect Álvaro Siza Vieira. The delightful, pink **Casa de Serralves** is a prime example of art deco, bearing the imprint of French architect Charles Siclis. One ticket gets you into both museums.

The museums sit within the marvellous 18-hectare **Parque de Serralves**. Lily ponds, rose gardens, formal fountains and whimsical touches – such as a bright-red sculpture of oversized pruning shears – make for a bucolic outing in the city. The estate is located 6km west of the city centre; take bus 201 from in front of Praça Dom João I, one block east of Avenida dos Aliados.

Tattva Design Hostel HOSTEL €
(Map p366; ☎220 944 622; www.tattvadesignhostel.com; Rua do Cativo 26-28; dm €15-25, d/q from €56/80; @📶) Tattva knows precisely what makes backpackers tick – the facilities are superb and the attractive rooms have thoughtful touches, including big lockers, good lighting, privacy curtains and a bathroom and balcony in every room. The open-air rooftop lounge is a great place for a sundowner.

★**Guest House Douro** BOUTIQUE HOTEL €€€
(Map p366; ☎222 015 135; www.guesthousedouro.com; Rua da Fonte Taurina 99-101; r from €140; ❄@📶) In a restored relic overlooking the Douro, these eight rooms have been blessed with gorgeous wooden floors, plush queen beds and marble baths; the best have dazzling river views. But it is the welcome that makes this place stand out from the crowd – your charming hosts Carmen and João bend over backwards to please.

★**Porto River** BOUTIQUE HOTEL €€€
(Map p366; ☎223 401 210; www.portoriver.pt; Rua dos Canastreiros 50; apt €175-300; ❄📶) Down by the Rio Douro and right in the thick of the action, Porto River is a class act. The owners have waved a magic wand over this old stone warehouse to transform it into a hotel of understated luxury. The bustle outside fades in bright, minimalist Scandi-style apartments done out in natural fabrics and with attention-grabbing details.

Aliados & Bolhão

Rivoli Cinema Hostel HOSTEL €
(Map p366; ☎968 958 637, 220 174 634; www.rivolicinemahostel.com; Rua Dr Magalhães Lemos 83; dm/d/tr from €20/54/69; @📶) Easygoing staff, spotless dorms and rooms jazzed up with cool movie-themed decor, a chilled lounge with DVDs, a roof terrace and an inflatable pool in summer – this hostel, lodged in a converted art deco building, really nails it. The atmosphere is nicely laid back and homemade treats appear at breakfast.

Residencial Santo André GUESTHOUSE €
(Map p366; ☎222 000 115; www.residencialsantoandre.pt; Rua Santo Il Defonso 112; s €22.50, d €30-35, q €40; 📶) A charming four-floor walk-up with spiralled staircase and 10 oddly curvaceous rooms, some with bathrooms. They're all spick and span, but it's the smaller rooms that catch the most light. Set on a quiet street, this is a splendid cheapie.

Magnólia Hostel HOSTEL €
(Map p366; ☎222 014 150; www.magnoliaporto.com; Av Rodrigues de Freitas 387; dm/d/tr/q from €17/55/75/85; @📶) You'll find a good vibe at this attractive, well-maintained hostel with a range of rooms spread over three floors of a converted townhouse. There's a lounge with a spooky, out-of-tune piano, and a leafy outdoor space that sometimes hosts concerts. Breakfast is included.

★**Canto de Luz** B&B €€
(Map p366; ☎225 492 142; www.cantodeluz.com; Rua do Almada 539; r €70-95; 📶) *Ah oui*, this French-run guesthouse, just a five-minute walk from Trindade metro, is a delight. Rooms are light, spacious and make the leap between classic and contemporary, with vintage furnishings used to clever effect. Your kindly hosts André and Brigitte prepare delicious breakfasts, with fresh-squeezed juice,

pastries and homemade preserves. There's also a pretty garden terrace.

★6 Only GUESTHOUSE €€
(Map p366; ☎926 885 187, 222 013 971; www.6only.pt; Rua Duque de Loulé 97; r €60-80, ste €75-100; 📶) This beautifully restored guesthouse has just six rooms – so get in your booking early. All flaunt simple but stylish details that effortlessly blend traditional elements (such as high stucco ceilings and polished-wood floors) with understated contemporary design. There's a lounge, a Zen-like courtyard and friendly staff. Fresh pastries and juice and eggs to order feature at breakfast.

Vintage Guest House GUESTHOUSE €€
(Map p366; ☎916 052 529; www.portovintageguesthouse.pt; Rua do Almada 580; d €75-85, tr/q €140/160; 🍴📶) *Bemvindo* (welcome) to one of Porto's most adorable new digs – a townhouse lovingly restored to seamlessly unite the vintage (antique furnishings, stucco, *azulejos*, even the odd four-poster) with chic modernity (fancy linens, slick bathrooms, polished concrete). It sits on one of the city's most up-and-coming, characterful streets.

B The Guest GUESTHOUSE €€
(Map p366; ☎222 011 989; www.btheguest.com; Rua Formosa 331; d €89-120; ❄📶) Opposite Mercado do Bolhão, this boutique-chic guesthouse subtly fuses 19th-century architecture and 21st-century design. Splashes of colour and eye-catching fabrics lend warmth to the pared-down interiors. Opt for the front for views or the back for peace. The staff are incredibly friendly and breakfasts generous. The one drawback? There's no lift and stairs are steep.

In Porto Gallery GUESTHOUSE €€
(Map p366; ☎222 011 805; www.inporto.pt; Rua do Bonjardim 358; d €100-120; ❄📶) Architects and artists have pitched in to create this guesthouse, dotted with original works. Muted colours, luxuriant fabrics and one-of-a-kind wall coverings dominate in rooms with names such as 'imagination', 'fantasy' and 'illusion'. Breakfast is served in the garden on fine days.

★InterContinental Porto HISTORIC HOTEL €€€
(Map p366; ☎220 035 600; www.ihg.com; Praça da Liberdade 25; d/ste from €225/338; P❄@📶) In a painstakingly restored former palace on the central Praça da Liberdade, this is a top choice for business and leisure visitors, with classic decor that nods to the building's history, a full spectrum of amenities, including a restaurant, fitness centre and spa treatments, and outstanding service.

Miragaia

★Gallery Hostel HOSTEL €
(Map p366; ☎224 964 313; www.gallery-hostel.com; Rua Miguel Bombarda 222; dm/d/tr/ste from €22/64/80/90; ❄📶) A true travellers' hub, this hostel-gallery has clean and cosy dorms and doubles, a sunny, glass-enclosed back patio, a grassy terrace, a cinema room, a shared kitchen and a bar-music room. Throw in its free walking tours, homemade dinners on request, port-wine tastings and concerts, and you'll see why it's booked up so often – reserve ahead.

Poets Inn B&B €
(Map p366; ☎223 324 209; www.thepoetsinn.com; Rua dos Caldeireiros 261; d/apt from €42/72; 📶) This laid-back B&B has a central but tucked-away location. Decorated by local artists, each of the doubles has a theme and some have fine city views. Most rooms share a bathroom. There's also a garden complete with hammock, a guest kitchen and a lounge with DVDs, plus a decent breakfast included in the price.

★Maison Nos B&B B&B €€
(Map p366; ☎927 537 457, 222 011 683; www.maisonnos.com; Rua Dr Barbosa de Castro 36; d €70-90; 📶) Stéphane and Baris go the extra mile to make you feel at home at their sweet, understatedly stylish B&B, nuzzled in among 14th-century walls in the Vitória district. The parquet-floored rooms are light and uniquely furnished – some with petite balconies, others with free-standing tubs. Fresh juice, homemade cake and strong coffee at breakfast kick-start the day perfectly.

Casa dos Caldeireiros B&B €€
(Map p366; ☎914 573 774; www.caldeireirosportoflats.com; Rua dos Caldeireiros 191; d €75-85; ❄📶) Wow, what a view! Snuggled down a Miragaia backstreet and occupying a 17th-century townhouse, Casa dos Caldeireiros affords lofty vistas over Porto's historic centre from many of its well-equipped studios, which retain original features such as beams and stone walls. Cartolina and Patio, with their private terraces, have the edge. There's a minimum two-night stay.

Yours Guesthouse GUESTHOUSE €€
(Map p366; ☎222 033 082; www.yoursguesthouse.com; Rua dos Caldeireiros 135; d/q from €60/100) Squirrelled away in one of the loveliest streets of old Porto, this guesthouse has bags of originality, with antiques speckling cheerfully decorated rooms, reached by a spiral staircase – the best have fine city views. Enjoy breakfast in the walled garden when the sun's out.

Pensão Favorita GUESTHOUSE €€
(Map p366; ☎220 134 157; www.pensaofavorita.pt; Rua Miguel Bombarda 267; d/tr/q from €70/85/110; 📶) An artful addition to Porto, Pensão Favorita has inviting rooms of ample size with big windows, mid-century furnishings and wide plank floors. The rooms in the red-brick addition out the back overlook the garden; there's also a lounge and restaurant with outdoor seating, which does great lunch specials.

★ROSA ET AL Townhouse BOUTIQUE HOTEL €€€
(Map p366; ☎916 000 081; www.rosaetal.pt; Rua do Rosário 233; ste €118-228; 📶) This gorgeously done-up townhouse in the thick of Porto's art district has six suites with hardwood floors and free-standing claw-foot tubs, a lovely garden out back, and spa treatments on request. The restaurant serves one of Porto's finest brunches and afternoon tea at weekends. There are also rotating exhibits, themed retreats, and terrific cookery workshops in conjunction with Taste Porto (p370).

Vila Nova de Gaia

Gaia Porto Hostel HOSTEL €
(Map p364; ☎224 968 282; www.hostelgaiaporto.pt; Rua Cândido dos Reis 374; dm €20, d €48-60; 📶) Down by the river and just a cork-pop away from the port-wine lodges, this hostel has fabulous views of the Rio Douro and Ribeira and a secluded garden. A glass of port on arrival, generous breakfasts and bright dorms and doubles spruced up with murals seal the deal.

Charm Guesthouse GUESTHOUSE €€€
(Map p366; ☎223 752 362; www.charmguesthouse.com; Rua Cândido dos Reis 40; d from €120; P❄📶) Charming indeed, these Gaia digs have boutiquey flavour, with eye-catching fabrics, design elements and bursts of fuchsia and aquamarine in the stone-walled, wood-floored rooms. Little touches such as Castelbel toiletries and fluffy bathrobes ramp up the comfort factor. The best views are from the Douro Suite terrace. Regional produce lands on the breakfast table.

Massarelos

Porta Azul GUESTHOUSE €€
(Map p366; ☎224 037 706; www.porta-azul.com; Rua Dom Manuel II 204; d from €70; 📶) Pedro and Marta make you feel instantly at home at their neatly tended guesthouse, located in a 19th-century townhouse opposite the Jardim do Palácio Cristal. The wood-floored rooms are bright and well-kept – upgrade to a junior suite for extra space – and homemade goodies feature at breakfast.

Boavista

Hospedaria Boavista GUESTHOUSE €
(Map p364; ☎226 098 376; Av da Boavista 880; d €35-45; 📶) Eight spacious budget rooms await in your Porto grandma's house. The carpet may be industrial, but the furniture is antique, the ceilings are high, the bathrooms gleaming and the beds are firm. Rooms overlook *senhora's* blooming veggie garden.

Casa do Conto DESIGN HOTEL €€
(Map p364; ☎222 060 340; www.casadoconto.com; Rua da Boavista 703; ste from €100; P❄📶) Porto architects, artists and storytellers have pooled their creativity to totally make over a 19th-century townhouse in an upcoming corner of town. The result is the 'House of Tales', with a clever mix of stark concrete and granite interiors, and vintage furnishings. The higher you go, the better the view. Breakfast is superb, with fresh fruit, pastries and eggs.

Foz do Douro

Pousada da Juventude HOSTEL €
(☎226 163 059, 925 664 983; www.pousadasjuventude.pt; Rua Paulo da Gama 551; dm/d/apt €15/40/70; P@📶) In a bright, modern building above the Rio Douro, this hostel offers handsome doubles with balconies and sweeping river views, well-maintained four-person dorms, and apartments. There's a restaurant and a supermarket nearby, but no kitchen. The hitch: it's 4km from central Porto. Take bus 207 from Campanhã station or bus 500 from Aliados.

Casa das Laranjas GUESTHOUSE €€
(☎965 445 624; www.facebook.com/casadaslaranjas; Travessa das Laranjeiras 33; d €85-100; 📶)

PORTO WITH CHILDREN

Exploring Porto with kids in tow can be child's play with a little know-how. What could be more family-friendly, after all, than screeching through the streets on a vintage tram, devising your own Harry Potter trail in the city that once inspired JK Rowling, hitting the beaches in Foz, or finding adventure in the footsteps of great Portuguese navigators?

Marionettes

Puppets on strings are in the spotlight at Ribeira's **Museu das Marionetas** (Map p366; www.marionetasdoporto.pt; Rua das Flores 22; €2; 11am-1pm & 2-6pm;).

Hands-on Activities

Check out the activity-driven family weekend workshops at Serralves' **Museu de Arte Contemporânea** (p374). The expansive gardens are also kid-friendly.

Shoreline Adventures

Hop aboard tram 1 to Foz for ice cream, lighthouse snapshots, a paddle in the Atlantic, and marine life encounters at the whopping **Sealife Porto** (www.visitsealife.com; 1 Rua Particular do Castelo do Queijo; adult/child €13/9; 10am-6pm Mon-Fri, to 7pm Sat & Sun;).

Budding Seafarers

Slip into the shoes of a swashbuckling explorer at the **World of Discoveries** (Map p366; www.worldofdiscoveries.com; Rua de Miragaia 106; adult/child €14/8; 10am-6pm Mon-Fri, to 7pm Sat & Sun;).

Day at the Park

Kids love letting off steam in Parque da Cidade (p370), Porto's biggest park, and it's also perfect picnic territory.

This squat, mint-hued townhouse resides in the heart of Foz, just a short amble from the sea. Its bright, wood-floored, beautifully refurbished rooms sport naturalistic wall coverings and are kept immaculate; the best of the bunch have balconies. Homemade treats and fresh-pressed juice appear at breakfast.

Eating

Taberna São Pedro SEAFOOD €

(Map p364; 220 993 883; Rua Agostinho Albaño 84, Afurada; mains €6-10; noon-4pm & 7.30-11pm) Fado drifts over the *azulejo*-clad walls, toddlers tear through the dining room, plump and oily sardines (and other fresh fish) are roasted on sidewalk grills, and you can almost smell the tart snap of *vinho verde* (young wine) in the air. There's much to love in this forever-packed, salt-of-the-earth local seafood house. It's located one block inland from the ferry pier.

★O Paparico PORTUGUESE €€

(225 400 548; www.opaparico.com; Rua de Costa Cabral 2343; mains €15-20; 7.30-11pm) It's worth the taxi hop north of town to O Paparico. Portuguese authenticity is the name of the game here, from the romantically rustic interior of stone walls, beams and white linen to the menu that sings of the seasons. Dishes such as veal with wild mushrooms and monkfish are cooked with passion, served with precision and expertly paired with wines.

Dom Peixe SEAFOOD €€

(224 927 160; www.dompeixe.com; Rua Heróis de França 241; mains €8-20; noon-11pm) Out of all the authentic indoor-outdoor places on Matosinhos' 'fish restaurant row', Dom Peixe stands out as being one of the best. Snag a table on the terrace and go for the catch of the day grilled simply on an open-air barbecue. You won't be disappointed.

Boa Nova Tea House GASTRONOMIC €€€

(Casa de Cha; 229 940 066, 932 499 444; www.ruipaula.com; Avenida da Liberdade, Leça da Palmeira, Matosinhos; menus €80-120; 7.30-11pm Mon, 12.30-3pm & 7.30-11pm Tue-Sat) Designed by Portuguese architect titan Álvaro Siza Vieira and completed in 1963, this cliffside teahouse and restaurant perches alluringly above a crashing sea. Massive boulders frame the white, low-rise building, while the light-flooded interior is Zen-like. The ingredients-driven menu goes with the seasons, but might include, say, crayfish, oyster and apple, or Wagyu beef with amaranth and chanterelles.

The restaurant is 20 minutes north of Porto along the coast. It's best reached by car or taxi.

Ribeira

Da Terra VEGETARIAN €
(Map p366; ☎223 199 257; www.daterra.pt; Rua Mouzinho da Silveira 249; buffet €9.90; ⏲noon-3.30pm & 7.30-11pm; ☑) Porto's shift towards lighter, super-healthy food is reflected in the buffet served at Da Terra. This popular, contemporary bistro puts its own spin on vegetarian and vegan food – from creative salads to Thai-style veggies and tagines. It also does a fine line in fresh-pressed juices and desserts. The website posts details of upcoming workshops and cookery courses.

Taberna do Largo PORTUGUESE €
(Map p366; ☎222 082 154; Largo de São Domingos 69; petiscos €2-14; ⏲5pm-midnight Tue-Thu, to 1am Fri, noon-1am Sat, noon-midnight Sun; 📶) Lit by wine-bottle lights, this sweet grocery store, deli and tavern is run with passion by Joana and Sofia. Tour Portugal with your tastebuds with their superb array of hand-picked wines, which go brilliantly with tasting platters of smoked tuna, Alentejo *salpicão* sausage, Azores São Jorge cheese, Beira *morcela* (blood sausage), *tremoços* (lupin beans) and more.

Mercearia das Flores DELI €
(Map p366; Rua das Flores 110; petiscos €2.50-7.50; ⏲9am-8pm Mon-Thu, 10am-10pm Fri & Sat, 1-8pm Sun; 📶) This rustic-chic delicatessen/food store serves all-day *petiscos* made with organic regional products on the three tables and two counters of its bright and airy interior. You can also order wines by the glass, tea from the Azores and locally brewed Sovina beer. Try the spicy sardines and salad on dark, sweet *broa* cornbread.

★**Cantina 32** PORTUGUESE €€
(Map p366; ☎222 039 069; www.cantina32.com; Rua das Flores 32; petiscos €5-15; ⏲12.30-2.30pm & 7.30-11pm; 📶) Industrial-chic meets boho at this delightfully laid-back haunt, with its walls of polished concrete, mismatched crockery, verdant plants, and vintage knick-knacks ranging from a bicycle to an old typewriter. The menu is just as informal – *petiscos* such as *pica-pau* steak (bite-sized pieces of steak in a garlic-white-wine sauce), quail egg croquettes, and cheesecake served in a flower pot reveal a pinch of creativity.

Traça PORTUGUESE €€
(Map p366; ☎222 081 065; www.restaurantetraca.com; Largo de São Domingos 88; mains €16-20; ⏲noon-3pm & 7-11.30pm Mon-Thu, noon-3pm & 7.30pm-2am Fri, 11.30am-2pm & 7.30pm-2am Sat) Hip and happening Traça is tucked in a 17th-century building that once housed a drugstore. Its retro-cool interior has nods to its Portuguese roots and rustic soul – *azulejos,* wood panelling, mounted antlers. It's big on soul food, and the meaty picks are particularly outstanding: T-bone steaks, game sausage, venison with mushrooms and the like. Terrace seats are gold dust when it's sunny.

Taberna dos Mercadores PORTUGUESE €€
(Map p366; ☎222 010 510; Rua dos Mercadores 36; mains €14-22; ⏲noon-11pm Tue-Sun) The chefs run a tight ship in the open kitchen at this curvaceous, softly lit, bottle-lined tavern, sizzling, stirring and delivering superb Portuguese grub with a smile from noon to night. On the menu are spot-on dishes as simple as *açorda de mariscos* (garlicky bread-based stew with shellfish), *feijoada* (black bean one-pot), grilled fish and meats.

Jimão TAPAS €€
(Map p366; ☎220 924 660; www.jimao.pt; Praça da Ribeira 11; tapas €4-6.50; ⏲noon-midnight Wed-Mon) Many of the restaurants on Praça da Ribeira are tourist central, Jimão being the exception. Service is genuinely friendly, the upstairs dining room has a cracking view of Ribeira and the tapas – garlicky gambas, codfish and octopus salad, sardine toasts and the like – are prepared with care and served with great wines.

O Comercial MODERN EUROPEAN €€
(Map p366; ☎918 838 649; www.ocomercial.com; Palácio da Bolsa, Rua Ferreira Borges; 3-course set lunch/dinner €15/20; ⏲12.30-3pm & 7.30-10.30pm Mon-Fri, 7.30-11.30pm Sat) A touch of class in the Palácio da Bolsa, O Comercial has a whiff of romantic grandeur with its chandeliers, high ceilings and *azulejo*-clad walls. The service is polished and the menu places the accent on well-prepared Med-style classics, such as veal carpaccio with pesto and tuna steak with port wine and onion sauce.

Cantinho do Avillez GASTRONOMIC €€
(Map p366; ☎223 227 879; www.cantinhodoavillez.pt; Rua Mouzinho da Silveira 166; mains

€17-22.50; ⌚12.30-3pm & 7pm-midnight Mon-Fri, 12.30pm-midnight Sat & Sun) Rock star chef José Avillez' latest venture is a welcome fixture on Porto's gastro scene. A bright, contemporary bistro with a retro spin, Cantinho keeps the mood casual and buzzy. On the menu are seasonal Portuguese dishes with imagination: from flaked *bacalhau* with melt-in-the-mouth 'exploding' olives to giant red shrimps from the Algarve with Thai spices.

★DOP GASTRONOMIC €€€

(Map p366; ☎222 014 313; www.ruipaula.com; Largo de São Domingos 18; menus €20-56; ⌚7-11pm Mon, 12.30-3pm & 7-11pm Tue-Sat; 📶) Housed in the Palácio das Artes, DOP is one of Porto's most stylish addresses, with its high ceilings and slick, monochrome interior. Much-feted chef Rui Paula puts a creative, seasonal twist on outstanding ingredients, with dish after delicate, flavour-packed dish skipping from octopus carpaccio to cod with lobster rice. The three-course lunch is terrific value at €20.

Aliados & Bolhão

Stash SANDWICHES €

(Map p366; ☎914 567 616; Praça Guilherme Gomes Fernandes 60; sandwiches €3.50-8; ⌚noon-midnight Tue-Sat) If you don't want to crack open the piggy bank to dine at Michelin-starred Pedro Lemos, you can at least flirt with his flavours at his latest venture – Stash. On the menu are gourmet sandwiches for pocket-money prices. Happy days.

Cafe Santiago PORTUGUESE €

(Map p366; ☎222 055 797; Rua Passos Manuel 226; mains €8-12; ⌚noon-11pm Mon-Sat) This is hands down one of the best places to try Porto's classic gut-busting treat, the *francesinha* – a thick, open-faced sandwich, piled with cheese, sausage, egg and/or assorted other meats, plus a tasty, rich beer sauce.

Leitaria da Quinta do Paço BAKERY, CAFE €

(Map p366; www.leitariadaquintadopaco.com; Praça Guilherme Gomes Fernandes 47; éclairs €1.10; ⌚8.45am-8pm Mon-Thu, to 9pm Fri & Sat) Since 1920, this cafe-patisserie has given a pinch of Paris to Porto with its delectable sweet and savoury éclairs, which are now justifiably famous. Sit in the slick interior or on the plaza terrace for a *cimbalinho* (espresso) and feather-light, cream-filled éclairs in flavours from classic lemon to the more unusual blue cheese, apple and fennel or chocolate and port wine.

Cultura dos Sabores VEGETARIAN €

(Map p366; ☎222 010 556; Rua da Ceuta 80; buffet lunch/dinner €10.50/12.50; ⌚8am-11pm Sun-Wed, to 2am Thu-Sat; 📶🌿) A hip, healthy addition to central Porto, this vegetarian and vegan restaurant can easily be spotted by the swings in its window. You can help yourself to the lunch and dinner buffet, which often includes hearty soups, salads, wild rice or pasta dishes. Herbal teas and detox juices are available.

★Flor dos Congregados PORTUGUESE €€

(Map p366; ☎222 002 822; www.flordoscongregados.pt; Travessa dos Congregados 11; mains €8-16; ⌚7-10pm Mon, 10am-10pm Tue-Sat) Tucked away down a narrow alley, this softly lit, family-run restaurant brims with stone-walled, wood-beamed, art-slung nooks. The frequently changing blackboard menu goes with the seasons.

All In Porto PORTUGUESE €€

(Map p366; ☎220 993 829; www.facebook.com/allinporto; Rua Arquitecto Nicolau Nasoni 17; petiscos €7-22; ⌚10am-midnight) Wine barrel tables, lanterns and funky Porto murals create a hip, laid-back space for sampling a stellar selection of Portuguese wines and nicely prepared *petiscos*. These range from flame-grilled *chouriço* (spicy sausage) to spicy sardine roe, cheeses and *conservas* (canned fish). Quiet enough for conversing, it's also a chilled spot to begin or end an evening over drinks.

Tapabento TAPAS €€

(Map p366; ☎912 881 272, 222 034 115; www.tapabento.com; Rua da Madeira 222; tapas & sharing plates €4-16, mains €18-21; ⌚7pm-midnight Tue, noon-midnight Wed-Thu, to 2am Fri & Sat) There's a good buzz at split-level Tapabento, discreetly tucked behind São Bento train station. Stone walls, bright prints and cheek-by-jowl tables set the scene for outstanding tapas and Douro wines. Sharing is the way to go – be it fresh oysters with shallot vinaigrette, razor clams with garlic and coriander or Azores cheese with rocket and walnuts.

Dama Pé de Cabra CAFE €€

(Map p366; ☎223 196 776; Passeio de São Lázaro 5; mains €12-20; ⌚9.30am-3.30pm Tue-Thu, to 11pm Fri & Sat, to noon Sun) The *bemvindo* is heartfelt at this cute, bottle-lined grocery store turned cafe. It's a cheerful spot for breakfast, brunch, coffee and cake, or a laid-back lunch of homemade breads with Portuguese hams and tangy cheeses.

Camafeu MODERN PORTUGUESE €€

(Map p366; ☎937 493 557; www.facebook.com/camafeu83; Praça de Carlos Alberto 83; mains €12-19; ⏰6-11pm Tue-Thu, 6.30pm-midnight Fri & Sat;) Visiting Camafeu, which overlooks Praça Carlos Alberto, is like eating in a friend's stylish 1st-floor apartment. There's room for just a handful of lucky diners in the chandelier-lit salon, which boasts French windows, antique furnishings and a polished wooden floor. Dishes such as slow-cooked pork cheek with *alheira* (a light, garlicky sausage of poultry or game), hazelnut and mushroom crumble and green asparagus are prepared with love and served with flair.

Book PORTUGUESE €€

(Map p366; ☎917 953 387; www.restaurantebook.pt; Rua de Aviz 10; mains €16-23; ⏰noon-3pm & 7.30pm-2am) One of Porto's hottest tables, this place has a library theme and buzzes with a mix of well-heeled locals and tourists. The decor is a blend of industrial and classic, and dishes are modern takes on Portuguese mainstays, such as duck breast with sweet potato and port wine or creamy rice with prawns, lime and coriander. Service can be slow. Book ahead.

Miss'Opo PORTUGUESE €€

(Map p366; ☎222 082 179; www.missopo.com; Rua dos Caldeireiros 100; petiscos €2-9; ⏰8pm-midnight Tue-Sun) Don't miss dinner at this cool guesthouse in the maze of alleyways up from the Ribeira, with a stylishly rough-around-the-edges look and delicious small plates being churned out of the tiny kitchen. Reserve ahead, especially on weekends. There are six lovely apartments (up to three people €75 to €120, up to six people €145 to €200) upstairs, featuring blond wood and kitchenettes.

Miragaia

★A Sandeira SANDWICHES €

(Map p366; ☎223 216 471; Rua dos Caldeireiros 85; mains €4.50, lunch menu €5; ⏰11am-3pm Mon-Wed, to midnight Thu-Sat;) Charming, boho-flavoured and lit by fairy lights, A Sandeira is a great bolt-hole for an inexpensive lunch. Chipper staff bring to the table creative salads such as smoked ham, rocket, avocado and walnuts, and Porto's best sandwiches (olive, feta, tomato and basil, for instance). The lunch menu including soup, a salad or sandwich, and a drink is a steal.

Quintal Bioshop DELI €

(Map p366; www.blogdoquintal.blogspot.com.au; Rua do Rosário 177; snacks & mains €2-7; ⏰10.30am-8pm Mon-Sat;) Tucked at the back of an organic grocery store, this bright, cheery deli opens onto a terrace and serves healthy, wholesome vegetarian food. It does fresh-pressed juices, creative sandwiches (try the goat's milk cheese, apple, walnut and honey) and salads. Or stop by for an organic tea with a slice of homemade cake between gallery hopping on Rua de Miguel Bombarda.

As 7 Maravilhas INTERNATIONAL €

(Map p366; ☎222 032 116; www.as7maravilhas.com; Rua das Taipas 17C; tapas €2.50-6; ⏰1pm-midnight Tue-Sun;) A wood-floored gastropub with a pinch of boho flair, a dash of vintage charm and a generous helping of globetrotter, As 7 Maravilhas is a one-off. The friendly German-Portuguese owners keep the good vibes and international beers flowing. These go very well with the tapas on offer, which reflect their well-travelled tastes – felafel, onion bhajis, *currywurst* and the like.

Taberna de Santo António PORTUGUESE €

(Map p366; ☎222 055 306; Rua das Virtudes 32; mains €5-10; ⏰8am-2am Tue-Fri, 9am-2am Sat & Sun) This family-run tavern prides itself on serving up good honest Portuguese grub with a smile. It dishes up generous helpings of codfish, grilled sardines and *cozido* (meat and vegetable stew) to the lunchtime crowds. It's a friendly TV-and-tiles place in the traditional Portuguese mould, with pavement seating on warm days.

Taberna do Barqueiro PORTUGUESE €

(Map p366; ☎937 691 732; Rua de Miragaia 123-124; mains €8-12; ⏰11am-10.30pm Mon & Wed-Sat, to 4pm Tue) Down by the river, the Taberna do Barqueiro is a rustic, homely bolt-hole, with stone walls, cheek-by-jowl tables and a terrace on the cobblestones. Daily specials such as *bacalhau com natas* (baked saltcod with cream) and Portuguese-style tapas such as sardines, cured ham, cheese, and pork in red wine are served with a smile.

Atelier CAFE €

(Map p366; Rua Clemente Meneres 20; snacks €2-6, lunch menu €5; ⏰8am-7pm Mon-Fri, 9am-3pm Sat) Just around the corner from the Museu Nacional Soares dos Reis, this white-walled, high-ceilinged cafe lodges in a beautifully converted century-old building. The friendly couple that run the place rustle up great coffee, sandwiches, quiches, salads, homemade cakes (including a mean apple pie with almonds) and fresh juices.

O Caraças PORTUGUESE €
(Map p366; ☎220 174 505; Rua das Taipas 27; mains €7-10; ⊙11.30am-11pm Mon-Sat) Run with heart and soul by a mother and her two daughters, this quaint, stone-walled tavern is a homely gem. Generous helpings of market-fresh Portuguese soul food – from salt cod to perfectly cooked pork – feature on the well-edited menu.

★**Belos Aires** ARGENTINE €€
(Map p366; ☎223195661; www.facebook.com/belosairesrestaurante; Rua de Belomonte 104; mains €12-20; ⊙8-11.30am & 7pm-midnight Mon-Sat;) At the heart of this intimate part-Argentine, part-Portuguese restaurant is Mauricio, a chef with a big personality and an insatiable passion for his homeland, revealed as you watch him dashing around in the open kitchen. The market-fresh menu changes frequently, but you'll always find superb steaks and to-die-forempanadas (savoury turnovers). Save an inch for the chocolate brownie with *dulce de leche*.

Frida MEXICAN €€
(Map p366; ☎226 062 286; www.cocinamestiza.pt; Rua Adolfo Casais Monteiro 135; mains €12-20; ⊙8pm-midnight;) Named after the most flamboyant of Mexican painters, this restaurant spices up Porto's epicurean scene. Soft lamp light and walls plastered with Mexican newspaper cuttings and bold Frida Kahlo artworks create an intimate backdrop for punchy flavours ranging from beef tacos to *chile en nogada* (stuffed poblano chillies with walnut sauce) and zingy tequila-based cocktails.

Papavinhos PORTUGUESE €€
(Map p366; ☎222 000 204; Rua de Monchique 23; mains €10-17.50; ⊙noon-3pm & 7-10.30pm Tue-Sun) This no-frills, family-run tavern extends a warm welcome and dishes up generous portions of home-cooking. Try for a window table to see the river twinkle at night as you dig into classics such as clams in garlic and *bacalhau com broa* (codfish with maize bread) with a glass of crisp house white. The €6 lunch is a bargain.

Vila Nova de Gaia

Taberninha Do Manel PORTUGUESE €€
(Map p366; ☎223 753 549; www.taberninhadomanel.comportugal.com; Avenida de Diogo Leite 308; mains €11-18; ⊙11am-2am Sun-Thu, to 4am Fri & Sat) Super-friendly service, big views across the Douro to Ribeira and a menu crammed with well-executed Portuguese classics – Iberian pork, *petiscos*, *bacalhau* in different guises – reel folk into Taberninha Do Manel. There's pavement seating for warm days and a rustic interior jam-packed with what looks like the contents of your grandmother's attic.

De Castro Gaia INTERNATIONAL €€
(Map p366; ☎910 553 559; www.myportocruz.com; Largo Miguel Bombarda 23, Espaço Porto Cruz; petiscos €4.50-10, mains €9.50-16.50; ⊙12.30-3pm & 7.30-11pm Tue-Sat, 12.30-3pm Sun) Polished concrete, slatted wood and clean lines give this restaurant in the Espaço Porto Cruz a slick, contemporary look. The menu matches reasonably priced ports and wines with *petiscos* and mains such as octopus rice and pork cheeks cooked in red wine and cumin. There are fine views across the Douro to the houses of old Porto spilling down the hillside.

★**Yeatman** GASTRONOMIC €€€
(Map p364; ☎220 133 100; www.the-yeatman-hotel.com; Rua do Choupelo 88, Yeatman Hotel; tasting menus €90/145; ⊙7.30-11pm) With its polished service, elegant setting and dazzling views over river and city, the Michelin-starred restaurant at the five-star Yeatman hotel is sheer class. Chef Ricardo Costa puts his imaginative spin on seasonal ingredients from lobster to pheasant – all skilfully cooked, served with flair and expertly matched with wines from the 1000-bottle cellar that is among the country's best.

Massarelos

Taberna Cais das Pedras PORTUGUESE €
(Map p364; ☎222 017 198; Rua Monchique 65; petiscos €2.50-5; ⊙2pm-2am Tue-Sun) A warm, homely vision of chequered tablecloths and wood floors, this tavern rustles up an appetising assortment of *petiscos*, such as clams, flame-grilled *chouriço*, *pataniscas* (fish fritters) and *feijoada* (pork and bean casserole) – all for pocket-money prices. Sharing is the way to go.

O Antigo Carteiro PORTUGUESE €€
(Map p364; ☎937 317 523; Rua Senhor da Boa Morte 55; mains €9-16; ⊙noon-11pm Tue-Sat) Coyly tucked away on a lane back from the river, O Antigo Carteiro is as close as you'll get to eating in a Portuguese family home.

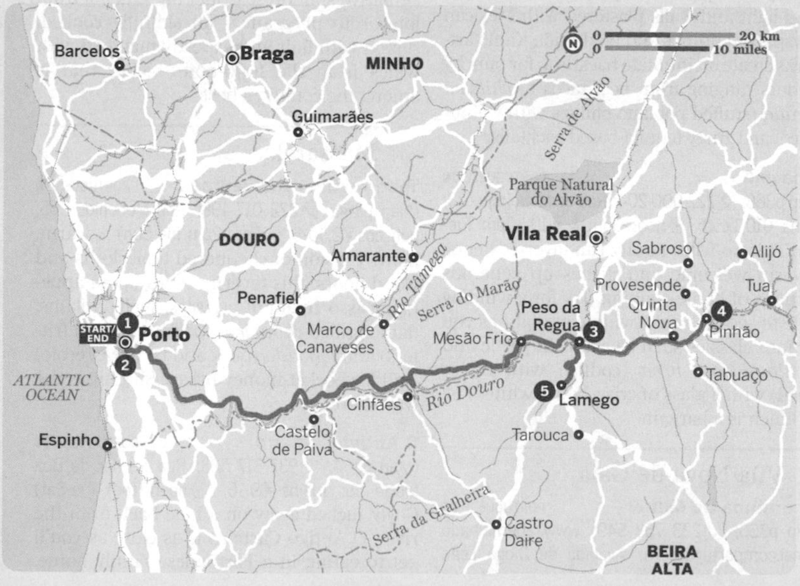

Barcelos
Braga
MINHO
0 20 km
0 10 miles
Guimarães
Serra de Alvão
Parque Natural do Alvão
DOURO
Vila Real
Sabroso
Alijó
Amarante
Rio Tâmega
Penafiel
Serra do Marão
Provesende
Tua
START/ END
1
Porto
2
Marco de Canaveses
Peso da Regua
3
Quinta Nova
4
Pinhão
Mesão Frio
ATLANTIC OCEAN
Tabuaço
5
Lamego
Cinfães
Rio Douro
Castelo de Paiva
Espinho
Tarouca
Serra da Gralheira
Castro Daire
BEIRA ALTA

1 WEEK Wines of the Douro

Wine lovers have their work cut out for them on a leisurely journey through the Douro Valley, Portugal's premier 'wine country'.

Not only is it the world's oldest demarcated wine region, bearing the title since 1756, it's also dazzling – steep terraced vineyards rise sharply from the banks of the Douro River, whitewashed *quintas* perch high up in the hills. Visitors are just as wowed by these dramatic vistas as they are by the area's viticulture, which has been turning out some of Portugal's premier wines for centuries.

Any self-respecting wine tour will begin in **Porto** (p359), gateway to the world's most famous port-wine region. Across the river is the historic **Vila Nova de Gaia** (p365), where you can sample countless varieties at its many port-wine lodges. Spend at least an afternoon tasting the sweet tipple in Gaia's lodges – the recently spruced up **Graham's** (p371) has a small museum and does excellent tours and tastings. Continue the journey east following the Douro, all the way to **Peso da Régua** (p402), a riverside town set in the heart of vineyard country. Make sure you stop by for a tasting at the nearby **Quinta do Vallado** (p403), a winery since 1716 and now a swank little rural hotel where you can have a fine wine-paired meal, and stay the night. Continue on to the quaint riverside village of **Pinhão** (p404), a great base for a few nights.

From the village head out to explore the **Alto Douro** (Upper Douro; p403), a spectacular area that Unesco designated a World Heritage site. A drive along the winding mountain roads reveals some of the most scenic views out to the vineyards, guesthouses and restaurants that sprinkle the area. Stop in for a tour and tasting at some of the wine estates; **Quinta Nova** (p404) and **Quinta do Crasto** (p404) are the most breathtaking, both offering a taste of their wines paired with magnificent views.

On the way back to Porto, visit the attractive food- and wine-loving town of **Lamego** (p399), a producer of fine sparkling wine.

Top: Vineyards, Douro Valley
Bottom: Barrel-lined cellars at Graham's (p371)

Attentive, clued-up staff pair regional wines with well-executed classics – garlicky octopus, pork tenderloin, *bacalhau com broa* and the like.

Boavista

Essência VEGETARIAN €
(☎228 301 813; www.essenciarestaurantevegetariano.com; Rua de Pedro Hispano 1190; 2-/3-course veg €7/9, nonveg €8/10; ⏰12.30-3pm & 8-10.30pm Mon-Thu, 12.30-3pm & 8pm-midnight Fri & Sat;) This bright, modern brasserie is famous Porto-wide for its generous vegetarian (and nonvegetarian!) menus, stretching from wholesome soups and salads to curries, pasta dishes and *feijoada*. There's a terrace for warm-weather dining.

Casinha Boutique Café CAFE €
(Map p364; ☎934 021 001; www.casinhaboutique.com; Avenida da Boavista 854; mains €4.50-12; ⏰9am-midnight Mon-Sat, 10am-10pm Sun;) All pretty pastel shades and hidden garden alcoves, this cafe lodged in a restored 19th-century townhouse is as cute as a button. The food impresses, too, with wholesome, locally sourced ingredients going into freshly prepared sandwiches, quiches, salads, crepes and totally divine desserts. There's also a deli for takeaway Portuguese olive oils, wines, preserves and more.

Em Carne Viva VEGETARIAN €€
(Map p364; ☎932 352 722, 220 925 598; www.emcarneviva.pt; Avenida da Boavista 868; 2-course menu €9.50, mains €11-20; ⏰noon-3pm & 7-10pm Mon-Fri, 12.30-3.30pm & 7-11pm Sat;) You can feel the love ooze out of Em Carne Viva like juice from a ripe peach. An elegant stucco-adorned parlour and a fabulously romantic garden set the scene for creative takes on vegetarian and vegan dishes – including the *francesinha* reinterpreted to chunky bean burgers with fries – all served on beautiful crockery. Save room for the scrumptious desserts.

Foz do Douro

Cafeína MODERN EUROPEAN €€
(☎226 108 059; www.cafeina.pt; Rua do Padrão 100; mains €17-19; ⏰12.30-6pm & 7.30pm-12.30am Sun-Thu, to 1.30am Fri & Sat;) Hidden coyly away from the seafront, Cafeína has a touch of class, with soft light casting a flattering glow across its moss-green walls, crisp tablecloths, lustrous wood floors and bookcases. The food is best described as modern European, simple as stuffed squid with saffron purée or rack of lamb in a herb and lemon crust, expertly matched with Portuguese wines.

Casa de Pasto da Palmeira PORTUGUESE €€
(☎226 168 244; Rua do Passeio Alegre 450; mains €6.50-14; ⏰noon-3pm & 7pm-midnight) An adorable restaurant right on the waterfront, with two small colourful rooms featuring contemporary artwork and a few tables on the front patio. The creative small-size dishes change daily – think hake and shrimp *moqueca* (Brazilian fish stew) with banana and coriander, and *alheira* rolls with turnip sprouts.

★**Pedro Lemos** GASTRONOMIC €€€
(☎220 115 986; www.pedrolemos.net; Rua do Padre Luís Cabral 974; tasting menus €80-120; ⏰12.30-3pm & 7.30-11pm Tue-Sun) One of Porto's two Michelin-starred restaurants, Pedro Lemos is sheer delight. With a love of seasonally sourced produce and robust flavours, the eponymous chef creates culinary fireworks using first-class ingredients from land and sea – be it ultra-fresh Atlantic bivalves or Alentejano black pork cooked to smoky deliciousness with wild mushrooms. Choose between the subtly lit, cosy-chic dining room or the roof terrace.

Drinking & Nightlife

Ribeira

★**Prova** WINE BAR
(Map p366; www.prova.com.pt; Rua Ferreira Borges 86; ⏰4pm-2am Wed-Mon;) Diogo, the passionate owner, explains the finer nuances of Portuguese wine at this chic, stone-walled bar, where relaxed jazz plays. Stop by for a two-glass tasting (€5), or sample wines by the glass – including beefy Douros, full-bodied Dãos and crisp Alentejo whites. These marry well with sharing plates of local hams and cheeses (€14). Diogo's port tonics are legendary.

Wine Quay Bar WINE BAR
(Map p366; www.winequaybar.com; Cais da Estiva 111; ⏰4-11pm Mon-Sat;) Sunset is prime-time viewing on the terrace of this terrific wine bar by the river. As you gaze across to the graceful arc of the Ponte Dom Luís I and over to the port cellars of Vila Nova de Gaia, you can sample some cracking Portuguese wines and appetisers (cured ham, cheese, olives and the like).

PORT WINE

With its intense flavours, silky textures and appealing sweetness, port wine is easy to love, especially when matched with its proper accompaniments: cheese, nuts, dried fruit and dark chocolate. Ports are wonderfully varied, and even non-connoisseurs can quickly learn to tell an aged tawny from a late-bottled vintage (LBV). For an insightful primer on port, hook onto a tasting at **Touriga** (p390) or **Vinologia** (Map p366; www.vinologia.pt; Rua de São João 28-30; ⊙11am-midnight), where the learned owners give an enlightening lesson with each glass they pour. Or sample fine ports by the glass at **Prova** (p384). From here, head across the Douro to Vila Nova de Gaia, the steep banks of which are speckled with grand port wine lodges – **Taylor's** (p373), **Graham's** (p371), **Croft** (Map p364; www.croftport.com; Rua Barão de Forrester 412; tours incl tasting €7; ⊙10am-6pm), **Ramos Pinto** (Map p366; ☎936 809 283; www.ramospinto.pt; Av Ramos Pinto 400; tours incl tasting €6; ⊙10am-6pm May-Oct, reduced hours Nov-Apr) and **Cálem** (p373) included.

History

It was probably Roman soldiers who first planted grapes in the Douro Valley some 2000 years ago, but tradition credits the discovery of port itself to 17th-century British merchants. With their own country at war with France, the British turned to their old ally Portugal to meet their drinking habits. The Douro Valley was a particularly productive area, though its wines were dark and astringent. According to legend, the British threw in some brandy with grape juice, both to take off the wine's bite and to preserve it for shipment back to England – and, hey presto, port wine was born. In fact, the method may already have been in use in the region, though what's certain is that the Brits took to the stuff with a passion. Their influence has been long and enduring, a fact that is still evidenced by some of port's most illustrious names including Taylor's, Graham's and Cockburn's.

The Grapes

Port-wine grapes are born out of adversity. They manage to grow on the rocky terraces of the Douro with hardly any water or even soil, and their roots must reach down as far as 30m, weaving past layers of acidic schist (shale-like stone) to find nourishment. Vines endure both extreme heat in summer and freezing temperatures in winter. These conditions produce intense flavours that stand up to the infusions of brandy. The most common varietals are hardy, dark reds such as *touriga, tinto cão* and *tinto barroca*.

The Wine

Grapes are harvested in autumn and immediately crushed (sometimes still by foot) and allowed to ferment until alcohol levels reach 7%. At this point, one part brandy is added to every five parts wine. Fermentation stops immediately, leaving the unfermented sugars that make port sweet. The quality of the grapes, together with the ways the wine is aged and stored, determines the kind of port you get. The most common include the following:

Ruby Made from average-quality grapes, and aged at least two years in vats; rich, red colours and sweet, fruity flavours.

Tawny Made from average-quality grapes, and aged for two to seven years in wooden casks; mahogany colours, drier than ruby, with nuttier flavours.

Aged tawny Selected from higher-quality grapes, then aged in wooden casks for 10, 20, 30 or 40 years (reflected in the price respectively). Subtler and silkier than regular tawny; drinks more like brandy or cognac than wine.

Vintage Made from the finest grapes from a single year (and only select years qualify), aged in barrels for two years, then aged in bottles for at least 10 years (and up to 100 or more); dark ruby colours, fruity yet extremely subtle and complex.

Late-bottled vintage (LBV) Made from very select grapes of a single year, aged for around five years in wooden casks, then bottled; similar to vintage, but ready for immediate drinking once bottled, and usually smoother and lighter bodied.

Wine Box WINE BAR

(Map p366; www.thewineboxporto.com; Rua dos Mercadores 72; ⌚1.30pm-midnight Thu-Tue; 📶) Wine cases turn the interior into quite a feature at this slinky, black-walled bar. The friendly staff will guide you through the 137 (at the last count) wines on the menu, most of which are available by the glass. They go nicely with tapas such as Padrón peppers and clams in a herby sauce.

Aliados & Bolhão

★Museu d'Avó BAR

(Map p366; Travessa de Cedofeita 54; ⌚8pm-4am Mon-Sat) The name translates as 'Grandmother's Museum' and indeed it's a gorgeous rambling attic of a bar, crammed with cabinets, old clocks, *azulejos* and gramophones, with curios hanging from its rafters. Lanterns and candles illuminate young *tripeiros* (Porto residents) locked in animated conversation as the house beats spin. If you get the late-night munchies, it also whips up tasty *petiscos* (€2 to €8).

★Aduela BAR

(Map p366; Rua das Oliveiras 36; ⌚3pm-2am Mon, 1pm-2am Tue-Sat, 2pm-midnight Sun) Retro and hip but not self-consciously so, chilled Aduela bathes in the nostalgic orange glow of its glass lights, which illuminate the green walls and mishmash of vintage furnishings. Once a sewing machine warehouse, today it's where friends gather to converse over wine and appetising *petiscos* (€3 to €8).

★Era Uma Vez No Paris BAR

(Map p366; Rua Galeria de Paris 106; ⌚11am-2am Mon-Thu, to 4am Fri & Sat) A little flicker of bohemian Parisian flair in the heart of Porto, Era Uma Vez No Paris time warps you back to the more decadent 1920s. Its ruby-red walls, retro furnishings and frilly lampshades spin a warm, intimate cocoon for coffee by day and drinks by night. DJs keep the mood mellow with indie rock and funk beats.

Terraplana CAFE

(Map p364; Avenida Rodrigues de Freitas 287; ⌚11am-midnight Tue-Thu, to 2am Fri & Sat, 5pm-midnight Sun) Totally relaxed and cool without trying, Terraplana takes you through from late-morning coffee to evening cocktails (around €7.50 a pop). Granite and tiles set the backdrop for the house special, the Terraplana Cafe, with coffee liqueur, vodka and an espresso shot. Or try the Living Dead Margarita, with a ginger and chilli kick.

Bonaparte Downtown PUB

(Map p366; www.facebook.com/bonapartedowntown; Praça Guilherme Gomes Fernandes 40; ⌚5pm-2am) This newcomer to downtown Porto's nightlife scene is a pleasingly relaxed number. Lanterns cast a warm glow across the cosy, knick-knack-crammed, wood-heavy interior, which morphs from a low-key spot to sip a pre-dinner beer to a much livelier haunt later in the evening.

La Bohème WINE BAR

(Map p366; www.laboheme.com.pt; Rua Galeria de Paris 40; ⌚3pm-2am Tue-Sun) With a high-ceilinged, Scandi-style pine interior, La Bohème is one of the most stylish, intimate bars on Rua Galeria de Paris. It's a nicely chilled choice for pairing fine wines with *petiscos*. DJs spin as the evening wears on.

Moustache CAFE

(Map p366; www.moustache.pt; Praça Carlos Alberto 104; ⌚10am-8pm Mon, to midnight Tue & Wed, to 2am Thu-Sat, 2-8pm Sun; 📶) 🍃 Ease into the day gently or wind it out over drinks and mellow beats at this urban-cool cafe with cultural edge. The armchairs are perfect for dawdling over a robust coffee or smoothie and snacks such as filled croissants and cakes. Products are mostly organic and fair trade and it also has lactose-free options.

Gin House BAR

(Map p366; www.facebook.com/theginhouse; Rua Cândido dos Reis 70; ⌚7pm-2am Sun-Thu, to 4am Fri & Sat) This slick, pared-down bar attracts an upbeat crowd with a splash of class, '80s and '90s pop and rock and 160 different kinds of gin. Try palate-awakening cocktails, a gin and tonic with cucumber and rose petals, for instance, but be aware that some come in fishbowl-sized glasses – more than a couple and the room might start to swim.

Wall BAR

(Map p366; www.facebook.com/thewallbar.baixa; Rua de Cândido dos Reis 90; ⌚5pm-4am Mon-Sat, 9pm-4am Sun) With backlit walls featuring a 3D cubist artwork of spirit bottles, high ceilings and a funky world map of names, the Wall has a dash of the urban sophisticate about it. Mingle with an effortlessly cool crowd enjoying the chilled DJ beats and expertly mixed cocktails (it boasts a mean mojito).

Café Candelabro CAFE

(Map p366; Rua da Conceição 3; ⌚10.30am-2am Mon-Fri, 2pm-2am Sat, 2.30pm-midnight Sun) Cool cafe-bar in a former bookstore, with a boho crowd and a retro vibe featuring black-and-white mosaic tile floors, bookcases with old books and magazines, and big windows opening out to the street. It gets busy, with blasting techno on weekend nights.

Café Au Lait BAR
(Map p366; www.facebook.com/aulait.cafe; Rua Galeria de Paris 44; ⌚9.30pm-4am Mon-Sat) Housed in a former textile warehouse, this narrow, intimate bar now stitches together a lively and unpretentious artistic crowd. Besides cocktails, there are snacks and salads, including vegetarian grub. DJs and occasional gigs amp up the vibe and add to the good cheer.

Galeria de Paris BAR
(Map p366; www.facebook.com/restaurantegaleriadeparis; Rua Galeria de Paris 56; ⌚8.30am-4am) The original on the strip that's now synonymous with the Porto party scene, this whimsically decorated spot has toys, thermos flasks, old phones and other assorted memorabilia lining the walls. In addition to cocktails and draught beer, you'll find tapas at night. Happy hour – with beer or wine for €2 – is from 5pm to 7pm.

Plano B BAR
(Map p366; www.planobporto.net; Rua Cândido dos Reis 30; ⌚10pm-2am Tue & Wed, to 4am Thu, to 6am Fri & Sat; 📶) This creative space has an art gallery in front, a tall-ceilinged cafe out back, and a cosy downstairs where DJs and live bands hold court. Much like the crowd, the programming is eclectic, with performance art, theatre and art openings held regularly.

Café Majestic CAFE
(Map p366; www.cafemajestic.com; Rua Santa Catarina 112; ⌚9.30am-midnight Mon-Sat) Yes, we know, it's pricey and rammed with tourists brandishing selfie sticks, but you should at least have a drink at Café Majestic just so you can gawp at its beaux arts interior, awash with prancing cherubs, opulently gilded woodwork and gold-braided waiters. Skip the so-so food and just go for coffee. There's a pavement terrace for sunny-day people-watching.

Livraria da Baixa CAFE
(Map p366; www.facebook.com/livrariadabaixa; Rua das Carmelitas 15; ⌚10am-2am; 📶) Part 1920s bookshop, part cafe-bar, this old-school charmer spills out onto the cobbled pavement – a terrific spot for people-watching and eavesdropping over tea or a glass of wine.

Bolhão Wine House WINE BAR
(Map p366; www.facebook.com/wine.house.bolhao; Mercado do Bolhão; ⌚10am-5pm Mon-Fri, 10am-1pm Sat) Bolhão Wine House is run with a passion by Patrícia and Hugo in their grandmother's old florist shop. With room for two, the tiny wine shop is a highly atmospheric spot to pick up a decent bottle of Portuguese *vinho* and sample a glass with sardines, a sharing plate of cheese and ham or delicious *queijadinhas* (mini cheesecakes).

Duas de Letra CAFE
(Map p366; www.duasdeletra.pt; Passeio de São Lázaro 48; ⌚10am-8pm Mon-Thu, to midnight Fri & Sat, 2-8pm Sun; 📶) Artsy cafe overlooking a leafy square, with a low-key vibe, wooden ceilings, an old bike hanging upside down, an exhibition space upstairs with rotating exhibits, and two patios. The snacks are delicious, and there's a great tea selection.

Casa de Ló CAFE
(Map p366; Travessa de Cedofeita 20A; ⌚2pm-2am Mon-Sat) Hidden off a narrow alley is this boho coffee house beloved by area hipsters. Think thick stone walls, old timber-beamed ceilings, a nice little patio out back, funky downbeat tunes and a pretty and pouty artsy crowd. DJs spin on Friday and Saturday.

GAY & LESBIAN PORTO

Note that while there are no exclusive women's bars or clubs, all the places listed here are at least somewhat mixed.

Zoom (Map p366; www.zoomporto.wix.com/zoomporto; Rua Passos Manuel 40; ⌚12.30am-6am Fri & Sat) Located in an old warehouse, this is the gay dance hall of the moment, with some of the best electronic dance music in town and an often mixed crowd.

Pride Bar (Map p364; Rua do Bonjardim 1121; ⌚11.30pm-6am Fri-Sun) Another favourite, with live music, drag shows and go-go boys. Open very late.

Café Lusitano (Map p366; www.cafelusitano.com; Rua José Falcão 137; ⌚10pm-3am Wed & Thu, to 4am Fri & Sat) In a handsomely designed throwback to 1950s Paris, this intimate space hosts a mixed gay-straight crowd. Live music on Wednesday nights.

Miragaia

Pinguim Café BAR

(Map p366; www.pinguimcafe.blogspot.co.uk; Rua de Belomonte 65; 9pm-4am Mon-Fri, 10pm-4am Sat & Sun) A little bubble of bohemian warmth in the heart of Porto, Pinguim attracts an alternative crowd. Stone walls and dim light create a cosy, intimate backdrop for plays, film screenings, poetry readings, rotating exhibitions of local art, and G&T sipping. It's full to the rafters at weekends.

Rota do Chá TEAHOUSE

(Map p366; www.rotadocha.pt; Rua Miguel Bombarda 457; tea €2.50; 11am-8pm Mon-Thu, to midnight Fri & Sat) This proudly bohemian cafe has a verdant but rustic back garden where students and the gallery crowd sit around low tables sampling from an enormous 300+ tea menu divided by region. Tasty snacks include quiches, muffins, scones and toast. It also serves weekend brunches and weekday lunch specials (€7).

Vila Nova de Gaia

360º Terrace Lounge WINE BAR

(Map p366; www.myportocruz.com; Largo Miguel Bombarda 23, Espaço Porto Cruz; 12.30pm-12.30am Tue-Thu, to 1.30am Fri & Sat, to 7pm Sun) From its perch atop the Espaço Porto Cruz, this decked terrace affords expansive views over both sides of the Douro and the city, fading into a hazy distance where the river meets the sea. As day softens into dusk, this is a prime sunset spot for sipping a glass of port or a cocktail while drinking in the incredible vista.

Boavista

Zenith Lounge Bar LOUNGE

(Map p364; Rua de Serralves 124; 10am-2am Tue-Sat May-Oct;) All of Porto spreads photogenically at your feet from this uber-hip rooftop lounge, which perches on the 15th floor of the HF Ipanema Park. Centred on a pool, the strikingly lit lounge attracts a good-looking, cocktail-sipping crowd, with regular live music, guest DJs and party nights in summer.

Bar Casa da Música BAR

(Map p364; www.casadamusica.com; Av da Boavista 604; 12.30-3pm & 7.30-11pm Mon-Thu, 12.30-3pm & 7.30pm-midnight Fri & Sat;) Situated on the top floor of Porto's most strikingly contemporary building, this bar is a fine place to sip a drink as the city starts to light up – the terrace commands great views. DJs occasionally work the decks at the twice-monthly Saturday clubbing sessions (11pm to 4am). See the website for more details.

Foz do Douro

Praia da Luz BAR

(www.praiadaluz.pt; Av do Brasil; 9am-2am) Praia da Luz is a worthwhile stop when out exploring Porto's coastline. It rambles over tiered wooden decks to its own private rocky cove, and while you could probably skip the food, you should definitely kick back and enjoy the view over a coffee or cocktail.

Bonaparte PUB

(www.bonaparteporto.net; Avenida do Brasil 130; 5pm-2am) Right on the seafront, this shipshape pub catapults you back to the age of great maritime discoveries, with its warm, woody, lantern-lit interior. It's a cosy, nicely relaxed spot for a pint of Guinness.

☆ Entertainment

Music & Theatre

★Casa da Música CONCERT VENUE

(House of Music; Map p364; 220 120 220; www.casadamusica.com; Avenida da Boavista 604; box office 9.30am-7pm Mon-Sat, to 6pm Sun) Grand and minimalist, sophisticated yet populist, Porto's cultural behemoth boasts a shoebox-style concert hall at its heart, meticulously engineered to accommodate everything from jazz duets to Beethoven's Ninth.

The hall holds concerts most nights of the year, from classical and blues to fado and electronica, with occasional summer concerts staged outdoors in the adjoining plaza.

Armazém do Chá LIVE MUSIC

(Map p366; www.armazemdocha.com; Rua José Falcão 180; 10pm-4am Tue, to 6am Wed-Fri, 4pm-6am Sat) This space downtown once housed a roasting company – it's called 'Tea Warehouse' – and now lives on as an alternative cafe-bar with an industrial-chic vibe and a weekly program of live concerts and DJ-spun tunes.

Breyner 85 LIVE MUSIC

(Map p366; 936 440 865; www.breyner85.com; Rua do Breiner 85; 5pm-2am Tue-Sun) This creative space in a two-floor townhouse features an eclectic line-up of bands covering rock, jazz and blues, as well as DJ nights, karaoke and pub quizzes. The large grassy

WORTH A TRIP

AFURADA & BEYOND

Sitting pretty on the banks of the Douro, the breezy fishing village of Afurada has remained charmingly oblivious to 21st-century trends. Houses are decked with *azulejos* (hand-painted tiles) and taverns such as **Taberna São Pedro** (p377) grill fish simply and deliciously on open-air grills. This old-fashioned way of life is depicted in Pedro Neves' 2007 documentary *A Olhar O Mar* (Gazing out to Sea).

There are several ways to get here. You can take a tram from Ribeira to the stop just west of the **Ponte da Arrábida** (Map p364), then catch a small **ferry** (one-way per person/bicycle €1/1; ⏱6am-midnight) across the river to the village. Alternatively, buses 93 and 96 from Cordoaria stop just across the bridge in Vila Nova de Gaia. From here, it's a short walk along the boardwalk to Afurada.

The lure of the sea is tangible in Afurada, with seabirds wheeling in the sky, washing strung out to dry in briny breezes and fishers tending to their nets and preparing their tackle. The river is the lifeblood for locals – stroll the waterfront for broad views of Foz across the water and the hazy smudge of the Atlantic on the horizon. If you arrive early you'll catch the **Mercado de Peixe** (Map p364; ⏱6am-7pm Mon-Fri, to 2pm Sat) fish market in full swing. For another snapshot of local life, nose around the **Lavadouro Público** (Public Laundry; Map p364; Rua da Praia), where *donas* (ladies) dish out local gossip with their arms immersed in soapsuds.

At the other end of the spectrum is the **Douro Marina** (Map p364; www.douromarina.com; Rua da Praia; ⏱9am-7pm) complex, designed by architects Barbosa & Guimarães. A striking vision in glass and steel with forms that resemble boat masts and sails, it harbours a sailing academy, shops, cafes and bike rental.

With your own set of wheels, you can roll along the riverfront to **Praia Nova do Cabedelo** in a matter of minutes. Afurada is just 1.5km from this lovely stretch of beach, hemmed by the dunes of the **Douro Estuary Nature Reserve**. Pedal on another 2km south and you'll reach the soft, golden, sheltered **Praia Estrela do Mar**, the best swimming beach in Porto.

Alternatively, it's around a 40-minute walk, or take bus 902 from Boa Vista bound for Lavadores (via Ponte Arrábida), get off at the pedestrian path and walk 800m south.

terrace is a treat. Concerts start at around 11pm and entry is free, apart from a €3 mininum spend. Sunday night jam sessions are particularly popular.

Maus Hábitos PERFORMING ARTS
(Map p366; www.maushabitos.com; 4th fl, Rua Passos Manuel 178; ⏱noon-midnight Tue & Sun, to 2am Wed & Thu, to 4am Fri & Sat) Maus Hábitos or 'Bad Habits' is an arty, nicely chilled haunt hosting a culturally ambitious agenda. Changing exhibitions and imaginative installations adorn the walls, while live bands and DJs work the small stage.

Hot Five Jazz & Blues Club JAZZ
(Map p366; ☎934 328 583; www.hotfive.pt; Largo Actor Dias 51; ⏱10pm-3am Wed-Sat) True to its name, this spot hosts live jazz and blues as well as the occasional acoustic, folk or all-out jam session. It's a modern but intimate space, with seating at small round tables, both fronting the stage and on an upper balcony. Concerts often start later than scheduled.

Hard Club LIVE MUSIC
(Map p366; www.hard-club.com; Praça do Infante Dom Henrique; ⏱10.30am-midnight Sun-Thu, to 2am Fri & Sat) Inside the converted Mercado Ferreira Borges, this happening music club with an industrial vibe hosts acts of great variety – from hip hop and house to rock and tango. There's also a restaurant on the gallery level and a lovely terrace with great views of the square.

Teatro Municipal Rivoli THEATRE
(Map p366; ☎223 392 200; www.teatromunicipaldoporto.pt; Praça Dom João I; 👪) This art deco theatre is one of the linchpins of Porto's evolving cultural scene. It traverses the whole spectrum from theatre to music, contemporary circus, cinema, dance and marionette productions.

Teatro Nacional São João THEATRE
(Map p366; ☎223 401 900; www.tnsj.pt; Praça da Batalha) The lavish, romantic Teatro Nacional São João was built in the style of Paris' Opéra Garnier. One of Porto's premier

performing-arts organisations, it hosts international dance, theatre and music groups. Set in an old synagogue-turned-church, shows are scheduled sporadically and take place in a spectacular interior courtyard framed by 15m stone walls.

TNSJ Mosteiro de São Bento da Vitória THEATRE
(Map p366; ☎223 401 900; www.tnsj.pt; Rua de São Bento da Vitória) Few theatre backdrops are more atmospheric than the Mosteiro de São Bento da Vitória, which harbours an offshoot of the Teatro Nacional de São João. See the website for the full line-up, which traverses the cultural spectrum from plays to ballet and readings. Tickets generally cost between €7.50 and €15.

Football

The flashy 52,000-seat Estádio do Dragão is home to heroes-of-the-moment **FC Porto** (Map p364; www.fcporto.pt). It's northeast of the centre, just off the VCI ring road (metro stop Estádio de Dragão).

Boavista FC (Map p364; www.boavistafc.pt; Rua 1º de Janeiro, Estádio do Bessa Século) is FC Porto's worthy cross-town rival. Its home turf is the Estádio do Bessa, which lies west of the centre just off Avenida da Boavista (take bus 3 from Praça da Liberdade). Check the local editions of *Jornal de Notícias* for upcoming matches.

Fado

Porto has no fado tradition of its own, but you can enjoy the Lisbon or Coimbra versions of 'Portuguese blues' into the wee hours at several places in town. **Restaurante O Fado** (Map p366; ☎222 026 937; www.ofado.com; Largo de São João Novo 16; ⏰8.30pm-1am Mon-Sat) is a decent option, but an even greater spot – also in Ribeira – is **Casa da Mariquinhas** (Map p366; www.casadamariquinhas.pt; Rua de São Sebastião 25; ⏰8pm-1am Wed & Thu, to 2am Fri & Sat), which has live fado nightly from Wednesday through Saturday.

Shopping

Ribeira

★Oliva & Co FOOD
(Map p366; www.olivaeco.com; Rua Ferreira Borges 60; ⏰10am-7pm Mon-Fri, to 8pm Sat) Everything you ever wanted to know about Portuguese olive oil becomes clear at this experiential store, which maps out the country's six PDO regions producing the extra-virgin stuff. Besides superb oils and olives, you'll find biscuits, chocolate and soaps made with olive oil. Try before you buy or join one of the in-depth tastings in collaboration with Taste Porto (p370).

43 Branco ARTS & CRAFTS
(Map p366; Rua das Flores 43; ⏰11am-7pm Mon-Sat) One-of-a-kind Portuguese crafts, fashion and interior design take centre stage at this new concept store, which brings a breath of fresh creativity to Rua das Flores. Here you'll find everything from filigree, gem-studded Maria Branco jewellery to funky sardine pencil cases, Porto-inspired Lubo T-shirts and beautifully packaged Bonjardim soaps.

Tradições GIFTS & SOUVENIRS
(Map p366; Rua das Flores 238; ⏰10am-7pm) For Portuguese souvenirs, Tradições is the real deal. In this friendly shop, the owner knows the story behind every item – from bags beautifully fashioned from Alentejo cork to Algarvian *flôr de sal* (hand-harvested sea salt), Lousã honey to Lazuli *azulejos*.

Aliados & Bolhão

★Workshops Pop Up ARTS & CRAFTS
(Map p366; ☎966 974 119; www.workshops-popup.com; Rua do Almada 275; ⏰1-7.30pm Mon-Fri, 10am-7.30pm Sat) Bringing a new lease of life to a restored smithy, this store is the brainchild of Nuno and Rita. It harbours an eclectic mix of pop-ups selling everything from original ceramics to vintage fashion, accessories and prettily wrapped Bonjardim soaps. It also runs English-speaking cookery workshops (followed by a meal with wine) for €30, or €42 including a market visit.

★Touriga WINE
(Map p366; ☎225 108 435; Rua da Fábrica 32; ⏰10am-1pm & 2.30-8pm Tue-Sat) Run with passion and precision by David Ferreira, this fabulous wine shop is a trove of well- and lesser-known ports and wines – many from small producers. Stop by for a wine or port-wine tasting (€3 to €12) or book ahead for the incredibly informative port-wine class (€25). Shipping can be arranged.

★A Pérola Do Bolhão FOOD & DRINKS
(Map p366; Rua Formosa 279; ⏰9.30am-7.30pm Mon-Sat) Founded in 1917, this delicatessen sports Porto's most striking art nouveau facade and is stacked high with sausages and cheeses, olives, dried fruits, wine and port.

STREET ART IN PORTO

If only walls could speak... Well, in Porto they do – volumes. Their narrative is that of Porto's growing tribe of street artists, whose bold, eye-catching works emblazon facades. Hurled across crumbling ancient walls, empty storefront glass and neglected stucco, they lend artistic edge, urban grit and an element of the unexpected to the everyday. A far cry from graffiti scrawls, the spray-paint wonders reveal artistic flair and creative expression that transcend the conventional and stop you dead in your tracks: a stencilled pilgrim here, a cloaked bodhisattva there.

Porto-born or Porto-based artists include the startlingly prolific Hazul Luza (a pseudonym), who works incognito under the cloak of darkness. His naturalistic, geometric-patterned, curlicue-embellished works dance across dilapidated city walls in the shape of flowers, exotic birds or religious motifs. Other home-grown talent includes Costah, known for his playful, brightly coloured murals; Frederico Draw, master of striking black-and-white graffiti portraits; and the ever-inventive Mr Dheo. Some of the artists are self-taught, others have backgrounds in architecture, digital art, illustration and design.

To plug into the scene today, arrange your own self-guided tour of Porto's must-see street art. High on any list should be the **Travessa de Cedeofeita** and **Escadas do Codecal**, as well as the car park at Trindade, with its large-scale murals. Lapa, just one metro stop north, is another hot spot, as is the gallery-dotted **Rua Miguel Bombarda**. Hazul has left his indelible stamp on **Rua São Pedro de Miragaia**, with a group of 10 artworks inspired by the name Florescer (to bloom or flourish). On **Rua das Flores**, clever graffiti sits side by side with beautifully restored historic buildings – look out for vibrantly patterned works by Hazul, glowing neon portraits by Costah and 15 electric boxes – each with its own burst of street-art colour. **Avenida dos Aliados** catches your attention with six telephone boxes bearing the imprint of well-known street artists such as Costah.

Coração Alecrim ARTS & CRAFTS
(Map p366; www.coracaoalecrim.com; Travessa de Cedofeita 28; ⊙noon-8pm Mon-Sat) 'Green, indie, vintage' is the strapline of this enticing store, accessed through a striking doorway painted with woodland animals (crickets chirrup a welcome as you enter). It stocks high-quality handmade Portuguese products, from pure wool blankets and beanies to one-off *azulejos*, shell coasters and beautiful ceramics.

Central Conserveira da Invicta FOOD
(Map p366; Rua Sá da Bandeira 115; ⊙10am-7pm) An ode to the humble tinned fish, this store is stacked to the rafters with bold, retro-wrapped cans of tuna, *bacalhau* and sardines plain and spicy. It stocks popular brands such as Santa Catarina, Tricana and Cego do Maio, which at between €2 and €4 a pop, make funky gifts. There are always free tastings.

A Vida Portuguesa GIFTS & SOUVENIRS
(Map p366; www.avidaportuguesa.com; Rua Galeria de Paris 20; ⊙10am-8pm Mon-Sat, 11am-7pm Sun) This lovely store in an old fabric shop showcases a medley of stylishly repackaged vintage Portuguese products – classic toys, old-fashioned soaps and retro journals, plus those emblematic ceramic Bordallo Pinheiro *andorinhas* (swallows).

Azulima ARTS & CRAFTS
(Map p366; www.azulima.pt; Rua do Bolhão 124; ⊙9.30am-12.30pm & 2.30-7pm Mon-Fri, 10am-12.30pm Sat) Heaven for the *azulejo* obsessed, this shop does a fine line in tiles of every shape, size and colour – from geometric to naturalistic, from slick and modern to classic blue-and-white numbers.

Almada 13 BOUTIQUE
(Map p366; Rua do Almada 13; ⊙10am-8pm Mon-Sat, 1-7pm Sun) This industro-glam emporium showcases the one-of-a-kind fashion, art and accessories of five different Porto-based designers and concept stores. Alongside ecofriendly Cork & Co, you'll find funky beach-themed creations from the Yellow Boat, quality teas from Rota do Chá, and quirky designs from Águas Furtadas that are an ode to Portuguese heritage.

Goodvibes FASHION & ACCESSORIES
(Map p366; Rua de José Falcão 107; ⊙2-7pm Mon, 11am-10pm Tue-Sat) Industro-cool Goodvibes is a boutique, gallery, concept store and cafe

rolled into one. Stop by to check out the latest exhibitions by Portuguese creatives and fashion and accessories – from bold, poppy prints by Hafu and sustainable street wear by Skunkfunk to backpacks by Eastpack and Ediel cork bags.

Casa Ramos FOOD

(Map p366; Rua Sá da Bandeira 347; ⏲9am-7pm Mon-Fri, 9am-1pm Sat) Old-world grocery stores like this one are a dying breed. Besides beans, *bacalhau* and *alheira* sausages by the kilo, you'll find everything from traditional sweets to teas and charcuterie here.

Arcádia CHOCOLATE

(Map p366; www.arcadia.pt; Rua do Almada 63; ⏲9.30am-7pm Mon-Fri, 9am-1pm Sat) Purveyors of handcrafted chocolates, Arcádia has been reeling in the sweet-toothed locals since 1933. This gloriously old-fashioned shop is a Wonka-like wonderland of confectionery, with gift-boxed pralines and flavoured bonbons, cocoa-rich bars, chocolates with Calém port or in the delicate form of hearts and flowers, and almond liqueur dragées – all made with care to traditional recipes.

Miragaia

★CC Bombarda MALL

(Map p366; Rua Miguel Bombarda 285; ⏲noon-8pm Mon-Sat) Amid the galleries along Rua Miguel Bombarda, this small, unique shopping mall is a highlight. Inside you'll find stores selling locally designed urban wear, gourmet teas, organic cosmetics, jewellery, vinyl, bonsai trees, stylish home knick-knacks and other hipster-pleasing delights. There's a cafe serving light bites in an internal courtyard.

Armazém CRAFTS, VINTAGE

(Map p366; Rua da Miragaia 93; ⏲11.30am-8pm) Bang on trend with Porto's thirst for new creative spaces is the hipsterish Armazém, located in a converted warehouse down by the river. A gallery, cafe and store all under one roof, with an open fire burning at its centre, it sells a pinch of everything – vintage garb, antiques, vinyl, artwork, ceramics and funky Portuguese-designed Mexxca bags and fashion.

águas furtadas ARTS, FASHION

(Map p366; www.aguasfurtadasdesign.blogspot.co.uk; Rua de Miguel Bombarda 285; ⏲10am-8pm Mon-Sat, 1-7pm Sun) This boutique is a treasure trove of funky Portuguese fashion, design, crafts and accessories, including born-again Barcelos cockerels in candy-bright colours and exquisitely illustrated pieces by influential Porto-based graphic designer Benedita Feijó.

CRU ARTS & CRAFTS

(Map p366; www.cru-cowork.com; Rua do Rosário 211; ⏲10am-8pm Mon-Fri, 2-8pm Sat) Allowing Portuguese designers to give flight to their fantasy, this unique gallery space crackles with creativity. What's on offer changes frequently, but at any one time you might find understated fashion, ceramics, accessories, art and beautifully handcrafted jewellery.

Flapper VINTAGE

(Map p366; Rua Miguel Bombarda 462; ⏲2.30-7.30pm) Nip into this diva's delight of a vintage and secondhand store to be time-warped back several decades. Besides clothing and glam accessories – rhinestone-studded clutch bags, pillbox hats, kitten heels etc – you'll find ceramics, clocks, dolls and more.

Foz do Douro

Yellow Boat FASHION & ACCESSORIES

(www.theyellowboatstore.com; Rua Rui Barbosa 21; ⏲11.30am-7.30pm Mon-Sat) A fashion boutique, interior design and concept store rolled into one urban-cool whole, the Yellow Boat sells – among other things – objects that are inspired by the sea, summer and beach, often with an emphasis on recycled materials.

Mercado da Foz MARKET

(Rua de Diu; ⏲7am-1pm Mon & Sat, to 7pm Tue-Fri) Stalls are piled high with fresh produce and flowers at this little covered market. For a bite to eat, stop by **Esquina do Mercado**, where you can sample (and buy) Trás-os-Montes cheeses and smoked sausages, Douro wines and meltingly tender *leitão* (suckling pig) from the Bairrada region.

Information

EMERGENCY

Police Station (☎222 092 000; Largo 1 de Dezembro)

Tourist Police (☎222 081 833; Rua Clube dos Fenianos 11; ⏲8am-2am) Multilingual station beside the main city *turismo*.

MEDICAL SERVICES

Santo António Hospital (☎222 077 500; www.chporto.pt; Largo Prof Abel Salazar) Has English-speaking staff.

ANDANTE CARD

➡ For maximum convenience, Porto's transport system offers the rechargeable **Andante Card** (www.linhandante.com), allowing smooth movement between tram, metro, funicular and many bus lines.

➡ The card itself costs only €0.60 and can be recharged for one year. Once you've purchased the card, charge it with credit according to which zones you will be travelling in.

➡ Purchase credit at metro ticket machines and staffed TIP booths at central hubs such as Casa da Música and Trindade, as well as the STCP office, the funicular, the electric tram museum and a scattering of other authorised sales points.

➡ Your time begins from when you first enter the vehicle or platform: just wave the card in front of a validation machine marked 'Andante'.

➡ Each trip allows you to move between methods of transport without additional cost.

POST

Post Office (Map p366; Praça General Humberto Delgado 320; ⏲8am-9pm Mon-Fri, 9am-6pm Sat) Across from the main tourist office

Post Office (Map p366; Praça da Batalha; ⏲9am-6pm Mon-Fri)

TOURIST INFORMATION

City Centre Turismo (Map p366; ☎223 393 472; www.visitporto.travel; Rua Clube dos Fenianos 25; ⏲9am-8pm May-Oct, to & 7pm Nov-Apr) The main city *turismo* has a detailed city map, a transport map and the *Agenda do Porto* cultural calendar, among other printed materials.

iPoint Campanhã (Map p364; www.visitporto.travel; Estação de Comboio de Campanhã; ⏲9.30am-6.30pm Jun-Aug) Seasonal information point run by the *turismo* at the Campanhã train station

iPoint Ribeira (Map p366; www.visitporto.travel; Praça da Ribeira; ⏲10am-7pm May-Sep, to 6pm Oct) Useful *turismo*-run information point on Praça da Ribeira, open seasonally.

Turismo (Gaia) (Map p366; ☎223 758 288; www.cm-gaia.pt; Av Diogo Leite 135; ⏲10am-8pm daily Apr-Sep, 9am-6pm Mon-Sat Oct-Mar) Gaia's *turismo* dispenses a good town map and a brochure listing all the lodges open for tours.

Turismo (Sé) (Map p366; ☎223 393 472; www.visitporto.travel; Terreiro da Sé; ⏲9am-8pm May-Oct, to 7pm Nov-Apr) Handy tourist office right next to the cathedral. Offers a ticket and hotel booking service.

Getting There & Away

AIR

Situated around 19km northwest of the city centre, the gleaming, ultra-modern **Francisco de Sá Carneiro Airport** (☎229 432 400; 4470-558 Maia) operates direct flights to major international hubs including London, Brussels, Madrid, Frankfurt and Toronto.

TAP (www.flytap.com) has multiple daily flights to/from Lisbon. There are also low-cost carriers, such as **easyJet** (www.easyjet.com) and **Ryanair** (www.ryanair.com), with nonstop services to London, Madrid, Paris, Frankfurt, Amsterdam and Brussels

BUS

As in many Portuguese cities, bus services in Porto are regrettably dispersed, with no central bus terminal. The good news is that there are frequent services to just about everywhere in northern Portugal, as well as express services to Coimbra, Lisbon and points south.

Domestic

Renex (Map p366; www.renex.pt; Rua Campo Mártires de Pátria 37) is the choice for Lisbon (€20, 3½ hours), with the most direct routes and eight to 12 departures daily, including one continuing on to the Algarve. Renex also has frequent services to Braga (€6, 1¼ hours). Buses depart from Campo dos á Mártires da Patria 37.

Rede Expressos (Map p366; ☎222 006 954; www.rede-expressos.pt; Rua Alexandre Herculano 366) has services to the entire country from the smoggy **Paragem Atlântico terminal** (Map p366).

For fast Minho connections, mainly on weekdays, three companies offer routes: **Transdev-Norte** (Map p366; www.transdev.pt; Garagem Atlântico, Rua de Alexandre Herculano 366) runs chiefly to Braga (€6, 1¼ hours) and Guimarães (€6, one hour); **AV Minho** (Map p366; www.avminho.pt) runs four times daily via Vila do Conde (€2.45, one hour) to Viana do Castelo (€5.60, 2¼ hours); and **Rodonorte** (Map p366; www.rodonorte.pt; Rua Ateneu Comercial do Porto 19) has multiple daily departures (fewer on Saturday) for Amarante (€6.30, one hour), Vila Real (€9, 1½ hours) and Bragança (€14, 3½ hours).

International

There are Eurolines (www.eurolines.com) departures from Interface Casa da Música (Rua Capitão

Henrique Calvão). Northern Portugal's own international carrier, **Internorte** (Map p364; www.internorte.pt; Praça da Galiza 96), departs from the same terminal. Most travel agencies can book outbound buses with either operator.

CAR & MOTORCYCLE

All major Portuguese and international car-hire companies have offices at the airport including **Cael** (☎229 964 269; www.cael.pt; Av Arquitecto Fernando Tavora 2021), while some, such as **Europcar** (☎222 057 737; www.europcar.com; Rua Antonio Bessa Leite 1478), also have offices downtown. Prices start at around €30 per day.

TRAIN

There are information points at both São Bento and Campanhã stations. Alternatively, call ☎707 210 220 or consult www.cp.pt.

Long-Distance Trains

Porto is the main rail hub for northern Portugal. Long-distance services start at **Campanhã** (Rua Monte da Estação) station, 3km east of the centre.

Direct IC destinations from Porto include Lisbon (2nd class €24.30, 3¼ hours, hourly).

Urbano, Regional & Interregional Trains

Most *urbano*, *regional* and *interregional* (IR) trains depart from the stunning indoor-outdoor **São Bento** (Praça Almeida Garrett) station, though all of these lines also pass through Campanhã.

For destinations on the Braga, Guimarães and Aveiro lines, or up the Douro Valley as far as Marco de Canaveses, take one of the frequent *urbano* trains. Don't spend extra money on *interregional, intercidade* (IC) or Alfa Pendular (AP) trains to these destinations as the *urbano* trains take around the same amount of time; Porto to Braga costs €14.20 by AP train, but around a fifth of that by *urbano*.

ℹ Getting Around

TO/FROM THE AIRPORT

- The Metro do Porto (http://en.metrodoporto.pt) violet line E (direction Estádio do Dragão) links the airport to downtown Porto; change at Trindade onto yellow line D (direction Santo Ovídio) for Aliados and São Bento stops. A one-way ticket costs €1.85 and the journey takes around 45 minutes.
- A daytime taxi costs €20 to €25 to/from the centre. Taxis authorised to run *from* the airport are labelled 'Maia' and/or 'Vila Nova de Telha'; the rank is just outside the Arrivals Hall. In peak-traffic time, allow an hour or more between the city centre and the airport.
- STCP (www.stcp.pt) runs a couple of public buses between the airport and the centre; the most useful is the 601 to Cordoaria, departing every 30 minutes from 5.30am to 11.30pm. A single costs €1.85.

BICYCLE

- Despite the narrow alleyways, steep hills and cobbled streets, cyclists are ubiquitous in Porto, and there are some particularly great rides along the Douro on dedicated bike paths from Ribeira to Foz or from Vila Nova de Gaia to Afurada and beyond.
- Bike rental outlets include **Fold 'n' Visit** (Map p366; ☎220 997 106; www.foldnvisit.com; Rua Alferes Malheiro 139; rental per half/full day from €13/17), **L&L** (Map p366; ☎223 251 722; www.lopesrentabike.wix.com/porto; 2nd fl, Largo São Domingos 13; bike hire per 1/24hr €2.50/15; ⏲10am-7pm) and **Porto Rent a Bike** (Map p366; ☎912 562 190, 222 022 375; www.portorentabike.com; Avenida Gustavo Eiffel 280; bikes per half-/full day from €10/15; ⏲10am-2pm & 3-7pm). A full day's rental will set you back around €15. Many also offer guided cycling tours.
- **Vieguini** (☎914 306 838; www.vieguini.pt; Rua Nova da Alfandega 7; bikes per half-/full day €8/12; ⏲9am-7.30pm) has a great selection of high-quality mountain bikes and also rents motor scooters (€28 per day).

BUS

- Porto's transport agency **STCP** (Sociedade de Transportes Colectivos do Porto; ☎808 200 166; www.stcp.pt) runs an extensive bus system, with central hubs at Praça da Liberdade (the south end of Av dos Aliados), Praça Almeida Garrett (in front of São Bento train station) and Cordoaria.
- Special all-night lines also run approximately hourly, leaving Aliados on the hour and returning on the half-hour from 1am to 5.30am.
- City *turismos* have maps and timetables for day and night routes.
- A ticket bought on the bus (one way to anywhere in the STCP system) costs €1.85, or €1.20 with an Andante Card.

CAR & MOTORCYCLE

- Driving in central Porto is stressful – avoid it if possible. Narrow one-way streets, construction and heavy traffic can turn 500m into half a morning.
- Street parking is tight, with a two-hour maximum stay on weekdays. There is no limit on weekends and parking spaces are more readily available.
- Most squares have underground, fee-charging lots – follow the blue Ps. Be aware that opportunistic locals may guide you into places and then expect tips. They can be very disagreeable if you don't comply. They may also direct you into an illegal spot – be sure to double-check signs.

FUNICULAR

The restored **Funicular dos Guindais** (one-way €2.50; ⌚8am-10pm May-Oct, to 8pm Nov-Apr) shuttles up and down a steep incline with tremendous river and bluff views from Av Gustavo Eiffel, opposite Ponte de Dom Luís I, to Rua Augusto Rosa, near Batalha and the cathedral. The funicular is part of the Andante Card scheme (www.linhandante.com).

METRO

- Porto's newish **metro system** (http://en.metrodoporto.pt) is compact and fairly easy to navigate – though not comprehensive. It comprises six metropolitan lines that all converge at the Trindade stop.
- Three lines – Linha A (blue, to Matosinhos), Linha B (red, to Vila do Conde and Póvoa de Varzim) and Linha C (green, to Maia) – run from Estádio do Dragão via Campanhã train station through the city centre, and then on to far-flung northern and western suburbs.
- Linha D (yellow) runs north–south from Hospital São João to João de Deus in Vila Nova de Gaia, crossing the upper deck of Ponte de Dom Luís I. Key stops include Aliados and São Bento station.
- Linha E (violet) connects Linha B with the airport.
- Linha F (orange) links Senhora da Hora to Fânzeres.
- Tickets cost €1.20/1.50/1.85 for zone 2/3/4 with an Andante Card (p393). Zone 2 covers the whole city centre east to Campanhã train station, south to Vila Nova de Gaia and west to Foz do Douro.
- Buy tickets from metro ticket machines, which have English-language menus. All stations also have maps.
- For timetables, maps and fares, visit the metro website.
- The metro runs from around 6am to 1am daily.

TAXI

There are taxi ranks throughout the centre, or you can call **Táxis Invicta** (☎225 076 400). Count on paying around €5 to €7 for trips within the centre during the day, with a 20% surcharge at night. There's an extra charge if you leave the city limits, which includes Vila Nova de Gaia.

TRAM

- Only three Porto tram lines remain, but they're very scenic.
- The Massarelos stop, on the riverfront near the foot of the Palácio de Cristal, is the tram system's hub. From here, line 1 trundles along the river to nearby Praça Infante Dom Henrique (Ribeira). Line 1E (appears as a crossed-out '1') heads down the river in the opposite direction, towards Foz do Douro.
- Line 18 heads uphill to the Igreja do Carmo and Jardim do Cordoaria.
- Line 22 makes a loop through the centre from Carmo to Batalha/Guindais.
- Trams run approximately every 30 minutes from 8am to 9pm.
- One-way tickets cost €2.50; a day pass costs €8.

Vila do Conde

POP 28,600

With its quaint historic heart, poetic folk hero, glassy river mouth, luscious beaches and salty past, you can understand why Vila do Conde is a popular weekend getaway for Porto residents. An important salt exporter during Roman times and a prime shipbuilding port during the Age of Discoveries, the town still drips history. Looming over it is the immense hilltop Mosteiro de Santa Clara, which, along with surviving segments of a long-legged medieval aqueduct, lends the town an air of monumentality. In addition to this, Vila do Conde's beaches are some of the best north of Porto, and a metro link makes getting here an easy afternoon jaunt from downtown Porto.

Vila do Conde sits on the north side of the Rio Ave, where it empties into the sea. From the metro station, look for the aqueduct (about 100m away) and follow it towards the large convent (another 400m). From here it's a few steep blocks downhill to the town's historic centre. From the centre it's another kilometre via Avenida Dr Artur Cunha Araújo or Avenida Dr João Canavarro to Avenida do Brasil and the 3km-long beach.

Sights

Alfândega Regia Museu da Construção Naval MUSEUM

(Museum of Shipbuilding; Largo da Alfândega; adult/child €1/0.50; ⌚10am-6pm Tue-Sun) Shipbuilding has been in Vila do Conde's bones since at least the 13th century. This museum on the banks of the Rio Ave, just west of Praça da República, has exhibits on trade and models of hand-built *nau* (a sort of pot-bellied caravel once used for cargo and naval operations). The real attraction, however, is the replica of a 16th-century *nau* moored opposite the museum.

Casa do Barco MUSEUM

(Cais das Lavandeiras; ⌚9am-7pm) FREE This glass-box museum on the southwest corner of Praça da República has a basement that offers up models, photo displays, old fishing gear and a full-sized boat that provide a glimpse into the city's shipbuilding past.

Museu das Rendas de Bilros MUSEUM
(Museum of Bobbin Lace; Rua São Bento 70; €1; ⏲10am-6pm Tue-Sun) It's no accident that seafaring fingers, so deft at making nets, should also be good at lace making. Vila do Conde is one of the few places in Portugal with an active school of the art, founded in 1918. Housed in a typical 18th-century townhouse in the town centre, the school includes the Museu das Rendas de Bilros, which displays eye-popping examples of work from Portugal and around the world.

Casa de José Régio MUSEUM
(Av José Régio; €1; ⏲10am-1pm & 2-6pm Tue-Sun) Religious art, antique furnishings, ceramics and early-20th-century contemporary art – including some stunning Julio canvases – can be glimpsed at the Casa de José Régio. Named after the distinguished local-born poet, playwright and healer José Régio (1901–69), who lived and worked here, admission includes a guided tour through each floor of the townhouse. The stunning upstairs office and library, and the rooftop garden, are highlights.

Beaches

Vila do Conde's two best beaches, **Praia da Forno** and **Praia de Nossa Senhora da Guia**, are wide, blond and picturesque even when the winds howl. Most of the year, seas are calm and suitable for young children. Buses marked 'Vila do Conde' from Póvoa de Varzim stop at the station and continue to the beach, about half-hourly all day from Monday to Friday (fewer on weekends).

Surfers can sometimes ride swells near the 17th-century Castelo de São João Baptista, at the river mouth. Once a castle, it's now a small deluxe hotel with a glamorous, hard-partying reputation.

Festivals & Events

Festa de São João RELIGIOUS
The town's biggest event takes place on the days leading up to 23 June, with fireworks, concerts, a traditional boat parade and a religious procession through the streets.

Curtas FILM
(www.curtas.pt) For over 20 years, this seaside hamlet has been hosting an edgy and popular short film fest each July.

Feira Nacional de Artesanato FAIR
(http://fna.vconde.org) A major fair showcasing Portuguese handicrafts is on during the last week of July through the first week of August.

Sleeping

Pensão Patarata GUESTHOUSE €
(☎252 631 894; Cais das Lavandeiras 18; s/d €30/40; 📶) Looking over the river, off the southwest corner of the square, this place has simple but sweet rooms with high ceilings and wooden furnishings, and all have river views. Breakfast is served at extra cost.

Parque de Campismo da Árvore CAMPGROUND €
(☎252 633 225; www.cnm.org.pt; Rua do Cabreiro, Árvore; sites per adult/tent €7.50/6; 📶🏊) Tightly packed and well shaded, this campsite is 3km from town, right next to Praia da Árvore.

Forte São João Baptista HOTEL €€
(☎918 894 486; www.fortesaojoao.pt; Avenida Brasil; s/d €80/105; P📶) Hidden within the forbidding, metres-thick stone walls of a 17th-century fort is this oasis of luxury. The hotel's eight rooms are cosy but plush, and popular on party nights (p397), even if you do have to forfeit your keys until 6am.

Hotel Brazão HOTEL €€
(☎252 642 016; www.hotelbrazao.pt; Avenida Dr João Canavarro; s/d €50/66; P❄@📶) Set in a restored 16th-century nobleman's house, this guesthouse has been added onto at various times over the years, making it a patchwork of old and new. Rooms are spacious and comfortable, with sea-green carpeting and crown mouldings. Situated 200m west of the Rua 25 de Abril *turismo*, it's excellent low-season value.

Eating

Around the corner from the *turismo*, Praça José Régio, a rather ugly modern plaza in the middle of the quaint old town, has an assortment of outdoor cafes, bars and restaurants.

Adega Gavina SEAFOOD €
(☎917 834 517; Rua Cais das Lavandeiras 56; mains €5-7; ⏲noon-3.30pm & 7.30pm-midnight Tue-Sat, noon-3.30pm Sun) The top choice in town offers tremendous roast-chicken lunches for a song, and burns good steaks, but first and foremost it's a seafood grill. Stroll into the kitschy interior and peruse the chalkboard menu, then choose your catch and watch the

chef grill it perfectly on the street-side barbecue. Excellent-value lunch specials come with potatoes, rice and steamed greens.

Restaurante Le Villageois PORTUGUESE €€
(Praça da República 94; mains €9-18; ⏰ noon-3pm & 7-10pm Tue-Sun) The popular Villageois has been preparing terrific steaks and fresh seafood in French-Portuguese style since 1977. The airy dining room is appointed with *azulejos*, the appealing sun-drenched patio is classy, and the bar is full. It hosts live fado on Friday and Saturday nights.

O Cangalho SEAFOOD €€
(☎ 252 110 898; Rua Cais das Lavandeiras 48; mains €10-15; ⏰ noon-3pm & 7-10pm Mon-Sat) The funky, tricked-out vintage Land Rover parked out front may catch your eye, and as you come close you'll notice the stylish bistro interior and fresh fish on ice. Great style, great vibe, tasty seafood.

Drinking & Nightlife

Forte São João Baptista CLUB
(www.fortesaojoao.pt; Avenida Brasil; ⏰ Jul-Sep) The best party spot in Vila do Conde: think mighty, seasonal blinged-out electronica throw-downs with international DJs, Bedouin tents, spinning disco balls and up to 2000 people spilling onto the windswept sands and dancing on the ancient fortress walls. Parties last until 6am. Make arrangements in advance to get on the door list.

Cacau BAR
(www.facebook.com/cacaucafebar; Praça da República 42; ⏰ 9am-2am) Running deep into the hollowed-out ground floor of an old stone relic, Cacau is a cafe by day and a bar by night, with electro tunes and a young crowd.

Information

Interactive Tourism Store (☎ 252 248 445; Cais das Lavandeiras; ⏰ 9am-7pm Jun-Sep, to 6pm Oct-May) This new interactive *turismo* has a wealth of materials and helpful staff.

Turismo (☎ 252 248 473; www.cm-viladoconde.pt; Rua 25 de Abril 103; ⏰ 9.30am-12.30pm & 2-6pm Mon-Fri) This friendly *turismo* has maps and some nice examples of local lace, but the staff do not speak much English.

Getting There & Away

Vila do Conde is 33km from Porto, and is a straight shot on the IC1 Hwy. It's served by Porto's Linha B (red) metro line to Póvoa de Varzim, stopping about 400m from the town centre. A one-way trip from central Porto costs €2.30 and takes about an hour – the trip is a little faster if you catch the express service.

Buses stop on Rua 5 de Outubro, near the *turismo*. AV Minho express buses stop hourly (fewer on weekends) en route to Porto (€3, 50 minutes) and Viana do Castelo (€4, one hour).

Amarante

POP 11,260

Handsomely set on a bend in the Rio Tâmega, the sleepy village of Amarante is dominated by a striking church and monastery, which sit theatrically beside a rebuilt medieval bridge that still bears city traffic. The willow-lined riverbanks lend a pastoral charm, as do the balconied houses and switchback lanes that rise quickly from the narrow valley floor.

The town enjoys some small degree of fame for being the hometown of São Gonçalo. Portugal's St Valentine, he is the target for lonely hearts who make pilgrimages here in the hope of finding true love. Surrounded by prized vineyards, Amarante is also something of a foodie mecca. As well as wine, the region produces excellent cheeses, *fumeiros* (smoked meats) and rich pastries.

History

The town may date back as far as the 4th century BC, though Gonçalo, a 13th-century hermit, is credited with everything from the founding of the town to the construction of its first bridge.

Amarante's strategically placed bridge (Ponte de São Gonçalo) almost proved to be its undoing in 1809, when the French lost their brief grip on Portugal. Marshal Soult's troops retreated to the northeast after abandoning Porto, plundering as they went. A French detachment arrived here in search of a river crossing, but plucky citizens and troops held them off, allowing residents to escape to the far bank. The French retaliated by burning down much of the town.

Amarante has also suffered frequent natural invasions by the Tâmega. Little *cheia* (high-water level) plaques in Rua 31 de Janeiro and Largo Conselheiro António Cândido tell the harrowing story.

Sights

Ponte de São Gonçalo BRIDGE
A symbol of the town's heroic defence against the French (marked by a plaque at

the southeastern end), the granite Ponte de São Gonçalo is Amarante's visual centrepiece. The original bridge, allegedly built at Gonçalo's urging in the 13th century, collapsed in a flood in 1763; this one was completed in 1790.

Museu Amadeo de Souza-Cardoso MUSEUM
(Alameda Teixeira de Pascoaes; adult/child €1/free; ⏲10am-12.30pm & 2-6pm Tue-Sun Jun-Sep, 9.30am-12.30pm & 2-5.30pm Oct-May) Hidden in one of the Mosteiro de São Gonçalo's cloisters is this delightfully eclectic collection of modernist and contemporary art, a pleasant surprise in a town of this size. The museum is named after Amarante's favourite son, artist Amadeo de Souza-Cardoso (1889–1918) – one of the best-known Portuguese artists of the 20th century, who abandoned naturalism for home-grown versions of Impressionism and cubism. The museum is full of his sketches, cartoons, portraits and abstracts.

Mosteiro de São Gonçalo MONASTERY
(⏲9am-7pm Jun-Sep, to 5.30pm Oct-May) Founded in 1543 by João III, the Mosteiro de São Gonçalo and **Igreja de São Gonçalo** weren't completed until 1620. Above the church's photogenic, Italian Renaissance side portal is an arcaded gallery, 30m high, with 17th-century statues of Dom João and the other kings who ruled while the monastery was under construction: Sebastião, Henrique and Felipe I.

The bell tower was added in the 18th century. The best view of the royal statues is from the steep lane just west of the church entrance. Within the lofty interior is an impressive gilded baroque altar, pulpits, an organ casing held up by fishtailed giants, and Gonçalo's tomb in a tiny chapel (to the left of the altar). Tradition has it that those in search of a partner will have their wish granted within a year if they touch the statue above his tomb. Sure enough, its limestone toes, fingers and face have been all but rubbed away by hopefuls.

Igreja de São Domingos CHURCH
(Praça da República; cloister €1; ⏲3-7pm Jun-Sep, to 5.30pm Oct-May) Rising beside São Gonçalo are several impressively steep switchbacks topped by this round, 18th-century church. The views from here are stunning.

Solar dos Magalhães RUINS
This burned-out skeleton of an old manor house situated above Rua Cândido dos Reis, near the train station, has been left in ruins – a stark and uncaptioned memento from Napoleon's troops.

Activities

Rio Tâmega BOATING, WALKING
(boat hire per 30min/1hr €5/10; ⏲boat hire 9am-8pm) For an idyllic river stroll, take the cobbled path along the north bank. A good picnic or daydreaming spot is the rocky outcropping overlooking the rapids 400m east of the bridge. You can also potter about the peaceful Rio Tâmega in a paddle or row boat; boat hire is available along the riverbank.

Festivals & Events

Festas de Junho RELIGIOUS
Held during the first weekend in June, *festa* highlights include an all-night drumming competition, a livestock fair, a handicrafts market and fireworks, all rounded off with Sunday's procession in honour of the main man – São Gonçalo.

Sleeping

Residencial Estoril GUESTHOUSE €
(☎255 431 291; mnestoril@hotmail.com; Rua 31 de Janeiro 150-152; s €30, d €35-50; 📶) Jutting out over the riverbank, Estoril has basic wood-floor rooms with small bathrooms, a couple of them with sweet views of São Gonçalo's bridge. It is one of the only spots to offer rooms year-round. Breakfast is charged extra.

Parque de Campismo de Penedo da Rainha CAMPGROUND €
(☎255 437 630; ccporto@sapo.pt; Rua Pedro Alvellos; sites per adult/tent/car €2.50/3.20/3.70; ⏲Feb-Nov; 🏊) A big, shady site that cascades down to the river, this campground has a *minimercado* (grocery shop) and bar. It's about 1km upstream (and uphill) from the town centre.

Casa da Calçada HISTORIC HOTEL €€€
(☎255 410 830; www.casadacalcada.com; Largo do Paço 6; s/d €175/185; P❄📶🏊) Oozing class and boasting every creature comfort, this 16th-century palace (rebuilt following Napoleon's destructive campaign) rises royally above the Ponte de São Gonçalo. Past the antique-filled parlours lie spacious, elegantly furnished rooms with marble bathrooms. The jacuzzi and pool overlook the hotel's vineyards. This Relais & Châteaux property is easily Amarante's top choice.

Eating & Drinking

Open-air cafes and bars pop up every summer along the riverside on Avenida General Silveira, opposite Mosteiro de São Gonçalo.

Confeitaria da Ponte BAKERY €
(255 432 034; Rua 31 de Janeiro 186; pastries €1.10-1.50; 8.30am-8.30pm) Boasting a peaceful, shaded terrace overlooking the bridge, this traditional bakery has the best ambience for enjoying Amarante's famous pastries and eggy custards.

Principe CAFE €
(255 431 009; Largo Conselheiro António Cândido 83; sandwiches €3-5; noon-10pm) If you're hankering to try the smoked meats Amarante is famous for, you might consider this modernised bar and cafe, where the barman treats his sandwiches like a gentleman and keeps his Sintra beer icy.

Mercado Municipal MARKET €
(Rua Capitão Augusto Casimiro; 8.30am-1pm) You can get picnic fixings at the mercado municipal (municipal market) , the big days of which are Wednesday and Saturday.

Adega Regional Quelha PORTUGUESE €€
(255 425 786; Rua de Olivença; mains €5-14.50; 11.30am-2pm & 7-10pm Mon-Thu, 11.30am-10pm Fri-Sun) One of several low-key *adegas* (wine taverns) proffering Amarante's fine smoked meats and cheese, Adega Regional Quelha is a good place to sample the local delicacies among locals. Grab a bite and a jug of red wine at the bar, or sit down to a simple but filling meal.

Zé da Calçada PORTUGUESE €€
(255 426 814; Rua 31 de Janeiro 83; mains €8-12; noon-10pm) Excellent northern cuisine served in an elegant country-style dining room or on a verandah with idyllic views of the *moistero* and the bridge. Top picks here include duck rice and grilled goat. Weekday lunch specials are great value.

Information

Turismo (255 420 246; www.amarante.pt/turismo; Alameda Teixeira de Pascoaes; 9am-5.30pm Mon-Fri) Next to the museum, in the former cloisters of São Gonçalo. It offers city maps, but very little English is spoken.

Getting There & Away

Self-drivers can use Amarante as an alternative base to explore the *quintas* (estates) of the Alto Douro.

There is free parking just east of the *turismo* where the *mercado municipal* is held; avoid parking there overnight before crowded market days (Wednesday and Saturday).

Lamego

POP 26,690

Most people come to Lamego – a prim, prosperous town 10km south of the Rio Douro – to see (and possibly to climb) the astonishing baroque stairway that zigzags its way up to the Igreja de Nossa Senhora dos Remédios. The old town centre itself has a mix of winding narrow lanes and tree-lined boulevards, with spotlit medieval landmarks looming from almost every angle. Connoisseurs also swear by Lamego's *raposeira,* the town's famously fragrant sparkling wine, which provides a fine break between bouts of port.

Lamego is a natural base for exploring the half ruined monasteries and chapels in the surrounding environs, one of which dates back to the time of the Visigoths.

History

Lamego was an important centre even in the time of the Visigoths and has had a cathedral since at least the 6th century. The city fell to the Moors in the 8th century and remained in their hands until the 11th century. In 1143 Portugal's first *cortes* (parliament) was convened here to confirm Afonso Henriques as Portugal's first king. The little town grew fat thanks to its position on trading routes between the Douro and the Beiras and, thanks to its wine, was already famous in the 16th century.

Sights

Museu de Lamego MUSEUM
(Largo de Camões; adult/student €3/1.50; 10am-6pm Tue-Sun) Occupying a grand, 18th-century episcopal palace, the Museu de Lamego is one of Portugal's finest regional museums. The collection features five entrancing works by renowned 16th-century Portuguese painter Vasco Fernandes (Grão Vasco), richly worked Brussels tapestries from the same period, and an extraordinarily diverse collection of heavily gilded 17th-century chapels rescued in their entirety from the long-gone Convento das Chagas.

Igreja de Nossa Senhora dos Remédios CHURCH
(7.30am-8pm May-Sep, to 6pm Oct-Apr) One of the country's most important pilgrimage sites, this twin-towered 18th-century church

has a trim blue-and-white stucco interior with a sky-blue rococo ceiling and a gilded altar. The church, however, is quite overshadowed by the zigzagging monumental **stairway** that leads up to it. The 600-plus steps are resplendent with *azulejos,* urns, fountains and statues, adding up to one of the greatest works in Portuguese rococo style.

It's a dramatic sight at any time, but the action peaks in late summer when thousands of devotees arrive and ascend the steps in search of miracles during the Festa de Nossa Senhora dos Remédios. Most offerings are made at the rear altar where Mother Mary reigns supreme. If you can't face the climb by foot, a road (turn-off 1km out on the Viseu road) winds up the hill for about 3km before reaching the top.

Sé CATHEDRAL
(Largo da Sé; ⌚9am-1pm & 3-6.30pm) Older than Portugal itself, Lamego's striking *sé* has been declared a national monument. There is little left of the 12th-century original except the base of its square belfry. The rest of the structure, including the brilliantly carved Gothic triple portal, dates mostly from the 16th and 18th centuries. Arresting biblical frescoes and the high choir stalls are the work of 18th-century Italian baroque architect Nicolau Nasoni, who left his mark all over Porto. With luck you will find the door open to the peaceful 16th-century cloisters, located just around the corner.

Castelo CASTLE
(Rua do Castelo; admission by donation; ⌚10am-12.30pm & 2-5.30pm) Climb the narrow, winding Rua da Olaria to this modest medieval castle, encircled by a clutch of ancient stone houses. What little remains – some walls and a tower – has belonged to the Boy Scouts ever since their mammoth 1970s effort to clear the site after years of use as a glorified rubbish tip. Unfortunately, it isn't always open. Still, walk through narrow stone lanes and you'll be treated to glorious views from the castle's perch.

Igreja Santa Maria de Almacave CHURCH
(Rua das Cortes 2; ⌚8am-noon & 4-7pm) This unassuming little church is Lamego's oldest surviving building, much of it dating back to the 12th century. It's thought that after winning independence from Spain, Portugal's first king assembled his initial *cortes* (an early version of Portugal's proto-democratic assembly of nobles and clergy) here from 1142 to 1144. It occupies the site of a Moorish cemetery; some of its grave markers are now in the Museu de Lamego.

Festivals & Events

Festa de Nossa Senhora dos Remédios RELIGIOUS
Lamego's biggest party runs for several weeks from late August to mid-September. In an afternoon procession on 8 September, ox-drawn carts rattle through the streets carrying *tableaux vivants* (religious scenes represented by costumed people), and devotees slowly ascend the stairway on their knees. Less-pious events in the run-up include rock concerts, folk dancing, car racing, parades and at least one all-night party.

Sleeping

Residencial Solar da Sé GUESTHOUSE €
(☎254 612 060; Avenida Visconde Guedes Teixeira 7; s/d €25/45; ❄📶) There are great deals to be had on rooms with French windows opening onto the *sé*. The carpet is a bit aged, but there's a funky modernist groove you might like. Or love.

Hotel Solar dos Pachecos HOTEL €€
(☎254 600 300; Avenida Visconde Guedes Teixeira 27; s/d €50/75; P❄📶) Occupying an impressive 18th-century nobleman's city home, this central place offers clean, carpeted rooms with exposed stone walls, ample light, high ceilings and wide terraces out the back.

Casa de Santo António de Britiande GUESTHOUSE €€€
(☎254 699 346; www.casasantoantoniobritiande.com; Largo de São Sebastião, Britiande; s/d/studio €90/220/240; P❄📶🏊) A stellar option just 5km southeast of Lamego in the village of Britiande, this lovely historic manor surrounded by fruit orchards has gorgeously landscaped gardens with a swimming pool. It's a great base for exploring the Alto Douro, and tops for birdwatching tours. The friendly owner prepares delicious meals on request.

Eating

Pastelaria Scala CAFE €
(Avenida Visconde Guedes Teixeira 31; pastries €1-2; ⌚8am-10pm) The charming wooden booths and tables are almost always crammed with locals who descend for great coffee and better pastries.

Trás da Sé PORTUGUESE €
(☎254 614 075; Largo da Sé; mains €5-6; ⏲noon-10pm) Congratulations to the chef line the walls at this *adega*-style place, where the atmosphere is friendly, the menu short and simple, the food good and the *vinho maduro* (matured wine) list long.

Mercado Municipal MARKET €
(Avenida 5 de Outubre; ⏲7.30am-6pm Mon-Fri, to 5pm Sat) The *mercado municipal* sells Lamego's famous hams and wines – ideal picnic food.

Drinking & Nightlife

Old Rock Caffe BAR
(Rua da Olaria; ⏲2pm-2am) One of the town's most inviting bars, with an alternative vibe and great cocktails.

Casa do Castelo BAR
(Rua do Castelinho 25; ⏲noon-2am Tue-Sun) A hidden drinking spot lies inside the walls of the *castelo*. This atmospheric landmark bar is subdued during the week, but packs in a festive student crowd on weekends.

Entertainment

Teatro Ribeiro Conceição THEATRE
(☎254 600 070; www.teatroribeiroconceicao.pt; Largo de Camões; tickets €5-20) This handsomely restored theatre and cultural space hosts a wide range of programs throughout the year, from children's puppet shows to classical concerts, orchestral concerts and ballets. There is also a cafe that has outdoor seating.

Information

Turismo (☎254 099 000; www.cm-lamego.pt; Rua Regimento de Infantaria 9; ⏲10am-7.30pm) This fantastic tourist office is full of solid suggestions from warm, knowledgeable, English-speaking staff.

Getting There & Away

The most appealing route to Lamego from anywhere in the Douro valley is by train to Peso da Régua and by bus or taxi from there. A taxi from Régua costs about €15 to €20.

From Lamego's bus station, Joalto/EAVT and Rede Expressos are the only operators. Buses travel about hourly to Peso da Régua (€2.30, 30 minutes) and daily to Viseu (€8.90, 1¼ hours) and Lisbon (€18.50, 5¾ hours). The Lisbon bus also passes through Vila Real (€6, one hour) and Chaves (€11.40, 2¼ hours). **Copy Print** (☎254 619 447; Avenida Visconde Guedes Teixeira; ⏲8am-8pm), a newsagent beside the *turismo*, sells tickets for these services.

Self-drivers take note: parking can be tight in Lamego.

Around Lamego

Capela de São Pedro de Balsemão

Older than Portugal itself, this mysterious little **chapel** (Balsemão; ⏲2-5.30pm Mon & Tue, 10am-12.30pm & 2-5.30pm Wed-Sun) was probably built by Visigoths as early as the 6th century. With Corinthian columns, round arches and intriguing symbols etched into the walls, it certainly pre-dates the introduction of even Romanesque architecture to Portugal. More ornate 14th-century additions were commissioned by the Bishop of Porto, Afonso Pires, who is buried under a slab in the floor. Check out the ancient casket dominating the entrance chamber: supported by lions and intricately engraved, it depicts the Last Supper on one side and the Crucifixion on the other.

The chapel is tucked away in the hamlet of Balsemão, 3km northeast of Lamego above the Rio Balsemão. It's a pleasant downhill walk from Lamego through an old-world village, then a riparian corridor full of flowers, grapevines and wild shrubs, though it is a rather steep return trip. From the 17th-century Capela do Desterro at the end of Rua da Santa Cruz, head southeast over the river and follow the road to the left.

Mosteiro de São João de Tarouca

The stunning, massive yet skeletal, remains of Portugal's first Cistercian monastery, the **Mosteiro de São João de Tarouca** (Tarouca; ⏲10am-12.30pm & 2-6pm May-Sep, 9.30am-12.30pm & 2-5.30pm Oct-Apr), founded in 1124, stand eerily in the wooded Barosa valley below the Serra de Leomil, 15km southeast of Lamego. There is beauty in the decay, as a stream bisects the walls backed by a bowl of terraced hills. The monastery fell into ruin after religious orders were abolished in 1834.

Only the church, considerably altered in the 17th century, stands intact among the ghostly ruins of the monks' quarters. Its treasures include the gilded choir stalls, 18th-century *azulejos*, and the church's pride and joy – a luminous *São Pedro* painted by Gaspar Vaz, contemporary and colleague of Grão Vasco.

From Lamego, Joalto/EAVT has several services each weekday (fewer on weekends) to Tarouca (€2.30).

Mosteiro de Salzedas

With pink stone arches picturesquely mouldering in the sun, the Cistercian **Mosteiro de Salzedas** (Salzedas; €3; ⌚2.30-6pm Mon & Tue, 9.30am-1pm & 2.30-6pm Wed-Sun) is located 3km up the Barosa valley from Ucanha in Salzedas. This was one of the grandest monasteries in the land when it was built in 1168 with funds from Teresa Afonso, governess to Afonso Henriques' five children. The enormous church, which was extensively remodelled in the 18th century, is today a bit scruffy with decay, particularly its roofless cloisters next door; the faux crystal chandeliers are an odd sight, too.

Across from the church lies the old *judiaria*, with dark narrow lanes skirting around the gloomy centuries-old dwellings.

Peso da Régua

POP 10,000

Lamego's business-like alter ego, the sun-bleached town of Régua abuts the Rio Douro at the western edge of the demarcated port-wine region. As the region's largest riverside town, it grew into a major port-wine entrepôt in the 18th century, and remains an important transport junction – thanks in part to the hulking IP3 bridge that soars above the river valley.

The town itself, set along a busy highway above the river, doesn't have a lot of charm – most visitors stop in just long enough to get recommendations, maps and directions to nearby wineries – but it makes a convenient base to visit the port-wine country, cruise the Rio Douro and and take a scenic riverside train ride. Most tourists stick to the scenic riverfront, but the quaint old town one block uphill is an almost exclusively local scene, and well worth a wander.

Sights

Museu do Douro MUSEUM
(www.museudodouro.pt; Rua Marquês de Pombal; adult/concession €6/3; ⌚10am-6pm) It's not all about the wine. Sometimes it's about contemporary canvases, Impressionist landscapes, old leather-bound texts, vintage port-wine posters and the remains of an old flat-bottomed port hauler. You'll find it all in a gorgeous converted riverside warehouse, with a restaurant and bar on-site. The gift shop, stocked with wine, handmade soaps and some terrific silver, is brilliant.

Activities

Steam Train to Tua RAIL
(Comboio Vapor; www.cp.pt; one-way €4; ⌚Jun-Oct) While the gorgeous Linha da Tua line remains out of service, you can still ride in this lovingly restored steam train, which travels four times daily along the Douro from Régua to Tua, making a 20-minute stop in Pinhão.

Tomaz do Douro CRUISE
(☎222 082 286; www.tomazdodouro.pt; cruises from €10) Tomaz do Douro offers a set of different cruises along the Douro, with different departure points.

Sleeping

Residencial Columbano GUESTHOUSE €
(☎254 320 710; Rua Sacadura Cabral 5050; s/d €30/55; P ❄ 📶 🏊) Located 1.5km west of the *turismo,* about a 20-minute walk or a short cab ride away, the modern Columbano is arguably Régua's best budget option. It offers simple and smallish but comfortable rooms, basic breakfast and an outdoor pool.

Quinta de Marrocos GUESTHOUSE €€
(☎254 322 680; www.quintademarrocos.com; Estrada Nacional 222, Valdigem; s/d €65/75; ❄ 📶) Housed in an old Franciscan monastery just 4km south of Régua on the left bank of the Douro, this estate has four comfortable rooms in a 17th-century house filled with family heirlooms. It is one of the oldest estates in the Douro, which has maintained viticultural activity for over four generations.

Hotel Régua Douro HOTEL €€
(☎254 320 700; www.hotelreguadouro.pt; Largo da Estação; s/d from €75/95; P ❄ @ 📶 🏊) This industrial-sized hotel sits by the river and is steps from the train station. It has plush, carpeted rooms in ruby (or is that tawny?) colour schemes and windows overlooking the Douro. The pool is much appreciated on hot days. Rooms with river views are pricier, as are weekend stays.

★ **Six Senses Douro Valley** HOTEL €€€
(☎254 660 600; www.sixsenses.com; Quinta de Vale Abraão, Samodães; r €500-600; P ❄ 📶 🏊) The first European property of the Six Senses group, this gorgeously renovated 19th-century manor house is nestled on an

idyllic bend in the river 5km from Régua. The rooms, suites and villas are chic and sleek, the spa is extraordinary, and the restaurant is one of the region's best, with veggies from the on-site organic gardens and wine as the centrepiece.

Quinta da Pacheca HERITAGE HOTEL €€€
(☎254 331 229; www.quintadapacheca.com; Rua do Relógio do Sol 261, Cambres; s/d from €160/170; P 📶) One of the Douro's best *quintas* for both wine tastings and overnight stays, Quinta da Pacheca is a short drive from Régua and has 15 rooms inside a restored 18th-century manor, a top-notch restaurant and guided wine tours hourly (€9, including tastings). Guests get complimentary bikes to use during their stay.

Quinta do Vallado HERITAGE HOTEL €€€
(☎254 323 147; www.quintadovallado.com; Vilarinho dos Freires; r €120-200; P ❄ 📶 ≋) This 70-hectare winery brings together five rooms in an old stone manor and eight swank rooms in an ultramodern slate building, decked out with chestnut and teak wood, each complete with a balcony. They all share a gorgeous pool. Guests get a free tour of the winery, with a tasting. Cycling, hiking, fishing, canoeing – whatever your interest, just ask.

Eating

A Tasquinha PORTUGUESE €€
(☎254 318 070; Rua Branca Martinho; mains €6-15; ⏱10am-10pm) Small and cosy, this tavern dishes out well-prepared regional mainstays with a focus on meat dishes. The portions are generous and the house wine of good quality.

Taberna do Jéréré PORTUGUESE €€
(Rua Marquês de Pombal 38; mains €9-16; ⏱noon-3pm & 7-11pm Mon-Sat, noon-3pm Sun) Excellent Portuguese dishes, including *bacalhau á Jéréré* (dried salt-cod with shrimp, mushroom and spinach), served in a tastefully rustic dining room with a beamed ceiling and granite floors. Great-value lunch specials.

Castas e Pratos PORTUGUESE €€€
(☎254 323 290; www.castasepratos.com; Avenida José Vasques Osório; mains €20-30; ⏱10.30am-11pm) The coolest dining room in town is set in a restored wood-and-stone railyard warehouse with exposed original timbers. You can order grilled *alheira* sausage or octopus salad from the tapas bar downstairs, or have the locally caught cod in an almond crust with Lamego ham or kid goat in port with fava beans in the mezzanine.

Information

Turismo (☎254 312 846; www.cm-pesoregua.pt; Avenida do Douro; ⏱9.30am-12.30pm & 2-6.30pm Mon-Sat) The new high-tech *turismo* office facing the Douro river supplies information about the town and the region, including the accommodation options and vineyards in the area.

Getting There & Away

Transdev buses run regularly to/from Lamego (€2.30, 20 minutes), and Tâmega/Rodonorte has five daily departures to Vila Real (€6, 30 minutes).

There are around 13 trains daily from Porto (€10, two hours); some continue up the valley to Pinhão (€2.80, 25 minutes, five daily). Around five trains depart daily for Tua (€4, 40 minutes). If you've taken a train this far and suddenly realise you need a car to visit the vineyards, your best bet is **Europcar** (☎254 321 146; www.europcar.com; Avenida João Franco; rental per day from €82).

To get to the *cais fluvial* (river terminal) from the *turismo*, bear left at the Residencial Império.

There is a public car park at the eastern end of the riverfront promenade.

ALTO DOURO

Heading upriver from Peso da Régua, terraced vineyards blanket every hillside, with whitewashed *quintas* perched high above the Douro. This dramatic landscape is the jaw-dropping by-product of over 2000 years of winemaking. While villages are small and architectural monuments few and far between, it's worth the trip simply for the panoramic ride itself (by car, train or boat). Its allure has clearly not gone unnoticed. In 2001 Unesco designated the entire Alto Douro wine-growing region a World Heritage Site.

Further east towards Spain, the soil is drier, with the sculpted landscape giving way to more rugged terrain. But despite the aridity – and the blisteringly hot summers – the land around Vila Nova de Foz Côa produces fine grapes and excellent olives and nuts.

Most recently, the construction of the Foz-Tua dam just metres from the Alto Douro has sparked controversy among Portuguese environmental groups and the region's wine producers. Regardless, the construction is in its final stages.

Pinhão & Around

POP 100

Encircled by terraced hillsides that produce some of the world's best port – and some stellar table wines, too, pretty little Pinhão sits on a particularly lovely bend of the Rio Douro, 25km upriver from Peso da Régua. Wineries and their competing signs dominate the scene. Even the delightful train station has *azulejos* (hand-painted tiles) depicting the grape harvest.

Activities

Quinta Nova HIKING, WINERY

(☎254 730 430; www.quintanova.com; Covas do Douro; wine tours €7, tastings €8-48; ⏲tours 11am, 12.45pm, 3.30pm, 4.45pm) Set on a stunning ridge, surrounded by luscious, ancient vineyards, overlooking the deep green Douro river with mountains layered in the distance, the Quinta Nova estate is well worth an in-depth exploration. The three hiking and biking trails (the longest is 2½ hours) are the best in the region. To get here, head 9km west of Pinhão, along the north bank of the Douro (EN322-2).

Quinta do Crasto VINEYARD

(☎934 920 024; www.quintadocrasto.pt; Sabrosa; tours incl tasting €18; ⏲by appointment) Perched like an eyrie on a promontory above the Rio Douro and a spectacular ripple of terraced vineyards – amid the lyrical landscapes of the Alto Douro – Quinta do Crasto quite literally takes your breath away. Stop by for a tour and tasting (of five wines) or lunch (€61 with wine). Call ahead, as groups sometimes storm the place.

Quinta do Bomfim WINE

(☎254 730 350; www.symington.com/news/quinta-do-bomfim; tours €7.50, incl tasting €10; ⏲10.30am-7pm daily Apr-Oct, 9.30am-5.30pm Tue-Sun Nov-Mar) Symington's swank *quinta* showcases a small museum inside a restored old winery. Guided tours (in several languages) include a visit to the lodge dating back to 1896 where young wine is still aged in old wooden vats. The tour ends in the gorgeous tasting room with a terrace featuring beautiful vistas of the Douro, where wines are available by the glass. The vineyard walks offer a great chance to immerse yourself in the ancient vineyard terraces (€5 with a map, hat and a bottle of water).

Quinta das Carvalhas WINE

(☎254 738 050; carvalhas@realcompanhiavelha.pt; tours bus/jeep €12.50/35) This *quinta* excels at 'vintage' tours, guided by the in-house agriculturalist, who takes you on a two-hour jeep tour around the gorgeous vineyards and to the top of the estate's ridge (book ahead). The cheaper alternative is with a bus that picks people up from the train station (10am, noon, 3pm and 5pm), with a tasting of three wines at the end.

It also offers walks around the vineyards (€10) and picnics in ruins on-site (€45).

Quinta da Roêda WINE

(☎223 742 800; www.croftport.com; tours incl tasting €10; ⏲10am-6pm) This recently opened *quinta* by Croft sits 1km from Pinhão. Housed in old stables, it's traditional – all wood, stone and planks from the old lodges in Gaia – and surrounded by 110 hectares of vineyards. During harvest, it offers grape treading in three granite tanks called *lagares* (€22).

If you are staying at Vintage House Hotel, there's free pick-up from town, or you can get one of the free electric bikes and ride up to the *quinta*.

Quinta do Tedo WINE

(☎254 789 165; www.quintadotedo.com; Folgosa; tours incl tasting €8; ⏲10am-7pm) Blessed with sublime real estate carved by two rivers – the Douro and Tedo – this American-French-Portuguese–owned 14-hectare estate offers short 20-minute tours of the winery (which is certified organic), followed by a tasting of port, table wine and organic olive oil. There are also certified hiking trails on the property that are especially wonderful for birdwatching.

Douro-a-Vela Boat Trips BOATING

(☎918 793 792; www.douroavela.pt; Folgosa; 2hr cruise €50) One of the sweetest thrills in the area demands that you simply lie back and cruise upriver into the heart of the Alto Douro aboard a sail boat. Catch the boat from the Folgosa do Douro pier, just outside DOC restaurant. The price listed is based on a six-person minimum (or pay €180 for two).

Train to Pocinho TOUR

(www.cp.pt; one-way €4.70) With the Linha do Tua still out of service, the most beautiful train trip in the area is this one-hour chug upriver along the most stunning section of the Tua line. Trains depart from the Pinhão train station (and return from Pocinho) five times per day.

Quinta do Portal WINE
(☎259 937 000; www.quintadoportal.com; tours incl tasting €7.50; ⊙10am-1pm & 2-6pm) This award-winning vineyard produces ports, red and white table wines, and a little-known muscatel wine. The surrounding region is one of the only places in the country producing muscatel (the other is Setúbal). Tours include a visit to the cellar with a tasting of three wines.

There's also a restaurant and guesthouse (doubles from €120). The winery lies about 12km north of Pinhão, along EN323, in the direction of Vila Real. Call ahead.

Quinta do Panascal WINE
(☎254 732 321; www.fonseca.pt; Valença do Douro; tours incl tasting €7; ⊙10am-6pm daily May-Oct, 10am-6pm Mon-Fri Nov-Apr) Producer of Fonseca ports, this lovely estate offers self-guided audio tours (in nine languages) through some beautifully situated vineyards, with a tasting of three wines. It's located about 15 minutes' drive west of Pinhão, well signed from the N222.

Sleeping

★Casa Cimeira RURAL INN €
(☎254 732 320; www.casacimeira-douro.com; Rua do Cimo do Povo, Valença do Douro; s/d €50/60; P❄📶🏊) Set in a 200-year-old home at the top of the hilltop town of Valença – its cobbled streets wrapped with vineyards and olive tree groves and alive with old country warmth – this is the domain of the charming Nogueira family. Rooms are quaint and spotless, there's a small pool, a sun deck and family-style dinners featuring their own house wine.

Hotel Douro HOTEL €
(☎254 732 404; www.hotel-douro.pt; Rua António Manuel Saraiva 39; s/d €50/60; ❄@📶) This cheery, well-kept hotel – the nicest of its kind in Pinhão – has several river-facing rooms, other large rooms facing a quiet rear courtyard, and a miniterrace covered with flowering vines.

★Morgadio da Calçada HERITAGE HOTEL €€
(☎254 732 218; www.morgadiodacalcada.com; Rua Cabo de Vila 18, Provesende; r €110-135; P❄📶🏊) Housed in a 17th-century manor estate in the gorgeous hillside village of Provesende, a 20-minute drive from Pinhão, this stunning guesthouse has eight minimalist rooms inside old stables, with skylights, pine-wood floors and original details. Run by the 19th-generation owner who also produces wine and soaps based on an old family recipe, this special hideaway serves up heritage and stories aplenty.

Quinta de la Rosa B&B €€
(☎254 732 254; www.quintadelarosa.com; Pinhão; d/ste from €90/115; P📶🏊) Sitting on the banks of the Douro, 2km west of Pinhão, this charming vineyard and winery runs hour-long tours (€10) followed by tastings at 11am daily. The bright, appealing rooms straddle different buildings, and private villas are available for weekly rental. Three-course dinners (€30) are perfectly matched with wines.

Quinta de Santo António INN €€
(☎254 789 177; www.quintasantoantonio.pt; Adorigo; s/d €85/95; P❄@📶🏊) This stunning 25-hectare property is owned by the former winemaker for Sandeman. The drive up the steep, rutted dirt road is exciting, the perch high, the river and mountain views jaw-dropping, and the price fair. Don't leave until you've sipped their 25-year-old tawny. Get here via the road to Tabuaço.

Casa de Casal de Loivos INN €€
(☎254 732 149; www.casadecasaldeloivos.com; Casal de Loivos; s/d €93/114; @🏊) For dreamy views, stay the night in one of the elegant rooms of this house that has been in this winemaking family for nearly 350 years. The halls are enlivened by museum-level displays of folkloric dresses, and the perch – high above the Alto Douro – is spectacular. Swim laps in the pool while peering down across the vines spreading in all directions.

★Quinta Nova INN €€€
(☎254 730 420; www.quintanova.com; Covas do Douro; s €175-205, d €190-220; 📶🏊) Set on a ridge, surrounded by 120 hectares of ancient vineyards, overlooking the Douro river with mountains layered in the distance, Quinta Nova is simply stunning. Besides plush lodging in a beautifully restored 19th-century manor, it offers romantic grounds, a pool looking out over vines, a restaurant, and wine tours and tastings.

Vintage House Hotel HOTEL €€€
(☎254 730 230; www.vintagehousehotel.com; Rua António Manuel Saraiva; s/d from €180/195; P❄@📶🏊) Occupying a string of 19th-century buildings right on the palm-lined riverfront, this luxurious sleep has just been revamped by the team behind the Yeatman in Porto. The result is a clutch of 50 beautifully redone rooms and suites, most with terraces or balconies with river views.

DON'T MISS

SAN SALVADOR DEL MUNDO

A series of small chapels dotting the hillside, San Salvador del Mundo makes for a stunning diversion between Pinhão and Foz Côa. Follow the signs to these stone turnouts with scenic hill, vineyard and river views. Some have stone slab tables and benches that demand a picnic, surrounded by wildflowers and serenaded by birdsong. After lunch continue to the top of the road and stroll to the chapel on the pinnacle. Spectacular.

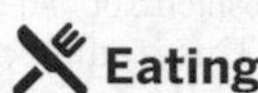

Eating

Veladouro PORTUGUESE €€

(☎254 738 166; Rua da Praia 3; mains €7-15; ⏲10am-midnight) Simple but tasty Portuguese food, such as wood-grilled meats and fish, is served inside this quaint schist building or outside under a canopy of vines. From the train station, turn left and go along the main road for 150m, then left again under a railway bridge, and right at the river.

★DOC PORTUGUESE €€€

(☎254 858 123; www.ruipaula.com; Estrada Nacional 222, Folgosa; mains €27.50-29; ⏲12.30-3.30pm & 7.30-11pm) Architect Miguel Saraiva's ode to glass-walled minimalism, DOC is headed up by Portuguese star chef Rui Paula. Its terrace peering out across the river is a stunning backdrop. Dishes give a pinch of imagination to seasonal, regional flavours, from fish *açordas* to game and wild mushrooms – all of which are paired with carefully selected wines from the cellar. The restaurant is in Folgosa, midway between Peso da Régua and Pinhão, on the south side of the river.

Information

The tiny *turismo* in Pinhão is almost never open and doesn't have much information when it is. For a wealth of info on the region, it's best to head to the *turismo* in **Sabrosa** (☎259 939 575; Rua do Loreto, Sabrosa; ⏲10am-1pm & 2-7pm Mon-Fri, 10am-1pm Sat & Sun) or in the nearby village of Provesende.

Getting There & Away

Regional trains go to and from Peso da Régua (€2.75, 25 minutes, five daily), where you can catch an onward train to Porto.

It's best to have your own wheels if you want to explore the area independently, as some of the best spots are not accessible by public transport.

Vila Nova de Foz Côa

In the heart of the Douro's *terra quente* (hot land), this once-remote, whitewashed town has been on the tourism map since the 1990s. That's when researchers – during an environmental impact study for a proposed dam – stumbled across an astounding collection of Palaeolithic art. These mysterious rock engravings, which number in the thousands, blanket the nearby Rio Côa valley. Archaeologists brought the petroglyphs to the world's attention, and the dam builders backed down when the whole valley was declared a Unesco World Heritage Site.

You may find the climate startlingly Mediterranean if you've just come from the mountains. Summers here are infernally hot, with temperatures regularly exceeding 45°C. But if you come in late March, you'll be treated to cooler climes, wildflowers and blooming almond trees.

Sights

Parque Arqueológico do Vale do Côa ARCHAEOLOGICAL SITE

(www.arte-coa.pt; Rua do Museu; park sites each €10, museum €5, park & museum €12; ⏲museum & park 9am-6pm Tue-Sun Mar-Oct, 9am-1pm & 2-6pm Tue-Sun Nov-Feb) Most visitors to Vila Nova de Foz Côa come for one reason: to see its world-famous gallery of rock art. Although the park is currently an active research zone, three sites are open to the public: Canada do Inferno, Ribeira de Piscos and Penascosa. While Penascosa has some of the most significant etchings, Canada do Inferno – which sits by the half-constructed dam – is the ideal place to understand just how close these aeons-old drawings came to disappearing.

Because the entire valley is a working archaeological site, all visitors must enter with a guided tour. Tours for Canada do Inferno depart at around 9.30am from the park museum in Vila Nova de Foz Côa; for Ribeira de Piscos at around 9.30am from the Muxagata visitor centre on the western side of the valley; and for Penascosa at around 9.30am from the Castelo Melhor visitor centre on the eastern side of the valley (which also offers €17 night tours departing from the museum).

Visitors gather at the various visitor centres, where they're taken, eight at a time, in the park's own 4WDs, for a guided tour of one of the sites (two hours at Canada do Inferno, which includes 1km of walking; one hour at Penascosa, with some walking;

2½ hours at Ribeira de Piscos, with 2km of walking). You can take in two sites in one day – one in the morning and one in the afternoon. Visitors with mountain bikes may go on guided bike tours (bring your own bike) in similar-sized groups.

Visitor numbers are strictly regulated, so from July to September book a tour through the park office well in advance or you may miss out; reservations are accepted from Tuesday to Sunday. You must book at least a few weeks ahead for bicycle trips at any time.

Make sure you bring comfortable shoes and a hat, sunscreen and water in summer months, as it gets extremely hot in the valley.

Old Town AREA

The sleepy old quarter makes for a pleasant stroll in the early evening. Highlights include the Praça do Município, with its impressive granite *pelourinho* (stone pillory), and the elaborately carved portal of the Manueline-style parish church. Just east off the square is the tiny Capela de Santa Quitéria, once the town's synagogue.

Museu da Casa Grande MUSEUM

(Rua Direita, Freixo de Numão; adult/student €2/1; 9am-noon & 2-6pm Tue-Sun) Archaeological finds from the Stone Age to the 18th century have been uncovered in the region around Freixo de Numão, 12km west of Vila Nova de Foz Côa. A good little display can be viewed in this baroque townhouse with Roman foundations. Some English and French is spoken. Guided tours are available by arrangement with the museum.

Sleeping

Hotel Vale do Côa HOTEL €

(279 760 010; www.hotelvaledocoa.net; Avenida Cidade Nova; s/d €42/55; P ❄) This modern hotel opposite the tourist office offers comfortable, air-conditioned rooms with clean-swept wooden floors. Most rooms have verandahs with views of the countryside.

Pousada da Juventude HOSTEL €

(279 764 041; www.pousadasjuventude.pt; Caminho Vicinal Currauteles 5; dm/d €13/32; P @) This hostel in a modern, pink-brick building is well worth the 800m-walk north from the town centre (1.4km by road). Its basic but handsome doubles have views over a rugged valley; four-bed dorms are clean and well maintained. Amenities include a bar, open kitchen, laundry, cafeteria, games room and large patio with sweeping views.

Casa do Rio GUESTHOUSE €€€

(279 764 339; www.quintadovallado.com; Quinta do Orgal, Castelo Melhor; r €190; P ❄) Set between the vineyards and the river, the all-wood Casa do Rio at Quinta do Orgal has six stunning suites offering river views and a full spectrum of amenities. There's a two-night minimum stay on weekends.

Eating

Cafeteria Ritz PORTUGUESE €

(Rua de São Miguel 14; mains €5-7; 8am-10pm Mon-Sat) Popular among the locals for locally styled roasts (and only roast-meat) dishes.

António & Julia SUPERMARKET €

(Rua de São Miguel 50; 9am-6pm Mon-Sat) Top-quality local hams, sausages, cheese and honey are available for picnics at this charming shop on the São Miguel strip.

Aldeia Douro PORTUGUESE €€

(279 094 403; Rua Dr José Augo Saraiva de Aguilar 19; mains €5-16; 11am-midnight Tue-Sun) Great regional food is prepared with a twist at this contemporary restaurant that plays with Portuguese classics. Great lunch menus daily and friendly staff.

Entertainment

Centro Cultural CONCERT VENUE

(279 760 324; Avenida Cidade Nova 2) Although there isn't a lot going on in Foz Côa, the Centro Cultural hosts concerts, temporary art exhibitions and films throughout the year. It's in the same building as the *turismo*.

Information

Miles Away (938 749 528; www.milesawaydouroandcoa.com; Avenida Dr Artur Máximo Saraiva de Aguilar 8) This top-notch agency does tailor-made tours around the Douro and Côa valleys (and to Porto), with a focus on wine, archaeology and nature experiences. It can arrange visits to wine estates not normally open to the public and to lesser-known areas such as the private Faia Brava Nature Reserve and the 200km-long Grande Rota do Vale Côa trail.

Turismo (279 760 329; www.cm-fozcoa.pt; Avenida Cidade Nova 2; 9am-5.30pm) Opposite Albergaria Foz Côa.

Getting There & Away

One daily bus connects Vila Nova de Foz Côa with Bragança (€8.30, 1¾ hours) and another with Miranda do Douro (€6, 2½ hours). Three buses per day travel via Trancoso (€4.40) to Viseu (€9.20, two hours).

Five daily trains run to Pocinho, at the end of the Douro valley line, from Porto (€10.65, 3½ hours) and Peso da Régua (€6), via Pinhão. A taxi between Pocinho and Vila Nova de Foz Côa costs about €6 to €8, and there are two daily buses (€2 to €4.40, 20 minutes).

Getting Around

A twice-daily bus passes the outskirts of Castelo Melhor (€1.90, 15 minutes); from there it's an easy walk to the Parque Arqueológico do Vale do Côa visitor centre. Alternatively, there is a taxi stand on the square in front of the park's office in Vila Nova de Foz Côa, and park guides often help organise carpools, too.

Long-distance coaches stop at the bus station about 150m north of the *turismo* at Avenida Gago Coutinho.

There is usually plenty of free parking along Avenida Gago Coutinho between the *turismo* and the Parque Arqueológico do Vale do Côa headquarters.

TRÁS-OS-MONTES

In Trás-os-Montes, despite its clutch of large towns, rural life is still the region's heart and soul, from the southwest's steep vineyard-clad hillsides, to the olive groves, almond orchards and rugged canyon-lands of the sun-baked east, and the chestnut-shaded, heathery highlands of the north.

Vila Real

POP 19,200 / ELEV 445M

Clinging to steep hillsides above the confluence of the Rios Corgo and Cabril, the university town of Vila Real in Trás-os-Montes is short on charm, although its historic centre, dotted with picturesque old churches, is pleasant enough. Its key attractions lie just beyond the city limits: the dramatically rugged highlands of the Parque Natural do Alvão; and the resplendent Casa de Mateus, one of Europe's most elegant country houses, surrounded by lovely vineyard country east of town.

Sights

★Casa de Mateus PALACE

(☎259 323 121; www.casadematеus.com; gardens €7.50, palace & gardens €11; ⏲9am-7.30pm May-Oct, to 6pm Nov-Apr) Famously depicted on bottles of Mateus rosé, the 18th-century Casa de Mateus is one of Portugal's great baroque masterpieces – probably the work of Italian-born architect Nicolau Nasoni. Guided tours of the mansion (in English, French, Spanish and German) take you through the main quarters, which combine rusticity with restrained grandeur.

Its granite wings shelter a forecourt dominated by an ornate stairway and guarded by rooftop statues. Surrounding the palace is a fantasy of a garden, with tiny boxwood hedges, prim statues and a fragrant cypress tunnel that's blissfully cool on even the hottest days. (Don't miss the fanciful 5m-tall curved ladders used to prune the tunnel's exterior branches!)

Inside, the library contains one of the first illustrated editions of Luís Vaz de Camões' *Os Lusíadas,* Portugal's most important epic poem, while another room houses an unintentionally droll collection of religious bric-a-brac, including three dozen macabre relics bought from the Vatican in the 18th century: a bit of holy fingernail, a saintly set of eyeballs, and the inevitable piece of the true cross – each with the Vatican's proof of authenticity.

Near the guided tour starting point, a wine shop offers tastings of three locally produced wines for €4. Especially interesting is the Alvarelhão, which is essentially the same fine rosé originally bottled by Mateus in the 1940s.

The palace is 3.5km east of the town centre. Take local Urbanos de Vila Real (€1, 20 minutes) towards the university (UTAD). It leaves from **Largo de Camões**, just north of the *turismo,* roughly half-hourly between 7.30am and 8pm, with fewer buses on weekends. Ask for 'Mateus' and the driver will set you down about 250m from the palace (if you don't ask, he may not stop).

Miradouro de Trás-do-Cemitério VIEWPOINT

For a fine view across the gorge of the Rio Corgo and Rio Cabril, walk south to this panoramic viewpoint, just beyond a small cemetery and chapel.

Museu Etnográfico de Vila Real MUSEUM

(Largo São Pedro 3; ⏲9am-noon & 2-5pm Mon-Fri, by appointment Sat & Sun) FREE This small but colourful museum documents the traditional culture of the surrounding highlands, with exhibits on linen-making, ceramics, farming techniques, games, musical instruments and local festivals.

Capela Nova CHAPEL

(cnr Ruas Central & Direita) Northeast of a cathedral is the magnificently over-the-top

Vila Real

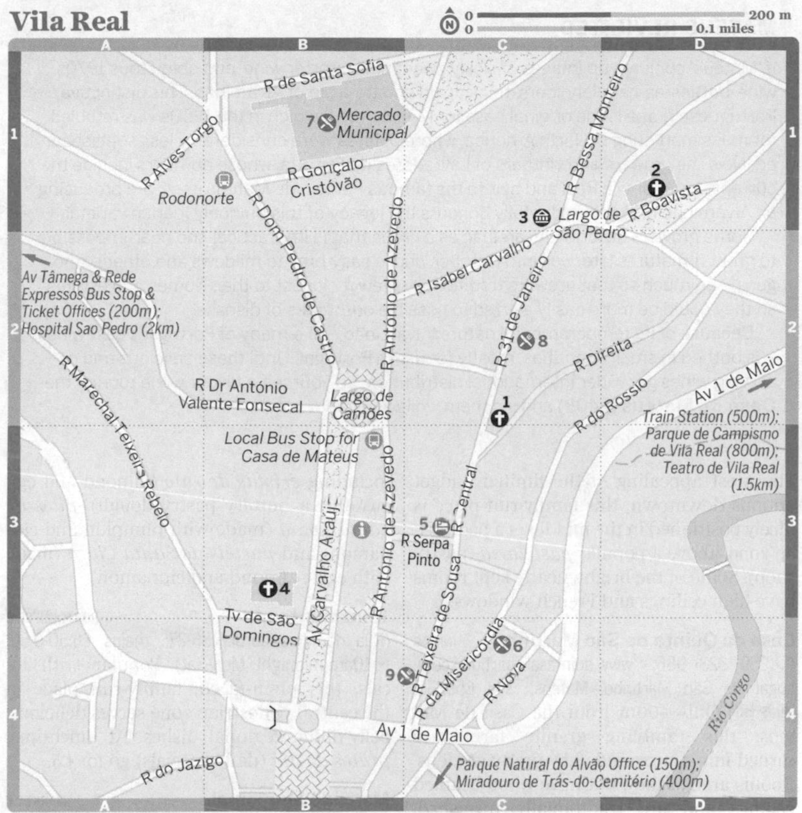

baroque facade of this 17th-century chapel. Inside are fine, 18th-century *azulejos* and large-headed cherubs with teddy-boy coifs.

Sé CATHEDRAL

(Travessa de São Domingos) Once part of a Dominican monastery, the Gothic *sé* has been given a lengthy facelift that has restored the 15th-century grandeur of its rather spare interior.

Igreja de São Pedro CHURCH

(Largo de São Pedro) Baroque architecture and *azulejos* are on view at the Igreja de São Pedro, one block north of Capela Nova.

Sleeping

Parque de Campismo de Vila Real CAMPGROUND €

(☎259 324 724; camping.vilareal@gmail.com; Rua Dr Manuel Cardona; sites per adult/child/tent/car €3.75/1.88/2.30/2.65; ⏱Mar-Nov; 🏊) This simple, shady hillside campsite above the Rio Corgo, 1.2km northeast of the centre, has a municipal pool nearby, which guests can use for €0.50.

Residencial Real GUESTHOUSE €

(☎259 325 879; www.residencialreal.com; Rua Combatentes da Grande Guerra 5; s/d €30/50)

Vila Real

Sights

1	Capela Nova	C2
2	Igreja de São Pedro	D1
3	Museu Etnográfico de Vila Real	C1
4	Sé	B3

Sleeping

5	Residencial Real	C3

Eating

6	Casa Lapão	C4
7	Mercado Municipal	B1
8	Terra de Montanha	C2
9	Transmontano	C4

MATEUS REVISITED

If 'Mateus' conjures up images of sickly sweet pink 'starter wine' and ubiquitous 1970s wine-bottles-as-candleholders, think again and try a sip of Alvarelhão. This distinctive Portuguese grape is the original base for Mateus rosé, which in the 1950s was retooled for mass marketing in North America, where palates were considerably less sophisticated. Now the growers and vintners of Lavradores de Feitoria, whose numbers include the current Count of Vila Real and heir to the famous Palácio de Mateus itself, are producing an Alvarelhão rosé that more fully honours the legacy of this uniquely Iberian varietal.

Some growers describe Alvarelhão as a grape that is impractical and near-impossible to grow. It matures late, well into October, and is easy prey to mildews and other pathogens – so much so that growers traditionally grew it closest to their homes and estates so they could be more easily alerted to possible outbreaks of disease.

Because of its temperamental nature, Alvarelhão – like many of Portugal's best wines – is bottled in small quantities, mostly for use in Portugal. Until these delicious and deserving wines get wider international distribution, do yourself a favour while touring the **Casa de Mateus** (p408) and sip them while you can!

The most appealing of the limited budget options downtown, this family-run place is nicely positioned in the middle of a pedestrian zone, above a popular *pastelaria* (pastry shop). Some of the bright, neatly kept rooms have high ceilings and French windows.

Casa da Quinta de São Martinho INN €€
(☎259 323 986; www.quintasaomartinho.com; Lugar de São Martinho, Mateus; s/d €55/65; P 📶 🏊) Only 400m from the Casa de Mateus, this rambling granite farmhouse turned inn is surrounded by pretty gardens. Rooms aren't fancy, but have wood-beamed ceilings and are traditionally furnished. Three-course dinners are served with advance notice.

Casa Agrícola da Levada INN €€
(☎259 322 190; www.casadalevada.com; Rua da Capela; s €54-70, d €60-80; P 📶 🏊) Just north of the centre, at the end of a long, shady drive lies this little gem of an inn. A collection of tastefully renovated old houses surrounds grounds that include rose gardens, a large grassy lawn and a swimming pool. The friendly, multilingual owners have deep roots in the region and are generous in sharing their knowledge of the area's highlights.

Eating

Numerous eateries are clustered in the historic centre, along the narrow streets just east of Avenida Carvalho Araújo.

Casa Lapão CAFE €
(www.casalapao.pt; Rua de Misericórdia 51-54; pastries from €1; ⏰8.30am-7pm) This spruce tearoom specialises in traditional local sweets, including *cristas de galo* (almond and egg paste in a buttery pastry dough), *pitos de Santa Luzia* (made with pumpkin and cinnamon) and *pastéis de Santa Clara* (made with eggs, almond and cinnamon).

Transmontano PORTUGUESE €
(Rua da Misericórdia 35-37; mains €6.50-9.50; ⏰10am-midnight Mon-Sat) Popular with locals, this plain-faced, family-run place in the central pedestrian zone serves delicious, belly-filling regional dishes. At lunchtime, *pratos do dia* (daily specials) go for €5.

Mercado Municipal MARKET €
(Rua de Santa Sofia; ⏰8am-3pm Mon-Sat) Self-caterers can stock up on rural produce at the market.

Chaxoila PORTUGUESE €€
(☎259 322 654; www.facebook.com/casadepastochaxoila; EN2; mains €7.50-16; ⏰10am-midnight) A traditional roadside restaurant a little outside town on the EN2 towards Chaves, convivial Chaxoila serves up great daily specials such as *cabrito* (kid goat) and *açorda* (bread and shellfish stew) from the open-plan kitchen. With its vine-covered terrace, it is popular with locals, so book ahead. Many of the portions are fit for two.

Terra de Montanha PORTUGUESE €€
(www.terramontanha.wix.com/terrademontanhavreal; Rua 31 de Janeiro 16-18; mains €10.50-13.50; ⏰12.30-2.30pm & 7.30-10.30pm Mon-Sat, 12.30-2.30pm Sun; 🍷) From the black crockery to the halved wine casks that serve as booths, everything here is rigorously *transmontana*. The hearty local cuisine includes specialities such as *posta barrosã* (grilled veal

steak). Weekday lunch specials are a great deal, plus they have vegetarian options – a rarity in these parts.

☆ Entertainment

Teatro de Vila Real PERFORMING ARTS

(☎259 320 009; www.teatrodevilareal.com; Alameda de Grasse) This slick, modern building, in a park-like area across the Corgo from the city centre, stages high-quality dance and theatre performances, as well as classical, jazz and world music. It also screens biweekly films. At the back, the theatre's bright cafe overlooking the Corgo is popular with Vila Real's beau monde.

ℹ Information

Parque Natural do Alvão Office (☎259 302 830; pnal@icnf.pt; Largo dos Freitas; ⏲9am-12.30pm & 2-5.30pm Mon-Fri)

Turismo (☎259 308 170; www.cm-vilareal.pt; Avenida Carvalho Araújo 94; ⏲9am-7pm Jun-Sep, reduced hours Oct-May) Located in a Manueline house in the town centre.

ℹ Getting There & Away

Several companies serve Vila Real. **Rodonorte** (☎259 340 710; www.rodonorte.pt) buses leave from a station on Rua Dom Pedro de Castro, 300m northwest of the *turismo*. **AV Tâmega** (☎259 322 928; www.avtamega.pt) and **Rede Expressos** (☎962 060 655; www.rede expressos.pt) both operate from a lot slightly west of the Rodonorte station, at the corner of Rua Dom António Valente da Fonseca and Avenida Cidade de Ourense. Destinations served by these companies include Bragança (€10.80, two hours), Chaves (€8, 70 minutes), Lamego (€6, 45 minutes), Lisbon (€20.50, five to 5½ hours), Miranda do Douro (€12.70, three to 3½ hours) and Porto (€9, 1½ hours).

Parque Natural do Alvão

With its rock-strewn highlands, schist villages, waterfalls and verdant pockets where cows graze in stone-walled pastures, the pristine Parque Natural do Alvão comes as a delightful revelation to travellers climbing from the hotter, drier country below. A drive of less than half an hour brings you from Vila Real to this extraordinary park straddling the central ridgeline of the Serra de Alvão, the highest peaks of which reach more than 1300m. The small (72-sq-km) protected area remains one of northern Portugal's best-kept secrets and shelters a remarkable variety of flora and fauna, thanks to its position in a transition zone between the humid coast and the dry interior.

Sights

The Rio Ôlo, a tributary of the Rio Tâmega, rises in the park's broad granite basin. A 300m drop above Ermelo gives rise to the spectacular Fisgas de Ermelo falls, the park's major tourist attraction.

Ermelo VILLAGE

The 800-year-old village of Ermelo is famous for its schist cottages capped with fairy-tale slate roofs that seem to have been constructed from broken blackboards. Once the main village of the region, it boasts traditional *espigueiros* (stone granaries), an ancient chapel, a sturdy granite *pelourinho*, a workshop that still practises the ancient local art of linen-making, and **Ponte de Várzea** – a Roman bridge rebuilt in medieval times.

The Ermelo turn-off is about 16km south of Mondim de Basto on the N304. The heart of town is about 1km uphill.

Lamas de Ôlo VILLAGE

Set in a wide, verdant valley some 1000m above sea level, somnolent Lamas de Ôlo is the park's highest village, best known for its photogenic thatched roofs, as well as a nearby mill that was long driven by water from a crude aqueduct.

Fisgas de Ermelo WATERFALL

Just north of the town of Ermelo, on the N304 between Vila Real and Mondim de Basto, is a turn-off to the dramatic Fisgas de Ermelo waterfalls. From this junction, the road climbs 4km to an overlook with picture-perfect views of the falls and the rugged terrain surrounding them.

To see the falls from above, return to the main road and climb to a T-junction with a right-hand turn marked Varzigueto. Follow the Varzigueto road a short distance until you see signs on the right-hand side for Piocas de Cima. There are actually two footpaths: the first is marked '1.5km', the second is marked '600m'. Either path leads down into the river gorge, where you'll find not only hair-raising views of the river plunging off a cliff face, but also (further up) a natural water slide and a series of pools perfect for cooling off on a hot day.

Activities

There are a number of fine hikes in the park. A 7km, three-hour jaunt around the southern village of Arnal is described in the Portuguese-language leaflet *Guia do Percurso Pedestre,* available at park offices. The signposted hike delivers views east beyond Vila Real to the Serra do Marão. While you're in Arnal, track down the slate-roofed centre for traditional handicraft techniques.

Another popular route is the 13km, five-hour loop through the high country starting just north of the Cimeira dam along the Vila Real–Lamas de Ôlo road. The trail, marked with red and yellow blazes, traverses the rock-strewn *planalto* (high plateau) for 8km to the village of Barreiro. From here, you can return 5km by road to your starting point, passing through Lamas de Ôlo en route.

Sleeping

Dona Benedita GUESTHOUSE €
(☎ 255 381 221; s/d €25/50) In Ermelo, Dona Benedita rents out three rooms, one of which has an en suite.

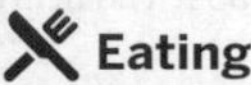

Eating

Sabores do Alvão PORTUGUESE €
(☎ 255 386 531; Lugar do Eido, Ermelo; mains €7-11; ⏲ noon-3.30pm & 7-10pm) A good option for food in Ermelo is Sabores do Alvão, a family-run restaurant by the church with nice valley views and hearty staples such as spare ribs cooked in wine and garlic, and served with rice.

Tasquinha d'Alice PORTUGUESE €
(☎ 255381381; Bobal; snacks €2.50-6; ⏲ 8.30am-midnight) In Bobal, halfway between Lamas de Ôlo and Mondim de Basto, Tasquinha d'Alice is recommended for its all-day snacks, such as great *alheira* as well as *salpicão* (small rounds of baked ham) omelette. It can also arrange full meals for groups of six or more with advance notice. The back room has lovely vistas.

Information

Exploring the park on your own is not simple, as maps, accommodation and public transport are limited. Whether you plan to walk or drive in the park, it's worth visiting one of the park offices, located in Vila Real and Mondim de Basto beforehand.

Getting There & Away

Public transport within the park is extremely limited; having your own wheels is preferable.

Auto Mondinense (☎ 255 381 296) runs from Mondim de Basto to Ermelo (€2.35, one hour) three times each weekday, and to Lamas de Ôlo (€3.20, 50 minutes) twice on Tuesdays and Fridays.

Rodonorte (☎ 259 340 710; www.rodonorte.pt) operates weekday buses from Vila Real to Lamas de Ôlo three times per day (€2.45, 30 minutes); the last bus back to Vila Real is at 2.10pm.

Mondim de Basto

POP 7495

Sitting in the Tâmega valley at the intersection of the Douro, Minho and Trás-os-Montes regions, low-lying Mondim de Basto has no compelling sights beyond a few flowery squares, but it makes an attractive base from which to explore the heights of the Parque Natural do Alvão. The vineyards surrounding town cultivate grapes used in the fine local *vinho verde.*

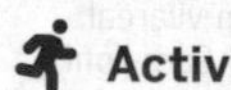

Activities

Hiking

Hikers wanting to feel a little burn in their thighs should consider the long haul up to the 18th-century **Capela da Senhora da Graça** on the summit of pine-clad Monte Farinha (996m). It takes about two hours to reach the top. The path starts east of town on the N312 (the *turismo* has a rough map). By car, turn off the N312 3.5km from Mondim towards Cerva; from there it's a twisting 9.5km to the top.

Swimming

At **Senhora da Ponte**, 2km south of town on the N304, there's a rocky swimming spot by a disused watermill on the Rio Cabril. Follow the signs to the Parque de Campismo de Mondim de Basto and then take the track to the right.

Wine Tasting

Casa Santa Eulália WINE
(☎ 255 386 111; www.casasantaeulalia.pt; Atei) Eight kilometres north of town in Atei, the 17th-century Casa Santa Eulália, set amid 32 hectares of vineyards, offers tastings of its refreshing local *vinho verde* with advance notice.

Sleeping

Quinta do Fundo INN €
(☎ 255 381 291; www.quintadofundo.com; Vilar de Viando; s/d/ste €40/50/75; P 📶 🏊) This pleasant spot, set amid a sea of vineyards 2km south of town on the N304, has decent

rooms (if you can overlook the shiny, vinyl-like flowered bedspreads), fine mountain vistas, a tennis court, bikes for rent and a swimming pool. The *quinta* also produces its own *vinho verde*. Ask about discounts for multinight stays.

Mondim Hotel & Spa HOTEL €€
(☎255 386 708; www.mondimhotelespa.pt; Av da Igreja 19; d €50-70, apt €68-120; P ❄ ☜) Smack in the heart of town, this place offers a set of clean if soulless rooms with good amenities. The on-site spa has a jacuzzi, sauna and gym. Prices go up on weekends.

Casa do Campo INN €€
(☎255 361 231; www.casadocampo.pt; Molares, Celorico de Basto; s/d/ste €75/90/110; P ❄ ☜ ≋) If you have wheels, consider this antique-packed, whitewashed 17th-century manor house with its own crenellated stone tower, chapel and extravagant topiary gardens. Rooms are modest but pleasant, with wood floors and plain country furnishings. Suites include a small living room with TV and *frigobar*. It is located 7km west of Mondim. There's an outdoor pool and tennis court.

Eating

O Transmontano PORTUGUESE €€
(☎255 381 682; Avenida da Igreja; mains €6-15; ⊙10am-3pm Mon, to midnight Tue-Sun) O Transmontano showcases a traditional Portuguese menu with a focus on meat specialities.

Adega Sete Condes PORTUGUESE €€
(☎255 382 342; Rua Velha; mains €7.50-12; ⊙9am-5pm Mon, to 11pm Tue-Sun) Tucked into a tiny corner near the *turismo*, this rustic, granite-walled spot has a small menu of well-prepared traditional dishes, including *bacalhau* and a very tasty *feijoada* (pork and bean stew).

Information

Parque Natural do Alvão Office (☎255 381 209; www.natural.pt; Lugar do Barrio; ⊙9am-12.30pm & 2-5.30pm Mon-Fri) About 700m west of the *turismo*.

Turismo (☎255 389 370; www.cm-mondimdebasto.pt; Praça do Municipio; ⊙9am-1pm & 2-5pm Mon-Fri, 9am-1pm Sat & Sun) Has loads of local information and rents bikes (per hour/day €1/5).

Getting There & Away

Buses stop behind the *mercado municipal*, 150m east of the *turismo* and what remains of the old town. **Auto Mondinense** (p412) has seven weekday and two to three weekend buses to Porto (€6.05, 2¾ hours) via Guimarães (€4, 1½ hours). For Vila Real, take a Mondinense bus to Campeã (€3.40, 50 minutes, three daily) and change there for the short-hop Rodonorte bus to Vila Real.

Chaves

POP 18,000 / ELEV 340M

A spa town with a long and fascinating history, Chaves (*shahv*-sh) is a pretty and engaging place, straddling the mountain-fringed banks of the Rio Tâmega only a few kilometres south of the Spanish border. Its well-preserved historic centre is anchored at the edges by a 16-arched Roman bridge dating back to Trajan's reign, a medieval tower and the rock-solid Forte de São Francisco.

All of these remnants testify to Chaves' earlier strategic importance in controlling the small but fertile plain that surrounds it. Romans built a key garrison here, that was subsequently contested by the Visigoths, Moors, French and Spanish. The city saw particularly fierce fighting during the Napoleonic invasion, when it was at the forefront of the resistance against French domination.

Nowadays Chaves is a placid backwater, where the Portuguese come to pamper themselves in the natural hot springs that bubble up in the city's heart.

The backbone of Chaves' old town is Rua de Santo António, which runs southeast from the *turismo* to the Roman bridge. The spa is near the river, just south of the centre.

There's plenty of free public parking below the Torre da Menagem and around Jardim do Tabolado.

Sights

Forte de São Francisco FORT
Reached by a drawbridge and bordered by a park with floral designs, hedges and grand old oaks, the 17th-century Forte de São Francisco is the centrepiece of Chaves' old town. The fort, with its thick walls, was completed in 1658 around a 16th-century Franciscan convent. These days it's a top-end hotel (p415), though nobody minds if you snoop around inside the walls.

Ponte Romana BRIDGE
Chaves' handsome, 140m-long, Roman-era bridge makes a lovely place for a car-free stroll. The span was completed in AD 104 by order of Emperor Trajan (hence its other name, Ponte Trajano). It likely served as a

Chaves

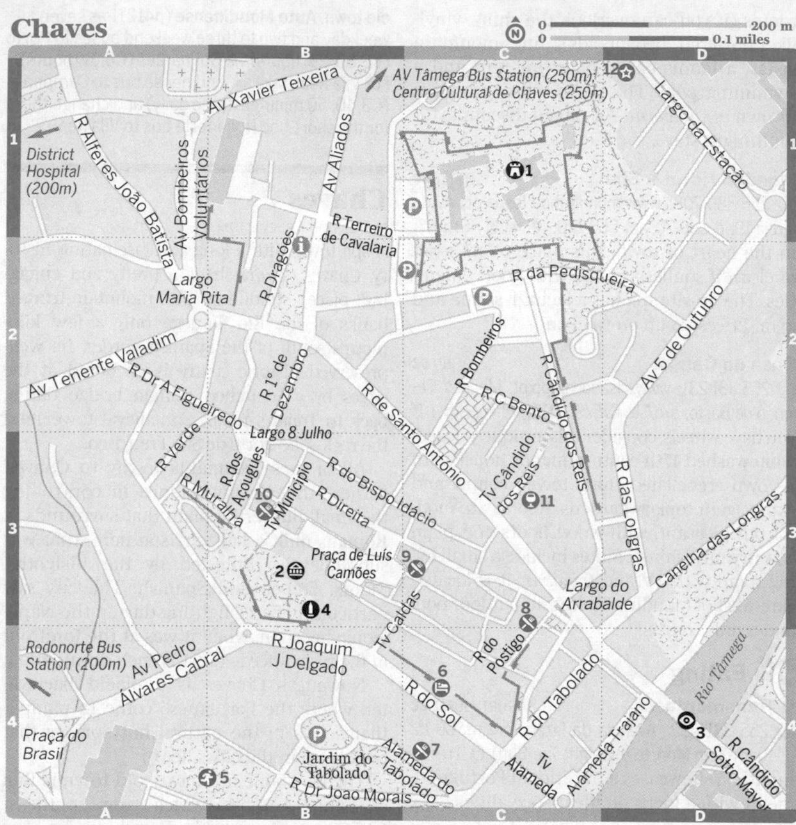

Chaves

Sights

1 Forte de São Francisco C1
2 Museu da Região Flaviense B3
Museu Militar .... (see 4)
3 Ponte Romana D4
4 Torre de Menagem B3

Activities, Courses & Tours

5 Termas de Chaves B4

Sleeping

Forte de São Francisco .... (see 1)
6 Hotel Kátia C4

Eating

7 Carvalho C4
8 João Padeiro C3
9 Maria C3
10 Paprika & Cacau B3

Drinking & Nightlife

11 Adega Faustino C3

Entertainment

12 Centro Cultural de Chaves D1

key link on the important road between Braga and Astorga (Spain), as two engraved Roman milestones on the centre of the bridge indicate.

Museu da Região Flaviense MUSEUM
(Praça de Luís Camões; admission incl Museu Militar €1; ⏲9am-12.30pm & 2-5.30pm) Small but interesting, this archaeological-ethnographic museum has lots of Roman artefacts, plus a collection of pre-Roman jewellery, bronze tools, grinding stones and menhirs, some dating back over 2500 years. There are also temporary art displays upstairs.

Torre de Menagem TOWER

The lovely Torre de Menagem (castle keep) stands alone on a grassy embankment behind the town's main square, the only major remnant of a 14th-century castle built by Dom Dinis. Around the tower are attractive manicured flowerbeds and a stretch of old defensive walls, with views over the town and countryside.

The *torre* now houses a motley collection of military gear in the **Museu Militar** (admission incl Museu da Região Flaviense €1; ⏲9am-12.30pm & 2-5.30pm), accessed via a series of creaky stairs.

Activities

Termas de Chaves SPA

(☎276 332 445; www.termasdechaves.com; Largo das Caldas; ⏲9am-7pm Mon-Sat, to 1pm Sun) The warm waters of the Termas de Chaves, which emerge from the ground at 73°C, are said to relieve everything from rheumatism to obesity. After shelling out the initial €40 medical consultation fee, you have access to a plethora of reasonably priced treatments (€5 to €23), ranging from steam baths to massage.

In the rotunda just outside the baths, spa employees distribute free glasses of the warm, bicarbonate-heavy waters, though they taste pretty awful.

Sleeping

Budget accommodation is clustered along Rua do Sol in the historic centre. For a bit more character and charm, consider the slew of attractive rural inns in the hills surrounding town. Book ahead in summer, when the spa is in full swing. Most places offer big discounts from September to May.

Hotel Kátia HOTEL €

(☎276 324 446; Rua do Sol 28; s/d €35/45; ❄📶) Recently upgraded from guesthouse to hotel, this family-run place offers small stylish rooms – some with verandahs – plus a decent restaurant downstairs. Get one of the rooms facing the street.

Quinta do Rebentão CAMPGROUND €

(☎276 322 733; www.ccchaves.com; Vila Nova de Veiga; sites per adult/child/tent/car €3.20/2.20/2.60/3, 2-/4-person bungalows €40/52; ⏲Jan-Nov; @📶🏊) Six kilometres southwest of Chaves, just off the N2, is this grassy, partly shaded, suburban camping facility with free hot showers, pool access and basic supplies.

Quinta de Santa Isabel INN €€

(☎276 351 818; www.quintadesantaisabel.com.pt; Santo Estevão; 2-/4-person apt €60/90; P📶🐾) This cluster of lovely stone houses – some dating back to the 16th century and converted from haylofts or stables – sits at the foot of a vineyard-covered hillside in the tiny town of Santo Estevão, 7km northeast of Chaves. The five apartments – each with a fireplace or woodstove, plus kitchenette or kitchen – are filled with historic charm, including ancient wood floors, stone walls and antique furniture.

Quinta da Mata INN €€

(☎276 340 030; www.quintadamata.net; Estrada Nacional 213, Vilar de Nantes; s/d €70/80; P@📶🏊) This isolated, family-friendly country haven, just 4.5km southeast of Chaves off the N213, centres on a lovingly restored and elegantly appointed 17th-century manor house with terracotta tile floors and stone walls. The grounds include tennis courts, a sauna and beautiful, flower-filled gardens on the lush hills overlooking the city. The excellent breakfast includes local ham and other regional treats. Bikes are free for guests.

★ **Pedras Salgadas** BUNGALOW €€€

(☎259 437 140; www.pedrassalgadaspark.com; Bornes de Aguiar; d/q €180/190; P❄📶🏊) Fully equipped eco-bungalows and a couple of treehouses are scattered around the woodlands of a spa park on the edge of Bornes de Aguiar, 30km south of Chaves. Shaded by tall trees, each spare and stylish cabin comes with grey slate tiled walls, private decks and lots of glass surfaces.

Vidago Palace HOTEL €€€

(☎276 990 920; www.vidagopalace.com; Parque de Vidago, Vidago; s/d €220/240; P❄@📶🏊) This salmon-pink grand palace in the spa town of Vidago, 12km south of Chaves, sits in the top rungs of Portugal's luxury hotels. The belle epoque grand dame showcases opulent rooms and suites, a gourmet restaurant in a ballroom, an 18-hole golf course, and a white-marble spa for taking in the natural spring waters.

Forte de São Francisco HISTORIC HOTEL €€€

(☎276 333 700; www.fortesaofrancisco.com; Rua do Terreiro da Cavalaria; s/d/ste from €88/98/168; P❄@🏊) For stylish digs in downtown Chaves, look no further than this remarkable historic inn. Housed in a 16th-century convent within the walls of the city's

17th-century fort, this extraordinary blend of four-star hotel and national monument has flawless rooms, as well as tennis courts and a sauna, plus a rare-bird aviary, a centuries-old private chapel and an upscale restaurant and bar.

Eating

Maria BAKERY €
(Largo do Municipio 4; snacks €0.55; 6.30am-6.30pm Mon-Sat, 1-6.30pm Sun) Look for the bright blue door of this tiny bakery, which whips up the best *pasteis de Chaves* (flaky turnovers filled with ground meat) in town.

João Padeiro BAKERY €
(www.facebook.com/padariajoaopadeirochaves; Rua do Postigo 8; pastries from €1; 8.30am-7pm) Snack on tasty regional treats at this corner bakery, including the trademark *folar de Chaves* (big pillowy loaves filled with bacon, *linguiça* and local *salpicão* sausage).

Paprika & Cacau PORTUGUESE €€
(276 402 137; www.facebook.com/paprikaecacau; Rua da Infantaria 19; mains €7-16; 10am-midnight Tue-Sun) Right at the historic heart of Chaves, with great views of the castle, this quaint restaurant serves up Portuguese dishes with a twist. The daily lunch specials are a steal.

Carvalho PORTUGUESE €€
(276 321 727; www.restaurante-carvalho.com; Largo das Caldas 4; mains €8-17; noon-3pm & 7-11pm Tue-Sat, noon-3pm Sun) Carvalho's top-notch regional dishes have earned recognition as some of Portugal's best. It is hidden away amid the cluster of parkside cafes opposite the Jardim do Tabolado.

Drinking & Nightlife

Adega Faustino WINE BAR
(Travessa Cândido dos Reis; noon-11pm Mon-Sat) Resembling a fire station from the outside, this cavernous ex-winery oozes atmosphere inside, with cobblestoned floors and gigantic wine casks lined up behind the bar. The menu features a long list of carefully prepared regional snacks (€4 to €9), from *salpicão* to pig's ear in vinaigrette sauce, plus an excellent selection of quaffable local wines.

Entertainment

Centro Cultural de Chaves PERFORMING ARTS
(276 333 713; Largo da Estação) Chaves' cultural centre stages regular concerts, plays and other events, most of them free of charge. For details on current shows, see the monthly *Agenda Cultural,* available at the *turismo.*

Information

Turismo (276 348 180; turismo@portoenorte.pt; Rua Terreiro de Cavalaria; 9am-12.30pm & 2-5.30pm Mon-Sat;) Helpful multilingual tourist office.

Getting There & Away

AV Tâmega (276 332 384; www.avtamega.pt) and **Rodonorte** (276 328 123; www.rodonorte.pt; Av de Santo Amaro) have terminals just north and west of the centre respectively. Only Tâmega serves all of the following destinations: Bragança (€11.60, three hours, one daily at 4pm), Coimbra (€13.40, 3¾ hours, three daily), Lisbon (€21.60, six to seven hours, three daily), Porto (€13.40, 2¼ hours, several daily) and Vila Real (€8, 1¼ hours, several daily).

Bragança

POP 30,000

The historical capital of Trás-os-Montes, Bragança is at once a modern city of broad sterile avenues and suburban high-rises, and a medieval village from whose crenellated heights one can still survey the surrounding countryside and see small farms, fields and oak-chestnut forest. While many streets – especially some in the older *centro* – give the appearance of a town down on its luck, new construction and civic projects express Bragança's enduring pride and dynamism. Recent additions to the city's cultural life include a municipal theatre, museums dedicated to contemporary art and regional folk traditions, and eye-catching public sculptures such as the bronze postman outside the *correio* (post office) and the massive fighting bulls in the Rotunda do Lavrador Transmontano.

History

Known as Bragantia to the Celts and Juliobriga to the Romans, Bragança is an ancient city. Its location, mere kilometres from the Spanish border, made it an important post in the centuries-long battles between Spain and Portugal. The walled citadel was built in 1130 by Portugal's first king, Afonso Henriques I. His son and successor, Sancho I, improved the fortifications by building Bragança's castle, with its watchtowers, dungeons and keep, in 1187, after reclaiming the city from the king of León.

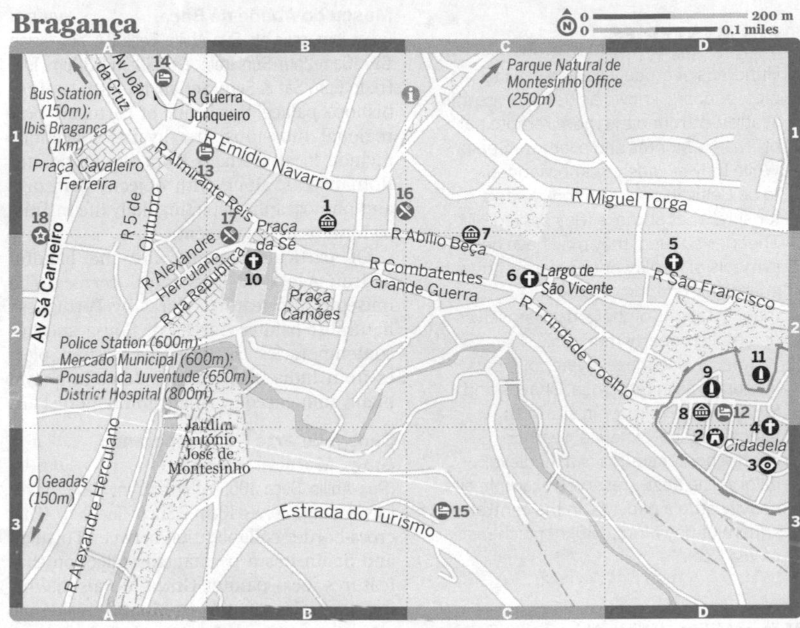

Bragança

Sights

1 Centro de Arte Contemporânea Graça Morais B1
2 Cidadela D3
3 Domus Municipalis D3
4 Igreja de Santa Maria D3
5 Igreja de São Bento D2
6 Igreja de São Vicente C2
7 Museu do Abade de Baçal C2
8 Museu Ibérico da Máscara e do Traje D2
Museu Militar .... (see 11)
9 Pelourinho D2
10 Sé B2
11 Torre de Menagem D2

Sleeping

12 Arco da Velha D2
13 Hotel Tic Tac A1
14 Hotel Tulipa A1
15 Pousada de São Bartolomeu C3

Eating

16 Restaurante Lá Em Casa B1
17 Solar Bragançano B2

Entertainment

18 Teatro Municipal A2

In 1442 Afonso V created the Duchy of Bragança for his uncle, an illegitimate son of the first Avis king João I, thus launching one of Portugal's wealthiest and most powerful noble families. The Braganças assumed the Portuguese throne in 1640, ending Spain's 60-year domination of Portugal. The family went on to reign in Portugal until the dissolution of the monarchy in 1910.

During the Napoleonic Wars, Bragança again served as an important strategic point against foreign invaders: it was from here that Sepúlveda launched his call to resistance against French forces.

Sights

Cidadela FORTRESS

Climb uphill from Largo de São Vicente and you'll soon set foot inside the astonishingly well-preserved 12th-century citadel. People still live in its narrow, atmospheric lanes, unspoilt by the few, low-key handicrafts shops and cafes that have crept in.

Within the ruggedly ramparted walls is the original castle – built by Sancho I in 1187 and beefed up in the 15th century by João I, then heavily restored in the 1930s. The stout **Torre de Menagem** was garrisoned up until the early 20th century. It now houses a

PIG MYSTERIES

Hundreds of crudely carved granite pigs, or boars, known as *berrões* are still scattered around the more remote parts of Trás-os-Montes and over into Spain. While they're widely acknowledged to be Celtic in origin, nobody knows for sure what purpose they served. Theories abound: they may have been symbols of fertility or prosperity, grave guardians, offerings to Iron Age gods, manifestations of the gods themselves or simply property markers.

You can see these mysterious pigs in museums in Bragança, Chaves and Miranda do Douro, or in situ in Bragança's citadel, where a weather-beaten porker supports a medieval pillory. The best-preserved example sits heavily atop a pedestal in the central square of tiny Murça, 30km northeast of Vila Real.

Museu Militar (Military Museum; €2, Sun morning free; ⏲9-noon & 2-5pm Tue-Sun), the four floors of which are filled with swords, guns and suits of armour spanning several centuries, from medieval times to WWI and the Salazar dictatorship's colonial exploits. The price of admission is well worth the chance to climb to the top of the crenellated tower, with great views all around. In front of the *torre* is an extraordinary, primitive **pelourinho** atop a granite boar similar to the *berrões* found around the province.

Squatting at the rear of the citadel is an odd pentagonal building known as the **Domus Municipalis** (Town House; ⏲9am-5pm Tue-Sun), the oldest town hall in Portugal (although its precise age is a matter of scholarly disagreement) and one of the few examples of civil Romanesque architecture on the Iberian Peninsula. Bragança's medieval town council once met upstairs in an arcaded room studded with weathered stone faces of man and beast and scratched with symbols of the stonemasons.

Beside the Domus Municipalis is the early-16th-century **Igreja de Santa Maria**. Of particular interest are its brick Mudéjar columns, vividly painted ceiling, and a 17th-century Santa Maria Madalena at the high altar, with her traditional long hair and ragged garb.

Museu do Abade de Baçal MUSEUM
(www.ipmuseus.pt; Rua Abílio Beça 27; admission €3, 10am-2pm Sun free; ⏲9.30am-5.30pm Tue-Fri, to 6pm Sat & Sun) Set in an 18th-century bishop's palace, this is one of Portugal's best regional museums. Its diverse collections include local artefacts from the Celtic and Roman eras, along with objects, paintings and photographs depicting daily life in Trás-os-Montes to the present.

Of particular interest are the handful of Iron Age stone pigs called *berrões*. The museum also features works by Portuguese naturalist painter Aurelia de Sousa and her contemporaries, as well as Christian pieces from India, which depict Jesus in a style highly influenced by Hindu and Buddhist art.

Centro de Arte Contemporânea Graça Morais MUSEUM
(Rua Abílio Beça 105; adult/student €2/1, mornings & Sun free; ⏲10am-6.30pm Tue-Sun) This cross-border collaboration between Portugal and Spain has a permanent collection that features local painter Graça Morais' haunting portraits of Trás-os-Montes residents, alongside more abstract work. The modern annexe showcases rotating special exhibitions, and there's a cafe with a lovely patio.

Museu Ibérico da Máscara e do Traje MUSEUM
(Iberian Mask & Costume Museum; Rua Dom Fernão o Bravo 24/26; adult/child €1/free; ⏲9am-1pm & 3-6pm Tue-Sun Jun-Sep, 9am-12.30pm & 2-5.30pm Tue-Sun Oct-May) This visually appealing little museum displays a colourful and fascinating collection of masks and costumes from the ancient pagan-based solstice and Carnaval festivities celebrated in Trás-os-Montes and neighbouring Zamora (Spain). Costumes are displayed across three floors, with the upper exhibits dedicated to the work of local artisans.

Sé CATHEDRAL
(Praça da Sé) Bragança's old cathedral started out in 1545 as the Igreja de São João Baptista, but moved up the ranks to become a cathedral in 1770 when the bishopric moved here from Miranda do Douro. It was then downgraded again when Bragança's contemporary cathedral, the **Igreja de Nossa Senhora Rainha**, opened just west of the centre.

Igreja de São Vicente CHURCH
(Largo de São Vicente) Romanesque in origin but rebuilt in the 17th century, this church may have played host to a chapter in Portu-

gal's favourite (and grisliest) love story. Tradition has it that the future Dom Pedro secretly married Inês de Castro here around 1354.

Igreja de São Bento CHURCH
(Rua São Francisco) Bragança's most attractive church has a Renaissance stone portal, a wonderful trompe l'œil ceiling over the nave and an Arabic-style inlaid ceiling above the chancel.

Festivals & Events

Feira das Cantarinhas FAIR
Bragança's biggest annual market, Feira das Cantarinhas, runs for three days in early May. It's a huge street fair of traditional handicrafts (a *cantarinha* is a small terracotta pitcher) held around the centre and Praça da Sé.

Sleeping

Hotel Tic Tac HOTEL €
(☎273 331 373; www.hoteltictac.pt; Rua Emídio Navarro 85; s/d €35/49; P ❄ 📶 🐾) This no-frills hotel is the best of the basic options smack in the city centre. Rooms are small but clean, complimentary amenities include wi-fi, parking and air-con, and the on-site restaurant serves good-value lunches.

Hotel Tulipa HOTEL €
(☎273 331 675; www.tulipaturismo.com; Rua Dr Francisco Felgueiras 8-10; s/d €35/45; ❄ 📶) The Tulipa offers clean and comfortable contemporary rooms, most with flat-screen TVs, and some adapted for visitors with disabilities. An additional plus is the central location between the bus station and downtown. The downstairs restaurant serves great-value weekday lunch specials.

Pousada da Juventude HOSTEL €
(☎273 329 231; www.pousadasjuventude.pt; Avenida 22 de Maio; dm €13, d with shared/private bathroom €28/32; P @ 📶) This modern – if sometimes inattentively run – hostel offers self-service laundry, free wi-fi, comfy common areas, and an on-site bar and restaurant. The two-bedroom apartment (€60) with its own kitchen and washer-dryer is a great option for families. It's located in the nondescript suburbs west of the centre, about a 30-minute walk from the Cidadela.

Arco da Velha APARTMENT €€
(☎966 787 208; www.turismobraganca.com; Rua Dom Fernão o Bravo; 2-bedroom apt €90; P 🐾) The only place to stay within Bragança's atmospheric medieval citadel, this comfy split-level apartment sleeps up to four, allows pets and has its own parking spot just outside. The original stone-walled building has been thoroughly remodelled, with modern furniture and a wood-pellet stove for chilly winter evenings. Minimum stay two nights.

Pousada de São Bartolomeu POUSADA €€€
(☎273 331 493; www.pousadas.pt; Estrada do Turismo; s/d €150/160; P ❄ @ 📶 🏊) This whitewashed modern affair may not be the most arresting *pousada* (upmarket inn) in Portugal, but its views over the Cidadela and countryside are way up there. It sits proudly alone, on a hilltop 1.5km southeast of the centre, and boasts lots of creature comforts, including a great restaurant and bright contemporary rooms with balconies overlooking the pool and the castle.

Eating

Restaurante Lá Em Casa PORTUGUESE €
(Rua Marquês de Pombal 7; mains €6-12.50; ⏱noon-3pm & 7-11pm Mon-Fri, noon-4pm & 7-10pm Sat & Sun) This place serves platters heaped with excellent, wood-grilled local meats in a stone-walled, pine-panelled dining room with fireplace. The veal and lamb are especially savoury. Daily lunch specials are well priced.

★**Don Roberto** PORTUGUESE €€
(☎273 302 510; www.facebook.com/restaurantd.roberto; Rua Coronel Álvaro Cepeda 1, Gimonde; mains €9-15; ⏱9am-10.30pm) It's worth catching a cab out to this traditional roadside tavern 7km from town, in the village of Gimonde en route to Montesinho. The ambience is down-home rural – think wooden beams and smoked hams hanging off the walls – and the food is the real deal. Try the D Roberto steak, starters such as *alheira* and *salpicão,* and the delicious *milho doce* dessert.

O Abel PORTUGUESE €€
(☎273 382 555; www.oabel.pt; Rua do Sabor, Gimonde; mains €10-14; ⏱noon-2.30pm & 7.15-10pm Mon-Wed, Fri & Sat, noon-2.30pm Sun) Well-known for top-notch barbecues prepared by Mr Abel himself, locals from all over the region flock to this simple restaurant for the delicious veal steaks and other grilled meats.

O Geadas PORTUGUESE €€
(☎273 324 413; www.geadas.net; Rua do Loreto; mains €13-19; ⏱noon-4pm & 7pm-midnight Mon-Sat, noon-4pm Sun) The unassuming roadside exterior can be deceptive, but the food is stellar at this traditional restaurant with a spacious dining room. Run by the same family

BUSES FROM BRAGANÇA

DESTINATION	COST (€)	TIME (HR)	COMPANY	FREQUENCY
Braga	13.50	4	Rodonorte	daily
Guimarães	13.50	3½	Rodonorte	daily
Lisbon	18.50	7	Rede Expressos	3 times a week
Nice, France	112	23	Eurolines	daily, except Sunday
Paris, France	86	19	Eurolines	daily
Porto	12	3	Rodonorte & Rede Expressos	daily
Vila Nova de Foz Côa	7.50	1¾	Rede Expressos	daily
Vila Real	9.10	2	Rodonorte	daily
Viseu	13	3¼	Rede Expressos	daily
Trancoso	9.80	2¼	Rede Expressos	daily

as the Pousada, it has a long family tradition of hospitality, hence the great service.

Solar Bragançano PORTUGUESE **€€**
(☎ 273 323 875; Praça da Sé 34; mains €9.50-14.50; ⊙ noon-3pm & 7-10pm Tue-Sun) Upstairs in a manor house opposite the cathedral square, this eatery boasts oak-panelled rooms, chandeliers, wide plank floors, a leafy and sun-dappled outdoor terrace and a seasonal menu weighted towards local game, with specialities including wild boar, partridge with grapes and pheasant with chestnuts.

Drinking & Nightlife

Mercado Club CLUB
(www.facebook.com/mercadoclub; Mercado Municipal) The most popular club in town, right inside the market building.

Entertainment

Teatro Municipal PERFORMING ARTS
(☎ 273 302 744; http://teatromunicipal.cm-braganca.pt; Praça Professor Cavaleiro Ferreira) The boxy Teatro Municipal has given the city's cultural life a great boost by hosting high-quality music, theatre and dance shows, plus afternoon performances for children. There's a multi-screen cinema next door.

Information

Parque Natural de Montesinho Office (☎ 273 329 135; www.icnf.pt; Parque Florestal de Bragança; ⊙ 9am-5.30pm Mon-Fri) Northeast of the *turismo*.

Turismo (☎ 273 381 273; www.cm-braganca.pt; Avenida Cidade Zamora; ⊙ 9.30am-12.30pm & 2-6pm Mon-Sat Jun-Sep, reduced hours Oct-May) An extremely helpful office.

Getting There & Away

BUS

Bragança's spiffy modern bus station, housed in the former train depot at the top of Avenida João da Cruz, is served by **Rede Expressos** (☎ 966 482 215; www.rede-expressos.pt), **Rodonorte** (☎ 273 300 180; www.rodonorte.pt) and **Eurolines** (☎ 273 326 211, 273 327 122; www.eurolines.com). Station offices tend to be open only at departure times. See table above. for further details

CAR & MOTORCYCLE

Parking is generally not difficult. There are lots of paid spots in the square just south of the *sé*, with free overnight parking for motor homes in the lot just east of the Cidadela.

Parque Natural de Montesinho

The peaceful highlands along Portugal's northeastern border with Spain constitute one of Trás-os-Montes' most appealing natural and cultural landscapes – it's a patchwork of rolling grasslands, giant chestnut trees, oak forests and deep canyons, sprinkled with ancient stone villages, where an ageing population still ekes out a hard-scrabble existence.

The 750-sq-km Parque Natural de Montesinho was established to protect the area's 88 lean villages as much as their natural setting. This harsh, remote *terra fria* (cold land) inspired early Portuguese rulers to establish a system of collective land tenure and then leave the villagers to their own devices, allowing for a remarkably democratic, communal culture, which persists today.

Sights

Unfortunately, remote villages of the park continue to be deserted by their young people, and many have not a single resident under the age of 60. However, these settlements – mostly just small clusters of granite houses roofed in slate and sheltering in deep valleys – retain an irresistible charm, especially in late April, when cherry and chestnut trees are in flower. In some towns, the government has helped preserve traditional slate-roofed stone houses as well as churches, forges, mills and the characteristic, charming *pombals* (dovecotes). Villages that retain lashings of character include Pinheiro Novo, Sernande, Moimenta and Dine in the west, and Montesinho, Varge, Rio de Onor and Guadramil in the east.

Moimenta VILLAGE

Moimenta has a lovely core of granite houses roofed in terracotta, plus a small baroque church – a rare dose of luxury in this austere corner of Portugal. The pretty 7km Calçada loop trail descends from town into the nearby river gorge, following sections of an old stone roadway across a remarkably well-preserved medieval bridge with a single impressive arch.

Dine VILLAGE

Dine and Moimenta, two of the prettiest villages in the western half of the park, are connected by a high-altitude road with panoramic views of the windmill-speckled hills along the Spanish border. In well-preserved Dine, you can visit a tiny **archaeological museum**, which documents the 1984 find by a Danish diplomat of Iron Age remains in a nearby cave.

The museum is usually locked, but just ask around and someone will rustle up the French-speaking caretaker, Judite, who may also lead you around to the cave itself – pointing out traditional lime kilns and wild-growing medicinal herbs along the way.

Montesinho VILLAGE

Hidden at the end of the road in a narrow valley wedged between forbidding granite heights, this tiny village is one of the park's best-preserved, thanks to a program to restore old dwellings and stop construction of new ones. The village is also the jumping-off point for the 8km Porto Furado hiking trail through the rugged hills to a nearby dam.

STUB bus 7 runs from Bragança to Montesinho (€1.20, one hour) at least once daily.

Rio de Onor VILLAGE

This lovely little town of 70 souls situated in the eastern half of the park is entirely unfazed by the Spanish–Portuguese border splicing it down the middle. It's interesting not just for its rustic stone buildings, the ground floors of which still house straw-filled stables for goats, sheep and donkeys, but also for its staunch maintenance of the communal lifestyle once typical of the region.

Spend an afternoon here and you'll see elderly locals trundling wheelbarrows from the well-tended community gardens surrounding town, pitchforking hay onto horse-drawn carts, stopping in at the local cafe – the communally shared proceeds of which are used to fund town festivals – or trading jobs with each other – one cousin staying to mind the store while the other goes to bring in

Parque Natural de Montesinho

the sheep. The twinned village also has one other claim to fame – a hybrid Portuguese-Spanish dialect known as Rionorês.

The border runs east–west through the middle of the village, while the Rio de Onor trickles along perpendicular to it. The road from Bragança continues north through town into Spain, branching right just before the border to cross an old stone bridge to the prettiest part of the village, where you'll find the community cafe.

From Bragança, STUB bus 5 heads to Rio de Onor (€1.20, 45 minutes) three times daily.

Activities

There are plenty of cycling and hiking opportunities. Park offices in Bragança (p420) and Vinhais (p423) offer free brochures detailing 11 marked hiking trails around the park (although some of these seem to be chronically out of print!).

If you come here in the summer, you can cool off in the park's plentiful (if chilly) rivers and streams. Look for signs pointing to *praias fluviais* (river beaches) throughout the park; one of the nicest such swimming spots is near the centre of the park, just northwest of the town of Fresulfe.

Sleeping

The natural base from which to explore the park is Bragança. Smaller villages within the park also offer accommodation, but public transport is patchy. For a pretty complete list of local sleeping options, check out the *Alojamento* (lodging) section of the free *Nordeste Transmontano* booklet available from Bragança's tourist office (p420).

Eastern Park

There are a number of self-catering stone cottages available in the village of Montesinho. Note that rooms book up in July and August.

Casa de Onor INN €€
(273 927 163; www.casadeonor.com; Rio de Onor; s €40, d €60-75) In a pretty stone house overlooking the river in the centre of Rio de Onor, Senhora Rita Rego rents five rooms sleeping one to six people, each with private bathroom. Breakfast is included, and additional meals are available upon request for €15 per person.

★ A Lagosta Perdida B&B €€€
(273 919 031; www.lagostaperdida.com; Rua do Cimo 4, Montesinho; s/d €94/125; P) The region's most upscale accommodation is this refurbished stone-walled house, run by a friendly Anglo-Dutch couple. It retains numerous period features, including high, beamed ceilings and an old stone water trough downstairs. The comfortable rooms come equipped with internet, tea-making facilities, flat-screen TVs and beautifully tiled modern bathrooms with tubs.

Western Park

Casa dos Marrões INN €
(273 999 550; www.casadosmarroes.com; Vilarinho; s/d €45/60, house €100; P) In Vilarinho, 17km northwest of Bragança, this 18th-century home built of oak, chestnut and schist has lovely beamed ceilings and exposed-stone walls. Across the street is a self-catering house sleeping up to six. A spring-fed outdoor pool, plus nearby hiking trails and riverside beaches, enhance its appeal.

Casa da Bica INN €
(273 323 577; www.montesinho.com/casadabica; Rua do Lameiro 9, Gondesende; d/house €39/165; P) In Gondesende, 12km northwest of Bragança, this schist cottage offers five rather spartan rooms upstairs (three of those with a private bathroom), plus a downstairs sitting area with fireplace, where breakfast is served.

Parque de Campismo Cepo Verde CAMPGROUND €
(273 999 371; www.montesinho.com; Gondesende; sites per adult/child/tent/car €4.25/2.10/3.95/2.65; P) This medium-sized rural facility is 9km west of Bragança near the tiny village of Gondesende on the park's southern border. Sixty campsites, some shaded and some in full sun, are set on a hillside above a central cafe and swimming pool (€1.50).

Casa de Casares RENTAL HOUSE €€
(934 346 673; www.casas-de-casares.pt; Casares; houses €75-85; P) Four lovingly restored traditional houses in the tiny village of Casares, featuring seven rooms and lots of original detail. Perfect if you're looking for a remote stay, with great countryside walks outside your door. There's a two-night minimum stay, and breakfast is included.

GHOST TOWNS: THE TRANSMONTANA EXODUS

Portugal is one of the few European countries to experience mass emigration well into the 20th century. In the 1970s alone, it's estimated that 775,000 people left the country – nearly 10% of the total population.

With difficult agricultural conditions and little industry, it's little surprise that Trás-os-Montes (along with neighbouring Minho) contributed more than its share to the exodus. The region's population shrank by nearly 33% between 1960 and 2001. To get an idea of the kinds of conditions they were fleeing, consider this: 60% of the region's workforce was engaged in agriculture into the 1990s – a figure higher than in many developing nations.

At the turn of the 20th century, the lion's share of emigrants headed to Brazil, which was undergoing a coffee boom. Later, many left for Portugal's African possessions, which received increased investment and interest during Salazar's regime. Then as Europe's postwar economy heated up in the 1960s and '70s, *transmontanas* began to stick closer to home, finding work as labourers in Germany, Belgium, Switzerland and especially France.

The effect of this exodus is still visible, especially in rural areas. Many villages have been abandoned wholesale, left to a few widows and a clutch of chickens. Around others you'll find a ring of modern construction, almost always paid for not by the fruit of the land but by money earned abroad. And don't be surprised to meet a villager, scythe in hand and oxen in tow, who speaks to you in perfect Parisian argot.

Casa do Parâmio COTTAGE €€
(☎938 331 942; www.montesinho.com/casa-do-paramio; Largo do Outeiro, Parâmio; house with/without breakfast €85/70) Right at the geographic heart of the park, this restored rural house features two doubles each with a private bathroom, a fireplace in the living room, and a traditional wood oven in the kitchen. The owner Cristiana treats guests like friends and makes homemade breakfasts and traditional pies.

Moinho do Caniço RENTAL HOUSE €€
(☎273 323 577; www.montesinho.com/moinho; N103, km 251, Castrelos; house with/without breakfast €80/70; P 🐾) This tastefully refurbished watermill – complete with centuries-old kitchen and open fireplace – is 12km west of Bragança on the N103. The rustically furnished stone-floored cottage sleeps up to six people, with trout fishing in the Rio Baceiro just outside the door. STUB bus 2 (€1.20, 55 minutes) stops nearby.

Eating

Café Montesinho CAFE €
(Montesinho; snacks €3-12) A cosy spot in the hub of the village, stone-walled Café Montesinho serves snacks and drinks, and also rents an upstairs two-bedroom apartment (€50) that sleeps up to four people, complete with kitchen and a pleasant verandah.

Taberna do Capelas PORTUGUESE €€
(Parâmio; mains €9-13) This recently opened restaurant in the tiny village of Parâmio serves simple meals featuring smoked sausages and local veggies, and tender meats such as lamb and cock (order ahead). Its homemade sweet rice is a great finale.

O Careto PORTUGUESE €€
(☎273 919 112; www.facebook.com/restauranteocareto; Varge; mains €10-15; ⊙noon-3pm & 7-10pm) Inside a traditional house in Varge village, this family-run restaurant has been in business for 20 years, serving delicious dishes showcasing local meats (cow or lamb).

Information

Parque Natural de Montesinho Office (☎273 770 309; cipnm@cm-vinhais.pt; Rua das Freiras, Vinhais; ⊙9am-1pm & 2-5pm Mon-Fri, 10am-1pm & 2-5pm Sat & Sun)

Getting Around

Exploring the park is difficult without a car, a bike or sturdy feet. The free park map clearly indicates which roads are paved – unpaved roads can be dicey both during and after rains.

Only some parts of the park are served by bus. For up-to-date schedules, check with Bragança's municipal bus company, STUB (www.stub.com.pt). Trips to towns within the park cost €1.20 and generally take an hour or less.

Miranda do Douro

POP 7480

A fortified frontier town hunkering on the precipice of the gorgeous Rio Douro canyon, Miranda do Douro was long a bulwark of Portugal's 'wild east'. With its crumbling castle lending an air of medieval charm, modern-day Miranda has taken on a decidedly different role – receiving Spanish tourists on short breaks, as opposed to repelling Castilian attacks.

The town's beautifully hulking, 16th-century church may seem all out of proportion to the rest of the town, but it once served as cathedral for the entire region. Visitors shouldn't miss Miranda's ethnographic museum, which sheds light on the region's border culture, including ancient rites such as the 'stick dancing' of the *pauliteiros*.

Street signs around town are written in Mirandês, an ancient language that developed during Miranda's long centuries of isolation from the rest of Portugal. Romance-language buffs will enjoy names such as Rue de la Santa Cruç, which read like a fantastical blend of French, Spanish and Portuguese.

History

Miranda was a vital stronghold during Portugal's first centuries of independence, and the Castilians had to be chucked out at least twice: in the early days by Dom João I, and again in 1710, during the War of the Spanish Succession. In 1545, perhaps as a snub to the increasingly powerful House of Bragança, a diocese was created here – hence the oversized cathedral.

During a siege by French and Spanish troops in 1762, the castle's powder magazine exploded, pulverising most of the castle and killing some 400 people. Twenty years later, shattered Miranda lost its diocese to Bragança. No one paid much attention to Miranda again until the nearby dam was built on the Douro in the 1950s.

Sights

Barragem de Miranda — LANDMARK

A road crawls across this 80m-high dam about 1km east of town, and on to Zamora, 55km away in Spain. Even dammed, the gorge is dramatic. You can take a one-hour boat trip through the gorge with Europarques.

Old Town — AREA

The backstreets in the old town hide some dignified 15th-century facades on Rua da Costanilha (which runs west off Praça de Dom João III) and a Gothic gate at the end of it.

Museu da Terra de Miranda — MUSEUM

(Praça de Dom João III 2; €2, 9am-1pm Sun free; 9am-1pm & 2-6pm Wed-Sun, 2-6pm Tue) This

SPEAKING MIRANDÊS

France has Provençal, Britain has Welsh and Gaelic, and Italy has dozens of distinct regional dialects. Portugal, by contrast, is one of Europe's most monolingual countries, thanks both to its long-stable borders (unchanged since the 13th century) and to the fact that it was conquered and consolidated within a very short period of time (less than 200 years).

The region around Miranda do Douro is a significant exception. Because of its proximity to Spain and long isolation from the rest of Portugal, residents of the towns and villages around Miranda still speak what linguists now recognise as an entirely distinct language. Closely related to Astur-Leonese – the regional language of the adjacent Spanish province – Mirandês is in fact closer to Iberian Latin, the language spoken during the Roman period, than it is to either Portuguese or Spanish.

While Mirandês has largely died out in the city of Miranda do Douro itself, it's still the first language of some 10,000 people in the surrounding villages. The Portuguese government officially recognised it as a second language in 1998, and increasingly the region's road signs are bilingual.

In 1882 Portuguese linguist José Leite de Vasconcelos described Mirandês as 'the language of the farms, of work, of home and love'. The same is true today.

Resurgent local pride in the language is evident in the window display of Miranda do Douro's **Papelaria Andrade**, the collection of Mirandês-language titles which includes translations of *Asterix* comic books.

modest but attractive museum sheds light on a unique culture that has preserved age-old traditions into the 21st century. The handsome 17th-century building (formerly Miranda's city hall) houses a fascinating collection of local artefacts: ceramics, textiles, furniture, musical instruments and tribal-looking masks, along with recreations of a traditional kitchen and a blacksmith's forge.

Sé CATHEDRAL
(hours vary) Inside the right transept of this handsomely severe 16th-century cathedral, look for the doll-like Menino Jesus da Cartolinha, a Christ child in a becoming top hat whose wardrobe rivals Imelda Marcos', thanks to deft local devotees.

Activities

Douro Pula Canhada ADVENTURE
(273 431 340; www.douropulacanhada.com; Apartado 11; tours from €25) Offers guided tours by jeep, mountain bike, donkey and on foot, as well as birdwatching.

Europarques BOATING
(273 432 396; www.europarques.com; adult/child under 10yr €16/8; trips 4pm daily, plus 11am Sat & Sun) Offers one-hour boat trips on the Miranda Dam. Boats leave from beside the dam on the Portuguese side. Occasional two-hour trips (€20) are also offered, but for larger groups only; check with the company for details.

Sleeping

Hotel Turismo HOTEL €
(273 438 030; www.hotelturismomiranda.pt; Rua 1 de Maio 5; s/d €30/50;) Offering terrific comfort for a modest price, this place opposite the *turismo* features large, spotless rooms – most including a separate sitting room – with cable TV, minibars and marble bathrooms. Front rooms have large windows with views across to the castle ruins, while the back rooms are quieter.

Hotel A Morgadinha HOTEL €
(273 438 050; www.hotelmorgadinha.pt; Rua do Mercado 57/59; s/d €20/40;) This simple hotel – one of several budget options along the same street – features spacious rooms with parquet wood floors and bathtubs. There are nice river views from the upstairs breakfast area and from many of the rooms; avoid those facing the street, which are noisier and more claustrophobic.

Hotel Parador Santa Catarina HOTEL €€
(273 431 005; www.hotelparadorsantacatarina.pt; Largo da Pousada; s/d €50/80; P) Every guest gets a private verandah with spectacular views of the gorge at this luxurious hotel perched on the canyon's edge. Rooms are a handsome mix of traditional and contemporary, with hardwood floors, flat-screen TVs and large marble bathrooms. The attached restaurant is the most upmarket in town.

Eating

O Moinho PORTUGUESE €
(273 431 116; http://miranda.restaurantemoinho.com; Rua do Mercado 47; pizzas €4.50-7, mains €6.50-10.50; 11am-11pm) Despite lacklustre service, this new-town spot serves up glorious Douro views along with a wide-ranging menu featuring pizza, pasta, salads and Portuguese standards.

Capa d'Honras PORTUGUESE €€
(Travessa do Castelo 1; mains €10-15; noon-3pm & 7-10pm) Named after the sinister-looking cape that is traditional to the region, this upmarket place just inside the old town gates serves local specialities such as *posta* (veal steak) as well as very good *bacalhau*.

São Pedro PORTUGUESE €€
(273 431 321; Rua Mouzinho de Albuquerque 20; mains €7.50-12.50; noon-3pm Mon, noon-3pm & 7-10pm Tue-Sun) This spacious restaurant, just in from the main old-town gate, serves up a fine *posta á São Pedro* (grilled veal steak dressed with garlic and olive oil). The €11 tourist menu comes with soup, main, dessert, wine and coffee.

O Mirandês PORTUGUESE €€
(www.omirandes.net; Rua Dom Dinis 7; mains €7-14; 7.30am-11pm) Below the castle, just to the right of the main road leading into the old town, this unassuming light-filled spot is popular with locals for its great-value lunch specials and tasty dinners.

Information

Parque Natural do Douro Internacional Office (273 431 457; Largo do Castelo; 8am-1pm & 2-5pm Mon-Fri) Around the block from the cathedral and across from a baroque church that has been converted into a public library.

Turismo (273 430 025; www.rt-nordeste.pt; Largo do Menino Jesus da Cartolinha; 9am-12.30pm & 2-5.30pm Mon-Sat)

THE HILLS ARE ALIVE: STRANGE WAYS IN TRÁS-OS-MONTES

For centuries, the remoteness of Trás-os-Montes has insulated it from central authority, helping its people preserve nonconformist ways that sometimes raise eyebrows in other parts of Portugal.

A number of licentious – and blatantly pagan – traditions still survive in the countryside. Witness the antics of the **Caretos of Podence** (near Macedo de Cavaleiros) – where gangs of young men in *caretos* (leering masks) and vividly striped costumes invade the town centre, bent on cheerfully humiliating everyone in sight. Prime targets are young women, at whom they thrust their hips and wave the cowbells hanging from their belts. Similar figures are to be seen in Varge, in the Parque Natural de Montesinho.

Colourful festivals derived from ancient Celtic solstice rituals take place in many villages in the two weeks between Christmas Eve and Dia dos Reis (Epiphany). During the so-called **Festa dos Rapazes** (Festival of the Lads), unmarried men over 16 light all-night bonfires and rampage around in robes of rags and masks of brass or wood. Un-Christian indeed!

Then there are the *pauliteiros* (stick dancers) of the Miranda do Douro region, who look and dance very much like England's Morris dancers. Local men deck themselves out in kilts and smocks, black waistcoats, bright flapping shawls, and black hats covered in flowers and ribbons, and do a rhythmic dance to the complex clacking of *paulitos* (short wooden sticks) – a practice that likely survives from Celtic times. The best time to see *pauliteiros* in Miranda is during the **Festas de Santa Bárbara** (also called Festas da Cidade, or City Festival), which is held on the third weekend in August.

Finally, there are the region's so-called crypto-Jews. During the Inquisition, Jews from Spain and Portugal found that they could evade ecclesiastical authorities here. Many families continued to observe Jewish practices in secrecy well into the 20th century.

Getting There & Away

BUS

Rodonorte (☎273 432 667; www.rodonorte.pt) offers service daily except Saturday to Mogadouro (€6.20, 45 minutes), with onward connections to Vila Nova de Foz Côa (€7.40, 2½ hours), Vila Real (€12.70, three to four hours) and Porto (€14.90, 4½ to six hours).

CAR & MOTORCYCLE

The quickest road from Bragança to Miranda do Douro is the N218 and N218-2, a winding 70km trip. The slower but lovelier 100km route (N216/N221) from Macedo de Cavaleiros via Mogadouro crosses a *planalto* (high plateau) dotted with olive, almond and chestnut groves and includes a dramatic switchbacking descent into the Rio Sabor valley. Miranda has plenty of free parking around Largo do Menino Jesus da Cartolinha.

Parque Natural do Douro Internacional

Tucked into Portugal's northeastern corner, this 870-sq-km, Chile-shaped park runs for 120km along the Rio Douro and the monumental canyon it has carved along the border with Spain. The canyon's towering, granite cliffs are the habitat for several threatened bird species, including black storks, Egyptian vultures, griffon vultures, peregrine falcons, golden eagles and Bonelli's eagles.

The human population is equally fragile. In the plains that run up to the canyon lip, there are some 35 villages, some inhabited by descendants of banished medieval convicts, as well as Jews who fled the Inquisition. The region's isolation has enabled its people to preserve even more ancient roots, such as the Celtic *dança dos paulitos*. A few hundred villagers still speak Mirandês; you'll see town names written in Portuguese and Mirandês throughout the park's northern reaches.

Sights

Miranda do Douro and Mogadouro are the best places from which to explore the park.

For fabulous, near-aerial views of the gorge and its birdlife, you can visit seven panoramic overlooks throughout the park. North to south, with the nearest village in parentheses, these are **Penha das Torres** (Paradela), **São João das Arribas** (Aldeia Nova), **Fraga do Puio** (Picote), **Carrascalinho** (Fornos), **Penedo Durão** (Poiares), **Sapinha** (Escalhão) and **Santo André** (Almofala).

As you move south along the river, the terrain gains a distinctly Mediterranean air, with rolling orchards of olives and almonds and, in the southernmost reaches, land demarcated for port-wine grapes.

Activities

There are four marked **hiking trails** in the park. The most convenient for nondrivers – and one of the most beautiful – is the 19km **Miranda do Douro to São João das Arribas loop**, starting and ending at Miranda do Douro's cathedral. The trail – open to hikers, cyclists and horses – passes through mixed oak woodlands and small villages, and includes striking vistas of the river at São João. Another stunning option is the **Vale da Ribeira do Mosteiro loop**, which passes through vineyards and rugged canyon country along a small tributary of the Douro.

Tours

Without your own transport, the easiest way to see the Douro gorge is on an hour-long cruise from Miranda do Douro with Europarques (p425).

From Miranda do Douro, Douro Pula Canhada (p425) offers guided tours by jeep, mountain bike, donkey and on foot, as well as birdwatching. **Naturisnor** (☎969 031 894; www.naturisnor.com) offers 2½-hour boat tours (€20) that take in the park's flora and fauna.

Sleeping

With its impressive views of the river gorge, Miranda do Douro is the most attractive base for exploring the park. Mogadouro also offers tourist services, but at nearly 15km from the Douro, it's a far less scenic option. Several rural house rental options are also available.

Casa dos Edras INN €€

(☎961 039 516; www.casadosedras.pt; Rua Principal, Aldeia Nova; r €70-75; P ❄ ≋) This gorgeously restored country house in Aldeia Nova, 5.5km from Miranda do Douro, is inside the park borders. The eight rooms come with flat-screen TVs, pinewood floors and garden or village vistas. The shared area features a fireplace, and there's a lawn with outdoor seating and a small swimming pool. A hearty breakfast is included and guests can use the bikes for free.

Casa de I Bárrio RENTAL HOUSE €€

(☎273 738 088; www.casadelbarrio.com; Rua de I Bárrio 7, Picote; d/house €60/120; P ❄ ᯤ) This great rural option in the village of Picote, 17km southwest of Miranda do Douro, is run by a linguist and a biologist, who offer free guided nature walks for their guests. The cosy solar-energy-powered house sleeps up to five and features lots of pine wood, a fireplace and a small patio. Breakfast is delivered every morning, and there are free bikes for guests.

Eating

A Lareira PORTUGUESE €€

(☎279 342 363; Av Nossa Senhora do Caminho 58-62, Mogadouro; mains €8-13; ⏲noon-3pm & 7-10pm) This recommended restaurant offers outstanding local beef, veal and mushrooms grilled on an open fireplace by the French-trained proprietor. The small, well-equipped rooms upstairs (single/double €25/30) are also excellent value.

Information

The most informative park office is in **Miranda do Douro** (p425), with another in **Mogadouro** (☎279 341 596; www.icnf.pt/portal/naturaclas/ap/p-nat/pndi; Rua Dr Francisco António Vicente 4, Mogadouro; ⏲10am-1pm & 2.30-5.30pm Mon-Fri).

Getting There & Away

Rodonorte (☎273 432 444; www.rodonorte.pt), **Santos** (☎273 432 444; www.santosviagensturismo.pt) and **Rede Expressos** (☎707 223 344; www.rede-expressos.pt) offer regular bus services to Miranda do Douro and Mogadouro from most major towns and cities in the region.

Getting Around

Public transport to smaller villages within the park is extremely limited, and mostly designed to serve schoolchildren; check with the park offices for current schedule information.

The Minho

Includes ➡

Best Places to Eat

- Casa de Pasto das Carvalheiras (p435)
- Le Babachris (p442)
- Taberna do Valentim (p449)
- O Abocanhado (p468)

Best Places to Sleep

- Margarida da Praça (p448)
- Casa do Juncal (p441)
- Carmo's Boutique Hotel (p457)
- Pousada do Gerês-Caniçada/São Bento (p467)

Why Go?

The Minho delivers world-class natural beauty with a knowing smile. Here are lush river valleys, sparkling beaches and granite peaks patrolled by locals – who, whether they are charging 2m waves along the Costa Verde or shepherding their flock into high mountain meadows, seem particularly in tune with their homeland. This is, after all, the birthplace of the Portuguese kingdom, and it would be hard to find better-preserved landmarks than those uplit and on display in the Minho's gorgeous old cities.

Then there's the bold, sharp and fruity *vinho verde* to consider. This young wine is fashioned from the fruit of kilometres of vineyards that wind along rivers, over foothills and into Minho mountain villages. The crops are eventually crushed and bottled in community *adegas* (wineries), giving each destination its own flavour. Of course, if you sip enough along the way, they may all blend into one delicious memory.

When to Go

Braga

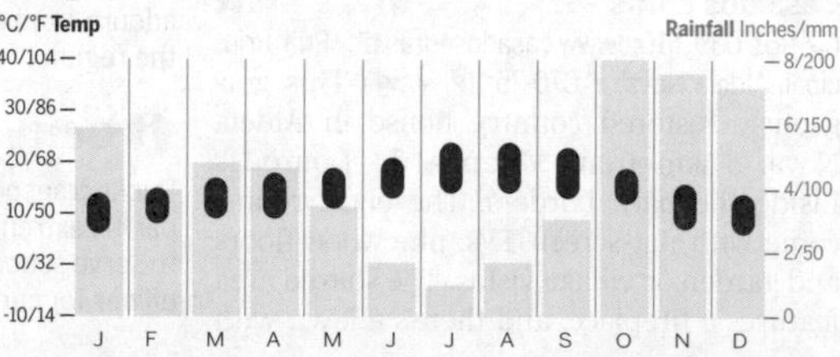

May In the first week of the month, Festa das Cruzes turns Barcelos into a fairground.

Jun Braga's Festas de São João bursts with pagan energy and fireworks.

Sep Festas de Senhora, Peneda, features candlelit processions and a gushing waterfall.

The Minho Highlights

1. Visit historic monuments, followed by dinner at a top restaurant in **Braga** (p430).

2. Stroll the atmospheric streets of **Viana do Castelo** (p444), then catch sunset on the beach.

3. Lounge at a cafe overlooking the medieval bridge and lush countryside beyond in **Ponte de Lima** (p454).

4. Explore the contemporary art and culture in buzzing **Guimarães** (p438).

5. Hike the boulder-strewn peaks and gorse-clad moorlands of **Parque Nacional da Peneda-Gerês** (p460).

Braga

POP 136,885

Portugal's third-largest city is an elegant town laced with ancient narrow lanes closed to vehicles, strewn with plazas and a splendid array of baroque churches. The constant chiming of bells is a reminder of Braga's age-old devotion to the spiritual world. Its religious festivals – particularly the elaborately staged Semana Santa (Holy Week) – are famous throughout Portugal. But don't come expecting piety alone: Braga's upscale old centre is packed with lively cafes and trim boutiques, some excellent restaurants and low-key bars catering to students from the Universidade do Minho. In fact, it's such a young city that in 2012 it was pronounced the European Youth Capital.

Just outside the city stands the magnificent, much-visited hillside church and sanctuary of Bom Jesus do Monte.

History

Founded by Romans, Braga was settled in the 1st century BC, named Bracara Augusta and made the capital of the Roman province of Gallaecia. Braga's position situated at the intersection of five Roman roads helped it grow fat on trade, but it fell to the Suevi around AD 410, and was sacked by the Visigoths 60 years later. The Visigoths' conversion to Christianity in the 6th century and the founding of an archbishopric in the next century put the town atop the Iberian Peninsula's ecclesiastical pecking order.

The Moors moved in around 715, sparking a long-running tug of war that ended when Fernando I, king of Castilla y León, definitively reconquered the city in 1040. The archbishopric was restored in 1070, though prelates bickered with their Spanish counterparts for the next 500 years over who was Primate of All Spain. The pope finally ruled in Braga's favour, though the city's resulting good fortune began to wane in the 18th century when a newly anointed Lisbon archdiocese stole much of its thunder.

Not surprisingly, it was from conservative Braga that António de Oliveira Salazar, with his unique blend of Catholicism and fascism, gave the speech that launched his 1926 coup, introducing Portugal to half a century of dictatorship.

Sights

GNRation CULTURAL CENTRE

(www.gnration.pt; Praça Conde de Agrolongo 123; 9.30am-6.30pm Mon-Fri, 2.30-6.30pm Sat) FREE Braga's newest cultural centre lives inside an 18th-century building that once housed police headquarters. Enter through the modern entrance with a glass sliding door and you're inside an incubator of the city's creative industry, with concerts, film screenings, workshops and theatre performances.

Sé Cathedral Choir CHURCH

(adult/child €2/1) The guided tour of the choir inside the Sé (cathedral) gives an up-close look at the mesmerising organs and gilded choir stalls. Visitors are led downstairs and into the cathedral's showpiece Capela dos Reis (Kings' Chapel), home to the tombs of Henri of Burgundy and Dona Teresa, parents of the first king of Portugal, Afonso Henriques.

You'll also visit the *azulejo* (hand-painted tile)-covered Capela de São Geraldo (dating from the 12th century but reworked over the years) and the 14th-century Capela da Glória, whose interior was painted in unrepentantly Moorish geometric motifs in the 16th century.

Museu dos Biscainhos MUSEUM

(Rua dos Biscainhos; adult/student €2/1, first Sun of the month free; 9.30am-12.45pm & 2-5.30pm Tue-Sun) An 18th-century aristocrat's palace is home to the enthusiastic municipal museum, with a nice collection of Roman relics and 17th- to 19th-century pottery and furnishings. The palace itself is the reason to come, with its polychrome, chestnut-panelled ceilings and 18th-century *azulejos* depicting hunting scenes. The ground floor is paved with deeply ribbed flagstones on which carriages would have once rattled through to the stables.

Sé CATHEDRAL

(www.se-braga.pt; Rua Dom Paio Mendes; 9am-7pm high season, 9am-6.30pm low season) Braga's extraordinary cathedral, the oldest in Portugal, was begun when the archdiocese was restored in 1070 and completed in the following century. It's a rambling complex made up of differing styles, and architecture buffs could spend half a day happily distinguishing the Romanesque bones from Manueline musculature and baroque frippery.

The original Romanesque style is the most interesting and survives in the cathedral's overall shape, the southern entrance and the marvellous west portal, which is carved with scenes from the medieval legend of Reynard the Fox (now sheltered inside a Gothic porch). The most appealing external features are the filigree Manueline towers and roof – an early work by João de Castilho, who went on to build Lisbon's Mosteiro dos Jerónimos.

You can enter the cathedral through the west portal or via a courtyard and cloister that's lined with Gothic chapels on the north side. The church itself features a fine Manueline carved altarpiece, a tall chapel with *azulejos* telling the story of Braga's first bishop, and fantastic twin baroque organs (held up by formidable satyrs and mermen), which are played at mass every Sunday at 11.30am.

Connected to the church is the **treasury** (adult/child €3/2; ⏲9am-12.30pm & 2.30-7pm high season, 9am-12.30pm & 2-6.30pm low season), housing a goldmine of ecclesiastical booty, including the lovely Nossa Senhora do Leite of the Virgin suckling Christ, attributed to 16th-century French sculptor Nicolas Chanterène. Other highlights are the iron cross that was used in 1500 to celebrate the very first Mass in Brazil.

To visit the choir (p430), visitors must purchase a separate ticket and join a guided tour (some guides speak English), which gives an up-close look at the mesmerising organs and gilded choir stalls. Visitors will then be led downstairs and into the cathedral's showpiece **Capela dos Reis** (Kings' Chapel), home to the tombs of Henri of Burgundy and Dona Teresa, parents of the first king of Portugal, Afonso Henriques. You'll also visit the *azulejo*-covered **Capela de São Geraldo** (dating from the 12th century but reworked over the years) and the 14th-century **Capela da Glória**, whose interior was painted in unrepentantly Moorish geometric motifs in the 16th century.

Centro Interpretativo das Memórias da Misericórdia de Braga MUSEUM

(Rua do Raio 400; ⏲10am-1pm & 2.30-6.30pm Tue-Sat) FREE Braga's newest museum is housed inside Palácio do Raio, the extroverted work by André Soares, its rococo face covered in *azulejos*. The gorgeous interiors, also filled with *azulejos*, showcase works of sacred art, textiles, paintings, sculptures, jewellery and pottery, all bearing witness to 500 years of the building's history.

Check out the collection of old medical instruments (weighing scales, pharmacy vials, tincture bottles); the building housed São Marcos hospital from 1884.

Museu da Imagem MUSEUM

(Campo das Hortas 35-37; ⏲11am-7pm Tue-Fri, 2.30-6.30pm Sat) FREE A minimalist, ancient and beautiful stone relic, outfitted tastefully with steel and wood stairs, this museum shows off impeccably lit, international photography exhibits on three floors.

Fonte do Ídolo RUINS

(Idol Spring; Rua do Raio; adult/student €1.85/0.95; ⏲9am-1pm & 2-6pm Tue-Fri, 10am-5pm Sat & Mon) A Roman ruin opened to the public, this spring is set underneath a mod lobby. An essential community water source, it was carved into a fountain during pre-Roman times by Celicus Fronto, an immigrant from the city-state of Arcobriga. One carving is of a toga-clad pilgrim thought to be holding the horn of plenty. There's an introductory video, too.

Termas Romanas do Alto Cividade RUINS

(Rua Dr Rocha Peixoto; adult/student €1.85/0.95; ⏲9am-1pm & 2-6pm Tue-Fri, 10am-5pm Sat & Mon) These ruins of an extensive bathing complex – with an attached theatre – dating from the 2nd century AD, were probably abandoned in the 5th century. See the seven-minute introductory video in English or Portuguese.

Museu Dom Diogo de Sousa MUSEUM

(Rua dos Bombeiros Voluntários; adult/student €3/1.50, Sun free; ⏲9.30am-6pm Tue-Sun May-Sep, 9.30am-5.30pm Tue-Sun Oct-Apr) The archaeological museum houses a nicely displayed collection of fragments from Braga's earliest days. The four rooms feature pieces from Palaeolithic times (arrowheads, funerary objects and ceramics) through the days of Roman rule and on up to the period dominated by the Suevi-Visigoth kingdom (5th through 7th centuries).

Praça da República SQUARE

The cafes and restaurants on this broad plaza are a pleasant place to start or finish your day. An especially mellow atmosphere descends in the evening, when coloured lights spring up and people of all ages congregate to enjoy the night air.

The square-shaped, crenellated tower behind the cafes is the walled-up **Torre de**

Braga

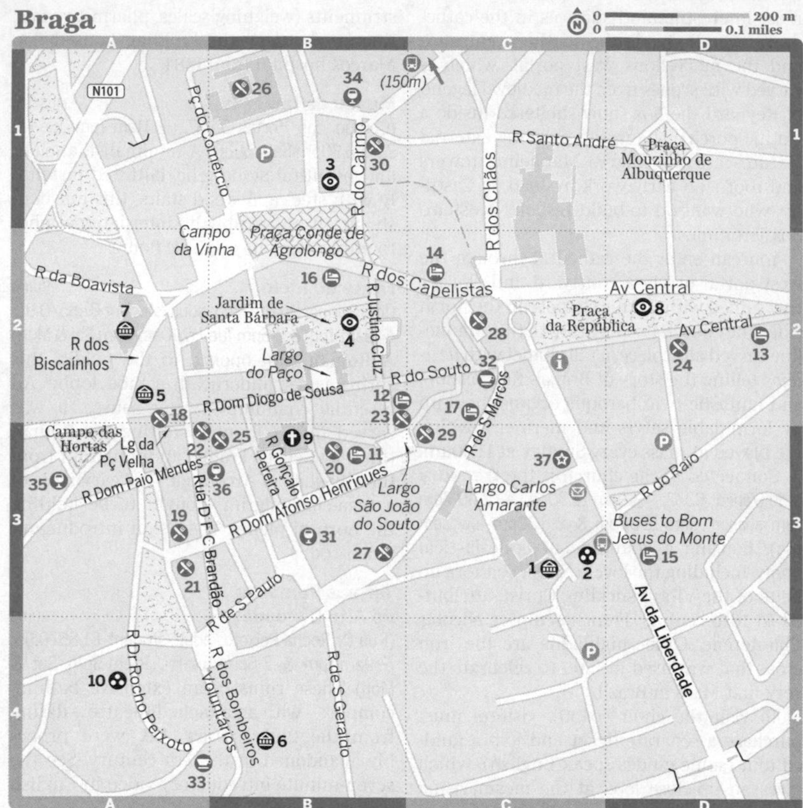

Menagem, which is all that survives of a fortified medieval palace.

Jardim de Santa Bárbara GARDENS

(Rua Justino Cruz) FREE This 17th-century square has narrow paths picking their way through a sea of flowers and topiary. On sunny days the adjacent pedestrianised Rua Justino Cruz and Rua Francisco Sanches fill with buskers and cafe tables.

Activities

Tourists' Affairs TOURS

(253 253 169; www.thetouristsaffairs.com) Excellent tour agency run by a pair of young, enthusiastic locals, an architect and an archaeologist, it specialises in all things Minho. Their focus is on tailor-made à la carte tours of Minho and beyond, but they also offer free walking tours of Braga – call a day ahead to reserve a spot.

Festivals & Events

Festas de São João CULTURAL

A pre-Christian solstice bash dressed up to look like holy days, this festival still bursts with pagan energy. Held for 10 days every June, it features medieval folk plays, processions, dancing, bonfires, fireworks – and thousands of little pots of basil. Basil is the symbol of São João (John the Baptist), and traditionally people write poems to loved ones and conceal them in their pots.

Locals also bust out squeaky plastic hammers and whack each other mercilessly.

Sleeping

★Collector's Hostel HOSTEL €

(253 048 124; www.collectorshostel.com; Rua Francisco Sanches 42; dm €19-22, s/d €26/30) A lovely hostel, lovingly run by two well-travelled women who met in Paris (one of whom was born in the hostel's living room),

Braga

Sights

1 Centro Interpretativo das Memórias da Misericórdia de Braga ... C3
2 Fonte do Ídolo ... C3
3 GNRation ... B1
4 Jardim de Santa Bárbara ... B2
5 Museu da Imagem ... A2
6 Museu Dom Diogo de Sousa ... B4
7 Museu dos Biscainhos ... A2
8 Praça da República ... D2
9 Sé ... B3
Sé Cathedral Choir ... (see 9)
Sé Cathedral Treasury ... (see 9)
10 Termas Romanas do Alto Cividade ... A4

Sleeping

11 Casa de Santa Zita ... B3
12 Collector's Hostel ... B2
13 Hotel Bracara Augusta ... D2
14 Hotel dos Terceiros ... C2
Hotel Ibis ... (see 3)
15 Just Go Hostel ... D3
16 Tea 4 Nine ... B2
17 Truthotel ... C2

Eating

18 Anjo Verde ... A2
19 Brac ... A3
20 Caldo Entornado ... B3
21 Casa de Pasto das Carvalheiras ... A3
Copo e Meio ... (see 18)
22 Cozinha da Sé ... A3
Félix Taberna ... (see 18)
23 Frigideiras do Cantinho ... B2
24 Livraria Centésima Página ... D2
25 Mercado da Saudade ... B3
26 Mercado Municipal ... B1
27 Retro Kitchen ... B3
28 Silvas ... C2
29 Spirito Cupcakes & Coffee ... C3
30 Taberna Velhos Tempos ... B1

Drinking & Nightlife

31 Barhaus ... B3
32 Café A Brasileira ... C2
33 Colinatrum ... A4
34 Convento do Carmo ... B1
35 Domus Vinum ... A3
36 Estúdio 22 ... B3
Sé La Vie ... (see 25)
Taberna Svbvra ... (see 22)

Entertainment

37 Teatro Circo de Braga ... C3

restored the family house and all the furniture inside, and turned the three floors into a cosy hideaway where guests feel like they're in their grandparents' home, with a twist.

Just Go Hostel HOSTEL €
(253 066 166; www.justgohostelbraga.com; Avenida da Liberdade 546; dm €15-16, d €36-42;) Don't be deceived by the unassuming entrance to what appears an office building. Occupying the top two floors, this swank, colourful hostel showcases well-appointed dorms and doubles, and great city views from the shared living room and kitchen.

Hotel Ibis HOTEL €
(253 204 800; www.ibis.com; Rua do Carmo 38; r €35-55; P @) The rooms in this smart, modern hotel all have wood floors, floating desks, bathtubs and queen beds. They aren't huge, but have all the mod cons, and those on the upper reaches have panoramic views of surrounding monuments. Walk-in prices dip as low as €35, at which it's a steal. Breakfast is charged extra (€6.50).

Hotel dos Terceiros HOTEL €
(253 270 466; www.terceiros.com; Rua dos Capelistas 85; s/d €30/43;) On a quiet pedestrian street near Praça da República, this simple hotel has recently updated rooms overlooking a small square, some with tiny balconies. Most rooms have one full and single bed each, and can sleep up to three people.

Truthotel HOTEL €
(253 277 177; www.truthotel.com; Rua de São Marcos 80; s/d €45/55; P @) This friendly hideaway in a fine old town house has individually decked-out rooms with high ceilings and parquet floors. Five of the rooms are decorated by artists; a few have terraces. There are rotating art exhibits in the lobby, and the staff are welcoming and friendly.

Casa de Santa Zita GUESTHOUSE €
(253 618 331; braga@osz.pt; Rua São João 20; s/d €25/36;) This impeccably kept pilgrims lodge has an air of palpable serenity. The sweet sisters offer bright, spotless rooms with hardwood floors, and breakfast is served in a stone arched dining room. The only drawback is a midnight curfew.

EASTER IN BRAGA

Braga hosts the most elaborate Easter celebrations in Portugal. It kicks off with **Semana Santa**, when Gregorian chants are piped throughout the city centre and makeshift candlelit altars light the streets at night. The action heats up during Holy Thursday's Procissão do Senhor Ecce Homo, when barefoot, hooded penitents – members of private Catholic brotherhoods – march through the streets spinning their eerie rattles.

The Good Friday celebration in the cathedral is a remarkable, elaborately staged drama with silk canopies, dirge-like hymns, dozens of priests and a weeping congregation. On Saturday evening, the Easter Vigil Mass begins dourly, the entire cathedral in shadow, only to explode in lights and jubilation. Finally, on Sunday, the people of Braga blanket their thresholds with flowers, inviting passing priests to enter and give their home a blessing.

Tea 4 Nine GUESTHOUSE €€
(☎914 004 606; www.tea4nine.pt; Praça Conde Agrolongo 49; s/d €80/105) A swish new guest house with four stunning suites featuring clean-lined contemporary decor, pine floors and a full range of top-of-the-line amenities. Two face the square, two are out back, and three more sit in another building facing the square. Note that there's no elevator. The sweet downstairs bistro with a garden does great lunch menus and a Sunday brunch (€7.50).

Hotel Bracara Augusta BOUTIQUE HOTEL €€
(☎253 206 260; www.bracaraaugusta.com; Avenida Central 134; s/d €79/99; P ❄ @) This stylish, grand town house offers bright, modern rooms with parquet floors, classic decor and marble bathrooms. The suites have French doors opening onto decorative balconies. Its restaurant offers an excellent breakfast buffet, with open-air dining by a gurgling fountain out back.

Eating

Retro Kitchen PORTUGUESE €
(☎253 267 023; Rua do Anjo 96; mains €8.50-12; noon-2.30pm & 8-10.30pm Mon & Wed-Sat) A vintage theme runs through this funky, laidback restaurant featuring tasty daily specials and a display of eclectic retro items curated by the friendly owner couple. The lunch menu is a steal at €6.

Spirito Cupcakes & Coffee ICE CREAM €
(Largo São João do Souto 19; cup €2-3.50, cone €2-4; 1.30-7pm Mon-Thu, 1.30-7pm & 9pm-midnight Fri & Sat) Don't miss the artisanal gelato at this always buzzing shop, where lines form out the door for a cup or cone of oatmeal-, cookie- or bubblegum-flavoured ice creams, and great cupcakes and coffees, too.

Taberna Velhos Tempos PORTUGUESE €
(☎253 214 368; Rua do Carmo 7; mains €7.50-11; noon-2.30pm & 8-10.30pm Mon-Sat) A rustic tavern with wooden beams, lots of bric-a-brac and a menu of tasty mainstays. Try the *bacalhau com nata* (baked codfish) or duck rice. The portions are huge so order only half sizes.

Mercado da Saudade CAFE €
(Rua Dom Paio Mendes 59; snacks €2-3.50; 11am-8pm Thu, 11am-2am Fri & Sat, 11am-10pm Sun) A colourful little grocery store-cafe, with a few storefront and sidewalk tables, where you can buy a variety of Portuguese products – from cork items, shoes and soaps to edibles such as chocolates and sardines. Its snacks are delicious; try the Portuguese pork sandwich and wash it down with a glass of wine or Sovina, the local handcrafted beer.

Livraria Centésima Página CAFE €
(Avenida Central 118-120; snacks €2.60-4.90; 9am-7.30pm Mon-Sat) Tucked inside Centésima Página, an absolutely splendid bookshop with foreign-language titles, this charming cafe serves a rotating selection of tasty quiches along with salads and desserts, and has outdoor tables in the pleasantly rustic garden. Its lunch specials are a steal.

Anjo Verde VEGETARIAN €
(Largo da Praça Velha 21; mains €7.50-8.60; noon-3pm & 7.30-10.30pm Mon-Sat;) Braga's vegetarian offering serves generous, elegantly presented plates in a lovely, airy

dining room. Vegetarian lasagne, risotto and vegetable tarts are among the choices. Mains can be bland, but the spiced chocolate tart is a superstar.

Silvas PORTUGUESE €
(Largo do Terreiro do Castelo; mains €6.50-8; noon-3.30pm & 7-11pm) A cosy little spot in the shadow of Torre de Menagem, this has a narrow glass-enclosed interior with a counter and a few tables outside. The well-prepared dishes change daily and include duck rice, rolled veal and always a fresh fish dish.

Frigideiras do Cantinho CAFE €
(Largo São João do Souto 1; mains €4-7; 8am-10pm) Set on a sweet, quiet plaza, with pleasant indoor and outdoor seating, this humble cafe is favoured by loyal locals for its *frigideiras* (€1.50 per pop): meat pies with pork and veal, a tradition dating from 1796.

Mercado Municipal MARKET €
(Praça do Comércio; 8am-3pm Mon-Fri, 6am-1pm Sat) The *mercado municipal* buzzes on weekdays and Saturday mornings, and is ideal for self-caterers.

Casa de Pasto das Carvalheiras FUSION €€
(253 046 244; Rua Dom Afonso Henriques 8; mains €4.50-14; noon-3pm & 7pm-midnight) This funky eatery with lots of colourful details and a long bar serves up flavourful fusion food served as *pratinhos* (small plates). The menus change weekly and feature dishes like salmon ceviche, *alheira* (a light garlicky sausage of poultry or game) rolls with turnip sprouts and black octopus polenta. Weekday lunch menus are a great deal (€8 or €12, depending on the number of dishes you order).

Caldo Entornado PORTUGUESE €€
(253 065 578; www.caldoentornado.com; Rua São João 8; mains €11-15; noon-3pm & 7-11pm Tue-Sat, noon-3pm Mon & Sun) Run by a friendly couple, this minimalist eatery with contemporary decor and pine-wood details serves great-value weekday lunches (€8) and a range of well-prepared mains like cod puff pastries, prawn curries and *picanhas* (rump steaks).

Brac PORTUGUESE €€
(253 610 225; Campo das Carvalheiras; snacks €3-9, mains €13-17; 11am-midnight Mon-Sat) Braga's gourmet hotspot offers tasty *petiscos* (tapas) at the backlit bar and more elaborate dishes like prawn curry and roasted black pork in the swank dining room with stone columns and exposed stone walls. Happy hour is every night from 5.30pm to 7pm.

Félix Taberna PORTUGUESE €€
(253 617 701; Largo da Praça Velha 18-19; mains €10.75-16.75; noon-3pm & 7pm-1am Mon-Fri, 7pm-1am Sat) Savour terrific Portuguese dishes in this attractive country-style tavern with two cosy dining rooms showcasing lots of bric-a-brac. The menu is small but dishes are delicious, including breaded sardines, duck rice and codfish *a minha moda*.

Copo e Meio PORTUGUESE €€
(253 265 475; Rua Dom Frei Cateano Brandão 120; tapas €2-9, mains €11-19; noon-2am Mon-Sat) This swanky, gourmet tapas bar-restaurant with two cute upstairs stone dining rooms and a streetside deck gets packed with local moneyed types. Come for the tapas and wine.

Cozinha da Sé PORTUGUESE €€
(253 277 343; Rua Dom Frei Caetano Brandão 95; mains €10-14; noon-3pm & 7-11pm Wed-Sun, 7-11pm Tue) Contemporary artwork hangs from the exposed stone walls at this intimate, cheery place. Traditional standouts include baked *bacalhau* (dried salt-cod) and *açorda de marisco* (seafood stew in a bread bowl).

Drinking & Nightlife

Convento do Carmo BAR
(929 255 229; Travessa do Carmo; 9pm-2am Thu, 6pm-6am Fri & Sat) This gorgeous bar-restaurant-performance-space, housed in a restored convent, has a flowery garden patio featuring a pool. A great place for a glass of wine and a taste of Braga's cultural repertoire – it hosts concerts, exhibits and theatre performances.

Barhaus BAR
(Rua Dom Gonçalo Pereira 58; 3pm-2am Mon-Thu, 3pm-4am Fri & Sat) A popular spot with two indoor bars and a huge open-air patio, which draws a crowd with posh pretensions. DJs spin '80s music on weekends, when there's a €3 cover.

Domus Vinum WINE BAR
(www.domus-vinum.com; Largo da Nossa Senhora da Boa Luz 12; tapas €4-7; 6pm-2am Tue-Sun) With Brazilian beats, a lantern-lit front patio and excellent wines by the glass, Domus Vinum draws a stylish crowd. The Portuguese

and Spanish tapas are excellent. It's just west of the old-town entrance portal, Arco da Porta Nova.

Café A Brasileira CAFE
(Largo do Barão de São Marinho 17; ⌚7am-8pm Mon-Sat) A Braga classic, this 19th-century cafe is a converging point for old and new generations. Try the *café de saco* (a small shot of filtered coffee).

Sé La Vie BAR
(Rua Dom Paio Mendes 37; ⌚3pm-2am Mon-Thu, 3pm-3am Fri & Sat) A fun little cafe-bar with an alternative vibe that puts on great shows and has a good selection of beers and snacks.

Taberna Svbvra BAR
(Rua Dom Frei Caetano Brandão 101; ⌚9pm-2am) Buzzy bar hidden behind a saloon-like wooden door, with a local low-key vibe and occasional live music. If the door is locked, knock and you'll be let into the smoky interior with guitars gracing the walls.

Estúdio 22 BAR
(Rua Dom Paio Mendes 22; ⌚6pm-2am Mon-Thu & Sun, 6pm-4am Fri & Sat) Loungey cafe-bar on a bustling strip by the cathedral, great for coffee drinking during the day, and sampling the speciality gin and tonics at night to the sound of live bands or DJs spinning funk and bossa.

Sardinha Biba CLUB
(www.sardinhabiba.com; Praça Dr Cândido da Costa Pires; ⌚11pm-6am Wed, Fri & Sat) One of Braga's oldest disco clubs, southeast of the historical centre, in the Mercado do Carandá. It churns out house and techno tunes to a party-happy crowd.

Colinatrum CAFE
(☎253 215 630; Rua Damião de Góis 11; ⌚8am-12.30am Mon-Thu, 8am-2am Fri & Sat, 8.30am-12.30am Sun; 📶) Situated on a hill that overlooks the countryside, this sleek cafe of glass and wood is a fine meeting spot for a coffee or two, sunset cocktails or late-night bites. From the muslin-shaded outdoor terrace you'll have a splendid view of Bom Jesus do Monte.

☆ Entertainment

Teatro Circo de Braga THEATRE
(☎253 203 800; www.theatrocirco.com; Avenida da Liberdade 697) One of the most dazzling theatres in the country, inside a grand fin de siècle building, where you can catch concerts, theatre and dance, with offerings ranging from the staid to the truly avant-garde.

ℹ Information

Biblioteca Lúcio Craveiro da Silva (www.blcs.pt; Rua de São Paulo 1; ⌚9am-6pm Mon-Fri summer, 9-8pm Mon-Fri, 9.30am-12.30pm & 2-6pm Sat rest of year; 📶) Free wi-fi and internet access on public computers.

Hospital Escala Braga (☎253 027 000; Sete Fontes – São Victor) A block west of Avenida da Liberdade.

Police Station (☎253 200 420; Campo de São Tiago 6)

Post Office (Rua do Raio 175A; ⌚8.30am-6pm Mon-Fri) Just off Avenida da Liberdade.

Turismo (☎253 262 550; www.cm-braga.pt; Avenida da Liberdade 1; ⌚9am-7pm Mon-Fri, 9am-12.30pm & 2-5.30pm Sat & Sun Jun-Sep, shorter hours in low season) Braga's helpful tourist office is in an art-deco-style building facing the fountain.

ℹ Getting There & Away

BUS

Braga has a centralised bus station that serves as a major regional hub.

Airport Bus (☎253 262 371; www.getbus.eu) About 10 buses daily do the 50-minute run between the Porto airport and Braga, in each direction. The one-way fare is €8 (€4 for children), return is €14 (€8 for children).

Empresa Hoteleira do Gerês (☎253 262 033) Serves Vila do Gerês (€4.30, 1½ hours) about hourly during the week, five times on Saturday and three times on Sunday.

Rede Expressos (www.rede-expressos.pt) Has up to 15 daily buses to Lisbon (€21, 4½ hours).

Transdev Norte/Arriva (☎253 209 401) Has at least eight buses per day to Viana do Castelo (€4.45, 1½ hours), Barcelos (€2.65, one hour), Guimarães (€3.20, 50 minutes), Ponte de Lima (€3.85, one hour) and Porto (€4.80, one hour), plus four per day to Campo do Gerês (€4.20, 1½ hours). Service drops by half at weekends.

CAR & MOTORCYCLE

The A3 motorway makes Braga an easy day trip from Porto. The N101 from Braga to Guimarães is a good road for a slow ride.

Avic (☎253 203 910; Rua Gabriel Pereira de Castro 28; ⌚9am-7pm Mon-Fri, 9am-12.30pm Sat) An efficient agency for several car-rental companies, with prices starting at €35 per day.

TRAIN

Braga is at the end of a branch line from Nine and also within Porto's *suburbano* network, which means commuter trains travel every hour or so from Porto (€3.10, about one hour); don't waste €32.80 on an Alfa Pendular (AP) train.

Useful AP links include Coimbra (€19.80, 2¼ hours, five to seven daily) and Lisbon (€31, four hours, two to four daily).

Barcelos

POP 20,000

The Minho is famous for its sprawling outdoor markets, but the largest, oldest and most celebrated is the Feira de Barcelos, held every Thursday in this ancient town. Tour buses arrive by the dozen, spilling their contents into the already brimming marketplace. Even if you don't come on a Thursday, you'll find that Barcelos has a pleasant medieval core, with old stone towers perched over the river. It also harbours an ancient but still-thriving pottery tradition.

Sights

Feira de Barcelos MARKET

(Campo da República; sunrise-sunset Thu) The largest, oldest and most celebrated of the Minho's markets is the Feira de Barcelos, held every Thursday in Barcelos on the banks of the Rio Cávado. Despite attracting travellers, the market retains its rural soul. Villagers hawk everything from scrawny chickens to hand-embroidered linen, and Roma women bellow for business in the clothes section. Snack on sausages and homemade bread as you wander among the brass cowbells, hand-woven baskets and carved ox yokes. Pottery is what most outsiders come to see.

Especially popular is the yellow-dotted *louça de Barcelos* ware and the gaudy figurines à la Rosa Ramalho, a local potter known as the Grandma Moses of Portuguese pottery – her work put Barcelos on the map in the 1950s.

You'll need at least a couple of hours to see all the goods.

Sleeping

Quinta do Convento da Franqueira INN €€

(253 831 606; www.quintadafranqueira.com; Carvalhal; s €70-85, d €90-110; Apr-Oct; P) This remarkable *quinta* (estate) is housed in a 16th-century convent turned vineyard and inn, 6km north of town. There's a two-night minimum stay during the high season.

ROOSTER RESCUE

His colourful crest adorns a thousand souvenir stalls – and you will notice the great and brilliant cocks sprinkled along the Barcelos streets like bigger-than-life chess pieces – but just how and why did the proud Portuguese cockerel become a national icon? It seems that a humble pilgrim, plodding his way to Santiago de Compostela in the 16th (some say 14th) century, stopped to rest in Barcelos, only to find himself wrongfully accused of theft and then swiftly condemned to be hanged. The outraged pilgrim told the judge that the roast on the judge's dinner table would affirm the pilgrim's innocence. And, just as the judge was about to tuck in, the cooked cock commenced to crow. The pilgrim was set free.

Hotel do Terço HOTEL €€

(253 808 380; www.hoteldoterco.com; Rua de São Bento 7; s/d €50/65; P) In the town centre, stay in one of the stylish rooms at this sleek, modern option sitting atop its namesake shopping centre.

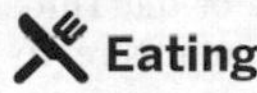

Eating

Galliano PORTUGUESE €€

(253 815 104; www.restaurantegalliano.com; Campo 5 de Outubro 20; mains €9-17; noon-3pm & 7.30pm-midnight Mon-Sat, noon-3pm Sun) The best food in Barcelos is to be had at Galliano, which features regional delicacies like *barrosã grelhado* (grilled steak), plus great-value lunch specials (€7).

Information

Turismo (253 811 882; turismo@cm-barcelos.pt; Largo Dr José Novais 27; 9.30am-6pm Mon-Fri, 10am-1pm & 2-5pm Sat, 10am-1pm & 2-4pm Sun mid-Mar–Sep) Hands out brochures and maps, and doles out useful info.

Getting There & Away

Transdev Norte/Arriva (253 209 401; Avenida Dr Sidónio País 445) has the only reliable bus service to/from Barcelos, with at least eight buses to Braga (€2.60, one hour) on weekdays and about four on weekends. It also has services to Ponte de Lima (€3.10, one hour).

Barcelos' train station is on the Porto–Valença do Minho line. There are three to five direct trains a day to/from Porto (€4.70, one hour), and commuter trains every hour or two that change at Nine (€4, 1¼ hours). There is similar service via Nine to Braga (€2.90, 45 to 60 minutes).

Bom Jesus do Monte

The goal of legions of penitent pilgrims every year, Bom Jesus do Monte is one of Portugal's most recognisable icons. A rather windswept and glamorous pilgrimage site, lying 5km east of central Braga, the sober neoclassical church stands atop a forested hill that offers grand sunset views across the city. But most people don't come simply for the church or even the view. They come to see the extraordinary baroque staircase, Escadaria do Bom Jesus.

Sights

The photogenic climb up to Bom Jesus is made up of tiered staircases, dating from different decades of the 18th century. The lowest is lined with chapels representing the Stations of the Cross. **Escadaria dos Cinco Sentidos** (Stairway of the Five Senses) features allegorical fountains with water gurgling from the ears, eyes, nose and mouth of different statues. Highest is **Escadaria das Três Virtudes** (Stairway of the Three Virtues), with chapels and fountains representing faith, hope and charity.

The area around the church has become something of a resort, with fancy hotels, tennis courts, flower gardens and a lake. It's choked with tourists on summer weekends, who come to explore the church, cobblestone roads and trails on foot or bicycle.

Sleeping

Grande Hotel HOTEL €€
(☎253 281 222; www.grande-hotel.com; Largo Mãe da Água, Tenões; s/d €45/70; P ❄ ☰) This sleek hotel, with its minimalist exterior and nouveau Renaissance interior, is 1km from the church (at the fork before reaching Bom Jesus, veer left). Its spacious doubles, most complete with balconies, are by far the best choice in the area.

Hotel do Elevador HOTEL €€
(☎253 603 400; www.hoteisbomjesus.pt; Monte do Bom Jesus; s/d €85/104; P ❄ @ ☰) Set in an antiquated villa, this is one of four Bom Jesus hotels owned by the same company. Its rooms have romantic old-world touches and magical views. The restaurant (mains €10 to €16) has a stunning perch.

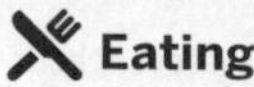

Eating

Adega Regional de Tenões PORTUGUESE €
(☎253 678 263; Rua Álvaro Vieira Nogueira 7, Tenões; mains €5-10; ⏲lunch & dinner) For good homemade food, try this traditional tavern on the road to Bom Jesus.

Getting There & Away

City bus 2 runs from Braga's Avenida da Liberdade to the bottom of the Bom Jesus steps (€1.65, 20 minutes) – the end of the line – every half-hour all day (hourly on Sunday). From here you can hoof it up the steps or hop aboard the newly restored **ascensor** (Funicular; Largo Mãe da Água; one way €1.20; ⏲9am-8pm summer, 9am-1pm & 2-6pm winter), which whisks visitors to the top every half hour. Alternatively, a taxi from central Braga to the top of the steps costs €7 to €10.

Guimarães

POP 65,000

The proud birthplace of Afonso Henriques, the first independent king of Portugal (born here in 1110, he later used the city to launch the main thrust of the Reconquista against the Moors), and, thus, the Portuguese kingdom, Guimarães has beautifully preserved its illustrious past. Its medieval centre is a warren of labyrinthine lanes and picturesque plazas framed by 14th-century edifices, while on an adjacent hill stands a 1000-year-old castle and the massive palace built by the first duke of Bragança in the 15th century. Guimarães' glory was recognised in 2001, when Unesco declared its old centre a World Heritage Site. In 2012, the city was the European Capital of Culture, which has given it a more creative edge.

On top of the city's historical treasures, museums and cultural institutions, there are cafe-filled plazas, atmospheric guest houses and delightful restaurants. Plus, Guimarães is a university town, its students lending much vitality to the place.

Sights

Platform for Arts and Creativity NOTABLE BUILDING
(Avenida Conde de Margaride 175; adult/student €4/3, free Sun mornings; ⏲10am-7pm Tue-Sun) For the 2012 European Capital of Culture the old market square was revamped into a multipurpose cultural centre inside a shimmering three-floor metallic building that looks like a bunch of stacked-up boxes. Inside is

Guimarães

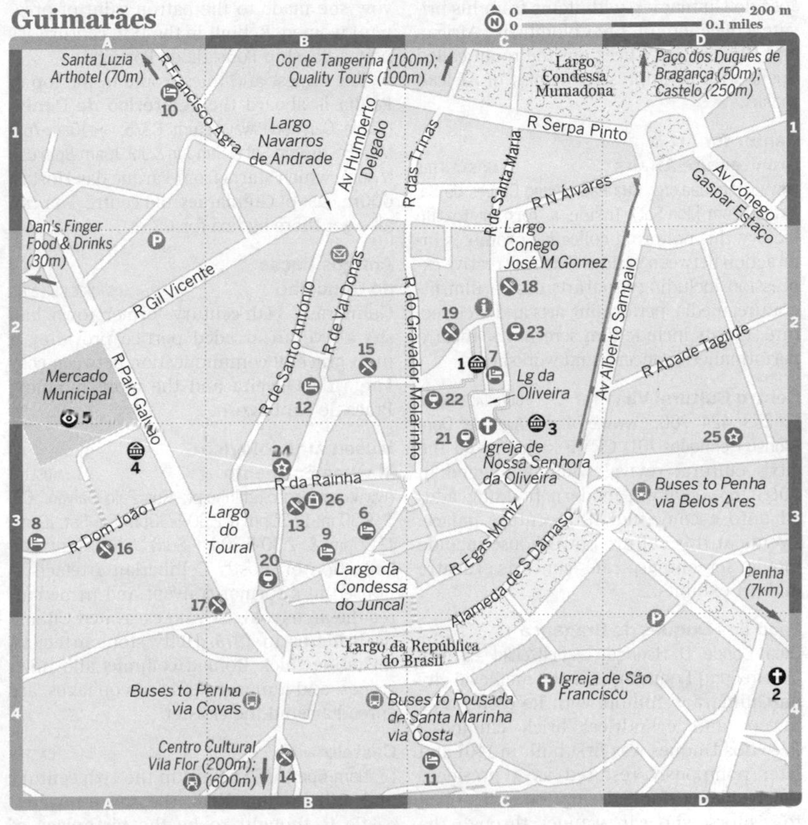

Guimarães

Sights
1 Antigos Paços do Concelho........ C2
2 Igreja de São Gualter........ D4
3 Museu Alberto Sampaio........ C3
4 Museu Arqueológico Martins Sarmento........ A3
5 Platform for Arts and Creativity........ A2

Sleeping
6 Casa do Juncal........ B3
7 Hotel da Oliveira........ C2
8 Hotel Mestre de Avis........ A3
9 Hotel Toural........ B3
10 My Hostel........ A1
11 Pousadas da Juventude........ C4
12 TM Guest House........ B2

Eating
13 Adega dos Caquinhos........ B3
14 Danúbio Bar........ B4
15 Histórico by Papaboa........ B2
16 Le Babachris........ A3
17 Pastelaria Clarinha........ B3
18 Solar do Arco........ C2
19 Tapas e Manias........ C2

Drinking & Nightlife
20 Cervejaria Martins........ B3
21 Coconuts........ C3
22 El Rock........ C2
23 Tásquilhado........ C2
Tunel 29........ (see 22)

Entertainment
24 Convívio Associação........ B3
25 São Mamede CAE........ D3

Shopping
26 Livraria Ideal........ B3

a permanent exhibit by Portuguese painter José de Guimarães, with items from his private collection of pre-Colombian, African and Chinese art. Check out the room called Spells with its impressive display of African masks.

Center for Art & Architecture Affairs ARTS CENTRE
(www.centroaaa.org; Rua Padre Augo Borges de Sá; ⌚2.30-7pm Mon-Sat) Inside a former textile factory, this nonprofit collective promotes interaction between various fields of creative expression, including visual arts, design, film, literature, media, performing arts and architecture. Events include film screenings, theatre performances, concerts and workshops.

Centro Cultural Vila Flor CULTURAL CENTRE
(☎253 424 700; www.ccvf.pt; Avenida Dom Afonso Henriques 701) CCVF kick-started the city's cultural revival when it opened in 2005 in a striking modern building added onto a converted 18th-century palace. Events at this culture powerhouse include movie screenings, cafe concerts, theatre and art exhibits.

Paço dos Duques de Bragança PALACE
(Rua Conde D Henrique; adult/child €5/free; ⌚9am-6pm) Looming over the medieval city on Guimarães' hilltop, with its crenellated towers and cylindrical brick chimneys, Paço dos Duques was first built in 1401 and later pompously restored as a presidential residence for Salazar. Today it's open to visitors who can wander through the rooms, which house a collection of Flemish tapestries, medieval weapons, a chapel with glittering stained-glass windows and enormous tapestries that relate various episodes in the Portuguese attempt to conquer North Africa.

Penha VIEWPOINT
Some 7km southeast up a twisting, cobbled road – or a short ride on an ageing cable car – is the wooded summit of Penha (617m) overlooking Guimarães, the highest point for kilometres. Its cool woods make it a wonderful escape from the city and summer heat. Kids love losing themselves amid the massive boulders, many cut with steps, crowned with flowers and crosses, or hiding in secret grottoes.

On the lower slopes of the hill lies the **Mosteiro de Santa Marinha da Costa**, 1.5km east of Penha's centre. It dates from 1154, when Dona Mafalda, wife of Afonso Henriques, commissioned it to honour a vow she made to the patron saint of pregnant women. Rebuilt in the 18th century, it's now a flagship Pousada de Portugal.

The easiest and finest route to the top of Penha is aboard the **Teleférico de Penha** (Cable Car; one way/return €3/5; ⌚10am-7pm Mon-Fri, to 8pm Sat & Sun Jun & Jul, 10am-8pm daily Aug), which starts from Parque das Hortas, 600m east of Guimarães' old centre. You can also get there by taxi for €8.

Antigos Paços do Concelho HISTORIC BUILDING
Guimarães' 14th-century former town hall sits above an arcaded portico providing a most graceful communication between cosy Largo da Oliveira and the more rambling Praça de Santiago.

Museu Arqueológico Martins Sarmento MUSEUM
(www.csarmento.uminho.pt; Rua Paio Galvão; €3; ⌚9.30am-12.30pm & 2.30-5.30pm Tue-Sat, 10am-12.30pm & 2.30-5.30pm Sun) This fantastic collection of mostly Celtiberian artefacts is housed in a former convent and named after the archaeologist who excavated Citânia de Briteiros in 1875. Hefty stone artefacts, including thick Roman columns and milestones, and a mossy Celtic sarcophagus, are spread around the cloister.

Castelo CASTLE
(⌚9am-6pm) FREE Built in the 11th century and still in fine form, the seven-towered castle is thought to be the birthplace of the great man himself, Afonso Henriques. Walk around the windswept ramparts of the castle and scale the narrow steps to the bird's-nest heights of Countess Mumadona's keep.

Igreja de Nossa Senhora da Oliveira CHURCH
(Largo da Oliveira; ⌚8.30am-noon & 3.30-7.30pm Mon-Sat, 9am-1pm & 5-8pm Sun) Founded by Countess Mumadona in the 12th century and rebuilt four centuries later, the beautiful Largo da Oliveira is dominated by the convent church of Igreja de Nossa Senhora da Oliveira. The monument outside the church is a Gothic canopy and cross, reputedly marking the spot where the great Wamba the Visigoth, victorious over the Suevi, drove his spear into the ground beside an olive tree and refused to reign unless a tree sprouted from the handle. In true legendary fashion, it did just that.

Igreja de São Gualter CHURCH
(Church of St Walter; Largo da República do Brasil; 7.30am-noon & 3-5pm Mon-Sat, 7.30am-noon Sun) This slender 18th-century construction with its 19th-century twin spires and blooming run-up from central Guimarães has the most striking appeal of all of the city's churches.

Museu Alberto Sampaio MUSEUM
(Rua de Alfredo Guimarães; adult/child €3/free, Sun morning free; 9am-6pm Tue-Sun, plus 8.30-11.30pm Wed-Sat Jun) Built around the serene Romanesque cloister of Igreja de Nossa Senhora da Oliveira, this museum has an excellent collection of ecclesiastical art and religious finery. Highlights include the tunic reputedly worn by João I at the Battle of Aljubarrota (1385).

Igreja de São Francisco CHURCH
This 13th-century church has a striking interior, along with a lovely Renaissance cloister and 18th-century *azulejos* depicting scenes from the saint's life.

Activities

Quality Tours TOURS
(253 527 144; www.qualitytours.pt; Largo Martins Sarmento 89; 9am-7pm) Quality Tours rents bikes (€15 per day) as well as scooters and four-wheelers; it also organises guided walking tours (€25 per person).

Festivals & Events

Guimarães Jazz MUSIC
One of the country's top festivals, this jazz extravaganza runs for about three weeks in November.

Festas de Cidade e Gualterianas CULTURAL
(www.aoficina.pt) Marked by a free fair (held in Guimarães since 1452 to honour its patron saint), this festival features folk dancing, rock concerts, fireworks and parades. It takes place on the first weekend in August.

Sleeping

My Hostel HOSTEL €
(253 414 023; www.myhostel-guimaraes.webnode.pt; Rua Francisco Agra 135; dm €15-19, €38-42;) Stylish hostel with eight colourful, bright rooms that include dorms and doubles with swank shared and private bathrooms. There's a nice shared kitchen/living room and a terrace. Towels cost €1 but breakfast is included. You can also order food and massages.

Pousadas da Juventude HOSTEL €
(253 421 380; www.pousadasjuventude.pt; Largo da Cidade 8; dm/d/apt €14/38/70; @) Set in the palatial 18th-century home of a prosperous factory owner, this terrific hostel in the historic Couros district has hardwood floors, bright six-bed dorms and spacious doubles that are downright stylish. It also has kitchen and laundry facilities and a huge living room with pool tables.

1720 Quinta da Cancela GUESTHOUSE €€
(919 199 299; www.quintadacancela.com; Rua da Liberdade, S Lourenço de Sande; r/cottage €99/145; P) A lovingly run 18th-century country estate halfway between Braga and Guimarães, Quinta da Cancela has six rooms filled with family antiques and heirlooms, and a cosy four-person cottage. Rates include breakfast and a bottle of the estate's own *vinho verde* (young wine). Meals are available on request, prepared by the gracious live-in owners. There's a natural pool on-site. A great choice for families.

Casa do Juncal GUESTHOUSE €€
(252 042 168; www.casajuncal.com; Rua Dr Avelino Germano 65; s€90-120, d €105-135) This gorgeously restored town house smack in the heart of town features six swish suites, each different in layout and with thoughtful original details. Prices include breakfast and a welcome drink. They have bikes for rent and a beautiful little garden in the back.

Santa Luzia Arthotel HOTEL €€
(253 071 800; Rua Francisco Agra 100; s/d €105/115; P) This brand-new hotel steps from the city centre has a string of stylish rooms and suites, artfully done and featuring the full range of amenities. On-site facilities include an outdoor and an indoor pool, as well as a spa and restaurant.

Hotel da Oliveira HOTEL €€
(253 514 157; www.hoteldaoliveira.com; Rua de Santa Maria 433; s/d €91/105;) The location of this contemporary hotel in a historic building in the heart of town is unbeatable. The rooms and suites are tastefully done up and jam-packed with amenities. Top choice while in town.

Hotel Toural HOTEL €€
(253 517 184; www.hoteltoural.com; Largo AL Carvalho; s/d €65/86; P@) In a complex of two connected historic buildings, this four-star hotel accessed through a leafy alleyway entrance has well-appointed rooms

overlooking the square, the patio or the mountains in the distance.

TM Guest House GUESTHOUSE €€
(☎253 433 504; www.tmhostels.com; Rua de Val Donas 11; apt €70-110;) This former fashion-inspired hostel has been converted into apartments, where some rooms come with balconies and terraces. Breakfast isn't available. Reserve ahead.

Hotel de Guimarães HOTEL €€
(☎253 424 800; www.hotel-guimaraes.com; Rua Eduardo Manuel de Almeida; s/d €80/90;) This business hotel near the train station has large rooms with lush linens, chic paint jobs and flat-screen TVs, along with a health club and spa. It's a bit removed from the old town, but still excellent value and an easy two-minute walk to the train.

Hotel Mestre de Avis HOTEL €€
(☎253 422 770; www.hotelmestredeavis.pt; Rua Dom João I 40; s/d €50/80;) Fronted by curlicue ironwork, this renovated hotel has bright rooms on a quiet cobbled street in the centre. The contemporary rooms come in three categories – standard, superior and deluxe. Some have balconies and alcoves; all feature a dash of style.

Pousada de Santa Marinha POUSADA €€€
(☎253 511 249; www.pousadas.pt; Largo Domingos Leite de Castro, Lugar da Costa; s/d €258/272;) This former monastery overlooking the city from the slopes of Penha is a magnificent, sprawling structure. The gardens are stunning and you'll want to wander around the cloister, past dribbling fountains and masterful *azulejos*. The rooms inside the former monks' cells feel cramped, so book a room in the modern wing.

Buses to Pousada de Santa Marinha run via Costa.

Eating

Dan's Finger Food & Drinks BURGERS €
(Avenida de São Gonçalo 171; burgers €5-8; noon-4pm & 7-11pm) People line out the door at this swank burger joint that does *picanha* burgers and tasty finger food like chicken and fish nuggets. Great craft beer, too.

Adega dos Caquinhos PORTUGUESE €
(Rua da Arrochela; mains €6-9; noon-11pm Mon-Thu, noon-2am Fri & Sat) A family-run tavern with a small menu of two to three dishes daily, prepared the home-style way. Whatever is fresh at the market you'll get served on your plate in this down-home cash-only spot with bits of broken ceramics gracing the walls. Try the homemade cookies ice cream.

Danúbio Bar CAFE €
(Avenida Dom Afonso Henriques 15; snacks €1-3.50; noon-11pm) This corner kiosk draws in a local crowd (of mostly old men) for its simple but tasty snacks at low prices. Try the delicious *pregos* (meat sandwiches) and *pataniscas* (fish fritters). Wash them down with beer either inside or on the tiny cobblestone square in front.

Pastelaria Clarinha BAKERY €
(Largo do Toural 86-88; pastries €0.70-3.20; 8am-10pm Tue-Sun) Since 1953 Guimarães' best pastry shop has filled its window with fresh-baked tarts and cakes to tempt passers-by. There are a few pavement tables and a heavenly *toucinho do ceu* (almond cake).

★**Le Babachris** PORTUGUESE €€
(☎964 420 548; Rua Dom João I 39; lunch €9.75, dinner €15.50-21.50; noon-3.30pm & 6-11pm Tue-Sat) The decor of this long and narrow two-floor restaurant is so simple and unassuming that you wouldn't expect such top-notch food to come out of its tiny kitchen. But top-notch it is – inventive, seasonal and market-fresh. They serve set menus only, featuring a meat and a fish option. Book ahead.

Tapas e Manias PORTUGUESE €€
(☎253 161 009; Praça de Santiago 13; tapas €3.60-8, mains €10.50-13.50; noon-3pm & 7-10pm Mon & Wed-Sun) Tasty tapas-style Portuguese dishes with a twist are served at this cosy restaurant on Praça de Santiago, with alfresco tables tended to by friendly staff.

Cor de Tangerina VEGETARIAN €€
(Largo Martins Sarmento 89; mains €6-12; noon-3pm & 7-10pm Tue-Thu, noon-3pm & 7-11pm Fri, noon-11pm Sat, noon-4pm Sun;) This charming restaurant whips up a good selection of cuisine you won't find elsewhere in Guimarães. Changing art exhibitions decorate the walls, while the wild, jazz-washed garden (with tangerine tree) produces much of the herbs used in the ancient stone kitchen. The chef is something of a herbal alchemist capable of brewing all manner of teas and tonics, too.

Histórico by Papaboa PORTUGUESE €€
(www.papaboa.pt; Rua de Val Donas 4; mains €9.50-14; noon-3pm & 7-11pm) The setting – in a

medieval fort with breezy courtyard seating and glassed-in stone dining room – is tremendous. Service is top-notch and the fare is dressed up yet traditional, such as black pork with prawns and mustard sauce. The weekday lunch menu is a steal. They have live music some nights.

Solar do Arco PORTUGUESE €€
(☎253 035 233; Rua de Santa Maria 48-50; mains €9.50-13; ⊙noon-10.30pm; ❄) With a handsomely panelled dining room under a graceful arcade, this is a top, central choice. Portuguese classics made with straight-from-the-market ingredients add to the allure. Touristy it is though, and hence pricier.

Drinking & Nightlife

Cervejaria Martins BEER HALL
(Largo do Toural 32-35; ⊙10am-2am Mon-Sat) An always bustling cafe-bar where sports blast on TV and lots of men sit around the circular counter. A long-standing favourite, going strong since the 1950s. It serves food until late (it's cheaper if you eat at the counter).

Coconuts BAR
(www.coconuts.com.pt; Largo da Oliveira 1-3; ⊙8am-2am Wed-Sat, 8am-midnight Sun & Tue) A popular bar with *azulejo*-filled interiors and tables on the cobblestone square. It has coffee, snacks and a low-key vibe during the day and turns into a happening hotspot at night, with DJs on Fridays and Saturdays.

Tunel 29 BAR
(www.tunel29.com; Praça de Santiago 29; ⊙6pm-late) A reggae- and electronica-infused, mosaic-tiled cave that sees its share of Guimarães party people.

El Rock BAR
(Praça de Santiago 31; ⊙2pm-2am) Dug into a narrow stone room and spreading onto the plaza is this funky beer bar. It hosts occasional live bands, and is the destination for many a pretty, wild-haired hipster when night falls.

Tásquilhado BAR
(Rua de Santa Maria 42; ⊙9pm-2am Wed-Sat, to midnight Sun) One of a swath of bar-hopping venues in the historic centre, this cosy, ever-popular bar plays alternative sounds and offers enticing drink specials during the week.

☆ Entertainment

Convívio Associação PERFORMING ARTS
(Largo da Misericórdia 7-8; ⊙3-7pm Mon-Fri, 9pm-midnight Mon-Thu, 9pm-2am Fri & Sat) Started 52 years ago, this creative cultural association – also a jazz school – is still going strong. Its program includes classical music concerts, jazz sessions, exhibits, theatre and workshops. Fridays and Saturdays are the busiest nights, when an older boho crowd descends on the bar and small open-air patio.

São Mamede CAE PERFORMING ARTS
(www.sao-mamede.com; Rua Dr José Sampaio 17-25; ⊙2-8pm Mon, 2pm-2am Tue-Sat, 3pm-midnight Sun) This converted old cinema/cultural centre draws a student crowd for its range of events, from performances to film screenings, cheap weekday lunches served at the funky 1st-floor cafe and a loungey wine bar on the top floor.

Shopping

Livraria Ideal BOOKS, MAPS
(Rua da Rainha 34; ⊙10am-7pm Mon-Sat) The city's best bookshop has a terrific selection of area maps.

Information

There's free wi-fi on the main squares in town.

Hospital (☎253 540 330; Rua dos Cutileiros, Creixomil) Opposite the bus station.

Police Station (☎253 540 660; Alameda Dr Alfredo Pimenta) Next to the fire department.

Post Office (Rua Teixeira dos Pascoais; ⊙8.30am-6.30pm Mon-Fri, 9am-12.30pm Sat)

Turismo (☎253 421 221; www.guimaraesturismo.com; Praça de Santiago; ⊙9.30am-7pm Mon-Fri, 10am-1pm & 2-7pm Sat, 10am-1pm Sun) The excellent, informative staff speak English, French and Spanish.

Getting There & Away

BUS

Transdev (☎253 516 229) has buses leaving at least hourly for Braga (€3.15, 50 minutes) Monday through Saturday, and eight buses on Sunday. It also has services to Porto (€5.10, 50 minutes) running approximately hourly on weekdays but less often on weekends, and to Lisbon (€20.50, five hours) daily.

Rodonorte (☎253 423 500; www.rodonorte.pt) heads for Amarante (€7.60, one hour), Vila Real (€8.50, two hours) and Bragança (€14.50, four hours).

Get Bus (www.getbus.eu) has six buses daily that do the 50-minute run between the Porto airport and Guimarães, in each direction. The one-way fare is €8 (€4 for children); return is €14 (€8 for children).

TRAIN

Guimarães is the terminus of a branch of Porto's wide *suburbano* network. Commuter trains potter out to Guimarães from Porto (€3.10, 75 minutes) 11 to 16 times daily. Try to avoid the once-daily *intercidade* (express) train, which costs €11.70 and departs at 7.43am.

Getting Around

There is street parking in front of the Convento do Carmo at the foot of the Paço dos Duques. If you wish to explore Guimarães and surrounds on two wheels or four, go to Quality Tours, which rents bikes (€15 per day) as well as scooters and four-wheelers; it also organises guided walking tours (€25 per person).

To get to Penha, the easiest and finest route to the top is aboard the Teleférico de Penha, which starts from Parque das Hortas, 600m east of Guimarães' old centre. You can get there by taxi (€8), and there are also buses to Penha via Belos Ares and via Covas.

Buses to Pousada de Santa Marinha run via Costa.

Citânia de Briteiros

One of the most evocative archaeological sites in Portugal, **Citânia de Briteiros** (admission incl museum €3; 9am-6pm Apr-Sep, to 5pm Oct-Mar), 15km north of Guimarães, is the largest of a liberal scattering of northern Celtic hill settlements, called *citânias* (fortified villages), dating back at least 2500 years. It's also likely that this sprawling 3.8-hectare site, inhabited from about 300 BC to AD 300, was the Celtiberians' last stronghold against the invading Romans.

When archaeologist Dr Martins Sarmento excavated the site in 1875, he discovered the foundations and ruins of more than 150 rectangular, circular and elliptical stone huts, linked by paved paths and a water-distribution system, all cocooned by multiple protective walls. Highlights include two reconstructed huts that evoke what it was like to live in the settlement and, further down the hill, a bathhouse with a strikingly patterned stone doorway.

Some artefacts are on display in the Sede e Museu Arqueológico in Guimarães, but the **Museu da Cultura Castreja** (Museum on Pre-Roman Culture; Solar da Ponte; €3; 9.30am-12.30pm & 2-6pm Apr-Sep, 9.30am-12.30pm & 2-5pm Oct-Mar) also has important artefacts from various sites housed in Sarmento's 18th- and 19th-century manor house. It's about 2km back down the hill towards Guimarães in the village of Briteiros Salvador.

From Guimarães, Transdev has about eight weekday buses that pass within 1km of the site; get off between the towns of Briteiros Salvador and Santa Leocádia. Check at the bus station for current schedule information.

Viana do Castelo

POP 15,600

The jewel of the Costa Verde, Viana do Castelo is blessed with both an appealing medieval centre and lovely beaches just outside the city. The old quarters showcase leafy, 19th-century boulevards and narrow lanes crowded with Manueline manors and rococo palaces. The town's setting just by the Rio Lima estuary means that Viana do Castelo is only a short hop from some excellent beaches, and also makes it a handy base for exploring the lower Lima valley and the nearby Serra d'Arga mountain.

History

The remains of Celtic hill settlements on Monte de Santa Luzia, overlooking the contemporary town centre, and the name Viana – a nod to its Roman past when this once-humble settlement was called Diana – convey Viana do Castelo's deep historical roots, while its Manueline mansions and monasteries recall its 16th-century prosperity as a major cod-fishing port. In fact, by the mid-17th century it had bloomed into Portugal's biggest overall port, with merchants trading as far afield as Russia.

More riches arrived in the 18th century, with the advent of the Brazilian sugar and gold trade. But with Brazil's independence and the rising importance of Porto, Viana's golden age stuttered and faded. These days Viana earns much of its current living and reputation as the Minho's favourite resort town.

Sights

Praia do Cabedelo BEACH

(ferry 9am-6pm) This is one of the Minho's best beaches: a 1km-long arch of blond, powdery sand that folds into grassy dunes backed by a grove of wind-blown pines. It's

SURFING & KITESURFING IN MINHO

Praia do Cabedelo is an excellent kitesurfing destination, with consistent on-shore wind year-round. It's a great teaching site, but also fun for intermediate surfers thanks to the lagoon-like conditions created by the southern headland and harbour breakwater, which is a full kilometre north. There's good kiting and some traditional surfing at **Esposende** 17km south of Cabedelo, but conditions are iffy.

Among the fine beaches strung north along the 25km of coast between Viana do Castelo and Caminha, **Afife** has the best surf breaks, with waves topping out at 2m during peak swells. Four daily regional trains (€1.40, 13 minutes) make their way up the coast to Afife from Viana. Advanced kitesurfers will want to drive a bit further north to **Moledo**, where the wind and waves are at their fiercest and finest.

For tips and gear rental, stop by **Viana Locals** (p447) at Praia do Cabedelo.

across the river from town, best reached on a five-minute ferry trip (p450) from the pier south of Largo 5 de Outubro.

Monte de Santa Luzia HILL

There are two good reasons to visit Viana's 228m eucalyptus-clad hill. One is the wondrous view down the coast and up the Lima valley. The other is the fabulously over-the-top, 20th-century, neo-Byzantine **Templo do Sagrado Coração de Jesus** (Temple of the Sacred Heart of Jesus; 9am-6pm). You can get a little closer to heaven on its graffiti-covered roof, via a lift, followed by an elbow-scraping stairway – take the museum entrance on the ground floor.

Behind the Pousada do Monte de Santa Luzia is another attraction, the **Ruinas da Cidade Velha** (€2, free for children under 12; 9am-noon & 2-6pm), ruins of a Celtiberian *citânia* (fortified village) from around the 4th century BC. You'll see the stones peeking above the wind-blown savannah. Most of the site is accessible via a boardwalk.

You can get up the mountain by the restored funicular (p450), which departs from near the train station every 15 minutes. You can also drive or take a taxi (3.5km) to the top, or hike 2km of steps (only for the fit and/or penitent). The road starts by the hospital, and the steps begin about 200m up the road.

Gil Eannes SHIP

(258 809 710; www.fundacaogileannes.pt; Navio Gil Eannes, Doca Comercial; €3.50, free for children under 6; 9.30am-7pm summer, 9.30am-6pm winter) Demanding attention on the waterfront near Largo 5 de Outubro is a pioneering naval hospital ship, the *Gil Eannes (zheel yanish)*. Now restored, the ship once provided on-the-job care for those fishing off the coast of Newfoundland. Visitors can clamber around the steep decks and cabins, though a scattering of old clinical equipment may make your hair stand on end.

Fábrica do Chocolate MUSEUM

(www.fabricadochocolate.com; Rua do Gontim 70-76; adult/child €8/6; 10am 6pm;) The town's newest attraction is this small five-room museum devoted to chocolate. It's fun and interactive, treating you to tidbits of facts and curiosities, but it's also often packed with school groups. There's a free audioguide to take you through the exhibits, and you get to put on a white coat and make a bar of chocolate at the end.

Museu do Traje MUSEUM

(Costume Museum; Praça da República; €2; 10am-6pm Tue-Fri, 10am-1pm & 3-6pm Sat & Sun) This attractive museum houses the traditional wear used for farming, fishing and seaweed harvesting in centuries past. You'll see costumes worn during the Romaria de Nossa Senhora d'Agonia and cool antique looms. The then-and-now mural-sized photos on the 2nd floor are pretty special, too.

Museu de Arte e Arqueologia MUSEUM

(Largo de São Domingos; 10am-6pm Tue-Fri, 10am-1pm & 3-6pm Sat & Sun) FREE The 18th-century Palacete Barbosa Maciel bears witness to Viana's affluent past. It houses this impressive collection of 17th- and 18th-century ceramics (especially blue Portuguese china) and furniture. Most impressive are three 2nd-floor rooms lined with *azulejos,* depicting scenes of hunting and palace life.

Praça da República SQUARE

This fine hub of seven narrow laneways is at the heart of the old town's zone of mansions and monuments. An especially elegant

Viana do Castelo

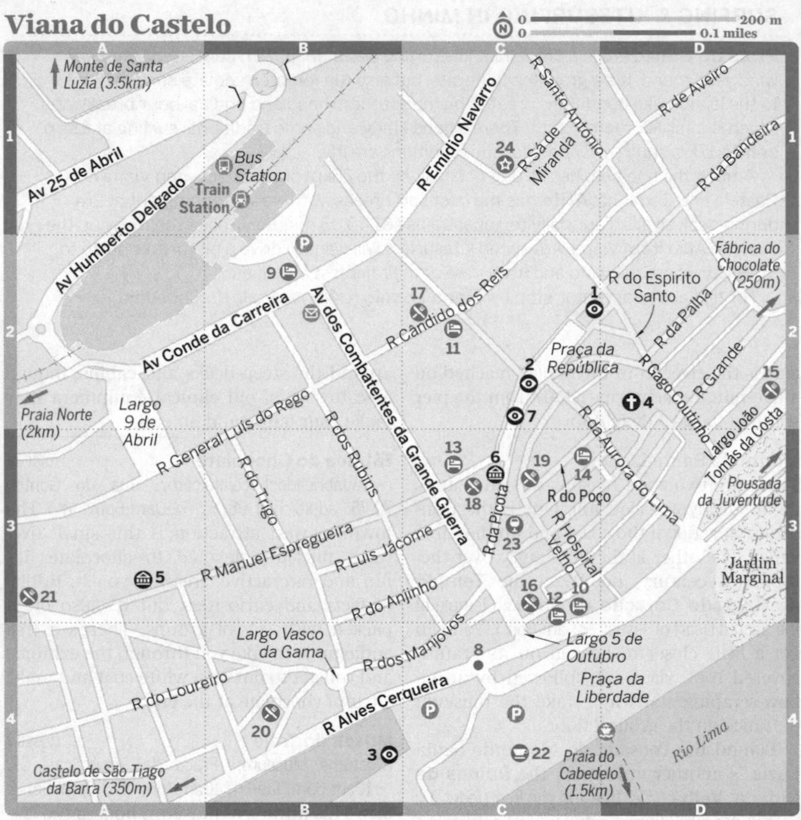

Viana do Castelo

Sights
- 1 Antigos Paços do Concelho ... C2
- 2 Chafariz ... C2
- 3 Gil Eannes ... B4
- 4 Igreja Matriz ... D2
- 5 Museu de Arte e Arqueologia ... A3
- 6 Museu do Traje ... C3
- 7 Praça da República ... C2

Activities, Courses & Tours
- 8 Viana Welcome Centre ... C4

Sleeping
- 9 Casa Melo Alvim ... B2
- 10 Hotel Jardim ... C3
- 11 Hotel Laranjeira ... C2
- 12 Margarida da Praça ... C3
- 13 O Laranjeira ... C3
- 14 Ó Meu Amor ... C3

Eating
- 15 À Moda Antiga ... D2
- 16 Casa de Pasto Maria de Perre ... C3
- 17 Casinha Boutique Café ... C2
- 18 Confeitaria Natário ... C3
- 19 Dolce Vianna ... C3
- 20 O Marques ... B4
- 21 O Pescador ... A3

Drinking & Nightlife
- 22 Foz ... C4
- 23 Republica ... C3

Entertainment
- 24 Teatro Municipal Sá de Miranda ... C1

example is the **Chafariz**, a Renaissance fountain built in 1554. The fountain is topped with Manueline motifs of an armillary sphere and the cross of the Order of Christ. The fortress-like **Antigos Paços do Concelho** is the old town hall – a 16th-century creation that sometimes hosts contemporary art exhibitions.

Castelo de São Tiago da Barra CASTLE
(9am-12.30pm & 2-5.30pm Mon-Fri) You can still scoot around the ramparts of this squat castle, a short walk west of the centre, which began in the 15th century as a smallish fort. It was integrated into a larger fort, commissioned by Felipe II of Spain (Felipe I of Portugal) in 1592, to guard the prosperous port against pirates.

Igreja Matriz CHURCH
(Largo Instituto Histórico do Minho; 9am-6pm Mon-Fri) This elegant parish church – also known as the *sé* – dates from the 15th century, although it has since been through several reincarnations. Check out its unusually sculpted Romanesque towers and Gothic doorway, carved with figures of Christ and the Evangelists.

Activities

Viana Welcome Centre TOURS
(258 098 415; www.vivexperiencia.pt; Praça do Eixo Atlântico; 10am-7pm Jul & Aug, 10am-1pm & 2-6pm Tue-Sun Sep-Jun) This private outfit offers creative city tours (€15 on foot, €20 by bike) in multiple languages, as well as regional food, wine and culture itineraries in the Douro and Minho. Canyoning, kayaking, surfing and hiking are also available, as is bike rental (€3/12 per hour/day) and rickshaw carts (€10 per hour).

Descubra Minho TOURS
(969 220 704; www.descubraminho.pt) Donkey tours, hikes and cycling trips to the nearby mountain of Serra d'Arga, just a 25-minute drive away, with its eight scenic villages and protected nature that includes diverse fauna such as the Iberian frog and the Garrano horse. The local guides can even take you on full-moon night treks. Reserve ahead.

Viana Locals SURFING
(258 325 168; www.vianalocals.com; Praia do Cabedelo) A friendly, full-service board-sports outfitter and school right on Praia do Cabedelo. It has surfboards, kite gear and paddle boards for rent and sale, and also does overnight repairs.

River Trips TOURS
(962 305 595; www.passeiofluvial.com; May-Sep) If there are enough passengers, boats run up and down the Rio Lima daily in summer, from the pier south of Largo 5 de Outubro (the same dock where ferries depart to Praia do Cabedelo). The most common trip takes 40 minutes (adult/child €7.50/4). Longer excursions (adult/child €12/6.50) take in the old shipyards; these must be booked at least a day ahead.

Festivals & Events

Viana has a knack for celebrations. The Romaria de Nossa Senhora d'Agonia, held in August, is the region's biggest annual bash, and **Carnaval** festivities here are considered northern Portugal's best. The town also goes a little nuts in mid-May during **Semana Acadêmica** (or Queima das Fitas), a week of end-of-term student madness. The *turismo* has details of other annual events.

Encontros de Viana FILM
A week-long festival of documentaries and short films; held in the first half of May.

Festival Maio CULTURAL
A national folk-dance extravaganza that takes place at the end of May.

Sleeping

★**Ó Meu Amor** GUESTHOUSE €
(258 406 513; www.omeuamor.com; Rua do Poço 19; s/d without bathroom €25/45; @) Top choice in town right in the historic centre, this hideaway in a rambling town house full of nooks and crannies has nine adorable

CELEBRATION OF SORROWS

Streets decorated with coloured sawdust, women decked out in traditional finery of scarlet and gold, men drinking till they keel over. Viana do Castelo's **Romaria de Nossa Senhora d'Agonia** (Festival of Our Lady of Sorrows; www.festas-agonia.com) is one of the Minho's most spectacular festivals. It takes place for three or four days around 20 August. Accommodation is very tight at this time, so book well ahead.

Expect everything from emotive religious processions to upbeat parades with deafening drums and lumbering carnival *gigantones* (giants) and *cabeçudos* (big heads).

rooms with shared bathrooms. Guests can use the kitchen and cosy living room. Each room has a theme – such as the India and Africa rooms in the attic – and some have tiny balconies with rooftop and mountain views.

O Laranjeira GUESTHOUSE €
(258 822 258; www.olaranjeira.com; Rua Manuel Espregueira 24; s €40-55, d €45-60;) This bright town house is a fantastic choice in the old centre, a cosy family-run spot with seven small but soulful rooms, each with a theme and some with patios. There's an attractive restaurant on the ground floor, where guests can enjoy discounted meals.

Hotel Jardim HOTEL €
(258 828 915; www.hoteljardimviana.pt; Largo 5 de Outubro 68; s/d €40/55;) In a stately 19th-century town house, this quirky place has spacious rooms with wooden floors, sizeable bathrooms and stone-framed French windows overlooking the historic centre or the river. For better views nab one of the lighter rooms on the top floors.

Orbitur CAMPGROUND €
(258 322 167; www.orbitur.com; Praia do Cabedelo; per site/person €25/6.90; Apr-Oct;) Nestled on the inland side of lovely sand dunes, this shady site is within walking distance of the ferry pier (and is a two-minute walk to the sea), and also has two- to six-person bungalows (€93 to €123). It heaves with holidaymakers in summer.

Pousada da Juventude HOSTEL €
(258 838 458; www.pousadasjuventude.pt; Rua da Lima; dm €13, d without/with bathroom €65/72;) The exterior may need a paint job, but the interiors of this Carrilho Graça–designed hostel, overlooking the marina 1km from the centre, are swank. Think black concrete floors and chic marble baths. Four-bed dorms have lockers.

★ **Margarida da Praça** GUESTHOUSE €€
(258 809 630; www.margaridadapraca.com; Largo 5 de Outubro 58; s €60-75, d €78-88;) Fantastically whimsical, this boutique inn offers thematic rooms in striking pinks, sea greens and whites, accented by stylish floral wallpaper, candelabra lanterns and lush duvets. The equally stylish lobby glows with candlelight in the evening.

Hotel Laranjeira HOTEL €€
(258 822 261; www.hotelaranjeira.com; Rua Cândido dos Reis 45; s/d €60/70;) This well-managed place was recently upgraded to hotel status and now has 26 contemporary if poky rooms with pine floors and glass-partitioned bathrooms. Some have balconies, and others great views of Santa Luzia.

Flôr de Sal BOUTIQUE HOTEL €€€
(258 800 100; www.hotelflordesal.com; Avenida de Cabo Verde 100, Praia Norte; s €140-170, d €170-235;) Perched on a windswept stretch of rocky coastline, this sleek designer offering has whitewashed rooms, all the modern touches and huge balconies with ocean views. There's a spa, gym, indoor pool and pleasant restaurant on-site. It's 2km west of the centre.

Casa Melo Alvim HOTEL €€€
(258 808 200; www.meloalvimhouse.com; Avenida Conde da Carreira 28; s/d €117/130;) Deluxe rooms in a stately 16th-century mansion, individually decked out with hardwood floors, four-poster beds, original stone accents and marble bathrooms. No two rooms are alike, but it is worth paying the extra €9 for the deluxe rooms, which have more space, huge ceilings and ornately carved beds.

Fábrica do Chocolate HOTEL €€€
(258 244 000; www.fabricadochocolate.com; Rua do Gontim 70-76; r from €130) Housed in a former chocolate factory, this recently opened hotel sports 18 themed rooms and suites with a choco theme running throughout. The on-site restaurant serves dishes with chocolate ingredients and the downstairs museum (p445) is free to visit for hotel guests. It's all a little gimmicky but great for families.

Pousada do Monte de Santa Luzia POUSADA €€€
(258 800 370; www.pousadas.pt; Monte de Santa Luzia; s/d €272/282;) This regal 1918 hotel sits squarely atop Monte de Santa Luzia, peering down at the basilica's backside and beyond it to some of the best coastal views in Portugal. Common areas are splendid, while the rooms themselves are comfortable, if less inspired than the views.

Eating

Viana do Castelo whips up some excellent seafood – among the region's best. Although you can find fresh fish at restaurants throughout the old town, the best joints are around the old fishing quarter on the west side of town.

À Moda Antiga PORTUGUESE €
(☎258 023 229; www.amodaantiga.pt; Largo João Tomás da Costa 63; mains €6-10; ⊙9am-11pm Tue-Sun) Right on the waterfront opposite the Jardim Marginal, this retro market and bistro serves great weekday lunch menus for just €6, as well as all-day dishes such as handmade burgers. The industrial space has high ceilings and exposed stone walls and a curated selection of old-fashioned Portuguese brands, plus there are a couple of tables outside.

Confeitaria Natário BAKERY €
(☎258 822 376; Rua Manuel Espregueira 37; pastries €2-3; ⊙9am-9pm Mon & Wed-Sat, 9am-1pm & 3.30-9pm Sun) This popular bakery is the place to try delicious *bolas de Berlim* (cream-filled doughnuts), which are so good that you may have to wait in line to get some.

Casinha Boutique Café CAFE €
(☎258 822 147; Rua Cândido dos Reis 20; dishes €4.25-6; ⊙9am-8pm Mon-Thu, 9am-11pm Fri & Sat, 10am-8pm Sun) This swank cafeteria-style cafe serves up tasty sandwiches, crêpes, quiches and salads in an airy light-flooded space with exposed stone walls and on a sweet little stone courtyard in the back. It also has brunch menus (from €9.95).

O Marques PORTUGUESE €
(Rua do Marques 72; meals from €5.50; ⊙noon-3.30pm & 7-10pm Mon-Fri, noon-3.30pm Sat) A tremendous backstreet find, this place is absolutely jammed with locals for the *platos do dia* (plates of the day; €5.50). Think baked cod with white beans or roasted turkey leg with potatoes and salad. It's a friendly, satisfying, family-run affair.

Dolce Vianna PIZZA €
(☎258 824 860; Rua do Poço 44; pizzas €6-7) This popular pizzeria buzzes for lunch, when there's a special weekday menu for €5.50 and a range of cheesy thick-crust pizzas churned out of the wood-burning oven in the corner. Service can be spotty.

Casa de Pasto Maria de Perre PORTUGUESE €€
(☎258 822 410; Rua de Viana 118; mains €9.50-15; ⊙noon-3pm & 6.30-10.30pm Tue-Sat, noon-3pm Sun) A convivial two-floor restaurant with exposed stone walls in a tiny side street off the waterfront, it gets very busy at lunchtime. The focus is on daily specials featuring fresh fish dishes and also hearty meat options.

Zefa Carqueja GRILL €€
(☎258 828 284; Campo do Castelo; mains €8-25; ⊙9.30am-3.30pm & 5.30-11.30pm) Barbecue aficionados should find this grill house for some of the best barbecue chicken and ribs in northern Portugal. You can also get barbecued seafood – including lobster. Dine in or line up at the grill and take it away.

Taberna do Valentim SEAFOOD €€
(Campo do Castelo; mains €9.75-12.50; ⊙12.30-3pm & 7.30-10pm Mon-Sat) This bright and buzzing seafood restaurant serves fresh grilled fish by the kilo and rich seafood stews – *arroz de tamboril* (monkfish rice) and *caldeirada* (fish stew).

O Pescador SEAFOOD €€
(☎258 826 039; Largo de São Domingos 35; mains €9.50-15.50; ⊙noon-3pm & 7-10pm Tue-Sat, noon-3pm Sun) A friendly, family-run restaurant admired by locals for its good seafood, and tasty lunch specials (from €6.50).

Drinking & Nightlife

Republica BAR
(Praça da Erva 17-19; ⊙9pm-2am daily summer, closed Sun & Mon rest of year) This is where the action happens on weekend nights, at this cosy bar on the old town's main square. Tables spill out and crowds hang out till closing time.

Norte Beach Club CLUB
(Avenida de Cabo Verde 36, Praia Norte; ⊙11pm-8am Thu-Sat) A good choice if you're looking to groove into the wee hours. This boxy space has a spacious dance floor ringed by an upstairs gallery for checking out the scene below. It's next door to the Flôr de Sal hotel.

Foz CAFE
(☎258 808 060; Praça da Liberdade; ⊙11am-2am) This glass-box cafe with a massive menu and even better views is a gathering point for locals late in the evening. It's a good place for a sundowner, a crêpe or even an ice cream. The wine list is substantial.

Entertainment

Teatro Municipal Sá de Miranda THEATRE
(☎258 809 382; www.cm-viana-castelo.pt; Rua Sá de Miranda) The cultural epicentre of Viana do

Castelo, this pink-washed neoclassical theatre hosts a regular line-up of music, theatre, dance and the occasional opera.

Information

Hospital (☎258 802 100; Estrada de Santa Luzia) North of the train station.
Police Station (☎258 809 880; Rua de Aveiro)
Post Office (Avenida dos Combatentes da Grande Guerra 318; ⏲9am-12.30pm & 2.30-6pm Mon-Fri)

Getting There & Away

BUS

Long-distance *expresso* buses operate from the shiny, centralised bus station, which is just across the tracks from the train station.
AV Cura/Transcolvia (☎258 806 830) Runs up the Lima valley to Ponte de Lima (€3.40, one hour), Ponte da Barca (€4.20, one hour) and Arcos de Valdevez (€4.30, one hour) at least hourly on weekdays (less at weekends).
AV Minho (☎258 800 340) Runs a line from Porto (€6.50, two hours) at least four times daily, passing through Esposende (€3.70, 40 minutes); one to three daily buses run to Valença do Minho (€4, one hour) and Monção (€5.50, one hour).
Transdev Norte (☎258 825 047) Has at least eight weekday and four weekend runs to Braga (€4.75, 1½ hours).

TRAIN

Daily direct services from Porto include five IR/international trains (€6.65, two hours) and five regional services (€4.95, two hours). For Braga (€5.50, 1½ to two hours, 14 daily), change at Nine. There are also seven to 11 daily trains to Valença do Minho (€4.55, 45 minutes to one hour).

Getting Around

Parking can be a challenge – most locals opt for paid underground car parks sprinkled about the centre (including car parks on either end of Avenida dos Combatentes da Grande Guerra). There's ample free parking next to the Castelo de São Tiago da Barra. If you need wheels to hit the beaches north of Viana, **Orbita** (☎258 813 513; www.orbitaviagens.com; Rua Alves Cerqueria 216-218; ⏲9am-6pm) rents cars from €29 per day, but they must be reserved at least one day in advance.

To get up to Monte de Santa Luzia, take the **funicular** (one way/return €2/3; ⏲9am-8pm high season, 10am-noon & 1-5pm Mon-Fri, 9am-6pm Sat & Sun low season), which departs from near the train station every 15 minutes.

Praia do Cabedelo is best reached via the **ferry** (one way/return adult €1.40/2.80, half-price/free under-12/under-six; ⏲to Praia do Cabedelo 9am-6pm) from the pier south of Largo 5 de Outubro.

Valença do Minho

POP 3400

Now you're really in the Minho, where all is green, fertile and rustling in shared Spanish–Porto winds and waters. And no place has a better view of it all than this atmospheric fort village occupying strategic heights above the picturesque Rio Minho. Valença do Minho (Valença) sits just a cannonball shot from Spain, and its impressive pair of citadels long served as the Minho's first line of defence against Spanish aggression. But history insists on repeating itself, and these days the town is regularly overrun by Spanish hordes.

Sights & Activities

The Spanish tourists come armed with wallets and make away with volumes of towels and linens from the high stacks that line the cobbled streets. The good news is that on even the busiest days (which tend to be Wednesdays and the weekends), you can sidestep the towel touts and discover that the two interconnected forts also contain a fully functioning village where locals shop, eat, drink and gossip among pretty squares and narrow, medieval lanes. And when, in the evening, the weary troops retreat to Spain with their loot, the empty watchtowers return to silent contemplation of their ancient enemy – the glowering Spanish fortress of Tui situated just across the river.

Visitors can easily see the sights of Valença as a day trip, but there are two atmospheric places to sleep situated within the fortress walls that allow you to see and feel peaceful Valença when it empties at sunset. That's when you can hear the footsteps of kittens in the laneways while birdsong echoes off the ancient stone walls.

There are two **fortresses**, bristling with bastions, watchtowers, massive gateways and defensive bulwarks, connected by a single bridge. The old churches and Manueline mansions inside testify to the success of the fortifications against several sieges, some as late as the 19th century. The earliest fortifications date from the 13th-century reign of Dom Afonso III, although largely what you see today was built in the 17th century, its design inspired by the French military architect Vauban.

Zip past the tacky gift shops and towel merchants, and follow the cobbled lanes to the far end of the larger northern fortress, which incorporates Dom Afonso's original stronghold and contains almost everything else that's of interest. From Praça da República bear right, then left, into Rua Guilherme José da Silva (which turns into Rua Dr Pedro Augusto Dias). On the left, opposite the post office, is the **Casa da Eira**, with a handsome Manueline window somewhat marred by a horrendous corrugated tin room that peeks above the crenallated walls. The 14th-century **Igreja de Santo Estevão**, with its neoclassical facade, is at the end of the street. From the church, take a left and you'll see the 1st-century Roman milestone from the old Braga–Astorga road.

From the milestone continue north to the end of Rua José Rodrigues and the now-decrepit Romanesque parish church, **Igreja de Santa Maria dos Anjos** (Church of St Mary of the Angels), dating from 1276. At the back is a tiny **chapel** with Romano-Gothic inscriptions on the outside. To the left of the parish church is the **Capela da Misericórdia** and beyond it the Pousada de São Teotónio.

But the best fun can be had rambling on and around the series of exterior walls. In fact, if you turn right by the *pousada* you'll descend the atmospheric lane through one of the **original gates**, with a trickling stream running below, and an impressive echo. Keep going and you'll pass through several thick, mossy layers to the outside world.

Sleeping

Residencial Portas do Sol GUESTHOUSE €
(☎964 607 915; www.residencialportasdosol.com; Rua Conselheiro Lopes da Silva 51; s/d €30/45; ❄@📶) This place, one of two options in the fortress, is set in an antiquated stone building that has been refurbished and outfitted with all things IKEA-esque, but that's not necessarily a bad thing. The ceilings are high, and the old stone window frames lend enough old-world panache. It's located in the north fort, about a half block away from the bridge.

Pousada de São Teotónio POUSADA €€€
(☎251 800 260; www.pousadas.pt; Baluarte do Socorro; s/d €135/145; P❄📶) Perched on the outermost post of the fortress and surrounded by green ramparts, this bright, modern *pousada* has large, luxurious rooms, most with prime views overlooking the walls and river to Spain; a few have balconies.

Eating

The restaurants inside the fortress serve the usual menu of grilled meats and fish, some paired with lovely views of the surrounding countryside. In springtime, don't miss the river-eel specialities.

Churrasqueira Valenciana PORTUGUESE €
(Rua Maestro Sousa Morais 6-8; mains €5-14; ⏲8am-10pm Tue-Sun) Come to this cavernous and always bustling dining room if you're looking for tasty and cheap grilled chicken. There's no patio dining, which means there's no view, but the local scene inside is worthy of your contemplation.

O Limoeiro PORTUGUESE €€
(Rua da Oliveira 23; mains €6.50-14; ⏲noon-3pm & 7-10pm) A lunch-only spot situated on the outer ramparts, popular with locals for its good codfish on the grill and seafood rice. Downstairs is a tiny bar area with a few tables, upstairs has a rustic dining room accessed along a vine-covered staircase. Tables spill onto the esplanade on warm days.

Fortaleza PORTUGUESE €€
(Rua Apolinário da Fonseca 5; meals €9-15; ⏲8am-10pm) Set in the south fortress, with tables inside and on a wide patio with views overlooking the edge of the fort, this place does decent grilled meats and fish, and rice with river eel in springtime. They have another more modern restaurant, Fortaleza 2, down the street at number 29.

Information

Turismo (☎251 823 329; www.cm-valenca.pt; Paiol de Marte, Praça Forte de Valença; ⏲9.30am-12.30pm & 2-5.30pm Mon-Sat) Helpful tourism office to the left of the main entrance into the old town, right by the main car park.

Getting There & Away

BUS

AV Minho (☎258 800 340) has three buses each weekday and two buses each on Saturday and Sunday, with runs beginning in Monção (€2, 20 minutes) and going all the way to Porto (€9, 3½ hours) via Viana do Castelo (€6, 1¼ hours).

TRAIN

Five to 10 trains run daily to Valença from Porto (€9.30, 3½ hours), two of which continue as far as Vigo in Spain.

Getting Around

An uninspiring new town sprawls at the foot of the fortress. From the bus station it's 800m north via Avenida Miguel Dantas (the N13) and the Largo da Trapicheira roundabout (aka Largo da Esplanada) to the *turismo*. The train station is just east of Avenida Miguel Dantas.

There are free car parks just west of the fortresses, though they can fill to capacity at weekends. If you're spending the night inside the town, you should be able to find free street parking within the fort.

Monção

Like Valença do Minho to the west, Monção (mohng-*sowng*) was once an important fortification along the border with Spain. It has a modest but attractive historic centre – which includes the remains of its 14th-century fortifications still watching over the river – that sees far fewer visitors than Valença's. The town's big claim to fame is its fine *vinho verde,* with signs touting Monção as the cradle of the refreshing Alvarinho wine (Spain's Galicia makes similar claims).

It is said that during a siege by Castilian soldiers in 1368, a local townswoman named Deu-la-Deu Martins managed to scrabble together enough flour from starving citizens to make a few loaves of bread, and in a brazen show of plenty tossed them to the enemy with the message, 'if you need any more, just let us know'. The disheartened Spaniards immediately withdrew to Spain.

Sights

Old Monção AREA

FREE The best part of Monção's old town is the utter lack of tourism. It's almost exclusively a local scene in chestnut-shaded **Praça Deu-la-Deu**, where a hand-on-breast statue of its namesake tops a **fountain** and looks hungrily down over the surrounding cafes.

The **Senhora da Vista** bastion at the northern end offers a gentle view across the sinuous Rio Minho into Spain. The **Capela da Misericórdia** at the square's southern end has a coffered ceiling painted with cherubs.

East of the square is the snug, cobbled old quarter. Two blocks along Rua da Glória is the pretty little Romanesque **igreja matriz** (parish church), where Deu-la-Deu is buried (look for the stone-carved alcove to the left of the entrance).

Palácio da Brejoeira PALACE

(☎251 666 129; www.palaciodabrejoeira.pt; Quinta da Brejoeira, Pinheiros; tour €3-7.50, wine tasting €2.50; ⌚9am-noon & 2-5.30pm Apr-Sep, 9am-noon & 2-5.30pm Tue-Sun Oct-Mar) On the N101 towards Arcos de Valdevez, this grand neoclassical palace built in the early 19th century has been open to the public since 2010, even though the current owner, a 95-year-old heir, still lives inside. Visits are by guided tour only, which run every 30 minutes.

You can choose the half-hour tour that takes in the opulent interiors (€5), such as the Empire-furniture-filled king's room and the dining room where Franco and Salazar had a meeting in 1950, as well as the family's chapel and the gardens with 20 species of camellia. Or you can opt for the half-hour tour of the surroundings (€3) that include a forest, a plane-tree avenue, a romantic lake and the vineyards – the estate has 18 hectares of vineyards planted with Alvarinho. The hour-long tour (€7.50) takes in all of the highlights.

Activities

Termas de Monção THERMAL BATHS

(www.tesal.com; Avenida das Caldas; entry €12-15; ⌚9am-8pm Mon-Sat, to 6pm Sun; 👪) Monção's *termas* (thermal springs) have a large aquatic area with jacuzzis, tiny waterfalls and a children's swimming area. In addition to dips in the warm springs, a wide variety of spa treatments are available, with day packages starting at €55.

Those wanting the aquatic experience without the fuss can head across the road to the *piscina municipal*, a handsomely designed 25m indoor pool, with a smaller pool for younger swimmers.

Adega Cooperativa de Monção WINE

(☎251 652 167; www.adegademoncao.pt; Cruzes – Macedo; ⌚8.30am-12.30pm & 2-6pm Mon-Fri,

GOING GREEN IN VINHO VERDE COUNTRY

Outside Portugal, *vinho verde* (literally 'green wine') gets a bum rap, but often for good reason – exports tend to sit on shelves far too long. The stuff is made to be drunk 'green' – that is, while it is still very young, preferably less than one year old.

While the wine is made from fully ripe rather than still-green grapes, as is sometimes believed, the straw-coloured whites can indeed achieve greenish tints – a visual reminder of the green landscape from which they come. Served well chilled on a hot summer day, its fruity nose, fine bubbles and acidic bite make *vinho verde* one of the great delights of travelling in northern Portugal.

Vinho verde is grown in a strictly demarcated region of the Minho that occupies the coastal lowlands between the Rio Douro and the Spanish border. There are actually more vines here than in the Douro, but the *quintas* (estates) are subdivided to such a degree that most growers simply sell their fruit, or their wine, to community *adegas* (wineries).

Traditionally, the vines are trained high, both to conserve land and to save the grapes from rot, and you can still see great walls of green in the summer months. Like German wines, *vinho verde* tends to be aromatic, light-bodied and low in alcohol. There are red *vinho verdes*, though you may find them chalky and more of an acquired taste. White is both the most common and the easiest to appreciate. Alvarinho grapes, grown around Monção, are also used to make a delightful *vinho verde*.

For more information about the wine, its history, and visiting particular regions and vineyards, check out www.vinhoverde.pt. **Wine Tourism in Portugal** (www.winetourismportugal.com) is another useful resource; it offers curated information about wine experiences all over Portugal, which can be booked on its website directly.

9am-1pm Sat) Alvarinho is the delicious, tart and full-bodied variety of white *vinho verde* produced around Monção and neighbouring Melgaço. If you'd like a tasting, stop by this *adega* (winery) 1.8km south of Monção on the N101 to Arcos de Valdevez. Otherwise, the clutch of bars around Monção's principal squares will be happy to oblige.

Festivals & Events

Festa da Nossa Senhora das Dores RELIGIOUS

A big five-day celebration in the third week of August, headed by a pious procession.

Festa do Corpo de Deus RELIGIOUS

The town's biggest party is held on Corpus Christi, the eighth Thursday after Easter. Events include a religious procession and medieval fair, with a re-enactment of St George battling the dragon.

Feira do Alvarinho CULTURAL

(www.feiraalvarinho.pt.vu) The self-described cradle of Alvarinho, Monção hosts a three-day fair in honour of its wine in the first weekend of July. It features music, folk dancing and much eating and drinking.

Sleeping

Hospedaria Beco da Matriz GUESTHOUSE €

(☎251 651 909; hospedariabecomatriz@sapo.pt; Beco da Matriz; r €35) Just left of the facade of the *igreja matriz*, this place offers simple but impeccable rooms, with comfortable beds and spotless tile floors. Some rooms have excellent views over the adjacent ramparts to Spain. Check in at the bar downstairs if there's no answer at the door.

Solar de Serrade INN €€

(☎251 654 008; www.solardeserrade.pt; Mazedo; d €70, ste €90-95; P 📶) One of two manor houses on area estates producing Alvarinho grapes and delicious wines, this rather magnificent 17th-century mansion on the road toward Arcos de Valdevez has whimsical gardens and eight rooms and suites with elaborately furnished digs. Good for romantic getaways.

Fonte da Vila BOUTIQUE HOTEL €€

(☎251 640 050; www.hotelfontedavila.com; Estrada de Melgaço; s/d €65/80; P ❄ 📶) The Spanish-owned Fonte da Vila has cheerfully painted rooms with wooden floors and a clean-lined contemporary look in a renovated and remodelled manor house with a garden patio. There's an upscale seafood restaurant on the ground floor. It's in the new town, right across from the petrol station.

Convento dos Capuchos BOUTIQUE HOTEL €€€
(☎251 640 090; www.conventodoscapuchos.com; Quinta do Convento de São António, Estrada de Melgaço; s/d from €90/147; P 📶 🏊) Monção's most captivating property is situated in a restored 18th-century hilltop monastery with a glimmering infinity pool overlooking the river below. The deluxe rooms have wooden floors and French doors opening onto a splendid riverfront terrace. Less-expensive rooms are set in a newly constructed annexe; they are large with chic furnishings, but lack the former's majesty and views.

Eating

Bard Rock Cafe CAFE €
(Rua da Boavista; snacks €3-5; ⊙10am-2am) Right on the ramparts is this two-floor music-themed cafe-bar with a few plastic chairs outside taking in views of Spain out across the river. Snacks like sandwiches, burgers and *francesinhas* (overstuffed sandwiches) are served all day; at night-time come for beers and cocktails. From the main square, go all the way to the river and then turn left.

Cabral PORTUGUESE €€
(☎251 651 775; Rua 1 de Dezembro; mains €6-18; ⊙10am-4.30pm & 7-11.30pm) Cabral grills fresh fish and also does a tasty *arroz de marisco* (rice and seafood stew). It's all served in an attractive stone-walled dining room, almost always packed at lunch, down a narrow lane from Praça Deu-la-Deu.

Sete á Sete PORTUGUESE €€
(☎251 652 577; Rua Conselheiro João da Cunha; mains €8.50-15; ⊙noon-3pm & 7.30-10pm Tue-Sun) At the entrance to the old centre, this stone-walled dining room serves top-notch Minho specialities made with the finest, freshest ingredients, such as the seasonal river eel and *cabrito* (kid).

Drinking & Nightlife

Lés-a-Lés CAFE
(Praça da República; ⊙8.30am-midnight Mon-Thu, 9am-4am Fri & Sat, 2pm-midnight Sun) A lovely new cafe-bar on the main square, with globally inspired finger food (snacks €3 to €7) and a cosy vibe for a drink at night.

Information

Turismo (☎251 649 013; www.cm-moncao.pt; Praça Deu-la-Deu; ⊙9.30am-12.30pm & 1.30-6pm) Housed in the Museu do Alvarinho, the *turismo* also sells a small but high-quality selection of pottery and lacework from artisans of northern Portugal.

Getting There & Away

AV Minho (☎258 800 341) operates one weekend and two weekday buses that stop here en route from Melgaço (€3.70, 35 minutes) to Porto (€9, four hours) via Viana do Castelo (€5.50, 1½ hours).

Getting Around

From the bus station it's 600m east to the defunct train station, then another two blocks north up Rua General Pimenta de Castro to the first of the town's two main squares, Praça da República. Praça Deu-la-Deu and the heart of the old town lie just one block further.

You'll find street parking around Praça da República and Praça Deu-la-Deu.

Ponte de Lima

POP 2800

This photogenic town by the sweet and mellow Rio Lima springs to life on weekends, when Portuguese tourists descend in droves, and every other Monday, when a vast market spreads along the riverbank. All the action happens within sight of Portugal's finest medieval bridge. Even if you can't make the market, Ponte de Lima's small, historic centre dotted with cafes and vast riverside gardens and greenways is well worth visiting. Even the outskirts are romantic: vineyards tumble to bustling avenues, and at sunset swallows take flight, singing and diving until night finally falls.

Sights

Ponte Romana LANDMARK
FREE The city's *pièce de résistance*, this elegant 31-arched bridge across the Rio Lima is now limited to foot traffic. Most of it dates from the 14th century, though the segment on the north bank by the village of Arcozelo is bona fide Roman. Largo de Camões, with a fountain resembling a giant bonbon dish, makes a fine spot to watch the sun set over the bridge.

Parque Temático do Arnado GARDENS
(⊙10am-7pm) FREE Green space is abundant in Ponte de Lima, but this small, intriguing

garden with rose bushes and lemon-filled trellises next to a public swimming pool on the west side of the river is notable because each May it hosts a competition where 12 artists create temporary gardens built around a theme. The winning garden is chosen in October and remains rooted for the year.

Town Walls LANDMARK

Fragments of the town walls survive behind and between the Torre da Cadeia Velha and the Torre de São Paulo (part of the fortifications made in the 14th century).

Museu do Brinquedo Português MUSEUM

(Casa do Arnado, Largo da Alegria, Arcozelo; adult/student & over 3yr €3/1.50; 10am-12.30pm & 2-6pm Tue-Sun;) In a gorgeous red mansion right after the Roman bridge in Arcozelo is this museum dedicated to Portuguese toys. The focus is on toys made from the late 19th century through to 1986. Displays in different rooms include raw materials and manufacturing techniques, and toys arranged by decade, from brightly painted wooden beach buckets to papier-mâché dolls and tinplate cannons.

There's also a play room, and a toy workshop accessed through the garden.

Museu dos Terceiros MUSEUM

(Avenida 5 de Outubro; €2.50; 10am-12.30pm & 2-6pm Tue-Sun) Downriver, the 18th-century Igreja de São Francisco dos Terceiros is now a rambling museum full of ecclesiastical and folk treasures, although the highlight is the church itself, with its gilded baroque interior. The Renaissance-style Igreja de Santo António dos Frades, once a convent church, is now a wing of the museum.

Lagoas de Bertiandos e São Pedro de Arcos NATURE RESERVE

(www.lagoas.cm-pontedelima.pt; Arcos; 9am-12.30pm & 2-5.30pm Mon-Fri, 2.30-5.30pm Sat & Sun) FREE This 350-hectare nature reserve is set in a wildlife-rich humid zone just north of the Rio Lima. There's a wildlife interpretation centre and eight hiking trails, ranging from an easy lakeside loop (1.6km) to a longer 12.5km hike. Get there on the A27 4km west from Ponte de Lima, taking exit 3.

Torre de São Paulo TOWER

Along with the Torre da Cadeia Velha, this tower constitutes the only standing remains of Ponte de Lima's medieval walls. Note the somewhat bizarre *azulejo* image on its front wall, entitled *Cabras são Senhor!* (They're goats m'lord!) – a reference to a local story in which Dom Afonso Henriques almost attacked a herd of goats, apparently mistaking them for Moors.

Torre da Cadeia Velha TOWER

(Old Prison Tower; 9.30am-12.30pm & 2-6pm) FREE Two crenellated towers (part of the fortifications made in the 14th century) face the river at the end of Rua Cardeal Saraiva. The Torre da Cadeia Velha now houses temporary art exhibitions and the *turismo*, plus a host of pigeons on its window ledges.

Activities

Ecovia do Rio Lima CYCLING

On both sides of the Rio Lima you'll find riverside bike paths – part of the Ecovia do Rio Lima network. For more info and maps, enquire at the *turismo* or check out www.ciclovia.pt.

Village Walks WALKING

There are several charming walks through the countryside, past ancient monuments and along cobbled lanes trellised with vines. The *turismo* has literature on routes ranging from 5km to 14km. Pack water and a picnic – cafes and restaurants are rare.

A steep 5km climb north of Arcozelo yields panoramic views up and down the Lima valley from a tiny and bizarre chapel (open irregular hours) dedicated to Santo Ovídio, patron saint of ears. Yes, you read that right. The interior is covered with ear-shaped

ROMAN BRIDGE

When a Roman regiment first passed through Ponte de Lima, soldiers were convinced that the Rio Lima was Lethe itself – the mythical 'river of oblivion'. Alas, no such luck. Decimus Junius Brutus forced his men to plunge ahead, but they still remembered all their sins upon reaching the far side. The impressive **Ponte Romana** (p454) – part of the Roman road from Braga to Astorga in Spain, and the town's namesake – supposedly marks their crossing. Though largely rebuilt in medieval times, it still contains traces of its Roman antecedent.

votive candles offered in hope of, or as thanks for, the cure of an ear affliction. You can also drive up; the turn-off from the N202 is located about 2.5km upstream of the N201 bridge.

Clube Náutico de Ponte de Lima WATER SPORTS
(☎258 944 899; www.cnplima.com; São Gonçalo, Arcozelo; kayak & canoe per 1½ hr €3; ⏰9.30am-12.30pm & 2-8pm) Across the river and 400m downstream from town, this aquatic outfitter rents canoes and plastic kayaks for exploring the mellow river as it spreads over willowed sand bars, glistens blue in the sun and fades to deep green at dusk. It also rents bicycles (€5 per 1½ hours).

Festivals & Events

Feiras do Cavalo CULTURAL
Held annually in the third week of June, this horse fair is one of the town's most raucous festivals, when the Expo Lima (the riverside fairgrounds) becomes a race track and stage for horses, carriages and musicians.

Vaca das Cordas & Corpus Christi CULTURAL
The ninth Friday after Easter is the date for a tradition that probably dates back at least to Roman times and possibly has Phoenician origins. It features a kind of bull-running in which young men goad a hapless bull (restrained by a long rope) as it runs through the town.

It's followed the next day by the more pious Festa do Corpo de Deus, with religious processions and flowers carpeting the streets.

Feiras Novas CULTURAL
(New Fairs) Held here since 1125, this is one of Portugal's oldest ongoing events. Stretching over three days during the third week of September, it centres on the riverfront, with a massive market and fair, and features folk dances, fireworks, brass bands and all manner of merrymaking. Book accommodation well ahead.

Sleeping

Quinta de Pentieiros CAMPGROUND €
(☎258 240 202; www.lagoas.cm-pontedelima.pt; site adult/child €3.50/2, casas €80-90; P 🏊) Inside the Lagoas nature reserve, this estate has campsites and more comfortable bungalows and *casas* (houses) with kitchen units that work well for families. There's also an inviting swimming pool (€2/3 on weekdays/weekends), horse riding and bike rental. Prices are lower (and crowds fewer) on weekdays.

Residencial São João GUESTHOUSE €
(☎258 941 288; alojamento_s.joao@sapo.pt; Largo de São João; s/d €35/40; 📶) This welcoming, family-run guest house offers a decent collection of clean, serviceable and mostly bright rooms with wooden floors. Most have private bathrooms. Quarters are tight and there's no TV but the location can't be beat.

Pousada da Juventude HOSTEL €
(☎258 751 321; www.pousadasjuventude.pt; Rua Papa João Paulo II; dm €12, d €26-30; P @ 📶) Built of concrete, wood and glass, this striking, contemporary youth hostel is a pleasant 10-minute walk south from the centre of town along the river. Facilities are limited, but the dorms and doubles (with private and shared bathroom) are clean and attractive.

Mercearia da Vila GUESTHOUSE €€
(☎258 753 562; www.merceariadavila.pt; Rua Cardeal Saraiva 34-36; d/ste €65/80; 📶) Six rooms hide above this charming old grocery-store-turned-cafe. Each comes with a theme (from green tea to chocolate), as well as hardwood floors and original furniture. Some have balconies, and the top-floor suite has a window overlooking the river. There's also a shared living room and kitchen. Don't miss the delicious *petiscos* and homemade cakes downstairs.

Casa do Pinheiro GUESTHOUSE €€
(☎258 943 971; www.casadopinheiro.pt; Rua General Norton de Matos 629; s/d €55/65; ❄ 📶 🏊) A stunning place set in a painstakingly restored private house from the 1700s, whose seven elegant rooms boast high ceilings, antique beds, hardwood floors and touches of religious art. Some rooms have balconies, while others open onto the splendid back garden with a small pool and fruit trees. Breakfast is fabulous.

Casa do Arrabalde INN €€
(☎258 742 442; www.casadoarrabalde.com; Arcozelo; s/d €65/80, cottage €100-140; P 📶 🏊) This terrific option sits conveniently just across the Ponte Romana in Arcozelo. The main quarters are still inhabited by the family who built the place in the 18th century. Rooms are grand and furnished with period antiques; the cottages are more contemporary.

There are huge verdant grounds and an inviting pool. Book ahead, as the family is often away.

Casa do Barreiro INN €€
(☎258 948 137; Gemieira; s/d €45/75, apt €70-120; P 📶 🏊) Particularly elegant, this 17th-century yellow manor house about halfway between Ponte de Lima and Ponte da Barca features original details, including stone mantles and *azulejos*. The six rooms and two apartments are spare but lovely, and the grounds gush with fountains, are surrounded by vineyards and include a pool and tennis courts. It's open May through September.

★**Carmo's Boutique Hotel** BOUTIQUE HOTEL €€€
(☎258 938 743; www.carmosboutiquehotel.com; Rua Santiago da Gemieira 10, Gemieira; d/ste €223/322; P ❄ 📶 🏊) This nouveau-romantic boutique hideaway in the village of Gemieira, 6.5km east of Ponte de Lima, has 15 sublime rooms, two pools, a cosy wine bar and a small basement spa inside a contemporary two-wing structure. Inside is all about casual and cosy chic, breakfast is served until noon and rates include dinner at the restaurant, which whips up great regional dishes. Worth a splurge.

Quinta do Ameal INN €€€
(☎258 947 172; www.quintadoameal.com; Refóios do Lima; ste €195-250; P 📶 🏊) Known for its top-notch whites made with the local *loureiro* grape, this gorgeous estate just outside Ponte de Lima recently unveiled five luxurious suites with a range of top-notch comforts, kitchenettes and original details. Three suites are in the main house and two more are in a separate villa, with outside showers backed by bamboo forests.

Eating

Açude PORTUGUESE €€
(☎258 944 158; Centro Náutico de Ponte de Lima, Arcozelo; mains €10.50-17; ⏰noon-3pm & 7-10pm Tue-Sat, noon-3pm Sun) A great option right on the riverfront in Arcozelo, a short walk from town, this boat-themed upstairs restaurant clad in wood serves tasty *posta a açude* steak and great *lagareiro* octopus (with potates, garic and olive oil).

A Carvalheira PORTUGUESE €€
(☎258 742 316; Rua do Eido Velho, Eido Velho; mains €12-18; ⏰12.30-3pm & 7-10pm Tue-Sun; P ❄) It's generally agreed that country-style A Carvalheira, a short ride southeast of town, serves the area's best food. Order ahead if you want the regional favourite – *arroz de sarrabulho* (stewed rice with pork and pork blood).

Manuel Padeiro PORTUGUESE €€
(☎258 941 649; Rua do Bonfim 20; mains €7.50-14; ⏰11.30am-3pm & 6.30-10pm Mon & Wed-Sun) The speciality at this simple local tavern with a 60-year tradition is *arroz de sarrabulho*. Other dishes are well prepared too, including the daily weekday lunch specials, which are a steal.

Muralha PORTUGUESE €€
(☎258 741 997; Largo da Picota; mains €8.50-12; ⏰lunch & dinner Wed-Mon, lunch Tue) Tucked into an alcove behind one of the town's old towers, this somewhat divey dining room serves tasty octopus and meat dishes. It brags about its *cabrito*, too.

Sabores do Lima PORTUGUESE €€
(☎258 931 121; Largo de António Magalhães 64; mains €8-13; ⏰9.30am-2am Tue-Sun) A few steps from the river, the inviting Sabores do Lima has exposed stone walls that give a dash of style to its open dining room. The first-rate cooking features grilled meats, cod dishes and a few assorted seafood plates.

A Tulha PORTUGUESE €€
(☎258 942 879; Rua Formosa; mains €6-15; ⏰noon-3pm & 7-10pm Tue-Sat, noon-3pm Sun; ❄) All dark wood, stone and terracotta tiles inside, this restaurant serves excellent meat and fish dishes with plenty of vegetables. Try the *medalhão á Tulha* – a thick steak wrapped in bacon.

Drinking & Nightlife

Arte e Baco WINE BAR
(Rua Formosa 19; ⏰7pm-2am Mon-Thu, 7pm-4am Fri & Sat, 8.30pm-2am Sun) The hippest bar in town is a black-floored, chalkboard-walled lounge featuring rotating art exhibitions, the finest wine from the Minho (mostly *vinho verde*) and Douro, fine cigars, better port and occasional live music.

Bar Che BAR
(Rua Formosa 37; ⏰2pm-2am Mon-Thu & Sun, 2pm-4am Fri & Sat) Images of the bar's namesake revolutionary decorate this cosy place, which has long attracted alternative types.

Entertainment

Teatro Diogo Bernardes THEATRE
(☎258 900 414; www.cm-pontedelima.pt; Rua Agostinho José Taveira) Behind the Museu dos Terceiros, the galleried Teatro Diogo Bernardes, built in 1893, is the pride of the town, with interesting music and theatre performances throughout the year.

Information

Hospital (☎258 909 500; Rua Conde de Bertiandos)

Police Station (☎258 900 380; Rua Dr Luís da Cunha Nogueira)

Post Office (Praça da República; ⊙8.30am-5.30pm Mon-Fri)

Turismo (☎258 240 208; www.cm-pontedelima.pt; Torre da Cadeia Velha; ⊙9.30am-1pm & 2-5.30pm) This exceptionally friendly and well-organised tourist office shares space with a small handicrafts gallery. The lower floor has glass walkways over the excavated layers of an ancient tower.

Getting There & Away

There is street parking uphill from Praça da República; higher up still, it's free.

Board long-distance buses on Avenida António Feijó (buy tickets on board) or at the bus station. All services thin out on Sunday.

AV Cura/Transcolvia (☎258 800 340) has a service to Viana do Castelo (€3.50, 50 minutes). **Rede Expressos** (☎258 942 870; www.rede-expressos.pt) has one daily run to Braga (€4, 30 minutes), Valença do Minho (€7, 25 minutes) and Lisbon (€19, 6½ hours) via Porto (€8, 2¼ hours).

Ponte da Barca

POP 2300

Peaceful and friendly Ponte da Barca, named after the *barca* (barge) that once ferried pilgrims and others across the Rio Lima, has an idyllic, willow-shaded riverfront (perfect for cycling into the wooded valley), a handsome 16th-century bridge, a tiny old centre and the best source of information on the Parque Nacional da Peneda-Gerês.

The old town, just east of the bridge, is packed into narrow lanes on both sides of the main road, Rua Conselheiro Rocha Peixoto. Wednesday is market day.

Sights & Activities

The riverfront is the focal point of the town (and a good place for a picnic), with picturesque weeping willows lining the banks of the Rio Lima, and a green lawn that beckons sunbathers. The lovely, 10-arched **ponte** (bridge) originally dated from the 1540s. Beside it is the old arcaded marketplace and a little garden, **Jardim dos Poetas**, dedicated to two 16th-century poet brothers, Diogo Bernardes and Agostinho da Cruz, who were born in Ponte da Barca.

Hiking

The *turismo* has a booklet called *Historia, Patrimonia & Cultura*, with regional information, including details of **hikes** in the surrounding valley, some of them punctuated with ancient sites. A simple stroll west for 4km leads to **Bravães**, a village famous for its lovely, small Romanesque **Igreja de São Salvador**. Its west portal is adorned with intricate carved animals, birds and human figures; its interior shelters simple frescoes of the Virgin and the Crucifixion.

Festivals & Events

Festa de São Bartolomeu CULTURAL
Held from 19 to 24 August, this festival sees folk music and dancing aplenty, not to mention parades and fireworks.

Sleeping

Hotel Os Poetas HOTEL €
(☎258 488 152; www.hotelospoetas.com; Rua Dr Alberto Cruz 9; s €35-45, d €50-60; P 📶) A riverfront hotel steps away from the historic centre, with simple but lovely rooms, many of which showcase views of the river.

Pensão Gomes GUESTHOUSE €
(☎258 452 288; Rua Conselheiro Rocha Peixoto 13; s/d with shared bathroom €20/25) Welcome to your sweet Barca granny's house. Incredibly cheap, old-world rooms have worn wooden floors, sloping ceilings and tonnes of charm, and there are fabulous river and bridge views from the rooftop terrace.

Casa Nobre do Correio Mor INN €€
(☎919 440 801; www.laceme.pt; Rua Trás do Forno 1; s/d from €60/80; 📶 🏊) Lovingly restored, this 17th-century manor house on the street above the town hall offers 10 gorgeous rooms, most with wide timber floors, antique furnishings and stone-framed French windows with city and river views.

Eating & Drinking

Beside the old bridge is the old arcaded marketplace and a little garden, Jardim dos

Poetas, which has a strip of occasionally happening bars with ample, shady park-bench riverside seating.

Vai à Fava PORTUGUESE €

(☎258 027 769; Rua Dr Alberto Cruz 13; mains €6-15; ⊙3-11pm Thu, 11.30am-11pm Fri & Sat, 11.30am-6pm Sun) A recently revamped spot with an upgraded menu and a repertoire of evening events, too. The terrace with the bridge view is a winner.

Varanda do Lima PORTUGUESE €€

(Campo do Cúrro; mains €9-18; ⊙lunch & dinner) This is one of Barca's grandest options, with fresh fish and all the traditional meat dishes served on pressed tablecloths. If you want something lighter, pop into the restaurant's popular cafe next door.

Information

ADERE Peneda-Gerês (☎258 452 250; www.adere-pg.pt; Rua Dom Manuel I; ⊙9am-12.30pm & 2.30-6pm Mon-Fri) ADERE Peneda-Gerês is the booking agent for many shelters and rural houses located in Parque Nacional da Peneda-Gerês.

Municipal Library (Rua Atrás do Forno 33; ⊙9am-12.30pm & 2-5.30pm Mon-Fri, 9am-1pm Sat;) Free internet access.

Post Office (Rua Com José de Oliveira Carneiro Bouças; ⊙9am-12.30pm & 2-5.30pm Mon-Fri) Main post office.

Turismo (☎258 455 246; www.pontedabarca.com.pt; Rua Conselheiro Rocha Peixoto 9; ⊙10am-1pm & 2-6pm Tue-Sat) The tourist office is 100m from the medieval bridge, and has a town map and accommodation information.

Getting There & Away

You'll find free parking in the shady square at the western end of the bridge.

AV Cura buses run to Arcos de Valdevez (€1.35, 10 minutes), Ponte de Lima (€2.80, 40 minutes) and Viana do Castelo (€4.20, two hours) a number of times daily; they stop either in front of São João fountain on Rua Diogo Bernardes or in front of Churasqueira Barquense restaurant on Rua Dr Francisco Sá Carneiro.

Salvador (www.salvador-transportes.com) buses depart for Arcos de Valdevez regularly every day (€1.35, 10 minutes); they stop at Churasqueira Barquense restaurant. Buses also travel through Ponte da Barca twice a day Monday to Friday on their way from Arco de Valdevez to Soajo (€2.80, 45 minutes) in Parque Nacional da Peneda-Gerês. Buses stop in front of D António Hotel. Enquire at the *turismo* for the current schedule. Salvador buses also travel to Braga daily (€3.85, one hour); buses stop next to Magalhães Hostel and the kiosk in the Bairro Santo António.

Renex (www.renex.pt) has three buses to Porto daily (€7, 2½ hours); buy tickets beforehand at Varela cafe; buses stop on Rua Dr Carlos Araújo in front of the pink buildings.

Arcos de Valdevez

POP 2300

Drowsy little Arcos de Valdevez is home to a couple of interesting old churches and several stately homes in a small, almost tourist-free old centre. It also has a vibrant, willow-shaded riverfront. While it doesn't merit a special trip, it's a handy gateway to the northern end of Parque Nacional da Peneda-Gerês.

Sleeping

Arcos Hotel Nature & Spa HOTEL €€

(☎258 093 600; www.arcoshotelnature.com; Lugar de Requeijo; s/d €75/95;) The views from the rooms and suites are the drawing card at this modern hotel a short walk away from the centre. There's a small on-site spa, too, and a restaurant.

Casa da Breia COTTAGE €€

(☎258 751 751; www.casadabreia.com; São Paio de Jolda; cottage €60-110;) This sweeping 17th-century *quinta* nestled in a village just 10km from Arcos is owned by a sweet family who offer the charming, historic stone cottages (former staff quarters) to guests. The hosts have terrific tips for visiting the nearby national park.

Eating

Doçaria Central BAKERY €

(☎258 515 215; Rua General Norton de Matos 47; pastries €1; ⊙9am-7pm Mon-Fri & Sun, 9am-1pm Sat) Founded in 1830, this wonderful confectioner stocks the town's favourite sweet, *rebuçados dos arcos* (enormous, jaw-breaking, hard-boiled sweets), and pastry, *charutos dos arcos* (preserved egg wrapped in a sugary dough). To get here take the street to the right of the tourist office, past the post office.

Casa Real Matadouro STEAK €€

(☎258 522 216; Pedrosas, Guilhadeses; mains €9-18; ⊙lunch & dinner) Set in a stately house on the riverside, Matadouro serves some of the best steaks in the Minho. It's located about 500m south of the *turismo*.

Minho Verde PORTUGUESE €€
(☎258 516 296; Rua Mário Júlio Almeida Costa 37; mains €6-16; ⊙lunch & dinner Mon-Sat) One of Arcos' finest restaurants is in an unlikely location in an ugly block down the waterfront from the *turismo*. However, it serves excellent Minho specialities ranging from *posta de vitela* (veal steak) to *arroz de sarrabulho*. On Saturdays in spring and summer it serves *feijão terrestre*, a local bean, with Barrosã beef.

Information

Turismo (☎258 520 530; Rua Prof Mário Júlio BA Costa; ⊙9.30am-12.30pm & 2-6pm Mon-Sat) This helpful, English-speaking tourist office is across from the town fountains (with the legless horses).

Getting There & Away

The bus station is almost 1km north of the town centre, but regional buses will stop on request in front of the *turismo*.

AV Cura buses run to Ponte da Barca (€1.35, 15 minutes), Ponte de Lima (€3.35, 50 minutes) and Viana do Castelo (€4, 1½ hours) eight times daily Monday to Friday, and once or twice on weekends.

Salvador buses roll at least twice on weekdays to Soajo (€2.75, 40 minutes) in Parque Nacional da Peneda-Gerês. There is no weekend service into the park.

Parque Nacional da Peneda-Gerês

Spread across four impressive granite massifs in Portugal's northernmost reach, this 703-sq-km park encompasses boulder-strewn peaks, precipitous valleys and lush forests of oak and fragrant pine. It also shelters more than 100 granite villages that, in many ways, have changed little since Portugal's founding in the 12th century. Established in 1971, Parque Nacional da Peneda-Gerês – Portugal's first and only national park – has helped preserve not just a unique set of ecosystems but also an endangered way of life for its human inhabitants.

Sights

Many of the park's oldest villages are found in the **Serra da Peneda** and remain in a time warp, with oxen being trundled down cobbled streets by black-clad widows, and horses shod in smoky blacksmith shops. The ancient, remote granite villages, still inhabited by farmers and shepherds (and now small doses of tourists), are the park's real treasures. So are their distinctive *espigueiros* (stone granaries). You can get lost (the good kind) amid the hard-handed, open-hearted shepherds of old Portugal who still maintain the practice of moving livestock, and even entire villages, to high pastures for up to five months each year. Yet, despite joint governmental and private initiatives, this rustic scene is in danger of fading away, as young people head for the cities and village populations continue to shrink.

The steeper, more pristine **Serra do Gerês** sees the most tourism, in the form of hiking and water sports such as kayaking and rafting.

There is a scattering of **Stone Age dolmens** and **antas** (megaliths) on the high plateaux of the Serra da Peneda and Serra do Gerês, near Castro Laboreiro, Mezio, Paradela, Pitões das Júnias and Tourém. Not all are easily accessible, but there is a good road from the park gateway in Mezio to **Gião**. Once home to the Mezio people, it's considered to be one of the most important rock compounds in the northwest Iberian peninsula.

Activities

The park is alive with adventure options. Hiking trails ranging from 1km to 30km long abound in all sections of the park. Signage is solid, mountain-bike rental is easy to source, and swimming holes beckon. Rio Caldo is the water-sports centre, and the thermal springs of Vila do Gerês are worth a dip.

Água Montanha Lazer WATER SPORTS
(☎253 391 779; www.aguamontanha.com; Lugar de Paredes) English-run Água Montanha Lazer rents single/double kayaks for €6/9 per hour, plus pedal boats and small motorboats. It will also take you wakeboarding (€50 per 20 minutes), or organise kayaking trips along the Albufeira de Salamonde. AML also rents three attractively furnished cottages, all with verandahs, kitchen units and water views.

Equi Campo HORSE RIDING
(☎253 161 405; www.equicampo.com; ⊙9am-7pm Jun-Aug, 9am-7pm weekends Sep-May) One of two Campo-based outfitters that are located on the right just before you arrive in the

Parque Nacional da Peneda-Gerês

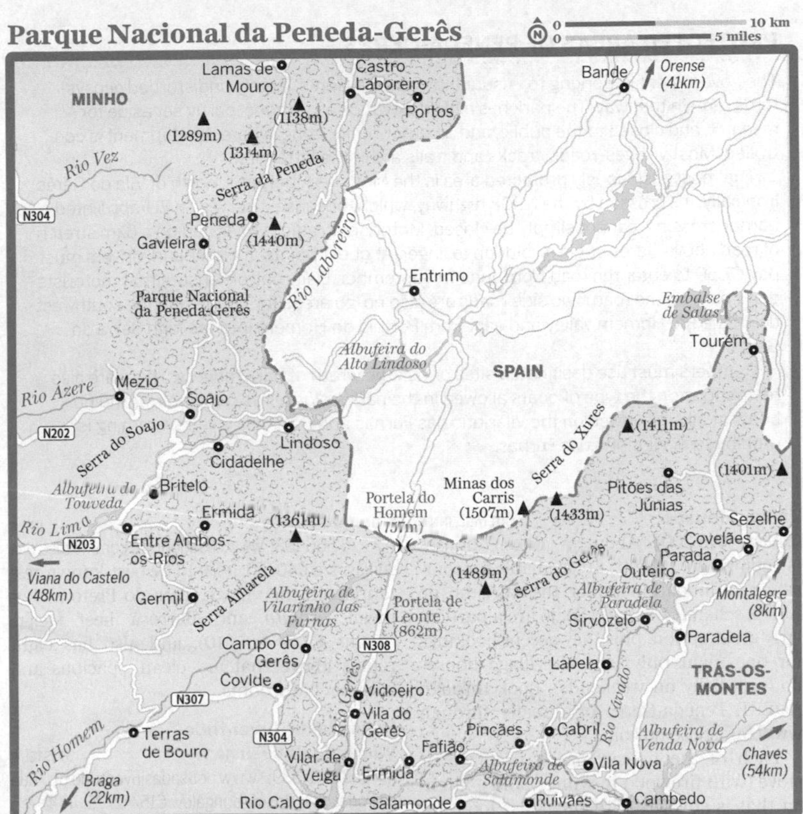

town. Guides lead horse-riding trips (one/two hours €17/30), hikes (half-day €80 per person) as well as treetop adventures (€12). You can also rent mountain bikes here if you would like to head off on your own (€5/17 per hour/day). The wooden shack also has a few tables outside where snacks are served.

Wildlife Watching

In the more remote areas there are a few wolves that still roam, as do wild boar, badgers and otters. With luck, you may catch a quick glimpse of roe deer and a few wild ponies. Closer to the ground are grass snakes and the rare, venomous black viper. Birders should look out for red kites, buzzards, goshawks, golden eagles as well as several species of owl.

The park's domestic animals are also of interest – and they don't tend to run away so quickly. In particular, primitive local breeds of long-horned cattle (the mahogany-coloured *barrosã* and darker *cachena*), goats, sheep, and the huge, sturdy Castro Laboreiro sheepdog are all unique to the area.

Sheltered valleys hold stands of white oak, arbutus, laurel and cork oak. Forests of black oak, English oak and holly give way at higher elevations to birch, yew and Scots pine, and in alpine areas to juniper and sandwort. The endemic Gerês iris grows in a small patch of the Serra do Gerês.

Sleeping

ADERE Peneda-Gerês (p459) in Porte da Barca is the booking agent for many shelters and rural houses located in the park. You can peruse pictures, read about and book accommodation online at www.go2nature.pt, the recently launched travel-agency outfit by ADERE-Peneda Gerês.

PROTECTED AREAS OF PENEDA-GERÊS

The government is working to ensure that Peneda-Gerês' largely undisturbed ecosystems remain that way. The park has a high-elevation inner zone, partly set aside for research and closed to the public, and an outer buffer zone, where development is controlled. Most villages, roads, tracks and trails are in the latter area.

The most assiduously protected area is the Mata de Albergaria, north of Vila do Gerês. Ironically, it's crossed by the N308 highway, which, because it serves an EU-appointed border crossing, cannot simply be closed. Motorised traffic is tolerated on a 6km stretch of road above Gerês but is forbidden to linger. At checkpoints at either end, drivers must pay €1.50 to enter the road from June to September. Daily patrols ensure that motorists don't park on the road. Two side roads are also no-go areas for non-residents: southwest down the Rio Homem valley and east from Portela do Homem into the high Serra do Gerês.

Campers must use designated sites or risk the wrath of park rangers. There are also restrictions on the type of boats allowed in the park's *albufeiras* (reservoirs), and no boats at all are allowed on the Vilarinho das Furnas and Paradela. Even swimming is prohibited in Vilarinho das Furnas.

Village Houses COTTAGE, INN €

(cottage €45-200) About a dozen houses (sleeping two to eight) are available for tourist accommodation under the Turismo de Aldeia scheme. Casas de Soajo are a particularly great option, plus they accept bookings for one night only; not all village houses do (especially on weekends). Book through ADERE Peneda-Gerês or directly through www.casasdesoajo.com.

Each of the houses has a fireplace or stove (with firewood in winter) and a kitchen that is stocked with breakfast food, including fresh bread on the doorstep each morning.

Miracastro GUESTHOUSE €

(☎251 460 020; www.albergariamiracastro.com; Castro Laboreiro; s/d €25/40; P ❄ wi-fi) A friendly, family-run guest house in the village of Castro Laboreiro, with simple rooms blessed with lots of light and gorgeous vistas from the balconies. The restaurant serves huge portions of tasty traditional dishes (€5 to €10), such as oven-baked *cabrito* and codfish with *broa* cornbread.

Miradouro do Castelo GUESTHOUSE €

(☎251 466 041; www.miradourodocastelo.com; Castro Laboreiro; d €45-55; P wi-fi) The sweeping views from the simple rooms with hardwood floors steal the show at this simple guest house situated in Castro Laboreiro. Of the seven rooms, three have the wow view, and cost €10 more. The downstairs restaurant serves up good local staples (€7 to €12).

Casa do Preto INN €

(☎276 566 158; www.casadopreto.com; Pitões das Júnias; s/d €40/50; P wi-fi) The best-known restaurant in the village, Casa do Preto makes mean *cabrito* and Barrosã beef steaks (mains €7.50 to €10), and also has eight rooms above that are clean, spacious and with big bathrooms.

Pousada da Juventude Vilarinho das Furnas HOSTEL €

(☎253 351 339; www.pousadasjuventude.pt; Rua da Pousada 1; dm/d/bungalow €15/42/75; P @ wi-fi) Campo's woodland hostel offers a spotless selection of spartan four-bed dormitories, some stylish double rooms (with bathrooms) and roomier bungalows that have kitchen units.

Casa dos Braganças INN €€

(☎276 579 138; www.casadosbragancas.com; Rua dos Braganças 8-10, Tourém; s/d €45/60; P wi-fi) Casa dos Braganças in the village of Tourém is a delightful rural inn run by a friendly live-in family. Inside this 18th-century house, rooms feature original details such as handpainted ceilings, stone walls, custom-made wood furniture and countryside views. There are free bikes, great birdwatching in the area (featuring some rare birds) and dinners on request.

Beleza da Serra GUESTHOUSE €€

(☎253 391 457; www.bserra.com; Lugar do Bairro 25, Vilar da Veiga; d €49-63, tr €63-79; P ❄ wi-fi) A great base for hiking and kayaking, this friendly waterfront guest house overlooks the Caniçada Reservoir, 4.5km south of Vila do Gerês. It has simple, clean, comfortable rooms and a restaurant dishing up regional food.

Drinking & Nightlife

Taberna Terra Celta BAR

(Rua dos Caldeireiros 2, Pitões das Júnias; ⏲9am-midnight Tue-Sun) Don't miss Taberna Terra Celta situated on the main village square, in an old wooden and stone home with an upstairs fireplace. On weekends it serves *fumeiro* (smoked meats), soups and salads; it's also a great stop for a drink.

Information

An EU-assisted consultancy, ADERE Peneda-Gerês, which was formed to spur ecotourism in the region, is the best resource for the park. Materials available include pamphlets on the park's natural, architectural and human landscapes, as well as on village-to-village walks using marked trails. There's also a booklet on accommodation.

The park has five information gateways, each created to welcome visitors in the five municipalities of the park, with a thematic display about an aspect of the park, and maps to take away. **Lindoso** (☎258 578 141; portalindoso@cmpb.pt; ⏲10am-6pm Apr-Sep, 10am-12.30pm & 2-5pm Oct-Mar) is the gateway for the Ponte da Barca municipality. Campo do Gerês represents the Terras de Bouro municipality. **Lamas de Mouro** (☎251 465 010; portadelamas@cm-melgaco.pt; ⏲10am-12.30pm & 2.30-7pm Apr-Sep, 10am-1pm & 2-5pm Oct-Mar), on the way to Castro Laboreiro, has info for Melgaço municipality. Another info point is at **Mezio** (☎258 510 100; portadomezio@ardal.pt; ⏲9.30am-8pm Jul & Aug, 9.30am-1pm & 2-6pm Apr-Jun & Sep, 9.30am-12.30pm & 2-5pm Oct-Mar), 13km from Arcos de Valdevez. Lastly, the gateway for the eastern part of the park is at Montalegre.

Getting There & Away

Empresa Hoteleira do Gerês (☎253 262 033) has bus services running from Braga to Vila do Gerês (€4.25, 1½ hours) hourly during the week, five times on Saturday and four times Sunday.

On weekdays there are eight Salvador bus services from Braga to Arcos de Valdevez (€4, one hour), three on weekends. Two Salvador buses also go on weekdays from Arcos de Valdevez to Soajo (€2.75, 50 minutes) and Lindoso (€3.55, one hour) in Parque Nacional da Peneda-Gerês; there are no bus services on weekends.

Serra da Peneda

The lesser-visited, northernmost end of the park is ripe for exploration. Lower-lying forested hills fade into massive glacially formed peaks, some topped with powerful 21st-century windmills, others sit idly watching over vast boulder fields. Old stone houses huddle in the shadows, wild horses and cattle gather and wander free, and stone fences sprout haphazardly and wind through wildflower prairies.

Sights & Activities

Hiking is the principal activity in this end of the park, but there's a certain amount of old-world history to explore on these trails too. The easiest walk can be found opposite the Lamas de Mouro gate. This **interpretative trail** winds past watermills, stone churches and community ovens, and along a stream for 4km.

Driving from here, bear right at the intersection and you'll head into the somewhat sprawling village of **Castro Laboreiro**, named for its endemic sheepdogs but more notable for the picturesque ruins of its 16th-century **castle**, built in 1505 on the foundations of a 12th-century Moorish castle. You can access it from a short and faint 800m trail. Views are stunning.

Castro Laboreiro has three other trails to explore. The shortest is a moderate 3km **interpretative trail**, but the more strenuous and spectacular are the **Trilho Castrejo**, a 17km ramble over some of the oldest trails in these mountains, and the equally beautiful but less demanding **Pertinho do Céu** from the village of Gavieira. Maps and brochures with trail descriptions are available in Lamas de Mouro, but you can also download the brochures for free from the website www.cm-melgaco.pt.

Further south, almost halfway between Lamas de Mouro and Soajo, is one of the park's most stunning mountain villages, and the *serra's* namesake. Set on both sides of a deep ravine, and backed by a domed mountain and gushing waterfall, **Peneda** is a stunner. The village's only hotel, a former pilgrims' lodge, is set next to the historic **Igreja Senhora da Peneda**. This historic church is the centre of the **Festas de Nossa Senhora da Peneda**, which takes place during the first week of September when villagers converge on the plaza for candlelit

ESPIGUEIROS

They look hauntingly like mausoleums, but *espigueiros* are in fact the stuff of life. New World corn was a great innovation in these low-yielding lands when it was introduced in the 18th century. But there was a catch – it ripened late, when autumn rains threatened harvests with rot. *Espigueiros* – granite caskets on stilts with slotted sides – were created to dry and store the valuable kernels. Usually built in clusters, covered with moss and topped with little crosses, they look like the village graveyard. Neither the washing lines lashed to them nor the squat, long-horned cattle grazing at their feet can entirely dispel their eerie charm.

processions and long nights of music, dance and prayer.

It's possible to **climb** the face of Peneda's gorgeous domed peak, but you'll need to bring your own climbing gear. Otherwise, a short but steep **1km trail** begins from behind the church and winds past, up and over the dome to an artificial but still scenic **lake** high in the hills where wild horses graze the savannah. If you stay on the trail past the lake you can make an 8km loop that leads back to the main highway just uphill from Peneda.

Sleeping

Parque Campismo Lamas de Mouro CAMPGROUND €
(☎251 466 041; www.camping-lamas.com; Lamas de Mouro; per adult/tent/car €4.20/3.70/3, bungalow for 2 people €65; ⏲Jul-Sep) This tremendous private campground near boulder fields and flowering meadows has shady creekside pitch sites plus four cosy pine-clad bungalows with kitchenettes. It rents out mountain bikes and offers treetop adventures, canyoning and hikes with shepherds. There are a couple of restaurants not too far away in the Lamas de Mouro village northwest of the park gate.

Hotel Castrum Villae HOTEL €€
(☎251 460 010; www.hotelcastrumvillae.pt; Castro Laboreiro; s/d €53/63; P 📶) A fairly modern, comfy hotel in Castro Laboreiro, a short hoof to the village's *castro* (castle). The tiled rooms are bright and have accent wallpaper but are just a cut above basic. However, the hotel also has a restaurant and rents bikes.

Peneda Hotel HOTEL €€
(☎251 460 040; www.penedahotel.pt; Lugar da Peneda; s/d €70/75; P 📶) Once a nest for Igreja Senhora da Peneda's pilgrims, this mountain lodge features a waterfall backdrop, a gushing creek beneath and ultracosy rooms with blond-wood floors, French windows and views of quaint Peneda village across the ravine. There's also a decent restaurant.

Getting There & Around

This is self-driving country. The five park offices provide general park information and can supply a map, but you'll get more specific hiking advice at the brilliant Lamas de Mouro gate.

Serra do Soajo

Sturdy Soajo (soo-*ahzh*-oo), high above the upper Rio Lima, is best known for its photogenic *espigueiros* (stone granaries). It has splendid views over the surrounding countryside, with scenic walks providing a fine opportunity to take in the beauty of this protected region. Although it lacks the majesty of the Serra da Peneda high country, it's accessible by public transport and, thanks to village enterprise and the Turismo de Aldeia, you can stay in one of Soajo's restored stone houses and glimpse a vanishing way of life.

Sights

Soajo's small main square, Largo do Eiró – with a *pelourinho* (stone pillory) topped by what can only be described as an ancient smiley face – is down a lane in the opposite direction from the bus stop.

Activities

Soajo is filled with the sound of rushing water, a resource that has been painstakingly managed over the centuries. A steep walk on the eastern slopes shows just how important these streams once were.

Located on the N304, about 250m north of the bus stop, is the signed trailhead for the **Trilho do Ramil**. Initially paved with immense stones and grooved by centuries of ox-cart traffic, it ascends though a landscape shaped by agriculture, taking in granite cottages, *espigueiros* and superb views. Further up are three derelict **watermills** for grinding corn, stone channels that once funnelled the stream from one mill to the next, and the reservoir that fed them. Once you reach the old guardhouse at 500m, the trail parallels Laceiras Creek and runs through oak and pine groves to **Branda Ramil** (a *branda* was a settlement of summer houses for villagers, who drove their livestock to high pastures and lived with them all summer).

Another walk, located along the **Caminho do Pão** and **Caminho da Fé**, takes you downhill from Soajo village to the **Ponte da Ladeira**, a simple medieval bridge. Hike another 500m upstream and you'll find perfect swimming holes at **Poço do Luzio**, an ideal antidote for Soajo's soaring summer mercury. Ask for a map at the information gate.

Sleeping

About a dozen houses (sleeping two to eight) are available for tourist accommodation under the Turismo de Aldeia scheme. Each has a fireplace or stove (with firewood in winter) and a kitchen that is stocked with breakfast food, including fresh bread on the doorstep each morning. Stays of more than one night are preferred on the weekends. Book through ADERE Peneda-Gerês (p459) in Ponte da Barca or directly through www.casasdesoajo.com.

Casa do Adro INN €
(☎258 576 327; Largo do Eiró; r from €50; P ❄ @) This manor house (rather than a cottage), located off Largo do Eiró by the parish church, dates back to the 18th century. Rooms are huge, furnished with antiques and blessed with sweet vineyard and village vistas. There is a minimum two-night stay in August.

Casa Do Mezio Aromatic & Nature Hotel HOTEL €€
(☎258 322 066; www.casadomezionaturehotel.pt; Vilar do Suente; P ❄ 📶 🏊) The best thing about this upscale countryside hotel 4km west of Soajo is the stunning mountain view from the contemporary light-flooded rooms. It's a good spot from which to explore the park, with all the facilities you may wish for – restaurant, pool, spa etc.

Eating

Casa do Videira PORTUGUESE €
(☎258 576 205; Eiró; mains €8.50-10; ⏲lunch Thu-Mon Jul-Sep, Fri-Mon Oct-Jun) Locals rave about Videira's authentic regional smoked meats and sausage and the homemade mainstays. The shady, arched patio of this family-run tavern is outfitted with sturdy, polished wooden tables. Most of the portions easily feed two, so order less. Try the delicious *cachena* beef and the *feijão terrestre* bean stew. Videira is situated by the bus stop.

Saber ao Borralho PORTUGUESE €€
(☎258 577 296; www.saberaoborralho.com; plates for 2 €18-20; ⏲lunch & dinner Wed-Sun) This handsomely set place features excellent local dishes like the Minho *barrosã* steak as well as three codfish dishes and a tempting dessert counter. Village house rentals are available here (€50 per night).

Espigueiro de Soajo PORTUGUESE €€
(☎258 576 136; Avenida 25 de Abril 1425; mains €8-13; ⏲lunch & dinner Tue-Sat, lunch Sun) This modern place serving terrific Minho meat has outdoor seating on a vine-covered terrace. Management is English-speaking (local by way of Boston) and very friendly. It's about 200m north of Soajo's centre on the N304.

Information

There's an ATM below the parish council office, off the far side of the square – it's the only one in the entire park.

Getting There & Around

Soajo is 21km northeast of Ponte da Barca on the N203 and N530, or the same distance from Arcos de Valdevez via the scenic N202 and N304. Buses stop by Casa do Videira at the intersection of these two roads. A few hundred metres down the N530 towards Lindoso are Soajo's trademark *espigueiros*.

On weekdays there are one to two Salvador buses from Arcos de Valdevez (€2.75, 50 minutes) via Ponte da Barca (€2.20, 35 minutes). A taxi from Arcos or Ponte da Barca costs €20 to €25.

Serra do Gerês

Big nature rises in steep wooded pinnacles, gushes with cold streams, and pools into crystalline swimming holes in the Gerês end of the park. This is the busiest section, which in summer months sees droves of tourists, and car traffic can jam up the roads. Its beating heart is the tourist resort town of Vila do Gerês, commonly referred to simply as Gerês. It is the park's busiest, most developed and unseemly settlement.

VILA DO GERÊS

Sandwiched tightly into the Rio Gerês valley, this spa town has a rather charming fin de siècle core that is surrounded by a ring of less appealing, modern *pensões* (guest houses).

The town is built on an elongated, one-way loop, with the *balneário* (spa centre) in the pink buildings on the lower road. The original hot spring and some baths are in the staid colonnade at the northern end (where the road takes a sharp U-turn).

Activities

There are several hiking trails within a short drive.

Cascata do Arado HIKING

This scenic and somewhat challenging 12km trail penetrates a gorgeous highland boulder field and thick fern gullies to a waterfall. It begins in Pedra Bela, 200m north of the park office.

Trilho da Preguiça HIKING

This park-maintained loop trail starts on the N308 about 3km above Gerês. For 5km it rolls through the valley's oak forests. A leaflet about the walk is available from the park office (€0.60). You can also carry on – or hitch – to the Portela de Leonte, 6km north of Gerês.

Roman Road Trails HIKING

There are several trails that link to an old Roman road that once stretched 320km between Braga and Astorga (in Spain), and now has World Heritage status. Most are marked only as Trilho da Geira.

The trail at Portela de Homem is an out-and-back 6km round-trip in the steep, wooded Mata de Albergaria range. Milestones – inscribed with the name of the emperor during whose rule they were erected – remain at miles XXIX, XXX and XXXI. Another Trilho de Geira, in the Terras de Bouro region, leaves from São Sebastião, roughly 6km from Campo do Gerês.

Águas do Gerês THERMAL BATHS

(www.aguasdogeres.pt; €3; 8am-noon & 2.30-6pm May-Oct) After a long hike, finish the day by soaking away your aches and pains in the town's thermal springs. In addition to the sauna, steam bath and pool (available with basic admission), you can indulge with a full range of treatments, including massages and facials.

Sleeping

Gerês has a good selection of hotels and plenty of *pensões,* though in summer you may find some are block-booked for spa patients and other visitors. Outside July and August (when it's packed), prices plummet.Most accommodation remains shuttered from November to April (as does the spa).

Adelaide Hotel HOTEL €

(253 390 020; www.adelaidehotel.pt; Rua de Arnaçó 45; s/d €45/59;) This big, modern, lemon-yellow hotel wins for value. The rooms are spacious, with parquet floors and new beds. Make sure you get a room with a balcony and views. It is uphill from the southern end of the town loop, and has a swimming pool on the other side of town and a shuttle to take you there.

Parque de Campismo de Vidoeiro CAMPGROUND €

(253 391 289; www.adere-pg.pt; per adult/tent/car €4/3.60/3.75; mid-May–mid-Oct) This cool and shady park-run facility is on a hillside next to the river, about 1km north of Vila do Gerês. Reception is open from 8am until noon and 3pm to 7pm. Avoid it in August, when screaming school children descend in droves.

Hotel Águas do Gerês HOTEL €€

(253 390 190; www.aguasdogeres.pt; Avenida Manuel F Costa 136; s €55, d €69-75;) In a grand fin de siècle building, this slightly upmarket place has decent, spacious, carpeted rooms with high ceilings and modern decor, although they don't live up to the exterior. The hotel also runs the hot springs and offers special packages.

Hotel Universal HOTEL €€

(253 615 896; www.hoteisgeres.com; Avenida Manuel F Costa 115; s/d €48/63;) Yes, it's kitschy, but it's still got class. The mosaic stone atrium is leafy and filled with light; rooms are large and sport headboard radios from a bygone era.

Hotel Baltazar HOTEL €€

(253 391 131; www.baltazarhotel.com; Rua Lagrifa Mendes 6; s/d €60/85;) In a fine old gran-

WORTH A TRIP

BEAUTY BEYOND: BARROSO

This small northeast region of upper Trás-os-Montes, shared by the Montalegre and Boticas municipalities, packs a punch with its pretty villages where time seems to have stood still for centuries and endangered Iberian wolves roam the thick oak forests. It's known to have some of the best *fumeiro* (smoked meats) in the entire region, mainly due to the cold and dry climate and the food the villagers give the pigs, such as chestnuts, pumpkin and cabbage. Particularly good are the *alheira, chouriço de abóbora* and *sangueira* sausages. Also look out for *feijoada à transmontana* or *leitão à transmontana,* both traditional dishes involving pork.

Of the villages in the region, **Pitões das Júnias** is the most scenic, set on a plateau surrounded by endless mountain vistas. It has an ancient monastery nearby, Santa Maria das Júnias, and a pretty waterfall, both an easy hike away. Several village houses have rooms to rent, including the best-known restaurant, **Casa do Preto** (p462). Don't miss **Taberna Terra Celta** (p463) on the main village square and make sure you grab some rye bread at the village bakery and some jars of heather honey, available for sale in restaurants. Another great lodging option in Barroso is **Casa dos Braganças** (p462) in the village of **Tourém**.

ite building, this friendly, family-run hotel just up from the hot springs has spacious rooms, many of which look onto a pleasant wooded park. The downstairs restaurant is excellent.

Eating

Lurdes Capela PORTUGUESE €
(Rua Dr Manuel Gomes de Almeida 77; mains €6-13; 11.30am-10pm) Family owned and operated, and almost always packed. Expect top-end service and even better food. We're talking massive fresh-fish platters with buttered potatoes and vegetables, fluffy, savoury omelettes and all the beef and cod dishes, too.

Adega Regional PORTUGUESE €€
(253 390 220; Avenida Manuel F Costa 115; mains €10-18; noon-2.30pm & 7-9.30pm Tue-Sun) Set behind Hotel Universal, and just above a roaring stream, this historic stone *adega* serves tapas and wine. Saturday-night karaoke kicks off at 10pm.

Information

Park Office (253 390 110; www.adere-pg.pt; Centro de Educação Ambiental do Vidoeiro; 9am-noon & 2-5.30pm Mon-Fri) About 1km north of the village on the track leading to the campground. There are several tour operators nearby, too, that offer water sports, bike rental, horseback riding, canoeing and canyoning.

Turismo (253 391 133; www.portoenorte.pt; Avenida 20 de Junho 45A; 9.30am-12.30pm & 2-6pm summer, 9am-12.30pm & 2-5.30pm winter) On the road into town, right where the road forks.

Getting There & Away

Buses stop at a traffic circle just south of the loop.

Empresa Hoteleira do Gerês (253 390 220; www.ehgeres.com) runs between six and 10 buses daily from Braga to Gerês (€4.25, 1½ hours), passing through Rio Caldo (€1.25, 1¼ hours). Buy tickets at Hotel Universal.

RIO CALDO

Just below Vila do Gerês, this tiny town sits on the back of the stunning *albufeira* de Caniçada, making it the park's centre for water sports.

English-run Água Montanha Lazer (p460) rents kayaks, pedal boats and small motorboats, and organises wakeboarding and kayaking trips.

Sleeping

Pousada do Gerês-Caniçada/ São Bento POUSADA €€€
(210 407 650; www.pousadas.pt; Caniçada; s/d €180/190;) This lovely place has a spectacular setting. High above the Albufeira, it offers a splendid retreat at eagle's-nest heights. The rooms have wood-beamed ceilings and comfy furnishings; some have verandahs with magnificent views. There's a pool, gardens, tennis court, and excellent

restaurant serving local delicacies (trout, roasted goat). To get here head south 3km from Rio Caldo along the N304, following signs to Caniçada.

CAMPO DO GERÊS

Campo do Gerês (called São João do Campo on some maps, and just Campo by most) is a humble huddle of stone houses high in the mountains in the middle of a wide, grassy basin. It sees more hikers than shepherds once the weather turns warm, thanks to easy access to some spectacular trails.

Coming from Vila do Gerês, you first arrive at a little traffic circle. The tiny village centre is another 1.5km straight on.

Sights

The **Museu Etnográfico** (adult/student €2/1; 9am-5.30pm Tue-Sun) is a moving memorial for the village of **Vilarinho das Furnas** that was submerged by the building of a dam in 1972.

In late summer and autumn when the reservoir level falls, the empty village walls rise like spectres from the water. You can visit the spooky remains about 2.5km beyond the dam, which is a comfortable three-hour return hike.

Activities

There are several well-marked hiking trails that are around Campo do Gerês; hikes last from three to six hours. You can pick up maps and trail information (€0.90 to €1.50) at the information desk located at the Museu Etnográfico.

Trilho da Cidade da Calcedónia HIKING
A narrow, sealed road snakes over the ridge from Vila do Gerês to Campo do Gerês, offering short but spectacular high-elevation walks from just about anywhere along its upper reaches. One of these is the Cidade da Calcedónia trail, a moderate, signposted, 7km (four-hour) loop that climbs up to a 912m viewpoint called the **Cabeço Calcedónia**, with views that will knock your socks off.

Trilho dos Currais HIKING
The 'Corrals Trail' is a moderate 10km loop that takes about four hours to complete. Along the way you'll wind beneath oak and pine and glimpse boulder fields, sublime valley views and – if you leave early enough and get lucky – resident deer, wolf or wild boar. The trailhead is located and signposted in Vidoeiro.

Sleeping

Parque Campismo de Cerdeira CAMPGROUND €
(253 351 005; www.parquecerdeira.com; Rua de Cerdeira 400; per person/tent/car €6.50/23/5, bungalow €70-110; P) Located in Campo do Gêres, this place has oak-shaded sites, a laundry, a pool, a mini-market and a particularly good restaurant . The ecofriendly bungalows open onto unrivalled mountain views.

Albergaria Stop GUESTHOUSE €
(253 350 040; www.albergariastop.com; Rua de São João 915; s €45, d €48-70; P) More mountain motel than lodge, this guest house has spotless rooms, wooden floors and mountain views. Most rooms have balconies, plus there is a pool and tennis courts. It's located just before the village. There is a two-night minimum stay in high season.

Eating

★ **O Abocanhado** PORTUGUESE €€
(253 352 944; www.abocanhado.com; Lugar de Brufe, Brufe; mains €15-18; 12.30-3.30pm & 7.30-9.30pm) This beautifully situated restaurant is a temple to the finest ingredients that the surrounding countryside has to offer, including *javali* (wild boar), *veado* (venison) and *coelho* (rabbit), as well as beef and goat raised in the adjacent fields. Finish with *requeijão* – a soft goat's cheese so fresh it's actually sweet.

The only drawback: in low season the restaurant keeps irregular hours, so call ahead before making the trip. It's located 9km east of Campo do Gerês (across the dam), in the village of Brufe, on a panoramic spot above the Rio Homem.

Information

Campo do Gerês (253 351 888; museu@cm-terrasdebouro.pt; Campo do Gerês; 9-12.30pm & 1.30-5.30pm Tue-Sun) The Campo do Gerês gate represents the Terras de Bouro municipality.

Getting There & Away

From Braga, Transdev has four daily bus services (€4.10, 1½ hours, fewer at weekends) stopping at the museum crossroad and the village centre.

Eastern Peneda-Gerês

Cabril, on the eastern limb of the national park, and Montalegre, just outside the park, are actually in Trás-os-Montes, but you're unlikely to visit either unless you're coming in or out of the park.

CABRIL

Although it hardly looks the part, peaceful Cabril – set with its outlying hamlets in a wide, fertile bowl backed by soaring peaks – is the administrative centre of Portugal's biggest *freguesia* (parish), stretching up to the Spanish border. Your best reference point is **Largo do Cruzeiro**, with its old *pelourinho*. To one side is the squat but stately **Igreja de São Lourenço**, said to have been moved five centuries ago, brick by brick, by villagers of nearby São Lourenço.

Activities

Javsport ADVENTURE
(☎252 850 621; www.javsport.pt) In Fafião you'll find the adventure outfitter Javsport, which operates popular canyoning expeditions down the Rio Arado and Rio Conho for €50 per person.

Eating

Restaurante Ponte Nova PORTUGUESE €
(Rua 25 de Abril 30; mains €7-13; ⏱9am-10pm) At a picturesque spot next to the bridge, this place does good river trout and, if you order ahead, *cabrito* or *javali assada* (roast wild boar). There's an outdoor deck right over the water that makes a great destination for an afternoon pick-me-up.

MONTALEGRE

Montalegre is the park's eastern gateway, and if ever there was a hamlet with a castle on the hill this is it. The small but particularly striking castle, part of Dom Dinis' 14th-century ring of frontier outposts, looms over the town and the surrounding fertile plains fed by so many rivers. The future Duke of Wellington made use of it in his drive to rid Portugal of Napoleon's troops in 1809. Today visitors can only wander around its perimeter, taking in the lovely views. Just below the castle lies the old town centre.

Sights

Barroso Eco Museu MUSEUM
(www.ecomuseu.org; Terreiro do Açougue 11; ⏱10am-12.30pm & 2-6pm) FREE Next to Montalegre's castle, this museum hosts exhibits that showcase regional history, rural traditions and folklore. There are also exhibits highlighting local flora and fauna, and a gallery rotating contemporary canvases from local artists.

Festivals & Events

The town comes alive each Friday the 13th for the **Noite das Bruxas**, a night-long celebration that attracts thousands for a raucous feast involving street performances and much drinking of *queimada*, a slow-brewed drink with strong *bagaço* (Portuguese firewater) and honey, said to wash away the evil spirits.

Sleeping

Casa de Campo O Castelo GUESTHOUSE €
(☎276 511 237; Terreiro do Açougue 1; s/d €35/45; P 📶) A simple family-run guest house right by Montalegre's castle, with rooms featuring hardwood floors and stone walls; some have terraces with views of the castle. Rates include breakfast.

Casa Zé Maria GUESTHOUSE €
(☎276 512 457; www.casazemaria.com; Rua Dr Victor Branco 21; d from €40; P 📶) This converted 19th-century granite manor features old-fashioned charm in its wooden-floored rooms with lacy bedspreads and dark-wood furnishings. It's located one block east and one block south of the *turismo*.

Eating

Pastelaria São Paulo BAKERY €
(Rua Direita 25; pastries €0.75-2; ⏱8am-8pm) If you're just in town long enough for a cup of something strong and a nibble of something sweet, then search out this bakery.

Tasca do Açougue PORTUGUESE €
(Terreiro do Açougue 7; mains €7-10, snacks €3-7; ⏱noon-10pm) In a charming stone cottage just below the castle, Tasca do Açougue serves tasty Iberian tapas dishes, including grilled octopus and smoked meats, as well as heartier plates. It's a lively place for a drink in the evening.

Information

Montalegre (☎ 276 518 320; Terreiro do Açougue; ⏲ 9am-12.30pm & 2-5.30pm Mon-Fri) The gateway for the eastern part of the park is at Montalegre.

Park Information Office (☎ 276 518 320; www.adere-pg.pt; Praça do Municipal; ⏲ 9am-12.30pm & 2-5.30pm Mon-Fri) Next door to the Barroso Eco Museu.

Turismo (☎ 276 510 203; www.cm-montalegre.pt; Terreiro do Açougue 11; ⏲ 10am-12.30pm & 2-6pm) Located in the Barroso Eco Museu complex.

Getting There & Away

Transdev (☎ 253 209 400; www.transdev.pt) runs three buses per day from Braga to Montalegre (€6.40, 2½ hours) from Monday to Thursday, and four on Friday; they run less frequently on weekends.

From the bus station it's 500m uphill on Rua General Humberto Delgado to a five-way roundabout, beside which you'll find the town hall and *turismo*. Keep heading uphill to reach the crown.

Understand Portugal

Portugal Today

The Portuguese have been through some tough times. Cuts to pensions and social programs, privatisation of government industries – all were part of the austerity package imposed by a conservative government and the EU powers holding the purse strings. Change, however, is on the horizon, as a new left-wing government takes the reins. Economic challenges aside, one of Portugal's biggest slow-brewing crises is its shrinking population. On a sunnier note, Portugal has become an EU leader in the realm of renewable energy.

Best on Film

A Lisbon Story (1994) Wim Wenders' love letter to Lisbon.

Letters from Fontainhas (1997–2006) Pedro Costa's art-house trilogy set in Lisbon.

Capitães de Abril (Captains of April; 2000) Overview of the 1974 Revolution of the Carnations.

Best in Print

O Manual dos Inquisidores (The Inquisitor's Manual; António Lobo Antunes, 1996) Story about life under the Salazar dictatorship.

Memorial do Convento (Baltasar and Blimunda; José Saramago, 1982) Darkly comic 18th-century love story.

Livro do Desassossego (The Book of Disquiet; Fernando Pessoa, 1982) Literary masterpiece by Portugal's greatest poet.

Best Albums

Moura (2015) Latest album by fado superstar Ana Moura.

Art of Amália (1998) Compilation by one of fado's greats, Amália Rodrigues.

Best of Rui Veloso (2000) Portugal's legendary rock-balladeer.

A New Way Forward

After four years of austerity measures under Prime Minister Pedro Passos Coelho, Portugal was ready to turn the page. And it did so in rather dramatic fashion. Following an inconclusive election in 2015, Coelho's conservative government failed to gain an overall majority in parliament. Seizing an opportunity, Socialist Party leader António Costa formed an anti-austerity coalition with two other left-wing parties and voted down the new centre-right government in an extraordinary parliamentary move. Kicked to the kerb after just 11 days in power, the centre-right administration would go down as the shortest in Portugal's history.

The rise of António Costa, a former mayor of Lisbon and the son of a communist poet from Goa, suggests a new era in Portuguese politics. In fact, the mere existence of a left-wing coalition is something unusual – unseen since the arrival of democracy at the end of the military dictatorship in the 1970s. The challenges, however, are substantial: unemployment stands at 12% (though markedly down from an all-time high of 17.5% in early 2013). And although the economy showed signs of life (growing 0.9% in 2014, then 1.5% in 2015), it appeared to have stalled in early 2016. And pressure was mounting from the EU for Portugal to rein in its budget deficit.

Most Portuguese, however, have clearly tired of receiving ultimatums from Brussels. In exchange for an €78-billion loan package from 'the Troika' – the International Monetary Fund, the European Central Bank and the European Commission – Portugal went through a draconian period of belt tightening. The conservative government raised taxes, cut wages and pensions, and clipped spending on social welfare. Critics of the measures say that the cuts only drove more people into poverty, caused further erosion of the middle class and sent job-seeking Portuguese out of the country in droves. Costa's objective now is clear: achieve economic growth and reduce the deficit, while reversing painful austerity measures – a daunting challenge, particularly given the fragile left-wing alliance holding his administration together.

Population Crisis

It's been called a 'perfect demographic storm' that could have catastrophic effects on society and the economy. The population in Portugal has been shrinking – falling year on year since 2010 – and unless things change, demographers estimate that the population could fall to just six million by 2060. The fertility rate has sunk to an all-time low, averaging 1.2 children per woman in 2013, compared to three per woman back in 1970. According to European statistics office Eurostat, Portugal has the lowest fertility rate in the EU.

Meanwhile, the population is greying; lurking in the background is the danger that communities will no longer be self-sustaining. The effect is visible to anyone who travels around the small villages in the interior, where elderly residents are the norm and local children are a rare sight. Toy shops and schools are closing while more businesses are being transformed into nursing homes.

The former Prime Minister Pedro Passos Coelho described the situation as one of Portugal's biggest problems. Some municipalities have begun offering incentives of up to €1000 for babies born to local mothers, and some business owners are offering financial incentives to their workers to have offspring.

Going Green

For four days in May 2016, Portugal did something astonishing. Over the course of 107 hours, the country was powered solely by renewable energy: biofuels, solar panels, wind turbines and hydropower created enough electricity to run the entire country. Portugal has invested heavily in renewable energy in recent years, and it now meets more than 50% of its needs with sustainable power, making it one of the leaders in Europe (behind only Austria, Sweden, Iceland and Norway). The Alentejo is home to one of the world's largest solar farms, with 376,000 panels spread across a 130-hectare site with a peak capacity of 46 megawatts. The nation has come a long way since 2007, when a coal-powered plant in Sines was named by the WWF as one of the largest CO_2 producers in all of Europe.

POPULATION: **10.5 MILLION**

AREA: **88,323 SQ KM**

UNEMPLOYMENT: **12%**

HIGHEST POINT: **TORRE (1993M)**

PER CAPITA GDP: **€25,900**

if Portugal were 100 people

85 would be Roman Catholic
9 would be other
4 would be no religion
2 would be other Christian

occupation of workforce

(% of population)

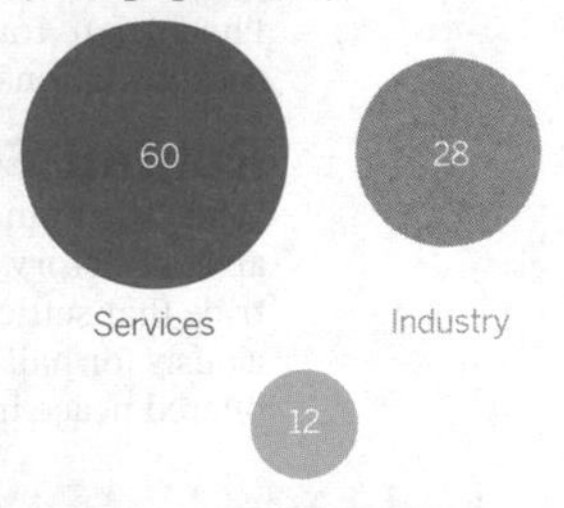

population per sq km

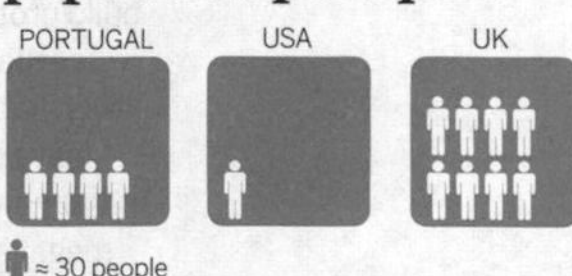

History

The small nation on the edge of Europe has seen a long line of conquerors and foreign rulers over the last 3000 years. Celts, Romans, Visigoths, Moors and Christian crusaders all made contributions to Portugal's early identity. In the 15th century, sea captains and explorers helped transform Portugal into a global empire. The centuries that followed saw devastation (the 1755 Lisbon earthquake) and great changes (industrialisation, dictatorship, decolonisation) before Portugal became a stable democracy in the 1980s.

Prehistoric Sites

- *Vila Nova de Foz Côa (Douro)*
- *Citânia de Briteiros (Minho)*
- *Cromeleque dos Almendres (Alentejo)*
- *Anta Grande do Zambujeiro (Alentejo)*
- *Cromeleque do Xerez (Alentejo)*

Early Peoples

One of Europe's earliest places of settlement, the Iberian Peninsula was first inhabited many millennia ago, when hominids wandered across the landscape some time before 200,000 BC. During the Palaeolithic period, early Portuguese ancestors left traces of their time on earth in stone carvings in the open air near Vila Nova de Foz Côa in the Alto Douro. These date back some 30,000 years and were only discovered by accident, during a proposed dam-building project in 1992. Other signs of early human artistry lie hidden in the Alent-ejo, in the Gruta do Escoural, where cave drawings of animals and humans date back to around 15,000 BC.

Homo sapiens weren't the only bipeds on the scene. Neanderthals coexisted alongside modern humans in places like Portugal for as long as 10,000 years. Some of the last traces of their existence were found in Iberia.

Neanderthals were only the first of a long line of inhabitants to appear (and later disappear) from the Iberian stage. In the 1st millennium BC Celtic people started trickling into the peninsula, settling northern and western Portugal around 700 BC. Dozens of *citânias* (fortified villages) popped up, such as the formidable Citânia de Briteiros. Further south, Phoenician traders, followed by Greeks and Carthaginians, founded coastal stations and mined metals inland.

Roman Settlement

When the Romans swept into southern Portugal in 197 BC, they expected an easy victory. But they hadn't reckoned on the Lusitani, a Celtic warrior tribe that settled between the Rio Tejo and Rio Douro and resisted ferociously for half a century. Unable to subjugate the Lusitani, the Romans offered peace instead and began negotiations with Viriato, the Lusitani-

TIMELINE

5000 BC

Little-understood Neolithic peoples build protected hilltop settlements in the lower Tejo valley. They leave behind stone monuments, including megaliths scattered around Évora in present-day Alentejo.

700 BC

Celtic peoples, migrating across the Pyrenees with their families and flocks, sweep through the Iberian Peninsula. They settle in fortified villages, known as *castros,* and intermarry with local tribes.

197 BC

After defeating Carthage in the Second Punic War, the Romans invade Iberia, expanding their empire west. They face fierce resistance from local tribes, including the Lusitani, but eventually conquer them.

an leader. Unfortunately for Viriato and his underlings, the peace offer was a ruse, and Roman agents, posing as intermediaries, poisoned him. Resistance collapsed following Viriato's death in 139 BC.

For a vivid glimpse into Roman Portugal, you won't see a better site than Conímbriga, or the remains of the so-called Temple of Diana, in Évora.

By the 5th century, when the Roman Empire had all but collapsed, Portugal's inhabitants had been under Roman rule for 600 years. So what did the Romans ever do for them? Most usefully, they built roads and bridges. But they also brought wheat, barley, olives and vines; large farming estates called *latifúndios*; a legal system; and, above all, a Latin-derived language. In fact, no other invader proved so useful.

Roman Sites

Conímbriga (Beiras)

Milreu (Algarve)

Termas Romanas (Évora)

Núcleo Arqueológico (Lisbon)

Cidade de Ammaia (Alentejo)

Moors & Christians

The gap left by the Romans was filled by barbarian invaders from beyond the Pyrenees: Vandals, Alans, Visigoths and Suevi, with Arian Christian Visigoths gaining the upper hand in 469.

Internal Visigothic disputes paved the way for Portugal's next great wave of invaders, the Moors – North African Muslims invited in 711 to help a Visigoth faction. They quickly occupied parts of Portugal's southern coast.

Southerners enjoyed peace and productivity under the Moors, who established a capital at Shelb (Silves). The new rulers were tolerant of Jews and Christians. Christian smallholding farmers, called Mozarabs, could keep their land and were encouraged to try new methods and crops, especially citrus and rice. Arabic words filtered into the Portuguese language, such as *alface* (lettuce), *arroz* (rice) and place names (including Fátima, Silves and Algarve), and locals became addicted to Moorish sweets.

THE MYSTERY OF THE NEANDERTHALS

Scientists have never come to an agreement about the fate of the Neanderthals – stout and robust beings who used stone tools and fire, buried their dead and had brains larger than those of modern humans. The most common theory is that *Homo sapiens* drove Neanderthals to extinction (perhaps in some sort of genocidal warfare). A less-accepted theory is that Neanderthals and humans bred together and produced a hybrid species. This idea gained credence when Portuguese archaeologists found a strange skeleton – the first complete Palaeolithic skeleton ever unearthed in Iberia – just north of Lisbon in 1999. The team, led by João Zilhão, director of the Portuguese Institute of Archaeology, discovered the 25,000-year-old remains of a young boy with traits of both early humans (pronounced chin and teeth) and of Neanderthals (broad limbs). The boy had been interred in what was clearly a ritual burial. Some believe this kind of relationship (lovemaking rather than war making) happened over the span of thousands of years and that some Neanderthal elements entered the modern human gene pool.

AD 100

Romans collect taxes to build roads, bridges and other public works. They cultivate vineyards, teach the natives to preserve fish by salting and drying, and grant local communities much autonomy.

400

Rome crumbles as German tribes run riot in southern Europe. The Suevi, peasant farmers from the Elbe, settle in present-day Porto. Christian Visigoths follow suit, conquering the land in 469.

711

Visigoth King Witiza is assassinated. When his eldest son, Agila, is blocked from the throne he seeks help from North African Berbers. The Muslim force arrives, establishes peace and puts down roots.

800

The Umayyad dynasty rules the Iberian Peninsula. The region flourishes under the tolerant caliphate. The Arabs introduce irrigation, bring new crops (including oranges and rice) and establish schools.

Islamic Sites

Alcáçova (Mértola)

Núcleo Islâmico (Tavira)

Castelo de São Jorge (Lisbon)

Mouraria (Moura)

Museu Municipal de Arqueologia (Silves)

Meanwhile, in the north, Christian forces were gaining strength and reached as far as Porto in 868. But it was in the 11th century that the Reconquista (the Christian reconquest) heated up. In 1064 Coimbra was taken and, in 1085, Alfonso VI thrashed the Moors in their Spanish heartland of Toledo; he is said to have secured Seville by winning a game of chess with its emir. But in the following year, Alfonso's troops were driven out by ruthless Moroccan Almoravids who answered the emir's distress call.

Alfonso called for help and European crusaders came running – rallying against the 'infidels'. With the help of Henri of Burgundy, among others, Alfonso made decisive moves towards victory. The struggle continued in successive generations, and by 1139 Afonso Henriques (grandson of Alfonso VI) won such a dramatic victory against the Moors at Ourique (Alentejo) that he named himself Dom – King of Portugal – a title confirmed in 1179 by the Pope (after extra tribute was paid, naturally). Afonso also retook Santarém and Lisbon from the Moors.

By the time he died in 1185, the Portuguese frontier was secure to the Rio Tejo, though it would take another century before the south was torn from the Moors.

Burgundian Era

During the Reconquista, people faced more than just war and turmoil: in the wake of Christian victories came new rulers and settlers.

The church and its wealthy clergy were the greediest landowners, followed by aristocratic fat cats. Though theoretically free, most common people remained subjects of the landowning class, with few rights. The first hint of democratic rule came with the establishment of the *cortes* (parliament). This assembly of nobles and clergy first met in 1211 at Coimbra, the then capital. Six years later, the capital moved to Lisbon.

Afonso III (r 1248–79) deserves credit for standing up to the church, but it was his son, the 'Poet King' Dinis (r 1279–1325), who really shook Portugal into shape. A far-sighted, cultured man, he took control of the judicial system, started progressive afforestation programs and encouraged internal trade. He suppressed the dangerously powerful military order of the Knights Templar, refounding them as the Order of Christ. He cultivated music, the arts and education, and he founded a university in Lisbon in 1290, which was later transferred to Coimbra.

Dom Dinis' foresight was spot on when it came to defence: he built or rebuilt some 50 fortresses along the eastern frontier with Castile and signed a pact of friendship with England in 1308, the basis for a future long-lasting alliance.

It was none too soon. Within 60 years of Dinis' death, Portugal was at war with Castile. Fernando I helped provoke the clash by playing a game of alliances with both Castile and the English. He dangled promis-

The word Portugal comes from Portus Cale, a name the Romans gave to a town near present-day Porto. The word morphed into Portucale under Visigoth rule and expanded significantly in meaning.

1147

The Reconquista is under way as Christians attain decisive victories over the Moors. Portugal's first king, Afonso Henriques (crowned 1139), leads the attack, laying siege to Lisbon.

1242

The last remaining Moors are driven out in the battle of Tavira. Portugal later establishes its border with Castile (Spain), aided by Dom Dinis: 50 fortresses line the eastern frontier.

1297

The boundaries of the Portuguese kingdom – much the same as they are today – are formalised with neighbouring Castile. The kingdom of Portugal has arrived.

1348

The Plague reaches Portugal (most likely carried on ships that dock in Porto and Lisbon). As in other parts of Europe, the disease devastates, killing one in three.

es of marriage to his daughter Beatriz in front of both nations, eventually marrying her off to Juan I of Castile, thus throwing Portugal's future into Castilian hands.

On Fernando's death in 1383, his wife, Leonor Teles, ruled as regent. But she too was entangled with the Spanish, having long had a Galician lover. The merchant classes preferred unsullied Portuguese candidate João, son (albeit illegitimate) of Fernando's father. João assassinated Leonor's lover, Leonor fled to Castile and the Castilians duly invaded.

The showdown came in 1385 when João faced a mighty force of Castilians at Aljubarrota. Even with Nuno Álvares Pereira (the Holy Constable) as his military right-hand man and English archers at the ready, the odds were stacked against him. João vowed to build a monastery if he won – and he did. Nuno Álvares, the brilliant commander-in-chief of the Portuguese troops, deserves much of the credit for the victory. He lured the Spanish cavalry into a trap and, with an uphill advantage, his troops decimated the invaders. Within a few hours the Spanish were retreating in disarray and the battle was won.

The victory clinched independence and João made good his vow by commissioning Batalha's stunning Mosteiro de Santa Maria da Vitória (aka the Mosteiro da Batalha or Battle Abbey). It also sealed Portugal's alliance with England, and João wed John of Gaunt's daughter. Peace was finally concluded in 1411.

Historic Collections

Museu do Oriente (Lisbon)

Museu Nacional de Machado de Castro (Coimbra)

Casa Museu Passos Canavarro (Santarém)

Age of Discoveries

João's success had whetted his appetite and, spurred on by his sons, he soon turned his military energies abroad. Morocco was the obvious target, and in 1415 Ceuta fell easily to his forces. It was a turning point in Portuguese history, a first step into its golden age.

It was João's third son, Henry, who focused the spirit of the age – a combination of crusading zeal, love of martial glory and lust for gold –

UNFORGETTABLE RIVER

When Roman soldiers reached the Rio Lima in 137 BC, they were convinced they had reached the Lethe, the mythical river of forgetfulness that flowed through Hades and from which no one could return. Unable to persuade his troops to cross waters leading (they thought) to certain oblivion, the Roman general Decimus Junius Brutus Callaicus forded the river alone. Once on the other side he called out to his troops, shouting each of their names. Stunned that the general could remember them, they followed him and continued their campaign. Incidentally, Brutus, who led legions to conquer Iberia after Viriato's death, was later named proconsul of Lusitania.

1385

Intermarriage between Castilian and Portuguese royal families leads to complications. Juan I of Castile, claiming the throne, invades. The Portuguese, with English help, rout the invaders at Aljubarrota.

1411

Newly crowned Dom João builds an elaborate monastery to commemorate his victory at Aljubarrota. João marries John of Gaunt's daughter, ushering in an English alliance lasting centuries.

1415

Dom João's third son, Prince Henry the Navigator, joins his father in the conquest of Ceuta in North Africa. Thus begins the colonial expansion of Portugal.

1418

Shipbuilding advances lead to the development of the caravel, a fast, agile ship that changes the face of sailing. Portuguese mariners put it to brilliant use on long voyages of exploration.

into extraordinary explorations across the seas. These explorations were to transform the small kingdom into a great imperial power.

The biggest breakthrough came in 1497 during the reign of Manuel I, when Vasco da Gama reached southern India. With gold and slaves from Africa and spices from the East, Portugal was soon rolling in riches. Manuel I was so thrilled by the discoveries (and resultant cash injection) that he ordered a frenzied building spree in celebration. Top of his list was the extravagant Mosteiro dos Jerónimos in Belém, later to become his pantheon. Another brief boost to the Portuguese economy at this time came courtesy of an influx of around 150,000 Jews, who had been expelled from Spain in 1492.

Spain, however, had also jumped on the exploration bandwagon and was soon disputing Portuguese claims. Christopher Columbus' 1492 'discovery' of America for Spain led to a fresh outburst of jealous conflict. It was resolved by the Pope in the bizarre 1494 Treaty of Tordesillas, by which the world was divided between the two great powers along a line 370 leagues west of the Cape Verde islands. Portugal won the lands east of the line, including Brazil, officially claimed in 1500.

The rivalry spurred the first circumnavigation of the world. In 1519 Portuguese navigator Fernão Magalhães (Ferdinand Magellan), his allegiance transferred to Spain after a tiff with Manuel I, set off in an effort to prove that the Spice Islands (today's Moluccas) lay in Spanish 'territory'. He reached the Philippines in 1521 but was killed in a skirmish there. One of his five ships, under the Basque navigator Juan Sebastián Elcano, reached the Spice Islands and then sailed home via the Cape of Good Hope, proving the Earth was round.

As its explorers reached Timor, China and eventually Japan, Portugal cemented its power with garrison ports and trading posts. The monarchy, taking its 'royal fifth' of profits, became stinking rich – indeed the wealthiest monarchy in Europe, and the lavish Manueline architectural style symbolised the exuberance of the age.

It couldn't last, of course. By the 1570s the huge cost of expeditions and maintaining an empire was taking its toll. The final straw came in 1578. Young, idealistic Sebastião was on the throne and, determined to bring Christianity to Morocco, he rallied a force of 18,000 and set sail from Lagos. He was disastrously defeated at the Battle of Alcácer Quibir (also known as the Battle of Three Kings): Sebastião and 8000 others were killed, including much of the Portuguese nobility. Sebastião's aged successor, Cardinal Henrique, drained the royal coffers ransoming those captured.

On Henrique's death in 1580, Sebastião's uncle, Felipe II of Spain (Felipe I of Portugal), fought for and won the throne. This marked the end of centuries of independence, Portugal's golden age and its glorious moment at the centre of the world stage.

Former Portuguese Colonies & Year of Independence

Brazil, 1822

Goa, 1961

Guinea-Bissau, 1974

Angola, 1975

Cape Verde, 1975

Mozambique, 1975

São Tomé e Príncipe, 1975

East Timor, 1975

Macau, 1999

1419

Portuguese sailors discover Madeira. More discoveries follow, including those of the Azores in 1427 and the Cape Verde islands in 1460. Explorers also chart the west coast of Africa.

1443

Explorers bring the first African slaves to Portugal, marking the beginning of a long, dark era of slavery in Europe and later the New World.

1494

The race for colonial expansion is on: Spain and Portugal carve up the world, with the Treaty of Tordesillas drawing the line 370 leagues west of Cape Verde.

1497

Facing pressure from the church, Dom Manuel I expels commercially active Jews. Those staying must convert or face persecution. By 1536 the Inquisition is under way, with thousands executed.

Exploration by the Portuguese

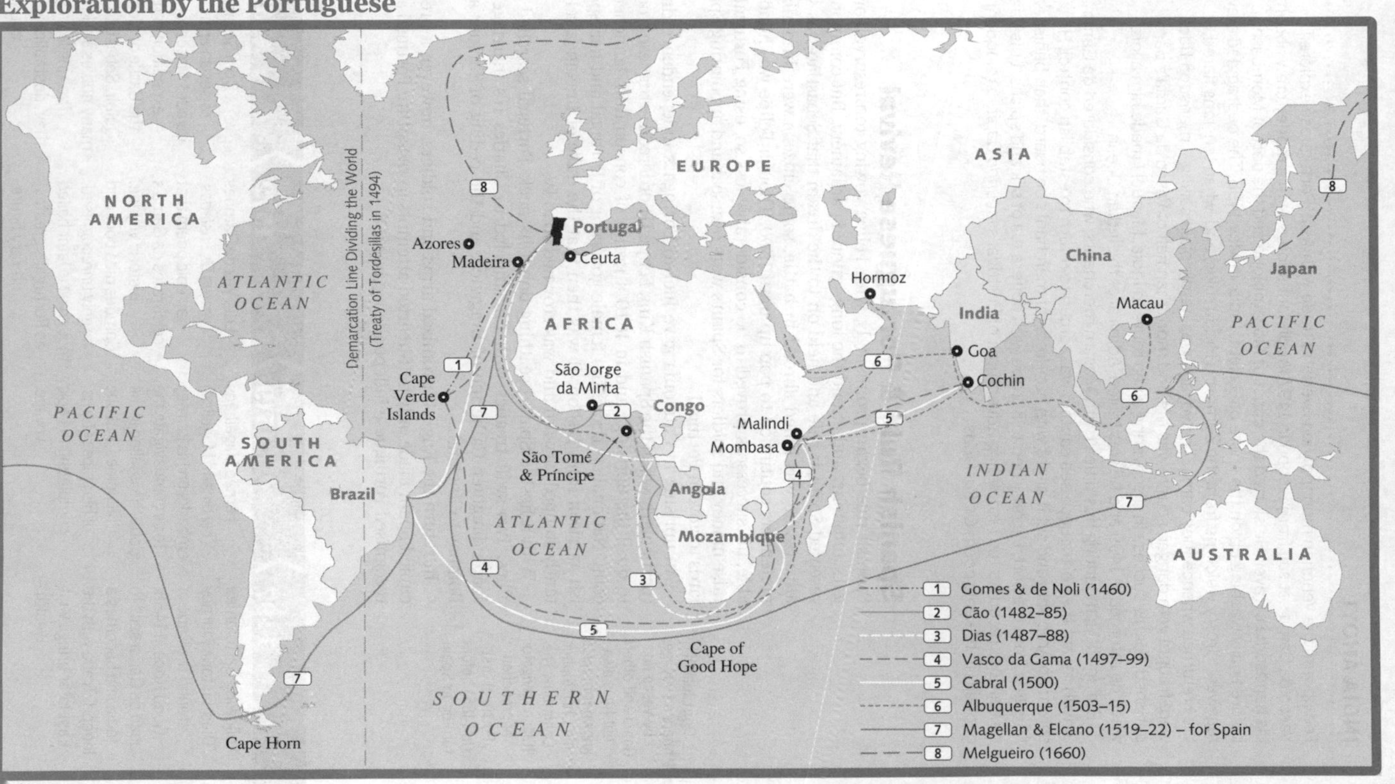

INDIA AHOY!

Fed up with the Venetian monopoly on overland trade with Asia, Portuguese explorer Vasco da Gama set sail from Lisbon in 1497 for distant shores, with a motley crew aboard his handsome caravel. He skirted the coast of Mozambique and the port of Mombasa before finally washing up on the shore of Calicut, India, in May 1498. The bedraggled crew received a frosty welcome from the Zamorin (Hindu ruler) and, when tensions flared, they returned whence they came. The voyage was hardly plain sailing – monsoon tides were fraught with danger, scurvy was rife and more than half of Vasco da Gama's party perished. For his success in discovering a sea route to India, Manuel I made him a lord when he returned in 1499 and he was hailed 'Admiral of the Indian Ocean'.

But, in 1502, mounting hostilities (with Muslim merchants, who considered da Gama a rival) meant the Portuguese sea captain was forced to return to establish control. He seized an Arab ship and set it alight with hundreds of merchants on board, then banished Muslims from the port. He returned to Europe with coffers full of silk and spices. Luís Vaz de Camões recounts the fascinating adventures of Portugal's *facundo Capitão* (eloquent captain) in the epic poem *Os Lusíadas*.

Spanish Rule & Portuguese Revival

Spanish rule began promisingly, with Felipe vowing to preserve Portugal's autonomy and attend the long-ignored parliament. But commoners resented Spanish rule and held on to the dream that Sebastião was still alive (as he was killed abroad in battle, some citizens were in denial); pretenders continued to pop up until 1600. Though Felipe was honourable, his successors proved to be considerably less so, using Portugal to raise money and soldiers for Spain's wars overseas and appointing Spaniards to govern Portugal.

An uprising in Catalonia gave fuel to Portugal's independence drive (particularly when the Spanish King Felipe III ordered Portuguese troops to quell the uprising) and in 1640 a group of conspirators launched a coup. Nationalists drove the female governor of Portugal and her Spanish garrison from Lisbon. It was then that the duke of Bragança reluctantly stepped forward and was crowned João IV.

With a hostile Spain breathing down its neck, Portugal searched for allies. Two swift treaties with England led to Charles II's marriage to João's daughter, Catherine of Bragança, and the ceding of Tangier and Bombay to England.

In return the English promised arms and soldiers: however, a preoccupied Spain made only half-hearted attempts to recapture Portugal and recognised Portuguese independence in 1668.

Dom João II financed voyages by Vasco da Gama and others, but he is also known for rejecting Christopher Columbus. The Italian navigator approached Portugal first (in 1485) before turning to Spain.

1497

Following Bartolomeu Dias' historic journey around the Cape of Good Hope in 1488, Vasco da Gama sails to India and becomes a legend. Trade with the East later brings vast wealth.

1519

Fernão Magalhães (Ferdinand Magellan) embarks on his journey to circumnavigate the globe. He is killed in the Philippines, but one of his ships returns, completing the epic voyage.

1572

Luís Vaz de Camões writes *Os Lusíadas*, an epic poem that celebrates da Gama's historic voyage. Camões dies poor and largely unrecognised, though he is later hailed as Portugal's greatest literary figure.

1578

Dom Sebastião raises an army and invades Morocco. The expedition ends at the Battle of Alcácer Quibir. Sebastião and many nobles are killed; the king leaves no heir, destabilising the country.

João IV's successors pursued largely absolutist policies (particularly under João V, an admirer of French King Louis XIV). The crown hardly bothered with parliament, and another era of profligate expenditure followed, giving birth to projects such as the wildly extravagant monastery-palace in Mafra.

Cementing power for the crown was one of Portugal's most revered (and feared) statesmen – the Marquês de Pombal, chief minister to the epicurean Dom José I (the latter more interested in opera than political affairs). Described as an enlightened despot, Pombal dragged Portugal into the modern era, crushing opposition with brutal efficiency.

Pombal set up state monopolies, curbed the power of British merchants and boosted agriculture and industry. He abolished slavery and distinctions between traditional and New Christians (Jews who had converted), and overhauled education.

When Lisbon suffered a devastating earthquake in 1755, Pombal swiftly rebuilt the city. He was by then at the height of his power, and he dispensed with his main enemies by implicating them in an attempt on the king's life.

He might have continued had it not been for the accession of the devout Dona Maria I in 1777. The anticlerical Pombal was promptly sacked, tried and charged with various offences, though he was never imprisoned. While his religious legislation was repealed, his economic, agricultural and educational policies were largely maintained, helping the country back towards prosperity.

But turmoil was once again on the horizon, as Napoleon was sweeping through Europe.

The Treaty of Windsor (1386), which established a pact of mutual assistance between Portugal and England, began what is widely considered to be the oldest surviving alliance in the world.

Dawn of a Republic

French Invasion Unleashes Royal Chaos

In 1793 Portugal found itself at war again when it joined Britain in sending naval forces against revolutionary France. Before long, Napoleon gave Portugal an ultimatum: close your ports to British shipping or be invaded.

There was no way Portugal could turn its back on Britain, upon which it depended for half of its trade and the protection of its sea routes. In 1807 Portugal's royal family fled to Brazil (where it stayed for 14 years), and Napoleon's forces marched into Lisbon, sweeping Portugal into the Peninsular War (France's invasion of Spain and Portugal, which lasted until 1814).

To the rescue came Sir Arthur Wellesley (later Duke of Wellington), Viscount Beresford and their seasoned British troops, who eventually drove the French back across the Spanish border in 1811.

Free but weakened, Portugal was administered by Beresford while the royals dallied in Brazil. In 1810 Portugal lost a profitable intermediary

It was the Portuguese who started England's obsession with tea: their explorers introduced it to Europe in the mid-17th century and tea enthusiast Catherine of Bragança did the rest.

1580

Sebastião's weak successor, the former Cardinal Henrique, dies. King Felipe II of Spain invades Portugal and becomes king. Spain will rule for 80 years, draining Portugal's coffers and ending its golden age.

1622

Portugal's empire is slipping out of Spain's grasp. The English seize Hormoz. Later, in the 1650s, the Dutch take Malacca, Ceylon (Sri Lanka) and part of Brazil.

1640

When Catalonia rebels against the oppressive monarchy, Felipe III sends Portuguese troops to quell the uprising. Portuguese nobles stage a coup and overthrow Spain. Dom João IV is crowned.

1690

With the economy in tatters and the empire fading, the Portuguese pray for a miracle. The prayer is answered when gold is discovered in Brazil; incredible riches soon flow into the royal coffers.

A DEVASTATING EARTHQUAKE

Lisbon in the 1700s was a thriving city, with gold flowing in from Brazil, a thriving merchant class and grand Manueline architecture. Then, on the morning of 1 November 1755, a devastating earthquake levelled much of the city, which fell like a pack of dominoes, never to regain its former status; palaces, libraries, art galleries, churches and hospitals were razed to the ground. Tens of thousands died, crushed beneath falling masonry, drowned in the tsunami that swept in from the Tejo or killed in the fires that followed.

Enter the formidable, unflappable, geometrically minded Marquês de Pombal. As Dom José I's chief minister, Pombal swiftly set about reconstructing the city, true to his word to 'bury the dead and heal the living'. In the wake of the disaster, the autocratic statesman not only kept the country's head above water as it was plunged into economic chaos but also managed to propel Lisbon into the modern era.

Together with military engineers and architects Eugenio dos Santos and Manuel da Maia, Pombal played a pivotal role in reconstructing the city in a simple, cheap, earthquake-proof way that created today's formal grid, and the Pombaline style was born. The antithesis of rococo, Pombaline architecture was functional and restrained: *azulejos* (hand-painted tiles) and decorative elements were used sparingly, building materials were prefabricated, and wide streets and broad plazas were preferred.

Dom José I, for his part, escaped the earthquake unscathed. Instead of being in residence at the royal palace, he had ridden out of town to Belém with his extensive retinue. After seeing the devastation, the eccentric José I refused to live in a masonry building ever again, and he set up a wooden residence outside town, in the hills of Ajuda, north of Belém. What was known as the Real Barraca (Royal Tent) became the site of the Palácio Nacional de Ajuda after the king's death.

role by giving Britain the right to trade directly with Brazil. The next humiliation was João's 1815 proclamation of Brazil as a kingdom united with Portugal – he did this to bring more wealth and prestige to Brazil (which he was growing to love) and, in turn, to him and the rest of the royal family residing there. With soaring debts and dismal trade, Portugal was at one of the lowest points in its history, reduced to a de facto colony of Brazil and a protectorate of Britain.

To 'relive' the Lisbon earthquake, visit the Lisbon Story Centre (p65), located near the heart of where so much destruction occurred.

Meanwhile, resentment simmered in the army. Rebel officers quietly convened parliament and drew up a new liberal constitution. Based on Enlightenment ideals, it abolished many rights of the nobility and clergy, and instituted a single-chamber parliament.

Faced with this fait accompli, João returned and accepted its terms – though his wife and his son Miguel were bitterly opposed to it. João's elder son, Pedro, had other ideas: left behind to govern Brazil, he snubbed

1703

France and Britain are at war. Facing (disastrous!) wine shortages, the English sign a new treaty with Portugal and become a major player in the Portuguese economy, with port production growing exponentially.

1717

Brazilian gold extraction nears its peak, with over 600,000oz imported annually. Dom João V becomes Europe's richest monarch, lavishing resources on ostentatious projects like the Palácio Nacional de Mafra.

1755

Lisbon suffers what was Europe's biggest natural disaster in recorded history. On All Saints' Day, three massive earthquakes destroy the city, followed by a tsunami and ravaging fires that kill tens of thousands.

1770

The king's powerful prime minister, the Marquês de Pombal, rebuilds Lisbon following a modern grid. He abolishes slavery, builds schools and develops the economy, crushing those in his way.

the constitutionalists by declaring Brazil independent in 1822 and himself its emperor. When João died in 1826, the stage was set for civil war.

Offered the crown, Pedro dashed out a new, less liberal charter and then abdicated in favour of his seven-year-old daughter, Maria, on the provisos that she marry uncle Miguel and that uncle Miguel accept the new constitution. Miguel took the oath but promptly abolished Pedro's charter and proclaimed himself king. A livid Pedro rallied the equally furious liberals and forced Miguel to surrender at Évoramonte in 1834.

After Pedro's death, his daughter Maria, now queen of Portugal at just 15, kept his flame alive with fanatical support of his 1826 charter. The radical supporters of the liberal 1822 constitution grew vociferous over the next two decades, bringing the country to the brink of civil war. The Duke of Saldanha, however, saved the day, negotiating a peace that toned down Pedro's charter while still radically modernising Portugal's infrastructure.

The Portuguese were the first Westerners to reach Japan, in 1543. They founded Nagasaki, introduced the mosquito net and brought new words to the Japanese language, including *pan* (bread) and, possibly, *arrigato* (thank you).

A Hopeful New Era

The latter half of the 19th century was a remarkable period for Portugal, and it became known as one of the most advanced societies in southern Europe. Casual visitors to Lisbon, such as Hans Christian Andersen, were surprised to find tree-lined boulevards with gas street lamps, efficient trams and well-dressed residents. Social advances were less anecdotal. The educational reformer João Arroio dramatically increased the number of schools, doubling the number of boys' schools and quadrupling the number of girls' schools. Women gained the right to own property; slavery was abolished throughout the Portuguese empire, as was the death penalty; and even the prison system received an overhaul – prisoners were taught useful trades while in jail so they could integrate into society upon their release.

Professional organisations, such as the Literary Guild, emerged and became a major force for the advancement of ideas in public discourse, inspiring debate in politics, religious life and the art world.

As elsewhere in Europe, this was also a time of great industrial growth, with a dramatic increase in textile production, much of it to be exported. Other significant undertakings included the building of bridges and a nationwide network of roads, as well as the completion of major architectural works such as the Palácio Nacional da Pena above Sintra.

Some historians believe Portuguese explorers reached Australia in the 1500s, 250 years before England's James Cook. For the inside scoop, read Kenneth McIntyre's *The Secret Discovery of Australia* (1977).

Dark Days & A King's Death

However, by 1900, discontent among workers began to grow. With increased mechanisation, workers began losing their jobs (some factory owners began hiring children to operate the machines), and their demands for fair working conditions went unanswered. Those who went on strike were simply fired and replaced. At the same time, Portugal

1803

Britain and France are again at war. Portugal sides with Britain and refuses Napoleon's call to close its ports to the British. French troops are on the march across Iberia.

1807

Napoleon invades Portugal. The Portuguese royal family and several thousand in their retinue pack up their belongings and set sail for Brazil. British warships guard their passage.

1815

Having fallen hard for Brazil, Dom João VI declares Rio de Janeiro the capital of the United Kingdom of Portugal and Brazil and the Algarves, relegating Lisbon to second-class status.

1822

In Brazil, Prince Regent Pedro leads a coup d'état and declares Brazilian independence, with himself th[illegible] new 'emperor'. D[illegible] João VI, his fat[illegible] returns to Portu[illegible] reclaim his [illegible]

experienced a demographic shift: rural areas were increasingly depopulated in favour of cities, and emigration (especially to Brazil) snowballed.

Much was changing, and more and more people began to look towards socialism as a cure for the country's inequalities. Nationalist republicanism swept through the lower-middle classes, spurring an attempted coup in 1908. It failed, but the following month Dom Carlos and Crown Prince Luís Filipe were brutally assassinated in Lisbon.

Carlos' younger son, Manuel II, tried feebly to appease republicans, but it was too little, too late. On 5 October 1910, after an uprising by military officers, a republic was declared. Manuel, dubbed 'the Unfortunate', sailed into exile in Britain, where he died in 1932.

Rise & Fall of Salazar

After a landslide victory in the 1911 elections, hopes were high among republicans for dramatic changes, but the tide was against them. The economy was in tatters, an issue only exacerbated by a financially disastrous decision to join the Allies in WWI. In the postwar years the chaos deepened: republican factions squabbled, unions led strikes and were repressed, and the military grew more powerful.

The new republic soon had a reputation as Europe's most unstable regime. Between 1910 and 1926 there were an astonishing 45 changes of government, often resulting from military intervention. Another coup in 1926 brought forth new names and faces, most significantly António de Oliveira Salazar, a finance minister who would rise through the ranks to become prime minister in 1932 – a post he would hold for the next 36 years.

Salazar hastily enforced his 'New State' – a corporatist republic that was nationalistic, Catholic, authoritarian and essentially repressive. All political parties were banned except for the loyalist National Union, which ran the show, and the National Assembly. Strikes were forbidden and propaganda, censorship and brute force kept society in order. The sinister new Polícia Internacional e de Defesa do Estado (PIDE) secret police inspired terror and suppressed opposition using imprisonment and torture. Various attempted coups during Salazar's rule came to nothing. For a chilling taste of life as a political prisoner under Salazar, you could visit the 16th-century Fortaleza at Peniche – used as a jail by the dictator.

The Inquisitor's Manual (2003), by António Lobo Antunes, is a brilliantly written depiction of the dark days under Salazar, seen through the eyes of Faulknerian characters such as 'the minister', Senhor Francisco.

The only good news was the dramatic economic turnaround. Through the 1950s and 1960s, Portugal experienced an annual industrial growth rate of 7% to 9%.

Internationally, the wily Salazar played two hands, unofficially supporting Franco's nationalists in the Spanish Civil War and, despite official neutrality, allowing the British to use Azores airfields during WWII and engaging in illegal sales of tungsten to Germany. It was later

1832

Now king, Pedro I returns to Portugal, where he must contest his throne against his brother, Miguel. Two years of civil war end with Miguel's banishment. Dom Pedro's daughter becomes queen.

1865

Portugal enjoys a period of peace and prosperity. Railways connect villages with Lisbon and Porto, now cities enriched by maritime trade. Advancements are made in industry, agriculture, health and education.

1890

Portugal takes a renewed interest in its African colonies. Britain wants control of sub-Saharan Africa and threatens Portugal with war. Cowed, Portugal withdraws, causing a crisis at home.

1900

The republican movement gains force. The humiliating Africa issue is one among many grievances against the crown. Others include rising unemployment and growing social inequalities.

SALAZAR & THE ECONOMY

When General António Carmona was named Portugal's president in 1926, he inherited a country in serious debt. Fearing economic catastrophe, Carmona called in an expert, a man by the name of António de Oliveira Salazar. At the time, Salazar was a 37-year-old bachelor, sharing spartan quarters with a priest (who would later become cardinal of Lisbon). Salazar himself was no stranger to religious life. He spent eight years studying to become a priest, and some residents of his small native village even called him 'father' on his visits. Only a last-minute decision led him to veer into law instead.

One of the country's first economists, Salazar garnered wide respect for his articles on public finance. When General Carmona approached him with the job of finance minister, Salazar accepted on one condition: that the spending of all government ministries fall under his discretion. The general agreed.

Salazar achieved enormous success in firing up the national economy. He severely curtailed government spending, raising taxes and balancing the budget during his first year. Unemployment decreased significantly. Salazar quickly became one of Carmona's star ministers. He also took on additional posts as other ministers resigned. In this way he consolidated power until Carmona eventually named him prime minister.

Salazar set a tone for civilian life that would last for many decades. Under his authoritarian rule, the country knew stability and prosperity, though at enormous cost: censorship, imprisonment and – in some cases – torture of political opponents. Among his most damning attributes was his attitude towards the working class. He believed in giving them a diet of 'fado, Fátima and football' to keep them happily compliant, but he had no intention of bettering their lot; at the end of his rule in 1968, Portugal had the highest rates of illiteracy and tuberculosis in Western Europe, and women were still not allowed to vote. Given the socially backward condition of the nation when Salazar relinquished power, the advancements of the last 40 years are all the more startling.

discovered that Salazar had also authorised the transfer of Nazi-looted gold to Portugal – 44 tonnes, according to Allied records.

But it was something else that finally brought the Salazarist era to a close – decolonisation. Refusing to relinquish the colonies, he was faced with ever more costly and unpopular military expeditions. In 1961 Goa was occupied by India, and nationalists rose up in Angola. Guerrilla movements also appeared in Portuguese Guinea and Mozambique.

Salazar, however, didn't have to face the consequences. In 1968 he had a stroke, and he died two years later.

His successor, Marcelo Caetano, failed to ease unrest. Military officers sympathetic to African freedom fighters grew reluctant to fight colonial wars – the officers had seen the horrible conditions in which the colonies lived beneath the Portuguese authorities. Several hundred officers

1908

The royal family fails to silence antimonarchist sentiment by shutting down newspapers, exiling dissidents and brutally suppressing demonstrations. Dom Carlos and his eldest son, Luís Filipe, are assassinated.

1910

Dom Carlos' younger son, 18-year-old Manuel, takes the throne but is soon ousted. Portugal is declared a republic. Chaos rules, and the country will see 45 governments in 16 years.

1916

Despite initial neutrality, Portugal gets drawn into WWI and sends 55,000 troops; nearly 10,000 perish. The war effort is devastating for the economy, creating a long postwar recession.

1932

António de Oliveira Salazar seizes power. The Portuguese economy grows but at enormous human cost. Salazar uses censorship, imprisonment and torture to silence his opponents.

formed the Movimento das Forças Armadas (MFA), which on 25 April 1974 carried out a nearly bloodless coup in Lisbon, later nicknamed the Revolution of the Carnations (after victorious soldiers stuck carnations in their rifle barrels). Carnations are still a national symbol of freedom.

From Revolution to Democracy

Despite the coup's popularity, the following year saw unprecedented chaos. It began where the revolution had begun: in the African colonies. Independence was granted immediately to Guinea-Bissau, followed by the speedy decolonisation of the Cape Verde islands, São Tomé e Príncipe, Mozambique and Angola.

Officially neutral in WWII, Portugal was a major intersection of both Allied and Nazi spying operations. British secret-service agents based there included Graham Greene, Ian Fleming and double agent Kim Philby.

The transition wasn't smooth: civil war racked Angola, and East Timor, freshly liberated in 1975, was promptly invaded by Indonesia. Within Portugal, too, times were turbulent, with almost a million refugees from African colonies flooding into the country.

The nation was an economic mess, with widespread strikes and a tangle of political ideas and parties. The communists and a radical wing of the MFA launched a revolutionary movement, nationalising firms and services. Peasant farmers seized land to establish communal farms that failed because of infighting and poor management. While revolutionaries held sway in the south, the conservative north was led by Mário Soares and his Partido Socialista (PS; Socialist Party).

In the early post-Salazar days, radical provisional governments established by the military failed one after the other, as did an attempted coup led by General António de Spínola in 1975. A period of relative calm finally arrived in 1976, when Portugal adopted a new constitution and held its first elections for a new parliament. General António Ramalho Eanes was elected president the same year and helped steer the country toward democracy. He chose as his prime minister Soares, who took the reins with enormous challenges facing Portugal, including soaring inflation, high unemployment and downward-spiraling wages.

Rocky Road to Stability

Portugal was soon committed to a blend of socialism and democracy, with a powerful president, an elected assembly and a Council of the Revolution to control the armed forces.

Mário Soares' minority government soon faltered, prompting a series of attempts at government by coalitions and nonparty candidates, including Portugal's first female prime minister, Maria de Lourdes Pintasilgo. In the 1980 parliamentary elections, a new political force took the reins: the conservative Aliança Democrática (AD; Democratic Alliance), led by Francisco Sá Carneiro.

1935

The largely unpublished 47-year-old poet Fernando Pessoa dies, leaving a trunk containing a staggering collection of writing. Critics later describe him as one of the greatest poets of the 20th century.

1943

Portugal, neutral during WWII, becomes a crossroads for the intelligence activities of Allied and Axis operatives. Salazar works both sides, selling tungsten to the Nazis while allowing Britain the use of airfields.

1961

The last vestiges of Portugal's empire begin to crumble as India seizes Goa. Independence movements are under way in Portugal's former African colonies of Angola, Mozambique and Guinea-Bissau.

1974

Army officers overthrow Salazar's successor in the Revolution of the Carnations. Portugal veers to the left, and communists and moderates struggle for power in the unstable country.

After Carneiro's almost immediate (and suspicious) death in a plane crash, Francisco Pinto Balsemão stepped into his shoes. He implemented plans to join the European Community (EC).

It was partly to keep the EC and the International Monetary Fund (IMF) happy that a new coalition government under Soares and Balsemão implemented a strict program of economic modernisation. Not surprisingly, the belt-tightening wasn't popular. The loudest critics were Soares' right-wing partners in the Partido Social Democrata (PSD; Social Democrat Party), led by the dynamic Aníbal Cavaco Silva. Communist trade unions organised strikes, and the appearance of urban terrorism by the radical left-wing Forças Populares 25 de Abril (FP-25) deepened unrest.

In 1986, after nine years of negotiations, Portugal joined the EC. Flush with new funds, it raced ahead of its neighbours with unprecedented economic growth. The new cash flow also gave prime minister Cavaco Silva the power to push ahead with radical economic plans. These included labour-law reforms that left many workers disenchanted. The 1980s were crippled by strikes – including one involving 1.5 million workers – though they were to no avail: the controversial legislation was eventually passed.

The economic growth, however, wouldn't last. In 1992 EC trade barriers fell and Portugal suddenly faced new competition. Fortunes dwindled as a recession set in, and disillusionment grew as Europe's single market revealed the backwardness of Portugal's agricultural sector.

Strikes, crippling corruption charges and student demonstrations over rising fees only undermined the PSD further, leading to Cavaco Silva's resignation in 1995. The general elections that year brought new faces to power, with the socialist António Guterres running the show. Despite hopes for a different and less conservative administration, it was business as usual, with Guterres maintaining the budgetary rigour that qualified Portugal for the European Economic & Monetary Union (EMU) in 1998. Indeed, for a while Portugal was a star EMU performer, with steady economic growth that helped Guterres win a second term. But corruption scandals, rising inflation and a faltering economy soon spelt disaster. Portugal had slipped into economic stagnation by the dawn of the 21st century. The next 10 years were ones of hardship for the Portuguese economy, which saw little or negative GDP growth, and rising unemployment from 2001 to 2010. As elsewhere in Europe, Portugal took a huge hit during the global financial crisis. Ultimatums from the EU governing body to rein in its debt (to avoid a Greece-style meltdown) brought unpopular austerity measures – pension reform, increased taxes, public-sector hiring freezes – that led to protests and strikes.

Portugal only narrowly missed claiming Europe's first female prime minister: in 1979 Margaret Thatcher snatched the honour just three months before Maria de Lourdes Pintasilgo (1930–2004).

1986

In a narrow second-round victory, Mário Soares is elected president of Portugal, becoming its first civilian head of state in 60 years. The same year, Portugal joins the EC, along with Spain.

1998

Lisbon hosts Expo '98, showcasing new developments, including Santiago Calatrava's cutting-edge train station and Europe's largest oceanarium and longest bridge (the Ponte de Vasco da Gama).

1998

José Saramago receives the Nobel Prize in Literature for his darkly humorous tales about ordinary characters facing fantastical obstacles. A lifelong communist, Saramago's work was condemned by the church.

1999

Legendary *fadista* (performer of traditional song) Amália Rodrigues dies aged 79. Three days of mourning are declared. Her extraordinary 40-year career is credite[illegible] with helping to revi[illegible] the dying ger[illegible]

Hard Times

Portugal: A Traveller's History (2004), by Harold Livermore, explores some of the richer episodes of the country's past, taking in cave paintings, vineyards and music, among other topics.

Portugal's economy wasn't particularly strong in the years before the economic crisis, making the economic fire all the more destructive. Lumped in with other economically failing eurozone nations, the group of them collectively known as PIIGS (Portugal, Italy, Ireland, Greece and Spain), Portugal – in dire financial straits – accepted an EU bailout worth €78 billion in 2011. The younger generation has borne the heaviest burden following the crisis, with unemployment above 40% for workers under the age of 25. In addition, there are the underemployed and those scraping by on meagre wages.

The EU bailout came with the stipulation that Portugal improve its budget deficit by reducing spending and increasing tax revenues. Austerity measures followed and the public took to the streets to protest against higher taxes and slashed pensions and benefits, in the context of record-high unemployment. Mass demonstrations and general strikes have grown, with the largest attracting an estimated 1.5 million people nationwide in 2013 – an astounding figure given Portugal's small size. Those in industries most affected by government policy – including education, healthcare and transportation – have joined ranks with the unemployed and pensioners to amass in the largest gatherings since the Revolution of the Carnations in 1974.

Despite the bailout package, Portugal remained in its most severe recession since the 1970s. Every day, Portuguese were confronted with depressing headlines announcing freezes on public spending, cuts in healthcare, removal of free school lunches, curtailing of police patrols and rising suicides, among other issues. Pensioners living on 200-odd euros a month struggled to feed themselves without family financial support, and poverty and hunger affected untold millions; according to TNS Global, roughly three out of four people in Portugal struggled to make their money last through the month.

What began as a financial crisis soon turned into a political crisis, as successive government ministers failed to ameliorate the growing problems. With anger mounting on the streets, the public clamoured for the resignation of prime minister Pedro Passos Coelho. Indeed, his time in power would come to an abrupt end in 2015, with a new left-wing government taking control.

2004

Hosting the UEFA European Championship, Portugal makes it to the final only to suffer an agonising loss to Greece. Over €600 million is spent remodelling and constructing stadiums.

2007

Portugal takes over the rotating EU presidency. The Treaty of Lisbon, an agreement that aims to give new coherence to the EU, is drafted.

2010

Portugal legalises same-sex marriage, becoming the sixth country in Europe (and the eighth in the world) to do so. A media firestorm ensues as the church condemns the law.

2013

Fed up with rising unemployment, soaring taxes and a proposed €4 billion in government spending cuts, 1.5 million protestors take to the streets of Portugal.

Religion

Christianity has been a powerful force in shaping Portugal's history, and religion still plays an important role in the lives of its people. Churches and cathedrals are sprinkled about every town and city across the country, and Portugal's biggest celebrations revolve around religious events, with a packed calendar of colourful parades and concerts held on important feast days. Portugal is also home to a number of pilgrimage sites, the most important of which, Fátima, attracts several million pilgrims each year.

Church & State

Portugal has a deep connection to the church. Even during the long rule of the Moors, Christianity flourished in the north – which provided a strategic base for Christian crusaders to retake the kingdom. Cleric and king walked hand in hand, from the earliest papal alliances of the 11th century through to the 17th century, when the church played a role both at home and in Portugal's expanding empire.

Things ran smoothly until the 18th century, when the Marquês de Pombal, a man of the Enlightenment, wanted to curtail the power of the church – specifically that of the Jesuits, whom he expelled in 1759. He also sought to modernise the Portuguese state (overseeing one of the world's first urban 'grid' systems) and brought education under the state's control. State–church relations seesawed over the next 150 years, with power struggles including the outright ban of religious orders in 1821 and the seizing by the state of many church properties.

The separation of church and state was formally recognised during the First Republic (1910–26). But in practice the church remained intimately linked to many aspects of people's lives. Health and education were largely under religious auspices, with Catholic schools and hospitals the norm. Social outlets for those in rural areas were mostly church related. And the completion of any public-works project always included a blessing by the local bishop.

In 1932 António de Oliveira Salazar swept into power, establishing a Mussolini-like Estado Novo (New State) that lasted until the 1974 Revolution of the Carnations. Salazar had strong ties to the Catholic church – he spent eight years studying for the priesthood before switching to law. His college roommate was a priest who later became the Cardinal Patriarch of Lisbon. Salazar was a ferocious anticommunist, and he used Roman Catholic references to appeal to people's sense of authority, order and discipline. He described the family, the parish and the larger institution of Christianity as the foundations of the state. Church officials who spoke out against him were silenced or forced into exile.

Following the 1974 revolution, the church found itself out of favour with many Portuguese; its support of the Salazar regime spelt its undoing in the topsy-turvy days following the government's collapse. The new constitution, ratified in 1976, again emphasised the formal separation of church and state, although this time the law had teeth, and Portugal quickly transitioned into a more secular society. Today, only about half of all weddings happen inside a church. Divorce is legal, as is abortion (up to 10 weeks; the

Religious Events

- *Semana Santa (Braga)*
- *Festa de São João (Porto & Braga)*
- *Festa de Santo António (Lisbon)*
- *Fátima Romaris (Fátima)*
- *Romaria de Nossa Senhora d'Agonia (Viana do Castelo)*
- *Festa de Nossa Senhora dos Remédios (Lamego)*

LIFE UNDER MUSLIM RULE

The Moors ruled southern Portugal for almost 400 years, and some scholars describe that time as a golden age. The Arabs introduced irrigation, previously unknown in Europe. Two Egyptian agronomists came to Iberia in the 10th century and wrote manuals on land management, animal husbandry, plant and crop cultivation, and irrigation designs. They introduced bananas, rice, coconuts, maize and sugar cane. They also encouraged food markets and small-scale cooperatives in olive-oil and wine production, which are still embraced in many parts of Portugal.

The Moors opened schools and set campaigns to achieve mass literacy (in Arabic, of course), as well as the teaching of mathematics, geography and history. Medicine reached new levels of sophistication. There was also a degree of religious tolerance, but this evaporated when Christian crusaders came to power. Much to the chagrin of Christian slave owners, slavery was not permitted in the Islamic kingdom – making it a refuge for runaway slaves. Muslims, Christians and Jews all peacefully coexisted, and at times even collaborated, creating one of the most scientifically and artistically advanced societies the world had ever known.

law went into effect following a 2007 referendum). In 2010 same-sex marriage was legalised, making Portugal the sixth European nation to permit it (with several other nations joining the ranks in recent years).

One of the more unusual rituals celebrated around Easter is the *enterro do bacalhau* (burying of the codfish), which marks the end of Lent.

The Inquisition

'After the earthquake, which had destroyed three-quarters of the city of Lisbon, the wise men of that country could think of no means more effectual to preserve the kingdom from utter ruin than to entertain the people with an auto-da-fe...'

Voltaire (*Candide*)

One of the darkest episodes in Portugal's history, the Inquisition was a campaign of church-sanctioned terror and execution that began in 1536 and lasted for 200 years, though it was not officially banned until 1821. It was initially aimed at Jews, who were either expelled from Portugal or forced to renounce their faith. Those who didn't embrace Catholicism risked facing the auto-da-fé (act of faith), a church ceremony consisting of a Mass, a procession of the guilty, reading of the sentences and, later, burning at the stake.

'Trials' took place in public squares in Lisbon, Porto, Évora and Coimbra in front of crowds sometimes numbering in the thousands. At the centre, atop a large canopied platform, sat the Grand Inquisitor, surrounded by a staff of aristocrats, priests, bailiffs, torturers and scribes, who meticulously recorded the proceedings.

The last auto-da-fé (act of faith; execution by burning at the stake) was held in 1765. Ironically enough, it was levied against 10 Jesuit priests who dared oppose the autocratic and anticlerical Marquês de Pombal.

The victims usually spent years in prison, often undergoing crippling torture, before seeing the light of day. They stood accused of a wide variety of crimes – such as skipping meals on Jewish fast days (signs of 'unreformed' Jews), leaving pork uneaten on the plate, failing to attend Mass or observe the sabbath, as well as blasphemy, witchcraft and homosexuality. No matter how flimsy the 'evidence' – often delivered to the tribunal by a grudge-bearing neighbour – very few were found not guilty and released. After a decade or so in prison, the condemned were finally brought to their auto-da-fé. Before meeting their judgement, they were dressed in a *san benito* (yellow penitential gown painted with flames) and a *coroza* (high conical cap) and brought before the tribunal.

After the sentence was pronounced, judgement was carried out in a different venue. By dawn the next morning, for instance, executioners would lead the condemned to a killing field outside town. Those who repented were strangled before being burnt at the stake. The unrepentant were simply burnt alive.

During the Inquisition years, the church executed over 2000 victims and tortured or exiled thousands more. The Portuguese even exported the auto-da-fé to the colonies, burning Hindus at the stake in Goa, for instance.

As Voltaire sardonically suggested, superstition played no small part in the auto-da-fé. Some believers thought that the earthquake of 1755 was the wrath of God upon them, and that they were being punished – not for their bloody autos-da-fé but because the Holy Office hadn't done quite enough to punish the heretics.

Apparitions at Fátima

For many Portuguese Catholics, Fátima represents one of the most momentous religious events of the 20th century, and it transformed a tiny village into a major pilgrimage site for Catholics across the globe. On 13 May 1917, 10-year-old Lúcia Santos and her two younger cousins, Jacinta and Francisco Marto, were out tending their parents' flocks in the fields outside the village of Fátima. Suddenly a bolt of lightning struck the earth, and a woman 'brighter than the sun' appeared before them. According to Santos, she came to them with a message exhorting people to pray and do penance to save sinners. She asked the children to pray the rosary every day, which she said was key to bringing peace to one's own life and to the world. At the time, peace was certainly on the minds of many Portuguese, who were already deeply enmeshed in WWI. She then told the children to come again on the 13th of each month, at the same time and place, and that in October she would reveal herself to them.

Word of the alleged apparition spread, although most who heard the tale of the shepherd children reacted with scepticism. Only a handful of observers came to the field for the 13 June appearance, but the following month several thousand showed up. That's when the apparition apparently entrusted the children with three secrets. In the weeks that followed, a media storm raged, with the government accusing the church of fabricating an elaborate hoax to revive its flagging popularity. The church, for its part, didn't know how to react. The children were even arrested and interrogated at one point, but the three refused to change their story.

On 13 October 1917 some 70,000 people gathered for what was to be the final appearance of the apparition. Many witnesses there experienced the so-called Miracle of the Sun, where the sun seemed to grow in size and dance in the sky, becoming a whirling disc of fire, shooting out multicoloured rays. Some spoke of being miraculously healed; others were frightened by the experience; still others claimed they saw nothing at all. The three children claimed they saw Mary, Jesus and Joseph in the

Fátima Books & Films

The Fourth Secret of Fátima (2006), written by Antonio Socci

The 13th Day (2009), directed by Ian and Dominic Higgins

Miracle of Our Lady of Fátima (1952), directed by John Brahm

CRYPTO JEWS

When Manuel I banned Judaism, most Jews fled or converted. Some, however, simply hid their faith from public view and wore the facade of being a New Christian (the name given to Jewish converts). Religious ceremonies were held behind closed doors, with the sabbath lamp placed at the bottom of a clay jar so that it could not be seen from outside. Within their Catholic prayer books Jews composed Jewish prayers, and they even overlaid Jewish prayers atop Catholic rituals (like the making of the sign of the cross). Clever food preparation – such as eating pork-free *alheiras* (seasoned garlicky sausages made of a mixture of chicken, rabbit, partridge or veal mixed with bread dough for consistency) – also helped hide their faith.

One Crypto-Jewish community in Belmonte managed to maintain its faith in hiding for over 400 years and was only revealed in 1917. Due to centuries of endogamy (intermarriage), many of the 200 Jews in this community suffer from hereditary diseases. No longer underground (Belmonte now has its own synagogue and Jewish cemetery), members of the community remain quite secretive about the practices they maintained in hiding.

FAITH ON THE DECLINE

The percentage of Portuguese who consider themselves Catholics (around 85%) ranks among the highest in Western Europe. The number of the faithful, however, has been on a steady decline since the 1970s, when over 95% of the nation was Catholic. Today nearly half a million residents describe themselves as agnostic, and less than 20% of the population are practising Catholics. Regional differences reveal a more complicated portrait: around half of northern Portugal's population still attend Sunday Mass, as do more than a quarter in Lisbon – with noticeably fewer churchgoers on the southern coast.

sky. Newspapers across the country reported on the event, and soon a growing hysteria surrounded it.

Only Lúcia made it into adulthood. Jacinta and Francisco, both beatified by the church in 2000, were two of the more than 20 million killed during the 1918 influenza epidemic. Lúcia later became a Carmelite nun and died at the age of 97 on 13 February 2007.

Three Secrets

Much mystery surrounds the three secrets told to the children at Fátima on 13 July 1917. Lúcia revealed the first two in 1941 at the request of the bishop of Leira, who was publishing a book on Jacinta. The first secret depicted a vision of demons and human souls suffering in the fires of hell. The second secret predicted that an even more disastrous war would follow WWI should the world – and in particular Russia – not convert. Disclosed months before the Bolshevik takeover in St Petersburg, this secret was considered particularly inflammatory, as it went on to say that, if Mary's call for repentance went unheeded, Russia would spread its terrors through the world, causing wars and persecution of the church. Lúcia was reluctant to reveal the third secret, claiming that she was told by the Virgin Mary never to reveal it. Stricken with illness and convinced she was going to die, Lúcia finally agreed to write the secret down in 1944.

> Portugal still has a few good old-fashioned pagan celebrations. The most famous is the Festa dos Rapazes (Festival of the Lads), which features young men in rags and wooden masks rampaging around Miranda do Douro.

The bishop who received the secret then passed it on to the Vatican, who kept it hidden away for decades. Lúcia requested that the last secret be revealed in 1960 or upon her death, whichever came first. She picked 1960 as she figured that by then the secret would be more understood. The Vatican, however, had other plans and announced in 1960 that the secret would probably remain sealed forever. Fátima followers, meanwhile, offered wild speculations on what the third secret might reveal – from nuclear holocaust to WWIII, global financial crisis, famine, the apocalypse. The church kept them in suspense until 2000, when it was finally revealed.

The last secret was the most mystical and controversial of the three. Lúcia described seeing an angel holding a flaming sword who pointed at the earth and cried out 'penance'. Then she saw a ruined city full of corpses and beyond that a mountain, up which climbed a bishop dressed in white – whom she took to be the pope. At the top he knelt before a cross made of hewn tree trunks and was killed by soldiers, who gunned him down.

Some claim that this predicted the assassination attempt on Pope John Paul II in 1981. The attempt happened on 13 May (the anniversary of the first apparition) and the Pope himself claimed that the Virgin of Fátima saved him from death. (According to some reconstructions of the shooting, the assassin's bullet followed an elliptical path rather than a straight line, thereby avoiding the Pope's vital organs.) Conspiracy theorists claim that the church was hiding the 'real' third secret, which related to the apocalypse and an apostasy within the church – a breakdown that would begin at the top. Recent scandals, including the Catholic sex-abuse cases in various parts of the world, have only fuelled speculation among some 'Fátimists' that the third secret has yet to be revealed.

Art & Architecture

Portugal has a long and storied art history. Neolithic tribes, Celtic peoples, Romans, Visigoths, Moors and early Christian crusaders have all left their mark on the Iberian nation. The Age of Discoveries – a rich era of grand cathedrals and lavish palaces – began around 1500. In the 500 years that followed, Portugal became a showcase for a dizzying array of architectural styles – Manueline, mannerist, baroque, art nouveau, modernist and postmodernist. Meanwhile, painters, sculptors, poets and novelists all made contributions to Portugal's artistic heritage.

Palaeolithic Palette

The Cromeleque dos Almendres, a most mysterious group of 95 huge monoliths, forms a strange circle in an isolated clearing among Alentejan olive groves near Évora. It's one of Europe's most impressive prehistoric sites.

All over Portugal, but especially in the Alentejo, you can visit such ancient funerary and religious structures, built during the Neolithic and Mesolithic eras. Most impressive are the dolmens: rectangular, polygonal or round funerary chambers, reached by a corridor of stone slabs and covered with earth to create an artificial mound. King of these is Europe's largest dolmen, the Anta Grande do Zambujeiro, near Évora, with six 6m-high stones forming a huge chamber. Single monoliths, or menhirs, often carved with phallic or religious symbols, also dot the countryside like an army of stone sentinels. Their relationship to promoting fertility seems obvious.

With the arrival of the Celts (800–200 BC) came the first established hilltop settlements, called *castros*. The best-preserved example is the Citânia de Briteiros, in the Minho, where you can literally step into Portugal's past. Stone dwellings were built on a circular or elliptical plan, and the complex was surrounded by a drystone defensive wall. In the *citânias* (fortified villages) further south, dwellings tended to be rectangular.

Prehistoric Relics

Vila Nova de Foz Côa (Douro)

Citânia de Briteiros (Minho)

Cromeleque dos Almendres (Alentejo)

Romans

The Romans left Portugal their typical architectural and engineering feats – roads, bridges, towns complete with forums (marketplaces), villas, public baths and aqueducts. These have now largely disappeared from the surface, though the majority of Portugal's cities are built on Roman foundations. Today you can descend into dank subterranean areas under new buildings in Lisbon and Évora, and see Roman fragments around Braga. At Conímbriga, the country's largest Roman site, an entire town is under excavation. Revealed so far are some spectacular mosaics, along with structural or decorative columns, carved entablatures and classical ornamentation, giving a sense of the Roman high life.

Portugal's most famous and complete Roman ruin is the Templo Romano, the so-called Temple of Diana in Évora, with its flouncy-topped Corinthian columns nowadays echoed by the complementary towers of Évora's cathedral. This is the finest temple of its kind on the Iberian Peninsula, its preservation the result of having been walled up in the Middle Ages and later used as a slaughterhouse.

Roman Ruins

Conímbriga (Beiras)

Temple of Diana (Évora)

Teatro Romano (Lisbon)

Milreu (Algarve)

A SERENDIPITOUS DISCOVERY

In 1989 researchers were studying the rugged valley of the Rio Côa, 15km from the Spanish frontier, to understand the environmental impact of a planned hydroelectric dam that was to flood the valley. In the course of their work, they made an extraordinary discovery: a number of petroglyphs (rock engravings) dating back tens of thousands of years.

Yet it wasn't until 1992, after the dam's construction was under way, that the importance of the find began to be recognised. Archaeologists came across whole clusters of petroglyphs, mostly dating from the Upper Palaeolithic period (10,000 to 40,000 years ago). Local people joined the search and the inventory of engravings soon grew into the thousands. In 1998 the future of the collection was safeguarded when Unesco designated the valley a World Heritage Site.

Today Rio Côa holds one of the largest-known collections of open-air Palaeolithic art in the world. Archaeologists are still puzzling over the meaning of the engravings – and why this site was chosen. Most of the petroglyphs depict animals: stylised horses, aurochs (extinct ancestors of domesticated cattle) and long-horned ibex (extinct species of wild goat). Some animals are depicted with multiple heads – as if to indicate the animal in motion – while others are drawn so finely that they require artificial light to be seen. Later petroglyphs begin to depict human figures as well. The most intriguing engravings consist of overlapping layers, with successive artists adding their touches thousands of years after the first strokes were applied – a kind of Palaeolithic palimpsest in which generations of hunters worked and reworked the engravings of their forebears.

Architectural Movements

Great Gothic

Cistercians introduced the Gothic trend, which reached its pinnacle in Alcobaça, in one of Portugal's most ethereally beautiful buildings. The austere abbey church and cloister of the Mosteiro de Santa Maria de Alcobaça, begun in 1178, has a lightness and simplicity strongly influenced by Clairvaux Abbey in France. Its hauntingly simple Cloisters of Silence were a model for later cathedral cloisters at Coimbra, Lisbon, Évora and many other places. This was the birth of Portuguese Gothic, which flowered and transmuted over the coming years as the country gained more and more experience of the outside world after centuries of being culturally dominated and restricted by Spain and the Moors.

By the 14th century, when the Mosteiro de Santa Maria da Vitória (commonly known as Mosteiro da Batalha or Battle Abbey) was constructed, simplicity was a distant, vague memory. Portuguese, Irish and French architects worked on this breathtaking monument for more than two centuries. The combination of their skills and the changing architectural fashions of the times, from Flamboyant (late) Gothic to Renaissance and then Manueline, turned the abbey into a seething mass of carving, organic decorations, lofty spaces and slanting stained-glass light. A showcase of High Gothic art, it exults in the decorative (especially in its Gothic Royal Cloisters and Chapter House) and its flying buttresses tip their hat to English Perpendicular Gothic.

Secular architecture also enjoyed a Gothic boom, thanks to the need for fortifications against the Moors and to the castle-building fervour of 13th-century ruler Dom Dinis. Some of Portugal's most spectacular, huddled, thick-walled castles – for example, Estremoz, Óbidos and Bragança – date from this time, many featuring massive double-perimeter walls and an inner square tower.

Gothic Sites

Mosteiro de Santa Maria de Alcobaça (Estremadura)

Convento do Carmo (Lisbon)

Mosteiro de Santa Maria da Vitória (Estremadura)

Manueline Sites

Mosteiro dos Jerónimos (Belém)

Torre de Belém (Belém)

Chapter House (Tomar)

[Igr]eja de Jesus ([S]etúbal)

Manueline

Manueline is a uniquely Portuguese style: a specific, crazed flavour of late Gothic architecture. Ferociously decorative, it coincided roughly with the reign of Dom Manuel I (r 1495–1521) and is interesting not just because of its extraordinarily imaginative designs, burbling with life, but also because this dizzyingly creative architecture skipped hand in hand with the era's booming confidence.

During Dom Manuel's reign, Vasco da Gama and fellow explorers claimed new overseas lands and new wealth for Portugal. The Age of Discoveries was expressed in sculptural creations of eccentric inventiveness that drew heavily on nautical themes: twisted ropes, coral and anchors in stone, topped by the ubiquitous armillary sphere (a navigational device that became Dom Manuel's personal symbol) and the cross of the Order of Christ (symbol of the religious military order that largely financed and inspired Portugal's explorations).

Manueline first emerged in Setúbal's Igreja de Jesus, designed in the 1490s by French expatriate Diogo de Boitaca, who gave it columns like trees growing into the ceiling and ribbed vaulting like twisted ropes. The style quickly caught on, and soon decorative carving was creeping, twisting and crawling over everything (aptly described by 19th-century English novelist William Beckford as 'scollops and twistifications').

Outstanding Manueline masterpieces are Belém's Mosteiro dos Jerónimos, masterminded largely by Diogo de Boitaca and João de Castilho; and Batalha's Mosteiro de Santa Maria da Vitória's otherworldly Capelas Imperfeitas (Unfinished Chapels).

Other famous creations include Belém's Torre de Belém, a Manueline-Moorish cake crossed with a chess piece by Francisco de Arruda; his brother Diogo de Arruda's fantastical organic, seemingly barnacle-encrusted window in the Chapter House of Tomar's Convento de Cristo; and the convent's fanciful 16-sided Charola – the Templar church, resembling an eerie *Star Wars* set. Many other churches sport a Manueline flourish against a plain facade.

The style was enormously resonant in Portugal, and reappeared in the early 20th century in exercises in mystical romanticism, such as Sintra's Quinta da Regaleira and Palácio Nacional da Pena, and Luso's over-the-top and extraordinary neo-Manueline Palace Hotel do Buçaco.

Memorial do Convento (Baltasar and Blimunda; 1982) is José Saramago's Nobel Prize–winning novel about the Mafra, a convent-palace dreamed up by size junkies and compulsive builders.

Baroque

With independence from Spain re-established and the influence of the Inquisition on the wane, Portugal burst out in a fever of baroque – an architectural style that was exuberant and theatrical and fired straight at the senses. Nothing could rival the Manueline flourish, but the baroque style – named after the Portuguese word for a rough pearl, *barroco* – cornered the market in flamboyance. At its height during the 18th century (almost a century later than in Italy), it was characterised by curvaceous forms, huge monuments, spatially complex schemes and lots and lots and lots of gold.

Financed by the 17th-century gold and diamond discoveries in Brazil, and encouraged by the extravagant Dom João V, local and foreign (particularly Italian) artists created mind-bogglingly opulent masterpieces. Prodigious *talha dourada* (gilded woodwork) adorns church interiors all over the place, but it reached its extreme in Aveiro's Mosteiro de Jesus, Lisbon's Igreja de São Roque and Porto's Igreja de São Francisco.

The baroque of central and southern Portugal was more restrained. Examples include the chancel of Évora's cathedral and the massive Palácio Nacional de Mafra. Designed by the German architect João Frederico Ludovice to rival the palace-monastery of San Lorenzo de El Escorial (near Madrid), the Mafra version is relatively sober, apart from its size – which is such that at one point it had a workforce of 45,000, looked after by a police force of 7000.

Portugal has few Renaissance buildings, but some examples of the style are the Great Cloisters in Tomar's Convento de Cristo, designed by Spanish Diogo de Torralva in the late 16th century; the nearby Igreja de Nossa Senhora da Conceição; and the Convento de Bom Jesus at Valverde, outside Évora.

Baroque Sites

Palácio Nacional de Mafra

Igreja de São Roque (Lisbon)

Igreja de São Francisco (Porto)

Palácio de Mateus (Vila Real)

Meanwhile, Tuscan painter and architect Nicolau Nasoni (who settled in Porto around 1725) introduced a more ornamental baroque style to the north. Nasoni is responsible for Porto's Torre dos Clérigos and Igreja da Misericórdia, and the whimsical Palácio de Mateus near Vila Real (internationally famous as the image on Mateus rosé wine bottles).

In the mid-18th century a school of architecture evolved in Braga. Local artists such as André Soares built churches and palaces in a very decorative style, heavily influenced by Augsburg engravings from southern Germany. Soares' Casa do Raio, in Braga, and much of the monumental staircase of the nearby Bom Jesus do Monte, are typical examples of this period's ornamentation.

Only when the gold ran out did the baroque fad fade. At the end of the 18th century, architects flirted briefly with rococo (best exemplified by Mateus Vicente's Palácio de Queluz, begun in 1747, or the palace at Estói) before embracing neoclassicism.

Modern Era

Modern Sites

Casa da Música (Porto)

Casa das Histórias Paula Rego (Cascais)

Gare do Oriente (Lisbon)

Torre Vasco da Gama (Lisbon)

The Salazar years favoured decidedly severe, Soviet-style state commissions (eg Coimbra university's dull faculty buildings, which replaced elegant 18th-century neoclassical ones). Ugly buildings and apartment blocks rose on city outskirts. Notable exceptions dating from the 1960s are Lisbon's Palácio da Justiça in the Campolide district and the gloriously sleek Museu Calouste Gulbenkian. The beautiful wood-panelled Galeto cafe-restaurant is a time capsule from this era.

The tendency towards urban mediocrity continued after the 1974 revolution, although architects such as Fernando Távora and Eduardo Souto de Moura have produced impressive schemes. Lisbon's postmodern Amoreiras shopping complex, by Tomás Taveira, is another striking contribution.

Portugal's most prolific contemporary architect is Álvaro Siza Vieira. A believer in clarity and simplicity, he takes an expressionist approach

TWO LEGENDARY ARCHITECTS

Porto is home to not one but two celebrated contemporary architects: Álvaro Siza Vieira (born 1933) and Eduardo Souto de Moura (born 1952). Both remain fairly unknown outside their home country, which is surprising given their loyal following among fellow architects and their long and distinguished careers. Both have earned the acclaimed Pritzker Prize, the Nobel of the architecture world (Siza Vieira in 1992, Souto de Moura in 2011). The two men are quite close, and they even have offices in the same building. They have collaborated on a handful of projects and, prior to going out on his own, Souto de Moura also worked for Siza Vieira.

On the surface, Siza Vieira's work may seem less than dazzling. Stucco, stone, tile and glass are his building materials of choice. Place means everything in Siza Vieira's work, with geography and climate carefully considered before any plans are laid, regardless of the size or scale of the project. Many of his works are outside the country, although the Serralves Museu de Arte Contemporânea in Porto and the cliffside Boa Nova Casa Chá near Matosinhos are two of his most famous works in Portugal.

Like Siza Vieira, Souto de Moura spurns flashy designs. His works feature minimalist but artful structures that utilise local building materials. The Estádio Municipal de Braga, built for the 2004 European football championship, is set in a former granite quarry (granite from the site was used to make concrete for the stadium). The rock walls of the quarry lie behind one goal; the other side opens to views of the city. Better known is Souto de Moura's design for the Casa das Histórias Paula Rego in Cascais. The red-concrete museum is distinguished by its two pyramid-shaped towers, providing a modern reinterpretation of classic Portuguese shapes (which appear in chimneys, lighthouses, towers and old palaces such as the Palácio Nacional de Sintra).

that is reflected in projects such as the Pavilhão de Portugal for Expo '98, Porto's splendid Museu de Arte Contemporânea and the Igreja de Santa Maria at Marco de Canavezes, south of Amarante. He has also restored central Lisbon's historic Chiado shopping district with notable sensitivity, following a major fire in 1988.

Spanish architect Santiago Calatrava designed the lean, organic monster Gare do Oriente for Expo '98, architecture that is complemented by the work of many renowned contemporary artists. The interior is more state-of-the-art spaceship than station. In the same area lies Lisbon's architectural trailblazer the Parque das Nações, with a bevy of unique designs, including a riverfront park and Europe's largest aquarium. The longest bridge in Europe, the Ponte de Vasco da Gama, built in 1998, stalks out across the river from nearby.

Since the turn of the millennium, Portugal has seen a handful of architecturally ambitious projects come to fruition. One of the grander projects is Rem Koolhaas' Casa da Música in Porto (2005). From a distance, the extremely forward-looking design appears to be a solid white block of carefully cut crystal. Both geometric and defiantly asymmetrical, the building mixes elements of tradition – like *azulejos* (hand-painted tiles) hidden in one room – with high modernism, such as the enormous curtains of corrugated glass flanking the concert stage.

Álvaro Siza: Complete Works 1952–2013, by Philip Jodidio, is an excellent monograph on the great contemporary architect and includes a full catalogue of his work both in Portugal and abroad.

Literary Giants

In 2010 Portugal lost one of its greatest writers when José Saramago died at the age of 87. Known for his discursive, cynical and darkly humorous novels, Saramago gained worldwide attention after winning the Nobel Prize in 1998. His best works mine the depths of the human experience and are often set in a uniquely Portuguese landscape. Sometimes his quasi-magical tales revolve around historic events – like the Christian Siege of Lisbon or the building of the Palácio Nacional de Mafra – while at other times he takes on grander topics (writing, for instance, of Jesus' life as a fallible human being) or even creates modern-day fables (in *Blindness*, everyone on earth suddenly goes blind). As a self-described libertarian communist, Saramago had political views that sometimes landed him in trouble. After his name was removed from a list of nominees for a European literary prize, he went into self-imposed exile, spending the last years of his life in the Canary Islands.

In the shadow of Saramago, António Lobo Antunes is Portugal's other literary great – and many of his admirers say the Nobel committee gave the prize to the wrong Portuguese writer. Antunes produces magical, fast-paced prose, often with dark undertones and vast historical sweeps; some critics compare his work to that of William Faulkner. Antunes' writing reflects his harrowing experience as a field doctor in Angola during Portugal's bloody colonial wars, and he often turns a critical gaze on Portuguese history – setting his novels around colonial wars, the dark days of the Salazar dictatorship and the 1974 revolution. Slowly gaining an international following, Antunes is still active today, and many of his earlier novels have finally been translated into English.

O Crime do Padre Amaro (The Sin of Father Amaro) is a powerful 19th-century novel by José Maria de Eça de Queiroz. The book is set in Portugal, though it was relocated for a popular Mexican film, *El Crimen del Padre Amaro* (2002).

Art of the Tile

Portugal's favourite decorative art is easy to spot. Polished painted tiles called *azulejos* (after the Arabic *al zulaycha*, meaning polished stone) cover everything from churches to train stations. The Moors introduced the art, having picked it up from the Persians, but the Portuguese wholeheartedly adopted it.

Portugal's earliest tiles are Moorish, from Seville. These were decorated with interlocking geometric or floral patterns (figurative representations aren't an option for Muslim artists for religious reasons). After the

PESSOA'S MANY PERSONALITIES

'There's no such man known as Fernando Pessoa', swore Alberto Caeiro, who, truth be told, didn't really exist himself. He was one of more than a dozen heteronyms (identities) adopted by Fernando Pessoa (1888–1935), Portugal's greatest 20th-century poet.

Heralded by literary critics as one of the icons of modernism, Pessoa was also among the stranger characters to wander the streets of Lisbon. He worked as a translator by day (having learned English while living in South Africa as a young boy) and wrote poetry by night – but not just Pessoa's poetry. He took on numerous personas, writing in entirely different styles, representing different philosophies, backgrounds and levels of mastery. Of Pessoa's four primary heteronyms, Alberto Caeiro was regarded as the great master by other heteronyms Alvaro de Campos and Ricardo Reis. (Fernando Pessoa was the fourth heteronym, but his existence, as alluded to earlier, was denied by the other three.) Any one style would have earned Pessoa renown as a major poet of his time, but considered together, the variety places him among the greats of modern literature.

Pessoa for many is inextricably linked to Lisbon. He spent his nights in cafes, writing, drinking and talking until late into the evening, and many of his works are set in Lisbon's old neighbourhoods. Among Pessoa's phobias: lightning and having his photograph taken. You can see a few of the existing photos of him at the Café Martinho da Arcada, one of his regular haunts.

Despite his quirks and brilliance, Pessoa published very little in his lifetime, with his great work *Livro do Desassossego* (Book of Disquiet) only appearing in 1982, 50 years after it was written. In fact, the great bulk of Pessoa's writing was discovered after his death: thousands of manuscript pages lay hidden away inside a wooden trunk. Scholars are still poring over his elusive works.

Portuguese captured Ceuta in Morocco in 1415, they began exploring the art themselves. The 16th-century Italian invention of majolica, in which colours are painted directly onto wet clay over a layer of white enamel, gave works a fresco-like brightness and kicked off the Portuguese *azulejo* love affair.

The earliest homegrown examples, polychrome and geometric, date from the 1580s and may be seen in churches such as Lisbon's Igreja de São Roque, providing an ideal counterbalance to fussy, gold-heavy baroque.

The late 17th century saw a fashion for huge panels depicting everything from saints to seascapes. As demand grew, mass production became necessary and the Netherlands' blue-and-white Delft tiles started appearing.

Portuguese tile makers rose to the challenge of this influx, and the splendid work of virtuosos António de Oliveira Bernardes and his son Policarpo in the 18th century springs from this competitive creativity. You can see their work in Évora, in the impressive Igreja de São João.

By the end of the 18th century, industrial-scale manufacture began to affect quality. There was also massive demand for tiles after the 1755 Lisbon earthquake. (Tiling answered the need for decoration and was cheap and practical – a solution for a population that had felt the ground move beneath its feet.)

From the late 19th century, the art-nouveau and art-deco movements took *azulejos* by storm, providing fantastic facades and interiors for shops, restaurants and residential buildings. Today, *azulejos* still coat contemporary life, and you can explore the latest in *azulejos* in the Lisbon metro. Maria Keil (1914–2012) designed 19 of the stations, from the 1950s onwards – look out for her wild modernist designs at the stations of Rossio, Restauradores, Intendente, Marquês de Pombal, Anjos and Martim Moniz. Oriente also showcases extraordinary contemporary work by artists from five continents.

The Lisbon metro is not just about transport – it's an art gallery, showcasing the best of Portuguese contemporary art and architecture, with especially wonderful *azulejos*. Check out Metro Lisboa's website, www.metrolisboa.pt.

Fine Arts

Early Masters

As Gothic art gave way to more humanistic Renaissance works, Portugal's 15th-century painters developed their own style. Led by the master Nuno Gonçalves, the *escola nacional* (national school) took religious subjects and grounded them against contemporary backgrounds. In Gonçalves' most famous painting, the panels of Santo Antonio (in Lisbon's Museu Nacional de Arte Antiga), he includes a full milieu of Portuguese society – nobles, Jews, fisherfolk, sailors, knights, priests, monks and beggars.

Some of Portugal's finest early paintings emerged from the 16th-century Manueline school. These artists, influenced by Flemish painters, developed a style known for its incredible delicacy, realism and luminous colours. The most celebrated painter of his time was Vasco Fernandes, known as Grão Vasco (1480–1543). His richly hued paintings (still striking five centuries later) hang in a museum in Viseu dedicated to his work – as well as that of his Manueline school colleague Gaspar Vaz. Meanwhile, sculptors including Diogo de Boitaca went wild with Portuguese seafaring fantasies and exuberant decoration on some of Portugal's icons.

Top Art Museums

Museu Nacional do Azulejo (Lisbon)

Casa das Histórias Paula Rego (Cascais)

Museu Nacional de Arte Antiga (Lisbon)

Museu Amadeo de Souza-Cardoso (Amarante)

Museu Grão Vasco (Viseu)

Star of Óbidos

The 17th century saw a number of talented Portuguese artists emerge. One of the best was Josefa de Óbidos, who enjoyed success as a female artist – an extreme rarity in those days. Josefa's paintings were unique in their personal, sympathetic interpretations of religious subjects and for their sense of innocence. Although she studied at an Augustine convent as a young girl, she left without taking the vows and settled in Óbidos (where she got her nickname). Still she maintained close ties to the church, which provided many of her commissions, and remained famously chaste until her death in 1684. Josefa left one of the finest legacies of work of any Portuguese painter. She excelled in richly coloured still lifes and detailed religious works, ignoring established iconography.

Naturalism

In the 19th century naturalism was the dominant trend, with a handful of innovators pushing Portuguese art in new directions. Columbano Bordalo Pinheiro, who hailed from a family of artists, was a seminal figure among the Portuguese artists of his time. He played a prominent role in the Leã d'Ouro, a group of distinguished artists, writers and intellectuals

THE FANTASTICAL WORLD OF PAULA REGO

The conservative Salazar years of the mid-20th century didn't create the ideal environment to nurture contemporary creativity, and many artists left the country. These include Portugal's best-known living artist, Paula Rego, who was born in Lisbon in 1935 but has been a resident of the UK since 1951. Rego's signature style developed around fairy-tale paintings with a nightmarish twist. Her works deal in ambiguity and psychological and sexual tension, such as *The Family* (1988), where a seated businessman is either being tortured or smothered with affection by his wife and daughter. Domination, fear, sexuality and grief are all recurring themes in Rego's paintings, and the mysterious and sinister atmosphere, heavy use of chiaroscuro (stark contrasting of light and shade) and strange distortion of scale are reminiscent of the work of surrealists Max Ernst and Giorgio de Chirico.

Rego is considered one of the great early champions of painting from a female perspective and she continues to add to a substantial volume of work. Her acclaim is growing, particularly with the opening of the Casa das Histórias Paula Rego, in Cascais, which showcases her work.

who gathered in the capital and were deeply involved in the aesthetic trends of the day. A prolific artist, Pinheiro painted some of the luminaries of his time, including the novelist Eça de Queirós and Teófilo Braga (a celebrated writer who later became president of the early republic). One of his best-known works is a haunting portrait of the poet Antero de Quental, who later died by suicide.

20th Century

Building on the works of the naturalists, Amadeo de Souza-Cardoso lived a short but productive life, experimenting with new techniques emerging in Europe. Raised in a sleepy village outside Amarante, he studied architecture at the Academia de Belas Artes in Lisbon but soon dropped out and moved to Paris. There he found his calling as a painter and mingled with the leading artists and writers of the time, including Amedeo Modigliani, Gertrude Stein, Max Jacob and many others. He experimented with impressionism, and later cubism and futurism, and created a captivating body of work, though he is little known outside Portugal.

José Sobral de Almada Negreiros delved even deeper into futurism, inspired by the Italian futurist Filippo Tommaso Marinetti. His work encompassed richly hued portraits with abstract geometrical details – an example is his famous 1954 portrait of Fernando Pessoa – and he was also a sculptor, writer and critic. He managed to walk a fine line during the Salazar regime, creating large-scale murals by public commission as well as socially engaged works critical of Portuguese society.

Saudade: the Portuguese Blues

The Portuguese psyche is a complicated thing, particularly when it comes to elusive concepts like *saudade*. In its purest form, *saudade* is the nostalgic, often deeply melancholic longing for something: a person, a place or just about anything that's no longer obtainable. *Saudade* is profoundly connected to the seafaring nation's history and remains deeply intertwined with Portuguese identity. The emotion has played a starring role in some of Portugal's great works of art – in film, in literature and, most importantly, in music.

Roots of Saudade

Scholars are unable to pinpoint exactly when the term *saudade* first arose. Some trace it back to the grand voyages during the Age of Discoveries, when sailors, captains and explorers spent many months at sea, and the term gave voice to the longing for the lives they left behind. Yet even before the epic voyages across the ocean, Portugal was a nation of seafarers, and *saudade* probably arose from those on terra firma – the women who longed for the men who spent endless days out at sea, some of whom never returned.

In Brazil, 30 January is set aside as the Dia de Saudade (Saudade Day). It's a fine day to engage in a bit of nostalgic longing for past lovers, distant homelands and better days.

Naturally, emigration is also deeply linked to *saudade*. Long one of Europe's poorest peoples, the Portuguese were often driven by hardship to seek better lives abroad. Until recently, this usually meant the men leaving behind their families to travel to northern Europe or America to find work. Families sometimes waited years before being reunited, with emigrants experiencing years of painful longing for their homeland – for the familiar faces and foods, and village life. Many did eventually return, but of course things had changed and so *saudade* reappeared, this time in the form of longing for the way things were in the past.

Nation of Emigrants

The great discoveries of Portuguese seafarers had profound effects on the country's demographics. With the birth and expansion of an empire, Portuguese settled in trading posts in Africa and Asia, but the colony of Brazil drew the biggest numbers of early Portuguese emigrants. They cleared the land (harvesting the Brazil wood that gave the colony its name), set up farms and went about the slow, steady task of nation building – with help, of course, from the millions of slaves brought forcibly from Africa. Numbers vary widely, but an estimated half-a-million Portuguese settled in Brazil during the colonial period, prior to independence in 1822, and over 400,000 flooded in during the second half of the 19th century.

Goa, India, still has vestiges of its Portuguese colonial past. In Margão, on the street named Rua das Saudades, there are Christian and Muslim cemeteries and a Hindu cremation ground.

By the 1900s, Portuguese began emigrating in large numbers to other parts of the world. The US and Canada received over half-a-million immigrants, with huge numbers heading to France, Germany, Venezuela and Argentina. The 1960s saw another surge of emigrants, as young men fled the country in order to avoid the draft that would send them to fight bloody colonial wars in Africa. The 1974 revolution also preceded a big exodus, as those associated with the Salazar regime went abroad rather than face reprisals.

What all these emigrants had in common was the deep sadness of leaving their homeland to struggle in foreign lands. Those left behind were also in a world of heartache – wives left to raise children alone, villages deserted of young men, families torn apart. The numbers are staggering: over three million emigrants between 1890 and 1990; no other European country apart from Ireland lost as many people to emigration.

The most famous Portuguese emigrant to Brazil was the future king himself. When Napoleon invaded in 1807, the royal family and their extensive retinue fled to Brazil, where they installed themselves in Rio de Janeiro. Many royal retainers never returned home; Dom João VI returned only in 1822.

Saudade in Literature

One of the first great Portuguese works of literature that explores the theme of *saudade* is *Os Lusíadas* (The Lusiads; The Portuguese). Luís Vaz de Camões mixes mythology with historical events in his verse epic about the Age of Discoveries of the 15th and 16th centuries. The heroic adventurer Vasco da Gama and other explorers strive for glory, but many never return, facing hardships such as sea monsters and treacherous kings along the way. First-hand experience informed Camões' work: he served in the overseas militia, lost an eye in Ceuta in a battle with the Moors, served prison time in Portugal and survived a shipwreck in the Mekong (swimming ashore with his unfinished manuscript held aloft, according to legend).

The great 19th-century Portuguese writer Almeida Garrett wrote an even more compelling take on the Age of Discoveries. In his book *Camões*, a biography of the poet, he describes the longing Camões felt for Portugal while in exile. He also captured the greater sense of *saudade* that so many experienced as Portugal's empire crumbled in the century following the great explorations.

More recent writers also explore the notion of *saudade*, though they take radically different approaches from their predecessors. Contemporary writer António Lobo Antunes deconstructs *saudade* in cynical tales that expose the nostalgic longing for something as a form of neurotic self-delusion. In *As Naus* (The Return of the Caravels; 1988), he turns the discovery myth on its head when, four centuries after da Gama's voyage, the great explorers, through some strange time warp, become entangled with the *retornados* (who returned to Portugal in the 1970s, after the loss of the country's African empire) as Renaissance-era achievements collapse in the poor, grubby, lower-class neighbourhoods of Lisbon.

Saudade in Film

The national music of Cape Verde, a former Portuguese colony, is *morna*, a distant cousin of fado, with plaintive songs revolving around lost loves and homesickness. Renowned 'barefoot diva' Cesária Évora (1941–2011) produced many hits, including 'Sodade' (Creole for '*saudade*').

Portugal's most prolific film-maker, Manoel de Oliveira (1908-2015), was making films well past his 100th birthday. In a career that spanned 75 years, he became known for carefully crafted, if slow-moving, films that delve deep into the world of *saudade* – of growing old, unrequited loves and longing for things that no longer exist. In *Viagem ao Princípio do Mundo* (Voyage to the Beginning of the World; 1997), several companions make a nostalgic tour of the rugged landscapes and traditional villages of the north – one in search of a past that he knows only in his dreams (having heard of his ancestral land from his Portuguese-born father), another haunted by a world that no longer exists (the places of his childhood having been uprooted). Past and present, nostalgia and reality collide in this quiet, meditative film. It stars a frail, 72-year-old Marcello Mastroianni as Oliveira's alter ego; this was the actor's final film before he died.

One of the finest love letters to the capital is the sweet, meandering *Lisbon Story* (1994), directed by German film-maker Wim Wenders. The story follows a sound engineer who goes in search of a missing director, discovering the city through the footage his friend left behind. Carefully crafted scenes conjure up the mystery and forlorn beauty of Lisbon (and other parts of Portugal, including a wistful sequence on the dramatic cliffs of Cabo Espichel). *Saudade* here explores many different realms, inspired in large part by the ethereal soundtrack by Madredeus – band members also play supporting roles in the film.

Fado

'I don't sing fado. It sings me.'

Amália Rodrigues

Portugal's most famous style of music, fado (Portuguese for 'fate'), couldn't really exist without *saudade*. These melancholic songs are dripping with emotion – and they revel in stories of the painful twists and turns of fate, of unreachable distant lovers, fathomless yearning for one's homeland and wondrous days that have come and gone. The emotional quality of the singing plays just as important a role as technical skill, helping fado to reach across linguistic boundaries. Listening to fado is perhaps the easiest way of understanding *saudade*, in all its evocative variety.

Although fado is something of a national treasure – in 2011 it was added to Unesco's list of the World's Intangible Cultural Heritage – it's really the music of Lisbon. (In the university town of Coimbra, fado exists in a different, slightly more cerebral form: it's exclusively men, often students or alumni, who sing of love, bohemian life and the city itself.) No one quite knows fado's origins, though African and Brazilian rhythms, Moorish chants and the songs of Provençal troubadors may have influenced the sound. What is clear is that, by the 19th century, fado could be heard all over the traditional working-class neighbourhoods of Mouraria and Alfama, usually in brothels and seedy taverns. It was the anthem of the poor, and it maintained an unsavoury reputation until the late 19th century, when the upper classes took an interest in the music and brought it into the mainstream.

Fado remained an obscure, mostly local experience until the 20th century, when it received national and later international attention. One singer who played a major role in its popularisation was Amália Rodrigues, the 'queen of fado', who became a household name in the 1940s. Born to a poor family in 1920, Amália took the music from the tavern to the concert hall, and then into households via radio and onto film screens, starring in the 1947 film *Capas Negras* (Black Capes). She had some of Portugal's best poets and writers of the day writing songs for

The film *Fados* (2007) is Spanish director Carlos Saura's love letter to the great Portuguese music. The film features the singing of fado legends like Camané and Mariza as well as genre-defying singers not often associated with the art – Brazilian singers Caetano Veloso and Chico Buarque, among others.

SAUDADE OF THE JEWS

Until the end of the 15th century, Jews enjoyed a prominent place in Portuguese society. The treasurer of Dom Afonso V (1432–81) was Jewish, as were others who occupied diplomatic posts and worked as trade merchants, physicians and cartographers. Jews from other countries were welcomed in Portugal, including those expelled from Spain in 1492. Eventually, pressure from the church and from Spain forced the king's hand, and in 1497 Manuel I decreed that all Jews convert to Christianity or leave the country. A catalogue of horrors followed, including the massacre of thousands of Jews in 1506 by mobs run riot and two centuries of the bloody Inquisition that kicked off in 1536.

Aside from a secretive Crypto-Jewish group in Belmonte that managed to preserve their faith, the Judaic community slowly withered and perished. Those who converted felt the heart-rending *saudade* of deep loss – essentially the loss of their identity. Once flourishing Jewish neighbourhoods died as residents went into exile or perhaps suffered arrest, torture and even execution. The personal losses paralleled the end of a flourishing and tolerant period in Portugal's history and effectively ended the Jewish presence in Portugal.

BRAZILIAN SAUDADE & BOSSA NOVA

Brazilian identity is also deeply connected to *saudade*, which isn't surprising given the influence Portugal has had on the country – nearly every inhabitant in Brazil can trace Portuguese roots somewhere in the family tree. In Brazil, *saudade* means much the same thing, and it has played a role in shaping the country's music – in particular, bossa nova. The 1958 hit 'Chega de Saudade' (often poorly translated as 'No More Blues'), by legendary songwriting team Tom Jobim and Vinícius de Moraes, is considered one of the first bossa nova songs ever recorded. In it, the singer pines for his lover, who has left him, and commands his sadness to go out and bring her back. Melancholic chords and a slow, wistful singing style are hallmarks here, as they are of nearly all bossa nova tunes. And even if you can't understand Portuguese, you'll still feel the sadness and deep sense of loss.

her. Yet, along the way, she had her share of ups and downs – depression, illness, failed love affairs – and her heart-rending fado was more than an abstraction.

Amália enjoyed wide acclaim, although her reputation was sullied following the 1974 revolution when she was criticised for tacitly supporting the Salazar regime (although there is little evidence of that). Fado's popularity slipped in the postrevolution days, when the Portuguese were eager to make a clean break with the past. (Salazar spoke of throwing the masses the three F's – fado, football and Fátima – to keep them happily occupied.) The 1990s, however, saw a resurgence of fado's popularity, with the opening of new fado houses and the emergence of new fado voices. Amália's reputation was also rehabilitated. Upon her death at age 79 in 1999, Portugal declared three days of national mourning and suspended the general-election campaign in her honour. She is buried in the Panteão Nacional (National Pantheon).

For more on Amália Rodrigues, check out the fine documentary *The Art of Amália* (2000), directed by Bruno de Almeida. The biopic *Amália* (2008), by Carlos Coelho da Silva, provides an in-depth portrait of a Rodrigues that few ever saw.

While fado may bring to mind dark bars of the Salazar years, this is not a musical form stuck in time. Contemporary performers and exponents of a new fado style include the dynamic *fadista* Mísia, who experimented with full band instrumentation. The Mozambique-born singer Mariza has earned accolades for her extraordinary voice and fresh, eclectic approach. She continues to break new ground in albums like *Terra* (2008) that bring in world music – African rhythms, flamenco, Latin sounds and jazz. Another one to watch is Carminho, a young singer with a powerful and mournful voice. Fado runs deep in her veins – her mother was the owner of one of Lisbon's most traditional fado houses (now closed), where as a young girl she heard the best *fadistas* of the time. The men aren't outdone: one of the great male voices in traditional fado these days is Camané.

Fados are traditionally sung by one performer accompanied by a 12-string Portuguese *guitarra* (pear-shaped guitar). When two *fadistas* perform, they sometimes engage in *desgarrada*, a bit of improvisational one-upmanship where the singers challenge and play off one another. At fado houses there are usually a number of singers, each one traditionally singing three songs.

Survival Guide

Directory A–Z

Accommodation

Seasons

In popular tourist destinations prices rise and fall with the seasons. Mid-June to mid-September are firmly high season (book well ahead); May to mid-June and mid-September to October are midseason; and other times are low season, when you can get some really good deals. Outside the resorts, prices don't vary much between seasons.

In the Algarve, you'll pay the highest premium for rooms from mid-July to the end of August, with slightly lower prices from June to mid-July and in September, and substantially less (as much as 50%) if you travel between November and April. Note that a handful of places in the Algarve close in winter.

We list July (high-season) prices in reviews.

Guesthouses

Guesthouses are small-scale budget or midrange accommodations, with a personal feel that can be lacking in larger hotels. Most of them are family-run places.

There are various types of guesthouses; prices typically range from €50 to €90 for a double room with private bathroom (and as little as €35 for the simplest lodgings with shared bathrooms).

Hostels

Portugal has scores of hostels, particularly in Lisbon and Porto. If you're thinking bare-bones, smelly, backpacker lodging, think again. Lisbon's hostels are among the best in Europe, with stylish design, often in heritage buildings, and excellent amenities.

- High-season dorm beds typically cost around €20. Many hostels also offer simple doubles with shared bathrooms, and some have small apartments.
- Bed linen and breakfast are usually included in the price. Standard features include kitchens, lounges with wi-fi access and computers for guest use.
- In summer reserve ahead, especially for doubles.
- Many of the hostels outside Lisbon are part of the **Pousadas da Juventude network** (www.pousadasjuventude.pt) affiliated with Hostelling International (HI).
- If you don't have a HI card, you can get a guest card, which requires six stamps (€2 per time) – one from each hostel you stay at – after which you have paid for your membership.

Pousadas

In 1942 the government started the Pousadas de Portugal (www.pousadas.pt), turning castles, monasteries and palaces into luxurious hotels, roughly divided into rural and historic options. Today the *pousadas* are run by Pestana, a Portuguese company and member of the Historic Hotels of Europe. July prices range from €120 to €250; prices in August are €10 to €20 more. Most *pousadas* are cheaper during the week; they have lots of discounts and deals, plus reduced prices for those aged over 55.

SLEEPING PRICE RANGES

The following price ranges refer to a double room with bathroom in high season. Unless otherwise stated breakfast is included in the price.

CATEGORY	COST
€	less than €60
€€	€60–€120
€€€	more than €120

Turihab Properties

These charming properties are part of a government scheme, through which you can stay in a farmhouse, manor house, country estate or rustic cottage as the owner's guest.

High-season rates for two people, either in a double room or a cottage, range from €70 to €140. Some properties have swimming pools, and most include breakfast (often provided with fresh local produce).

There are three types of Turihab lodgings:

Aldeias de Portugal (www.aldeiasdeportugal.pt) Lodging in rural villages in the north, often in beautifully converted stone cottages.

Casas no Campo (www.casasnocampo.net) Country houses, cottages and luxury villas.

Solares de Portugal (www.solaresdeportugal.pt) Grand manor houses, some of which date from the 17th or 18th century.

BOOK YOUR STAY ONLINE

For more accommodation reviews by Lonely Planet authors, check out http://lonelyplanet.com/hotels/. You'll find independent reviews, as well as recommendations on the best places to stay. Best of all, you can book online.

Camping & Holiday Parks

Camping is popular in Portugal; there are many campgrounds, often in good locations and situated near beaches. Prices for sites are typically calculated per person, per tent and per vehicle – usually €4.50 to €6.50 for each. Keep in mind that many sites get crowded and noisy at busy times (especially during July and August).

- Nearly all campgrounds have hot showers, electrical hookups and a cafe. The best campgrounds also have a pool, restaurant, laundry service, children's playgrounds and perhaps a tennis court.
- Generally, campgrounds that are run by **Orbitur** (☎226 061 360; www.orbitur.pt) offer the best services. Some towns have municipal campsites, which can vary in quality.
- For detailed listings of some 228 campsites nationwide, pick up the *Roteiro Campista* (€8; www.roteiro-campista.pt) publication, updated annually and sold at *turismos* and bookshops. It contains details of most of the Portuguese campgrounds, with maps and directions.

Private Rooms

In coastal resorts, mostly in summer, you can often rent a *quarto* (private room) in a

PRACTICALITIES

Weights & measures Portugal uses the metric system. Decimals are indicated by commas, thousands by points.

Newspapers Main newspapers include *Diário de Noticias, Público, Jornal de Noticias* and the tabloid bestseller *Correio da Manhã*. English-language newspapers include the long-running daily, the *Portugal News* (www.theportugalnews.com), and the weekly *Algarve Resident* (www.algarveresident.com).

Radio Portugal's national radio stations include state-owned Rádiodifusão Portuguesa (RDP), which runs the stations Antena 1, 2 and 3 and plays Portuguese broadcasts and evening music (Lisbon frequencies are 95.7, 94.4 and 100.3). For English-language radio there is the BBC World Service (Lisbon 90.2) and Voice of America (VOA), or a few Algarve-based stations, such as Kiss (95.8 and 101.2).

Television TV channels in Portugal include Rádio Televisão Portuguesa (RTP-1 and RTP-2), Sociedade Independente (SIC) and TV Independente (TV1), with RTP-2 providing the best selection of foreign films and world-news coverage. Other stations fill the airwaves with a mix of Portuguese and Brazilian soaps, game shows and dubbed or subtitled foreign films.

Video system Portugal uses the PAL video system, incompatible with both the French SECAM system and the North American NTSC system.

Smoking Allowed in some restaurants and most bars. Restaurants that allow smoking are supposed to have separate smoking sections, but inadequate ventilation means nonsmokers will be breathing in the fumes. Many hotels still offer smoking rooms.

private house. These usually have a shared bathroom, are cheap and clean, and might remind you of a stay with an elderly aunt. Prices generally run from €35 to €45 per double.

Rental Accommodation

Plenty of villas and cottages are available for rent. Choose Portugal (www.chooseportugal.com) lists hundreds of private houses and apartments that are for rent.

Customs Regulations

You can bring as much currency as you like into Portugal, though €10,000 or more must be declared.

The duty-free allowance for travellers more than 17 years old from non-EU countries:

➡ 200 cigarettes or the equivalent in tobacco

➡ 1L of alcohol that's more than 22% alcohol, or 2L of wine or beer.

Allowance for nationals of EU countries:

➡ 800 cigarettes or the equivalent

➡ 10L of spirits, 20L of fortified wine, 60L of sparkling wine or a mind-boggling 90L of still wine or 110L of beer.

Discount Cards

➡ Portugal's network of *pousadas da juventude* (youth hostels) is part of the Hostelling International (HI) network. An HI card from your hostelling association at home entitles you to the standard cheap rates.

➡ A student card will get you reduced admission to almost all sights. Likewise, those aged over 65 with proof of age will save cash.

➡ If you plan to do a lot of sightseeing in Portugal's main cities, the Lisboa Card and Porto Card are sensible investments. Sold at tourist offices, these cards allows discounts or free admission to many attractions and free travel on public transport.

Electricity

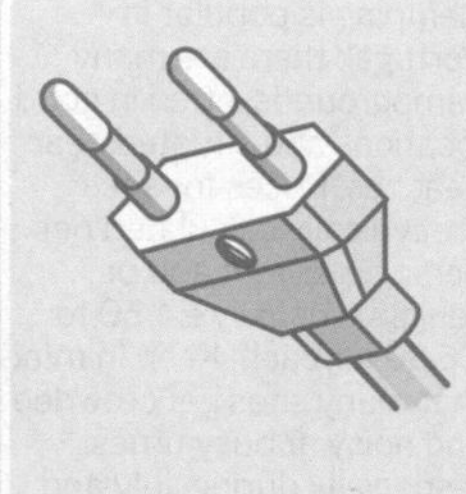

230V/50Hz

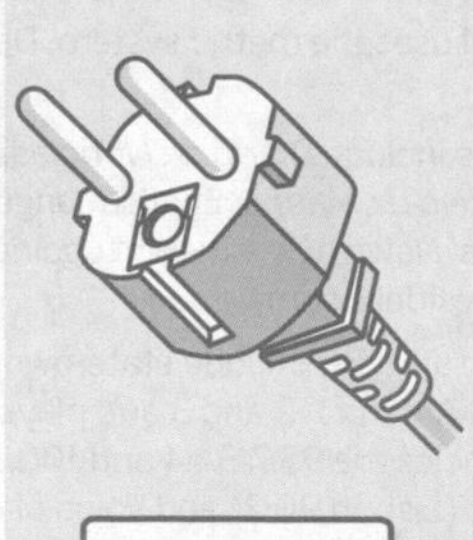

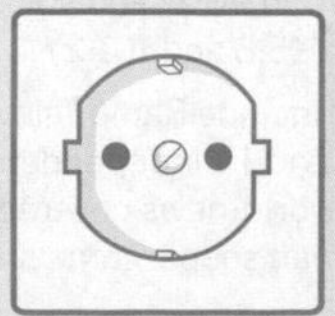

230V/50Hz

Embassies & Consulates

There's no New Zealand consulate in Portugal. The nearest New Zealand embassy is in **Madrid** (☎91 523 02 26; www.mfat.govt.nz/en/embassies; 3rd fl, Calle de Pinar 7, Madrid). The following embassies are in Lisbon; the Spanish consulate is in Porto and the UK Consulate is in Portimão.

Australian Embassy (☎213 101 500; www.portugal.embassy.gov.au; Av da Liberdade 200, 2nd fl)

Canadian Embassy (☎213 164 600; www.canadainternational.gc.ca; Avenida da Liberdade 198-200, Edifício Victoria; ⊙8.30am-12.30pm & 1-5.15pm Mon-Thu, 8.30am-1pm Fri)

French Embassy (☎213 939 294; www.ambafrance-pt.org; Rua Santos-o-Velho 5)

German Embassy (☎218 810 210; www.lissabon.diplo.de; Campo dos Mártires da Pátria 38)

Irish Embassy (☎213 308 200; www.embassyofireland.pt; Av da Liberdade 200, 4th fl)

Netherlands Embassy (☎213 914 900; http://portugal.nlembaixada.org; Av Infante Santo 43)

Spanish Consulate (☎225 363 915; Rua de Dom João IV 341; ⊙9am-2pm Mon-Fri)

Spanish Embassy (☎213 472 384; www.exteriores.gob.es; Rua do Salitre 1; ⊙9am-2pm Mon-Fri)

UK Consulate (☎282 490 750; www.gov.uk/government/world/portugal; Avenida Guanaré; ⊙9.30am-2pm Mon, Wed & Fri)

UK Embassy (☎213 924 000; www.gov.uk/government/world/portugal; Rua de Saõ Bernardo 33)

US Embassy (☎217 273 300; http://portugal.usembassy.gov; Av das Forças Armadas)

GLBTI Travellers

In 2010 Portugal legalised gay marriage, becoming the sixth European country to do so. Most Portuguese profess a laissez-faire attitude about same-sex couples, although how out you can be depends on where you are in Portugal. In Lisbon, Porto and the Algarve, acceptance has increased, whereas in most other areas, same-sex couples would be met with incomprehension. In this conservative Catholic country, homosexuality is still outside the norm. And while homophobic violence is extremely rare, discrimination has been reported in schools and workplaces.

Lisbon has the country's best gay and lesbian network and nightlife. Lisbon and Porto hold Gay Pride marches, but outside these events the gay community keeps a discreet profile.

Health

Portugal has a high-quality healthcare system, with pharmacies and doctors readily available countrywide.

Before You Go

HEALTH INSURANCE

Citizens of the EU are eligible for free emergency medical treatment if they have a European Health Insurance Card (EHIC), which replaces the no-longer-valid E111 certificate. It will not cover you for nonemergencies or emergency repatriation.

Citizens from other countries should find out if there is a reciprocal arrangement for free medical care between their country and Portugal. If you do need health insurance, consider a policy that covers you for the worst possible scenario, such as an accident requiring an emergency flight home. Find out in advance if your insurance plan will make payments directly to providers or reimburse you later for overseas health expenditures.

RECOMMENDED VACCINATIONS

The WHO recommends that all travellers should be covered for diphtheria, tetanus, measles, mumps, rubella and polio, regardless of their destination. Since most vaccines don't produce immunity until at least two weeks after they're given, visit a physician at least six weeks before departure.

In Portugal

AVAILABILITY & COST OF HEALTH CARE

Good health care is readily available and for minor illnesses pharmacists can give valuable advice and sell over-the-counter medication. Most pharmacists speak some English. They can also advise when more specialised help is required and point you in the right direction.

HEAT EXHAUSTION & HEAT STROKE

Be mindful of heat exhaustion, particularly on hot summer days in the Algarve, and when engaging in vigorous outdoor activities anywhere in the country during the hottest months. Heat exhaustion occurs following excessive fluid loss with inadequate replacement of fluids and salt. Symptoms include headache, dizziness and tiredness. To treat heat exhaustion, replace lost fluids by drinking water and/or fruit juice or an oral rehydration solution, such as Dioralyte, and cool the body with cold water and fans.

Heat stroke is much more serious, resulting in irrational and hyperactive behaviour and eventually loss of consciousness and death. Medical treatment should be sought. Rapid cooling by spraying the body with water and fanning is ideal. Emergency fluid and electrolyte replacement by intravenous drip is recommended.

JELLYFISH & SEA URCHINS

In general, jellyfish aren't a major problem in Portuguese waters, though there are rare sightings along the southern beaches. Stings from jellyfish are painful but not dangerous. Douse the wound in vinegar to deactivate any stingers that haven't 'fired'. Applying calamine lotion, antihistamines or analgesics may reduce the reaction and relieve the pain.

Watch for sea urchins around rocky beaches. If needles become embedded in skin, immerse the limb in hot water to relieve the pain. To avoid infection visit a doctor and have the needles removed.

RABIES

Rabies, though rare in Portugal, is a risk, and it is transmitted via the bite of an infected animal. It can also be transmitted if the animal's saliva comes in contact with an open wound. If you've been bitten by a wild animal, begin a treatment of shots at once.

TAP WATER

Tap water is generally safe to drink in Portugal.

TRAVEL HEALTH WEBSITES

It's a good idea to consult your government's travel-health website before departure, if one is available:

Australia (www.smarttraveller.gov.au)

Canada (www.travel.gc.ca)

UK (www.fitfortravel.nhs.uk)

USA (http://wwwnc.cdc.gov/travel)

GOVERNMENT TRAVEL ADVICE

The following government websites offer travel advisories and information on current hot spots.

Australian Department of Foreign Affairs (www.smarttraveller.gov.au)

British Foreign Office (www.gov.uk/foreign-travel-advice)

Canadian Department of Foreign Affairs (www.travel.gc.ca)

US State Department (http://travel.state.gov)

Insurance

Don't leave home without a travel-insurance policy to cover theft, loss and medical problems. You should get insurance for the worst-case scenario; for example, an accident or illness requiring hospitalisation and a flight home.

Check the small print in your insuance policy as some policies contain terms that specifically exclude 'dangerous activities' such as scuba diving, motorcycling or even trekking. If these activities are in your sights, either find another policy or ask about an amendment (usually available for an extra premium) that includes them.

Make sure you keep all documentation for any claims later on. Some policies ask you to call back (reverse charges) to a centre in your home country, where an immediate assessment of your problem is made.

Worldwide travel insurance is available at www.lonelyplanet.com/travel-insurance. You can buy, extend and claim online any time – even if you're already on the road.

Internet Access

Wi-fi access is widespread in Portugal. If you have your own laptop, most hotels, hostels and midrange guesthouses offer free wireless access. Many cafes and some restaurants also offer free wi-fi. Cybercafes are now rare.

We use the icon @ to indicate places that have a physical computer where guests can access the internet; the wi-fi icon indicates where wireless access is available.

Other options:

Bibliotecas municipais Municipal libraries.

Rede de Espaços Internet (www.rededeespacosinternet.pt) Municipally run spaces where you can get online for free.

Legal Matters

➡ Fines for illegal parking are common. If you're parked illegally you'll be towed and will have to pay around €100 to get your car back. Be aware of local road rules, as fines for other transgressions will also be enforced.

➡ It's illegal in Portugal to drive while talking on a mobile phone.

➡ Narcotic drugs were decriminalised in 2001 in an attempt to clear up the public-health problems among drug users and to address the issue as a social rather than a criminal one. You may be brought before a commission and subject to fines or treatment if you are caught with up to 10 doses of a drug.

➡ Drug dealing is still a serious offence and suspects may be held for up to 18 months before coming to trial. Bail is at the court's discretion.

Maps

National and natural park offices usually have simple park maps, though these are of little use for trekking or cycling. The following offer a good range of maps:

Omni Resources (www.omnimap.com) US company that sells excellent maps, including 1:25,000 topographic maps.

Stanfords (www.stanfords.co.uk) Good selection of Portugal maps and travel products in the UK.

Money

Portugal uses the euro, along with most other European nations.

ATMs & Eftpos

ATMs are the easiest way to get cash in Portugal, and they are easy to find in most cities and towns. Tiny rural villages probably won't have ATMs, so it's wise to get cash in advance. Most banks have a Multibanco ATM, with menus in English (and other languages), that accepts Visa, Access, MasterCard, Cirrus and so on. You just need your card and PIN. Keep in mind that the ATM limit is €200 per withdrawal, and many banks charge a foreign transaction fee (typically around 2% to 3%).

Credit & Debit Cards

Most hotels and smarter restaurants accept credit cards; smaller guesthouses, budget hotels and smaller restaurants might not, so it's wise to have cash with you.

Money Changers

Note that banks and *bureaux de change* are free to set their own rates and commissions, so a low commission might mean a skewed exchange rate.

Taxes & Refunds

Prices in Portugal almost always include 23% VAT (some basic foodstuffs and services carry reduced rates of 6% and 13%, respectively). Non-EU passport holders can claim back the VAT on goods from participating retailers – be sure to ask for the tax-back forms and get them stamped by customs. Refunds are processed at the airport or via post.

Opening Hours

Opening hours vary throughout the year. We provide high-season opening hours; hours will generally decrease in the shoulder and low seasons.

Banks 8.30am–3pm Monday to Friday

Bars 7pm–2am

Cafes 9am–7pm

Clubs 11pm–4am Thursday to Saturday

Restaurants noon–3pm & 7–10pm

Shopping malls 10am–10pm

Shops 9.30am–noon & 2–7pm Monday to Friday, 10am–1pm Saturday

Post

Post offices are called CTT (www.ctt.pt). *Correio normal* (ordinary mail) goes in the red letterboxes, *correio azul* (airmail) goes in the blue boxes. Automated red postal stands dispense stamps, saving you the hassle of waiting in line at the post office. Post to Europe takes up to five working days, and up to seven for the rest of the world. Economy mail (or surface airlift) is about a third cheaper but takes a week or so longer.

Public Holidays

Banks, offices, department stores and some shops close on the public holidays listed here. On New Year's Day, Easter Sunday, Labour Day and Christmas Day, even *turismos* close.

New Year's Day 1 January

Carnaval Tuesday February/March – the day before Ash Wednesday

Good Friday March/April

Liberty Day 25 April

Labour Day 1 May

Corpus Christi May/June – ninth Thursday after Easter

Portugal Day 10 June – also known as Camões and Communities Day

Feast of the Assumption 15 August

Republic Day 5 October

All Saints' Day 1 November

Independence Day 1 December

Feast of the Immaculate Conception 8 December

Christmas Day 25 December

Safe Travel

➡ Once behind the wheel of a car, the otherwise mild-mannered Portuguese change personality. Aggressive driving, such as tailgating at high speeds and overtaking on blind corners, is all too common. Portugal has one of the highest road accident rates in Europe. Police have responded by aggressively patrolling certain dangerous routes, such as on the cheerfully named 'highway of death' from Salamanca in Spain.

➡ Compared with other European countries, Portugal's crime rate remains low, but some types of crime – including car theft – are on the rise. Crime against foreigners is of the usual rush-hour-pickpocketing, bag-snatching and theft-from-rental-cars variety. Take the usual precautions: don't flash your cash; keep valuables in a safe place; and, if you're challenged, hand it over – it's not worth taking the risk.

➡ Take care in the water; the surf can be strong, with dangerous ocean currents.

Telephone

To call Portugal from abroad, dial the international access code (☎00), then Portugal's country code (☎351), then the number. All domestic numbers have nine digits, and there are no area codes. Most public phones accept phonecards only – available at most news stands – though a few coin-operated phones are still around. You can also make calls from booths in Portugal Telecom offices and some post offices – pay when your call is finished.

Long-distance and international calls have cheaper rates from 9pm to 9am weekdays, all weekend and on holidays.

Mobile Phones

Portugal uses the GSM 900/1800 frequency, the same as found in Australia, the UK and the rest of the EU. Mobile-phone usage is widespread in Portugal, with extensive coverage provided in all but the most rural areas. The main domestic operators are Vodafone, Optimus and TMN. All of them sell prepaid SIM cards that you can insert into a GSM mobile phone and use as long as the phone is not locked by the company providing you service. If you need a phone, you can buy one at the airport or at shops throughout the country with a package of minutes for under €20. This is generally cheaper than renting a phone.

Time

Portugal, like Britain, is on GMT/UTC in winter and GMT/UTC plus one hour in summer. This puts it an hour earlier than Spain year-round. Clocks are set forward by an hour on the last Sunday in March and back on the last Sunday in October.

Toilets

Finding public toilets in major cities such as Lisbon and Porto can be difficult. Most towns and villages that draw tourists have free public toilets. The *mercado municipal* (municipal market) often has free toilets. These are generally fairly clean and adequately maintained. In more built-up areas, your best bet is to look for a toilet in a shopping centre or simply duck into a cafe.

Tourist Information

➡ Turismo de Portugal, the country's national tourist board, operates a handy website: www.visitportugal.com.

➡ Locally managed *postos de turismo* (tourist offices, usually signposted '*turismo*') are everywhere, offering brochures and varying degrees of infomation and help with sights and accommodation.

Travellers with Disabilities

➡ The term *deficientes* (Portuguese for 'disabled') gives some indication of the limited awareness of disabled needs. Although public offices and agencies are required to provide access and facilities for people with disabilities, private businesses are not.

➡ Lisbon airport is wheelchair accessible, while Porto and Faro airports have accessible toilets.

➡ Parking spaces are allotted in many places, but are frequently occupied. The EU parking card entitles visitors to the same street-parking concessions given to disabled residents.

➡ Newer and larger hotels tend to have some rooms which have been adapted, though the facilities may not be up to scratch; ask at the local *turismo*.

➡ Most campgrounds have accessible toilets and some hostels have facilities for people with disabilities.

➡ Lisbon, with its cobbled streets and hills, may be difficult for some travellers with disabilities, but not impossible. The Baixa's flat grid and Belém are fine, and all the sights at Parque das Nações are accessible.

Download Lonely Planet's free Accessible Travel guide from http://lptravel.to/AccessibleTravel, or to obatin more information, contact one of the following listed organisations:

Accessible Portugal (☎926 910 989; www.accessibleportugal.com; Rua Jorge Barradas 50, 4th fl) This Lisbon-based tour agency offers a wide range of itineraries and can arrange accommodation, transfers, overnight trips and outdoor activities such as tandem skydiving and hot-air balloon trips.

Cooperativa Nacional de Apoio Deficientes (☎218 595 332; www.facebook.com/cooperativa.deficientes; Praça Dr Fernando Amado, Lote 566-E, Lisbon) This private organisation can help with travel needs.

Secretaria do Nacional de Reabilitação (☎217 929 500; www.inr.pt; Av Conde de Valbom 63, Lisbon) The national governmental organisation representing people with disabilities supplies information, provides links to useful operations and publishes guides (in Portuguese) that advise on barrier-free accommodation, transport, shops, restaurants and sights.

Visas

Nationals of EU countries don't need a visa for any length of stay in Portugal. Those from Canada, New Zealand, the USA and (by temporary agreement) Australia can stay for up to 90 days in any six months without a visa. Others, including nationals of South Africa, need a visa unless they're the spouse or child of an EU citizen.

The general requirements for entry into Portugal also apply to citizens of other signatories of the 1990 Schengen Convention (Austria, Belgium, Denmark, Finland, France, Germany, Greece, Iceland, Italy, Luxembourg, the Netherlands, Norway, Spain and Sweden). A visa issued by one Schengen country is generally valid for travel in all the others, but unless you're a citizen of the UK, Ireland or a Schengen country, you should check visa regulations with the consulate of each Schengen country you plan to visit. You must apply for any Schengen visa while you are still in your country of residence.

Volunteering

Online resources such as **Global Volunteers** (www.globalvolunteers.org/portugal), **Go Abroad** (www.goabroad.com) and **Transitions Abroad** (www.transitionsabroad.com) list opportunities that are offered to volunteers in Portugal – including teaching English and helping out on social projects.

World Wide Opportunities on Organic Farms (WWOOF; www.wwoof.pt) sometimes has opportunities in Portugal. In exchange for your volunteer help, you'll receive food and lodging, and learn about organic farming as well.

Women Travellers

➡ Women travelling alone in Portugal report few serious problems. Women should take the same precautions they'd take when travelling anywhere – be cautious where you walk after dark and don't hitch.

➡ If you're travelling with a male partner, people will expect him to do all the talking and ordering, and pay the bill. In some conservative pockets of the north, unmarried couples will save hassle by saying they're married.

➡ If you're a victim of violence or rape while you're in Portugal, you can contact the **Associação Portuguesa de Apoio à Vítima** (APAV, Portuguese Association for Victim Support; ☎213 587 900; www.apav.pt; Rua José Estêvão 135), which offers assistance for rape victims. Visit the website for the locations of offices nationwide.

Work

The most likely kind of work you will be able to find is teaching English, if you have Teaching English as a Foreign Language (TEFL) certification. If you're in the UK, contact the British Council, or get in touch with language schools in the area where you want to teach as possible avenues of work.

Bar work is a possibility in the Algarve, particularly in Lagos; ask around. You can also try looking in the local English press for job advertisements.

Transport

GETTING THERE & AWAY

Entering the Country

An increasingly popular destination, Portugal is well connected to North America and European countries by air. There are also handy overland links by bus and train to and from Spain, from where you can continue on to other destinations on the continent.

Flights, cars and tours can be booked online at lonelyplanet.com/bookings.

Air

Most international flights arrive in Lisbon, though Porto and Faro also receive some. For more information, including live arrival and departure schedules, see www.ana.pt. TAP (www.flytap.com) is Portugal's international flag carrier as well as its main domestic airline. Major airports:

Faro Airport (FAO; ☎289 800 800; www.ana.pt; 📶)

Lisbon Airport (Lisbon Airport; ☎218 413 700; www.ana.pt; Alameda das Comunidades Portuguesas)

Porto Airport (OPO; ☎229 432 400; www.ana.pt)

Land

Portugal shares a land border only with Spain, but there is both bus and train service linking the two countries, with onward connections to the rest of mainland Europe.

Bus

The major long-distance carriers that serve European destinations are **Busabout** (www.busabout.com) and **Eurolines** (www.eurolines.com); though these carriers serve Portugal, the country is not currently included in the multicity travel passes of either company.

For some European routes, Eurolines is affiliated with the big Portuguese operators **Internorte** (☎707 200 512; www.internorte.pt) and **Eva Transportes** (☎289 899 760; www.eva-bus.com).

CONTINENTAL EUROPE

Eurolines has services to Portugal from destinations all across Europe, typically running about twice a week. From Paris, hefty surcharges apply to one-way or return tickets for most departures from July to mid-August and also on Saturday year-round.

UK–Portugal and France–Portugal Eurolines services cross to Portugal via northwest Spain. These Spanish lines offer services to Portugal:

Alsa (www.alsa.es)

Avanza (☎968 056 080; www.avanzabus.com)

Damas (www.damas-sa.es)

CLIMATE CHANGE & TRAVEL

Every form of transport that relies on carbon-based fuel generates CO_2, the main cause of human-induced climate change. Modern travel is dependent on aeroplanes, which might use less fuel per kilometre per person than most cars but travel much greater distances. The altitude at which aircraft emit gases (including CO_2) and particles also contributes to their climate change impact. Many websites offer 'carbon calculators' that allow people to estimate the carbon emissions generated by their journey and, for those who wish to do so, to offset the impact of the greenhouse gases emitted with contributions to portfolios of climate-friendly initiatives throughout the world. Lonely Planet offsets the carbon footprint of all staff and author travel.

CONTINENTAL EUROPE BUSES TO PORTUGAL

FROM	TO	COST (€)	DURATION (HR)	FREQUENCY
Amsterdam	Faro	185	36	3 times weekly
Amsterdam	Porto	155	32	3 times weekly
Barcelona	Lisbon	90	19	3 times weekly
Brussels	Faro	175	32	3 times weekly
Brussels	Porto	140	28	3 times weekly
Hamburg	Faro	190	42	3 times weekly
Hamburg	Lisbon	165	40	3 times weekly
Hamburg	Porto	160	38	3 times weekly
Madrid	Lisbon	30-60	8	daily
Madrid	Porto	30-65	8½	daily
Paris	Faro	98-130	27	3 times weekly
Paris	Lisbon	91-120	26	daily
Paris	Porto	91-108	22	daily
Seville	Faro	18-26	?	daily
Seville	Lisbon	30-46	7	daily

UK

Eurolines runs several services to Portugal from Victoria coach station in London, with a stopover and change of bus in France and sometimes Spain. These include two buses a week to Viana do Castelo (34 hours), five to Porto (33 hours), five via Coimbra to Lisbon (35 hours) and two via Faro to Lagos (38 hours). These services cost around £85 one way.

Car & Motorcycle

If you're driving your own car or motorcycle into Portugal, you need the following:

- vehicle registration (proof of ownership)
- insurance documents
- motor vehicle insurance with at least third-party cover.

CONTINENTAL EUROPE

Of more than 30 roads that cross the Portugal–Spain border, the best and biggest do so near Valença do Minho (E01/A3), Chaves (N532), Bragança (E82/IP4), Vilar Formoso (E80/IP5), Caia (E90/A6/IP7), Serpa (N260) and Vila Real de Santo António (E1/IP1). There are no longer any border controls.

UK

The quickest driving route from the UK to Portugal is by taking a car ferry to northern Spain. **Brittany Ferries** (www.brittany-ferries.co.uk) runs three routes, each of which depart twice weekly from mid-March through October:

- Portsmouth to Santander (from £794 return, 24 hours)
- Portsmouth to Bilbao (from £1100 return, 24 to 32 hours)
- Plymouth to Santander (from £1008 return; 20 hours).

From Bilbao or Santander it's roughly 1000km to Lisbon, 800km to Porto and 1300km to Faro.

An alternative is to catch a ferry across the Channel, or take the Eurotunnel (www.eurotunnel.com) vehicle train beneath it, to France and motor down the coast. The fastest sea crossings are between Dover and Calais, and are operated by **P&O Ferries** (www.poferries.com).

Train

Trains are a popular way to get around Europe – comfortable, frequent and generally on time. But unless you have a rail pass the cost can be higher than flying.

You will have few problems buying long-distance tickets as little as a day or two ahead, even in the summer. For those intending to do a lot of European rail travel, the **European Rail Timetable** (www.europeanrailtimetable.co.uk) is updated monthly and is available for sale as a digital download on the website. Another excellent resource for train travel around Europe (and beyond) is the website **Man in Seat Sixty-One** (www.seat61.com).

CONTINENTAL EUROPE

There are several ways to travel to Portugal by train. The fastest way coming from Paris is to take the TGV Atlantique from Montparnasse station to Irún (in Spain). From there, change to the overnight Lisbon-bound train, which crosses into Portugal at Vilar Formoso (Fuentes de Oñoro in Spain), continuing to Coimbra and Lisbon;

TRAINS TO PORTUGAL

FROM	TO	COST (€)	DURATION (HR)	FREQUENCY
Madrid	Lisbon	61-88	10½	daily
Paris	Lisbon	137-190	21	daily
Vigo	Porto	15	3¼	twice daily

change at Coimbra for Porto. If heading south, change trains at Lisbon. You can also travel via Madrid and other parts of Spain, but aside from Galicia, all trains take the same journey into Portugal.

The only other train route into Portugal is via Vigo, Galicia, which heads on to Valença do Minho and Porto, where you can change to other destinations in Portugal. This latter route is handy if you're including a trip to Santiago de Compostela in your itinerary.

The train journey from Paris (Gare de Montparnasse) to Lisbon takes 21 hours and stops in a number of Spanish cities along the way. You can buy tickets direct from **SNCF** (www.voyages-sncf.com).

If travelling by train from Spain, you can purchase tickets online through **Renfe** (www.renfe.com).

UK

The fastest and most convenient route to Portugal from the UK is with **Eurostar** (www.eurostar.com) from London Waterloo to Paris, and then onward by TGV.

TRAIN PASSES

Many of the passes listed here are available through **Rail Europe** (www.raileurope.com); most travel agencies also sell them, though you will save a little by buying directly from the issuing authority. Note that even with a pass you must still pay for seat and couchette reservations and express-train supplements.

InterRail Pass (www.interrail.eu) Allows a certain number of travel days within a set time frame. The network includes 30 countries. A pass for five days of travel over 15 days costs €264 for 2nd class and €413 for 1st class. A month of unlimited travel costs €626 for 2nd class and €983 for 1st class. The InterRail Pass is available to European citizens and official residents residing in Europe for six months before starting their travels. You cannot use it in your home country (save for one outbound journey and one inbound one).

Eurail (www.eurail.com) Sells passes to non-European residents. The Global pass is valid for unlimited travel in 28 European countries, including Portugal, and ranges from 5 days (adult/under 26 US$533/348) to three months (US$1867/1216). The Select pass allows you to travel between two, three or four of your chosen Eurail countries. You can choose from five to 10 travelling days, which can be taken at any point within a two-month period.

Portugal-Spain rail pass (www.raileurope.com) Available only to non-European residents and valid for a specified period of travel in Spain and Portugal during a two-month period, from four days (US$294) to 10 days (US$480). First-class tickets cost about 25% more.

River

Transporte Fluvial del Guadiana (www.rioguadiana.net) operates car ferries across the Rio Guadiana between Ayamonte in Spain and Vila Real de Santo António in the Algarve every hour (half-hourly in the summer) from 8.30am to 7pm Monday to Saturday, and from 9.30am to 6pm on Sunday. Buy tickets from the waterfront office (€1.80/5.50/1.15 per person/car/bike).

Sea

There are no scheduled seagoing ferries to Portugal, but many to Spain. The closest North African ferry connections are from Morocco to Spain; contact **Trasmediterranea** (www.trasmediterranea.es) for details. Car ferries also run from Tangier to Gibraltar.

GETTING AROUND

Air

Flights within mainland Portugal are expensive and, for the short distances involved, not really worth considering. Nonetheless, **TAP** (www.flytap.com) has multiple daily Lisbon–Porto and Lisbon–Faro flights (taking less than one hour) year-round. For Porto to Faro, change in Lisbon.

Bicycle

Cycling is popular in Portugal, even though there are few dedicated bicycle paths. Possible itineraries are numerous in the mountainous national/natural parks of the north (especially Parque Nacional da Peneda-Gerês), along the coast or across the Alentejo plains. Coastal trips are easiest from north to south, with the prevailing winds. More demanding is the Serra da Estrela (which serves as the Tour de Portugal's 'mountain run'). You could also try the Serra do Marão between Amarante and Vila Real.

Local bike clubs organise regular Passeio BTT trips; check their flyers at rental agencies, bike shops and *turismos* (tourist offices). Guided trips are often available in popular tourist destinations.

Cobbled roads in some old-town centres may jar your teeth loose if your tyres aren't fat enough; they should be at least 38mm in diameter.

Documents

If you're cycling around Portugal on your own bike, proof of ownership and a written description and photograph of it will help police in case it's stolen.

Hire

There are numerous places to rent bikes, especially in the Algarve and other touristy areas. Prices range from €8 to €25 per day.

Information

For listings of events and bike shops, buy the bimonthly Portuguese-language *Bike Magazine*, available from larger newsagents.

For its members, the UK-based **Cycling UK** (www.cyclinguk.org) publishes useful and free information on cycling in Portugal, plus notes for half a dozen routes around the country. It also offers tips, maps, topography guides and other publications by mail order.

Transport

Boxed or bagged-up bicycles can be taken free on all *regional* and *interregional* trains as accompanied baggage. They can also go unboxed on a few suburban services on weekends or for a small charge outside the rush hour. Most domestic bus lines won't accept bikes on board.

Boat

Other than river cruises along the Rio Douro from Porto and the Rio Tejo from Lisbon, Portugal's only remaining waterborne transport are cross-river ferries. Commuter ferries include those across the Rio Tejo to/from Lisbon and across the mouth of the Rio Sado between Setúbal and Tróia.

Bus

A host of small private bus operators, most amalgamated into regional companies, run a dense network of services across the country. Among the largest are **Rede Expressos** (☎707 223 344; www.rede-expressos.pt), **Rodonorte** (☎259 340 710; www.rodonorte.pt) and the Algarve line **Eva Transportes** (www.eva-bus.com).

Bus services are of four general types:

Alta Qualidade A fast deluxe category offered by some companies.

Carreiras Marked 'CR'; slow, stopping at every crossroads.

Expressos Comfortable, fast buses between major cities.

Rápidas Quick regional buses.

Even in summer you'll have little problem booking an *expresso* ticket for the same or next day. A Lisbon–Faro express bus takes about four hours and costs €18.50; Lisbon–Porto takes about 3½ hours for around €19. By contrast, local services can thin out to almost nothing on weekends, especially in summer when school is out.

Don't rely on *turismos* for accurate timetable information. Most bus-station ticket desks will give you a little computer printout of fares and services.

Except in Lisbon or Porto, there's little reason to take municipal buses, as most attractions are within walking distance.

Car & Motorcycle

Portugal's modest network of *estradas* (highways) is gradually spreading across the country. Main roads are sealed and generally in good condition. The downside is your fellow drivers: the country's per-capita death rate from road accidents has long been one of Europe's highest, and drinking, driving and dying are hot political potatoes. The good news is that recent years have seen a steady decline in the road toll, thanks to a zero-tolerance police crackdown on accident-prone routes and alcohol limits.

Driving can be tricky in Portugal's small walled towns, where roads may taper to donkey-cart size before you know it and fiendish one-way systems can force you out of your way.

A common occurrence in larger towns is people who lurk around squares and car parks, waving you into the parking space you've just found for yourself and asking for payment for this service. It's wise to do as Portuguese do and hand over some coins (€0.50) to keep your car out of 'trouble' (scratches, broken windows etc).

Driving Licences

Nationals of EU countries, the USA and Brazil need only their home driving licence to operate a car or motorcycle in Portugal. Others should get an International Driving Permit (IDP) through an automobile licensing department or automobile club in their home country.

Fuel

Fuel is expensive – about €1.50 for a litre of *sem chumbo* (unleaded petrol) at the time of writing. There are plenty of self-service stations, and credit cards are accepted at most. If you're near the border, you can save money by filling up in

Spain, where it's around 20% cheaper.

Highways & Toll Roads

Top of the range roads are *auto-estradas* (motorways), all of them *portagens* (toll roads); the longest of these are Lisbon–Porto and Lisbon–Algarve. Toll roads charge cars and motorcycles a little over €0.06 per kilometre (around €20 from Lisbon to Porto and €19 from Lisbon to Faro).

Nomenclature can be baffling. Motorway prefixes indicate the following:

A Portugal's toll roads.

E Europe-wide designations.

N Main two-lane *estradas nacionais* (national roads); prefix letter used on some road maps only.

IC (itinerário complementar) Subsidiary highways.

IP (itinerário principal) Main highways.

Hire

➡ To rent a car in Portugal you should be at least 25 years old and have held your driving licence for more than a year (some companies allow younger drivers at higher rates). The widest choice of car-hire companies is at Lisbon, Porto and Faro airports. Competition has driven Algarve rates lower than elsewhere.

➡ Some of the best advance-booking rates are offered by internet-based brokers such as **Holiday Autos** (www.holidayautos.com). Other bargains come as part of 'fly/drive' packages. The worst deals tend to be those done with international firms on arrival, though their prepaid promotional rates are competitive. Book at least a few days ahead in high season. For on-the-spot rental, domestic firms such as **Auto Jardim** (www.auto-jardim.com) have some of the best rates.

➡ The average price for renting the smallest and cheapest available car for a week in high season is around €300 (with tax, insurance and unlimited mileage) if booked from abroad, and a similar amount when booked through a Portuguese firm.

➡ For an additional fee you can get personal insurance through the rental company, unless you're covered by your home policy. A minimum of third-party coverage is compulsory in the EU.

ROAD DISTANCES (KM)

	Aveiro	Beja	Braga	Bragança	Castelo Branco	Coimbra	Évora	Faro	Guarda	Leiria	Lisbon	Portalegre	Porto	Santarém	Setúbal	Viana do Castelo	Vila Real	Viseu
Aveiro	---																	
Beja	383	---																
Braga	129	504	---															
Bragança	287	566	185	---														
Castelo Branco	239	271	366	299	---													
Coimbra	60	329	178	314	191	---												
Évora	305	78	426	488	191	251	---											
Faro	522	166	643	732	437	468	244	---										
Guarda	163	369	260	197	102	161	291	535	---									
Leiria	126	273	244	402	179	72	195	412	233	---								
Lisbon	256	183	372	530	264	202	138	296	402	146	---							
Portalegre	276	178	403	390	93	222	100	344	193	172	219	---						
Porto	71	446	58	216	308	123	368	585	202	189	317	339	---					
Santarém	188	195	309	464	181	134	117	346	295	78	80	147	251	---				
Setúbal	299	143	420	575	316	246	105	256	406	189	47	186	362	123	---			
Viana do Castelo	144	519	56	241	382	191	441	658	275	262	387	412	73	324	435	---		
Vila Real	169	528	94	120	261	199	450	683	159	282	412	352	98	349	460	150	---	
Viseu	86	415	185	228	177	86	366	554	75	158	288	268	127	220	331	241	113	---

AUTOMATED TOLLS

Note that Portugal's main toll roads now have automated tollbooths, meaning you won't be able to simply drive through and pay an attendant. You'll need to hire an electronic tag to pay for the tolls. Many car-rental agencies hire out the small electronic devices (for around €6 per week, less on subsequent weeks), and it's worth inquiring if one is available before renting a car. If you don't use the device and go through a toll, you may receive a fine (via your car-hire agency) after your trip. The other option is simply to avoid the *auto-estradas*, which isn't always easy to do, especially when travelling across the Algarve.

For more information, including locations where you can hire electronic tag devices throughout the country (useful if your car hire doesn't have them or you're driving your own vehicle), contact government-run **Via Verde** (☎707 500 900; www.viaverde.pt)

➡ Rental cars are especially at risk of break-ins or petty theft in larger towns, so don't leave anything of value visible in the car.

➡ Motorcycles and scooters can be rented in larger cities and all over coastal Algarve. Expect to pay from €30/60 per day for a scooter/motorcycle.

Insurance

Your home insurance policy may or may not be extendable to Portugal, and the coverage of some comprehensive policies automatically drops to third party outside your home country unless the insurer is notified.

If you hire a car, the rental firm will provide you with registration and insurance papers, plus a rental contract.

If you are involved in a minor collision with no injuries, the easiest way for drivers to sort things out with their insurance companies is to fill out a Constat Aimable (the English version is called a European Accident Statement). There's no risk in signing this: it's just a way to exchange the relevant information and there's usually one included in rental-car documents. Make sure it includes any details that may help you prove that the accident was not your fault. To alert the police, dial ☎112.

Parking

Parking is often metered within city centres but free on Saturday evening and Sunday. Lisbon has car parks, but these can get expensive (upwards of €20 per day).

Road Rules

➡ Despite the sometimes chaotic relations between drivers, there are rules. To begin with, driving is on the right, overtaking is on the left and most signs use international symbols. An important rule to remember is that traffic from the right usually has priority. Portugal has lots of ambiguously marked intersections, so this is more important than you might think.

➡ Except when marked otherwise, speed limits for cars (without a trailer) and motorcycles (without a sidecar) are 50km/h in towns and villages, 90km/h outside built-up areas and 120km/h on motorways. By law, car safety belts must be worn in the front and back seats, and children under 12 years may not ride in the front. Motorcyclists and their passengers must wear helmets, and motorcycles must have their headlights on day and night.

➡ The police can impose steep on-the-spot fines for speeding and parking offences, so save yourself a big hassle and remember to toe the line.

➡ The legal blood-alcohol limit is 0.5g/L, and there are fines of up to €2500 for drink-driving. It's also illegal in Portugal to drive while talking on a mobile phone.

Hitching & Ride-Sharing

Hitching is never entirely safe, and we don't recommend it. Travellers who hitch should understand that they are taking a small but potentially serious risk. In any case it isn't an easy option in Portugal. Almost nobody stops on major highways, and on smaller roads drivers tend to be going short distances so you might only advance from one field to the next.

Local Transport

Bus

Except in Lisbon or Porto, there's little reason to take municipal buses, as most attractions are within walking distance. Most areas have regional bus services, for better or worse.

Metro

Both Lisbon and Porto have ambitious underground systems that are still growing.

Tram

Tram lovers shouldn't miss the charming relics rattling through the narrow streets of Lisbon and Porto.

Taxi & Ride-share Services

➡ Taxis offer fair value over short distances and are

Train Routes

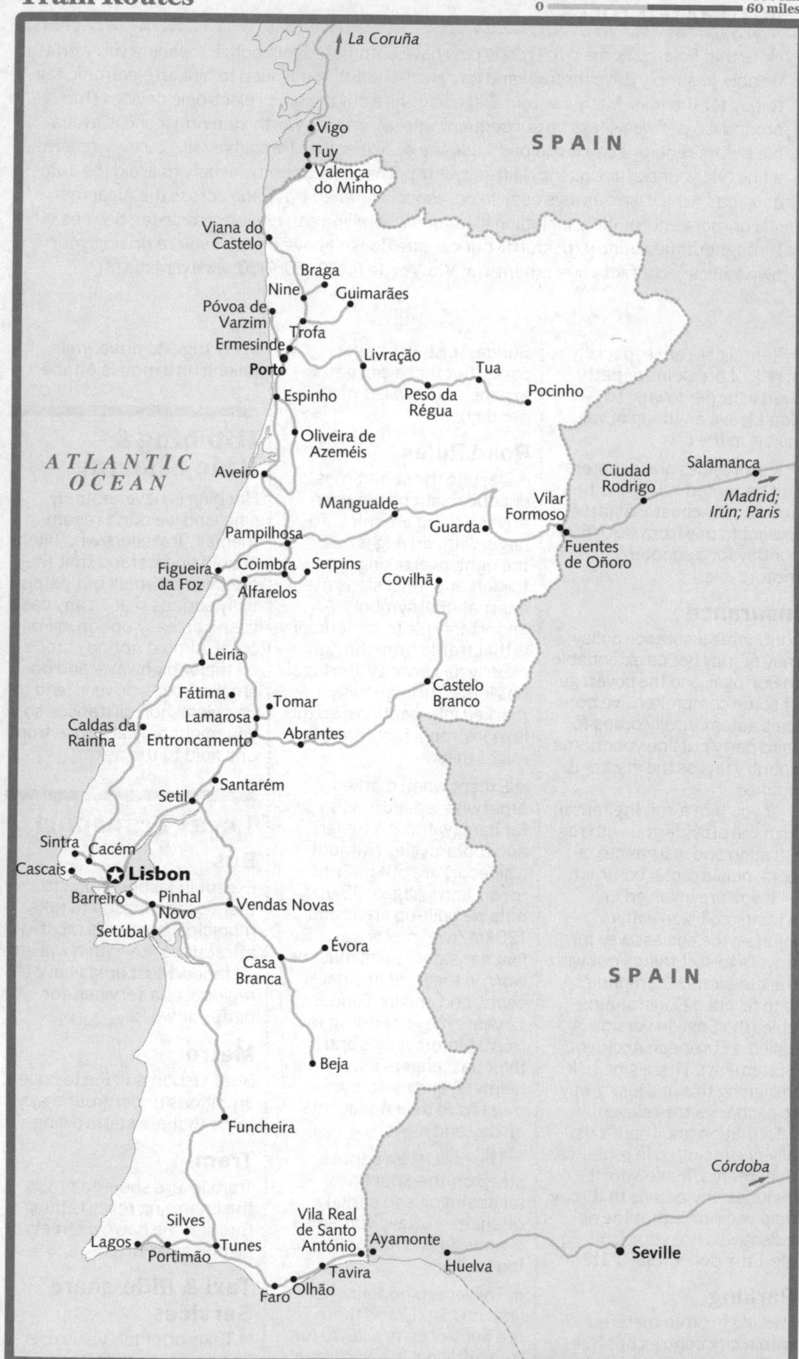

plentiful in large towns and cities. Ordinary taxis are usually marked with an 'A' (which stands for *aluguer*, for hire) on the door, number plate or elsewhere. They use meters and are available on the street and at taxi ranks, or by telephone for a surcharge of €0.80.

➡ The fare on weekdays during daylight hours is about €3.25 *bandeirada* (flagfall) plus around €0.80 per kilometre, and a bit more for periods spent idling in traffic. A fare of €6 will usually get you across bigger towns. It's best to insist on the meter, although it's possible to negotiate a flat fare. If you have a sizeable load of luggage you'll pay a further €1.60.

➡ Rates are about 20% higher at night (9pm to 6am), on weekends and on holidays. Once a taxi leaves the city limits you also pay a surcharge or higher rate.

➡ In larger cities, including Lisbon and Porto, meterless taxis marked with a T (for *turismo*) can be hired from private companies for excursions. Rates for these are higher but standardised; drivers are honest and polite, and generally speak foreign languages.

➡ Uber is available in Lisbon and Porto.

Tours

If you're short on time, an organised tour can be a good way to take in the highlights of a destination.

Bus

AVIC (☎258 820 360; www.avic.pt) Runs tours in Porto, the Douro and the Minho.

Diana Tours (☎217 998 540; www.dianatours.pt) Specialises in Lisbon and Sintra.

Train

Comboios de Portugal (☎707 210 220; www.cp.pt), the state railway company, organises Saturday day trips up the Douro valley on an old steam engine during the summer months.

Specialist Tours

For special-interest tours, try **Martin Randall Travel** (www.martinrandall.com), a UK cultural specialist that arranges first-rate escorted tours, including a historical and architectural tour of central Portugal, or **Naturetrek** (www.naturetrek.co.uk), which specialises in birdwatching and botanical tours and runs an eight-day excursion around southern Portugal.

Train

Portugal has an extensive railway network, making for a scenic way of travelling between destinations, see www.cp.pt.

Discounts

➡ Children aged under five travel free; those aged five to 12 go for half price.

➡ A youth card issued by Euro26 member countries gets you a 20% discount on *regional* and *interregional* services on any day. For distances above 100km, you can also get a 20% discount on *intercidade* (express) services and a 10% discount on Alfa Pendular (AP) trains – though the latter applies only from Tuesday to Thursday.

➡ Travellers aged 65 and over can get 50% off any service by showing ID.

Information & Reservations

➡ You can get hold of timetable and fare information at all stations and from www.cp.pt.

➡ You can book *intercidade* and Alfa Pendular tickets up to 30 days ahead, though you'll have little trouble booking for the next or even the same day. Other services can only be booked 24 hours in advance.

➡ A seat reservation is mandatory on most *intercidade* and Alfa trains; the booking fee is included in the price.

Train Passes

The One Country Portugal Pass from **InterRail** (www.interrail.eu) gives you unlimited travel on any three, four, six or eight days over a month (2nd class costs per three/four/six/eight days €78/95/125/148; 1st class costs about 35% more). It's available to all travellers who hail from outside of Portugal and can be purchased from many travel agents in Portugal or in advance from the website.

Types & Classes of Service

There are four main types of long-distance service. Note that international services are marked IN on timetables.

Regional (R) Slow, stop everywhere.

Interregional (IR) Reasonably fast.

Intercidade (IC) *Rápido* or express trains.

Alfa Pendular Deluxe This service is marginally faster than express and much pricier.

Only the Faro–Porto Comboio Azul and international trains such as *Sud-Expresso* and Talgo *Lusitânia* have restaurant cars, though all IC and Alfa trains have aisle service and most have bars.

Lisbon and Porto have their own *urbano* (suburban) train networks. Lisbon's network extends to Sintra, Cascais, Setúbal and up the lower Tejo valley. Porto's network takes the definition of 'suburban' to new lengths, running all the way to Braga, Guimarães and Aveiro. *Urbano* services also travel between Coimbra and Figueira da Foz. The distinction matters where long-distance services parallel the more convenient, plentiful and considerably cheaper *urbanos*.

Language

Portuguese pronunciation is not difficult because most sounds are also found in English. The exceptions are the nasal vowels (represented in our pronunciation guides by ng after the vowel), which are pronounced as if you're trying to make the sound through your nose; and the strongly rolled *r* (represented by rr in our pronunciation guides). Also note that the symbol zh sounds like the 's' in 'pleasure'. The stress generally falls on the second-last syllable of a word. In our pronunciation guides stressed syllables are indicated with italics. If you keep these few points in mind and read our coloured pronunciation guides as if they were English, you won't have problems being understood.

Portuguese has masculine and feminine forms of nouns and adjectives. Both forms are given in this chapter where necessary, and indicated with 'm' and 'f' respectively.

BASICS

Hello.	*Olá.*	o·*laa*
Goodbye.	*Adeus.*	a·de·*oosh*
How are you?	*Como está?*	*ko*·moo shtaa
Fine, and you?	*Bem, e você?*	beng e vo·*se*
Excuse me.	*Faz favor.*	faash fa·*vor*
Sorry.	*Desculpe.*	desh·*kool*·pe
Yes.	*Sim.*	seeng
No.	*Não.*	nowng
Please.	*Por favor.*	poor fa·*vor*
Thank you.	*Obrigado.* *Obrigada.*	o·bree·*gaa*·doo (m) o·bree·*gaa*·da (f)
You're welcome.	*De nada.*	de *naa*·da

WANT MORE?

For in-depth language information and handy phrases, check out Lonely Planet's *Portuguese Phrasebook*. You'll find it at **shop.lonelyplanet.com**, or you can buy Lonely Planet's iPhone phrasebooks at the Apple App Store.

What's your name?
Qual é o seu nome? kwaal e oo *se*·oo *no*·me

My name is ...
O meu nome é ... oo *me*·oo *no*·me e ...

Do you speak English?
Fala inglês? *faa*·la eeng·*glesh*

I don't understand.
Não entendo. nowng eng·*teng*·doo

ACCOMMODATION

Do you have a single/double room?
Tem um quarto de solteiro/casal? teng oong *kwaar*·too de sol·*tay*·roo/ka·*zal*

How much is it per night/person?
Quanto custa por noite/pessoa? *kwang*·too *koosh*·ta poor *noy*·te/pe·*so*·a

Is breakfast included?
Inclui o pequeno almoço? eeng·*kloo*·ee oo pe·*ke*·noo aal·*mo*·soo

air-con	*ar condicionado*	aar kong·dee·syoo·*naa*·doo
bathroom	*casa de banho*	*kaa*·za de *ba*·nyoo
bed	*cama*	*ka*·ma
campsite	*parque de campismo*	*paar*·ke de kang·*peezh*·moo
cot	*cama de grades*	*ka*·ma de *graa*·desh
guesthouse	*casa de hóspedes*	*kaa*·za de *osh*·pe·desh
hotel	*hotel*	o·*tel*
youth hostel	*pousada de juventude*	poh·*zaa*·da de zhoo·veng·*too*·de
window	*janela*	zha·*ne*·la

DIRECTIONS

Where's (the station)?
Onde é (a estação)? ong·de e (a shta·sowng)

What's the address?
Qual é o endereço? kwaal e oo eng·de·re·soo

Could you please write it down?
Podia escrever isso, por favor? poo·dee·a shkre·ver ee·soo poor fa·vor

Can you show me (on the map)?
Pode-me mostrar (no mapa)? po·de·me moosh·traar (noo maa·pa)

at the corner	*na esquina*	na shkee·na
at the traffic lights	*nos semáforos*	noosh se·maa·foo·roosh
behind ...	*atrás de ...*	a·traash de ...
in front of ...	*em frente de ...*	eng freng·te de ...
far	*longe*	long·zhe
left	*esquerda*	shker·da
near	*perto*	per·too
next to	*ao lado do ...*	ow laa·doo de ...
opposite ...	*do lado oposto ...*	doo laa·doo oo·posh·too ...
right	*direita*	dee·ray·ta
straight ahead	*em frente*	eng freng·te

EATING & DRINKING

What would you recommend?
O que é que recomenda? oo ke e ke rre·koo·meng·da

What's in that dish?
Quais são os ingredientes daquele prato? kwaish sowng oosh eeng·gre·dee·eng·tesh da·ke·le praa·too

I don't eat ...
Eu não como ... e·oo nowng ko·moo ...

Cheers!
Saúde! sa·oo·de

That was delicious.
Isto estava delicioso. eesh·too shtaa·va de·lee·see·o·zoo

Bring the bill/check, please.
Pode-me trazer a conta. po·de·me tra·zer a kong·ta

I'd like to reserve a table for ...	*Eu queria reservar uma mesa para ...*	e·oo ke·ree·a rre·zer·vaar oo·ma me·za pa·ra ...
(eight) o'clock	*as (oito da noite)*	ash (oy·too da noy·te)
(two) people	*(duas) pessoas*	(doo·ash) pe·so·ash

KEY PATTERNS

To get by in Portuguese, mix and match these simple patterns with words of your choice:

When's (the next bus)?
Quando é que sai (o próximo autocarro)? kwang·doo e ke sai (oo pro·see·moo ow·to·kaa·rroo)

Where do I (buy a ticket)?
Onde é que eu (compro o bilhete)? ong·de e ke e·oo (kong·proo oo bee·lye·te)

I'm looking for (a hotel).
Estou à procura de (um hotel). shtoh aa proo·koo·ra de (oong o·tel)

Do you have (a map)?
Tem (um mapa)? teng (oong maa·pa)

Please bring (the bill).
Pode-me trazer (a conta). po·de·me tra·zer (a kong·ta)

I'd like (the menu).
Queria (um menu). ke·ree·a (oong me·noo)

I'd like (to hire a car).
Queria (alugar um carro). ke·ree·a (a·loo·gaar oong kaa·rroo)

I have (a reservation).
Eu tenho (uma reserva). e·oo ta·nyoo (oo·ma rre·zer·va)

Could you please (help)?
Pode (ajudar), por favor? po·de (a·zhoo·daar) poor fa·vor

Do I need (a visa)?
Preciso de (um visto)? pre·see·zoo de (oong veesh·too)

Key Words

appetisers	*aperitivos*	a·per·ee·tee·voosh
bar	*bar*	baar
bottle	*garrafa*	ga·rraa·fa
bowl	*tigela*	tee·zhe·la
breakfast	*pequeno almoço*	pe·ke·noo aal·mo·soo
children's menu	*menu das crianças*	me·noo dash kree·ang·sash
cold	*frio*	free·oo
delicatessen	*charcutaria*	shar·koo·ta·ree·a
dinner	*jantar*	zhang·taar
food	*comida*	koo·mee·da
fork	*garfo*	gar·foo
glass	*copo*	ko·poo
hot (warm)	*quente*	keng·te
knife	*faca*	faa·ka

Signs

Aberto	Open
Encerrado	Closed
Entrada	Entrance
Fechado	Closed
Informação	Information
Lavabos/WC	Toilets
Proibido	Prohibited
Saída	Exit

lunch	*almoço*	aal·*mo*·soo
main course	*prato principal*	*praa*·too preeng·see·*paal*
market	*mercado*	mer·*kaa*·doo
menu (in English)	*menu (em inglês)*	me·*noo* (eng eeng·*glesh*)
plate	*prato*	*praa*·too
restaurant	*restaurante*	rresh·tow·*rang*·te
spicy	*picante*	pee·*kang*·te
spoon	*colher*	koo·*lyer*
vegetarian food	*comida vegetariana*	koo·*mee*·da ve·zhe·ta·ree·*aa*·na
wine list	*lista dos vinhos*	*leesh*·ta doosh *vee*·nyoosh
with/without	*com/sem*	kong/seng

Meat & Fish

beef	*carne de vaca*	*kaar*·ne de *vaa*·ka
chicken	*frango*	*frang*·goo
duck	*pato*	*paa*·too
fish	*peixe*	*pay*·she
lamb	*cordeiro*	kor·*day*·roo
pork	*porco*	*por*·koo
turkey	*peru*	pe·*roo*
veal	*novilho*	noo·*vee*·lyoo

Fruit & Vegetables

apple	*maçã*	ma·*sang*
apricot	*alperce*	aal·*per*·se
artichoke	*alcachofra*	aal·ka·*sho*·fra
asparagus	*espargos*	*shpar*·goosh
beetroot	*beterraba*	be·te·*rraa*·ba
cabbage	*couve*	*koh*·ve
capsicum	*pimento*	pee·*meng*·too
carrot	*cenoura*	se·*noh*·ra
celery	*aipo*	*ai*·poo
cherry	*cereja*	se·*re*·zha
corn	*milho*	*mee*·lyoo
cucumber	*pepino*	pe·*pee*·noo
fruit	*fruta*	*froo*·ta
grapes	*uvas*	*oo*·vash
lemon	*limão*	lee·*mowng*
lettuce	*alface*	aal·*faa*·se
mushrooms	*cogumelos*	koo·goo·*me*·loosh
nut	*oleaginosa*	o·lee·a·zhee·*no*·za
onion	*cebola*	se·*bo*·la
orange	*laranja*	la·*rang*·zha
peach	*pêssego*	*pe*·se·goo
peas	*ervilhas*	er·*vee*·lyash
pineapple	*ananás*	a·na·*naash*
plum	*ameixa*	a·*may*·sha
potato	*batata*	ba·*taa*·ta
prune	*ameixa seca*	a·*may*·sha *se*·ka
pumpkin	*abóbora*	a·*bo*·boo·ra
spinach	*espinafres*	shpee·*naa*·fresh
strawberry	*morango*	moo·*rang*·goo
tomato	*tomate*	too·*maa*·te
turnip	*nabo*	*naa*·boo
vegetable	*hortaliça*	or·ta·*lee*·sa
watermelon	*melancia*	me·lang·*see*·a

Other

bread	*pão*	powng
butter	*manteiga*	mang·*tay*·ga
cheese	*queijo*	*kay*·zhoo
egg	*ovo*	*o*·voo
honey	*mel*	mel
lentils	*lentilha*	leng·*tee*·lya
noodles	*massas*	*maa*·sash
oil	*óleo*	*o*·lyoo
pepper	*pimenta*	pee·*meng*·ta
rice	*arroz*	a·*rrosh*
salt	*sal*	saal
sugar	*açúcar*	a·*soo*·kar
vinegar	*vinagre*	vee·*naa*·gre

Drinks

beer	*cerveja*	ser·*ve*·zha
coffee	*café*	ka·*fe*
juice	*sumo*	*soo*·moo
milk	*leite*	*lay*·te
red wine	*vinho tinto*	*vee*·nyoo *teeng*·too

tea	*chá*	shaa
(mineral) water	*água (mineral)*	*aa*·gwa (mee·ne·*raal*)
white wine	*vinho branco*	*vee*·nyoo *brang*·koo

EMERGENCIES

Help!	*Socorro!*	soo·*ko*·rroo
Go away!	*Vá-se embora!*	*vaa*·se eng·*bo*·ra
Call ...!	*Chame ...!*	*shaa*·me ...
a doctor	*um médico*	oong *me*·dee·koo
the police	*a polícia*	a poo·*lee*·sya

I'm lost.
Estou perdido. — shtoh per·*dee*·doo (m)
Estou perdida. — shtoh per·*dee*·da (f)

I'm ill.
Estou doente. — shtoh doo·*eng*·te

It hurts here.
Dói-me aqui. — *doy*·me a·*kee*

I'm allergic to ...
Eu sou alérgico/alérgica a ... — e·oo soh a·*ler*·zhee·koo/a·*ler*·zhee·ka a ... (m/f)

Where are the toilets?
Onde é a casa de banho? — *ong*·de e a *kaa*·za de *ba*·nyoo

SHOPPING & SERVICES

I'd like to buy ...
Queria comprar ... — ke·*ree*·a kong·*praar* ...

I'm just looking.
Estou só a ver. — shtoh so a ver

Can I look at it?
Posso ver? — *po*·soo ver

I don't like it.
Não gosto. — nowng *gosh*·too

How much is it?
Quanto custa? — *kwang*·too *koosh*·ta

It's too expensive.
Está muito caro. — shtaa *mweeng*·too *kaa*·roo

Can you lower the price?
Pode baixar o preço? — *po*·de bai·*shaar* oo *pre*·soo

Question Words

How?	*Como?*	*ko*·moo
What?	*Quê?*	ke
When?	*Quando?*	*kwang*·doo
Where?	*Onde?*	*ong*·de
Who?	*Quem?*	keng
Why?	*Porquê?*	poor·*ke*

There's a mistake in the bill.
Há um erro na conta. — aa oong *e*·rroo na *kong*·ta

ATM	*caixa automático*	*kai*·sha ow·too·*maa*·tee·koo
credit card	*cartão de crédito*	kar·*towng* de *kre*·dee·too
internet cafe	*café da internet*	ka·*fe* da eeng·ter·*ne*·te
post office	*correio*	koo·*rray*·oo
tourist office	*escritório de turismo*	shkree·*to*·ryoo de too·*reezh*·moo

TIME & DATES

What time is it?
Que horas são? — kee o·rash sowng

It's (10) o'clock.
São (dez) horas. — sowng (desh) o·rash

Half past (10).
(Dez) e meia. — (desh) e *may*·a

morning	*manhã*	ma·*nyang*
afternoon	*tarde*	*taar*·de
evening	*noite*	*noy*·te
yesterday	*ontem*	*ong*·teng
today	*hoje*	*o*·zhe
tomorrow	*amanhã*	aa·ma·*nyang*
Monday	*segunda-feira*	se·*goong*·da·*fay*·ra
Tuesday	*terça-feira*	*ter*·sa·*fay*·ra
Wednesday	*quarta-feira*	*kwaar*·ta·*fay*·ra
Thursday	*quinta-feira*	*keeng*·ta·*fay*·ra
Friday	*sexta-feira*	*saysh*·ta·*fay*·ra
Saturday	*sábado*	*saa*·ba·doo
Sunday	*domingo*	doo·*meeng*·goo
January	*Janeiro*	zha·*nay*·roo
February	*Fevereiro*	fe·*vray*·roo
March	*Março*	*maar*·soo
April	*Abril*	a·*breel*
May	*Maio*	*maa*·yoo
June	*Junho*	*zhoo*·nyoo
July	*Julho*	*zhoo*·lyoo
August	*Agosto*	a·*gosh*·too
September	*Setembro*	se·*teng*·broo
October	*Outubro*	oh·*too*·broo
November	*Novembro*	no·*veng*·broo
December	*Dezembro*	de·*zeng*·broo

TRANSPORT

Public Transport

boat	*barco*	baar·koo
bus	*autocarro*	ow·to·*kaa*·roo
plane	*avião*	a·vee·*owng*
train	*comboio*	kong·*boy*·oo
tram	*eléctrico*	ee·*le*·tree·koo

I want to go to (Braga).
Queria ir a (Braga). — ke·*ree*·a eer a (*braa*·ga)

Does it stop at (Amarante)?
Pára em (Amarante)? — *paa*·ra eng (a·ma·*rang*·te)

What time does it leave/arrive?
A que horas sai/chega? — a ke o·rash sai/*she*·ga

Please tell me when we get to (Évora).
Por favor avise-me quando chegarmos a (Évora). — poor fa·*vor* a·*vee*·ze·me *kwang*·doo she·*gaar*·moosh a (*e*·voo·ra)

Please stop here.
Por favor pare aqui. — poor fa·*vor paa*·re a·*kee*

aisle seat	*lugar na coxia*	loo·*gaar* na koo·*shee*·a
cancelled	*cancelado*	kang·se·*laa*·doo
delayed	*atrasado*	a·tra·*zaa*·doo
platform	*plataforma*	pla·ta·*for*·ma

Numbers

1	*um*	oong
2	*dois*	doysh
3	*três*	tresh
4	*quatro*	*kwaa*·troo
5	*cinco*	*seeng*·koo
6	*seis*	saysh
7	*sete*	*se*·te
8	*oito*	*oy*·too
9	*nove*	*no*·ve
10	*dez*	desh
20	*vinte*	*veeng*·te
30	*trinta*	*treeng*·ta
40	*quarenta*	kwa·*reng*·ta
50	*cinquenta*	seeng·*kweng*·ta
60	*sessenta*	se·*seng*·ta
70	*setenta*	se·*teng*·ta
80	*oitenta*	oy·*teng*·ta
90	*noventa*	no·*veng*·ta
100	*cem*	seng
1000	*mil*	meel

ticket office	*bilheteira*	bee·lye·*tay*·ra
timetable	*horário*	o·*raa*·ryoo
train station	*estação de caminhos de ferro*	shta·*sowng* de ka·*mee*·nyoosh de *fe*·rroo
window seat	*lugar à janela*	loo·*gaar* aa zha·*ne*·la

a ... ticket	*um bilhete de ...*	oong bee·*lye*·te de ...
1st-class	*primeira classe*	pree·*may*·ra *klaa*·se
2nd-class	*segunda classe*	se·*goong*·da *klaa*·se
one-way	*ida*	*ee*·da
return	*ida e volta*	*ee*·da ee *vol*·ta

Driving & Cycling

I'd like to hire a ...	*Queria alugar ...*	ke·*ree*·a a·loo·*gaar* ...
bicycle	*uma bicicleta*	*oo*·ma bee·see·*kle*·ta
car	*um carro*	oong *kaa*·rroo
motorcycle	*uma mota*	*oo*·ma *mo*·ta

bicycle pump	*bomba de bicicleta*	*bong*·ba de bee·see·*kle*·ta
child seat	*cadeira de criança*	ka·*day*·ra de kree·*ang*·sa
helmet	*capacete*	ka·pa·*se*·te
mechanic	*mecânico*	me·*kaa*·nee·koo
petrol/gas	*gasolina*	ga·zoo·*lee*·na
service station	*posto de gasolina*	*posh*·too de ga·zoo·*lee*·na

Is this the road to ...?
Esta é a estrada para ...? — *esh*·ta e a *shtraa*·da *pa*·ra ...

(How long) Can I park here?
(Quanto tempo) Posso estacionar aqui? — (*kwang*·too *teng*·poo) *po*·soo shta·see·oo·*naar* a·*kee*

The car/motorbike has broken down (at ...).
O carro/A mota avariou-se (em ...). — oo *kaa*·rroo/a *mo*·ta a·va·ree·*oh*·se (eng ...)

I have a flat tyre.
Tenho um furo no pneu. — *ta*·nyoo oong *foo*·roo noo pe·*ne*·oo

I've run out of petrol.
Estou sem gasolina. — shtoh seng ga·zoo·*lee*·na

I'd like my bicycle repaired.
Queria consertar a minha bicicleta. — ke·*ree*·aa kong·ser·*taar* a *mee*·nya bee·see·*kle*·ta

GLOSSARY

For terms for food, drinks and other culinary vocabulary, see p529. For additional terms and information about the Portuguese language, see the Language chapter on p522.

adegas – wineries
Age of Discoveries – the period during the 15th and 16th centuries when Portuguese sailors explored the coast of Africa and finally charted a sea route to India
albergaria – upmarket inn
albufeira – reservoir, lagoon
aldeia – village
alta – upper
anta – see dolmen
arco – arch
armillary sphere – celestial sphere used by early astronomers and navigators to chart the stars; a decorative motif in Manueline architecture and atop *pelourinhos*
arrayal, arraiais (pl) – street party
artesanato – handicrafts shop
avenida – avenue
azulejo – hand-painted tile, typically blue and white, used to decorate buildings

bairro – town district
baixa – lower
balneário – health resort, spa
barcos rabelos – colourful boats once used to transport port wine from vineyards
barragem – dam
beco – cul de sac
biblioteca – library
bilhete diário/turístico – day pass/tourist ticket

câmara municipal – city or town hall
caldas – hot springs
Carnaval – Carnival; festival that takes place just before Lent
casa de hóspedes – boarding house, usually with shared showers and toilets
casais – huts
castelo – castle
castro – fortified hill town
cavaleiro – horseman
CCI – Camping Card International
Celtiberians – descendants of Celts who arrived in the Iberian Peninsula around 600 BC
centro de saúde – state-administered medical centre
cidade – town or city
citânia – Celtic fortified village
claustro – cloisters
concelho – municipality, council
cortes – Portugal's early parliament
CP – Caminhos de Ferro Portugueses (the Portuguese state railway company)
cromeleque – circle of prehistoric standing stones
cruz – cross

direita – right; abbreviated as D, dir or Dta
dolmen – Neolithic stone tomb (*anta* in Portuguese)
Dom, Dona – honorific titles (like Sir, Madam) given to royalty, nobility and landowners; now used more generally as a very polite form of address

elevador – lift (elevator), funicular
espigueiros – stone granaries
esplanada – terrace, seafront promenade
estação – station (usually train station)
estalagem – inn; more expensive than an *albergaria*
expressos – comfortable, fast buses between major cities
estradas – highways

fadista – singer of *fado*
fado – traditional, melancholic Portuguese style of singing
feira – fair
festa – festival
fortaleza – fortress

GNR – Guarda Nacional Republicana, the national guard (the acting police force in rural towns without PSP police)
guitarra – guitar
gruta – cave

hospedaria – see *casa de hóspedes*

IC (intercidade) – express intercity train
ICEP – Investimentos, Comércio e Turismo de Portugal, the government's umbrella organisation for tourism
igreja – church
igreja matriz – parish church
ilha – island
IR (interregional) – fairly fast train that doesn't make too many stops

jardim – garden
judiaria – quarter in a town where Jews were once segregated

largo – small square
latifúndios – Roman system of large farming estates
litoral – coastal
livraria – bookshop
Lisboêtas – Lisbon dwellers
loggia – covered area or porch on the side of a building
lugar – neighbourhood, place

Manueline – elaborate late Gothic/Renaissance style of art and architecture that emerged during the reign of Dom Manuel I in the 16th century
mantas alentejanas – handwoven woollen blankets
marranos – 'New Christians', ie Jews who converted during the Inquisition
menhir – standing stone monument typical of the late Neolithic Age
mercado municipal – municipal market
mesa – table
minimercado – grocery shop or small supermarket
miradouro – viewpoint
Misericórdia – derived from Santa Casa da Misericórdia (Holy House of Mercy), a charitable

institution founded in the 15th century to care for the poor and the sick; it usually designates an old building that was founded by this organisation
moliceiro – high-prowed, shallow-draft boats traditionally used for harvesting seaweed in the estuaries of Beira Litoral
mosteiro – monastery
mouraria – the quarter where Moors were segregated during and after the Christian *Reconquista*
museu – museum

paço – palace
parque de campismo – camping ground
parque nacional – national park
parque natural – natural park
pelourinho – stone pillory, often ornately carved; erected in the 13th to 18th centuries as symbols of justice and sometimes as places where criminals were punished
pensão, pensões (pl) – guesthouse, the Portuguese equivalent of a B&B, though breakfast is not always served
planalto – high plain
pombal – dovecote, a structure for housing pigeons
ponte – bridge
portagem – toll road
pousada – government-run upmarket inn, often a converted castle, convent or palace
pousada da juventude – youth hostel; usually with kitchen, common rooms and sometimes rooms with private bathroom
praça – square
praia – beach
PSP – Polícia de Segurança Pública, the local police force

quinta – country estate or villa; in the Douro wine-growing region it often refers to a wine lodge's property

R (regional) – slow train
Reconquista – Christian reconquest of Portugal (718–1249)
reservas naturais – nature reserves
residencial, residenciais (pl) – guesthouse; slightly more expensive than a *pensão* and usually serving breakfast
ribeiro – stream
rio – river
romaria – religious pilgrimage
rua – street

saudade – melancholic longing for better times
sé – cathedral
sem chumbo – unleaded (petrol)
senhor – man
senhora – woman
serra – mountain, mountain range
solar – manor house

tasca – tavern
termas – spas, hot springs
terra quente – hot country
torre de menagem – castle tower, keep
Turihab – short for Turismo Habitação, a scheme for marketing private accommodation (particularly in northern Portugal) in cottages, historic buildings and manor houses
turismo – tourist office

vila – town

FOOD GLOSSARY

a conta – the bill

açorda – bread-based stew, usually served with mixed *mariscos* (shellfish) or *camarão* (prawn)

agua – water, usually offered *sem gas* (still) or *com gas* (bubbly)

amêijoas – clams

arroz – rice

arroz de marisco – rich shellfish and rice mixture

arroz de tamboril – monkfish rice

atum – tuna

azeite – olive oil

azeitonas – olives

bacalhau – salted codfish

bacalhau à brás – shredded fried cod with potato and scrambled egg

bacalhau com – shredded cod with cream and potatoes

bica – espresso

bife – steak

borrego – lamb

caldeirada – fish and shellfish stew, not unlike bouillabaisse

camarão/camarões – prawn/ prawns

carapau – a type of (small) mackerel

carne – meat

carne de porco – pork

carne de vaca – beef

cataplana – seafood stew cooked in a copper pot

cerveja – beer

choco – cuttlefish

chorіço – smoked pork sausage

couvert – bread, cheese, olives brought to you table before your meal

cozido à portuguesa – stew of sausages, meats and vegetables

dose – a portion, usually big enough for two

ementa – menu

entradas – appetizers

espadarte – swordfish

especialidade da casa – house speciality

espetada – kebab

feijoada – bean and sausage stew, usually made with white beans

frango – chicken

frutos do mar – seafood

galão – tall weak coffee with milk

lula – squid

mariscos – shellfish

meia de leite – coffee with milk

meia dose – half-portion, usually serves one

migas – fried breadcrumbs flavoured with sausage

pão – bread

pastel de nata – custard tart

pastelaria – pastry shop and bakery

peixe – fish

pernil no forno – roast leg of pork

petiscos – small (tapas-sized) plates

piri piri – spicy chilli sauce

polvo – octopus

prato do dia – plate of the day

prato principal – main course

queijada – cheesecake

queijo – cheese

salmão – salmon

sandes – sandwiches

sardinhas – sardines

sobremesa – dessert

vinho – wine

vinho blanco – white wine

vinho tinto – red wine

vinho verde – semi-sparkling young wine

vitela – veal

Behind the Scenes

SEND US YOUR FEEDBACK

We love to hear from travellers – your comments keep us on our toes and help make our books better. Our well-travelled team reads every word on what you loved or loathed about this book. Although we cannot reply individually to your submissions, we always guarantee that your feedback goes straight to the appropriate authors, in time for the next edition. Each person who sends us information is thanked in the next edition – the most useful submissions are rewarded with a selection of digital PDF chapters.

Visit **lonelyplanet.com/contact** to submit your updates and suggestions or to ask for help. Our award-winning website also features inspirational travel stories, news and discussions.

Note: We may edit, reproduce and incorporate your comments in Lonely Planet products such as guidebooks, websites and digital products, so let us know if you don't want your comments reproduced or your name acknowledged. For a copy of our privacy policy visit lonelyplanet.com/privacy.

OUR READERS

Many thanks to the travellers who used the last edition and wrote to us with helpful hints, useful advice and interesting anecdotes:
Alfredo Mager, Andrew Porteous, Anke Brock, Anne van Riesen, Anne-Maria van Hilst, Annick Beausejour, Brent Shaphren, Catherine Rolland, Chris Poullaos, Christopher McDonald, David Curtis, David Owen, Dennis Gowans, Diego Ures, Dominik Witzigmann, Dor Wegman, Edward Goldobin, Elijah Lovkoff, Eva Fernandez, Ewen & Heidi Mcleish, François de Pitray, Geert Van de Wiele, Giovanni Bonvento, Gunilla Possenius, Harold Wever, Jack Bouer, Janis Packham, Johann Tournebize, John Field, Jona Knoke, Jörg Falkenberg, José Henrique Rodrigues dos Santos, Julia van den Berg, Julie Woods, Kieran Aylward, Liz Vaughan, Maria Ramos, Michiel van Dam, Mong-Yang Loh, Muzz Shapiro, Nick Gurney, Nick Hassey, Paolo Campegiani, Pascal Leutenegger, Paul Starkey, Pedro Oliveira, Priscila Annibal, Richard Price, Rosanette Alonso, Sibylla Lane, Solveig Moe, Stephen Freedman

WRITER THANKS

Regis St Louis

I'm grateful to many folks – innkeepers, baristas, *tourismo* staff and fellow travellers alike – who shared tips on their favourite places in the Alentejo. Special thanks to João Teixeira and Kevin Raub for a fine finale to the trip. As always, hugs to Cassandra and daughters Magdalena and Genevieve, who make this whole enterprise worthwhile.

Kate Armstrong

Muito obrigada to Manuela Fonseca and her colleagues at Turismo de Portugal, Antonio Belo (Tomar), Raquel (Porto de Mos) and José Conde from CISE. At LP, thank you Brana Vladisavljevic for your guidance and patience. Special shout out to 'the-main-thing-is-we-go-in-the-right-direction-Sally', partner in crime for some of the way whose 'can do' attitude and eventual off-piste preparedness made for one hell of an adventure. Finally, as always, to my Portuguese family, Dom Antonio Pedro and Dona Mina, and my amiga Portuguesa and woman-in-the-know about everything, Ana Palma.

Kerry Christiani

I could not have written this guide without a little help from Porto amigos. I am *muito obrigada* to 'gourmet guru' André for his delicious insights, to Diogo at Prova and David at Touriga for opening up my eyes to Portuguese wine, and to Nuno and Rita at Workshops Pop Up for their juicy tips. Big thanks also to Sandra Lorenz at Porto CVB.

Marc Di Duca

Big *obrigado* goes to all who helped me in the Algarve, especially the staff at tourist information centres in Silves, Faro, Lagos and Tavira. Also thanks to my parents-in-law for looking after the kiddies while I was on the road, and to my wife for her support during my long trips abroad.

Anja Mutić

Obrigada, Hoji & Kweli, for coming along for the ride and making life on and off the road a lot more fun. Thanks to all the great people I crossed paths with in Portugal over the years; you've been the reason I keep coming back. Finally, *hvala* to my always-laughing mom and the inspiring memory of my father.

Kevin Raub

Thanks to my wife, Adriana Schmidt Raub, who is sharing this Portuguese adventure with me after eight years in Brazil! Brana Vladisavljevic, Regis St Louis, Anja Mutić, Kate Armstrong and all my partners-in-crime at LP. On the road, Filipa Achega, Jayme Simões, Vitor Carriço, Marina da Costa, Celia Pedroso, Lucy Pepper, André Oliveira, Inês Brandling, Randy Paul, Misha Pinkhasov and Rui Matias.

ACKNOWLEDGEMENTS

Climate map data adapted from Peel MC, Finlayson BL & McMahon TA (2007) 'Updated World Map of the Köppen-Geiger Climate Classification', *Hydrology and Earth System Sciences*, 11, 1633–44.
Cover photograph: Palácio Nacional da Pena, Sintra, Malachit, Shutterstock©

THIS BOOK

This 10th edition of Lonely Planet's *Portugal* guidebook was researched and written by Regis St Louis, Kate Armstrong, Kerry Christiani, Marc Di Duca, Anja Mutić and Kevin Raub. The previous edition was written by Regis St Louis, Kate Armstrong, Anja Mutić and Andy Symington.

This guidebook was produced by the following:

Destination Editor Brana Vladisavljevic (thanks to Lorna Parkes)

Product Editor Alison Ridgway

Senior Cartographer Anthony Phelan

Book Designer Wibowo Rusli

Assisting Editors Sarah Bailey, Imogen Bannister, Kate Chapman, Nigel Chin, Gabrielle Innes, Sandie Kestell, Kellie Langdon, Korina Miller, Anne Mulvaney, Genna Patterson, Jessica Ryan, Saralinda Turner

Assisting Cartographer Julie Dodkins

Cover Researcher Naomi Parker

Thanks to Daniel Corbett, Andi Jones, Lauren Keith, Claire Naylor, Karyn Noble, Lauren O'Connell, Kirsten Rawlings, Tony Wheeler

Index

Map Pages **000**
Photo Pages **000**

N

Map Pages **000**
Photo Pages **000**

Map Legend

Sights

- Beach
- Bird Sanctuary
- Buddhist
- Castle/Palace
- Christian
- Confucian
- Hindu
- Islamic
- Jain
- Jewish
- Monument
- Museum/Gallery/Historic Building
- Ruin
- Shinto
- Sikh
- Taoist
- Winery/Vineyard
- Zoo/Wildlife Sanctuary
- Other Sight

Activities, Courses & Tours

- Bodysurfing
- Diving
- Canoeing/Kayaking
- Course/Tour
- Sento Hot Baths/Onsen
- Skiing
- Snorkelling
- Surfing
- Swimming/Pool
- Walking
- Windsurfing
- Other Activity

Sleeping

- Sleeping
- Camping

Eating

- Eating

Drinking & Nightlife

- Drinking & Nightlife
- Cafe

Entertainment

- Entertainment

Shopping

- Shopping

Information

- Bank
- Embassy/Consulate
- Hospital/Medical
- Internet
- Police
- Post Office
- Telephone
- Toilet
- Tourist Information
- Other Information

Geographic

- Beach
- Gate
- Hut/Shelter
- Lighthouse
- Lookout
- Mountain/Volcano
- Oasis
- Park
- Pass
- Picnic Area
- Waterfall

Population

- Capital (National)
- Capital (State/Province)
- City/Large Town
- Town/Village

Transport

- Airport
- Border crossing
- Bus
- Cable car/Funicular
- Cycling
- Ferry
- Metro station
- Monorail
- Parking
- Petrol station
- S-Bahn/Subway station
- Taxi
- T-bane/Tunnelbana station
- Train station/Railway
- Tram
- Tube station
- U-Bahn/Underground station
- Other Transport

Note: Not all symbols displayed above appear on the maps in this book

Routes

- Tollway
- Freeway
- Primary
- Secondary
- Tertiary
- Lane
- Unsealed road
- Road under construction
- Plaza/Mall
- Steps
- Tunnel
- Pedestrian overpass
- Walking Tour
- Walking Tour detour
- Path/Walking Trail

Boundaries

- International
- State/Province
- Disputed
- Regional/Suburb
- Marine Park
- Cliff
- Wall

Hydrography

- River, Creek
- Intermittent River
- Canal
- Water
- Dry/Salt/Intermittent Lake
- Reef

Areas

- Airport/Runway
- Beach/Desert
- Cemetery (Christian)
- Cemetery (Other)
- Glacier
- Mudflat
- Park/Forest
- Sight (Building)
- Sportsground
- Swamp/Mangrove

Anja Mutić

Porto, the Douro & Trás-os-Montes; The Minho Croatia-born New York–based writer Anja has had a full-blown love affair with Portugal for over a decade. On her first visit in 2005, she fell head over heels; on the second visit in 2006, she met her partner in life and travel and has been returning ever since for stints and longer stays. Anja has covered many a city and corner of Portugal for various publications but has a particularly soft spot for the north. Anja is online at www.everthenomad.com.

Kevin Raub

Lisbon & Around Kevin grew up in Atlanta and started his career as a music journalist in New York, working for *Men's Journal* and *Rolling Stone* magazines. He ditched the rock 'n' roll lifestyle for travel writing and recently relocated to Lisbon after eight years in Brazil – and is certainly feeling the quirky language effects on his Portuguese fluency! This is Kevin's 39th Lonely Planet guide. Follow him on Twitter and Instagram at @RaubOnTheRoad.

OUR STORY

A beat-up old car, a few dollars in the pocket and a sense of adventure. In 1972 that's all Tony and Maureen Wheeler needed for the trip of a lifetime – across Europe and Asia overland to Australia. It took several months, and at the end – broke but inspired – they sat at their kitchen table writing and stapling together their first travel guide, *Across Asia on the Cheap*. Within a week they'd sold 1500 copies. Lonely Planet was born.

Today, Lonely Planet has offices in Franklin, London, Melbourne, Oakland, Dublin, Beijing and Delhi, with more than 600 staff and writers. We share Tony's belief that 'a great guidebook should do three things: inform, educate and amuse'.

OUR WRITERS

Regis St Louis

The Alentejo Regis' longtime admiration for wine, rugged coastlines and soulful music made him easy prey for Portugal – a country he has travelled extensively over the past decade. Favourite memories from recent trips include negotiating sheep-filled lanes near Alvito, feasting on *percebes* (goose barnacles) along the Costa Vicentina and exploring mesmerising industrial ruins in Portalegre and São Domingos. Regis has contributed to more than 50 Lonely Planet guidebooks, and he has also written for the BBC, the *Telegraph* and the *Chicago Tribune*. Follow his latest posts on Twitter or Instagram at @regisstlouis.

Kate Armstrong

Estremadura & Ribatejo; The Beiras A regular visitor to Portugal, Kate first backpacked around the country over 25 years ago and fell for central Portugal's fortified villages (and their ghosts), coastal seafood and Portuguese hospitality. Lured by the language of fado, she later returned to study Portuguese. For this edition Kate hiked in the Serra da Estrela, entered more castles than a soldier in medieval times, and consumed quantities (ahem, kilos) of convent cakes. She is published regularly in Australian and international publications – see www.katearmstrong.com.au and @nomaditis.

Kerry Christiani

Porto, the Douro & Trás-os-Montes Ever since Kerry first clapped eyes on Porto: the historic centre's houses piled higgledy-piggledy like Jenga blocks above the Rio Douro, and the pure Atlantic light – she knew it was love. That love has intensified over the years, and now goes way beyond the city's looks and straight to its soul – the wonderfully hospitable *tripeiros*. Kerry studied Portuguese translation to MA level before going on to author more than a dozen Lonely Planet titles, including *Pocket Lisbon* and *Pocket Porto*. She tweets @kerrychristiani.

Marc Di Duca

The Algarve A long-established travel guide author, Marc cut his Portuguese teeth hiking the *levadas* of Madeira, a tiny piece of paradise to which he wrote the first edition of Lonely Planet's guide in 2015. Swapping samba for fado and bananas for oranges, Marc traversed the Algarve for this edition of Lonely Planet's *Portugal*, by far his favourite region of the mainland. When not on the road for Lonely Planet, Marc can be found in Sandwich, Kent, with his wife and two sons.

OVER PAGE MORE WRITERS

Published by Lonely Planet Global Limited
CRN 554153
10th edition – March 2017
ISBN 978 1 78657 322 3

10 9 8 7 6 5 4 3 2 1
Printed in China